THE BIG PICTURE.

A rich, poster-worthy display in each chapter grabs students' attention and broadens their understanding of big processes, big concepts, and big data.

SNAPSHO...

Graphics focused on demographic data help students understand the meaning behind the numbers.

INFOGRAPHICS MAKE THIS A VISUAL TEXT FOR TODAY'S STUDENTS.

SNAPSHOT OF AMERICA: WHAT DO WE BELIEVE?

Catholic **25.1%**
Baptist **15.8%**
Unaffiliated **15.0%**
Generic Christian **14.2%**
Mainline Protestant **12.9%**
Refused/Don't Know **5.2%**
Pentecostal/Charismatic **3.5%**
Protestant Denominations **3.1%**
2.7%
Mormon **1.4%**
Jewish **1.2%**

U.S. tax burden compared to other countries:

 29% of Americans feel that their religion is "the one true faith"

 **53%** of Americans feel that it is necessary to believe in God to be moral

...9% ...America ...freedom

 40% of Americans stated that they attend church services weekly; religious leaders report only 20% actually attend

Source: Lorem ipsum dolor sit amet, consectetur adipiscing elit. Suspendisse consequat neque lectus, non fermentum lectus facilisis vel. Lorem ipsum dolor sit amet, consectetur adipiscing elit.

Source: Lorem ipsum dolor sit amet, consectetur adipiscing elit. Suspendisse consequat neque lectus, non fermentum lectus facilisis vel. Lorem ipsum dolor sit amet, consectetur adipiscing elit.

...an Bodies, 2012; 2010 U.S. Religion Census: Religious Congregations & Membership Study, Created by ...ious Identification Survey 2008," Table 3, commons.trincoll.edu/aris/files/2011/08/ARIS_Report_2008.pdf.

SNAPSHOT OF AMERICA: HOW DO WE PARTICIPATE IN CIVIC LIFE?

How we engage in our civic life

48% of adults directly take part in a civic group or activity.

39% of adults recently contacted a government official or spoke out in a public forum via offline methods.

34% did those things via online methods.

39% of adults do political or civic activities on social networking sites.

How *much* we engage in our civic life

10%
Very Engaged
(10 activities +)

15%
Engaged
(6–10 activities)

46%
Moderately Engaged
(1–5 activities)

28%
Disengaged
(0 activities)

BEHIND THE NUMBERS

Some people are much more engaged in politics and society than others. It is the voice of the people. What does politics look like if most of us are like the "Disengaged" in the figure, or alternatively if the majority of us become "Very Engaged"? Who wins and who loses with different levels of civic engagement?

Source: In a 2012 survey, the Pew Research Center asked about whether people had participated in a series of 29 offline and online activities. "Aaron Smith, "Civic Engagement in the Digital Age," www.pewinternet.org/2013/04/25/civic-engagement-in-the-digital-age/. Some of the values for the figures were derived by the authors from the Pew data set.

Every element of **Keeping the Republic** is crafted to provide the tools students need to be thoughtful, savvy consumers of political information.

IN YOUR OWN WORDS.

Learning objectives help students organize chapter material. A "Who, What, How" summary in every major chapter section reinforces these goals so students can relay what they've read in their own words.

WHAT'S AT STAKE...?

Chapter-opening vignettes ask students to think about what people are struggling to get from politics and how the rules affect the outcome of who wins and who loses.

IN YOUR OWN WORDS   After you've read this chapter, you will be able to

>> Describe the role of each branch of government.

>> Explain why the founders chose to structure each of the three branches of government as they did.

>> Identify the ways in which federalism divides power between national and state governments.

>> Demonstrate how the flexibility built in to the Constitution has allowed it to change with the times.

>> Discuss whether the Constitution fosters or limits citizen participation in government.

PAUSE AND REVIEW:

WHO, WHAT, HOW

The founders' goal was to devise a legislature, an executive, and a judiciary that would correct the flaws of the Articles of Confederation while balancing the rights and powers of citizens against the need for the government to be secure from abuse and corruption. The means they employed were unusual—they had the unique opportunity to write the rule book, the Constitution, from scratch, constrained only by the necessity of gaining the approval of sufficient states to allow the Constitution to be ratified and thus seen as legitimate.

IN YOUR OWN WORDS >> Describe the role of each branch of government.

Denver: A Mile High in More Ways Than One
Former marine Steve Azzariti served two tours in Iraq and suffers posttraumatic stress disorder, which he says is eased by using marijuana. He was also first in line to buy recreational pot when it became legal under Colorado law in January 2014. While laws have changed in many states, consuming cannabis remains an illegal substance in most other states, and marijuana use is still a federal offense. The resulting patchwork of state laws and changing federal enforcement from one administration to the next make for a confusing pot market. The options are for Congress to act, for the Courts to clear things up, or for Steve and his fellow users to be left in (a pleasant?) limbo.

WHAT'S AT STAKE...WHEN A STATE TAKES MARIJUANA LAWS INTO ITS OWN HANDS?

IF YOU ARE READING THIS FROM
Washington State, Colorado, or a state that has legalized some form of marijuana for medical use, be careful—very careful—how you exercise your newfound rights. Due to the crazy patchwork nature of America's marijuana laws, what is legal in your home state might get you a year or more in jail and a hefty fine if you take it on the road.

Of course, everyone knows that smoking marijuana is against the law in the United States. Among other things, the United States federal Controlled Substances Act says so. Under that law, passed in 1970, marijuana is a "schedule one drug," equivalent, in legal terms, to heroin and LSD. But most people also know that, although the U.S. government considers marijuana a drug for which there is "no currently accepted medical use," twenty-three states beg to differ, and two (Colorado and Washington) say who cares, it's just plain fun. Voters in both of those states voted to legalize recreational marijuana in 2012.

So if you live in one of those states and have a prescription or buy the pot legally for recreational use, you are okay, right?

Not so fast.

Consider the case of B. J. Patel, a thirty-one-year-old man from Arizona who was traveling through Idaho and was stopped for failing to signal by a police officer who was using license plate recognition software to target out-of-state drivers. The officer saw the medical marijuana card in his wallet, asked where the pot was and, when shown by Patel, promptly arrested him. No matter how law-abiding Patel had been when he bought the pot, he was breaking the law in Idaho.

Idaho law provides for up to a year imprisonment and a $1,000 fine for under three ounces of pot and up to five years in jail and a $10,000 fine for more than three ounces. The state haul has gone from 131.2 pounds of pot in 2011 to 645 pounds in 2012 to 721.5 pounds in 2103. "Come on vacation, leave on probation," says a Coeur d'Alene lawyer.[1]

Or consider the case of the five brothers in Colorado who sell an oil made from a strain of marijuana that doesn't even get you high. The plant is rich in a substance, CBD, that is used to treat seizures. It's legal in Colorado, of course, but there is a global demand for the oil and the brothers want to expand to meet that demand. The fly in their ointment is that, even though the oil is not an intoxicant, it is made from marijuana and marijuana is illegal under federal law. Generally, federal law trumps state law when there is a conflict, but Attorney General Eric Holder has said that as long as the sale of marijuana is regulated, the federal government won't prosecute its use in the states where it is legal.[2] But try to sell that marijuana, or any product made from it, across state lines and the feds will seize it and possibly put the seller in jail.

So the brothers are trying to get their product classified as "industrial hemp," which is okay by Colorado, but not necessarily by the United States. If the federal government doesn't buy their argument, they are ready to do battle. "We are hoping the enforcement agencies have bigger fish to fry and don't want to take a bunch of medicine away from sick kids," said one of the brothers. "But if they are going to do it, we're all in. If you are going to be locked up, it's a thing worth getting locked up for."[3]

Finally, consider the case of a Minnesota mom who was recently arrested in 2014 for giving her fifteen-year-old son marijuana oil on a doctor's advice to relieve chronic pain and muscle spasms from a brain injury. The pot was purchased legally in Colorado but administered in Minnesota, which has passed a law allowing medical marijuana. The catch? It doesn't come into effect until July 2015. Said Bob Capecchi, who works for the Marijuana Policy Project in Washington D.C., "Stunned was my initial reaction. I can't think of an instance where an individual has been brought up on charges like this simply because the effective date hasn't come around yet for the law that has already been passed. Let's not forget, there is a medical marijuana law that has been endorsed by the legislature and by the Governor."[4]

So why is there so much legal turmoil about the use of marijuana, something that a majority of Americans now think should be legal?[5] Why can an activity that is legal in one state get you fined and thrown in jail in another? Why can the federal government forbid an activity, but turn a blind eye to it unless you carry it across state lines? How do the laws get so complicated and tangled that you can get yourself arrested in one state for an activity that is legal in the state in which you took part in it, even if it is soon to be legal in the place where you are arrested? What is at stake when states decide to pass their own laws legalizing marijuana? We will return to this question at the end of the chapter, when we have a better grasp on the complex relationships that are generated by American federalism. <<

DON'T BE FOOLED BY...
PUBLIC OPINION POLLS

In the heat of the Clinton impeachment hearings, angry conservative Republicans could not believe the polls: over 65 percent of Americans still approved of the job the president was doing and did not want to see him removed from office. Their conclusion? The polls were simply wrong. "The polls are targeted to get a certain answer," said one Floridian. "There are even T-shirts in South Florida that say 'I haven't been polled'."[1]

Do we need to know people personally who have been polled in order to trust poll results? Of course not. But there are lots of polls out there, not only those done carefully and responsibly by reputable polling organizations but also polls done for marketing and overtly political purposes—polls with an agenda, we might say. How are we, as good scholars and citizens, to know which results are reliable indications of what the public thinks, and which are not? One thing we can do is bring our critical thinking skills to bear by asking some questions about the polls reported in the media.

WHAT TO WATCH OUT FOR[2]

- **Who is the poll's sponsor?** Even if the poll was conducted by a professional polling company, it may still have been commissioned on behalf of a candidate or company. Does the sponsor have an agenda? How might that agenda influence the poll, the question wording, or the sponsor's interpretation of events?

- **Is the sample representative?** That is, were proper sampling techniques followed? What is the margin of error?

- **From what population was the sample taken?** There is a big difference, for instance, between the preference of the general public for a presidential candidate and the preference of likely voters, especially if we are interested in predicting the election's outcome! Read the fine print. Sometimes a polling organization will weight responses according to the likelihood that the respondent will actually vote in order to come up with a better prediction of the election result. Some polls survey only the members of one party, or the readers of a particular magazine, or people of a certain age, depending on the information they are seeking to discover. Be sure the sample is not self-selected. Always check the population being sampled, and do not assume it is the general public.

- **How are the questions worded?** Are loaded, problematic, or vague terms used? Could the questions be confusing to the average citizen? Are the questions available with the poll results? If not, why not? Do the questions seem to lead you to respond one way or the other? Do they oversimplify issues or complicate them? If the survey claims to have detected change over time, be sure the same questions were used consistently. All these things could change the way people respond.

- **Are the survey topics ones that people are likely to have information and opinions about?** Respondents rarely admit that they don't know how to answer a question, so responses on obscure or technical topics are likely to be more suspect than others.

- **What is the poll's response rate?** A lot of "don't knows," "no opinions," or refusals to answer can have a decided effect on the results.

- **Do the poll results differ from those of other polls, and if so, why?** Check out elections.huffingtonpost.com/pollster, www.fivethirtyeight.com, or www.realclearpolitics.com for some context. Don't necessarily assume that a change in individual poll numbers means that public opinion has changed. What is it about this poll that might have caused the discrepancy?

- **What do the results mean?** Who is doing the interpreting? What are that person's motives? For instance, pollsters who work for the Democratic Party will have an interpretation of the results that is favorable to Democrats, and a Republican interpretation will favor Republicans. Try interpreting the results yourself.

1. Melinda Henneberger, "Where G.O.P. Gathers, Frustration Does Too," New York Times, February 1, 1999, 3.
2. Some of these questions are based in part on similar advice given to poll watchers in Herbert Asher, Polling and the Public: What Every Citizen Should Know, 7th ed. (Washington, DC: CQ Press, 2007), 206–209.

DON'T BE FOOLED BY.

These boxes encourage students to be analytical and skeptical consumers of political information.

CLUES TO CRITICAL THINKING

- **Consider the source**
- **Lay out the argument**
- **Uncover the evidence**
- **Evaluate the conclusion**
- **Sort out the political implications**

CLUES TO CRITICAL THINKING.

Brief readings with CLUES questions help students acquire the habit of active and close reading.

PROFILES IN CITIZENSHIP:
JOE BIDEN

In the cold December that followed the 2010 midterm elections—with the 111th Congress in the waning days of its lame-duck session before the members headed home for their holiday break—the Obama administration still had a long Christmas wish list. Senate ratification of the New START Treaty with Russia was on its agenda, as were extending the tax cuts for those making under $250,000 a year and getting unemployment insurance extended for those especially hard hit by the recession. The administration wanted to repeal the "don't ask, don't tell" policy in the military and get the DREAM Act passed, which would allow kids brought to this country by parents who entered illegally to find a path to citizenship through education or military service. After what President Obama described as the "shellacking" the Democrats took in the elections, no one thought he had a chance of getting any of those things done, but his administration was scrambling to end the year on a positive note.

Our interview with Vice President Joe Biden took place in the thick of the administration's negotiations with congressional Republicans over extending the tax cuts, and Biden was the negotiator-in-chief. We were slotted in for an appointment in his White House office between cabinet members who wanted to discuss the implications of agreeing to extend the Bush tax cuts for the country's wealthiest citizens, and Nancy Pelosi, then the Speaker of the House, and Harry Reid, the Senate majority leader, who were adamantly opposed to extending the tax cuts for the wealthy. The air in his White House office fizzed with power and excitement as Biden waited for a call from Senate minority leader Mitch McConnell to cement a deal that would, he argued, "save the economy from a double dip recession, make a compromise where the working poor continue to get their tax cuts even though we have to give temporarily on the upper end, where you see an increase in the stimulus that you'll end up with a million and a half more jobs than you would've next year, and where in the process we get the arms control treaty ratified and the trade deal."

Though the call didn't come while we were there, by late afternoon it would be announced that, due in large part to Biden's bargaining, the White House had gotten much of what it wanted in the tax cut deal. The repeal of "don't ask, don't tell" followed days later, as did ratification of the New START Treaty and passage of several other key pieces of legislation. While the administration didn't get everything it wanted—the tax cuts were extended for the wealthiest Americans as well as for those in the middle class and the DREAM Act did not pass—no one argued when President Obama hailed the lame-duck session as the most productive in decades.

That day in early December, the vice president clearly relished his role in brokering the deal that would make it possible for the rest to follow, and he was eloquent and hopeful about the possibilities of using power to good purpose. It's a great time to be in service, he says, what he calls "the single greatest opportunity" in his forty years of public life. "We are in one of those inflection points in history," he says, "I don't think it's occurred in American history but three times, where . . . if we do nothing, the momentum is going to drag us in the direction that makes it increasingly more difficult to correct the course." He discusses some of the biggest challenges we face—global warming, inequalities in education, our changing economy, and our standing in the world. "So you are at one of those moments where if we get it right, this can be a truly transformational moment where you look back twenty years from now and say, we had set the course of the nation, we put it on a trajectory that puts us in

PROFILES IN CITIZENSHIP.

Author interviews with inspiring public figures offer students insight and advice for getting involved in political action.

THINKING OUTSIDE THE BOX

Why does critical thinking feel like so much more work than "regular thinking"?

THINKING OUTSIDE THE BOX.

These questions challenge students' assumptions and provoke thoughtful responses.

FLEXIBILITY AND INTERACTIVITY.
An eBook with video and multimedia assets in every chapter.

With purchase of a new print copy with an access code, students can take advantage of a free mobile-friendly **Interactive eBook** anywhere, anytime, with easy access across desktop, smartphone, and tablet devices. By simply clicking on icons in the eBook, students experience a broad array of video, audio, data, primary sources, and *CQ Researcher* reports that deepen their learning as they explore key topics.

SAGE edge™
for CQ Press

SAGE edge for Students provides a personalized approach to help students accomplish their coursework goals in an easy-to-use learning environment.

- Mobile-friendly **eFlashcards** and **quizzes** provide self-assessment and practice.

- A customized **action plan** includes tips and feedback on progress through course materials.

- **Chapter summaries** with **learning objectives** reinforce the most important material.

- **Video** and **multimedia content** enhance exploration of key topics.

- EXCLUSIVE! Access to full-text **SAGE journal articles** that expand on chapter concepts.

SAGE edge for Instructors supports teaching by making it easy to integrate quality content.

- **Test Bank**, with 400 additional questions (more than 1,800 items total), is linked to Bloom's Taxonomy and tied to learning objectives and page references. Also with **Respondus** test generation capabilities.

- **Sample course syllabi**.

- Editable, chapter-specific **PowerPoint® slides**.

- **Instructor's manual** with lecture starters, ideas for class activities, and discussion questions.

- All **graphics from the text** for class presentations.

- **Video** and **multimedia content** that appeal to different learning styles.

- **Video questions** that track student usage of the Interactive eBook.

- All instructor and student assessment material on a **common course cartridge**.

- **Transition guide** of chapter-by-chapter key changes in the new edition.

COMING SUMMER 2015!

for CQ Press

Available with an **access code:**

- **Diagnostic pre-tests** tie to chapter learning objectives.

- **Personalized study plans** address specific knowledge gaps.

- **Interactivities** with simulations and review questions challenge students to apply concepts and work through scenarios.

- **Post-tests** track student mastery of key learning objectives.

- Course Management System **gradebook integration**.

KEEPING THE REPUBLIC

THE ESSENTIALS

EDITION **7**

KEEPING THE REPUBLIC

POWER AND CITIZENSHIP IN AMERICAN POLITICS

THE ESSENTIALS

EDITION **7**

CHRISTINE BARBOUR
INDIANA UNIVERSITY

GERALD C. WRIGHT
INDIANA UNIVERSITY

Los Angeles | London | New Delhi
Singapore | Washington DC | Boston

Los Angeles | London | New Delhi
Singapore | Washington DC

FOR INFORMATION:

CQ Press
An Imprint of SAGE Publications, Inc.
2455 Teller Road
Thousand Oaks, California 91320
E-mail: order@sagepub.com

SAGE Publications Ltd.
1 Oliver's Yard
55 City Road
London, EC1Y 1SP
United Kingdom

SAGE Publications India Pvt. Ltd.
B 1/I 1 Mohan Cooperative Industrial Area
Mathura Road, New Delhi 110 044
India

SAGE Publications Asia-Pacific Pte. Ltd.
3 Church Street
#10–04 Samsung Hub
Singapore 049483

Acquisitions Editor: Sarah Calabi
Senior Developmental Editor: Nancy Matuszak
Developmental Editor: Ann Kirby-Payne
Digital Content Editor: Allison Hughes
Editorial Assistant: Raquel Christie
Production Editor: David. C. Felts
Typesetter: C&M Digitals (P) Ltd.
Copy Editor: Amy Marks
Proofreader: Theresa Kay
Indexer: Will Ragsdale
Cover Designer: Rose Storey
Marketing Manager: Amy Whitaker

Printed in Canada

A catalog record of this book is available from the Library of Congress.

ISBN 978-1-4833-5274-9 (pbk.)

LCCN: 2014957044

This book is printed on acid-free paper.

MIX
Paper from
responsible sources
FSC® C011825

15 16 17 18 10 9 8 7 6 5 4 3 2

We dedicate this book with love to our parents,

Patti Barbour and John Barbour and

Doris and Gerry Wright,

To our kids, Andrea and Darrin, Monica and Michael,

To our grandkids, Amelia, Elena, Paloma, and Asher,

And to each other.

ABOUT THE AUTHORS

CHRISTINE BARBOUR

Christine Barbour teaches in the Political Science Department and the Hutton Honors College at Indiana University, where she has become increasingly interested in how teachers of large classes can maximize what their students learn. At Indiana, Professor Barbour has been a Lilly Fellow, working on a project to increase student retention in large introductory courses, and a member of the Freshman Learning Project, a university-wide effort to improve the first-year undergraduate experience. She has served on the *New York Times* College Advisory Board, working with other educators to develop ways to integrate newspaper reading into the undergraduate curriculum. She has won several teaching honors, but the two awarded by her students mean the most to her: the Indiana University Student Alumni Association Award for Outstanding Faculty and the Indiana University Chapter of the Society of Professional Journalists Brown Derby Award. When not teaching or writing textbooks, Professor Barbour enjoys playing with her dogs, traveling with her coauthor, and writing about food. She is the food editor for *Bloom Magazine* of Bloomington and is a coauthor of *Indiana Cooks!* (2005) and *Home Grown Indiana* (2008). She is currently working on another cookbook and a book about local politics, development, and the fishing industry in Apalachicola, Florida.

GERALD C. WRIGHT

Gerald C. Wright has taught political science at Indiana University since 1981. An accomplished scholar of American politics, and the 2010 winner of the State Politics and Policy Association's Career Achievement Award, his books include *Statehouse Democracy: Public Opinion and Policy in the American States* (1993), coauthored with Robert S. Erikson and John P. McIver, and he has published more than fifty articles on elections, public opinion, and state politics. Professor Wright has long studied the relationship among citizens, their preferences, and public policy. He is currently conducting research with grants from the National Science Foundation and the Russell Sage Foundation on the factors that influence the equality of policy representation in the states and in Congress. He is also writing a book about representation in U.S. legislatures. He has been a consultant for Project Vote Smart in the past several elections. Professor Wright is a member of Indiana University's Freshman Learning Project, a university-wide effort to improve the first-year undergraduate experience by focusing on how today's college students learn and how teachers can adapt their pedagogical methods to best teach them. In his nonworking hours, Professor Wright also likes to spend time with his dogs, travel, eat good food, and play golf.

BRIEF CONTENTS

BRIEF CONTENTS

CONTENTS

11 PUBLIC OPINION 397

12   POLITICAL PARTIES   433

PREFACE

WHEN one of us was a freshman journalism major in college, more years ago now than she cares to remember, she took an introduction to American politics course—mostly because the other courses she wanted were already full. But the class was a revelation. The teacher was terrific, the textbook provocative, and the final paper assignment an eye opener. "As Benjamin Franklin was leaving Independence Hall," the assignment read, "he was stopped by a woman who asked, 'What have you created?' Franklin replied, 'A Republic, Madam, if you can keep it'." Have we succeeded in keeping our republic? Had we been given a democracy in the first place? These questions sparked the imagination, the writing of an impassioned freshman essay about the limits and possibilities of American democracy, and a lifetime love affair with politics. If we have one goal in writing this textbook, it is to share the excitement of discovering humankind's capacity to find innovative solutions to those problems that arise from our efforts to live together on a planet too small, with resources too scarce, and with saintliness in too short a supply. In this book we honor the human capacity to manage our collective lives with peace and even, at times, dignity. And, in particular, we celebrate the American political system and the founders' extraordinary contribution to the possibilities of human governance.

WHERE WE ARE GOING

Between the two of us, we have been teaching American politics for way more than half a century. We have used a lot of textbooks in that time. Some of them have been too difficult for introductory students (although we have enjoyed them as political scientists!), and others have tried excessively to accommodate the beginning student and have ended up being too light in their coverage of basic information. We wanted our students to have the best and most complete treatment of the American political system we could find, presented in a way that would catch their imagination, be easy to understand, and engage them in the system about which they were learning.

This book is the result of that desire. It covers essential topics with clear explanations, but it is also a thematic book, intended to guide students through a wealth of material and to help them make sense of the content both academically and personally. To that end we develop two themes that run throughout every chapter: an analytic theme to assist students in organizing the details and connecting them to the larger ideas and concepts of American politics and an evaluative theme to help them find personal meaning in the American political system and develop standards for making judgments about how well the system works. Taken together, these themes provide students a framework on which to hang the myriad complexities of American politics.

The analytic theme we chose is a classic in political science: politics is a struggle over limited power and resources, as gripping as a sporting event in its final minutes, but much more vital. The rules guiding that struggle influence who will win and who will lose, so that often the struggles with the most at stake are over the rule making itself. In short, and in the words of a famous political scientist, *politics is about who gets what, and how they get it*. To illustrate this theme, we begin and end every chapter with a feature called *What's at Stake . . . ?* that poses a question about what people want from politics—what they are struggling to get and how the rules affect who gets it. At the end of every major chapter section, we stop to revisit Harold Laswell's definition in context and ask *Who, What, How*. This periodic analytic summary helps solidify the conceptual work of the book and gives students a sturdy framework within which to organize the facts and other empirical information we want them to learn. For the evaluative theme, we focus on the "who" in the formulation of "who gets what, and how." Who are the country's citizens? What are the ways they engage in political life? To "keep" a republic, citizens must shoulder responsibilities as well as exercise their rights. We challenge students to view democratic participation among the diverse population as the price of maintaining liberty.

Working in concert with the Who, What, How summary are the new *In Your Own Words* goals that provide each chapter's major points up front to help students organize the material they read. Who, What, How summaries provide the opportunity for students to pause and review these goals and gauge how well they're understanding and retaining the information.

Our citizenship theme has three dimensions. First, in our *Profiles in Citizenship* feature, present in every chapter, we introduce students to important figures in American politics and ask the subjects why they are involved in public service or some aspect of political life. Based on personal interviews with these people, the profiles model republic-keeping behavior for students, helping them to see what is expected of them as members of a democratic polity. We feel unabashedly that a primary goal of teaching introductory politics is not only to create good scholars but also to create good citizens. Second, at the end of nearly every chapter, the feature *The Citizens and . . .* provides a critical view of what citizens can or cannot do in American politics, evaluating how democratic various aspects of the American system actually are and what possibilities exist for change. Third, we premise this book on the belief that the skills that make good students and good academics are the same skills that make good citizens: the ability to think critically about and process new information and the ability to be actively engaged in one's subject. Accordingly, in our *CLUES to Critical Thinking* feature, we help students understand what critical thinking looks like by modeling it for them, and guiding them through the necessary steps as they examine current and classic readings about American politics. Similarly, the *Don't Be Fooled by . . .* feature assists students to critically examine the various kinds of political information they are bombarded with—from information in textbooks like this one, to information from social networks, to information from their congressional representative or political party. *Thinking Outside the Box* questions prompt students to take a step back and engage in some big-picture thinking about what they are learning.

The book's themes are further illustrated through two unique features that will enhance students' visual literacy and critical thinking skills. Each chapter includes a rich, poster-worthy display called *The Big Picture* that focuses on a key element in the book, complementing the text with a rich visual that grabs students' attention and engages them in understanding *big processes* like how cases get to the Supreme Court, *big concepts* such as when the law can treat people differently, and *big data*, including who has immigrated to the U.S. and how they have assimilated. In addition, an innovative feature called *Snapshot of America,* reimagined from the Who Are We feature of past editions, describes through graphs, charts, and maps just who we Americans are and where we come from, what we believe, how educated we are, and how much money we make. This recurring feature aims at exploding stereotypes, and *Behind the Numbers* questions lead students to think critically about the political consequences of America's demographic profile. These visual features are the result of a new partnership with award-winning designer, educator, and artist Mike Wirth, who has lent his expert hand in information design and data visualization to craft these unique, informative, and memorable graphics.

Marginal glosses of the key terms as they occur and chapter summary material—vocabulary, summaries, quizzes, and suggestions for further study (books, films, and web sites)—help to support the book's major themes and to reinforce the major concepts and details of American politics.

HOW WE GET THERE

In many ways this book follows the path of most American politics texts: there are chapters on all the subjects that instructors scramble to cover in a short amount of time. But in keeping with our goal of making the enormous amount of material here more accessible to our students, we have made some changes to the typical format. After our introductory chapter, we have included a chapter not found in every book: "American Citizens and Political Culture." Given our emphasis on citizens, this chapter is key. It covers the history and legal status of citizens and immigrants in America and the ideas and beliefs that unite us as Americans as well as the ideas that divide us politically.

Another chapter that breaks with tradition is Chapter 4, "Federalism and the U.S. Constitution," which provides an analytic and comparative study of the basic rules governing this country—highlighted up front because of our emphasis on the *how* of American politics. This chapter covers the essential elements of the Constitution: federalism, the three branches, separation of powers and checks and balances, and amendability. In each case we examine the rules the founders provided, look at the alternatives they might have chosen, and ask what difference the rules make to who wins and who loses in America. This chapter is explicitly comparative. For each rule change considered, we look at a country that does things differently. We drive home early the idea that understanding the rules is crucial to understanding how and to whose advantage the system works. Throughout the text we look carefully at alternatives to our system of government as manifested in other countries—and among the fifty states.

Because of the prominence we give to rules—and to institutions—this book covers Congress, the presidency, the bureaucracy, and the courts before looking at public opinion, parties, interest groups, voting, and the media—the inputs or processes of politics that are shaped by those rules. While this approach may seem counterintuitive to instructors who have logged many miles teaching it the other way around, we have found that it is not counterintuitive to students, who have an easier time grasping the notion that the rules make a difference when they are presented with those rules in the first half of the course. We have, however, taken care to write the chapters so that they will fit into any organizational framework.

We have long believed that teaching is a two-way street, and we welcome comments, criticisms, or just a pleasant chat about politics or pedagogy. You can email us directly at barbour@indiana.edu and wright1@indiana.edu.

ENHANCING PEDAGOGY WITH TECHNOLOGY

Students today are connected, wired and networked in ways previous generations could not have imagined, and they process information in ways that go way beyond reading the printed word on a paper page. To keep up with them and their quickly evolving world, *Keeping the Republic* is now a full-fledged, integrated media experience. When students purchase a new print copy of the book, they receive **FREE access** to an enhanced ebook. Through a series of annotated icons, opposite the marginal glossary definitions at the foot of each page, students can quickly link to multimedia on the page where a topic is discussed, pointing to articles and background pieces, to audio clips of interviews, to video clips of news stories or satirical commentary, to reference and biography material, to *CQ Researcher* policy backgrounder reports, to important and current data on such topics as approval ratings and public opinion polls. This allows students to explore an important concept or idea while reading—a reinforcing exercise as well as vetted content that provides depth and added context. It's an enhanced, enriching, and interactive learning experience.

WHAT'S NEW IN THE SEVENTH EDITION

The 2008 election turned some of the conventional wisdom about who gets what in American politics upside down. Americans elected an African American to the presidency and seriously entertained the idea of a woman president or vice president. Young people, traditionally nonvoters, turned out for the primaries and caucuses, and again for the general election. Changing demographics and the passing of time had blurred the distinction between red states and blue states. Although in 2010, politics looked more like business as usual, by 2012 what one observer calls "the coalition of the ascendant" was back in place, with growing demographic groups such as young people and minorities taking a larger share of the electorate than they traditionally have. As was expected, the 2014 midterm elections marked a return to the lower turnout, older, whiter, and more Republican electorate, giving a majority to Republicans in both houses, with candidates already positioning for a 2016 run for the presidency. We have updated the text throughout to reflect the current balance of power in the House and Senate and tried to put the election results into historical perspective.

And that's not all. Writing the seventh edition gave us an opportunity to reimagine the book's graphics. We worked closely with Mike Wirth, an award-winning designer, educator, and artist who specializes in information design and data visualization, to translate the book's abstract concepts and data into concrete knowledge. Together, we've created *The Big Picture* and *Snapshot of America* graphics, which are designed to enhance students' visual literacy and critical thinking skills and bring the book's themes to life. These two unique and exciting features are key to creating a more visual text for today's students. They explore a range of topics, from how the founders from the Articles of Confederation to the U.S.

Constitution and what must have been in Madison's mind as he wrote *Federalist* no. 51 to how we voted in recent elections. As always, graphs in every chapter reflect the newest data available, and the book now features over 200 images and cartoons, the majority of them brand new. New *What's at Stake . . . ?* vignettes examine such topics as immigration reform, the legalization of marijuana in some states, marriage equality, and the president's use of executive power.

The *In Your Own Words* objectives help students organize the material they read and keep chapter goals in the forefront. Encouraging information understanding and retention, these goals are reinforced at the end of every major chapter section so that, in the end, students can make learning an objective and relay that knowledge *in their own words*.

ANCILLARIES

We know how important good resources can be in the teaching of American government. Our goal has been to create resources that not only support but also enhance the text's themes and features. **SAGE edge** offers a robust online environment featuring an impressive array of tools and resources for review, study, and further exploration, keeping both instructors and students on the cutting edge of teaching and learning. SAGE edge content is open access and available on demand. Learning and teaching has never been easier! We gratefully acknowledge Ann Kirby-Payne; Susannah Prucka, University of Maryland Baltimore County; Angela Narasimhan, Keuka College; and Alicia Fernandez, California State University, Fullerton, for developing the ancillaries on this site.

SAGE edge for Students at **http://edge.sagepub. com/barbour7e** provides a personalized approach to help students accomplish their coursework goals in an easy-to-use learning environment.

- Mobile-friendly **eFlashcards** strengthen understanding of key terms and concepts.

- Mobile-friendly practice **quizzes** allow for independent assessment by students of their mastery of course material.

- A customized online **action plan** includes tips and feedback on progress through the course and materials, which allows students to individualize their learning experience.

- **Chapter summaries** with **learning objectives** reinforce the most important material.

- Carefully selected chapter-by-chapter **video and multimedia content** which enhance classroom-based explorations of key topics

- EXCLUSIVE! Access to certain full-text **SAGE journal articles** have been carefully selected for each chapter. Each article supports and expands on the concepts presented in the chapter. This feature also provides questions to focus and guide your interpretation.

SAGE edge for Instructors at http://edge.sagepub.com/barbour7e supports teaching by making it easy to integrate quality content and create a rich learning environment for students.

- **Test banks** that provide a diverse range of pre-written options as well as the opportunity to edit any question and/or insert personalized questions to effectively assess the students' progress and understanding.

- **Sample course syllabi** for semester and quarter courses provide suggested models for structuring one's course.

- Editable, chapter-specific **PowerPoint® slides** offer complete flexibility for creating a multimedia presentation for the course

- An **instructor's manual** features chapter overviews and learning objectives, lecture starters, ideas for class activities, and discussion questions.

- A set of all the **graphics from the text**, including all of the maps, tables, and figures, in PowerPoint, .pdf, and .jpg formats for class presentations.

- Carefully selected chapter-by-chapter **video and multimedia content** which enhance classroom-based explorations of key topics

- Comprehensive **video questions** based on the interactive ebook and multimedia videos per chapter to prompt class activities and discussions.

- A **common course cartridge** includes all of the instructor resources and assessment material from the student study site, making it easy for instructors to upload and use these materials in LMS such as Blackboard™, Angel®, Moodle™, Canvas, and Desire2Learn™.

- **Transition guide** provides a chapter-by-chapter outline of key changes to the seventh edition.

ACKNOWLEDGMENTS

The Africans say that it takes a village to raise a child—it is certainly true that it takes one to write a textbook! We could not have done it without a community of family, friends, colleagues, students, reviewers, and editors who supported us, nagged us, maddened us, and kept us on our toes. Not only is this a better book because of their help and support, but it would not have been a book at all without them.

On the home front, we thank our families, who have hung in there with us even when they thought we were nuts (and even when they were right). Our friends, old and new, have all listened to endless progress reports (and reports of no progress at all) and cheered the small victories with us. We are forever grateful for the unconditional love and support, not to mention occasional intellectual revelation (Hobbes was wrong: it is not a dog-eat-dog world after all!), offered up gladly by Ollie, Gracie, and Giuseppe. (Though we lost Max, Clio, Daphne, Gina, Zoë, Ginger, Bandon, Maggie, and Spook along the way, they were among our earliest and strongest supporters and we miss them still.)

Colleagues now or once in the Political Science Department at Indiana University have given us invaluable help on details beyond our ken: Yvette Alex Assensoh, Bill Bianco, Jack Bielasiak, Doris Burton, Ted Carmines, Dana Chabot, Mike Ensley, Chuck Epp, Judy Failer, Russ Hanson, Margie Hershey, Bobbi Herzberg, Virginia Hettinger, Jeff Isaac, Fenton Martin, Burt Monroe, Lin Ostrom, Rich Pacelle, Karen Rasler, Leroy Rieselbach, Jean Robinson, Steve Sanders, Pat Sellers, and the late John Williams. IU colleagues from other schools and departments have been terrific: Trevor Brown, Dave Weaver, and Cleve Wilhoit from the Journalism School; Bill McGregor and Roger Parks from the School of Public and Environmental Affairs; John Patrick from the School of Education; and Julia Lamber and Pat Baude from the Law School have all helped out on substantive matters. Many IU folks have made an immeasurable contribution by raising to new levels our consciousness about teaching: Joan Middendorf and David Pace, as well as all the Freshman Learning Project people. James Russell and Bob Goelhert, and all the librarians in the Government Publications section of our library have done yeoman service for us. We are also grateful to colleagues from other institutions: Joe Aistrup, Shaun Bowler, Bob Brown, Tom Carsey, Kisuk Cho, E. J. Dionne, Todd Donovan, Bob Erikson, David Hobbs, Kathleen Knight, David Lee, David McCuan, John McIver, Dick Merriman, Glenn Parker, Denise Scheberle, John Sislin, Dorald Stoltz, and Linda Streb. Rich Pacelle and Robert Sahr were particularly helpful.

Special thanks to all our students—undergraduate and graduate, past and present—who inspired us to write this book in the first place. Many students helped us in more concrete ways, working tirelessly as research assistants. On previous editions these former students, now colleagues at other universities, helped enormously: Nate Birkhead, Tom Carsey, Jessica Gerrity, Dave Holian, Tracy Osborn, Brian Schaffner, and Mike Wagner. Jon Winburn, Laura Bucci, Trish Gibson, Katelyn Stauffer, and Ben Toll have been super helpful in the creation of the electronic version of the book, and Katelyn has been a gem of a research assistant. We are also grateful to Hugh Aprile, Liz Bevers, Christopher McCollough, Rachel Shelton, Jim Trilling, and Kevin Willhite for their help with the earliest editions of the book.

Thanks also to Mike Stull, for taking us seriously in the first place; and to Jean Woy, for the vision that helped shape the book. Ann West in particular was a friend, a support, and a fabulous editor. We will love her forever.

We have also benefited tremendously from the help of the folks at Project Vote Smart and the many outstanding political scientists across the country who have provided critical reviews of the manuscript at every step of the way. We'd like to thank the following people who took time away from their own work to critique and make suggestions for the improvement of ours. They include all the candy reviewers—Sheldon Appleton, Paul Babbitt, Harry Bralley, Scott Brown, Peter Carlson, David Holian, Carol Humphrey, Glen Hunt, Marilyn Mote-Yale, and Craig Ortsey—and also:

Yishaiya Abosch, California State University, Fresno
Amy Acord, Lone Star College, Cy-Fair
Danny M. Adkison, Oklahoma State University
Craig Douglas Albert, Georgia Regents University Augusta
Ellen Andersen, Indiana University–Purdue University, Indianapolis
Alicia Andreatta, Cisco College
Don Arnold, Laney College
Kevin Bailey, former member, Texas House of Representatives, District 140
Jeffrey A. Bosworth, Mansfield University
Ralph Edward Bradford, University of Central Florida
James Bromeland, Winona State University
Jenny Bryson Clark, South Texas College
Scott E. Buchanan, Columbus State University
John F. Burke, University of St. Thomas
Charity Butcher, Kennesaw State University
Anne Marie Cammisa, Georgetown University
David Campbell, University of Notre Dame
Francis Carleton, University of Nevada, Las Vegas
Michael Ceriello, Clark College
Jennifer B. Clark, South Texas Community College
Diana Cohen, Central Connecticut State University
Kimberly H. Conger, Colorado State University
Renee Cramer, Drake University
Paul Davis, Truckee Meadows Community College
Christine L. Day, University of New Orleans
Mary C. Deason, University of Mississippi
William Delehanty, Missouri Southern State University
Robert E. DiClerico, West Virginia University
Robert L. Dion, University of Evansville
Price Dooley, University of Central Arkansas
Lois Duke-Whitaker, Georgia Southern University
Johanna Dunaway, Louisiana State University
Richard Ellis, Willamette University
C. Lawrence Evans, William and Mary College
Victoria Farrar-Myers, University of Texas at Arlington

Femi Ferreira, Hutchinson Community College
Daniel Franklin, Georgia State University
Heidi Getchell-Bastien, Northern Essex Community College
Savanna Garrity, Madisonville Community College
Dana K. Glencross, Oklahoma City Community College
Abe Goldberg, University of South Carolina Upstate
Larry Gonzalez, Houston Community College-Southwest
Eugene Goss, Long Beach City College
Richard Haesly, California State University, Long Beach
Bill Haltom, University of Puget Sound
Victoria Hammond, Austin Community College–Northridge
Patrick J. Haney, Miami University
Sally Hansen, Daytona State College
Charles A. Hantz, Danville Area Community College
Virginia Haysley, Lone Star College–Tomball
David M. Head, John Tyler Community College
Paul Herrnson, University of Maryland
Erik Herzik, University of Nevada–Reno
Ronald J. Hrebenar, University of Utah
Tseggai Isaac, Missouri University of Science and Technology
William G. Jacoby, Michigan State University
W. Lee Johnston, University of North Carolina Wilmington
Kelechi A. Kalu, Ohio State University
Joshua Kaplan, University of Notre Dame
John D. Kay, Santa Barbara City College
Ellen Key, Appalachian State University
Richard J. Kiefer, Waubonsee College
Kendra A. King, Oglethorpe University
Tyson King-Meadows, University of Maryland–Baltimore County
Elizabeth Klages, Augsburg College
Bernard D. Kolasa, University of Nebraska at Omaha
John F. Kozlowicz, University of Wisconsin–Whitewater
Geoffrey Kurtz, Borough of Manhattan Community College–CUNY
Lisa Langenbach, Middle Tennessee State University
Jeff Lee, Blinn College–Bryan
Angela K. Lewis, University of Alabama at Birmingham
Ted Lewis, Naval Postgraduate School
Kara Lindaman, Winona State University
Brad Lockerbie, East Carolina University
Paul M. Lucko, Angelina College
Vincent N. Mancini, Delaware County Community College
Jonathan Martin, Texas Tech University
Tom McInnis, University of Central Arkansas
Amy McKay, Georgia State University
Tim McKeown, University of North Carolina at Chapel Hill
Sam Wescoat McKinstry, East Tennessee State University
Utz Lars McKnight, University of Alabama

David McCuan, Sonoma State University

Lauri McNown, University of Colorado at Boulder

Bryan McQuide, University of Idaho

Lawrence Miller, Collin County Community College–
    Spring Creek

Maureen F. Moakley, University of Rhode Island

Sarah Moats, West Virginia University

Theodore R. Mosch, University of Tennessee at Martin

T. Sophia Mrouri, Lone Star College, Fairbanks Center

Melinda A. Mueller, Eastern Illinois University

Steven Neiheisel, St. Mary's University

Adam Newmark, Appalachian State University

David Nice, Washington State University

Zane R. Nobbs, Delta College

James A. Norris, Texas A&M International University

Susan Orr, College at Brockport, SUNY

Gerhard Peters, Citrus College

Mike Pickering, University of New Orleans

Darrial Reynolds, South Texas College

David Robinson, University of Houston–Downtown

Jason Robles, Colorado State University

Dario Albert Rozas, Milwaukee Area Technical College

Trevor Rubenzer, University of South Carolina, Upstate

Raymond Sandoval, Richland College

Thomas A. Schmeling, Rhode Island College

Paul Scracic, Youngstown State University

Todd Shaw, University of South Carolina

Daniel M. Shea, Allegheny College

Neil Snortland, University of Arkansas at Little Rock

Michael W. Sonnleitner, Portland Community
    College–Sylvania

Robert E. Sterken Jr., University of Texas at Tyler

Atiya Kai Stokes-Brown, Bucknell University

Ruth Ann Strickland, Appalachian State University

Tom Sweeney, North Central College

Bill Turini, Reedley College

Richard S. Unruh, Fresno Pacific University

Anip Uppal, Alpena Community College

Lynn Vacca, Lambuth University

Jan P. Vermeer, Nebraska Wesleyan University

Elizabeth A Wabindato, Northern Arizona University

Julian Westerhout, Illinois State University

Matt Wetstein, San Joaquin Delta College

Cheryl Wilf, Kutztown University

Shawn Williams, Campbellsville University

David C. Wilson, University of Delaware

David E. Woodard, Concordia University–St. Paul

Shoua Yang, St. Cloud State University

Kimberly Zagorski, University of Wisconsin–Stout

David J. Zimny, Los Medanos College

We are also incredibly indebted to the busy public servants who made the *Profiles in Citizenship* possible. We are gratified and humbled that they believed in the project enough to give us their valuable time. Thanks also to Matthew Brandi for sharing his thoughts and insights on his Occupy experience.

There are several people in particular without whom this edition would never have seen the light of day. Mike Wirth has been an enormously talented and enthusiastic partner on the book's infographics, for which we are endlessly thankful. Pat Haney the provider of the nuts and bolts of the foreign policy chapter, has been a cheerful, tireless collaborator, a good friend and colleague for twenty years now, and we are so grateful to him. Chuck McCutcheon, a huge help and a delight to work with, lent his expertise to the social and economic policy chapters. And for helping us to find all of the great multimedia assets for the interactive ebook, we are grateful for the work of Angela Narasimhan (Keuka College), Charles Jacobs (St. Norbert College), and Kimberly Turner (College of DuPage) and to our own Ann Kirby-Payne.

Finally, it is our great privilege to acknowledge and thank all the people at CQ Press who believed in this book and made this edition possible. In this day and age of huge publishing conglomerates, it has been such a pleasure to work with a small, committed team dedicated to top-quality work. Brenda Carter, more than anyone, saw the potential of this book and made it what it is today. Charisse Kiino earned our instant gratitude for so thoroughly and immediately "getting" what this book is about. They have both worked tirelessly with us and we have relied heavily on their good sense, their wisdom, their patience, and their friendship. Thanks to Linda Trygar and her team of field reps across the country who sometimes seem to know the book better than we do ourselves. We appreciate their enthusiasm and commitment. For putting this beautiful book together and drawing your attention to it, we thank the folks on the design, production, editorial, and marketing teams: Gail Buschman, Sarah Calabi, Raquel Christie, Catherine Forrest, Davia Grant, Allison Hughes, Paul Pressau, and especially David Felts for his good production management, and to Amy Marks, for her always gentle and miraculous copyediting. We are also more grateful than we can say to Nancy Matuszak, who has pulled out all the stops to make this book happen. She's a gem.

Very special mention goes to two people on this edition. The amazing Sarah Calabi jumped right in to this project as a new acquisitions editor, found herself immediately in the weeds, and bailed us out with style, smarts, and laughter. We are not sure how we got so lucky but we want her always on our side.

Lastly, huge hugs and thanks to Ann Kirby-Payne, who has been our development editor for multiple editions of this book. She has been a stalwart support, a firm hand, and an unflaggingly cheerful presence on FaceTime in the dark hours of the early morning. We are in awe of her gritty courage, grace, and integrity. We also thank Owen and Josie for sharing their mom during their summer vacations. You guys are awesome, too.

Christine Barbour
Gerald C. Wright

TO THE STUDENT

SUGGESTIONS ON HOW TO READ THIS TEXTBOOK

1. As they say in Chicago about voting, do it **early and often**. If you open the book for the first time the night before the exam, you will not learn much from it and it won't help your grade. Start reading the chapters in conjunction with the lectures, and you'll get so much more out of class.

2. Pay attention to the **chapter headings** and **In Your Own Words** goals. They tell you what we think is important, what our basic argument is, and how all the material fits together. Often, chapter subheadings list elements of an argument that may show up on a quiz. Be alert to these clues.

3. **Read actively.** Constantly ask yourself: Why is this important? How do these different facts fit together? What are the broad arguments here? How does this material relate to class lectures? How does it relate to the broad themes of the class? When you stop asking these questions, you are merely moving your eyes over the page, and that is a waste of time.

4. **Highlight or take notes.** Some people prefer highlighting because it's quicker than taking notes, but others think that writing down the most important points helps in recalling them later. Whichever method you choose (and you can do both), be sure you're doing it properly.

   - **Highlighting.** An entirely highlighted page will not give you any clues about what is important. Read each paragraph and ask yourself: What is the basic idea of this paragraph? Highlight that. Avoid highlighting all the examples and illustrations. You should be able to recall them on your own when you see the main idea. Beware of highlighting too little. If whole pages go by with no marking, you are probably not highlighting enough.

   - **Outlining.** Again, the key is to write down enough, but not too much. Go for key ideas, terms, and arguments.

5. **Note all key terms,** and be sure you understand the definition and significance.

6. Do not skip **tables and figures.** These things are there for a purpose, because they convey crucial information or illustrate a point in the text. After you read a chart or graph or *Big Picture* infographic, make a note in the margin about what it means.

7. **Do not skip the boxes.** They are not filler! The *Don't Be Fooled by . . .* boxes provide advice on becoming a critical consumer of the many varieties of political information that come your way. Each *Profile in Citizenship* box highlights the achievements of a political actor pertinent to that chapter's focus. They model citizen participation and can serve as a beacon for your own political power long after you've completed your American government course. And the *Snapshot of America* boxes help you understand who Americans are and how they line up on all sorts of dimensions.

8. Make use of the book's web site at **http://edge.sage pub.com/barbour7e**. There you will find chapter summaries, flashcards, and practice quizzes that will help you prepare for exams.

CQ Press, an imprint of SAGE, is the leading publisher of books, periodicals, and electonic products on American government and international affairs. CQ Press consistently ranks among the top commercial publishers in terms of quality, as evidenced by the numerous awards its products have won over the years. CQ Press owes its existence to Nelson Poynter, former publisher of the St. Petersburg Times, and his wife Henrietta, with whom he founded Congressional Quarterly in 1945. Poynter established CQ with the mission of promoting democracy through education and in 1975 founded the Modern Media Institute, renamed The Poynter Institute for Media Studies after his death. The Poynter Institute (www.poynter.org) is a nonprofit organization dedicated to traning journalists and media leaders.

In 2008, CQ Press was acquired by SAGE, a leading international publisher of journals, books, and electronic media for academic, educational, and professional markets. Since 1965, SAGE has helped inform and educate a global community of scholars, practitioners, researchers, and students spanning a wide range of subject areas, including business, humanities, social sciences, and science, technology, and medicine. A privately owned corporation, SAGE has offices in Los Angeles, London, New Delhi, Singapore, and Boston in addition to the Washington DC office of CQ Press.

1 POLITICS: WHO GETS WHAT, AND HOW?

© Daily News, L.P. (New York). Used with permission.

IN YOUR OWN WORDS After you've read this chapter, you will be able to

» Describe the role politics plays in determining how power and resources are distributed in a society.

» Compare different economic and political systems in terms of how power is distributed between citizens and government.

» Explain the historical origins of American democracy.

» Describe the enduring tension in the United States between self-interested human nature and public spirited government.

» Apply the five steps of critical thinking to this book's themes of power and citizenship in American politics.

WHAT'S AT STAKE...IN TAKING IT TO THE STREETS?

LIKE SO MANY OTHERS, TWENTY-FOUR- year-old Matthew Brandi heard the call through the Internet. "I actually decided to go protest after seeing online videos of protesters being arrested, with the caption, 'for each one they take away, two will replace them!'" He says, "It's like it was my duty to go. I owed it to the person who got arrested. They stepped up and got taken out, so someone had to replace them. I called three friends to come with me as well."[1]

And so on October 1, 2011, Matt and his friends marched across the Brooklyn Bridge as a part of Occupy Wall Street—soon to be shortened to just "Occupy," as the movement spread from New York's Zuccotti Park to other locations—to protest the growing income gap between the top 1 percent of income earners in this country and everyone else. By the end of the day, Matt and seven hundred other marchers found themselves under arrest—an official response that only galvanized them to further action.

What was especially striking about the Occupy movement was the clear assumption that the economic inequality it lamented was the result of a rigged system, that

politicians by themselves could not solve the problem because they were a central part of it. Said Matt Brandi, "When action is left to politicians, the end result is often no action at all." So the Occupy people took matters into their own hands, protesting what they saw as corruption that kept the system from working to the benefit of everyone, and criticizing the growing inequality of income in the United States. What they did not do was issue a list of "demands" or specify certain policies that would satisfy them.

While the movement had many supporters—even President Barack Obama spoke words of encouragement, noting that the movement reflected a broad-based frustration about how our financial system works[2]—critics immediately attacked the movement for being "anti-capitalist," "disorganized," and "unfocused." CNN's Erin Burnett, reporting on the protests, said, "What are they protesting? No one seems to know."[3]

As the rallying cry "We are the 99%" swept through the nation—through cities, smaller towns, and college campuses—it was particularly attractive to young

Americans, struggling in the difficult economy and frustrated with the status quo that seemed to enrich the few at the expense of the many. As those most tied into social media, they were also most likely to hear about the protests and to spread the word. Like the protests that fueled the Arab Spring in the Middle East, Occupy was an Internet-generation movement, fired up and sustained by Twitter, Facebook, and YouTube.

Young people are notoriously uninvolved in politics, often seeing it as irrelevant to their lives and the things they really care about. Knowing that they pay little attention and tend not to vote in large numbers, politicians feel free to ignore their concerns, reinforcing their cynicism and apathy. Young people did turn out in larger-than-usual numbers in 2008 (51 percent of those under thirty turned out, and they made up 17 percent of the electorate, an increase of 2.2 million voters over 2004), breaking decisively (66 to 39 percent) for President Obama over his opponent, Sen. John McCain of Arizona. But the recession had dampened their enthusiasm, and it was not at all clear that they would turn out in such numbers again.[4]

But the Occupy movement spoke to many of them, and to their disillusion with the political system. Again, Matt Brandi: "The people lose their power once they commit to supporting a particular policy, politician, or party. Their energy and efforts are co-opted for political power wrangling and electioneering."

Our founders were no fans of political parties (they aren't even mentioned in the Constitution), but they did value political engagement and they knew that democracies needed care and attention in order to survive. In 1787, when Benjamin Franklin was asked by a woman what he and other founders of the Constitution had created, he replied, "A republic, madam, if you can keep it." Many contemporary writers worry that we are not keeping the republic, that as new generations find politics a turn-off they will become disaffected adults and the system will start to unravel. As one writer says, "a nation that hates politics will not long thrive as a democracy."[5]

Yet protesters like Matt Brandi sound as committed to democracy as Benjamin Franklin could have wished, even though his efforts are not focused on voting or traditional methods of political engagement. Is a nation of Matt Brandis a nation in trouble, or does his brand of activism, and the whole protest ethic of the Occupy movement, help

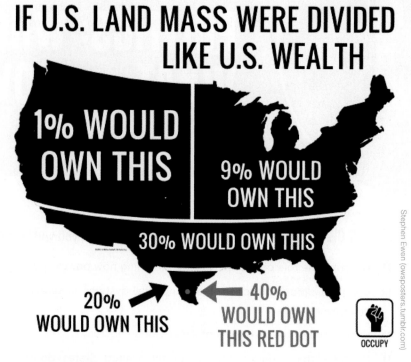

IF U.S. LAND MASS WERE DIVIDED LIKE U.S. WEALTH

1% WOULD OWN THIS

9% WOULD OWN THIS

30% WOULD OWN THIS

20% WOULD OWN THIS

40% WOULD OWN THIS RED DOT

OCCUPY

Stephen Ewen (owsposters.tumblr.com)

A Powerful Message

The Occupy Wall Street movement used vivid posters like this one to focus America's attention on the vastly increased inequalities of income and wealth that have transpired since the 1970s.

to keep the republic? What, exactly, is at stake in taking one's views to the street? We return to this question after we learn more about the meaning of politics and the difference it makes in our lives. ◀◀

HAVE you got grand ambitions for your life? Do you want a powerful position in business, influence in high places, money to make things happen? Perhaps you would like to make a difference in the world, heal the sick, fight for peace, feed the poor. Or maybe all you want from life is a good education; a well-paying job; a comfortable home; and a safe, prosperous, contented existence. Think politics has nothing to do with any of those things? Think again.

All the things that make those goals attainable—a strong national defense, education loans or tax deductions for tuition money, economic prosperity, full employment, favorable mortgage rates, policies that let us take time off from work to have kids, secure streets and neighborhoods, cheap and efficient public transportation—are influenced by or are the products of politics.

Yet, if you listen to the news, politics may seem like one long campaign commercial: eternal bickering and finger-pointing by public servants who seem more interested in feathering their own nests than in helping voters secure theirs. Public policy often seems to focus on bailouts for banks and powerful industries like automobile manufacturers at the expense of those everyday citizens who politicians like to refer to as "Main Street." Politics, which we would like to think of as a noble and even morally elevated activity, takes on all the worst characteristics of the business world, where we expect people to take advantage of each other and pursue their own private interests. Can this really be the heritage of Thomas Jefferson and Abraham Lincoln? Can this be the "world's greatest democracy" at work?

In this chapter we get to the heart of what politics is, how it relates to other concepts such as power, government, rules, economics, and citizenship. We propose that politics can best be understood as the struggle over who gets power and resources in society. Politics produces winners and losers, and much of the reason it can look so ugly is that people fight desperately not to be losers.

Contrary to their depictions in the media, and maybe even in our own minds, the people who are doing that desperate fighting are not some special breed who are different—more corrupt or self-interested or greedy—from the rest of us. They *are* us—whether they are officials in Washington or mayors of small towns, corporate CEOs or representatives of labor unions, local cops or soldiers in the Middle East, churchgoers or atheists, doctors or lawyers, shopkeepers or consumers, professors or students, they are the people that in a democracy we call *citizens*.

As we will see, it is the beauty of a democracy that all the people, including the everyday people like us, get to fight for what they want. Not everyone can win, of course, and many never come close. There is no denying that some people bring resources to the process that give them an edge, and that the rules give advantages to some groups of people over others. But the people who pay attention and who learn how the rules work can begin to use those rules to increase their chances of getting what they want, whether it is a lower personal tax bill, greater pollution controls, a more aggressive foreign policy, safer streets, a better-educated population, or more public parks. If they become very skilled citizens, they can even begin to change the rules so that they can fight more easily for the kind of society they think is important, and so that people like them are more likely to end up winners in the high-stakes game we call politics.

The government our founders created for us gives us a remarkable playing field on which to engage in that game. Like any other politicians, the designers of the American system were caught up in the struggle for power and

resources, and in the desire to write laws that would maximize the chances that they, and people like them, would be winners in the new system. Nonetheless, they crafted a government remarkable for its ability to generate compromise and stability, and also for its potential to realize freedom and prosperity for its citizens.

WHAT IS POLITICS?
A peaceful means of determining who gets power and influence in society

Over two thousand years ago, the Greek philosopher Aristotle said that we are political animals, and political animals we seem destined to remain. The truth is that politics is a fundamental and complex human activity. In some ways it is our capacity to be political—to cooperate, bargain, and compromise—that helps distinguish us from all the other animals out there. Politics may have its baser moments—Watergate comes to mind—but it also allows us to reach more exalted heights than we could ever achieve alone, from the dedication of a new public library, to the building of a national highway system, to the stabilization of a crashing economy, to the guarantee of health care to all U.S. citizens.

Since this book is about politics, in all its glory as well as its shame, we need to begin with a clear definition. One of the most famous definitions, put forth by the well-known political scientist Harold Lasswell, is still one of the best, and we use it to frame our discussion throughout this book. Lasswell defined **politics** as "who gets what when and how."[6] Politics is a way of determining, without recourse to violence, who gets power and resources in society, and how they get them. **Power** is the ability to get other people to do what you want them to do. The resources in question here might be governmental jobs, tax revenues, laws that help you get your way, or public policies that work to your advantage.

The tools of politics are compromise and cooperation; discussion and debate; even, sometimes, bribery and deceit. Politics is the process through which we try to arrange our collective lives in some kind of **social order** so that we can live without crashing into each other at every turn, and to provide ourselves with goods and services we could not obtain alone. But politics is also about getting our own way. Our way may be a noble goal for society or pure self-interest, but the struggle we engage in is a political struggle. Because politics is about power and other scarce resources, there will always be winners and losers in politics. If we could always get our own way, politics would disappear. It is because we cannot always get what we want that politics exists.

What would a world without politics be like? There would be no resolution or compromise between conflicting interests, because those are certainly political activities. There would be no agreements struck, bargains made, or alliances formed. Unless there were enough of every valued

---

politics who gets what, when, and how; a process of determining how power and resources are distributed in a society without recourse to violence

power the ability to get other people to do what you want

social order the way we organize and live our collective lives

POLITICS AND GOVERNMENT

Although the words *politics* and *government* are sometimes used interchangeably, they refer to different things. Politics is a process or an activity through which power and resources are gained and lost. **Government**, on the other hand, is a system or organization for exercising authority over a body of people.

American *politics* is what happens in the halls of Congress, on the campaign trail, at Washington cocktail parties, and in neighborhood association meetings. It is the making of promises, deals, and laws. American *government* is the Constitution and the institutions set up by the Constitution for the exercise of authority by the American people, over the American people.

Authority is power that citizens view as legitimate, or "right"—power to which we have given our implicit consent. You can think of it this way: As children, we probably did as our parents told us, or submitted to their punishment if we didn't, because we recognized their authority over us. As we became adults, we started to claim that our parents had less authority over us, that we could do what we wanted. We no longer saw their power as wholly legitimate or appropriate. Governments exercise authority because people recognize them as legitimate even if they often do not like doing what they are told (paying taxes, for instance). When governments cease to be regarded as legitimate, the result may be revolution or civil war, unless the state is powerful enough to suppress all opposition.

RULES AND INSTITUTIONS

Government is shaped by the process of politics, but it in turn provides the rules and institutions that shape the way politics continues to operate. The rules and institutions of government have a profound effect on how power is distributed and who wins and who loses in the political

The Best Medicine

The political parties and their candidates frequently clash on issues and ideology. Norms of courtesy have evolved so that competing elites continue to work together to reach the compromises that make democratic politics possible. Here, President Barack Obama and then–Republican presidential candidate Mitt Romney share a moment of hilarity with a laughing Cardinal Timothy Dolan at the 2012 Alfred E. Smith Dinner, a humorous respite in the midst of an otherwise acrimonious political campaign.

resource to go around, or unless the world were big enough that we could live our lives without coming into contact with other human beings, life would be constant conflict— what the philosopher Thomas Hobbes (1588–1679) called a "war of all against all." Individuals, unable to cooperate with one another (because cooperation is essentially political), would have no option but to resort to brute force to settle disputes and allocate resources.

Our capacity to be political saves us from that fate. We do have the ability to persuade, cajole, bargain, promise, compromise, and cooperate. We do have the ability to agree on what principles should guide our handling of power and other scarce resources and to live our collective lives according to those principles. Because there are many potential theories about how to manage power—who should have it, how it should be used, how it should be transferred— agreement on which principles are **legitimate**, or accepted as "right," can break down. When agreement on what is legitimate fails, violence often takes its place. Indeed, the human history of warfare attests to the fragility of political life.

Although one characteristic of government is that it has a monopoly on the legitimate use of force, politics means that we have alternatives, that bloodshed is not the only way of dealing with human conflict. Interestingly, the word *politics* comes from the Greek word *polis*, meaning "city-state." Similarly, the word *civilization* comes from the Latin word *civitas*, meaning "city" or "state." Thus our Western notions of politics and civilization share similar roots, all tied up with what it means to live a shared public life.

> **legitimate** accepted as "right" or proper
>
> **government** a system or organization for exercising authority over a body of people
>
> **authority** power that is recognized as legitimate

arena. Life is different for people in other countries not only because they speak different languages and eat different foods but also because their governments establish rules that cause life to be lived in different ways.

Rules can be thought of as the *how* in the definition "who gets what...and *how*." They are directives that determine how resources are allocated and how collective action takes place—that is, they determine how we try to get the things we want. We can do it violently, or we can do it politically, according to the rules. Those rules can provide for a single dictator, for a king, for rule by God's representative on Earth or by the rich, for rule by a majority of the people, or for any other arrangement. The point of the rules is to provide some framework for us to solve without violence the problems that are generated by our collective lives.

Because the rules we choose can influence which people will get what they want most often, understanding the rules is crucial to understanding politics. Consider for a moment the impact a change of rules would have on the outcome of the sport of basketball, for instance. What if the average height of the players could be no more than 5'10"? What if the baskets were lowered? What if foul shots counted for two points rather than one? Basketball would be a very different game, and the teams recruited would look quite unlike the teams for which we now cheer. So it is with governments and politics: change the people who are allowed to vote or the length of time a person can serve in office, and the political process and the potential winners and losers change drastically.

We can think of institutions as the *where* of the political struggle, though Lasswell didn't include a "where" component in his definition. They are the organizations where governmental power is exercised. In the United States, our rules provide for the institutions of a representative democracy—that is, rule by the elected representatives of the people, and for a federal political system. Our Constitution lays the foundation for the institutions of Congress, the presidency, the courts, and the bureaucracy as a stage on which the drama of politics plays itself out. Other systems might call for different institutions—perhaps an all-powerful parliament, or a monarch, or even a committee of rulers.

> **rules** directives that specify how resources will be distributed or what procedures govern collective activity
>
> **institutions** organizations in which governmental power is exercised
>
> **economics** production and distribution of a society's material resources and services
>
> **capitalist economy** an economic system in which the market determines production, distribution, and price decisions, and property is privately owned

These complicated systems of rules and institutions do not appear out of thin air. They are carefully designed by the founders of different systems to create the kinds of society they think will be stable and prosperous, but also where people like themselves are likely to be winners. Remember that not only the rules but also the institutions we choose influence who most easily and most often get their own way.

POLITICS AND ECONOMICS

Whereas politics is concerned with the distribution of power and resources in society, **economics** is concerned specifically with the production and distribution of society's wealth—material goods such as bread, toothpaste, and housing, and services such as medical care, education, and entertainment. Because both politics and economics focus on the distribution of society's resources, political and economic questions often get confused in contemporary life. Questions about how to pay for government, about government's role in the economy, and about whether government or the private sector should provide certain services have political and economic dimensions. Because there are no clear-cut distinctions here, it can be difficult to keep these terms straight.

The sources of the words *politics* and *economics* suggest that their meanings were once more distinct than they are today. We already saw that the Greek source of the word *political* was *polis*, or "city-state," the basic political unit of ancient Greece. For the free male citizens of the city-state of Athens (by no means the majority of the inhabitants), politics was a prestigious and jealously restricted activity. However, the public, political world of Athens was possible only because a whole class of people (slaves and women) existed to support the private world, the *oikonomia*, or "household." This early division of the world into the political and the economic clearly separated the two realms. Political life was public, and economic life was private. Today that distinction is not nearly so simple. What is public and private now depends on what is controlled by government. The various forms of economic systems are shown in Figure 1.1.

CAPITALISM In a pure **capitalist economy,** all the means used to produce material resources (industry, business, and land, for instance) are owned privately, and decisions about production and distribution are left to individuals operating through the free-market process. Capitalist economies rely on the market—the process of supply and demand—to decide how much of a given item to produce or how much to charge for it. In capitalist countries, people do not believe that the government is capable of making such judgments (like how much toothpaste to produce), and they want to keep such decisions out of the hands of government and in the hands of individuals who they believe know best about what they want. The philosophy that corresponds

FIGURE 1.1 A COMPARISON OF ECONOMIC SYSTEMS

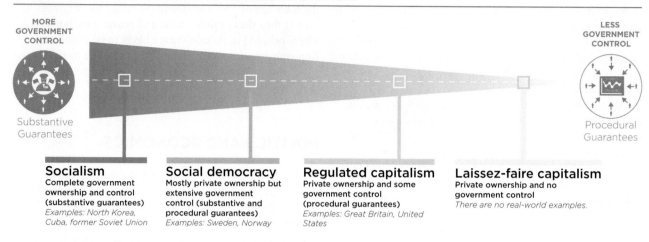

MORE GOVERNMENT CONTROL

LESS GOVERNMENT CONTROL

Substantive Guarantees

Procedural Guarantees

Socialism
Complete government ownership and control (substantive guarantees)
Examples: North Korea, Cuba, former Soviet Union

Social democracy
Mostly private ownership but extensive government control (substantive and procedural guarantees)
Examples: Sweden, Norway

Regulated capitalism
Private ownership and some government control (procedural guarantees)
Examples: Great Britain, United States

Laissez-faire capitalism
Private ownership and no government control
There are no real-world examples.

Economic systems are defined largely by the degree to which government owns the means by which material resources are produced (for example, factories and industry) and controls economic decision making. On a scale ranging from socialism—complete government ownership and control of the economy (on the left)—to laissez-faire capitalism—complete individual ownership and control of the economy (on the right)—social democracies would be located in the center. These hybrid systems are characterized by mostly private ownership of the means of production but considerable government control over economic decisions.

with this belief is called **laissez-faire capitalism**, from a French term that, loosely translated, means "let people do as they wish." The government has no economic role at all in such a system. However, no economic system today maintains a purely unregulated form of capitalism, with the government completely uninvolved.

Like most other countries today, the United States has a system of **regulated capitalism**. It maintains a capitalist economy and individual freedom from government interference remains the norm, but it allows government to step in and regulate the economy to guarantee individual rights and to provide **procedural guarantees** that the rules will work smoothly and fairly. Although in theory the market ought to provide everything that people need and want, and should regulate itself as well, sometimes the market breaks down, or fails. In regulated capitalism, the government steps in to try to fix it.

Markets have cycles, with periods of growth often followed by periods of slowdown or recession. Individuals and businesses look to government for protection from these cyclical effects. For example, President Franklin D. Roosevelt created the Works Progress Administration to get Americans back to work during the Great Depression, and more recently, Congress acted to stabilize the economy in the wake of the financial collapse caused by the subprime mortgage crisis in the fall of 2008. Government may also act to ensure the safety of the consumer public and of working people, or to encourage fair business practices (like prevention of monopolies), or to provide goods and services that people have no incentive to produce themselves.

Highways, streetlights, libraries, museums, schools, Social Security, national defense, and a clean environment are some examples of the goods and services that many people are unable or unwilling to produce privately. Consequently, government undertakes to provide these things (with money provided by taxpayers) and, in doing so, becomes not only a political but an economic actor as well. To the extent that government gets involved in a capitalist economy, we move away from laissez-faire to regulated capitalism.

SOCIALISM In a **socialist economy** like that of the former Soviet Union (based loosely on the ideas of German economist Karl Marx), economic decisions are made not by individuals through the market but rather by politicians, based on their judgment of what society needs. Rather than allowing the market to determine the proper distribution of material resources, politicians decide what the distribution

> **laissez-faire capitalism** an economic system in which the market makes all decisions and the government plays no role
>
> **regulated capitalism** a market system in which the government intervenes to protect rights and make procedural guarantees
>
> **procedural guarantees** government assurance that the rules will work smoothly and treat everyone fairly, with no promise of particular outcomes
>
> **socialist economy** an economic system in which the state determines production, distribution, and price decisions, and property is government owned

ought to be and then create economic policy to bring about that outcome. In other words, they emphasize not procedural guarantees of fair rules and process, but rather **substantive guarantees** of what they believe to be fair outcomes.

According to the basic values of a socialist or communist system (although the two systems have some theoretical differences, for our purposes they are similar), it is unjust for some people to own more property than others and to have power over them because of it. Consequently, the theory goes, the state or society—not corporations or individuals—should own the property (like land, factories, and corporations). In such systems, the public and private spheres overlap, and politics controls the distribution of all resources. The societies that have tried to put these theories into practice have ended up with very repressive political systems, but Marx hoped that eventually socialism would evolve to a point where each individual had control over his or her own life—a radical form of democracy.

Many theories hold that socialism is possible only after a revolution that thoroughly overthrows the old system to make way for new values and institutions. This is what happened in Russia in 1917 and in China in the 1940s. Since the socialist economies of the former Soviet Union and Eastern Europe have fallen apart, socialism has been left with few supporters, although some nations, such as China, North Korea, and Cuba, still claim allegiance to it. Even China, however, introduced market-based reforms in the 1970s and by 2010 ranked as the world's second largest economy, after the United States.

SOCIAL DEMOCRACY Some countries in Western Europe, especially the Scandinavian nations of Norway, Denmark, and Sweden, have developed hybrid economic systems. As noted in Figure 1.1, these systems represent something of a middle ground between socialist and capitalist systems. Primarily capitalist, in that they believe most property can be held privately, proponents of **social democracy** argue nonetheless that the values of equality promoted by socialism

Patrick T. Fallon/Bloomberg via Getty Images

Building a Better Rocket?
Entrepreneur Elon Musk is CEO of Tesla Motors, makers of the all-electric car, but he is also CEO of SpaceX, a private company that develops launch vehicles and spacecraft. His Dragon unmanned shuttle has been delivering cargo to the International Space Station since 2012. While capitalism enables ambitious entrepreneurs like Musk, it is also true that his achievements in space travel would not be possible (or profitable) without the years (and billions of dollars) of previous government investment in space technology.

are attractive and can be brought about by democratic reform rather than revolution. Believing that the economy does not have to be owned by the state for its effects to be controlled by the state, social democratic countries attempt to strike a difficult balance between providing substantive guarantees of fair outcomes and procedural guarantees of fair rules.

Since World War II, the citizens of many Western European nations have elected social democrats to office, where they have enacted policies to bring about more equality—for instance, the elimination of poverty and unemployment, better housing, and adequate health care for all. Even where social democratic governments are voted out of office, such programs have proved so popular that it is often difficult for new leaders to alter them.

IN YOUR OWN WORDS » Describe the role politics plays in determining how power and resources are distributed in a society.

POLITICAL SYSTEMS AND THE CONCEPT OF CITIZENSHIP
Different ideas about power and the social order, different models of governing

Just as there are different kinds of economic systems, there are different sorts of political systems, based on different

---

substantive guarantees government assurance of particular outcomes or results

social democracy a hybrid system combining a capitalist economy and a government that supports equality

Too Small?

If the U.S. Postal Service is forced to make a profit, small rural sites like this one in Bradley, Michigan, would probably be shut down. As a public corporation, the Postal Service has to be accessible and deliver mail everywhere, from the icy slopes of Alaska to the swamps of Florida, for the cost of one first-class stamp.

ideas about who should have power and what the social order should be—that is, how much public regulation there should be over individual behavior. For our purposes, we can divide political systems into two types: those in which the government has the power to impose a particular social order, deciding how individuals ought to behave, and those in which individuals exercise personal power over most of their own behavior and ultimately over government as well. These two types of systems are not just different in a theoretical sense. The differences have very real implications for the people who live in them. Thus the notion of citizenship (or the lack of it) is tied closely to the kind of political system a nation has.

Figure 1.2 offers a comparison of these systems. One type of system, called authoritarian government, potentially has total power over its subjects; the other type, nonauthoritarian government, permits citizens to limit the state's power by claiming rights that the government must protect. Another way to think about the distinction is that, in authoritarian systems, government makes substantive decisions about how people ought to live their lives; in nonauthoritarian systems, government merely guarantees that there are fair rules and leaves the rest to individual control. Sometimes governments that exercise substantive decision making in the economic realm also do so with respect to the social order. But, as Figure 1.3 shows, there are several possible combinations of economic and political systems.

FIGURE 1.2   **A COMPARISON OF POLITICAL SYSTEMS**

LESS GOVERNMENT CONTROL

Procedural Guarantees

Anarchy
No government or manmade laws; individuals do as they please.
There are no real-world examples.

Nonauthoritarian system
(such as democracy)
Individuals (citizens) decide how to live their lives. Government role is limited to procedural guarantees of individual rights.
Examples: United States, Sweden, Japan, South Korea, India

Authoritarian system
Government decides how individuals (subjects) should live their lives and imposes a substantive vision.
Examples: China, North Korea, Cuba, Saudi Arabia

MORE GOVERNMENT CONTROL

Substantive Guarantees

Political systems are defined by the extent to which individual citizens or governments decide what the social order should look like—that is, how people should live their collective, noneconomic lives. Except for anarchies, every system allots a role to government to regulate individual behavior—for example, to prohibit murder, rape, and theft. But beyond such basic regulation, they differ radically on who gets to determine how individuals live their lives, and whether government's role is simply to provide procedural guarantees that protect individuals' rights to make their own decisions or to provide a much more substantive view of how individuals should behave.

Inclusive Capitalism ● Nationalized Facebook? ●

FIGURE 1.3   POLITICAL AND ECONOMIC SYSTEMS

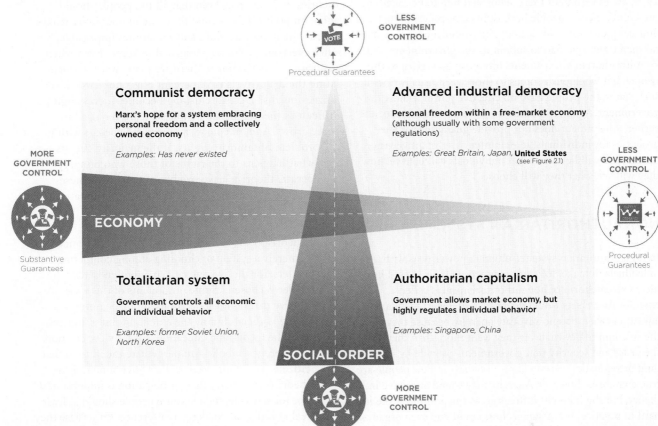

Political systems work in conjunction with economic systems, but government control over the economy does not necessarily translate into tight control over the social order. We have identified four possible combinations of these systems, signified by the labeled points in each quadrant. These points are approximate, however, and some nations cannot be classified so easily. Sweden is an advanced industrial democracy by most measures, for instance, but because of its commitment to substantive economic values, it would be located much closer to the vertical axis.

AUTHORITARIAN SYSTEMS

Authoritarian governments give ultimate power to the state rather than to the people to decide how they ought to live their lives. By "authoritarian governments," we usually mean those in which the people cannot effectively claim rights against the state; where the state chooses to exercise its power, the people have no choice but to submit to its will.

Authoritarian governments can take various forms: sovereignty can be vested in an individual (dictatorship or monarchy), in God (theocracy), in the state itself (fascism), or in a ruling class (oligarchy). When a system combines an authoritarian government with a socialist economy, we say that the system is **totalitarian**. As in the earlier example of the former Soviet Union, a totalitarian system exercises its power over every part of society—economic, social, political, and moral—leaving little or no private realm for individuals.

But an authoritarian state may also limit its own power. In such cases, it may deny individuals rights in those spheres where it chooses to act, but it may leave large areas of society, such as a capitalist economy, free from governmental interference. Singapore is an example of this type of **authoritarian capitalism**, where people have considerable

> **authoritarian governments** systems in which the state holds all power over the social order
>
> **totalitarian** a system in which absolute power is exercised over every aspect of life
>
> **authoritarian capitalism** a system in which the state allows people economic freedom but maintains stringent social regulations to limit noneconomic behavior

economic freedom but stringent social regulations limit their noneconomic behavior. When American teenager Michael Fay was caught vandalizing cars in Singapore in 1994, the government there sentenced him to be caned. In the United States, people have rights that prevent cruel and unusual punishment like caning, but in Singapore, Fay had no such rights and had to submit to the government's will.

Authoritarian governments often pay lip service to the people, but when push comes to shove, as it usually does in such states, the people have no effective power against the government. Again, to use the terminology we introduced earlier, government does not provide guarantees of fair processes for individuals; it guarantees a substantive vision of what life will be like—what individuals will believe, how they will act, what they will choose.

NONAUTHORITARIAN SYSTEMS

In nonauthoritarian systems, ultimate power rests with individuals to make decisions concerning their lives. The most extreme form of nonauthoritarianism is called **anarchy**. Anarchists would do away with government and laws altogether. People advocate anarchy because they value the freedom to do whatever they want more than they value the order and security that governments provide by forbidding or regulating certain kinds of behavior. Few people are true anarchists, however. Anarchy may sound attractive in theory, but the inherent difficulties of the position make it hard to practice. For instance, how could you even organize a revolution to get rid of government without some rules about who is to do what and how decisions are to be made?

DEMOCRACY A less extreme form of nonauthoritarian government, and one much more familiar to us, is **democracy** (from the Greek *demos*, meaning "people"). In democracies, government is not external to the people, as it is in authoritarian systems; in a fundamental sense, government *is* the people. Recognizing that collective life usually calls for some restrictions on what individuals may do (laws forbidding murder, for instance, or theft), democracies nevertheless try to maximize freedom for the individuals who live under them. Although they generally make decisions through some sort of majority rule, democracies still provide procedural guarantees to preserve individual rights—usually protections of due process and minority rights. This means that if individuals living in a democracy feel their rights have been violated, they have the right to ask government to remedy the situation.

Democracies are based on the principle of **popular sovereignty**; that is, there is no power higher than the people and, in the United States, the document establishing their authority, the Constitution. The central idea here is that no government is considered legitimate unless the governed consent to it, and people are not truly free unless they live under a law of their own making.

THEORIES OF DEMOCRACY Generally, as we indicated, democracies hold that the will of the majority should prevail. This is misleadingly simple, however. Some theories of democracy hold that all the people should agree on political decisions. This rule of unanimity makes decision making very slow, and sometimes impossible, since everyone has to be persuaded to agree. Even when majority rule is the norm, there are many ways of calculating the majority. Is it 50 percent plus one? Two-thirds? Three-fourths? Decision making becomes increasingly difficult as the number of people who are required to agree grows. And, of course, majority rule brings with it the problem of minority rights. If the majority gets its way, what happens to the rights of those who disagree? Democratic theorists have tried to grapple with these problems in various ways, none of them entirely satisfactory to all people:

- Theorists of **elite democracy** propose that democracy is merely a system of choosing among competing leaders; for the average citizen, input ends after the leader is chosen.[7] Some proponents of this view believe that political decisions are made not by elected officials but by the elite in business, the military, the media, and education. In this view, elections are merely symbolic—to perpetuate the illusion that citizens have consented to their government. Elite theorists may claim that participation is important, if not for self-rule, then because people should at least feel as if they are making a difference. Otherwise they have no stake in the political system.

- Advocates of **pluralist democracy** argue that what is important is not so much individual participation but rather membership in groups that participate in government decision making on their members' behalf.[8] As a way of trying to influence a system that gives them a limited voice, citizens join groups of people with whom they share an interest, such as labor unions, professional associations, and environmental or business groups. These groups represent their members' interests and try to influence government to enact policy that carries out the group's will. Some pluralists argue that individual citizens have

---

anarchy the absence of government and laws

democracy government that vests power in the people

popular sovereignty the concept that the citizens are the ultimate source of political power

elite democracy a theory of democracy that limits the citizens' role to choosing among competing leaders

pluralist democracy a theory of democracy that holds that citizen membership in groups is the key to political power

little effective power and that only when they are organized into groups are they truly a force for government to reckon with.

- Supporters of **participatory democracy** claim that more than consent or majority rule in making governmental decisions is needed. Individuals have the right to control all the circumstances of their lives, and direct democratic participation should take place not only in government but in industry, education, and community affairs as well.[9] For advocates of this view, democracy is more than a way to make decisions: It is a way of life, an end in itself.

These theories about how democracy should (or does) work locate the focus of power in individuals, groups, and elites. Real-world examples of democracy probably include elements of more than one of these theories; they are not mutually exclusive.

The people of many Western countries have found the idea of democracy persuasive enough to found their governments on it. In recent years, especially since the mid-1980s, democracy has been spreading rapidly through the rest of the world as the preferred form of government. No longer the primary province of industrialized Western nations, attempts at democratic governance now extend into Asia, Latin America, Africa, Eastern Europe, and the republics of the former Soviet Union. There are many varieties of democracy other than our own. Some democracies make the legislature (the representatives of the people) the most important authority; some retain a monarch with limited powers; some hold referenda at the national level to get direct feedback on how the people want them to act on specific issues.

Most democratic forms of government, because of their commitment to procedural values, practice a capitalist form of economics. Fledgling democracies may rely on a high degree of government economic regulation, but advanced industrial democracies combine a considerable amount of personal freedom with a free-market (though still usually regulated) economy. It is rare to find a country that is truly committed to individual political freedom that also tries to regulate the economy heavily. The philosopher Karl Marx believed that radical democracy would coexist with communally owned property, in a form of **communist democracy**, but such a system has never existed, and most real-world systems fall somewhere along the horizontal continuum shown in Figure 1.3.

THE ROLE OF THE PEOPLE

What is important about the political and economic systems we have been sorting out here is that they have direct impact on the lives of the people who live in them. So far we have given a good deal of attention to the latter parts of Lasswell's definition of politics. But easily as important as the *what* and the *how* in Lasswell's formulation is the *who*. Underlying the different political theories we have looked at are fundamental differences in the powers and opportunities possessed by everyday people.

THE PEOPLE AS SUBJECTS In authoritarian systems, the people are **subjects** of their government. They possess no rights that protect them from that government; they must do whatever the government says or face the consequences, without any other recourse. They have obligations to the state but no rights or privileges to offset those obligations. They may be winners or losers in government decisions, but they have very little control over which it may be.

THE PEOPLE AS CITIZENS Everyday people in democratic systems have a potentially powerful role to play. They are more than mere subjects; they are **citizens**, or members of a political community with rights as well as obligations. Democratic theory says that power is drawn from the people, that the people are sovereign, that they must consent to be governed, and that their government must respond to their will. In practical terms, this may not seem to mean much, since not consenting doesn't necessarily give us the right to disobey government. It does give us the option of leaving, however, and seeking a more congenial set of rules elsewhere. Subjects of authoritarian governments rarely have this freedom.

In democratic systems the rules of government can provide for all sorts of different roles for citizens. At a minimum, citizens can usually vote in periodic and free elections. They may be able to run for office, subject to certain conditions, like age or residence. They can support candidates for office, organize political groups or parties, attend meetings, write letters to officials or the press, march in protest or support of various causes, even speak out on street corners.

---

participatory democracy a theory of democracy that holds that citizens should actively and directly control all aspects of their lives

advanced industrial democracy a system in which a democratic government allows citizens a considerable amount of personal freedom and maintains a free-market (though still usually regulated) economy

communist democracy a utopian system in which property is communally owned and all decisions are made democratically

subjects individuals who are obliged to submit to a government authority against which they have no rights

citizens members of a political community with both rights and responsibilities

Theoretically, democracies are ruled by "the people," but different democracies have at times been very selective about whom they count as citizens. Beginning with our days as colonists, Americans have excluded many groups of people from citizenship: people of the "wrong" religion, income bracket, race, ethnic group, lifestyle, and gender have all been excluded from enjoying the full rights of colonial or U.S. citizenship at different times. In fact, American history is the story of those various groups fighting to be included as citizens. Just because a system is called a democracy is no guarantee that all or even most of the residents under that system possess the status of citizen.

CITIZEN RIGHTS AND RESPONSIBILITIES

Citizens in democratic systems are said to possess certain rights, or powers to act, that government cannot limit. Just what these rights are varies in different democracies, but they usually include freedoms of speech and the press, the right to assemble, and certain legal protections guaranteeing fair treatment in the criminal justice system. Almost all of these rights are designed to allow citizens to criticize their government openly without threat of retribution by that government.

Citizens of democracies also possess obligations or responsibilities to the public realm. They have the obligation to obey the law, for instance, once they have consented to the government (even if that consent amounts only to not leaving); they may also have the obligation to pay taxes, serve in the military, or sit on juries. Some theorists argue that virtuous citizens should put community interests ahead of personal interests. A less extreme version of this view holds that while citizens may go about their own business and pursue their own interests, they must continue to pay attention to their government. Participating in its decision-making process is the price of maintaining their own liberty and, by extension, the liberty of the whole. Should citizens abdicate this role by tuning out of public life, the safeguards of democracy can disappear, to be replaced with the trappings of authoritarian government. There is nothing automatic about democracy. If left unattended by nonvigilant citizens, the freedoms of democracy can be lost to an all-powerful state, and citizens can become transformed into subjects of the government they failed to keep in check.

IN YOUR OWN WORDS >> Compare different economic and political systems in terms of how power is distributed between citizens and government.

ORIGINS OF DEMOCRACY IN AMERICA
From divine right to social contract

Government in the United States is the product of particular decisions the founders made about the who,

what, and how of American politics. There was nothing inevitable about those decisions, and had the founders decided otherwise, our system would look very different indeed.

Given the world in which the founders lived, democracy was not an obvious choice for them, and many scholars argue that in some respects the system they created is not really very democratic. We can see this more clearly if we understand the intellectual heritage of the early Americans, the historical experience, and the theories about government that informed them.

THE ANCIENT GREEK EXPERIENCE

The heyday of democracy, of course, was ancient Athens, from about 500 to 300 BCE. Even Athenian democracy, as we have already indicated, was a pretty selective business. To be sure, it was rule by "the people," but "the people" was defined narrowly to exclude women, slaves, youth, and resident aliens. Athenian democracy was not built on values of equality, even of opportunity, except for the 10 percent of the population defined as citizens. With its limited number of citizens and its small area of only one thousand square miles, Athens was a participatory democracy in which all citizens could gather in one place to vote on political matters. While this privileged group indulged its passion for public activity, the vast majority of residents were required to do all the work to support them. We can see parallels to early American democracy, which restricted participation in political affairs to a relatively small number of white men.

POLITICS IN THE MIDDLE AGES

Limited as Athenian democracy was, it was positively wide open compared to most of the forms of government that existed during the Middle Ages, from roughly AD 600 to 1500. During this period, monarchs gradually consolidated their power over their subjects, and some even challenged the greatest political power of the time, the Catholic Church. Some earthly rulers claimed to take their authority from God, in a principle called the **divine right of kings**. Privileged groups in society, like the clergy or the nobles, had some rights, but ordinary individuals were quite powerless politically. Subjects of authoritarian governments and an authoritarian church, they had obligations to their rulers but no rights they could claim as their own. If a ruler is installed by divine mandate, who, after all, has any rights

> **divine right of kings** the principle that earthly rulers receive their authority from God

Democracy May Be Popular, But It's Not Easy

Although democracy has been spreading, getting there is often rough, and even deadly. Here we see a mild, civilized protest by a Scot backing the movement for more autonomy from Britain in 2012. Things were a bit more tense in the Ukrainian parliament in 2014, where a fistfight broke out between the right-wing Svoboda (Freedom) Party and communists while Russia was encouraging separatists in the countries' eastern provinces. In Egypt, protests against the entrenched regime of Syrian president Bashar al-Assad in 2011 marked the beginnings of a civil war that has claimed an estimated 220,000 lives, a third of them civilians, and with no end in sight.

against God? Education was restricted, and most people in the Middle Ages were dependent on political and ecclesiastical leaders for protection and information, as well as salvation.

THE PROTESTANT REFORMATION AND THE ENLIGHTENMENT

Between 1500 and 1700, important changes took place in the ways that people thought about politics and their political leaders. The *Protestant Reformation* led the way in the 1500s, claiming essentially that individuals could pray directly to God and receive salvation on faith alone,

without the church's involvement. In fact, Martin Luther, the German priest who spearheaded the Reformation, argued that the whole complex structure of the medieval church could be dispensed with. His ideas spread and were embraced by a number of European monarchs, leading to a split between Catholic and Protestant countries. Where the church was seen as unnecessary, it lost political as well as religious clout, and its decline paved the way for new ideas about the world.

Those new ideas came with the *Enlightenment* period of the late 1600s and 1700s, when ideas about science and the possibilities of knowledge began to blow away the shadows and cobwebs of medieval superstition. A new and refreshing understanding of human beings and their place in the

Courtesy of Christine Barbour

You don't hear college students say this every day, but Meagan Szydlowski loves politics. Her imagination was captured by her father's election to the city council. "I went to everything I could with him, like meetings, talking to newspapers and stuff, and I loved it! It was so exciting," she says of her dad's campaign.

She calls that election her "jump start"—she has been hooked on politics ever since. A term as the chair of the Illinois College Republicans followed, and internships in her local state representative's office as well as in her congressman's office—a congressman who just happened to be Dennis Hastert, then–Speaker of the House of Representatives. When we caught up with her, she was spending a summer in Washington, D.C., having been selected as one of five participants in Northern Illinois's Congressional Internship Program, working on Capitol Hill, and loving it.

Szydlowski says she always knew she was a Republican. "My dad and I talked about these things," she says. "Our conversations were always political."

So once she got to college at Northern Illinois University (NIU) and saw a sign that said, "Join the NIU College Republicans," she knew it was for her.

"I went to the first meeting, and it was perfect," she says. "It was a great way to meet people. . . . So I volunteered for everything they had and went to all the meetings." And then the chair at the time asked her to run for chair for next year. "And I was like, I've only been here a year, there's people that's been here longer than me, he's like—no, you are active, you are involved in things and I want you to do this." So she ran and she won, and spent her sophomore year running the NIU College Republicans.

Within the year she was being approached to run as chair of the statewide organization. She did some research and decided to take it on, contacting all the different campus chairs around the state and developing relationships with them. It all paid off: "We had a big convention in downtown Chicago and had a campaign and I got elected to chairman of the statewide convention." She served from January

natural world, based on human reasoning, took hold. Enlightenment philosophy said that human beings were not at the mercy of a world they could not understand, but rather they could learn the secrets of nature and, with education as their tool, harness the world to do their bidding.

Not only did scientific and economic development take off, but philosophers applied the intoxicating new theories about the potential of knowledge to the political world. Thomas Hobbes (who slightly preceded the Enlightenment) and John Locke, both English philosophers, came up with theories about how government should be established that discredited divine right. Governments are born not because God ordains them, but because life without government is "solitary, poor, nasty, brutish, and short" in Hobbes's words, and "inconvenient" in Locke's. The foundation of government is reason, not faith, and reason leads people to consent to being governed because they are better off that way.

The idea of citizenship that was born in the Enlightenment constituted another break with the past. People have freedom and rights before government exists, declared

Locke. When they decide they are better off with government than without it, they enter into a **social contract**, giving up a few of those rights in exchange for the protection of the rest of their rights by a government established by the majority. If that government fails to protect their rights, then it has broken the contract and the people are free to form a new government, or not, as they please. But the key element here is that for authority to be legitimate, citizens must *consent* to it. Note, however, that nowhere did Locke suggest that all people ought to participate in politics, or that people are necessarily equal. In fact, he was concerned mostly with the preservation of private property, suggesting that only property owners would have cause to be bothered with government because only they have something concrete to lose.

> **social contract** the notion that society is based on an agreement between government and the governed in which people agree to give up some rights in exchange for the protection of others

2008 to April 2009, also getting to sit on the national College Republicans' Executive Committee and serving as a member of the Illinois Republican Party's State Central Committee as a result.

That position involved her in Republican Party politics around the state, but maybe the best part of the job included attending the 2008 Republican National Convention in Minneapolis that September as an alternate. She had a blast. The most exciting event was the night of Sarah Palin's speech. Rudy Giuliani spoke first, and Meagan had been a big supporter of his, working on his primary campaign, so she was already fired up, and then Palin's speech electrified the crowd. While disappointed in the outcome of that election, she's philosophical, knowing that in American politics no party stays on top forever.

Meagan managed to fit a few more activities into her college career before she graduated—she studied in Oxford, England; held a variety of student government posts; and was a student research assistant for one of her professors. She is thinking graduate school might lie in her future. "I got a great education at NIU, and I want to have that influence on other people," she says.

> "DON'T THINK YOU ARE TOO YOUNG OR YOUR VOICE DOESN'T MATTER. DURING CAMPAIGNS THEY LOVE YOUNG PEOPLE AND THEIR ENERGY AND EXCITEMENT, AND YOU WILL BE WELCOMED...."

What? Not running for office herself? At least right now, Meagan is pretty sure that's not for her. The scrutiny of public officials turns her off. But whatever she ends up doing, she's confident that it will involve politics.

Here's some of her advice for fellow students:

On majoring in political science:

I'm just really, really happy that I found something I love so much, and that I've been able to turn it into my area of study and hopefully a career. I love this—political science is not just my major, it is my life—I read all the newspapers every day, check the web sites, and watch the news every day. It's pretty rewarding.

On keeping the republic:

Keeping the republic is all about involvement and interest. Don't be afraid to get involved right away—don't think you are too young or your voice doesn't matter. During campaigns they love young people and their energy and excitement, and you will be welcomed.... Alexander Hamilton in the *Federalist Papers* said, "The ingredients which constitute safety in the republican sense are a due dependence on the people, and a due responsibility." That basically sums up how important I think it is for people to be active and engaged.

Source: Meagan Szydlowski spoke with Christine Barbour in July 2010.

THINKING OUTSIDE THE BOX

Do subjects enjoy any advantages that citizens don't have?

SOURCES OF DEMOCRACY CLOSER TO HOME

While philosophers in Europe were beginning to explore the idea of individual rights and democratic governance, there had long been democratic stirrings on the founders' home continent. The Iroquois Confederacy was an alliance of five (and eventually six) East Coast Native American nations whose constitution, the "Great Law of Peace," impressed American leaders such as Benjamin Franklin with its suggestions of federalism, separation of powers, checks and balances, and consensus building. Although historians are not sure that these ideas had any direct influence on the founders' thinking about American governance, they were clearly part of the stew of ideas that the founders could dip in to, and some scholars make the case that their influence was significant.[10]

IN YOUR OWN WORDS >> Explain the historical origins of democracy in America.

>> CITIZENSHIP IN AMERICA
The tension between a self-interested nature and a public-interested ideal

For our purposes, the most important thing about these ideas about politics is that they were prevalent at the same time the American founders were thinking about how to build a new government. Locke particularly influenced the writings of James Madison, a major author of our Constitution. The founders wanted to base their new government on popular consent, but they did not want to go too far. Madison, as we will see, was particularly worried about a system that was too democratic.

DON'T BE FOOLED BY...
YOUR TEXTBOOK

Consider these two passages describing the same familiar event: Christopher Columbus's arrival in the Americas.[1]

From a 1947 textbook:

At last the rulers of Spain gave Columbus three small ships, and he sailed away to the west across the Atlantic Ocean. His sailors became frightened. They were sure the ships would come to the edge of the world and just fall off into space. The sailors were ready to throw their captain into the ocean and turn around and go back. Then, at last they all saw the land ahead. They saw low green shores with tall palm trees swaying in the wind. Columbus had found the New World. This happened on October 12, 1492. It was a great day for Christopher Columbus—and for the whole world as well.

And from a 1991 text:

When Columbus stepped ashore on Guanahani Island in October 1492, he planted the Spanish flag in the sand and claimed the land as a possession of Ferdinand and Isabella. He did so despite the obvious fact that the island already belonged to someone else—the "Indians" who gathered on the beach to gaze with wonder at the strangers who had suddenly arrived in three great, white-winged canoes. He gave no thought to the rights of the local inhabitants. Nearly every later explorer—French, English, Dutch and all the others as well as the Spanish—thoughtlessly dismissed the people they encountered. What we like to think of as the discovery of America was actually the invasion and conquest of America.

Which one of these passages is "true"? The first was the conventional textbook wisdom through the 1950s and 1960s in America. The latter reflects a growing criticism that traditional American history has been told from the perspective of history's "winners," largely white middle-class males of European background. Together they highlight the point that history does vary depending on who is telling it, and when they are telling it, and even to whom they are telling it. The telling of history is a potent political act, as one recent study explains, citing George Orwell's 1984 that "who controls the past controls the future."[2] What this means to you is that the critical vigilance we urge you to apply to all the information that regularly bombards you should be applied to your textbooks as well. And, yes, that means this textbook, too.

There is some truth to the idea that history is written by the winners, but it is also true that the winners change over time. If history was once securely in the hands of the white European male, it is now the battleground of a cultural war between those who believe the old way of telling (and teaching) history was accurate, and those who believe it left out the considerable achievements of women and minorities and masked some of the less admirable episodes of our past in order to glorify our heritage.[3] For instance, one author in the 1990s studied twelve high school history textbooks and documented areas where he felt the "history" was inaccurate or misleading. His criticism includes claims that history textbooks create heroic figures by emphasizing the positive aspects of their lives and ignoring their less admirable traits; that they create myths about the American founding that glorify Anglo-European settlers at the expense of the Native Americans and Spanish settlers who were already here; that they virtually ignore racism and its opponents, minimizing its deep and lasting effects on our culture; that they neglect the recent past; and that they idealize progress and the exceptional role America plays in the world, skipping over very real problems and issues of concern.[4]

The question of bias in textbooks is not reserved for history books; this textbook itself has a point of view. In these pages we have an interest in highlighting the issues of power and citizenship, and in focusing on the impact of the rules in American politics. In addition, we take a multicultural approach. We do not ignore or disparage the achievements of the traditional heroes of American history, but we do not think that their outstanding political accomplishments warrant ignoring the contributions, also substantial, of people who have not traditionally been politically powerful.

The fact that all textbooks have some sort of bias means you must be as critically careful in what you accept from textbook authors as you are (or should be) in what you accept from any other scholars, newspaper writers, or other media commentators.

WHAT TO WATCH OUT FOR

Here are some things you can think about when you are reading a textbook.

- **The author's point of view.** Where is the author coming from? Does he or she promote particular values or ideas? Are any points of view left out of the story being told?

- **The book's audience.** If it is a big, colorful book, it is probably aimed at a wide market. If so, what might that say about its content? If it is a smaller book with a narrower focus, who is it trying to appeal to?

- **Use of evidence.** If it backs up an argument with plenty of facts from reputable sources, then perhaps its claims are true, even if they are surprising or unfamiliar to you. Do the authors make an effort to cover both sides of an issue or a controversy? Read the footnotes, and if something troubles you, locate the primary source (the one the authors relied on) and read it yourself.

- **Your own reactions.** Did the book cause you to look at a subject in a new way? Are its conclusions surprising? Exciting? Troublesome? What is the source of your reaction? Is it intellectual, or emotional? What caused you to react this way?

1. These two passages were cited in a chart accompanying Sam Dillon, "Schools Growing Harsher in Scrutiny of Columbus," *New York Times*, October 12, 1992, 4, web version. The first paragraph is from Merlin M. Ames, *My Country* (Sacramento: California State Department of Education, 1947); the second is from John A. Garraty, *The Story of America* (New York: Holt Rinehart Winston, Harcourt Brace Jovanovich, 1991).

2. Laura Hein and Mark Seldon, eds., *Censoring History: Citizenship and Memory in Japan, Germany, and the United States* (Armonk, NY: M. E. Sharpe, 2000).

3. Frances Fitzgerald, *America Revised* (New York: Vintage Books, 1979).

4. James W. Loewen, *Lies My Teacher Told Me* (New York: New Press, 1995).

THE DANGERS OF DEMOCRACY

Enthusiastic popular participation under the government established by the Articles of Confederation—the document that tied the colonies together before the Constitution was drafted—almost ended the new government before it began. Like Locke, Madison thought government had a duty to protect property, and if people who didn't have property could get involved in politics, they might not care about protecting the property of others. Worse, they might form "factions," groups pursuing their own self-interests rather than the public interest, and even try to get some of that property for themselves. So Madison rejected notions of "pure democracy," in which all citizens would have direct power to control government, and opted instead for what he called a "republic."

A **republic**, according to Madison, differs from a democracy mainly in that it employs representation and can work in a large state. Most theorists agree that democracy is impossible in practice if there are a lot of citizens and all have to be heard from. But we do not march to Washington or phone our legislator every time we want to register a political preference. Instead, we choose representatives—members of the House of Representatives, senators, and the president—to represent our views for us. Madison thought this would be a safer system than direct participation (all of us crowding into town halls or the Capitol) because public passions would be cooled off by the process. You might be furious about health care costs when you vote for your senator, but he or she will represent your views with less anger. The founders hoped that the representatives would be older, wealthier, and wiser than the average American, and that they would be better able to make cool and rational decisions.

> **republic** a government in which decisions are made through representatives of the people

MADISON'S VISION OF CITIZENSHIP

The notion of citizenship that emerges from Madison's writings is not a very flattering one for the average American, and it is important to note that it is not the only ideal of citizenship in the American political tradition. Madison's low expectations of the American public were a reaction to an earlier tradition that had put great faith in the ability of democratic man to put the interests of the community ahead of his own, to act with what scholars call "republican virtue." According to this idea, a virtuous citizen could be trusted with the most serious of political decisions because if he (women were not citizens at that time, of course) were properly educated and kept from the influence of scandal and corruption, he would be willing to sacrifice his own advancement for the sake of the whole. His decisions would be guided not by his self-interest but by his public-interested spirit. At the time of the founding, hope was strong that, although the court of the British monarch had become corrupt beyond redemption, America was still a land where virtue could triumph over greed. In fact, for many people this was a crucial argument for American independence: severing the ties would prevent that corruption from creeping across the Atlantic and would allow the new country to keep its virtuous political nature free from the British taint.[11]

When democratic rules that relied on the virtue, or public interestedness, of the American citizen were put into effect, however, especially in the days immediately after independence, these expectations seemed to be doomed. Instead of acting for the good of the community, Americans seemed to be just as self-interested as the British had been. When given nearly free rein to rule themselves, they had no trouble remembering the rights of citizenship but ignored the responsibilities that come with it. They passed laws in state legislatures that canceled debts and contracts and otherwise worked to the advantage of the poor

AP Photo/Bebeto Matthews

Citizenship Through Volunteerism

Although Americans emphasize the individual, they don't always shun collective action. Black Girls Code (BGC) is an organization that focuses on educating girls and women of color about computer engineering and technology, a growing and high-paying field in which they are underrepresented. Here, volunteers Ashley Tolbert and Nagita Sykes help the Ostrun sisters, Jessica (11) and Jayda (7), in an app-building session at Google.

majority of farmers and debtors—and that seriously threatened the economic and political stability of the more well-to-do. It was in this context of national disappointment that Madison devised his notion of the republic. Since people had proved, so he thought, not to be activated by virtue, a government was needed that would produce virtuous results, regardless of the character of the citizens who participated in it.

IN YOUR OWN WORDS » Describe the enduring tension in the United States between self-interested human nature and public-spirited government.

AMERICAN CITIZENSHIP TODAY

Today, two competing views of citizenship still exist in the United States. One, echoing Madison, sees human nature as self-interested and holds that individual participation in government should be limited, that "too much" democracy is a bad thing. The second view continues to put its faith in the citizen's ability to act virtuously, not just for his or her own good but for the common good. President John F. Kennedy movingly evoked such a view in his inaugural

address in 1960, when he urged Americans to "ask not what your country can do for you—ask what you can do for your country." The *Snapshot of America* illustrates the kinds of citizenship activity in which Americans engage.

These opposing views of citizenship have coexisted throughout our history. Especially in times of crisis such as war or national tragedy, the second view of individual sacrifice for the public good has seemed more prominent. In the wake of September 11, 2001, citizens freely gave their time and money to help their fellow countrypeople and were more willing to join the military and volunteer for community service. At other times, and particularly at the national level of politics, the dominant view of citizenship has appeared to be one of self-interested actors going about their own business with little regard for the public good, especially at moments such as the one in 2011 when a stand-off between the president and Congress brought the nation to the brink of economic default for the sake of a political dispute. When observers claim, as they often do today, that there is a crisis of American citizenship, they usually mean that civic virtue is taking second place to self-interest as a guiding principle of citizenship.

These two notions of citizenship do not necessarily have to be at loggerheads, however. Where self-interest and public spirit meet in democratic practice is in the process of deliberation, collectively considering and evaluating goals and ideals for communal life and action. Individuals bring their own agendas and interests, but in the process of discussing them with others holding different views, parties can find common ground and turn it into a base for collective action. Conflict can erupt, too, of course, but the process of deliberation at least creates a forum from which the possibility of consensus might emerge. Scholar and journalist E. J. Dionne reflects on this possibility: "At the heart of republicanism [remember that this is not a reference to our modern parties] is the belief that self-government is not a drab necessity but a joy to be treasured. It is the view that politics is not simply a grubby confrontation of competing interests but an arena in which citizens can learn from each other and discover an 'enlightened self-interest' in common." Despite evidence of a growing American disaffection for politics, Dionne hopes that Americans will find again the "joy" in self-governance because, he warns, "A nation that hates politics will not long thrive as a democracy."[12]

SNAPSHOT OF AMERICA: HOW DO WE PARTICIPATE IN CIVIC LIFE?

How We Engage in Our Civic Life

48% of adults directly take part in a civic group or activity.

39% of adults recently contacted a government official or spoke out in a public forum via offline methods.

34% did those things via online methods.

39% of adults do political or civic activities on social networking sites.

How *Much* We Engage in Our Civic Life

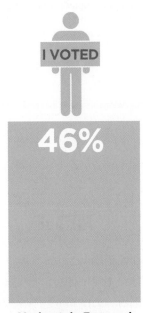

10%

15%

46%

28%

Very Engaged
(10 activities +)

Engaged
(6–10 activities)

Moderately Engaged
(1–5 activities)

Disengaged
(0 activities)

BEHIND THE NUMBERS

Some people are much more engaged in politics and society than others. It is the voice of the people. What does politics look like if most of us are like the "Disengaged" in the figure, or alternatively if the majority of us become "Very Engaged"? Who wins and who loses with different levels of civic engagement?

Source: In a 2012 survey, the Pew Research Center asked about whether people had participated in a series of 29 offline and online activities. *Aaron Smith, "Civic Engagement in the Digital Age," www.pewinternet.org/2013/04/25/civic-engagement-in-the-digital-age/. Some of the values for the figures were derived by the authors from the Pew data set.

CLUES
TO CRITICAL THINKING

Thinking Like a Political Scientist

This book is an introduction to American politics, and in a way it is also an introduction to political science. Political science is not exactly the same kind of science as biology or geology. Not only is it difficult to put our subjects (people and political systems) under a microscope to observe their behavior, but we are somewhat limited in our ability to test our theories. We cannot replay World War II to test our ideas about what caused it, for example. A further problem is our subjectivity; we are the phenomena under investigation, and so we may have stronger feelings about our research and our findings than we would, say, about cells and rocks.

These difficulties do not make a science of politics impossible, but they do mean we must proceed with caution. Even among political scientists, disagreement exists about whether a rigorous science of the political world is a reasonable goal. We can agree, however, that it is possible to advance our understanding of politics beyond mere guessing or debates about political preferences. Although we use many methods in our work (statistical analysis, mathematical modeling, case studies, and philosophical reasoning, to name only a few), what political scientists have in common is an emphasis on critical thinking about politics.

Critical thinking means challenging the conclusions of others, asking why or why not, turning the accepted wisdom upside down, and exploring alternative interpretations. It means considering the sources of information—not accepting an explanation just because someone in authority offers it, or because you have always been told that it is the true explanation, but because you have discovered independently that there are good reasons for accepting it. You may emerge from reading this textbook with the same ideas about politics that you have always had; it is not our goal to change your mind. But as a critical thinker, you will be able to back up your old ideas with new and persuasive arguments of your own, or to move beyond your current ideas to see politics in a new light.

Becoming adept at critical thinking has a number of benefits:

- We learn to be good democratic citizens. Critical thinking helps us sort through the barrage of information that regularly assails us, and it teaches us to process this information thoughtfully. Critical awareness of what our leaders are doing and the ability to understand and evaluate what they tell us is the lifeblood of democratic government.

- We are better able to hold our own in political (or other) arguments: we

---

THINKING OUTSIDE THE BOX

When, if ever, should individuals be asked to sacrifice their own good for that of their country?

THINKING CRITICALLY ABOUT AMERICAN POLITICS
How to use the themes and features in this book

Our primary goal in this book is to get you thinking critically about American politics. Critical thinking is a crucial skill to learn, no matter what training your major or career plans call for. As we discuss in the *CLUES to Critical Thinking* box in this chapter, and as we show you graphically in this chapter's *Big Picture*, *critical thinking* is the analysis and evaluation of ideas and arguments based on reason and evidence—it means digging deep into what you read and what you hear and asking tough questions. Critical thinking is what all good scholars do, and it is also what savvy citizens do.

Our analytic and evaluative tasks in this book focus on the twin themes of power and citizenship. We have adopted the classic definition of politics proposed by the late political scientist Harold Lasswell that politics is "who gets what when and how." We simplify his understanding by dropping the *when* and focusing on politics as the struggle by citizens over who gets power and resources in society and how they get them, although we do occasionally use timelines to illustrate how the struggle for power and resources can change dramatically over time.

think more logically and clearly, we are more persuasive, and we impress people with our grasp of reason and fact. There is not a career in the world that is not enhanced by critical thinking skills.

- We become much better students. The skills of the critical thinker are not just the skills of the good citizen; they are the skills of the scholar. When we read critically we figure out what is important quickly and easily, we know what questions to ask to tease out more meaning, we can decide whether what we are reading is worth our time, and we know what to take with us and what to discard.

Although it may sound a little dull and dusty, critical thinking can be a vital and enjoyable activity. When we are good at it, it empowers and liberates us. We are not at the mercy of others' conclusions and decisions. We can evaluate facts and arguments for ourselves, turning conventional wisdom upside down and exploring the world of ideas with confidence.

How does one learn to think critically?

The trick to learning how to think critically is to do it. It helps to have a model to follow, however, and we provide one in *The Big Picture*. The focus of critical thinking here is on understanding political argument. Argument in this case refers not to a confrontation or a fight, but rather to a political contention, based on a set of assumptions, supported by evidence, leading to a clear, well-developed conclusion with consequences for how we understand the world.

Critical thinking involves constantly asking questions about the arguments we read: Who has created it, what is the basic case and what values underlie it, what evidence is used to back it up, what conclusions are drawn, and what difference does the whole thing make? To help you remember the questions to ask, we have used a mnemonic device that creates an acronym from the five major steps of critical thinking. Until asking these questions becomes second nature, thinking of them as CLUES to critical thinking about American politics will help you keep them in mind. To help you develop the critical thinking habit, readings featured in each chapter of this book will provide a CLUES model for you to follow.

This is what CLUES stands for:

- Consider the source and the audience
- Lay out the argument and the underlying values and assumptions
- Uncover the evidence
- Evaluate the conclusion
- Sort out the political implications

When you read each of the *CLUES to Critical Thinking* features in the book, keep in mind *The Big Picture*'s graphic imagery that traces out this process.

Source: Adapted from the authors' "Preface to the Student," in Christine Barbour and Matthew J. Streb, eds., *Clued in to Politics: A Critical Thinking Reader in American Government*, 3rd ed. (Washington, DC: CQ Press, 2010).

ANALYSIS

Lasswell's definition of politics gives us a framework of *analysis* for this book; that is, it outlines how we break down politics into its component parts in order to understand it. Analysis helps us understand how something works, much like taking apart a car and putting it back together again helps us understand how it runs. Lasswell's definition provides a strong analytic framework because it focuses our attention on questions we can ask to figure out what is going on in politics.

Accordingly, in this book, we analyze American politics in terms of three sets of questions:

- **Who** are the parties involved? What resources, powers, and rights do they bring to the struggle?

- **What** do they have at stake? What do they stand to win or lose? Is it power, influence, position, policy, or values?

- **How** do the rules shape the outcome? Where do the rules come from? What strategies or tactics do the political actors employ to use the rules to get what they want?

If you know who is involved in a political situation, what is at stake, and how (under what rules) the conflict over resources will eventually be resolved, you will have a pretty good grasp of what is going on, and you will probably be able to figure out new situations, even when your days of taking a course in American government are far behind you. To get you in the habit of asking those questions, we have designed several features in this text explicitly to reinforce them.

As you found at the start of your reading, each chapter opens with key tasks that we expect you to be able to perform, *In Your Own Words*, to reinforce what you learn as you read, and a *What's at Stake...?* feature that analyzes a political situation in terms of what various groups of citizens

THE BIG PICTURE: HOW TO THINK CRITICALLY

Follow the CLUES to Critical Thinking

START
Your Comfort Zone

CONSIDER THE SOURCE

ASK YOURSELF

- Where does this information come from?
- Who is the author?
- Who is he or she talking to?
- How do the source and the audience shape the author's perspective?

LAY OUT THE ARGUMENT

ASK YOURSELF

- What argument is the author asking you to accept?
- If you accept the argument, what values are you also buying?
- Does the argument hold together logically?

UNCOVER THE EVIDENCE

ASK YOURSELF

- Did the author do research to back up the conclusions?
- Is there any evidence or data that is not provided that should be there?
- If there is no evidence provided, does there need to be?

I read it on the Internet. It must be true.

My parents always watch this TV station. Of course it's reliable.

OCEAN OF EXCUSES

Arguments sound like conflict. I hate conflict.

Values are private. It's rude to pry.

Logic gives me hives!

Data means numbers. Numbers freak me out.

BRIDGE to

What, do I look like some kind of detective?

Who cares? What do I need to know for the test?

SEA OF CONFUSION

There is no way to know what conclusions are right.

Ouch! Thinking is hard work. Wake me up when it's over.

How would I know?

These ideas make me really uncomfortable. They don't click with anything I think I know. Time for a beer!

I don't like this person's values. Why should I care about his or her conclusions?

ENLIGHTENMENT

WISDOM HAPPINESS

GOAL

SUCCESS BIG BUCKS

ASK YOURSELF

- What difference does this argument make to your understanding of the political world?
- How does it affect who gets what and how they get it?
- Was getting this information valuable to you or did it waste your time?

SORT OUT THE POLITICAL SIGNIFICANCE

- What's the punch line here?
- Did the author convince you that he or she is correct?
- Does accepting the conclusion to this argument require you to change any of your ideas about the world?

EVALUATE THE CONCLUSIONS

stand to win or lose. Each chapter ends with a *Let's Revisit . . .* feature, in which we return to the issues raised in the introduction, once you have the substantive material of the chapter under your belt. We also focus our analysis along the way by closing each major chapter section, beginning in Chapter 2, with a *Pause and Review: Who, What, How* feature that explicitly addresses the questions of who gets what, and how they get it, concisely summarizes what you have learned, and asks you to put your understanding *in your own words.* We reinforce the task of analysis with a *Don't Be Fooled by . . .* feature that discusses ways you can improve your critical thinking skills by analyzing (that is, taking apart) different kinds of sources of information about politics. Similarly, *CLUES to Critical Thinking* features in each chapter provide a text that is central to the substantive material you are learning to give you some practice in using the critical thinking model we described on pages 20–21. New to this edition, *The Big Picture* infographics relate the book's themes to the big concepts, big processes, and big data that will help you make sense of American politics. *Snapshots of America* provide you with a lot more data to help you understand who the American people are, and *Behind the Numbers* boxes help you dig into the question of what challenges our diversity poses for the task of governance. Finally, *Thinking Outside the Box* questions, found throughout each chapter, help you take the analysis one step further: What if the rules or the actors or the stakes were different? What would be the impact on American politics? How would it work differently?

EVALUATION

As political scientists, however, we not only want to understand *how* the system works, we also want to assess *how well* it works. A second task of critical thinking is *evaluation*, or seeing how well something measures up according to a standard or principle. We could choose any number of standards by which to evaluate American politics, but the most relevant, for most of us, is the principle of democracy and the role of citizens.

We can draw on the two traditions of self-interested and public-interested citizenship we have discussed to evaluate the powers, opportunities, and challenges presented to American citizens by the system of government under which they live. In addition to the two competing threads of citizenship in America, we can also look at the kinds of action that citizens engage in and whether they take advantage of the options available to them. For instance, citizen action might be restricted by the rules, or by popular interest, to merely choosing between competing candidates for office, as in the model of *elite democracy* described earlier. Alternatively, the rules of the system might encourage citizens to band together in groups to get what they want, as they do in *pluralist democracy.* Or the system might be open and offer highly motivated citizens a variety of opportunities to get

involved, as they do in *participatory democracy.* American democracy has elements of all three of these models, and one way to evaluate citizenship in America is to look at what opportunities for each type of participation exist and whether citizens take advantage of them.

THINKING OUTSIDE THE BOX

Why does critical thinking feel like so much more work than "regular thinking"?

To evaluate how democratic the United States is, we include in most chapters a section called *The Citizens and. . . ,* which looks at the changing concept and practice of citizenship in this country with respect to the chapter's subject matter. That feature looks at citizenship from many angles, considering the following types of questions: What role do "the people" have in American politics? How has that role expanded or diminished over time? What kinds of political participation do the rules of American politics (formal and informal) allow, encourage, or require citizens to take? What kinds of political participation are discouraged, limited, or forbidden? Do citizens take advantage of the opportunities for political action that the rules provide them? How do they react to the rules that limit their participation? How have citizens in different times exercised their rights and responsibilities? What do citizens need to do to "keep" the republic? How democratic is the United States?

To put all this in perspective, the book includes two other features that give you a more concrete idea of what citizen participation might mean on a personal level. Found in each chapter, *Profiles in Citizenship* introduce you to individuals who have committed a good part of their lives to public service and focus on what citizenship means to those people and what inspired them to take on a public role. The *Snapshots of America* provide some demographic data to bring the diversity of the American citizenry front and center and to highlight the difficulties inherent in uniting into a single nation individuals and groups with such different and often conflicting interests.

We have outlined nine features that recur throughout this book. Remember that each is designed to help you to think critically about American politics, either by analyzing power in terms of who gets what, and how, or by evaluating citizenship to determine how well we are keeping Benjamin Franklin's mandate to keep the republic. And remember that further exploration of the book's themes is always available on the companion web site at http://edge.sagepub.com/barbour7e.

IN YOUR OWN WORDS » Apply the five steps of critical thinking to this book's themes of power and citizenship in American politics.

LET'S REVISIT: WHAT'S AT STAKE...

We began this chapter looking at the problem of youthful disengagement from politics and the rise of the Occupy movement in 2011 and asked, What is at stake in taking it to the streets? Does getting oneself arrested marching across the Brooklyn Bridge count as "keeping the republic"? Since then, we have covered a lot of ground, arguing that politics is fundamental to human life and, in fact, makes life easier for us by giving us a nonviolent way to resolve disputes. We pointed out that politics is a method by which power and resources get distributed in society: politics is who gets what and how they get it. Citizens who are aware and involved stand a much better chance of getting what they want from the system than those who check out or turn away. One clear consequence when young people disregard politics, then, is that they are far less likely to get what they want from the political system. This is exactly what happens.

So what does that mean for the Occupy protesters in Zuccotti Park and across the nation? Were they really the disorganized, leaderless bunch of radicals their critics implied they were, or were they engaged in something more intentional and, perhaps, democratic?

As Occupy protester Matt Brandi says:

> The objective of Occupy was to change the direction of the national dialogue and debate. . . . By appearing in strong numbers and generating media interest (both new/social and commercial/mass), Occupy was able to influence the national dialogue. We protested about inequality and exploitation, the corruption of our government by wealth and influence; and while we did not make "demands," people began to talk about inequality, exploitation, and the corruption of democracy. The very way people talked and thought about these issues changed.

What Matt is suggesting was at stake for the Occupy protesters was, in the language of political scientists, agenda setting. A problem not defined as a problem, or not on the national agenda, cannot be solved by public action. By defining income inequality, which many of us simply took for granted, as a problem in need of a solution, Occupy did indeed change the conversation.

In fact, it is arguable that the Occupy protesters had as much or more power than they would have had if they had confined their participation to voting, since they actually helped set the choices that people faced at the ballot box. Because many Republicans and even quite a few Democrats are heavily indebted to the financial industry, neither was likely to point out the problems generated by it unless prodded by some external event or action. By doing that prodding, Occupy convinced at least the Democrats that they needed to respond to these constituent concerns.

You only needed to listen to the debates between President Obama and his 2012 Republican challenger, Mitt Romney, to see that both candidates were participating in the conversation Occupy had begun. The two disagreed on how the federal tax burden should be distributed, with the president arguing that the wealthy should pay a higher share and Romney maintaining that higher taxes would inhibit the ability of "job creators" to grow the economy. Romney's comment, caught on a video of a fundraiser, that 47 percent of Americans paid no taxes and could not be convinced to take responsibility for themselves only underscored the two parties' different views of income inequality.

© Nancy Siesel/Demotix/Corbis

Taking It to the Flood-Ravaged Streets?

Occupy Wall Street protests focused national attention on income inequality and earned the participants jeers as slackers who would rather lay around Zuccotti Park and complain than work. But when Hurricane Sandy wiped out much of the New York/New Jersey coast in October 2012, the reconstituted movement—now called Occupy Sandy—was among the first and most vigorous responders. Here, Occupy volunteers provide much needed labor in Rockaway Beach, Queens, two weeks after a fourteen-foot storm swell devastated the community.

By the time the ballots were counted on November 7, the answer to whether young people would turn out in 2012 as they had in 2008 was answered. Early estimates were that youth turnout had gone up—19 percent of the electorate was eighteen to twenty-nine years of age, and they split for Obama 60 to 36 percent. But the commitment to more conventional forms of participation did not mean the spirit of Occupy had been lost. When Hurricane Sandy hit the East Coast just days before the election, the movement, reborn as Occupy Sandy, was at the forefront of the relief efforts. Without the cumbersome bureaucracy of organizations like the Red Cross and the Federal Emergency Management Agency (FEMA), Occupy Sandy was lighter on its feet and better able to get supplies to those in need.[13]

Perhaps the lesson of the Occupy movement, and the answer to the question of what is at stake in taking it to the streets, is that there is no one-size-fits-all answer to keeping the republic. Voting, indeed, is an essential part of the equation. Knowing how dependent he was on the votes of young people, President Obama was attentive to issues like student loans and Obamacare regulations that allowed those under twenty-six to stay on their parents' health insurance. And having seen, for two elections in a row, that the youth turnout can be decisive, Republicans will also likely try to be more youth-friendly in their policy positions.

But Occupy highlights the value of grassroots action, and the power of stepping outside the system to put pressure on the status quo to respond to unmet and even previously unvoiced needs. It might not have been what Benjamin Franklin had in mind, but occupying the republic may very well be another means of keeping it.

TO SUM UP

for CQ Press

Sharpen your skills with **SAGE edge** at **http://edge.sagepub.com/ barbour7e. SAGE edge for students** provides a personalized approach to help you accomplish your coursework goals in an easy-to-use learning environment.

REVIEW

What Is Politics?

Politics may appear to be a grubby, greedy pursuit, filled with scandal and backroom dealing. In fact, despite its shortcomings and sometimes shabby reputation, politics is an essential means for resolving differences and determining how power and resources are distributed in society. Politics is about who gets power and resources in society— and how they get them.

Government, on the other hand, is the system established for exercising authority over a group of people. In the United States the government is embodied in the Constitution and the institutions set up by the Constitution. Government is shaped not only by politics but also by economics, which is concerned specifically with the distribution of wealth and society's resources.

politics (p. 3)
power (p. 3)
social order (p. 3)
legitimate (p. 4)
government (p. 4)
authority (p. 4)
rules (p. 5)
institutions (p. 5)
economics (p. 5)
capitalist economy (p. 5)
laissez-faire capitalism (p. 6)
regulated capitalism (p. 6)
procedural guarantees (p. 6)
socialist economy (p. 6)
substantive guarantees (p. 7)
social democracy (p. 7)

Political Systems and the Concept of Citizenship

Political systems dictate how power is distributed among leaders and citizens, and these systems take many forms. Authoritarian governments give ultimate power to the state. Nonauthoritarian systems, like democracy, place power largely in the hands of the people. Democracy is based on the principle of popular sovereignty, giving the people the ultimate power to govern. The meaning of citizenship is key to the definition of democracy. Citizens are believed to have rights protecting them from government as well as responsibilities to the public realm.

authoritarian government (p. 9)
totalitarian (p. 9)
authoritarian capitalism (p. 9)
anarchy (p. 10)
democracy (p. 10)
popular soveignty (p. 10)
elite democracy (p. 10)
pluralist democracy (p. 10)
participatory democracy (p. 11)
advanced industrial democracy (p. 11)
communist democracy (p. 11)
subjects (p. 11)
citizens (p. 11)

Origins of Democracy in America

Democracy was not an obvious choice for the founders—their decisions were based on their own intellectual heritage and the historical experiences that informed them.

divine right of kings (p. 12)
social contract (p. 14)
republic (p. 17)

American Citizenship Today

At the time of our nation's founding, two competing views of citizenship emerged. The first view, articulated by James Madison, sees the citizen as fundamentally self-interested; this view led the founders to fear too much citizen participation in government. The second view puts faith in citizens' ability to act for the common good, to put their obligation to the public ahead of their own self-interest. Both views are still alive and well today, and we can see evidence of both sentiments at work in political life.

Thinking Critically About American Politics

In this textbook, we rely on two underlying themes to analyze how our American political system works, and to evaluate how well it works. The first theme is power, and how it functions in our system: we look at political events in term of who the actors are, what they have to win or lose, and how the rules shape the way these actors engage in their struggle. The second theme is citizenship: specifically, how diverse citizens participate in political life to improve their own individual situations and to promote the interests of the community at large. Throughout this book, we will evaluate citizenship carefully as a means to determine how well the American system is working.

Delve into democracy.
The Kettering Foundation is a nonprofit organization devoted to the study of democracy. Check out their website for informative videos, news coverage, and podcasts focused on the question of what it takes to make democracy work as it should. Even better, follow them on social media to stay on top of what's happening in democracy as events unfold.

Get up to speed on politics.
A great place to start is **Politix .com**, a youth-oriented, interactive political news and discussion site that invites participants to test their political knowledge with online quizzes, to register their opinions in online polls, and to engage in debates about current events. Want to go further? The **American Association of State College and Universities Political Engagement Project** is focused on increasing the level of civic engagement among students at public colleges and universities. Visit their site to see what they do, how they do it—and whether your school is involved.

Volunteer!
Get involved with your community—or any community!—by devoting your time and talent to a cause you believe in. **Volunteermatch.org** connects people with organizations, nonprofits, and people in need.

Rethink your fiction.
Political themes are the backbone of dystopian novels like George Orwell's **1984,** Suzanne Collins's **Hunger Games trilogy**, and Aldous Huxley's **Brave New World**. Try reading (or rereading) these popular stories (or watching their film adaptations) armed with what you now know about politics, and consider what each has to say about the ways in which power can be distributed, abused, and perhaps even challenged.

ENGAGE

Dalton, Russell J. 2009. The Good Citizen: How a Younger Generation Is Reshaping American Politics, revised ed. Washington, DC: CQ Press. Dalton shows that trends in participation and policy priorities reflect a younger generation that is more engaged, more tolerant, and more supportive of social justice, leading to new norms of citizenship.

Lasswell, Harold. 1936. *Politics: Who Gets What, When, and How.* New York: McGraw-Hill. Lasswell's classic work on politics, originally published in 1911, lays out the definition of politics that is used throughout this textbook.

Van Belle, Douglas A., and Kenneth M. Mash. 2016. *A Novel Approach to Politics: Introducing Political Science Through Books, Movies, and Popular Culture,* 4th ed. Washington, DC: CQ Press. Drawing on examples from popular culture and the media, the authors explain essential political theory in a way that will entertain and enlighten.

***Erin Brockovich.* 2000.** A woman down on her luck manages to find a job as a legal assistant and works toward the good of the community by exposing a power company that has been dumping toxic waste. This popular film exposes what's at stake when an everyday citizen takes an interest and gets involved.

2

AMERICAN CITIZENS AND POLITICAL CULTURE

IN YOUR OWN WORDS   After you've read this chapter, you will be able to

» Analyze the role of immigration in American politics and what it takes to become a U.S. citizen.

» Explain how shared core values define the United States as a country and a culture.

» Describe the political debates that drive partisan divisions in American politics.

» Describe the gap between the American democratic ideal and its practice.

WHAT'S AT STAKE...IN PASSING IMMIGRATION REFORM?

IT LOOKED LIKE THE BIGGEST LEGISLATIVE no-brainer on earth. The Republicans had lost the 2012 presidential election by almost five million votes and the powers that be in the party were gathered for what one of them called an "autopsy" on the results. One of their conclusions: immigration reform was central to a future presidential win for the party.

After all, Mitt Romney had won the votes of only 27 percent of Latinos—a group that was 10 percent of the electorate in 2012 and sure to get bigger. Immigration reform is an important issue to the Latino community but, unfortunately for the Republican Party, blocking any reform that attempts to do other than return the estimated twelve million undocumented immigrants in the United States to their homes is a major issue for the Republican base, especially those identifying as Tea Partiers. To get the presidential nomination, Romney had run so far to the right that he was never able to find his way back to the middle. The party leadership, meeting after the election to assess the damage, determined that that had to change.

Their report said, in part, "we must embrace and champion comprehensive immigration reform. If we do not, our Party's appeal will continue to shrink to its core constituencies only. . . . In essence, Hispanic voters tell us

our Party's position on immigration has become a litmus test, measuring whether we are meeting them with a welcome mat or a closed door."[1]

Other Republicans echoed that message. Just a few days after the election, Speaker of the House John Boehner, previously lukewarm on the chances of getting his caucus to tackle immigration reform, said, "This issue has been around far too long and while I believe it's important for us to secure our borders and to enforce our laws, I think a comprehensive approach is long overdue, and I'm confident that the president, myself, others, can find the common ground to take care of this issue once and for all."[2]

Business leaders were on board too. Early in 2013 they had met with labor groups to hammer out agreement on a guest worker program with Grover Norquist, the head of Americans for Tax Reform, and other Republican heavyweights, all of whom were concerned that without reform, the party's 2016 presidential prospects would be grim.

Democrats were eager to agree and in June 2013, the Senate, with a bipartisan majority scarcely heard of in these polarized times, passed an extensive immigration reform bill with a vote of 68–32.[3] The bill provided for tougher

A Dream That Unites, Divides

A student lights a candle at a rally for undocumented "Dreamers" in Santa Ana, California. Core American values like democracy, freedom, and equality have lured immigrants to American shores for more than two centuries. But for undocumented young people who were brought to this country as children, American citizenship remains elusive. The debate over their fate is a divisive one in American politics.

border security measures but also for a thirteen-year path to citizenship for those in this country without proper documentation. The ball was in Speaker Boehner's court.

And there it sat. Any path to citizenship for those who had initially broken the law by their arrival in this country was too much for conservative Republicans who had scuttled Boehner's legislative plans many times before. The House determined to write its own bill but nothing happened.

By year's end, supporters of immigration reform were beginning to despair. Still, Boehner kept hope alive that the House would pass something until it became obvious in late summer of 2014, with an election on the horizon, that it would not. President Obama was so frustrated that one of his biggest goals was still unmet that he single-handedly deferred the deportation of young undocumented immigrants who had been brought to this country as small children. He declared that he would take further executive action to reform immigration laws on his own. Yet by the time fall rolled around, at the request of fellow Democrats running for reelection, he had not done so either.

How had it come to this? How can immigration reform go from a win-win sure thing to a no-win risk? Had the Republicans changed their minds about the importance of immigration reform or were they committing electoral

suicide? And why weren't the Democrats ready to pick up the torch? What was at stake for all these actors in passing—or not passing—immigration reform? **«**

OVER the years, American schoolchildren have grown up hearing two conflicting stories about who we are as a nation. The first, that we are a melting pot, implies that the United States is a vast cauldron into which go many cultures and ethnicities, all of which are boiled down into some sort of homogenized American stew. The other story, that we are a multicultural nation, tells us that each cultural, ethnic, and religious identity should be preserved and celebrated, lest its distinctive nature be lost. Reality, as is often the case, falls somewhere between these two competing images of the American people.

The rich diversity of the American people is one of the United States' greatest strengths, combining talents, tradition, culture, and custom from every corner of the world. But our diversity, far from being uniformly celebrated, has also contributed to some of the nation's deepest conflicts. We cannot possibly understand the drama that is American politics without an in-depth look at who the actors are: the *who* in many ways shapes the *what* and *how* of politics.

Our politics—what we want from government and how we try to get it—stems from who we are. Who Americans are—where they have come from and what they have brought with them, what their lives look like and how they spend their time and money, what they believe and how they act on those beliefs—helps determine what they choose to fight for politically and how they elect to carry out the fight. It is critically important, as we approach the study of American politics, that we understand who American citizens are: where their roots lie, what their lives are like, and what sorts of things they need and value.

Since we cannot, of course, meet all the Americans who are out there, we settle for the next best thing: we use statistics to provide us with relevant details about a large and unwieldy population. Throughout this book we use statistics, in the form of charts and graphs, to examine the demographic trends that shape our national culture—political and otherwise—in a feature called *Snapshots of America*. We'll use this information not only to understand better who we are but also to consider how the characteristics, habits, and lives of real people relate to the political issues that shape our society. (Be sure to read *Don't Be Fooled by… Visual Presentations of Data* for a discussion of the uses and limits of statistics in politics. It will serve you well as you read this book.)

In this chapter's *Snapshots of America*, you will see that our population is aging gradually; older people demand more money for pensions and nursing home care, and they compete for scarce resources with younger families, who

© Cindy Yamanaka/ZUMA Press/Corbis

want better schools and health care for children. You will see that the white population in the United States will soon be outnumbered by ethnic and racial minority populations that traditionally support affirmative action and other policies (less popular with whites) designed to raise them up from the lower end of the socioeconomic scale. Our population is in constant flux, and every change in the make-up of the people brings a change in what we try to get from government and how we try to get it.

As you look at these depictions of the American people and American life, try to imagine the political problems that arise from such incredible diversity. How can a government represent the interests of people with such varied backgrounds, needs, and preferences? How does who we are affect what we want and how we go about getting it?

WHO IS AN AMERICAN?
Native-born and naturalized citizens

In Chapter 1 we said that citizenship exacts obligations from individuals and also confers rights on them, and that the American concept of citizenship contains both self-interested and public-spirited elements. But citizenship is not only a prescription for how governments ought to treat residents and how those residents ought to act; it is also a very precise legal status. A fundamental element of democracy is not just the careful specification of the rights and obligations of citizenship but also an equally careful legal description of just who is a citizen and how that status can be acquired by immigrants who choose to switch their allegiance to a new country. In this section we look at the legal definition of American citizenship and at the long history of immigration that has shaped our body politic.

AMERICAN CITIZENSHIP

American citizens are usually born, not made. If you are born in any of the fifty states or in most overseas U.S. territories, such as Puerto Rico or Guam, you are an American citizen, whether your parents are Americans or not. This follows the principle of international law called *jus soli*, which means literally "the right of the soil." The exceptions to this rule in the United States are children born to foreign diplomats serving in the United States and children born on foreign ships in U.S. waters. These children would not be considered U.S. citizens. According to another legal principle, *jus sanguinis* ("the right by blood"), if you are born outside the United States to American parents, you are also an American citizen (or you can become one if you are adopted by American parents). Interestingly, if you are born in the United States but one of your parents holds citizenship in another country, depending on that country's laws, you may be able to hold dual citizenship. Most countries, including the United States, require that a child with dual citizenship declare allegiance to one country on turning age eighteen. It is worth noting that requirements for U.S. citizenship, particularly as they affect people born outside the country, have changed frequently over time.

So far, citizenship seems relatively straightforward. But as we know, the United States since before its birth has been attractive to **immigrants**, who are citizens or subjects of another country who come here to live and work. The *Big Picture* in this chapter helps us to understand some characteristics of the foreign-born population of the United States. Today there are strict limitations on the numbers of immigrants who may legally enter the country. There are also strict rules governing the criteria for entry. If immigrants come here legally on permanent resident visas—that is, if they follow the rules and regulations of the U.S. Citizenship and Immigration Services (USCIS)—they may be eligible to apply for citizenship through a process called **naturalization**.

THINKING OUTSIDE THE BOX

Should it be possible to lose one's citizenship under any circumstances?

> **immigrants** citizens or subjects of one country who move to another country to live or work
>
> **naturalization** the legal process of acquiring citizenship for someone who has not acquired it by birth

J.B. Handelsman/The New Yorker Collection/ The Cartoon Bank

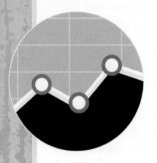

DON'T BE FOOLED BY...
VISUAL PRESENTATIONS OF DATA

When we talk about American politics, we frequently talk about large numbers—of people, of votes, of incomes, of ages, of policy preferences or opinions. Thinking about thousands, millions, even billions of things can boggle the mind, but charts, graphs, and other visual depictions can help us think about numbers and numerical relationships without getting tangled up in the sheer size of the quantities involved. As savvy consumers of American politics, we need to be able to sort through the barrage of numbers that are thrown at us daily, and the ways in which they are displayed.

Data and Statistics

Political scientists, in fact all scientists, are focused on the empirical results of their research. When those data are in numerical or quantitative terms, like how many people say they voted for Democrats or Republicans, or how much of the federal budget is devoted to various programs like welfare and education, the result can look like one gigantic, unorganized mass of numbers.

To help bring order to the chaos, scientists use statistical analysis. Whereas a statistic, such as the population of the United States, is a numerical fact, statistics is the science of collecting, organizing, and interpreting numerical data. At its simplest, statistics allows us to calculate the mean, or average, of a bunch of numbers, and to see how far individual datapoints fall away from, or deviate from, the mean. For instance, instead of having to deal with income figures for all Americans, we can talk about the average income, and we can compare averages for different groups, and make intelligent observations about the distribution of income in the United States. When we do this, the numbers start to take on shape and organization, and we can talk about them in a useful way.

Statistical techniques allow us to compare groups and characteristics of groups with one another and over time, to discern relationships among characteristics that we might not otherwise be able to see, to look at the distribution of characteristics across a population, and to see how a part relates to the whole group. Although statistics can be used in almost any discipline, from economics to medicine, it is interesting to note that the word comes from the Latin for "state" or "government." Statistics might have been tailor-made for investigating political puzzles.

Displaying the Data

Scientists need a way to show other people the data they have gathered and analyzed. It is here that a picture can often be worth a thousand words. Among the most common ways to display data are tables, which present data in columns and rows; bar charts, which compare data across various categories; line graphs, which typically track changes over time; and pie charts, which break down a total number, such as a population or a budget, by percentage to show how the whole is divided proportionally. All of these types of graphs are used frequently by scientists, journalists, and, yes, by textbook authors, to display data quickly and clearly. Increasingly, data-driven artists are offering attractive displays of quantitative information in rich infographics that combine statistics, graphs, tables, and text with inviting and innovative art. The *Big Picture* and *Snapshots of America* features in this book are examples of such infographics, and chances are you've seen lots more in the media and on the Web.

WHAT TO WATCH OUT FOR

Charts and graphs are a boon to our ability to communicate information about large numbers, but they can also be easily manipulated. Some common distortions include the following:

- **Altering the baseline.** When looking at a line graph or bar chart, take time to scrutinize the way numbers are plotted on the axes. Typically the numbers that go up the vertical axis begin at zero and move up at regularly scheduled intervals. The real relationship between the numbers on each axis can be disguised, however, if the baseline is not zero—especially if it is below zero. Do not take for granted that you know what the baseline is until you check. Check the scale or timeframe plotted on the axes, too. A set of numbers (for example, the Dow Jones Industrial Average) can look very erratic over a series of hours, days, or even weeks; but when plotted over years, patterns seem more predictable and far less volatile.

- **Using misleading averages or means.** The mean, calculated by adding up a series of values and dividing by the number of values, generally gives us a good midrange estimate. However, sometimes the outlying values, the ones at the top or bottom, are so far from the middle that they skew the mean, giving a false impression of what the "average" is. When this happens, we often prefer to use the median, calculated by arranging all the values numerically and then finding the one in the physical middle.

- **Breaking down data selectively.** Statisticians typically break down data into chunks for comparison: you might divide a population into five or seven or ten segments, to see how they differ in terms of earnings, grades, and so on. But the way those data are chunked can skew the graphic one way or another. For example, when looking at the tax burden of Americans by income, the data will look dramatically different if you break down the set into five even segments (or quintiles) than it will if you look at much smaller segments, or if you plot data for outliers (the super rich and the super poor) separately from others in the sample.

- **Not showing populations as a percentage of the base.** Often charts and graphs will show growth in the numbers of a group without relating the group to the population as a whole. Always ask yourself if a graph removes data from some context that would help you understand it better.

- **Not using constant dollars.** Nominal dollar values cannot be compared over time because inflation means that a dollar today buys far less than it did, say, fifty years ago. Put simply, $1.00 in 1980 had the purchasing power of $2.89 in 2014. So, for an accurate comparison, constant dollars—that is, dollars that have been adjusted for changing price levels over time—should always be used. If the values have not been adjusted, think twice about the graph. (See figure on the minimum wage.)

- **Making poor design choices.** Sometimes infographic and data visualization designers make aesthetic choices that may skew the perception of particular data. The way in which color is used, the choice of chart or graph type, and the inclusion of additional effects or visual ornamentation can imply meaning beyond what the numbers actually say. Any one or a combination of these can intentionally or unintentionally influence the perception of that data when they are visualized. In accounting terms, for example, the color red denotes debt, whereas the color black denotes a favorable balance; using those colors in certain graphs may convey an unintended meaning.

- **Implying causality where none exists.** The fact that two variables shift at the same time does not mean that one has caused the other. Causality is very difficult to show, and generally the best we can do is to show that two things are correlated. Beware of cause-and-effect claims.

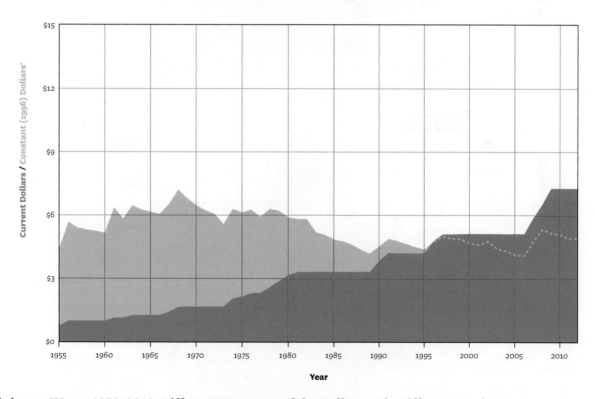

Minimum Wage, 1970–2010: Different Measures of the Dollar Imply Different Stories

Nominal dollars are the actual dollar amount Congress sets for the minimum wage. Constant dollars are nominal dollars adjusted to reflect purchasing power (set in terms of a base year, here 2010). Notice that the minimum wage goes up in fits and starts as Congress has periodically made adjustments, suggesting an increasing minimum wage (if one relies on nominal dollars). However, those adjustments did not keep up with inflation. Thus, when measured in terms of purchasing power (constant dollars), the minimum wage has been allowed to drop rather dramatically.

SNAPSHOT OF AMERICA: WHO ARE WE AND WHO WILL WE BE BY 2050?

■ White (Non-Hispanic)   ■ Hispanic   ■ Black   ■ Asian

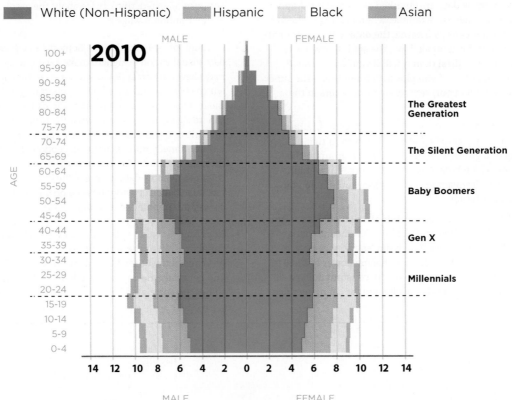

2010

MALE   FEMALE

AGE
100+
95-99
90-94
85-89
80-84
75-79
70-74
65-69
60-64
55-59
50-54
45-49
40-44
35-39
30-34
25-29
20-24
15-19
10-14
5-9
0-4

14 12 10 8 6 4 2 0 2 4 6 8 10 12 14

The Greatest Generation

The Silent Generation

Baby Boomers

Gen X

Millennials

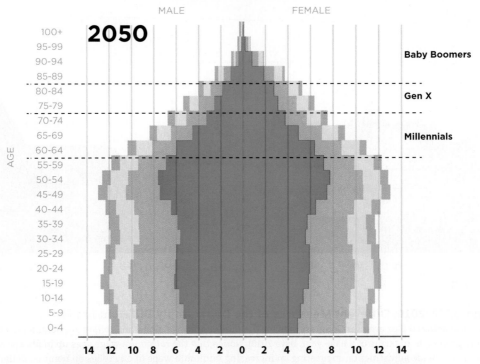

2050

MALE   FEMALE

AGE
100+
95-99
90-94
85-89
80-84
75-79
70-74
65-69
60-64
55-59
50-54
45-49
40-44
35-39
30-34
25-29
20-24
15-19
10-14
5-9
0-4

14 12 10 8 6 4 2 0 2 4 6 8 10 12 14

Baby Boomers

Gen X

Millennials

BEHIND THE NUMBERS

By 2050 most of the Baby Boomers will have died, and today's younger generations will be collecting Social Security. And the working population will be predominately non-white. What will this increasing racial and ethnic diversity mean for American politics? What do you think the two political parties will look like in 2050?

Source: Pew Research Center Social & Demographic Trends, U.S. Population Projections: 2005–2050.

NONIMMIGRANTS

Many people who come to the United States do not come as legal permanent residents. The USCIS refers to these people as nonimmigrants. Some arrive seeking **asylum**, or protection. These are political **refugees**, who are allowed into the United States if they face or are threatened with persecution because of their race, religion, nationality, membership in a particular social group, or political opinions. Not everyone who feels threatened is given legal refugee status, however. The USCIS requires that the fear of persecution be "well founded," and it is itself the final judge of a well-founded fear. Refugees may become legal permanent residents after they have lived here continuously for one year (although there are annual limits on the number who may do so). At that time, they can begin accumulating the in-residence time required to become a citizen, if they wish to do so.

Other people who may come to the United States legally but without official permanent resident status include visitors, foreign government officials, students, international representatives, temporary workers, members of foreign media, and exchange visitors. These people are expected to return to their home countries and not take up permanent residence in the United States.

Undocumented immigrants have arrived here by avoiding the USCIS regulations, usually because they would not qualify for one reason or another. American laws have become increasingly harsh with respect to undocumented immigrants, but people continue to come anyway. Many undocumented immigrants act like "citizens," obeying the laws, paying taxes, and sending their children to school. Nonetheless, some areas of the country, particularly those near the Mexican-American border, like Texas and California, often have serious problems brought on by undocumented immigration. Even with border controls to regulate the number of new arrivals, communities can find themselves swamped with new residents, often poor and unskilled, looking for a better life. Because their children must be educated and they themselves may be entitled to receive social services, they can pose a significant financial burden on those communities without necessarily increasing the available funds. Although many undocumented immigrants pay taxes, many also work off the books, meaning they do not contribute to the tax base. Furthermore, most income taxes are federal, and federal money is distributed back to states and localities to fund social services based on the population count in the census.

Since undocumented immigrants are understandably reluctant to come forward to be counted, their communities are typically underfunded in that respect as well.

Even people who are not legal permanent residents of the United States have rights and responsibilities here, just as when we travel in other countries we have rights and obligations there. The rights that immigrants enjoy are primarily legal protection. Not only are they entitled to due process in the courts (guarantee of a fair trial, right to a lawyer, and so on), but the U.S. Supreme Court has ruled that it is illegal to discriminate against immigrants in the United States.[4] Nevertheless, their rights are limited. They cannot, for instance, vote in our national elections (although some localities, in the hopes of integrating immigrants into their communities, allow them to vote in local elections[5]) or decide to live here permanently without permission (which may or may not be granted). In addition, immigrants, even legal ones, are subject to the decisions of the USCIS, which is empowered by Congress to exercise authority in immigration matters.

U.S. IMMIGRATION POLICY

Immigration law is made by Congress (with the approval of the president) and implemented by the federal agency we discussed in the previous section, the U.S. Citizenship and Immigration Services. The 1996 Illegal Immigration Reform and Immigrant Responsibility Act had granted the agency, then known as the Immigration and Naturalization Service (INS), considerable power to make nonappealable decisions at the border that can result in the deportation of an immigrant who may have quite innocently violated an immigration rule and then cannot reenter the country for five years. In the wake of September 11, 2001, security issues have come to play a central role in deciding who may enter the country, and new legislation took the INS out of the Department of Justice, where it was formerly located, renamed it the U.S. Citizenship and Immigration Services, and placed it under the jurisdiction of the newly formed Department of Homeland Security.

WHOM TO ADMIT No country, not even the huge United States, can manage to absorb every impoverished or threatened global resident who wants a better or safer life. Deciding whom to admit is a political decision—like all political decisions, one that results in winner and losers. Every job given to an immigrant means one less job for an American citizen, and jobs are just the sort of scarce resource over which political battles are fought. If times are good and unemployment is low, newcomers, who are often willing to do jobs Americans reject in prosperous times, may be welcomed with open arms, but when the economy hits hard times, immigration can become a bitter issue among jobless Americans. Immigrants, especially the very young and the very old, are also large consumers of social services and community resources. Immigrants do

---

asylum protection or sanctuary, especially from political persecution

refugees individuals who flee an area or a country because of persecution on the basis of race, nationality, religion, group membership, or political opinion

BIG PICTURE: HOW IMMIGRATION HAS CHANGED THE FACE OF AMERICA

Immigration to the U.S. reflects both historical events outside our borders and policy decisions made within them. Each wave of arrivals triggered public anxiety about changing demographics, prompting policies that limited the number of incoming immigrants and often targeted specific ethnic or racial groups. We may be a nation of immigrants, but immigrants quickly assimilate, often closing the door behind them.

Immigrants, Their Children, and Everyone Else

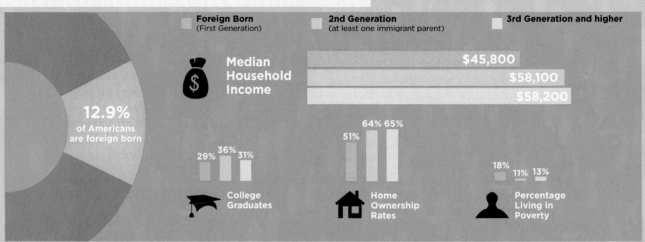

Foreign Born (First Generation)   **2nd Generation** (at least one immigrant parent)   **3rd Generation and higher**

12.9% of Americans are foreign born

Median Household Income
$45,800
$58,100
$58,200

College Graduates
29%   36%   31%

Home Ownership Rates
51%   64%   65%

Percentage Living in Poverty
18%   11%   13%

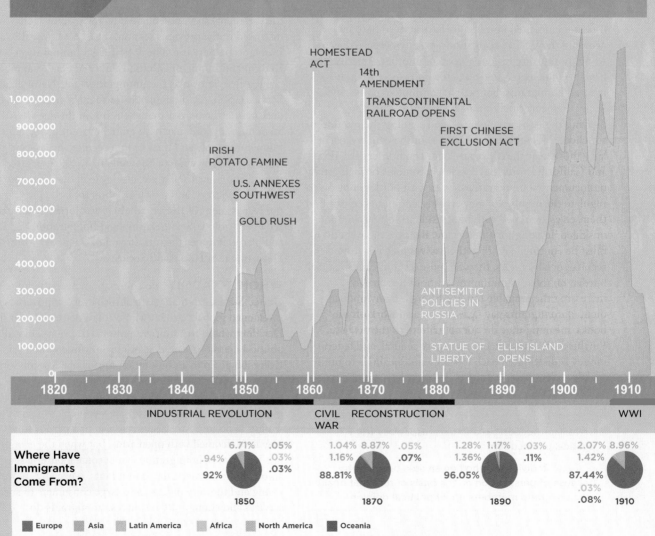

HOMESTEAD ACT
14th AMENDMENT
TRANSCONTINENTAL RAILROAD OPENS
FIRST CHINESE EXCLUSION ACT
IRISH POTATO FAMINE
U.S. ANNEXES SOUTHWEST
GOLD RUSH
ANTISEMITIC POLICIES IN RUSSIA
STATUE OF LIBERTY
ELLIS ISLAND OPENS

1,000,000
900,000
800,000
700,000
600,000
500,000
400,000
300,000
200,000
100,000
0

1820   1830   1840   1850   1860   1870   1880   1890   1900   1910

INDUSTRIAL REVOLUTION   CIVIL WAR   RECONSTRUCTION   WWI

Where Have Immigrants Come From?

1850: 6.71%, .05%, .94%, .03%, .03%, 92%
1870: 1.04%, 8.87%, 1.16%, .05%, .07%, 88.81%
1890: 1.28%, 1.17%, 1.36%, .03%, .11%, 96.05%
1910: 2.07%, 8.96%, 1.42%, .03%, .08%, 87.44%

■ Europe   ■ Asia   ■ Latin America   ■ Africa   ■ North America   ■ Oceania

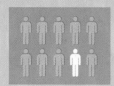

Nine out of ten Hispanic children in the United States under the age of 18 were born in the United States and are citizens.

40%
FORTUNE 500

About 40% of Fortune 500 firms were founded by immigrants or their children.

1/4
TECH STARTUPS

A quarter of high-tech startups have an immigrant founder.

Foreign-Born Population as a Percentage of State Population: 2010

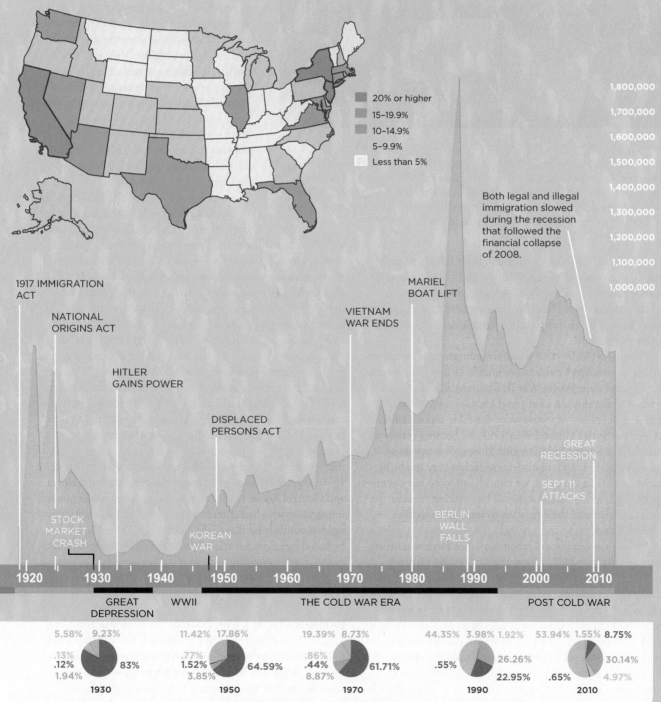

Legend:
- 20% or higher
- 15–19.9%
- 10–14.9%
- 5–9.9%
- Less than 5%

Both legal and illegal immigration slowed during the recession that followed the financial collapse of 2008.

1,800,000
1,700,000
1,600,000
1,500,000
1,400,000
1,300,000
1,200,000
1,100,000
1,000,000

1917 IMMIGRATION ACT

NATIONAL ORIGINS ACT

HITLER GAINS POWER

DISPLACED PERSONS ACT

STOCK MARKET CRASH

KOREAN WAR

VIETNAM WAR ENDS

MARIEL BOAT LIFT

BERLIN WALL FALLS

SEPT 11 ATTACKS

GREAT RECESSION

1920   1930   1940   1950   1960   1970   1980   1990   2000   2010

GREAT DEPRESSION   WWII   THE COLD WAR ERA   POST COLD WAR

	1930	1950	1970	1990	2010
	5.58% 9.23%	11.42% 17.86%	19.39% 8.73%	44.35% 3.98% 1.92%	53.94% 1.55% 8.75%
	.13%	.77%	.86%		
	.12% 83%	1.52% 64.59%	.44% 61.71%	.55% 26.26%	.65% 30.14%
	1.94%	3.85%	8.87%	22.95%	4.97%

Source: Pew Research Center, "Latino Children: A Majority Are U.S. Born Offspring of Immigrants" May 28, 2009
www.pewhispanic.org/2009/05/28/ii-the-legal-and-generational-status-of-hispanic-children/.

© Mike Segar/Reuters/Corbis

To Support and Defend

Immigrants may serve in the U.S. military regardless of their citizenship. When becoming naturalized, they renounce their former home and vow to "support and defend" the United States "against all enemies." Here, foreign-born military personnel congratulate one another after taking the oath of allegiance during a naturalization ceremony held at the Statue of Liberty in 2011.

contribute to the economy through their labor and their taxes, but because they are distributed disproportionately throughout the population, some areas find their social service systems more burdened than others, and immigration can be a much more controversial issue in places where immigrants settle.

Nations typically want to admit immigrants who can do things the country's citizens are unable or unwilling to do. During and after World War II, when the United States wanted to develop a rocket program, German scientists with the necessary expertise were desirable immigrants. When the Soviet Union fell in 1991, we became concerned that former Soviets familiar with Moscow's weapons of mass destruction and other defense technology might be lured to work in countries we considered to be our enemies. In 1992 Congress passed a special law making it easier for such scientists and their families to immigrate to the United States.

At times in our history when our labor force was insufficient for the demands of industrialization and railroad building and when western states wanted larger populations, immigrants were welcomed. Today, immigration law allows for temporary workers to come to work in agriculture when our own labor force falls short or is unwilling to work for low wages. As a rule, however, our official immigration policy expects immigrants to be skilled and financially stable so that they do not become a burden on the American social services system. Remember that politics is

about how power and resources are distributed in society; who gets to consume government services is a hotly contested issue.

Whether motivated by cultural stereotypes, global events, or domestic economic circumstances, Americans have decided at times that we have allowed "enough" immigrants to settle here, or that we are admitting too many of the "wrong" kind of immigrants, and we have encouraged politicians to enact restrictions. When this happens, immigrants are scapegoated for the nation's problems and demonized as a threat to American culture. From 1882 to 1943, legislation outlawed Chinese immigration because westerners saw it as an economic and a cultural threat. Similarly, reacting to the large numbers of southern and eastern Europeans who began flooding into the country in the very late 1800s and early 1900s, legislation in the 1920s limited immigration by individual nationalities to a small percentage of the total number of immigrants already in residence from each country. This quota system favored the northern and western nationalities, seen as more desirable immigrants, who had arrived in larger numbers earlier, allowing Great Britain and Ireland to send 65,721 immigrants yearly, for instance, but Italy only 5,802.[6] As we will see, today's debate over undocumented immigration taps into some of the same emotions and passions as earlier efforts to limit legal immigration.

Congress abolished the existing immigration quota system in 1965 with the Immigration and Nationality Act. This act doubled the number of people allowed to enter the country, set limits on immigration from the Western Hemisphere, and made it easier for families to join members who had already immigrated. More open borders meant immigration was increasingly harder to control. Reacting to the waves of undocumented immigrants who entered the country in the 1970s and 1980s, Congress passed the Immigration Reform and Control Act in 1986, granting amnesty to undocumented immigrants who had entered before 1982 and attempting to tighten controls on those who came after. Although this law included sanctions for those who hired undocumented immigrants, people continued to cross the border illegally from Mexico looking for work. In the 1990s, legislation under President Clinton strengthened the power of the INS.

IMMIGRATION LAW TODAY As we saw in *What's at Stake. . . ?*, in recent years the immigration debate has come to be defined by the tension between two opposing political camps. On the one hand are those who seek to grapple with the issue of the estimated 12 million undocumented immigrants already in this country and the demands of American business for the cheap labor that immigrants provide; on the other hand are those who prioritize the rule of law and believe undocumented immigrants should be sent home and the borders tightened against the arrival of any more. From former president George W. Bush's futile efforts to pass immigration reform in the early 2000s, to President Barack Obama's more recent, equally frustrated efforts, immigration reform has been a political job that has stymied politicians on both sides of the aisle.

Despite the trend of tightening immigration laws, President George W. Bush, a former governor of Texas and well familiar with the challenges of immigration policy, had indicated early in his first administration that he was considering giving amnesty—freedom from punishment, including deportation—to Mexicans living illegally in the United States. Confronted with opposition from the president's own party, the White House soon reported that its real interest was in an expanded guest worker program, in which workers could enter the country from Mexico to work temporarily in industries that needed low-wage labor. These plans were put on hold in the face of tougher enforcement of immigration laws and heightened scrutiny of immigrants after September 11, 2001, but Bush revived his call for a guest worker program immediately after the 2004 election. He claimed it would help fill jobs Americans were unwilling to take and bolster homeland security by providing a record of who was in the United States. Democrats and moderate Republican legislators hailed the proposals, but conservatives again vowed to block passage of any such legislation, demanding instead new laws to crack down on undocumented immigrants. In Bush's last term in office, Congress tried repeatedly to pass reform that emphasized border security and more stringent enforcement of legislation on the books. Immigrants pushed back. Between March and May 2006, several million immigrants protested anti-immigrant sentiment in Congress, marching in 120 American cities under banners proclaiming, "We Are America." Another proposal, in 2007, to create a guest worker program and to allow undocumented immigrants already here to remain and eventually earn citizenship status, also failed to pass, and Bush had to confront the fact that what he had hoped to make a signature piece of domestic policy in his administration was not to be.

With the support of the Obama administration, Democrats hoped to pass the Development, Relief and Education for Alien Minors (DREAM) Act, which would have allowed undocumented immigrants who had arrived in this country as minors to earn legal residency through higher education or military service. The House passed the bill in 2009, but conservative Republicans blocked it in the Senate. When the

THE BALANCE OF TRADE WITH GREAT BRITAIN SEEMS TO BE STILL AGAINST US.
650 Paupers arrived at Boston in the Steamship *Nestoria*, April 15th, from Galway, Ireland, shipped by the British Government.

Library of Congress

Anti-immigrant Sentiment Is Nothing New

Americans often claim to be a nation of immigrants, but that does not mean they always welcome new arrivals—some might argue that anti-immigrant backlash is as American as apple pie. This 1883 cartoon, which critically points to the arrival of poor immigrants from Ireland, is one of many nativist cartoons from that era.

Senate attempted to vote on it one last time in December 2010, Republicans (with the help of a few more conservative Democrats) blocked the vote; and when Republicans took the House majority in 2011, the bill was essentially dead for the foreseeable future. In response, President Obama took the step in 2012 of using executive action to defer the deportment of the so-called Dreamers. In the Republican presidential primary that year, however, most of the candidates competed for the toughest immigration stance. One exception was Rick Perry, who as governor of Texas had supported the Texas policy of offering in-state college tuition to the children of undocumented immigrants, but his impassioned defense of this policy during the debates sunk his hopes with the conservative base of his party. In fact, as we saw in *What's at Stake…?*, it was the Republican Party's dismal showing with Latino voters in 2012 that caused the party to urge the passage of legislation addressing the immigration issue, although Republican leaders were unable to pull it off.

Viewing federal efforts to control undocumented immigration as insufficient, some states have decided to take matters into their own hands. In 2010 the Arizona legislature passed a law that made it a crime for immigrants to fail to carry their documentation on them, and authorized police to

● **Second-Generation Americans**

Who Is an American? **41**

PROFILES IN CITIZENSHIP: ESMERALDA SANTIAGO

© Stan Godlewski/ZUMA Press/Corbis

The weird thing about meeting a person whose memoirs you have read is that you know the intimate details of her life, and yet you don't know her at all. She's an old friend and a stranger, at once familiar and unknown.

But Esmeralda Santiago's voice is as warm as her writing, lilting with the echoes of her Puerto Rican childhood, curling around you, drawing you in. Welcomed into her home, offered a cup of tea, you don't stay a stranger for long. Santiago's fast grin dissolves into a rich, delicious chuckle, her huge brown eyes crinkle up, her soft dark hair, laced with silver, waves back from a face gently lined with a life generously lived.

It's an amazing journey she has made from the metal shack in Macun with the rude privy out back, where ripe, luscious guavas hang from the trees, free for the picking, to the tony hills of suburban New York, where the houses look like mansions and the indoor plumbing is elegant but the imported guavas in the grocery store are hard and expensive. It's an immigrant's journey that has taken every bit of strength and pluck and intelligence she could muster, and it has left her suspended between two cultures, at home in both, but belonging entirely to neither.

Sitting in her bright, light dining room, she describes how this cultural odyssey has shaped her allegiances. "When I talk about my community—depending on who's listening—they respond to different things. And so if I say 'my community' in a roomful of Latinos they think I'm speaking about Puerto Ricans, and if I'm in a roomful of women they think I'm talking about women, and of course in Westchester County they think I'm talking about Westchester."

Like all Puerto Ricans, she is an American citizen, but her faint accent and exotic beauty make it clear she is not "from here." But when she goes back to Puerto Rico, a place that means home even though she left when she was thirteen, she is not from there either. On the island she has been told that she is too American—that her accent is not right, her personality too assertive.

And so, in a voice that belongs to all immigrants, she says, "It's a constant flux of—Where is my culture? Which culture do I belong to? Which is my community? Who am I representing now? And is there a point at which I represent just me? And who is that person? That's why I write memoirs. To answer those questions."

demand that documentation if they had any reason to suspect that a person was in the country illegally. Critics immediately claimed that the law would lead to racial profiling, but its proponents said that Arizona was only trying to deal with a leaky border that the federal government had failed to police.[7] Since the passage of the Arizona law, several other states led by conservative legislatures have followed suit, often with unintended consequences. One Alabama study, for instance, found that in the wake of the passage of a strict immigration bill, 40,000 to 80,000 workers had left the state, reducing demand for goods and services and costing the state between 70,000 and 140,000 jobs.[8] In May 2012 the Supreme Court struck down much of the Arizona law, with repercussions for immigration laws in Alabama, South Carolina, and Utah.[9] The Court said that although the state was within its rights to require police officers to verify the status of those they stop, it could not infringe on the federal right to set immigration policy.[10]

PAUSE AND REVIEW:

WHO, WHAT, HOW

Immigration and citizenship are issues in which the political and humanitarian stakes are very high. For non-Americans who are threatened or impoverished in their native countries, the stakes are sanctuary, prosperity, and improved quality of life, which they seek to gain through acquiring asylum or by becoming legal or undocumented immigrants.

People who are already American citizens have a stake here as well. At issue is the desire to be sensitive to humanitarian concerns, as well as to fill gaps in the nation's pool of workers and skills, and to meet the needs of current citizens. These often-conflicting goals are turned into law

And it is why her memoirs resonate so thoroughly with so many people who themselves have launched a new life in a new place, while not entirely releasing their grip on the old.

> **"THE MINUTE THAT I REALIZED THAT I WOULD NOT BE SILENCED, THEN I KNEW I HAD TO SPEAK."**

In all her communities, Santiago has become a voice for those who cannot speak for themselves. She says, "I think it comes from having to accompany my mother to the welfare office where I saw that somebody had to help these people, you know. And I would go there with my mother, but we would frequently spend the whole day because there were no translators for the other women and men there and so I would be the translator. I would be this little fifteen year old with really broken English, but I was the only one who could be an intermediary, and I think that that experience is one that I still live. I really feel like I'm out there speaking for people who, for whatever reasons, are not able to do that."

So today she is actively involved in issues she cares about, ranging from the protection of battered women, to the artistic development of adolescents, to the support of public libraries. Of the latter, she says, it is essential for the survival of democracy in an information age that there be places where people can go to get "the knowledge of the world" without having to spend the grocery money to get it. "That, to me," she says, "is democracy."

On why she speaks out:

With gifts comes responsibility. If you have a gift, it's not just a gift. If you're a painter, then it's not just a talent that you have. You have the responsibility to then express the soul of a people—of your community, whatever that community is. And for me, the minute that I realized that I would not be silenced, then I knew I had to speak. It was really that simple. I couldn't sleep, I couldn't look at myself in the mirror if I didn't speak about these things. . . . No matter what the personal cost and no matter what other people think. . . . I want to let them lose sleep over it [laughs]. I would like that better. I love it when I get calls the next day, saying, "I was up all night thinking about what you said yesterday," and I'm going, "Oh, good!" [laughs].

On the American founders and the job of keeping the republic:

Well, we forget about them. They're these old guys in funny costumes. We don't think of them as great thinkers and people who had a passion. . . . I mean they were humanists. They were not [just] creating a government, they were creating a community. We go back to that word . . . and they saw this as a community of people, of human beings, and that to me is what a country is. It's not the institutions; it's the people living there.

[Students] have to stop thinking about patriotism in terms of the country, the nation. . . . They have to think of it in terms of the guy sitting next to them. Patria is the people who make up a country. When it all changed for me was when I had to help somebody. . . . That's when I became patriotic. Because that human being needed help. And I could give it.

Source: Esmeralda Santiago spoke with Christine Barbour and Gerald Wright on March 25, 2005.

---

by policymakers in Congress and the White House, and their solutions are implemented by the bureaucracy of the USCIS.

IN YOUR OWN WORDS » Analyze the role of immigration in American politics and what it takes to become a U.S. citizen.

> **political culture** the broad pattern of ideas, beliefs, and values about citizens and government held by a population
>
> **values** central ideas, principles, or standards that most people agree are important

THE IDEAS THAT UNITE US
A common culture based on shared values

Making a single nation out of such a diverse people is no easy feat. It is possible only because, despite all our differences, most Americans share some fundamental attitudes and beliefs about how the world works and how it should work. These ideas, our political culture, pull us together and, indeed, provide a framework in which we can also disagree politically without resorting to violence and civil war.

Political culture refers to the general political orientation or disposition of a nation—the shared values and beliefs about the nature of the political world that give us a common language in which to discuss and debate political ideas. **Values** are ideals or principles that most people agree are important, even if they disagree on exactly how the value—such as "equality" or "freedom"—ought to be defined. Political culture is shared, although certainly some individuals find themselves at odds with it. When we say, "Americans think…," we mean that most Americans hold those views, not that there is unanimous agreement on them. Political culture is handed down from generation to generation, through families, schools, communities, literature, churches and synagogues, and so on, helping to provide stability for the nation by ensuring that a majority of citizens are well grounded in and committed to the basic values that sustain it. We talk about the process through which values are transferred in Chapter 11, "Public Opinion."

Note that statements about values and beliefs are not descriptive of how the world actually *is*, but rather are prescriptive, or **normative**, statements about how the value-holders believe the world *ought* to be. Our culture consists of deep-seated, collectively held ideas about how life *should* be lived. Normative statements aren't true or false but depend for their worth on the arguments that are made to back them up. Often we take our own culture (that is, our common beliefs about how the world should work) so much for granted that we aren't even aware of it. We don't think we have a culture or a normative view of the world; we just think we have the right outlook and those who differ from us are simply mistaken. Just as anyone who has traveled in another country has probably noticed that that country's citizens have different ideas about how the world should work and define their core values differently than we do, visitors to the United States can sometimes see our culture more clearly than we can. For that reason, it is often easier to see our own political culture by contrasting it to another, and we engage in some comparisons in the rest of this chapter.

FAITH IN RULES AND INDIVIDUALS

In American political culture, our expectations of government focus on rules and processes rather than on results. For example, we think government should guarantee a fair playing field but not guarantee equal outcomes for all the players. In addition, we believe that individuals are responsible for their own welfare and that what is good for them is good for society as a whole. Our insistence on fair rules, as we saw in Chapter 1, is an emphasis on **procedural guarantees**, while the belief in the primacy of the individual citizen is called **individualism**. American culture is not wholly procedural and individualistic—indeed, differences on these matters constitute some of the major partisan divisions in American politics—but these characteristics are more prominent in the United States than they are in most other nations.

To illustrate this point, we can compare American culture to the more social democratic cultures of Scandinavia, such as Sweden, Denmark, and Norway. In many ways, the United States and the countries in Scandinavia are more similar than they are different: they are all capitalist democracies, and they essentially agree that individuals ought to make most of the decisions about their own lives. Recall our

comparison of political and economic systems from Chapter 1. The United States and Scandinavia, which reject substantial governmental control of both the social order and the economy, would all fit into the upper-right quadrant of Figure 1.3, along with other advanced industrial democracies like Japan and Great Britain.

They do differ in some important ways, however. All advanced industrial democracies repudiate the wholehearted substantive guarantees of communism, but the Scandinavian countries have a greater tolerance for some substantive economic policy than does the more procedural United States. We explore these differences here in more detail so that we can better understand what American culture supports and what it does not.

PROCEDURAL GUARANTEES As we have noted, when we say that American political culture is procedural, we mean that Americans generally think government should guarantee fair processes—such as a free market to distribute goods, majority rule to make decisions, due process to determine guilt and innocence—rather than specific outcomes. The social democratic countries of Sweden, Denmark, and Norway, however, as we saw in Chapter 1, believe that government should actively seek to realize the values of equality—perhaps to guarantee a certain quality of life to all citizens or to increase equality of income. Government can then be evaluated by how well it produces those substantive outcomes, not just by how well it guarantees fair processes.

While American politics does set some substantive goals for public policy, Americans are generally more comfortable ensuring that things are done in a fair and proper way, and trusting that the outcomes will be good ones because the rules are fair. Although the American government is involved in social programs and welfare, it aims more at helping individuals get on their feet so that they can participate in the market (fair procedures) than at cleaning up slums or eliminating poverty (substantive goals).

INDIVIDUALISM The individualistic nature of American political culture means that individuals are seen as responsible for their own well-being. This contrasts with a collectivist point of view, which gives government or society some responsibility for individual welfare, and holds that what is good for society may not be the same as what is in the interest of individuals.

> **normative** describes beliefs or values about how things should be or what people ought to do rather than what actually is
>
> **procedural guarantees** government assurance that the rules will work smoothly and treat everyone fairly, with no promise of particular outcomes
>
> **individualism** belief that what is good for society is based on what is good for individuals

Thus our politics revolves around the belief that individuals are usually the best judges of what is good for them; we assume that what is good for society will follow automatically. For contrast, let's look again at Sweden, a democratic capitalist country like the United States, but one with a more collectivist political culture. At one time, Sweden had a policy that held down the wages of workers so that more profitable and less profitable industries would be more equal, and society, according to the Swedish view, would be better off. Americans would reject this policy as violating their belief in individualism (and proceduralism, as well). American government rarely asks citizens to make major economic sacrifices for the public good, although individuals often do so privately and voluntarily. Where Americans are asked to make economic sacrifices, like paying taxes, such requests are unpopular and more modest than in most other countries. A collective interest that supersedes individual interests is generally invoked in the United States only in times of war or national crisis. This echoes the two American notions of self-interested and public-interested citizenship we discussed in Chapter 1.

CORE AMERICAN VALUES: DEMOCRACY, FREEDOM, AND EQUALITY

We can see our American procedural and individualistic perspective when we examine the different meanings of three core American values: democracy, freedom, and equality.

DEMOCRACY Democracy in America, as we have seen, means representative democracy, based on consent and majority rule. Basically, Americans believe democracy should be a procedure to make political decisions, to choose political leaders, and to select policies for the nation. It is seen as a fundamentally just or fair way of making decisions because every individual who cares to participate is heard in the process, and all interests are considered. We don't reject a democratically made decision because it is not fair; it is fair precisely *because* it is democratically made. Democracy is valued primarily not for the way it makes citizens feel, or the effects it has on them, but for the decisions it produces. Americans see democracy as the appropriate procedure for making public decisions—that is, decisions about government—but generally not for decisions in the private realm. Rarely do employees have a binding vote on company policy, for example, as they do in some Scandinavian countries.

FREEDOM Americans also put a very high premium on the value of freedom, defined as freedom for the individual from restraint by the state. This view of freedom is procedural in the sense that it holds that no unfair restrictions should be put in the way of your pursuit of what you want, but it does not guarantee you any help in achieving those things. For instance, when Americans say, "We are all free to get a job," we mean that no discriminatory laws or other legal barriers are stopping us from applying for any particular position; a substantive view of freedom would ensure us the training to get a job so that our freedom meant a positive opportunity, not just the absence of restraint.

Americans have an extraordinary commitment to procedural freedom, perhaps because our values were forged during the Enlightenment, when liberty was a guiding principle. This commitment can be seen nowhere so clearly as in the Bill of Rights, the first ten amendments to the U.S. Constitution, which guarantees our basic civil liberties, the areas where government cannot interfere with individual action. Those civil liberties include freedom of speech and expression, freedom of belief, freedom of the press, and the right to assemble, just to name a few. (See Chapter 5, "Fundamental American Liberties," for a complete discussion of these rights.)

But Americans also believe in economic freedom, the freedom to participate in the marketplace, to acquire money and property, and to do with those resources pretty much as we please. Americans believe that government should protect our property, not take it away or regulate our use of it too heavily. Our commitment to individualism is apparent here, too. Even if society as a whole would benefit if we paid off the federal debt (the amount our government owes from spending more than it brings in), our individualistic view of economic freedom means that Americans have one of the lowest tax rates in the industrialized world (for a comparison, see "*Snapshot of America:* How Much Do We Pay?"). This reflects our national tendency in normal times to emphasize the rights of citizenship over its obligations.

EQUALITY Another central value in American political culture is equality. Of all the values we hold dear, equality is probably the one we cast most clearly in procedural versus substantive terms. Equality in America means government should guarantee equality of treatment, of access, of opportunity, not equality of result. People should have equal access to run the race, but we don't expect everyone to finish in the same place. Thus we believe in political equality (one person, one vote) and equality before the law—that the law shouldn't make unreasonable distinctions among people the basis for treating them differently, and that all people should have equal access to the legal system.

One problem the courts have faced is deciding what counts as a reasonable distinction. Can the law justifiably discriminate between—that is, treat differently—men and women, minorities and white Protestants, rich and poor, young and old? When the rules treat people differently, even if the goal is to make them more equal in the long run, many Americans get very upset. Witness the controversy surrounding affirmative action policies in this country. The point of such policies is to allow special opportunities to members of groups that have been discriminated against in the past, to remedy the long-term effects of that discrimination. For many Americans, such policies violate our commitment to procedural solutions. They wonder how treating people unequally can be fair.

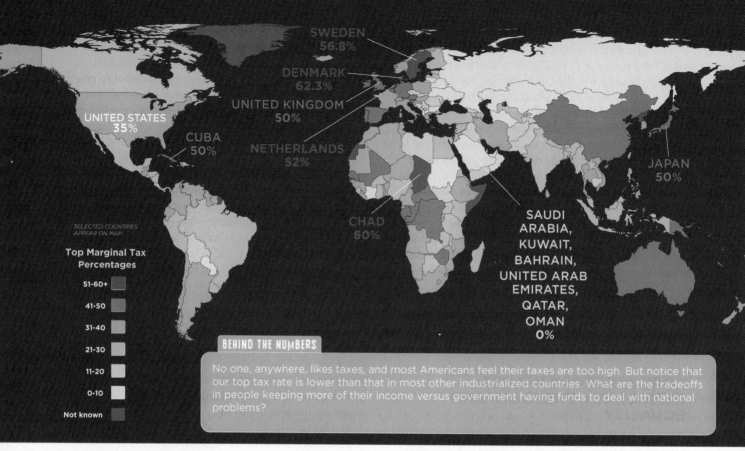

SWEDEN
56.8%

DENMARK
62.3%

UNITED KINGDOM
50%

UNITED STATES
35%

CUBA
50%

NETHERLANDS
52%

JAPAN
50%

CHAD
60%

SAUDI
ARABIA,
KUWAIT,
BAHRAIN,
UNITED ARAB
EMIRATES,
QATAR,
OMAN
0%

SELECTED COUNTRIES
APPEAR ON MAP

**Top Marginal Tax
Percentages**

51-60+
41-50
31-40
21-30
11-20
0-10

Not known

BEHIND THE NUMBERS

No one, anywhere, likes taxes, and most Americans feel their taxes are too high. But notice that our top tax rate is lower than that in most other industrialized countries. What are the tradeoffs in people keeping more of their income versus government having funds to deal with national problems?

Source: Organization for Economic Cooperation and Development, Revenue Statistics 2008, Table A, p. 19. OECD Publishing, dx.doi.org/10.1787/rev_stats-2008-en-fr.

PAUSE AND REVIEW:

WHO, WHAT, HOW

To live as a nation, citizens need to share a view of who they are, how they should live, and what their world should be like. If they have no common culture, they fragment and break apart, like the divided peoples of Ireland and the former Yugoslavia. Political cultures provide coherence and national unity to citizens who may be very different in other ways.

Americans achieve national unity through a political culture based on procedural and individualistic visions of democracy, freedom, and equality.

IN YOUR OWN WORDS >> Explain how shared core values define the United States as a country and a culture.

THE IDEAS THAT DIVIDE US

Differences over how much government control there should be in our lives

Most Americans are united in their commitment at some level to a political culture based on proceduralism and individualism and to the key values of democracy, freedom, and equality.

This shared political culture gives us a common political language, a way to talk about politics that keeps us united even though we may disagree about many specific ideas and issues.

That's a good thing since, human nature being what it is, we are likely to disagree about politics, and disagree often. Although Americans have much in common, there are more than 300 million of us, and the *Snapshots of America* features demonstrate graphically how dramatically different we are in terms of our religious, educational, geographic, and professional backgrounds. We have different interests, different beliefs, different prejudices, different hopes and dreams.

With all that diversity, we are bound to have a variety of beliefs and opinions about politics, the economy, and society that help us make sense of our world but that can divide us into opposing camps. These camps, or different belief systems, are called **ideologies**. Sharing a political culture doesn't mean we don't have ideological differences, but because we share core values about how the world should be, we have a common language in which to debate, and resolve our differences, and a set of boundaries that keeps those differences from getting out of hand. Again, like the values and beliefs that underlie our culture, our ideologies are based on normative prescriptions. Remember that one of the

ideologies sets of beliefs about politics and society that help people make sense of their world

Ten American Values ● Things Americans Do ●

SNAPSHOT OF AMERICA: HOW MUCH DO WE EARN?

The Size of Our Paychecks

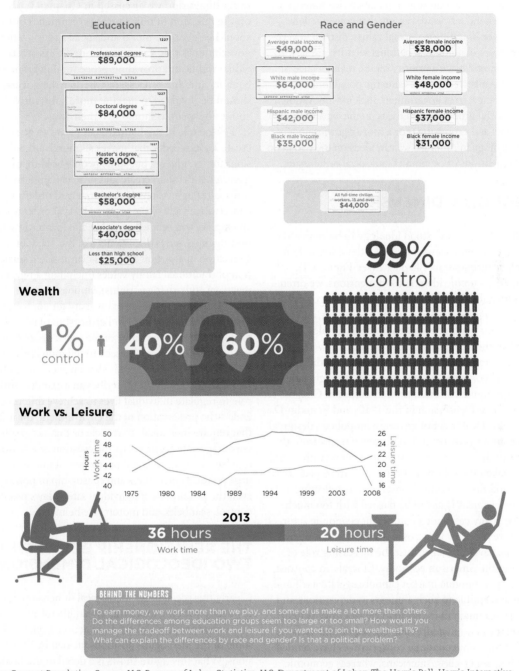

Education

Professional degree
$89,000

Doctoral degree
$84,000

Master's degree
$69,000

Bachelor's degree
$58,000

Associate's degree
$40,000

Less than high school
$25,000

Race and Gender

Average male income
$49,000

Average female income
$38,000

White male income
$64,000

White female income
$48,000

Hispanic male income
$42,000

Hispanic female income
$37,000

Black male income
$35,000

Black female income
$31,000

All full-time civilian
workers, 15 and over
$44,000

Wealth

1%
control

40%   60%

99%
control

Work vs. Leisure

Hours — Work time: 40, 42, 44, 46, 48, 50
Leisure time: 16, 18, 20, 22, 24, 26
1975 1980 1984 1989 1994 1999 2003 2008

2013
36 hours — Work time
20 hours — Leisure time

BEHIND THE NUMBERS

To earn money, we work more than we play, and some of us make a lot more than others. Do the differences among education groups seem too large or too small? How would you manage the tradeoff between work and leisure if you wanted to join the wealthiest 1%? What can explain the differences by race and gender? Is that a political problem?

Source: Current Population Survey, U.S. Bureau of Labor Statistics, U.S. Department of Labor; The Harris Poll, Harris Interactive.

Note: Work includes working for pay, keeping house, and going to school.

---

reasons we can disagree so passionately on political issues is that normative statements about the world are not true or false, good or bad—instead, they depend for their force on the arguments we make to defend them. It might seem clear as a bell to us that our values are right and true, but to a person who disagrees with our prescriptions, we are as wrong as they think we are. So we debate and argue.

But because we share that political culture, our range of debate in the United States is fairly narrow, compared with the ideological spectrum of many countries. We have no successful communist or socialist parties here, for instance, because the ideologies on which those parties are founded seem to most Americans to push the limits of procedural and individualistic culture too far, especially in the economic realm. The two main ideological camps in the United States are the liberals (associated, since the 1930s, with the Democratic Party) and the conservatives (with the Republicans), with many Americans falling somewhere in between.

There are lots of different ways to characterize American ideologies. In general terms, we can say that **conservatives** tend to be in favor of traditional social values, distrust government action except in matters of national security, are slow to advocate change, and place a priority on the maintenance of social order. **Liberals**, in contrast, value the possibilities of progress and change, trust government, look for innovations as answers to social problems, and focus on the expansion of individual rights and expression. For a more rigorous understanding of ideology in America, we can focus on the two main ideological dimensions of economics and social order issues.

THE ECONOMIC DIMENSION

Traditionally we have understood ideology to be centered on differences in economic views, much like those located on our economic continuum in Chapter 1 (see Figure 1.1). Based on these economic ideological dimensions, we often say that the liberals who advocate a large role for government in regulating the economy are on the far left, and those conservatives who think government control should be minimal are on the far right. Because we lack any widespread radical socialist traditions in the United States, both American liberals and conservatives are found on the right side of the broader economic continuum we discussed in Chapter 1.

Since the Great Depression in the 1930s and Franklin D. Roosevelt's New Deal (a set of government policies designed to get the economy moving and to protect citizens from the worst effects of the Depression), American conservatives and liberals have taken the following positions with respect to government and the economy. Conservatives, reflecting a belief that government is not to be trusted with too much power and is, in any case, not a competent economic actor, and that private property is sacrosanct and should remain wholly private, have reacted against the increasing role of government in the American economy. Liberals, in contrast, arguing that the economic market cannot regulate itself and, left alone, is susceptible to such ailments as depressions and recessions, have a much more positive view of government and the good it can do in addressing economic and social problems. Historically, economic conservatives have tended to be wealthier, upper-class Americans, whereas economic liberals have been more likely to be lower-paid, blue-collar workers. See "*Snapshot of America:* How Much Do We Earn?" to see how much American incomes vary.

THE SOCIAL ORDER DIMENSION

In the 1980s and 1990s another ideological dimension became prominent in the United States. Perhaps because, as some researchers have argued, most people are able to meet their basic economic needs and more people than ever before are identifying themselves as middle class, many Americans began to focus less on economic questions and more on issues of morality and quality of life. The new ideological dimension, which is analogous to the social order dimension we discussed in Chapter 1, divides people on the question of how much government control there should be over the moral and social order—whether government's role should be limited to protecting individual rights and providing procedural guarantees of equality and due process, or whether the government should be involved in making more substantive judgments about how people should live their lives.

Few people in the United States want to go so far as to create a social order that makes all moral and political decisions for its subjects, but some people hold that it is the government's job to create and protect a preferred social order, although visions of that preferred order may differ. A conservative view of the preferred social order usually includes an emphasis on religion in public life (prayer in school, public posting of religious documents like the Ten Commandments), a rejection of abortion and physician-assisted suicide, promotion of traditional family values (including a rejection of gay marriage and other gay rights), emphasis on the "American Way" (rejecting the value of diversity for conformity and restricting immigration), and censorship of materials that promote alternative visions of the social order. Conservatives are not the only ones who seek to tell individuals how to live their lives, however. There is also a newer, more liberal vision of the social order that prescribes an expanded government role to regulate individual lives to achieve different substantive ends—the preservation of the environment, for instance (laws that require individuals to recycle or that tax gasoline to encourage conservation), or the creation of a sense of community based on equality and protection of minorities (rules that urge political correctness and censorship of pornography), or even the promotion of individual safety (laws promoting gun control, seat belts, and motorcycle helmets).

THE RELATIONSHIP BETWEEN THE TWO IDEOLOGICAL DIMENSIONS

Clearly this social order ideological dimension does not dovetail neatly with the more traditional liberal and conservative orientations toward government action. Figure 2.1 shows some of the ideological positions yielded by these two dimensions. What this figure shows is a detail of the broader political spectrum we saw in Chapter 1, focused on the narrower spectrum commonly found in an advanced industrial

conservatives people who generally favor limited government and are cautious about change

liberals people who generally favor government action and view change as progress

economic liberals those who favor an expanded government role in the economy but a limited role in the social order

FIGURE 2.1 IDEOLOGICAL BELIEFS IN THE UNITED STATES

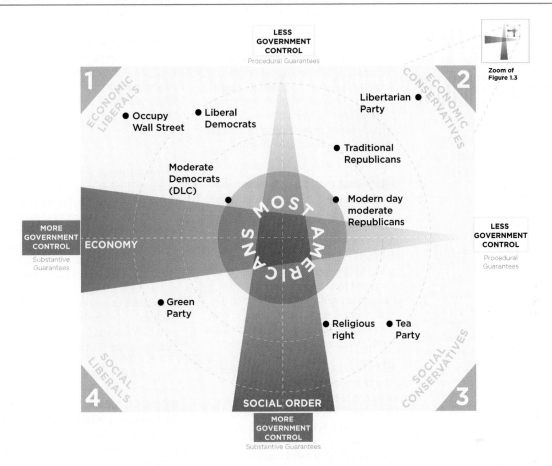

1. Economic Liberals

Expanded government role in economy and limited government role in social order
Examples: welfare, national health care, maximum individual freedom (pro-choice, pro-gay rights, right to die), civil rights for immigrants, regulation of Wall Street

2. Economic Conservatives

Limited government role in economy and in social order
Examples: low taxes, laissez-faire capitalism, maximum individual freedom (pro-choice, anti–gun control), guest worker program

3. Social Conservatives

Limited government role in economy and expanded government role in social order
Examples: low taxes, prayer in school, censorship of books that violate traditional values, anti-gay rights, tight restriction on immigration

4. Social Liberals

Expanded government role in economy and in social order
Examples: welfare, social programs, censorship of pornography, strict pollution controls, affirmative action

Although committed generally to a procedural and individualistic political culture (this entire figure would fit in the upper-right quadrant of Figure 1.3), Americans still find plenty of room for political disagreement. This figure outlines the two main dimensions of that conflict: beliefs about government's role in the economy and beliefs about government's role in establishing a preferred social order. Those ideological beliefs on the right side of the figure are conservative beliefs, and those on the left side are more liberal. The axes in these figures are continuums and do not represent all-or-nothing positions; most Americans fall somewhere in between.

democracy. For instance, **economic liberals**, who are willing to allow government to make substantive decisions about the economy, tend to embrace the top procedural individualistic position on the social order dimension, and so they fall into the upper-left quadrant of the figure. Some economic policies they favor are job training and housing subsidies for the poor, taxation to support social programs, and affirmative action to ensure that opportunities for economic success are truly

● Wealth Distribution   **●** U.S. Middle Class

CLUES
TO CRITICAL THINKING

"Will the 2012 Election Be a Contest of Whole Foods vs. Cracker Barrel Shoppers?"

By David Wasserman
Washington Post,
December 9, 2011

A writer for the Washington Post *cast the 2012 election as a battle "between alternate universes of culture and cuisine," noting how political beliefs and the cultural divide are reflected in the clientele of two popular food sources. We chose this article because it demonstrates nicely the pervasiveness of political culture—it can even influence what we choose to put on our plates.*

"You can't find this place out where I live," laments a middle-aged man from Arlington to a white-haired shopkeeper at Manassas's Cracker Barrel on a recent Saturday. Over the store's speaker system, a country singer croons about going back to the way things were. In the dining room, a heaping plate of the restaurant's signature "Chicken n' Dumplins" sells for $7.39. More than a dozen pickup trucks—and just six European cars—dot the parking lot less than a mile from the Civil War battlefield.

The same day, 26 miles closer to Washington, an attendant herds four Toyota Priuses and eight German

luxury cars around a parking lot at Clarendon's Whole Foods, the nerve center of a posh neighborhood that has spawned three boutique cupcakeries and two frozen-yogurt shops in the past two years. Inside, a quart of organic pomegranate juice runs $10.99. Large placards celebrate Whole Foods' seven "core values," its five-step animal-welfare rating system and a three-color "eco-scale" for household cleaning products.

Whole Foods and Cracker Barrel—the former founded in 1980 in Austin, the latter in 1969 in Lebanon, Tenn.—have grown into multibillion-dollar empires, each with hundreds of locations. If Whole Foods follows through on plans to develop new stores in Idaho, Iowa and New Hampshire next year, each chain will count locations in 42 states. But even as these stores appear everywhere, their cultural orbits could hardly be more politically divergent.

Every election has its cultural divides. The 1896 presidential contest, for instance, is remembered as a battle between William Jennings Bryan's populists and William McKinley's industrialist supporters. The 1972 election pitted Richard Nixon's "silent majority" against George McGovern and the counterculture.

In 2012, the campaign might be a contest between these alternate universes of culture and cuisine: Whole Foods Markets and Cracker Barrel Old Country Stores.

In 2008, candidate Barack Obama carried 81 percent of counties with a Whole Foods and just 36 percent of counties with a Cracker Barrel—a record

45-point gap. In 2000, Vice President Al Gore won 58 percent of counties now containing a Whole Foods and 26 percent of those now boasting a Cracker Barrel, a 32-point difference. And in 1992, Gov. Bill Clinton won 60 percent of Whole Foods counties and 40 percent of Cracker Barrel counties—a mere 20-point margin.

. . .

In the 2010 midterm elections, the culinary divide was even more apparent: Eighty-two percent of congressional districts that flipped from Democratic to Republican were home to a Cracker Barrel, and just 20 percent of these districts had a Whole Foods. Though Whole Foods refused to comment for this story, Cracker Barrel says there's no connection. "Politics don't play any role in our site selection process," said Julie Davis, a spokeswoman for the company.

"Politics is aligned with lifestyle right now, not policy," says Texas journalist Bill Bishop, author of "The Big Sort: Why the Clustering of Like-Minded America Is Tearing Us Apart." "Food used to be political because it represented a class of farmers or workers. Now it represents certain tastes."

. . . Whole Foods means "liberal elite" in the minds of many. In 2007, Obama undermined his campaign's efforts to move beyond his professorial image when he asked an Iowa farm crowd: "Anybody gone into Whole Foods lately and see what they charge for arugula?" Iowa didn't have a Whole Foods—yet.

. . .

equal. As far as government regulation of individuals' private lives goes, however, these liberals favor a hands-off stance, preferring individuals to have maximum freedom over their noneconomic affairs. They are willing to let government regulate such behaviors as murder, rape, and theft, but they believe that most moral issues (such as abortion and the right to die) are questions of individual responsibility. They have an

expansive vision of individual rights, valuing diversity and including in the system people who historically have been left out—women, minorities, gays, and immigrants. Their love for their country is tempered by the view that the government should be held to the same strict procedural standard to which individuals are held—laws must be followed, checks and balances adhered to in order to limit government power,

Pollsters and corporate marketers increasingly think alike. The expansion of Whole Foods and Cracker Barrel in the 1990s coincided with a marketing craze that divided America into small, targetable groups of like-minded people. . . . Political microtargeting, a technique that President George W. Bush's team pioneered to pinpoint persuadable voters in 2004 and Obama adapted in 2008, is an extension of this thinking. Whether you're selling kale or a political candidate, the strategy is the same: Divide and conquer.

"There's an increasing alignment between brand personality and political personality," says Alex Lundry, vice president and director of research for TargetPoint, a GOP microtargeting firm. "That's what makes the microtargeting we do so powerful."

And it becomes self-sustaining. After Whole Foods and Cracker Barrel locate near consumers who can make stores profitable, "those stores become a magnet for consumers who think alike," Lundry says.

How could each party bridge the gap? Should Democrats spend time courting evangelical environmentalists who might shop at Whole Foods in Colorado Springs, Colo., or Mason, Ohio? Should Republicans reach out to growing Latino communities in Cracker Barrel towns such as Sanford, N.C., or Allentown, Pa.?

. . .

In the quest to attract independent voters who make or break close elections, 2012 could become a showdown over the rare suburban outposts where Whole Foods and Cracker Barrel coexist. One such place is Plymouth Meeting, Pa., a Philadelphia suburb where the two stores face off near Exit 20 of the Pennsylvania Turnpike.

Who lives there? According to Nielsen's market analysis of this Zip code, it's "Domestic Duos": middle-income, older, married couples who shop at Kohl's to save cash and drive moderately priced Chevy Impalas, but who also have disposable income to sail Norwegian Cruise Line. Next year, both parties will spend millions to win this persuadable segment of voters—and bridge the organic-nostalgic divide. But as that divide widens, they may find that the persuadable slice of the electorate is narrower than ever.

Source: Reprinted by permission of the author.

Consider the source and the audience: This article, written by an analyst for the Cook Report, which charts trends in public opinion, appeared in the *Washington Post*. Why is Wasserman writing for a source that is read by politicians and others involved in the business of government?

Lay out the argument and the underlying values and assumptions: There are many other ways of characterizing the ideological differences in the United States than the procedural-versus-substantive dimensions we use in this chapter. What does Wasserman mean by suggesting that the sides are the "organic" Whole Foods Democrats versus the "nostalgic" Cracker Barrel Republicans? Which people fall into each camp, and what values do they hold? Where do you fall?

Uncover the evidence: Wasserman's argument relies on the overlay of voting results on the patterns of store openings by Whole Foods and Cracker Barrel. What other evidence could support Wasserman's argument?

Evaluate the conclusion: Wasserman suggests that the prevalence of microtargeting makes it tough for each party to cross the cultural divide represented by the Whole Foods–Cracker Barrel split. Does the divide exist? Is it bridgeable? How?

Sort out the political significance: What does it mean for the future of American political culture if we are divided not only along political lines but also along cultural lines so fundamental that they are reflected in the way we like to eat? What is the "divide and conquer" strategy of microtargeters likely to mean for us politically?

and individual rights protected, even when the individuals are citizens of another country.

> **economic conservatives** those who favor a strictly procedural government role in the economy and the social order

Economic conservatives share their liberal counterparts' reluctance to allow government interference in people's private lives, but they combine this with a conviction that government should limit involvement in the economy as well. In the upper-right quadrant of the figure, these economic conservatives prefer government to limit its role in economic decision making to regulation of the market (like changing interest rates and cutting taxes to end recessions), elimination of "unfair" trade practices (like monopolies), and provision of some public goods (like highways and national defense). When it comes to immigration they favor more open policies since immigrants often work more cheaply and help keep the labor market competitive for business. The most extreme holders of economic conservative views are called **libertarians**, people who believe that only minimal government action in any sphere is acceptable. Consequently, economic conservatives also hold the government accountable for sticking to the constitutional checks and balances that limit its own power.

In the lower-left quadrant of the figure, people tend to favor a substantive government role in achieving a more equal distribution of material resources (such as welfare programs and health care for the poor) but want that equality carried into the social order as well. They are willing, at least to some extent, to allow government to regulate individual behavior to create what they see as a better society. While they continue to want the freedom to make individual moral choices that economic liberals want, **social liberals** are happy to see some government action to realize a substantive vision of what society should be like. This liberal vision is forward looking and adaptive to changing social roles and technological progress. It seeks to regulate the effects of that progress, protecting the physical environment and individual well-being from the hazards of modern life. Government is valued for how well it realizes this vision of substantive fairness, and it is criticized when it falls short.

The most extreme adherents of social liberalism are sometimes called **communitarians** for their strong commitment to a community based on radical equality of all people. It is a collectivist, community-based vision that holds that individuals should be expected to make some sacrifices for the betterment of society. Because collectivism is not very popular in the American individualist culture, strong adherents to this view are relatively few in number. Many economic liberals, however, pick up some of the policy prescriptions of social liberals, like environmentalism and gun control.

To the right of them, and below economic conservatives on the figure, are **social conservatives**. These people share economic conservatives' views on limited government involvement in the economy, but with less force and perhaps for different reasons (in fact, following the Great Depression, social conservatives, many of whom were members of the working class, were likely to be New Deal liberals). Their primary concern is with their vision of the moral tone of life, not economics, and it does not seem incongruous to

them that they should want a limited economic role for government while requiring that politicians enact a fairly substantive set of laws to create a particular moral order. Their vision of that order includes an emphasis on fundamentalist religious values and traditional family roles, and a rejection of change or diversity that they see as destructive to the preferred social order. Immigration is threatening because it brings into the system people who are different and threatens to dilute the majority that keeps the social order in place. Social conservatives seek to protect people's moral character rather than their physical or economic well-being, and they embrace a notion of community that emphasizes a hierarchical order (everyone in his or her proper place) rather than equality for all. Since limited political power is not valued here, a large and powerful state is appreciated as being a sign of strength on the international stage. Patriotism for social conservatives is not a matter of holding the government to the highest procedural standards, as it is for those in the top half of Figure 2.1. Less worried about limiting government power over individual lives, they adopt more of a "my country right or wrong," "America First" view that sees criticism of the United States as unpatriotic.

libertarians those who favor a minimal government role in any sphere

social liberals those who favor greater control of the economy and the social order to bring about greater equality and to regulate the effects of progress

communitarians those who favor a strong, substantive government role in the economy and the social order so that their vision of a community of equals may be realized

social conservatives those who endorse limited government control of the economy but considerable government intervention to realize a traditional social order; based on religious values and hierarchy rather than equality

WHO FITS WHERE?

Many people, indeed most of us, might find it difficult to identify ourselves as simply "liberal" or "conservative," because we consider ourselves liberal on some issues, conservative on others. The framework in Figure 2.1 allows us to see ourselves and major groups in society as we might line up if we distinguish between economic and social-moral values. We can see, for instance, the real spatial distances that lie among (1) *the religious right* (as social conservatives are known), who are very conservative on political and moral issues but who were once part of the coalition of southern blue-collar workers who supported Roosevelt on the New Deal; (2) *traditional Republicans*, who are very conservative on economic issues but often more libertarian on political and moral issues, wanting government to guarantee procedural fairness and keep the peace, but otherwise to leave them alone; and (3) *moderate Republicans*, who are far less conservative economically and morally. As both John McCain in 2008 and Mitt Romney in 2012 discovered, it can be difficult or impossible for a Republican candidate on the national stage to hold such an unwieldy coalition together.

In the summer of 2009, as debate over health care reform dragged on in Washington and unemployment continued to rise, a wave of populist anger swept the nation. The so-called Tea Party movement (named after the Boston Tea Party rebellion against taxation in 1773) was antigovernment (except for programs like Medicare that benefit the Tea Partiers, who tended to be older Americans), anticorporation, and pro-American. Mostly it was angry, fed by emotional appeals of conservative talk show hosts and others, whose rhetoric took political debate out of the range of logic and analysis and into the world of emotional drama and angry invective. Although many of the Tea Partiers are social conservatives, many are also libertarians. They are largely conservative, wanting to return to what they remember as a more gloried past. A *New York Times* poll found that Americans who identified as Tea Party supporters were more likely to be Republican, white, married, male, and over forty-five, and to hold views that were more conservative than Republicans generally.[11] In fact, they succeeded in shaking up the Republican Party in 2010 and 2012, as they supported primary challenges to officeholders who did not share their antigovernment ideology.

The members of Congress elected by the Tea Party wave took a no-compromise stance toward policymaking, demanding the fulfillment of their wish list and refusing to negotiate with the Democrats or President Obama to get things done. That is, rather than participate in the give-and-take, compromise-oriented process of American politics, they held out for their substantive policy ends, presenting Speaker of the House John Boehner with serious challenges to his leadership, bringing the country to the brink of economic disaster over their refusal to raise the debt ceiling so that the United States could pay its bills in the summer of 2011, and even, in October 2013, shutting down the federal government for more than two weeks.

The Tea Partiers are tough to fit neatly on to the scheme depicted in Figure 2.1 precisely because their appeal is largely emotionally based and not internally consistent. What is clear is that they are outside the circle that defines mainstream American beliefs, posing a challenge to Republicans who run statewide or nationally as they need to satisfy two divergent constituencies. Mitt Romney discovered this during the Republican primary season in 2012, when Tea Party members supported first Rick Perry, then Newt Gingrich, and then Rick Santorum in their effort to pick "anybody but Mitt," who they viewed as too moderate. Whether they pack a similar political punch in 2016 is yet to be seen. Although there were signs in 2014 that their influence was waning, as more conventional economic conservatives pushed back against them, they remained a potent electoral force.

Similarly, the Democrats must try to respond to the *economic liberals* in the party, very procedural on most political and moral issues (barring affirmative action) but relatively (for Americans) substantive on economic concerns; to *social liberals*, substantive on both economic and social issues; and to more middle-of-the-road Democratic groups that are fairly procedural on political and moral issues but not very substantive on economic matters at all. It was President Bill Clinton, as a founder of the now-defunct Democratic Leadership Council (DLC), who helped move his party closer to the mainstream from a position that, as we can see in Figure 2.1, is clearly out of alignment with the position taken by most Americans. Ironically, in the 2000 election, Al Gore's commitment to the DLC position left him vulnerable to attack from Ralph Nader, who, as a representative of the Green Party, came from the lower-left quadrant. This position does not draw huge numbers of supporters, but in an election as close as the one in 2000, it probably drew sufficient support from Gore to cost him the election. In 2004 Democratic candidate John Kerry did not have to worry as much about appealing to voters in that lower-left quadrant since many of them disliked George W. Bush so much that they were willing to vote for a candidate with whom they did not completely agree in order to try to oust Bush from office. Democrat Barack Obama had the same advantage in 2008, drawing support from across his party's ideological spectrum in large part because of Bush's deep unpopularity. When the Occupy movement rose on the president's left flank in 2011, Obama was quick to adopt some of the movement's anti–Wall Street, anti-inequality rhetoric and made it a central part of his campaign, helping to ensure that we would not face an interparty challenge from the left.

PAUSE AND REVIEW:

WHO, WHAT, HOW

Although most Americans share a political culture, deep political differences can remain about whose view of government should prevail and who should benefit from its actions. These differences have traditionally centered on government's economic role but increasingly also involve views on establishing a preferred social order, and on what the preferred social order should be. In the United States, ideologies generally go by the umbrella labels *liberalism* and *conservatism,* although many differences exist even within these broad perspectives. Ideological conflict can be contentious since what is at stake are fundamental views of what the political world ought to look like.

IN YOUR OWN WORDS >> Describe the political debates that drive partisan divisions in American politics.

>> THE CITIZENS AND AMERICAN POLITICAL BELIEFS

The gap between the ideal and the practice of American democracy

One of the core values of American political culture is democracy, an ideal that unites citizens—both those who are born here as well as more newly minted naturalized citizens—in the activity of self-governance. The American notion of democracy is a procedural one, a representative democracy valued for making decisions in which all voices are heard. It doesn't ask much of us except that we pay attention to the news of the day and come together periodically and vote to elect our public officials.

Keeping in mind that James Madison's "republican government" was not meant to be a "pure" democracy, it is interesting to note that it has grown more democratic in some ways in the past two hundred years. For one thing, more people can participate now—such as women and African Americans—and, since eighteen-year-olds won the right to vote, the electorate is younger than ever before. But in many ways government remains removed from "the people," even if the definition of "the people" has expanded over time. While more people *can* participate in American politics, the truth is that not very many *do.* American turnout rates (the percentages of people who go to the polls and vote on election days) are abysmally low

compared to those of other Western industrialized democracies, and surveys show that many Americans are apathetic toward politics. Even in 2008, a year of unusually high turnout, only about 60 percent of eligible voters cast a vote.

How does American democracy work with such low rates of participation or interest on the part of the citizenry? One theory, based on the elite notion of democracy described in Chapter 1, claims that it doesn't really matter whether people participate in politics because all important decisions are made by elites—leaders in business, politics, education, the military, and the media. People don't vote because their votes don't really matter.

Drawing on the pluralist theory of democracy, another explanation claims that Americans don't need to participate individually because their views are represented in government sufficiently through their membership in various groups. For instance, a citizen may be a member of an environmental group, a professional association or labor union, a parent-teacher organization, a veterans' group, a church, or a political party. That citizen may not bother to vote on Election Day, but his or her voice is heard nonetheless because all the groups to which he or she belongs have political influence.

By contrast, some educators and social scientists argue that falling levels of involvement, interest, and trust in politics are not something to be explained and dismissed with complacency, but instead signal a true civic crisis in American politics. They see a swing from the community-minded citizens of republican virtue to the self-interested citizens of Madisonian theory so severe that the fabric of American political life is threatened. These scholars argue that democracies can survive only with the support and vigilance of citizens, and that American citizens are so disengaged as to put democracy itself in danger. They would place the responsibility for low levels of participation in the United States not just on the system but also on the citizens themselves for not availing themselves of the opportunities for engagement that exist.

For instance, Benjamin Barber, discussing the tendency of Americans to take their freedoms for granted and to assume that since they were born free they will naturally remain free, says that citizenship is the "price of liberty."[12] For all the importance of presidents and senators and justices in the American political system, it is the people, the citizens, who are entrusted with "keeping the republic." The founders did not have great expectations of the citizens of the new country, and they feared the ravages of mob rule if there were "too much" democracy, but they knew well that the ultimate safeguards of free government are free citizens. Government whose citizens abdicate their role is government whose freedom, fragile at the best of times, is in jeopardy. We live in an age of overwhelming cynicism about and distrust in government.

One manifestation of that cynicism and distrust is that citizens are opting out of government participation, not only not voting but not even paying attention.

The question of how democratic the United States is may seem to be largely an academic one—that is, one that has little or no relevance to your personal life—but it is really a question of who has the power, who is likely to be a winner in the political process. Looked at this way, the question has quite a lot to do with your life, especially as government starts to make more demands on you and you on it. Are you likely to be a winner or a loser? Are you going to get what you want from the political system? How much power do people like you have to get their way in government?

IN YOUR OWN WORDS » Describe the gap between the American democratic ideal and its practice.

THINKING OUTSIDE THE BOX

Does it matter to the success of a democracy if relatively few people take an active political role (by paying attention, voting, exchanging political views, and the like)?

LET'S REVISIT: WHAT'S AT STAKE...

We began this chapter with a look at the political circus surrounding the issue of immigration reform between the 2012 and 2014 elections. Initially the Republican leadership determined that they had to pass immigration reform in order to improve their chances with Latino voters, but the Tea Party Republican base scuttled those plans. Meanwhile, Democrats, who began almost universally on board with reform, ended up asking their president to hold off on fulfilling his promise to try to sort out the situation with executive action. What had seemed like a slam dunk for everyone had become too toxic to touch before the midterm elections. How on earth had this happened? What was really at stake in passing immigration reform in 2014?

Part of the problem is that, for the Republican Party, the stakes were mixed. For business leaders, a guest worker program meant affordable labor for jobs Americans were not always willing to do. They argued that undocumented workers came here because there were jobs for them and that policies that punished employers for hiring them benefited no one and damaged the economy.

For Republican Party leaders, passing reform meant getting a difficult issue off the agenda, one that portrayed the party in a divisive, unflattering light and sent a negative message to an important and growing voting bloc. They knew that Latinos were key to carrying the vote in battleground states like Colorado, Nevada, and Florida. Furthermore, they believed that the policies of economic individualism and social conservatism they advocated should be attractive to Latino voters but that until immigration was off the table, they would not get a hearing. The party's post-election

"autopsy" report concluded that "[I]f Hispanic Americans hear that the GOP doesn't want them in the United States, they won't pay attention to our next sentence. It doesn't matter what we say about education, jobs or the economy; if Hispanics think that we do not want them here, they will close their ears to our policies."[13]

But there is another segment of the Republican Party for whom immigration reform is not a good thing. Many conservatives in the party, including those branding themselves as the Tea Party, think reform means giving a pass to law-breakers who would be rewarded for coming here illegally. By not sending them back home, they say we would be condoning a crime, and they dub most immigration reform efforts "amnesty" bills. According to them, reform will be expensive and will cost American jobs. At its worst, the rhetoric on this side of the argument, with its references to an "illegal invasion," "third world diseases," and "access to terrorists," begins to sound like xenophobia and even racism,[14] part of the reason why the party leadership want to get it behind them. As we will see in Chapters 7 and 12, the Tea Partiers exercise disproportionate influence over their Republican colleagues, and fear of being branded as pro-amnesty or soft on criminals keeps many other Republicans from speaking up in favor or reform.

But while frustrating to its leadership, the reluctance of some Republicans to pass reform is nothing new—as we saw in this chapter, even Republican President George W. Bush ran into the buzz saw of his own party when he tried to make it happen. The fact that Democrats have backed off is less easy to explain at first glance. After all, Democrats were so pumped after the 2012 election that they vowed to make immigration a key issue in 2014. But something happened on the way from one election to the other; children from Central America began crossing the border in huge numbers, citing fears for their safety in the drug- and crime-infested countries of El Salvador, Honduras, and Guatemala. Defenders of the kids say that they are political refugees; critics say they are just after economic opportunity and the chance to be reunited with relatives.

Republicans have seized on the wave of immigration to blame Obama's 2012 decision not to deport the so-called "dreamers"—kids who were brought here by their parents years ago when they were little. They say that Obama's unilateral executive action, which they decried from the beginning as an executive power grab, sent a message to these other children that it is okay to come here illegally. The situation caught the media's attention, and public opinion on immigration began to swing against the Democrats.[15]

And the Democrats were worried. For those who were up for reelection in 2014, the stakes were their jobs, but party leaders feared that the issue might cost them control of the Senate, although that was something that was likely in the cards anyway. They asked the president to hold off on taking any action, and reluctantly he agreed, convinced by the argument that ultimately what was at stake was the possibility of getting any reform done at all.

Of course, the final major stakeholder in the battle over immigration reform is the Latino community itself, which feels dissed by the Republicans and, increasingly, ignored by the Democrats. Shortly after the 2012 election, Eliseo Medina, the secretary-treasurer of the Service Employees International Union and a leader of efforts to mobilize Latino voters, said "The Latino giant is wide awake, cranky and taking names."[16]

After 2014, there will be plenty on the list.

TO SUM UP

for CQ Press

Sharpen your skills with **SAGE edge** at http://edge.sagepub.com/barbour7e. **SAGE edge for students** provides a personalized approach to help you accomplish your coursework goals in an easy-to-use learning environment.

REVIEW

Who Is an American?

Citizenship in the United States is both a concept promising certain rights and responsibilities, and a precise legal status. U.S. immigrants are citizens or subjects of another country who come here to live and work. To become full citizens, they must undergo naturalization by fulfilling requirements designated by the U.S. Citizenship and Immigration Services.

Some people come to the United States for other reasons and do not seek permanent residency. In recent years the influx of undocumented immigrants, particularly in the southwestern

states, has occupied national debate. Advocates of strict immigration policy complain that undocumented immigrants consume government services without paying taxes. Opponents of these policies support the provision of basic services for people who, like our ancestors, are escaping hardship and hoping for a better future. Congress, with the president's approval, makes immigration law, but these rules change frequently.

immigrants (p. 33)
naturalization (p. 33)
asylum (p. 37)
refugees (p. 37)

The Ideas That Unite Us

Americans share common values and beliefs about how the world should work that allow us to be a nation despite our diversity. The American political culture is described as both procedural and individualistic. Because we focus more on fair rules than on the outcomes of those rules, our culture has a procedural nature. In addition, our individualistic nature means that we assume that individuals know what is best for them and that individuals, not government or society, are responsible for their own well-being.

Democracy, freedom, and equality are three central American values. Generally, Americans acknowledge democracy as the most appropriate way to make public decisions. We value freedom for the individual from government restraint, and we value equality of opportunity rather than equality of result.

political culture (p. 43)
values (p. 43)
normative (p. 44)
procedural guarantees (p. 44)
individualism (p. 44)

The Ideas That Divide Us

While the range of ideological debate is fairly narrow in America when compared to other countries, there exists an ideological division among economic liberals, social liberals, economic conservatives, and social conservatives based largely on attitudes toward government control of the economy and of the social order.

ideologies (p. 46)
conservatives (p. 48)
liberals (p. 48)
economic liberals (p. 49)
economic conservatives (p. 51)
libertarians (p. 52)
social liberals (p. 52)
communitarians (p. 52)
social conservatives (p. 52)

The Citizens and American Political Beliefs

America's growing political apathy is well documented. Yet despite abysmal voting rates, the country continues to function, a fact that may be explained by several theories. However, many people claim that such apathy may indeed signal a crisis of democracy.

Learn the Gettysburg Address. The words spoken by Abraham Lincoln at Gettysburg in 1863 sum up both the promise and the challenge of the United States in less than 280 words. Documentary filmmaker Ken Burns invited celebrities, filmmakers, and everyday citizens to take a little time to memorize this powerful speech, and record their recitations for the world to see. Check out **learntheaddress.org** to see them.

Find your immigrant roots. Trace your family history to find out when and how you came to be an American. Begin your search at **FamilySearch.org,** a nonprofit genealogy organization that can open doors to your family tree. You can also visit **Ellis Island online,** which offers virtual tours to get a glimpse of what was once America's main immigrant entry facility. Their free archives include passenger searches, immigrant experiences, timelines, and photos.

Take a look at your census tract. Just how diverse is your hometown? Visit the **U.S. Census Bureau** for vast amounts of data—current, historical, and future projections—on the American people and businesses. You can look at the nation as a whole, or just at your state, city, or census tract. Check out the Census Bureau's reports for help deciphering the numbers.

Wander through the Pluralism Project. Harvard University's two-decade-long study of ways in which religious diversity impacts and is impacted by American life has yielded a wealth of resources. Click through them for videos, slideshows, and case studies, or to get involved in any of a number of civic engagement projects focused on respecting and embracing the diverse tapestry of religious beliefs in the United States.

Ferguson, Craig. 2009. *American on Purpose: The Improbable Adventures of an Unlikely Patriot.* New York: Harper Perennial. Scottish-born comedian Craig Ferguson details his journey to American citizenship, with musings on what it means to be American.

Schrag, Peter. 2010. *Not Fit for Our Society: Immigration and Nativism in America.* Berkeley: University of California Press. This ironically titled volume offers a thorough history of immigration in the United

States from the colonial era through the present day, noting the similarities in anti-immigrant rhetoric that has been directed at each new group to come to our shores.

Schudson, Michael. 2011. *The Good Citizen: A History of American Civil Life.* **New York: Free Press.** In this provocative analysis of how this country's definition of what makes "a good citizen" has changed over time, Schudson argues that we expect too much from our citizens.

Borderland: Dispatches From the U.S.-Mexico Border. This National Public Radio series offers insightful reports on life on both sides of the U.S.-Mexico border.

30 Days. 2005–2008, FX television series. Documentarian Morgan Spurlock offers real-world glimpses into different pockets of American culture—challenging himself and others to live the life of someone of vastly different circumstances for thirty straight days—while cameras roll.

Dreamer: A True American Story. 2013. This independent film tells the story of a young Mexican American man whose life, career, and sense of who he is fall apart when it is revealed that he was brought to the country illegally when he was very young.

3

POLITICS OF THE AMERICAN FOUNDING

IN YOUR OWN WORDS   After you've read this chapter, you will be able to

» Describe the competition among different colonial powers for control of America.

» Describe the events and political motivations that led to the colonies' split with England.

» Explain what the Articles of Confederation did and what it failed to do.

» Identify the goals, divisions, and compromises that shaped the Constitution.

» Summarize the debate over ratification of the Constitution.

» Explain the role of everyday citizens in the founding of the United States.

WHAT'S AT STAKE...IN CHALLENGING THE LEGITIMACY OF THE U.S. GOVERNMENT?

IT MIGHT HAVE BEEN 1773 ALL OVER AGAIN. Antitax and antigovernment, the 2010 Tea Partiers were angry, and if they didn't go as far as to empty shiploads of tea into Boston Harbor, they made their displeasure known in other ways. Though their ire was directed at government in general, they found specific targets in the George W. Bush administration's Troubled Asset Relief Program (TARP) bailouts of big financial institutions in 2008 and other measures taken in response to the economic crisis that began that year, including mortgage assistance for people facing foreclosure, the stimulus bill, and the health reform act, all passed by Congress in 2009 and 2010 with the strong backing of President Barack Obama.

Many of the Tea Partiers were simply focused on airing their aversion to the agenda of President Obama and the Democrats who had swept into office after the 2008 election, and they signaled their intention to vote for more conservative replacements in 2010 and 2012. Other messages were more ominous, rejecting the very legitimacy of the U.S. government—by doubting the citizenship of the

president, by claiming that the election that brought him to power had been rigged by groups like ACORN, or by arguing that the government in Washington was tyrannical and it was the job of patriotic citizens to resist it.

The Tea Party movement is a decentralized mix of many groups—most simply frustrated Republicans (the major party that most Tea Partiers identify with or lean toward) but others more extreme. David Barstow of the *New York Times* wrote in early 2010 that a "significant undercurrent within the Tea Party movement" was less like a part of the Republican Party than it was like "the Patriot movement, a brand of politics historically associated with libertarians, militia groups, anti-immigration advocates and those who argue for the abolition of the Federal Reserve."[1] He quotes a Tea Party leader so worried about the impending tyranny threatening her country that she can imagine being called to violence in its defense: "I don't see us being the ones to start it, but I would give up my life for my country. . . . Peaceful means are the best way of going about it. But sometimes you are not given a choice."

AP Photo/Joel Page

Is That a Gun in Your Pocket?

Outside a 2009 Obama town hall meeting in New Hampshire, this armed demonstrator's sign refers to the Thomas Jefferson quote, "The tree of liberty must be refreshed from time to time with the blood of patriots and tyrants." He grabs our attention because the pistol seems to threaten a readiness to political action that extends well beyond the voting booth or peaceful protest.

Reflecting these same feelings, Tea Party members in Oklahoma City in April 2010 declared their intention to pass a state law to create a militia to defend their state against the federal government.[2] Their announcement came just days before the fifteenth anniversary of the day Timothy McVeigh, holding many similar views about the illegitimacy of the federal government, attacked the federal building in Oklahoma City, killing 168 people, including 19 children.

Like the extreme Tea Partiers quoted above and even McVeigh and his associates, Patriot and militia group members are everyday men and women who say they are the ideological heirs of the American Revolution. They liken themselves to the colonial Sons of Liberty, who rejected the authority of the British government and took it upon themselves to enforce the laws they thought were just. The Sons of Liberty instigated the Boston Massacre and the Boston Tea Party, historical events that we celebrate as patriotic but that would be considered treason or terrorism if they took place today—and were considered as such by the British back when they occurred.

More conventional Republicans hoped that the Tea Party's grip on their party had started to weaken in the wake of some well-publicized Tea Party defeats—namely, the Republicans' loss in the 2012 election, when presidential candidate Mitt Romney had been forced to swing sharply to the right to win the primaries, and the negative public reaction to the government shutdown that followed House Republicans' inability to approve an appropriations bill in October 2013. Nonetheless, the revolutionary rhetoric and the goals stayed put.

In 2014, self-identified patriots launched Operation American Spring, promoted on teaparty.org and billed on operationamericanspring.com this way:

> The goal is restoring the US Constitution as the law of the land, removing the lawless leadership. Will this be a cake-walk? No, it will be painful, and some people may die because the government will not be non-violent; some of us will end up in a cell, and some may be injured. If that's what it will take to save our nation, do we have any choice? Freedom loving Americans will say there is no choice, we must begin the second American Revolution. Not with guns, but with millions of Americans demanding a return to constitutional government and the resignation of Obama, Biden, Reid, McConnell, Boehner, Pelosi, and Holder as a start...then the constitutional restoration process can begin. An AMERICAN SPRING can be avoided only if the above mentioned officials resign.[3]

To the disappointment of organizers, only a tiny fraction of the hoped-for 10–30 million participants actually showed up (attendance was in the hundreds, not millions). But any flagging Tea Party spirits were uplifted in June, when House majority leader Eric Cantor, a conservative Republican, was defeated in his primary by an even more conservative Tea Party candidate.

Today's so-called Patriot groups claim that the federal government has become as tyrannical as the British government ever was, that it deprives citizens of their liberty and over-regulates their everyday lives. They go so far as to claim that federal authority is illegitimate. Militia members reject federal laws that do everything from limiting the weapons that individual citizens can own, to imposing taxes on income, to requiring the registration of motor vehicles, to creating the Federal Reserve Bank, to reforming the health care system. They maintain that government should stay out of individual lives, providing security at the national level, perhaps, but allowing citizens to regulate and protect their own lives.

Some militias go even further. They may blend their quests for individual liberty with rigid requirements about who should enjoy that liberty. White supremacist or anti-Semitic groups aim at achieving an all-white continent or see Jewish collaboration behind ominous plots to destroy America. Many militia members are convinced that the United Nations is seeking to take over the United States (and that top U.S. officials are letting this happen). In August 2012, with the November election in the offing, a Texas judge, Tom Head, actually called for a tax increase so that police could be prepared for what he anticipated would happen if President Obama were reelected. He said, "He's going to try to hand over the sovereignty of the United States to the UN, and what is going to happen when that happens? . . . I'm thinking the worst. Civil unrest, civil disobedience, civil war maybe. And we're not just talking a few riots here and demonstrations, we're talking Lexington, Concord, take up arms and get rid of the guy."[4]

Although there are some indications that militia membership was down in the wake of the negative publicity surrounding the 1995 Oklahoma City bombing, membership in such groups surged after Obama's first election.[5] The groups base their claim to legitimate existence on the Constitution's Second Amendment, which reads, "A well regulated Militia, being necessary to the security of a free State, the right of the people to keep and bear Arms, shall not be infringed." Members of state militias, and other groups like them, take this amendment literally and absolutely. The website teaparty.org, though not representative of all Tea Party groups, says "gun ownership is sacred."[6]

The federal government has reacted strongly to limit the threat presented by state militias and others who believe that its authority is not legitimate. Partly in response to the Oklahoma City bombing, Congress passed an antiterrorism bill signed by President Bill Clinton in 1996 that would make it easier for federal agencies to monitor the activities of such groups. Those powers were broadened in the wake of the September 11, 2001, attacks on the United States by foreign terrorists. President George W. Bush gave the Department of Homeland Security a broad mandate to combat terrorism, including the homegrown variety. And in June 2014, in reaction to the surging numbers of radicalized people within the country, Attorney General Eric Holder announced that he would revive the domestic terrorism task force that had been formed after the Oklahoma City bombings but failed to meet once September 11, 2001, turned the nation's attention to terrorism overseas.

Is the federal government responding appropriately to these threats? Are these groups, as they claim, the embodiment of revolutionary patriotism? Do they support the Constitution, or sabotage it? And where do we draw the line between a Tea Party member who wants to sound off against elected officials and policies she doesn't like, and one who advocates resorting to violence to protect her particular reading of the Constitution? Think about these questions as you read this chapter on the founding of the United States. Think about the consequences and implications of revolutionary activity then and now. At the end of this chapter we revisit the question of what's at stake for American politics in the militia movement's challenge to the legitimacy of American government. «

FROM the moment students start coloring in pictures of grateful Pilgrims and cutting out construction paper turkeys in grade school, the founding of the United States is a recurring focus of American education, and with good reason. Democratic societies, as we saw in Chapter 1, rely on the consent of their citizens to maintain lawful behavior and public order. To be committed to the rules and the goals of the American system requires that we feel good about that system. What better way to stir up good feelings and patriotism than by recounting thrilling stories of bravery and derring-do on the part of selfless heroes dedicated to the cause of American liberty? We celebrate the Fourth of July with fireworks and parades, displaying publicly our commitment to American values and our belief that our country is special, in the same way that other nations celebrate their origins all over the world. Bastille Day (July 14) in France, May 17 in Norway, October 1 in China, July 6 in Malawi, Africa—all are days on which people rally together to celebrate their common past and their hopes for the future.

Of course people feel real pride in their countries and of course many nations, not only our own, do have amazing stories to tell about their earliest days. But as political scientists, we must separate myth from reality. For us, the founding of the United States is central not because it inspires warm feelings of patriotism but because it can teach us about American politics, the struggles for power that forged the political system that continues to shape our collective struggles today.

The history of the American founding has been told from many points of view. You are probably most familiar with this account: The early colonists escaped to America to avoid religious persecution in Europe. Having arrived on the shores of the New World, they built communities that allowed them to practice their religions in peace and to govern themselves as free people. When the tyrannical British king made unreasonable demands on the colonists, they had no choice but to protect their liberty by going to war and by establishing a new government of their own.

But sound historical evidence suggests that the story is more complicated, and more interesting, than that. A closer look shows that the early Americans were complex beings with economic and political agendas as well as religious and philosophical motives. After much struggle among themselves, the majority of Americans decided that those agendas could be carried out better and more profitably if they broke their ties with England.[7]

Just because a controversial event like the founding is recounted by historians or political scientists one or two hundred years after it happens does not guarantee that there is common agreement on what actually took place. People write history not from a position of absolute truth but from particular points of view. When we read a historical account, as critical thinkers we need to ask probing questions: Who is telling the story? What point of view is being represented? What values and priorities lie behind it? If I accept this interpretation, what else will I have to accept?

In this chapter we talk a lot about history—the history of the American founding and the creation of the Constitution. As we point out in the Chapter 1 *Don't Be Fooled by . . .* feature, we, like all other authors, have a particular point of view that affects how we tell the story. True to the first basic theme of this book, we are interested in power and politics. We want to understand American government in terms of who the winners and losers are likely to be. It makes sense for us to begin by looking at the founding to see who the winners and losers were then. We are also interested in how rules and institutions make it more likely that some people will win and others lose. Certainly an examination of the early debates about rules and institutions will help us understand that. Finally, because we are interested in winners and losers, we are interested in understanding how people come to be defined as players in the system in the first place, the focus of the second theme of this book—citizenship. It was during the founding that many of the initial decisions were made about who "We the People" would actually be.

POLITICS IN THE ENGLISH COLONIES
Power struggles in the new world

America was a battlefield—both political and military—long before the war for independence from Britain was fought. Not only did the English settlers have to struggle with brutal winters, harsh droughts, disease, and other unanticipated natural disasters, but they quickly came into conflict with the people who already inhabited the New World when they arrived—Native Americans and Spanish and French colonists.

Declaring that they had a legitimate right to colonize unoccupied territory, the British set about populating the eastern coast of America. Many Native Americans initially helped the British overcome the rigors of life in the New World. But cultural differences between the Indians and the British—and the latter's conviction that their beliefs and practices were superior to Indian ways—made the relationship between the two unpredictable. Some Indians engaged in political dealings with the Europeans, forming military coalitions (partnerships), trade alliances, and other arrangements. Others were more hostile, particularly in the face of the European assumption that the New World was theirs to subdue and exploit.

The Spanish, too, were an obstacle to English domination. Spain in the sixteenth century seemed to be well on its way to owning the New World. Spanish explorers had laid claim to both eastern and western North America as well as key parts of Central and South America. The ancestors of many of the 21 million Spanish-speaking people in America today were living in what is now New Mexico, California, Colorado, and Texas, for instance, before many people were speaking English in America at all. But the monarchs of England liked the idea of getting a piece of the treasure that was being exported regularly from the Americas. Spain and England were already in conflict in Europe, and Spain was vulnerable. Despite treaties, Spanish spies, intrigue with Native Americans, and occasional military action, Britain edged Spain out of the colonial picture in eastern America. Had Spain been able to enforce the treaties Britain had signed, or had it been able to form a more constant and productive alliance with France, it might have been able to reverse its fortunes. In due time, the English would have to fend off the Dutch and the French, as well, but by the late 1700s the eastern seaboard colonies were heavily English. Though Spain maintained its presence in the West and the Southwest, those territories did not figure in American politics until much later.

REASONS FOR LEAVING ENGLAND

Many British subjects were eager and willing to try their luck across the Atlantic. They came to America to make their fortunes, to practice their religions without interference, to become landowners—to take advantage of a host of opportunities that England, still struggling out of the straightjacket of feudalism, could not offer. **Feudalism** was a

> **feudalism** a social system in which a rigid social and political hierarchy was based on the ownership of land

social system in which a rigid social and political hierarchy was based on the ownership of land, but land ownership was restricted to the very few. Individuals lived out their lives in the class to which they were born; it was unheard of to work one's way up from peasant to landowner.

Although the colonists did not know it, life in England in the 1600s was on the brink of major change. Within the century, political thinkers would begin to reject the idea that monarchs ruled through divine right, would favor increasing the power of Parliament at the expense of the king, and would promote the idea that individuals were not merely subjects but citizens, with rights that government could not violate. Civil war and revolution in England would give teeth to these fresh ideas. The new philosophy, a product of the Enlightenment, was open to religious tolerance, giving rise to more reformist and separatist sects. Commerce and trade would create the beginnings of a new middle class with financial power independent of the landed class of feudalism, a class that would blossom with the rise of industry in the 1700s.

But in the early 1600s, settlers came to America in part because England seemed resistant to change. It would be a mistake to think, however, that the colonists, having been repressed in England, came to America hoping to achieve liberty for all people. The colonists emigrated in order to practice their religions freely (but not necessarily to let others practice theirs), to own land, to engage in trade, to avoid debtors' prison. England also had a national interest in sending colonists to America. Under the economic system of mercantilism, nations competed for the world's resources through trade, and colonies were a primary source of raw materials for manufacturing. Entrepreneurs often supported colonization as an investment, and the government issued charters to companies, giving them the right to settle land as English colonies.

POLITICAL PARTICIPATION IN THE COLONIES

It shouldn't surprise us, therefore, to find that the settlers often created communities that were in some ways as restrictive and repressive as the ones they had left behind in England. The difference, of course, was that *they* were now the ones doing the repressing rather than the ones being repressed. In other ways, life in America was more open than life in Britain. Land was widely available. Although much of it was inhabited by Native Americans, the Indians believed in communal or shared use of property. The Europeans arrived with notions of private property and the sophisticated weaponry to defend the land they claimed. Some colonies set up systems of self-rule, with representative assemblies such as Virginia's House of Burgesses, Maryland's

slavery the ownership, for forced labor, of one people by another

House of Delegates, and the town meetings of the northern colonies. Though they had governors, often appointed by the king, at least until the late 1600s the colonies were left largely, though not exclusively, to their own devices.

Although the colonies offered more opportunities than did life in Britain, they also continued many of the injustices that some colonists had hoped to escape. A useful way to understand who had power in the colonies is to look at the rules regulating political participation—that is, who was allowed to vote in colonial lawmaking bodies, who wasn't, and why. Each colony set its own voting rules, based on such factors as property, religion, gender, and race.

- *Property.* Although voting laws varied in England by locality as well, there they had in common an emphasis on property-holding requirements. Very simply, conventional British wisdom held that if you didn't own property, you were unlikely to take a serious interest in government (whose job was largely to protect property, after all), and you were equally unlikely to share the values and virtues attached to rural life, which formed the core of British upper-class culture. Gradually the colonies too began to require of voters some degree of property ownership or, later, tax-paying status. This requirement did not exclude as many people from voting in America as in England since property owning was so much more widespread among the settlers.

- *Religion.* More pervasive than property-owning or tax-paying requirements, at least in the earliest days of colonial government, were moral or religious qualifications. The northern colonies, especially, were concerned about keeping the ungodly out of government. By 1640, for instance, religious tests for voting prevented three-fourths of the Massachusetts population from having any political power. By 1691, however, Massachusetts had moved into line with Virginia and the other colonies that based an individual's political rights on his wealth rather than his character.

- *Gender.* Women weren't officially excluded from political participation in America until the Revolution. Until then, as in England, they occasionally could exercise the vote when they satisfied the property requirement and when there were no voting males in their households. In some localities, widows, in particular, or daughters who had inherited a parent's property, could vote or participate in church meetings (which sometimes amounted to the same thing). Some colonies allowed women to vote, whereas others, notably Pennsylvania, Delaware, Virginia, Georgia, New York, and South Carolina, excluded them, at least for some period of time.[8]

- *Race.* Before slavery took hold as an American institution at the end of the 1600s, Africans were subjected

A Political Divide
Under English rule, some women in the American colonies were able to participate in politics. Once the United States was formed, however, the states crafted a strict political divide that restricted voting primarily to wealthy, landowning men.

to the same laws and codes of behavior as Europeans living in America.[9] The colonies required tremendous amounts of cheap labor to produce the raw materials and goods needed for trade with England under the mercantilist system, and when English people from the Caribbean island of Barbados settled in South Carolina in 1670, they brought with them the institution of slavery. Slavery proved economically profitable even in the more commercial areas of New England, but it utterly transformed the tobacco plantations of Maryland and Virginia.[10]

Not surprisingly, as slavery became accepted in the colonies, the rights of blacks were gradually stripped away. In the 1640s Maryland denied blacks the right to bear arms. A 1669 Virginia law declared that if a slave "should chance to die" when resisting his or her master or the master's agent, it would not be a felony—a crime that legally required malice—because no one would destroy his own property with malice. Most politically damaging, by the 1680s free blacks were forbidden to own property, the only access to political power that colonial society recognized.[11] Reasons for these legal changes are not hard to find. Slavery can work only if slaves are dependent, defenseless, and afraid to escape. Also, an institution as dehumanizing as slavery requires some justification that enables slaveholders to live with themselves, especially in the Enlightenment era, when words like "natural rights" and "liberty" were on everyone's

The Granger Collection, New York

tongue. It was said that the Africans were childlike, lazy, and undisciplined, and that they needed the supervision of slave owners. The worse slaves were treated, the more their humanity was denied. Racism, the belief that one race is superior to another, undoubtedly existed before slavery was well established in America, but the institution of slavery made it a part of American political culture. We discuss the issue of race in American politics in more detail in Chapter 6.

PAUSE AND REVIEW:

WHO, WHAT, HOW

The English colonists wanted, first and foremost, to find new opportunities in America. But those opportunities were not available to all. Religious and property qualifications for the vote, and the exclusion of women and blacks from political life, meant that the colonial leaders did not feel that simply living in a place or obeying the laws or even paying taxes carried with it the right to participate in government. Following the rigid British social hierarchy, they wanted rules to ensure that the "right kind" of people could participate, people who could be depended on to make the kind of rules that would ensure their status and maintain the established order. The danger of expanding the vote, of course, is that the new majority might want something very different from what the old majority wanted.

IN YOUR OWN WORDS » Describe the competition among different colonial powers for control of America.

THE SPLIT FROM ENGLAND
Making the transition from British subjects to American citizens

Both England and America accepted as perfectly normal the relationships of colonial power that initially bound them together. Americans, as colonists, were obliged to make England their primary trading partner, and all goods they traded to other countries had to pass through Britain, where a tax was collected on them. The benefits of being a colony, however, including financial support by British corporations, military defense by the British army and navy, and a secure market for their agricultural products, usually

Slavery in Colonial America ● Native American Ideas About Property ●

outweighed any burdens of colonial obligation. Eventually the relationship started to sour as the colonists developed an identity as Americans rather than as transplanted English people, and as the British became a more intrusive political presence. Even then, they searched painstakingly for a way to fix the relationship before they decided to eliminate it altogether. Revolution was not an idea that occurred readily to either side.

BRITISH ATTEMPTS TO GAIN CONTROL OF THE COLONIES

Whether the British government had actually become oppressive in the years before 1776 is open to interpretation. Certainly the colonists thought so. Britain was deeply in debt, having won the **French and Indian War**, which effectively forced the French out of North America and the Spanish to vacate Florida and retreat west of the Mississippi. The war, fought to defend the British colonies and colonists in America, turned into a major and expensive conflict across the Atlantic as well. Britain, having done its protective duty as a colonial power and having taxed British citizens heavily to finance the war, turned to its colonies to help pay for their defense. It chose to do that by levying taxes on the colonies and by attempting to enforce more strictly the trade laws that would increase British profits from American resources.

The irony is that, with the British victory in the war, the colonies were largely free of Spanish, French, and Indian threat. No longer in need of British protection, they could afford to resist British efforts to make them help pay for it.[12] The series of acts the British passed infuriated the colonists. The Sugar Act of 1764, which imposed customs taxes, or duties, on sugar, was seen as unfair and unduly burdensome in a depressed postwar economy, and the Stamp Act of 1765 incited protests and demonstrations throughout the colonies. Similar to a tax in effect in Great Britain for nearly a century, it required that a tax be paid, in scarce British currency, on every piece of printed matter in the colonies, including newspapers, legal documents, and even playing cards. The colonists claimed that the law was an infringement on their liberty and a violation of their rights not to be taxed without their consent. Continued protests and political changes in England resulted in the repeal of the Stamp Act in 1766. The Townshend Acts of 1767, taxing goods imported from England such as paper, glass, and tea, followed by the Tea Act of 1773, were seen by the colonists as intolerable violations of their rights. To show their displeasure they hurled 342 chests of tea into Boston Harbor in the infamous Boston Tea Party. Britain responded by passing the

> **French and Indian War** a war fought between France and England, and allied Indians, from 1754 to 1763; resulted in France's expulsion from the New World

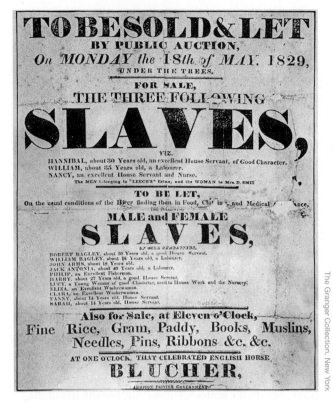

The Granger Collection, New York

Human Trade
Slaves were used to meet the needs of the South's burgeoning economy in tobacco and cotton, which required plentiful, cheap labor. They were shipped from Africa and sold to farmers alongside rice, books, and other goods. In the eighteenth century, approximately 275,000 slaves were shipped to the American colonies. Many did not survive the harsh conditions of the passage.

Coercive Acts of 1774, designed to punish the citizens of Massachusetts. In the process, Parliament sowed the seeds that would blossom into revolution in just a few years.

CHANGING IDEAS ABOUT POLITICS

The American reluctance to cooperate with Britain was reinforced by the colonists' changing worldview. Philosophical ideas that were fermenting in England and the European Enlightenment as a whole, especially those of John Locke, were finding a natural home in America. Bernard Bailyn, a scholar of early American history, says that American thinking challenged and broke with British ideology on the interpretation of three major concepts: representation, constitution, and sovereignty.[13]

With respect to representation, Americans came to believe that elected representatives should do precisely what the people who elected them told them to do. This was very different from the British notion of "virtual representation," in which the representative followed his conscience, acting in the best interests of the country as a whole and thus, by definition, of the citizens who lived there. The colonists also began to understand the notion of a constitution as a specific grant of powers to and limitations on government, including Parliament itself. This idea was in turn directly connected to the notion of sovereignty. For the British, the sovereign authority was Parliament, which established the rule of law and constitutional principles. But the colonists held fast to the principle of popular sovereignty; that is, the ultimate authority, the power to govern, belonged in the hands of the people.

These philosophical changes meant that any British colonial authority had begun to seem illegitimate to many of the colonists. Much has been made in American school-books about the colonists' defiant rejection of British taxation without representation. The British had offered Americans representation in Parliament, however, and they had rejected it in the assemblies of South Carolina and Virginia.[14] It wasn't just taxation the colonists objected to; it was the British parliament itself.

Some loyalists to the Crown continued to support British authority because they were involved in British administration of the colonies, because they had commercial ties to Britain, because they believed that America still needed British military protection, or because they were committed to the notion of monarchy. For the rest of the colonists, however, it became harder and harder to recognize British power over them as legitimate authority.

REVOLUTION

From the moment that the unpopularly taxed tea plunged into Boston Harbor in December 1773, it became apparent that the Americans were not going to settle down and behave like proper and orthodox colonists. Even before the Tea Party, mobs in many towns were demonstrating and rioting against British control. Calling themselves the Sons of Liberty, and under the guidance of the eccentric Samuel Adams, cousin to the future president John Adams, rebellious colonists routinely caused extensive damage and, in early 1770, provoked the so-called Boston Massacre, an attack by British soldiers that left six civilians dead and further inflamed popular sentiments.

By the time of the Boston Tea Party, also incited by the Sons of Liberty, passions were at a fever pitch. The American patriots called a meeting in Philadelphia in September 1774. Known as the First Continental Congress, the meeting declared the Coercive Acts void, announced a plan to stop trade with England, and called for a second meeting in May 1775. Before they could meet again, in the early spring of 1775, the king's army went marching to arrest Samuel Adams and another patriot, John Hancock, and to discover the hiding place of the colonists' weapons. Roused by the silversmith Paul Revere, Americans in Lexington and Concord fired the first shots of rebellion at the British, and revolution was truly under way.

THE DECLARATION OF INDEPENDENCE

Even in the midst of war, the colonists did not at first clearly articulate a desire for independence from England. But publication of the pamphlet *Common Sense*, written by the English-born Thomas Paine, turned their old ideas upside-down. In this immensely popular pamphlet, which sold more than 150,000 copies in just a few weeks,[15] Paine called for the rejection of the king, for independence, and for republican government, and his passionate writing crystallized the thinking of the colonial leaders.[16]

In 1776, at the direction of a committee of the Continental Congress, thirty-four-year-old Thomas Jefferson sat down to write a declaration of independence from England. His training as a lawyer at the College of William and Mary, and his service as a representative in the Virginia House of Burgesses, helped prepare him for his task, but he had an impressive intellect in any case. President John Kennedy once announced to a group of Nobel Prize winners he was entertaining that they were "the most extraordinary collection of talents that has ever gathered at the White House, with the possible exception of when Thomas Jefferson dined alone."[17] A testimony to Jefferson's capabilities is the strategically brilliant document that he produced.

The Declaration of Independence is first and foremost a political document. Having decided to make the break from England, the American founders had to convince themselves, their fellow colonists, and the rest of the world that they were doing the right thing. Revolutions are generally frowned on politically, unless the revolutionaries can convince the world that they have particularly good and legitimate reasons for their actions. Other national leaders don't like them because they upset the status quo and give ideas to the politically discontent in their own countries. In addition, revolutionaries face the problem of justifying *their* revolution, but no other ones. After all, they presumably intend to set up a new government after the revolution, and they don't want people revolting against *it*. The story told to justify a revolution has to guard against setting off a chain reaction. The Declaration of Independence admirably performs all these tasks.

Jefferson did not have to hunt further than the writing of John Locke for a good reason for his revolution. Recall

popular sovereignty the concept that the citizens are the ultimate source of political power

Common Sense 1776 pamphlet by Thomas Paine that persuaded many Americans to support the Revolutionary cause

Declaration of Independence the political document that dissolved the colonial ties between the United States and Britain

from Chapter 1 that Locke said that government is based on a contract between the rulers and the ruled. The ruled agree to obey the laws as long as the rulers protect their basic rights to life, liberty, and property. If the rulers fail to do that, they break the contract and the ruled are free to set up another government. This is exactly what the second paragraph of the Declaration of Independence says, except that Jefferson changed "property" to "the pursuit of happiness," perhaps to garner the support of those Americans who didn't own enough property to worry about. Having established that the breaking of the social contract was a good reason for revolution, Jefferson could justify the American Revolution if he could show that Britain had broken such a contract by violating the colonists' rights.

Consequently, he spelled out all the things that King George III had allegedly done to breach the social contract. Take a look at the Declaration in the *CLUES to Critical Thinking* feature in this chapter and notice the extensive list of grievances against the king. For twenty-seven paragraphs, Jefferson documented just how badly the monarch had treated the colonists. Note, however, that many of the things the colonists complained of were the normal acts of a colonial power. No one had told the king that he was a party to a Lockean contract, so it isn't surprising that he violated it at every turn. Furthermore, some of the things he was blamed for were the acts of Parliament, not of the king at all. Perhaps because the colonists intended to have some sort of parliament of their own, or perhaps, as some scholars have argued, because they simply did not recognize Parliament's authority over them, George III was the sole focus of their wrath and resentment. But the clear goal of the document was to so thoroughly discredit George III that this revolution became inevitable in the eyes of every American, and the world.

THINKING OUTSIDE THE BOX

Are there any circumstances in which it would be justifiable for groups in the United States to rebel against the federal government today?

"...THAT ALL MEN ARE CREATED EQUAL"

The Declaration of Independence begins with a statement of the equality of all men. Since so much of this document relies heavily on Locke, and since clearly the colonists did *not* mean that all men are created equal, it is worth turning

to Locke for some help in seeing exactly what they did mean. In his most famous work, *A Second Treatise on Government*, Locke wrote,

Though I have said above that all men are by nature equal, I cannot be supposed to understand all sorts of equality. Age or virtue may give men a just precedency. Excellency of parts and merit may place others above the common level. Birth may subject some, and alliance or benefits others, to pay an observance to those whom nature, gratitude, or other respects may have made it due.[18]

Men are equal in a natural sense, said Locke, but society quickly establishes many dimensions on which they may be unequal. A particularly sticky point for Locke's ideas on equality is his treatment of slavery, which he did not endorse but ultimately failed to condemn. Here, too, our founders would have been in agreement with him.

The founders' ambivalence about slavery and equality can be seen in a passage that Jefferson included in the original draft of the Declaration, as part of the political indictment of George III. He wrote:

He [George III] has waged cruel war against human nature itself, violating its most sacred rights of life and liberty in the persons of a distant people who never offended him, captivating and carrying them into slavery in another hemisphere or to incur miserable death in their transportation thither.[19]

Blaming King George for the institution of slavery, and including it on a list of behaviors so horrible that they justify revolution, was an amazing act on the part of a man who not only owned slaves himself, but also was writing on behalf of many other slave owners. His action shows just how politically confusing and morally ambiguous the issue was at that time. Reflecting the political realities of the time, the passage was eventually deleted.

AFRICAN AMERICANS AND THE REVOLUTION The Revolution was a mixed blessing for American slaves. On the one hand, many slaves won their freedom as a result of the war; slavery was outlawed north of Maryland, and many slaves in the Upper South also were freed. The British offered freedom in exchange for service in the British army, although the conditions they provided were not always a great improvement over enslavement. The abolitionist, or antislavery, movement gathered steam in some northern cities, expressing moral and constitutional objections to the institution of slavery. Whereas before the Revolution only about 5 percent of American blacks were free, the number grew tremendously with the coming of war.[20]

Many African Americans served in the war. There were probably about twelve blacks in the first battle at Lexington

CLUES
TO CRITICAL THINKING

The Declaration of Independence

By Thomas Jefferson, July 4, 1776

We discuss the Declaration of Independence at length in this chapter, but it is often a good idea to read for yourself the primary sources by which our history has been shaped.

IN CONGRESS, JULY 4, 1776
The unanimous Declaration of the thirteen United States of America

When in the Course of human events it becomes necessary for one people to dissolve the political bands which have connected them with another and to assume among the powers of the earth, the separate and equal station to which the Laws of Nature and of Nature's God entitle them, a decent respect to the opinions of mankind requires that they should declare the causes which impel them to the separation.

We hold these truths to be self-evident, that all men are created equal, that they are endowed by their Creator with certain unalienable Rights, that among these are Life, Liberty and the pursuit of Happiness. — That to secure these rights, Governments are instituted among Men, deriving their just powers from the consent of the governed, — That whenever any Form of Government becomes destructive of these ends, it is the Right of the People to alter or to abolish it, and to institute new Government, laying its foundation on such principles and organizing its powers in such form, as to them shall seem most likely to effect their Safety and Happiness. Prudence,

indeed, will dictate that Governments long established should not be changed for light and transient causes; and accordingly all experience hath shewn that mankind are more disposed to suffer, while evils are sufferable than to right themselves by abolishing the forms to which they are accustomed. But when a long train of abuses and usurpations, pursuing invariably the same Object evinces a design to reduce them under absolute Despotism, it is their right, it is their duty, to throw off such Government, and to provide new Guards for their future security. — Such has been the patient sufferance of these Colonies; and such is now the necessity which constrains them to alter their former Systems of Government. The history of the present King of Great Britain is a history of repeated injuries and usurpations, all having in direct object the establishment of an absolute Tyranny over these States. To prove this, let Facts be submitted to a candid world.

He has refused his Assent to Laws, the most wholesome and necessary for the public good.

He has forbidden his Governors to pass Laws of immediate and pressing importance, unless suspended in their operation till his Assent should be obtained; and when so suspended, he has utterly neglected to attend to them.

He has refused to pass other Laws for the accommodation of large districts of people, unless those people would relinquish the right of Representation in the Legislature, a right inestimable to them and formidable to tyrants only.

He has called together legislative bodies at places unusual, uncomfortable, and distant from the depository of their Public Records, for the sole purpose of fatiguing them into compliance with his measures.

He has dissolved Representative Houses repeatedly, for opposing with manly firmness his invasions on the rights of the people.

He has refused for a long time, after such dissolutions, to cause others to be elected, whereby the Legislative Powers,

incapable of Annihilation, have returned to the People at large for their exercise; the State remaining in the mean time exposed to all the dangers of invasion from without, and convulsions within.

He has endeavoured to prevent the population of these States; for that purpose obstructing the Laws for Naturalization of Foreigners; refusing to pass others to encourage their migrations hither, and raising the conditions of new Appropriations of Lands.

He has obstructed the Administration of Justice by refusing his Assent to Laws for establishing Judiciary Powers.

He has made Judges dependent on his Will alone for the tenure of their offices, and the amount and payment of their salaries.

He has erected a multitude of New Offices, and sent hither swarms of Officers to harass our people and eat out their substance.

He has kept among us, in times of peace, Standing Armies without the Consent of our legislatures.

He has affected to render the Military independent of and superior to the Civil Power.

He has combined with others to subject us to a jurisdiction foreign to our constitution, and unacknowledged by our laws; giving his Assent to their Acts of pretended Legislation:

For quartering large bodies of armed troops among us:

For protecting them, by a mock Trial from punishment for any Murders which they should commit on the Inhabitants of these States:

For cutting off our Trade with all parts of the world:

For imposing Taxes on us without our Consent:

For depriving us in many cases, of the benefit of Trial by Jury:

For transporting us beyond Seas to be tried for pretended offences:

For abolishing the free System of English Laws in a neighbouring Province, establishing therein an Arbitrary government, and enlarging its Boundaries so as to render it at once an example and fit instrument for introducing the same absolute rule into these Colonies:

For taking away our Charters, abolishing our most valuable Laws and altering fundamentally the Forms of our Governments:

For suspending our own Legislatures, and declaring themselves invested with power to legislate for us in all cases whatsoever.

He has abdicated Government here, by declaring us out of his Protection and waging War against us.

He has plundered our seas, ravaged our coasts, burnt our towns, and destroyed the lives of our people.

He is at this time transporting large Armies of foreign Mercenaries to compleat the works of death, desolation, and tyranny, already begun with circumstances of Cruelty & Perfidy scarcely paralleled in the most barbarous ages, and totally unworthy the Head of a civilized nation.

He has constrained our fellow Citizens taken Captive on the high Seas to bear Arms against their Country, to become the executioners of their friends and Brethren, or to fall themselves by their Hands.

He has excited domestic insurrections amongst us, and has endeavoured to bring on the inhabitants of our frontiers, the merciless Indian Savages whose known rule of warfare, is an undistinguished destruction of all ages, sexes and conditions.

In every stage of these Oppressions We have Petitioned for Redress in the most humble terms: Our repeated Petitions have been answered only by repeated injury. A Prince, whose character is thus marked by every act which may define

a Tyrant, is unfit to be the ruler of a free people.

Nor have We been wanting in attentions to our British brethren. We have warned them from time to time of attempts by their legislature to extend an unwarrantable jurisdiction over us. We have reminded them of the circumstances of our emigration and settlement here. We have appealed to their native justice and magnanimity, and we have conjured them by the ties of our common kindred to disavow these usurpations, which would inevitably interrupt our connections and correspondence. They too have been deaf to the voice of justice and of consanguinity. We must, therefore, acquiesce in the necessity, which denounces our Separation, and hold them, as we hold the rest of mankind, Enemies in War, in Peace Friends.

We, therefore, the Representatives of the united States of America, in General Congress, Assembled,

appealing to the Supreme Judge of the world for the rectitude of our intentions, do, in the Name, and by Authority of the good People of these Colonies, solemnly publish and declare, That these united Colonies are, and of Right ought to be Free and Independent States, that they are Absolved from all Allegiance to the British Crown, and that all political connection between them and the State of Great Britain, is and ought to be totally dissolved; and that as Free and Independent States, they have full Power to levy War, conclude Peace, contract Alliances, establish Commerce, and to do all other Acts and Things which Independent States may of right do. — And for the support of this Declaration, with a firm reliance on the protection of Divine Providence, we mutually pledge to each other our Lives, our Fortunes, and our sacred Honor.

Source: National Archives, http://www .archives.gov/exhibits/charters/declaration_ transcript.html.

Consider the source and the audience: Thomas Jefferson is writing here to rally American colonists as well as to justify the American Revolution to the world. How do those twin goals affect his writing?

Lay out the argument and the underlying values and assumptions: Jefferson painstakingly lays out an argument here that, if the logic holds, leads inescapably to the conclusion that Americans must declare independence. What is that argument? What values about equality, rights, and political legitimacy underlie his argument about the social contract?

Uncover the evidence: What evidence does Jefferson offer for the premise of his argument, that all men are created equal and possess certain rights? To show that George III has broken the social contract, he offers certain "facts" to a "candid world." What are those facts? Are they all evidence of George III's misdeeds?

Evaluate the conclusion: Jefferson concludes that the argument he has made and the facts he has presented mean that the colonies are "absolved from allegiance to the British crown." Assuming the facts he presents are true, was it possible to come to any other conclusion?

Sort out the political implications: The political implications of Jefferson's work were obvious and immediate: The colonies launched a war of independence that created the United States. How did this declaration smooth the way for that to happen? What if Jefferson had failed in his task—where would we be today?

The Granger Collection, New York

Women at War

Deborah Sampson and a few other women disguised themselves as males and served in the colonial army. Sampson served under George Washington's command but was dishonorably discharged after the war when it became known she was a woman. Ten years later, after Washington's intervention, she became the first woman in the U.S. Army to receive a soldier's pension.

and Concord, in Massachusetts. The South feared the idea of arming slaves, for obvious reasons, but by the time Congress began to fix troop quotas for each state, southerners were drafting slaves to serve in their masters' places.

In the aftermath of war, however, African Americans did not find their lot greatly improved, despite the ringing rhetoric of equality that fed the Revolution. The economic profitability of slave labor still existed in the South, and slaves continued to be imported from Africa in large numbers. The explanatory myth—that all men were created equal but that blacks weren't quite men and thus could be treated unequally—spread throughout the new country, making even free blacks unwelcome in many communities. By 1786 New Jersey prohibited free blacks from entering the state, and within twenty years northern states had started passing laws specifically denying free blacks the right to vote.[21] No wonder the well-known black abolitionist Frederick Douglass said, in 1852: "This Fourth of July is yours, not mine. You may rejoice, I must mourn."

NATIVE AMERICANS AND THE REVOLUTION

Native Americans were another group the founders did not consider to be prospective citizens. Not only were they already considered members of their own sovereign

nations, but their communal property holding, their nonmonarchical political systems, and their divisions of labor between women working in the fields and men hunting for game were not compatible with European political notions. Pushed farther and farther west by land-hungry colonists, the Indians were actively hostile to the American cause in the Revolution. Knowing this, the British hoped to gain their allegiance in the war. But the colonists, having asked in vain for the Indians to stay out of what they called a "family quarrel," were able to suppress early on the Indians' attempts to get revenge for their treatment at the hands of the settlers.[22] There was certainly no suggestion that the claim of equality at the beginning of the Declaration of Independence might include the peoples who had lived on the continent for centuries before the white man arrived.

WOMEN AND THE REVOLUTION Neither was there any question that "all men" might somehow be a generic term for human beings that would include women. Politically the Revolution proved to be a step backward for women. It was after the war that states began specifically to prohibit women, even those with property, from voting.[23] That doesn't mean, however, that women did not get involved in the war effort. Within the constraints of society, they contributed what they could to the American cause. They boycotted tea and other British imports, sewed flags, made bandages and clothing, nursed and housed soldiers, and collected money to support the Continental Army. Under the name Daughters of Liberty, women in many towns met publicly to discuss the events of the day, spinning and weaving to make the colonies less dependent on imported cotton and woolens from England, and drinking herbal tea instead of tea that was taxed by the British. Some women moved beyond such mild patriotic activities to outright political behavior, writing pamphlets urging independence, spying on enemy troops, carrying messages, and even, in isolated instances, fighting on the battlefields.[24]

Men's understanding of women's place in early American politics is nicely put by Thomas Jefferson, writing from Europe to a woman in America in 1788:

> But our good ladies, I trust, have been too wise to wrinkle their foreheads with politics. They are contented to soothe & calm the minds of their husbands returning ruffled from political debate. They have the good sense to value domestic happiness above all others. There is no part of the earth where so much of this is enjoyed as in America.[25]

Women's role with respect to politics is plain: they may be wise and prudent, but their proper sphere is the domestic, not the political, world. They are almost "too good" for politics, representing peace and serenity, moral happiness rather than political dissension, the values of the home over the values of the state. This explanation provides a flattering reason for keeping women in "their place," while allowing men to reign in the world of politics.

PAUSE AND REVIEW:

WHO, WHAT, HOW

By the mid-1700s the interests of the British and the colonists were clearly beginning to separate. If the colonists had played by the rules of imperial politics, England would have been content. It would have taxed the colonies to pay its war debts, but it also would have continued to protect them and rule benignly from across the sea.

The colonial leaders, however, changed the rules. Rejecting British authority, they established new rules based on Enlightenment thought. Then they used impassioned rhetoric and inspiring theory to engage the rest of the colonists in their rebellion. Finally, they used revolution to sever their ties with England.

The Revolution dramatically changed American fortunes, but not everyone's life was altered for the good by political independence. Many of those who were not enfranchised before the war—slaves and free blacks, American Indians, and women—remained powerless afterward, and in some cases voting rules became even more restrictive.

IN YOUR OWN WORDS » Describe the events and political motivations that led to the colonies' split with England.

THE ARTICLES OF CONFEDERATION
Political and economic instability under the nation's first constitution

In 1777 the Continental Congress met to try to come up with a framework or constitution for the new government. We use the word *constitution* in this country almost as if it could refer only to one specific document. In truth, a **constitution** is any establishment of rules that "constitutes"—that is, makes up—a government. It may be written, as in our case, or unwritten, as in Great Britain's. One constitution can endure for over two hundred years, as ours has, or it can

constitution the rules that establish a government

Articles of Confederation the first constitution of the United States (1777) creating an association of states with weak central government

confederation a government in which independent states unite for common purpose but retain their own sovereignty

change quite frequently, as the French constitution has. What's important about a constitution is that it defines a political body, the rules and institutions for running a government. As we have said before, those rules have direct consequences for how politics works in a given country, who the winners are and who the losers will be.

The **Articles of Confederation**, our first constitution, created the kind of government the founders, fresh from their colonial experience, preferred. The rules set up by the Articles of Confederation show the states' jealousy of their own power. Having just won their independence from one large national power, the last thing they wanted to do was create another. They were also extremely wary of one another, and much of the debate over the Articles of Confederation reflected wide concern that the rules not give any states preferential treatment. (See the Appendix for the text of the Articles of Confederation.)

The Articles established a "firm league of friendship" among the thirteen American states, but they did not empower a central government to act effectively on behalf of those states. The Articles were ultimately replaced because, without a strong central government, they were unable to provide the economic and political stability that the founders wanted. Even so, under this set of rules, some people were better off, and some problems, namely the resolution of boundary disputes and the political organization of new territories, were handled extremely well.

THE PROVISIONS OF THE ARTICLES

The government set up by the Articles was called a **confederation** because it established a system in which each state would retain almost all of its own power to do what it wanted. In other words, in a confederation, each state is sovereign, and the central government has only the job of running the collective business of the states. It has no independent source of power and resources for its operations. Another characteristic of a confederation is that, because it is founded on state sovereignty (authority), it says nothing about individuals. It creates neither rights nor obligations for individual citizens, leaving such matters to be handled by state constitutions.

Under the Articles of Confederation, Congress had many formal powers, including the power to establish and direct the armed forces, to decide matters of war and peace, to coin money, and to enter into treaties. Its powers, however, were quite limited. For example, while Congress controlled the armed forces, it had no power to draft soldiers or to tax citizens to pay for its military needs. Its inability to tax put Congress—and the central government as a whole—at the mercy of the states. The government could ask, but it was up to the states to contribute or not as they chose. Furthermore, Congress lacked the ability to regulate commerce between states, and between states and foreign powers. It could not establish a common and stable

DON'T BE FOOLED BY...
YOUR SOCIAL NETWORKS

Pity your poor grandparents. When they were your age, communicating with someone who wasn't in the same place meant picking up the telephone (in those days inconveniently attached to a wall) or writing a letter—the old-fashioned kind that required an envelope and a stamp. Today we live in a Web 2.0 world—a world in which the social, collaborative, and user-centered aspects of the Internet have changed our lives in untold ways. Sites like Twitter and Facebook allow us to connect to friends, follow popular figures, and share content and opinions on the news of the day with ease. Chances are you already engaged in some form of social networking today: 65 percent of adult Internet users are involved with social networking; even Grandma is sharing photographs of her grandchildren with her Facebook friends.[1]

But social networking is not just about being social. Technologies that enable citizens to connect with one another, to engage in lively debate, and to organize hold great promise for democracy. Around the world, the power to communicate on a massive scale—once held only by governments and those with access to print or broadcast media outlets—is now in the hands of anyone who can afford or has access to a cell phone. During the impeachment trial of Philippine president Joseph Estrada in 2001, activists were able to organize millions for demonstrations in a matter of hours via forwarded text messages.[2] A decade later, social networking sites like Twitter and Facebook played an integral role in organizing massive protests in Moldova (2009) and Iran (2009–2010), and full-on revolutions in Tunisia (2010–2011) and Egypt (2011). Here in the United States, social networking sites have fostered civic engagement, providing platforms for organizing massive grassroots movements like the Tea Party and Occupy Wall Street and enabling citizens to lobby their leaders at every level and to help to set political agendas on everything from local stop signs to same-sex marriage. Imagine the impact that social networking might have had on the American founding!

But that political upside of social networking has a downside as well. Free to speak our minds on every issue, we can find ourselves in virtual fistfights with friends and acquaintances whose political feelings differ from our own. And of course, the unfettered freedom to post and repost stories can be harmful. It's always been hard to put a stop to the circulation of an unfounded rumor, but before

information moved at Internet speed, you had a fighting chance. In the era of instant, mass communication, anyone with a computer or smartphone can pass on a piece of information or misinformation—and not just to one friend, but to thousands—with the touch of a button. Much like the spread of a real infectious disease, once a story "goes viral" via electronic channels, it can be difficult, if not impossible, to contain.

WHAT TO WATCH OUT FOR

- **Don't create your own echo chamber.** With social networking sites (like Facebook and Twitter), social news sites (like Digg and Reddit), and tools like RSS feeds and Google Alerts, it's easy to create your own custom news channel, ensuring that you only have to read stories from the sources you like, about subjects that interest you. But your information is only as good as the sources it comes from—be sure to cast a wide net to ensure you're getting all sides of the story, not just the one that you want to hear.

- **Beware the re-tweet.** On the Web, gossip and lies spread much more quickly than verified facts. Case in point: in 2012 a blogger posted a false claim that South Carolina governor Nikki Haley was about to be indicted. The lie went viral, tweeted to a national audience within two minutes, and made its way to several national news organizations, including the *Washington Post* and CBS News, within twenty.[3] So, when something comes up in your Facebook or Twitter feed, think twice before passing it along yourself. Is the information good? Is there a link to a reputable source? Does the original source appear to have verified the story?

- **Verify forwarded email.** When you open up an email and read a story that seems unbelievable, chances are you shouldn't believe it. Email chain letters are the urban legends of the Internet age, and like the legends of yore, they refuse to die. When one shows up in your inbox, take a moment to see if the claims made in it are legit. A number of fact-checking sites, including Snopes.com and TruthOrFiction.com, are dedicated to investigating and evaluating Internet rumors.

- **All your friends and followers may not be on the same page as you are.** You may be surprised to learn that your friends' political stands on issues are not your own. Although a majority of social network users usually just ignore posts with which they disagree, others say they've "defriended" individuals because of their political posts.[4] If you choose to engage in a political debate on your Facebook page, be prepared for the consequences.

- **Remember, nothing's really private on the Web.** No privacy protections are perfect; once you post something, you no longer control it. Other people can repost your comments, and even your deleted posts might live on in cyberspace. Anything you share—from a status update to a comment on a news article—may find its way to future employers, partners, in-laws, or even your as-yet unborn children. Think twice before airing controversial views, and don't post pictures you aren't willing to have the whole world gaze upon!

1. Mary Madden and Kathryn Zickuhr, "65 Percent of Online Adults Use Social Networking Sites," The Pew Internet and American Life Project, August 26, 2011, pewinternet. org/Reports/2011/Social-Networking-Sites.aspx.

2. Clay Shirky, "The Political Power of Social Media: Technology, the Public Sphere, and Political Change," *Foreign Policy,* January/ February 2011, www.foreignaffairs.com/articles/67038/clay-shirky/the-political-power-of-social-media.

3. Jeremy W. Peters, "A Lie Races Across Twitter Before the Truth Can Boot Up," *New York Times*, April 9, 2012, www .nytimes.com/2012/04/10/us/politics/false-nikki-haley-twitter-report-spreads-fast.html?hp.

4. Lee Rainie and Aaron Smith, "Social Networking Sites and Politics," The Pew Internet and American Life Project, March 12, 2012, pewinternet.org/Reports/2012/Social-networking-and-politics.aspx.

monetary system. In essence, the Articles allowed the states to be thirteen independent units, printing their own currencies, setting their own tariffs, and establishing their own laws with regard to financial and political matters. In every critical case—national security, national economic prosperity, and the general welfare—the U.S. government had to rely on the voluntary goodwill and cooperation of the state governments. That meant that the success of the new nation depended on what went on in state legislatures around the country.

SOME WINNERS, SOME LOSERS

The era of American history following the Revolution was dubbed "this critical period" by John Quincy Adams, nephew of patriot Samuel Adams, son of John Adams, and himself a future president of the country. During this time, while the states were under the weak union of the Articles, the future of the United States was very much up in the air. The lack of an effective central government meant that the country had difficulty conducting business with other countries and enforcing harmonious trade relations and treaties. Domestic politics was equally difficult. Economic conditions following the war were poor. Many people owed money and could not pay their debts. State taxes were high and the economy was depressed, offering farmers few opportunities to sell their produce, for example, and hindering those with commercial interests from conducting business as they had before the war.

> popular tyranny the unrestrained power of the people
>
> Shays's Rebellion a grassroots uprising (1787) by armed Massachusetts farmers protesting foreclosures

The radical poverty of some Americans seemed particularly unjust to those hardest hit, especially in light of the rhetoric of the Revolution about equality for all. Having used "equality" as a rallying cry during the war, the founders were afterward faced with a population that wanted to take equality seriously and eliminate the differences that existed between men.[26]

One of the ways this passion for equality manifested itself was in some of the state legislatures, where laws were passed to ease the burden of debtors and farmers. Often the focus of the laws was property, but rather than preserving property, as Lockean theory said laws should do, these laws frequently were designed to confiscate or redistribute property instead. The have-nots in society, and the people acting on their behalf, were using the law to redress what they saw as injustices in early American life. To relieve postwar suffering, they printed paper money, seized property, and suspended "the ordinary means for the recovery of debts."[27] In other words, in those states, people with debts and mortgages could legally escape or postpone paying the money they owed. With so much economic insecurity, naturally those who owned property would not continue to invest and lend money. The Articles of Confederation, in their effort to preserve power for the states, had provided for no checks or limitations on state legislatures. In fact, such action would have been seen under the Articles as infringing on the sovereignty of the states.

The political elite in the new country started to grumble about **popular tyranny**. In a monarchy, one feared the unrestrained power of the king, but perhaps in a republican government one had to fear the unrestrained power of the people. The final straw was **Shays's Rebellion**. Massachusetts was a state whose legislature, dominated by wealthy and secure citizens, had not taken measures to aid the debt-ridden population. In an effort to keep their land from foreclosure (seizure by those to whom they owed money), a mob of angry musket-wielding farmers from western Massachusetts, led by a former officer of the Continental Army, Daniel Shays, stormed a federal armory in Springfield that housed 450 tons of military supplies in January 1787. The mob was turned back after a violent clash with state militia, but the attack frightened and embarrassed the leaders of the United States, who feared that the rebellion foreshadowed the failure of their grand experiment in self-governance. In their minds, it underscored the importance of discovering what James Madison would call "a republican remedy for those diseases most incident to republican government."[28] In other words, the leaders had to find a way to contain and limit the will of the people in a government that was to be based on the will of the people. If the rules of government were not producing the "right" winners and losers, then the rules would have to be changed before the elite lost the power to change them.

THINKING OUTSIDE THE BOX

How would American politics be different today if we had retained the Articles of Confederation instead of adopting the Constitution?

PAUSE AND REVIEW:

WHO, WHAT, HOW

The fledgling states had an enormous amount at stake as they forged their new government after the Revolution. Perceiving that alarming abuses of power by the British king had come from a strong national government, they were determined to limit the central power of the new nation. The solution was to form a "firm league of friendship" among the several states but to keep the power of any central institutions as weak as possible.

With widespread land ownership possible and with the need for popular support, most farmers and artisans enjoyed the status of citizenship. Given easy access to the state legislatures under the Articles of Confederation, they were able to use the rules of the new political system to take the edge off the economic hardships they were facing.

But the same rules that made it so easy for the new citizens to influence their state governments made it more difficult for the political and economic leaders of the former colonies to protect their own economic security. In their eyes, new rules were needed that would remove government from the rough-and-ready hands of the farmers and protect it from what they saw as unreasonable demands.

IN YOUR OWN WORDS >> Explain what the Articles of Confederation did and what it failed to do.

THE CONSTITUTIONAL CONVENTION
Division and compromise over state power and representation

Even before Shays and his men attacked the Springfield armory, delegates from key states had met in Annapolis, Maryland, to discuss the nation's commercial weaknesses. There they adopted a proposal to have each state send delegates to a national convention to be held in Philadelphia in May 1787. The purpose of the meeting would be to make the national government strong enough to handle the demands of united action.

The Philadelphia Convention was authorized to try to fix the Articles of Confederation, but it was clear that many of the fifty-five state delegates who gathered in May were not interested in saving the existing framework at all. Many of the delegates represented the elite of American society, and thus they were among those being most injured under the terms of the Articles. When it became apparent that the **Constitutional Convention** was replacing, not revising, the Articles, some delegates refused to attend, declaring that such a convention was outside the Articles of Confederation and therefore illegal—in fact, it was treason. The convention was in essence overthrowing the government.

"AN ASSEMBLY OF DEMIGODS"

When Thomas Jefferson, unable to attend the convention because he was on a diplomatic mission to Europe, heard about the Philadelphia meeting, he called it "an assembly of demigods."[29] As you'll see from "*Snapshot of America:* Who Were the Founders?", the delegates were among the most educated, powerful, and wealthy citizens of the new country. Some leading figures were absent. Not only was Jefferson in Paris, but John Adams was also in Europe. Samuel Adams had not been elected but had declared his general disapproval of the "unconstitutional" undertaking, as had Patrick Henry, another hotheaded revolutionary patriot and advocate of states' rights. But there was George Washington, from Virginia, the general who had led American troops to victory in the Revolution. Also from Virginia were George Mason, Edmund Randolph, and James

> **Constitutional Convention** the assembly of fifty-five delegates in the summer of 1787 to recast the Articles of Confederation; the result was the U.S. Constitution

SNAPSHOT OF AMERICA: WHO WERE THE FOUNDERS?

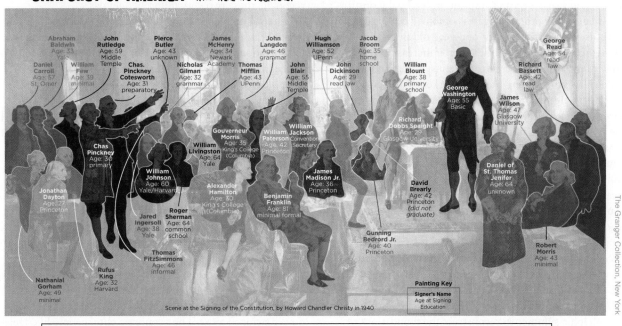

Scene at the Signing of the Constitution, by Howard Chandler Christy in 1940

The Granger Collection, New York

Painting Key

Signer's Name
Age at Signing
Education

■ CT ■ DE ■ GA ■ MD ■ MA NH NJ NY ■ NC ■ PA RI ■ SC ■ VA

Occupations of the Founders

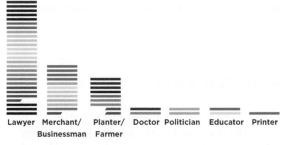

Lawyer | Merchant/ Businessman | Planter/ Farmer | Doctor | Politician | Educator | Printer

Religions of the Founders

20 Episcopalian
12 Presbyterian
7 Congregationalist
3 Quaker
2 Methodist
2 Roman Catholic
2 Anglican

1 Lutheran
1 Christian Reformed
1 Dutch Reformed
1 Calvinist
1 Deist
1 Unknown

Ratification by State

New Hampshire - Jun. 21, 1788
New York - Jul. 26, 1788
Massachusetts - Feb. 7, 1788
(including Maine)
Connecticut - Jan. 9, 1788
Rhode Island - May 29, 1790
Pennsylvania - Dec. 12, 1787
New Jersey - Dec. 18, 1787
Delaware - Dec. 7, 1787
Maryland - Apr. 28, 1788
Virginia - Jun. 26, 1788
North Carolina - Nov. 21, 1789
South Carolina - May 23, 1788
Georgia - Jan. 2, 1788

How Many Signed and How Many Didn't?

40   **16**

Walked out and didn't sign

Oliver Ellsworth (CT)
James McClurg (VA)
George Wythe (VA)
Alexander Martin (NC)
William R Davie (NC)
Robert Yates (NY)
John Lansing Jr. (NY)
William Houstoun (GA)
William Pierce (GA)
Caleb Strong (MA)
John F Mercer (MD)
Luther Martin (MD)
William Houston (NJ)

Abstained from signing

Elbridge Gerry (MA)
George Mason (VA)
Edmund J Randolph (VA)

BEHIND THE NUMBERS

The founders were clearly an elite group of men. They attended the top schools, and most were successful and wealthy. In general, how does one's economic and social status affect one's political views? Are your views shaped by your own circumstances? Can a government created by "an assembly of demigods" work for the rest of us mortals?

Madison, the sickly and diminutive but brilliant politician who would make a greater imprint on the final Constitution than all the other delegates combined. Other delegates were also impressive: eighty-one-year-old Benjamin Franklin, as mentally astute as ever, if increasingly feeble in body; Gouverneur Morris from Pennsylvania; and Alexander Hamilton among the New Yorkers.

These delegates represented the very cream of American society. They were well educated in an age when most of the population was not, about 50 percent having gone to schools like Harvard, William and Mary, Columbia (called King's College until 1784), and other institutions that are still at the top of the educational hierarchy. They were also wealthy; they were lawyers, land speculators, merchants, planters, and investors. Even though they were, on the whole, a young group (over half were under forty, and James Madison, just thirty-six), they were politically experienced. Many had been active in Revolutionary politics, and they were well read in the political theories of the day, like the ideas of Enlightenment thinker John Locke.

Members of the delegations met through a sweltering Philadelphia summer to reconstruct the foundations of American government. The heat and humidity were heightened because the windows of Convention Hall were kept closed against listening ears and, consequently, the possibility of a cooling breeze. So serious was the convention about secrecy that when a delegate found a copy of one of the major proposals, apparently dropped by another delegate, he turned it over to presiding officer George Washington. Washington took the entire convention to task for its carelessness and threw the document on the table, saying, "Let him who owns it take it." No one dared.[30] We owe most of what we know about the convention today to the notes of James Madison, which he insisted not be published until after the deaths of all the convention delegates.[31]

As the delegates had hoped, the debates at the Constitutional Convention produced a very different system of rules than that established by the Articles of Confederation. Many of these rules were compromises to resolve the conflicting interests brought by delegates to the convention.

Imagine that you face the delegates' challenge—to construct a new government from scratch. You can create all the rules, arrange all the institutions, just to your liking. The only hitch is that you have other delegates to work with. Delegate A, for instance, is a merchant with a lot of property; he has big plans for a strong government that can ensure secure conditions for conducting business and can adequately protect property. Delegate B is a planter. In Delegate B's experience, big governments are dangerous. Big governments are removed from the people, and it is easy for corruption to take root when people can't keep a close eye on what their officials are doing. People like Delegate B think that they do better when power is broken up and localized and there is no strong central government. In fact, Delegate B would prefer a government like that

provided by the Articles of Confederation. How do you reconcile these two very different agendas?

The solution adopted under the Articles of Confederation had basically favored Delegate B's position. The new Constitution, given the profiles of the delegates in attendance, was moving strongly in favor of Delegate A's position. Naturally the agreement of all those who followed Delegate B would be important in ratifying, or getting approval for, the final Constitution, so their concerns could not be ignored. The compromise chosen by the founders at the Constitutional Convention was called **federalism**. Unlike a confederation, in which the states retain the ultimate power over the whole, federalism gives the central government its own source of power, in this case the Constitution of the people of the United States. But unlike a unitary system, which we discuss in Chapter 4, federalism also gives independent power to the states.

Compared to how they fared under the Articles of Confederation, the advocates of states' rights were losers under the new Constitution, but they were better off than they might have been. The states could have had *all* their power stripped away. The economic elite, people like Delegate A, were clear winners under the new rules. This proved to be one of the central issues during the ratification debates. Those who sided with the federalism alternative, who mostly resembled Delegate A, came to be known as **Federalists**. The people like Delegate B, who continued to hold on to the strong state–weak central government option, were called **Anti-Federalists**. We will return to them shortly.

LARGE STATES, SMALL STATES

Once the convention delegates agreed that federalism would provide the framework of the new government, they had to decide how to allot power among the states. Should all states count the same in decision making, or should the larger states have more power than the smaller ones? The rules chosen here could have a crucial impact on the politics of the country. If small states and large states had equal amounts of power in national government, residents of large states such as Virginia, Massachusetts, and New York would effectively have less voice in the government than would residents of small states, like New Jersey and Rhode Island, since they would have proportionately less influence on how their power was wielded. If power were allocated

---

federalism a political system in which power is divided between the central and regional units

Federalists supporters of the Constitution who favored a strong central government

Anti-Federalists advocates of states' rights who opposed the Constitution

on the basis of size, however, the importance of the small states would be reduced.

Two plans were offered by convention delegates to resolve this issue. The first, the **Virginia Plan**, was created by James Madison and presented at the convention by Edmund Randolph. The Virginia Plan represented the preference of the large, more populous states. This plan proposed that the country would have a strong national government, run by a bicameral (two-house) legislature. One house would be elected directly by the people, one indirectly by a combination of the state legislatures and the popularly elected national house. But the numbers of representatives would be determined by the taxes paid by the residents of the state, which would reflect the free population in the state. In other words, large states would have more representatives in both houses of the legislature, and national law and policy would be weighted heavily in their favor. Just three large states, Virginia, Massachusetts, and Pennsylvania, would be able to form a majority and carry national legislation their way. The Virginia Plan also called for a single executive, to see that the laws were carried out, and a national judiciary, both appointed by the legislature, and it gave the national government power to override state laws.

A different plan, presented by William Paterson of New Jersey, was designed by the smaller states to offer the convention an alternative that would better protect their interests. The **New Jersey Plan** amounted to a reinforcement, not a replacement, of the Articles of Confederation. It provided for a multiperson executive, so that no one person could possess too much power, and for congressional acts to be the "supreme law of the land." Most significantly, however, the Congress was much like the one that had existed under the Articles. In a unicameral (one-house) legislature, each state got only one vote. The delegates would be chosen by state legislatures. The powers of Congress were stronger than under the Articles, but the national government was still dependent on the states for some of its funding. The large states disliked this plan because small states together could block what the larger

states wanted, even though the larger states had more people and contributed more revenue.

The prospects for a new government could have foundered on this issue. The stuffy heat of the closed Convention Hall shortened the tempers of the weary delegates, and frustration made compromise difficult. Each side had too much to lose by yielding to the other's plan. The solution finally arrived at was politics at its best. The **Great Compromise** kept much of the framework of the Virginia Plan. It was a strong federal structure headed by a central government with sufficient power to tax its citizens, regulate commerce, conduct foreign affairs, organize the military, and exercise other central powers. It called for a single executive and a national judicial system. The compromise that allowed the smaller states to live with it involved the composition of the legislature. Like the Virginia Plan, it provided for two houses. The House of Representatives would be based on state population, giving the large states the extra clout they felt they deserved, but in the Senate each state had two votes. This gave the smaller states relatively much more power in the Senate than in the House of Representatives. Members of the House of Representatives would be elected directly by the people, members of the Senate by the state legislatures. Thus the government would be directly binding on the people as well as on the states. A key to the compromise was that most legislation would need the approval of both houses, so that neither large states nor small states could hold the entire government hostage to their wishes. The smaller states were sufficiently happy with this plan that most of them voted to approve, or ratify, the Constitution quickly and easily. *The Big Picture* compares the Constitution with the Articles of Confederation, and shows how we got there via a number of compromises.

NORTH AND SOUTH

The compromise reconciling the large and small states was not the only one crafted by the delegates. The northern and the southern states, which is to say the non-slave-owning and the slave-owning states, were at odds over how population was to be determined for purposes of representation in the House of Representatives. The southern states wanted to count slaves as part of their populations when determining how many representatives they got, even though they had no intention of letting the slaves vote. Including slaves would give them more representatives and, thus, more power in the House. For exactly that reason, the northern states said that if slaves could not vote, they should not be counted. The compromise, also a triumph of politics if not humanity, is known as the **Three-fifths Compromise**. It was based on a formula developed by the Confederation Congress in 1763 to allocate tax assessments among the states. According to this compromise, for representation purposes, each slave would count as three-fifths of a person, every five slaves counting as

---

Virginia Plan a proposal at the Constitutional Convention that congressional representation be based on population, thus favoring the large states

New Jersey Plan a proposal at the Constitutional Convention that congressional representation be equal, thus favoring the small states

Great Compromise the constitutional solution to congressional representation: equal votes in the Senate, votes by population in the House

Three-fifths Compromise the formula for counting five slaves as three people for purposes of representation, which reconciled northern and southern factions at the Constitutional Convention

THE BIG PICTURE: HOW WE GOT TO THE CONSTITUTION FROM THE ARTICLES OF CONFEDERATION

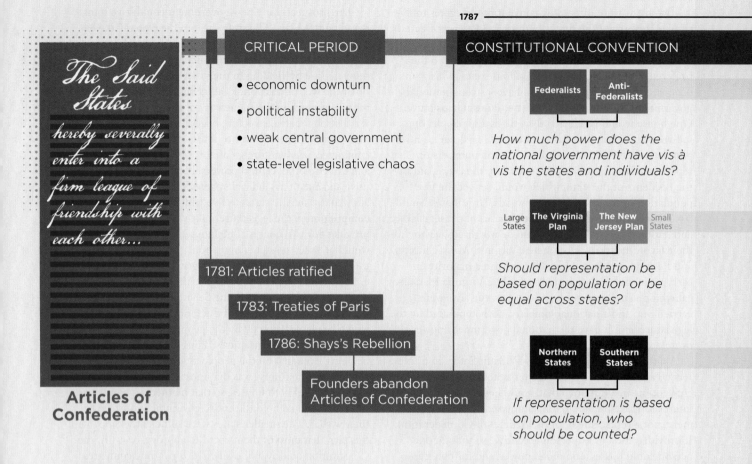

1787

The Said States hereby severally enter into a firm league of friendship with each other...

Articles of Confederation

CRITICAL PERIOD

- economic downturn
- political instability
- weak central government
- state-level legislative chaos

1781: Articles ratified

1783: Treaties of Paris

1786: Shays's Rebellion

Founders abandon Articles of Confederation

CONSTITUTIONAL CONVENTION

Federalists | Anti-Federalists

How much power does the national government have vis à vis the states and individuals?

Large States | The Virginia Plan | The New Jersey Plan | Small States

Should representation be based on population or be equal across states?

Northern States | Southern States

If representation is based on population, who should be counted?

Articles of Confederation	The Virginia Plan
State sovereignty	Popular sovereignty
State law is supreme	National law is supreme
Unicameral legislature; equal votes for all states	Bicameral legislature; representation in both houses based on population
Two-thirds vote to pass important laws	Majority vote to pass laws
No congressional power to levy taxes, regulate commerce	Congressional power to regulate commerce and tax
No executive branch; laws executed by congressional committee	No restriction on strong single executive
No national judiciary	National judiciary
All states required to pass amendments	Popular ratification of amendments

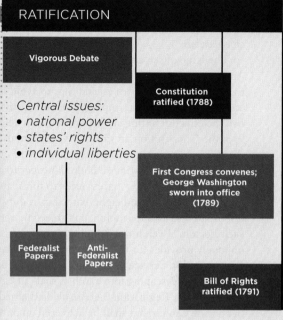

1787   **1788**   **1789**   **1791**

Federal Compromise

Both state and national sovereignty preserved. Flexible balance of power between the levels. Protections for individuals come later in the Bill of Rights.

Connecticut Compromise

Two legislative chambers, one based on population, one on equality across states.

3/5 Compromise

Representation in the House to be based on population, counting all "free Persons" and "three fifths of all other Persons."

The Constitution

RATIFICATION

Vigorous Debate

Central issues:
- *national power*
- *states' rights*
- *individual liberties*

Federalist Papers

Anti-Federalist Papers

Constitution ratified (1788)

First Congress convenes; George Washington sworn into office (1789)

Bill of Rights ratified (1791)

The New Jersey Plan

State sovereignty

State law is supreme

Unicameral legislature; one vote per state

Extraordinary majority to pass laws

Congressional power to regulate commerce and tax

Multiple executive

No national judiciary

All states required to pass amendments

The Constitution

People are sovereign

National law is supreme

Bicameral legislature; equal votes in Senate; representation by population in House

Simple majority to pass laws in Congress; presidential veto

Congressional power to regulate commerce and tax

Strong executive

Federal court system

Amendment process is complex

three people. Interestingly, the actual language in the Constitution is a good deal cagier than this. It says that representatives and taxes shall be determined according to population, figured "by adding to the whole Number of free Persons, including those bound to Service for a Term of Years, and excluding Indians not taxed, three fifths of *all other persons.*"

The issue of slavery was divisive enough for the early Americans that the most politically safe approach was not to mention it explicitly at all and thus to avoid having to endorse or condemn it. Implicitly, of course, their silence had the effect of letting slavery continue. Article I, Section 9, of the Constitution, in similarly vague language, allows that "The Migration or Importation of such Persons as any of the States now existing shall think proper to admit, shall not be prohibited by Congress prior to the Year one thousand eight hundred and eight, but a Tax or duty may be imposed on such Importation, not exceeding ten dollars for each Person." Even more damning, Article IV, Section 2, obliquely provides for the return of runaway slaves: "No Person held to Service or Labour in one State under the Laws thereof, escaping into another, shall, in Consequence of any Law or Regulation therein, be discharged from such Service or Labour, but shall be delivered up on Claim of the Party to whom such Service or Labour may be due." The word *slavery* does not appear in the Constitution until it is expressly outlawed in the Thirteenth Amendment, passed in December 1865, over eighty years after the writing of the Constitution.

PAUSE AND REVIEW:

WHO, WHAT, HOW

Not only the political and economic elite but also the everyday citizens who did not attend the Constitutional Convention stood to gain or lose dramatically from the proceedings. At stake that summer were the very rules that would provide the framework for so many political battles in the future.

Differences clearly existed among the founding elites. Those representing large states, of course, wanted rules that would give their states more power, based on their larger population, tax base, and size. Representatives of small states, on the other hand, wanted rules that would give the states equal power, so that they would not be squashed by the large states. North and South also differed on the rules. The North wanted representation to be based on the population of free citizens, while the South wanted to include slaves in the population count. The Great Compromise and the Three-fifths Compromise solved both disagreements.

Finally, the people at the convention were divided along another dimension as well. The Federalists

sought to create a strong central government more resistant to the whims of popular opinion. Opposing them, the Anti-Federalists wanted a decentralized government, closer to the control of the people. It was the Federalists who controlled the agenda at the convention and who ultimately determined the structure of the new government.

IN YOUR OWN WORDS >> Identify the goals, divisions, and compromises that shaped the Constitution.

RATIFICATION
Selling the Constitution to Americans

For the Constitution to become the law of the land, it had to go through the process of ratification—being voted on and approved by state conventions in at least nine of the states. As it happens, the Constitution was eventually ratified by all thirteen states, but not until some major political battles had been fought.

FEDERALISTS VERSUS ANTI-FEDERALISTS

So strongly partisan were the supporters and opponents of the Constitution that if the battle were taking place today we would probably find them sniping at each other on shows like *The Sean Hannity Show* and *Hardball With Chris Matthews*, and Stephen Colbert would be busy mocking both sides. It was a fierce, lively battle that produced, instead of high television ratings, some of the finest writings for and against the American system.

Those in favor of ratification called themselves the Federalists. The Federalists, like Delegate A in our hypothetical constitution-building scenario, were mostly men with a considerable economic stake in the new nation. Having fared poorly under the Articles, they were certain that if America were to grow as an economic and world power, it needed to be the kind of country in which people with property would want to invest. Security and order were key values, as was popular control. The Federalists thought people like themselves should be in charge of the government, although some of them did not object to an expanded suffrage if government had enough built-in protections. Mostly, these students of the Enlightenment were convinced that a good government could be designed if the underlying principles of human behavior were known. If people were ambitious and tended toward corruption,

> ratification the process through which a proposal is formally approved and adopted by vote

then government should make use of those characteristics to produce good outcomes.

The Anti-Federalists, on the other hand, rejected the notion that ambition and corruption were inevitable parts of human nature. If government could be kept small and local, and popular scrutiny truly vigilant, then Americans could live happy and contented lives without getting involved in the seamier side of politics. If America did not stray from its rural roots and values, it could permanently avoid the creeping corruption that they believed threatened it. The Articles of Confederation were more attractive to the Anti-Federalists than was the Constitution because they did not call for a strong central government that, tucked away from the voters' eyes, could become a hotbed of political intrigue. Instead, the Articles vested power in the state governments, which could be more easily watched and controlled.

Writing under various aliases as well as their own names, the Federalists and Anti-Federalists fired arguments back and forth in pamphlets and newspaper editorials, aimed at persuading undecided Americans to come out for or against the Constitution. The Federalists were far more aggressive and organized in their "media blitz," hitting New York newspapers with a series of eloquent editorials published under the pen name Publius, but really written by Alexander Hamilton, James Madison, and John Jay. These essays were bound and distributed in other states where the ratification struggle was close. Known as *The Federalist Papers*, they are one of the main texts on early American politics today. In response, the Anti-Federalists published essays written under such names as Cato, Brutus, and The Federal Farmer.[32]

THE FEDERALIST PAPERS

There were eighty-five essays written by Publius. These essays are clever, they are well thought out and logical, but they are also tricky and persuasive examples of the hard sell. We take a close look at two of the most important of the essays, numbers 10 and 51, in Chapters 4 and 13, respectively (you can find links to all *The Federalist Papers* in the Engage section at the end of this chapter). Their archaic language makes *The Federalist Papers* generally difficult reading for contemporary students. However, the arguments in support of the Constitution are laid out so beautifully that taking the trouble to read them is worthwhile. It would be a good idea to turn to them and read them carefully now.

> *The Federalist Papers* a series of essays written to build support for ratification of the Constitution
>
> factions groups of citizens united by some common passion or interest and opposed to the rights of other citizens or to the interests of the whole community

In *Federalist* No. 10, Madison tried to convince Americans that a large country was no more likely to succumb to the effects of special interests than a small one (preferred by the Anti-Federalists). He explained that the greatest danger to a republic came from factions—what we might call interest groups. Factions are groups of people motivated by a common interest, but one different from the interest of the country as a whole. Farmers, for instance, have an interest in keeping food prices high, even though that would make most Americans worse off. Businesspeople prefer high import duties on foreign goods, even though they make both foreign and domestic goods more expensive for the rest of us. Factions are not a particular problem when they constitute a minority of the population because they are offset by majority rule. They become problematic, however, when they are a majority. Factions usually have economic roots, the most basic being between the haves and have-nots in society. One of the majority factions that worried Madison was the mass of propertyless people whose behavior was so threatening to property holders under the Articles of Confederation.

To control the *causes* of factions would be to infringe on individual liberty. But Madison believed that the *effects* of factions were easily managed in a large republic. First of all, representation would dilute the effects of factions, and it was in this essay that Madison made his famous distinction between "pure democracy" and a "republic." In addition, if the territory were sufficiently large, factions would be neutralized because there would be so many of them that no one would be likely to become a majority. Furthermore, it would be difficult for people who shared common interests to find one another if some lived in South Carolina, for instance, and others lived in New Hampshire. Clearly Madison never anticipated the invention of Twitter. We discuss Madison's argument about factions again in Chapter 13, when we take up the topic of interest groups. In the meantime, however, notice how Madison relied on mechanical elements of politics (size and representation) to remedy a flaw in human nature (the tendency to form divisive factions). This is typical of the Federalists' approach to government, and it reflects the importance of institutions as well as rules in bringing about desired outcomes in politics.

We see the same emphasis on mechanical solutions to political problems in *Federalist* No. 51. Madison argued here that the institutions proposed in the Constitution would lead to neither corruption nor tyranny. The solution was the principles of checks and balances and separation of powers. We discuss these at length in Chapter 4, but it is worth looking at Madison's interesting explanation of why such checks work. Again building his case on a potential defect of human character, he said, "Ambition must be made to counteract ambition."[33] If men tend to be ambitious, give two ambitious men the job of watching over each other, and neither will let the other have an advantage.

The eighty-fourth *Federalist Paper* was written by Hamilton. It doesn't reflect great principles, but it is interesting politically because it failed dismally. The Constitution was ratified in spite of it, not because of it. In this essay, Hamilton argued that a **Bill of Rights**—a listing of the protections against government infringement of individual rights guaranteed to citizens by government itself—was not necessary in a constitution.

The original draft of the Constitution contained no Bill of Rights. Some state constitutions had them, and so the Federalists argued that a federal Bill of Rights would be redundant. Moreover, the limited government set up by the federal Constitution didn't have the power to infringe on individual rights anyway, and many of the rights that would be included in a Bill of Rights were already in the body of the text. To the Anti-Federalists, already afraid of the invasive power of the national government, this omission was more appalling than any other aspect of the Constitution.

Hamilton argued that a Bill of Rights was unnecessary, even dangerous. As it stood, Hamilton said, the national government didn't have the power to interfere with citizens' lives in many ways, and any interference at all would be suspect. But if the Constitution were prefaced with a list of things government could *not* do to individuals, then government would assume it had the power to do anything that wasn't expressly forbidden. Therefore, government, instead of being unlikely to trespass on its citizens' rights, would be more likely to do so with a Bill of Rights than without. This argument was so unpersuasive to Americans at that time that the Federalists were forced to give in to Anti-Federalist pressure during the ratification process. The price of ratification exacted by several states was the Bill of Rights, really a Bill of "Limits" on the federal government, added to the Constitution as the first ten amendments. We look at those limits in detail in Chapter 5, on fundamental American liberties.

THE FINAL VOTE

The smaller states, gratified by the compromise that gave them equal representation in the Senate, and believing they would be better off as part of a strong nation, ratified the Constitution quickly. The vote was unanimous in Delaware, New Jersey, and Georgia. In Connecticut (128–40) and Pennsylvania (46–23), the convention votes, though not unanimous, were strongly in favor of the Constitution. This may have helped to tip the balance for Massachusetts, voting much more closely to ratify (187–168). Maryland (63–11) and South Carolina (149–73) voted in favor of ratification in the spring of 1788, leaving only one more state to supply the requisite nine to make the Constitution law.

The battles in the remaining states were much tighter. When the Virginia convention met in June 1788, the Federalists felt that it could provide the decisive vote and threw much of their effort into securing passage. Madison and his Federalist colleagues debated with such Anti-Federalist advocates as George Mason and Patrick Henry, promising as they had in Massachusetts to support a Bill of Rights. Virginia

ratified the Constitution by the narrow margin of 89 to 79, preceded by a few days by New Hampshire, voting 57 to 47. Establishment of the Constitution as the law of the land was ensured with approval of ten states. New York also narrowly passed the Constitution, 30 to 27, but North Carolina defeated it (193–75) and Rhode Island, which had not sent delegates to the Constitutional Convention, refused to call a state convention to put it to the vote. Later both North Carolina and Rhode Island voted to ratify and join the union, in November 1789 and May 1790, respectively.[34] The *Snapshot* on page 77 summarizes the voting on the Constitution.

Again we can see how important rules are in determining outcomes. The Articles of Confederation had required the approval of all the states. Had the Constitutional Convention chosen a similar rule of unanimity, the Constitution may very well have been defeated. Recognizing that unanimous approval was not probable, however, the Federalists decided to require ratification by only nine of the thirteen, making adoption of the Constitution far more likely.

THINKING OUTSIDE THE BOX

Would we have more freedoms today, or fewer, without the Bill of Rights?

PAUSE AND REVIEW:

WHO, WHAT, HOW

The fight over ratification of the Constitution not only had the actual form of government at stake but also represented a deep philosophical difference about the nature of human beings and the possibilities of republican government. The Federalists favored the new Constitution. For the Anti-Federalists, the Constitution seemed to present innumerable opportunities for corruption to fester. Knowing they had lost the battle for public opinion and for votes, they made the attachment of a Bill of Rights a condition of their acquiescence.

IN YOUR OWN WORDS ⟫ Summarize the debate over ratification of the Constitution.

> **Bill of Rights** a summary of citizen rights guaranteed and protected by a government; added to the Constitution as its first ten amendments in order to achieve ratification

» THE CITIZENS AND THE FOUNDING
New rights bring obligations

As we said at the beginning of this chapter, there are different stories to be told about the American founding. We did not want to fall into the oversimplification trap, portraying the founding as a headlong rush to liberty on the part of an oppressed people. Politics is always a good deal more complicated than that, and this is a book about politics. We also wanted to avoid telling a story that errs on the other end of one-sidedness, depicting the American founding as an elite-driven period of history, in which the political, economic, and religious leaders decided they were better off without English rule, inspired the masses to revolt, and then created a Constitution that established rules that benefited people like themselves. Neither of these stories is entirely untrue, but they obscure two very important points.

The first point is that there was not just one "elite" group at work during the founding period. Although political and economic leaders might have acted together over the matter of the break with England (and even then, important elites remained loyal to Britain), once the business of independence was settled, it was clear that competing elite groups existed: leaders of big states and small states, leaders of the northern and southern states, merchant elites and agricultural elites, elites who found their security in a strong national government and those who found it in decentralized power. The power struggle between all those adversaries resulted in the compromises that form the framework of our government today.

THE RISE OF THE "ORDINARY" CITIZEN

The second point is that not all the actors during the founding period were among the top tier of political, economic, and religious leadership. Just because the Revolution and the government-building that followed it were not the product of ordinary citizens zealous for liberty does not mean that ordinary citizens had nothing to do with it.

Citizenship as we know it today was a fledgling creation at the time of the founding. The British had not been citizens of the English government but subjects of the English Crown. There is a world of difference between a subject and a citizen, as we pointed out in Chapter 1. The subject has a personal tie to the monarch; the citizen has a legal tie to a national territory. The subject has obligations; the citizen has both obligations and rights. One writer identifies three elements of American citizenship that were accepted in principle (though hard to put into practice) after the Revolution: (1) citizenship should rest on consent, (2) there should not be grades or levels of citizenship, and (3) citizenship should confer equal rights on all citizens.[35] The source for these new ideas about citizenship was Enlightenment thinking. We have seen in the ideas of John Locke the concept of the social contract—that citizenship is the product of a contractual agreement between rulers and ruled that makes obeying the law contingent on having one's rights protected by the state.

These new ideas were not all equally easy to put into practice. The notion of citizenship based on consent was relatively straightforward. In a way, the Declaration of Independence constituted a withdrawal of colonial consent to be ruled by George III, and the ratification of the Constitution was a collective consent to the new government. It was more difficult for Americans to work out how to avoid different levels of citizenship and to confer equal rights on all citizens.

In the European tradition, people born into different orders of society (based largely on their families' ownership of land) had, if not different levels of citizenship, then different social and political status. In America, the abundance of land meant that people who in Europe would have been at the bottom of the social and political order were catapulted into the landowner class and were thus eligible to be citizens in the new republic. Under the Articles of Confederation especially, Americans embraced this new definition of mass citizenship, but their experience during the critical period led the founders to mistrust it profoundly. To some extent, the writing of the Constitution was about reining in the power of the citizens, checking and balancing the power of the people as well as the power of the government.

The final element of the new definition of citizenship was the notion that citizenship conferred equal rights. Here principle clashed with profound prejudice. We saw throughout this chapter that the rights of citizenship were systematically denied to Native Americans, to African Americans, and to women. The ideals of citizenship that were born during the founding are truly innovative and inspiring,

NEWT GINGRICH

Chip Somodevilla/Getty Images

History is anything but dull when it comes from the mouth of the man who has made so much of it. Newt Gingrich is the architect of the "Contract With America," a document that helped propel the Republicans into the majority in Congress in 1994 for the first time in forty years, and made him Speaker of the U.S. House of Representatives from 1995 to 1998. As you will see in Chapter 7, his ideas and the policies they generated still inform the terms of political debate in this country nearly two decades later, a fact that no doubt encouraged him to make his unsuccessful run for the presidency in 2012.

But sitting at his desk at the American Enterprise Institute, with his distinguished gray head tilted slightly as he listens to a question, his fingertips pressed lightly together as he thinks over the answer, it is hard to forget that long before he revolutionized American politics in the 1990s, Newt Gingrich was a history professor at Western Georgia College. For the last six years he has resumed the work of a scholar in the rarified atmosphere of the American Enterprise Institute, a conservative Washington think tank where, in addition to being a media commentator and adviser to his party, he can play with ideas and talk to other smart people to his heart's content.

Clearly, life as an intellectual suits him. Does it mean Gingrich has given up politics for good? Clearly not. The media had a field day speculating on the possibility that he'd run for president in 2008, and of course, he gave it a shot in 2012. His 2010 book, *To Save America: Stopping Obama's Secular-Socialist Machine*, certainly hints at his intention to stay active in public life.

It seems to be part of who he is. When he was as young as ten years old, he was flexing his civic muscles by petitioning the Harrisburg (Pennsylvania) City Council to build a zoo. They didn't, but only, he claims with a smile, because his military family moved away before he could persuade them. Given his extraordinary record of public achievement since, it is a good bet he'd have gotten his zoo if the Gingrich family had stayed put.

But they did not. Throughout his junior-high years the Gingriches lived in a number of post–World War II European cities—gracious, civilized cities-turned-battlefields that still bore the scars of combat. There was no pretending that the atrocities of war "couldn't happen there"; they had happened, and it was apparent to Gingrich that they could happen at home, too, if serious steps weren't taken. He says, "Out of all that experience I concluded that citizenship was central to our freedom and our safety, and that having civilian leaders who thought about it every day was central to our survival. I spent the

but they were unavailable in practice to a major portion of the population for well over a hundred years. It is conventional today to be appalled at the failure of the founders to practice the principles of equality they preached, and certainly that failure *is* appalling in light of today's values, but we should remember that the whole project of citizenship was new to the founders and that in many ways they were far more democratic than any who had come before

them. One of our tasks in this book will be to trace the evolving concept and practice of American citizenship, as the conferral of equal rights so majestically proclaimed in the Declaration slowly becomes reality for all Americans.

IN YOUR OWN WORDS » Explain the role of everyday citizens in the founding of the United States.

LET'S REVISIT: **WHAT'S AT STAKE...**

Having read the history of Revolutionary America, what would you say is at stake in the modern militia movement? The existence of state militias and similar groups poses a troubling dilemma for the federal government; and

groups whose members are mostly benign, like the Tea Partiers, are even trickier for the government to deal with. Bill Clinton, who was president when Timothy McVeigh bombed the federal building in Oklahoma City, warned

summer of 1958 praying about it, and then in August of 1958 [when he was 15] I decided to do what I've been doing ever since."

What he does—the short answer—is to study history and glean from it insights about human motivation and behavior, and then use those historical insights to make things happen today. He is committed to crafting new ideas out of old lessons, leading his fellow citizens on a mission he believes will restore the country to its fundamental principles.

Ask him to explain just why it's important to study history and he pauses so long you wonder if he's forgotten the question or perhaps thinks it's so obvious that he won't deign to give it an answer. But no, he's just assembling his thoughts; you can almost hear the clicks and whirls of the processors. He opens his mouth and gracefully constructed sentences tumble out, fully formed. No umms, no stumbles; just perfect, elegant prose. Here's what he says:

On why students should study history:

If you've never run out of gas, you may not understand why filling your gas tank matters. And if you've never had your brakes fail, you may not care about having your brakes checked. And if you've never slid on an icy road, you may not understand why learning to drive on ice really matters. For citizens, if you haven't lived in a bombed-out city like Beirut or Baghdad, if you haven't seen a genocidal massacre like Rwanda, if you haven't been in a situation where people were starving to death, like Calcutta, you may not understand why you ought to study history. Because your life is good and it's easy and it's soft.

But for most of the history of the human race, most people, most of the time, have lived as slaves or as subjects to other people. And they lived lives that were short and desperate and where they had very little hope. And the primary breakthroughs have all been historic. It was the Greeks discovering the concept of self-governance, it was the Romans creating the objective sense of law, it was the Jewish tradition of being endowed by God—those came together and fused in Britain with the Magna Carta, and created a sense of rights that we take for granted every day. Because we have several hundred years of history protecting us. And the morning that history disappears, there's no reason to believe we'll be any better than Beirut or Baghdad.

On keeping the republic:

Be responsible, live out your responsibilities as a citizen, dedicate some amount of your time every day or every week to knowing what is going on in the world, be active in campaigns, and if nobody is worthy of your support, run yourself. . . . The whole notion of civil society [is] doing something as a volunteer, doing something, helping your fellow American, being involved with human beings. America only works as an organic society. . . . We're the most stunningly voluntaristic society in the world. And so if voluntarism dries up, in some ways America dries up.

Source: Newt Gingrich spoke with Christine Barbour on March 21, 2005.

at the time of the fifteenth anniversary of those attacks that "There can be real consequences when what you say animates people who do things you would never do." There are those out there, like McVeigh, who "were profoundly alienated, disconnected people who bought into this militant antigovernment line."[36]

The dilemma is that, on the one hand, the purpose of government is to protect our rights, and the Constitution surely guarantees Americans freedom of speech and assembly. On the other hand, government must hold the monopoly on the legitimate use of force in society or it will fall, just as the British government fell to the American colonies. If groups are allowed to amass weapons and forcibly resist or even attack U.S. law enforcers, then they constitute "mini-governments," or competing centers of authority, and

life for citizens becomes chaotic and dangerous.

The American system was designed to be relatively responsive to the wishes of the American public. Citizens can get involved, they can vote, run for office, change the laws, and amend the Constitution. By permitting these legitimate ways of affecting American politics, the founders hoped to prevent the rise of groups, like the Hutaree, that would promote and act toward violence. The founders intended to create a society characterized by political stability, not by revolution, which is why Jefferson's Declaration of Independence is so careful to point out that revolutions should occur only when there is no alternative course of action.

Some militia members reject the idea of working through the system; they say, as did McVeigh, that they consider themselves at war with the federal government. We call disregard for the law at the individual level "crime," at the group level "terrorism" or "insurrection," and at the majority level "revolution." It is the job of any government worth its salt to prevent all three kinds of activities. Thus it is not the existence or the beliefs but the activities of the militia groups that government seeks to control.

What's at stake in the challenges to the legitimacy of government are the very issues of government authority and the rights of individual citizens. It is difficult to draw the line between the protection of individual rights and the exercise of government authority. In a democracy, we want to respect the rights of all citizens, but this respect can be thwarted when a small number of individuals reject the rules of the game agreed on by the vast majority.

TO SUM UP

Sharpen your skills with **SAGE edge** at http://edge.sagepub.com/barbour7e. **SAGE edge for students** provides a personalized approach to help you accomplish your coursework goals in an easy-to-use learning environment.

REVIEW

Politics in the English Colonies

The politics of the American founding shaped the political compromises embodied in the Constitution. This in turn defined the institutions and many of the rules that do much to determine the winners and losers in political struggles today.

The battle for America involved a number of different groups, including American Indians, the Spanish, the French, and the British colonists. The English settlers came for many reasons, including religious and economic, but then duplicated many of the politically restrictive practices in the colonies that they had sought to escape in England. These included restrictions on political participation and a narrow definition of citizenship.

feudalism (p. 64)
slavery (p. 65)

The Split From England

The Revolution was caused by many factors, including British attempts to get the colonies to pay for the costs of the wars fought to protect them. The pressures from the Crown for additional taxes coincided with new ideas about the proper role of government among colonial elites. These ideas are embodied in Jefferson's politically masterful writing of the Declaration of Independence.

French and Indian War (p. 67)
popular sovereignty (p. 68)
Common Sense (p. 68)
Declaration of Independence (p. 68)

The Articles of Confederation

The government under the Articles of Confederation granted too much power to the states, which in a number of cases came to serve the interests of farmers and debtors. The Constitutional Convention was called to design a government with stronger centralized powers that would overcome the weaknesses elites perceived in the Articles.

constitution (p. 73)
Articles of Confederation (p. 73)

confederation (p. 73)
popular tyranny (p. 75)
Shays's rebellion (p. 75)

The Constitutional Convention

The new Constitution was derived from a number of key compromises: federalism was set as a principle to allocate power to both the central government and the states; the Great Compromise allocated power in the new national legislature; and the Three-fifths Compromise provided a political solution to the problem of counting slaves in the southern states for purposes of representation in the House of Representatives.

Constitutional Convention (p. 76)
federalism (p. 78)
Federalist (p. 78)
Anti-Federalists (p. 78)
Virginia Plan (p. 79)
New Jersey Plan (p. 79)

Great Compromise (p. 79)
Three-fifths Compromise (p. 79)

Ratification

The politics of ratification of the Constitution provides a lesson in the marriage between practical politics and political principle. *The Federalist Papers* served as political propaganda to convince citizens to favor ratification, and they serve today as a record of the reasoning behind many of the elements of our Constitution.

ratification (p. 82)
The Federalist Papers (p. 83)
factions (p. 83)
Bill of Rights (p. 84)

The Citizens and the Founding

The American founding reflects competition among elites as well as the establishment of a new form of citizenship.

See where it all happened. Travelers can walk Boston's Freedom Trail, tour historic Philadelphia, or have an immersive colonial experience in Williamsburg, Virginia.

Take a virtual tour. You don't really have to leave home to get a glimpse of America's history. **The Museum of the American Revolution**, currently under construction in Philadelphia, offers a glimpse of what's to come at their web site. Armchair tourists can also explore revolutionary battlefields like the one in Saratoga, New York.

Read *Common Sense*. Just about everyone in Colonial America took the time to read Thomas Paine's seminal essay, and history changed because of it.

You can read it, too, or download it to your e-reader or smartphone for free from most e-book providers.

Read *The Federalist Papers*. They're among the most important documents related to the founding of the United States. You can read them online (or download them for free) from the Library of Congress.

Loewen, James W. 2007. *Lies My Teacher Told Me: Everything Your American History Textbook Got Wrong.* **New York: Touchstone.** This is a stimulating book even for those who find history boring. Loewen explains why some of what you read for your high school history class may have been just plain wrong.

McCullough, David. 2005. *1776.* **New York: Simon & Schuster.** McCullough captured the human story of those who marched with General George Washington in the year of the Declaration of Independence.

Roberts, Cokie. 2008. *Ladies of Liberty: The Women Who Shaped Our Nation.* The noted American journalist investigates the influence of female patriots, and their impact on our nation's politics and history.

Turn. American Movie Classic's series explores the founding with the same dramatic, character-driven flair that made *The Walking Dead* and *Breaking Bad* such binge-worthy viewing.

Constitution USA With Peter Sagal. 2013. The host of National Public Radio's Wait, Wait, Don't Tell Me hits the road to explore the Constitution: how we got it, how we kept it, and how it plays out in our lives today.

Liberty! The American Revolution. 1998. The acclaimed PBS documentary covers the political maneuverings of the American War for Independence in six episodes.

4 FEDERALISM AND THE U.S. CONSTITUTION

IN YOUR OWN WORDS   After you've read this chapter, you will be able to

» Describe the role of each branch of government.

» Explain why the founders chose to structure each of the three branches of government as they did.

» Identify the ways in which federalism divides power between national and state governments.

» Demonstrate how the flexibility built in to the Constitution has allowed it to change with the times.

» Discuss whether the Constitution fosters or limits citizen participation in government.

WHAT'S AT STAKE...WHEN A STATE TAKES MARIJUANA LAWS INTO ITS OWN HANDS?

IF YOU ARE READING THIS FROM Washington State, Colorado, or a state that has legalized some form of marijuana for medical use, be careful—very careful—how you exercise your newfound rights. Due to the crazy patchwork nature of America's marijuana laws, what is legal in your home state might get you a year or more in jail and a hefty fine if you take it on the road.

Of course, everyone knows that smoking marijuana is against the law in the United States. Among other things, the United States federal Controlled Substances Act says so. Under that law, passed in 1970, marijuana is a "schedule one drug," equivalent, in legal terms, to heroin and LSD. But most people also know that, although the U.S. government considers marijuana a drug for which there is "no currently accepted medical use," twenty-three states beg to differ, and two (Colorado and Washington) say who cares, it's just plain fun. Voters in both of those states voted to legalize recreational marijuana in 2012.

So if you live in one of those states and have a prescription or buy the pot legally for recreational use, you are okay, right?

Not so fast.

Consider the case of B. J. Patel, a thirty-one-year-old man from Arizona who was traveling through Idaho and was stopped for failing to signal by a police officer who was using license plate recognition software to target out-of-state drivers. The officer saw the medical marijuana card in his wallet, asked where the pot was and, when shown by Patel, promptly arrested him. No matter how law-abiding Patel had been when he bought the pot, he was breaking the law in Idaho.

Idaho law provides for up to a year imprisonment and a $1,000 fine for under three ounces of pot and up to five years in jail and a $10,000 fine for more than three ounces. The state haul has gone from 131.2 pounds of pot in 2011 to 645 pounds in 2012 to 721.5 pounds in 2103. "Come on vacation, leave on probation," says a Coeur d'Alene lawyer.[1]

Courtesy Ann Kirby-Payne

to do battle. "We are hoping the enforcement agencies have bigger fish to fry and don't want to take a bunch of medicine away from sick kids," said one of the brothers. "But if they are going to do it, we're all in. If you are going to be locked up, it's a thing worth getting locked up for."[3]

Finally, consider the case of a Minnesota mom who was recently arrested in 2014 for giving her fifteen-year-old son marijuana oil on a doctor's advice to relieve chronic pain and muscle spasms from a brain injury. The pot was purchased legally in Colorado but administered in Minnesota, which has passed a law allowing medical marijuana. The catch? It doesn't come into effect until July 2015. Said Bob Capecchi, who works for the Marijuana Policy Project in Washington D.C., "Stunned was my initial reaction. I can't think of an instance where an individual has been brought up on charges like this simply because the effective date

Denver: A Mile High in More Ways Than One

Former marine Steve Azzariti served two tours in Iraq and suffers posttraumatic stress disorder, which he says is eased by using marijuana. He was also first in line to buy recreational pot when it became legal under Colorado law in January 2014. While laws have changed in many states, consuming cannabis remains an illegal substance in most other states, and marijuana use is still a federal offense. The resulting patchwork of state laws and changing federal enforcement from one administration to the next make for a confusing pot market. The options are for Congress to act, for the Courts to clear things up, or for Steve and his fellow users to be left in (a pleasant?) limbo.

Or consider the case of the five brothers in Colorado who sell an oil made from a strain of marijuana that doesn't even get you high. The plant is rich in a substance, CBD, that is used to treat seizures. It's legal in Colorado, of course, but there is a global demand for the oil and the brothers want to expand to meet that demand. The fly in their ointment is that, even though the oil is not an intoxicant, it is made from marijuana and marijuana is illegal under federal law. Generally, federal law trumps state law when there is a conflict, but Attorney General Eric Holder has said that as long as the sale of marijuana is regulated, the federal government won't prosecute its use in the states where it is legal.[2] But try to sell that marijuana, or any product made from it, across state lines and the feds will seize it and possibly put the seller in jail.

So the brothers are trying to get their product classified as "industrial hemp," which is okay by Colorado, but not necessarily by the United States. If the federal government doesn't buy their argument, they are ready

hasn't come around yet for the law that has already been passed. Let's not forget, there is a medical marijuana law that has been endorsed by the legislature and by the Governor."[4]

So why is there so much legal turmoil about the use of marijuana, something that a majority of Americans now think should be legal?[5] Why can an activity that is legal in one state get you fined and thrown in jail in another? Why can the federal government forbid an activity, but turn a blind eye to it unless you carry it across state lines? How do the laws get so complicated and tangled that you can get yourself arrested in one state for an activity that is legal in the state in which you took part in it, even if it is soon to be legal in the place where you are arrested? What is at stake when states decide to pass their own laws legalizing marijuana? We will return to this question at the end of the chapter, when we have a better grasp on the complex relationships that are generated by American federalism. «

IMAGINE that you are playing Monopoly but you've lost the rule book. You and your friends decide to play anyway and make up the rules as you go along. Even though the game still looks like Monopoly, and you're using the Monopoly board, and the money, and the game pieces, and the little houses and hotels, if you aren't following the official Monopoly rules, you aren't really playing Monopoly.

In the same way, imagine that America becomes afflicted with a sort of collective amnesia so that all the provisions of the Constitution are forgotten. Or perhaps the whole country gets fed up with politics as usual in America and votes to replace our Constitution with, say, the French Constitution. Even if we kept all our old politicians, and the White House and the Capitol, and the streets of Washington, what went on there would no longer be recognizable as American politics. What is distinctive about any political system is not just the people or the buildings, but also the rules and the ideas that lie behind them and give them life and meaning.

In politics, as in games, rules are crucial. The rules set up the institutions and the procedures that are the heart of the political system, and these institutions and procedures help determine who will be the winners and losers in politics, what outcomes will result, and how resources will be distributed. Political rules are themselves the product of a political process, as we saw in Chapter 3. Rules do not drop from the sky, all written and ready to be implemented. Instead they are created by human beings, determined to establish procedures that will help them, and people like them, get what they want from the system. If you change the rules, you change the people who will be advantaged and disadvantaged by those rules.

The founders were not in agreement about the sorts of rules that should be the base of American government. Instead they were feeling their way, balancing historical experience against contemporary reality. They had to craft new rules to achieve their goal of a government whose authority comes from the people but whose power was limited so as to preserve the liberty of those people. The questions that consumed them may surprise us. We know about the debate over how much power should belong to the national government and how much to the states. But discussions ranged far beyond issues of federalism versus states' rights. How should laws be made, and by whom? Should the British parliament be a model for the new legislature, with the "lords" represented in one house and the "common people" in the other? Or should there even be two houses at all? What about the executive? Should it be a king, as in England? Should it be just one person, or should several people serve as executive at the same time? How much power should the executive have, and how should he or they be chosen? And what role would the courts play? How could all these institutions be designed so that no one could become powerful enough to destroy the others? How could the system change with the times and yet still provide for stable governance?

Their answers to those questions are contained in the official rule book for who gets what, and how, in America, which is of course the Constitution. In Chapter 3 we talked about the political forces that produced the Constitution, the preferences of various groups for certain rules, and the compromises these groups evolved to get the document ratified. In this chapter we look at the Constitution from the inside. Since rules are so important in producing certain kinds of outcomes in the political system, it is essential that we understand not only what the rules provide for, but also what the choice of those rules means, what other kinds of rules exist that the founders did *not* choose, and what outcomes the founders rejected by not choosing those alternative rules.

Scholars spend whole lifetimes studying the Constitution. We can't achieve their level of detail here, but fortunately we don't need to. In this chapter, we'll focus on the founders' concerns, the constitutional provisions they established, the alternatives they might have chosen, and how their choices affect who gets what, and how, in American politics.

THE THREE BRANCHES OF GOVERNMENT
Making, executing, and interpreting the laws

All governments must have the power to do three things: (1) legislate, or make the laws; (2) administer, or execute the laws; and (3) adjudicate, or interpret the laws. The kinds of institutions they create to manage those powers vary widely. Because of our system of separation of powers, which we discuss later in this chapter, separate branches of government handle the legislative, executive, and judicial powers. Article I of the Constitution sets up Congress, our legislature; Article II establishes the presidency, our executive; and Article III outlines the federal court system, our judiciary.

THE LEGISLATIVE BRANCH

Legislative power is lawmaking power. Laws can be created by a single ruler or by a political party, they can be divined from natural or religious principles, or they can be made by the citizens who will have to obey the laws or by representatives working on their behalf. Most countries that claim to be democratic choose the last method of lawmaking. The body of government that makes laws is called the **legislature**.

> **legislature** the body of government that makes laws

Legislatures themselves can be set up in different ways: they can have one or two chambers, or houses; members can be elected, appointed, or hereditary; and if elected, they can be chosen by the people directly or by some other body. A variety of electoral rules can apply. The U.S. Congress is a **bicameral legislature**, meaning there are two chambers, and the legislators are elected directly by the people for terms of two or six years, depending on the house.

THINKING OUTSIDE THE BOX

Are there any advantages to living under Calvinball rules?

THE CASE FOR REPRESENTATION In *Federalist No. 10*, James Madison argued that American laws should be made by representatives of the people rather than by the people themselves. He rejected what he called "pure democracies," small political systems in which the citizens make and administer their own laws. Instead Madison recommended a **republic**, a system in which a larger number of citizens delegate, or assign, the tasks of governing to a smaller body. A republic claims two advantages: the dangers of factions are reduced, and the people running the government are presumably the best equipped to do so. Representation, said Madison, helps to "refine and enlarge the public views by passing them through the medium of a chosen body of citizens," distinguished by their wisdom, patriotism, and love of justice.[6]

Of course, Americans were already long accustomed to the idea of representation. All the states had legislatures. The Articles of Confederation had provided for representation as well, and even Britain had representation of a sort in Parliament.

WHAT DOES THE CONSTITUTION SAY? Article I sets out the framework of the legislative branch of government.

> **bicameral legislature** a legislature with two chambers
>
> **republic** a government in which decisions are made through representatives of the people

Since the founders expected the legislature to be the most important part of the new government, they spent the most time specifying its composition, the qualifications for membership, its powers, and its limitations.

The best known part of Article I is the famous Section 8, which spells out the specific powers of Congress. This list is followed by the provision that Congress can do anything "necessary and proper" to carry out its duties. The Supreme Court has interpreted this clause so broadly that there are few effective restrictions on what Congress can do.

The House of Representatives, where representation is based on population, was intended to be truly the representative of all the people, the "voice of the common man," as it were. To be elected to the House, a candidate need be only twenty-five years old and a citizen for seven years. Since House terms last two years, members run for reelection often and can be ousted fairly easily, according to public whim. The founders intended this office to be accessible to and easily influenced by citizens and to reflect frequent changes in public opinion.

The Senate is another matter. Candidates have to be at least thirty years old and citizens for nine years—older, wiser, and, the founders hoped, more stable than the representatives in the House. Because senatorial terms last for six years, senators are not so easily swayed by changes in public sentiment. In addition, senators were originally elected not directly by the people, but by members of their state legislatures. Election by state legislators, themselves already a "refinement" of the general public, would ensure that senators were a higher caliber of citizen: more in tune with "the commercial and monied interest," as Massachusetts delegate Elbridge Gerry put it at the Constitutional Convention.[7] The Senate would thus be a more aristocratic body; that is, it would look more like the British House of Lords, where members are admitted on the basis of their birth or achievement, not by election.

POSSIBLE ALTERNATIVES: A UNICAMERAL LEGISLATURE?

The Congress we have is not the only Congress the founders could have given us. Instead of establishing the House of Representatives and the Senate, for instance, they could have established one legislative chamber only, what we call a unicameral legislature. Many countries today have unicameral legislatures—Malta, New Zealand, Denmark, Sweden, Spain, Israel, North Korea, Kuwait, Syria, Malawi, and Cameroon, to name a few. And while most of the fifty United States have followed the national example with bicameral state legislatures, Nebraska has chosen a unicameral, nonpartisan legislature.

> unicameral legislature a legislature with one chamber

The Washington Post/Getty Images

Protect and Educate
The National Archives house much of the documentary history of the nation, including copies of the Declaration of Independence, the Constitution, and the Gettysburg Address. Here Special Archive Police Officer Euril Perry answers a tourist's questions, making education as much a part of his job as policing.

Proponents of such institutions claim that lawmaking is faster and more efficient when laws are debated and voted on in only one chamber. They say such laws are also more responsive to changes in public opinion, which at least theoretically is a good thing in a democracy.

On the national level, a unicameral system can help encourage citizens to feel a sense of identity with their government, since it implies that the whole country shares the same fundamental interests and can thus be represented by a single body. Originally in Europe, governments had different legislative chambers to represent different social classes or estates in society. We can see the remnants of this system in the British parliament, whose upper chamber is called the House of Lords, and lower, the House of Commons, or the common people. The French once had five houses in their legislature, and the Swedish four. As countries become more democratic—that is, as their governments become more representative of the people as a whole and not of social classes—the legislatures become more streamlined. Sweden eventually moved to two legislative houses, and in 1971 it adopted a unicameral legislature. France now has two. Britain still has the Lords and the Commons, but increasing democratization has meant less legislative power for the House of Lords, which now can only delay, not block, laws made by the House of Commons.[8] In that sense, the fewer chambers a legislature has, the more representative it is of the people as a whole.

A unicameral system has several clear disadvantages, however. For one thing, such a system makes it difficult for the legislature to represent more than one set of interests. Although the United States did not have the feudal history of Europe, with its remnants of nobility and commons, it was still a country with frequently conflicting economic interests, as politics under the Articles of Confederation had made painfully evident. Our founders preferred bicameralism in part because the two houses could represent different interests in society—the people's interests in the House and the more elite interests in the Senate.

In addition to providing for representation of different interests, another advantage of a bicameral legislature was its ability to represent the different levels of the federal government in the legislative process. Federal governments that preserve a bicameral structure typically do so with the intention of having the "people" represented in one house and the individual regions—in our case, the states—in another. In the United States, representation in the House is based on the state's population, and representation in the Senate is based simply on statehood, with each state getting two votes. The fact that the senators used to be elected by the state legislatures reinforces the *federal* aspect of this arrangement. In the German *Bundesrat*, the members are chosen by the governments of each state.

A final reason the founders were convinced that bicameralism was better than unicameralism for the young republic is that they believed the more they divided the power of government into smaller units, the safer the government would be from those who would abuse its power. Two legislative chambers would keep a watch over each other and check their tendencies to get out of hand. The quick legislative responsiveness of a unicameral legislature can have some drawbacks. Changes in public opinion are often only temporary, and perhaps a society in a calmer moment would not want the laws to be changed so hastily. Rapid-response lawmaking can also result in excessive amounts of legislation, creating a legal system that confuses and baffles the citizenry. When asked by Thomas Jefferson, who had been in France during the Constitutional Convention, why the delegates had adopted a bicameral legislature, George Washington explained that, just as one would pour one's coffee into the saucer to cool it off (a common practice of the day), "we pour legislation into the senatorial saucer to cool it." As Professor Richard Fenno points out, legislation has as often been cooled by pouring it into the House of Representatives. Each chamber has served to cool the passions of the other; this requirement that laws be passed twice has helped keep the American legislature in check.[9]

THE EXECUTIVE BRANCH

The **executive** is the part of government that "executes" the laws, or sees they are carried out. Although technically executives serve in an administrative role, many end up with some decision-making or legislative power as well. National executives are the leaders of their countries, and they participate, with varying amounts of power, in making laws and policies. That role can range from the U.S. president, who, while not a part of the legislature itself, can propose, encourage, and veto legislation, to European prime ministers, who are part of the legislature and may have, as in the British case, the power to dissolve the entire legislature and call a new election.

FEARS OF THE FOUNDERS That the Articles of Confederation provided for no executive power at all was a testimony to the founders' conviction that such a power threatened their liberty. The chaos that resulted under the Articles, however, made it clear that a stronger government was called for—not only a stronger legislature, but a stronger executive as well. The constitutional debates reveal that many of the founders were haunted by the idea that they might inadvertently reestablish that same tyrannical power over themselves that they had escaped only recently with the Revolution. The central controversies focused on whether the executive should be more than one person, whether he should be able to seek reelection as many times as he wanted, and whether he should be elected directly by the people or indirectly by the legislature.

The founders were divided. On one side were those like Alexander Hamilton, who insisted that only a vigorous executive could provide the stability necessary to preserve liberty. Hamilton recommended an executive appointed for life so that he would be independent of the political process. Others, like Edmund Randolph of Virginia, were unwilling to entertain the notion of a single executive, let alone one chosen for life. Randolph proposed instead three executives, representing various regions of the country, as a safer repository of power.[10]

Those fearing a strong executive believed its power could be limited by dividing it among several officeholders, but they eventually lost to those who believed there should be a single president. The issue of whether the executive should be allowed to run for reelection for an unlimited number of terms got tangled up with the question of just how the president was to be elected. If, as some founders argued, he were chosen by Congress rather than by the people, then he should be limited to one term. Since he would be dependent on Congress for his power, he might fail to provide an adequate check on that body, perhaps currying favor with Congress in order to be chosen for additional terms.

On the other hand, the founders had no great trust in "the people," as we have seen, so popular election of the

---

executive the branch of government responsible for putting laws into effect

president was considered highly suspect, even though it would free the executive from dependence on Congress and allow him to be elected for multiple terms. Alexander Hamilton wanted to go so far as to have the president serve for life, thereby eliminating the problem of being dependent on Congress *or* on the popular will.

That these diverse ideas were resolved and consensus was achieved is one of the marvels of the American founding. The final provision of presidential authority was neither as powerful as Hamilton's kinglike lifetime executive nor as constrained as Randolph's multiple executive. Still, it was a much stronger office than many of the founders, particularly the Anti-Federalists, wanted.

WHAT DOES THE CONSTITUTION SAY? The solution chosen by the founders was a complicated one, but it satisfied all the concerns raised at the convention. The president, a single executive, would serve an unlimited number of four-year terms. (A constitutional amendment in 1951 limited the president to two elected terms.) But in addition, the president would be chosen neither by Congress nor directly by the people. Instead the Constitution provides for his selection by an intermediary body called the Electoral College. Citizens vote not for the presidential candidates, but for a slate of electors, who cast their votes for the candidates about six weeks after the general election. The founders believed that this procedure would ensure a president elected by well-informed delegates who, having no other lawmaking power, could not be bribed or otherwise influenced by candidates. We will say more about how this process works in Chapter 14, on elections.

Article II of the Constitution establishes the executive. The four sections of that article make the following provisions:

- Section 1 sets out the four-year term and the manner of election (that is, the details of the Electoral College). It also provides for the qualifications for office: that the president must be a natural-born citizen of the United States, at least thirty-five years old, and a resident of the United States for at least fourteen years. The vice president serves if the president cannot, and Congress can make laws

---

Electoral College an intermediary body that elects the president

presidential system government in which the executive is chosen independently of the legislature and the two branches are separate

parliamentary system government in which the executive is chosen by the legislature from among its members and the two branches are merged

---

about the succession if the vice president is incapacitated.

- Section 2 establishes the powers of the chief executive. He is commander-in-chief of the armed forces and of the state militias when they are serving the nation, and he has the power to grant pardons for offenses against the United States. With the advice and consent of two-thirds of the Senate, the president can make treaties, and with a simple majority vote of the Senate the president can appoint ambassadors, ministers, consuls, Supreme Court justices, and other U.S. officials whose appointments are not otherwise provided for.

- Section 3 says that the president will periodically tell Congress how the country is doing (the State of the Union address given every January) and will propose to the members those measures he thinks appropriate and necessary. Under extraordinary circumstances the president calls Congress into session or, if the two houses of Congress cannot agree on when to end their sessions, may adjourn them. The president also receives ambassadors and public officials, executes the laws, and commissions all officers of the United States.

- Section 4 specifies that the president, vice president, and other civil officers of the United States (such as Supreme Court justices) can be impeached, tried, and convicted for "Treason, Bribery, or other High Crimes and Misdemeanors."

POSSIBLE ALTERNATIVES: A PARLIAMENTARY SYSTEM? As the debates over the American executive clearly show, many options were open to the founders as they designed the executive office. They chose what is referred to today as a presidential system, in which a leader is chosen independently of the legislature to serve a fixed term of office that is unaffected by the success or failure of the legislature. The principal alternative to a presidential system among contemporary democracies is called a parliamentary system, in which the executive is a member of the legislature, chosen by the legislators themselves, not by a separate national election. When the founders briefly considered the consequences of having a president chosen by Congress, they were discussing something like a parliamentary system. The fundamental difference between a parliamentary system and a presidential system is that in the former the legislature and the executive are merged, but in the latter they are separate. In parliamentary systems the executive is accountable to the legislature, but in a presidential system he or she is independent.

Generally speaking, the executive or prime minister in a parliamentary system is the chosen leader of the majority party in the legislature. This would be roughly equivalent

© Reuters TV/Reuters

No "Hail to the Chief" Here

When the president of the United States appears before Congress, it is usually a formal and relatively respectful affair. But in the United Kingdom the prime minster is afforded no such luxury. Here, British prime minister David Cameron is heckled by members of the opposing party during a typical parliamentary session.

to allowing the majority party in the House of Representatives to install its leader, the Speaker of the House, as the national executive. What is striking about the parliamentary system is that most of the citizens of the country never vote for the national leader. Only members of the prime minister's legislative district actually cast a vote for him or her. If the parliament does not think the prime minister is doing a good job, it can replace him or her without consulting the country's voters.

This process is very different from the American provision for impeachment of the president for criminal activity. Parliaments can remove executives for reasons of political or ideological disagreement. Although there may be political disagreement over the grounds for impeachment in the American case, as there was in the impeachment of President Bill Clinton, there must be at least an allegation of criminal activity, which need not exist for removal in a parliamentary system. (If the United States had a parliamentary system, then a legislative vote of "no confidence" could have ousted the president at the beginning of the process.) Consequently the executive in a parliamentary system is dependent on the legislature and cannot provide any effective check if the legislature abuses its power. In Germany's parliamentary government, an independent court can restrain the legislature and keep it within the bounds of the constitution, but the British system has no check at all. The upper house of Parliament, the House of Lords, is the highest court and even it

cannot declare an act of the House of Commons unconstitutional. The French system is a curious hybrid. It is parliamentary since the prime minister is chosen from the majority party in the legislature, but there is *also* a strong president who is independent of the legislature. Because the French split the executive functions, there is an executive check on the legislature, even though it is a parliamentary system.

Politics is very different in a parliamentary system than it is in a presidential system. Leadership is clearly more concentrated in the former case. Because the prime minister usually chooses his or her cabinet from the legislature, the executive and legislative truly overlap. It is much easier for a prime minister to get his or her programs and laws passed by the legislature because, under normal circumstances, he or she already has the party votes to pass them. If the party has a serious loss of faith or "confidence" in the prime minister, it can force the prime minister out of office. Thus the prime minister has a strong incentive to cooperate with the legislature. In some cases, like the British, the prime minister has some countervailing clout of his or her own. The British prime minister has the power to call parliamentary elections at will within a five-year period and consequently can jeopardize the jobs of members of parliament, or at least threaten to do so. This does not necessarily result in more frequent elections in Britain than in the United States with its fixed elections (from 1900 to 2004 Britain held twenty-seven general elections to the United States' twenty-four), but it does mean the prime minister can time the elections to take place when the party's fortunes are high. One result of this close relationship between executive and legislative is that the ties of political party membership seem to be stronger in a parliamentary system, in which a party's domination of national politics depends on block voting along party lines. As we will see in Chapter 12, party discipline, as this is called, is much reduced in the U.S. system.

THE JUDICIAL BRANCH

Judicial power is the power to interpret the laws and to judge whether the laws have been broken. Naturally, by establishing how a given law is to be understood, the courts (the agents of judicial power) end up making law as well. Our constitutional provisions for the establishment of the judiciary are brief and vague; much of the American federal judiciary under the Supreme Court is left to Congress to arrange. But the founders left plenty of clues as to how they felt about judicial power in their debates and their writings, particularly in *The Federalist Papers*.

THE "LEAST DANGEROUS" BRANCH
In *Federalist* No. 78, Hamilton made clear his view that the judiciary was the least threatening branch of power. The executive and the legislature might endanger liberty, but not so the judiciary. Hamilton said that, as long as government functions are separate from one another (that is, as long as the judiciary is not part of the executive or the legislature), then the judiciary "will always be the least dangerous to the political rights of the Constitution; because it has the least capacity to annoy or injure them." The executive "holds the sword," and the legislature "commands the purse." The judiciary, controlling neither sword nor purse, neither "strength nor wealth of the society," has neither "FORCE nor WILL but merely judgment."[11]

Although the founders were not particularly worried, then, that the judiciary would be too powerful, they did want to be sure it would not be too political—that is, caught up in the fray of competing interests and influence. The only federal court they discussed in much detail was the Supreme Court, but the justices of that Court were to be appointed for life, provided they maintain "good behavior," in part to preserve them from politics. Once appointed they need not be concerned with seeking the favor of the legislature, the executive, or the people. Instead

---

judicial power the power to interpret laws and judge whether a law has been broken

judicial review the power of the Supreme Court to rule on the constitutionality of laws

---

of trying to do what is popular, they can concentrate on doing what is just, or constitutional.

Even though the founders wanted to keep the Court out of politics, they did make it possible for the justices to get involved when they considered it necessary. The practice of judicial review is introduced through the back door, first mentioned by Hamilton in *Federalist* No. 78 and then institutionalized by the Supreme Court itself, with Chief Justice John Marshall's 1803 ruling in *Marbury v. Madison*, a dispute over presidential appointments. **Judicial review** allows the Supreme Court to rule that an act of Congress or the executive branch (or of a state or local government) is unconstitutional, that it runs afoul of constitutional principles. This review process is not an automatic part of lawmaking; the Court does not examine every law that Congress passes or every executive order to be sure that it does not violate the Constitution. Rather, if a law is challenged as unconstitutional by an individual or a group, and if it is appealed all the way to the Supreme Court, then the justices may decide to rule on it.

This remarkable grant of power to the "least dangerous" branch to nullify legislation is *not* itself in the Constitution. In *Federalist* No. 78, Hamilton argued that it was consistent with the Constitution, however. In response to critics who objected that such a practice would place the unelected Court in a position superior to that of the elected representatives of the people, Hamilton wrote that, on the contrary, it raised the people, as authors of the Constitution, over the government as a whole. Thus judicial review enhanced democracy rather than diminished it.

In 1803 Marshall agreed. As the nation's highest law, the Constitution sets the limits on what is acceptable legislation. As the interpreter of the Constitution, the Supreme Court has a duty to determine when laws fall outside those limits. Interestingly, this gigantic grant of power to the Court was made by the Court itself and remains unchallenged by the other branches. The irony is that the sort of empire-building the founders hoped to avoid appears in the branch they took the least care to safeguard. We return to *Marbury v. Madison* and judicial review in Chapter 10, on the court system.

WHAT DOES THE CONSTITUTION SAY?
Article III of the Constitution is very short. It says that the judicial power of the United States is to be "vested in one Supreme Court, and in such inferior courts as the Congress may from time to time ordain and establish," and that judges serve as long as they demonstrate "good behavior." It also explains that the Supreme Court has original jurisdiction in some types of cases and appellate jurisdiction in others. That is, in some cases the Supreme Court is the only court that can rule; much more often, inferior courts try cases, but their rulings can be appealed to the Supreme Court. Article III provides for jury trials in all criminal cases except impeachment, and it defines the practice of and punishment

© Nate Beeler/Cagle Cartoons Inc.

When Is a Mandate a Tax?
When the Supreme Court says it is. The Court upheld President Obama's health care plan based on a majority ruling that the individual mandate is a tax—and completely within Congress's constitutional powers. Ironically, the president pitched the plan as anything but a tax in order to get the support of tax-wary members of Congress.

for acts of treason. Because the Constitution is so silent on the role of the courts in America, that role has been left to be defined by Congress and, in some cases, by the courts themselves.

POSSIBLE ALTERNATIVES: LEGISLATIVE SUPREMACY? Clearly one alternative to judicial review is to allow the legislature's laws to stand unchallenged. This system of **legislative supremacy** underlies British politics. The British have no written constitution. Acts of Parliament are the final law of the land and cannot be reviewed or struck down by the courts. They become part of the general collection of acts, laws, traditions, and court cases that make up the British "unwritten constitution." Our Court is thus more powerful, and our legislature correspondingly less powerful, than the same institutions in the British system. We are accustomed to believing that judicial review is an important limitation on Congress and a protection of individual liberty. Britain is not remarkably behind the United States, however, in terms of either legislative tyranny or human rights. Think about how much difference judicial review really makes, especially if you consider the experience of a country like Japan, where judicial review usually results in upholding government behavior *over* individual rights and liberties.[12]

Yet another alternative to our system would be to give judicial review *more* teeth. The German Constitutional Court also reviews legislation to determine if it fits with the German Basic Law, but it does not need to wait for

cases to come to it on appeal. National and state executives, the lower house of the legislature (the *Bundestag*), or even citizens can ask the German high court to determine whether a law is constitutional. Like the U.S. Supreme Court, the Constitutional Court is flooded with far more cases than it can accept and must pick and choose the issues on which it will rule.

PAUSE AND REVIEW:

WHO, WHAT, HOW

The founders' goal was to devise a legislature, an executive, and a judiciary that would correct the flaws of the Articles of Confederation while balancing the rights and powers of citizens against the need for the government to be secure from abuse and corruption. The means they employed were unusual—they had the unique opportunity to write the rule book, the Constitution, from scratch, constrained only by the necessity of gaining the approval of sufficient states to allow the Constitution to be ratified and thus seen as legitimate.

IN YOUR OWN WORDS >> Describe the role of each branch of government.

SEPARATION OF POWERS AND CHECKS AND BALANCES
Mechanical arrangements to limit abuses of power

Separation of powers means that the legislature, the executive, and the judicial powers are not exercised by the same person or group of people, lest they abuse the considerable amount of power they hold. We are indebted to the French Enlightenment philosopher the Baron de Montesquieu for explaining this notion. In his massive book *The Spirit of the Laws*, Montesquieu wrote that liberty could be threatened only if the same group that enacted tyrannical laws also executed them. He said, "There would be an end of everything, were the same

> **legislative supremacy** an alternative to judicial review, the acceptance of legislative acts as the final law of the land
>
> **separation of powers** the institutional arrangement that assigns judicial, executive, and legislative powers to different persons or groups, thereby limiting the powers of each

FIGURE 4.1 SEPARATION OF POWERS AND CHECKS AND BALANCES

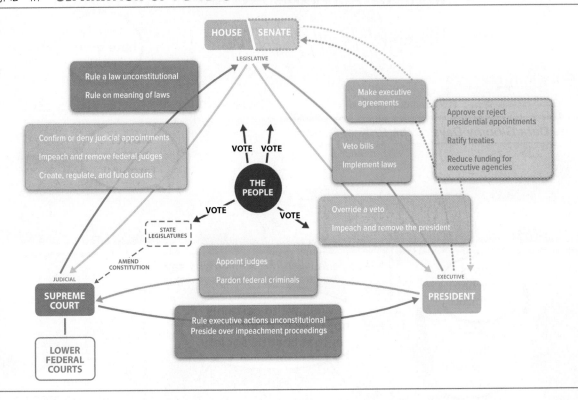

man or the same body, whether of nobles or of the people, to exercise those three powers, that of enacting laws, that of executing the public resolutions, and of trying the causes of individuals."[13] Putting all political power into one set of hands is like putting all our eggs in one basket. If the person or body of people entrusted with all the power becomes corrupt or dictatorial, the whole system will go bad. If, on the other hand, power is divided so that each branch is in separate hands, one may go bad while leaving the other two intact. The principle of separation of powers gives each of the branches authority over its own domain.

A complementary principle, **checks and balances**, allows each of the branches to police the others, checking any abuses and balancing the powers of government. The purpose of this additional authority is to ensure that no branch can exercise power tyrannically. In our case, the president can veto an act of Congress, Congress can override a veto, the Supreme Court can declare a law of Congress unconstitutional, Congress can—with the help of the states—amend the Constitution itself, and so on. Figure 4.1 illustrates these relationships.

> **checks and balances** the principle that allows each branch of government to exercise some form of control over the others

Which really is the least dangerous branch of the federal government?

REPUBLICAN REMEDIES

As we see in this chapter's *The Big Picture*, James Madison wrote in *Federalist* No. 51 that "If men were angels, no government would be necessary. If angels were to govern men, neither external nor internal controls on government would be necessary."[14] Alas, we are not angels, nor are we governed by angels. Since human nature is flawed and humans are sometimes ambitious, greedy, and corruptible, precautions must be taken to create a government that will make use of human nature, not be destroyed by it. A republic, which offers so many opportunities to so many people to take advantage of political power, requires special controls. The job, according to Madison, was to find a "republican remedy for those diseases most incident to republican government."[15] He said, "In framing a government which is to be administered by men over men, the great difficulty is this: you must first enable the government to control the governed; and in the next place oblige it to

control itself."[16] The founders used separation of powers and checks and balances to oblige government to control itself, to impose internal limitations on government power in order to safeguard the liberty of the people.

The founders were generally supportive of separation of powers, some form of which appeared in all the state governments. Not so readily accepted was the notion of checks and balances, that once power was separated, it should be somehow shared. Having carefully kept the executive from taking on a legislative role, the founders were reluctant, for example, to give the president veto power.

In *Federalist* No. 47, Madison explained the relationship of separation of powers to checks and balances. Rather than damaging the protection offered by separation of powers, sharing some control over each branch reinforced security because no branch could wield its power without some check. The trick was to give people in each branch an interest in controlling the behavior of the others. This is how human nature, flawed though it might be, could be used to limit the abuses of power. As Madison put it, in *Federalist* No. 51: "Ambition must be made to counteract ambition."[17] Thus there was no danger in sharing some control over the branches because jealous humans would always be looking over their shoulders for potential abuses.

WHAT DOES THE CONSTITUTION SAY?

The Constitution establishes separation of powers with articles setting up a different institution for each branch of government. We have already examined Article I, establishing Congress as the legislature; Article II, establishing the president as the executive; and Article III, outlining the court system. Checks and balances are provided by clauses within each of those articles.

- Article I sets up a bicameral legislature. Because both houses must agree on all legislation, each can check the other. Article I also describes the presidential veto, with which the president can check Congress, and the override provision, by which two-thirds of Congress can check the president. Congress can also use impeachment to check abuses of the executive or judicial branch.

- Article II empowers the president to execute the laws and to share some legislative function by "recommending laws." He has some checks on the judiciary through his power to appoint judges, but his appointment power is checked by the requirement that a majority of the Senate must confirm his choices. The president can also check the judiciary by granting pardons. The president is commander-in-chief of the armed forces, but his ability to exercise his authority is checked by the Article I provision that only Congress can declare war.

- Article III creates the Supreme Court. The Court's ruling in the case of *Marbury v. Madison* fills in some of the gaps in this vague article by establishing judicial review, a true check on the legislative and executive branches. Congress can countercheck judicial review by amending the Constitution (with the help of the states).

The Constitution wisely ensures that no branch of the government can act independently of the others, yet none is wholly dependent on the others, either. This approach results in a structure of separation of powers and checks and balances that is distinctly American.

POSSIBLE ALTERNATIVES: FUSION OF POWERS?

An alternative way to deal with the different branches of government is to fuse rather than separate them. We have already discussed what this might look like when we compared a parliamentary system with a presidential system. A parliamentary system involves a clear **fusion of powers**. Because the components of government are not separate, no formal internal checks can curb the use of power. That is not to say that the flaws in human nature might not still encourage members of the government to keep a jealous eye on one another, but no deliberate mechanism exists to bring these checks into being. In a democracy, external checks may still be provided by the people, through either the ballot box or public opinion polls. Where the government is not freely and popularly elected, or, more rarely these days, when all the components are fused into a single monarch, even the checks of popular control are missing.

PAUSE AND REVIEW:

WHO, WHAT, HOW

The founders wanted, for themselves and the public, a government that would not succumb to the worst of human nature. The viability and stability of the American system would be jeopardized if they could not find a way to tame the jealousy, greed, and ambition that might threaten the new republic. The remedy they chose to save the American Constitution from its own leaders and citizens is the set of rules called separation of powers and checks and balances. Whether the founders were right or wrong about human nature, the principles of government

fusion of powers an alternative to separation of powers, combining or blending branches of government

they established have been remarkably effective at guaranteeing the long-term survival of the American system.

IN YOUR OWN WORDS » Explain why the founders chose to structure each of the three branches of government as they did.

FEDERALISM
Balancing power between national and state governments

Federalism, as we said in Chapter 3, is a political system in which authority is divided between different levels of government. In the United States, federalism refers to the relationship between the national government (also frequently, but confusingly, called the *federal* government) and the states. Each level has some power independent of the other levels so that no level is entirely dependent on another for its existence. For the founders, federalism was a compromise in the bitter dispute between those who wanted stronger state governments and those who preferred a stronger national government. Both sides knew that the rules dividing power between the states and the federal government were crucial to determining who would be the winners and losers in the new country.

Today the effects of federalism are all around us. We pay income taxes to the national government, which parcels out the money to the states, under certain conditions, to be spent on programs such as welfare, highways, and education. In most states, local schools are funded by local property taxes and run by local school boards (local governments are created under the authority of the state), and state universities are supported by state taxes and influenced by the state legislatures. Even so, both state and local governments are subject to national legislation, such as the requirement that schools be open to students of all races, and both can be affected by national decisions about funding various programs. Sometimes the lines of responsibility can be extremely unclear. Witness the simultaneous presence, in many areas, of city police, county police, state police, and, at the national level, the Federal Bureau of Investigation (FBI), all coordinated, for some purposes, by the national Department of Homeland Security.

> **enumerated powers of Congress** congressional powers specifically named in the Constitution (Article I, Section 8)
>
> **necessary and proper clause** constitutional authorization for Congress to make any law required to carry out its powers
>
> **supremacy clause** constitutional declaration (Article VI) that the Constitution and laws made under its provisions are the supreme law of the land

Even when a given responsibility lies at the state level, the national government frequently finds a way to enforce its will. For instance, it is up to the states to decide on the minimum drinking age for their citizens. In the 1970s many states required people to be only eighteen or nineteen before they could legally buy alcohol; today all the states have a uniform drinking age of twenty-one. The change came about because interest groups persuaded officials in the federal (that is, national) government that the higher age would lead to fewer alcohol-related highway accidents and greater public safety. The federal government couldn't pass a law setting a nationwide drinking age of twenty-one, but it could control the flow of highway money to the states. By withholding 5 percent of federal highway funds, which every state wants and needs, until a state raised the drinking age to twenty-one, Congress prevailed. Similar congressional pressure led states to lower the legal standard for drunk driving to a 0.08 percent blood alcohol level by the fall of 2003.[18] These examples show how the relations between levels of government work when neither level can directly force the other to do what it wants.

WHAT DOES THE CONSTITUTION SAY?

No single section of the Constitution deals with federalism. Instead the provisions dividing up power between the states and the national government appear throughout the Constitution. Local government is not mentioned in the Constitution at all, because it is completely under the jurisdiction of the states. Most of the Constitution is concerned with establishing the powers of the national government. Since Congress is the main lawmaking arm of the national government, many of the powers of the national government are the powers of Congress. The strongest statement of national power is a list of the **enumerated powers of Congress** (Article I, Section 8). This list is followed by a clause that gives Congress the power to make all laws that are "necessary and proper" to carry out its powers. The **necessary and proper clause** (also called the "elastic clause" because the Supreme Court has interpreted it broadly) has been used to justify giving Congress many powers never mentioned in the Constitution. National power is also based on the **supremacy clause** of Article VI, which says that the Constitution and laws made in accordance with it are "the supreme law of the land." This means that when national and state laws conflict, the national laws will be followed. The Constitution also sets some limitations on the national government. Article I, Section 9, lists some specific powers not granted to Congress, and the Bill of Rights (the first ten amendments to the Constitution) limits the power of the national government over individuals.

The Constitution says considerably less about the powers granted to the states. The Tenth Amendment says that all powers not given to the national government are reserved for the states, although, as we will soon see, the Court's interpretation of the necessary and proper clause as

FIGURE 4.2 THE CONSTITUTIONAL DIVISION OF POWERS BETWEEN THE NATIONAL GOVERNMENT AND THE STATES

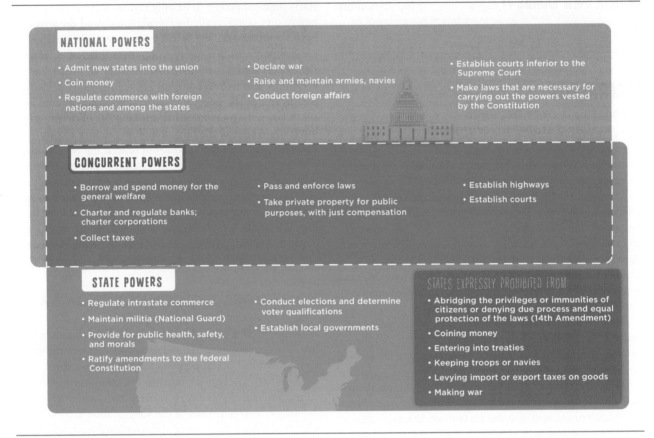

NATIONAL POWERS

- Admit new states into the union
- Coin money
- Regulate commerce with foreign nations and among the states
- Declare war
- Raise and maintain armies, navies
- Conduct foreign affairs
- Establish courts inferior to the Supreme Court
- Make laws that are necessary for carrying out the powers vested by the Constitution

CONCURRENT POWERS

- Borrow and spend money for the general welfare
- Charter and regulate banks; charter corporations
- Collect taxes
- Pass and enforce laws
- Take private property for public purposes, with just compensation
- Establish highways
- Establish courts

STATE POWERS

- Regulate intrastate commerce
- Maintain militia (National Guard)
- Provide for public health, safety, and morals
- Ratify amendments to the federal Constitution
- Conduct elections and determine voter qualifications
- Establish local governments

STATES EXPRESSLY PROHIBITED FROM:

- Abridging the privileges or immunities of citizens or denying due process and equal protection of the laws (14th Amendment)
- Coining money
- Entering into treaties
- Keeping troops or navies
- Levying import or export taxes on goods
- Making war

---

elastic makes it difficult to see which powers are withheld from the national government. The states are given the power to approve the Constitution itself and any amendments to it. The Constitution also limits state powers. Article I, Section 10, denies the states certain powers, mostly the kinds they possessed under the Articles of Confederation. The Fourteenth Amendment limits the power of the states over individual liberties, essentially a Bill of Rights that protects individuals from state action, since the first ten amendments apply only to the national government.

What these constitutional provisions mean is that the line between the national government and the state governments is not clearly drawn. We can see from Figure 4.2 that the Constitution designates specific powers as national, state, or concurrent. **Concurrent powers** are those that both levels of government may exercise. But the federal relationship is a good deal more complex than this figure would lead us to believe. The Supreme Court has become crucial to establishing the exact limits of such provisions as the necessary and proper clause, the supremacy clause, the Tenth Amendment, and the Fourteenth Amendment. The Court's interpretation has

changed over time, especially as historical demands have forced it to think about federalism in new ways.

TWO VIEWS OF FEDERALISM

Political scientists have also changed the way they think about federalism. For many years the prevailing theory was known as **dual federalism**, basically arguing that the relationship between the two levels of government was like a layer cake. That is, the national and state governments were to be understood as two self-contained layers, each essentially separate from the other and carrying out its functions independently. In its own area of power, each level was supreme. Dual federalism reflects the formal distribution of powers in the Constitution, and perhaps it was an accurate

concurrent powers powers that are shared by both the federal and state governments

dual federalism the federal system under which the national and state governments are responsible for separate policy areas

Elastic Clause ●

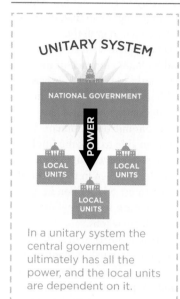

UNITARY SYSTEM

In a unitary system the central government ultimately has all the power, and the local units are dependent on it.

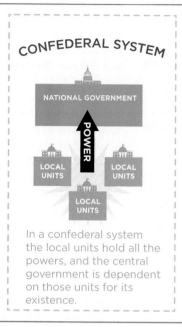

CONFEDERAL SYSTEM

In a confederal system the local units hold all the powers, and the central government is dependent on those units for its existence.

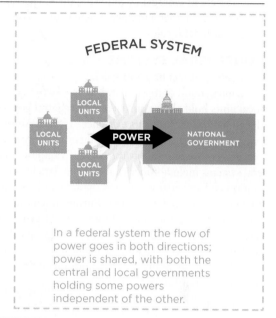

FEDERAL SYSTEM

In a federal system the flow of power goes in both directions; power is shared, with both the central and local governments holding some powers independent of the other.

portrayal of the judicial interpretation of the federal system for our first hundred years or so.

But this theory was criticized for not realistically describing the way the federal relationship was evolving in the twentieth century. It certainly did not take into account the changes brought about by the New Deal. The layer cake image was replaced by a new bakery metaphor. According to the new theory of **cooperative federalism**, rather than being two distinct layers, the national and state levels were swirled together like the chocolate and vanilla batter in a marble cake.[19] National and state powers were interdependent, and each level required the cooperation of the other to get things done. In fact, federalism came to be seen by political scientists as a partnership in which the dominant partner was, more often than not, the national government.

POSSIBLE ALTERNATIVES TO FEDERALISM

The federal system was not the only alternative available to our founders for organizing the relationship between the central government and the states. In fact, as we know, it wasn't even their first choice as a framework for government.

> **cooperative federalism** the federal system under which the national and state governments share responsibilities for most domestic policy areas
>
> **unitary system** government in which all power is centralized

The Articles of Confederation, which preceded the Constitution, handled the relationship quite differently. We can look at federalism as a compromise system that borrows some attributes from a unitary system and some from a confederal system, as shown in Figure 4.3. Had the founders chosen either of these alternatives, American government would look very different today.

UNITARY SYSTEMS In a **unitary system** the central government ultimately has all the power. Local units (states or counties) may have some power at some times, but basically they are dependent on the central unit, which can alter or even abolish them. Many contemporary countries have unitary systems, among them Britain, France, Japan, Denmark, Norway, Sweden, Hungary, and the Philippines.

Politics in Britain, for example, works very differently from politics in the United States, partly due to the different rules that organize central and local government. Most important decisions are made in London, from foreign policy to housing policy—even the details of what ought to be included in the school curriculum. Even local taxes are determined centrally. When Margaret Thatcher, then the British prime minister, believed that some municipal units in London were not supportive of her government's policies, she simply dissolved the administrative units. Similarly, in 1972, when the legislature in Northern Ireland (a part of Great Britain) could not resolve its religious conflicts, the central government suspended the local lawmaking body and ruled Northern Ireland from London. These actions are tantamount to a Republican president's dissolving a Democratic state that disagreed with his policies, or the national government's deciding during the days of segregation to suspend the state legislature in Alabama and run the state from Washington. Such an arrangement has been impossible in the United States except during the chaotic state of emergency following the Civil War. What is commonplace under a unitary system is unimaginable under our federal rules.

CONFEDERAL SYSTEMS Confederal systems provide an equally sharp contrast to federal systems, even though the names sound quite similar. In a **confederal system** the local units hold all the power, and the central government is dependent on them for its existence. The local units remain sovereign, and the central government has only as much power as those units allow it to have. Examples of confederal systems include America under the Articles of Confederation and associations such as the United Nations and the European Union, twenty-eight European nations that have joined economic and political forces. The European Union has been experiencing problems much like ours after the Revolutionary War, debating whether it ought to move in a federal direction. Some of the nations involved, jealous of their sovereignty, have been reluctant.

WHAT DIFFERENCE DOES FEDERALISM MAKE?

That our founders settled on federalism, rather than a unitary or a confederal system, makes a great deal of difference to American politics. Federalism gave the founders a government that could take effective action, restore economic stability, and regulate disputes among the states, while still allowing the states considerable autonomy. Several specific consequences of that autonomy deserve discussion.

CREATING COMPETITION AMONG THE STATES The federal relationship has an impact on state politics by placing the states in competition with one another for scarce resources. For example, consider the so-called race to the bottom that some observers and academics fear results when states have discretion over benefit levels and eligibility requirements for social programs such as welfare. The concern is that the states will cut benefits because they worry that being more generous than neighboring states will cause poor people to move into their states. That is, some policymakers fear that if they don't cut payments, their states will become "welfare magnets." When benefits and program requirements are set by the national government, states have fewer incentives to cut benefits in the race to the bottom.[20]

A second consequence of competition among the states is their competition for industry. "Smokestack chasing" happens as states bid against one another to get industries to locate within their borders by providing them with property and corporate income tax breaks, loan financing, and educational training for workers, and by assuming the costs of roads, sewers, and other infrastructure that new industries

would otherwise have to pay for themselves. For instance, in the early 1980s, Tennessee outbid other states for a Nissan automobile plant by paying roughly $11,000 per job. After that, the stakes became increasingly higher so that, in 1993, Alabama "won" a thirty-five-state race to grab the Mercedes-Benz sport utility vehicle plant with an incentive plan that cost the state around $200,000 for each of the expected 1,500 jobs.[21] More recently, as economic experts have concluded that these bidding wars benefit the industries much more than they do the states, the states have developed other strategies for economic development.[22] Nevertheless, the states don't seem able to kick the smokestack-chasing habit entirely. Consider, for example, the effort by local governments in Florida, even in the midst of recession-driven belt tightening, to use $31 million in incentives to lure from its Ohio home a solar panel manufacturing plant that promised 1,800 new jobs.[23]

While states continue to pursue industries, they increasingly have turned attention to getting non-U.S. companies to invest in their states. This effort at "foreign direct investment" has resulted in thousands of projects landed by the states. Nevertheless, there is continuing controversy about the extent to which such projects pay off, given the costs to the states. One thing is clear: governors who land such enterprises are rewarded by job-hungry voters at the polls, thus giving us reason to expect the states to continue competing.[24]

PROVIDING INCREASED ACCESS TO GOVERNMENT Federalism also makes a difference in the lives of citizens. It provides real power at levels of government that are close to the citizens. Citizens can thus have access to officials and processes of government that they could not have if there were just one distant, effective unit. Federalism also enhances the power of interest groups in that it provides a variety of government levels at which different groups can try to gain political advantage. Often a group that is not successful at one level can try again at another and "shop" for institutions or agencies that are more receptive to its requests. The states vary considerably in their political ideologies and thus in the policies they are likely to adopt. (See "*Snapshot of America*: How Do We Differ From State to State?".) For example, African Americans were unable to achieve significant political influence in the South as long as the southern states, with their segregationist traditions, were allowed to control access to the voting booths. When the national government stepped in to stop segregation with the Civil Rights Act of 1964, the balance of power began to become less lopsided. Conversely, when women were unable to get the vote at the national level, they turned their attention to the states and won their suffrage there first. Today we can see the effects of group power in the area of the environment. Without the action

---

confederal system government in which local units hold all the power

SNAPSHOT OF AMERICA: HOW DO WE DIFFER FROM STATE TO STATE?

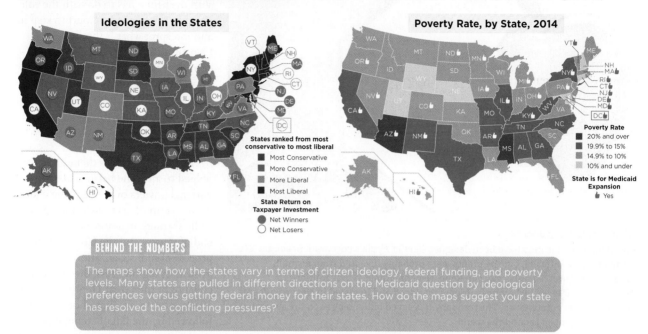

Ideologies in the States

States ranked from most conservative to most liberal
- Most Conservative
- More Conservative
- More Liberal
- Most Liberal

State Return on Taxpayer Investment
- Net Winners
- Net Losers

Poverty Rate, by State, 2014

Poverty Rate
- 20% and over
- 19.9% to 15%
- 14.9% to 10%
- 10% and under

State is for Medicaid Expansion
- Yes

BEHIND THE NUMBERS

The maps show how the states vary in terms of citizen ideology, federal funding, and poverty levels. Many states are pulled in different directions on the Medicaid question by ideological preferences versus getting federal money for their states. How do the maps suggest your state has resolved the conflicting pressures?

Source: Based on Robert S. Erikson, Gerald C. Wright, and John McIver, *Statehouse Democracy* (New York: Cambridge University Press, 1993), and updated by authors; WalletHub (http://wallethub.com/edu/states-most-least-dependent-on-the-federal-government/2700/#methodology

of the federal government, many of the states in the American West would adopt much more lenient rules for use of federal lands for grazing, farming, and oil exploration, all of which can be quite profitable for them. Although environmentalists have little clout in places like Utah or Alaska, they are far more influential in Washington, D.C., where policy is currently made.

ALLOWING FLEXIBILITY AT THE LOCAL LEVEL

Federalism gives government considerable flexibility to preserve local standards and to respond to local needs—that is, to solve problems at the levels at which they occur. Examples include local traffic laws, community school policies, and city and county housing codes. Federalism also allows experimentation with public policy. If all laws and policies need not be uniform across the country, then different states may try different solutions to common problems and share the results of their experiments. For instance, in 1993, policymakers in Georgia, hoping to stem the loss of their brightest young people to out-of-state colleges and universities, developed a way to fund higher education that would make going to school in Georgia more attractive. Using funds from the state lottery, Georgia's Hope Scholarships pay for tuition, mandatory fees, and a book allowance for any Georgia resident who completes high school with a "B" average, a program that one close observer calls "probably the most successful public initiative in Georgia history." The program has been so successful

that other states, including Florida, Kentucky, Nevada, Maryland, and Texas, have adopted versions tailored to meet their own particular needs.[25]

The flexibility that federalism provides can also be helpful when Congress cannot or will not act. As recent polarization in the nation's capital has essentially paralyzed legislative action for most purposes, enterprising states can take advantage of the resulting power vacuum. For example, in the face of congressional gridlock over the development of fossil fuel resources, the states have leapt into the breach with their own energy policies, many times reflecting the political proclivities of the dominant party in the states. For example, Republican-controlled Pennsylvania has encouraged fracking (the process of pumping water and chemicals into subterranean rock formations to free bound-up natural gas and oil), whereas neighboring New York and, to a lesser extent, Ohio—which share the giant Marcellus Shale Deposit—have taken a much more environmentally cautious approach to the development of shale deposits.[26]

The flexibility that federalism offers states has disadvantages as well. Where policies are made and enforced locally, all economies of scale are lost. Many functions are also repeated across the country as states locally administer national programs. Making and enforcing laws can be troublesome as well under federalism. Different penalties for the same crime can make it difficult to gauge the consequences of one's behavior across states. For example, being caught with an ounce of recreational marijuana will get an

AP Photo/Paul Sakuma

iTax Games Anyone?

Your iPhone or Mac may have been designed here at Apple's corporate headquarters in Cupertino, California, but the profits were probably invested from a small, nondescript office 200 miles away in Reno, Nevada. Apple avoids millions in California state taxes by having its profits managed and invested in Nevada, where there are no corporate taxes. The company has saved billions by such tax avoidance strategies employed around the world.

offender a $5,000 fine and up to five years in jail in Florida, but in California it draws only a $100 fine, and in Colorado and Washington State, as we have seen, there is no penalty at all.[27] Most problematic is the fact that federalism permits, even encourages, local prejudices to find their way into law. To the degree that states have more rather than less power, the uniform enforcement of civil rights cannot be guaranteed. Gay Americans, for example, do not have the same rights in all localities of the United States today.

Even though federalism is not a perfect system, overall it has proved to be a flexible and effective compromise for American government. The United States is not the only nation with a federal system, although other countries may distribute power among their various units differently than we do. Germany, Canada, Mexico, Australia, and Switzerland are all examples of federal systems.

THE CHANGING BALANCE: AMERICAN FEDERALISM OVER TIME

Although the Constitution provides for both national and state powers (as well as some shared powers), several factors have caused the balance between the two to change considerably since it was written. First, because of the founders' disagreement over how power should be distributed in the new country, the final wording about national and state powers was kept vague intentionally, which probably helped the Constitution get ratified. Because it wasn't clear how much power the different levels held, it has been possible ever since for both ardent Federalists and states' rights advocates to find support for their positions in the document.

Another factor that has caused the balance of national and state powers to shift over time has to do with the role given to the Supreme Court to step in and interpret what it thinks the Constitution really means when conflict exists over which level of government should have the final say on a given issue. Those interpretations have varied along with the people sitting on the Court and with historical circumstances.

The circumstances themselves have helped to alter the balance of state and national powers over time. The context of American life is transformed periodically through major events such as the end of slavery and the Civil War, the process of industrialization and the growth of big business, the economic collapse of the Great Depression in the 1930s, world wars (both hot and cold) followed by the fall of communism in the 1980s, and the devastating terrorist attacks of September 11, 2001. The most recent of these events was the huge economic recession that began in 2008 with the mortgage crisis and that has resulted in massive federal government economic stimulus programs to stem the economy's downward spiral. With these events come shifts in the demands made on the different levels of government. When we talk about federalism in the United States, we are talking about specific constitutional rules and provisions, but we are also talking about a continuously changing context in which those rules are understood.

Two trends are apparent when we examine American federalism throughout our history. One is that American government in general is growing in size, at both the state and national levels. We make many more demands than did, say, the citizens of George Washington's time, or Abraham Lincoln's, and the apparatus to satisfy those demands has grown accordingly. But within that overall growth, a second trend has been the gradual strengthening of the national government at the expense of the states.

The increase in the size of government shouldn't surprise us. One indisputable truth about the United States is that, over the years, it has gotten bigger, more industrialized, more urban, and more technical. As the country has grown, so have our expectations of what the government will do for us. We want to be protected from the fluctuations of the market, from natural disasters, from terrorists, from unfair business practices, and from unsafe foods and drugs. We want government to protect our "rights," but our concept of those rights has expanded beyond the first ten amendments to the Constitution to include things like economic security in old age, a minimum standard of living for all citizens, a safe interstate highway system, and crime-free neighborhoods. These new demands and expectations create larger government at all levels but particularly at the national level, where the resources and will to accomplish such broad policy goals are more likely to exist.

Traditionally, liberals have preferred to rely on a strong central government to solve many social problems that the states have not solved, such as discrimination and poverty. Conservatives have tended to believe that "big government" causes more problems than it solves. Like the Anti-Federalists at the founding, they have preferred to see power and government services located at the state or local level, closer to the people being governed. From 2000 to 2006, however, with Republicans holding the reins of power in both the legislative and executive branches, the conservative distaste for big government waned somewhat as they were the ones dictating the actions of that government. President Bush's No Child Left Behind Act, for instance, took away many of the prerogatives of local school districts to decide whether to engage in regular testing of students, and yet it enjoyed the support of many conservatives. Some Republicans themselves noted that, once they come to Washington, conservatives can be "as bad as liberals" about enforcing the national will on states.[28] Once President Obama was elected and the Democrats passed the economic stimulus bill and health care reform, however, Republicans quickly returned to their traditional views and decried the return of "big government." Both Democrats and Republicans are more willing to entertain the possibility of national government action when they are the ones controlling the national government.

The growth of the national government's power over the states can be traced by looking at four moments in our national history: the early judicial decisions of Chief Justice John Marshall, the Civil War, the New Deal, and the civil rights movement and the expanded use of the Fourteenth Amendment from the 1950s through the 1970s. Since the late 1970s we have seen increasing opposition to the growth of what is called "big government" on the part of citizens and officials alike, but most of the efforts to cut it back in size and to restore power to the states have been mixed.

JOHN MARSHALL: STRENGTHENING THE CONSTITUTIONAL POWERS OF THE NATIONAL GOVERNMENT

John Marshall, the third chief justice of the United States (1801–1835), was a man of decidedly Federalist views. His rulings did much to strengthen the power of the national government both during his lifetime and after. The 1819 case of *McCulloch v. Maryland* set the tone. In resolving this dispute about whether Congress had the power to charter a bank and whether the state of Maryland had the power to tax that bank, Marshall had plenty of scope for exercising his preference for a strong national government. Congress did have the power, he ruled, even though the Constitution didn't spell it out, because Congress was empowered to do whatever was necessary and proper to fulfill its constitutional obligations.

Marshall did not interpret the word *necessary* to mean "absolutely essential," but rather he took a looser view, holding that Congress could do whatever was "appropriate" to execute its powers. If that meant chartering a bank, then the necessary and proper clause could be stretched to include chartering a bank. Furthermore, Maryland could not tax the federal bank because "the power to tax involves the power to destroy."[29] If Maryland could tax the federal bank, that would imply the state had the power to destroy the bank, making Maryland supreme over the national government and violating the Constitution's supremacy clause, which makes the national government supreme.

Marshall continued this theme in *Gibbons v. Ogden* in 1824.[30] In deciding that New York did not have the right to create a steamboat monopoly on the Hudson River, Marshall focused on the part of Article I, Section 8, that allows Congress to regulate commerce "among the several states." He interpreted commerce very broadly to include almost any kind of business, creating a justification for a national government that could freely regulate business and that was dominant over the states.

Gibbons v. Ogden did not immediately establish national authority over business. Business interests were far too strong to meekly accept government authority, and subsequent Court decisions recognized that strength and a prevailing public philosophy of laissez-faire. The national government's power in general was limited by cases such as *Cooley v. Board of Wardens* of Port of Philadelphia (1851),[31] which gave the states greater power to regulate commerce if local interests outweigh national interests, and *Dred Scott v. Sanford* (1857),[32] which held that Congress did not have the power to outlaw slavery in the territories.

THE CIVIL WAR: NATIONAL DOMINATION OF THE STATES

The Civil War represented a giant step in the direction of a stronger national government. The war itself was fought for a variety of reasons. Besides the issue of slavery and the conflicting economic and cultural interests of the North and South, the war was fought to resolve the question of national versus state supremacy. When the national government, dominated by the northern states, passed legislation that would have furthered northern interests, the southern states tried to invoke the doctrine of nullification. **Nullification** was the idea that states could render national laws null if they disagreed with them, but

---

McCulloch v. Maryland Supreme Court ruling (1819) confirming the supremacy of national over state government

Gibbons v. Ogden Supreme Court ruling (1824) establishing national authority over interstate business

nullification declaration by a state that a federal law is void within its borders

the national government never recognized this doctrine. The southern states also seceded, or withdrew from the United States, as a way of rejecting national authority, but the Union's victory in the ensuing war showed decisively that states did not retain their sovereignty under the Constitution.

THE NEW DEAL: NATIONAL POWER OVER BUSINESS The Civil War did not settle the question of the proper balance of power between national government and business interests. In the years following the war, the courts struck down both state and national laws regulating business. For example, *Pollock v. Farmer's Loan and Trust Company* (1895) held that the federal income tax was unconstitutional[33] (until it was legalized by the Sixteenth Amendment in 1913). *Lochner v. New York* (1905) said that states could not regulate working hours for bakers.[34] This ruling was used as the basis for rejecting state and national regulation of business until the middle of the New Deal in the 1930s. *Hammer v. Dagenhart* (1918) said that national laws prohibiting child labor were outside Congress' power to regulate commerce and therefore were unconstitutional.[35]

Throughout the early years of Franklin Roosevelt's New Deal, designed amid the devastation of the Great Depression of the 1930s to recapture economic stability through economic regulations, the Supreme Court maintained its antiregulation stance. But the president berated the Court for striking down his programs, and public opinion backed the New Deal and Roosevelt himself against the interests of big business. Eventually the Court had a change of heart. Once established as constitutional, New Deal policies redefined the purpose of American government and thus the scope of both national and state powers. The relationship between the nation and the states became more cooperative as the government became employer, provider, and insurer of millions of Americans in times of hardship. Our Social Security system was born during the New Deal, as were many other national programs designed to get America back to work and back on its feet. A sharper contrast to the laissez-faire policies of the turn of the century can hardly be imagined.

THINKING OUTSIDE THE BOX

What would the U.S. government be like today if states had the power of nullification?

CIVIL RIGHTS: NATIONAL PROTECTION AGAINST STATE ABUSE The national government picked up a host of new roles as American society became more complex, including that of guarantor of individual rights against state abuse. The Fourteenth Amendment to the Constitution was passed after the Civil War to make sure southern states extended all the protections of the Constitution to the newly freed slaves. In the 1950s and 1960s the Supreme Court used the amendment to strike down a variety of state laws that maintained segregated, or separate, facilities for whites and African Americans, from railway cars to classrooms. By the 1970s the Court's interpretation of the Fourteenth Amendment had expanded, allowing it to declare unconstitutional many state laws that it said deprived state citizens of their rights as U.S. citizens. For instance, the Court ruled that states had to guarantee those accused of state crimes the same protections that the Bill of Rights guaranteed those accused of federal crimes. As we will see in more detail in Chapter 5, the Fourteenth Amendment has come to be a means for severely limiting the states' powers over their own citizens.

The trend toward increased national power has not put an end to the debate over federalism, however. In the 1970s and 1980s Presidents Richard Nixon and Ronald Reagan tried hard to return some responsibilities to the states, mainly by giving them more control over how they spend federal money. In the next section, we look at recent efforts to alter the balance of federal power in favor of the states.

FEDERALISM TODAY

Clearly federalism is a continually renegotiated compromise between advocates of strong national government on the one hand and advocates of state power on the other. Making the job of compromise more complex, however, is that, as we have suggested, federalism is not a purely ideological issue, but also reflects pragmatic politics. If a party dominates the federal government for a long time, its members become accustomed to looking to that government to accomplish their aims. Those whose party persists in the minority on the federal level tend to look to the states.[36] In short, most of the time people will fight to have decisions made in the arena (national or state) where they are most likely to prevail, or where the opposition will have the greatest difficulty achieving their policy goals.

Although the Supreme Court, since the days of *Marbury v. Madison*, had endorsed an extension of the range of the national government, the conservative Supreme Court under Chief Justice William Rehnquist passed down a set of decisions beginning in 1991 that signaled a rejection of congressional encroachment on the prerogatives of the states—a power shift that was dubbed **devolution**. However, that movement came to an abrupt stop in 2002 following the attacks of September 11, 2001. The Court continues to

> **devolution** the transfer of powers and responsibilities from the federal government to the states

DON'T BE FOOLED BY...
THE OP-ED PAGES

"All the news that's fit to print," proclaims the banner of the *New York Times*. But news isn't the only thing you'll find in what readers fondly refer to as "the old gray lady." Some of the most informative, entertaining, and, frequently, infuriating "news" printed in the *New York Times*—and most other newspapers today—can be found in the op-ed pages, where opinion pieces, editorials, and letters to the editor reign supreme. Often the last two inside pages of the first section, the op-ed pages need to be read differently from the rest of the paper. Writers of the standard news pages try to be objective, and while their values and beliefs may sneak in, they attempt to minimize the influence of their opinions on their work.

Writers on the op-ed pages, in contrast, flaunt their opinions, proudly display their biases, and make value-laden claims with abandon. This can make for fascinating reading, and can help you to formulate your own opinions, if you know what you are reading. Op-ed writers include

- **The newspaper's editorial board**—editors employed by the paper who take stands on public matters, recommend courses of action to officials, and endorse candidates for office. On the whole, editorial boards are more conservative than liberal (for example, they have endorsed Republican presidential candidates far more often than they have endorsed Democrats)—but they often reflect the ideological tendencies of their reader base. The editors of the *New York Times*, which is read by a liberal urban population, take stances that are on the more liberal side, while the *Wall Street Journal*, subscribed to by the national business community, is more conservative. *USA Today*, which aspires to a broad national circulation, attempts to be more moderate in its outlook.

- **Columnists**—writers employed by the paper or by a news syndicate (whose work is distributed to many newspapers) who analyze current events from their personal ideological point of view. Columnists can be liberal, like the *Washington Post's* E. J. Dionne or the *New York Times's* Nicholas Kristof, or conservative, like David Brooks and Ross Douthat (*New York Times*) and George Will (*Washington Post*). Maureen Dowd and Tom Friedman,

both of the *New York Times*, are cogent observers and critics of the political scene who defy precise placement on an ideological scale. While their values tend toward the liberal, they are equally hard on both parties.

- **Guest columnists**—ranging from the country's elite in the *New York Times* to everyday Americans in *USA Today*—who expound their views on a wide range of issues.

- **Readers of the newspaper**—who write letters to the editor, responding either to points of news coverage in the newspaper or to other items on the op-ed pages.

WHAT TO WATCH OUT FOR

- **Who is the author?** What do you know about him or her? As you get used to reading certain newspaper editorial pages and columnists, you will know what to expect from them. Guest columnists are harder to gauge. The paper should tell you who they are, but you can always do further research on the Web or elsewhere. Figure out how the author's job or achievements might influence his or her views.

- **What are the values underlying the piece you are reading?** Does the author make his or her values clear? If not, can you figure them out based on what the person writes? Unless you know the values that motivate an author, it is difficult to judge fairly what he or she has to say, and it can be difficult not to be hoodwinked as well.

- **Is the author building an argument?** If so, are the premises or assumptions that the author makes clear? Does the author cite adequate evidence to back up his or her points? Does the argument make sense? Notice that these are versions of the same questions we set out in our CLUES model of critical thinking. Always think critically when you are reading an op-ed piece, or you are in danger of taking someone's opinions and preferences as fact!

- **What kinds of literary devices does the author use that you might not find in a straight news story?** Opinion writers, especially columnists, might use sarcasm or irony to expose what they see as the absurdities of politics or political figures, and they might even invent fictional characters. What is the point of these literary devices? Are they effective?

- **Has the author persuaded you?** Why or why not? Has the author shown you how to look at a familiar situation in a new light, or has he or she merely reinforced your own opinions? Do you feel inspired to write a letter to the editor on the subject? If so, do it!

Redefining American Government

This highly partisan contemporary cartoon shows President Franklin Roosevelt cheerfully steering the American ship of state toward economic recovery, despite detractors in big business. New Deal policies redefined the scope of both national and state powers.

have a conservative majority under Chief Justice John Roberts, but its inclinations have tended more toward favoring business than resurrecting federalism.[37]

Whether or not the Supreme Court's decisions give the federal government greater latitude in exercising its powers, the states are still responsible for the policies that most affect our lives. For instance, the states retain primary responsibility for everything from education to regulation of funeral parlors, from licensing physicians to building roads and telling us how fast we can drive on them. Most questions of contemporary federalism involve the national government trying to influence how the states and localities go about providing the goods and services and regulating the behaviors that have traditionally been within their jurisdictions.

Why should the national government care so much about what the states do? There are several reasons. First, from a Congress member's perspective, it is easier to solve many social and economic problems at the national level, especially when those problems, like race discrimination or air pollution, affect the populations of multiple states. In some instances, national problem solving involves redistributing resources from one state or region to another, which individual states, on their own, would be unwilling or unable to do. Second, members of Congress profit electorally by passing laws and regulations that bring to their states resources, such as highway funds; welfare benefits; urban renewal money; and assistance to farmers, ranchers, miners, and educators. Doing well by constituents gets incumbents reelected.[38] Third, sometimes members of

Congress prefer to adopt national legislation to preempt what states may be doing or planning to do. In some cases they might object to state laws, as Congress did when it passed civil rights legislation against the strong preferences of the southern states. In other cases they might enact legislation to prevent states from making fifty different regulatory laws for the same product. If Congress makes a set of nationally binding regulations, businesses or corporations—generally large contributors to politicians—do not have to incur the expense of altering their products or services to meet different state standards.

To deliver on their promises, national politicians must have the cooperation of the states. Although some policies, such as Social Security, can be administered easily at the national level, others, such as changing educational policy or altering the drinking age, remain under state authority and cannot be legislated in Washington. Federal policymakers face one of their biggest challenges in this regard: how to get the states to do what federal officials have decided they should do.

HOW THE NATIONAL GOVERNMENT TRIES TO INFLUENCE THE STATES Congress makes two key decisions when it attempts to influence what the states are doing. The first concerns the character of the rules and regulations that are issued: will they be broad enough to allow the states flexibility, or narrow and specific to guarantee that policy is executed as Washington wishes? The other is about whether the cost of the new programs will be paid for by the national government and, if so, by how much. The combination of these two decisions yields the four general congressional strategies for influencing the states that we see in Table 4.1.

- *Option One: No National Government Influence.* In the period of dual federalism, the federal government left most domestic policy decisions to the states. When it chooses to leave a state's authority unchallenged, it provides no instructions (either broad or specific) and no funding (bottom row in Table 4.1). When there is no national government influence, states can act as they wish in the given policy area.

- *Option Two: Categorical Grants.* Sometimes Congress decides that the nation's interests depend on all the states taking actions to solve some particular problem—perhaps the provision of early childhood education, food security for the disadvantaged, or health care for low income individuals. The most popular tool Congress has devised for this purpose is the **categorical grant** (upper left in Table 4.1), which provides very detailed instructions, regulations, and

> **categorical grant** federal funds provided for a specific purpose, restricted by detailed instructions, regulations, and compliance standards

TABLE 4.1

HOW THE NATIONAL GOVERNMENT INFLUENCES THE STATES

	DOES CONGRESS PROVIDE FEDERAL FUNDS?	
	YES, FEDERAL GRANTS AS INCENTIVES	**NO FEDERAL FUNDING**
STRICT AND SPECIFIC REQUIREMENTS	**Categorical grants:** • Good for congressional credit taking. • Ensures state compliance and policy uniformity. • Heavy federal regulatory burden ("red tape"). • National policy requirements may not be appropriate for local conditions.	**Unfunded mandates:** • Very cheap for the federal government. • Easy way for members of Congress to garner favor. • States complain about unfairness and burdensome regulations. • Undermines state cooperation.
NO RULES, OR BROAD GRANTS OF POWER WITHIN PROGRAM AREAS	**Block grants:** • Greater state flexibility, program economy. • State politicians love money without "strings." • Greater program innovation. Undermines congressional credit taking. • Grants become highly vulnerable to federal budget cuts. • Leads to policy diversity and inequality, meeting state rather than national goals.	**No federal influence:** • States have autonomy and pay for their own programs. • Results in high diversity of policies, including inequality. Promotes state competition and its outcomes. • Calls for congressional and presidential restraint in exercising their powers.

(Row axis label: HOW STRICT ARE THE RULES?)

compliance requirements for the states (and sometimes for local governments, as well) in specific policy areas. If a state complies with the requirements, federal money is released for those specified purposes. If a state doesn't comply with the detailed provisions of the categorical grant, it doesn't get the money. In many cases the states have to provide some funding themselves.

The states, like most governments, never have enough money to meet all their citizens' demands, so categorical grants can look very attractive, at least on the surface. The grants can be refused, but that rarely happens. In fact, state and local governments have become so dependent on federal grants that these subsidies now make up 27 percent of all state and local spending.[39] State politicians, however, chafe

> **block grant** federal funds provided for a broad purpose, unrestricted by detailed requirements and regulations

under the requirements and all the paperwork that the federal government imposes with categorical grants. States and localities also frequently argue that federal regulations prevent them from doing a good job. They want the money, but they also want more flexibility. Most members of Congress, on the other hand, like to use categorical grants—they receive credit for sponsoring specific grant programs, which in turn helps establish them as national policy leaders, building their reputations with their constituents for bringing "home" federal money.

• *Option Three: Block Grants.* State politicians understandably want the maximum amount of freedom possible. They want to control their own destinies, not just carry out political deals made in Washington, and they want to please the coalitions of interests and voters that put them in power in the states. Their preferred policy tool, the **block grant** (lower left in Table 4.1), combines broad (rather than detailed) program requirements and regulations with funding

Federalism **115**

You Can Do It Your Way . . . But Do It!
The Affordable Care Act provides for insurance exchanges, or marketplaces, but consistent with the American tradition of federalism, the states have options: they could develop their own exchanges, or leave it to the federal government. Kentucky was one of the more successful state exchanges, and part of that was developing Kynect, an outreach program. Here, a Kentucky health professional answers residents' questions about the options available under the Kentucky exchange.

from the federal treasury. Block grants give the states considerable freedom in using the funds in broad policy areas. State officials find support here from conservative politicians at the national level who, despite the electoral advantages to be gained from them, have long balked at the detailed, Washington-centered nature of categorical grants.

Block grants were promoted by Republican presidents Nixon, Reagan, Gerald Ford, and George W. Bush. However, the largest and most significant block grant was instituted under Democratic president Bill Clinton in 1996 with the passage of the welfare reform act. This reform changed a categorical grant program called Aid to Families with Dependent Children (AFDC) to a welfare block grant to the states, Temporary Assistance to Needy Families (TANF). Under TANF, the states have greater leeway in defining many of the rules of their welfare programs, such as qualifications and work requirements. Under AFDC, all families who qualified were guaranteed benefits—just as people who qualify for Social Security are assured coverage. This guarantee is not part of TANF. If the states run short of money—as they have since the onset of the 2008 Great Recession—families that might otherwise qualify may not receive welfare benefits even as the states divert the federal money to

other programs.[40] Such decisions, and their repercussions, are left to the individual states.

Congress has generally resisted the block grant approach for both policy and political reasons. In policy terms, many members of Congress fear that the states will do what they want instead of what Congress intends. One member characterized the idea of putting federal money into block grants as "pouring money down a rat hole,"[41] because it is impossible to control how the states deal with particular problems under block grants. Congress also has political objections to block grants. When federal funds are not attached to specific programs, members of Congress can no longer take credit for the programs. From their standpoint, it does not make political sense to take the heat for taxing people's income, only to return those funds to the states as block grants, leaving governors and mayors to get the credit for how the money is spent. In addition, interest groups contribute millions of dollars to congressional campaigns when members of Congress have control over program specifics. If Congress allows the states to assume that control, interest groups have less incentive to make congressional campaign contributions. As a result, the tendency in Congress has been to place more conditions on block grants with each annual appropriation,[42] and categorical grants remain the predominant form of federal aid, amounting to about 80 percent of all aid to state and local governments.

- *Option Four: Unfunded Mandates.* The politics of federalism yields one more strategy, shown in the upper right of Table 4.1. When the federal government issues an **unfunded mandate**, it imposes specific policy requirements on the states but does not provide a way to pay for those activities. Rather, Congress forces states to comply either by threatening criminal or civil penalties or by promising to cut off other, often unrelated, federal funds if the states do not follow its directions. A recent example has nearly caused a rebellion in the states. The REAL ID Act was passed by Congress in 2005 following a recommendation of the White House Office of Homeland Security and the 9/11 Commission. This law required regulation of state driver's licenses,

> **unfunded mandate** a federal order mandating that states operate and pay for a program created at the national level

typically under control of the states, including verification of an applicant's identity, as well as standardization of watermarks, holograms, and a machine-readable code. These would be required for identification by any citizen doing business with a federal agency, including travelers passing through security at airports. The cost of the program's implementation was estimated to be about $11 billion through 2016, with the vast majority of it to be shouldered by the states. Although virtually no one opposes the overall goal of national security, the requirements of the law and its cost led to a potential showdown. In March 2011 the Office of Homeland Security delayed for the third time the implementation of the law, this time postponing it until January 2013, citing states' inability to comply due to the recession as well as uncertainty about proposals in Congress to change the law. Finally, the first phase of the law was deferred until January 2014, with some states getting an even later deferment.[43]

Unfunded mandates are more attractive to members of Congress in periods of ballooning national deficits.[44] Whereas Congress passed unfunded mandates only eleven times from 1931 through the 1960s, it passed fifty-two such mandates in the 1970s and 1980s, a trend that continued into the 1990s.[45] In large part due to complaints from the states, Congress passed the Unfunded Mandate Act of 1995, which promised to reimburse the states for expensive unfunded mandates or to pass a separate law acknowledging the cost of an unfunded mandate. This act has limited congressional efforts to pass "good laws" that cost the U.S. Treasury nothing. However, because Congress can define what the states see as an unfunded mandate in several different ways—as a simple "clarification of legislative intent," for example—Congress has continued to push some policy costs on to the states, as in the REAL ID legislation discussed above and the No Child Left Behind Act, which required extensive tests and intervention for failing students and schools.[46] In addition, fears of large unfunded mandates played a role in the debates leading up to health care reform. For instance, a version of the reform that expanded Medicaid for low-income people prompted instant criticism from governors because significant portions of Medicaid (varying from about 25 to 50 percent) are paid for from the state treasuries.[47] Congress later backed down and provided assistance to the states to meet the new policy, but that did not stop the states from challenging the act in court, which resulted in the Supreme Court's ruling that states could not be forced to expand coverage under the Medicaid program.

THE CONTINUING TENSION BETWEEN NATIONAL AND STATE GOVERNMENT The current status of federalism is a contradictory mix of

rhetoric about returning power to the states and new national initiatives (and program requirements) in the areas of health, education, and the environment. Although many in the states and even the national government say they want the states to have more power, or simply that they want all levels of government to do *less*, the imperatives of effective policy solutions and congressional and presidential electoral calculations combine to create strong pressures for national solutions to our complex problems.

Advocates for the national government and supporters of the states are engaged in a constant struggle for power, as they have been since the days of the Articles of Confederation. The power of the federal government is enhanced through the mechanisms of cooperative federalism, which give the federal government an increasing role in domestic policy. As the federal government has used the restrictive rules of categorical grants and the economic threats that provide the muscle of unfunded mandates, critics have claimed that cooperative federalism has been transformed into "coercive federalism," in which the states are pressured to adopt national solutions to their local problems with minimal state input.

Remember, however, that members of Congress who pass the laws are elected in the states and have their primary loyalties to their local constituencies, not to any national audience. Their states have traditionally been only too happy to accept federal funds to meet the needs of their residents (and voters) for everything from education to highways to welfare and health care for the poor. However, they also chafe under the rules and regulations that typically come with federal dollars, and especially since 2009, the powerful antigovernment rhetoric emerging from the Republican Party and its Tea Party wing strongly opposes the growth of the federal government. All of this opposition can override even the electoral incentives that members of Congress have for supporting policies that bring federal money to their states, as evidenced by the nearly half of the states that have refused federal funds to expand Medicaid under the Affordable Care Act (see *CLUES to Critical Thinking*). This is happening at the same time that the United States has been enduring slower growth following its longest and worst economic recession since the Great Depression. The states were particularly hard hit as revenues from sales, income, and property taxes dropped dramatically. Federal stimulus funds helped the states deal with about 40 percent of their budget shortfalls, but those funds began drying up in 2010, leaving the states with continuing insufficient funds and forcing them to lay off workers to make up the difference.[48] Education, the largest item in most state budgets, has been hit hard as thousands of teachers were let go. In 2012 the number of teachers (per 1,000 population) was the lowest it has been since 1999. Other government layoffs were even more severe. For example, the number of noneducation state and local employees dipped to its lowest level since 1986.[49] The recovery of the states is likely to lag behind that of the

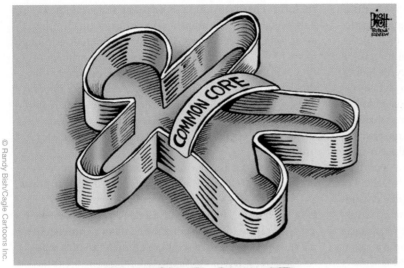

THE COOKIE CUTTER

grants and devolution, and the national government holds out for a cooperative federalism in which it can award categorical grants and exact unfunded mandates. Underlying the ideological battle is the political truth that the contestants generally favor the level of government that is most likely to give them what they want.

IN YOUR OWN WORDS ›› Identify the ways in which federalism divides power between national and state governments.

State and Local Prerogatives Versus National Needs

The push for adoption of the Common Core educational standards was reinforced by the Obama administration, which allowed states that adopt the program to compete for "Race to the Top" federal grants. While most states have joined, some argue that the effort is a federal power grab to appropriate the traditional primary role of the states and localities in K–12 education.

general economy for years, with the result that many citizens will continue to face substantially decreased services from the states in the areas of education, health, and public security.[50] Still, many states led by conservative governors and legislatures rejected stimulus funds, seeing them not as necessary help in hard times but as encroachments by a power-hungry federal government.[51]

The level of conflict is not going to drop any time soon. Indeed, such conflict is almost built in to the state-federal relationship as it has evolved under cooperative federalism, and this conflict has been exacerbated by the recession, which led to big shortfalls in state revenues and increased federal efforts to deal with the ongoing economic crisis.[52]

PAUSE AND REVIEW:

WHO, WHAT, HOW

Where decisions are made—in Washington, D.C., or in the state capitals—makes a big difference in who gets what, and how they get it. The compromise of federalism as it appears in the Constitution, and as it has been interpreted by the Supreme Court, allows the nation, the states, and the citizens to get political benefits that would not be possible under either a unitary or a confederal system, but the balance of power has swung back and forth over the years. Much of the current battle is fought in the halls of Congress, where states pull for a dual federalist interpretation that would give them block

AMENDING THE CONSTITUTION
Making it difficult but not impossible

If a constitution is a rule book, then its capacity to be changed over time is critical to its remaining a viable political document. A rigid constitution runs the risk of ceasing to seem legitimate to citizens who have no prospect of changing the rules according to shifting political realities and visions of the public good. A constitution that is revised too easily, however, can be seen as no more than a political tool in the hands of the strongest interests in society. A final feature of the U.S. Constitution that deserves mention here is its **amendability**—that is, the founders' provision for a method of amendment, or change, that allows the Constitution to grow and adapt to new circumstances. In fact, the founders provided for two methods: the formal amendment process outlined in the Constitution, and an informal process that results from the vagueness of the document and the evolution of the role of the courts.

In the more than two hundred years since the U.S. Constitution was written, more than 10,000 amendments have been introduced, but it has been formally amended only twenty-seven times. We have passed amendments to expand the protections of civil liberties and rights—to protect freedom of speech and religion; to provide guarantees against abuses of the criminal justice system; to guarantee citizenship rights to African Americans; and to extend the right to vote to blacks, women, and eighteen-year-olds.

We have also passed amendments on more mechanical matters—to tinker with the rules of the political institutions the Constitution sets up in order to better control the outcomes. To that end, we have made senatorial elections direct, we have limited a president to two terms in office, and we have provided for a succession if the president is unable to serve out his term.

> **amendability** the provision for the Constitution to be changed, so as to adapt to new circumstances

FIGURE 4.4 AMENDING THE CONSTITUTION

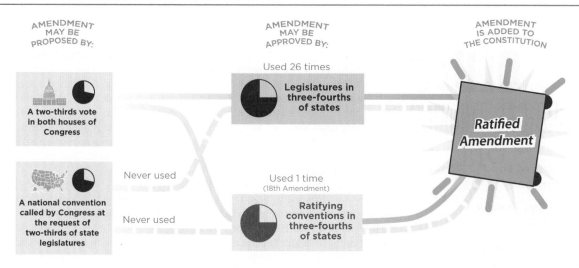

AMENDMENT MAY BE PROPOSED BY:

A two-thirds vote in both houses of Congress

A national convention called by Congress at the request of two-thirds of state legislatures

Never used

Never used

AMENDMENT MAY BE APPROVED BY:

Used 26 times

Legislatures in three-fourths of states

Used 1 time
(18th Amendment)

Ratifying conventions in three-fourths of states

AMENDMENT IS ADDED TO THE CONSTITUTION

Ratified Amendment

On at least one occasion we have also used the Constitution to make a policy that could more easily have been made through normal legislative channels. With the ratification of the Eighteenth Amendment in 1919 we instituted Prohibition, making the production and sale of alcohol illegal. When our national views on temperance changed, we repealed the amendment in 1933, having to pass a new amendment to do so.

But the Constitution can be changed in more subtle ways by the Supreme Court without an amendment's ever being passed. In the name of interpreting the Constitution, for example, the Supreme Court has extended many Bill of Rights protections to state citizens via the Fourteenth Amendment, permitted the national government to regulate business, prohibited child labor, and extended equal protection of the laws to women. In some cases, amendments had earlier been introduced to accomplish these goals but failed to be ratified (like the child labor amendment and the Equal Rights Amendment), and sometimes the Court has simply decided to interpret the Constitution in a new way. Judicial interpretation is at times quite controversial. Many scholars believe that the literal word of the founders should be adhered to, while others claim that the founders could not have anticipated all the opportunities and pitfalls of modern life and that the Constitution should be understood to be a flexible or "living" document.

But these views about whether the Constitution should be changed by amendment or by interpretation are not just matters for academics to solve—they also have political implications and tend to break down along partisan lines. For instance, many recent calls to amend the Constitution have focused on banning abortion, banning gay marriage, banning flag burning, or permitting prayer in school. For the most part, people split into partisan camps in their support of or opposition to those amendments. Democrats tend to

oppose such amendments, believing they curtail fundamental individual rights, and Republicans tend to support them, claiming that they promote important traditional values.

But one can go even further in drawing partisan lines around this issue. Democrats, in general, as liberals who believe that change is inevitable and probably a good thing, are more willing to see the Constitution as a flexible, living document that can be altered continually in small, nonpermanent ways by judicial interpretation. Republicans, on the other hand, share, for the most part, the conservative suspicion of change and a belief that the words of the founders ought not to be tampered with by unelected judges. They are willing to change the Constitution, and even to change it in deep and fundamental ways, but they prefer to do it by amendment. We return to this controversy when we look more closely at the courts in Chapter 10.

WHAT DOES THE CONSTITUTION SAY?

The Constitution is silent on the subject of judicial interpretation, but in part because it is so silent, especially in Article III, the courts have been able to evolve their own role. On the other hand, Article V spells out in detail the rather confusing procedures for officially amending the Constitution. These procedures are federal; that is, they require the involvement and approval of the states as well as the national government. The procedures boil down to this: amendments may be proposed either by a two-thirds vote of the House and the Senate or, when two-thirds of the states request it, by a constitutional convention. Amendments must be approved either by the legislatures of three-fourths of the states or by conventions of three-fourths of the states. (See Figure 4.4.) Two interesting qualifications are contained in Article V. No amendment affecting slavery

CLUES
TO CRITICAL THINKING

"Two Sides of the Medicaid Expansion Coin"

**By Tom Miller, *The Hill*,
June 11, 2014,**

As of this writing, twenty-four states had refused to expand their Medicaid programs (a categorical grant to the states to provide health care coverage to the poor) as made possible by the Patient Protection and Affordable Care Act. Since the Supreme Court, while upholding most of the law, ruled in 2012 that no state had to expand its Medicaid program, states have a lot of flexibility here. This article evaluates an effort by Republican governor of Indiana, Mike Pence, to expand Medicaid in a way that is consistent with Republican dislike for the idea of guaranteed health care coverage but that is close enough to the act's requirements that the federal government will grant them a waiver to do it their way. How does this effort show the strengths and weaknesses of American federalism?

Is it possible for more Republican-led state governments to expand their Medicaid programs without politically endorsing the extension of ObamaCare under the Affordable Care Act (ACA)? Indiana Gov. Mike Pence (R) says he can, but he hasn't convinced a number of conservative Republican critics.

Last month, the state of Indiana unveiled its latest request for a federal Medicaid waiver from the Centers for Medicare and Medicaid Services (CMS) that would allow it to expand its Healthy Indiana Plan (HIP) to cover as many as 559,000 uninsured Hoosiers. For several years, Pence has been seeking Obama administration approval of a modified (HIP 2.0) version of the much smaller

HIP experiment that was first launched in 2008.

The original HIP was quite popular in the state and received positive evaluations by several outside reviewers. It was constructed very differently from traditional Medicaid, relying on a combination of a high-deductible health insurance policy (HDHP) and a generously funded individual Personal Wellness and Responsibility (POWER) account for participating enrollees. The coverage package was somewhat akin to private-sector HDHPs combined with tax-advantaged Health Savings Accounts (HSAs), but with more state government money on the table.

Healthy Indiana Plan members demonstrated decreased levels of inappropriate hospital emergency care use. They increased utilization of primary and preventive care. Average per-member, per-month costs grew at a slower rate than projected Medicaid spending and met the initial waiver's requirement of five-year budget neutrality.

The proposed HIP 2.0 waiver would be on a much larger scale. The original HIP (as subsequently amended to gain an earlier waiver extension) targeted non-elderly, non-disabled adults with household incomes less than 100 percent of the Federal Poverty Level (FPL) and who were not otherwise eligible for Medicaid. Enrollment also was capped to stay within the limits of Indiana's own funds (from an increased cigarette tax) needed to finance the enhanced coverage expansion.

The Indiana proposal needs to be placed within an updated political context. Although the Affordable Care Act aimed to mandate all states to expand their Medicaid program eligibility up to 138 percent of the FPL, the Supreme Court ruled in June 2012 that each state must be allowed to choose whether it will do so, without being penalized for opting out. As of earlier this year, up to 24 states had declined the ACA's

Medicaid coverage offer. For many states led by Republican governors and/or Republican state legislatures, expanding Medicaid in compliance with the Obama administration's wishes was seen not just as a bad deal that their future state budgets could not afford, but also little more than a negotiated surrender after years of pledging opposition to, and eventual repeal of, ObamaCare as a whole.

Nevertheless, the Obama administration has pressed forward this year to try to expand its ACA-brand-of-Medicaid's "market share" in Republican-leaning states. Several states have warmed to the idea of Medicaid waivers that would allow them to increase subsidized healthcare coverage for their citizens in a manner that looks a bit more like private insurance than traditional Medicaid. In states like Arkansas, Iowa and Michigan, Republican state lawmakers have signed on to Medicaid expansions, even though they appear to offer less market-based, private option reform than promised.

Will Indiana's HIP 2.0 be different? As a former chairman of the House Republican Study Committee and the House Republican Conference, as well as an outspoken opponent of ObamaCare, Pence certainly brings strong conservative credentials to the table.

However, gaining a federal waiver for his state's Medicaid expansion requires working within the boundaries set by Obama administration officials. Hence, Medicaid's mandatory benefits must be guaranteed for HIP 2.0 enrollees (and even sweetened further). Medicaid's cost-sharing restrictions are maintained for those with incomes up to the FPL, and they remain unlikely to be collected in any case. Moreover, some of HIP's strongest incentives for beneficiaries to monitor their healthcare utilization closely had to be watered down. Copayments for improper use of hospital emergency department care are limited, and forfeiture penalties for not contributing to one's POWER account with personal funds apply only to enrollees between 100 percent and 138 percent of the FPL.

A proposal to link HIP 2.0 funding to premium assistance subsidies for employer-based coverage and add some soft-work requirements still lacks much evidence of past success elsewhere and may, in the immortal words of the late Sen. Daniel Patrick Moynihan (D-N.Y.), mostly constitute "boob bait for the Bubbas." Finally, the HIP 2.0 promise of budget neutrality appears to be, in a May 14 draft analysis, back-loaded toward the end of its five-year waiver period, and relies to some extent on enrollees' annual rollovers of first-year POWER account contributions from taxpayers, with potential loss of remaining balances when the waiver ends.

The positive case for the Indiana experiment begins with acknowledging that the ACA remains at little risk of full repeal, particularly for the next two and a half years. If one assumes that its Medicaid expansion will become increasingly entrenched, and extended, into the future, the political challenge becomes how to make somewhat privatized lemonade out of another health entitlement's lemons. Although one might accuse some would-be conservative policy advocates as believing that healthcare reform sentences consist only of a noun, a verb and "HSA," the Indiana plan may offer a more credible approach to improving Medicaid than thinly structured block-grant proposals alone provide.

Of course, the political reality is that at least some conservative state policymakers prefer to use "Other People's Money" via the federal treasury rather than reallocate funds within their less open-ended state budgets. Although Indiana funded a good bit of its initial HIP experiment with an increase in its cigarette taxes on state residents, there just aren't enough

smokers there to hit more ambitious enrollment goals. The state's hospital industry has been willing to kick in more funds through a special tax assessment, but only within the limits of getting even more revenue back in newly insured patients.

The overriding judgment call is whether Indiana is sending a signal of counterrevolutionary resolve, or disguised take-the-money-and-run capitulation, to the remaining states holding out against Medicaid expansion as part of broader efforts to overturn ObamaCare. The evidence for the former would be stronger if Indiana officials truly were still prepared to walk away from a bad waiver deal. But at this point, it appears that Pence and his state allies need even a watered down version of HIP 2.0 more than the Obama administration needs to add another red-state political trophy to its list of ACA-compliant jurisdictions. Moreover, assurances that the state

later can back out of the expansion if federal funding comes up short ring hollow, as a matter of either current law or practical politics.

The HIP 2.0 Medicaid expansion does mean a substantial expansion of the ACA coverage entitlement to a broader slice of the "able-bodied" lower income population (it also conveniently excludes the most costly "medically frail" from its non-disabled-population eligibility criteria). Will it provide a new pathway both to better health and heightened cost consciousness? Or just the lure of an HSA-like wrapper to sell an additional layer of dependency on politically mediated benefits?

Indiana is flipping the Medicaid expansion coin and hoping its latest bet with taxpayer dollars pays off.

Miller is a resident fellow at the American Enterprise Institute.

Source: Copyright 2014 The Hill

Consider the source and the audience: *The Hill* is a Washington newspaper that covers Congress. It is read by Washington insiders and publishes both conservative and liberal columnists. The signature line on the article tells us that Tom Miller is at the American Enterprise Institute, a conservative think tank. How would a conservative probably feel about the Medicaid expansion under the Affordable Care Act, also known as Obamacare?

Lay out the argument and the underlying values and assumptions: What does Miller think about the entire idea of the Affordable Care Act? What does he think constitutes a conservative health care plan and how does Indiana's HIP program have to potential to fit the bill?

Uncover the evidence: Miller is looking for evidence that HIP would provide coverage while keeping health care costs down and avoiding personal dependency on the federal government. Does he find any?

Evaluate the conclusion: Miller feels that Indiana governor Pence's effort to "make somewhat privatized health care out of another health care entitlement's lemons" is a coin toss. Are the odds better or worse than that? Is it a project worth trying?

Sort out the political significance: How does federalism affect the outcome of Miller's speculation here? Could you have experimentation like this at the state level without it? Does this flexibility strengthen or weaken our national policymaking?

PROFILES IN CITIZENSHIP: SUSANA MARTINEZ

Courtesy of the office of Governor Susana Martinez

It has always been important to Susana Martinez that everyone play by the same rules. As a child, when she and her family played a game, she assembled all the cousins and said, "We're going to play this game and these are the rules. This is how you play and you're not allowed to cheat and if you cheat you're not going to play." Her grandmother called her *abogadita*—the little lawyer. When she was senior class president she called in the janitorial staff and told them that "first impressions are huge," so they had best up their game and keep the grounds ship shape. When the principal called her out and told her it wasn't her job to dress down the janitors, she stuck to her guns and the school grounds stayed trimmed and tidy. That is pretty much what you need to know about how Governor Martinez runs the state of New Mexico today.

Being governor isn't on everyone's list of childhood aspirations, but it had been on Martinez's since she was about 14. From the time that the teachers at school had the students do an exercise where they imagined where they would be in five years, in ten, and in fifteen, she has had an eye on the bigger picture, and it involved public service. "I enjoyed watching the news where we would watch senators and congressmen debate each other and argue their points. That I really enjoyed; who would make the better point, and why. I loved watching the news." But being a senator didn't appeal. She says, "I knew that as one of a hundred, how much change can you bring when you have to convince so many more? I thought the best place to cause the greatest change was being a governor, so that became my goal."

Raised in a conservative Catholic family in Texas by a dad in law enforcement and an office worker mom, she kept her focus on those goals (being a future governor meant "I had to keep my closet clean. I had to not do those dumb things that teenagers do."). From college at University of Texas at El Paso she headed to law school in Oklahoma and into the courtroom, working for the district attorney. "I was a talker, so I knew I wanted to be in the courtroom. . . . I went to court every day for twenty-five years because that's where the action is. . . . I loved it. I loved the ability to debate and argue my position." She carved out a niche for herself as a tough prosecutor, specializing in cases of child murder and abuse. "I fought hard for these kids. Putting someone in prison for a hundred years didn't bother me one bit after the damage they had done to these kids."

She began to think of running for the office of district attorney herself. But just a year or so before that she and her husband had had an epiphany. Although she had been raised as a Democrat she realized after a lunch with local Republicans that her values aligned more closely with theirs. She got into the car with her husband after the lunch and said, "I'll be damned, we're Republicans!" For a woman with political ambitions in New Mexico, a blue state, this was not necessarily a good thing. But she ran for D.A., against

could be made before 1808, and no amendment can deprive a state of its equal vote in the Senate without that state's consent. We can easily imagine the North-South and large state–small state conflicts that produced those compromises.

POSSIBLE ALTERNATIVES: MAKING THE CONSTITUTION EASIER OR HARDER TO AMEND

The fifty states provide some interesting examples of alternative rules for amending constitutions. Compared to the national government, some states make it harder to amend their own constitutions. For instance, twelve states require that the amendment pass in more than one session of the legislature—that is, in successive years.

Rules can also make it much easier to amend constitutions. Some states require only simple legislative majorities (50 percent plus one) to propose amendments, and unlike the national Constitution, some states give their citizens a substantial role in the process through mechanisms called referenda and initiatives, which we discuss in the next section. The method by which an amendment is proposed can affect the success of the amendment itself. For instance, amendments limiting the number of terms legislators can serve have been passed in several states with the citizen-controlled initiative, but they have not fared well in states that depend on state legislatures to propose amendments. With opinion polls showing large public majorities favoring

her old boss, and won the way she had done most things in her life—by doing her homework, being prepared, and having a clear vision of where she wanted to go.

When the opportunity came around to run for governor in 2010, she took the same approach. Martinez worked hard, ran hard, and won, determined to clean up a state government that she felt had gotten sloppy. When you talk to her about it, it is clear she is enjoying every minute.

> ... IF WE ARE DISCUSSING IMPORTANT ISSUES, WE CAN HAVE MORE CONTROL OVER DETERMINING OUR OWN FUTURE AND CRAFTING OUR DESTINIES AS INDIVIDUALS, AS A COMMUNITY AND AS A NATION

What is fun about it?

"I like fighting about things that matter. I am a fighter. I'm also a negotiator, because as a D.A. you cannot take every case to court, you just can't. There aren't enough days in the year or enough judges or enough prosecutors to do that.

So you learn the skills of advocacy, you learn to negotiate, you learn the skills of fighting for a cause... and then enjoy the fruits... of the hard work, of the teamwork. I've always believed that you are nothing alone but you can be great with a fabulous team."

And by the way, the grounds at the New Mexico statehouse are looking pretty fabulous too!

On patriotism:

I would define patriotism as love of one's country and being loyal to it. I also believe it is important to acknowledge our history and God's providence. I think believing in something and having faith is very important. When I was a prosecutor, I remember before I went into the courtroom and after studying all the information—I believed in the case I was prosecuting and in the facts I had collected, and in the end, everything just gelled. Sure there were moments when things weren't always perfect, maybe a piece of information just didn't fit as neatly as we would like or something was said by someone that changed things slightly, but I would assemble all the available information and evidence, and have confidence in what we were pursuing. In the end though, I always remember praying and saying, "If I'm wrong, say 'not guilty.' If I'm right, say 'guilty.'"

On keeping the republic:

I think to keep the republic, people must stay informed, particularly youth. With the world of technology, it can play both ways as there is an abundance of information, but also a dearth of attention. On my iPhone and iPad, I can access every piece of news I could ever want. From what's happening in the Middle East in *The New York Times* to developments in Congress in *The Washington Post* to our local newspapers, it's all at my fingertips. But at the same time, all that access to information, including movies and other things can take away from—for instance—watching the six o'clock news, which is very important to stay informed. Consuming information is not enough, in that discussion is required, whether you agree with someone's viewpoint or not. A cup of coffee at Starbucks, where the kids hang out, can go a long way to receiving a diversity of opinion. In the end, if we are discussing important issues, we can have more control over determining our own future and crafting our destinies as individuals, as a community and as a nation.

Source: Susana Martinez spoke with Christine Barbour and Gerald C. Wright on September 23, 2014.

term limits, we can safely assume that term limits for Congress would pass much faster if the U.S. Constitution had a provision for a national constitutional initiative. Congress has proven, not surprisingly, reluctant to put restrictions on congressional careers.

One problem with making it too easy to amend a constitution is that public opinion can be fickle, and we might not always want the constitution to respond too hastily to changes in public whim. A second problem is that where amendments can be made easily, special interests push for amendments that give them tax breaks or other protections. Constitutional status of their special treatment protects those interests from having to periodically justify that treatment to the public and the legislature.

Finally, where constitutions can be amended more easily, they are amended more frequently. The initiative process in California permits relatively easy translation of citizen concerns into constitutional issues. Compared to just twenty-seven amendments of our national Constitution, California's constitution has been amended more than five hundred times with everything from putting a cap on taxes, to limiting legislative terms, to withholding public services from undocumented immigrants. Such matters would be the subject of ordinary legislation in states where amending is more difficult and thus would not have "higher law" status. Some critics feel that the fundamental importance of a constitution is trivialized by cluttering it with many additions that could be dealt with in other ways.

Two good reasons, then, why the U.S. Constitution has weathered the passing of time so well are (1) it is not too detailed and explicit, and (2) its amendment procedure, in Madison's words, "guards equally against that extreme facility, which would render the Constitution too mutable; and the extreme difficulty, which might perpetuate its discovered faults."[53]

PAUSE AND REVIEW:

WHO, WHAT, HOW

The founders and the American public had an enormous stake in a Constitution that would survive. The founders had their own reputations as nation-builders at stake, but they and the public also badly wanted their new experiment in self-governance to prove successful, to validate the Enlightenment view of the world. For the Constitution to survive, it had to be able to change, but to change judiciously. The amendment process provided in the Constitution allows for just such change. But occasionally this process is too slow for what the courts consider justice, and they use their broad powers to interpret the existing words of the Constitution in light of the changed circumstances of the modern day. That is, they focus not so much on what the founders meant at the time, but on what they would intend if they were alive today. The founders would have been as mixed in support of this practice as are contemporary scholars. Perhaps the focus of so many critical eyes on the Court has served as an informal check on this power.

IN YOUR OWN WORDS ≫ Demonstrate how the flexibility built in to the Constitution has allowed it to change with the times.

≫ THE CITIZENS AND THE CONSTITUTION
Limited participation at the national level, enhanced opportunities beyond

Remember Benjamin Franklin's reply to the woman who asked him what he and his colleagues had created? "A Republic, Madam, if you can keep it." In fact, however, the Constitution assigns citizens only the slimmest of roles in keeping the republic. The founders wrote a constitution that in many respects profoundly limits citizen participation.

The political role available to "the people" moved from "subject" to "citizen" with the writing of the Constitution, and especially with the addition of the Bill of Rights, but the citizens' political options were narrow. It is true that

they could vote if they met the tight restrictions that the states might require. Their roles as voters, however, were and are confined to choosing among competing political elites, in the case of the Senate or the presidential electors, or among competing people like themselves who are running for the House, but who will be constrained once in power by a system of checks and balances and the necessity of running for reelection in two years.

The Constitution is not a participatory document. It does not create a democratic society in which individuals take an active part in their own governance. The national political system is remote from most individuals, as the Anti-Federalists claimed it would be, and the opportunities to get involved in it are few and costly in terms of time, energy, and money. In fact, the founders preferred it that way. They did not trust human beings, either to know their own best interests or to handle power without being corrupted. They wanted popular power to serve as a potential check on the elected leaders, but they wanted to impose strict checks on popular power as well, to prevent disturbances like Shays's Rebellion from springing up to threaten the system. The Constitution was the republic's insurance policy against chaos and instability.

But in two crucial ways the Constitution does enhance opportunities for participation. First, because it creates a federal system, participation can flourish at the state and local levels even while it remains limited at the national level. We will see that a variety of less formal options are available to citizens, but three of the formal mechanisms of direct democracy at the state level deserve special mention: the initiative, the referendum, and the recall.

With the **initiative**, citizens can force a constitutional amendment or state law to be placed on the ballot. This is accomplished by getting a sufficient number of signatures on petitions, typically between 3 and 15 percent of those voting in the last election for governor. Once on the ballot, an initiative is adopted with a majority vote and becomes law, *completely bypassing the state legislature*. About half of the states have provisions for the initiative, and in California it has become the principal way to make significant changes to state law, most notably, in recent years when the state passed Proposition 8 in 2008, negating the state supreme court's ruling allowing gay marriage. (Proposition 8 has since been overturned by a federal court and an appeal to that ruling is likely to be heard by the Supreme Court.)

The **referendum** is an election in which bills passed by the state legislatures are submitted to the voters for their approval. In most states, constitutional amendments have to be submitted for a referendum vote, and in some states

---

initiative citizen petitions to place a proposal or constitutional amendment on the ballot, to be adopted or rejected by majority vote, bypassing the legislature

referendum an election in which a bill passed by the state legislature is submitted to voters for approval

questions of taxation do also. A number of states allow citizens to call for a referendum (by petition) on controversial laws passed by the state legislature, and in many cases the state legislatures themselves can ask for a referendum on matters they believe the voters should decide directly. Referenda are often very complicated and difficult to understand, but they can have large consequences for the citizens who must decipher them and vote on them.

Recall elections are a way for citizens to remove elected officials from office before their terms are up. These, too, require petitions, usually with more signatures than are needed for an initiative (frequently 25 percent of the electorate). Statewide recalls are infrequent, but some are quite notable, like the one that removed Gray Davis as governor of California in 2003, clearing the way for Arnold Schwarzenegger's election, and the 2012 recall challenge to both state legislators and Governor Scott Walker in Wisconsin. While enough of the recalls were successful to switch control of the Wisconsin Senate to the Democrats, Governor Walker held on to his office.

The record of these three measures of direct democracy is mixed. They do enhance opportunities for individuals to participate, and they give citizens more control over what their government does. However, many citizens do not take advantage of these opportunities, leaving greater power concentrated in the hands of those who do. Furthermore, many of the details of lawmaking can be complicated and hard to understand without careful study—something most citizens don't have time to give them. As a result, the people who do vote can be misled or manipulated by complex or obscure wording, and it is hard for them to know exactly what they are voting on. Finally, direct democracy, by eliminating the checks the founders thought important, makes government more responsive to short-term fluctuations in public opinion, sometimes denying politicians the necessary time to take a long-term approach to problem solving and policymaking.

A second way that the Constitution enhances opportunities for citizen participation, even though it makes such activity difficult at the national level, is by providing political stability. It is precisely because the Constitution has protected the United States from the kind of chaos and instability that existed under the Articles of Confederation

> **recall elections** votes to remove elected officials from office

© David J. & Janice L. Frent Collection/Corbis

Not So Happy Hours
Amending the U.S. Constitution is no easy task, but Americans' love-hate relationship with alcohol was intense enough to do it twice in a mere fourteen years. Temperance advocates succeeded in banning the sale of "intoxicating liquors" with the Eighteenth Amendment in 1919; prohibition opponents, many of whom voiced their opinions with pins like these, managed to have it repealed in 1933.

that citizens have the luxury of developing a host of citizenship roles that are not prescribed in the Constitution. Citizens participate in local government, on school boards and in parent-teacher organizations, in charitable groups, and in service organizations. They volunteer in congressional and presidential election campaigns, they run for office, and they serve as magistrates. They circulate petitions, take part in fundraising drives, and participate in neighborhood associations. They file lawsuits, they belong to interest groups, and they march in parades and demonstrations. They read papers and watch the news, they call in to radio talk shows, and they write letters to the editor. They surf political sites on the Internet and register their opinions through web site polling.

In twenty-first-century America, the opportunities for community, local, and state participation are only likely to increase, and this at a time when the Internet brings even the national government closer to many homes. All these activities are acts of citizenship, albeit a kind of citizenship on which the Constitution is silent. Our founding document does not endorse a role for citizens, other than that of watchful voter, but it creates a political environment in which a variety of forms of civic participation can flourish.

IN YOUR OWN WORDS ≫ Discuss whether the Constitution fosters or limits citizen participation in government.

LET'S REVISIT: **WHAT'S AT STAKE...**

As we have seen in this chapter, the issue of what powers go to the federal government and what powers are reserved to the states has been a hotly contested one since the founding, and one that has no clean, crisp,

right answer. As the country and the composition of the Supreme Court have changed, so too have interpretations of states' rights and federal power. All of that means that the issue of medical marijuana, which currently is

● Legalize It?

legal in twenty-three states and the District of Columbia, and recreational marijuana, which is legal in two, is an excellent example of the messiness that can characterize federal issues in the United States, where national law dictates that any kind of marijuana at all is illegal.

The states and the national government both have a stake in protecting their turf against the other when it comes to marijuana laws. One of the chief virtues of federalism is that it gives the states the flexibility to experiment and to respond to their citizens' demands for policy change. Policies are frequently incubated in the states before they are ready for launching on the national stage, or before the national stage is ready to receive them. The trouble when it comes to legalizing marijuana—medical or recreational— is that there is already a binding federal policy in place. The federal government under the George W. Bush administration claimed that its law trumped state laws because of the commerce clause, the part of Article I, Section 8, of the Constitution that gives Congress the power to regulate commerce among the states. In 2005 the Supreme Court backed that view, voting six to three in *Gonzales v. Raich*, a case concerning a California medical marijuana law.[54] Occasionally, federal agents raided local distribution centers, seizing and confiscating quantities of the drug.[55] Defenders of the laws responded that growing, selling, or smoking marijuana for personal medical use within a single state has nothing to do with interstate commerce. Fourteen states passed laws decriminalizing the use of marijuana for medical purposes by prescription, and slowly, federal law swung in their direction. In May 2009 the Supreme Court refused to hear a case challenging the California law, essentially handing a victory to medical marijuana proponents, and that October, the Justice Department, now under the Barack Obama administration, signaled that, as long as use was consistent with state laws, marijuana use by those holding a prescription for it would not be prosecuted.[56] Reading these cues, more states followed suit, only to see the Obama administration reverse course, cracking down on growers, dispensers, and state regulators, even those in strict compliance with state law.[57]

State law can conflict, of course, not just with national law but with the laws of other states, and here it is the states that have a stake in enforcing their own marijuana laws—either because their citizens deeply disagree with the laws of other states or because there is profit to be had in prosecuting people from other states who violate the law. As the Idaho example in our opener suggested, states with different laws and policies can provide treacherous terrain for their citizens, and nice cash cows for the states collecting fines for violations of their laws. The flip side of federalism's ability to permit experimentation and innovation is that on some issues you can end up with fifty different policies regulating the same behavior. As the Idaho example indicates, citizens from one state can

be caught flat-footed when visiting another if they don't take care to learn the laws of their destination. Marriage equality is another example of the incongruity of state laws—a gay couple married in one state might find themselves unmarried if they travel or move to a state that doesn't recognize same-sex marriages. The Constitution says that states have to give full faith and credit to the "public acts, records, and judicial proceedings of every other state," but that doesn't include laws providing for criminal penalties for outlawed behavior or even, necessarily, those that create a legal state like marriage.

It is not just states that have a stake in setting their own laws on things like marijuana policy; businesses also have a stake in what states do and in resolving the legal confusion that can result from federalism. As is evident in the experience of the brothers who want to grow nonintoxicating marijuana for medical purposes, but who face barriers against transporting the medicinal oil across state lines, businesses can face expensive and exasperating delays and roadblocks when they have to accommodate fifty separate state laws. Throw the federal law into the mix as well, and federalism can be an entrepreneur's nightmare.

And finally, citizens have a stake in how the states manage their policies on marijuana. For some supporters of the medical marijuana laws, what is at stake is the ability of ill patients to receive the most effective treatment possible. But they are allied with those who want to put limits on national power, some of whom might not approve of medical marijuana on its own merits. In his dissent in *Gonzales v. Raich*, Justice Clarence Thomas said, "No evidence from the founding suggests that 'commerce' included the mere possession of a good or some purely personal activity that did not involve trade or exchange for value. In the early days of the Republic, it would have been unthinkable that Congress could prohibit the local cultivation, possession, and consumption of marijuana." If the national government can regulate this, it can regulate anything.[58]

Opponents of the medical marijuana laws say that as long as the Court has ruled that the state laws violate the commerce clause, the national law should be enforced. Further, some argue that it does touch the issue of interstate commerce because the provision and purchase of medical marijuana "affects the marijuana market generally," and they worry that if the federal government cannot regulate this, then perhaps the government will be hampered in other areas, like child pornography, as well.[59]

That there is no clear constitutional resolution of such issues, that it is possible for the Court to produce conflicting rulings on this policy, and that the Bush and Obama administrations would take such variable stances on it explains both how our federal system has found the flexibility to survive so long and so well, and why the debates over where power resides can be so bitterly fought.

TO SUM UP

SAGE edge™
for CQ Press

Sharpen your skills with **SAGE edge** at http://edge.sagepub.com/ barbour7e. **SAGE edge for students** provides a personalized approach to help you accomplish your coursework goals in an easy-to-use learning environment.

REVIEW

The Three Branches of Government

The Constitution is the rule book of American politics. The great decisions and compromises of the founding were really about the allocation of power among the branches of the government, between the national and state governments, and between government and citizens.

Congress is given broad lawmaking responsibilities in the Constitution. It is composed of two houses, the House of Representatives and the Senate, each with different qualifications, terms of office, and constituencies. Having two houses of the legislature that are constitutionally separated from the president means that more interests are involved in policymaking and that it takes longer to get things done in the United States than under a parliamentary system.

The president is elected indirectly by the Electoral College. Compared to the chief executive of parliamentary systems, the U.S. president has less power.

The Supreme Court today has much greater powers than those named in the Constitution. This expansion derives from the adoption of the principle of judicial review, which gives the Court much more power than its counterparts in most other democracies and also acts as a check on the powers of the president, Congress, and the states.

legislature (p. 93)
bicameral legislature (p. 94)
republic (p. 94)
unicameral legislature (p. 95)
executive (p. 96)
Electoral College (p. 97)
presidential system (p. 97)
parliamentary system (p. 97)
judicial power (p. 99)
judicial review (p. 99)
legislative supremacy (p. 100)

Separation of Powers and Checks and Balances

The scheme of checks and balances prevents any branch from overextending its own power. It grew out of the founders' fears of placing too much trust in any single source. The system provides a great deal of protection from abuses of power, but it also makes it difficult to get things done.

separation of powers (p. 100)
checks and balances (p. 101)
fusion of powers (p. 104)

Federalism

The Constitution is ambiguous in defining federalism, giving "reserved powers" to the states but providing a "necessary and proper clause" that has allowed tremendous growth of national powers. Our understanding of federalism in the United States has evolved from a belief in dual federalism, with distinct policy responsibilities for the national and state governments, to the more realistic cooperative federalism, in which the different levels share responsibility in most domestic policy areas.

Alternatives to our federal arrangement are unitary systems, which give all effective power to the central government, and confederal systems, in which the individual states (or other subunits) have primary power. The balance of power adopted between central and subnational governments directly affects the national government's ability to act on large policy problems and the subnational units' flexibility in responding to local preferences.

Federalism creates competition among the states, connects citizens with government, and offers flexibility in governing at the local level. The growth of national power can be traced to the early decisions of Chief Justice John Marshall, the constitutional consequences of the Civil War, the establishment of national supremacy in economics with the New Deal, and new national responsibilities in protecting citizens' rights that are associated with the civil rights movement.

Devolution has required new, and sometimes difficult, agreements between state governments and their citizens. For the most part, state institutions (legislature, courts, governor) have become stronger and more efficient in the process.

enumerated powers of Congress (p. 105)
necessary and proper clause (p. 105)

supremacy clause (p. 105)
concurrent powers (p. 106)
dual federalism (p. 106)
cooperative federalism (p. 107)
unitary system (p. 107)
confederal systems (p. 108)
McCulloch v. Maryland (p. 111)
Gibbons v. Ogden (p. 111)
nullification (p. 111)
devolution (p. 112)
categorical grant (p. 114)
block grant (p. 115)
unfunded mandate (p. 116)

ENGAGE

Carry the Constitution in your pocket.
The **Library of Congress's Constitution App** lets you download the U.S. Constitution, along with useful analysis and interpretation, right to your smartphone.

Consider your state constitution.
The **Cornell University Law School** web site provides useful links to each state's constitution in addition to the U.S. Constitution. These documents provide useful points of comparison to our national "rule book."

See federalism in action.
The **National Conference of State Legislatures** is dedicated to state-federal issues. Their site includes loads of information on national policies implemented at the state level.

EXPLORE

Beer, Samuel H. 1993. *To Make a Nation: The Rediscovery of American Federalism*. Cambridge, MA: Harvard University Press. This book is an exceptional historical examination of American federalism with an emphasis on contrasting nation-centered and state-centered federalism.

Ketcham, Ralph (ed.). 2003. *The Antifederalist Papers and the Constitutional Convention Debates*. New York: Signet Classics. The debate over ratification, conducted in newspaper editorials and on the floor of the Constitutional Convention, was an unprecedented experiment in government by the people. This volume presents the arguments of Anti-Federalists, among them Patrick Henry, who were concerned that a strong national government would pose a threat to the liberties for which they had fought so hard in the revolution.

Madison, James, Alexander Hamilton, and John Jay. 1961. *The Federalist Papers*. New York: New American Library. Madison, Hamilton, and Jay presented compelling arguments for ratification of the proposed Constitution under the pseudonym Publius. *The Federalist Papers* may be a bit difficult to understand, but they are some of the most important works ever written in the history of the United States.

Rossiter, Clinton. 1966. *1787: The Grand Convention*. New York: Macmillan. In a marvelous account of the Constitutional Convention, Rossiter goes into great detail describing the convention's participants, the debate over ratification, and the early years of the new republic.

***Constitution USA With Peter Sagal*. 2013.** The host of National Public Radio's *Wait, Wait, Don't Tell* Me hits the road to explore the Constitution: how we got it, how we kept it, and how it plays out in our lives today.

***Iron-Jawed Angels*. 2004.** Hilary Swank and Frances O'Connor play two fiery young suffragettes, working for a constitutional amendment guaranteeing women the right to vote. Along the way, they incur the wrath of President Woodrow Wilson and anger other suffragette leaders.

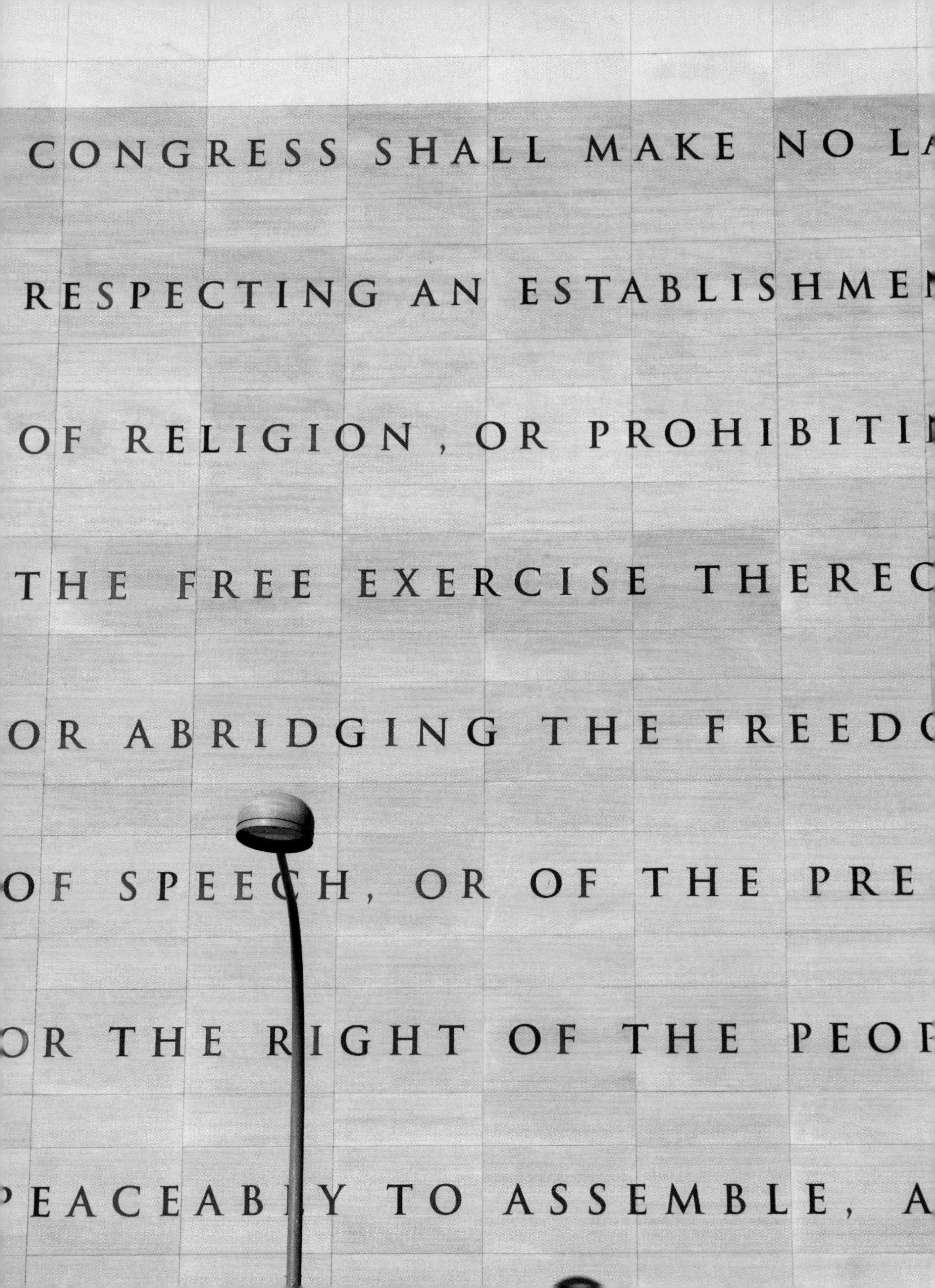

CONGRESS SHALL MAKE NO LA

RESPECTING AN ESTABLISHMEN

OF RELIGION, OR PROHIBITIN

THE FREE EXERCISE THEREO

OR ABRIDGING THE FREEDO

OF SPEECH, OR OF THE PRE

OR THE RIGHT OF THE PEOP

PEACEABLY TO ASSEMBLE, A

FUNDAMENTAL AMERICAN LIBERTIES

IN YOUR OWN WORDS   After you've read this chapter, you will be able to

» Define rights and liberties and their role in a democratic society.

» Explain how the Bill of Rights relates to the federal government and to the states.

» Describe how the First Amendment protects both church and state, as well as individuals' religious freedom.

» Demonstrate how the protections of freedom of speech and of the press have been tested.

» Give examples of different interpretations of the Second Amendment's meaning.

» Describe the protections afforded criminal defendants under the Constitution.

» Discuss the extent of an individual's right to privacy.

» Compare the idea of civil rights with that of civil obligations.

WHAT'S AT STAKE...IN REGULATING GUN OWNERSHIP?

THE NATION'S PILLOWS WERE SOAKED WITH tears on the night of December 14, 2012, after a day of watching the horrific footage from Sandy Hook Elementary School, in Newtown, Connecticut. Cameras captured huddled parents, stunned, waiting for news, and small bodies, faces covered, being carried out of the school on stretchers, along with those of the brave teachers who had tried to protect and shelter them. Twenty first graders, only six to seven years old, were killed, shot multiple times, along with six adults. Reports said the shooter, clad in black, had had three weapons, including a semiautomatic XM-15 assault rifle that had enabled him to shoot at least 154 times in less than five minutes without having to reload.

The nations' leaders—from President Obama, newly reelected with the wind at his back, to Governor Dannel P. Malloy of Connecticut—swore that this time would be different. They would push Congress to pass legislation

outlawing the assault weapons that had made the shooter's job easier. Murder of children on this scale, in the place they were supposed to be safe and secure, would never happen again.

The public was galvanized. Vigils were held remembering the dead, petitions were signed demanding action, and donations poured in to gun control advocacy groups. Polls showed 52 percent of Americans favored major restrictions on guns, and higher percentages favored lesser controls.[1]

Speaking at a prayer vigil for the victims, President Obama said bluntly:

> Since I've been president, this is the fourth time we have come together to comfort a grieving community torn apart by mass shootings, fourth time we've hugged survivors, the fourth time we've consoled the families of victims.

And in between, there have been an endless series of deadly shootings across the country, almost daily reports of victims, many of them children, in small towns and in big cities all across America, victims whose—much of the time their only fault was being at the wrong place at the wrong time.

We can't tolerate this anymore. These tragedies must end. And to end them, we must change. . . . [2]

By early January, he had formed a task force on gun violence, with Vice President Joe Biden at the helm, and he had proposed that Congress pass legislation banning assault weapons, requiring universal background checks on gun purchases, and limiting magazine capacity to ten cartridges.

Interest groups rallied to pressure members of Congress to follow up. Congresswoman Gabrielle Giffords, herself shot in the head in a mass shooting in Tucson, Arizona, announced the formation of Americans for Responsible Solutions, which raised $6 million in its first year. The newly formed Moms Demand Action for Gun Sense organized chapters across the country. Former New York City mayor Michael Bloomberg founded Everytown for Gun Safety, an umbrella group that quickly claimed more than two million members. The Brady Campaign to Prevent Gun Violence and the Law Center to Prevent Gun Violence also kicked into high gear, reporting record donations. Altogether, gun control groups said they spent five times as much in federal lobbying in 2013 as they had the year before.[3]

And yet. Anyone who pays attention to the news in the United States knows that nothing happened. Several states passed gun reforms, but from Congress there was nothing. Even in the emotion-filled days after the attacks, Speaker of the House John Boehner expressed regret, but promised no action. A Senate compromise bill on background checks failed on what President Obama called "a pretty shameful day for Washington."[4]

And in answer to those who had pledged this would never happen again, it happened again. And again. By one count, "Newtown-like" shootings—that is, shootings near or at a school—happened on average *every five weeks* in the eighteen months after Sandy Hook, and that number didn't include all the other shootings that took place in locations other than near school grounds.[5] Just in the space of time it took to write this *What's at Stake . . .?*, another school shooting took place in Seattle. One girl dead, plus the shooter, and several more seriously injured.

How could it be that a nation so moved after the Newtown shootings, could be so unable to move their representatives to action on this issue? Just what was at stake in the issue of gun safety? It turns out, in the United States, gun issues are as much about how we define our rights as how we define our welfare. We will return to these questions after we have learned more about the political battles Americans wage over their civil liberties. «

"GIVE me liberty," declared patriot Patrick Henry at the start of the Revolutionary War, "or give me death." "Live Free or Die," proudly proclaims the New Hampshire license plate. Americans have always put a lot of stock in their freedom. Certain that they live in the least restrictive country in the world, Americans celebrate their freedoms and are proud of the Constitution, the laws, and the traditions that preserve them.

And yet, living collectively under a government means that we aren't free to do whatever we want. Limits on our freedoms allow us to live peacefully with our fellows, minimizing the conflict that would result if we all did exactly what we pleased. John Locke said that liberty does not equal license; that is, the freedom to do some things doesn't mean the freedom to do everything. Deciding what rights we give up to join civilized society, and what rights we retain, is one of the great challenges of democratic government.

What are these things called "rights" or "liberties," so precious that some Americans are willing to lay down their lives to preserve them? On the one hand, the answer is very simple. *Rights* and *liberties* are synonyms; they mean freedoms or privileges to which one has a claim. In that respect, we use the words more or less interchangeably. But when prefaced by the word *civil*, both rights and liberties take on a more specific meaning, and they no longer mean quite the same thing.

Our **civil liberties** are individual freedoms that place limitations on the power of government. In general, civil liberties protect our right to think and act without governmental interference. Some of these rights are spelled out in the Constitution, particularly in the Bill of Rights. These include the rights to express ourselves and to choose our own religious beliefs. Others, like the right to privacy, rest on the shakier ground of judicial decision making. Although government is prevented from limiting these freedoms per se, we will see that sometimes one person's freedom—to speak or act in a certain way—may be limited by another person's rights. Government does play a role in resolving the conflicts between individuals' rights.

> **civil liberties** individual freedoms guaranteed to the people primarily by the Bill of Rights

Whereas civil liberties refer to restrictions on government action, **civil rights** refer to the extension of government action to secure citizenship rights to all members of society. When we speak of civil rights, we most often mean that the government must treat all citizens equally, apply laws fairly, and not discriminate unjustly against certain groups of people. Most of the rights we consider civil rights are guaranteed by the Thirteenth, Fourteenth, Fifteenth, Nineteenth, and Twenty-sixth Amendments. These amendments lay out fundamental rights of citizenship, most notably the right to vote but also the right to equal treatment before the law and the right to due process of law. They forbid government from making laws that treat people differently on the basis of race, and they ensure that the right to vote cannot be denied on the basis of race or gender.

Not all people live under governments whose rules guarantee them fundamental liberties. We argued in Chapter 1 that one way of distinguishing between authoritarian and nonauthoritarian governments is that nonauthoritarian governments, including democracies, give citizens the power to challenge government if they believe it has denied their basic rights. When we consider our definition of politics as "who gets what, and how," we see that rights are crucial in democratic politics, where a central tension is the power of the individual pitted against the power of the government. What's at stake in democracy is the resolution of that tension. In fact, democracies depend on the existence of rights in at least two ways. First, civil liberties provide rules that keep government limited, so that it cannot become too powerful. Second, civil rights help define who "we, the people" are in a democracy, and they give those people the power necessary to put some controls on their governments.

We will take two chapters to explore the issues of civil liberties and civil rights in depth. In this chapter we begin with a general discussion of the meaning of rights or liberties in a democracy, and then focus on the traditional civil liberties that provide a check on the power of government. In Chapter 6 we focus on civil rights and the continuing struggle of some groups of Americans—like women, African Americans, and other minorities—to be fully counted and empowered in American politics.

> **civil rights** citizenship rights guaranteed to the people (primarily in the Thirteenth, Fourteenth, Fifteenth, Nineteenth, and Twenty-sixth Amendments) and protected by the government

© 2013 Jerry Holbert. Dist. by Universal Uclick

RIGHTS IN A DEMOCRACY
Limiting government to empower people

The freedoms we consider indispensable to the working of a democracy are part of the everyday language of politics in America. We take many of them for granted: we speak confidently of our freedoms of speech, of the press, of religion, and of our rights to bear arms, to a fair trial, and to privacy. There is nothing inevitable about these freedoms, however.

In fact there is nothing inevitable about the idea of rights at all. Until the writing of Enlightenment figures such as John Locke, it was rare for individuals to talk about claiming rights against government. Governments were assumed to have all the power, giving their subjects only such privileges as government was willing to bestow. Locke argued that the rights to life, liberty, and the pursuit of property were conferred on individuals by nature, and that one of the primary purposes of government was to preserve the natural rights of its citizens.

This notion of natural rights and limited government was central to the founders of the American system. In the Declaration of Independence, Thomas Jefferson wrote that men are "endowed by their Creator with certain inalienable rights; that among these are life, liberty, and the pursuit of happiness; that, to secure these rights, governments are instituted among men." John Locke could not have said it better himself.

Practically speaking, of course, any government can make its citizens do anything it wishes, regardless of their rights, as long as it is in charge of the military and the police. But in nonauthoritarian governments like the United States, public opinion is usually outraged at the invasion of individual rights. Unless the government is willing to dispense with its reputation as a democracy, it must respond in some way to pacify public opinion. Public opinion can be a powerful guardian of citizens' rights in a democracy.

RIGHTS AND THE POWER OF THE PEOPLE

Just as rights limit government, they also empower its citizens. To claim a right is to claim a power—power over a government that wants to collect data on its citizens for security purposes; power over a school board that wants children to say a Christian prayer in school, regardless of their religious affiliation; power over a state legal system that wants to charge suspects with a crime without guaranteeing that a lawyer can be present; power over a state legislature that says residents can't vote because of the color of their skin or the fact that they were born female.

A person who can successfully claim that he or she has rights that must be respected by government is a citizen of that government; a person who is under the authority of a government but cannot claim rights is merely a subject, bound by the laws but without any power to challenge or change them. This does not mean, as we will see, that a citizen can always have things his or her own way. Nor does it mean that noncitizens have no rights in a democracy. It *does* mean that citizens have special protections and powers that allow them to stand up to government and plead their cases when they believe an injustice is being done.

The power of citizenship is nowhere so clearly illustrated as in the Supreme Court case of *Dred Scott v. Sanford*. Dred Scott was an African American slave who, through a transfer of ownership in 1834, was taken from Missouri, a slave state, into Illinois and the Wisconsin Territory, which Congress had declared to be free areas. Scott argued that living in a free territory made him a free man. The Court's decision, handed down in 1857, denied Scott the legal standing to bring a case before the Supreme Court because, according to the Court, Dred Scott, as an African American and as a slave, could not be considered a citizen of the United States. Although several northern states had extended political rights to African Americans by this time, the ruling declaring Scott a noncitizen denied him access to the courts, one of the primary arenas in which the battle for rights is fought.

WHEN RIGHTS CONFLICT

Because rights represent power, they are, like all other forms of power, subject to conflict and controversy. Often

for one person to get his or her own way, someone else must lose out.

People clash over rights in two ways. The first type of rights conflict occurs between individuals. One person's right to share a prayer with classmates at the start of the school day conflicts with another student's right not to be subjected to a religious practice against his or her will. Our right as citizens to know about the individuals we elect to office might conflict with a given candidate's right to privacy. What is at stake in these disputes might be an inevitable conflict of interest (for instance, candidate versus voter). Or it might be a more fundamental issue—like the role of religion in society, gay rights, or the death penalty—that reflects not just differences in preferences or interests, but deeply held visions of the "right" kind of society. These visions are often so firmly embedded in people's minds that any challenge is intolerable.

The second way rights conflict is when the rights of individuals are pitted against the needs of society and the demands of collective living. The decision to wear a motorcycle helmet or a seat belt, for instance, might seem like one that should be left up to individuals. But society also has an interest in regulating these behaviors because the failure to wear helmets or seat belts is costly to society in more ways than one. The death or serious injury of its citizens deprives society of productive members who might have lived to make important contributions. Through public education and other social programs, society makes a considerable investment in its citizens, which is lost if those citizens die prematurely. In addition, accident victims might require expensive, long-term medical treatment, usually taking place eventually at public expense. The decision about whether to wear a motorcycle helmet might seem to be a private one, but it has many public repercussions. Similarly, individual acts such as carrying a gun or publishing pornography can have consequences for society.

WHEN RIGHTS CONFLICT—THE CASE OF NATIONAL SECURITY

One very clear example of how individual rights can conflict with the needs of society is the case of national security. After the terrorist attacks of September 11, 2001, Americans were deeply afraid. Determined to prevent a repeat of the horrific attacks, the government federalized airport security and began screening passengers, searching luggage, and allowing armed agents on airplanes. Officials scrutinized the backgrounds of tourists and students from the Middle East and kept a close eye on Arab Americans they suspected of having ties to terrorist organizations.

In October 2001 Congress passed and President George W. Bush signed the USA Patriot Act, which, among other things, made it easier for law enforcement to

Patriot or Traitor?

Edward Snowden, who fled the United States after leaking federal documents that revealed the extent of government spying and data mining, addresses a panel at the 2013 South By Southwest Music Conference and Festival in Austin, Texas, via satellite link from an undisclosed location. The Snowden case has tested the limits of American civil liberties and divided the public.

intercept email and conduct roving wiretaps, gave it access to library records and bookstore purchases, and allowed immigrants suspected of terrorist activity to be held for up to seven days (and sometimes indefinitely) without being charged. The Bush administration, fearful that the evidence required in a U.S. court of law might not be forthcoming to convict a suspected terrorist, issued an executive order that non-U.S. citizens arrested on grounds of terrorism could be subject to trial in a military tribunal, where usual rules of due process need not apply. And, as we know now, the national Security Agency (NSA) began to collect enormous amounts of data from the phone and electronic communications of both foreign and domestic individuals.

All these measures may have increased the security of U.S. citizens, but they also reduced their civil liberties. In the immediate aftermath of September 11, such a trade-off struck most Americans as worthwhile. In times of national danger, we are susceptible to calls for locking down our liberties if we believe that doing so can help lock out threats. Somehow a reduction in freedom does not seem like an unreasonable price to pay for a reduction in fear.

But not all Americans were quick to endorse the sacrifice of their rights in favor of a potentially safer society. Immediately after the Patriot Act was passed, organizations such as the American Civil Liberties Union (ACLU) criticized the legislation for infringing on Americans'

privacy, violating due process, and being discriminatory. Although their efforts failed, some members of Congress tried to repeal sections of the act. Even support among the public began to wane as the events of September 11 became more distant. In January 2002 the country was evenly split when asked whether government should take steps to prevent terrorism even if civil liberties were violated. By November 2003, 64 percent of the public responded that government should take steps to prevent additional terrorist attacks but not violate civil liberties; only 31 percent said that steps should be taken even if civil liberties were violated.[6] Nonetheless, in 2006 Congress voted to reauthorize the 2001 Patriot Act and President Bush signed the bill. In 2011 President Barack Obama signed a three-year extension of some of the act's surveillance measures, despite the objections of civil libertarians who had hoped to find in Obama a stronger supporter of individual rights. The furor over the amassing of data on U.S. citizens by the NSA hit such a fever pitch, especially as disclosures by whistleblower Edward Snowden made clear the scope of the operation, that in January 2014, President Obama said he wanted to end the NSA's data collection and called on Congress to pass legislation, something the House did that June.

American citizens are not the only ones whose rights may be traded off for greater national security, but Americans are more willing to tolerate the reduction in liberties when they come at the expense of non-U.S. citizens. Those accused of terrorism or of being enemy combatants have been tortured by the U.S. government, imprisoned in ways that violate the Geneva Conventions on the treatment of prisoners of war, and denied the rights of due process that Americans accused of crimes are guaranteed. While large numbers of Americans object to torture, support for providing terrorists with trials in civilian courts is far less widespread.

The balancing of public safety with individuals' rights is complex. We could ensure our safety from most threats, perhaps, if we were willing to give up all our freedom. With complete control over our movements, with the ability to monitor all our communications, and with information on all our spending decisions, government could keep itself informed about which of us was likely to endanger others. The ultimate problem, of course, is that without our civil liberties, we have no protection from government itself.

THINKING OUTSIDE THE BOX

In the delicate balance between security and freedom, on which side should we err?

HOW DO WE RESOLVE CONFLICTS ABOUT RIGHTS?

Because we are fortunate enough to be political and, we hope, rational beings, we can resolve disputes over rights without necessarily resorting to violence. But that doesn't make their resolution easy or necessarily "fair." Much of the conflict over rights in this country is between competing visions of what is fair. Because so much is at stake, the resulting battles are often politics at its messiest. Adding to the general political untidiness is the fact that so many actors get involved in the process: the courts, Congress, the president, and the people themselves. Although we focus on these actors in depth later in this book, we now look briefly at the role each one plays in resolving conflicts over rights.

THE COURTS One of the jobs of the judiciary system is to arbitrate disputes among individuals about such things as rights. In this country, the highest you can go in seeking justice through the courts—that is, the highest court of appeal—is the U.S. Supreme Court. For legal and practical reasons, the Supreme Court can hear only a fraction of the cases that are appealed to it, so the Court agrees to hear cases when it wants to send a message to lower courts about how the Constitution should be interpreted. As we discussed in Chapter 4, the Supreme Court may exercise a power called judicial review, which enables it to decide if laws of Congress or the states are consistent with the Constitution and, if they are not, to invalidate them. Judicial

review is generally used sparingly by the Court, but it can offer a remedy when rights conflict.

Even though we typically think of the Supreme Court as the ultimate judge of what is fair in the United States, the truth is that its rulings have varied as the membership of the Court has changed. There is no guarantee that the Court will reach some unarguably "correct" answer to a legal dilemma; as we will see in Chapter 10, the justices are human beings influenced by their own values, ideals, and biases in interpreting and applying the laws. In addition, although the founders had hoped that the Supreme Court justices would be above the political fray, they are in fact subject to all sorts of political pressures, from the ideology of the presidents who appoint them to the steady influence of public opinion and the media. How else can we account for the fact that the same institution that denied Dred Scott his right to use the court system was responsible a century later for breaking down the barriers between blacks and whites in the South? At times in our history the Court has championed what seem like underdog interests that fight the mainstream of American public opinion—for example, ruling in favor of those who refuse to salute the American flag on religious grounds.[7] It has also tempered some of the post–September 11 legislation by ruling, for instance, that U.S. citizens held as enemy combatants do have some due process rights.[8] The Court also rejected the Bush administration's argument that the Supreme Court had no jurisdiction over military tribunals for foreign-born enemy combatants, holding that such tribunals must be authorized by Congress, not executive order.[9] At other times the Supreme Court has been less expansionary in its interpretation of civil liberties, and its rulings have favored the interests of big business over the rights of ordinary Americans, have blocked the rights of racial minorities, and have even put the stamp of constitutional approval on the World War II incarceration of Japanese Americans in internment camps,[10] an action for which we, as a nation, have since apologized.

CONGRESS Another actor involved in the resolution of conflicts over rights in this country is Congress. Sometimes Congress has chosen to stay out of disputes about rights. At other times it has taken decisive action either to limit or to expand the rights of many Americans. For example, the Smith Act, passed by Congress in 1940, made it illegal to advocate the overthrow of the U.S. government by force or to join any organization that advocated government subversion. A decade later, in the name of national security, the House Un-American Activities Committee investigated and ruined the reputations of many Americans suspected of having sympathy for the Communist Party, sometimes on the flimsiest of evidence.[11] But Congress has also acted on the side of protecting rights. When the courts became more conservative in the 1980s and 1990s, with appointments made by Republican presidents Ronald Reagan and George H. W. Bush, for example, the judiciary narrowed its protections of civil rights issues. The Democratic-led Congress of

Spying on Gamers ● NSA Spying ●

the time countered with the Civil Rights Act of 1991, which broadened civil rights protection in the workplace. Similarly, Congress held hearings in 2010 on "don't ask, don't tell," a policy that prevented gay men and lesbians from serving openly in the military, and the legislation was repealed in December of that year.

THE PRESIDENT Presidents as well can be involved in resolving disputes over rights. They can get involved by having administration officials lobby the Supreme Court to encourage outcomes they favor. Popular presidents can also try to persuade Congress to go along with their policy initiatives by bringing public pressure to bear. Their influence can be used to expand or contract the protection of individual rights. In the 1950s President Dwight Eisenhower was reluctant to enforce desegregation in the South, believing that it was the job of the states, not the federal government.[12] President John Kennedy chose more active involvement when he sent Congress a civil rights bill in 1963 (it was signed by Lyndon Johnson in 1964). More recently, President Obama moved to close the detention center at Guantánamo Bay that had been the center of so much controversy, but logistical and political difficulties, including action by Congress to block the funds for the transfer of detainees to mainland prisons, have left the center open, and Obama turned his attention to making some improvements in the prisoners' lives, including the banning of brutal interrogations.

THE PEOPLE Finally, the American people themselves are actors in the struggle over rights. Individual Americans may use the courts to sue for what they perceive as their rights, but more often individuals act in groups. One of the best known of these groups is the ACLU. The ACLU's goal is to defend the liberties of Americans, whatever their ideological position. Thus the ACLU would be just as likely to fight for the right of the American Nazi Party to stage a march as it would be to support a group of parents and students challenging the removal of books with gay themes from a high school library, and in fact it has been critical of both the Bush administration and the Obama administration for their support of wiretapping and surveillance of individuals.[13] Other interest groups that get involved in the effort to resolve rights conflicts include the National Association for the Advancement of Colored People (NAACP), the National Organization for Women (NOW), the Christian Coalition, Common Cause, environmental groups like the Sierra Club, AARP (formerly the American Association of Retired Persons), and the National Rifle Association (NRA). These groups and many others like them engage in fundraising and public relations activities to publicize their views and work to influence government directly, by meeting with lawmakers and testifying at congressional hearings. Even though individuals may not feel very effective in trying to change what government does, in groups their efforts are magnified, and the effects can be considerable.

The Granger Collection, New York

Un-American Activity

Preying on American anxieties about communism, Senator Joseph McCarthy led an aggressive investigation of suspected communists in the government during the 1950s. Though his investigations, with their sensational and clever tactics, ruined many careers, McCarthy failed to find evidence of even one "card-carrying communist" in the government. He was censured by the Senate in 1954 and died in disgrace in 1957.

PAUSE AND REVIEW:

WHO, WHAT, HOW

Citizens of democracies have a vital stake in the issue of fundamental rights. What they stand to gain is more power for themselves and less for government. But citizens also have at stake the resolution of the very real conflicts that arise as all citizens try to exercise their rights simultaneously. And as citizens try to maximize their personal freedoms, they are likely to clash with governmental rules that suppress some individual freedom in exchange for public order.

The means for resolving these conflicts are to be found in the Constitution, in the exercise of judicial review by the Supreme Court, in congressional legislation and presidential persuasion, and in the actions of citizens themselves, engaging in interest group activities and litigation.

IN YOUR OWN WORDS » Define rights and liberties and their role in a democratic society.

THE BILL OF RIGHTS AND INCORPORATION
Keeping Congress and the state governments in check

The Bill of Rights looms large in any discussion of American civil liberties, but the document that today seems so inseparable from American citizenship had a stormy birth. Controversy raged over whether a bill of rights was necessary in the first place, deepening the split between Federalists and Anti-Federalists during the founding. And the controversy did not end once it was firmly established as the first ten amendments to the Constitution. Over a century passed before the Supreme Court agreed that at least some of the restrictions imposed on the national government by the Bill of Rights should be applied to the states as well.

WHY IS A BILL OF RIGHTS VALUABLE?

Recall from Chapter 3 that we came very close to not having any Bill of Rights in the Constitution at all. The Federalists had argued that the Constitution itself was a bill of rights, that individual rights were already protected by many of the state constitutions, and that to list the powers that the national government did *not* have was dangerous, as it implied that it *did* have every other power. Alexander Hamilton had spelled out this argument in *Federalist* No. 84, and James Madison agreed, at least initially, calling the effort to pass such "parchment barriers," as he called the first ten amendments, a "nauseous project."[14]

But Madison, in company with some of the other Federalists, came to agree with such Anti-Federalists as Thomas Jefferson, who wrote, "A bill of rights is what the people are entitled to against every government on earth."[15] Even though, as the Federalists argued, the national government was limited in principle by popular sovereignty (the concept that ultimate authority rests with the people), it could not hurt to limit it in practice as well. A specific list of the rights held by the people would give the judiciary a more effective check on the other branches.

To some extent Hamilton was correct in calling the Constitution a bill of rights in itself. Protection of some very specific rights is contained in the text of the document. The national government may not suspend writs of **habeas corpus**, which means that it cannot fail to bring prisoners, at their request, before a judge and inform them why they are being held and what evidence is against them. This provision protects people from being imprisoned solely for political reasons. Both the national and state governments are forbidden to pass **bills of attainder**, which are laws that single out a person or group as guilty and impose punishment

without trial. Neither can they pass **ex post facto laws**, which are laws that make an action a crime after the fact, even though it was legal when carried out. States may not impair or negate the obligation of contracts; here the founders obviously had in mind the failings of the Articles of Confederation. And the citizens of each state are entitled to "the privileges and immunities of the several states," which prevents any state from discriminating against citizens of other states. This provision protects a nonresident's right to travel freely, conduct business, and have access to state courts while visiting another state.[16] Of course, nonresidents are discriminated against when they have to pay a higher nonresident tuition to attend a state college or university, but the Supreme Court has ruled that this type of "discrimination" is not a violation of the privileges and immunities clause.

For the Anti-Federalists, these rights, almost all of them restrictions on the national and state governments with respect to criminal laws, did not provide enough security against potential abuse of government power. The first ten amendments add several more categories of restrictions on government. Although twelve amendments had been proposed, two were not ratified: one concerned the apportionment of members of Congress, and the other barred midterm pay raises for them. (The congressional pay raise amendment, which prevents members of Congress from voting themselves a salary increase effective during that term of office, was passed as the Twenty-seventh Amendment in 1992.) Amendments One through Ten were ratified on December 15, 1791. See *The Big Picture* for details on the provisions of the Bill of Rights.

APPLYING THE BILL OF RIGHTS TO THE STATES

If you look closely at the Bill of Rights, you'll see that most of the limitations on government action are directed toward Congress. "Congress shall make no law . . . ," begins the First Amendment. Nothing in the text of the first ten amendments would prevent the Oregon legislature, for instance, from passing a law restricting the freedoms of Oregon newspaper editors to criticize the government. Until about the turn of the twentieth century, the Supreme Court clearly stipulated that the Bill of Rights applied only to the national government and not to the states.[17]

habeas corpus the right of an accused person to be brought before a judge and informed of the charges and evidence against him or her

bills of attainder laws under which specific persons or groups are detained and sentenced without trial

ex post facto laws laws that criminalize an action after it occurs

TABLE 5.1
APPLYING THE BILL OF RIGHTS TO THE STATES

AMENDMENT	ADDRESSES	CASE	YEAR
Fifth	Just compensation	*Chicago, Burlington & Quincy v. Chicago*	1897
First	Freedom of speech	*Gilbert v. Minnesota*	1920
		Gitlow v. New York	1925
		Fiske v. Kansas	1927
	Freedom of the press	*Near v. Minnesota*	1931
Sixth	Counsel in capital cases	*Powell v. Alabama*	1932
First	Religious freedom (generally)	*Hamilton v. Regents of California*	1934
	Freedom of assembly	*DeJonge v. Oregon*	1937
	Free exercise	*Cantwell v. Connecticut*	1940
	Religious establishment	*Everson v. Board of Education*	1947
Sixth	Public trial	*In re Oliver*	1948
Fourth	Unreasonable search and seizure	*Wolf v. Colorado*	1949
	Exclusionary rule	*Mapp v. Ohio*	1961
Eighth	Cruel and unusual punishment	*Robinson v. California*	1962
Sixth	Counsel in felony cases	*Gideon v. Wainwright*	1963
Fifth	Self-incrimination	*Malloy v. Hogan*	1964
Sixth	Impartial jury	*Parker v. Gladden*	1966
	Speedy trial	*Klopfer v. North Carolina*	1967
	Jury trial in serious crimes	*Duncan v. Louisiana*	1968
Fifth	Double jeopardy	*Benton v. Maryland*	1969
Second	Right to bear arms	*McDonald v. Chicago*	2010

Not until the passage of the Fourteenth Amendment in 1868 did the Constitution make it possible for the Court to require that states protect their citizens' basic liberties. That post–Civil War amendment was designed specifically to force southern states to extend the rights of citizenship to African Americans, but its wording left it open to other interpretations. The amendment says, in part,

> No state shall make or enforce any law which shall abridge the privileges and immunities of citizens of the United States; nor shall any state deprive any person of life, liberty, or property, without due process of law; nor deny to any person within its jurisdiction the equal protection of the laws.

In 1897 the Supreme Court tentatively began the process of nationalization, or **incorporation**, of most (but not all) of the protections of the Bill of Rights into the states' Fourteenth Amendment obligations to guarantee their citizens due process of law.[18]

Not until the case of *Gitlow v. New York* (1925), however, did the Court begin to articulate a clear theory of incorporation. In *Gitlow*, Justice Edward Sanford wrote, "We may and do assume that freedom of speech and of the press . . . are among the fundamental rights and liberties protected . . . from impairment by the states."[19] Without

incorporation Supreme Court action making the protections of the Bill of Rights applicable to the states

THE BIG PICTURE: WHAT THE BILL OF RIGHTS MEANS TO YOU

Americans like to think that the founders were so concerned with our personal freedoms that they created a bedrock of liberty for us to stand on. But of course, the Bill of Rights is a political document and the founders weren't motivated so much by concern for us as by fear of a powerful national government that might use the coercive power of the state for its own ends. Notice that not one of our liberties—even the right to life—is absolute.

GOVERNMENT **CONGRESS**
RELIGION FREE
SPEECH REDRESS
LAW
ASSEMBLE
PROHIBITING **PRESS**

1ST FREEDOM OF PRESS, RELIGION, ASSEMBLY & PETITION

YOU CAN go to a church of your own choosing, observe your religious traditions, express your opinions, publish them as you wish, get together with like-minded people, and convey your collective sentiment to the government.

BUT YOU CAN'T...

practice religion in conflict with the law or in the public sphere with public support, taunt people to pick fights with them, threaten national security, or maliciously ruin a reputation.

FREE
MILITIA
PEOPLE REGULATED
INFRINGED
ARMS
SECURITY **STATE**
NECESSARY

2ND RIGHT TO BEAR ARMS

YOU CAN own a gun, just in case the government should find itself in the need of a well-trained militia.

BUT YOU CAN'T...

own a gun without background checks or registration (in some places). Can't just shoot at random, either. Murder and mayhem are still against the law.

PEACE
PRESCRIBED
SOLDIER
LAW HOUSE
INFRINGED
QUARTERED
CONSENT **OWNER**

3RD QUARTERING OF SOLDIERS

YOU CAN be free from the government forcing you to let soldiers stay in your house without permission.

BUT YOU CAN'T...

get off so easily if your relatives overstay their welcome. ☺

OATH
SECURE
SEARCHES CAUSE
ARMS WARRANTS
VIOLATED
UNREASONABLE **PEOPLE**

4TH ARRESTS AND SEARCHES

YOU CAN be protected from unreasonable searches and seizures by the police

BUT YOU CAN'T...

be protected from all searches. Generally, police need a warrant to search your stuff. But be darned careful what you carry in your car or say on your phone.

FREE
PROPERTY
PROCESS INFAMOUS
LIFE **CRIMINAL**
INFRINGED
JEOPARDY
LIBERTY **PUBLIC**

5TH RIGHTS OF PERSONS ACCUSED OF CRIMES

YOU CAN be safe from arrest, imprisonment, self-incrimination, having your stuff confiscated, and being put to death without due process of law.

BUT YOU CAN'T...

take back a confession given before you were read your Miranda rights. The cat's out of the bag and the confession usually counts.

GOVERNMENT
WITNESSES
IMPARTIAL PROCESS
SPEEDY CRIMINAL
LAW
ACCUSATION
CONFRONTED DEFENSE

6TH RIGHTS OF PERSONS ON TRIAL FOR CRIMES

YOU CAN expect a speedy trial, to be told what you are accused of, and to have a lawyer to help you sort it all out.

BUT YOU CAN'T...

assume a "speedy trial" won't take years, or that your overworked public defendant lawyer won't be something less than crackerjack.

RE-EXAMINED
COMMON
SUITS COURT
LAW TRIAL
ASSEMBLE
STATES JURY

7TH JURY TRIALS IN CIVIL CASES

YOU CAN have a trial by jury.

BUT YOU CAN'T...

avoid jury duty forever. It's an obligation implied by the right to a jury trial.

PUNISHMENT
EXCESSIVE
UNUSUAL FINES
CRUEL INFRINGED
INFLICTED
SECURITY BAIL

8TH AVOID CRUEL AND UNUSUAL PUNISHMENT

YOU CAN hope you never have to ponder what "cruel" and "unusual" mean. Even SCOTUS isn't entirely sure.

BUT YOU CAN'T...

avoid punishments if you've earned them. So don't push your luck.

ENUMERATION
RIGHTS
OTHERS RETAINED
DENY CERTAIN
DISPARAGE
CONSTITUTION
PEOPLE

9TH RIGHTS KEPT BY THE PEOPLE

YOU CAN have more rights than just the ones listed here (this is what Hamilton was talking about in *Federalist* 78).

BUT YOU CAN'T...

rely on that completely. Some Supreme Court justices think you have only the rights listed here and no more.

STATES
CONSTITUTION
PEOPLE PROHIBITED
UNITED
RESERVED
SECURITY POWERS

10TH POWERS KEPT BY THE STATES OR THE PEOPLE

YOU CAN, if you're a state, get all powers not needed by Congress to carry out its duties (see Article 1, Section 8).

BUT YOU CAN'T...

avoid being subject to 50 sets of state laws, which means that joint you packed in Colorado could get you arrested when you're back in Indiana.

any great fanfare, the Court reversed almost a century of ruling by assuming that some rights are so fundamental that they deserve protection by the states as well as the federal government. This approach meant that all rights did not necessarily qualify for incorporation; the Court had to consider each right on a case-by-case basis to see how fundamental it was. This was a tactic that Justice Benjamin N. Cardozo called **selective incorporation**. Over the years the Court has switched between a theory of selective incorporation and total incorporation. As a result, almost all the rights in the first ten amendments have been incorporated, with some notable exceptions, such as the Second Amendment (see Table 5.1).

Keep in mind that since incorporation is a matter of interpretation rather than an absolute constitutional principle, it is a judicial creation. What justices create they can also uncreate if they change their minds or if the composition of the Court changes. Like all other judicial creations, the process of incorporation is subject to reversal, and it is possible that such a reversal may currently be under way as today's more conservative Court narrows its understanding of the rights that states must protect.

PAUSE AND REVIEW:

WHO, WHAT, HOW

Because rights are so central to a democracy, citizens clearly have a stake in seeing that they are guaranteed these rights at every level of government. The Bill of Rights guarantees them at the federal level, but it is through the process of incorporation into the Fourteenth Amendment that they are guaranteed at the state level unless the state constitution also provides guarantees. Incorporation, as a judicial creation, is not on as firm ground as the Bill of Rights because it can be reversed if the Supreme Court changes its mind.

The Supreme Court also has a stake here. It has considerably expanded its power over the states and within the federal government by virtue of its interpretation of the Fourteenth Amendment and its creation of the process of incorporation.

IN YOUR OWN WORDS >> Explain how the Bill of Rights relates to the federal government and to the states.

FREEDOM OF RELIGION
Limiting Congress to protect both church and state, as well as the individual's right to believe

The First Amendment reads, "Congress shall make no law respecting an establishment of religion, or prohibiting the

free exercise thereof; or abridging the freedom of speech, or of the press; or the right of the people peaceably to assemble, and to petition the government for a redress of grievances." These are the "democratic freedoms," the liberties that the founders believed to be necessary to maintain a representative democracy by ensuring a free and unfettered people. For all that, none of these liberties has escaped controversy, and none has been interpreted by the Supreme Court to be absolute or unlimited. Beginning with freedom of religion, we will look at each clause of the First Amendment, the controversy and power struggles surrounding it, and the way the courts have interpreted and applied it.

The briefest look around the world tells us what happens when politics and religion are allowed to mix. When it comes to conflicts over religion, over our fundamental beliefs about the world and the way life should be lived, the stakes are enormous. Passions run deep, and compromise is difficult.

So far the United States has been spared the sort of violent conflict that arises when one group declares its religion to be the one true faith for the whole polity. One reason for this is that Americans are largely Christian, although they belong to many different sects (see "*Snapshot of America:* What Do We Believe?"), so there hasn't been too much disagreement over basic beliefs. But another reason that violent conflict over religion is limited in the United States is the First Amendment, whose first line guarantees that "Congress shall make no law respecting an establishment of religion or prohibiting the free exercise thereof." Although this amendment has generated a tremendous amount of controversy, it has at the same time established general guidelines with which most people can agree and a venue (the courts) where conflicts can be aired and addressed. The establishment clause and the free exercise clause, as the two parts of that guarantee are known, have become something of a constitutional battleground in American politics, but they have kept the United States from becoming a battleground of a more literal sort by deflecting religious conflict to the courts.

WHY IS RELIGIOUS FREEDOM VALUABLE?

Not all the founders endorsed religious freedom for everyone, but some of them, notably Jefferson and Madison, cherished the notion of a universal freedom of conscience, the right of all individuals to believe as they pleased. Jefferson wrote that the First Amendment built "a wall of separation between church and state."[20] They based their view of religious freedom on three main arguments.

> **selective incorporation** incorporation of rights on a case-by-case basis

First, history has shown, from the Holy Roman Empire to the Church of England, that when church and state are linked, all individual freedoms are in jeopardy. After all, if government is merely the arm of God, what power of government cannot be justified?

A second argument for practicing religious freedom is based on the effect that politics can have on religious concerns. Early champions of a separation between politics and religion worried that the spiritual purity and sanctity of religion would be ruined if it mixed with the worldly realm of politics, with its emphasis on power and influence.[21] Further, if religion became dependent on government, in Madison's words, it would result in "pride and indolence in the clergy; ignorance and servility in the laity; in both, superstition, bigotry and persecution."[22]

Finally, as politics can have negative effects on religion, so too can religion have negative effects on politics, dividing society into the factions that Madison saw as the primary threat to republican government. Religion, Madison feared, could have a divisive effect on the polity only if it became linked to government.

THE ESTABLISHMENT CLAUSE: SEPARATIONISTS VERSUS ACCOMMODATIONISTS

The beginning of the First Amendment, forbidding Congress to make laws that would establish an official religion, is known as the **establishment clause**. Americans have fought over the meaning of the establishment clause almost since its inception. While founders like Jefferson and Madison were clear on their position that church and state should be separate realms, other early Americans were not. After independence, for instance, all but two of the former colonies had declared themselves to be "Christian states."[23] Non-Christian minorities were rarely tolerated or allowed to participate in politics. Jews could not hold office in Massachusetts until 1848.[24] It may be that the founders were sometimes less concerned with preserving the religious freedom of others than with guaranteeing their own.

A similar division continues today between the **separationists**, who believe that a "wall" should exist between church and state, and the nonpreferentialists, or **accommodationists**, who contend that the state should not be separate from religion but rather should accommodate it, without showing a preference for one religion over another.

> **establishment clause** the First Amendment guarantee that the government will not create and support an official state church
>
> **separationists** supporters of a "wall of separation" between church and state
>
> **accommodationists** supporters of government nonpreferential accommodation of religion

These accommodationists argue that the First Amendment should not prevent governmental aid to religious groups, prayer in school or in public ceremonies, public aid to parochial schools, the posting of religious documents such as the Ten Commandments in public places, or the teaching of the Bible's story of creation along with evolution in public schools. Adherents of this position claim that a rigid interpretation of separation of church and state amounts to intolerance of their religious rights or, in the words of Supreme Court Justice Anthony Kennedy, to "unjustified hostility to religion."[25] President Reagan, both Presidents Bush, and many Republicans have shared this view, as have many powerful interest groups such as the Christian Coalition.

A lot is clearly at stake in the battle between the separationists and the accommodationists. On one side of the dispute is the separationists' image of a society in which the rights of all citizens, including minorities, receive equal protection by the law. In this society, private religions abound, but they remain private, not matters for public action or support. Very different is the view of the accommodationists, which emphasizes the sharing of community values, determined by the majority and built into the fabric of society and political life.

MIDCENTURY RULINGS ON THE ESTABLISHMENT CLAUSE Today U.S. practice stands somewhere between these two images. Sessions of Congress open with prayers, for instance, but a schoolchild's day does not. Religion is not kept completely out of our public lives, but the Court has generally leaned toward a separationist stance. In the 1960s the Court tried to cement this stance, refining a test that made it unconstitutional for the government to pass laws that affect religion unless the laws have a "secular intent" (that is, a nonreligious intent) and "a primary effect that neither advances nor inhibits religion."[26] In two separate cases the Court decided that laws requiring prayer or the reading of biblical verses in public schools violated the Constitution, and that permitting children to be excused did not reduce the unconstitutionality of the original laws.[27] In an earlier case the Court had ruled that even nondenominational prayer could not be required of children in public schools,[28] and in 1968 the Court struck down an Arkansas law prohibiting the teaching of evolution in public schools.[29] With these rulings the Court was aligning itself firmly with the separationist interpretation of the establishment clause.

THE *LEMON* TEST But the Court in the 1960s, under the leadership of Chief Justice Earl Warren, was known for its liberal views, even though Warren, himself a Republican, had been appointed to the Court by President Eisenhower. As the more conservative appointments of Republican presidents Richard Nixon and Reagan began to shape the Court, the Court's rulings moved in a more accommodationist direction. In *Lemon v. Kurtzman* (1971), the Court added to the old test a third provision that a law not foster

SNAPSHOT OF AMERICA: WHAT DO WE BELIEVE?

Our Religious Identities

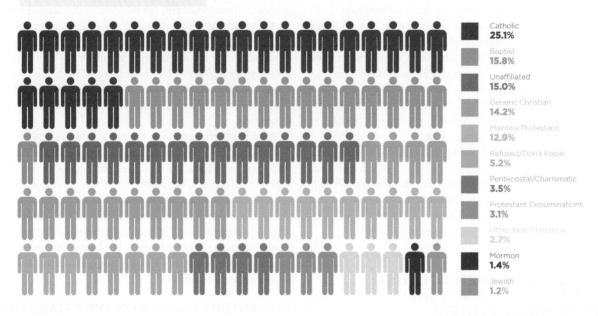

Catholic
25.1%

Baptist
15.8%

Unaffiliated
15.0%

Generic Christian
14.2%

Mainline Protestant
12.9%

Refused/Don't Know
5.2%

Pentecostal/Charismatic
3.5%

Protestant Denominations
3.1%

Other Non-Christians
2.7%

Mormon
1.4%

Jewish
1.2%

My Religion Is the One Religion

65% of Americans feel that many religions can lead to eternal life

29% of Americans feel that their religion is "the one true faith"

53% of Americans feel that it is necessary to believe in God to be moral

29% of Americans feel that America has too little religious freedom

40% of Americans stated that they attend church services weekly; religious leaders report only 20% actually attend

Source: © Association of Statisticians of American Religious Bodies, 2012; 2010 U.S. Religion Census: Religious Congregations & Membership Study, Created by Research Services using ESRI ArcMap 10.0; "American Religious Identification Survey 2008," Table 3, commons.trincoll.edu/aris/files/2011/08/ARIS_Report_2008.pdf.

Where Religious Majorities Live

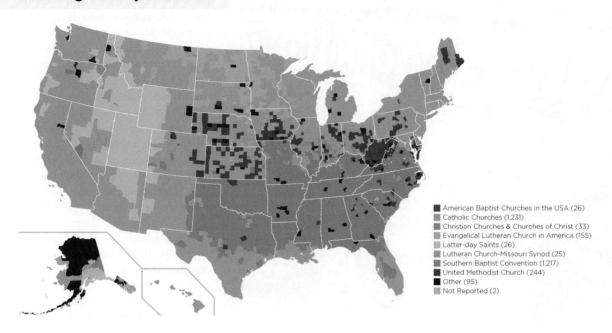

■ American Baptist Churches in the USA (26)
■ Catholic Churches (1,231)
■ Christian Churches & Churches of Christ (33)
■ Evangelical Lutheran Church in America (155)
■ Latter-day Saints (26)
■ Lutheran Church-Missouri Synod (25)
■ Southern Baptist Convention (1,217)
■ United Methodist Church (244)
■ Other (95)
■ Not Reported (2)

Where Religious Minorities Live

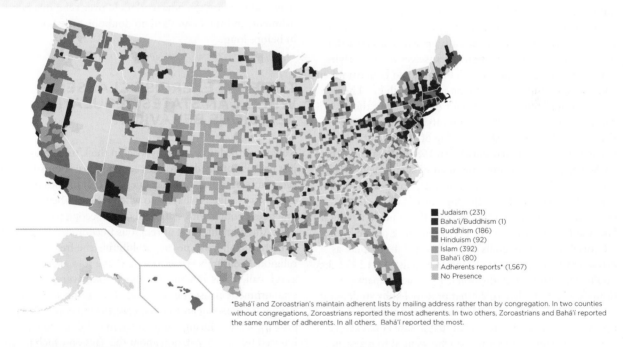

■ Judaism (231)
■ Baha'i/Buddhism (1)
■ Buddhism (186)
■ Hinduism (92)
■ Islam (392)
■ Baha'i (80)
■ Adherents reports* (1,567)
■ No Presence

*Bahá'í and Zoroastrian's maintain adherent lists by mailing address rather than by congregation. In two counties without congregations, Zoroastrians reported the most adherents. In two others, Zoroastrians and Bahá'í reported the same number of adherents. In all others, Bahá'í reported the most.

BEHIND THE NUMBERS

America has always been a religious nation, and as the infographic shows we are an overwhelmingly Christian nation, but also that we practice in many other traditions as well. Is there a danger as religious views make their way into politics, or is this just healthy exercise of First Amendment freedoms?

© Adam Zyglis/Cagle Cartoons Inc.

"an excessive government entanglement with religion."[30] Under the new *Lemon* test the justices had to decide how much entanglement there was between politics and religion, leaving much to their own discretion.

As the current rule in deciding establishment cases, the *Lemon* test is not used consistently, primarily because the justices have not settled among themselves the underlying issue of whether religion and politics should be separate, or whether state support of religion is permissible.[31] The justices still lean in a separationist direction, but their rulings occasionally nod at accommodationism. In 1984 they allowed a Rhode Island display of a crèche at Christmas (accommodationist);[32] in 1985 they struck down an Alabama law requiring a moment of silence before the public school day began (separationist);[33] in 1987 they rejected a Louisiana law requiring schools to teach creationism (separationist);[34] in 1990 they upheld a federal law (the Equal Access Act of 1984) requiring public high schools to permit religious and political clubs to meet as extracurricular activities (accommodationist);[35] in 1992 they disallowed prayer at graduation ceremonies (separationist);[36] in 2000 they ruled that prayers led by students at high school football games were unconstitutional (separationist);[37] and in 2004 they ruled that a state could keep a state scholarship from a student who wanted to major in pastoral ministries (separationist).[38] Also in 2004, the Supreme Court heard a case on the inclusion of the phrase "one nation under God" in the Pledge of Allegiance. The Court failed to rule on the merits of the case this time, making its decision on other grounds.

THE GAP BETWEEN CONSTITUTIONAL LAW AND STATE PRACTICE
Clearly, religion is a subject about which people feel strongly; however, and despite the separationist tilt of the Court's rulings, many Americans have found a way to bring their religions into their public lives, even into the schoolroom. Some communities simply ignore the law, allowing children to begin the school day with prayer or to gather in religious clubs and associations at school. In addition, many state legislatures are testing the limits by passing laws that blur the lines between secular and nonsecular activities at school. A Florida law, signed in 2012, allows school boards to encourage students to give "inspirational messages" at school events; other states are considering similar bills. Georgia, Texas, Tennessee, and South Carolina passed bills allowing schools to offer Bible classes, but setting no parameters to ensure that the teachers of such courses are qualified or that the courses offered are academic rather than religious in nature. And some states, like Louisiana and Tennessee, have passed legislation that requires that teachers clarify the "strengths and weaknesses" of evolution and other subjects held to be controversial by some in the religious community.[39] These practices and laws are the new battlefield over religious establishment, and the Court will no doubt be called on to weigh in before long.

THE FREE EXERCISE CLAUSE: WHEN CAN STATES REGULATE RELIGIOUS BEHAVIOR?

Religious freedom is controversial in the United States not just because of the debate between the separationists and the accommodationists. Another question that divides the public and justices alike is what to do when religious beliefs and practices conflict with state goals. The second part of the First Amendment grant of religious freedom guarantees that Congress shall make no law prohibiting the free exercise of religion. Seemingly straightforward, the **free exercise clause**, as it is called, has generated as much controversy as the establishment clause. For example, what is the solution when a religious belief against killing clashes with compulsory military service during a war, or when religious holy days are ignored by state legislation about the days on which individuals should be expected to work? When is the state justified

> **Lemon test** three-pronged rule used by the courts to determine whether the establishment clause is violated
>
> **free exercise clause** the First Amendment guarantee that citizens may freely engage in the religious activities of their choice

Burwell v. Hobby Lobby ●

in regulating religions? The Court decided in 1940 that there is a difference between the freedom to believe and the freedom to act on those beliefs.[40] Americans have an absolute right to believe whatever they want, but their freedom to act is subject to government regulation. The state's **police power** allows it to protect its citizens, providing social order and security. If it needs to regulate behavior, it may. These two valued goods of religious freedom and social order are bound to conflict, and the Court has had an uneasy time trying to draw the line between them.

The Court's ambivalence can be seen in two cases, three years apart, concerning the obligation to salute the flag. In *Minersville School District v. Gobitis* (1940), two children of a Jehovah's Witness family were expelled from school for violating a rule that required them to salute the flag each day.[41] For a Jehovah's Witness, saluting the flag would amount to worshiping a graven image (idol), which their religion forbids. Their father brought suit, claiming that the rule violated his children's freedom of religion. The Court rejected his claim, arguing that children are required to salute the flag to promote national unity, which in turn fosters national security. Within three years, however, the composition of the Court had changed, and several members had changed their minds. In *West Virginia State Board of Education v. Barnette* (1943), children of Jehovah's Witnesses were again expelled for refusing to salute the flag, but this time the Court overturned the school board's rule requiring the salute.[42]

While *Barnette* still holds, the Court has gone back and forth on other religious freedom issues as it has struggled to define what actions the state might legitimately seek to regulate. Under their police power, states have been allowed to require that businesses close on Sundays, or that certain merchandise not be sold then. In *The Blue Law Cases*, the Court argued that the states are within their rights to require Sunday closings as a provision for a day of rest, and that the Sunday closing laws, while religious in origin, no longer contain religious intent.[43] In *Sherbert v. Verner* (1963), however, the Court seemed to contradict itself. A Seventh Day Adventist, for whom Saturday is the Sabbath, was fired from a company for refusing to work on Saturday and was denied unemployment compensation when she refused to take other jobs with compulsory Saturday hours. A lower court ruled in favor of the woman, and the case was appealed to the Supreme Court. The Court upheld *Sherbert*, finding the denial of benefits to be a clear violation of her constitutional rights. The Court wrote that any incidental burden placed on religious freedom must be justified by a **compelling state interest**; that is, the

state must show that it is absolutely necessary for some fundamental state purpose that the religious freedom be limited.[44] How the Court determines what is and what is not a compelling state interest is examined in Chapter 6.

The Court rejected this compelling state interest test, however, in *Employment Division, Department of Human Resources v. Smith* (1990), when it upheld a law denying state unemployment benefits to employees of a drug rehabilitation organization who were fired for using peyote, a hallucinogenic drug, for sacramental purposes in religious ceremonies.[45] Here the Court abandoned its ruling in *Sherbert* and held that if the infringement on religion is not intentional but is rather the byproduct of a general law prohibiting socially harmful conduct, applied equally to all religions, then it is not unconstitutional. It found that the compelling state interest test, while necessary for cases dealing with matters of race and free speech, was inappropriate for religious freedom issues. Under the *Smith* ruling, a number of religious practices have been declared illegal by state laws on the grounds that the laws do not unfairly burden any particular religion.

Religious groups consider the *Smith* ruling a major blow to religious freedom because it places the burden of proof on the individual or church to show that its religious practices should not be punished, rather than on the state to show that the interference with religious practice is absolutely necessary. In response to the *Smith* decision, Congress in 1993 passed the Religious Freedom Restoration Act (RFRA). This act, supported by a coalition of ninety religious groups, restored the compelling state interest test for state action limiting religious practice and required that when the state did restrict religious practice, it be carried out in the least burdensome way. However, in the 1997 case of *City of Boerne v. Flores*, the Court held that the RFRA was an unconstitutional exercise of congressional power.[46] Congress amended the act in 2003 to apply only to the federal government, and many states passed their own RFRAs to protect religious practices at the state level. The Supreme Court in 2006 affirmed the amended federal RFRA when it ruled that the act protected a New Mexico church's use of tea containing an illegal substance for sacramental purposes, reinstating the compelling state interest test.[47]

Supporters of greater freedom for religious institutions were heartened greatly in 2012, when the Supreme Court issued a unanimous ruling in *Hosanna-Tabor Evangelical Lutheran Church and School v. Equal Employment Opportunity Commission*, a ruling the *New York Times* called perhaps "its most significant religious liberty decision in two decades."[48] In *Hosanna-Tabor*, the Court held that the hiring practices of religious groups could not be regulated by federal employment law (in this case, law that prohibited discrimination against an employee with a disability), because that would essentially give government the right to tell such groups whom they could hire. Chief Justice John Roberts wrote the unanimous opinion, saying, "The Establishment Clause prevents the government from appointing ministers and the Free Exercise Clause prevents it from interfering with the

---

police power the ability of the government to protect its citizens and maintain social order

compelling state interest a fundamental state purpose, which must be shown before the law can limit some freedoms or treat some groups of people differently

freedom of religious groups to select their own." Still, the sweeping decision has not stopped critics of the Court's earlier *Boerne* ruling from arguing that to really protect religious freedom, the Constitution should be amended to make RFRA the law of the land.[49]

Concern over religious freedom among church members grew after the full implementation of the Affordable Care Act (ACA) in 2014. The Obama administration interpreted the ACA requirements as meaning that employer-based health insurance should provide birth control coverage, but the Supreme Court later ruled, in a case brought by the owners of the Hobby Lobby chain of crafts stores, that corporations that are not publicly traded (so-called closely held corporations) did not have to provide such coverage if it violated the owners' religious beliefs.

WHEN IS A RELIGION A RELIGION?

Finally, religious freedom is controversial because it raises some thorny questions: What *is* religion? Can any group call itself a religion? If it does so, is it entitled to constitutional protection? Are all its practices protected? Should nonreligion (like atheism or agnosticism) be similarly protected?

In *Reynolds v. U.S.* (1878) and subsequent cases, the Court has upheld a congressional statute prohibiting polygamy against a Mormon who claimed that his religion required him to marry many wives.[50] In *Reynolds*, the Court said that because religion is not defined in the Constitution, the justices must look elsewhere to determine the founders' intentions. A historical analysis led them to the conclusion that, as the Mormon Church did not exist at the time of the founding, and polygamy was not associated with any religion practiced then, it was not a behavior the founders would have meant to protect. The law was constitutional, given government's right to enforce standards of "civilized society."

The Court also confronted the question of what constitutes religion in a number of cases dealing with conscientious objections to serving in war. Here the question was not whether Congress could force someone to go to war against his religious beliefs. Congress had already passed several laws exempting the conscientious objector from military service—first members of well-recognized religious sects like the Quakers and then, in 1940, anyone whose objection was based on "religious training and belief." The Court has had to decide what claims to exemptions under this law were legitimate, and what Congress could and could not exempt without violating anyone's rights. The Court eventually came to argue that "religious training and belief" could be understood broadly, and that even nonreligious objectors could be exempt if they held ethical and moral beliefs parallel to and just as strong as religious convictions.[51] Thus, in some cases, the Court protected the rights of atheists and agnostics as well as members of organized religious groups.

WHO, WHAT, HOW

All citizens have a stake in a society where they are not coerced to practice a religion in which they do not believe, and where they cannot be prevented from practicing the religion in which they do believe. The rules that help them get what they want here are the establishment clause and the free exercise clause of the First Amendment. There is, however, an inherent conflict between those two clauses. If there truly is a wall of separation between church and state, as the separationists want, then restrictions on religious practice are permissible, which is the opposite of what the accommodationists seek. The only solution is to find a level of separation that the separationists can tolerate that is compatible with a level of protection to which accommodationists can agree.

IN YOUR OWN WORDS >> Describe how the First Amendment protects both church and state, as well as individuals' religious freedom.

FREEDOM OF EXPRESSION
Checking government by protecting speech and the press

Among the most cherished of American values is the right to free speech. The First Amendment reads that "Congress shall make no law . . . abridging the freedoms of speech, or of the press" and, at least theoretically, most Americans agree.[52] When it comes to actually practicing free speech, however, our national record is less impressive. In fact, time and again, Congress *has* made laws abridging freedom of expression, often with the enthusiastic support of much of the American public. As a nation we have never had a great deal of difficulty restricting speech we don't like, admire, or respect. The challenge of the First Amendment is to protect the speech we despise.

The ongoing controversy surrounding free speech has kept the Supreme Court busy. On the one hand are claims that the right to speak freely should be absolute, that we should permit no exceptions whatsoever. On the other hand are demands that speech should be limited—perhaps because it threatens national security or unity or certain economic interests; because it is offensive, immoral, or hurtful; because it hinders the judicial process; or because it injures reputations. The Supreme Court has had to navigate a maze of conflicting arguments as it has assessed the constitutionality of a variety of congressional and state laws that do, indeed, abridge the freedom of speech and of the press.

WHY IS FREEDOM OF EXPRESSION VALUABLE?

It is easier to appreciate what is at stake in the battles over when and what kind of speech should be protected if we think about just why we value free speech so much in the first place. Four arguments for keeping speech free of restrictions deserve our particular attention:

- *An informed citizenry.* In a democracy, citizens are responsible for participating in their government's decisions. Democratic theory holds that, to participate wisely, citizens must have information about what their government is doing. This requires, at the least, a free press, able to report fully on government's activities. Otherwise, citizens are easily manipulated by those people in government who control the flow of information.

- *A watchdog for government.* By being free to voice criticism of government, to investigate its actions, and to debate its decisions, both citizens and journalists are able to exercise an additional check on government that supplements our valued principle of checks and balances. This watchdog function of freedom of expression helps keep government accountable and less likely to step on our other rights. A perfect example of this was the investigation into the Watergate activities by reporters from the *Washington Post* and other newspapers. Had we not had a free press that allowed the investigation of Watergate, the unscrupulous politics or so-called dirty tricks of the Nixon administration would have continued unchecked.

- *A voice for the minority.* Another reason for allowing free speech in society—even (or especially) speech of which we do not approve—is the danger of setting a precedent of censorship. Censorship in a democracy usually allows the voice of the majority to prevail. One of the reasons to support minority rights as well as majority rule, however, is that we never know when we may fall into the minority on an issue. If we make censorship a legitimate activity of government, we too will be potentially vulnerable to it.

- *Preservation of the truth.* Political theorist John Stuart Mill argued that the free traffic of all ideas, those known to be true as well as those suspected to be false, is essential in a society that values truth. By allowing the expression of all ideas, we discover truths that we had previously believed to be false (the world is not flat, after all), and we develop strong defenses against known falsehoods like racist and sexist ideas.

> sedition **speech that criticizes the government to promote rebellion**

If free speech is so valuable, why is it so controversial? Like freedom of religion, free speech requires tolerance of ideas and beliefs other than our own, even ideas and beliefs that we find personally repugnant. Those who are convinced that their ideas are eternally true see no real reason to practice toleration, especially if they are in the majority. It is clear to them that language they view as offensive should be silenced, to create the sort of society they believe should exist. In addition, as the country saw in the controversial case of Edward Snowden, who leaked federal documents he had obtained to show the scope of the government's electronic spying operation, sometimes conflicting ideas about what constitutes the public interest can lead reasonable people to disagree about whether speech ought to be protected or restricted. Many people argued that Snowden was a hero showing uncommon courage as he "blew the whistle" on the extent of federal surveillance; others considered him a traitor to his country for releasing classified information that weakened us internationally.[53]

It is the Supreme Court that generally has to balance the claims of those who defend the rights of all speakers and those who think they should be limited. The Court has had to make difficult decisions about how to apply the First Amendment to speech that criticizes government, symbolic speech, obscenity, and other offensive speech, as well as about freedom of the press. How the Court arrived at the very complex and rich interpretation that it generally uses today is a political tale.

SPEECH THAT CRITICIZES THE GOVERNMENT

Speech that criticizes the government to promote rebellion, called **sedition**, has long been a target of restrictive legislation, and most of the founders were quite content that it should be so. Of course, all the founders had engaged daily in the practice of criticizing their government when *they* were in the process of inciting their countrymen to revolution against England, so they were well aware of the potential consequences of seditious activity. Now that the shoe was on the other foot, and they were the government, many were far less willing to encourage dissent. It was felt that criticism of government undermined authority and destroyed patriotism, especially during wartime.

EARLY RESTRICTIONS ON SPEECH It didn't take long for American "revolutionaries" to pass the Alien and Sedition Act of 1798, which outlawed "any false, scandalous writing against the government of the United States." In the early 1800s, state governments in the South punished speech advocating the end of slavery and even censored the mail to prevent the distribution of abolitionist literature. Throughout that century and into the next, all levels of government, with the support and encouragement of public

CLUES
TO CRITICAL THINKING

"Strip Searches: The Supreme Court's Disturbing Decision"

By Adam Cohen
Time, April 6, 2012

A Yale University Law School professor is troubled by a 2012 Supreme Court ruling that allows police to strip search citizens suspected of minor offenses. We chose this reading because it highlights effectively the political nature of questions related to what civil liberties we can claim.

TIME

It might seem that in the United States, being pulled over for driving without a seat belt should not end with the government ordering you to take off your clothes and "lift your genitals." But there is no guarantee that this is the case—not since the Supreme Court ruled this week that the Constitution does not prohibit the government from strip-searching people charged with even minor offenses. The court's 5–4 ruling turns a deeply humiliating procedure— one most Americans would very much like to avoid—into a routine law-enforcement tactic.

This case arose when a man named Albert Florence was pulled over by New Jersey state troopers while he was driving to his parents' house with his wife and young son. The trooper arrested him for failing to pay a fine—even though, it turned out, he actually had paid it. Florence was thrown into the Essex County Correctional Facility, which has a strip-search policy for all new arrestees.

Florence, who had not even violated the law, was subjected to one of the more degrading interactions a citizen can have with his government. He was made to disrobe, lift his genitals for the guards to show that he was not hiding anything and cough in a squatting position. Florence said he was strip-searched twice.

After he was released, Florence sued, arguing that strip searches of people arrested for minor offenses violate the Fourth Amendment. There is a lot of support for the view that strip searches are an extreme measure that should be used only when the government has reason to believe that the specific person they want to search is concealing weapons, drugs or other contraband. The American Correctional Association, the oldest and largest correctional association in the world, has a standard saying that strip searches should take place only when there is individualized suspicion. Law-enforcement groups including the U.S. Marshals Service and Immigration and Customs Enforcement adhere to this standard.

Many courts have said just what Florence argued—that the Constitution prohibits strip searches of people arrested on minor offenses unless there is individualized suspicion. That includes at least seven U.S. Courts of Appeals, the powerful federal courts that are just one rung below the Supreme Court. Ten states, including Florida and Michigan, actually make suspicionless strip searches illegal.

But the Supreme Court, by a 5–4 vote, has given its blessing to strip searches of people who are charged with minor crimes even if the government has no specific reason to believe they are concealing anything. The majority focused on how hard jailers have it. "The difficulties of operating a detention center must not be underestimated by the courts," the majority opinion said. Strip searches can help keep weapons— and disease and lice—out of prisons.

But the dissenters make a much more compelling case. Justice Stephen Breyer made the most important argument: that being forced to get naked and be stared at by strangers is inherently "humiliating and degrading." He then set out some of the many disturbing ways in which the government has used this power— including to strip naked a nun, who had served for 50 years as a Sister of Divine Providence, when she was arrested during an anti–Vietnam War protest. Breyer also noted the kinds of offenses that people have committed that have led to their being strip searched: driving with a noisy muffler, failing to use a turn signal and riding a bicycle without an audible bell.

---

opinion, squashed the views of radical political groups, labor activists, religious sects, and other minorities.[54]

By World War I (1914–1918), freedom of speech and of the press were a sham for many Americans, particularly those holding unorthodox views or views that challenged the status quo. War in Europe was seen as partly due to the influence of evil ideas, and leaders in America were determined to keep those ideas out of the United States. Government clamped down hard on people promoting socialism, anarchism, revolution, and even labor unions. By the end of World War I, thirty-two of forty-eight states had laws against sedition, particularly prohibiting speech that advocated the use of violence or force to bring about industrial or political change. In 1917 the U.S. Congress had passed the Espionage Act, which made it a crime to "willfully obstruct the recruiting or enlistment service of the United States," and a 1918 amendment to the act spelled out what that meant. It became a crime to engage in "any

The dissent also demolishes the main point made in favor of strip-searching every arrestee: that it is necessary to keep prisons secure. In fact, there are many ways of keeping weapons and contraband out that are far less degrading. The prison to which Florence was admitted also does pat-frisks of inmates and makes them go through metal detectors. One of these detectors is the Body Orifice Screening System chair, which can detect metal hidden in the body when inmates sit on it.

People do not like being physically humiliated by their government. The outraged reactions of many Americans to the TSA's post-9/11 airport screening procedures show how deeply people feel about the matter, even when the purpose is the very important one of stopping armed terrorists from getting onto airplanes. The Supreme Court majority, however, does not seem to get it—or to appreciate the fact that when the government can strip-search people who do not wear a seat belt, it can strip-search any of us.

The conservative Supreme Court majority has been on a crusade in the past few years on behalf of its very peculiar ideal of freedom. In 2010, in *Citizens United v. FEC*, the court upheld the freedom of large corporations to spend unlimited amounts of money to decide federal elections. During the health care arguments in March, the Justices seemed inclined to stand up for people's freedom to not participate in a government health care plan. But when

there is a case in which the freedom at stake is crystal clear—the right to not be forced to needlessly lift one's genitals or squat while coughing for a law-enforcement official—this court is firmly focused on the government's important interests in taking it away.

Cohen, the author of *Nothing to Fear*, teaches at Yale Law School. The views expressed are solely his own.

Consider the source and the audience: Adam Cohen is a law professor at Yale University. A quick Internet search will tell you he was also once a staff attorney for the American Civil Liberties Union, a libertarian group that focuses on the protection of civil liberties. How is a libertarian perspective reflected in this article? Why would a law professor with those views want to publish in a mainstream media outlet like the *Time* magazine web site?

Lay out the argument and the underlying values and assumptions: How does Cohen define *freedom*? How does he suggest the majority on the Supreme Court defines that value, and what do they balance it against? How does Cohen believe the dissenting opinion on the Court refutes the majority's case? Where does he come down, and why?

Uncover the evidence: When making an argument about values, what kind of evidence can be brought to bear? If the goal is to be persuasive rather than to prove an empirical case, what kinds of arguments does each side offer to support its case?

Evaluate the conclusion: Cohen clearly believes that the Court's majority opinion is wrong and that it allows law enforcement to humiliate and degrade individuals without cause. Apart from the individual's discomfort and embarrassment, what is wrong with giving law enforcement that power? How might it be abused?

Sort out the political significance: Cohen is labeling the five justices who decided this case "the conservative Supreme Court majority." In what way might the choice to support the needs of law enforcement over the rights of individuals be seen as a conservative choice? Might not conservatives also have easily come down in favor of the rights of the individual? How do you place these arguments on the chart on page xx?

disloyal . . . scurrilous, or abusive language about the form of government of the United States, . . . or any language intended to bring the form of government of the United States . . . into contempt, scorn, contumely, or disrepute."[55] Such sweeping prohibitions made it possible to arrest people on the flimsiest of pretexts.

THE ROLE OF THE SUPREME COURT Those arrested and imprisoned under the new sedition laws

looked to the Supreme Court to protect their freedom to criticize their government, but they were doomed to disappointment. The Court did not dispute the idea that speech criticizing the government could be punished. The question it dealt with was just how bad the speech had to be before it could be prohibited. The history of freedom of speech cases is a history of the Court's devising tests for itself to determine if certain speech should be protected or could be legitimately outlawed. In four cases upholding the

© Mark Godfrey/The Image Works

Freedom of the Press in Action

The reporting of *Washington Post* journalists Bob Woodward (center) and Carl Bernstein (second from left) on the Watergate break-in and cover-up resulted in congressional investigations and, ultimately, President Richard Nixon's 1974 resignation on the brink of his impeachment. Woodward and Bernstein's work drives home the importance of a free press. Here they discuss story developments with publisher Katherine Graham, managing editor Howard Simons, and executive editor Benjamin Bradlee.

Espionage Act, the Court used a measure it called the **bad tendency test**, which simply required that, for the language to be regulated, it must have "a natural tendency to produce the forbidden consequences." That is, if Congress has the right to outlaw certain actions, it also has the right to outlaw speech that is likely to lead to those actions. This test is pretty easy for prosecutors to meet, so most convictions under the act were upheld.[56]

But in two of those cases, *Schenck v. United States* (1919) and *Abrams v. United States* (1919), Justice Oliver Wendell Holmes began to articulate a new test, which he called the **clear and present danger test**. This test, as Holmes conceived it, focused on the circumstances in which language was used.[57] If no immediately threatening circumstances existed, then the language in question would be protected and Congress could not regulate it. But Holmes's views did not represent the majority opinion of the Court, and the clear and present danger test was slow to catch on.

With the tensions that led to World War II, Congress again began to fear the power of foreign ideas, especially communism, which was seen as a threat to the American way of life. The Smith Act of 1940 made it illegal to advocate the violent overthrow of the government or to belong to an organization that did so. Similarly, as the communist scare picked up speed after the war, the McCarran Act of 1950 required members of the Communist Party to register with the U.S. attorney general. At the same time, Senator Joseph McCarthy was conducting investigations of American citizens to search out communists, and the House Un-American Activities Committee was doing the same thing. The suspicion or accusation of being involved in communism was enough to stain a person's reputation irreparably, even if there were no evidence to back up the claim. Many careers and lives were ruined in the process.

Again the Supreme Court did not weigh in on the side of civil liberties. Convictions under both the Smith and McCarran Acts were upheld. The Court had used the clear and present danger test intermittently in the years since 1919, but usually not as originally intended, to limit speech only in the rarest and most dire of occasions. Instead the clear and present danger test came to be seen as a kind of balancing test in which society's interests in prohibiting the speech were weighed against the value of free speech; consequently, the emphasis on an obvious and immediate danger was lost.

> **bad tendency test** rule used by the courts that allows speech to be punished if it leads to punishable actions
>
> **clear and present danger test** rule used by the courts that allows language to be regulated only if it presents an immediate and urgent danger

The Court's record as a supporter of sedition laws finally ended with the personnel changes that brought Earl Warren to the position of chief justice. In 1969 the Court overturned the conviction of Charles Brandenburg, a Ku Klux Klan leader who had been arrested under Ohio's criminal syndicalism law. In this case the Court ruled that abstract teaching of violence is not the same as incitement to violence. In other words, political speech could be restricted only if it was aimed at producing or was likely to produce "imminent lawless action." Mere advocacy of specific illegal acts was protected unless it led to immediate illegal activity. In a concurring opinion, Justice William O. Douglas pointed out that it was time to get rid of the clear and present danger test because it was so subject to misuse and manipulation. Speech, except when linked with action, he said, should be immune from prosecution.[58] The **imminent lawless action test** continues to be the standard for regulating political speech today.

SYMBOLIC SPEECH

The question of what to do when speech *is* linked to action, of course, remained. Many forms of expression go beyond mere speech or writing. Should they also be protected? No one disputes that government has the right to regulate actions and behavior if it believes it has sufficient cause, but what happens when that behavior is also expression? When is an action a form of expression? Is burning a draft card, or wearing an armband to protest a war, or torching the American flag an action or an expression? All these questions, and more, have come before the Court, which generally has been more willing to allow regulation of symbolic speech than of speech alone, especially if the regulation is not a direct attempt to curtail the speech.

We already saw, in the discussion of freedom of religion, that the Court has decided that some symbolic expression, such as saluting or not saluting the American flag, is a protected form of speech. But drawing the line between what is and is not protected has been extremely difficult for the Court. In *United States v. O'Brien* (1968), the Court held that burning a draft card at a rally protesting the Vietnam War was *not* protected speech because the law against burning draft cards was legitimate and not aimed at restricting expression. In that case, Chief Justice Earl Warren wrote, "We think it clear that a government regulation is sufficiently justified if it is within the constitutional power of the Government; if it furthers an important or

substantial governmental interest; if the governmental interest is unrelated to the suppression of free expression; and if the incidental restriction on alleged First Amendment freedoms is no greater than is essential to the furtherance of that interest."[59] Following that reasoning, in 1969 the Court struck down a school rule forbidding students to wear black armbands as an expression of their opposition to the Vietnam War, arguing that the fear of a disturbance was not a sufficient state interest to warrant the suppression.[60]

One of the most divisive issues of symbolic speech that has confronted the Supreme Court, and indeed the American public, concerns that ultimate symbol of our country, the American flag. There is probably no more effective way of showing one's dissatisfaction with the United States or its policies than burning the Stars and Stripes. In 1969 the Court split five to four when it overturned the conviction of a person who had broken a New York law making it illegal to deface or show disrespect for the flag (he had burned it).[61] Twenty years later, with a more conservative Court in place, the issue was raised again by a similar Texas law. Again the Court divided five to four, voting to protect the burning of the flag as symbolic expression.[62] Because the patriotic feelings of so many Americans were fired up by this ruling, Congress passed the federal Flag Protection Act in 1989, making it a crime to desecrate the flag. In *United States v. Eichman*, the Court declared the federal law unconstitutional for the same reasons it had overturned the New York and Texas laws: all were aimed specifically at "suppressing expression."[63] The only way to get around a Supreme Court ruling of unconstitutionality is to amend the Constitution. Efforts to pass an amendment failed by a fairly small margin in the House and the Senate, meaning that despite the strong feeling of many, flag burning is still considered protected speech in the United States.

The Court has recently proved willing to restrict symbolic speech, however, if it finds that the speech goes beyond expression of a view. In a 2003 ruling, the Court held that cross burning, a favored practice of the Ku Klux Klan and other segregationists that it had previously held to be protected speech, was not protected under the First Amendment if it was intended as a threat of violence. "When a cross burning is used to intimidate, few if any messages are more powerful," wrote Justice Sandra Day O'Connor, speaking for a six-to-three majority. "A state may choose to prohibit only those forms of intimidation that are most likely to inspire fear of bodily harm," if the intent to stir up such fear is clear.[64] The Court noted that cross burning would still be protected as symbolic speech in certain cases, such as at a political rally.

Closely related to symbolic speech is an additional First Amendment guarantee, **freedom of assembly**, or "the right of the people peaceably to assemble, and to petition the government for a redress of grievances." The courts have interpreted this provision to mean not only that people can meet and express their views collectively, but also that their very association is protected as a form of political expression.

> **imminent lawless action test** rule used by the courts that restricts speech only if it is aimed at producing or is likely to produce imminent lawless action
>
> **freedom of assembly** the right of the people to gather peacefully and to petition government

PROFILES IN CITIZENSHIP: BILL MAHER

MAXX/Landov

Bill Maher is a big fan of the First Amendment. That's because he says what few of us dare to say, what most of us dare not even think. The gasp of laughter that follows the comedian's one-liners is not just shocked amusement; it's shocked recognition that, uncomfortable, unflattering, and unpalatable as his observations are, they're often right on target. Maher has made a career out of mocking the emperor's anatomy, while most of us are still oohing and aahing over the splendor of his new clothes. Usually the First Amendment saves his bacon.

And sometimes it doesn't. On September 17, 2001, he went on his ABC comedy show, *Politically Incorrect*, and said, about the suicide bombing of the World Trade Center: "We have been the cowards, lobbing cruise missiles from miles away. That's cowardly. Staying in the airplane when it hits the building—say what you want about it, it's not cowardly."

Predictably, in those shaky days of national trouble, all hell broke loose.

Asked about Maher's comment at a White House press briefing, then–press secretary Ari Fleischer replied: "All Americans . . . need to watch what they say, watch what they do." Advertisers balked, and Maher's show was canceled.

He's back now, with a cable show called *Real Time With Bill Maher*, where he continues to speak his mind. Still, there are limits. He says: "I can't get up there every week and just rail about the environment and global warming and whatever is going on that I think is most important. But I push it as far as I can. You've got to try to find entertaining ways to get the message through. I always say, in America if you want to teach somebody something, it's got to be like a pill in the dog's food. You've got to wrap it in the bologna . . . stick it right at the back of his throat so he doesn't even know it's there."

The trouble, as he sees it, is that Americans want to fit their beliefs into tidy categories of "liberal" and

So, for instance, they have ruled that associations like the NAACP cannot be required to make their membership lists public[65] (although groups deemed to have unlawful purposes do not have such protection) and that teachers do not have to reveal the associations to which they belong.[66] In addition, the Court has basically upheld people's rights to associate with whom they please, although it held that public[67] and, in some circumstances, private groups cannot discriminate on the basis of race or sex.[68]

OBSCENITY AND PORNOGRAPHY

Of all the forms of expression, obscenity has probably presented the Court with its biggest headaches. In attempting to define it in 1964, Justice Potter Stewart could only conclude, "I know it when I see it."[69] The Court has used a variety of tests for determining whether material is obscene, but until the early 1970s, only the most hard-core pornography was regulated.

Coming into office in 1969, however, President Nixon made it one of his administration's goals to control pornography in America. Once the Court began to reflect the ideological change that came with Nixon's appointees,

rulings became more restrictive. In 1973 the Court developed the **Miller test**, which returned more control over the definition of obscenity to state legislatures and local standards. Under the *Miller* test, the Court asks "whether the work depicts or describes, in a patently offensive way, sexual conduct specifically defined by state law" and "whether the work, taken as a whole, lacks serious literary, artistic, political or scientific value" (called the SLAPS test).[70] These provisions have also been open to interpretation, and the Court has tried to refine them over time. The emphasis on local standards has meant that pornographers can look for those places with the most lenient definitions of obscenity in which to produce and market their work, and the Court has let this practice go on.

The question of whether obscenity should be protected speech raises some fundamental issues, and has created some unlikely alliances. Justice John Marshall Harlan was quite right when he wrote that "one man's vulgarity is another man's lyric."[71] People offended by what they

> **Miller test** rule used by the courts in which the definition of obscenity must be based on local standards

"conservative" as if that sums up the whole debate. Maher wants us to dig our way out of our comfortable platitudes to reach new truths, even if they're unpopular. He recalls getting booed once on the *Tonight Show* after he berated an animal trainer who had appeared with his tiger. "They're like, please, Mr. Comedown. We just enjoyed a delightful animal show, and I pointed out that animals really don't want to be in show business." New rule, as Maher would say today.

"...IF YOU WANT TO TEACH SOME-BODY SOMETHING, IT'S GOT TO BE LIKE A PILL IN THE DOG'S FOOD."

Maher is a libertarian, but, true to his own creed, he is also a bit of everything else, believing fiercely in causes like animal rights, the environment, personal responsibility, and civic education. Today, he says,

we've lost the thread to the things that matter. Raised by parents who served in World War II, Maher grew up thinking that there was a common good worth sacrificing for, "that the world had been to the brink and good citizenship was responsible for saving it. And we have nothing like that today. Nothing." Here's more Maher:

On patriotism:

Well, it means being loyal to your country above other countries. And I am . . . . [But] it has to be put in context and also it has to be put side by side with a greater humanity . . . . Americans who say, "This is the greatest country in the world," without having any clue what goes on in any other countries, are just pulling it out of nowhere. There are many things that I'm proud of in this country. I'm proud of how my parents and other people stopped fascism and communism. I'm certainly proud of what we started in 1776. It was a new dawn of freedom and liberty in the world. But I'm not

proud of slavery. I'm not proud of the genocide of the Indians. I'm not proud of much of what goes on today. So I still believe in the promise of America, but most of America looks at itself through rose-colored glasses. And that's not healthy.

On keeping the republic:

Take it upon [yourself] to learn the basics . . . . [K]ids need . . . to learn history. Because kids say to me all the time when I say something from history: "How should I know about that? I wasn't born." Oh, really? So nothing happened before you were born? . . . Kids need to learn history so they can put themselves in the proper place, which is of great insignificance . . . . The problem with kids today is not too little self-esteem, it's too much. And history, I think, learning a big picture, is very important in that.

Source: Bill Maher spoke with Christine Barbour and Gerald C. Wright on May 9, 2005.

---

consider to be obscenity believe that their values should be represented in their communities. If that means banning adult bookstores, nude dancing at bars, and naked women on magazine covers at the supermarket, then so be it. But opponents argue that what is obscene to one person may be art or enjoyment to another. The problem of majorities enforcing decisions on minorities is inescapable here. A second issue that has generated debate over these cases is the feminist critique of pornography: that it represents aggression toward women and should be banned primarily because it perpetuates stereotypes and breeds violence. Thus radical feminists, usually on the left end of the political spectrum, have found themselves in alliance with conservatives on the right. There is a real contradiction here for feminists, who are more often likely to argue for the expansion of rights, particularly as they apply to women. Feminists advocating restrictions on pornography reconcile the contradiction by arguing that the proliferation of pornography ultimately limits women's rights by making life more threatening and fundamentally unequal.

---

fighting words **speech intended to incite violence**

FIGHTING WORDS AND OFFENSIVE SPEECH

Among the categories of speech that the Court has ruled may be regulated is one called **fighting words**, words whose express purpose is to create a disturbance and incite violence in the person who hears the speech.[72] However, the Court rarely upholds legislation designed to limit fighting words unless the law is written very carefully and specifically. Consequently it has held that threatening and provocative language is protected unless it is likely to "produce a clear and present danger of serious substantive evil that rises far above public inconvenience, annoyance, or unrest."[73]

The Court has also ruled that offensive language, while not protected by the First Amendment, may occasionally contain a political message, in which case constitutional protection applies. For instance, the Court overturned the conviction of a young California man named Paul Cohen who was arrested for violating California's law against "maliciously and willfully disturb[ing] the peace or quiet of any neighborhood or person . . . by . . . offensive conduct." Cohen had worn a jacket in a Los Angeles courthouse that had "Fuck the Draft" written across the back, in protest of the Vietnam

Public Salute

Remains of military personnel arrive at Dover Air Force Base, in an undated photo released by the U.S. Air Force in response to a Freedom of Information Act request. The Obama administration reversed the policy of former president George W. Bush, which blocked photographs of returning caskets. Supporters of the policy reversal claim that banning photographs allowed the government to suppress evidence of the human costs of the wars in Iraq and Afghanistan and violated freedom of the press, while critics say the ban allowed families to mourn in private and preserved the dignity of the fallen.

War. The Court held that this message was not directed to any specific person who was likely to see the jacket and, further, there was no evidence that Cohen was in fact inciting anyone to a disturbance. Those who were offended by the message on Cohen's jacket did not have to look at it.[74]

These cases have taken on modern-day significance in the wake of the **political correctness** movement that swept the country in the late 1980s and 1990s, especially on college campuses. Political correctness refers to an ideology, held primarily by some liberals, including some civil rights activists and feminists, that language shapes society in critical ways, and therefore racist, sexist, homophobic, or any other language that demeans any group of individuals should be silenced to minimize its social effects. An outgrowth of the political correctness movement was the passing of speech codes on college campuses that ban speech that might be offensive to women and ethnic and

other minorities. Critics of speech codes, and of political correctness in general, argue that such practices unfairly repress free speech, which should flourish, of all places, on college campuses. In 1989 and 1991, federal district court judges agreed, finding speech codes on two campuses, the University of Michigan and the University of Wisconsin, in violation of students' First Amendment rights.[75] Neither school appealed. The Supreme Court spoke on a related issue in 1992 when it struck down a Minnesota "hate crime law." The Court held that it is unconstitutional to outlaw broad categories of speech based on its content. The prohibition against activities that "arouse anger, alarm or resentment in others on the basis of race, color, creed, religion or gender" was too sweeping and thus unconstitutional.[76]

FREEDOM OF THE PRESS

The First Amendment covers not only freedom of speech but also freedom of the press. Many of the controversial issues we have already covered apply to both of these areas, but some problems are confronted exclusively, or primarily, by the press: the issue of prior restraint, libel restrictions, and the conflict between a free press and a fair trial.

PRIOR RESTRAINT The founders modeled their ideas about freedom of expression on British common law, which held that it is acceptable to censor writing and speech about the government as long as the censorship occurs *after* publication. **Prior restraint**, a restriction on the press before its message is actually published, was seen as a more dangerous form of censorship since the repressed ideas never entered the public domain and their worth could not be debated. The Supreme Court has shared the founders' concern that prior restraint is a particularly dangerous form of censorship and almost never permits it. Two classic judgments illustrate their view. In *Near v. Minnesota*, the Court held that a Minnesota law infringed on a newspaper publisher's freedom of the press. Jay Near's newspaper *The Saturday Press* was critical of African Americans, Jews, Catholics, and organized labor. His paper was shut down in 1927 under a state law that prohibited any publication of "malicious, scandalous and defamatory" materials. If he continued to publish the paper, he would have been subject to a $1,000 fine or a year in jail. While an extreme emergency, such as war, might justify previous restraint on the press, wrote Justice Charles Evans Hughes, the purpose of the First Amendment was to limit it to those rare circumstances.[77] Similarly, and more recently, in *New York Times Company v.*

> **political correctness** the idea that language shapes behavior and therefore should be regulated to control its social effects
>
> **prior restraint** censorship of or punishment for the expression of ideas before the ideas are printed or spoken

Times v. Sullivan ●

United States, the Court prevented the Nixon administration from stopping the publication by the *New York Times* and the *Washington Post* of a "top secret" document about U.S. involvement in Vietnam. These so-called Pentagon Papers were claimed by the government to be too sensitive to national security to be published. The Court held that "security" is too vague to be allowed to excuse the violation of the First Amendment; to grant such power to the president, it ruled, would be to run the risk of destroying the liberty that the government is trying to secure.[78]

LIBEL   Freedom of the press also collides with the issue of **libel**, the written defamation of character (verbal defamation is called *slander*). Obviously it is crucial to the watchdog and information-providing roles of the press that journalists be able to speak freely about the character and actions of those in public service. But at the same time, because careers and reputations are easily ruined by rumors and innuendo, journalists ought to be required to "speak" responsibly. The Supreme Court addressed this issue in *New York Times v. Sullivan*. In 1960 a Montgomery, Alabama, police commissioner named Sullivan claimed he had been defamed by an advertisement that had run in the *Times*. The ad, paid for by the Committee to Defend Martin Luther King, had alleged that various acts of racism had taken place in the South, one in particular supported by police action on a Montgomery college campus. Sullivan, claiming that as police commissioner he was associated with the police action and was thus defamed—and arguing that there were factual errors in the story (although only minor ones)—sued the *Times* for libel and won.

The *Times* was convinced that officials illegally resisting desegregation in the South would use libel cases to deflect attention from the northern press if this judgment were not challenged. The paper brought a unique defense to the case when it appealed to the Supreme Court. It argued that if government officials could claim personal damages when institutions they controlled were portrayed negatively in the press, and if any inaccuracy at all in the story were sufficient to classify the story as false and thus libelous, then libel law would have the same effect that antisedition laws had once had: neither citizens nor the press could criticize the government—dramatically weakening the protection of the First Amendment.[79]

The Supreme Court accepted the *New York Times* argument, and libel law in the United States was revolutionized. No longer simply a state matter, libel became a constitutional issue under the First Amendment. The Court held that public officials, as opposed to private individuals, when suing for libel, must show that a publication acted with "actual malice," which means not that the paper had an evil intent but only that it acted with "knowledge that [what it printed] was false or with reckless disregard for whether it

was false or not."[80] Shortly afterward, the Court extended the ruling to include public figures such as celebrities and political candidates—anyone whose actions put them in a public position.

The Court's rulings attempt to give the press some leeway in its actions. Without *Sullivan*, investigative journalism would never have been able to uncover the U.S. role in Vietnam, for instance, or the Watergate cover-up. Freedom of the press, and thus the public's interest in keeping a critical eye on government, is clearly the winner here. The Court's view is that when individuals put themselves into the public domain, the public's interest in the truth outweighs the protection of those individuals' privacy.

THE RIGHT TO A FAIR TRIAL   Freedom of the press also confronts head-on another Bill of Rights guarantee, the right to a fair trial. Media coverage of a crime can make it very difficult to find an "impartial jury," as required by the Sixth Amendment. On the other side of this conflict, however, is the "public's right to know." The Sixth Amendment promises a "speedy and public trial," and many journalists interpret this provision to mean that the proceedings ought to be open. The courts, on the other hand, have usually held that this amendment protects the rights of the accused, not of the public. But while the Court has overturned a murder verdict because a judge failed to control the media circus in his courtroom,[81] on the whole it has ruled in favor of media access to most stages of legal proceedings. Likewise, courts have been extremely reluctant to uphold gag orders, which would impose prior restraint on the press during those proceedings.[82]

CENSORSHIP ON THE INTERNET

Lawmakers do not always know how to deal with new outlets for expression as they become available. Modern technology has presented the judiciary with a host of free speech issues the founders never anticipated. The latest to make it to the courts is the question of censorship on the Internet. Some web sites contain explicit sexual material, obscene language, and other content that many people find objectionable. Since children often find their way onto the Internet on their own, parents and groups of other concerned citizens have clamored for regulation of this medium. Congress obliged in 1996 with the Communications Decency Act (CDA), which made it illegal to knowingly send or display indecent material over the Internet. In 1997 the Supreme Court ruled that such provisions constituted a violation of free speech, and that communication over the Internet, which it called a modern "town crier," is subject to the same protections as nonelectronic expression.[83] When Congress tried again with a more narrowly tailored bill, the Child Online Protection Act, the Court struck it down, too.[84]

> **libel**   written defamation of character

DON'T BE FOOLED BY...
THE WORLD WIDE WEB

P. T. Barnum said there's a sucker born every minute—and that was decades before the advent of the Internet. He would have rubbed his hands in glee over the gullibility of people in the electronic age. While freedom of speech is a powerful liberty, as we have seen in this chapter, one consequence is that it makes it very difficult to silence those making fraudulent or misleading claims. Anyone who has the small amount of money needed to set up a web page or a blog can get on the Internet and disseminate information. All of us, of course—professors, students, politicians, journalists, doctors, lawyers, CEOs, and anyone else with access to the web—are potential suckers.

Americans expect the government to regulate radio and television, of course, because, before the days of cable and satellites, these media were held to be scarce resources that belonged to the public. Private publishers can also enforce standards—of excellence, or accuracy, or style—on what they publish. But lawmakers and judges have been hesitant to regulate free speech on the Internet.[1] That's because when a medium is quasi-public, like the Internet, and access to it is easy and cheap, it is impossible to restrict the views and ideas that are published without also doing some serious damage to the freedom of speech. Today we have access to more information than we could ever have imagined, but we are not trained to use it critically and competently. It is up to us as consumers to sort the grain from the chaff. Of the many fascinating sources of information that you can find online, here are a few worthy of special consideration:

- *"Official" Web Sites.* Just about any organization, corporation, or political figure of note is likely to have a web site, from which they present news and information about themselves, their services, or their product. Looking for the text of the president's last speech? Visit whitehouse.gov. Want to know how many miles to the gallon that Prius gets? Toyota.com will be happy to provide facts and figures. It's good to get information from official sources, but always bear in mind that the information they provide may be tailored to meet the site owner's needs, not those of the readers. It's unlikely that you'll find a critique of the U.S. president's policies on his official site, nor will you get a thoughtful review from Toyota of the ups *and* downs of driving a Prius.

- *Blogs.* A blog is an online "weblog," a forum in which you can keep a public journal of sorts on any subject you want to talk about, from cooking to travel to politics. Political blogs present a particular challenge to the reader because bloggers from the left and right battle daily, crossing the line between journalism and activism, with no requirement that they meet the ethical obligations of either. That doesn't necessarily make blogs unreliable sources of information (and it doesn't mean you shouldn't set up your own blog if you are so inclined). It does mean, however, that you should be wary of information you find on a blog, and you should always try to figure out where the blogger is coming from so that you can see what impact his or her ideological perspective has on the news he or she conveys.

- *Wikipedia.* On first glance Wikipedia looks like a researcher's dream come true—a free online encyclopedia that seems to cover every subject under the sun. What could be better for a harried student writing a term paper or just for a curious person seeking to verify the date of a historical event or a person's name? The only catch with Wikipedia is that it is a communal encyclopedia, written, edited, and fact-checked by the people who use it. See something that seems questionable in a Wikipedia entry? You can edit it yourself, or tag it as potentially offensive, untrue, or libelous, in hopes that someone else in the community will address it. The check on what you might add or say are the thousands of eyes watching over your shoulder, correcting your mistakes even as you correct theirs. The self-policing, collaborative power of Wikipedia creates an amazing resource, but one you need to use warily because the information there is only as good as the last person who edited it. Never rely on it without double-checking!

- *Search Engines.* When you want to verify information you received from any source—a rant on a blog, an interesting Tweet, even a juicy bit of political news you just overheard while waiting in line for your morning coffee—chances are the first thing you'll do is enter a few keywords into a search engine to find out the real story. Search engines like Google, Bing, and Yahoo scan the Internet for content related to specific terms: type in "Congress," for example, and the first thing that comes up is the United States House of Representative's website (www.house.gov). However, most search engines use specific tools and a battery of information—including your past searches and your browsing history—to determine what results are best for you. That means that when it comes to political news, your own political leanings, as gleaned from what you've clicked on in the past, can have an impact on your search results—and influence what you click on in the future. Further, web writers are careful to pepper their stories with key words that will increase traffic to their sites, so the "best" information might not be what comes in at the top of your search results.[2]

WHAT TO WATCH OUT FOR

The Internet is clearly the source of endless possibilities and scary scenarios. What allows us to rely on what we find on the Internet is our own hard work and careful scrutiny. Here are some tips to help you become a savvy surfer of the World Wide Web:

- **Find out the source of the web site.** Examine the web address, or URL, for clues. Although these days there are many domains, web addresses that end with .com, .org, .gov, .net, or .edu indicate, respectively, commercial, nonprofit, government, network, or educational sites. Sites from other countries end with abbreviations of the nation (for example, .kr indicates the site is from Korea and .fr indicates France). Remember, however, that anyone can purchase rights to a web address, and an official-looking address does not necessarily confer legitimacy on a site.

- **Follow the money.** Commercial interests can shape the content of what we find on the web in any number of ways: links to sponsors' pages may appear prominently on a web page, web sites may promote the products of their advertisers as if they were objectively recommending them without making the financial relationship clear, or the commercial bias may be even more subtle. One author says that "trusting an Internet site to navigate the World Wide Web . . . is like following a helpful stranger in Morocco who offers to take you to the best rug store. You may very well find what you are looking for, but your guide will get a piece of whatever you spend."[3]

- **Check out the author.** You can find out who runs a site by going to www.internic.net and using the "whois" search function. This will give you names and contact information but is not, warns Tina Kelly of the *New York Times,* conclusive. Similarly, she suggests running authors' names through a search engine to see what you can find out about them. Some browsers will tell you when a site was last updated. And remember that you can always email authors of a site and ask for their credentials.[4] If no contact information for the author is available on the site itself, that alone can tell you something about its reliability. For more information on how to evaluate various types of web sites, check out the Cornell University Library's site at olinuris.library.cornell.edu/ref/research/webeval.html.

- **Note the other kinds of information the site directs you to.** If you are in doubt about a site's legitimacy, check some of its links to external sites, as well as any footnotes or citations. Are they up to date and well maintained? Do the sources to which they lead help you identify the ideological, commercial, or other bias the site may contain? If there are no notes or links to other sites, ask yourself what this might mean.

- **Watch out for Internet vandalism.** The open market of the Internet leaves it vulnerable to attacks from vandals who—for reasons ranging from satire to partisanship to outright maliciousness—create deliberately misleading content, or edit existing content in a misleading way. Wikipedia editors have had to scramble to keep up with partisans and pranksters who have vandalized entries on everything from George W. Bush to Islam to stingrays and bananas.[5] Look for very recent posts, or footnotes that don't link to real articles or research, to weed out imposters. Similarly, it's easy for the unscrupulous to create a Twitter account in a name that is not his or her own—and even real Twitter feeds belonging to prominent politicians have been known to be hacked. If a politician's feed seems out of character, or is riddled with profanity or absurdity, check to be sure it's real.

- **If something about a site does not look right, investigate more closely.** One author calls this the J.D.L.R. (Just Doesn't Look Right) test.[6] Be suspicious if, for example, you notice lots of misspellings or grammatical errors, or if the site has an odd design. Analyze the site's tone and approach. When a familiar site doesn't look the way you expect it to, consider the possibility that hackers have broken in to it and changed its content. Ultimately, remember this: anyone can put up a web site—even you. Are you a reliable enough source to be quoted in a college student's research paper?

1. Jonathan Weisman, "After an Online Firestorm, Congress Shelves Antipiracy Bills," *New York Times,* January 20, 2012, www.nytimes.com/2012/01/21/technology/senate-postpones-piracy-vote.html?_r=1&ref=global; and Declan McCulagh, "Supreme Court Deals Death Blow to Antiporn Law," CNET News, January 21, 2009, news.cnet.com/8301-13578_3-10147171-38.html.

2. Farhad Manjoo, "HuffPo's Achilles' Heel: Search Engine Optimization Won't Work Forever," *Slate,* February 8, 2011, www.slate.com/articles/technology/technology/2011/02/huffpos_achilles_heel.2.html.

3. Saul Hansell and Army Harmon, "Caveat Emptor on the Web: Ad and Editorial Lines Blur," *New York Times,* February 26, 1999, A1.

4. Tina Kelly, "Whales in the Minnesota River? Only on the Web, Where Skepticism Is a Required Navigational Aid," *New York Times,* March 4, 1999, D1.

5. Jenny Kleeman, "Wiki Wars," *The Observer,* March 24, 2007, www.guardian.co.uk/technology/2007/mar/25/wikipedia.web20.

6. Tina Kelly, "Whales in the Minnesota River," *New York Times,* March 4, 1999, http://www.nytimes.com/1999/03/04/technology/whales-in-the-minnesota-river.html

The Court has not always ruled on the side of a completely unregulated Internet. While not restricting the creation of content, in 2003 the Supreme Court did uphold the Children's Internet Protection Act, which required public libraries that received federal funds to use filtering software to block material that is deemed harmful to minors, such as pornography.[85] However, these filters can create some problems. Many companies and institutions use them to screen offensive incoming email, but such filters often have unwanted consequences. Since the filters cannot evaluate the material passing through, they can end up blocking even legitimate messages and publications. One editor of a newsletter on technology has resorted to intentionally misspelling words (for example, writing "sez" instead of "sex") to avoid the automatic sensors that screen many of his readers' mail.[86]

The Internet can also have the effect of freeing people from censorship, however. As many people who have worked on their high school newspapers know, the Court has ruled that student publications are subject to censorship by school officials if the restrictions serve an educational purpose. The Internet, however, offers students an alternative medium of publication that the courts say is not subject to censorship. As a result, students have been able to publish such matters as the results of investigations into school elections and campus violence that have been excluded from the hard-copy newspaper.[87]

We can probably expect some flux in the laws on Internet censorship as the courts become more familiar with the medium itself and the issues surrounding it, including issues not only about open access to information, but also about the protection of the rights of those who create the intellectual property people seek to share on the Internet. In fact, the increasing use of the Internet not just as a source of information but also as a mechanism for people to download books, music, movies, and other forms of entertainment has set up another clash of rights. This conflict is between authors and creators—even the manufacturers of medication—who claim a copyright to their works, and the public, who wants to access those works, frequently without paying full fare for their use. In 2012 two bills, one in the House (the Stop Online Piracy Act, or SOPA) and one in the Senate (the Protect IP Act, or PIPA), attempted to address this issue by requiring Internet providers to monitor their users and block access to international sites that share files. Companies like Google, Yahoo, Bing, Facebook, Twitter, and Tumblr, which depend on open Internet access, opposed the legislation, claiming it would require them to censor their users' practices and stifle free speech and innovation. Many of them went dark or threatened to do so in protest of the bills, and leaders in both houses postponed votes, effectively killing the proposed legislation in its current form.[88] The issue of the protection of intellectual property rights on the Internet remains unresolved. (See *Don't Be Fooled by . . . the World Wide Web* for some tips on how to evaluate what you find on the Internet.)

THINKING OUTSIDE THE BOX

How much free speech do we need on our college campuses?

PAUSE AND REVIEW:

WHO, WHAT, HOW

No less than the success of free democratic government is at stake in the issue of freedom of expression. This First Amendment liberty, we have argued, produces information about government, limits corruption, protects minorities, and helps maintain a vigorous defense of the truth. But something else is at stake as well—preservation of social order; stable government; and protection of civility, decency, and reputation.

It has been left to the courts, using the Constitution, to balance these two desired goods: freedom of expression on the one hand, and social and moral order on the other. The courts have devised several rules, or tests, to try to reconcile the competing claims. Thus we have had the bad tendency test, the clear and present danger test, the *Miller* test, and revised libel laws. The tension between freedom and order lends itself not to a permanent solution, since the circumstances of American life are constantly in flux, but rather to a series of uneasy truces and revised tests.

IN YOUR OWN WORDS » Demonstrate how the protections of freedom of speech and of the press have been tested.

THE RIGHT TO BEAR ARMS
Providing for militias to secure the state or securing an individual right?

The Second Amendment to the Constitution reads, "A well-regulated militia, being necessary to the security of a free state, the right of the people to keep and bear arms, shall not be infringed." As we saw in *What's at Stake . . . ?*, this amendment has been the subject of some of the fiercest debates in American politics. Originally it was a seemingly straightforward effort by opponents of the Constitution to keep the federal government in check by limiting the power of standing, or permanent, armies. Over time it has become a rallying point for those who want to engage in

SNAPSHOT OF AMERICA: WHO OWNS THE GUNS?

Gun Laws by State

Number of regulations on gun ownership and possession

6
5
4
3
2
1
None

Carry in Public

◖ Open
◗ Concealed
◉ Both

Regulations on gun ownership and possession include: missing firearms, locking device, private sales, gun shows, long guns or rifles, and handguns.

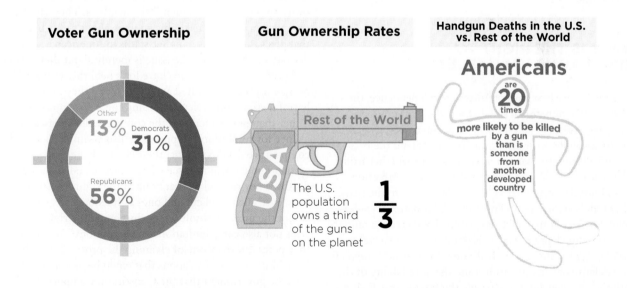

Voter Gun Ownership

Other
13%

Democrats
31%

Republicans
56%

Gun Ownership Rates

Rest of the World

USA

The U.S. population owns a third of the guns on the planet

$\frac{1}{3}$

Handgun Deaths in the U.S. vs. Rest of the World

Americans
are
20
times
more likely to be killed by a gun than is someone from another developed country

BEHIND THE NUMBERS

Liberals generally believe that more guns lead to more crime and killing, while conservatives tend to hold that guns are necessary for one's safety and to deter criminals. Notice that the states vary in regulating fire arms. Where would you feel safer? And how does comparison of the U.S. to the world inform this debate?

Source: Pew Research Center American Trends Panel April 29-May 27, 2014; Wall Street Journal, "Where is 'Open Carry' Legal?" Aug 22, 2014, blogs.wsj.com/numbers/map-where-is-open-carry-legal-1715/.

sporting activities involving guns, those who believe that firearms are necessary for self-defense, those who believe an armed citizenry is necessary to check government that might become tyrannical, and those who simply don't believe that it is government's business to make decisions about who can own guns. (See "*Snapshot of America: Who Owns the Guns?*".)

Although various kinds of gun control legislation have been passed at the state and local levels, powerful interest groups like the NRA have kept it to a minimum at the federal level. The 1990s, however, saw the passage of three federal bills that affect the right to bear arms: the 1993 Brady Bill, requiring background checks on potential handgun purchasers; the 1994 Crime Bill, barring semiautomatic assault weapons; and a 1995 bill making it illegal to carry a gun near a school. The 1995 law and the interim provisions of the Brady Bill, which imposed a five-day waiting period for all gun sales, with local background checks until a national background check system could be established, were struck down by the Supreme Court on the grounds that they were unconstitutional infringements of the national government into the realm of state power.[89] In September 2004 Congress let the ban on semiautomatic weapons expire, largely at the urging of then–House majority leader Tom DeLay. While some Democrats in Congress promised to reintroduce the ban, many members have been reluctant to act, possibly because the NRA continues to target gun control candidates for defeat in reelections.

WHY IS THE RIGHT TO BEAR ARMS VALUABLE?

During the earliest days of American independence, the chief source of national stability was the state militia system—armies of able-bodied men who could be counted on to assemble, with their own guns, to defend their country from external and internal threats, whether from the British, the Native Americans, or local insurrection. Local militias were seen as far less dangerous to the fledgling republic than a standing army under national leadership. Such an army could seize control and create a military dictatorship, depriving citizens of their hard-won rights. Madison, Hamilton, and Jay devoted five *Federalist Papers* to the defense of standing armies and the unreliability of the militia, but they did not persuade the fearful Anti-Federalists. The Second Amendment was designed to guard against just that tyranny of the federal government.

ARGUMENTS IN DEFENSE OF THE SECOND AMENDMENT TODAY The restructuring of the U.S. military, and the growing evidence that under civilian control it did not pose a threat to the liberties of American citizens, caused many people to view the Second Amendment as obsolete. But although the militia system that gave

rise to the amendment is now defunct, supporters of rights for gun owners, like the NRA, argue that the amendment is as relevant as ever. They offer at least four reasons the right to bear arms should be unregulated. First, they argue that hunting and other leisure activities involving guns do not hurt anybody (except, of course, the hunted) and are an important part of American culture. They are concerned that even the restriction of weapons not used for hunting, such as assault weapons, will harm their sport by making the idea of regulation more acceptable to Americans and starting society down the slippery slope of gun control. Second, gun rights advocates claim that possession of guns is necessary for self-defense. They believe that gun control means that only criminals, who get their guns on the black market, will be armed, making life even more dangerous. Their third argument is that citizens should have the right to arm themselves to protect their families and property from a potentially tyrannical government, just as the American revolutionaries did. Finally, advocates of unregulated gun ownership say that it is not government's business to regulate gun use. The limited government they insist the founders intended does not have the power to get involved in such questions, and any federal action is thus illegitimate.

ARGUMENTS AGAINST THE RIGHT TO BEAR ARMS Opponents of these views—such as Handgun Control, Inc., and the Coalition to Stop Gun Violence—counter that none of these claims has anything to do with the Second Amendment, which refers only to the use and ownership of guns by state militia members. They say that gun owners want to make this an issue about rights because that gives their claims a higher status in American discourse, when in fact the issue is merely about their wants and preferences. Americans have long held that wants and preferences can be limited and regulated if they have harmful effects on society. Focusing the debate on rights rather than policy increases the conflict and decreases the chance for resolution.[90] Opponents also assemble facts and comparative data to support their claims that countries with stricter gun control laws have less violence and fewer gun deaths. They remind us that none of the rights of Americans, even such fundamental ones as freedoms of speech and of the press, is absolute, so why should the right to bear arms not also carry limitations and exceptions? And, finally, they point out the irony of claiming the protection of the Constitution to own weapons that could be used to overturn the government that the Constitution supports.[91]

JUDICIAL DECISIONS

Until 2008 the Supreme Court had ruled on only a handful of cases that had an impact on gun rights and the Second Amendment, mostly interpreting the Second Amendment as intending to arm state militias, and letting state gun-related legislation stand.[92] The Supreme Court did strike down the legislation concerning possession of guns near schools and reversed one provision of the Brady Bill on federalism, not Second Amendment, grounds. In the close Brady case, four dissenters argued that the burden put on the localities was not disproportionate to the good done by addressing what they called an "epidemic of gun violence."[93] In 2004 the Court let stand a lower court's ruling that supported a California ban on assault rifles on the grounds that the Second Amendment did not protect individual gun owners. The ruling applies only to those states in the Ninth Circuit, however, and does not require a state to ban assault rifles.

In 2008, however, the Supreme Court heard arguments for the first time since 1939 on whether the Constitution guarantees an individual the right to bear arms. In a five-to-four decision, the Court held that it did, striking down a Washington, D.C., law that banned handgun possession in the home. Although the Court held that the D.C. law violated an individual's right to own a gun for self-protection, the majority was careful to say that the right to own guns is not unlimited. For instance, it does not encompass military-grade weapons, and it does not extend to felons and the mentally ill.[94] In 2010 the Court took the ruling a step further, holding not only that the federal government could not violate an individual's right to bear arms, as it had in the D.C. case, but that neither could a state government.[95]

AP Photo/Mary Altaffer

Standing Up Against "Stand Your Ground"

The Million Hoodie March in New York City was a protest against the shooting of Trayvon Martin. Martin, a black teenager wearing a hoodie, was shot and killed by neighborhood watch captain George Zimmerman, whose supporters initially argued that the killing was justified under Florida's Stand Your Ground law. The law holds that deadly force is justified if a person feels threatened with bodily harm, though Martin was armed only with candy and a soft drink. Even though Zimmerman ended up using a more conventional claim of self-defense, the event brought new attention and scrutiny to a host of such laws passed recently in several states, where supporters argue that they are protected by the Second Amendment.

PAUSE AND REVIEW:

WHO, WHAT, HOW

Some citizens want a protected right to own whatever guns they choose, and others want some regulation on what guns can be owned by private citizens. The rule that should determine who wins and who loses here is the Second Amendment, but though the Supreme Court has been fairly clear that the amendment does not confer on Americans an unqualified right to gun ownership, it also has been reluctant to allow the federal government to impose its will on the states. Consequently, the battle is played out in state legislatures and in Congress.

IN YOUR OWN WORDS ≫ Give examples of different interpretations of the Second Amendment's meaning.

THE RIGHTS OF CRIMINAL DEFENDANTS
Protecting the accused from an arbitrary government

A full half of the amendments in the Bill of Rights, and several clauses in the Constitution itself, are devoted to protecting the rights of people who are suspected or accused of committing a crime. These precautions were a particular concern for the founders, who feared an arbitrary government that could accuse and imprison people without evidence or just cause. Governments tend to do such things to shore up their power and to silence their critics. The authors of these amendments believed that, to limit government power, people needed to retain rights against government throughout the process of being accused, tried, and punished for criminal activities. Amendments Four through Eight protect people against unreasonable searches and seizures, self-incrimination, and cruel and unusual punishment, and guarantee them a right to legal advice, a speedy and public trial, and various other procedural protections.

WHY ARE THE RIGHTS OF CRIMINAL DEFENDANTS VALUABLE?

As we indicated, a primary reason for protecting the rights of the accused is to limit government power. One way governments can stop criticism of their actions is by eliminating the opposition, imprisoning them or worse. The guarantees in the Bill of Rights provide checks on government's ability to prosecute its enemies.

Another reason for guaranteeing rights to those accused of crimes is the strong tradition in American culture, coming from our English roots, that a person is innocent until proven guilty. An innocent person, naturally, still has the full protection of the Constitution, and even a guilty person is protected to some degree, for instance, against cruel and unusual punishment. All Americans are entitled to what the Fifth and Fourteenth Amendments call due process of law. **Due process of law** means that laws must be reasonable and fair, and that those accused of breaking the law, and who stand to lose life, liberty, or property as a consequence, have the right to appear before their judges to hear the charges and evidence against them, to have legal counsel, and to present any contradictory evidence in their defense. Due process means essentially that those accused of a crime have a right to a fair trial.

During the 1960s and 1970s the Supreme Court expanded the protection of the rights of the accused and incorporated them so that the states had to protect them as well. And yet the more conservative 1980s and 1990s witnessed a considerable backlash against a legal system perceived as having gone soft on crime—overly concerned with the rights of criminals at the expense of safe streets, neighborhoods, and cities, and deaf to the claims of victims of violent crimes. We want to protect the innocent, but when the seemingly guilty go free because of a "technicality," the public is often incensed. The Supreme Court has had the heavy responsibility of drawing the line between the rights of defendants and the rights of society. We can look at the Court's deliberations on these matters in four main areas: the protection against unreasonable searches and seizures, the protection against self-incrimination, the right to counsel, and the protection against cruel and unusual punishment.

PROTECTION AGAINST UNREASONABLE SEARCHES AND SEIZURES

The Fourth Amendment says,

The right of the people to be secure in their persons, houses, papers, and effects, against unreasonable searches and seizures, shall not be violated, and no warrants shall issue but upon probable cause, supported by oath or affirmation, and particularly describing the place to be searched, and the persons or things to be seized.

The founders were particularly sensitive on this question because the king of England had had the right to order the homes of his subjects searched without cause, looking for any evidence of criminal activity. For the most part this amendment has been interpreted by the Court to mean that a person's home is private and cannot be invaded by police without a warrant, obtainable only if they have very good reason to think that criminal evidence lies within.

WHAT'S REASONABLE? Under the Fourth Amendment, there are a few exceptions to the rule that searches require warrants. Automobiles present a special case, for example, since by their nature they are likely to be gone by the time an officer appears with a warrant. Cars can be searched without warrants if the officer has probable cause to think a law has been broken, and the Court has gradually widened the scope of the search so that it can include luggage or closed containers in the car.

Modern innovations like wiretapping and electronic surveillance presented more difficult problems for the Court because previous law had not allowed for them. A "search" was understood legally to require some physical trespass, and a "seizure" involved taking some tangible object. Listening in on a conversation—electronically from afar—was simply not covered by the law. In fact, in the first case in which it was addressed, the Court held that bugging did not constitute a search.[96] That ruling held for forty years, until the case of *Katz v. United States* (1967), when it was overturned by a Court that required, for the first time, that a warrant be obtained before phones could be tapped.[97] In the same year, the Court ruled that conversations were included under Fourth Amendment protection.[98] A search warrant is thus needed in order to tap a phone, although, as we noted earlier, the 2001 Patriot Act makes it a good deal easier to get a warrant.

Physical searches of cell phones have also presented a modern conundrum for the courts, as cell phones have been considered to be part of the content of one's pockets, which the Supreme Court had determined could be legally searched. But in 2014, writing for a unanimous Court, Chief Justice John Roberts acknowledged that "[t]he average smartphone user has installed 33 apps which together can form a revealing montage of the user's life." Thus, our phones are "mini-computers" that contain the same kind of information about us that our houses have

> **due process of law** guarantee that laws will be fair and reasonable and that citizens suspected of breaking the law will be treated fairly

traditionally contained, and just as our houses cannot be searched without a warrant, now neither can our cell phones (at least most of the time). It bears repeating, however, that warrants are not that hard to come by, so people who store information they prefer to keep private on their cell phones or computers should in general be cautious.[99]

Yet another modern area in which the Court has had to determine the legality of searches is mandatory random testing for drug or alcohol use, usually by urine or blood tests. These are arguably a very unreasonable kind of search, but the Court has tended to allow them where the violation of privacy is outweighed by a good purpose, for instance, discovering the cause of a train accident,[100] preventing drug use in schools,[101] or preserving the public safety by requiring drug tests of train conductors and airline pilots.

Finally, in 2012 the Court held, five to four, that the Fourth Amendment is not violated by the requirement that someone arrested for a minor infraction and not suspected of concealing a weapon or drugs could nonetheless be subjected to an invasive strip search. In *Florence v. Board of Chosen Freeholders of County of Burlington*, the majority ruled that the plaintiff could be subject to a strip search even though he had been arrested for something that he had not in fact done and that would not have been a crime in any case. The key issue was that the plaintiff was going to be held in the general jail population, and correctional officers are rightly concerned with jail security, which outweighs an individual's privacy rights.[102]

THE EXCLUSIONARY RULE By far the most controversial part of the Fourth Amendment rulings has been the exclusionary rule. In a 1914 case, *Weeks v. United States*, the Court confronted the question of what to do with evidence that had, in fact, been obtained illegally. It decided that such evidence should be excluded from use in the defendant's trial.[103] This **exclusionary rule**, as it came to be known, meant that even though the police might have concrete evidence of criminal activity, if obtained unlawfully, it could not be used to gain a conviction of the culprit.

The exclusionary rule has been controversial from the start. In some countries, including England, illegally obtained evidence can be used at trial, but the defendant is allowed to sue the police in a civil suit or bring criminal charges against them. The object is clearly to deter misbehavior on the part of the police, while not allowing guilty people to go free. But the exclusionary rule, while it does serve as a deterrent to police, helps criminals avoid punishment. The Court itself has occasionally seemed uneasy about the rule. When the Fourth Amendment was incorporated, in *Wolf v. Colorado*, the exclusionary rule was not extended to the states. The Court ruled that it was a judicial creation, not a constitutionally protected right.[104] Not until the 1961 case of *Mapp v. Ohio* was the exclusionary rule finally incorporated into state as well as federal practice.[105]

But extending the reach of the exclusionary rule did not end the controversy. While the Warren Court (1953–1969) continued to uphold it, the Burger and Rehnquist Courts (1969–2005) cut back on the protections it offers. In 1974 they ruled that the exclusionary rule was to be a deterrent to abuse by the police, not a constitutional right of the accused.[106] The Court subsequently ruled that illegally seized evidence could be used in civil trials[107] and came to carve out what it called a *good faith exception*, whereby evidence is admitted to a criminal trial, even if obtained illegally, if the police are relying on a warrant that appears to be valid at the time or on a law that appears to be constitutional (though either may turn out to be defective),[108] or on a warrant that is obtained in error. In 2009 the Roberts Court ruled that to trigger the exclusionary rule, the police conduct must be deliberate.[109] The Court's

> **exclusionary rule** rule created by the Supreme Court that evidence seized illegally may not be used to obtain a conviction

more conservative turn on this issue has not silenced the debate, however. Some observers are appalled at the reduction in the protection of individual rights, whereas others do not believe that the Court has gone far enough in protecting society against criminals.

PROTECTION AGAINST SELF-INCRIMINATION

No less controversial than the rulings on illegally seized evidence are the Court's decisions on unconstitutionally obtained confessions. The Fifth Amendment provides for a number of protections for individuals, among them that no person "shall be compelled in any criminal case to be a witness against himself." The Supreme Court has expanded the scope of the protection against self-incrimination from criminal trials, as the amendment dictates, to grand jury proceedings, legislative investigations, and even police interrogations. It is this last extension that has proved most controversial.

Court rulings in the early 1900s ordered that police could not coerce confessions, but they did not provide any clear rule for police about what confessions would be admissible. Instead the Court used a case-by-case scrutiny that depended on "the totality of the circumstances" to determine whether confessions had been made voluntarily. This approach was not very helpful to police in the streets trying to make arrests and conduct investigations that would later hold up in court. In 1966 the Warren Court ruled, in *Miranda v. Arizona*, that police had to inform suspects of their rights to remain silent and to have a lawyer present during questioning to prevent them from incriminating themselves. The *Miranda* rights are familiar to viewers of police dramas: "You have the right to remain silent. Anything you say can and will be used against you . . . ." If a lawyer could show that a defendant had not been "read" his or her rights, information gained in the police interrogation would not be admissible in court. Like the exclusionary rule, the *Miranda* ruling could and did result in criminals going free even though the evidence existed to convict them.

Reacting to public and political accusations that the Warren Court was soft on crime, Congress passed the Crime Control and Safe Streets Act of 1968, which allowed confessions to be used in federal courts not according to the *Miranda* ruling but according to the old "totality of the circumstances" rule. *Miranda* was still effective in the states, however. Vowing to change the liberal tenor of the Warren Court, 1968 presidential candidate Richard Nixon pledged to appoint more conservative justices. True to his campaign promise, once elected he appointed Warren Burger as chief justice. Under the Burger Court, and later the Rehnquist Court, the justices have backed off the *Miranda* decision to some degree. In 2000, despite the fact that some justices had been highly

Rights of the Accused

Clarence Earl Gideon spent much of his time in prison studying the law. His handwritten appeal to the Supreme Court resulted in the landmark decision *Gideon v. Wainwright,* which granted those accused of state crimes the right to counsel.

critical of the *Miranda* ruling over the years, the Court upheld the 1966 decision, stating that it had become an established part of the culture, and held the 1968 Crime Control Act to be unconstitutional.[110]

RIGHT TO COUNSEL

Closely related to the *Miranda* decision, which upholds the right to have a lawyer present during police questioning, is the Sixth Amendment declaration that the accused shall "have the assistance of counsel for his defense." The founders' intentions on this amendment are fairly clear from the 1790 Federal Crimes Act, which required courts to provide counsel for poor defendants only in capital cases—that is, in those punishable by death. Defendants in other trials had a right to counsel, but the government had no obligation to provide it. The Court's

SNAPSHOT OF AMERICA: WHERE DO WE STAND ON CAPITAL PUNISHMENT?

U.S. Execution Rates

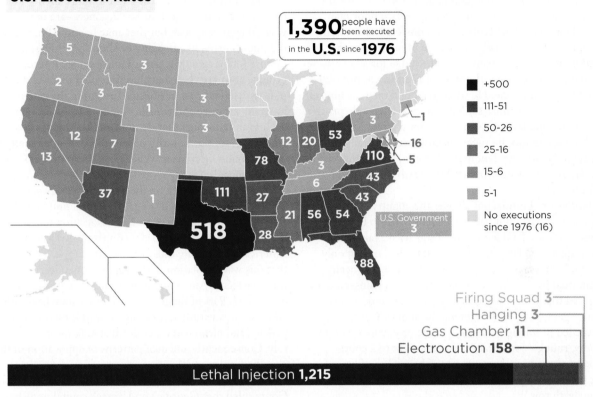

1,390 people have been executed in the **U.S.** since **1976**

■	+500
■	111-51
■	50-26
■	25-16
■	15-6
■	5-1
■	No executions since 1976 (16)

Firing Squad **3**
Hanging **3**
Gas Chamber **11**
Electrocution **158**

Lethal Injection **1,215**

For and Against Capital Punishment Over Time

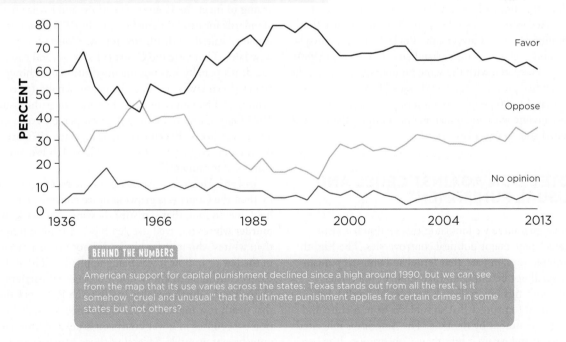

Favor

Oppose

No opinion

BEHIND THE NUMBERS

American support for capital punishment declined since a high around 1990, but we can see from the map that its use varies across the states: Texas stands out from all the rest. Is it somehow "cruel and unusual" that the ultimate punishment applies for certain crimes in some states but not others?

Source: Death Penalty Information Center, Facts about the Death Penalty, updated October 29, 2014, www.deathpenaltyinfo.org/documents/FactSheet.pdf.

decisions were in line with that act until 1938, when in *Johnson v. Zerbst* it extended the government's obligation to provide counsel to impoverished defendants in all criminal proceedings in federal courts.[111] Only federal crimes, however, carried that obligation, until 1963. In one of the most dramatic tales of courtroom appeals, a poor man named Clarence Earl Gideon was convicted of breaking and entering a pool hall and stealing money from the vending machine. Gideon asked the judge for a lawyer, but the judge told him that the state of Florida was not obligated to give him one. He tried to defend the case himself but lost to the far more skilled and knowledgeable prosecutor. Serving five years in prison for a crime he swore he did not commit, he filed a handwritten appeal with the Supreme Court. In a landmark decision, *Gideon v. Wainwright*, the Court incorporated the Sixth Amendment right to counsel.[112]

Not just in Florida, but all over the country, poor people in prison who had not had legal counsel had to be tried again or released. Gideon himself was tried again with a court-appointed lawyer, who proved to the jury not only that Gideon was innocent but that the crime had been committed by the chief witness against him. Conservatives believed that *Gideon* went far beyond the founders' intentions. Again, both the Burger and Rehnquist Courts succeeded in rolling back some of the protections won by *Gideon*, ruling—for instance, that the right to a court-appointed attorney does not extend beyond the filing of one round of appeals, even if the convicted indigent person is on death row.[113]

Though the right to counsel is now seen by most people as an essential right, many argue that this right is in reality often violated because of overworked public defenders or state laws that limit who can receive court-appointed counsel. According to a study by the National Association of Criminal Defense Lawyers, the Bucks County, Pennsylvania, public defender's office handled 4,173 cases in 1980. "Twenty years later, with the same number of attorneys, the office handled an estimated 8,000 cases." In Wisconsin, "more than 11,000 people go unrepresented annually because anyone with an annual income of more than $3,000 is deemed able to pay a lawyer."[114]

PROTECTION AGAINST CRUEL AND UNUSUAL PUNISHMENT

The final guarantee we look at in this section has also generated some major political controversies. The Eighth Amendment says, in part, that "cruel and unusual punishments" shall not be inflicted. Like some of the earlier amendments, this one reflects a concern of English law, which sought to protect British subjects from torture and inhumane treatment by the king. The Americans inherited the concern and wrote it into their Constitution. It is easy to see why it would be controversial, however. What is

"cruel"? And what is "unusual"? Can we protect American citizens from cruel and unusual punishment delivered in other countries?

The Court has ruled that not all unusual punishments are unconstitutional, because all new punishments—electrocution or lethal injection, for instance—are unusual when they first appear, but they may be more humane than old punishments like hanging or shooting.[115] Despite intense lobbying on the part of impassioned interest groups, however, the Court has not ruled that the death penalty itself is cruel or unusual (except in the case of mentally retarded individuals,[116] juveniles,[117] and crimes against an individual that do not result in the death of the victim[118]), and the majority of states have death penalty laws (see "*Snapshot of America:* Where Do We Stand on Capital Punishment?").

The strongest attack on the death penalty began in the 1970s, when the NAACP Legal Defense Fund joined with the ACLU and the American Bar Association to argue that the death penalty was disproportionately given to African Americans, especially those convicted of rape. They argued that this was a violation of the Eighth Amendment, and also the Fourteenth Amendment guarantee of equal protection of the laws. Part of the problem was that state laws differed about what constituted grounds for imposing the death penalty, and juries had no uniform standards on which to rely. Consequently, unequal patterns of application of the penalty developed.

In *Furman v. Georgia* (1972) and two related cases, the Court ruled that Georgia's and Texas's capital punishment laws were unconstitutional, but the justices were so far from agreement that they all filed separate opinions, totaling 231 pages.[119] Thirty-five states passed new laws trying to meet the Court's objections and to clarify the standards for capital punishment. By 1976 six hundred inmates waited on death row for the Court to approve the new laws. That year the Court ruled in several cases that the death penalty was not unconstitutional, although it struck down laws requiring the death penalty for certain crimes.[120] The Court remained divided over the issue. In 1977 Gary Gilmore became the first person executed after a ten-year break. Executions by state since 1976 are detailed in "*Snapshot of America*: Where Do We Stand on Capital Punishment?"

In 1987 *McClesky v. Kemp* raised the race issue again, but by then the Court was growing more conservative.[121] It held, five to four, that statistics showing that blacks who murder whites received the death penalty more frequently than whites who murder blacks did not prove a racial bias in the law or in how it was being applied.[122] The Rehnquist Court continued to knock down procedural barriers to imposing the death penalty. In 2006 the Roberts Court held that death row inmates could challenge state lethal injection procedures in lower courts on cruel and unusual punishment grounds. Several of those courts came to different conclusions. In 2008, in *Baze v. Rees*,[123] the

Supreme Court upheld Kentucky's lethal injection practice, and other states, waiting for a sign from the Court, went ahead with their own practices.

In recent years public support for capital punishment appears to be softening, not because of opposition in principle but because of fears that the system might be putting innocent people on death row. This feeling grew as DNA testing cleared some death row residents, and careful investigation showed that others, too, were innocent. After thirteen death row convicts in his state were exonerated between 1977 and 2000, Illinois governor George Ryan, a moderate Republican who supported the death penalty in principle, called for a statewide halt to executions. "I cannot support a system, which, in its administration, has proven so fraught with error," Ryan explained, "and has come so close to the ultimate nightmare, the state's taking of an innocent life."[124] Following his lead, then–Maryland governor Parris Glendening issued a moratorium in 2002, but that action was quickly reversed by the new governor, Robert Ehrlich, in January 2003. In 2007 the New Jersey legislature banned the death penalty in the state—the first state to do so since the Supreme Court declared capital punishment constitutional in 1976.[125]

Despite misgivings, the American public continues to favor capital punishment. In 2009 a Gallup poll found 65 percent of the public supporting the death penalty, with 31 percent opposed, even though only 57 percent thought that it was applied fairly.[126]

PAUSE AND REVIEW:

WHO, WHAT, HOW

Every citizen has a huge stake in the protection of the rights of criminal defendants. If the government were allowed to arrest, imprison, and punish citizens at will, without legal protections, in secrecy, and without record, then all of us, criminal or not, would be vulnerable to persecution, perhaps for who we are, how we vote, what we say, or what we believe. It is the rules of due process that protect us from an unpredictable and unaccountable legal system.

IN YOUR OWN WORDS »» Describe the protections afforded criminal defendants under the Constitution.

THE RIGHT TO PRIVACY
The personal meets the political

One of the most controversial rights in America is not even mentioned in the Constitution or the Bill of Rights: the right to privacy. This right is at the heart of one of the deepest divisions in American politics, the split over abortion rights, and is fundamental to two other controversial areas of civil liberties: gay rights and the right to die.

WHY IS THE RIGHT TO PRIVACY VALUABLE?

Although the right to privacy is not spelled out in the Bill of Rights, it goes hand in hand with the founders' insistence on limited government. Their goal was to keep government from getting too powerful and interfering with the lives and affairs of individual citizens. They certainly implied a right to privacy, and perhaps even assumed such a right, but they did not make it explicit.

The right to privacy, to be left alone to do what we want, is so obviously desirable that it scarcely needs a defense. The problem, of course, is that a right to privacy without any limits is anarchy, the absence of government altogether. Clearly governments have an interest in preventing some kinds of individual behavior—murder, theft, and rape, for example. But what about more subtle behaviors that do not directly affect the public safety but arguably have serious consequences for the public good, like prostitution, drug use, gambling, and even, to take the example we used earlier in this chapter, riding a motorcycle without a helmet? Should these behaviors fall under a right to privacy, or should the state be able to regulate them? The specific issues the Court has dealt with related to this topic are contraception use and abortion, laws restricting the behavior of homosexuals, and laws preventing terminally ill patients from ending their lives.

A right to privacy per se did not enter the American legal system until 1890, when an article called "The Right to Privacy" appeared in the *Harvard Law Review*.[127] In the years after the article appeared, states began to add a privacy right to their own bodies of statutory or constitutional law. The Supreme Court had dealt with privacy in some respects when it ruled on cases under the Fourth and Fifth Amendments, but it did not "discover" a right to privacy until 1965, and whether such a right exists remains controversial. None of the rights guaranteed by the first ten amendments to the Constitution is absolute. All, as we have seen, include limitations and contradictions. The right to privacy, without firm constitutional authority, is the least certain of all.

REPRODUCTIVE RIGHTS

Throughout the 1940s, people had tried to challenge state laws that made it a crime to use birth control, or even to give out information about how to prevent pregnancies. The Supreme Court routinely refused to hear these challenges until the 1965 case of *Griswold v. Connecticut*.

*"If I wanted the government in my body,
I would have asked it out on a date."*

Privacy Versus Morality

Many issues that deal with issues of privacy, such as abortion, sexual orientation, and the right to die, also engender strong moral values among people who want government to enforce those views. Thwarted by the Supreme Court in their attempt to outlaw abortion, conservative Republicans in the Virginia legislature passed a law requiring an invasive and medically unnecessary transvaginal ultrasound as a condition for obtaining an abortion. Privacy rights proponents objected.

Connecticut had a law on its books making it illegal to use contraceptive devices or to distribute information about them. Under that law, Estelle Griswold, the Connecticut director of Planned Parenthood, was convicted and fined $100 for counseling married couples about birth control.

The Court held that while the right to privacy is not explicit in the Constitution, a number of other rights, notably those in Amendments One, Three, Four, Five, and Nine, create a "zone of privacy" in which lie marriage and the decision to use contraception. It said that the specific guarantees in the Bill of Rights have "penumbras," or outlying shadowy areas, in which can be found a right to privacy. The Fourteenth Amendment applies that right to the states, and so Connecticut's law was unconstitutional.[128] In 1972 the Court extended the ruling to cover the rights of unmarried people to use contraception as well.[129]

Because of the Court's insistence that reproductive matters are not the concern of the government, abortion rights advocates saw an opportunity to use the *Griswold* ruling to strike down state laws prohibiting or limiting abortion. Until the Civil War, such laws were uncommon; most states allowed abortions in the early stages of pregnancy. After the war, however, opinion turned, and by 1910 every state except Kentucky had made abortions illegal. In the 1960s, legislation was again becoming more liberal, but abortions were still unobtainable in many places.

The Court had tried to avoid ruling on the abortion issue, but by 1973 it had become hard to escape. In *Roe v. Wade* the justices held that the right to privacy did indeed encompass the right to abortion. It tried to balance a woman's right to privacy in reproductive matters with the state's interest in protecting human life, however, by treating the three trimesters of pregnancy differently. In the first three months of pregnancy, it held, there can be no compelling state interest that offsets a woman's privacy rights. In the second three months, the state can regulate access to abortions if it does so reasonably. In the last trimester, the state's interest becomes far more compelling, and a state can limit or even prohibit abortions as long as the mother's life is not in danger.[130]

The *Roe* decision launched the United States into an intense and divisive battle over abortion. States continued to try to limit abortions by requiring the consent of husbands or parents, by outlawing clinic advertising, by imposing waiting periods, and by erecting other roadblocks. The Court struck down most of these efforts, at least until 1977, when it allowed some state limitations. But the battle was not confined to statehouses. Congress, having failed to pass a constitutional amendment banning abortions, passed over thirty laws restricting access to abortions in various ways. For instance, it limited federal funding for abortions through Medicaid, a move the Supreme Court upheld in 1980.[131] Presidents got into the fray as well. President Reagan and the first President Bush were staunch opponents of *Roe* and worked hard to get it overturned. Reagan appointed only antiabortion judges to federal courts, and his administration was active in pushing litigation that would challenge *Roe*.

The balance on the Supreme Court was crucial. *Roe* had been decided by a seven-to-two vote, but many in the majority were facing retirement. When Warren Burger retired, Reagan elevated William Rehnquist, one of the two dissenters, to chief justice, and appointed conservative Antonin Scalia in his place. Reagan's appointees did finally move the Court in a more conservative direction, but even they did not overturn *Roe*. The 1973 ruling has been limited in some ways, but Rehnquist did not succeed in gathering a majority to strike it down.[132] In 2007 the Roberts Court moved to uphold a ban on partial-birth abortion, but it has not signaled that it would overturn *Roe*.[133]

The debate over reproductive rights in this country is certainly not over. Indeed, all the vitriolic debate that surrounded the 2014 *Hobby Lobby* case shows that even the idea that contraception use is entirely a matter of private conscience is not wholly settled. Rejection of the notion that there is a constitutional right to privacy has long been a rallying point for the Christian Right, which has become a powerful part of the Republican Party. And while some Democrats also oppose abortion rights, abortion has become largely a partisan issue. Since 1980 the Republicans have included a commitment to a constitutional amendment banning abortion in their presidential party platform. Unable to effect change at a national level, many have directed their efforts to the states. One strategy, pursued by right-to-life groups in Colorado, Mississippi, Oklahoma, and others, is the attempt to pass personhood amendments that would define life as beginning from the moment of conception, creating a legal person possessing citizenship rights. Such amendments would have the effect of making abortion illegal, but also, opponents fear, some forms of birth control and the disposal of fertilized eggs after in vitro fertilization processes.[134] While no such amendment has yet passed, and while the Oklahoma Supreme Court declared the proposed amendment in that state to be unconstitutional, the strategy continues to have enthusiastic supporters. In addition, a number of state legislatures have focused on making abortions harder to obtain, or more emotionally difficult for women (for instance, by requiring them to view a mandatory ultrasound of the fetus).[135] With Americans nearly evenly split on the question of abortion, it is likely to remain a hot-button issue in American politics for some time to come.[136]

GAY RIGHTS

The *Griswold* and *Roe* rulings have opened up a variety of difficult issues for the Supreme Court. If there is a right to privacy, what might be included under it? On the whole, the Court has been very restrictive in expanding it beyond the reproductive rights of the original cases. Most controversial was its ruling in *Bowers v. Hardwick* (1986).[137]

Michael Hardwick was arrested under a Georgia law outlawing heterosexual and homosexual sodomy. A police officer, seeking to arrest him for failing to show up in court on a minor matter, was let into Hardwick's house by a friend and directed to his room. When the officer entered, he found Hardwick in bed with another man, and arrested him. Hardwick challenged the law (although he wasn't prosecuted under it), claiming that it violated his right to privacy. The Court disagreed. Looking at the case from the perspective of whether there was a constitutional right to engage in sodomy, rather than from the dissenting view that what took place between consenting adults was a private matter, the Court held five to four that the state of Georgia had a legitimate interest in regulating such behavior.

Justice Lewis Powell, who provided the fifth vote for the majority, said after his retirement that he regretted his vote in the *Bowers* decision, but by then, of course, it was too late. Several states were critical of the Court's ruling. Kentucky's Supreme Court went so far in 1992 as to strike down the state's sodomy law as unconstitutional on the grounds the U.S. Supreme Court refused to use.[138] The Georgia Supreme Court itself struck down Georgia's sodomy law in 1998 on privacy grounds, but in a case involving heterosexual rather than homosexual activity. Not until 2003, in *Lawrence v. Texas*, did the Court, in a six-to-three decision, finally overturn *Bowers* on privacy grounds.[139] Interestingly, despite its longtime reluctance to overturn *Bowers*, the Court in 1996 used the equal protection clause of the Fourteenth Amendment to strike down a Colorado law that would have made it difficult for gays to use the Colorado courts to fight discrimination, and it has used that logic in subsequent cases, as we will see in Chapter 6.[140] Thus the Court can pursue several constitutional avenues to expand the rights of gay Americans, should it want to do so.

THE RIGHT TO DIE

A final right-to-privacy issue that has stirred up controversy for the Court is the so-called right to die. In 1990 the Court ruled on the case of Nancy Cruzan, a woman who had been in a vegetative state and on life-support systems since she was in a car accident in 1983. Her parents asked the doctors to withdraw the life support and allow her to die, but the state of Missouri, claiming an interest in protecting the "sanctity of human life," blocked their request. The Cruzans argued that the right to privacy included the right to die without state interference, but the Court upheld Missouri's position, saying it was unclear that Nancy's wishes in the matter could be known for sure but that when such wishes were made clear, either in person or via a living will, a person's right to terminate medical treatment was protected under the Fourteenth Amendment's due process clause.[141]

The right-to-die issue surged back into national prominence in 2005 through a case involving Terri Schiavo, a young woman who had been in a persistent vegetative state for more than fifteen years. Claiming that Schiavo had not wished to be kept alive by artificial measures, her husband asked a state court to have her feeding tube removed. Her parents challenged the decision, but after numerous appeals the court ordered the tube removed in accordance with the precedent set in the Cruzan case. Social conservatives in Congress tried to block the action, but all federal courts, including the Supreme Court, refused to intervene and Schiavo died soon after. Angered by their inability to overturn the state court ruling, conservative groups vowed to fight for federal judicial appointees who would be more likely to intervene in such cases.

The Schiavo case did not change the prevailing legal principles—that this is a matter for individuals to decide and that when their wishes are known they should be respected by the doctors and the courts. In this matter, at least, public opinion seems to be consistent with the law. Polls showed the public strongly opposed to Congress' intervention to prevent Schiavo's death, and large majorities supported the removal of her feeding tube. In the wake of the case, 70 percent of Americans said they were thinking about getting their own living wills.[142]

The question of a person's right to suspend treatment is different from another legal issue—whether individuals have the right to have assistance ending their lives when they are terminally ill and in severe pain. Proponents of this right argue that patients should be able to decide whether to continue living with their conditions, and since such patients are frequently incapacitated or lack the means to end their lives painlessly, they are entitled to help if they want to die. Opponents, on the other hand, say a patient's right to die may require doctors to violate their Hippocratic Oath, and that it is open to abuse. Patients, especially those whose illnesses are chronic and costly, might feel obligated to end their lives out of concern for family or financial matters. In 1997 the Supreme Court ruled that the issue be left to the states and left open the possibility that dying patients might be able to make a claim to a constitutional right to die in the future.[143]

Oregon provided the first test of this policy. In 1997 it passed a referendum allowing doctors under certain circumstances to provide lethal doses of medication to enable terminally ill patients to end their lives. In late 2001 U.S. attorney general John Ashcroft effectively blocked the law by announcing that doctors who participated in assisted suicides would lose their licenses to prescribe federally regulated medications, an essential part of medical practice. In 2004 a federal appellate court ruled that Ashcroft overstepped his authority under federal law, and in early 2006 the Supreme Court upheld the Oregon law.

PAUSE AND REVIEW:

WHO, WHAT, HOW

What's at stake in the right to privacy seems amazingly simple, given the intensity of the debate about it. In short, the issue is whether citizens have the right to control their own bodies in fundamentally intimate matters like birth, sex, and death. The controversy arises when opponents argue that citizens do not have that right, but rather should be subject to religious rules, natural laws, or moral beliefs that dictate certain behaviors with respect to these matters. They promote legislation and constitutional amendments that seek to bring behavior into conformity with their beliefs. The founders did not act to protect this right, possibly because they did not anticipate that they had created a government strong enough to tell people what to do in such personal matters, or possibly because technology has put choices on the table today that did not exist more than two hundred years ago. In the absence of constitutional protection or prohibition of the right to privacy, the rule that provides for it today derives from a series of Court cases that could just as easily be overturned should the Court change its mind.

IN YOUR OWN WORDS » Discuss the extent of an individual's right to privacy.

» THE CITIZENS AND CIVIL LIBERTIES
Individual rights yield a collective benefit

In the United States we are accustomed to thinking about citizenship as a status that confers on us certain rights. We have explored many of those rights in detail in this chapter. But as we stand back and ask ourselves why each of these rights is valuable, an interesting irony appears. Even though these are *individual* rights, valued for granting freedoms to individuals and allowing them to make claims on their government, we value them also because they lead to *collective* benefits—we are better off as a society if individuals possess these rights. Democratic government is preserved if criticism is allowed; religion can prosper if it is not entangled in politics; militias may defend the security of a free state if individual citizens are armed; and justice will be available to all if it is guaranteed to each.

The collective as well as the individual nature of American civil liberties recalls the argument we made in Chapter 1 that there are two strands of thinking about citizenship in the United States—one focused on individual rights and the self-interest of citizens and the other emphasizing obligations or duties seen as necessary to protect the public interest. We said these traditions have existed side by side throughout our history. They have done so because neither can exist solely by itself in a democracy: obligation without rights is an authoritarian dictatorship, and rights without obligation lead to a state of nature, anarchy, with no government at all. Citizenship in a democracy plainly carries both rights and duties.

The final section of a chapter on civil liberties is an interesting place to speculate about the duties attached to American citizenship. We have explored the Bill of Rights. What might a Bill of Obligations look like? The Constitution itself suggests the basics. Obligations are very much the flip side of rights; for every right guaranteed, there is a corresponding duty to use it. For instance, the provisions for elected office and the right to vote imply a duty to vote. Congress is authorized to collect taxes, duties, and excises, including an income tax; citizens are obligated to pay those taxes. Congress can raise and support armies, provide and maintain a navy, provide for and govern militias; correspondingly, Americans have a duty to serve in the military. The Constitution defines treason as waging war against the states or aiding or abetting their enemies; citizens have an obligation not to betray their country or state. Amendments Five and Six guarantee grand juries and jury trials to those accused of crimes; it is citizens who must serve on those juries.

THINKING OUTSIDE THE BOX

Should the founders have provided a Bill of Obligations as well as a Bill of Rights?

As citizenship obligations around the world go, these are not terribly onerous. In Europe such obligations are explicitly extended to include providing for the welfare of those who cannot take care of themselves, for instance. Tax burdens are much higher in most other industrialized nations than they are in the United States. In some countries the obligation to vote is enforced legally, and others have mandatory military service for all citizens, or at least all male citizens.

Still, many people find the obligations associated with American citizenship to be too harsh. For instance, two *Wall Street Journal* reporters wrote, "We [Americans] are a nation of law breakers. We exaggerate tax-deductible expenses, lie to customs officials, bet on card games and sports events, disregard jury notices, drive while intoxicated . . . and hire illegal child care workers . . . . Nearly all people violate some laws, and many run afoul of dozens without ever being considered or considering themselves criminals."[144] While 90 percent of Americans value their right to a trial by jury, only 12 percent are willing to accept the jury duty that makes that right possible.[145] We have already seen that voter turnout in the United States falls far behind that in most other nations.

How much fulfillment of political obligation is enough? Most Americans clearly obey most of the laws, most of the time. When there is a war and a military draft, most draft-aged males have agreed to serve. If we do not pay all the taxes we owe, we pay much of them. If we do not vote, we get involved in our communities in countless other ways. As a nation, we are certainly getting by, at least for now. But perhaps we should consider the long-term political consequences to a democratic republic if the emphasis on preserving civil liberties is not balanced by a corresponding commitment to fulfilling political obligations.

IN YOUR OWN WORDS >> Compare the idea of civil rights with that of civil obligations.

LET'S REVISIT: WHAT'S AT STAKE...

We began this chapter with the mass shootings at Sandy Hook Elementary School. We asked how a concerted effort by a newly reelected president of the United States, with the backing of the public and multiple interest groups and, at least initially, much of Congress, could have yielded so little in the way of results at the national level.

For so much effort to have yielded so little, clearly the stakes must be very high indeed. We saw in this chapter that the advocates of gun ownership have been careful to couch their arguments in Second Amendment terms—if they are defending a fundamental right, their claims have more weight than if they are merely defending their right to participate in a hobby they enjoy but that has fatal consequences when it gets out of hand. Still, there are other staunch defenders of their right to do something—to keep

100 percent of their income, let's say, or to marry multiple spouses, or to drive their vehicles along the highway at 150 miles an hour—who have to give way to claims of public safety or the general welfare.

Why are gun owners not among these?

Let's go back to the days after Sandy Hook.

There was President Obama, standing before the families of the kids who had been shot, promising that:

> In the coming weeks, I'll use whatever power this office holds to engage my fellow citizens, from law enforcement, to mental health professionals, to parents and educators, in an effort aimed at preventing more tragedies like this, because what choice do we have? We can't accept events like this as routine.

"Are we really prepared to say that we're powerless in the face of such carnage, that the politics are too hard?" he asked. "Are we prepared to say that such violence visited on our children year after year after year is somehow the price of our freedom?"[146]

At the same time, the response of the leaders of the National Rifle Association (NRA) was to decry the violence and argue that there should be armed patrols at schools to prevent it. Said the group's CEO, Wayne LaPierre: "The only way to stop a bad guy with a gun is with a good guy with a gun. I call on Congress today to appropriate whatever is necessary to put armed police officers in every single school in this nation." Rather than accept the idea that easy access to assault weapons had made the Sandy Hook massacre possible, LaPierre instead blamed the entertainment industry, which he called, with no conscious irony, "a callous, corrupt, shadow industry that sows violence against its own people," specifically mentioning games like Grand Theft Auto and films like *Natural Born Killers* and *American Pyscho*.[147]

On the one hand, the president, the vice president, many of their party, and a majority of the public had at stake solving a public policy problem that has long plagued the United States. Deaths by handguns in this country, as we have seen, outpace those of most other places, and guns are so much a part of the culture that in some states they can now be carried legally in bars and churches.

For former congresswoman Gabby Giffords, and former mayor Michael Bloomberg, and for all of the others willing to put their time and their resources behind the push to end gun violence, the stakes were winning a fight that had been personally costly to them, or was deeply important for ideological reasons.

But for the NRA the stakes in this battle are existential—if the NRA is no longer seen as the stalwart and unyielding defender of Americans' inviolable right to own guns, it loses power over the bulk of the Republican Party and even some Democrats; and once it loses its appearance of power, it will have lost something irretrievable. As *Business Insider* says, the NRA is "a juggernaut of influence in Washington" because it is simultaneously "a lobbying firm, a campaign operation, a popular social club, a generous benefactor and an industry group."[148] In part, its strength comes from its members, not because they are a majority of Americans, but because they are an intense minority, passionately committed to their cause, ready to mobilize, and unwilling to tolerate any compromise in the protection of what they believe is an essential right.

In the end, the NRA prevailed, as it has consistently in the thirty years since becoming politically active in American politics. On April 17, 2013, the watered-down bill that had reached the Senate floor fell on the basis of its requirement to expand background checks on gun purchasers, to ensure that those with mental health issues or criminal backgrounds cannot purchase guns, and its provision to renew the ban on the purchase of assault weapons that expired in 2004. The NRA said the background checks would lead to the creation of a gun registry, something it adamantly opposes.

Frustrated and angry, President Obama pointed out that the bill explicitly banned the creation of such a registry, but added that members of Congress were "worried that the gun lobby would spend a lot of money and paint them as anti–Second Amendment. And obviously a lot of Republicans had that fear, but Democrats had that fear, too. And so they caved to the pressure. And they started looking for an excuse, any excuse to vote 'no.'"[149]

And so they did, as they had so many times before.

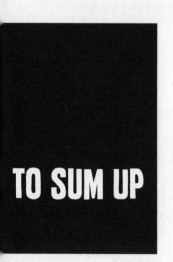

TO SUM UP

Sharpen your skills with **SAGE edge** at http://edge.sagepub.com/ barbour7e. **SAGE edge for students** provides a personalized approach to help you accomplish your coursework goals in an easy-to-use learning environment.

Rights in a Democracy

Our civil liberties are individual freedoms that place limitations on the power of government. Most of these rights are spelled out in the text of the Constitution or in its first ten amendments, the Bill of Rights, but some have developed over the years through judicial decision making.

Sometimes rights conflict, and when they do, government, guided by the Constitution and through the institutions of Congress, the executive, and the actions of citizens themselves, is called upon to resolve these conflicts.

civil liberties (p. 132)
civil rights (p. 132)

The Bill of Rights and Incorporation

For much our history the limitations on government outlined in the Bill of Rights applied only to Congress, meaning that while the federal government could not infringe on civil rights, state and local governments could. The passage of the Fourteenth Amendment began the process of nationalizing, or incorporating, the protections of the Bill of Rights at the state level, although not all of the amendments have been incorporated yet.

habeas corpus (p. 138)
bills of attainder (p. 138)
ex post facto laws (p. 138)
incorporation (p. 139)
selective incorporation (p. 142)

Freedom of Religion

According to the establishment and free exercise clauses of the First Amendment, citizens of the United States have the right not to be coerced to practice a religion in which they do not believe, as well as the right not to be prevented from practicing the religion they espouse. Because these rights can conflict, religious freedom has been a battleground ever since the founding of the country. The courts have played a significant role in navigating the stormy waters of religious expression since the founding.

establishment cause (p. 143)
separationists (p. 143)
accommodationists (p. 143)
Lemon **test** (p. 146)
free exercise clause (p. 146)
police power (p. 147)
compelling state interest (p. 147)

Freedom of Expression

Freedom of expression, also provided for in the First Amendment, is often considered the hallmark of our democratic government. Freedom of expression produces information about government, limits corruption, protects minorities, and helps maintain a vigorous defense of the truth. But this right may at times conflict with the preservation of social order and protection of civility, decency, and reputation. Again, it has been left to the courts to balance freedom of expression with social and moral order.

sedition (p. 149)
bad tendency test (p. 152)
clear and present danger test (p. 152)
imminent lawless action test (p. 153)
freedom of assembly (p. 153)
Miller **test** (p. 154)
fighting words (p. 155)
political correctness (p. 156)
prior restraint (p. 156)
libel (p. 157)

The Right to Bear Arms

The right to bear arms, supported by the Second Amendment, has also been hotly debated—more so in recent years than in the past, as federal gun control legislation has been enacted only recently. Most often the debate over gun laws is carried out in state legislatures.

The Rights of Criminal Defendants

The founders believed that to limit government power, people needed to retain rights against government throughout the process of being accused, tried, and punished for criminal activities. Thus they devoted some of the text of the Constitution as well as the Bill of Rights to a variety of procedural protections, including the right to a speedy and public trial, protection from unreasonable search and seizure, and the right to legal advice.

due process of law (p. 164)
exclusionary rule (p. 165)

The Right to Privacy

Though the right to privacy is not mentioned in either the Constitution or the Bill of Rights—and did not even enter the American legal system until the late 1800s—it has become a fiercely debated right on a number of different levels, including reproductive rights, gay rights, and the right to die. In the absence of constitutional protection, the series of court cases on these matters determines how they are to be resolved. Many of these issues are still on shaky ground, as the states create their own legislation and the courts hand down new rulings.

The Citizens and Civil Liberties

Our political system is concerned with protecting individual rights, which grant freedoms and allow us to make claims on our government. But citizens are also expected to act within certain restrictions—laws and limits designed to protect the collective good. The balance between the freedom to do as we wish with the obligations to do as we should is a continuing challenge.

ENGAGE

Know your rights.
The **American Civil Liberties Union** is devoted to fighting for individual rights. You can follow them on Twitter (@aclu) for frequent updates on civil liberties cases as they wind through the courts, or visit their fact-filled web site for a wealth of information on current events and the history of the organization.

Read a banned book.
From *Huckleberry Finn* to *Harry Potter*, books are often in the crosshairs of groups or individuals seeking to remove content they find offensive from libraries and school curricula. The American Library Association leads the fight for intellectual freedom. Visit their banned books page to see a list of the most frequently challenged books, to help them lobby Congress for legislation that promotes and protects your access to books and reading material, or to take part in Banned Books Week, the ALA's annual celebration of the "Freedom to Read."

Enter the Second Amendment debate.
Take some time to explore both sides of this pressing constitutional issue by following the loudest voices on both sides. The **National Rifle Association** is dedicated to firearms education and to ensuring that Americans' right to bear arms is not curtailed by the government; you can get frequent updates via Twitter at @NRA. **The Brady Campaign to Prevent Gun Violence** was founded by former Reagan press secretary Jim Brady after he was injured during the 1981 assassination attempt on the president, and is the most prominent gun control organization in the nation. Visit the organization's web site or follow them at @bradybuzz.

Visit the Newseum.
Located in Washington, D.C., the Newseum is a state-of-the-art experience that offers immersive exhibits dedicated to the history of the news. Its Newseum Institute is devoted to First Amendment study and exploration. If you can't make it to D.C., check out the Newseum's First Amendment Center site for research and news regarding First Amendment issues as well as to find commentary and analysis by legal specialists.

EXPLORE

Lewis, Anthony. 2007. *Freedom for the Thought That We Hate: A Biography of the First Amendment.* **New York: Basic Books.** Law professor and Pulitzer Prize–winning writer Lewis explores the history of the First Amendment and how its legal application and judicial rulings have allowed this liberty to evolve over time.

Prejean, Helen. 2004. *The Death of Innocents: An Eyewitness Account of Wrongful Executions.* **New York: Random House.** In this follow-up to her bestselling *Dead Man Walking*, Prejean tells the story of two men whom she believed to have been wrongfully convicted of, and executed for, crimes they did not commit. In telling their stories, Prejean, a Catholic nun who has counseled death row inmates for three decades and accompanied six men to their deaths, explores the inhumanity of the system and dismantles the legal and religious arguments that have been used to justify the death penalty.

Waldman, Steven. 2008. *Founding Faith: Providence, Politics, and the Birth of Religious Freedom in America.* **New York: Random House.** Waldman explores the intentions of the founding fathers and the foundations of religious freedom in early America.

The Central Park Five. **2012.** Noted documentary filmmaker Ken Burns recounts the decades-long tale of the 1989 Central Park jogger case, in which a young woman was brutally raped and assaulted. Five youths were arrested, coerced into making confessions, convicted, imprisoned, and eventually exonerated in the highly publicized and racially charged case.

Bowling for Columbine. **2002.** A controversial and, at times, humorous filmmaker, Michael Moore attempts to uncover why the United States has so many firearms-related deaths.

The People vs. Larry Flynt. **1996.** Director Milos Forman chronicles the notorious publisher's journey from "smut peddler" to champion of free speech, culminating in the Supreme Court's 1988 landmark decision in his favor.

Gideon's Trumpet. **1979.** This inspiring movie is about the 1963 Supreme Court case *Gideon v. Wainwright*. Based on Anthony Lewis's book published in 1964.

6 THE STRUGGLE FOR EQUAL RIGHTS

IN YOUR OWN WORDS After you've read this chapter, you will be able to

>> Outline the criteria used by the courts to determine if and when the law can treat people differently.

>> Summarize key events and outcomes in the struggle for equality of African Americans.

>> Explain the different paths to equality taken by other racial and ethnic groups.

>> Describe how women have fought for equality and the changing role of women in American politics.

>> Recognize examples of other groups that face discrimination.

>> Identify tools used by citizens to expand the promise of civil rights.

WHAT'S AT STAKE...IN THE ADOPTION OF MARRIAGE EQUALITY?

CIVIL RIGHTS GAINS ARE ALMOST ALWAYS a matter of small steps forward and small steps back. In moments of big social change, you can see both the gravitational pull of the old way of doing things and the growing momentum of the new. Take a step away and you can see how a civil rights movement unfolds, but when you are in the middle of it, the big picture is harder to see.

Consider the case of marriage equality—the idea that all Americans, regardless of sexual orientation, should be granted the same rights to be married in the eyes of the state. As this is being written, at the end of 2014, the writing is on the wall for marriage equality—it is happening. About 60 percent of Americans live in states where marriage equality is legal; 40 percent still do not. But the road to this point has been rocky indeed.

As little as twenty years ago, gays could not marry legally in any of the fifty United States. And just in case any state in the future should think that allowing gays to marry was a good idea, Congress had passed the Defense of Marriage Act (DOMA), which said that contrary to the "full faith and credit" clause in the Constitution, states do not have to recognize marriages performed in other states if they

would not be legal under the laws of their own, and that, furthermore, the federal government does not recognize such marriages either. The bill was signed, reluctantly, by Bill Clinton in 1996.

Big step back. But watch what happened after that.

In 1999, Vermont allows gays to form civil unions, but not to marry.

On *May 17, 2004, Massachusetts became the first state to allow gays to marry* when the state Supreme Court said the state constitution required it.

Small step forward.

And that same year, eleven states passed constitutional amendments to ban gay marriage. The number quickly rose to seventeen.

Small steps back.

In 2005, the California legislature passed a law allowing gay marriage (twice); the Republican governor vetoed it (twice).

Standing still.

In 2006, more states chose to ban gay marriage, even as others started to allow domestic partnerships.

Sign of the Times

In the summer of 2012, Representative Barney Frank married his longtime partner, James Ready. For many, like those attending the celebration, it was like any other wedding of two people in love. For others, same-sex marriage is an affront to the institution of marriage itself. The 2012 presidential candidates were on opposite sides of the issue, but marriage equality is becoming increasingly less controversial as public opinion swings in favor.

In May 2008 the California Supreme Court overturned a state law preventing gays from marrying. About 18,000 gay couples were married. Anti-marriage groups worked to put Proposition 8, banning gay marriage, on the ballot. It passed.

Forward steps, halted, and begun again.

Connecticut, 11/12/2008 (court decision)

Vermont, 9/1/2009 (state legislature)

Iowa, 4/24/2009 (court decision)

New Hampshire, 1/1/2010 (state legislature)

Washington, D.C., 3/3/2010 (legislature)

In 2010 polls began to show majority support for the right to marry, with younger people clearly leading the change.

February, 2011: The Obama administration announces that it doesn't believe that DOMA is constitutional and will no longer defend it in court.

New York, 7/24/2011 (state legislature)

2012 was a year of flux; many steps forward and many back.

Faced with a marriage equality bill passed by the legislature, New Jersey Republican governor Chris Christie vetoed the law, saying it should be voted on by the people.

A federal appeals court upheld a ruling by a lower federal court overturning California's Proposition 8. It headed to the Supreme Court.

The Colorado state Senate passed a law allowing civil unions. Republican opponents of the bill prevented it from coming up for a final vote.

North Carolina voters passed Proposition 1 banning same-sex marriage and ending domestic partner benefits, domestic violence, and child custody protections for unmarried couples.

In a televised interview, President Barack Obama defined his evolving position on marriage equality. Long a supporter of gay rights, Obama had nonetheless gotten stuck somewhere short of endorsing gay marriage. "I had hesitated on gay marriage in part because I thought that civil unions would be sufficient. . . . I was sensitive to the fact that for a lot of people, the word *marriage* was something that invokes very powerful traditions and religious beliefs. . . . At a certain point, I've just concluded that for me personally it is important for me to go ahead and affirm that I think same-sex couples should be able to get married."[1]

A federal appeals court ruled that DOMA unconstitutionally denied gay couples federal benefits. A district court judge ruled part of it unconstitutional in July, and another did so in October.[2]

In November 6, 2012, voters in Maine, Maryland, Washington, and Minnesota chose to legalize marriage equality, and voters in Minnesota defeated a constitutional amendment banning it.

Washington, 12/09/12 (popular vote)

Maine, 12/29/2012 (popular vote)

Maryland, 1/1/2013 (popular vote)

Delaware, 7/1/2013 (state legislature)

Minnesota, Rhode Island, 8/1/2013 (state legislature)

Hawaii, 12/2/2013 (state legislature)

In 2013 the Supreme Court struck down DOMA and let the lower court ruling against Proposition 8 stand.

California, 6/28/2013 (court decision)

New Jersey, 10/21/2013 (court decision)

New Mexico, 12/19/2013 (court decision)

Huge steps forward. And then still more.

Illinois, 6/1/2014 (state legislature)

Oregon, 5/19/2014 (court decision)

Pennsylvania, 5/20/2014 (court decision)

In late 2014 the Supreme Court refused to hear challenges to rulings by several district courts striking down state bans, allowing those rulings to stay.

Indiana, Oklahoma, Utah, Virginia, and Wisconsin 10/6/2013 (court decision)

And almost immediately, like dominos. . .

Colorado, 10/7/2014 (court decision)

Nevada, West Virginia, 10/09/2014 (court decision)

North Carolina, 10/10/2014 (court decision)

Idaho, 10/13/2014 (court decision)

Alaska, Arizona, 10/17/2014 (court decision)

Wyoming, 10/21/2014

As of this writing, eighteen states still ban gay marriage and the battle is headed back to the Supreme Court. Still, the progress has been remarkable—faster than anyone imagined ten years ago. What's the big deal here? Why the snarl of law, lawsuits, and confusion? What is actually at stake for this country in the issue of marriage equality? We return to this question after we learn more about what's involved in civil rights struggles for equal rights in this country. «

WHEN you consider where we started, the progress toward equality in the United States can look pretty impressive. Nowhere is the change more vivid than in the case of racial equality. Just over fifty years ago, it was illegal for most blacks and whites to go to the same schools in the American South or to use the same public facilities, like swimming pools and drinking fountains. Today, for most of us, the segregated South is a distant memory. On August 28, 2008, forty years from the day that civil rights leader Martin Luther King Jr. declared that he had a dream that one day a child would be judged on the content of his character rather than the color of his skin, the nation watched as Barack Obama, born of a white mother from Kansas and a black father from Kenya, accepted the Democratic Party's nomination to the presidency, an office he would go on to win. Such moments, caught in the media spotlight, illuminate a stark contrast between now and then.

But in some ways, the changes highlighted at such moments are only superficial. Though black cabinet members are not uncommon—George W. Bush had two African American secretaries of state, Colin Powell and Condoleezza Rice, and Obama appointed the first black attorney general, Eric Holder—there have been remarkably few blacks in national elected office. *USA Today* pointed out in 2002 that "if the U.S. Senate and the National Governors Association were private clubs, their membership rosters

> **civil rights** citizenship rights guaranteed to the people (primarily in the Thirteenth, Fourteenth, Fifteenth, Nineteenth, and Twenty-sixth Amendments) and protected by the government

would be a scandal. They're virtually lily white,"[3] and not much has changed since then. Since Reconstruction, only three elected governors and four elected U.S. senators have been African Americans. Ironically, Obama's election to the presidency in 2008 removed the only black senator serving at the time. There are two African American senators, Cory Booker (D-NJ) and Tim Scott (R-SC); both were elected to full terms in 2014.

Even though legal discrimination ended nearly fifty years ago, inequality still pervades the American system and continues to be reflected in economic and social statistics. On average, blacks are less educated and much poorer than whites, they experience higher crime rates, they live disproportionately in poverty-stricken areas, they score lower on standardized tests, and they rank at the bottom of most social measurements. Life expectancy is lower for African American men and women than for their white counterparts, and a greater percentage of African American children live in single-parent homes than do white or Hispanic children. The statistics illustrate what we suggested in Chapter 5—that rights equal power, and long-term deprivation of rights results in powerlessness. Unfortunately, the granting of formal **civil rights**, which we defined in Chapter 5 as the citizenship rights guaranteed by the Thirteenth, Fourteenth, Fifteenth, Nineteenth, and Twenty-sixth Amendments, does not immediately bring about change in social and economic status.

African Americans are not the only group that shows the effects of having been deprived of its civil rights. Native Americans, Hispanics, and Asian Americans have all faced or face unequal treatment in the legal system, the job market, and the schools. Women, making up over half the population of the United States, have long struggled to gain economic parity with men. People in America are also denied rights, and consequently power, on the basis of their sexual orientation, their age, their physical abilities, and their citizenship status. A country once praised by French observer Alexis de Tocqueville as a place of extraordinary equality, the United States today is haunted by traditions of unequal treatment and intolerance that it cannot entirely shake.

In this chapter we look at the struggles of these groups to gain equal rights and the power to enforce those rights. The struggles are different because the groups themselves, and the political avenues open to them, vary in important ways. We'll learn how groups can use different political strategies to change the rules and win power.

THE MEANING OF POLITICAL INEQUALITY
When is different treatment okay?

Despite the deeply held American expectation that the law should treat all people equally, laws by nature must treat some people differently from others. Not only are laws designed in the first place to discriminate *between* those who abide by society's rules and those who don't,[4] but the laws can also legally treat criminals differently once they are convicted. For instance, in all but two states, Maine and Vermont, felons are denied the right to vote for some length of time, and in ten states, felons forfeit voting rights permanently.[5] But when particular groups are treated differently because of some characteristic like race, religion, gender, sexual orientation, age, or wealth, we say that the law discriminates *against* them, that they are denied equal protection of the laws. Throughout our history, legislatures, both state and national, have passed laws treating groups differently based on characteristics such as these. Sometimes those laws have seemed just and reasonable, but often they have not. Deciding which characteristics may fairly be the basis of unequal treatment is the job of all three branches of our government, but especially of our court system.

WHEN CAN THE LAW TREAT PEOPLE DIFFERENTLY?

The Supreme Court has expended considerable energy and ink on this problem, and its answers have changed over time as various groups have waged the battle for equal rights against a backdrop of ever-changing American values, public opinion, and politics. Before we look at the struggles those groups have endured in their pursuit of equal treatment by the law, we should understand the Court's current formula for determining what sorts of discrimination need what sorts of legal remedy.

LEGAL CLASSIFICATIONS The Court has divided the laws that treat people differently into three tiers (see *The Big Picture*):

- The top tier refers to those ways of classifying people that are so rarely constitutional that they are immediately "suspect." Suspect classifications require that the government have a *compelling state interest* for treating people differently. Race is a **suspect classification**. To determine whether a law making a suspect classification is constitutional, the Court subjects it to a heightened standard of review called **strict scrutiny**. Strict scrutiny means that the Court looks very carefully at the law and the government interest involved. As we saw in Chapter 5, laws that deprived people of some fundamental religious rights were once required to pass the compelling state interest test; at that time, religion was viewed by the Court as a suspect category.

- Classifications that the Court views as less potentially dangerous to fundamental rights fall into the middle tier. These "quasisuspect" classifications may or may not be legitimate grounds for treating people differently. Such classifications are subject not to strict scrutiny but to an **intermediate standard of review**. That is, the Court looks to see if the law requiring different treatment of people bears a substantial relationship to an important state interest. An "important interest test" is not as hard to meet as a "compelling interest test." Laws that treat women differently than men fall into this category.

- Finally, the least-scrutinized tier of classifications is that of "nonsuspect" classifications; these are subject to the **minimum rationality test**. The Court asks whether the government had a *rational basis* for making a law that treats a given class of people differently. Laws that discriminate on the basis of age, such as a curfew for young people, or on the basis of economic level, such as a higher tax rate for those in a certain income bracket, need not stem from compelling or important government interests. The government must merely have had a rational basis for making the law, which is fairly easy for a legislature to show.

THE FIGHT FOR SUSPECT STATUS The significance of the three tiers of classifications and the three review standards is that all groups that feel discriminated against want the Court to view them as a suspect class so that they will be treated as a protected group. Civil rights laws might cover them anyway, and the Fourteenth Amendment, which guarantees equal protection of the laws, may also formally protect them. However, once a group is designated as a suspect class, the Supreme Court is unlikely to permit *any* laws to treat them differently. Thus gaining suspect status is crucial in the struggle for equal rights.

After over one hundred years of decisions that effectively allowed people to be treated differently because of their race, the Court finally agreed in the 1950s that race is a suspect class. Women's groups, however, have failed to convince the Court, or to amend the Constitution, to make gender a suspect classification. The intermediate standard of review was devised by the Court to express its view that it is a little more dangerous to classify people by gender than by age or wealth, but not as dangerous as classifying them by race or religion. Until recently, some groups in America—homosexuals, for instance—have struggled to get the Court to consider them in the quasisuspect category. Although the lower courts have flirted with changing that status, the Supreme Court didn't specify a standard of review when it struck down the Defense of Marriage Act in 2013. Some states and localities have passed legislation to prevent discrimination on the basis of sexual orientation, but gays can still be treated differently by law as long as the state can demonstrate a rational basis for the law.

suspect classification classification, such as race, for which any discriminatory law must be justified by a compelling state interest

strict scrutiny a heightened standard of review used by the Supreme Court to assess the constitutionality of laws that limit some freedoms or that make a suspect classification

intermediate standard of review standard of review used by the Court to evaluate laws that make a quasisuspect classification

minimum rationality test standard of review used by the Court to evaluate laws that make a nonsuspect classification

These standards of review make a real difference in American politics—they are part of the rules of politics that determine society's winners and losers. Americans who are treated unequally by the laws consequently have less power to use the democratic system to get what they need and want (like legislation to protect and further their interests), to secure the resources available through the system (like education and other government benefits), and to gain new resources (like jobs and material goods). People who cannot claim their political rights have little if any standing in a democratic society.

WHY DO WE DENY RIGHTS?

People deny rights to others for many reasons, although they are not always candid about what those reasons are. People usually explain their denial of others' rights by focusing on some group characteristic. They may say that the other group is not "civilized" or does not recognize the "true God," or that its members are in some other way unworthy or incapable of exercising their rights. People feel compelled to justify poor treatment by blaming the group they are treating poorly.

But usually there is something other than simple fault-finding behind the denial of rights. People deny the rights of others because rights are power. To deny people rights is to have power over them and to force them to conform to our will. Thus at various times in our history people with power in the United States have compelled slaves to work for their profit, they have denied wives the right to divorce their husbands, and they have driven Native Americans from their homes so that they could develop their land. Denying people their rights is an attempt to keep them dependent and submissive. When they find their voice to demand their rights and the laws change, they soon leave their subservience behind.

People also deny rights to others for another reason. Isolating categories of people—be they recent immigrants who speak English poorly, homosexuals whose lifestyle seems threatening, or people whose religious beliefs are unfamiliar—helps groups to define who they are, who their relevant community is, and who they are *not*. Communities can believe that they, with their culture, values, and beliefs, are superior to people who are different. This belief promotes cohesion and builds loyalty to "people who are like us"; it also intensifies dislike of and hostility to those who are "not our kind." It is only a small step from there to believing that people outside the community do not really deserve the same rights as those "superior" people within.

DIFFERENT KINDS OF EQUALITY

The notion of equality is controversial in America. The disputes arise in part because we often think that "equal" must mean "identical" or "the same." Thus equality can seem threatening to the American value system, which prizes people's freedom to be different, to be unique individuals. We can better understand the controversies over the attempts to create political equality in this country if we return briefly to a distinction we made in Chapter 2, between substantive and procedural equality.

In American political culture, we prefer to rely on government to guarantee fair treatment and equal opportunity (a *procedural* view), rather than to manipulate fair and equal outcomes (a *substantive* view). We want government to treat everyone the same, and we want people to be free to be different, but we do not want government to treat people differently in order to make them equal at the end. This distinction poses a problem for the civil rights movement in America, the effort to achieve equal treatment by the laws for all Americans. When the laws are changed, which is a procedural solution, substantive action may still be necessary to ensure equal treatment in the future.

PAUSE AND REVIEW:

WHO, WHAT, HOW

In the struggle for political equality, the people with the most at stake are members of groups who, because of some characteristic beyond their control, have been denied their civil rights. What they seek is equal treatment by the laws. The rules the Supreme Court uses to determine if they should have equal treatment are the three standards of strict scrutiny, the intermediate standard of review, and the minimum rationality test.

But minority groups are not the only ones with a stake in the battle for equal rights. Those who support discrimination want to maintain the status quo, which bolsters their own power and the power of those like them. The means open to them are maintaining discriminatory laws and intimidating those they discriminate against.

IN YOUR OWN WORDS » Outline the criteria used by the courts to determine if and when the law can treat people differently.

RIGHTS DENIED ON THE BASIS OF RACE
The battle to end the legacy of slavery and racism, fought mainly in the courts

We cannot separate the history of our race relations from the history of the United States. Americans have struggled for centuries to come to terms with the fact that citizens of African nations were kidnapped, packed into sailing vessels, exported to America, and sold, often at great profit, into a life that destroyed their families, their spirit, and their human dignity. The stories of white supremacy and black inferiority, told to numb the sensibilities of European Americans to the horror of their own behavior, have been almost as damaging as slavery itself and have lived on in the

THE BIG PICTURE: WHEN THE LAW CAN TREAT PEOPLE DIFFERENTLY

The Supreme Court has expended considerable energy and ink on this problem, and its answers have changed over time as various groups have waged the battle for equal rights against a backdrop of ever-changing American values, public opinion, and politics. Before we look at the struggles those groups have endured in their pursuit of equal treatment by the law, we should understand the Court's current formula for determining what sorts of discrimination need what sorts of legal remedy.

Hmmm. Does the government classify people into groups in this law?

How does the government classify people in this law?

Ah, that kind of classification is:

Yes, it is!

No, it isn't!

CASE   CASE   CASE

Yes, it does!

No, it doesn't!

Race

Gender

Age, wealth, sexual orientation
(Stay tuned! This one is in flux.)

Suspect

Quasi-suspect

Nonsuspect

EXAMPLE OF CLASSIFICATION UPHELD	**SUSPECT** Government had a compelling state interest (national security) in relocating Japanese Americans from the West Coast during World War II. *Korematsu v. United States* (1944)
CLASSIFICATION STRUCK DOWN	State government had no compelling reason to segregate schools to achieve state purpose of educating children. *Brown v. Board of Education* (1954)

So, what standard should I use?

No, you must use a higher standard!

No, you must use a lower standard!

That means I have to ask:

There IS a compelling interest.

There is NO compelling interest.

In that case, the government will...

Strict scrutiny standard of review

Is there a compelling state interest in this classification?

CITIZEN   GOVERNMENT

most likely lose, and the law will be struck down.

Intermediate standard of review

Is there an important state purpose for this classification?

CITIZEN   GOVERNMENT

often lose, and the law will be struck down.

Minimum rationality standard of review

Is there a rational basis for this classification?

CITIZEN   GOVERNMENT

probably prevail, and the law will be upheld.

QUASI-SUSPECT
Court upheld federal law requiring males but not females to register for military service (the draft). *Rostker v. Goldberg* (1981)

Court struck down an Alabama law requiring husbands but not wives to pay alimony after divorce. *Orr v. Orr* (1979)

NONSUSPECT
Court found a Missouri law requiring public officials to retire at age seventy to have a rational basis. *Gregory v. Ashcroft* (1991)

Court struck down an amendment to the Colorado constitution that banned legislation to protect people's rights on the basis of their sexual orientation because it had no rational relation to a legitimate state goal. *Romer v. Evans* (1996)

American psyche—and in political institutions—much longer than the practice they justified. **Racism**, institutionalized power inequalities in society based on the perception of racial differences, is not a "southern problem" or a "black problem"; it is an American problem, and one that we have not yet managed to eradicate from national culture.

Not only has racism had a decisive influence on American culture, it has also been central to American politics. From the start, those with power in America have been torn by the issue of race. The framers of the Constitution were so ambivalent that they would not use the word *slavery*, even while that document legalized its existence. Although some early politicians were morally opposed to the institution of slavery, they were, in the end, more reluctant to offend their southern colleagues by taking an antislavery stand. Even the Northwest Ordinance of 1787, which prohibited slavery in the northwestern territories, contained the concession to the South that fugitive slaves could legally be seized and returned to their owners. Sometimes in politics the need to compromise and bargain can cause people to excuse the inexcusable for political gain.

THINKING OUTSIDE THE BOX

What would a legal system that treated all people exactly the same look like?

BLACKS IN AMERICA BEFORE THE CIVIL WAR

At the time of the Civil War there were almost four million slaves in the American South and nearly half a million free blacks living in the rest of the country. Even where slavery was illegal, blacks as a rule did not enjoy full rights of citizenship. In fact, in *Dred Scott v. Sanford* (1857), the Supreme Court had ruled that blacks could not be citizens because the founders had not intended them to be citizens. "On the contrary," wrote Justice Roger Taney, "they were at that time considered as a subordinate and inferior class of beings, who had been subjugated by the dominant race, and whether emancipated or not, yet remained subject to their authority."[6]

Congress was no more protective of blacks than the Court was. Laws such as the Fugitive Slave Act of 1850 made life precarious even for free northern blacks. When national institutions seemed impervious to their demands for black rights, the abolitionists, a coalition of free blacks and northern whites working to end slavery altogether, tried other strategies. The movement put pressure on the Republican Party to take a stand on political equality and persuaded three state legislatures (Iowa, Wisconsin, and New York) to hold referenda (statewide votes) on black suffrage between 1857 and 1860. The abolitionists lost all three votes by large margins. Even in the North, on the eve of the Civil War, public opinion did not favor rights for blacks.

THE CIVIL WAR AND ITS AFTERMATH: WINNERS AND LOSERS

We can't begin to speculate here on all the causes of the Civil War. Suffice it to say that the war was not fought simply over the moral evil of slavery. Slavery was an economic and political issue as well as an ethical one. The southern economy depended on slavery, and when, in an effort to hold the Union together in 1863, President Abraham Lincoln issued the Emancipation Proclamation, he was not simply taking a moral stand. He was trying to use economic pressure to keep the country intact. The proclamation, in fact, did not free all slaves, only those in states rebelling against the Union.[7]

It is hard to find any real "winners" in the American Civil War. Indeed the war took such a toll on North and South that neither world war in the twentieth century would claim as many American casualties. The North "won" the war, in that the Union was restored, but the costs would be paid for decades afterward. Politically, the northern Republicans, the party of Lincoln, were in the ascendance, controlling both the House and the Senate, but their will was often thwarted by President Andrew Johnson, a Democrat from Tennessee who was sympathetic toward the South.

The Thirteenth Amendment, banning slavery, was passed and ratified in 1865. In retaliation, and to ensure that their political and social dominance of southern society would continue, the southern white state governments legislated **black codes**. Black codes were laws that essentially sought to keep blacks in a subservient economic and political position by restoring as many of the conditions of slavery as possible. As one scholar describes it, "Twenty years after freedom, a former slave was apt to be a black peasant, apathetically scratching a crop out of exhausted soil not his own, with scrawny mules and rusted plows and hoes that he had neither the incentive nor the means to improve."[8] In all likelihood, he was still working for, or at least on the land of, his former master. "Freedom" did not make a great deal of difference in the lives of most former slaves after the war.

RECONSTRUCTION AND ITS REVERSAL

Congress, led by northern Republicans, tried to check southern obstruction of its will by instituting a period of federal control of southern politics called **Reconstruction**, which began in 1865. In an attempt to make the black codes unconstitutional, the Fourteenth Amendment was passed,

> **racism** institutionalized power inequalities in society based on the perception of racial differences
>
> **black codes** a series of laws in the post–Civil War South designed to restrict the rights of former slaves before the passage of the Fourteenth and Fifteenth Amendments
>
> **Reconstruction** the period following the Civil War during which the federal government took action to rebuild the South

guaranteeing all people born or naturalized in the United States the rights of citizenship. Further, no state could deprive any person of life, liberty, or property without due process of the law, or deny any person equal protection of the law. As we saw in Chapter 5, the Supreme Court has made varied use of this amendment, but its original intent was to bring some semblance of civil rights to southern blacks. The Fifteenth Amendment followed in 1870, effectively extending the right to vote to all adult males.

At first Reconstruction worked as the North had hoped. Under northern supervision, southern life began to change. Blacks voted, were elected to some local posts, and cemented Republican dominance with their support. But soon southern whites responded with violence. Groups like the Ku Klux Klan terrorized blacks in the South and made them reluctant to claim the rights to which they were legally entitled for fear of reprisals. Lynchings, arson, assaults, and beatings made claiming one's rights or associating with Republicans a risky business. Congress fought back vigorously and suppressed the reign of terror for a while, but its efforts earned accusations of military tyranny, and the Reconstruction project began to run out of steam. Plagued by political problems of their own, the Republicans were losing electoral strength and seats in Congress. Meanwhile, the Democrats were gradually reasserting their power in the southern states. By 1876, Reconstruction was effectively over, and shortly after that, southern whites set about the business of disenfranchising blacks, or taking away their newfound political power.

SEGREGATION AND THE ERA OF JIM CROW

Without the protection of the northern Republicans, disenfranchisement turned out to be easy to accomplish. The strategy chosen by the Democrats, who now controlled the

© Bettmann/Corbis

Murderous Mob
After Reconstruction the fervor to reestablish and maintain white supremacy in southern and border states led to acts of terror. Between 1882 and 1951, 3,437 African Americans were lynched by mobs. Local authorities usually claimed the killers could not be identified, although the mobs often posed for photographs like this one that were then turned into postcards and saved as macabre souvenirs.

southern state governments, was a sly one. Under the Fifteenth Amendment the vote could not be denied on the basis of race, color, or previous condition of servitude, so they set out to deny it on other, legal, bases that would have the primary effect of targeting blacks. **Poll taxes**, which required the payment of a small tax before voters could cast their votes, effectively took the right to vote away from the many blacks who were too poor to pay, and **literacy tests**, which required potential voters to demonstrate some reading skills, excluded most blacks who, denied an education, could not read. Even African Americans who were literate were often kept from voting because a white registrar administered the test unfairly. To permit illiterate whites to vote, literacy tests were combined with **grandfather clauses**, which required passage of such tests only by those prospective voters whose grandfathers had not been allowed to vote before 1867. Thus, unlike the black codes, these new laws, called **Jim Crow laws**, obeyed the letter of the Fifteenth Amendment, never explicitly saying that they were denying blacks the right to vote because of their race, color, or previous condition of servitude. This strategy proved devastatingly effective, and by 1910, registration of black voters had dropped dramatically, and registration of poor, illiterate whites had fallen as well.[9] Southern Democrats were back in power and had eliminated the possibility of competition.

poll taxes taxes levied as a qualification for voting

literacy tests tests requiring reading or comprehension skills as a qualification for voting

grandfather clauses provisions exempting from voting restrictions the descendants of those able to vote in 1867

Jim Crow laws southern laws designed to circumvent the Thirteenth, Fourteenth, and Fifteenth Amendments and to deny blacks rights on bases other than race

Jim Crow laws were not just about voting but also concerned many other dimensions of southern life. The 1900s launched a half-century of **segregation** in the South—that is, of separate facilities for blacks and whites for leisure, business, travel, education, and other activities. The Civil Rights Act of 1875 had guaranteed that all people, regardless of race, color, or previous condition of servitude, were to have full and equal accommodation in "inns, public conveyances on land or water, theaters, and other places of public amusement," but the Supreme Court struck down the law, arguing that the Fourteenth Amendment only restricted the behavior of states, not of private individuals.[10] Having survived the legal test of the Constitution, Jim Crow laws continued to divide the southern world in two. But it was not a world of equal halves. The whites-only facilities were invariably superior to those intended for blacks; they were newer, cleaner, more comfortable. Before long, the laws were challenged by blacks who asked why equal protection of the law shouldn't translate into some real equality in their lives.

One Jim Crow law, a Louisiana statute passed in 1890, required separate accommodations in all trains passing through the state. Homer Plessy, traveling through Louisiana, chose to sit in the white section. Although Plessy often passed as a white person, he was in fact one-eighth black, which made him a black man according to Louisiana law. When he refused to sit in the "Colored Only" section, Plessy was arrested. He appealed his conviction all the way to the Supreme Court, which ruled against him in 1896. In *Plessy v. Ferguson*, the Court held that enforced separation of the races did not mean that one race was inferior to the other. As long as the facilities provided were equal, states were within their rights to require them to be separate. Rejecting the majority view, Justice John Marshall Harlan wrote in a famous dissent, "Our Constitution is color-blind, and neither knows nor tolerates classes among citizens."[11] It would be over fifty years before a majority on the Court shared his view. In the meantime, everyone immediately embraced the "separate," and forgot the "equal," part of the ruling. Segregated facilities for whites and blacks had received the Supreme Court's seal of approval.

THE LONG BATTLE TO OVERTURN *PLESSY*: THE NAACP AND ITS LEGAL STRATEGY

The years following the *Plessy* decision were bleak ones for African American civil rights. The formal rules of politics giving blacks their rights had been enacted at the national level, but no branch of government at any level was willing to enforce them. The Supreme Court had firmly rejected attempts to give the Fourteenth Amendment more teeth. Congress was not inclined to help since the Republican fervor for reform had worn off. Nor were the southern state governments likely to support black rights.

In the early days of the twentieth century, African Americans themselves did not agree on the best political strategy to follow. Booker T. Washington, president of the Tuskegee Institute, a black college, advocated an accommodationist approach. Blacks should give up demanding political and social equality, he said, and settle for economic opportunity. Through hard work and education they would gradually be recognized on their merits and accorded their rights. This philosophy, popular with whites because it asked so little and seemed so unthreatening, angered many other blacks who felt that they had accommodated whites long enough. People like W. E. B. Du Bois took a far more assertive approach. Only by demanding their rights and refusing to settle for second-class treatment, he argued, would blacks ever enjoy full citizenship in the United States.[12]

Du Bois was influential in starting one of a handful of African American groups born in the early 1900s to fight for civil rights. The **National Association for the Advancement of Colored People (NAACP)**, founded in 1910, aimed to help individual blacks; to raise white society's awareness of the atrocities of contemporary race relations; and most important, to change laws and court rulings that kept blacks from true equality. The NAACP, over time, was able to develop a legal strategy that was finally the undoing of Jim Crow and the segregated South.

By the 1930s, political changes suggested to the legal minds of the NAACP that the time might be right to challenge the Court's "separate but equal" decision. Blacks had made some major political advances in the North, not so much by convincing Republicans to support them again, but by joining the coalition that supported Democratic president Franklin Roosevelt's New Deal. Wanting to woo black voters from the Republican Party, the Democrats gave as much influence to blacks as they dared without alienating powerful southern Democratic congressmen. The Supreme Court had even taken some tentative steps in the direction of civil rights, such as striking down grandfather clauses in 1915.[13] But after four decades the *Plessy* judgment was still intact.

THE EARLY EDUCATION CASES The NAACP, with the able assistance of a young lawyer named Thurgood Marshall, decided to launch its attack in the area of education. Segregation in education was particularly disastrous for blacks because the poor quality of their schools limited their potential, which in turn reinforced southern beliefs

---

segregation the practice and policy of separating races

Plessy v. Ferguson Supreme Court case that established the constitutionality of the principle "separate but equal"

National Association for the Advancement of Colored People (NAACP) an interest group founded in 1910 to promote civil rights for African Americans

Will Counts Collections, Indiana University Archives

© Bettmann/Corbis

Apologies: Better Late Than Never

The scene was chaotic and ugly in 1957 when Elizabeth Eckford and eight other black students integrated Central High School in Little Rock, Arkansas. Forty years later, Eckford and a member of the mob that had taunted her, Hazel Bryan Massery, met again in front of the school, this time on friendly terms (Massery had telephoned Eckford in 1962 to apologize for her part in the disturbance).

about their inferiority. Knowing that a loss reinforcing *Plessy* would be a major setback, the lawyers at the NAACP chose their cases very carefully. Rather than trying to force the immediate integration of elementary schools, a goal that would have terrified and enraged whites, they began with law schools. Not only would this approach be less threatening, but law schools were clearly discriminatory (most states didn't even have black law schools) and were an educational institution the justices on the Court knew well. The NAACP decision to lead with law school cases was a masterful legal strategy.

The first education case the NAACP took to the Court was *Missouri ex rel Gaines v. Canada*. Lloyd Gaines, a black man, wanted to go to law school in Missouri. Missouri had no law school for blacks but promised to build one. In the meantime, they told him, they would pay his tuition at an out-of-state law school. Gaines sued the state of Missouri, claiming that the facilities open to him under Missouri law were not equal to those available to white students. The Court, in 1938, agreed. It argued that Missouri had failed in its obligation to provide equal facilities and that black students in Missouri had an equal right to go to law school in-state.[14] The *Gaines* case was significant because the Court was looking at something it had ignored in

Plessy: whether the separate facilities in question were truly equal.

Twelve years later, the *Gaines* decision was expanded in *Sweatt v. Painter*. Again a black law school candidate, Herman Sweatt, applied to a white law school, this time in Texas. The law school denied him admission, but mindful of the Missouri ruling, Texas offered to provide Sweatt with a school of his own in three downtown basement rooms, with a part-time faculty and access to the state law library. Again the NAACP argued before the Court that this alternative would not be an equal facility. But this time it went further and claimed that even if the schools *were* comparable, Sweatt's education would still be unequal because of the intangible benefits he would lose: the reputation of the school, talking with classmates, and making contacts for the future, for example. The justices agreed. Perhaps they were aware of how different their own legal educations would have been, isolated in three basement rooms by themselves. If the separate education was not equal, they said, it was unconstitutional under the Fourteenth Amendment.[15]

The ruling striking down "separate but equal" laws was aided by an unrelated case that, ironically, had the effect of depriving Japanese American citizens of many of their civil rights during World War II. In *Korematsu v. United States*

SNAPSHOT OF AMERICA: HOW WELL DO WE FARE, BY RACE AND ETHNICITY?

Educational Attainment

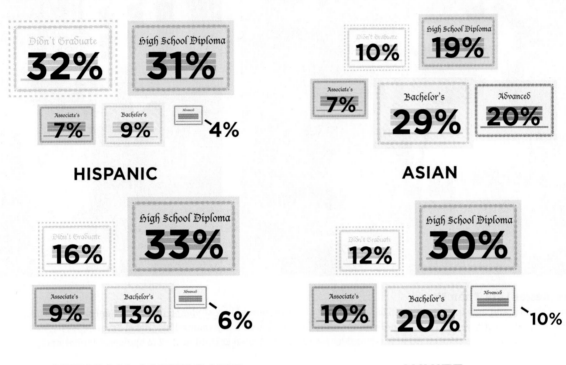

HISPANIC
- Didn't Graduate: **32%**
- High School Diploma: **31%**
- Associate's: **7%**
- Bachelor's: **9%**
- Advanced: **4%**

ASIAN
- Didn't Graduate: **10%**
- High School Diploma: **19%**
- Associate's: **7%**
- Bachelor's: **29%**
- Advanced: **20%**

AFRICAN AMERICANS
- Didn't Graduate: **16%**
- High School Diploma: **33%**
- Associate's: **9%**
- Bachelor's: **13%**
- Advanced: **6%**

WHITE
- Didn't Graduate: **12%**
- High School Diploma: **30%**
- Associate's: **10%**
- Bachelor's: **20%**
- Advanced: **10%**

Median Household Income

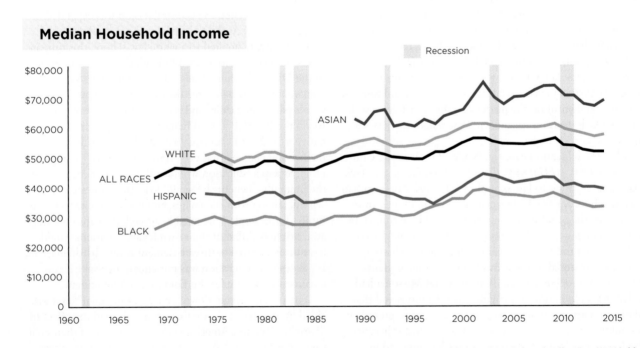

Source: U.S. Census Educational Attainment in the United States: 2013, Table 1 [https://www.census.gov/hhes/socdemo/education/data/cps/2013/tables.html]; Income and Poverty in the United States: 2013 [http://www.census.gov/content/dam/Census/library/publications/2014/demo/p60-249.pdf]

Poverty Rates

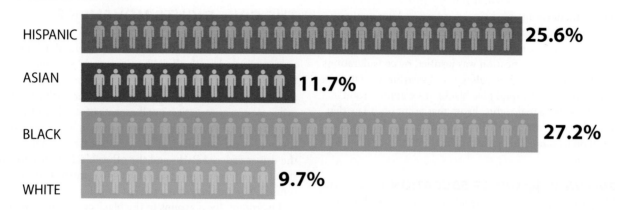

HISPANIC — 25.6%

ASIAN — 11.7%

BLACK — 27.2%

WHITE — 9.7%

Mean Earnings, by Education and Race/Ethnicity, 2010

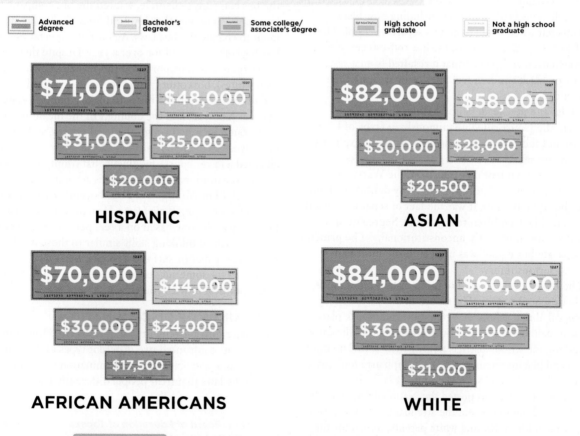

Advanced degree   Bachelor's degree   Some college/associate's degree   High school graduate   Not a high school graduate

HISPANIC
$71,000
$48,000
$31,000 $25,000
$20,000

ASIAN
$82,000
$58,000
$30,000 $28,000
$20,500

AFRICAN AMERICANS
$70,000
$44,000
$30,000 $24,000
$17,500

WHITE
$84,000
$60,000
$36,000 $31,000
$21,000

BEHIND THE NUMBERS

There are sizable racial and ethnic group differences in income and those living in poverty. Twice as many African Americans, Hispanics, and Native Americans live in poverty as whites and Asians. What explanations might account for these differences? Should government play a role in bringing about more equality?

(1944), Justice Hugo Black articulated the strict scrutiny test described earlier in this chapter: "All legal restrictions which curtail the civil rights of a single racial group are immediately suspect. That is not to say that all such restrictions are unconstitutional. It is to say that courts must subject them to the most rigid scrutiny."[16] After applying strict scrutiny, the Court allowed the laws that limited the civil rights of Japanese Americans to stand because it felt that the racial classification was justified by considerations of national security. The ruling was disastrous for Japanese Americans, but it would give blacks more ammunition in their fight for equal rights. From that point on, a law that treated people differently on the basis of race had to be based on a compelling governmental interest, or it could not stand.

BROWN V. BOARD OF EDUCATION By the early 1950s the stage was set for tackling the issue of education more broadly. The NAACP had four cases pending that concerned the segregation of educational facilities in the South and the Midwest. The Court ruled on all of them under the case name *Brown v. Board of Education of Topeka*. In its now-familiar arguments, the NAACP emphasized the intangible aspects of education, including how black students felt when made to go to a separate school. They cited sociological evidence of the low self-esteem of black schoolchildren and argued that it resulted from a system that made black children feel inferior by treating them differently.

Under the new leadership of Chief Justice Earl Warren, the Court ruled unanimously in favor of Linda Brown and the other black students. Without explicitly denouncing segregation or overturning *Plessy*, lest the South erupt in violent outrage again, the Warren Court held that separate schools, by their very definition, could never be equal because it was the fact of separation itself that made black children feel unequal. Segregation in education was inherently unconstitutional.[17] The principle of "separate but equal" was not yet dead, but it had suffered serious injury.

The *Brown* decision did not bring instant relief to the southern school system. The Court, in a 1955 follow-up to *Brown*, ruled that school desegregation had to take place "with all deliberate speed."[18] Such an ambiguous direction was asking for school districts to drag their feet. The most public and blatant attempt to avoid compliance took place in Little Rock, Arkansas, in September 1957, when Governor Orval Faubus posted the National Guard at the local high school to prevent the attendance of nine African American children. Rioting white parents, filmed for the nightly news, revealed the faces of southern bigotry. Finally, President Dwight Eisenhower sent one thousand federal troops to guarantee the safe passage of the nine black children through the angry mob of white parents who threatened to lynch them rather than let them enter the school. The *Brown* case, and the attempts to enforce it, proved to be a catalyst for a civil rights movement that would change the

whole country. See "*Snapshot of America:* How Well Do We Fare, by Race and Ethnicity?" for data on educational disparities that still exist.

THE CIVIL RIGHTS MOVEMENT

In the same year that the Court ordered school desegregation to proceed "with all deliberate speed," a woman named Rosa Parks sat down on a bus in Montgomery, Alabama, and started a chain of events that would end with a Court order to stop segregation in all aspects of southern life. As law required, Parks sat in the black section at the back of the bus. As the bus filled, all the white seats were taken, and the driver ordered Parks and the other blacks in her row to stand. Tired from a fatiguing day as a seamstress, Parks refused. She was arrested and sent to jail.

Overnight, local groups in the black community organized a **boycott** of the Montgomery bus system. A boycott seeks to put economic pressure on a business to do something by encouraging people to stop purchasing its goods or services. Montgomery blacks, who formed the base of the bus company's clientele, wanted the bus company to lose so much money that it would force the local government to change the bus laws. Against all expectations, the bus boycott continued for over a year. Despite their dependence on public transportation (fewer blacks owned cars than whites), boycotters found the stamina to walk, carpool, and otherwise avoid the buses to make a political statement that was heard around the country. In the meantime, the case wound its way through the legal system, and a little over a year after the boycott began, the Supreme Court affirmed a lower court's judgment that Montgomery's law was unconstitutional.[19] Separate bus accommodations were not equal. (The Montgomery bus boycott was portrayed in the movie *The Long Walk Home.* Watching a historical film—especially one based on a real person or an event—requires critical thinking skills similar to those needed to read a newspaper or surf the web. See *Don't Be Fooled by… the Movies* for some suggestions on how to get the most out of the political movies you view.)

TWO KINDS OF DISCRIMINATION

The civil rights movement launched by the Montgomery bus boycott confronted two different types of discrimination. **De jure discrimination** (discrimination by law) is created by laws that treat people differently based on some

> *Brown v. Board of Education of Topeka* **Supreme Court case that rejected the idea that separate could be equal in education**
>
> **boycott** refusal to buy certain goods or services as a way to protest policy or force political reform
>
> **de jure discrimination** discrimination arising from or supported by the law

DON'T BE FOOLED BY...
THE MOVIES

Throughout this book, we've suggested films that offer some insights into the political events that have shaped our history. Movies like 42 (2013), which tells the story of Jackie Robinson breaking baseball's racial barriers in the 1940s, and *Twelve Years a Slave* (2013), which tells a true story of a free black man from upstate New York who was abducted and sold into slavery in 1841, do indeed stir emotional responses and invite viewers to consider the more human aspects of the struggle for civil equality in America. But are they good history? Do they enhance the audience's understanding of events? Do they tell the whole truth?

Of course not. Movies are created to make money, to tell stories in a dramatic and compelling manner, and often to promote a particular cause or idea. Stories inspired by real events are retold through the eyes of producers, writers, directors, and actors who bend the truth to create a particular artistic and commercial vision. Even films with no commercial ambitions whatsoever—independent documentaries, for example—are shot (and, perhaps more important, edited) by filmmakers who inevitably have their own agenda. Thus even the most even-handed and objective treatment of an issue is bound to be informed somewhat by the filmmaker's basic feelings. Ken Burns's *Civil War* (1990), for example, is a critically acclaimed, thorough, and fact-based documentation of the war between the states. But it is colored by Burns's own feelings and by the culture in which it was produced. A different filmmaker, living at a different time or in a different place, might have used the same facts and materials to create a very different film.

WHAT TO WATCH OUT FOR

How then can you distinguish the well-established historical fact from the artist's fancy? Is it possible for a film to enhance our understanding of political events without manipulating us? It is—if you keep a critical eye. The next time you settle in for a movie about politics, history, or social movements, ask yourself the following questions:

- **What kind of film are you watching?** Big Hollywood releases are meant to draw in a huge audience and make lots of money. That often means that factual accuracy is less important than action, romance, or drama. Thus a film like *Charlie Wilson's War* (2007) might change some details and facts surrounding the Texas congressman's campaign to provide backing for the Afghan resistance against the Soviet Union in the 1980s. Even films that purport to be inspired by true stories often bend, gloss over, or ignore crucial facts, or even create new ones. *The Help* (2011), for example, reflects the realities of many women living and working in the South in the era of Jim Crow, but it is still a work of fiction.

- **Who made the movie?** Do the producers have a stake in a particular interpretation of events? Does the director have an axe to grind or some personal experience that might inspire or influence his vision? How might a film like *Twelve Years a Slave* (2013) have been different had it been made by a white director rather than Steve McQueen, an African American man? Would the story told by Gus Van Sant, a gay man, in the 2008 biopic *Milk* have been told differently by a straight director?

- **What is the filmmaker's reputation?** Some filmmakers are known for striving to be historically accurate, others for taking artistic license, and still others for using the medium to promote their own beliefs or philosophies. For example, Michael Moore is well known for using his movies, such as *Sicko* (2007) and *Capitalism: A Love Story* (2009), to promote his political views; and Mel Gibson used his film *The Passion of the Christ* (2004) to express his interpretation of particular religious events. Oliver Stone's reputation for making movies that dramatize his theories of the nefarious forces behind political and social events (like the 1991 film *JFK*) no doubt influenced how his 2008 movie *W.*, about President George W. Bush, was received.

- **Where and when was it made?** Films are informed by the times in which they were produced and must be viewed with that in mind. Movies that were considered progressive at the time they were released—such as *Woman of the Year* (1942) or *Guess Who's Coming to Dinner* (1967)—would likely seem sexist or racist to modern audiences.

- **What is the primary source for historical material?** Filmmakers often consult historians and other experts to add factual and dramatic accuracy to their movies. Steven Spielberg's acclaimed film *Lincoln* (2012) was adapted from the critically acclaimed book *Team of Rivals* by noted Civil War scholar Doris Kearns Goodwin.

- **Who is telling the story?** Consider the movie's perspective. Films about the civil rights movement as seen by the U.S. attorney general, a nonviolent protester, or a southern sheriff would prove very different from beginning to end.

- **What have the critics said about it?** Thorough reviews of films from reputable critics and historians can offer insights into any hidden agendas. *Mississippi Burning* (1988), for example, is a powerful film, but it has been widely criticized by historians for its grossly misleading account of the investigation into the murder of three civil rights workers in the rural South.

© Aristide Economopoulous/Star Ledger/Corbis

Random Checks Aren't Always Balanced

Police officers routinely stop and frisk individuals at random as a means of controlling criminal behavior in areas with high rates of crime and violence. Departments claim that because they stop individuals at random, checks like this one in Irvington, New Jersey, are not discriminatory in nature. But because black neighborhoods are more likely to be plagued by crime, African Americans are stopped at much higher rates than are other Americans—leading to concerns that the practice is essentially a form of de facto discrimination.

characteristic like race. This is the sort of discrimination most blacks in the South faced. Especially in rural areas, blacks and whites lived and worked side by side, but by law they used separate facilities. Although the process of changing the laws was excruciatingly painful, once the laws were changed and the new laws were enforced, the result was integration.

The second sort of discrimination, called **de facto discrimination** (discrimination in fact), however, produces a kind of segregation that is much more difficult to eliminate. Segregation in the North was of this type because blacks and whites did not live and work in the same places to begin with. It was not laws that kept them apart, but past discrimination, tradition, custom, economic status, and residential patterns. This kind of segregation is so hard to remedy because there are no laws to change; the segregation is woven more complexly into the fabric of society.

We can look at the civil rights movement in America as having two stages. The initial stage involved the battle to change the laws so that blacks and whites would be equally protected by the laws, as the Fourteenth Amendment guarantees. The second stage, and one that is ongoing today, is the fight against the aftereffects of those laws, and of centuries of discrimination, that leave many blacks and whites still living in communities that are worlds apart.

CHANGING THE RULES: FIGHTING DE JURE DISCRIMINATION Rosa Parks and the Montgomery bus boycott launched a new strategy in blacks' fight for equal rights. Although it took the power of a court judgment to move the city officials, blacks themselves had exercised considerable power through peaceful protest and massive resistance to the will of whites. One of the leaders of the boycott was a young Baptist minister named Martin Luther King Jr. A founding member of the Southern Christian Leadership Conference, a group of black clergy committed to expanding civil rights, King became known for his nonviolent approach to political protest. This philosophy of peacefully resisting enforcement of laws perceived to be unjust, and marching or "sitting in" to express political views, captured the imagination of supporters of black civil rights in both the South and the North. Black college students, occasionally joined by whites, staged peaceful demonstrations, called sit-ins, to desegregate lunch counters in southern department stores and other facilities. The protest movement was important not just for the practices it challenged directly—such as segregation in motels and restaurants, on beaches, and in other recreational facilities—but also for the pressure it brought to bear on elected officials and the effect it had on public opinion, particularly in the North, which had been largely unaware of southern problems.

The nonviolent resistance movement, in conjunction with the growing political power of northern blacks, brought about remarkable social and political change in the 1960s. The administration of Democratic president John F. Kennedy, not wanting to alienate the support of southern Democrats, tried at first to limit its active involvement in civil rights work. But the political pressure of black interest groups forced Kennedy to take a more visible stand. The Reverend King was using his tactics of nonviolent protest to great advantage in the spring of 1963. The demonstrations he led to protest segregation in Birmingham, Alabama, were met with extreme police violence. With an eye to the national media, King included children in the march. When the police turned on the demonstrators with swinging clubs, vicious dogs, and high-pressure hoses, the horror was brought to all Americans with their morning

> **de facto discrimination** discrimination that is the result not of law but rather of tradition and habit

newspapers. Kennedy responded to the political pressure, so deftly orchestrated by King, by sending to Birmingham federal mediators to negotiate an end to segregation, and then by sending to Congress a massive package of civil rights legislation.

Kennedy did not live to see his proposals become law, but they became the top priority of his successor, Lyndon Johnson. During the Johnson years, the president, majorities in Congress, and the Supreme Court were in agreement on civil rights issues, and their joint legacy is impressive. The Kennedy-initiated Civil Rights Bill of 1964 reinforced the voting laws, allowed the attorney general to file school desegregation lawsuits, permitted the president to deny federal money to state and local programs that practiced discrimination, prohibited discrimination in public accommodations and in employment, and set up the Equal Employment Opportunity Commission (EEOC) to investigate complaints about job discrimination. Johnson also sent to Congress the Voting Rights Act of 1965, which, when passed, disallowed discriminatory tests like literacy tests and provided for federal examiners to register voters throughout much of the South. The Supreme Court, still the liberal Warren Court that had ruled in *Brown*, backed up this new legislation.[20] In addition, the Twenty-fourth Amendment, outlawing poll taxes in federal elections, was ratified in 1964.

Because of the unusual cooperation among the three branches of government, by the end of the 1960s life in the South, though far from perfect, was radically different for blacks. In 1968, 18 percent of southern black students went to schools with a majority of white students; in 1970 the percentage rose to 39, and in 1972 to 46. The comparable figure for black students in the North was only 28 percent in 1972.[21] Voter registration had also improved dramatically: from 1964 to 1969, black voter registration in the South nearly doubled, from 36 to 65 percent of adult blacks.[22]

CHANGING THE OUTCOMES: FIGHTING DE FACTO DISCRIMINATION
Political and educational advances did not translate into substantial economic gains for blacks. As a group, they remained at the very bottom of the economic hierarchy, and ironically, the problem was most severe not in the rural South but in the industrialized North. Many southern blacks who had migrated to the North in search of jobs and a better quality of life found

AP Photo/Bill Hudson

Nonviolence as a Strategy for Change
In Birmingham, Alabama, a seventeen-year-old demonstrator is attacked by a police dog after defying a city antiparade ordinance on May 3, 1963. This photograph, running on the front page of the *New York Times* the next day, would draw the attention of President John F. Kennedy. As stories and images of such events spread across the country, more and more people demanded that the violence end and blacks be given equal rights and opportunities.

conditions not much different from those they had left behind. Abject poverty, discrimination in employment, and segregated schools and housing led to frustration and inflamed tempers. In the summers of 1966 and 1967, race riots flashed across the northern urban landscape, leaving death, destruction, and ashes in their wake. Impatient with the passive resistance of the nonviolent protest movement in the South, many blacks became more militant in their insistence on social and economic change. The Black Muslims, led by Malcolm X until his assassination in 1965; the Black Panthers; and the Student Nonviolent Coordinating Committee all demanded "black power" and radical change. These activists rejected the King philosophy of working peacefully through existing political institutions to bring about gradual change.

Northern whites who had applauded the desegregation of the South grew increasingly nervous as angry African Americans began to target segregation in the North. As we explained earlier, the de facto segregation in the North was not the product of laws that treated blacks and whites differently, but instead resulted from different residential patterns, socioeconomic trends, and years of traditions and customs that subtly discriminated against blacks. Black inner-city schools and white suburban schools were often as segregated as if the hand of Jim Crow had been at work.

In the 1970s the courts and some politicians, believing that they had a duty not only to end segregation laws in education but also to integrate the schools, instituted a policy of **busing** in some northern cities. Students from majority-white schools would be bused to mostly black schools, and vice versa. The policy was immediately controversial; riots in South Boston in 1974 resembled those in Little Rock seventeen years earlier.

Not all opponents of busing were reacting from racist motives. Busing students from their homes to a distant school strikes many Americans as fundamentally unjust. Parents who move to better neighborhoods so they can send their children to better schools do not want to see those children bused back to their old schools. Parents want their children to be part of a local community and its activities, which is hard when the children must leave the community for the better part of each day. And they fear for the safety of their children when they are bused into poverty-stricken areas with high crime rates. Even many African American families were opposed to busing because of fears for their children's safety and because of the often long bus rides into predominantly white neighborhoods.

The Supreme Court has shared America's ambivalence about busing. Although it endorsed busing as a remedy for segregated schools in 1971,[23] three years later it ruled that busing plans could not merge inner-city and suburban districts unless officials could prove that the district lines had been drawn in a racially discriminatory manner.[24] Since many whites were moving out of the cities, there were fewer white students to bus, and busing did not really succeed in integrating schools in many urban areas. Fifty years after the *Brown* decision, many schools, especially those in urban areas, remain largely segregated.[25]

EARLY EFFORTS AT AFFIRMATIVE ACTION

The example of busing highlights a problem faced by civil rights workers and policymakers: deciding whether the Fourteenth Amendment guarantee of equal protection simply requires that the states not sanction discrimination or imposes an active obligation on them to integrate blacks and whites. As the northern experience shows, the absence of legal discrimination does not mean equality. In 1965 President Johnson issued Executive Order 11246, which not only prohibited discrimination in firms doing business with the government but also ordered them to take **affirmative action** to compensate for past discrimination. In other words, if a firm had no black employees, it wasn't enough not to have a policy against hiring them; the firm now had to actively recruit and hire blacks. The test would not be federal law or company policy, but the actual racial mix of employees.

Johnson's call for affirmative action was taken seriously not only in employment situations but also in university decisions. Patterns of discrimination in employment and higher education showed the results of decades of decisions

by white males to hire or admit other white males. Blacks, as well as other minorities and women, were relegated to low-paying, low-status jobs. After Johnson's executive order, the EEOC decided that the percentage of blacks working in firms should reflect the percentage of blacks in the labor force. Many colleges and universities reserved space on their admissions lists for minorities, sometimes accepting minority applicants with grades and test scores lower than those of whites.

Like busing, affirmative action has proved controversial among the American public. We have talked about the tension in American politics between procedural and substantive equality, between equality of treatment and equality of results. That is precisely the tension that arises when Americans are faced with policies of busing and affirmative action, both of which are instances of American policy attempting to bring about substantive equality. The end results seem attractive, but the means to get there—treating people differently—seem inherently unfair in the American value system.

The Court reflected the public's unease with these affirmative action policies when it ruled in *Regents of the University of California v. Bakke* in 1978. A white applicant for admission, Alan Bakke, had been rejected from the medical school at the University of California, Davis, even though minorities with lower grades and scores had been accepted. He challenged Davis's policy, claiming that it denied him admission to medical school on account of his race—effectively resulting in "reverse discrimination." The Court agreed with him, in part. It ruled that a quota system like Davis's, holding sixteen of one hundred spots for minorities, was a violation of the equal protection clause. But it did not reject the idea of affirmative action, holding that schools can have a legitimate interest in having a diversified student body, and that they can take race into account in admissions decisions, just as they can take into account geographic location, for instance.[26] In this and several later cases, the Court signaled its approval of the intent of affirmative action, even though it occasionally took issue with specific implementations.[27]

Few of the presidents who immediately followed Kennedy and Johnson took strong pro–civil rights positions, but none effected a real reversal in policy until Ronald Reagan. The Reagan administration lobbied the Court strenuously to change its rulings on the constitutionality of affirmative action. In 1989 the Court fulfilled civil rights advocates' most pessimistic expectations. In a series of rulings, it struck down a variety of civil rights laws, holding that the Fourteenth Amendment did not protect

> **busing** achieving racial balance by transporting students to schools across neighborhood boundaries
>
> **affirmative action** a policy of creating opportunities for members of certain groups as a substantive remedy for past discrimination

workers from racial harassment on the job,[28] that the burden of proof in claims of employment discrimination was on the worker,[29] and that affirmative action was on shaky constitutional ground.[30] The Democratic-led Congress sought to undo some of the Court's late-1980s rulings by passing the Civil Rights Bill of 1991, which made it easier for workers to seek redress against employers who discriminate.

BLACKS IN CONTEMPORARY AMERICAN POLITICS

The Supreme Court's use of strict scrutiny on laws that discriminate on the basis of race has put an end to most de jure discrimination. However, de facto discrimination remains, with all the consequences that stem from the fact that tradition and practice in the United States endorse a fundamental inequality of power. In addition, African Americans continue to grapple with issues such as racial profiling, which, like the inequities in the criminal justice system that we discuss in Chapter 10, mean they often feel that the American political system treats them differently.

Race relations in this country are complicated by the growing diversity within the black community itself. Many blacks in America are in fact not native-born African Americans. They may come from Haiti, or the West Indies, or they may be African immigrants and not Americans at all. In Miami, 48 percent of the black population is West Indian, and a third of New York City blacks are foreign-born immigrants, as are a third of the blacks in Massachusetts and 8 percent of the blacks in Washington, D.C. One researcher points out that "the foreign-born African Americans and native-born African Americans are becoming as different from each other as foreign-born and native-born whites, in terms of culture, social status, aspirations, and how they think of themselves."[31]

This growing diversity signals problems for intraracial relations. Blacks born in other countries, where they were very likely not a minority, often have difficulty identifying with the experience of American blacks and seeing themselves as part of the same group with the same concerns and interests. Their primary identity might be nationality rather than race (they might see themselves as primarily Somali, or Ethiopian, or Jamaican, or Haitian). Native-born black Americans, for their part, often view black immigrants with the same general suspicion and stereotypes that Americans have traditionally directed toward immigrants. As this trend toward diversity grows, it will become even harder than it is now to characterize the "black experience" in America. In this section we examine some of the other critical issues facing blacks in contemporary American politics.

THE ECONOMIC OUTLOOK FOR BLACKS

We began this chapter noting that blacks fall behind whites on most socioeconomic indicators, although we should not disregard the existence of a growing black middle class. The median household income for African Americans in 2012 was $33,321; for whites, it was $57,009. Though blacks constituted about 13.1 percent of the U.S. population in 2012, in 2007 they owned only 7.1 percent of nonfarm U.S. businesses.[32] The racial income gap is blamed, in part, on lack of enforcement of antidiscrimination laws, showing that even when laws change, the results may not.[33] (See "*Snapshot of America:* How Well Do We Fare, by Racial and Ethnic Groups?" for more comparisons.)

But even when overt discrimination is not present, the differences persist. One study by two sociologists uncovered the dispiriting fact that, all other things being equal, African American doctors, lawyers, and real estate managers make less than their white counterparts. Those in securities and financial services fields make seventy-two cents for every dollar earned by a white man in the same job. They speculate that perhaps the gap is due to blacks tending to be assigned by employers to black clients, who are often less financially well off than whites.[34] Such studies show how subtle and yet how pervasive economic inequities can be.[35]

POLITICAL GAINS AND LOSSES

Because people of lower income and education levels are less likely to vote, African Americans' economic disadvantage has translated into a political limitation as well, especially in a country with a history of suppressing the black vote. The Voting Rights Act of 1965 put protections in place, but in 2013, in a five-to-four decision, the Supreme Court threw out a part of the law that it claims requires updating: the clause that requires nine southern states to "pre-clear" with the Department of Justice any changes they make to their voting laws to be sure they are race neutral. The ruling left the door open for new congressional legislation to qualify states for pre-clearance, but so far, while Democrats have pushed for such legislation, Republican stalling tactics have held it off.[36] Due in large part to President Obama's effective voter mobilization effort, African American turnout in 2012 was a robust 13 percent of the electorate, but it remains to be seen how Democrats will fare in future years in the face of more restrictive voting rules.

African Americans have had difficulty overcoming barriers not just on the voting side of the democratic equation. In terms of elected officials, progress has been mixed. By 2001 there were slightly more than nine thousand black elected officials in the United States, in posts ranging from local education and law enforcement jobs to the U.S. Congress. But the number of African Americans is much higher at local levels of government, where the constituents who elect them are more likely to be African American themselves. As the constituencies grow larger and more diverse, the task of black candidates gets tougher. In 2011 there were over 650 black mayors,[37] but only one African American governor (Deval Patrick of Massachusetts). In the 114th Congress, elected in 2014, 45 of 435 members of the House of Representatives were black, and there were two black senators.

Still, public opinion polls had indicated that more than 140 years after the end of the Civil War, Americans were ready to elect a black president,[38] and in 2008 and again in 2012, they did just that. Barack Obama (who previously served as just the sixth black member of the U.S. Senate) is the nation's first African American president, elected in a campaign that was remarkably free of racial overtones, although Obama did give one speech during the primary campaign that dealt explicitly with race. Obama's administration promised to usher in a much more relaxed attitude toward race (he jokingly referred to himself, in his first press conference after his election, as a "mutt"). Although that approach to a subject that has been difficult for Americans to talk about may help to create more ease in the long run, in the short term a disconcerting amount of criticism of the administration, especially from such right-wing entertainer-commentators as Rush Limbaugh and conservative provocateurs such as Ann Coulter and the late Andrew Breitbart, comes with a racial tinge.

It's an open question whether this dramatic movement at the top of the ticket will have an overall effect on the numbers of African Americans in American politics. In 2008 black turnout at the polls rose to 16.1 million voters, 2 million more than turned out in 2004.[39] That change, if lasting, might send more black candidates to political office. And in the wake of Obama's election, African Americans appeared to be more optimistic about black progress; a majority (53 percent) said life will be better for blacks in the future (compared to 44 percent who said so in 2007), and 54 percent of blacks said Obama's election has improved race relations, but by 2013, only 32 percent said that a lot of progress had been made toward Martin Luther King's dream of racial equality.[40]

In general, African American candidates continue to face a reality that is daunting. They attribute their difficulties achieving statewide and national office to four factors: the scarcity of blacks in lesser state offices, from which statewide candidates are often recruited; the fact that many good black politicians are mayors, who traditionally have trouble translating urban political success to statewide success; the fact that black politicians have fewer deep pockets from which to raise funds, since they often represent lower-income areas; and "old-fashioned prejudice"— their belief that nonblacks are less likely to vote for them and that party officials are less likely to encourage them to run for higher office because of that.[41]

AFFIRMATIVE ACTION TODAY Affirmative action continues to be a controversial policy in America. In 1996 voters in California declared affirmative action illegal in their state, and voters in Washington did the same in 1998. In 2006 Michigan voted to ban affirmative action in the state's public colleges and government contracting, and in 2008 affirmative action was on the ballot in Colorado and Nebraska. While the Nebraska ban passed with 58 percent of the vote, it was defeated narrowly in Colorado. In 2010

Arizona passed a constitutional ban on government-sponsored affirmative action programs. The American public remains divided: opinion polls show support for the ideals behind affirmative action, but not if it is perceived to be giving minorities preferential treatment.[42]

The federal courts have taken the notion that race is a suspect classification to mean that any laws treating people differently according to race must be given strict scrutiny. Even though strict scrutiny has traditionally been used to support the rights of racial minorities, when applied consistently across the board, it can also preclude laws that give them special treatment or preferences, even if those preferences are meant to create more equality. That doesn't necessarily mean that the courts throw out the laws, but they do hold them to a higher standard. In a 2001 case rejecting a University of Michigan Law School affirmative action policy, a federal district court judge stated the principle bluntly: "All racial distinctions are inherently suspect and presumptively invalid.... Whatever solution the law school elects to pursue, it must be race-neutral."[43] A few months later, a federal appeals court held that the University of Georgia's affirmative action policy was unconstitutional. It said that while a university can strive to achieve a diverse student body, race could not be the only factor used to define diversity.[44]

The University of Michigan Law School case eventually found its way to the Supreme Court, along with another that dealt with Michigan's undergraduate admissions policy. As in *Bakke*, students who had been rejected with higher grade point averages and test scores than some admitted students challenged the constitutionality of Michigan's policies, again on Fourteenth Amendment grounds. The Supreme Court handed down two decisions, the results of which were essentially in line with the *Bakke* decision. The Court threw out the university's undergraduate admissions policy because it was tantamount to racial quotas.[45] In a five-to-four decision, however, the Court held that the law school's holistic approach of taking into account the race of the applicant was constitutional because of the importance of creating a diverse student body.[46] Just ten years later, however, in 2013, a considerably more conservative Court than the one in 2003 held that race-based admissions standards had to be given strict scrutiny and, in a separate ruling, upheld a Michigan ban on using race in admissions decisions.[47]

Despite the controversy, there remains considerable support for affirmative action in the United States. Efforts to end affirmative action have previously failed in state legislatures in New Jersey, Michigan, Arizona, Colorado, and almost a dozen other states. As the 2006 success of the so-called Michigan Civil Rights Initiative, the 2008 defeat of affirmative action in Nebraska, and the 2010 vote on Arizona's Proposition 107 show, however, campaigns in the public can succeed where the legislature may balk.

The issues raised by the affirmative action debate in America deserve to be taken seriously by students of

American politics. Unlike many earlier debates in American civil rights politics, this one cannot be reduced to questions of racism and bigotry. What is at stake are two competing images of what America ought to be about. On one side is a vision of an America whose discriminatory past is past and whose job today is to treat all citizens the same. This view, shared by many minorities as well as many white Americans, argues that providing a set of lower standards for some groups is not fair to anybody. Ward Connerly, an African American businessman and a former member of the University of California Board of Regents, whose American Civil Rights Institute is a strong opponent of affirmative action, says that "people tend to perform at the level of competition. When the bar is raised, we rise to the occasion. That is exactly what black students will do in a society that has equal standards for all."[48] (See "Profiles in Citizenship: Ward Connerly.")

On the other side of the debate are those who argue that affirmative action programs have made a real difference in equalizing chances in society, and although they are meant to be temporary, their work is not yet done. These advocates claim that the old patterns of behavior are so ingrained that they can be changed only by conscious effort. New York Times writer David Shipler says, "White males have long benefited from unstated preferences as fraternity brothers, golfing buddies, children of alumni and the like—unconscious biases that go largely unrecognized until affirmative action forces recruiters to think about how they gravitate toward people like themselves."[49]

PAUSE AND REVIEW:

WHO, WHAT, HOW

All Americans have had a great deal at stake in the civil rights movement. Blacks have struggled, first, to be recognized as American citizens and, then, to exercise the rights that go along with citizenship. Lacking fundamental rights, they also lacked economic and social power. Those who fought to withhold their rights knew that recognizing them would inevitably upset the traditional power structure in both the South and the North.

The formal citizenship rights granted African Americans by way of the Thirteenth, Fourteenth, and Fifteenth Amendments should have changed the rules of American politics sufficiently to allow blacks to enter the political world on an equal footing with whites. Yet when Congress and the courts failed to enforce the Reconstruction amendments, southern blacks were at the mercy of discriminatory state and local laws for nearly a century. Those laws were finally changed by a combination of tactics that succeeded in eliminating much of the de jure discrimination that had followed the Civil War.

However, they were not very effective in remedying the de facto discrimination that persisted, particularly in the North. Efforts to get rid of de facto discrimination generally involve substantive remedies like affirmative action, which remain controversial with procedure-loving Americans. The remnants of past discrimination, in the form of greater poverty and lower education levels for blacks, mean that increased political rights are not easily translated into equal economic and social power.

IN YOUR OWN WORDS » Summarize key events and outcomes in the struggle for equality of African Americans.

RIGHTS DENIED ON THE BASIS OF RACE AND ETHNICITY
Different paths to equality for Native Americans, Hispanics, and Asian Americans

African Americans are by no means the only Americans whose civil rights have been denied on racial or ethnic grounds. Native Americans, Hispanics, and Asian Americans have all faced their own particular kind of discrimination. For historical and cultural reasons, these groups have had different political resources available to them, and thus their struggles have taken shape in different ways.

NATIVE AMERICANS

Native Americans of various tribes shared the so-called New World for centuries before it was discovered by Europeans. The relationship between the original inhabitants of this continent and the European colonists and their governments has been difficult, marked by the new arrivals' clear intent to settle and develop the Native Americans' ancestral lands, and complicated by the Europeans' failure to understand the Indians' cultural, spiritual, and political heritage. The lingering effects of these centuries-old conflicts continue to color the political, social, and economic experience of Native Americans today.

NATIVE AMERICANS AND THE U.S. GOVERNMENT The precise status of Native American tribes in American politics and in constitutional law is complicated. The Indians always saw themselves as sovereign independent nations, making treaties, waging war, and otherwise dealing with the early Americans from a position of strength and equality. But that sovereignty has not been recognized consistently by the United States. The commerce clause of the Constitution (Article I, Section 8) gives Congress the power to regulate trade "with foreign nations, among the several states, and with the Indian

AP Photo/Rich Pedroncelli

Ward Connerly is a reluctant warrior. He didn't set out to become the go-to guy in the battle against affirmative action; he didn't even want a political life. He wanted to leave the world a better place than he found it, but he was content to contribute to the political campaigns of others while building his successful California business and enjoying his family. For Connerly, a Republican, the agent of change should be the individual, not government—he was committed to private enterprise and hard work.

That's what he told his friend, Republican governor Pete Wilson, when Wilson asked Connerly to join his administration. Still, Wilson was persuasive, and in 1993 Connerly found himself beginning a twelve-year term as one of the eighteen people on the hugely powerful University of California Board of Regents.

To Connerly, service on the board was "an awesome responsibility." So when the issue of affirmative action came up, he took it seriously. Connerly had had reservations about the policy from the start. Although he grew up poor, his

Uncle James and his grandmother had taught him to value the dignity that comes from self-reliance and the pride that comes from hard work.

Still, he wasn't looking to launch a major controversy when he was approached by the parents of a highly qualified white student who could not gain admission to the UC system. Investigating, he found what he called a system-wide pattern of discrimination against whites and Asians. Affirmative action did not seem to him to be a program of outreach but rather a program of racial preferences, which he found as distasteful when offered to blacks as when offered to whites, and which he believed would weaken black students in the bargain.

The story of how he overturned the UC affirmative action policy is recounted in his book, *Creating Equal*. Although the battle left him feeling bruised, it also strengthened his belief that affirmative action was unfair to whites and debilitating to blacks, and he ended up leading the successful effort to pass Proposition 209, an initiative that

tribes." The U.S. perception of Indian tribes as neither foreign countries nor states was underscored by Chief Justice John Marshall in 1831. Denying the Cherokees the right to challenge a Georgia law in the Supreme Court, as a foreign nation would be able to do, Marshall declared that the Indian tribes were "domestic dependent nations."[50]

Until 1871, however, Congress continued to treat the tribes outwardly as if they were sovereign nations, making treaties with them to buy their land and relocate them. The truth is that regardless of the treaties, the commerce clause was interpreted as giving Congress guardianship over Indian affairs. The tribes were often forcibly moved from their traditional lands; by the mid-1800s, most were living in western territories on land that had no spiritual meaning for them, where their hunting and farming traditions were ineffective, leaving them dependent on federal aid. The creation of the Bureau of Indian Affairs in 1824 as part of the Department of War (moved, in 1849, to the Department of the Interior) institutionalized that guardian role, and the central issues became what the role of the federal government would be and how much self-government the Indians should have.[51]

Modern congressional policy toward the Native Americans has varied from trying to assimilate them into the broader, European-based culture to encouraging them to develop economic independence and self-government. The combination of these two strategies—stripping them of their native lands and cultural identity, and reducing their federal funding to encourage more independence—has resulted in tremendous social and economic dislocation in the Indian communities. Poverty, joblessness, and alcoholism have built communities of despair and frustration for many Native Americans. Their situation has been aggravated as Congress has denied them many of the rights promised in their treaties in order to exploit the natural resources so abundant in the western lands they have been forced onto, or as they have been forced to sell rights to those resources in order to survive.

POLITICAL STRATEGIES The political environment in which Native Americans found themselves in the mid-twentieth century was very different from the one faced by African Americans. What was at stake were Indians' civil rights and their enforcement, and the fulfillment of old

ended affirmative action statewide in California.

Undaunted, he took on another fight in 1997 over the issue of domestic partner benefits for gays. Originally "close to homophobic," he realized, meeting with long-term gay faculty couples, that "[it was] the real deal, you know. There was no difference except it was two women or two men rather than a man and woman, but it was clear to me that they loved each other, that families can come in different forms and . . . that I needed to rethink my position." Concluding that "if I believe in freedom, then it's got to be for everybody," he led the effort that secured the benefits.

> "...IF I BELIEVE IN FREEDOM THEN IT'S GOT TO BE FOR EVERYBODY."

Having infuriated liberals with his stance on affirmative action, Connerly was now annoying his fellow conservatives, including the governor who appointed him. "I was an equal opportunity offender," he says wryly. But the values that informed the one battle underlay the other as well—an abiding commitment to fair play and hard work, to procedural guarantees, not substantive results.

So today, his long term on the board finally ended, Connerly is back to running his own business full time, but also running the American Civil Rights Institute—a national, not-for-profit organization aimed at educating the public about the need to move beyond racial and gender preferences. Although he tried to leave the issue behind, he could not. "Once you get involved in race you can't extricate yourself from it. It's just something that begins to eat at you, and you can't finish until the job is done. And the job is never done." Here's what else he says:

On having the courage of your convictions:

It requires an awful lot of guts. An awful lot of courage. . . . There will be those who will question whether you're comfortable in your own skin and are you betraying your race and your gender and all of that stuff, which will require that you be very, very secure. . . . [I]t requires you to think hard about who you are, what you want to accomplish. . . . As my grandmother used to often say, "like a tree standing by the water, I shall not be moved." And that was the creed that I adapted and that served me well for those twelve years.

On keeping the republic:

Realize that you live in a great place. And it has been made great by a lot of people over the years who have worked hard to make it great. Every one of your ancestors has made some contribution along the way. . . . [I]t's not the elected official who's made it great, it's the people themselves. . . . That falls on the back of the ordinary citizen. Take it seriously because it's an awesome responsibility.

Source: Ward Connerly spoke with Christine Barbour and Gerald Wright on April 1, 2005.

promises and the preservation of a culture that did not easily coexist with modern American economic and political beliefs and practice. For cultures that emphasized the spirituality of living in harmony with lands that cannot really "belong" to anyone, haggling over mining and fishing rights seems the ultimate desecration. But the government they rejected in their quest for self-determination and tribal traditions was the same government they depended on to keep poverty at bay.

Essentially, Native American tribes find themselves in a relationship with the national government that mimics elements of federalism, what some scholars have called "frybread federalism."[52] Although that relationship has evolved over time, the gist of it is that American Indians are citizens of tribes as well as citizens of the United States, with rights coming from each. It was not clear what strategy the Native Americans should follow in trying to get their U.S. rights recognized. State politics did not provide any remedies, not merely because of local prejudice but also because the Indian reservations were separate legal entities under the federal government. Because Congress itself has been largely responsible for denying the rights of Native Americans, it

was not a likely source of support for their expansion. Too many important economic interests with influence in Congress have had a lot at stake in getting their hands on Indian-held resources. In 1977 a federal review commission found the Bureau of Indian Affairs guilty of failing to safeguard Indian legal, financial, and safety interests. Nor were the courts anxious to extend rights to Native Americans. Most noticeably in cases concerning religious freedom, the Supreme Court has found compelling state interests to outweigh most Indian claims to religious freedom. In 1988, for instance, the Court ruled that the Forest Service could allow roads and timber cutting in national forests that had been used by Indian tribes for religious purposes.[53] And in 1990 the Court held that two Native American drug counselors who had been dismissed for using peyote, a hallucinogenic drug traditionally used in Native American religious ceremonies, were not entitled to unemployment benefits from the state of Oregon.[54]

Like many other groups shut out from access to political institutions, Native Americans took their political fate into their own hands. Focusing on working outside the system to change public opinion and to persuade Congress to alter

AP Photo/Mike Groll

A Good Deal?

New York governor Andrew Cuomo (left) and Ray Halbritter of the Oneida Indian Nation talk while signing an agreement in 2013 guaranteeing the tribe exclusive rights to operate casinos in central New York. Casinos have become big business for Indian tribes and the states in which they operate, but despite the profits they generate, poverty and its consequences continue to be the norm on many reservations.

public policy, the Indians formed interest groups like the National Congress of American Indians (NCAI), founded in 1944, and the American Indian Movement (AIM), founded in 1968, to fight for their cause. AIM, for example, staged dramatic demonstrations, such as the 1969 takeover of Alcatraz Island in San Francisco Bay and the 1973 occupation of a reservation at Wounded Knee (the location of an 1890 massacre of Sioux Indians). AIM drew public attention to the plight of many Native Americans and, at the same time, to the divisions within the Indian community on such central issues as self-rule, treaty enforcement, and the role of the federal government.

CONTEMPORARY CHALLENGES But for all the militant activism of the sixties and seventies, Native Americans have made no giant strides in redressing the centuries of dominance by white people. They remain at the bottom of the income scale in America, earning less than African Americans on average, and their living conditions are often poor. In 2012, 29.1 percent of American Indians lived in poverty, compared to only 15.9 percent of the total U.S. population.[55] And in 2012 only 78.8 percent of adult Native Americans (aged twenty-five years or older) held a high school diploma, compared to 86.4 percent of the overall adult population.[56] Consider, for example, the individuals on the Pine Ridge Indian Reservation in Pine Ridge, South Dakota. Some 70 percent are unemployed, fewer than 10

percent have graduated from high school, and life expectancy is somewhere in the high forties, much lower than the national average, which approaches eighty years.[57]

Since the 1980s, however, an ironic twist of legal interpretation has enabled some Native Americans to parlay their status as semisovereign nations into a foundation for economic prosperity. As a result of two court cases,[58] and Congress' 1988 Indian Gaming Regulatory Act, if a state allows any form of legalized gambling at all, even a state lottery, then Indian reservations in that state may allow all sorts of gambling, subject only to the regulation of the Bureau of Indian Affairs. Many reservations now have casinos that rival Las Vegas in gaudy splendor, and the money is pouring into their coffers. Close to thirty states now allow Indian gambling casinos, which in 2010 brought in more than $26 billion, more than Native Americans received in federal aid.[59] In 2006 Native American gaming revenue represented 42 percent of all casino gambling revenue nationwide,[60] although many tribes and individuals have no share in it.

Casino gambling is controversial on several counts. Native Americans themselves are of two minds about it—some see gambling as their economic salvation and others as spiritually ruinous. The revenue created by the casinos has allowed Indian tribes to become major donors to political campaigns in states such as California, which has increased their political clout though leaving them open to criticism for making big money donations while many reservations remain poverty stricken. Many other Americans object for economic reasons. Opponents like casino owner Donald Trump claim that Congress is giving special privileges to Native Americans that may threaten their own business interests. Regardless of the moral and economic questions unleashed by the casino boom, for many Native Americans it is a way to recoup at least some of the resources that were lost in the past.

Politically, there is the potential for improvement as well. Although recent Supreme Court cases failed to support religious freedom for Native Americans, some lower court orders have supported their rights. In 1996 President Bill Clinton issued an executive order that requires federal agencies to protect and provide access to sacred religious sites of American Indians, which has been a major point of contention in Indian-federal relations. Until the Supreme Court ruled in 1996 that electoral districts could not be drawn to enhance the power of particular racial groups, Native Americans had been gaining strength at the polls, to better defend their local interests. Still, the number of American Indian state representatives has increased slightly in the past few years[61]; two American Indians, Tom Cole and Markwayne Mullin, both Republicans from Oklahoma, are currently serving in the House of Representatives. One American Indian, Democrat Elizabeth Warren of Massachusetts, currently serves in the Senate, although her ethnic identity became a campaign issue when her opponent suggested she was lying about it.

HISPANIC AMERICANS

Hispanic Americans, often also called Latinos, are a diverse group with yet another story of discrimination in the United States. They did not have to contend with the tradition of slavery that burdened blacks, and they don't have the unique legal problems of Native Americans, but they face peculiar challenges of their own in trying to fight discrimination and raise their standing in American society. Among the reasons that the Hispanic experience is different are the diversity within the Hispanic population; the language barrier that many face; and the political reaction to immigration, particularly undocumented immigration, from Mexico into the United States.

Hispanics are the largest minority group in the United States today, making up over 16 percent of the population. Their numbers have more than tripled in the past thirty years, from 14.6 million in 1980 to 52 million in 2011.[62] Between 2000 and 2010 the Hispanic population grew at a rate that is four times the U.S. average.[63] This population explosion means that the problems facing Hispanics will become much more central to the country as a whole as the twenty-first century unfolds.

DIVERSITY A striking feature of the Hispanic population is its diversity. Hispanics have in common their Spanish heritage, but they have arrived in the United States traveling different routes, at different times. As illustrated in *"Snapshot of America:* What Are Our Fastest-Growing Minority Groups?", the current Hispanic population is quite diverse, even though the vast majority is Mexican. Americans with Mexican backgrounds, called Chicanos or Chicanas, do not necessarily share the concerns and issues of more recent Mexican-born immigrants, so there is diversity even within this group. Immigrants from different countries have settled across the United States. Mexican Americans are concentrated largely in California, Texas, Arizona, and New Mexico; Puerto Ricans tend to settle in New York, New Jersey, and other northern states; and Cubans are clustered in South Florida.

> **English-only movements** efforts to make English the official language of the United States

These groups differ in more than place of origin and settlement. Cubans are much more likely to have been political refugees, escaping the communist government of Fidel Castro, whereas those from other countries tend to be economic refugees looking for a better life. Because educated, professional Cubans are the ones who fled, they have largely regained their higher socioeconomic status in this country. For instance, almost 24 percent of Cuban Americans are college educated, a percentage comparable to that found in the U.S. population as a whole, but only 9 percent of Mexican Americans and 16 percent of Puerto Ricans are college graduates.[64] Consequently, Cuban Americans also hold more professional and managerial jobs, and their standard of living, on average, is much higher. What this diversity means is that there is little reason for Hispanics to view themselves as a single ethnic group with common interests and thus to act in political concert. Their numbers suggest that if they acted together they would wield considerable clout, but their diversity has led to fragmentation and powerlessness.

THE ENGLISH-ONLY MOVEMENT Language has also presented a special challenge to Hispanics. The United States today ranks sixth in the world in the number of people who consider Spanish a first language, with an active and important Spanish-language media of radio, television, and press. This preponderance of Spanish speakers is probably due less to a refusal on the part of Hispanics to learn English than to the fact that new immigrants are continually streaming into this country.[65] Nonetheless, especially in areas with large Hispanic populations, white Anglos feel threatened by what they see as the encroachment of Spanish. Many communities have launched English-only movements to make English the official language, precluding foreign languages from appearing on ballots and official documents. The English-only controversy is clearly about more than language—it is about national and cultural identity, a struggle to lay claim to the voice of America.

THE CONTROVERSY OVER IMMIGRATION A final concern that makes the Hispanic struggle for civil rights unique in America is the reaction against immigration, particularly undocumented immigration from Mexico. As we saw in Chapter 2, undocumented immigration is a critical problem in some areas of the country. A backlash against undocumented immigration has some serious consequences for Hispanic American citizens, who may be indistinguishable in appearance, name, and language from recent immigrants. They have found themselves suspected, followed, and challenged by the police; forced to show proof of legal residence on demand; and subjected to unpleasant reactions from non-Hispanic citizens who blame an entire ethnic group for the perceived behavior of a few of its members. All this makes acceptance into American society more difficult for Hispanics; encourages segregation; and makes the subtle denial of equal rights in

SNAPSHOT OF AMERICA: WHAT ARE OUR FASTEST-GROWING MINORITY GROUPS?

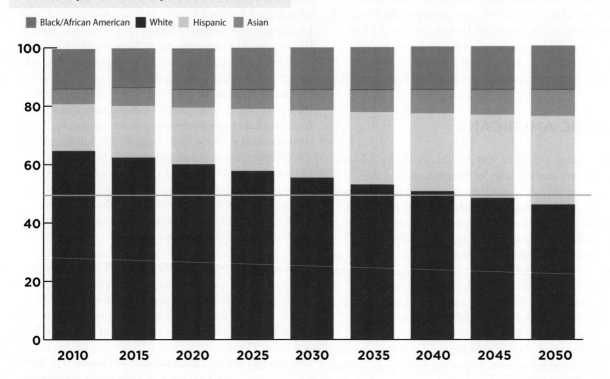

U.S. Population Projections to 2050

Legend: Black/African American | White | Hispanic | Asian

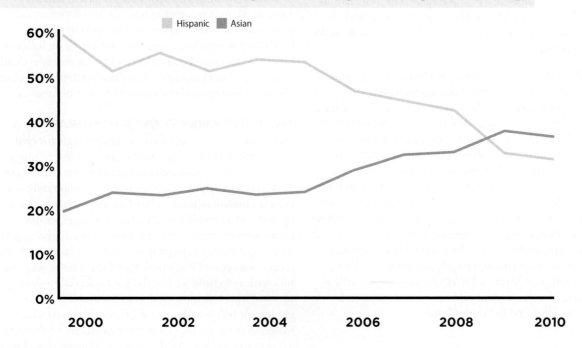

The Rise of Asian Americans as Largest Percentage of Immigrants Arriving

Legend: Hispanic | Asian

The Diversity of Latino Immigrants

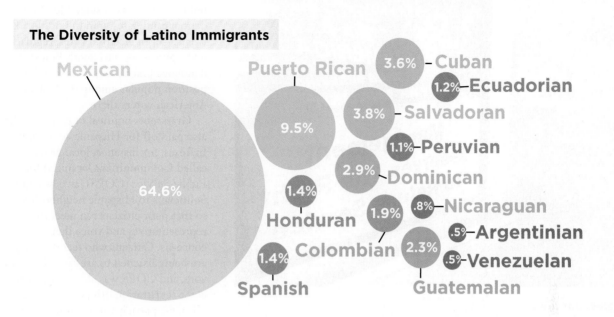

Mexican 64.6%

Puerto Rican 9.5%

Cuban 3.6%

Ecuadorian 1.2%

Salvadoran 3.8%

Peruvian 1.1%

Dominican 2.9%

Honduran 1.4%

Nicaraguan .8%

Colombian 1.9%

Argentinian .5%

Guatemalan 2.3%

Venezuelan .5%

Spanish 1.4%

The Diversity of Asian Immigrants

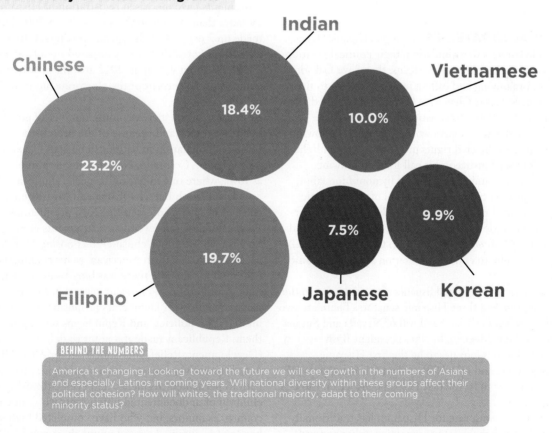

Chinese 23.2%

Indian 18.4%

Vietnamese 10.0%

Filipino 19.7%

Japanese 7.5%

Korean 9.9%

BEHIND THE NUMBERS

America is changing. Looking toward the future we will see growth in the numbers of Asians and especially Latinos in coming years. Will national diversity within these groups affect their political cohesion? How will whites, the traditional majority, adapt to their coming minority status?

Source: Pew Research Center Social & Demographic Trends, U.S. Population Projections: 2005–2050; Mark Hugo Lopez, Ana Gonzalez-Barrera and Danielle Cuddington, "Diverse Origins: The Nation's 14 Largest Hispanic-Origin Groups"; Pew Research Hispanic Trends Project, [http://www.pewhispanic.org/2013/06/19/diverse-origins-the-nations-14-largest-hispanic-origin-groups/]

Inglés, por favor
Though the United States has no official language, some people advocate an "English only" policy, which critics say would limit the rights of immigrants.

employment, housing, and education, for instance, easier to carry out.

POLITICAL STRATEGIES Though Hispanics face formidable barriers to assimilation, their political position is improving. Like African Americans, they have had some success in organizing and calling public attention to their circumstances. Cesar Chavez, as leader of the United Farm Workers in the 1960s, drew national attention to the conditions under which farm workers labored. Following the principles of the civil rights movement, he highlighted concerns of social justice in his call for a nationwide boycott of grapes and lettuce picked by nonunion labor, and in the process he became a symbol of the Hispanic struggle for equal rights. Groups like the Mexican American Legal Defense and Education Fund (MALDEF) and the League of United Latin American Citizens (LULAC) continue to lobby to end discrimination against Hispanic Americans.

There were twenty-nine Hispanic representatives in the 114th Congress and three Hispanic senators. There are two Hispanic governors (Brian Sandoval of Nevada and Susana Martinez of New Mexico). In 2004 President Bush appointed Alberto Gonzales to be the first Hispanic attorney general, and in 2009 President Obama appointed Sonia Sotomayor to be the first Hispanic justice on the U.S. Supreme Court.

The voter turnout rate for Hispanics has traditionally been low because they are disproportionately poor and poor people are less likely to vote, but this situation is changing. Where the socioeconomic status of Hispanics is

high and where their numbers are concentrated, as in South Florida, their political clout is considerable. Presidential candidates, mindful of Florida's twenty-seven electoral votes, regularly make pilgrimages to South Florida to denounce Cuba's communist policies, a position popular among the Cuban American voters there.

Grassroots political organization has also paid off for Hispanic communities. In Texas, for instance, local groups called Communities Organized for Public Service (COPS) have brought politicians to Hispanic neighborhoods so that poor citizens can meet their representatives and voice their concerns. Citizens who feel that they are being listened to are more likely to vote, and COPS was able to organize voter registration drives that boosted Hispanic participation. Similarly, the Southwest Voter Registration Education Project has led over one thousand voter registration drives in several states, including California, Texas, and New Mexico. Such movements have increased registration of Hispanic voters by more than 50 percent.[66] Nationally, in 2008 Hispanics made up 7 percent of all registered voters. Fifty percent of all Latinos voted that year, compared to only 45 percent in 2000.[67] Turnout was up in 2012 as well, with Latino voters comprising 10 percent of the electorate, up from 9 percent in 2008.

Because of the increase in the number of potential Hispanic voters, and because of the prominence of the Hispanic population in battleground states such as Florida, New Mexico, Colorado, Nevada, and even in places such as Iowa, where one might not expect a significant Hispanic population, both Barack Obama and Mitt Romney actively courted Hispanic voters in the 2012 presidential election. Each candidate ran several advertisements entirely in Spanish, and Romney considered choosing Florida senator Marco Rubio, a Cuban American, as his running mate. Although at one time there was bipartisan consensus on immigration reform, in recent years it has become a partisan issue, with Democrats proposing more generous immigration policies, and Republicans seeking to tighten them. Republicans made it a point to defeat the DREAM (Development, Relief, and Education for Alien Minors) Act, different versions of which would have provided a path to permanent residency and even citizenship for the children of undocumented immigrants who came to this country as minors, but who have completed high school here and maintained a good moral character. In 2012 President Obama took matters into his own hands, announcing that his administration would grant a special immigration status to young people who fit the DREAM profile, deferring any deportation action against them for two years. Ultimately, the 2012 Latino vote broke for Obama, 71 to 27 percent. In the immediate aftermath of the election Republicans held a "post-mortem" to see where their voter outreach efforts needed to be beefed up. The initial consensus was that they needed to join Democrats behind immigration reform if they were not to lose the Latino vote for a generation or more. Such a plan proved too much for the Tea Party faction of the party, however, and the efforts of more moderate party members came to nothing.

ASIAN AMERICANS

Asian Americans share some of the experiences of Hispanics, facing cultural prejudice as well as racism and absorbing some of the public backlash against immigration. Yet the history of Asian American immigration, the explosive events of World War II, and the impressive educational and economic success of many Asian Americans mean that the Asian experience is also in many ways unique.

by Dorothea Lange, accessed via Library of Congress

They Were Americans

During World War II, more than 120,000 Americans of Japanese descent—two thirds of whom were U.S. citizens—were forced by executive order to relocate to internment camps for the duration of the war. Here, a sign hung in a Japanese American–owned store remains after the shop owner, a University of California graduate, was forced to abandon his business and move to a War Relocation Authority center in 1942.

DIVERSITY Like Hispanics, the Asian American population is diverse. (See "*Snapshot of America:* What Are Our Fastest-Growing Minority Groups?".) There are Americans with roots in China, Japan, Korea, the Philippines, India, Vietnam, Laos, and Cambodia, to name just a few. Asian Americans vary not only by their country of origin but also by the time of their arrival in the United States. There are Chinese and Japanese Americans whose families have lived here for nearly two centuries, arriving in the early 1800s with the waves of immigrants who came to work in the frontier West. In part because of the resentment of white workers, whose wages were being squeezed by the low pay the immigrants would accept, Congress passed the Chinese Exclusion Act in 1882, halting immigration from China, and the National Origin Act of 1925, barring the entry of the Japanese. It was 1943 before Congress repealed the Chinese Exclusion Act, and 1965 before Asian immigrants were treated the same as those of other nationalities. Asians and Pacific Islanders are currently the fastest-growing immigrant group in America, arriving from all over Asia but in particular from the war-torn countries of Vietnam, Laos, and Cambodia.

Today Asian Americans live in every region of the United States. In 2012 Asians comprised 56.4 percent of the population in Hawaii, and six million were living in California.[68] As of 2012, Asians were the fastest growing racial or ethnic group in the country, with 60 percent of their growth coming from international migration. Los Angeles had the largest Asian population of any U.S. county. The more recent immigrants are spread unevenly throughout the country, with increasing numbers in the south.

DISCRIMINATION Asians have faced discrimination in the United States since their arrival. The fact that they are identifiable by their appearance has made assimilation into the larger European American population difficult. While most immigrants dream of becoming citizens in their new country, and eventually gaining political influence through the right to vote, that option was not open to Asians. The Naturalization Act of 1790 provided only for white immigrants to become naturalized citizens, and with few exceptions—for Filipino soldiers in the U.S. Army during World War II, for example—the act was in force until 1952. Branded "aliens ineligible for citizenship," not only were Asians permanently disenfranchised, but in many states they could not even own or rent property. Female citizens wishing to marry Asian "aliens" lost their own citizenship. The exclusionary immigration laws of 1882 and 1925 reflect this country's hostility to Asians, but at no other time was anti-Asian sentiment so painfully evident than in the white American reaction to Japanese Americans during World War II.

When the United States found itself at war with Japan, there was a strong backlash against Asian Americans. Because most Americans could not tell the difference between people from different Asian heritages, non-Japanese citizens found it necessary to wear buttons proclaiming "I am Korean" or "I am Filipino" to avoid having rocks and racial insults hurled at them.[69] In 1942, however, the U.S. government began to round up Japanese Americans, forcing them to abandon or sell their property, and putting them in detention camps for purposes of "national security." While the government was worried about security threats posed by those with Japanese sympathies, two-thirds of the 120,000 incarcerated were American citizens. Neither German Americans nor Italian Americans, both of whose homelands were also at war with the United States, were stripped of their rights. Remarkably, after they were incarcerated, young Japanese men were asked to sign oaths of loyalty to the American government so that they could be drafted into military service. Those who refused in outrage over their treatment were imprisoned. The crowning insult was the Supreme Court's approval of curfews and detention camps for Japanese Americans.[70] Though the government later backed down and, in fact, in 1988 paid $1.25 billion as reparation to survivors of the ordeal, the Japanese internment camps remain a major scar on America's civil rights record.

THE PRICE OF PROSPERITY One unusual feature of the Asian American experience is their overall academic success and corresponding economic prosperity. Although all Asian groups have not been equally successful (groups that have immigrated primarily as refugees—like the Vietnamese—have higher rates of poverty than do others), median household income in 2010 was $64,308 for Asian and Pacific Islanders, compared with $51,846 for whites, $37,759 for Hispanics, and $32,068 for blacks.[71] A number of factors probably account for this success. Forced out of wage labor in the West in the 1880s by resentful white workers, Asian immigrants developed entrepreneurial skills and many came to own their own businesses and restaurants. A cultural emphasis on hard work and high achievement lent itself particularly well to success in the American education system and culture of equality of opportunity. Furthermore, many Asian immigrants were highly skilled and professional workers in their own countries and passed on the values of their achievements to their children.

High school and college graduation rates are higher among Asian Americans than among other ethnic groups, and are at least as high as, and in some places higher than, those of whites. In 2013, 19.9 percent of the students at Harvard were Asian, as were 22 percent at Stanford, 30 percent at MIT, and 42.3 percent at the University of California, Berkeley.[72] What their high levels of academic success sometimes mean for Asian Americans is that they become the targets of racist attacks by resentful whites.[73] Asian Americans have accused schools like Stanford, Brown, Harvard, and Berkeley of "capping" the number of Asians they admit, and white alumni who feel that slots at these elite schools should be reserved for their children have complained about the numbers of Asians in attendance. Although the schools deny the capping charges, Asian American students won favorable judgments in sixteen out of forty complaints they filed with the Department of Education between 1988 and 1995, a much higher rate than that achieved by any other racial group.[74] Their success also means that Asian Americans stand in an odd relationship to affirmative action, a set of policies that usually helps minorities blocked from traditional paths to economic prosperity. While affirmative action policies might benefit them in hiring situations, they actually harm Asian Americans seeking to go to universities or professional schools. Because these students are generally so well qualified, more of them would be admitted if race were not taken into account to permit the admission of Hispanic and African American students. Policies that pit minority groups against each other in this way do not promote solidarity and community among them and make racist attitudes even harder to overcome.

POLITICAL STRATEGIES According to all our conventional understanding of what makes people vote in the United States, participation among Asian Americans ought to be quite high. Voter turnout usually rises along with education and income levels, yet Asian American voter registration and turnout rates have been among the lowest in the nation. Particularly in states with a sizable number of Asian Americans such as California, where they constitute 13.4 percent of the population, their political representation and influence do not reflect their numbers.[75]

Political observers account for this lack of participation in several ways. Until after World War II, as we saw, immigration laws restricted the citizenship rights of Asian Americans. In addition, the political systems that many Asian immigrants left behind did not have traditions of democratic political participation. Finally, many Asian Americans came to the United States for economic reasons and have focused their attentions on building economic security rather than learning to navigate an unfamiliar political system.[76]

Some evidence indicates, however, that this trend of nonparticipation is changing. Researchers have found that where Asian Americans do register, they tend to vote at rates higher than those of other groups.[77] In 2012 there were two Asian American governors (Bobby Jindal of

Louisiana and Nikki Haley of South Carolina). The 114th Congress saw seven Asian American members of the House of Representatives, and one Asian American senator. In the end, Asian Americans made up 3 percent of the electorate, and overwhelmingly supported Barack Obama in 2012, 73 to 26 percent.

One reason for the increasing participation of Asian Americans, in addition to the success of voter registration drives, is that many Asian Americans are finding themselves more and more affected by public policies. Welfare reform that strips many elderly legal immigrants of their benefits, changes in immigration laws, and affirmative action are among the issues driving Asian Americans to the polls. However, even continued efforts to register this group are unlikely to bring about electoral results as dramatic as those that we are starting to see for Hispanics, because Asian Americans tend to split their votes more or less equally between Democrats and Republicans.[78] Whereas African Americans vote for Democratic candidates over Republicans at a ratio of eight to one, and Hispanics, two to one, Asian Americans generally favor the Democrats only slightly.[79]

PAUSE AND REVIEW:

WHO, WHAT, HOW

Native Americans' rights have been denied through the Supreme Court's interpretation of the commerce clause, giving Congress power over them and their lands. Because neither Congress nor the courts have been receptive to the claims of Native Americans, they have sought to force the American government to fulfill its promises to them and to gain political rights and economic well-being by working outside the system and using the resources generated from running casinos.

Hispanics too have been denied their rights, partly through general discrimination but partly through organized movements such as the English-only movement and anti-immigration efforts. Because of their diversity and low levels of socioeconomic achievement, they have not been very successful in organizing to fight for their rights politically. Tactics that Hispanic leaders use include boycotts and voter education and registration drives.

Finally, Asian Americans, long prevented by law from becoming citizens and under suspicion during World War II, have also had to bear the collective brunt of Americans' discriminatory actions. As diverse as Hispanics, Asian Americans have also failed to organize politically. Their socio-economic fate, however, has been different from that of many Hispanic groups, and as a group, Asian Americans have managed to thrive economically in their own communities despite political discrimination.

IN YOUR OWN WORDS >> Explain the different paths to equality taken by other racial and ethnic groups.

RIGHTS DENIED ON THE BASIS OF GENDER
Fighting the early battles for equality at the state level

Of all the battles fought for equal rights in the American political system, the women's struggle has been perhaps the most peculiar, because women, while certainly denied most imaginable civil and economic rights, were not outside the system in the same way that racial and ethnic groups have been. Most women lived with their husbands or fathers, and many shared their view that men, not women, should have power in the political world. Women's realm, after all, was the home, and the prevailing belief was that women were too good, too pure, too chaste, to deal with the sordid world outside. As a New Jersey senator argued in the late 1800s, women should not be allowed to vote because they have "a higher and holier mission. . . . Their mission is at home."[80] Today there are still some women as well as men who agree with the gist of this sentiment. That means that the struggle for women's rights not only has failed to win the support of all women but also has been actively opposed by some, as well as by many men whose power, standing, and worldview it has threatened.

WOMEN'S PLACE IN THE EARLY NINETEENTH CENTURY

The legal and economic position of women in the early nineteenth century, though not exactly "slavery," in some ways was not much different. According to English common law, on which our legal system was based, when a woman married, she merged her legal identity with her husband's, which is to say in practical terms, she no longer had one. Once married, she could not be a party to a contract, bring a lawsuit, own or inherit property, earn wages for any service, gain custody of her children in case of divorce, or initiate divorce from an abusive husband. If her husband were not a U.S. citizen, she lost her own citizenship. Neither married nor unmarried women could vote. In exchange for the legal identity his wife gave up, a husband was expected to provide security for her, and if he died without a will, she was entitled to one-third of his estate. If he made a will and left her out of it, however, she had no legal recourse to protect herself and her children.[81]

CLUES
TO CRITICAL THINKING

"Ain't I a Woman?"

By Sojourner Truth, speaking at the Women's Rights Convention in Akron, Ohio, 1851

There were both women and men at the Women's Rights Convention in Akron in 1851, but the convention was dominated by impassioned arguments from men who believed that women were not capable of doing the things men did and were not made equal by God. Sojourner Truth was an emancipated slave from New York with a commanding presence and a spellbinding speaking voice. When she rose to speak, her listeners found themselves torn between cheers and tears. Though Truth herself has become the stuff of legend, her speech remains today a brief but powerful comment on gender roles.

Well, children, where there is so much racket there must be something out of kilter. I think that 'twixt the negroes of the South and the women at the North, all talking about rights, the white men will be in a fix pretty soon. But what's all this here talking about?

That man over there says that women need to be helped into carriages, and lifted over ditches, and to have the best place everywhere. Nobody ever helps me into carriages, or over mud-puddles, or gives me any best place! And ain't I a woman? Look at me! Look at my arm! I have ploughed and planted, and gathered into barns, and no man could head me! And ain't I a woman? I could work as much and eat as much as a man—when I could get it—and bear the lash as well! And ain't I a woman? I have borne thirteen children, and seen most all sold off to slavery, and when I cried out with my mother's grief, none but Jesus heard me! And ain't I a woman?

Then they talk about this thing in the head; what's this they call it? [member of audience whispers, "intellect"] That's it, honey. What's that got to do with women's rights or negroes' rights? If my cup won't hold but a pint, and yours holds a quart, wouldn't you be mean not to let me have my little half measure full?

Then that little man in black there, he says women can't have as much rights as men, 'cause Christ wasn't a woman! Where did your Christ come from? Where did your Christ come from? From God and a woman! Man had nothing to do with Him.

If the first woman God ever made was strong enough to turn the world upside down all alone, these women together ought to be able to turn it back, and get it right side up again! And now they is asking to do it, the men better let them.

Obliged to you for hearing me, and now old Sojourner ain't got nothing more to say.

Source: Sojourner Truth Institute, http://www.sojournertruth.org/Library/Speeches/AintIAWoman.htm.

Consider the source and the audience: How might Sojourner Truth's audience have affected how she presented her message? Most contemporary accounts of her speech come to us from her supporters. How might this fact shape the context in which we read her words today?

Lay out the argument, the values, and the assumptions: Truth was a slave until New York freed all its slaves in 1828, when she was approximately thirty years old. To what extent did her personal experience fit with the notions that women were too weak and needed too much pampering to be equal to men? What idea of equality does she seem to be working with? Does she think equal means identical? What is her image of God? Does God have a gender?

Uncover the evidence: What is Truth's evidence that women can be as strong and tough as men? Is it compelling? Can she prove God's will? Can her opponents? Can anyone win that part of the argument? If so, how?

Evaluate the conclusion: Is Truth's claim that all people should be allowed to develop to their capacity convincing today? Why would anyone ever have opposed it?

Sort out the political significance: Truth's contention that the mystique of feminine weakness and delicacy didn't apply to slave women and thus probably didn't apply to white women must have been shocking at the time. Do we still have different expectations of people according to gender and race?

Opportunities were not plentiful for women who preferred to remain unmarried. Poor women worked in domestic service and, later, in the textile industry. But most married women did not work outside the home. For unmarried women, the professions available were those that fit their supposed womanly nature and that paid too little to be attractive to men, primarily nursing and teaching. Women who tried to break the occupational barriers were usually rebuffed, and for those who prevailed, success was often a mixed blessing. When in 1847, after many rejections and a miserable time in medical school, Elizabeth Blackwell graduated at the top of her class to become the first woman doctor in the United States, the only way she could get patients was to open her own hospital for women and children. The legal profession did not welcome women either, because once women were married, they could no longer be recognized in court. In 1860 Belle Mansfield was admitted to the Iowa bar by a judge sympathetic to the cause of women's rights. But when Myra Bradwell became the first woman law school graduate ten years later, the Illinois bar refused to admit her. Rather than support her, the U.S. Supreme Court ruled that admission to the bar was the states' prerogative.[82]

THE BIRTH OF THE WOMEN'S RIGHTS MOVEMENT

The women's movement is commonly dated from an 1848 convention on women's rights held in Seneca Falls, New York. There, men and women who supported the extension of rights to women issued a Declaration of Principles that deliberately sought to evoke the sentiments of those calling for freedom from political oppression. Echoing the Declaration of Independence, it stated:

> We hold these truths to be self-evident: that all men and women are created equal; that they are endowed by their Creator with certain inalienable rights; that among these are life, liberty and the pursuit of happiness.

Against the advice of many of those present, a resolution was proposed to demand the vote for women. It was the only resolution not to receive the convention's unanimous support—even among supporters of women's rights, the right to vote was controversial. Other propositions were enthusiastically and unanimously approved, among them calls for the right to own property, to have access to higher education, and to receive custody of children after divorce. Some of these demands were realized in New York by the 1848 Married Women's Property Act, and still others in an 1860 New York law, but these rights were not extended to all American women, and progress was slow. (See *CLUES to Critical Thinking*.)

The women's movement picked up steam after Seneca Falls and the victories in New York, but it had yet to settle on a political strategy. The courts were closed to women, of course, much as had been for Dred Scott; women simply weren't allowed access to the legal arena. For a long time, women's rights advocates worked closely with the antislavery movement, assuming that when blacks received their rights, as they did with the passage of the Fourteenth Amendment, they and the Republican Party would rally to the women's cause. Not only did that fail to happen, but the passage of the Fourteenth Amendment marked the first time the word *male* appeared in the Constitution. There was a bitter split between the two movements, and afterward it was not unheard of for women's rights advocates to promote their cause, especially in the South, with racist appeals, arguing that giving women the right to vote would dilute the impact of black voters.

In 1869 the women's movement itself split into two groups, divided by philosophy and strategy. The National Woman Suffrage Association took a broad view of the suffrage issue and included among its goals the reform of job discrimination, labor conditions, and divorce law. It favored a federal suffrage amendment, which required work at the national level. Regularly, from 1878 to 1896 and again after 1913, the Susan B. Anthony Amendment, named after an early advocate of women's rights, was introduced into Congress but failed to pass. The American Woman Suffrage Association, on the other hand, took a different tack, focusing its efforts on the less dramatic but more practical task of changing state electoral laws. It was this state strategy that would prove effective and finally create the conditions under which the Susan B. Anthony Nineteenth Amendment would be passed and ratified in 1920.

THE STRUGGLE IN THE STATES

The state strategy was a smart one for women. Unlike the situation that blacks faced after the war, the national government did not support the women's cause. It was possible for women to have an impact on state governments, however. Different states have different cultures and traditions, and the Constitution allows them to decide who may legally vote. Women were able to target states that were sympathetic to them and gradually gain enough political clout that their demands were listened to on the national level.

Women had been able to vote since 1869 in the Territory of Wyoming. In frontier country, it wasn't possible for women to be as protected as they might be back East, and when they proved capable of taking on a variety of other roles, it was hard to justify denying them the same rights as men. When Wyoming applied for statehood in 1889, Congress tried to impose the disenfranchisement of women as the price of admission to the Union. The Wyoming legislature responded, "We will remain out of the Union a hundred years rather than come in without the women."[83] When Wyoming was finally admitted to the United States, it was the first state to allow women to vote.

That success was not to prove contagious, however. From 1870 to 1910, women waged 480 campaigns in thirty-three states, caused seventeen referenda to be held in eleven states, and won in only two of them: Colorado (1893) and

FIGURE 6.1 **WOMEN'S RIGHT TO VOTE BEFORE THE NINETEENTH AMENDMENT (1920)**

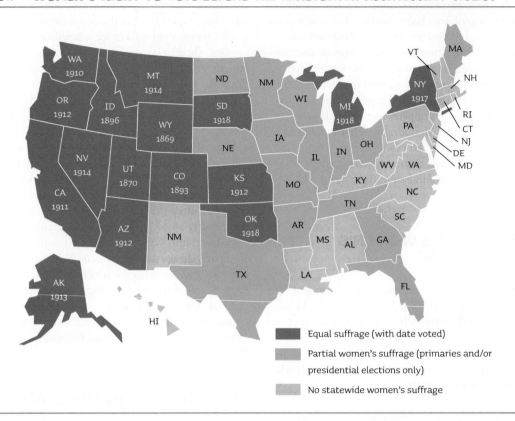

WA 1910
MT 1914
ND
NM
VT
MA
NH
OR 1912
ID 1896
WY 1869
SD 1918
WI
MI 1918
NY 1917
RI
CT
NJ
DE
MD
NV 1914
UT 1870
NE
IA
IL
IN
OH
PA
WV
VA
CA 1911
CO 1893
KS 1912
MO
KY
NC
AZ 1912
NM
OK 1918
AR
TN
SC
MS
AL
GA
AK 1913
TX
LA
FL
HI

■ Equal suffrage (with date voted)

■ Partial women's suffrage (primaries and/or presidential elections only)

■ No statewide women's suffrage

Idaho (1896). In 1890 the National and American Woman Suffrage Associations merged, becoming the National American Woman Suffrage Association (NAWSA), and began to refine their state-level strategy. By 1912, women could vote in states, primarily in the West, that controlled 74 of the total 483 Electoral College votes that decided the presidency, but the movement was facing strong external opposition and was being torn apart internally by political differences.

In 1914 an impatient, militant offshoot of NAWSA began to work at the national level again, picketing the White House and targeting the president's party, contributing to the defeat of twenty-three of forty-three Democratic candidates in the western states where women could vote. The appearance of political power lent momentum to the state-level efforts. In 1917 North Dakota gave women presidential suffrage; then Ohio, Indiana, Rhode Island, Nebraska, and Michigan followed suit. Arkansas and New York joined the list later that year. NAWSA issued a statement to members of Congress that if they would not pass the Susan B. Anthony Amendment, it would work to defeat every legislator who opposed it. The amendment passed in the House, but not the Senate, and NAWSA targeted four senators. Two were defeated, and two held on to their seats by only narrow margins. Nine

more states gave women the right to vote in presidential elections (see Figure 6.1).

In 1919 the Susan B. Anthony Amendment was reintroduced into Congress with the support of President Woodrow Wilson and passed by the necessary two-thirds majority in both houses. When, in August 1920, Tennessee became the thirty-sixth state to ratify the Nineteenth Amendment, for the required total of three-fourths of the state legislatures, women finally had the vote nationwide. Unlike the situation faced by African Americans, the legal victory ended the battle. Enforcement was not as difficult as enforcement of the Fifteenth Amendment, although many women were not inclined to use their newly won right. But until the end, the opposition had been petty and virulent, and the victory was only narrowly won.

WINNERS AND LOSERS IN THE SUFFRAGE MOVEMENT

The debate over women's suffrage, like the fight over black civil rights, hit bitter depths because so much was at stake. If women were to acquire political rights, opponents feared, an entire way of life would be over. And, of course, in many ways they were right.

The opposition to women's suffrage came from a number of different directions. In the South, white men rejected women's suffrage for fear that women would encourage enforcement of the Civil War amendments, giving political power to blacks. And if women could vote, then of course black women could vote, further weakening the white male position. Believing that women would force temperance on the nation, brewing and liquor interests fought the women's campaign vigorously, stuffing ballot boxes and pouring huge sums of money into antisuffrage efforts. In the East, industrial and business interests, concerned that voting women would pass enlightened labor legislation, also opposed suffrage. Antisuffrage women's groups, usually composed of upper-class women, claimed that their duties at home were more than enough for women, and that suffrage was unnecessary since men represented and watched out for the interests of women.[84] For some well-to-do women, the status quo was comfortable, and changing expectations about women's roles could only threaten that security.

Everything these opponents feared came to pass eventually, although not necessarily as the result of women voting. In fact, in the immediate aftermath of the Nineteenth Amendment, the results of women's suffrage were disappointing to supporters. Blacks and immigrants were still being discriminated against in many parts of the country, effectively preventing both males and females from voting. Political parties excluded women, and most women lacked the money, political contacts, and experience to get involved in politics. Perhaps most important, general cultural attitudes worked against women's political participation. Politically active women were ostracized and accused of being unfeminine, making political involvement costly to many women.[85] While the women's rights advocates were clear winners in the suffrage fight, it took a long time for all the benefits of victory to materialize. As the battle over the Equal Rights Amendment (ERA) was to show, attitudes toward women were changing at a glacial pace.

THE EQUAL RIGHTS AMENDMENT

The Nineteenth Amendment gave women the right to vote, but it did not ensure the constitutional protection against discrimination that the Fourteenth Amendment had provided for African Americans. Even though the Fourteenth Amendment technically applied to women as well as men, the courts did not interpret it that way. It was not unconstitutional to treat people differently on account of gender. Since the ratification of the Nineteenth

> **Equal Rights Amendment** constitutional amendment passed by Congress but never ratified that would have banned discrimination on the basis of gender

From the collection of Christine Barbour

Democrat: *May I have the Honor?*
Republican: *May I have the Honor?*

Going to the Dance
In 1919, with the Nineteenth Amendment headed toward final ratification, women began to sense the first signs of real political power.

Amendment in 1920, some women's groups had been working for the passage of an additional **Equal Rights Amendment** that would ban discrimination on the basis of sex and guarantee women the equal protection of the laws. Objections to the proposed amendment again came from many different directions. Traditionalists, both men and women, opposed changing the status quo and giving more power to the federal government. But there were also women, and supporters of women's rights, who feared that requiring laws to treat men and women the same would actually make women worse off by nullifying the variety of legislation that sought to protect women. Many social reformers, for instance, had worked for laws that would limit working hours or establish minimum wages for women, which now would be in jeopardy. Opponents also feared that an ERA would strike down laws preventing women from being drafted and sent into combat. Many laws in American society treat men and women differently, and few, if any, would survive under such an amendment. Nonetheless, an ERA was proposed to Congress on a fairly regular basis.

In the 1960s the political omens started to look more hopeful for expanding women's rights. Support for women's rights more generally came from an unlikely

Politics Matters—Title IX Evens the Score

Players from the University of Connecticut's men's and women's basketball teams—both of which would go on to NCAA titles in 2014—high five during an intersquad scrimmage. Title IX of the Higher Education Act, passed in 1972, sought to end discrimination in athletic programs at institutions receiving federal funding; it has resulted in more sports programs and scholarships for young women and a stronger field of female athletes. Since 1999, UConn's women Huskies have won the championship seven times; the men, four.

quarter, however. Title VII of the Civil Rights Act of 1964, intended to prohibit job discrimination on the basis of race, was amended to include discrimination on the basis of gender, as well, in the hopes that the addition would doom the bill's passage. Unexpectedly, the amended bill passed.

In 1967 the National Organization for Women (NOW) was organized to promote women's rights and lent its support to the ERA. Several pieces of legislation that passed in the early seventies signaled that public opinion was favorable to the idea of expanding women's rights. Title IX of the Education Amendments of 1972 banned sex discrimination in schools receiving federal funds, which meant, among other things, that schools had to provide girls with the equal opportunity and support to play sports in school. The Revenue Act of 1972 provided for tax credits for child care.

In 1970 the ERA was again introduced in the House, and this time it passed. But the Senate spent the next two years refining the language of the amendment, adding and removing provisions that would have kept women from being drafted. Arguing that such changes would not amount to true equality, advocates of equal rights for women managed to defeat them. Finally, on March 22, 1972, the ERA passed in the Senate. The exact language of the proposed amendment read:

1. Equality of rights under the law shall not be denied or abridged by the United States or by any State on account of sex.

2. The Congress shall have the power to enforce, by appropriate legislation, the provisions of this article.

3. This amendment shall take effect two years after the date of ratification.

When both houses of Congress passed the final version of the amendment, the process of getting approval of three-quarters of the state legislatures began. Thirty states had ratified the amendment by early 1973. But while public opinion polls showed support for the idea of giving constitutional protection to women's rights, the votes at the state level began to go the other way. By 1977 only thirty-five states had voted to ratify, three short of the necessary thirty-eight. Despite the extension of the ratification deadline from 1979 to 1982, the amendment died unratified.

Why did a ratification process that started out with such promise fizzle so abruptly? The ERA failed to pass for several reasons. First, while most people supported the idea of women's rights in the abstract, they weren't sure what the consequences of such an amendment would be, and people feared the possibility of radical social change. Second, the ERA came to be identified in the public's mind with the 1973 Supreme Court ruling in *Roe v. Wade* that women have abortion rights in the first trimester of their pregnancies. Professor Jane Mansbridge argued that conservative opponents of the ERA managed to link the two issues, claiming that the ERA was a rejection of motherhood and traditional values, and turning ERA votes into referenda on abortion.[86]

Finally, the Supreme Court had been striking down some (though not all) laws that treated women differently from men, using the equal protection clause of the Fourteenth Amendment.[87] This caused some people to argue that the ERA was unnecessary, which probably reassured those who approved of the principle of equality but had no desire to turn society upside-down.

THINKING OUTSIDE THE BOX

Is it possible to have too much equality?

GENDER DISCRIMINATION TODAY

Despite the failure of the ERA, today most of the legal barriers to women's equality in this country have been eliminated. But because the ERA did not pass, and there is no constitutional amendment specifically guaranteeing equal protection of the laws regardless of gender, the Supreme Court has not been willing to treat gender as a suspect classification, although it has come close at times. Laws that treat men and women differently are subject only to the intermediate standard of review, not the strict scrutiny test. There must be only an important government purpose for laws that discriminate against women, not a compelling interest. Examples of laws that have failed that test, and thus have been struck down by the Court, include portions of the Social Security Act that give benefits to widows but not to widowers, and laws that require husbands but not wives to be liable for alimony payments.[88] Some laws that do treat men and women differently—for instance, statutory rape laws and laws requiring that only males be drafted—have been upheld by the Court.

Having achieved formal equality, women still face some striking discrimination in the workplace. (See "*Snapshot of America:* How Equal Are We, by Gender?".) Women today earn seventy-seven cents for every dollar earned by men, and the National Committee on Pay Equity, a nonprofit group in Washington, calculates that that pay gap may cost women almost a half-million dollars over the course of their work lives.[89] Women's ability to seek remedies for this discrimination has been limited by law. In 2007 the U.S. Supreme Court ruled in a five-to-four decision that a female worker's right to sue for discrimination was constrained by the statutes of limitations in existing civil rights law.[90] On January 29, 2009, the first bill signed into law by President Obama was the Lilly Ledbetter Act, extending the time frame so that workers could still sue even if the wage discrimination against them revealed itself over time. A companion piece to this legislation, the Paycheck Fairness Act, would prohibit discrimination and retaliation against workers who bring discrimination claims. It passed in the House in 2009 but stalled in the Senate. As of 2014 it remains a controversial proposal, with Democrats claiming women should have increased legal protection in the workplace, and Republicans arguing that women make less money than men for reasons other than discrimination (like the decision to leave the labor market to have children), and that market forces ought to prevail without regulation.

In addition, women are tremendously underrepresented at the upper levels of corporate management, academic administration, and other top echelons of power. Some people argue that women fail to achieve levels of power and salary on a par with men because many women may leave and enter the job market several times or put their careers on hold to have children. Such interruptions prevent them from accruing the kind of seniority that pays

dividends for men. The so-called Mommy track has been blamed for much of the disparity between men's and women's positions in the world. Others argue, however, that there is an enduring difference in the hiring and salary patterns of women that has nothing to do with child-bearing, or else reflects male inflexibility when it comes to incorporating motherhood and corporate responsibility. These critics claim that there is a "glass ceiling" in the corporate world, invisible to the eye but impenetrable, that prevents women from rising to their full potential. The Civil Rights Act of 1991 created the Glass Ceiling Commission to study this phenomenon, and among the commission's conclusions was the observation that business is depriving itself of a large pool of talent by denying leadership positions to women.

Ever since President Johnson's executive order of 1965 was amended in 1968 to include gender, the federal government has had not only to stop discriminating against women in its hiring practices but also to take affirmative action to make sure that women are hired. Many other levels of government take gender into consideration when they hire, and the Supreme Court has upheld the practice.[91] But it is hard to mandate change in leadership positions when the number of jobs is few to begin with and the patterns of discrimination appear across corporations, universities, and foundations.

Some analysts have argued that the glass ceiling is a phenomenon that affects relatively few women, and that most women today are less preoccupied with moving up the corporate ladder than with making a decent living, or getting off what one observer has called the "sticky floor" of low-paying jobs.[92] While the wage gap between men and women with advanced education is narrowing, women still tend to be excluded from the more lucrative blue-collar positions in manufacturing, construction, communication, and transportation.[93]

Getting hired, maintaining equal pay, and earning promotions are not the only challenges women face on the job. They are often subject to unwelcome sexual advances, comments, or jokes that make their jobs unpleasant, offensive, and unusually stressful. Sexual harassment, brought to national attention during the Senate confirmation hearings for Clarence Thomas's appointment to the Supreme Court in 1991, often makes the workplace a hostile environment for women. Now technically illegal, it is often difficult to define and document, and women have traditionally faced retribution from employers and fellow workers for calling attention to such practices. In the late 1990s it became clear that even when the U.S. government is the employer, **sexual harassment** can run rampant. The much-publicized cases of sexual harassment in the military show that progress toward gender equality in the armed forces still has a long way to go, and cases like the 2004 lawsuit against such prominent private employers as Merrill Lynch, Morgan Stanley, and Boeing indicate that the problem continues to plague the private sector, too.

> **sexual harassment** unwelcome sexual speech or behavior that creates a hostile work environment

SNAPSHOT OF AMERICA: HOW EQUAL ARE WE, BY GENDER?

Gender Wage Gap for Different Professions: Annual Earnings

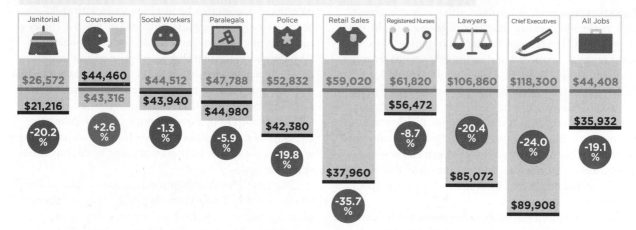

Janitorial	Counselors	Social Workers	Paralegals	Police	Retail Sales	Registered Nurses	Lawyers	Chief Executives	All Jobs
$26,572	$44,460	$44,512	$47,788	$52,832	$59,020	$61,820	$106,860	$118,300	$44,408
$21,216	$43,316	$43,940	$44,980	$42,380	$37,960	$56,472	$85,072	$89,908	$35,932
-20.2%	+2.6%	-1.3%	-5.9%	-19.8%	-35.7%	-8.7%	-20.4%	-24.0%	-19.1%

Women's Salary as a Percentage of Men's

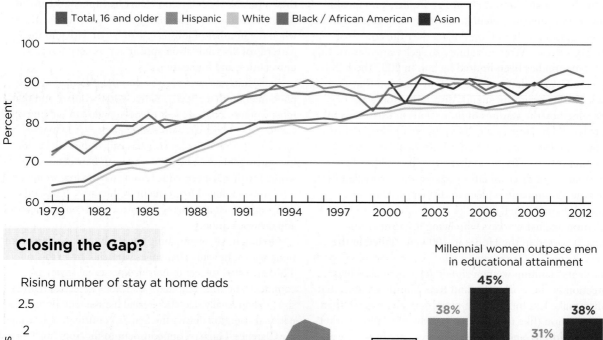

Legend: Total, 16 and older | Hispanic | White | Black / African American | Asian

Y-axis: Percent (60, 70, 80, 90, 100)
X-axis: 1979, 1982, 1985, 1988, 1991, 1994, 1997, 2000, 2003, 2006, 2009, 2012

Closing the Gap?

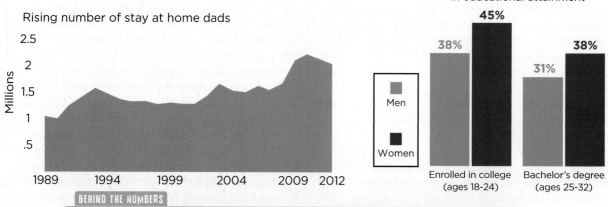

Rising number of stay at home dads

Y-axis: Millions (.5, 1, 1.5, 2, 2.5)
X-axis: 1989, 1994, 1999, 2004, 2009, 2012

Millennial women outpace men in educational attainment

- Men
- Women

Enrolled in college (ages 18-24): 38% / 45%
Bachelor's degree (ages 25-32): 31% / 38%

BEHIND THE NUMBERS

Men make more than women overall, but the size of the pay gap varies by profession and by racial and ethnic group. What factors might account for these differences in the pay gap? With more stay-at-home dads, and more women attending and finishing college, will this pay inequality be a concern for the millennial generation?

Source: U.S. Bureau of Labor Statistics, Highlights of Women's Earnings, October 2013, www.bls.gov/cps/cpswom2012.pdf.

Another form of employment discrimination is highlighted in the recent dramatic rise in the number of cases of discrimination reported by pregnant women. Between fiscal years 1992 and 2003, pregnancy discrimination complaints filed with the EEOC jumped 39 percent, outpacing sexual harassment claims.[94] Allegations of pregnant women being unfairly fired or denied promotion have been made against several companies, including Wal-Mart and Hooters. In one study, roughly half of the sample of pregnant women stated that their bosses had had negative reactions to the pregnancies.

WOMEN IN CONTEMPORARY POLITICS

Women still face discrimination not only in the boardroom but in politics as well. While more women today hold elected office than at any other time in history, women still remain the most underrepresented group in Congress and the state legislatures.

AP Photo/Steven Senne

A Game-Changing Lineup

The field of candidates vying for the Democratic presidential nomination in January 2008—Bill Richardson, who is Hispanic; Hillary Clinton; John Edwards; and Barack Obama—resembled the cast of a public service announcement about the opportunities for women and multicultural individuals in twenty-first-century America. A century earlier, not all the individuals pictured would have had the opportunity to vote, much less run for the nation's highest office.

Women have been underrepresented in government for many reasons. Some observers argue that women may be less likely to have access to the large amounts of money needed to run a successful campaign. A study of U.S. House candidates from the 1970s to the 1990s shows that women candidates raised and spent about three-fourths of what a male candidate did between 1974 and 1980. However, by 1990, women candidates for the House raised and spent *more* money than did male candidates; women candidates raised 111 percent of what male candidates did for the 1992 race.[95] Others argue that women are not as likely as men to want to go in to politics. For instance, more women candidates for state legislative office report waiting to wage a campaign until after they were asked to run by a party or legislative official.[96]

However, the representation of women in government is clearly better than it was. In 1971 women comprised only 2 percent of Congress members and less than 5 percent of state legislators. By 2014, 18.5 percent of Congress members and 24.2 percent of state legislators were female, both all-time highs. In the 114th Congress, 84 of 435 members of the House of Representatives were female and there were 20 female senators. In 2014 women held 22.6 percent of all statewide executive offices including five governorships, eleven lieutenant governorships,[97] and, 249, or 18.4 percent, of the cities with populations of more than 30,000 had female mayors.[98] In 2014 the state of New Hampshire had elected an all-female congressional delegation (two members of the House and two senators) as well as a female governor.

A January 2014 poll even showed that 77 percent of those surveyed think that the United States would have a woman president within the next ten years.[99] Indeed, Hillary Clinton came very close to winning the Democratic nomination for president back in 2008, and polls at the time indicated that she could have beaten Republican John McCain. In her concession speech, she reflected on the impact of her candidacy this way:

Now, on a personal note—when I was asked what it means to be a woman running for president, I always gave the same answer: that I was proud to be running as a woman but I was running because I thought I'd be the best president. But I am a

SNAPSHOT OF AMERICA: HOW DO AMERICAN WOMEN COMPARE?

The Global Gender Gap index provides a framework for capturing the scope of gender-based disparities through benchmarks of national gender gaps on economic, political, education, and health criteria.

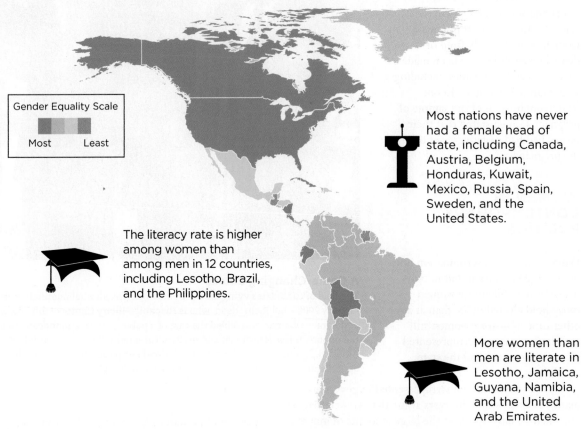

Gender Equality Scale

Most   Least

Most nations have never had a female head of state, including Canada, Austria, Belgium, Honduras, Kuwait, Mexico, Russia, Spain, Sweden, and the United States.

The literacy rate is higher among women than among men in 12 countries, including Lesotho, Brazil, and the Philippines.

More women than men are literate in Lesotho, Jamaica, Guyana, Namibia, and the United Arab Emirates.

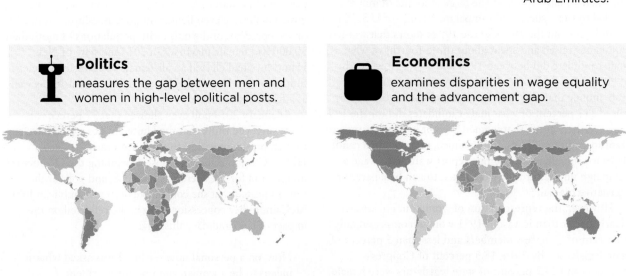

Politics
measures the gap between men and women in high-level political posts.

Economics
examines disparities in wage equality and the advancement gap.

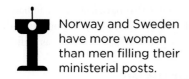 Norway and Sweden have more women than men filling their ministerial posts.

 There are only 24 women CEOs of Fortune 500 companies

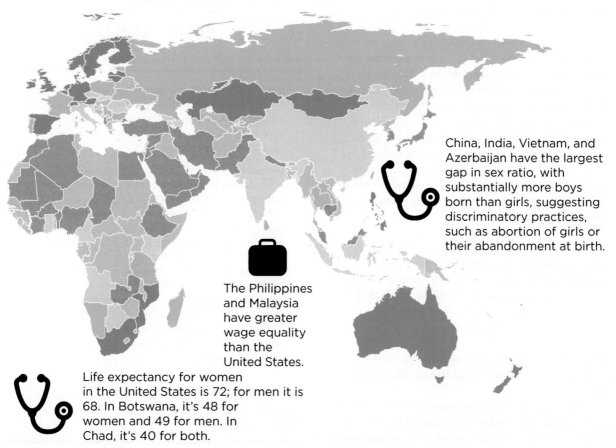

China, India, Vietnam, and Azerbaijan have the largest gap in sex ratio, with substantially more boys born than girls, suggesting discriminatory practices, such as abortion of girls or their abandonment at birth.

 The Philippines and Malaysia have greater wage equality than the United States.

 Life expectancy for women in the United States is 72; for men it is 68. In Botswana, it's 48 for women and 49 for men. In Chad, it's 40 for both.

Education
considers access to education, using the ratios of women to men in school.

Health
reflects sex ratio at birth and the life expectancy gap between men and women.

BEHIND THE NUMBERS

In the United States we are accustomed to thinking of ourselves on the forefront of civil rights, but when it comes to gender that is clearly not the case. We did not allow women the right to vote until 1920 and unlike many nations with worse records than ours we still have not elected a female chief executive. What might account for why some countries are so far ahead of others on all these dimensions of gender rights?

Source: World Economic Forum, "The Global Gender Gap Report 2013," [www3.weforum.org/docs/WEF_GenderGap_Report_2013.pdf].

woman, and like millions of women, I know there are still barriers and biases out there, often unconscious.

I want to build an America that respects and embraces the potential of every last one of us.

I ran as a daughter who benefited from opportunities my mother never dreamed of. I ran as a mother who worries about my daughter's future and a mother who wants to lead all children to brighter tomorrows. To build that future I see, we must make sure that women and men alike understand the struggles of their grandmothers and mothers, and that women enjoy equal opportunities, equal pay, and equal respect. Let us resolve and work toward achieving some very simple propositions: There are no acceptable limits and there are no acceptable prejudices in the twenty-first century.

You can be so proud that, from now on, it will be unremarkable for a woman to win primary state victories, unremarkable to have a woman in a close race to be our nominee, unremarkable to think that a woman can be the president of the United States. And that is truly remarkable.[100]

It's entirely likely that, barring some unforeseen circumstance, she will be a candidate for the presidency again in 2016.

Seeking to attract some of the women who were bitterly disappointed by Clinton's loss to Obama, McCain himself nominated a woman as his vice presidential running mate later in 2008. While no woman has yet attained the presidency, in 2006 Nancy Pelosi became the first female Speaker of the House, and three of the last four secretaries of state have been women. In fact, in 2010 the second and fourth officials in the line of succession to the president of the United States were women (the Speaker of the House follows the vice president, and the secretary of state comes after the president pro tempore of the Senate).

It is difficult to know if the underrepresentation of women throughout government has real policy consequences, but a variety of decisions affecting women ranging from issues concerning women in the marketplace to women's health are often without a significant female voice. In the past few years alone we have seen political battles over whether all women should be provided with services that help protect them against domestic violence, whether they should be able to sue easily for discrimination in the workplace, whether they should be guaranteed equal pay for equal work, whether they should have access to all forms of birth control, whether they are entitled to have that birth control covered by their health insurance policies, whether they should have to undergo an invasive form of ultrasound in order to have a legal abortion, and other similar issues. Some

research suggests that states that have a stronger female presence in the government may enact more "women-friendly" policies, although other political factors matter as well.[101]

PAUSE AND REVIEW:

WHO, WHAT, HOW

Supporters and opponents of the women's movement struggled mightily over the extension of rights to women. As in the battles we discussed earlier, at stake were not just civil rights but social and economic power as well.

Because the courts and Congress were at first off-limits to the women's movement, women took their fight to the states, with their more accepting cultures and less restrictive rules. Having finally gained the vote in enough states to put electoral pressure on national officials, women got the national vote in 1920. The Nineteenth Amendment, however, did not give them the same equal protection of the laws that the Fourteenth Amendment had given blacks. Today the courts give women greater protection of the law, but the failure of the ERA to be ratified means that laws that discriminate against them are still subject to only an intermediate standard of review.

IN YOUR OWN WORDS >> Describe how women have fought for equality and the changing role of women in American politics.

RIGHTS DENIED ON OTHER BASES
Challenging other classifications in the courts

Race, ethnicity, and gender, of course, are not the only grounds on which the laws treat people differently in the United States. Four other classifications that provide interesting insights into the politics of rights in America are sexual orientation, age, disability, and lack of citizenship.

SEXUAL ORIENTATION

Gays and lesbians have faced two kinds of legal discrimination in this country. On the one hand, overt discrimination simply prohibits some behaviors: until 2011 gays could not serve openly in the military, for instance, and in some states they cannot adopt children or teach in public schools. But a more subtle kind of discrimination doesn't forbid their actions or behavior; it simply fails to recognize them legally. Thus in many states gays still cannot marry or claim the rights that married people share, such as collecting their partner's Social Security, being covered by a partner's insurance plan, being each other's next of kin, or having a family. Some of these rights can be mimicked with complicated and expensive legal arrangements, some are possible because of the good will of particular companies toward their employees, but others, under the current laws, are out of reach. Being gay, unlike being black or female or Asian, is something that can be hidden from public view, and until the 1970s many gays escaped overt discrimination by denying or concealing who they were, but that too is a serious deprivation of civil rights.[102]

POLITICAL STRATEGIES: THE COURTS

As we discussed in Chapter 5, the case of *Bowers v. Hardwick* (1986) failed to advance the rights of gays and lesbians. The Court ruled that a Georgia statute against sodomy was a legitimate exercise of the state's power and that it met the minimum rationality test described earlier in this chapter.[103] The Court did not require that a law that treated people differently on the basis of sexual orientation had to fulfill either a compelling or an important state purpose; it merely had to be a reasonable use of state power. The four justices who dissented from that opinion did not want to tackle the issue of whether homosexuality was right or wrong. Rather they claimed that, as a privacy issue, what consenting adults do is none of the government's business.

Gay rights again took a hit in 1995, when the Court ruled that the South Boston Allied War Veterans Council did not have to let the Irish-American Gay, Lesbian and Bisexual Group of Boston march in its annual St. Patrick's Day parade under a banner proclaiming its sexual orientation. But the decision did not touch on the rights of homosexuals; it was based solely on the question of the veterans' group's right to freedom of expression.[104]

More recently, however, gays and lesbians have had some major victories in the courts. In 1996 a bitterly divided Court struck down an amendment to the Colorado constitution that would have prevented gays from suing for discrimination in housing and employment. The amendment had been a reaction on the part of conservative groups to legislation in several cities that would have made it illegal to discriminate against gays in housing, employment, and related matters. The Court ruled that gays could not be singled out and denied the fundamental protection of the laws, that "a state cannot deem a class of persons a stranger to its laws." While the majority on the Court did not rule in this case that sexual orientation was a suspect classification, it did hint at greater protection than the minimum rationality test would warrant.[105] For the first time, it treated gay rights as a civil rights issue.

In 2000 a bare majority on the Court relied on their precedent in the St. Patrick's Day parade case to rule on First Amendment grounds that the Boy Scouts of America had the right to exclude gay leaders because doing so was part of their "expressive message."[106] This ruling did not do anything to limit the more general civil rights issues that the Colorado case advanced.

The two biggest victories for gays and lesbians in a court of law, however, came in 2003. First, in *Lawrence v. Texas*, the Supreme Court overturned the *Bowers* decision, ruling that state sodomy laws were a violation of the right to privacy.[107] Even though many states had already repealed their sodomy laws, or failed to enforce them, the *Lawrence* decision was substantively and symbolically a break with previous judicial opinion that allowed the states to regulate the sexual behavior of gays and lesbians.

The gay and lesbian movement received another unexpected legal victory in 2003, when the Massachusetts Supreme Judicial Court ruled, in an extremely controversial four-to-three decision, that marriage was a civil right and that the state's law banning homosexual marriage violated the equal protection and due process clauses in the Massachusetts constitution.[108] The Massachusetts court ruling sent shockwaves throughout the country as the nation's first legal gay marriages were performed in Massachusetts. (Some local officials in California and New York began to conduct gay marriages as well, though these were later determined to be illegal.)

Critics on the right (and even some on the left) argued that the ruling was an example of judicial activism—of judges trying to legislate from the bench. They claimed that the court had overstepped its bounds and that decisions regarding marriage should be left to the state legislatures. Opponents of the decision also noted that the majority of the public opposed same-sex marriage. Almost immediately after the ruling, President Bush announced his support for an amendment to the Constitution defining marriage as a union between a man and a woman. However, because Congress had already passed a Defense of Marriage Act (DOMA) in 1996 asserting that states need not recognize gay marriages performed in other states, the amendment failed to garner much immediate congressional support.

The Supreme Court struck down DOMA as unconstitutional in 2013, but public opinion and state laws are changing so quickly on the subject, it is unlikely that such an amendment would gain traction. In reaction to the Massachusetts Supreme Court ruling, many states had taken measures to ban gay marriage by constitutional amendment or by statute, but in the wake of the Supreme Court's DOMA decision, many of those bans are being struck down in lower courts. Despite the popular backlash in some places, there has clearly been rapid movement toward an expansion of marriage rights at the state level. As we saw in *What's at Stake...in the Adoption of Marriage Equality?*, gay marriage is currently legal in thirty-two states and the District of Columbia, and is recognized by the federal government.

POLITICAL STRATEGIES: ELECTIONS

The courts are not the only political avenue open to gays in their struggle for equal rights. Gays have also been effective in parlaying their relatively small numbers into a force to be reckoned with electorally. Although it is difficult to gain an accurate idea of the size of the gay population in the United States,[109] between 4 and 5 percent of the electorate self-identifies as gay, lesbian, or bisexual—a larger portion of the electorate than Hispanics or Jews or other groups that are courted by the political parties.[110] It is not only as individuals that gays wield political power, however. Gays began to organize politically in 1969 after riots following police harassment at a gay bar in New York City, the Stonewall Inn. Today many interest groups are organized around issues of concern to the gay community. The largest, the Human Rights Campaign, made a total contribution to campaigns of nearly $4.5 million in 2008, with $1.3 million going to federal candidates.[111] While in the past gays have primarily supported the Democratic Party, a growing number identify themselves as independent, and a group of conservative gays calling themselves the Log Cabin Republicans have become active on the political right. Openly gay members of Congress have been elected from both sides of the partisan divide.

In 1992, acting on a campaign promise made to gays, President Clinton decided to end the ban on gays in the military with an executive order, much as President Truman had ordered the racial integration of the armed forces in 1948. Clinton, however, badly miscalculated the public reaction to his move. The Christian Right and other conservative and military groups were outraged. In the ensuing storm, Clinton settled instead for a "don't ask, don't tell" (DADT) policy: members of the armed forces did not need to disclose their sexual orientation, but if they revealed it, or the military otherwise found out, they could still be disciplined or discharged. For example, shortly after the September 11 attacks, at a time when the military was already facing a shortage of translators who could speak Arabic, six gay army linguists who spoke Arabic were dismissed.[112] In 2008 Barack Obama campaigned on the repeal of DADT, and in 2010 his administration signaled its intention to repeal the policy banning gays in the military.[113] Although down to the wire, a lame-duck session of Congress finally broke a Republican filibuster led by Sen. John McCain and voted to repeal the policy in December 2010. It finally ended in September 2011.

Gays have also tried to use their political power to fend off the earlier-mentioned legislation banning gay marriage. The legislation was prompted in the mid-1990s by a case in the Hawaiian courts that could have allowed gays to marry in that state. Under the Constitution's "full faith and credit" clause, the other states would have to recognize those marriages as legal. State legislators rushed to create laws rejecting gay marriage, and in 1996 Congress passed DOMA to prevent federal recognition of gay marriage and allow states to pass laws denying its legality. President Clinton, who opposed the idea of gay

marriage, signed the bill under protest, claiming that the bill was politically motivated and mean-spirited. Although the Obama administration continued to enforce the law, it stopped defending it in federal courts, arguing that it did not think part of the law is constitutional. Speaking for the Republican majority in the House, John Boehner said that they would hire the necessary staff to defend the law in court itself. The Supreme Court's decision in 2013 essentially agreeing with the Obama administration made the issue moot.

At the state level, policy on gay marriage is all over the map, so to speak. In 2000 Vermont passed a law creating civil unions that stop short of achieving the status of marriage but that allow same-sex couples to have all the rights and responsibilities of married couples. Although this law has been deeply divisive in the state, efforts at such measures short of full marriage are being superseded by court decisions in favor of same sex marriage. With the changes in public opinion and the direction of court decisions, this trend is likely to continue; however, differing ruling by lower federal courts, mean this will likely ultimately be decided by the Supreme Court.

Another issue of active concern to gays is workplace discrimination. The Employment Non-Discrimination Act (ENDA) would make it illegal to discriminate on the basis of sexual orientation in hiring, firing, pay, and promotion decisions. Despite repeated efforts to pass the bill (since 1994 it has been introduced in every Congress except one), it has so far failed to get through both houses. As it became clear that the 113th Congress would once again refuse to act, President Obama announced in 2014 that he was preparing an executive order that would make it illegal for federal contractors and subcontractors to discriminate against lesbian, bisexual, gay, or transgender (LBGT) employees.

The issue of gay rights has come to the forefront of the American political agenda not only because of gays' increasing political power but also because of the fierce opposition of the Christian Right. Their determination to banish what they see as an unnatural and sinful lifestyle—and their conviction that protection of the basic rights of homosexuals means that they will be given "special privileges"—has focused tremendous public attention on issues that most of the public would rather remained private. The spread of AIDS and the political efforts of gay groups to fight for increased resources to battle the disease have also heightened public awareness of gay issues. Public opinion remains mixed on the subject, but tolerance is increasing. In 2010, 70 percent or more of Americans favored lifting the ban on gays in the military,[114] and 54 percent favored permitting gays to adopt children (up from 46 percent in 1999).[115] Still, in 2012, 48 percent opposed gay marriage.[116] Interestingly, young people consistently support issues of gay and lesbian rights in far greater numbers than their elders, an indication that change may be on the horizon. For example, whereas 71 percent of those aged eighteen to twenty-nine supported same-sex marriage, only 21 percent of those aged eighty or over did so.[117]

AGE

In 1976 the Supreme Court ruled that age is not a suspect classification.[118] That means that if governments have rational reasons for doing so, they may pass laws that treat younger or older people differently from the rest of the population, and courts do not have to use strict scrutiny when reviewing those laws. Young people are often not granted the full array of rights of adult citizens, being subject to curfews or locker searches at school; nor are they subject to the laws of adult justice if they commit a crime. Some observers have argued that children should have expanded rights to protect them in dealings with their parents.

Older people face discrimination most often in the area of employment. Compulsory retirement at a certain age, regardless of an individual's capabilities or health, may be said to violate basic civil rights. The Court has generally upheld mandatory retirement requirements.[119] Congress, however, has sought to prevent age discrimination with the Age Discrimination Act of 1967, outlawing discrimination against people up to seventy years of age in employment or in the provision of benefits, unless age can be shown to be relevant to the job in question. In 1978 the act was amended to prohibit mandatory retirement before seventy, and in 1986 all mandatory retirement policies were banned except in special occupations.

Unlike younger people, who can't vote until they are eighteen and don't vote in great numbers after that, older people defend their interests very effectively. Voter participation rates rise with age, and older Americans are also extremely well organized politically. AARP (formerly the American Association of Retired Persons), a powerful interest group with over 30 million members, has been active in pressuring government to preserve policies that benefit older people. In the debates in the mid-1990s about cutting government services, AARP was very much present, and in the face of the organization's advice and voting power, programs like Social Security and Medicare (providing health care for older Americans) remained virtually untouched.

DISABILITY

People with physical and mental disabilities have also organized politically to fight for their civil rights. Advocates for the disabled include people with disabilities themselves, people who work in the social services catering to the disabled, and veterans' groups. Even though laws do not prevent disabled people from voting, staying in hotels, or using public phones, circumstances

AP Photo/Brian Nicholson, Standard-Examiner

A Minor Thing
School lockers can be searched without a warrant because discrimination on the basis of age is not considered a violation of civil rights. Because age is a nonsuspect classification, it is not unconstitutional to treat Americans under the age of eighteen differently from others.

often do. Inaccessible buildings, public transportation, and other facilities can pose barriers as insurmountable as the law, as can public attitudes toward and discomfort around disabled people.

The 1990 Americans with Disabilities Act (ADA), modeled on the civil rights legislation that empowers racial and gender groups, protects the rights of the more than 44 million mentally and physically disabled people in this country. Disabilities covered under the act need not be as dramatic or obvious as confinement to a wheelchair or blindness. People with AIDS, those recovering from drug or alcohol addiction, and patients with heart disease or diabetes are among those covered. The act provides detailed guidelines for access to buildings, mass transit, public facilities, and communication systems. It also guarantees protection from bias in employment; the EEOC is authorized to handle cases of job discrimination because of disabilities, as well as race and gender. The act was controversial because many of the required changes in physical accommodations, such as ramps and elevators, are extremely expensive to install. Advocates for the disabled respond that these expenses will be offset by increased business from disabled people and by the added productivity and skills that the disabled bring to the workplace. The reach of the act was limited in 2001, when the Supreme Court ruled that state employees could not sue their states for damages under the ADA because of the seldom discussed, but extremely important, Eleventh Amendment, which limits lawsuits that can be filed against the states.[120] The Court's five-to-four decision was criticized by disability rights advocates as severely limiting the ADA.

CITIZENSHIP

The final category of discrimination we discuss is discrimination against people who are not citizens. Should noncitizens have the same rights as U.S. citizens? Should all noncitizens have those rights? Illegal visitors as well as legal? Constitutional law has been fairly clear on these questions, granting both citizens and noncitizens most of the same constitutional rights, except the right to vote. (Even documented aliens who serve in the military are unable to vote.) Politics and the Constitution have not always been in sync on these points, however. Oddly for a nation of immigrants, the United States has periodically witnessed backlashes against the flow of people arriving from other countries, often triggered by fear that the newcomers' needs will mean fewer resources, jobs, and benefits for those who arrived earlier. During these backlashes, politicians have vied for public favor by cutting back on immigrants' rights. The Supreme Court responded in 1971 by declaring that alienage, like race and religion, is a suspect classification, and that laws that discriminate against aliens must be backed by a compelling government purpose.[121] To be sure, the Court has upheld some laws restricting the rights of immigrants, but it has done so only after a strict scrutiny of the facts. In light of the ruling, it has even supported the rights of undocumented immigrants to a public education.[122]

Among the groups who fight for the rights of immigrants are the Coalition for Humane Immigrant Rights and many politically active Hispanic groups. The people they represent, however, are often among the poorest, and the most politically silent, in society. Undocumented immigrants, especially, do not have much money or power, and they are thus an easy target for disgruntled citizens and hard-pressed politicians. However, considerable evidence suggests that while immigrants, particularly the larger groups like Mexicans, tend to be poor, they do become assimilated into American society. The average wages of second- and third-generation Mexican Americans, for instance, rise to about 80 percent of the wages of whites.[123] And their wage levels do not necessarily depress the overall wage levels. In the 1980s wages rose faster in parts of the country with higher immigrant populations.[124] Although many immigrant groups are certainly poor, and a gap remains between their average standards of living and those of longer-term residents, the reaction against immigration in this country may be out of proportion to the problem.

Even groups that already enjoy basic civil rights can face considerable discrimination. Opposition to the extension of more comprehensive rights to these groups comes from a variety of directions.

In the case of gays and lesbians, opponents claim that providing a heightened standard of review for laws that discriminate on the basis of sexual orientation would be giving special rights to gays. Gays and lesbians are politically sophisticated and powerful, however, and the techniques they use are often strategies that had originally been closed off to minorities and women. Both they and their opponents use the courts, form interest groups, lobby Congress, and support presidential candidates to further their agendas.

In terms of age discrimination, opponents are motivated not by moral concerns but by issues of social order and cost-efficiency. Older people are able to protect their rights more effectively than younger people because of their higher voter turnout.

People resist giving rights to the disabled generally out of concern for the expense of making buildings accessible and the cost-efficiency of hiring disabled workers. Organization into interest groups and effective lobbying of Congress have resulted in considerable protection of the rights of the disabled.

Finally, noncitizens seeking rights face opposition from a variety of sources. Although immigrants themselves are not usually well organized, the biggest protection of their rights comes from the Supreme Court, which has ruled that alienage is a suspect classification and, therefore, laws that discriminate on the basis of citizenship are subject to strict scrutiny.

IN YOUR OWN WORDS » Recognize examples of other groups that face discrimination.

» THE CITIZENS AND CIVIL RIGHTS
The power of group action

The stories of America's civil rights struggles are the stories of citizen action. But clearly, citizens acting individually have not been able to bring about all the changes that civil rights groups have achieved. Although great leaders and effective organizers have played an important role in the battles for rights, the battles themselves have been part of a group movement.

In Chapter 1 we discussed three models of democracy that define options for citizen participation: elite, pluralist, and participatory. Of the three, the pluralist model best describes the actions that citizens have taken to gain the government's protection of their civil rights. Pluralism emphasizes the ways that citizens can increase their individual power by organizing into groups. The civil rights movements in the United States have been group movements, and to the extent that groups have been unable to organize effectively to advance their interests, their civil rights progress has been correspondingly slowed.

As we will see in Chapter 13, what have come to be known as *interest groups* play an increasingly important role in American politics. In fact, from the 1960s through the end of the century, the number of national associations in the United States grew by over 250 percent, to about 23,000, and the number of groups organized specifically to advocate the rights of African Americans, Hispanics, Asian Americans, and women multiplied by six times during that period.[125] Scholars do not agree on whether this proliferation of groups increases the quality of democracy or skews its results. Groups that are well organized, well financed, and well informed and that have particularly passionate members (who put their votes where their hearts are) are likely to carry greater weight with lawmakers than are

groups that are less focused and less well to do. On the one hand, money, information, and intensity of opinion can make interest groups more powerful than their numbers, a fact that seems at odds with notions of political equality and democracy. On the other hand, as we have seen, individuals can accomplish things together in groups that they can only dream of doing alone. In the case of the civil rights movement, democracy would have clearly been impoverished without the power of groups to work on distributing citizenship rights more broadly. We return to the question of how democratic a pluralist society can be in Chapter 13, when we investigate in more depth the role of interest groups in American politics.

IN YOUR OWN WORDS >> Identify tools used by citizens to expand the promise of civil rights.

Can we end de facto discrimination without imposing substantive solutions?

LET'S REVISIT: **WHAT'S AT STAKE...**

As we have seen in this chapter, civil rights battles are hard fought—waged passionately by those trying to be included in the civic life of the country, resisted at every step by those who are invested in keeping things as they are. Since rights are power, it is not surprising to see such emotion and resources invested in these epic clashes.

What's at stake here for gay and lesbian Americans is obvious. Marriage is an officially sanctioned relationship that confers a host of legal and financial benefits. It allows you the right to participate in health decisions regarding your spouse, to file tax returns jointly, to raise a family and to share decision-making authority for your kids, to buy property jointly, and to inherit a certain amount of that property from your spouse without tax liability. And as anyone contemplating the institution knows, there are psychological, emotional, and social benefits as well. Not only does being able to get married confer a number of benefits, but being forbidden to do so is exclusionary. It singles out a group to deny them rights shared by other members of society, putting an unmistakable stigma on those who are shunned.

Not only do gay marriage advocates argue that gay people would be better off if such marriages were legal, but some believe that *everyone* would be better off. Andrew Sullivan, a longtime gay marriage advocate, argues that gay marriage is good for society because it gives people a stake and a way to build families. He also believes, as he wrote about his own marriage to his husband, Aaron, that marriage is part of the pursuit of happiness, and as such, is an integral part of the American Dream.[126]

Those who oppose gay marriage have at stake the maintenance of a worldview and social order that they believe is right—for either religious or moral reasons, whether because their particular interpretation of the Bible makes such relationships sinful, or because they feel that same-sex marriages somehow devalue heterosexual ones.[127] Not only do they hold personal beliefs that marriage equality should not be allowed, but they are on the substantive end of the continuum we laid out in Chapter 2—they believe that it is the role of government to enforce a social order that they believe is correct, by imposing those beliefs on others.

Politically, the stakes are less clear-cut, which is why we see such a hodgepodge of public action with respect to marriage equality. In fact, when it comes to marriage equality, we seem to have almost hit a tipping point. The public's opinion on the issue, like President Obama's, has evolved rapidly. For members of the younger generation, the idea of marriage equality is mostly a no-brainer. While about half the general population supports it, those supporters include two-thirds of those under age thirty.[128] So, for supporters of gay marriage, taking a favorable position is no longer as politically toxic as it might have been.

Objections to gay marriage have become the minority position, but those who hold such views hold them strongly, and vote accordingly. Hence, a politician like Gov. Chris Christie, who in all likelihood does not oppose gay marriage himself, didn't hesitate to veto a bill he knew would be unpopular with the Republican base. But as the older generation dies out and the views of today's under-thirties come to hold sway, all the efforts to put the issue directly to the people will likely yield much more expansive policies.

TO SUM UP

⑤SAGE edge™
for CQ Press

Sharpen your skills with **SAGE edge** at http://edge.sagepub.com/barbour7e. **SAGE edge for students** provides a personalized approach to help you accomplish your coursework goals in an easy-to-use learning environment.

REVIEW

The Meaning of Political Equality

Throughout U.S. history, various groups, because of some characteristic beyond their control, have been denied their civil rights and have fought for equal treatment under the law. All three branches of the government have played an important role in providing remedies for the denial of equal rights.

Groups that are discriminated against may seek procedural remedies, such as changing the law to guarantee equality of opportunity, or substantive remedies, such as the institution of affirmative action programs, to guarantee equality of outcome.

civil rights (p. 181)
suspect classification (p. 182)
strict scrutiny (p. 182)
intermediate standard of review (p. 182)
minimum rationality test (p. 182)

Rights Denied on the Basis of Race

African Americans have experienced both de jure discrimination, created by laws that treat people differently, and de facto discrimination, which occurs when societal tradition and habit lead to social segregation.

African Americans led the first civil rights movement in the United States. By forming interest groups such as the NAACP and developing strategies such as nonviolent resistance, African Americans eventually defeated de jure discrimination.

De facto discrimination persists in America, signified by the education and wage gap between African Americans and whites. Programs like affirmative action, which could remedy such discrimination, remain controversial. Although African Americans have made great strides in the past fifty years, much inequality remains.

racism (p. 186)
black codes (p. 186)
Reconstruction (p. 186)
poll taxes (p. 187)
literacy tests (p. 187)
grandfather clauses (p. 187)
Jim Crow laws (p. 187)

Rights Denied on the Basis of Race and Ethnicity

Native Americans, Hispanics, and Asian Americans have also fought to gain economic and social equality. Congressional control over their lands has led Native Americans to assert economic power through the development of casinos. Using boycotts and voter education drives, Hispanics have worked to stem the success of English-only movements and anti-immigration efforts. Despite their smaller numbers, Asian Americans also aim for equal political clout, but it is through a cultural emphasis on scholarly achievement that they have gained considerable economic power.

Rights Denied on the Basis of Gender

Women's rights movements represented challenges to power, to a traditional way of life, and to economic profit. Early activists found success through state politics because they were restricted from using the courts and Congress; efforts now focus on the courts to give women greater protection of the law.

Rights Denied on Other Bases

Gays, youth, the elderly, and the disabled enjoy the most fundamental civil rights, but they still face de jure and de facto discrimination. While laws concerning gays, lesbians, and transgender individuals are usually motivated by moral beliefs, social order and cost-efficiency concerns mark the restrictions against youth, the elderly, and disabled Americans. The rights of noncitizens, especially undocumented Americans, remain somewhat unclear, and discrimination on the basis of citizenship status continues to be an issue in the United States.

The Citizens and Civil Rights

The progression of civil rights in the United States has been propelled largely by group action, an example of the pluralist model of democracy. Through collective action, those seeking change and equality are able to putting pressure on lawmakers and on the courts to remedy unequal treatment.

ENGAGE

Take an online tour through Civil Rights history.
The Library of Congress's online exhibition **Voices of Civil Rights** provides photographs and first-person accounts from the movement.

Join a campaign for equality.
You can connect with many of the civil rights organizations mentioned in this chapter, as well as additional resources, from the Keeping the Republic web site. Just go to **http://edge.sagepub.com/barbour7e** and select the Chapter 6 Web Resources section. Among them are:

- **Human Rights Campaign,** which focuses on issues faced by the gay, lesbian, bisexual, and transgender communities, and includes a scorecard of how well members of Congress rate on these issues.
- **American Indian Movement,** which provides information, history, and insights into enduring issues in the American Indian community.
- **League of United Latin American Citizens (LULAC),** which works toward advancing the civil rights of the U.S. Hispanic population.
- **National Association for the Advancement of Colored People (NAACP),** the country's oldest civil rights organization.
- **National Organization for Women (NOW),** the preeminent women's rights organization, which publishes policy briefs on a wealth of issues relevant to bringing about equality for women.
- **Civilrights.org,** a collaboration of the Leadership Conference on Civil Rights and the Leadership Conference on Civil Rights Education Fund, whose mission is "to serve as the site of record for relevant and up-to-the-minute civil rights news and information."

Brown, Dee. 1971. *Bury My Heart at Wounded Knee: An Indian History of the American West.* **New York: Henry Holt.** An eloquent and meticulously documented account of the systematic destruction of the American Indian during the second half of the nineteenth century. Both the book and the 2007 documentary it inspired provide powerful insights into the Native American experience.

Colby, Tanner. 2012. *Some of My Best Friends Are Black: The Strange Story of Integration in America.* **New York: Penguin.** Fifty years after *Brown v. Board of Education* made de jure segregation illegal, de facto segregation is growing. In this book, journalist Tanner Colby explores the ways in which efforts to desegregate our classrooms, cities, and society have failed.

Sullivan, Andrew. 1996. *Virtually Normal: An Argument About Homosexuality.* **New York: Vintage.** Nearly a decade before same-sex marriages were first recognized in the state of Massachusetts, Sullivan investigated the debate over how homosexuals fit in to a predominantly heterosexual society, and presented his own conservative arguments in favor of same-sex marriage.

***Cesar Chavez.* 2014.** This epic biopic tells the story of the man who galvanized California's farm workers in an unprecedented strike in the 1960s.

***The Normal Heart.* 2014.** In the early 1980s, gay men in New York suddenly became sick, and were dying en masse from an unidentified disease. This stirring drama, based on the period play, captures the uncertainty of the early days of the AIDS crisis, and illuminates the struggles of the first activists as they tried to bring political attention to the issue.

***Miss Representation.* 2011.** This lively documentary explores the ways in which women in power are treated differently than men, particularly in the media, and the effects of that treatment on politics, education, and culture.

***American Experience: The Murder of Emmett Till.* 2003.** In 1955, a fourteen-year-old Chicago boy visiting relatives in Mississippi was brutally murdered after allegedly whistling at a white woman on the street. His mother's bold decision to make his funeral public opened much of America's eyes to the injustices being carried out against African Americans in the South. This PBS documentary and its accompanying web site tell Till's story.

***4 Little Girls.* 1997.** Director Spike Lee's documentary tells the story of the 1963 bombing of a black church in Birmingham, Alabama, that left four young girls dead and fueled the civil rights movement.

7 CONGRESS

IN YOUR OWN WORDS   After you've read this chapter, you will be able to

>> Describe the tensions between local representation and national lawmaking.

>> Explain how checks and balances work between Congress and the executive and judicial branches.

>> Identify the politics that influence how congressional districts are defined and who runs for Congress.

>> Summarize the central role that the parties play in Congress.

>> Describe the process of congressional policymaking.

>> Discuss the relationship between the people and Congress.

WHAT'S AT STAKE...IN USING THE NUCLEAR OPTION TO END A FILIBUSTER?

NOVEMBER 21, 2013, WAS A DAY OF HIGH-PITCHED emotion in the U.S. Senate as a major rules change was in the works. Each side said it was the other one's fault, and they had the facts to prove it. Republicans cited the Democrats' blocking of Robert Bork, the uber-conservative but eminently qualified nominee Ronald Reagan picked for the Supreme Court in 1987. Democrats pointed to Republicans' effort to block Chuck Hagel, himself a former senator, from becoming President Obama's defense secretary, and both sides had plenty of other examples besides. The target of all this angst was the filibuster, a parliamentary maneuver that essentially allows a minority of the Senate's one hundred members to bring the entire chamber to a halt if it is so inclined.

This is how it works: The filibuster, an informal senatorial agreement—it is not found in the Constitution—lets a group of senators prevent a vote from taking place on

the Senate floor by allowing them to hold an extended debate—essentially "talking a bill to death." And it is death, unless three-fifths of the chamber (that's sixty senators) votes for cloture, which ends the debate and allows the vote to proceed. The end result is that if a minority in the Senate is passionate or ornery enough, it can thwart the will of the majority, and of the voters who elected them.

The use of the filibuster—once reserved for the rarest and most controversial votes—had become commonplace by 2013, so commonplace in fact that almost any vote reaching the Senate floor needed sixty votes to pass. And no one bothered with the traditional trappings of the filibuster any more—no more Mr.-Smith-Goes-to-Washington-style talking marathons, no cots brought into the cloakroom to allow senators to sleep in between stints on the floor. No, the filibuster had become sadly routine:

Brendan Hoffman/Getty Images News/Getty Images

Congress   **231**

© CinemaPhoto/Corbis

Talk a Bill to Death

In the 1939 movie *Mr. Smith Goes to Washington*, a naïve man appointed to fill a vacant Senate seat soon finds himself amid the shortcomings of the political process. During a vote on a bill crafted by corrupt politicians, Mr. Smith takes to the Senate floor in a filibuster to defend himself against false charges and stop the bill's passage. The movie's idealistic portrayal of Mr. Smith's filibuster goals is a far cry from today's reality, where partisanship has become entrenched.

agencies were left unconfirmed, in part because the Republicans disapproved of their missions, and Democratic frustration hit a high pitch. The blocked votes that precipitated the crisis were three of Obama's nominees to the D.C. Court of Appeals. The court, intended to have eleven members, currently had eight—four Republicans and four Democrats, with the three vacancies that occurred during Obama's administration to be filled by him. Rather than let Obama's nominees through, giving the advantage to the Democrats, the Republicans insisted on referring to his nominations as "court packing" and wanted to keep the number at eight. Charles Grassley, a Republican senator, spoke for his party when he said, "The data overwhelmingly supports the conclusion that the D.C. Circuit is underworked. . . . Everyone knows this is true. That circuit does not need any more judges."[2]

It was the straw that broke the camel's back for Harry Reid, then Senate majority leader; after months of being lobbied by members of his party, Reid was ready to pull the trigger on the so-called nuclear option.

The minority leader simply informed the majority leader of the intention to filibuster and, if the majority leader couldn't summon sixty votes, the bill or the nomination would be dead.

In fact, then–Senate minority leader Mitch McConnell, R-Ky., shortly after the Republicans lost their majority in the Senate in 2008, spelled it out when he said, "I think we can stipulate once again for the umpteenth time that matters that have any level of controversy about it in the Senate will require 60 votes."[1] And sure enough, Republicans proceeded to foil as much of President Obama's agenda as they could, employing the filibuster to block votes on presidential appointments to the bureaucracy, on his judicial nominees, as well as on policies such as an extension of unemployment benefits, immigration, and gun regulation.

So on November 21, 2013, a year after the president had scored a decisive win over his Republican opponent, many of his judicial appointees were still stuck in the pipeline, unable to get a vote. The heads of federal

The dire-sounding name of the legislative measure dated back to 2005, when then-Republican Senate majority leader Bill Frist was so annoyed with Democratic filibusters of President George W. Bush's judicial nominees that he threatened to use what Republicans called the "nuclear option." Essentially, Frist would have called on the presiding officer of the Senate for a ruling on the constitutionality of the use of the judicial filibuster, and that officer (probably Bush's vice president, Dick Cheney) would have ruled it unconstitutional. Moderate Republicans warned that their party would not always be in the majority and that they would someday regret it if they eliminated the traditional protection for a Senate minority. Along with moderate Democrats, they crafted a compromise that averted the nuclear option.

Things had gotten so bad after the 2012 election, however, that Harry Reid said that his party was ready to reform the filibuster, and a number of his fellow Democrats were poised to support him.[3] Confronted with the fact that he had previously opposed reforming the filibuster, Reid said, "They have done everything they can to deny the fact that Obama has been elected and then reelected. I have a right to change how I feel about things."[4]

The nuclear option Reid crafted was not designed to do away with the filibuster entirely—he didn't have enough Democratic votes for that. The minority would still retain a veto over legislation and Supreme Court nominees. But for appointments to head up the federal bureaucracy or to fill the vacancies on the lower courts that were resulting in judicial bottlenecks, a simple majority would suffice.

Republicans were furious, calling Reid's move a "power grab" and warning Democrats that when they retook the Senate they would do away with the filibuster for everything, legislation and Supreme Court nominees as well, making the Democrats sorry they had ever thought to change the rules. Said Mitch McConnell, soon to be the majority leader again himself, "I say to my friends on the other side of the aisle: you'll regret this. And you may regret it a lot sooner than you think."[5]

Which side is right here? Is the filibuster a good thing, or a bad thing, or does it just depend on where you stand on any particular issue? What is at stake in the filibuster, anyway? We will be able to look at this issue more carefully after we have a better understanding of how Congress works. **«**

THE U.S. Congress is the world's longest-running and most powerful democratic legislature. If politics is all about who gets what, and how, then Congress is arguably also the center of American national politics. Not only does it often decide exactly who gets what, but Congress also has the power to alter many of the rules (or the how) that determine who wins and who loses in American political life.

The Capitol building in Washington, D.C., home to both the House of Representatives and the Senate, has become as much a symbol of America's democracy as are the Stars and Stripes or the White House. We might expect Americans to express considerable pride in their national legislature, with its long tradition of serving democratic government. But if we did, we would be wrong.

Congress is generally distrusted, seen by the American public as incompetent, corrupt, torn by partisanship, and at the beck and call of special interests.[6] Yet despite their

> **representation** the efforts of elected officials to look out for the interests of those who elect them
>
> **national lawmaking** the creation of policy to address the problems and needs of the entire nation

contempt for the institution of Congress as a whole, Americans typically like their representatives and senators and reelect them so often that critics have long been calling for term limits to get new people into office (see "*Snapshot of America:* How Do We Hate Congress? [Let Us Count the Ways.]"). How can we understand this bizarre paradox?[7]

There are two main reasons for America's love-hate relationship with Congress. The first is that the things that help a member of Congress keep his or her job—satisfied constituents and a supportive party—don't always make the institution as a whole look very good. Voters want their representatives in Washington to take care of their local or state interests and to ensure that their home district gets a fair share of national resources. Parties want their members to be loyal to the party itself and not to "go rogue"—voting with the other party, for instance, or being seen as independent. On the other hand, citizens also want Congress to take care of the nation's business, and to look like a mature, deliberative, and collegial body, a goal not necessarily furthered by individual legislators' efforts to keep their jobs.

The second reason for citizens' love-hate relationship with Congress is that the rules that determine how Congress works were designed by the founders to produce slow, careful lawmaking that can seem motionless to an impatient public. When citizens are looking to Congress to produce policies that they favor or to distribute national resources, the built-in slowness can look like intentional foot dragging and partisan bickering. That it is instead a constitutional safeguard is part of a civics lesson most Americans have long forgotten.

Keeping in mind these two dynamics, our legislators' struggle to meet our conflicting expectations and our own frustration with Congress' institutionalized slowness, will take us a long way toward understanding our mixed feelings about our national legislature. In this chapter we explore those dynamics as we look at who—including citizens, other politicians, and members of Congress themselves—gets the results they want from Congress, and how the rules of legislative politics help or hinder them.

UNDERSTANDING CONGRESS
The essential tensions among representation, lawmaking, and partisanship

We have traditionally counted on our elected representatives in both the House and the Senate to perform two major roles: representation and lawmaking. By **representation**, we mean that those we elect should represent, or look out for, our local interests and carry out our will. At the same time, we expect our legislators to address the country's social and economic problems by **national lawmaking**—passing laws that serve the interest of the entire nation.

Because the roles of representation and lawmaking often conflict (what is good for us and our local community may

SNAPSHOT OF AMERICA: HOW DO WE HATE CONGRESS? (LET US COUNT THE WAYS.)

The Popularity of Congress Today

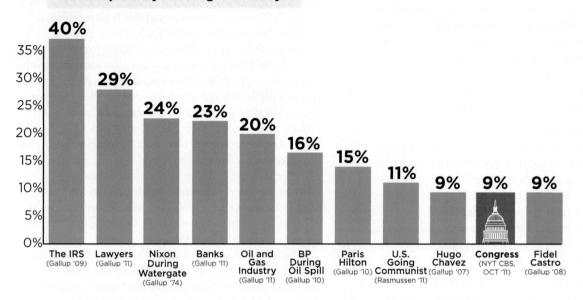

40%	The IRS (Gallup '09)
29%	Lawyers (Gallup '11)
24%	Nixon During Watergate (Gallup '74)
23%	Banks (Gallup '11)
20%	Oil and Gas Industry (Gallup '11)
16%	BP During Oil Spill (Gallup '10)
15%	Paris Hilton (Gallup '10)
11%	U.S. Going Communist (Rasmussen '11)
9%	Hugo Chavez (Gallup '07)
9%	Congress (NYT CBS, OCT '11)
9%	Fidel Castro (Gallup '08)

Approval Ratings of How Congress Is Handling Its Job

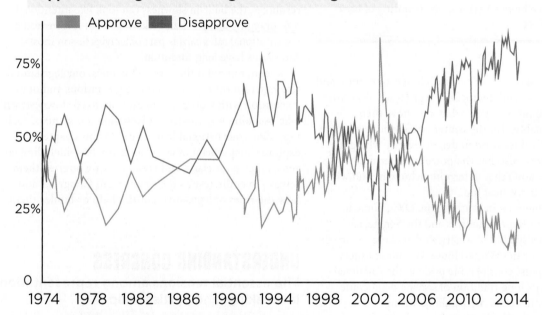

■ Approve ■ Disapprove

1974 1978 1982 1986 1990 1994 1998 2002 2006 2010 2014

BEHIND THE NUMBERS

Americans are proud of our form of government, but the data show, we do not approve of how Congress does its job. Moreover, this disapproval is at an all-time high. Why do you think we are so disappointed? What can Congress do to change the public's attitude?

Source: John R. Hibbing and Elizabeth Theiss-Morse, Congress as Public Enemy (New York: Cambridge University Press, 1995), 58; American National Election Studies Cumulative File, 1948–2004; National Elections Study 2008 Pre-Post Study; Ezra Klein, "2011 in 11 Charts," December 28, 2011, www.washingtonpost.com/blogs/ezra-klein/post/2011-in-11-charts/2011/08/25/gIQAXQXJMP_blog.html.

not serve the national good), scholars have long noted that members of Congress would usually favor their roles as representatives since the way they get reelected is by pleasing voters in their districts. Thus national problems go unaddressed while local problems get attention, resources, and solutions. This is partly why we tend to think poorly of the job done by Congress as a national policymaking institution, even if we like our own representatives.

The tension between representation and lawmaking, however, is complicated further by the fact that members of Congress have to be responsive not only to their constituents and the nation, but also to their parties. Since the early days of the republic, **partisanship**—the loyalty to a party that helps shape how members see the world, how they define problems, and how they determine appropriate solutions—has been an important part of how members of Congress identify and organize themselves. They have juggled a commitment to the party with the simultaneous need to represent voters and to solve national problems, usually creating some kind of balance among the three. As we will see in Chapter 12, party identification can be a useful guide for voters as well as politicians.

But the political parties in the United States have varied over time in their **polarization**—that is, in how great the ideological differences are between the two parties and in how much ideological agreement there is within them. We discuss this issue in more detail later in this chapter. For now the key point is that, in today's political climate, when the parties are deeply polarized, partisanship has turned into something more—**hyperpartisanship**, or a commitment to party so strong that it can transcend other commitments, leading members to choose party over constituents or over the national interest. In hyperpartisanship, the very fact that one side favors a solution to a problem can be enough for the other to declare it unacceptable, even if the party previously supported the same solution. Hyperpartisanship was last at play in the early 1900s (we discuss partisan eras in more detail in Chapter 12).

AP Photo/Steve Helber

Not the Speech He Was Planning For

House majority leader Eric Cantor, R-Va., delivers his concession speech after an unexpected primary defeat in June 2014. Polls showed that Cantor—an entrenched incumbent who outspent his Tea Party opponent, David Brat, by millions—was ultimately done in by his lack of attention to issues in his home district.

But everything old is new again, and since the mid-1990s partisanship has again become a fierce divider of the American public. In fact, a recent study found that the American public is more divided by party than by race, class, gender, or age,[8] and members of Congress have not been so polarized by party since the Civil War.[9] In practical terms this polarization has real implications for how laws get made in Congress. The districts from which members are elected are increasingly drawn by state legislatures (also in the grips of hyperpartisanship) so that they are safe for Democrats or safe for Republicans, with fewer members of the other party. This means the people running for Congress have little incentive to appeal to more moderate voters, as they used to do. If the hyperpartisan representative wants to keep his or her job and not face a primary election challenge from a candidate viewed by the party as more ideologically pure, he or she has to pick party over what's best for the district or the nation.[10] The results, as the *What's at Stake. . . ?* features in this chapter and Chapter 12 make clear, can slow government to a crawl or even bring it to the brink of disaster.

Being a hyperpartisan often conflicts with representation and lawmaking, but that is not always the case. For instance, if your district is drawn to be safe for members of your party, then your commitment to your constituents will reinforce rather than conflict with your commitment to the party; and if your party controls the White House and Congress, national problem solving can coincide with the party's program. But more often hyperpartisanship creates

partisanship loyalty to a party that helps shape how members see the world, define problems, and identify appropriate solutions

polarization the ideological distance between the parties and the ideological homogeneity within them

hyperpartisanship a commitment to party so strong it can transcend other commitments

DON'T BE FOOLED BY...
YOUR ELECTED OFFICIALS

Being a critical constituent means more than sitting around the dinner table griping about Congress. It means knowing what your representatives are doing so that you can evaluate how well they are representing your interests. How can you learn about your representatives' or senators' performance in Congress? There is an abundance of information, but not all of it is equally reliable or equally easy to find.

WHAT TO WATCH OUT FOR

- **Get to know your elected representatives.** Members regularly come home for long weekends in part to maintain contact with constituents. Staff will be happy to reply to your phone call or email to tell you of upcoming town meetings or visits to district offices to meet with constituents. This is harder to arrange for a U.S. senator from a large state, but most citizens can meet with their U.S. representative with just a bit of effort. Members of Congress also maintain their own web sites, and these are great starting points if you want to know what your representative is doing, how he or she voted, or what his or her family looks like. The coverage on these sites, understandably, is glowing, so you need to scrutinize it well.

- **Don't trust, verify.** Thanks to the Internet there are now several web sites that follow up on what our elected officials say and run fact-checks so that we can know when they are stretching, bending, or outright breaking with the truth. Notable here are politifact.com, run by the esteemed *Tampa Bay Times*, which rates politicians' claims on their "Truth-O-Meter," from "True" to "Half True," to "Pants on Fire." Also good is factcheck.org, operated by the University

of Pennsylvania's Annenberg Public Policy Center. One of the best sources for checking up on members of Congress comes from a nonpartisan organization, Project Vote Smart (PVS). PVS collects information on the background, issue positions, campaign finances, and voting records of more than 13,000 officeholders and candidates for president, governor, Congress, and the state legislatures. It also tracks performance evaluations for members of Congress from special interest groups that provide them. One big advantage of PVS is that it attempts to provide data on all candidates, not just incumbents, and it makes its information available during the campaign. All information is free and available online at www.votesmart.org.

- **For an overview of the debates going on in Congress**, you can find the detailed proceedings of past sessions in the *Congressional Record*, which is available in print at many university libraries and online (thomas.loc.gov/home/thomas.php) for the past few congressional sessions. The *Congressional Record* is informative, but it can be tedious to read. Moreover, it is not an exact transcript of congressional proceedings. Members are regularly given permission, by unanimous consent, to "extend and revise" their remarks, even to the extent of adding entirely new speeches they never gave. Read this source with some skepticism.

Congress on Your Computer
Every member of Congress has an official web site, where he or she can share information with constituents. Smart voters need to understand the obvious, that members of Congress are only going to share what puts them in a positive light. Of course, their political opponents do just the opposite.

a difficult tension with the other legislative roles, and what the American public often sees in the news is a Congress that cannot seem to function, whose members appear to be more interested in scoring points against each other than in taking care of the nation's business, who in the worst-case scenario are willing to blow up the country (figuratively) rather than compromise with the other side that they have demonized. The American people's opinion of Congress has been at an all-time low, and no wonder. At the same time, voters generally like their own members of Congress, either because they tend to the local business of the state or district, or because they share the voter's partisan identification.

FOUR KINDS OF REPRESENTATION

Representation means working on behalf of one's **constituency**, the folks back home in the district who voted for the member as well as those who did not. To help us understand this complex job, political scientists often speak about four types of representation.[11] Most members of Congress try to excel at all four functions so that constituents will rate them highly and reelect them.

POLICY REPRESENTATION Policy representation refers to congressional work for laws that advance the economic and social interests of the constituency. For example, House members and senators from petroleum-producing states can be safely predicted to vote in ways favorable to the profitability of the oil companies, members from the Plains states try to protect subsidies for wheat farmers, and so on. It is rarer for a member to champion a national interest, since it is in the local constituency that he or she will face reelection, but some members do focus on such issues as foreign policy, campaign finance reform, or the environment.

ALLOCATIVE REPRESENTATION Voters have also come to expect a certain amount of **allocative representation**, in which the congressperson gets projects and grants for the district. Such perks have traditionally been called "**pork barrel** projects" but more recently are referred to as "earmarks." These are provisions in various appropriations documents or the budget that direct funding for quite specific purposes (for example, highway construction or the establishment of a research institution) and are electorally popular because they appear free to the district while the costs are spread to all taxpayers.

CASEWORK Senators and representatives also represent their states or districts by taking care of the individual problems of constituents, especially problems that involve the federal bureaucracy. This kind of representation is called **casework**, or constituency service, and it covers things such as finding out why a constituent's Social Security check has not shown up, sending a flag that has flown over the U.S. Capitol to a high school in the district, or helping with immigration and naturalization problems. To promote their work for constituents, members maintain web pages and send information to the homes of voters through more traditional channels. (See *Don't Be Fooled*

---

constituency the voters in a state or district

policy representation congressional work to advance the issues and ideological preferences of constituents

allocative representation congressional work to secure projects, services, and funds for the represented district

pork barrel public works projects and grants for specific districts paid for by general revenues

casework legislative work on behalf of individual constituents to solve their problems with government agencies and programs

---

by . . . *Your Elected Officials* for some tips on how to be a savvy consumer of congressional information.) The congressional privilege of **franking** allows members to use the U.S. mail at no charge. This free postal service fulfills the democratic purpose of keeping citizens informed about their lawmakers' activities, but because only positive information about and images of the congressperson are sent out, it is also self-serving.

SYMBOLIC REPRESENTATION A fourth kind of representation is called **symbolic representation**. In this elusive but important function, the member of Congress tries to represent many of the positive values Americans associate with public life and government. Thus members are glad to serve as commencement speakers at high school graduations or attend town meetings to explain what is happening in Washington. Equally important are the ways members present themselves to their districts—for example, using colloquialisms such as "y'all" even if they are not from the South, or wearing a denim work shirt to the county fair. These appearances are part of a member's "home style" and help to symbolize the message "I am one of you" and "I am a person you can trust; I share your values and interests."[12]

THINKING OUTSIDE THE BOX

Does the local interest have to clash with the national interest?

NATIONAL LAWMAKING

As we explained earlier, representation is not the only business of our senators and representatives. A considerable part of their job involves working with one another in Washington to define and solve the nation's problems. We expect Congress to create laws that serve the common good. One scholar calls this view of effective lawmaking "collective responsibility."[13] By this he means that Congress should be responsible for the effectiveness of its laws in solving national problems. A variety of factors are involved in a representative's calculation of how to vote on matters of national interest. He or she might be guided by conscience or ideology, by the demands of constituents, by interest groups, or by party position. These considerations may very well be at odds with the four kinds of representation just described, which frequently makes it difficult, if not impossible, for members to fulfill their collective responsibility.

Imagine, for instance, the dilemma of a Democratic congresswoman representing an oil-producing district in Texas who has to vote yes or no on government support for the development of non-fossil-fuel technologies. What is good for the nation—to decrease our dependence on fossil fuels so that we are less reliant on foreign sources of oil and to reduce global warming—is not necessarily what is good for the economic interests of her district. The bill would mean higher taxes for her constituents to support a technology that makes their main industry less profitable. In deciding how to vote, our congresswoman would have to consider tough questions that affect the public good, her policy goals, and her reelection.

In this case, what's best for the local district clearly clashes with the national interest. And the scenario holds true again and again for every representative and senator. Thus the potential for conflict is great when one works for one's constituents as well as for the entire nation. We all want a Congress that focuses on the nation's problems, but as voters we tend to reward members for putting constituency concerns first.

PARTISANSHIP

As we noted in our introduction, complicating this already difficult balance between representation and lawmaking is a heightened commitment to party that we call hyperpartisanship. Party affiliations have always been an important part of the identities of members of Congress, but in recent years they have come to trump other considerations. In today's era of hyperpartisanship the parties are polarized, which means that the issue positions and ideological stances of Democrats and Republicans have been growing apart and each party has become more internally homogeneous. This means that bipartisanship (working with members of the opposite party) is increasingly rare, especially when the very act of cooperating with the other side can be seen as a betrayal of one's own.

Two influential political scientists, one at the Brookings Institution (a liberal think tank) and one at the American Enterprise Institute (a conservative think tank) but both with solid reputations as impartial scholars, wrote a book in 2012 in which they argued that the problem of hyperpartisanship in the first part of this century has not affected both parties equally. The title of a *Washington Post* article they wrote laying out their argument is "Let's Just Say It: The Republicans Are the Problem." (See *CLUES to Critical Thinking* in Chapter 12.)[14] Their argument is *not* that there is anything wrong with the substance of what Republicans want or with their policies or with conservative ideology; rather, they argue that the problem is that the recent Republican strategy of putting party first, not tolerating internal dissent, and refusing to compromise has ground

> **franking** the privilege of free mail service provided to members of Congress
>
> **symbolic representation** efforts of members of Congress to stand for American ideals or to identify with common constituency values

American government to a halt. They say, "We have been studying Washington politics and Congress for more than 40 years, and never have we seen them this dysfunctional. In our past writings, we have criticized both parties when we believed it was warranted. Today, however, we have no choice but to acknowledge that the core of the problem lies with the Republican Party."[15]

The consequence, they say, is that American government is in trouble: "Today, thanks to the GOP, compromise has gone out the window in Washington. In the first two years of the Obama administration, nearly every presidential initiative met with vehement, rancorous, and unanimous Republican opposition in the House and the Senate, followed by efforts to delegitimize the results and repeal the policies."[16] In fact, instead of taking the procedural position that we discussed in Chapter 1 as a part of American political culture—that the process of a free election legitimates the results—they took a more substantive stance—that what they wanted was the best policy and if the procedures of the government didn't endorse their plan, they would simply block them and hope that the failure of the system would frustrate the public sufficiently that people would vote Republicans into power. Instead, voters in 2012 delivered a rebuke to this effort—reelecting President Obama, increasing the Democratic majority in the Senate, and even adding Democrats to the House.

Obama believed that his reelection would cool the fervor of Republican opposition efforts, but instead, Tea Party Republicans only stiffened their resolve to block the president.[17] Their efforts culminated in a government shutdown in October 2013, when House Republicans refused to pass a continuing budget resolution (which would allow the government to continue operating) unless it defunded the Patient Protection and Affordable Care Act, also known as "Obamacare." The Senate Democrats would not agree to this killing of the administration's signature legislation. After sixteen days and an estimated $10 billion lost to the U.S. economy, the House Republicans agreed to a Senate bill, gaining only a token concession of trivial legislative importance.[18]

For very committed, very conservative Republicans who fundamentally disagree with liberal goals and policies, it may seem like a perfectly reasonable strategy to refuse to compromise with Democrats in an effort to hold out for what they want. That's what happened in the summer of 2011, when conservatives brought the country to the brink of default on its debts because they could not compromise on raising any taxes as a way to solve the nation's financial problems; and twice in 2013, when the debt ceiling needed to be raised again and then when a budget agreement was needed to allow the government to stay in business. In fact, there is an influential movement by some conservative organizations, including, for example, the Tea Party, the Club for Growth, and Americans for Tax Reform, to punish and replace Republican members who vote the "wrong way" or do not heed the party line.[19]

As a consequence, representatives and senators, especially Republicans, have been more worried about representing their party—and especially the most ideologically extreme members of their party—rather than the compromise and bipartisan activity that enables Congress to make laws that respond to policy needs at the local and particularly the national level. Sometimes this causes more moderate Republicans to try to satisfy their Tea Party critics, but it leads others to leave public service altogether. Republican senator Olympia Snowe of Maine retired in 2012, decrying the end of bipartisanship in the institution she had served since 1995 (see *CLUES to Critical Thinking*). Later that same year, Ohio Republican representative Steve LaTourette, who had already won his primary and was almost certainly going to be reelected, decided to leave the House, saying, "I have reached the conclusion that the atmosphere today, and the reality that exists in the House of Representatives, no longer encourages the finding of common ground."[20] In the 2014 midterm elections, however, Republicans kept the majority in the House and also took control of the Senate. While obstruction may be a functional goal for a minority party, it becomes self-defeating for a party in power, as it risks alienating its supporters. Recognizing this, President Obama invited congressional leadership to meet at the White House in the week after the election to determine whether common goals for action could be found. With an eye on 2016, perhaps Congress will find legislative incentives to prioritize over partisanship.

PAUSE AND REVIEW:

WHO, WHAT, HOW

Both citizens and their representatives have something serious at stake in the tensions among representation, lawmaking, and hyperpartisanship. Citizens want their local interests protected, and many partisan activists who have contributed time and money have strong policy preferences. But citizens also want sound national policy, and here they are often disappointed. The need to secure reelection by catering to local—and increasingly partisan—interests often means that their representatives have fewer incentives to concentrate on national lawmaking.

In fact, members of the House and the Senate face a true dilemma. On the one hand, they want to serve their constituents' local interests and needs, and they want to be reelected to office by those constituents. But they also must face personal, party, and special interest demands to take stands that might not suit the voters back home.

IN YOUR OWN WORDS » Describe the tensions between local representation and national lawmaking.

CLUES
TO CRITICAL THINKING

"Why I'm Leaving the Senate"

By Olympia Snowe, *Washington Post,* **March 1, 2012**

This statement was published in the Washington Post *on the occasion of Maine senator Olympia Snowe's decision to retire. It illustrates the frustration of some more moderate members of Congress at the institution's increasing dysfunction.*

Two truths are all too often overshadowed in today's political discourse: Public service is a most honorable pursuit, and so is bipartisanship.

I have been immeasurably honored to serve the people of Maine for nearly 40 years in public office and for the past 17 years in the United States Senate. It was incredibly difficult to decide that I would not seek a fourth term in the Senate.

Some people were surprised by my conclusion, yet I have spoken on the floor of the Senate for years about the dysfunction and political polarization in the institution. Simply put, the Senate is not living up to what the Founding Fathers envisioned.

During the Federal Convention of 1787, James Madison wrote in his Notes of Debates that "the use of the Senate is to consist in its proceedings with more coolness, with more system, and with more wisdom, than the popular branch." Indeed, the Founding Fathers intended the Senate to serve as an institutional check that ensures all voices are heard and considered, because while our constitutional democracy is premised on majority rule, it is also grounded in a commitment to minority rights.

Yet more than 200 years later, the greatest deliberative body in history is not living up to its billing. The Senate of today routinely jettisons regular order, as evidenced by the body's failure to pass a budget for more than 1,000 days; serially legislates by political brinkmanship, as demonstrated by the debt-ceiling debacle of August that should have been addressed the previous January; and habitually eschews full debate and an open amendment process in favor of competing, up-or-down, take-it-or-leave-it proposals. We witnessed this again in December with votes on two separate proposals for a balanced-budget amendment to the Constitution.

As Ronald Brownstein recently observed in National Journal, Congress is becoming more like a parliamentary system—where everyone simply votes with their party and those in charge employ every possible tactic to block the other side. But that is not what America is all about, and it's not what the Founders intended. In fact, the Senate's requirement of a supermajority to pass significant legislation encourages its members to work in a bipartisan fashion.

One difficulty in making the Senate work the way it was intended is that America's electorate is increasingly divided into red and blue states, with lawmakers representing just one color or the other. Before the 1994 election, 34 senators came from states that voted for a presidential nominee of the opposing party. That number has dropped to just 25 senators in 2012. The result is that there is no practical incentive for 75 percent of the senators to work across party lines.

The great challenge is to create a system that gives our elected officials reasons to look past their differences and find common ground if their initial party positions fail to garner sufficient

CONGRESSIONAL POWERS AND RESPONSIBILITIES
Expansive powers held in check by the Constitution

The Constitution gives the U.S. Congress enormous powers, although it is safe to say that the founders could not have imagined the scope of contemporary congressional power since they never anticipated the growth of the federal government to today's size. As we will see, they were less concerned with the conflict between local and national interests we have been discussing than they were with the representation of short-term popular opinion versus long-term national interests. The basic powers of Congress are laid out in Article I, Section 8, of the Constitution (see Chapter 4). They include the powers to tax, to pay debts, to regulate interstate commerce, and to provide for the common defense and welfare of the United States, among many other things.

DIFFERENCES BETWEEN THE HOUSE AND THE SENATE

The term *Congress* refers to the institution that is formally made up of the U.S. House of Representatives and the

support. In a politically diverse nation, only by finding that common ground can we achieve results for the common good. That is not happening today and, frankly, I do not see it happening in the near future.

For change to occur, our leaders must understand that there is not only strength in compromise, courage in conciliation and honor in consensus-building—but also a political reward for following these tenets. That reward will be real only if the people demonstrate their desire for politicians to come together after the planks in their respective party platforms do not prevail.

I certainly don't have all the answers, and reversing the corrosive trend of winner-take-all politics will take time. But as I enter a new chapter in my life, I see a critical need to engender public support for the political center, for our democracy to flourish and to find solutions that unite rather than divide us.

I do not believe that, in the near term, the Senate can correct itself from within. It is by nature a political entity and, therefore, there must be a benefit to working across the aisle.

But whenever Americans have set our minds to tackling enormous problems, we have met with tremendous success. And I am convinced that, if the people of our nation raise their collective voices, we can effect a renewal of the art of legislating—and restore the luster of a Senate that still has the potential of achieving monumental solutions to our nation's most urgent challenges.

I look forward to helping the country raise those voices to support the Senate returning to its deserved status and stature—but from outside the institution.

Source: Reprinted by permission of Olympia Snowe, LLC/Olympia's List.

Consider the source and the audience: Senator Snowe is choosing to publish her statement explaining her retirement in the *Washington Post,* a newspaper read by Washington insiders. What is her motive for publishing it there instead of, say, the *New York Times* or even a paper in Maine?

Lay out the argument, the values, and the assumptions: Why does Snowe say bipartisanship is an "honorable pursuit"? How does she think the framers intended the Senate to work and what does she think has thwarted those intentions? Why does she think senators are now less willing to compromise?

Uncover the evidence: Snowe offers examples from her own experience to document the Senate's dysfunction. Is that persuasive? To explain the increasing polarization of the institution, she offers data on how many senators now come from states that voted for a president of the opposite party. How would that lead senators to behave?

Evaluate the conclusion: Snowe blames increasing polarization and hyperpartisanship for the Senate's dysfunction. Could that dysfunction be caused by other factors?

Sort out the political implications: Snowe does not think the Senate can heal itself, and she calls on "the people of our nation [to] raise their collective voices"—what does she want them to do? Is there any effective way those outside the Senate can solve the problem?

U.S. Senate. Congresses are numbered so that we can talk about them over time in a coherent way. Each congress covers a two-year election cycle. The 113th Congress was elected in November 2012, and its term runs from January 2013 through the end of 2014. The **bicameral** (two-house) **legislature** is laid out in the Constitution. As we discussed in earlier chapters, the founders wanted two chambers so that they could serve as a restraint on each other, strengthening the principle of checks and balances. The

framers' hope was that the smaller, more elite Senate would "cool the passions" of the people represented in the House. Accordingly, while the two houses are equal in their overall power—both can initiate legislation (although tax bills must originate in the House) and both must pass every bill in identical form before it can be signed by the president to become law—there are also some key differences, particularly in the extra responsibilities assigned to the Senate. In addition, the two chambers operate differently, and they have distinct histories and norms of conduct (that is, informal rules and expectations of behavior).[21] Some of the major differences are outlined in Table 7.1.

> **bicameral legislature** legislature with two chambers

TABLE 7.1

DIFFERENCES BETWEEN THE HOUSE AND THE SENATE

DIFFERENCES	HOUSE	SENATE
Constitutional		
Term length	2 years	6 years
Minimum age	25	30
Citizenship required	7 years	9 years
Residency	In state	In state
Apportionment	Changes with population	Fixed; entire state
Impeachment	Impeaches official	Tries the impeached official
Treaty-making power	No authority	2/3 approval
Presidential appointments	No authority	Majority approval
Organizational		
Size	435 members	100 members
Number of standing committees	23	16
Total committee assignments per member	Approx. 6	Approx. 11
Rules Committee	Yes	No
Limits on floor debate	Yes	No (filibuster possible)
Electoral, 2012		
Average winners spent	$1,560,954	$11,474,819
Average losers spent	$507,907	$7,434,819
Most expensive campaign	$21,197,801	$49,496,249
Incumbency advantage	90% reelected	91% reelected
	(93.0% 54-year average)	(80.9% 54-year average)

Sources: Roger H. Davidson, Walter J. Oleszek, and Frances E. Lee, *Congress and Its Members*, 13th ed. (Washington, D.C.: CQ Press, 2008), 44, 187; Federal Election Commission data compiled by the Center for Responsive Politics: Election Stats 2012, www.opensecrets.org/bigpicture/incad .php?cycle=2012.

The single biggest factor determining differences between the House and the Senate is size. With 100 members, the Senate is less formal; the 435-person House needs more rules and hierarchy in order to function efficiently. The Constitution also provides for differences in terms: two years for the House, six for the Senate (on a staggered basis—all senators do not come up for reelection at the same time). In the modern context, this means that House members (also referred to as congresspersons or members of Congress, a term that sometimes applies to senators as well) never stop campaigning. Senators, in contrast, can suspend their preoccupation with the next campaign for the first four or five years of their terms and thus, at least in theory, have more time to spend on the affairs of the nation. The minimum age of the candidates is different as well: members of the House must be at least twenty-five years old, senators thirty. This again reflects the founders' expectation that the Senate would be older,

wiser, and better able to deal with national lawmaking. This distinction was reinforced in the constitutional provision that senators be elected not directly by the people, as were members of the House, but by state legislatures. Although this provision was changed by constitutional amendment in 1913, its presence in the original Constitution reflects the convictions of its authors that the Senate was a special chamber, one step removed from the people.

Budget bills are initiated in the House of Representatives. In practice this is not particularly significant since the Senate has to pass budget bills as well, and most of the time differences are negotiated between the two houses. The budget process has gotten quite complicated, as demonstrated by congressional struggles to deal with the deficit, which called for reductions in spending at the same time that constituencies and interest groups were pleading for expensive new programs. The budget process illustrates once again the constant tension for members of Congress between being responsive to local or particular interests, supporting the party leadership, and at the same time trying to make laws in the interest of the nation as a whole.

Other differences between the House and the Senate include the division of power on impeachment of public figures such as presidents and Supreme Court justices. The House impeaches, or charges the official with "Treason, Bribery, or other high Crimes and Misdemeanors," and the Senate tries the official. Both Andrew Johnson and Bill Clinton were impeached by the House, but in both cases the Senate failed to find the president guilty of the charges brought by the House. In addition, only the Senate is given the responsibility of confirming appointments to the executive and judicial branches, and of sharing the treaty-making power with the president, responsibilities we explore in more detail later in the chapter.

CONGRESSIONAL CHECKS AND BALANCES

The founders were concerned about the abuse of power by the executive and legislative branches, and even by the people. But, as we saw in Chapter 3, they were most anxious to avoid executive tyranny, and so they granted Congress an impressive array of powers. Keeping Congress at the center of national policymaking are the power to regulate commerce; the exclusive power to raise and to spend money for the national government; the power to provide for economic infrastructure (roads, postal service, money, patents); and significant powers in foreign policy, including the powers to declare war, to ratify treaties, and to raise and support the armed forces.

As we discussed in Chapter 4, the Supreme Court has generally interpreted the necessary and proper clause of the Constitution quite favorably for the expansion of congressional power. But the Constitution also limits congressional powers through the protection of individual rights and by the watchful eye of the other two branches of government, with which Congress shares power. We look briefly at those relationships here.

CONGRESS AND THE EXECUTIVE BRANCH

Our system of checks and balances means that to exercise its powers, each branch has to have the cooperation of the others. Thus Congress has the responsibility for passing bills, but the bills do not become law unless (1) the president signs them or, more passively, refrains from vetoing them, or (2) both houses of Congress are able to muster a

congressional oversight a committee's investigation of the executive and of government agencies to ensure they are acting as Congress intends

full two-thirds majority to override a presidential veto. While the president cannot vote on legislation or even introduce bills, the Constitution gives the chief executive a powerful policy formulation role in calling for the president's annual State of the Union address and in inviting the president to recommend to Congress "such measures as he shall judge necessary and expedient."

One of the most important functions of Congress is **congressional oversight** of the executive—of the president and the agencies of the bureaucracy that fall under the executive branch. This is usually done through hearings and selective investigations of executive actions whereby Congress attempts to ensure that the president and bureaucracy are carrying out the laws as Congress intended. Executive implementation of congressional legislation is often a point of friction between the two branches. Sometimes the conflict occurs because of differences in presidential and congressional intent. We know, for example, that the number of congressional investigations of executive behavior goes up sharply when the president faces a House of Representatives controlled by the opposition party.[22]

For example, as we will see in Chapter 8, when it implemented policy, the administration of George W. Bush frequently ignored or reinterpreted congressional intent when it believed that Congress' actions represented unconstitutional interference in the workings of the executive branch. Despite criticism for its creation of an energy policy with the confidential participation of oil industry executives, a rush to war in Iraq, and numerous alleged misuses of executive power, the Bush administration faced little congressional opposition.[23] Reluctant to press an administration that had for much of the time following the September 11, 2001, terror attacks enjoyed high public popularity and, moreover, that had returned the Republican Party to the White House after eight years of exile, the Republican-led Congress gave the Bush administration a lot of latitude.

Democrats, however, were chomping at the bit to investigate what they saw as executive excesses and abuse of power. When, in 2006, Republicans lost their majorities in both the House and the Senate, the new Democratic leadership of both houses got busy. "Congress Girds Up for Return to Oversight," read one early 2007 headline in a major paper. "Revival of Oversight Role Sought; Congress Hires More Investigators, Plans Subpoenas," read another.[24] Democrats are not quite as loath to investigate presidents of their own party as are Republicans, but the Obama administration has proved to be remarkably scandal-free. Though the GOP has tried hard to find a target to tarnish the administration,[25] investigations into Solyndra, "Fast and Furious," and the death of four Americans in Benghazi, Libya, yielded nothing of note before the 2012 election.[26]

Nevertheless, the Republican majority in Congress set out with a new series of investigations of the administration, including the creation in 2014 of a seven-person Select Committee on Benghazi with the goal, in the words of Speaker John Boehner, of "getting to the truth," about whether the Obama administration misled the public about the deadly attack in Libya. Not incidentally, several congressional Republicans noted that they expected the investigations would favor them going into the 2014 elections in November.[27] As we will see in the *What's at Stake. . . ?* in Chapter 8, in the summer of 2014 Speaker John Boehner also launched a lawsuit against the president, on the grounds that he had exceeded his legal authority when he allowed employers to hold off on providing health care coverage for one to two years, as required by the Affordable Care Act, as kinks in administering the law were worked out.

Oversight also comes into play when Congress delegates authority to regulatory agencies in the executive branch. Often the agencies do what they are supposed to do, which can make the job of keeping an eye on them boring and unrewarding. If Congress does not keep watch, however, the agencies can develop unhealthy relationships with those they are supposed to be regulating. This was the case with the Securities and Exchange Commission, which failed to protect us from the risky investment practices that resulted in the economic meltdown in late 2008, as well as with the Minerals Management Service, whose failure to adequately police offshore drilling procedures contributed to the ecological disaster in the Gulf of Mexico following the 2010 explosion of BP's *Deepwater Horizon* drilling platform. The Marine Mammal Protection Act and the National Environmental Policy Act were routinely violated by regulators seeking bonuses for encouraging offshore oil drilling.[28] Since these relationships develop far from public scrutiny, we rely on Congress to ensure, through oversight, that agencies do the job they were set up to do, though there is a strong temptation for members to slight congressional responsibility here in favor of splashier and more electorally rewarding activities.

Another congressional check on the executive is the requirement that major presidential appointments—for instance to cabinet posts, ambassadorships, and the federal courts—must be confirmed by the Senate. Historically, most presidential appointments have proceeded without incident, but in recent administrations, appointments have become increasingly political. Senators sometimes use their confirmation powers to do more than "advise and consent" on the appointment at hand. They frequently tie up appointments, either because they oppose the nominee on account of his or her ideology or because they wish to extract promises and commitments from the president. Senators may place a "hold" on presidential appointees, which by tradition means that the Senate will not consider the appointment until the hold is lifted. A hold can be suspended, but, like ending the filibuster we read about in *What's at Stake. . . ?*, that takes sixty votes. Although

senators often agree that the hold process gives undue weight to individual members, they tend to defer to each other, which makes getting the votes needed to break the hold very difficult. In today's highly polarized Congress, senators of the minority party are quick to object to many of a president's appointees. The result is that many appointments languish and high offices in the federal government go unfilled for months or even years. One example among hundreds is the case of Dawn Johnsen, President Obama's choice to head the Office of Legal Counsel at the Justice Department. She was one of the earliest Obama appointees, but her nomination languished for over a year as Republicans objected to work she had done in providing legal counsel to abortion rights groups twenty years earlier and to her criticism of the George W. Bush administration's interrogation and detention policies. She withdrew her name from consideration as it became clear her appointment was not going to get to the floor of the Senate for a vote.[29] The power to approve appointments can also be abused, as when, for instance, in 2012, freshman senator Rand Paul, R-Ky., put a hold on a highly qualified Obama court nominee to force the president's hand on an unrelated proposal to cut off aid to Egypt.[30]

Presidents can find the Senate's ability to block their appointments incredibly frustrating, as it gums up the works of the executive and judicial branches, preventing agencies and courts from taking care of their business. Stymied presidents have sometimes taken advantage of a constitutional provision that allows them to make temporary appointments without Senate approval if a vacancy occurs when the Senate is not in session. These so-called recess appointments were designed to let presidents fill vacancies in an era when it might take the Senate long weeks to convene, but modern-day presidents sometime use them to get around Senate opposition. Senators determined to deny a president the opportunity to make a recess appointment have taken to keeping the Senate in session on a technicality, even when they are not in Washington. President Obama, facing such obstruction, argued that Congress was really in recess when its members were not present and made several appointments, some of which were challenged in court. In 2014 the Supreme Court voided recess appointments that Obama had made while the Senate was technically in session, calling it an overreach of his authority because it is up to Congress to decide when it is or is not in session.[31]

A final built-in source of institutional conflict between Congress and the president is the difference in constituencies. The president looks at each policy in terms of a national constituency and his own policy program, whereas members of Congress necessarily take a narrower view. For example, the president may decide that clean air should be a national priority. For some members of Congress, however, a clean air bill might mean closing factories in their districts because it would not be profitable to bring them up to emissions standards, or shutting down soft coal mines because the bill would kill the market for high-sulfur coal. Increasingly within an era of hyperpartisanship, opposition members appear to oppose the president simply to deny the administration the appearance of policy effectiveness. Often, public policy looks very different from the perspective of congressional offices than it does from the presidential Oval Office at the other end of Pennsylvania Avenue.

CONGRESS AND THE JUDICIAL BRANCH The constitutional relationship between the federal courts and Congress is simple in principle: Congress makes the laws, and the courts interpret them. The Supreme Court also has the lofty job of deciding whether laws and procedures are consistent with the Constitution, although this power of judicial review is not actually mentioned in the Constitution.

We think of the judiciary as independent of the other branches, but this self-sufficiency is only a matter of degree. Congress, for example, is charged with setting up the lower federal courts and determining the salaries for judges, with the interesting constitutional provision that a judge's salary cannot be cut. Congress also has considerable powers in establishing some issues of jurisdiction—that is, deciding which courts hear which cases (Article III, Section 2). And, as we just indicated, in accepting and rejecting presidential Supreme Court and federal court nominees, the Senate influences the long-term operation of the courts.[32]

Congress also exerts power over the courts by passing laws that limit the courts' discretion to rule or impose sentences as judges think best. For example, in the 1980s, Congress passed strict drug laws that required mandatory sentences for offenders; judges could not sentence someone for less than the minimum time that Congress defined in legislation. And finally, though it is hard to do, Congress can remove the ability of federal courts and the Supreme Court to interpret constitutional issues by trying to amend the Constitution itself.

PAUSE AND REVIEW:

WHO, WHAT, HOW

The Constitution gives great power to both the House and the Senate, but it does so in the curiously backhanded way known as checks and balances. The House and the Senate share most lawmaking functions, but the fact that they *both* must approve legislation gives them a check over each other. They in turn are checked by the power of the president and

the courts. The legislature is unable to operate without the cooperation of the other two branches unless it can demonstrate unusual internal strength and consensus, allowing it to override presidential vetoes and, in more extreme circumstances, amend the Constitution and impeach presidents.

IN YOUR OWN WORDS » Explain how checks and balances work between Congress and the executive and judicial branches.

CONGRESSIONAL ELECTIONS
Political calculations to define districts and determine who will run

The first set of rules a future congressperson or senator has to contend with are those that govern congressional elections. These, more than any others, are the rules that determine the winners and losers in congressional politics. No matter what a legislator might hope to accomplish, he or she cannot achieve it as a legislator without winning and keeping the support of voters. With House elections every two years and Senate elections every six years, much of the legislator's life is spent running for reelection. In fact, one professor argues that most aspects of Congress are designed to aid the reelection goals of its members.[33] With elections so central, let us take a look at how the rules work, who runs for office, and how the electoral process shapes what members do in Washington.

THE POLITICS OF DEFINING CONGRESSIONAL DISTRICTS

As a result of the Great Compromise in 1787, the Constitution provides that each state will have two senators and that seats in the House of Representatives will be allocated on the basis of population. Two important political processes regulate the way House seats are awarded on this basis. One is **reapportionment**, in which the 435 House seats are reallocated among the states after each ten-year census. States whose populations grow gain seats, which are taken from those whose populations decline or remain steady. Figure 7.1 shows the current apportionment for each state through 2020. The winners are mostly in the rapidly growing Sun Belt states of the South and Southwest; the losers are largely in the Northeast and Midwest.

Since areas that lose population will also lose representatives, just how you count the population becomes critical. Democrats in 2000 proposed using what they claimed was a more precise statistical sampling technique that would allow census workers to get a better estimate of hard-to-count portions of the population such as poor people and immigrants. Fearing that this would add to the population

reapportionment a reallocation of congressional seats among the states every ten years, following the census

FIGURE 7.1 **HOUSE APPORTIONMENT FOR ELECTIONS IN 2012-2020**

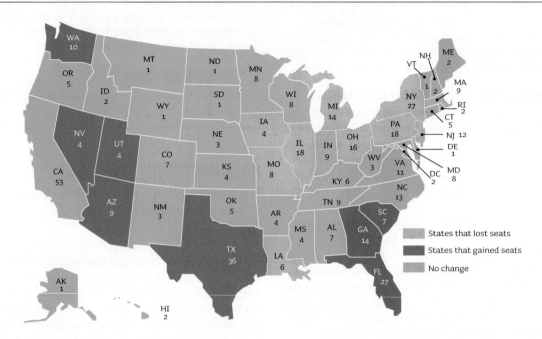

States that lost seats
States that gained seats
No change

Source: U.S. Census Bureau, "Apportionment Data," 2010.census.gov/2010census/data/apportionment-data-text.php.

of Democratic districts, and thus increase Democratic representation, Republicans balked. The Supreme Court sided with the Republicans, ruling that the Constitution and the legislation on the books required that, for purposes of reapportionment, the census had to reflect an actual count of the population.

Even more political, however, is the second process that regulates the way districts are drawn. Until the 1960s the states often suffered from malapportionment, the unequal distribution of population among the districts so that some had many fewer residents than others. This, in effect, gave greater representation to those living in lower population districts. This difference is built in to the Constitution in the case of the U.S. Senate, but the Supreme Court decided in 1964 that for the U.S. House of Representatives as well as for both houses of the state legislatures, Americans should be represented under the principle of "one person, one vote" and that the districts therefore must have equal populations.[34] The average size of a house district in the year 2010 was 710,767.[35] Districts are equalized following the census through a political process called **redistricting**, or the redrawing of district lines in states with more than one representative. This procedure, which is carried out by the state legislators (or by commissions they empower), can turn into a bitter political battle because how the district lines are drawn will have a lot to do with who gets elected.

Gerrymandering is the process of drawing district lines to benefit one group or another, and it can result in some extremely strange shapes by the time the state politicians

are through. Gerrymandering usually is one of three kinds. **Partisan gerrymandering** is the process in a particular state legislature whereby the majority party draws districts to maximize the number of House seats their party can win. Consequently, Democrats might draw districts that would split a historically Republican district and force an incumbent Republican to run in a new, more liberal district—a tactic called "cracking"—or even draw districts to concentrate as many opposition party voters as possible—called "packing"—so that the party drawing the districts can more easily win in surrounding districts. As a result of partisan gerrymandering, it is easily possible for a party to win a substantial majority of seats in the legislature while losing the statewide popular vote.

The Republican success in the 2010 elections gave the party control of the redistricting process in a majority of states. Artful districting in North Carolina resulted in Republicans winning nine of the state's thirteen congressional districts even though Democrats took 51 percent of

---

redistricting process of dividing states into legislative districts

gerrymandering redistricting to benefit a particular group

partisan gerrymandering redistricting controlled by the majority party in a state's legislature, to increase the number of districts that party can expect to carry

FIGURE 7.2   OF GERRYMANDERS AND EARMUFFS

Illinois Fourth Congressional District

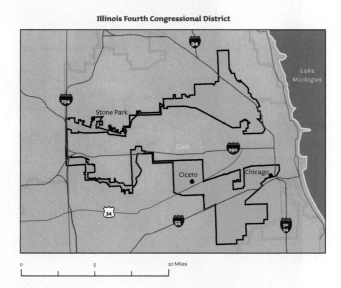

Back in 1812, district lines in the state of Massachusetts were drawn to concentrate Federalist support in a few key districts. A contemporary cartoon likened one particularly convoluted district to a long-necked monster, nicknamed the "Gerry-mander" after Massachusetts governor Eldbridge Gerry. Redistricting after the 2010 Census proved that the gerrymander is alive and well, as evidenced by the new map of the Illinois Fourth Congressional District, nicknamed the "earmuffs" district, which joins two predominantly Latino areas in Chicago.

Source: "Congressional District 4," NationalAtlas.gov; Library of Congress.

the two-party vote. Similar results occurred in Arizona, Michigan, Pennsylvania, and Wisconsin. All contributed to the odd outcome of the Republican's holding a majority in Congress (234 to 201 seats) while Democrats received 1.4 million more votes for the House.[36]

A second kind of gerrymandering is pro-incumbent gerrymandering. This happens when legislators agree to create districts to enhance the electoral security of the current members of both parties.[37] Such political outcomes tend to occur when a state legislature is divided so closely that neither party can dictate the redistricting process.

Finally, **racial gerrymandering** occurs when district lines are drawn to favor or disadvantage an ethnic or a racial group. For many years, states in the Deep South drew district lines to ensure that black voters would not constitute a majority that could elect an African American to Congress. Since the 1982 Voting Rights Act, the drawing of such lines has been used to maximize the likelihood that African Americans will be elected to Congress. Both Republicans and minority (African American and Latino) political activists have backed the formation of *majority-minority districts*, in

> **racial gerrymandering** redistricting to enhance or reduce the chances that a racial or an ethnic group will elect members to the legislature

which African Americans or Hispanics constitute majorities. This has the effect of concentrating enough minority citizens to elect one of their own, and at the same time, it takes these (usually Democratic) voters out of the pool of voters in other districts—a process aptly termed "bleaching"—thus making it easier for nonminority districts to be won by Republicans.[38] When sufficient numbers of minority voters are not concentrated in a geographic area, majority-minority districts take bizarre shapes. One of many examples is the Fourth Congressional District in Illinois, which joined two Hispanic communities (see Figure 7.2). The district has been named "earmuffs."[39]

Racial gerrymandering, however, remains highly controversial. While politicians and racial and ethnic group leaders continue to jockey for the best district boundaries for their own interests, the courts struggle to find a "fair" set of rules for drawing district lines. In recent cases the Supreme Court declared that race cannot be the predominant factor in drawing congressional districts. It can be taken into account, but so must other factors, such as neighborhood and community preservation. Since, as we discussed in Chapter 6, race is a suspect classification, it is subject to *strict scrutiny* whenever the law uses it to treat citizens differently, and the law must fulfill a compelling state purpose whether it penalizes them or benefits them.[40] After holding an earlier effort unconstitutional, the Court allowed a later redrawing of the North Carolina district to stand, arguing that where black voters are mostly Democrats, disentangling race from politics can be difficult, and that race can be a legitimate concern in redistricting as long as it is not the "dominant and controlling" consideration.[41] Partisan gerrymandering, on the other hand, is perfectly constitutional.

THINKING OUTSIDE THE BOX

Why is geography a better basis for congressional representation than, say, race, religion, gender, occupation, or socioeconomic group?

DECIDING TO RUN

The formal qualifications for Congress are not difficult to meet. In addition to the age and citizenship requirements listed in Table 7.1, the Constitution requires that a member live in the state he or she wants to represent, although state laws vary on how long or when. Custom dictates that if you are running for the House, you live in the actual district. There are no educational requirements for Congress—you don't even need to have graduated from college or high school. In many ways, the qualifications for Congress are lighter than for most jobs you might apply for when you graduate, but you do have to be prepared to expose yourself to the critical scrutiny of your prospective constituents— not a pleasant prospect if you value your privacy!

WHY WOULD ANYONE WANT THIS JOB? Given the low esteem in which Congress is held by most Americans, it's hard to imagine why anyone would want to be a part of that institution, let alone spend the money, resources, and public effort necessary to win. Some members of Congress, of course, are probably motivated by a desire to serve the public. These days they are also increasingly likely to be motivated by ideology—running for office from a sense of personal conviction and commitment to enact policy that represents strongly held values.

But low esteem aside, being a member of Congress is a very attractive job in its own right. First, there is all the fun of being in Washington, living a life that is undeniably exciting and powerful. The salary, $174,000 in 2014, puts representatives and senators among the top wage earners in the nation, and the "perks" of office include generous travel allowances, ample staff, franking privileges (free use of the U.S. mail), free parking at Reagan National Airport, health and life insurance, and a substantial pension.[42] Many of those benefits are designed to help members keep their jobs once they get them; franking privileges, videotaping services, and

© Ron Sachs/CNP/Corbis

From SNL to the Senate

Minnesota senator Al Franken majored in political science at Harvard, but he made his name as a writer and occasional performer on *Saturday Night Live* before graduating to a career as an astute—but always funny—political commentator and author. After winning his Senate seat in an extremely tight race in 2008, Franken settled down to serious business in Washington. Here, he attends a reception for newly confirmed Supreme Court justice Elena Kagan in 2010.

trips home were all designed by members of Congress to help them get reelected—all at taxpayer expense.

Offsetting the benefits, salary, power, and prestigious title ("The Honorable So-and-So") are the facts that the work is hard and the job security nonexistent. No matter how hard they work, members of Congress are sure to face an opponent in the next election who claims they did not do enough and declares that it's "time for a change." So they have to work all the harder, raise more money, and be even more popular than they were to begin with, just to keep their job. Also, despite the seemingly high salary, the job of being a member of Congress is expensive. Most members have to maintain two households, one in Washington and one at home, and many find it hard to manage on their congressional salaries.[43] It is also hard on families, who must either divide their time between two homes or live without one parent for part of the year. Finally, like Sen. Olympia Snowe (see *CLUES to Critical Thinking*), more and more members are becoming disenchanted with the job. The level of conflict in Congress is so high—especially the bitter partisan infighting—and the interest group pressure and fundraising needs so intense, that for some "the job just isn't any fun any more."[44]

WHAT IT TAKES TO WIN To have an outside chance of winning, nonincumbent candidates for Congress need political and financial assets. The key political asset for a potential candidate is experience, such as working for other candidates, serving as a precinct chair, or holding an office in the local party organization. Even more helpful is experience in elective office. Political amateurs without such experience are considered "low-quality" candidates for Congress because they almost never win—unless they happen to be famous sports stars, television personalities, or wealthy businesspeople who have personal resources that can help them beat the odds.[45]

"High-quality" candidates with the requisite political assets need to be careful not to squander them. They do not want to use up favors and political credibility in a losing effort, especially if they have to give up something valuable, like money or an office they currently hold, in order to run. **Strategic politicians** act rationally and carefully in deciding whether a race is worth running. They ask,

1. *Is this a district or state I can win?* People want to vote for and be represented by people like themselves, so potential candidates determine whether they and the district are compatible. Liberals do not do well in conservative parts of the South, African Americans have great difficulty getting elected in predominantly white districts, Republicans have a hard time in areas that are mostly Democratic, and so forth.

2. *Can I beat my opponent?* Whether an opponent is vulnerable is governed largely by the **incumbency advantage**, which refers to the edge in visibility, experience, organization, and fundraising ability possessed by the people who already hold the job. It can make them hard to defeat (see the box "The 114th Congress" on the next page). Three possibilities exist:

   a. An incumbent of the potential candidate's party already holds the seat. In this case, winning the nomination is a real long shot. In the postwar era,

only about 1 percent of incumbents are defeated in primaries, and even in the worst years, over 95 percent still get their party's nomination.[46]

   b. An incumbent of the opposite party holds the seat. In this case, winning the primary to get the party's nomination may be easier, but the odds are against winning in the general election unless the incumbent has been weakened by scandal, redistricting, or a challenge from within his or her party. Since 1954, incumbents have been reelected at a rate of 93 percent; in 2012 that figure dropped by just 2 percent.[47]

   c. The incumbent is not running. This is an "open seat," a potential candidate's best chance for success. However, because others know this as well, both the primary and the general elections are likely to be hard fought by high-quality candidates.

3. *Can I get the funds necessary to run a winning campaign?* Modern political campaigns are expensive, and campaigns that run on a budget and a prayer are hardly ever successful. Winning nonincumbents over the past decade have spent on average over four times as much as nonincumbents who did not win, and even then the winning nonincumbents could not keep up with the spending of incumbents.[48] Incumbents have access to a lot more political action committee (PAC) money and other contributions than do nonincumbents. (PACs are money-raising organizations devoted to a particular interest group, such as a labor union or trade association; they make donations to candidates that best represent their interests. We'll hear more about PACs in Chapter 13, on interest groups.)

4. *How are the national tides running?* Some years are good for Democrats, some for Republicans. These tides are a result of such things as presidential popularity, the state of the economy, and military engagements abroad. If it is a presidential election year, enthusiasm for a popular presidential candidate might sweep fellow party members to victory in what is known as the **coattail effect**, but this has been less significant in recent elections.

The strength of coattails might be declining, but there is no arguing with the phenomenon of the **midterm loss**. This is the striking regularity with which the presidential party loses seats in Congress in the midterm elections, also called "off-year" elections—those congressional elections that fall between presidential election years. Before 1998 the presidential party lost seats in the House of Representatives in every midterm election of the twentieth century except in 1934. The 1994 election that brought Republicans to power in Congress for the first time in forty years (see Figure 7.3) was a striking example of the midterm loss: Republicans won fifty-three seats previously held by Democrats, making it the largest change of this sort in the previous fifty years.[49] In general, the presidential party losses depend on the president's standing with the public and the state of the economy; an unpopular

---

strategic politicians office-seekers who base the decision to run on a rational calculation that they will be successful

incumbency advantage the electoral edge afforded to those already in office

coattail effect the added votes received by congressional candidates of a winning presidential party

midterm loss the tendency for the presidential party to lose congressional seats in off-year elections

THE 114TH CONGRESS

Going into the 2014 elections, the odds were not in the Democrats' favor. The presidential party almost always loses seats in the midterm elections, and even more so in a president's sixth year. Adding to this were Obama's relatively low approval ratings—an important predictor of the size of the midterm loss—and a sense of national unease stemming from events like the Ebola outbreak and advances by the Islamic State in the Middle East. Consistent with this, all of the (nonpartisan) election prognosticators predicted that the Republicans would take control of the Senate and add seats to their slim majority of the House. And that is what happened, but perhaps more so. What were expected to be tight races in a number of Senate contests turned out to be comfortable Republican wins. When the dust settled, however, the actual seat changes in both chambers were about

what the experts had been predicting. It was a low turnout election, even by midterm standards, and thus less of a "wave" of Republican support than what one expert called a "Democratic trough," referring to the low turnout of the young and some minorities, especially Latinos, compared to the electorates that brought Barack Obama to victory in 2008 and 2012.[50]

The makeup of the new Congress has shifted some. It will be more conservative, in part because there are more Republicans, but also, the newly elected Republicans are likely to side more with the Tea Party wing than with the leadership faction of the congressional parties. Both the House and the Senate have slightly increased the representation of women (84, up from 81 in the House; and 21, up from 20 in the Senate). There are

32 Hispanic members (3 senators and 29 representatives (up from 28). The number of Asians elected dropped to 8 from 10 (7 in the House, one in the Senate). Finally, the House has 2 Native Americans, both from Oklahoma, and 1 Pacific Islander, not surprisingly from Hawaii.

The past few years have been marked by inaction and extremely high levels of partisanship. Nothing in the new Congress suggests that there is a foundation for anything different. Although in the election's aftermath congressional leaders and President Obama talked about more bipartisan cooperation, realistically, the parties are farther apart than ever, with too many members unwilling to sacrifice their steadfast positions to expect a major change in the way Congress has done—and not done—its business in recent years.

FIGURE 7.3 PARTY CONTROL IN THE HOUSE OF REPRESENTATIVES, 1925-2012

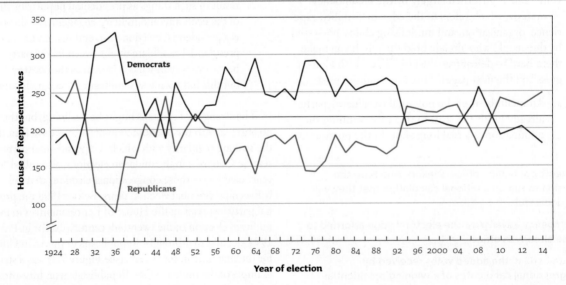

After a long period of uninterrupted dominance by the Democratic Party, Republicans controlled the House of Representatives for twelve years following the "Republican Revolution" of 1994. The Democrats won back control of both houses of Congress in 2006 and extended their control in 2008, but lost control of the House in the 2010 midterm elections and of the Senate in 2014.

president and a sour economy spell bad news for congressional candidates of the presidential party in an off-year election.[51]

In 1998 and again in 2002, unusual circumstances not only eliminated the midterm loss but also led the president's party to pick up seats. In 1998 the economy was sound and the public clearly did not agree with the impeachment of President Clinton, rejecting the Republican Party that was driving it. In 2002, following the terror attacks in 2001 and in the midst of the lead up to the Iraq War, President Bush's popularity was far higher than when he was elected, helping his party reverse the midterm loss. However, in 2006 the midterm loss returned true to form and Bush paid the price as the Democrats won back control of both houses of Congress. Similarly, in 2010 a sputtering economic recovery, high unemployment, and President Obama's correspondingly low approval ratings cost the Democrats the majority in the House. The GOP gain of sixty-three House seats was the largest for that party in six decades, eclipsing the historic 1994 victory and easily wiping out the Democrats' gains in the previous two election cycles. The Democrats were especially vulnerable because they had won in a large number of Republican districts in 2006 and again in 2008. With fewer seats at stake in the Senate, the Democrats lost only six seats, keeping majority control in that chamber, but not by much. In 2014 the Democrats again lost seats in the House, but this time lost control of the Senate as well, giving the coveted leadership spot to Senator Mitch McConnell from Kentucky.

WHO GETS ELECTED?

The founders intended that the House of Representatives, which was elected directly by the people, would be the "people's house," reflecting the opinions and interests of the mass of American citizenry. The Senate was to be a more elite institution, composed of older men of virtue, education, and property like the founders themselves, whom they believed

> descriptive representation the idea that an elected body should mirror demographically the population it represents

The Underrepresented Majority
More than half of all Americans are female, but women have been historically underrepresented in Congress. Between the two chambers, however, there are at least enough women to field an all-female softball team. Here, the Congressional Women's softball team celebrates after a 10–5 victory over female journalists in a charity event to help young women with breast cancer.

would have the wisdom to balance the impulses of the popularly elected House. In a way, the division of representational duties between the House and the Senate reflects the distinction between the dual tasks of constituent representation on the one hand and national lawmaking on the other that we have said forms the central dilemma for legislators today.

But today we no longer see the responsibility of making national policy as the sole province of the Senate, nor do we believe that responding to public opinion, interests, and demands is a lower order of representation belonging just to the House. In fact, our expectations about the House and the Senate have changed dramatically since the days of the founding. Most of us have more trust in the people and—as we saw at the outset of this chapter—considerably less regard for politicians, even those with education and property. In this section we look at what kind of legislature the people choose.

The first question we can ask is whether Congress measures up to the definition of what we call **descriptive representation**, in which the legislature is expected to mirror the demographics of those it represents. Founder and president John Adams said a representative assembly "should be in miniature an exact portrait of the people at large. It should think, feel, reason, and act like them."[52] In this regard, Congress fails quite miserably. Congress today, almost as much as the 1787 Constitutional Convention in Philadelphia, is dominated by relatively well-educated, well-to-do white males. The poor, the less educated, women, and minorities are not represented proportionately to their numbers in the population, although there are

SNAPSHOT OF AMERICA: WHO REPRESENTS US IN CONGRESS?

■ MALE ● FEMALE ☆ MILITARY SERVICE

■ AFRICAN AMERICAN ■ LATINO ■ ASIAN AMERICAN ■ ALASKAN/PACIFIC ISLANDER ■ NATIVE AMERICAN ■ WHITE

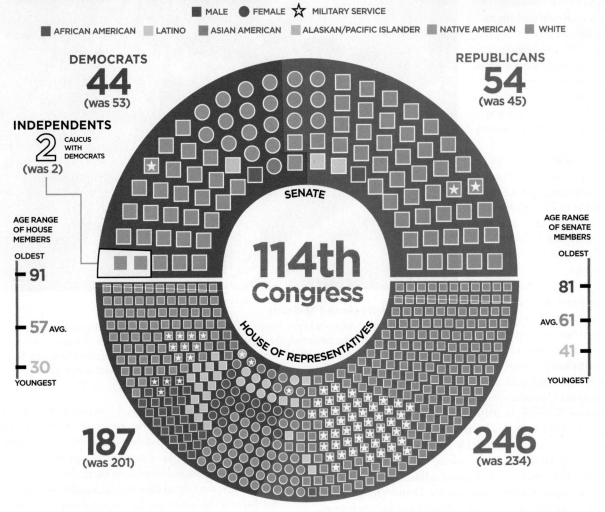

DEMOCRATS
44
(was 53)

INDEPENDENTS
2 CAUCUS WITH DEMOCRATS
(was 2)

REPUBLICANS
54
(was 45)

AGE RANGE OF HOUSE MEMBERS
OLDEST
91
57 AVG.
30
YOUNGEST

AGE RANGE OF SENATE MEMBERS
OLDEST
81
AVG. **61**
41
YOUNGEST

SENATE

114th Congress

HOUSE OF REPRESENTATIVES

187
(was 201)

246
(was 234)

NUMBER OF CONGRESSIONAL MEMBERS BY RACE AND GENDER SINCE 1900

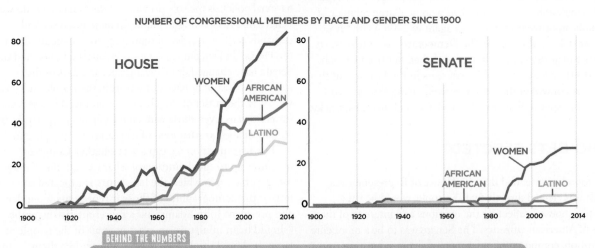

HOUSE

WOMEN
AFRICAN AMERICAN
LATINO

SENATE

WOMEN
AFRICAN AMERICAN
LATINO

BEHIND THE NUMBERS

Congress has been dominated by white males—and it still is, but less so than in the past (bottom line charts). What difference does it make if more minorities and females are elected to Congress? Does it matter which party they serve?

Source: CQ Weekly Guide to the New Congress, Nov. 6, 2014. Note: includes likely winners of races not settled at press time.

several trends in the direction of a more demographically representative Congress. (See "*Snapshot of America*: Who Represents Us in Congress?".)

OCCUPATIONS Americans work in many kinds of jobs. Only a relatively few have professional careers; far more are skilled and semiskilled workers, service economy workers, sales representatives, managers, and clerical workers. Yet this large bulk of the population does not send many of its own to Congress. Rather, Congress is dominated by lawyers and businesspeople and, not surprisingly, politicians. While the occupations tend to split more or less evenly between the parties, the Republicans draw much more heavily from business and banking, and the Democrats are more likely to have come from public service careers.

Although being an attorney or a state legislator is frequently listed as a member's prior occupation, many of those serving have more varied and surprising backgrounds. Former occupations of legislators include members of the clergy, sheriffs, a border patrol chief, scientists, radio talk show hosts, an astronaut, several with careers in the military, professional musicians, a comedian, professional athletes, organic farmers, a fruit picker, ski and driving instructors, a casino dealer and prison guard, a coroner, a taxi cab driver, and a former oil field worker. Thus while it is arguable that some *current* professions, especially law, are overrepresented, members also have had experience with many of the jobs of ordinary Americans.[53]

EDUCATION AND INCOME Even though members of Congress have collectively worked at an array of occupations before they got to Capitol Hill, the fact is that they are not representative of their fellow Americans when it comes to education and income. In the adult population at large, 26.7 percent graduated from college and only 8.9 percent have advanced degrees. In contrast, of Congress' 535 members, more than three-quarters have advanced degrees. Their income is well above the average American's income as well. Many House members—and an even greater percentage of senators—are millionaires.[54]

By these standards, Congress is an educational, occupational, and income elite. Those lower in the socioeconomic ranks do not have people like themselves in Washington working for them. A hard question to answer is whether it matters. Who can do a better job of representing, say, a working-class man who did not finish high school: people like himself, or those with the education and position to work in the halls of Congress on his behalf? The varied backgrounds of many members do suggest that congressmen and congresswomen probably have a good idea of what "ordinary" people's lives are like and the problems they face. We revisit this question when we look at the representation of women and minorities in Congress.

RACE, GENDER, AND INCOME Over the long haul, women and minorities have not been well represented in Congress (as indicated in "*Snapshot of America*: Who

Represents Us in Congress?"). Congress, however, is more representative today than it has been through most of our history. Until the civil rights movement in the 1960s, there were hardly any blacks or Hispanics in the House. Women seemed to have fared somewhat better, partly because of the once-common practice of appointing (and sometimes electing) a congressman's widow to office when the member died. This tactic was thought to minimize intraparty battles for the appointment. Not until the 1970s did female candidates begin to be elected and reelected on their own in significant numbers.

In the 1990s representation of all three groups, especially blacks and women, began to improve. The reasons, however, are quite different. Women have been coming into their own as candidates, a natural extension of their progress in education and the workplace. Women's political status has also been reinforced by the growing salience of issues that are of particular concern to them, from abortion to family leave policy to sexual harassment. In the 1992 congressional election, following Clarence Thomas's Supreme Court confirmation hearing, during which male legislators appeared tone-deaf to the issue of sexual harassment, women were phenomenally successful. In what has been dubbed the "Year of the Woman," women increased their representation in the House by two-thirds (from twenty-eight to forty-seven seats) and tripled their representation in the Senate (from two to six). This success is due in part to the large number of open seats created by retirements and redistricting following the 1992 census, which created opportunities to run in districts long held by incumbents.[55] Each election since has seen the addition of at least one new female senator, and they have come from both parties (nine Democrats and five Republicans). The House has had a similar increase.

Despite these dramatic changes in women's representation since the 1970s, the number of women in office has still not reached the levels that exist in many other countries and the percentage of women in the U.S. Congress still ranks comparatively low. These differences exist in part because election rules in some countries, such as Sweden, require parties to run a certain number of women candidates. But new research also highlights the role that the potential pool of candidates for Congress plays. In the United States there are fewer women in the pool of possible candidates than there are men because women tend to be less likely than men to be "self-starters" in running for office; that is, rather than just deciding to run for office and jumping into the campaign, women are more likely to wait to be asked by a party leader or the community. This difference exists even among a pool of potential women officeholders—like attorneys and local officeholders—that is similar to potential male candidates in all other characteristics. Because this is the case at the local and state legislative levels, these lower levels of government produce fewer women to run for office at higher levels like the U.S. Congress.[56]

The pattern of black representation showed steady increases during the 1970s and 1980s, followed by a comparatively large jump in the 1990s with the advent of racial gerrymandering. As we noted, the Supreme Court has

PROFILES IN CITIZENSHIP: JON TESTER

Tom Williams/CQ Roll Call Group/Getty Images

Thomas Jefferson, who had a soft spot for farmers, no doubt would have approved of Sen. Jon Tester. "Cultivators of the earth," to Jefferson's mind, were the "most virtuous" and "most valuable" of citizens. Senator Tester doesn't talk much about virtue, but he does think it's important that he leaves Washington every weekend, going home to Montana to get his hands dirty on the farm his family has worked for a century now.

"I think it keeps you real," he says about his determination to keep farming every week. "There's a lot of folks here who treat you, because you got a title in front of your name, they treat you different, they make you think you're special, when we're not. We're not different from anybody. When I go home, when I walk into my shop and I pull my swather out and it's got a flat tire, they don't give a damn if I am a senator or not. It keeps you real and also I think it keeps you grounded with what's going on economically in the country. If the farm quits working, I know that right away; if the market disappears, I know it; fuel prices go up, I know it; cost of equipment goes up or down, I know it."

If politics seems like an unusual occupation for a farmer, consider that Tester is also a former music teacher, holding a degree in music from the College of Great Falls. But he got caught up in public service early. During a high school trip to the state capital, his imagination had been fired by the state Senate—the grandeur of the building, the enthusiasm of the representatives, and a job that looked "very challenging but very fun." In the back of his mind was the idea that some day he might want to give it a try.

But in a rural community, he says, there is an expectation that citizens will serve on boards and committees. So Tester first did a stint on the school board and his local Soil Conservation Service Committee before following that high school ambition and running for, and winning, a seat in the Montana Senate. It was as much fun as he had thought it might be. "I like public service," says Tester. "It gives you positive vibes all the time. There is a lot of negative, sure there is, but there is a feeling of accomplishment different than working in a field, harvesting a field, picking hay bales or rocks or whatever you are doing on the farm."

In 2006, after eight years in the state Senate, he decided to make the leap to national politics. He was a long-shot candidate for the U.S. Senate, and the race was squeaky close—even the day after the election they weren't sure he had actually won—but Tester was

been reluctant to approve racially based districting, making the future of this pattern hard to predict.[57]

Hispanics have been even more underrepresented in Congress than have blacks because Hispanic populations do not tend to be as solidly concentrated as African Americans, they do not vote as consistently for a single party, and many do not vote at all. Underrepresentation of this group may be poised to change, however. Because the Hispanic population is growing so rapidly in America, both parties have pushed for Hispanics to run for office and have also worked hard to mobilize Hispanics to vote, although Democrats have been more successful recently, with the Obama campaign winning the Hispanic vote in the 2008 and 2012 elections by large margins, especially among the young. What might be a temporary Democratic support could be sealed as one-party loyalty, depending on how the issue of immigration plays out. In 1994 California Republicans backed Proposition 187, which sought to bar undocumented workers from receiving public services. Although it was later declared unconstitutional, that political move stimulated a rapid rise in Hispanic registration at an eight-to-one Democratic ratio and helped turn California to a solid blue (Democratic) state in national elections. The Republicans' continued support for tough, punitive immigration regulations, as evidenced in stringent immigration legislation passed by Arizona in 2010 (and subsequently in five other states, though the Supreme Court declared much of it unconstitutional in 2012); the strong anti-immigrant rhetoric of Mitt Romney, the Republican presidential nominee in 2012; and the Republican role in scuttling immigration reform in 2014 is likely to continue to push Hispanics toward the Democratic Party.[58]

It should surprise no one to know that members of Congress, who are more successful and more accomplished than the average citizen, also are wealthier by a fair amount than the average voter, but the income differences between most of us and those we send to Washington have grown

philosophical about it, figuring he had done his best and it was in the voters' hands. When the dust settled, he was the new senator from Montana, a job he finds good, but challenging. "This is a great job," he says. "It's a tremendous honor. There's all sorts of good stuff about it."

> "THE TRUTH IS THAT YOU CAN MAKE A DIFFERENCE AND IT MIGHT NOT TAKE NEAR AS MUCH WORK AS YOU THINK IT'S GOING TO TAKE. AND SECOND OF ALL, IF YOU GET INVOLVED, YOU'LL MAKE YOUR COMMUNITY, YOUR COUNTY, YOUR STATE, YOUR COUNTRY A BETTER PLACE."

Down sides? There are those, too, though "there isn't any job out there that doesn't have its ups and downs," he says. The most frustrating part, for him, is the excessive partisanship that the Senate is prone to these days, despite the fact that behind the scenes the senators are collegial and friendly. "I can tell you that there is no doubt in my mind that folks vote in some cases 'yes' or 'no' just to be partisan. That's not what's always best for the country. That's not always best for your constituents, not always what's best for your state." Watching a Senate vote take place along party lines from the television in his office, he points at the screen. "There is only one hope for what we see on that tube right there, and that's the next generation. They're the ones that can fix this, and if they are willing to allow this to happen, it will never get fixed. It just won't. They can fix it."

Hello, next generation? The ball is in your court. Here is some more of Tester's advice:

On taking risks:

[When I was running for the Senate] I was running in the primary against a guy who had already won statewide who was a millionaire—I'm not. I just thought, if we work hard, like the way I was brought up—if you work hard, and stick to it, to do what you want to do, the good Lord will open the door or he won't. And if you never try it, trust me—there were many times I wanted to get out of the race, many times. But if you never try it, you never know.

On keeping the republic:

[Benjamin] Franklin is right. This place won't work if everybody sits on their hands. And I think it's critically important and I think it's very rewarding for people to get involved. And there is all too many times that I hear people . . . say, 'Oh, I can't make a difference.' You know, 'I can't do this or I can't do that'—well, 'can't' shouldn't be a word in somebody's lexicon. The truth is that you can make a difference and it might not take near as much work as you think it's going to take. And second of all, if you get involved, you'll make your community, your county, your state, your country a better place. And I think that's the big issue. It takes some work, but it's very rewarding, and the time I'm talking about is that you don't have to do it eight hours a day. You can do it one evening a month in some cases. And it is very, very important. It's very important to the health of the country, it's very important for you to know what's going on in your community, and it makes life a whole helluva lot more fun.

Source: Senator Jon Tester spoke with Christine Barbour and Gerald Wright on July 27, 2010.

---

quite markedly in recent years. Between 1984 and 2009 the median net worth of members of the House of Representatives increased more than twofold (from $280,000 to $725,000) while the comparable figures for the average American family actually fell (from $20,600 to $20,500).[59] One of the reasons for this growing divide is the greatly increased cost of running for Congress; candidates who can bankroll a substantial portion of their campaign expenses stand a much better chance of getting party support and winning their election bids, so rich people are more likely to run and win.

DOES IT MATTER? Does descriptive representation of these traditionally underrepresented groups matter? For the poor, the answer is not hard to find; there is little or no descriptive representation for the poor, and this does appear to have a substantive effect on how well their interests are represented. Research suggests that the concerns of the poor do not have equal weight with those of the better off. Constituents with higher income and better educations have the resources and skills to communicate their policy preferences to their representatives, and they are more likely to vote and to participate in and contribute to campaigns. The result is that elected officials in general pay less attention to the concerns of the poor in their legislative work. In short, economic inequality carries over to the policymaking process of who gets what.[60]

For race and gender, the answer is that descriptive representation matters, at least at a symbolic level if not in substantive terms. Having "one of our own" as an active participant in the policy process has positive symbolic meaning for women, Hispanics, and African Americans.[61] Results are mixed, however, as to whether the presence of these groups in the legislative process produces better policies for these groups. Members of these demographic groups do tend to put issues of concern to those groups on the political agenda, but in terms of how they actually vote, the effect is muted. Women legislators do tend to vote for "women's issues," but they are also Democrats and Republicans, and partisan interest can override gender commitment.[62] The effect of descriptive representation is similarly mixed for minorities. As mentioned earlier, creating majority-minority districts through racial gerrymandering (typically at least 65 percent African American and Hispanic) has the effect of "bleaching" adjacent districts, particularly in the southern states. The result is whiter, more conservative districts that elect more Republicans and make it harder to pass legislation that is friendly to minority interests.[63] And, as is true for women, African American and Hispanic legislators add to the agenda new bills regarding their demographic groups and speak about their issues in floor debate. However, once one takes into account the character of districts, there is little difference in voting on bills between those legislators and their non-Hispanic, white counterparts. The increase in minority legislators elected to Congress has increased the number of bills concerning race, but passage of these bills is contingent on which party is in charge of the legislative process rather than simply the number of minority legislators.[64]

The primary policy effect of descriptive representation seems to be that it brings what might be otherwise neglected perspectives to the legislatures, raising minority-interest issues and anticipating the needs and concerns of fellow minorities when new issues arise.[65] For groups like the poor, who are not represented descriptively, even these limited benefits do not exist.

What limited evidence we have suggests, similarly, that the lack of many poor or working people in Congress probably leads to some of their concerns being left off the congressional agenda. While 50 to 60 percent of the population can be considered "working class" based on occupational status, only 2 percent of those elected to Congress fit this definition. The underrepresentation of working-class interests is reflected in how members vote on economic policies. On economic matters, working-class members are substantially more liberal than Congress as a whole, and if workers were represented proportionately in Congress, it is likely that each Congress would pass at least some significant additional legislation that favors their economic interests.[66]

PAUSE AND REVIEW:

WHO, WHAT, HOW

Congressional elections are the meeting ground for citizens and their representatives, where each brings his or her own goals and stakes in the process. Citizens want a congressperson who will take care of local affairs, mind the nation's business, and represent them generally on political and social issues. The rules of local representation and electoral politics, however, mean that citizens are more likely to get someone who takes care of local interests and affairs, and who sticks to a partisan line, at the expense of national interests and general representation.

Members of Congress want election, and then reelection. Because they make many of the rules that control electoral politics, the rules often favor those already in office. Many members may wish to turn to national affairs, to do what is best for the nation regardless of their local district or state, but they have to return continually to the local concerns and electoral supporters that are crucial to their reelection.

IN YOUR OWN WORDS » Identify the politics that influence how congressional districts are defined and who runs for Congress.

CONGRESSIONAL ORGANIZATION
The key role of political parties and congressional committees

Despite the imperatives of reelection and the demands of constituency service, the primary business of Congress is making laws. Lawmaking is influenced a great deal by the organization of Congress—that is, the rules of the institution that determine where the power is and who can exercise it. In this section we describe how Congress organizes itself and how this structure is influenced by members' goals.

THE CENTRAL ROLE OF PARTY

Political parties are central to how Congress functions for several reasons. First, Congress is organized along party lines. In each chamber, the party with the most members—the **majority party**—decides the rules for the chamber and gets the top leadership posts, such as the Speaker of the House, the majority leader in the Senate, and the chairs of all the committees and subcommittees.

Party is also important in Congress because it is the mechanism for members' advancement. Because all positions are determined by the parties, members have to advance within their party to achieve positions of power in the House or the Senate, whether as a committee chair or in the party leadership.

Finally, party control of Congress matters because the parties stand for very different things. Across a wide range of issues, Democrats embrace more liberal policies, whereas Republicans advocate more conservative ones. Figure 7.4 shows that on issues from abortion to oil exploration to affirmative action programs, Democratic House candidates are more liberal and Republican House candidates are much more conservative. Upon winning office, these candidates vote very differently from one another. As Figure 7.5

> **majority party** the party with the most seats in a house of Congress

FIGURE 7.4 PARTY DIFFERENCES AMONG HOUSE CANDIDATES ON POLICY STANCES, 2012

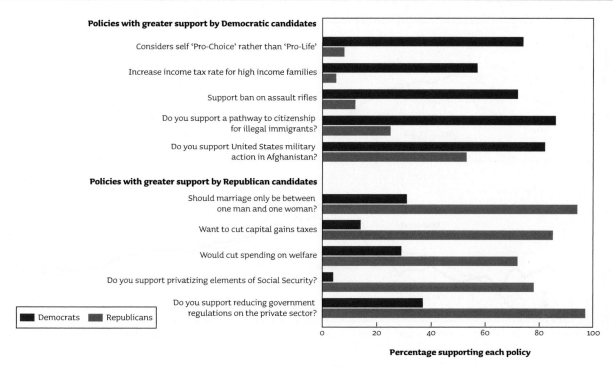

Policies with greater support by Democratic candidates

Considers self 'Pro-Choice' rather than 'Pro-Life'

Increase income tax rate for high income families

Support ban on assault rifles

Do you support a pathway to citizenship for illegal immigrants?

Do you support United States military action in Afghanistan?

Policies with greater support by Republican candidates

Should marriage only be between one man and one woman?

Want to cut capital gains taxes

Would cut spending on welfare

Do you support privatizing elements of Social Security?

Do you support reducing government regulations on the private sector?

■ Democrats ■ Republicans

0   20   40   60   80   100

Percentage supporting each policy

Source: Project Vote Smart, 2012, "Political Courage Test." Calculated by the authors.

FIGURE 7.5 PARTY VOTING IN CONGRESS, 1970–2013

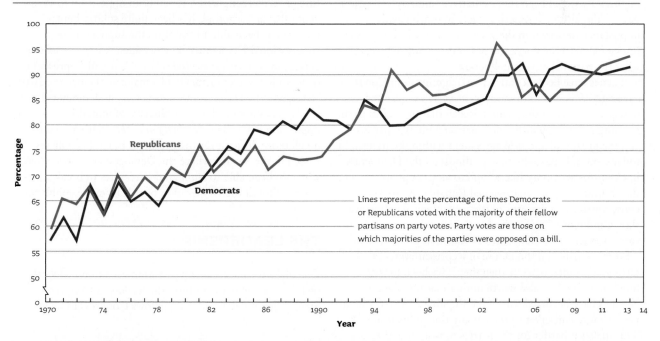

Republicans

Democrats

Lines represent the percentage of times Democrats or Republicans voted with the majority of their fellow partisans on party votes. Party votes are those on which majorities of the parties were opposed on a bill.

Percentage

1970   74   78   82   86   1990   94   98   02   06   09   11   13   14

Year

Sources: Roger H. Davidson, Walter J. Oleszek, and Frances E. Lee, *Congress and Its Members*, 12th ed. (Washington, D.C.: CQ Press, 2010), Figure 9-1; "The U.S. Congress Votes Data Base," *Washington Post*, projects.washingtonpost.com/congress/112/house/party-voters/ and updated by author with data from projects.washingtonpost.com/congress/113/house/members/.

FIGURE 7.6 IDEOLOGICAL POLARIZATION OF THE PARTIES IN CONGRESS, 1879–2012

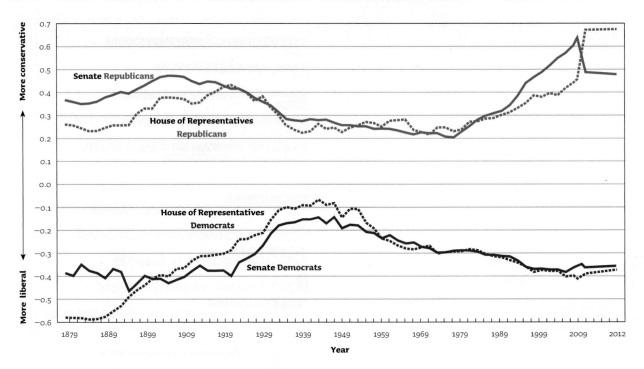

Source: Data on the liberal-conservative measures (DW-NOMINATE scores) developed by Keith Poole and Howard Rosenthal, "The Polarization of the Political Parties," May 10, 2012, voteview.com/political_polarization.asp.

illustrates, Democratic members of the House are increasingly likely to vote with the majority of their party and are opposed by Republican representatives similarly voting as a bloc. Thus, although Americans like to downplay the importance of parties in their own lives, political parties are fundamental to the operation of Congress and, hence, to what the national government does.

Parties have become much more significant in Congress in recent years due to the process of **party polarization**, described earlier in the chapter. Recall that this refers to the growing ideological differences between the two parties and the greater ideological agreement within the parties. In today's era of hyperpartisanship, almost all the Democrats in Congress are pretty liberal, and to an even greater extent the vast majority of congressional Republicans are very conservative. The patterns of party-ideological voting are shown in Figure 7.6. The higher the line, the more conservative the party is in its voting. Notice that the parties in both the Senate and the House of Representatives are farther apart ideologically than they have been for over a hundred years. It is also worth noting that the biggest changes have occurred within the Republican Party, which is now more conservative than at any time in its history.[67] This makes it harder for the parties to work together because the two parties' members are committed to such divergent positions across the whole range of issues with which Congress must deal.

Polarization has also been a significant factor in the growing intensity of conflict and rancor that is characteristic of recent congresses. Republican opposition to President Obama's proposals has been quite solid, whereas Obama has been able to count on the support of most congressional Democrats. The president was successful in getting his priorities enacted by the House of Representatives while the Democrats held a majority (before the 2010 election) only because there were enough Democrats there to get his bills passed even in the face of united Republican opposition. As we saw in *What's at Stake...?*, it has been much more difficult for the president to get his policies passed in the Senate, where the Democrats only occasionally have been able to command sixty votes to break a filibuster without the cooperation of at least one Republican.

THE LEADERSHIP

The majority and minority parties in each house elect their own leaders, who are, in turn, the leaders of Congress. Strong, centralized leadership allows Congress to be more

> **party polarization** greater ideological (liberal versus conservative) differences between the parties and increased ideological consensus within the parties

efficient in enacting party or presidential programs, but it gives less independence to members to take care of their own constituencies or to pursue their own policy preferences.[68] Although the nature of leadership in the House of Representatives has varied over time, the current era is one of considerable centralization of power. Because the Senate is a smaller chamber and thus easier to manage, its power is more decentralized.

LEADERSHIP STRUCTURE The Constitution provides for the election of some specific congressional officers, but Congress itself determines how much power the leaders of each chamber will have. The main leadership offices in the House of Representatives are the Speaker of the House, the majority leader, the minority leader, and the whips (see Figure 7.7). The real political choice about who the party leader should be occurs within the party groupings in each chamber. The Speaker of the House is elected by the majority party and, as the person who presides over floor deliberations, is the most powerful House member. The House majority leader, second in command, is given wide-ranging responsibilities to assist the Speaker.

The leadership organization in the Senate is similar but not as elaborate. The presiding officer of the Senate is the vice president of the United States, who can cast a tie-breaking vote when necessary but otherwise does not vote. When the vice president is not present, which is almost always the case, the presiding officer is the president pro tempore (an honorific given to the longest-serving senator of the majority party). In practice, however, the role is typically performed by a junior member. Because of the Senate's much freer rules for deliberation on the floor, the presiding officer has less power than in the House, where debate is generally tightly controlled. The locus of real leadership in the Senate is the majority leader and the minority leader. Each is advised by party committees on both policy and personnel matters, such as committee appointments.

In both chambers, Democratic and Republican leaders are assisted by party whips. (The term *whip* comes from an old English hunting expression; the "whipper in" was charged with keeping the dogs together in pursuit of the fox.) Elected by party members, whips find out how people intend to vote so that, on important party bills, the leaders can adjust the legislation, negotiate acceptable amendments, or employ favors (or, occasionally, threats) to line up support. Whips work to persuade party members to support the party on key bills, and they are active in making sure favorable members are available to vote when needed.

LEADERSHIP POWERS Leaders can exercise only the powers that their party members give them. From the members' standpoint, the advantage of a strong leader is that he or she can move legislation along, get the party program passed, do favors for members, and improve the party's standing. The disadvantage is that a strong party leader can pursue national party (or presidential) goals at the expense of members' pet projects and constituency interests, and he or she can withhold favors.

The power of the Speaker of the House has changed dramatically over time. At the beginning of the twentieth century, the strong "boss rule" of Speaker Joe Cannon (1903–1911) greatly centralized power in the House. Members rebelled at this in 1910 and moved to the seniority system, which vested great power in committee chairs instead of the Speaker. Power followed seniority, or length of service on a committee, so that once a person assumed the chair of a committee, business was run very much at his or her pleasure.[69] The seniority system itself was reformed in the 1970s by a movement that weakened the grip of chairs and gave some power back to the committees and subcommittees, but especially to the Speaker and the party caucuses.[70]

Speakers' powers were enhanced further with the Republican congressional victories in the 1994 election, when Rep. Newt Gingrich, R-Ga., became Speaker (see the *Profiles in Citizenship* in Chapter 3). Gingrich quickly became the most powerful Speaker since the era of boss rule. His House Republican colleagues were willing to give him new powers because his leadership enabled them to take control of the House and to enact the well-publicized conservative agenda that they called the "Contract With America."[71] Gingrich continued as the powerful Republican congressional spokesperson and leader until he resigned in the wake of the almost unprecedented reversal of the 1998 midterm loss, to be replaced by Dennis Hastert, a Republican from Illinois.

When the Democrats won control of the House in 2006, Nancy Pelosi was elected Speaker, the first woman to hold that position. In response to those who wondered if Pelosi could wield power as effectively as her male counterparts, Pelosi herself stated, "Anybody who's ever dealt with me knows not to mess with me."[72] Pelosi's role in passing Obama's health care reform bill was crucial, and she was effective at maintaining the support and discipline of her Democratic majority in the House, holding on to her leadership position in the party even after the Republicans regained the majority in 2010.[73] One early assessment by a longtime congressional watcher is that she is "entitled to be regarded among the best speakers."[74] John Boehner's lot as Speaker has been more difficult in many ways. His leadership skills are challenged by the effort of holding together a diverse caucus, divided between traditional Republicans and the newly elected Tea Partiers who come to Congress

> **Speaker of the House** the leader of the majority party who serves as the presiding officer of the House of Representatives
>
> **seniority system** the accumulation of power and authority in conjunction with the length of time spent in office

FIGURE 7.7 STRUCTURE OF THE HOUSE AND SENATE LEADERSHIP IN THE 114TH CONGRESS

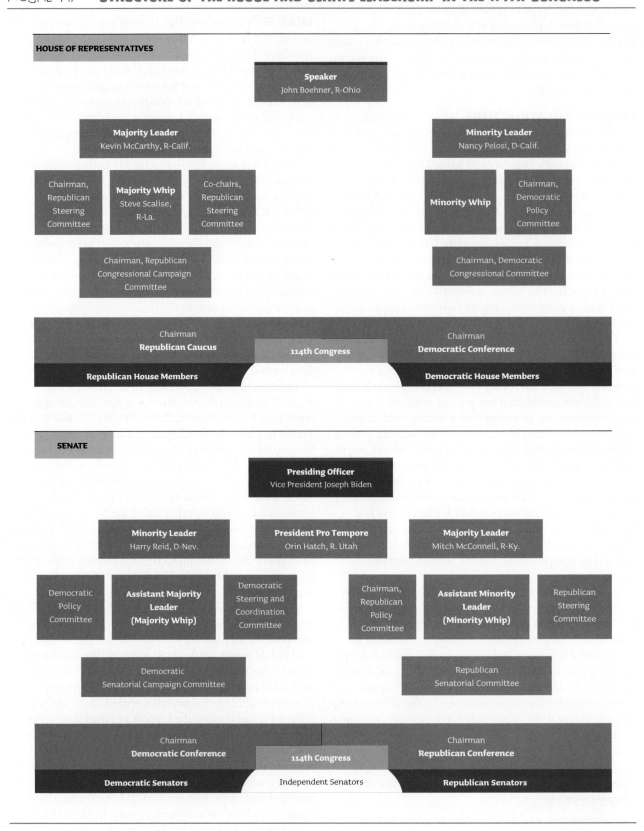

HOUSE OF REPRESENTATIVES

Speaker
John Boehner, R-Ohio

Majority Leader
Kevin McCarthy, R-Calif.

Minority Leader
Nancy Pelosi, D-Calif.

Chairman, Republican Steering Committee

Majority Whip
Steve Scalise, R-La.

Co-chairs, Republican Steering Committee

Minority Whip

Chairman, Democratic Policy Committee

Chairman, Republican Congressional Campaign Committee

Chairman, Democratic Congressional Committee

Chairman
Republican Caucus

114th Congress

Chairman
Democratic Conference

Republican House Members

Democratic House Members

SENATE

Presiding Officer
Vice President Joseph Biden

Minority Leader
Harry Reid, D-Nev.

President Pro Tempore
Orin Hatch, R. Utah

Majority Leader
Mitch McConnell, R-Ky.

Democratic Policy Committee

Assistant Majority Leader (Majority Whip)

Democratic Steering and Coordination Committee

Chairman, Republican Policy Committee

Assistant Minority Leader (Minority Whip)

Republican Steering Committee

Democratic Senatorial Campaign Committee

Republican Senatorial Committee

Chairman
Democratic Conference

114th Congress

Chairman
Republican Conference

Democratic Senators

Independent Senators

Republican Senators

The Johnson Treatment

As Senate majority leader (and later as president), Lyndon Johnson was legendary for his ability to cajole, charm, bully, and—by any means necessary—persuade others to see things his way. Here, the six foot, four inch tall Johnson makes a point or two, towering over colleagues while invading their personal space.

determined not to compromise in accomplishing their ambitious agenda. Indeed, Speaker Boehner was so battered during the fractious 113th Congress that there were continued calls for his resignation from both liberals and conservatives.[75]

The leaders of the Senate have never had as much formal authority as those in the House, and that remains true today. The traditions of the Senate, with its much smaller size, allow each senator to speak or to offer amendments when he or she wants. The highly individualistic Senate would not accept the kind of control that some Speakers wield in the House. But though the Senate majority leader cannot control senators, he or she can influence the scheduling of legislation, a factor that can be crucial to a bill's success. The majority leader may even pull a bill from consideration, a convenient exercise of authority when defeat would embarrass the leadership.

The current majority leader, Mitch McConnell of Kentucky, replaces Democrat Harry Reid, a highly effective manager in the biggest legislative victories of Obama's first years as president, shepherding the health care bill through the Senate and also helping to get major legislation passed in the lame-duck session after the 2010 election.[76] McConnell, who has hoped to win the majority's leader's seat for several elections in a row, only to see his chances slip away, immediately made conciliatory remarks about finding common ground with the Democrats, vowing that there would be no government shut downs or debt ceiling crises under his watch. Among his members, however, are at least three senators with 2016 presidential aspirations and Tea Party inclinations, which may complicate his job.

THE COMMITTEE SYSTEM

Meeting as full bodies, it would be impossible for the House and the Senate to consider and deliberate on all of the 10,000 bills and 100,000 nominations they receive every two years.[77] Hence, the work is broken up and handled by smaller groups called committees.

The Constitution says nothing about congressional committees; they are completely creatures of the chambers of Congress they serve. The committee system has developed to meet the needs of a growing nation as well as the evolving goals of members of Congress. Initially, congressional committees formed to consider specific issues and pieces of legislation; after they made their recommendations to the full body, they dispersed. As the nation grew, and with it the number of bills to be considered, this ad hoc system became unwieldy and Congress formed a system of more permanent committees. Longer service on a committee permitted members to develop expertise and specialization in a particular policy area, and thus bills could be considered more efficiently. Committees also provide members with a principal source of institutional power and the primary position from which they can influence national policy.

WHAT COMMITTEES DO It is at the committee and, even more, the subcommittee stages that the nitty-gritty details of legislation are worked out. Committees and subcommittees do the hard work of considering alternatives and drafting legislation. Committees are the primary information gatherers for Congress. Through hearings, staff reports, and investigations, members gather information on policy alternatives and discover who will support different policy options. Thus committees act as the eyes, ears, and workhorses of Congress in considering, drafting, and redrafting proposed legislation.

Committees do more, however, than write laws. Committees also undertake the congressional oversight we discussed earlier in this chapter; that is, they check to see that the executive and its agencies are carrying out the laws as Congress intended them to. Committee members gather information about agencies from the media, constituents, interest groups, staff, and special investigations (see the discussion of the Government Accountability Office, later in this chapter). A lot of what is learned in oversight is reflected in changes to the laws giving agencies their power and operating funds.

Members and the general public all strongly agree on the importance of congressional oversight; it is part of the "continuous watchfulness" that Congress mandated for itself in the Legislative Reorganization Act of 1946 and reiterated in its Legislative Reorganization Act of 1970. Nevertheless, oversight tends to be slighted in the congressional process. The reasons are not hard to find. Oversight takes a lot of time, and the rewards to individual members are less certain than from other activities like fundraising or grabbing a headline in the district with a new pork project. Consequently, oversight most often takes the form of "fire-alarm" oversight, in which some scandal or upsurge in public interest directs congressional attention to a problem in the bureaucracy, rather than careful and systematic reviews of agencies' implementation of congressional policies.[78]

TYPES OF COMMITTEES Congress has four types of committees: standing, select, joint, and conference. The vast majority of work is done by the **standing committees**. These are permanent committees, created by statute, that carry over from one session of Congress to the next. They review most pieces of legislation that are introduced to Congress. So powerful are the standing committees that they scrutinize, hold hearings on, amend, and, frequently, kill legislation before the full Congress ever gets the chance to discuss it.

The standing committees of the 113th Congress are listed in Table 7.2, and as their names indicate, most deal with issues in specific policy areas, such as agriculture, foreign relations, or justice. Each committee is typically divided into several subcommittees that focus on detailed areas of policy. There are twenty-three standing committees and 104 subcommittees in the House. The Senate has sixteen committees and seventy-two subcommittees. Not surprisingly, committees are larger in the House, with membership rising to more than seventy on some committees, compared to fewer than thirty on the Senate committees. The size of the committees and the ratio of majority to minority party members on each are determined at the start of each Congress by the majority leadership in the House

TABLE 7.2
STANDING COMMITTEES OF THE 113TH CONGRESS

HOUSE	SENATE
Agriculture	Agriculture, Nutrition, and Forestry
Appropriations	
Armed Services	Appropriations
Budget	Armed Services
Education and the Workforce	Banking, Housing, and Urban Affairs
Energy and Commerce	Budget
Ethics	Commerce, Science, and Transportation
Financial Services	
Foreign Affairs	Energy and Natural Resources
Homeland Security	
House Administration	Environment and Public Works
Judiciary	Finance
Natural Resources	Foreign Relations
Oversight and Government Reform	Health, Education, Labor, and Pensions
Rules	Homeland Security and Governmental Affairs
Science, Space, and Technology	
Select Intelligence	Indian Affairs
Small Business	Judiciary
Transportation and Infrastructure	Rules and Administration
Veterans' Affairs	Small Business and Entrepreneurship
Ways and Means	Veterans' Affairs
House Select Committee Intelligence	Senate Special or Select Committees Aging Ethics Intelligence

standing committees permanent committees responsible for legislation in particular policy areas

and by negotiations between the majority and minority leaders in the Senate. Standing committee membership is relatively stable as seniority on the committee is a major factor in gaining subcommittee or committee chairs; the chairs wield considerable power and are coveted positions.

The policy areas represented by the standing committees of the two houses roughly parallel each other, but the **House Rules Committee** exists only in the House of Representatives. (There is a Senate Rules and Administration Committee, but it does not have equivalent powers.) The House Rules Committee provides a "rule" for each bill that specifies when it will be debated, how long debate can last, how it can be amended, and so on. Because the House is so large, debate would quickly become chaotic without the organization and structure provided by the Rules Committee. Such structure is not neutral in its effects on legislation, however. Since the committees are controlled by the majority party in the House, and especially by the Speaker, the rule that structures a given debate will reflect the priorities of the majority party.

When a problem before Congress does not fall under the jurisdiction of a standing committee, a **select committee** may be appointed. These committees are usually temporary and do not recommend legislation per se. They are used to gather information on specific issues, like the Select Committee on Homeland Security did after the September 11 terror attacks, or to conduct an investigation, as did the Select Bipartisan Committee to Investigate the Preparation for and Response to Hurricane Katrina. In May 2014 the House of Representatives voted to establish the Select Committee on Benghazi to investigate further what happened in the attack in Benghazi, Libya, in which four Americans were killed.

Joint committees are made up of members of both houses of Congress. While each house generally considers bills independently (making for a lot of duplication of effort and staff), in some areas they have coordinated activities to

Alex Wong/Getty Images News/Getty Images

A Little Publicity Doesn't Hurt
Committee hearings often happen far from the public eye. In 2010 Stephen Colbert testified (in then-character) before a somewhat-obscure subcommittee of the House Judiciary Committee, offering a humorous but sincere plea on behalf of migrant farm workers. Colbert joked that he hoped his star power would bump coverage of this important issue "all the way up to C-Span 1." His testimony made the evening news.

expedite consideration of legislation. The joint committees in the 113th Congress were on printing, economics, and taxation, and will probably be similar in the 114th.

Before a bill can become law, it must be passed by both houses of Congress in exactly the same form. But because the legislative process in each house often subjects bills to different pressures, they may be very different by the time they are debated and passed. **Conference committees** are temporary committees made up of members of both houses of Congress commissioned to resolve these differences, after which the bills go back to each house for a final vote. Members of the conference committees are appointed by the presiding officer of each chamber, who usually taps the senior members, especially the chair, of the committees that considered the bill. Most often the conferees are members of those committees.

In the past, conference committees have tended to be small (five to ten members). In recent years, however, as Congress has tried to work within severe budget restrictions and across the divide of increased party polarization, it has taken to passing huge "megabills" that collect many proposals into one. Conference committees have expanded in turn, sometimes ballooning into gigantic affairs with many "subconferences."[79] This has given rise to a relatively new process of "omnibus" legislation in which the committees play a less central role and congressional leadership is much more involved, even at early stages. We discuss these changes later in this chapter when we talk about policymaking.

GETTING ON THE RIGHT COMMITTEES Getting on the right standing committee is vital for all members of Congress because so much of what members want to accomplish is realized through their work on these committees.

House Rules Committee the committee that determines how and when debate on a bill will take place

select committee a committee appointed to deal with an issue or a problem not suited to a standing committee

joint committees combined House-Senate committees formed to coordinate activities and expedite legislation in a certain area

conference committees temporary committees formed to reconcile differences in House and Senate versions of a bill

Political scientist Richard Fenno identified three goals for members—reelection, lawmaking (also called policymaking), and influence in Congress—and argued that committee memberships are the principal means for achieving these goals.[80] Because members are concerned with reelection, they try to get on committees that deal with issues of concern to constituents. Examples of good matches include the Agriculture Committee for farm states' legislators and the Defense Committee for members with military bases or contractors in their districts.

Members who like to focus on national lawmaking might try to get assigned to committees like Commerce or Foreign Affairs, which have broad jurisdictions and often deal with weighty, high-profile concerns. The House Ways and Means Committee and the Senate Finance Committee, because they deal with taxation—a topic of interest to nearly everyone—are highly prized committee assignments.

When it comes to committee assignments that serve the third goal, achieving power within Congress, an excellent choice is the House Rules Committee. Because it plays the central "traffic cop" role we discussed earlier, its members are in a position to do a lot of favors for members whose bills have to go through Rules. Almost all senators have the opportunity to sit on one of the four most powerful Senate committees: Appropriations, Armed Services, Finance, and Foreign Relations.[81]

Decisions on who gets on what committee vary by party and chamber. Although occasionally the awarding of committee assignments has been used by the parties to reward those who support party positions, in general both the Democrats and the Republicans accommodate their members when they can, since the goal of both parties is to support their ranks and help them be successful.

COMMITTEE CHAIRS

For much of the twentieth century, congressional power rested with the chairmen and chairwomen of the committees of Congress; their power was unquestioned under the seniority system. Seniority remains important today, but chairs serve at the pleasure of their party caucuses and the party leadership. The committees, under this system, are expected to reflect more faithfully the preferences of the average party member rather than just those of the committee chair or current members.[82]

CONGRESSIONAL RESOURCES

For Congress to knowledgeably guide government lawmaking, it needs expertise and information. Members find, however, that alone they are no match for the enormous amount of information generated by the executive branch, on the one hand, or the sheer informational demands of the policy process—economic, social, military, and foreign affairs—on the other. The need for independent, expert information, along with the ever-present reelection imperative, has led to a big growth in what we call the congressional bureaucracy. Congress has more than 22,000 employees, paid for by the federal government. This makes it by far the largest-staffed legislature in the world.

CONGRESSIONAL STAFF

The vast majority of congressional staff—about 14,000 secretaries, computer personnel, clericals, and professionals—work for individual members or committees. Representatives average about seventeen staff members; senators' staffs average around forty, but the numbers vary largely with the population of each senator's state. Staff members can be assigned to either legislative work or constituency service, at the member's discretion. Those doing primarily constituency work are usually located in the district or state, close to constituents, rather than in Washington. In fact, most offices employ interns, frequently college students, whose efforts supplement the full-time staff.

The committees' staffs (about 2,200 in the House and 1,200 in the Senate) do much of the committee work, from honing ideas, suggesting policy options to members, scheduling hearings, and recruiting witnesses, to actually drafting legislation.[83] In most committees each party also has its own staff. Following the 1994 election, committee staffs were cut by one-third; however, members did not force any cuts in the sizes of their personal staffs. Because of the huge workloads, members rely on staff a great deal, which can give them a great deal of influence.

CONGRESSIONAL BUREAUCRACY

Reflecting a reluctance dating from Vietnam and Watergate to be dependent on the executive branch for information, Congress has built its own research organizations and agencies to facilitate its work. Unlike personal or committee staffs, these are strictly nonpartisan, providing different kinds of expert advice and technical assistance. The Congressional Research Service (CRS), a unit of the Library of Congress, employs over eight hundred people to do research for members of Congress. For example, if Congress is considering a bill to relax air quality standards in factories, it can have the CRS determine what is known about the effects of air quality on worker health.

The Government Accountability Office (formerly the General Accounting Office but still known as the GAO), with its 3,200 employees, audits the books of executive departments and conducts policy evaluation and analysis. It issues reports such as *Defense Health Care: TRICARE Dental Services Contracts' Requirements and Structure; Airline Competition: The Average Number of Competitors in Markets Serving the Majority of Passengers Has Changed Little in Recent Years, but Stakeholders Voice Concerns about Competition;* and *Foster Care: HHS Needs to Improve Oversight of Fostering Connections Act Implementation.*[84] These studies are meant to help Congress determine the nature of policy problems, possible solutions, and what government agencies are actually doing. The GAO studies supplement the already substantial committee staffs working on legislation and oversight.

A third important congressional agency is the Congressional Budget Office (CBO). The CBO is Congress' economic adviser, providing members with economic estimates about the budget, the deficit or surplus, and the national debt, as well as forecasts of how they will be influenced by different tax and spending policies. The CBO's regularly updated estimates on the costs of various versions of the health care reform plans were a central element in congressional considerations of the bill. Congress has a stronger and more independent role in the policy process when it is not completely dependent on the executive branch for information and expertise.

PAUSE AND REVIEW:

WHO, WHAT, HOW

Members of Congress, the congressional leaders, and the parties are all vitally concerned with the rules of congressional organization. The members want autonomy to do their jobs and to respond to their constituents. But they are dependent on their leaders, and thus on their parties, for the committee assignments that enhance their job performance and help them gain expertise in areas that their constituents care about. Without party and leadership cooperation, the individual member of Congress is isolated and relatively powerless, especially in the House, where party control is stronger.

Congressional leaders want tight rules of organization so that they can control what their members do and say. Members of the House and the Senate make their own organizational rules, which give the dominant party in each house power over the internal rules and, consequently, over the policies produced.

IN YOUR OWN WORDS >> Summarize the central role that the parties play in Congress.

HOW CONGRESS WORKS
An already complex process, complicated further by internal and external forces

The policies passed by Congress are a result of both external and internal forces. The external environment includes the problems that are important to citizens at any given time—sometimes the economy, sometimes foreign affairs, at other times national security or the federal deficit or the plight of the homeless and so forth. The policy preferences of the president loom large in this external environment as well. It is often said, with some exaggeration but a

> **norms** informal rules that govern behavior in Congress

bit of truth, that "the president proposes, the Congress disposes" of important legislation. Parties, always important, have been increasing their influence in the policymaking arena, and organized interests play a significant role as well.

THE CONTEXT OF CONGRESSIONAL POLICYMAKING

Congress also has a distinct internal institutional environment that shapes the way it carries out its business. Three characteristics of this environment are especially important.

SEPARATE HOUSES, IDENTICAL BILLS First, the Constitution requires that almost all congressional policy has to be passed in identical form by both houses. This requirement, laid out by the founders in the Constitution, makes the policy process difficult because the two houses serve different constituencies and operate under different decision-making procedures. Interests that oppose a bill and lose in one chamber can often be successful at defeating a bill in the other chamber. The opposition has to stop a bill in only one place to win, but the proponents have to win in both. In Congress, it is much easier to play defense than offense.

FRAGMENTATION The second overriding feature of the institutional environment of Congress as a policy-making institution is its fragmentation. As you read the next section, on how a bill becomes a law, notice how legislation is broken into bits, each considered individually in committees. It is very difficult to coordinate what one bill does with those laws that are already on the books or with what another committee might be doing in a closely related area. Thus we do such seemingly nonsensical things as simultaneously subsidizing tobacco growers and antismoking campaigns.[85] This fragmentation increases opportunities for constituencies, individual members, and well-organized groups to influence policy in those niches about which they really care. The process also makes it very hard for national policymakers—the president or the congressional leaders—who would like to take a large-scale, coordinated approach to our major policy problems.

NORMS OF CONDUCT The third critical feature of the institutional environment of Congress is the importance of **norms**, or informal rules that establish accepted ways of doing things. These are sometimes called "folkways" and are quickly learned by newcomers when they enter Congress. Norms include the idea that members should work hard, develop a specialization, treat other members with the utmost courtesy, reciprocate favors generally, and take pride in their chambers and in Congress. The purpose of congressional norms is to constrain conflict and personal animosity in an arena where disagreements are inevitable, but they also aid in getting business done. Although congressional norms continue to be important, they are less constraining on members today than they were in the 1950s and 1960s.[86] The extent to which the norms of respect and decorum have been stretched in a hyperpartisan Congress was illustrated when Rep. Joe Wilson, R-S.C., yelled out "You lie!" during President Obama's nationally televised health care address before a joint session of Congress in 2009. Fortunately, the Wilson outburst was an exception. The norms of collegial deference are important, especially in the current era of intense partisan conflict. Without those norms, what is frequently tense partisan rhetoric would undoubtedly devolve quickly into some version of the rude and unpleasant vitriol common in the political blogosphere.[87]

HOW A BILL BECOMES A LAW— SOME OF THE TIME

When we see something that seems unfair in business or in the workplace, when disaster strikes and causes much suffering, when workers go on strike and disrupt our lives— whenever a crisis occurs, we demand that government do something to solve the problem that we cannot solve on our own. This means government must have a policy, a set of laws, to deal with the problem. Because so many problems seem beyond the ability of individual citizens to solve, there is an almost infinite demand for new laws and policies, often with different groups demanding quite contradictory responses from the government.

This section considers briefly how demands for solutions become laws. We consider two aspects of congressional policy here: (1) the agenda, or the source of ideas for new policies; and (2) the legislative process, or the steps a bill goes through to become law. Very few proposed policies, as it turns out, actually make it into law, and those that do have a difficult path to follow.

SETTING THE AGENDA Before a law can be passed, it must be among the things that Congress thinks it ought to do. There is no official list of actions that Congress needs to take, but when a bill is proposed that would result in a significant change in policy, it must seem like a reasonable thing for members to turn their attention to—a problem that is possible, appropriate, and timely for them to try to solve with a new policy. That is, it must be on the legislative agenda. Potential new laws can get on Congress' agenda in several ways. First, because public attention is focused so intently on presidential elections and campaigns, new presidents are especially effective at setting the congressional agenda. Later in their terms, presidents also use their yearly State of the Union addresses to outline the legislative agenda they would like Congress to pursue. Because the media and the public pay attention to the president, Congress does too. This does not guarantee presidential success, but it means the president can usually get Congress to give serious attention to his major policy proposals. His proposals may be efforts to fulfill campaign promises, to

pay political debts, to realize ideological commitments, or to deal with a crisis.

A second way an issue gets on the legislative agenda is when it is triggered by a well-publicized event, even if the problem it highlights is not a new one at all. For example, the 2010 explosion of BP's oil drilling platform *Deepwater Horizon* and the subsequent release of millions of barrels of crude oil into the Gulf of Mexico drew the nation's attention to energy policy, the adequacy of regulatory procedures, and the need to protect the environment. What leaders in Washington will actually do in response to such an event is hard to predict, especially in circumstances in which they are unable to do much of anything (the federal government had neither the technical know-how nor the equipment to plug the oil well, for instance). Nonetheless, such events create a public demand that the government "do something!"

A third way an idea gets on the agenda is for some member or members to find it in their own interests, either political or ideological, to invest time and political resources in pushing the policy. Many members of Congress want to prove their legislative skills to their constituents, key supporters, the media, and fellow lawmakers. The search for the right issue to push at the right time is called policy entrepreneurship. Most members of Congress to greater or lesser degrees are policy entrepreneurs. Those with ambition, vision, and luck choose the issues that matter in our lives and that can bring them significant policy influence and recognition, but most successful policy entrepreneurs are not widely recognized outside of the policy communities in which they operate.[88] Policy entrepreneurship by members is important in setting the congressional policy agenda, and it can reap considerable political benefits for those associated with important initiatives.

LEGISLATIVE PROCESS: BEGINNING THE LONG JOURNEY Bills, even those widely recognized as representing the president's legislative program, must be introduced by members of Congress. The formal introduction is done by putting a bill in the "hopper" (a wooden box) in the House, where it goes to the clerk of the House, or by giving it to the presiding officer in the Senate. The bill is then given a number (for example, HR932 in the House or S953 in the Senate) and begins the long journey that *might* result in its becoming law. Figure 7.8 shows the general route for a bill once it is introduced in either the House or the Senate, but the details can get messy, and there are exceptions (as

legislative agenda the slate of proposals and issues that representatives think it worthwhile to consider and act on

policy entrepreneurship practice of legislators becoming experts and taking leadership roles in specific policy areas

FIGURE 7.8   HOW A BILL BECOMES A LAW: SHORT VERSION

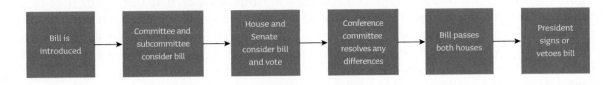

Bill is introduced → Committee and subcommittee consider bill → House and Senate consider bill and vote → Conference committee resolves any differences → Bill passes both houses → President signs or vetoes bill

The Big Picture on p. 268 shows). A bill introduced in the House goes first through the House and then on to the Senate, and vice versa. However, bills may be considered simultaneously in both houses.

LEGISLATIVE PROCESS: MOVING THROUGH COMMITTEE

The initial stages of committee consideration are similar for the House and the Senate. The bill first has to be referred to committee. This is largely automatic for most bills; they go to the standing committee with jurisdiction over the content of the bill. A bill to change the way agricultural subsidies on cotton are considered would start, for example, with the House Committee on Agriculture. In some cases, a bill might logically fall under more than one committee's jurisdiction, and here the Speaker exercises a good deal of power. He or she can choose the committee that will consider the bill or even refer the same bill to more than one committee. This gives the Speaker important leverage in the House because he or she often knows which committees are likely to be more or less favorable to different bills. Senators do not worry quite as much about where bills are referred because they have much greater opportunity to make changes later in the process than representatives do. We'll see why when we discuss floor consideration.

Bills then move on to subcommittees, where they may, or may not, get serious consideration. Most bills die in committee because the committee members either don't care about the issue (it isn't on their agenda) or actively want to block it. Even if the bill's life is brief, the member who introduced it can still campaign as its champion. In fact, a motivation for the introduction of many bills is not that the member seriously believes the bill has a chance of passing but that the member wants to be seen back home as taking some action on the issue.

Bills that subcommittees decide to consider will have hearings—testimony from experts, interest groups, executive department secretaries and undersecretaries, and even other members of Congress. The subcommittee deliberates and votes the bill back to the full committee. There the committee further considers the bill and makes changes and

> **filibuster** a practice of unlimited debate in the Senate in order to prevent or delay a vote on a bill

revisions in a process called *markup.* If the committee votes in favor of the final version of the bill, it goes forward to the floor. Here, however, a crucial difference exists between the House and the Senate.

GETTING TO THE FLOOR: HOUSE RULES

In the House, bills go from the standing committee to the Rules Committee. This committee, highly responsive to the Speaker of the House, gives each bill a "rule," which includes when and how the bill will be considered. Some bills go out under an "open rule," which means that any amendments can be proposed and added as long as they are germane, or relevant, to the legislation under consideration. More typically, especially for important bills, the House leadership gains more control by imposing rules that limit the time for debate and restrict the amendments that can be offered. For example, if the leadership knows that there is a lot of sentiment in favor of action on a tax cut, it can control the form of the tax cut by having a restrictive rule that prohibits any amendments to the committee's bill. In this way, even members who would like to vote for a different kind of tax cut face pressure to go along with the bill because they can't amend it; it is either this tax cut or none at all, and they don't want to vote against a tax cut. Thus, for some bills, not only can the House Rules Committee make or break the bill, but it can also influence the bill's final content.

GETTING TO THE FLOOR: SENATE RULES

The Senate generally guarantees all bills an "open rule" by default, and unlike in the House, there is no germane rule that says that an amendment must logically relate to the policy being considered. The majority leader, usually in consultation with the minority leader, schedules legislation for consideration. Their control, however, is fairly weak because any senator can introduce any proposal as an amendment to any bill, sometimes called a rider, and get a vote on it. Thus senators have access to the floor for whatever they want in a way that is denied to representatives. Furthermore, whereas in the House the rule for each bill stipulates how long a member can debate, the Senate's tradition of "unlimited debate," as we saw in the *What's at Stake...?* that opened this chapter, means that a member can talk indefinitely. Senators opposed to a bill can **filibuster** in an effort to tie up the floor of the Senate in nonstop debate to prevent the Senate from voting on a bill. A filibuster can

BIG PICTURE: HOW OUR LAWS ARE MADE

How does a bill become a law? Sometimes it seems like our lawmakers are playing some goofy game to which no one really understands the rules. In fact, it is not quite that bad, but the process is far more complicated than the Schoolhouse Rock cartoon version of poor, dejected Bill, sitting on Capitol Hill, would have you believe. Take a close look at this version of the lawmaking process, and you will not be surprised that so many bills fail to make it to the president's desk. The founders wanted a slow, incremental lawmaking process in which the brakes could be applied at multiple points, and that is exactly what they got.

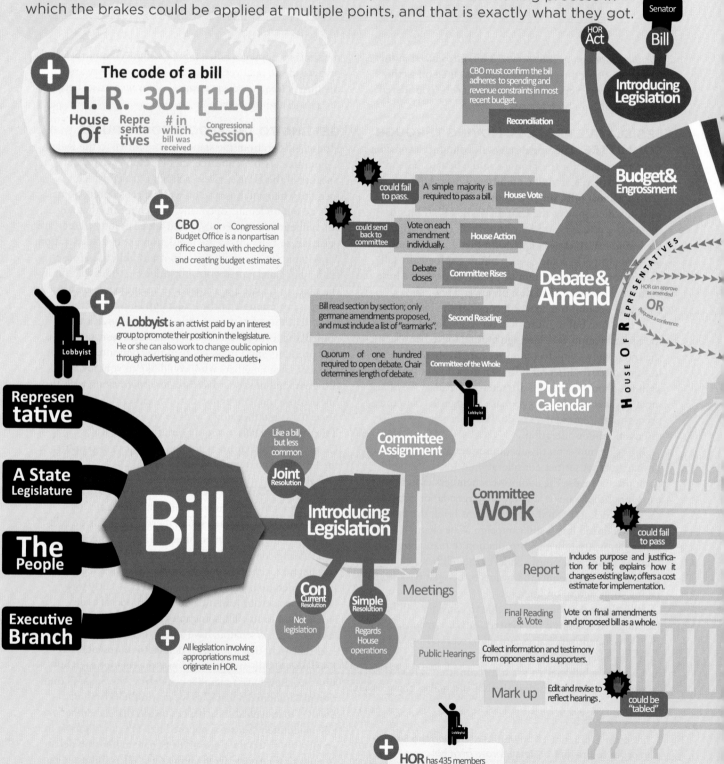

+ The code of a bill

H. R. 301 [110]

| House Of | Repre senta tives | # in which bill was received | Congressional Session |

+ CBO or Congressional Budget Office is a nonpartisan office charged with checking and creating budget estimates.

+ A Lobbyist is an activist paid by an interest group to promote their position in the legislature. He or she can also work to change oublic opinion through advertising and other media outlets †

Lobbyist

Represen tative

A State Legislature

The People

Executive Branch

+ All legislation involving appropriations must originate in HOR.

Bill

Like a bill, but less common

Joint Resolution

Introducing Legislation

Con Current Resolution — Not legislation

Simple Resolution — Regards House operations

+ HOR has 435 members and 23 standing committees.

Lobbyist

Committee Assignment

Committee Work

Meetings

Report — Indudes purpose and justification for bill; explains how it changes existing law; offers a cost estimate for implementation.

could fail to pass

Final Reading & Vote — Vote on final amendments and proposed bill as a whole.

Public Hearings — Collect information and testimony from opponents and supporters.

Mark up — Edit and revise to reflect hearings.

could be "tabled"

Put on Calendar

Quorum of one hundred required to open debate. Chair determines length of debate. — **Committee of the Whole**

Bill read section by section; only germane amendments proposed, and must include a list of "earmarks". — **Second Reading**

Debate closes — **Committee Rises**

Debate & Amend

Vote on each amendment individually. — **House Action**

could send back to committee

A simple majority is required to pass a bill. — **House Vote**

could fail to pass

Budget & Engrossment

CBO must confirm the bill adheres to spending and revenue constraints in most recent budget.

Reconciliation

Introducing Legislation

HOR Act

Senator Bill

HOUSE OF REPRESENTATIVES

HOR can approve as amended

OR

Request a conference

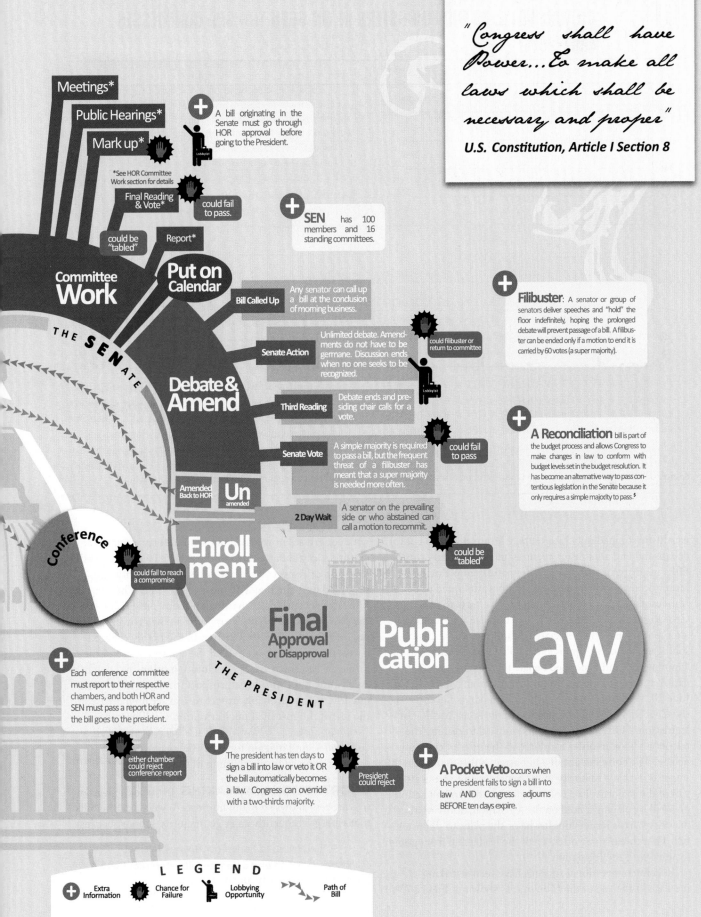

"Congress shall have Power...To make all laws which shall be necessary and proper"

U.S. Constitution, Article I Section 8

Meetings*

Public Hearings*

Mark up*

+ A bill originating in the Senate must go through HOR approval before going to the President.

*See HOR Committee Work section for details

Final Reading & Vote*

could fail to pass.

could be "tabled"

Report*

+ SEN has 100 members and 16 standing committees.

Committee Work

Put on Calendar

Bill Called Up — Any senator can call up a bill at the conclusion of morning business.

+ **Filibuster**: A senator or group of senators deliver speeches and "hold" the floor indefinitely, hoping the prolonged debate will prevent passage of a bill. A filibuster can be ended only if a motion to end it is carried by 60 votes (a super majority).

Debate & Amend

Senate Action — Unlimited debate. Amendments do not have to be germane. Discussion ends when no one seeks to be recognized.

could filibuster or return to committee

Third Reading — Debate ends and presiding chair calls for a vote.

+ **A Reconciliation** bill is part of the budget process and allows Congress to make changes in law to conform with budget levels set in the budget resolution. It has become an alternative way to pass contentious legislation in the Senate because it only requires a simple majority to pass.[5]

Senate Vote — A simple majority is required to pass a bill, but the frequent threat of a filibuster has meant that a super majority is needed more often.

could fail to pass

Amended Back to HOR

Un amended

2 Day Wait — A senator on the prevailing side or who abstained can call a motion to recommit.

could be "tabled"

Conference

could fail to reach a compromise

Enroll ment

Final Approval or Disapproval

Publi cation

Law

THE SENATE

THE PRESIDENT

+ Each conference committee must report to their respective chambers, and both HOR and SEN must pass a report before the bill goes to the president.

either chamber could reject conference report

+ The president has ten days to sign a bill into law or veto it OR the bill automatically becomes a law. Congress can override with a two-thirds majority.

President could reject

+ **A Pocket Veto** occurs when the president fails to sign a bill into law AND Congress adjourns BEFORE ten days expire.

LEGEND

+ Extra Information

Chance for Failure

Lobbying Opportunity

▶▶▶ Path of Bill

FIGURE 7.9 CLOTURE VOTES TO END FILIBUSTERS IN THE 66TH TO 113RD CONGRESSES (1917-2014)

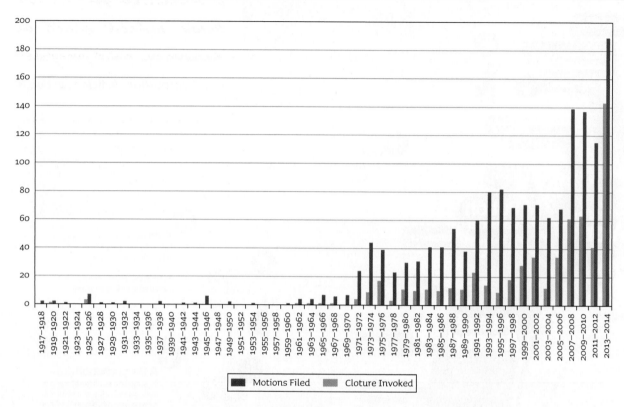

Motions Filed   Cloture Invoked

Source: U.S. Senate, "Senate Action on Cloture Motions," www.senate.gov/pagelayout/reference/cloture_motions/clotureCounts.htm.

usually be stopped only by **cloture**. Cloture, a vote to cut off debate and end a filibuster, requires an extraordinary three-fifths majority, or sixty votes. A dramatic example of a filibuster occurred when southern senators attempted to derail Minnesota senator Hubert Humphrey's efforts to pass the Civil Rights Act of 1964. First, they filibustered Humphrey's attempt to bypass the Judiciary Committee, whose chair, a southern Democrat, opposed the bill. This was known as the "minibuster," and it stopped Senate business for sixteen days.[89] It was considered "mini" because from March 30 to June 30, 1964, these same southern Democrats filibustered the Civil Rights Act and created a twenty-week backlog of legislation.[90] Often these senators resorted to reading the telephone book in order to adhere to the rules of constant debate. The consequence of a filibuster, as this example suggests, is that a minority in the Senate is able to thwart the will of the majority. Even one single senator can halt action on a bill by placing a hold on the legislation, notifying the majority party's leadership that he or she plans to filibuster a bill. That threat alone often keeps the leadership from going forward with the legislation.[91]

Recent congressional sessions have seen a striking increase in the use of the filibuster, as shown in Figure 7.9,

with congresses now averaging around forty attempts at cloture. Only about a third of these have been successful in mustering the necessary sixty votes, so a minority has prevailed over the majority most of the time. The use of the filibuster is considered "hardball politics"; its greater use in the past fifteen to twenty years reflects the growing party polarization we discussed earlier. In the highly charged partisan atmosphere of the U.S. Senate today, use of the filibuster and the consequent cloture motions has reached an all-time high with little prospect for change.[92] Consequently, we can probably expect to also see an increase in the use of the so-called nuclear option we discussed in *What's at Stake . . . ?* Now that it has been used we can count on seeing it again for votes the majority party considers crucial to the running of the government.

UNORTHODOX LAWMAKING Because the legislative process allows so many interests to weigh in, the bills that emerge frequently can't get majority support because

> **cloture** a vote to end a Senate filibuster; requires a three-fifths majority, or sixty votes

everyone can find some part to object to, because members anticipate a presidential veto, or because of partisan differences. Since the 1980s congressional leaders have dealt with the logjam of bills by packaging them all together in what is usually called **omnibus legislation**, a large bill that contains so many important elements, including the money necessary to fund the government, that members can't afford to defeat it and the president can't afford to veto it, even if the bill contains elements they dislike. This "unorthodox lawmaking"[93] has become the norm for most of the budget and many other difficult-to-pass bills. As a result (1) more power has been concentrated in the party leadership, (2) the White House is more involved than was traditionally the case, and (3) the traditional power of standing committees has waned as they are more frequently bypassed or overridden as the leadership moves legislation along. The overly large bills that sometimes result go unread by some members and are criticized by outsiders as an abuse of the legislative process. And the public, as we have seen, finds the entire process a turn-off (see "*Snapshot of America: How Do We Hate Congress? [Let Us Count the Ways.]*" on page 234). It is, nevertheless, an important mechanism that Congress has developed to pass needed legislation and to keep the government running.

FINAL CHALLENGES: A BILL BECOMES A LAW A bill must survive a number of challenges to get out of Congress alive. A bill can be killed, or just left to die, in a subcommittee, the full committee, the House Rules Committee, or any of the corresponding committees in the Senate; and, of course, it has to pass votes on the floors of both houses.

There are multiple ways for the House of Representatives to vote, including a simple voice vote ("all in favor say 'aye'"), but most important legislation requires each member to explicitly vote "yea" or "nay" in what are called **roll call votes**. These are a matter of public record and are monitored by the media, interest groups, and sometimes even constituents. A variety of influences come to bear on the senator or member of Congress as he or she decides how to vote. Studies have long shown that party affiliation is the most important factor in determining roll call voting, but constituency also plays a role, as does presidential politics.

Busy representatives often take cues from other members whom they respect and generally agree with.[94] They also consult with their staff, some of whom may be very knowledgeable about certain legislation. Finally, interest groups have an effect on how a member of Congress votes, but studies suggest that their impact is much less than we usually imagine. Lobbying and campaign contributions buy access to members so that the lobbyists can try to make their case, but they do not actually buy votes.[95]

The congressperson or senator who is committed to passing or defeating a particular bill cannot do so alone, however, and he or she looks to find like-minded members for political support. Once a representative or senator knows where he or she stands on a bill, there are a variety of methods for influencing the fate of that bill, many of them effective long before the floor vote takes place. Congressional politics—using the rules to get what one wants—can entail many complex strategies, including controlling the agenda (whether a bill ever reaches the floor), proposing amendments to a bill, influencing its timing, and forming coalitions with other members to pass or block a bill. Knowing how to use the rules makes a huge difference in congressional politics.

If a bill emerges from the roll call process in both houses relatively intact, it goes to the president, unless the chambers passed different versions. If the bills differ, then the two versions go to a conference committee made up of members of both houses, usually the senior members of the standing committees that reported the bills. If the conferees can reach an agreement on a revision, then the revised bill goes back to each house to be voted up or down; no amendments are permitted at this point. If the bill is rejected, that chamber sends it back to the conference committee for a second try.

Finally, any bill still alive at this point moves to the president's desk. He has several choices of action. The simplest choice is that he signs the bill and it becomes law. If he doesn't like it, however, he can veto it. In that case, the president sends it back to the originating house of Congress with a short explanation of what he does not like about the bill. Congress can then attempt a **veto override**, which requires a two-thirds vote of both houses. Because the president can usually count on the support of *at least* one-third of *one* of the houses, the veto is a powerful negative tool; it is hard for Congress to accomplish legislative goals that are opposed by the president. They can, however, bundle policies together, so that the bill that arrives on the president's desk contains elements that he would typically want to veto along with legislation that is very hard for him to turn down. To get around this practice, Congress introduced and passed in 1996 a controversial line-item veto bill, which would have allowed presidents to strike out spending provisions they didn't like, but the Supreme Court ruled in June 1998 that the line-item veto was unconstitutional.[96]

The president can also kill a bill with the **pocket veto**, which occurs when Congress sends a bill to the president

omnibus legislation a large bill that contains so many important elements that members can't afford to defeat it and the president can't afford to veto it, even if the bill contains elements they dislike

roll call votes publicly recorded votes on bills and amendments on the floor of the House or the Senate

veto override reversal of a presidential veto by a two-thirds vote in both houses of Congress

pocket veto presidential authority to kill a bill submitted within ten days of the end of a legislative session by not signing it

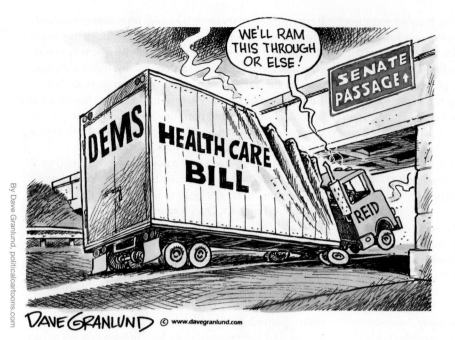

WE'LL RAM THIS THROUGH OR ELSE!

SENATE PASSAGE →

DEMS HEALTH CARE BILL

REID

DAVE GRANLUND © www.davegranlund.com

By Dave Granlund, politicalcartoons.com

He can influence the legislative agenda; try to persuade his fellow party members in Congress to support his policies; take his case to the people; or, once the process is under way, threaten to veto or, in fact, use several different veto techniques.

But it is Congress that has the most range and flexibility when it comes to passing or stopping legislation. Members want to satisfy constituents, build national reputations or platforms on which to run for future office, and accomplish ideological and partisan goals. They have a wealth of legislative tools and strategies at their disposal. But success is not just a matter of knowing the rules. It is personality, luck, timing, and context, as well as political skill in using the rules that make a successful legislator. Repeated filibusters may accomplish a political goal, but if they earn a party a reputation as excessively partisan and obstructionist, they could also cause voter backlash. Legislative politics is a complex balance of rules and processes that favors the skilled politician.

IN YOUR OWN WORDS » Describe the process of congressional policymaking.

within ten days of the end of a session and the president does not sign it. The bill fails simply because Congress is not in session to consider a veto override. The president might choose this option when he wants to veto a bill without drawing much public attention to it. Similarly, the president can do nothing, and if Congress remains in session, a bill will automatically become law in ten days, excluding Sundays. This seldom-used option signals presidential dislike for a bill but not enough dislike for him to use his veto power.

The striking aspect of our legislative process is how many factors have to fall into place for a bill to become law. At every step there are ways to kill bills, and a well-organized group of members in the relatively decentralized Congress has a good chance, in most cases, of blocking a bill to which these members strongly object. In terms of procedures, Congress is better set up to ensure that bills do not impinge on organized interests than it is to facilitate coherent, well-coordinated solutions to the nation's problems. Once again, we see a balance between representation, lawmaking, and partisanship, with the procedures of passage tilted against effective lawmaking.

PAUSE AND REVIEW:

WHO, WHAT, HOW

All American political actors, those in Washington and those outside, have something important at stake in the legislative process. The president has a huge stake in what Congress does in terms of fulfilling his own campaign promises, supporting his party's policy goals, and building his political legacy.

» THE CITIZENS AND CONGRESS
Public frustration with a slow-moving institution

Academics and journalists spend a great deal of time speculating about what the decline in public support for our political institutions means for American democracy.[97] In this final section we look at the implications for citizens of their increasingly negative views of the U.S. Congress. Although public approval of Congress spiked in the wake of September 11, from 1974 through the 1990s, periodic Gallup polls showed that less than a third of the public "approves of the way Congress is handling its job." In early 2012 this proportion dropped to just 10 percent! Part of the blame may be attributed to a general decline in respect for societal institutions ranging from government to organized religion to the media.[98] However, the intense partisanship of the contemporary Congress and its repeated legislative crises as the parties are unable to compromise is no doubt a major contributor to our generally low regard for the institution.

At least four factors help to explain why citizens are not always very happy with Congress. First, some candidates encourage a negative image of the institution they want to join—running for Congress by running against it, and declaring their intention to fight against special interests, bureaucrats, and the general incompetence of Washington.[99] Second, in the post-Watergate wave of investigative reporting, media coverage of Congress has become more negative, even though impartial observers say that Congress is probably less corrupt than ever before. Third, since the 1970s the law requires that information about how much campaigns cost and who contributes to them must be made public, casting a shadow of suspicion on the entire process and raising the concern that congressional influence can be bought. Finally, citizens are turned off by what they see as incessant bickering and partisanship in Congress.

THINKING OUTSIDE THE BOX

What difference does it make that Americans dislike Congress so much?

Given the reasons why many Americans are unhappy with Congress, most of the reforms currently on the agenda are not likely to change their minds. One of the most popular reforms being advocated is term limits. The specific proposals vary, but the intent is to limit the number of terms a member of Congress can serve, usually to somewhere between eight and twelve years. Term limits might work if there was evidence that serving in Congress corrupts good people, but there is no such evidence, and thus the reform would not be likely to bring about a "cleaner" institution. Other reforms, however, might make a difference in public support for Congress. Campaign finance reform, for instance, could have a significant impact. Institutional reforms might be able to speed up congressional lawmaking and reduce the need to compromise on details.

Such reforms, however, will probably not fundamentally change how the public feels about Congress. Congress does have the power to act, and when it is unified and sufficiently motivated, it usually does. When Congress reflects a sharply divided society, however, it has a harder time getting things done. It is unable to act *because it is a representative institution*, not because members are inattentive to their districts or in the grip of special interests. Furthermore, Congress has more incentives on a daily basis to be a representative institution than a national lawmaking body. It is important to remember, too, that this slow process is not entirely an accident. It was the founders' intention to create a legislature that would not move hastily or without deliberation. The irony is that the founders' mixed bag of incentives works so well that Congress today often does not move very much at all.

The truth is that democracy is messy. Bickering arises in Congress because members represent many different Americans with varied interests and goals. It has always been this way, and probably always will be. However, it seems worse today because the parties have come to represent warring ideological armies. The rhetoric is coarse, and bipartisan cooperation is increasingly viewed as a weakness by party activists and outside groups.

It is precisely our bickering, our inefficiency, and the need to compromise—even when that is hard to do—that preserve the freedoms Americans hold dear. It is the nature of our representative government. We conclude where we began. Congress has the conflicting goals of representing constituents, working together to solve national problems, and operating as members of opposing partisan teams. These goals often and necessarily conflict. The practice of congressional politics is fascinating to many close-up observers but looks rather ugly as we average citizens understand it, based on the nightly news and what we hear during campaigns. It is important to understand, however, that this view of Congress stems as much from the difficulties inherent in the conflicting incentives of the job as from the failings of the people we send to Washington.

IN YOUR OWN WORDS » Discuss the relationship between the people and Congress.

LET'S REVISIT: **WHAT'S AT STAKE...**

We've learned enough about politics to know that Congress is a rule-based institution, and as always, the rules determine who wins and who loses. One of the trickier rules is the filibuster, which has its ardent foes as well as its passionate defenders, as we saw in the *What's at Stake. . . ?* that opened this chapter.

But what is true here, of course, is that everyone in the Senate has a high stake in the fate of the filibuster—its opponents and defenders change sides with their electoral fortunes. Both parties love the filibuster when they are in the minority and it enables them to block an opposing majority, but not so much when it's the other way around. Thus despite their fury over the Republicans' attempt to stop them from filling federal court vacancies, the Democrats are not quite as opposed to the filibuster when they are in the minority.

But, as we have seen, the use of the filibuster has skyrocketed dramatically in the recent past, making it the norm even for routine legislation in the Senate. Rather than debating a bill and registering their disapproval by voting against it, opposing senators prevent the debate from happening in the first place. In the summer of 2010, Democratic senator Russ Feingold from Wisconsin actually joined a Republican filibuster of financial regulatory reform. Republicans were

opposed to the bill because they felt it infringed on the rights of business, and Feingold opposed it because he felt that it didn't infringe enough on the rights of business, but no matter. Politics makes strange bedfellows, and it wasn't until then–majority leader Harry Reid peeled off the support of a couple of Republicans that the vote went through.

Americans are advocates of the idea of supporting a downtrodden minority against a tyrannical majority, but in the case of the filibuster, it is the minority that threatens to become tyrannical, holding a majority of senators and, by implication, the voters who elected them, hostage. One of the reasons why Americans don't like their Congress is because legislative business so often gets mired down in partisan wrangling; the filibuster is one more rule by which this can take place.

In 2007, when the Democrats had only a 51–49 majority in the Senate, former Democratic congressman David Obey said, "They [the public] think we have control of the Senate while we merely have custody. They think that we can control the Senate when in fact we are nine votes short of having the 60 votes that you need to actually run the Senate. So the Senate is a choke point on everything."[100]

The use of the so-called nuclear option was an attempt by Democrats to break

through the choke point created by the use of the filibuster for nearly every vote that comes along. Whether Republicans make good on their threats to get rid of the filibuster for all votes now that they are in power remains to be seen, and we will never know if, as some Democrats have argued, they would have done so anyway. But what we do know is that politics is about trying to arrange the rules so that they give you an advantage. While both parties could benefit from the filibuster, even as they sometimes lost, it was to both parties' advantage to keep it. But once one party perceived itself to be at more of a disadvantage, as the Democrats did, all bets were off because they had very little to lose in changing the rules. If they thought they would end up losing anyway, they would be better off getting what they could before the rules changed against them.

Fearing rapid political change, the American founders built a good deal of gridlock into their constitutional design, with checks and balances slowing down the policymaking process to a snail's pace under the best of circumstances. The filibuster can grind the snail's pace to a complete halt. Norm Ornstein of the conservative American Enterprise Institute says, "The Senate is set up culturally not to act on anything quickly. That's a good thing. But there can be too much of a good thing."[101]

TO SUM UP

for CQ Press

Sharpen your skills with **SAGE edge** at http://edge.sagepub.com/ barbour7e. **SAGE edge for students** provides a personalized approach to help you accomplish your coursework goals in an easy-to-use learning environment.

Describe the tensions between local representation and national lawmaking.

Members of Congress are responsible for both representation and lawmaking. These two duties are often at odds because what is good for a local district may not be beneficial for the country as a whole. Representation style takes four different forms—policy, allocative, casework, and symbolic—and congresspersons attempt to excel at all four. However, since the legislative process designed by the founders is meant to be very slow, representatives have fewer incentives to concentrate on national lawmaking when reelection interests, and therefore local interests, are more pressing.

representation (p. 233)
national lawmaking (p. 233)
partisanship (p. 235)
polarization (p. 235)
hyperpartisanship (p. 235)
constituency (p. 237)
policy representation (p. 237)
allocative representation (p. 237)
pork barrel (p. 237)
casework (p. 237)
franking (p. 238)
symbolic representation (p. 238)

Explain how checks and balances work between Congress and the executive and judicial branches.

The founders created our government with a structure of checks and balances. In addition to checking each other, the House and the Senate may be checked by either the president or the courts. Congress is very powerful but must demonstrate unusual strength and consensus to override presidential vetoes and to amend the Constitution.

bicameral legislature (p. 241)
congressional oversight (p. 243)

Identify the politics that influence how congressional districts are defined and who runs for Congress.

Citizens and representatives interact in congressional elections, which in turn are profoundly affected by the way in which state legislatures define congressional districts. The incumbency effect is powerful in American politics because those in office often create legislation that makes it difficult for challengers to succeed.

reapportionment (p. 245)
redistricting (p. 246)
gerrymandering (p. 246)

partisan gerrymandering (p. 246)
racial gerrymandering (p. 247)
strategic politicians (p. 249)
incumbency advantage (p. 249)
coattail effect (p. 249)
midterm loss (p. 249)
descriptive representation (p. 251)

Summarize the central role that the parties play in Congress.

Representatives want autonomy and choice committee assignments to satisfy constituent concerns. They achieve these goals by joining together into political parties and obeying their leadership and party rules. House and Senate members make their own organizational rules, which means the dominant party in each house has great power over the internal rules of Congress and what laws are made.

majority party (p. 256)
party polarization (p. 258)
Speaker of the House (p. 259)
seniority system (p. 259)
standing committees (p. 262)
House Rules Committee (p. 263)
select committee (p. 263)
joint committees (p. 263)
conference committees (p. 263)

Describe the process of congressional policymaking.

The structure of our bicameral legislature and organization of each house can slow the legislative process, yet despite these obstructions, Congress has a wealth of tools and strategies for creating policy. Legislative politics is a complex balance of rules and processes that favors the skilled politician.

norms (p. 265)
legislative agenda (p. 266)
policy entrepreneurship (p. 266)
filibuster (p. 267)
cloture (p. 270)
omnibus legislation (p. 271)
roll call votes (p. 271)
veto override (p. 271)
pocket veto (p. 271)

Discuss the relationship between the people and Congress.

Citizens, interest groups, the president, and members of Congress all have a stake in the legislative process. Voters organized into interest groups may have a greater impact on legislative outcomes than may the individual. Yet Congress, with various legislative tools and strategies, holds the most sway over the fate of legislation.

ENGAGE

Get the PolitiFact app.
Chances are you're already reading political news on your smartphone or tablet, so it might be helpful to have a fact-checking app handy as well. The *Tampa Bay Times's* PolitiFact app is available for iOS and Android devices, and it will help you assess the news (and win political arguments).

Know your reps . . . and let them know who you are.
Take a moment to get in touch with your representative and senators. Let them know what concerns they need to be thinking about to better represent your local needs as well as national interests. You can find contact information for your representatives at the Senate and House web sites.

Take a look at your district map.
Reviewing the lines that define your district can be enlightening. Head to www.govtrack.us to see how your district has been gerrymandered, and consider whether or not that gerrymandering benefits you and your neighbors.

Join Olympia's List.
As we learned in the *CLUES* feature in this chapter, former senator Olympia Snowe left Congress in 2012, feeling that extreme partisanship had crippled the legislative body. She started Olympia's List to pressure her former colleagues to build consensus, seek compromise, and move the country forward.

EXPLORE

Caro, Robert A. 2002. *Master of the Senate: The Years of Lyndon Johnson.* **New York: Knopf.** The third in a planned series of four books about Johnson, this lengthy volume details Johnson's expert use of power to rise to the top leadership position in the Senate.

CQ Weekly. This publication is the best source for the most recent happenings in Congress. It has especially great election coverage.

Mann, Thomas E., and Norman J. Ornstein. 2008. *The Broken Branch: How Congress Is Failing America and How to Get It Back on Track.* **New York: Oxford University Press.** Two noted political scholars argue that relentless partisanship has led to a decline in deliberation, weakened checks and balances, and a legislature that fails to fulfill its obligations to the Constitution and the people of the United States.

McCutcheon, Chuck, and Christina L. Lyons. *CQ's Politics in America 2011.* **Washington, DC: CQ Press.** Make this your first stop when researching individual members of Congress, their districts, or their states. Contains voting records, campaign expenditures, state and district demographics, and more.

Alpha House. 2013–. This clever original sitcom from Amazon.com follows four fictional senators who share the same D.C. house rental, as they face reelection battles, looming indictments, and party politics, all with a sense of humor.

Charlie Wilson's War. 2007. Free-wheeling Texas congressman Charlie Wilson (played by Tom Hanks) circumnavigates the legislative process when he collaborates with a rogue CIA operative (Philip Seymour Hoffman) to assist Afghan rebels in their fight against the Soviet Union.

Mr. Smith Goes to Washington. 1939. This film is Frank Capra's classic story about a young politician who is appointed to the Senate and, defying his party's bosses, fights the leaders' corruption.

8

THE PRESIDENCY

IN YOUR OWN WORDS   After you've read this chapter, you will be able to

» Compare the president's roles as head of state and head of government.

» Compare the modern presidency with the founders' expectations for a limited executive.

» Identify strategies and tools presidents employ to overcome the constitutional limitations of the office.

» Describe the organization and functions of the executive office.

» Evaluate the importance of leadership style and image as they relate to presidential power.

» Give examples of ways in which public opinion affects the relationship between citizens and the president.

WHAT'S AT STAKE...IN A PRESIDENT'S USE OF EXECUTIVE POWER?

ON JULY 29, 2014, THE REPUBLICAN-LED House of Representatives took the unusual step of voting, on party lines, to sue the president of the United States for failing to enforce a law that, incidentally, they hated and had themselves tried more than fifty times to repeal.

The law in question, of course, was the Affordable Care Act (aka Obamacare), a target of Republican wrath since the day it passed in 2010. But still, when the Obama administration moved to delay for one year the implementation of part of the law that required employers to provide health insurance to employees, they were up in arms over what they called "executive overreach," arguing that Obama had overstepped his authority. While playing down the calls of some of the more conservative members of his party to actually impeach the president, Speaker of the House John Boehner said, "This isn't about Republicans and Democrats. It's about defending the Constitution we swore an oath to uphold."[1]

For his part, Obama replied that the vote was a stunt, and it is true that, six months later, no suit had yet been filed.

Still, as relations between this White House and Congress have become impossibly strained, the president has turned more and more to executive action to get his agenda accomplished, adding to his usual calls for bipartisanship during the 2014 State of the Union address a list of unilateral steps he could take during what he called a "Year of Action," saying, "Wherever and whenever I can take steps without legislation to expand opportunity for more American families, that's what I'm going to do."[2]

By October the journal *Politico* counted more than sixty executive actions taken by Obama since his January speech. Although it found that most of them would take some time to make their impact felt, they included higher minimum wage for federal workers and anti-discrimination measures in the federal workplace for gays, a new retirement savings plan, new workplace reforms, efforts to halt climate change by boosting fuel efficiency standards and reducing emissions, the creation of a marine sanctuary, assistance repaying student loans, regulation of for-profit colleges, small business assistance, and other similar programs that can be accomplished with the executive pen.[3]

President Obama isn't the first and he won't be the last president who tries to do an end run around a Congress who won't give him what he wants. The tension between the two institutions was built in intentionally by the founders, who wanted the legislature to check what might

iStockphoto

YOU'RE RUINING OUR OBSTRUCTION BY GETTING THINGS DONE! WE FIND THAT UNCONSTITUTIONAL! WE'RE SUING!

BOEHNER

SPEAKER OF THE HOUSE v. OBAMA

© John Darkow/Cagle Cartoons Inc.

be a too-strong executive, and the executive to check what might be a too-strong legislature. While they probably didn't envision a speaker of the House suing a sitting president, it's not inconsistent with Madison's idea that ambition must be made to counteract ambition, as he put it in *Federalist #51*. (See *The Big Picture* in Chapter 4.)

Strains in executive-legislative relations can come from other routes than simply executives carving their own paths through executive action. Another source of tension between the two branches can come via a document known as a **signing statement**, intended to "clarify" the president's understanding of what a bill means and how he believes it ought to be enforced. Since the 1800s, presidents have been issuing statements if they thought a part of a bill they signed unconstitutionally restricted executive power; but these signing statements had been used only sparingly. Much more typically, presidents objected to legislation by using the presidential veto, whereupon Congress could override the veto if the bill had sufficient support.

But President George W. Bush took signing statements to a new level. When he signed the newly passed reauthorization of the Patriot Act in March 2006, for instance, he did so with a public and patriotic flourish. Very quietly, without the public display that greeted the bill's signing, the White House also issued a document saying that the president reserved the right to withhold information from Congress if he deemed that it would "impair foreign relations, national security, the deliberative process of the executive, or the performance of the executive's constitutional duties."[4]

Most people in Congress didn't even notice that the signing statement had been added, but those who did were furious.

Democratic senator Patrick Leahy from Vermont unknowingly foreshadowed Speaker Boehner's accusation against Obama when he called the signing statement "nothing short of a radical effort to manipulate the constitutional separation of powers and evade accountability and responsibility for following the law."[5]

Bush did not invent the signing statement, but unlike his predecessors, Bush had not vetoed a single bill by the time he issued the Patriot Act signing statement, after more than five years in office. Instead he had issued a huge number of signing statements, over 750, compared to 232 by his father in his four years in the White House, and only 140 issued by Bill Clinton in his eight years. Comparatively, President Barack Obama would veto two bills and issue only about 20 signing statements by his fourth year in office (at which point in his first term Bush had issued 87).

The ways in which presidents and legislators can jockey for power are legion and can run headlong into each other, even when the executive and the legislators are in the same party. When Congress failed to enact immigration reform before the 2014 election, Obama, who had long promised the Latino community that he would see to it that some sort of reform passed, determined to do what he could with executive action. News reports of his determination to act, including the possibility of finding a path for citizenship for the nation's nearly 12 million undocumented immigrants, spooked members of his own party running for reelection in red states where Romney had won in 2012. Fearful of an electoral backlash among a public already nervous about an influx of young children crossing the border from Central America, they asked the president to postpone his actions on immigration until after the election, which he agreed to do, much to the dismay and anger of Latino voters.

What to make of this complicated relationship between president and Congress? We learned in the last chapter that law making is the legislators' job, with the executive merely charged with implementing the laws they make. Clearly the relationship is a good deal more complicated than that. What is at stake when a president takes unilateral action or reserves to himself the prerogative of a signing statement? We will return to that question after we have learned more about how the executive office works. **«**

> **signing statements** statements recorded along with signed legislation clarifying the president's understanding of the constitutionality of the bill

ASK just about anyone who the most powerful person in the world is and the answer will probably be "the president of the United States." He, or perhaps someday soon, she, is the elected leader of the nation that has one of the most powerful economies, one of the greatest military forces, and the longest-running representative government that the world has ever seen. Media coverage enforces this belief in the importance of the U.S. president. The networks and news services all have full-time reporters assigned to the White House. The evening news tells us what the president has been doing that day. Even if he only went to church or played a round of golf, his activities are news. This attention is what one scholar calls the presidency's "monopolization of the public space."[6] It means that the president is the first person the citizens and the media think of when anything of significance happens, whether it is a terrorist attack, a natural disaster, or a big drop in the stock market. We look to the president to solve our problems and to represent the nation in our times of struggle, tragedy, and triumph. The irony is that the U.S. Constitution provides for a relatively weak chief executive, and the American public's and, indeed, the world's expectations of the president constitute a major challenge for modern presidents.

The challenge of meeting the public's expectations is made all the more difficult because so many political actors have something at stake in the office of the presidency. Most obviously, the president himself wants to widen his authority to act so that he can deliver on campaign promises and extend the base of support for himself and his party. Although the formal rules of American politics create only limited presidential powers, informal rules help him expand them. Citizens, both individually and in groups, often have high expectations of what the president will do for them and for the country, and they may be willing to allow him more expanded powers to act. An unpopular president, however, will face a public eager to limit his options and ready to complain about any perceived step beyond the restrictive constitutional bounds. Congress, too, stands to gain or lose based on the president's success. Members of the president's party will share some of his popularity, but in general the more power the president has, the less Congress has. This is especially true if the majority party in Congress is different from the president's. So Congress has a stake in limiting what the president may do.

This chapter tells the story of who gets what from the American presidency and how they get it.

THE DOUBLE EXPECTATIONS GAP

Public expectations and the reality of what the president can actually do

Presidential scholars note that one of the most remarkable things about the modern presidency is how much the office has become intertwined with public expectations and perceptions. The implication, of course, is that we expect one thing and get something less—that there is a gap between our expectations and reality. In fact, we can identify two different expectations gaps when it comes to popular perceptions of the presidency. One is between the very great promises that presidents make, and that we want them to keep, on the one hand, and the president's limited constitutional power to fulfill those promises, on the other. The second gap is between two conflicting roles that the president is expected to play, between the formal and largely symbolic role of head of state and the far more political role of head of government. These two expectations gaps form a framework for much of our discussion of the American presidency.

THE GAP BETWEEN PRESIDENTIAL PROMISES AND THE POWERS OF THE OFFICE

The first gap between what the public expects the president to do and what he can actually accomplish is of relatively recent vintage. Through the 1930s the presidency in the United States was pretty much the office the founders had planned, an administrative position dwarfed by the extensive legislative power of Congress. During Franklin Roosevelt's New Deal, however, public expectations of the president changed. Roosevelt did not act like an administrator with limited powers; he acted like a leader whose strength and imagination could be relied on by an entire nation of citizens to rescue them from the crisis of the Great Depression. Over the course of Roosevelt's four terms in office, the public became used to seeing the president in just this light, and future presidential candidates promised similarly grand visions of policy in their efforts to win supporters. Rather than strengthening the office to allow presidents to deliver on such promises, however, the most significant constitutional change in the presidency weakened it. In reaction to Roosevelt's four elections, the Twenty-second Amendment was passed, limiting the number of terms a president can serve to two.

Today's presidents suffer the consequences of this history. On the one hand, we voters demand that they woo us with promises to change the course of the country, to solve our problems—by creating jobs, perhaps, or offering disaster assistance, or keeping the nation safe—and to enact visionary policy. On the other hand, we have not increased the powers of the office to meet those greatly expanded expectations. Thus, the president must wheel, deal, bargain, and otherwise gather the support needed to overcome his constitutional limitations. And if the president doesn't meet our expectations, or if the country doesn't thrive the way we think it should, even if it isn't his fault and there's nothing he could have done to change things, we hold him accountable and vote him out of office. Some evidence of this can be seen in the fates of the past nine presidents; only five have been reelected to a second term, and of those, Richard Nixon resigned after Watergate, Ronald Reagan faced the Iran-contra scandal and his party lost its majority in the Senate, Bill Clinton was impeached, and George W. Bush won reelection by the smallest margin of any

Head of Government, Head of State

The presidency is one office, but the president plays two roles. When President Obama announced a new policy on fuel and emissions standards (with the CEO of General Motors in attendance), he was leading on a potentially controversial government policy and thus acting as head of government. When he attended the graduation and commissioning ceremony of the U. S. Military Academy at West Point in 2014 to make a statement about the U.S. role in world politics, his goal was to unify us and speak for the nation as head of state.

reelected president and left office with the lowest level of public approval of any president finishing two full terms. Barack Obama faced a difficult reelection effort due to a slack economy and sluggish unemployment and won by a smaller margin than his initial victory in 2008. The inability of some of our most skilled politicians to survive for even two full terms of office suggests that our expectations of what can be done potentially outstrip the resources and powers of the position.

THE GAP BETWEEN CONFLICTING ROLES

The second expectations gap that presidents face is in part a product of the first. Since we now expect our presidents to perform as high-level legislators as well as administrators, holders of this office need to be adept politicians. That is, today's presidents need to be able to get their hands dirty in the day-to-day political activities of the nation or, as we just said, to wheel, deal, and bargain. But the image of their president as a politician, an occupational class not held in high esteem by most Americans, often doesn't sit well with citizens who want to hold their president above politics as a symbol of all that is good and noble about America. Thus not only must presidents contend with a job in which they are required to do far more than they are given the power to do, but they must also cultivate the talents to perform two very contradictory roles: the essentially political head of government, who makes decisions about who will get scarce resources, and the elevated and apolitical head of state, who should unify rather than divide the public. Few presidents are skilled enough to carry off both roles with aplomb; the very talents that make a president effective at one side of this equation often work against his success at the other.

HEAD OF STATE The **head of state** serves as the symbol of the hopes and dreams of a people and is responsible for enhancing national unity by representing that which is common and good in the nation. Most other nations separate the head-of-state role from the head-of-government role so that clearly acknowledged symbolic duties can be carried out without contamination by political considerations. One of the clearest examples is Great Britain's monarchy. As head of state, Queen Elizabeth remains a valued symbol of British nationhood. Her Christmas speech is listened to with great interest and pride by the nation, and, despite occasional family troubles, she continues to be an important symbol of what it means to be British. Meanwhile, the prime minister of England can get on with the political business of governing.

That the founders wanted the presidency to carry the dignity, if not the power, of a monarch is evident in George Washington's wish that the president might bear the title "His High Mightiness, the President of the United States and the Protector of Their Liberties."[7] While Americans were not ready for such a pompous title, we nevertheless do put presidents, as the embodiment of the nation, on a higher plane than other politicians. Consequently the American president's job includes a ceremonial role for activities like greeting other heads of state, attending state funerals, tossing out the first baseball of the season, hosting the annual Easter egg hunt on the White House lawn, and consoling survivors of national tragedies. The vice president can relieve the president of some of these responsibilities, but there are times when only the president's presence will do.

> **head of state** the apolitical, unifying role of the president as symbolic representative of the whole country

HEAD OF GOVERNMENT The president is elected to do more than greet foreign dignitaries, wage war, and give electrifying speeches, however. As **head of government**, he is also supposed to run the government, make law, and function as the head of a political party, all functions that will result in some citizens winning more than others, some losing, and some becoming angry—all of which work against the unifying image of the head of state. These political roles are the functions that have expanded so greatly since Roosevelt's presidency.

Running the country, as we shall see throughout this chapter, involves a variety of political activities. First, the president is uniquely situated to define the nation's policy agenda—that is, to get issues on the unofficial list of business that Congress and the public think should be taken care of. The media's constant coverage of the president, combined with the public's belief in the centrality of the office, means that modern presidents have great influence in deciding what policy issues will be addressed.

An effective head of government must do more than simply bring issues to national attention, however. We also expect him to broker the deals, line up the votes, and work to pass actual legislation. This may seem peculiar since Congress makes the laws, but the president is often a critical player in developing political support from the public and Congress to get these laws passed. Thus the president is also seen as the nation's chief lawmaker and coalition builder. An excellent example of the president's role in making law can be seen in Obama's efforts to pass his major domestic program, the Patient Protection and Affordable Care Act, also known as "Obamacare." The president brought congressional Democrats and Republicans together in a "health care summit" to try to build a bipartisan coalition in support of the bill. When that effort came to naught, he worked to bring more conservative Democrats aboard, and his White House helped craft the strategy that enabled Democrats to get the bill passed after Republican senator Scott Brown took over Ted Kennedy's seat and left the Democrats unable to break a Republican filibuster (see Chapter 7).

In addition to helping to make the laws, the president is supposed to make government work. When things go okay, no one thinks much about it. But when things go wrong, the president is the one who has to have an explanation—he is accountable. President Harry Truman kept a sign on his desk that read "The Buck Stops Here," which nicely summarizes this view of presidential responsibility, which generally holds that if something is wrong, it is the president's problem, even if it is something that lies outside of his control.

The president does not just lead the nation; he leads his political party as well. As its head, he appoints the chair of his party's national committee and can use his powers as

president—perhaps vetoing a bill, directing discretionary funds, or making appointments—to reward loyalty or punish a lack of cooperation. He also has considerable patronage at his disposal to reward the party faithful, although this practice is fading (see Chapter 9). The president can, if he wants, have a major influence on his party's platform. And, finally, the president is an important fundraiser for his party. By assisting in the election of party members, he helps to ensure support for the party's program in Congress.

We explore the president's powers in greater detail later in this chapter. What is important for our purposes here is that all these roles are *political* aspects of the president's job. Remember that "political" means allocating resources and benefits to some people over others, deciding who wins and who loses. Thus the responsibilities of the office place the president in an inherently and unavoidably contradictory position. On the one hand he is the symbol of the nation, representing all the people (head of state); and on the other he has to take the lead in politics that are inherently divisive (head of government). Thus the political requirements of the president as head of government necessarily undermine his unifying role as head of state.

The hyperpartisanship that has infected the U.S. Congress in recent years makes it even more difficult for the president to bridge these conflicting roles. The distinction depends on our ability as a nation to insist on respect for the office even when we disagree with the specific views or actions of the person holding it. When politics leads us to move from criticizing the policies of the president to insulting the office, it is more difficult for the president to act as unifying figure when he has to.

PAUSE AND REVIEW:

WHO, WHAT, HOW

Presidents want to leave a legacy, a reputation for having led the country in a meaningful way. To do this they make grand promises that they may not necessarily have the power to fulfill. Their job is complicated by the requirement that they serve as head of state, even as they are forced to act as head of government to accomplish their political goals. The people who hold the conflicting expectations of the president are, of course, the American voters. Citizens have a stake in having a successful president, but their expectations make it unlikely that he will succeed. Since voters choose among presidential candidates on the basis of their campaign promises, candidates are only encouraged to make grander promises, in the hopes of getting elected—ultimately increasing the expectations gaps as they are unable to deliver on their extravagant pledges.

IN YOUR OWN WORDS >> Compare the president's roles as head of state and head of government.

> **head of government** the political role of the president as leader of a political party and chief arbiter of who gets what resources

DON'T BE FOOLED BY...
POLITICAL CARTOONS

Political cartoons are not just for laughs. While they may often use humor as a way of making a political point, that point is likely to be sharp and aimed with uncanny accuracy at political targets. In fact, noted cartoonist Jeff MacNelly, who won a Pulitzer Prize for his work, once said that if cartoonists couldn't draw, most of them would probably have become hired assassins.[1]

Since the first days of our republic, Americans have been using drawings and sketches to say what mere words cannot. Benjamin Franklin and Paul Revere, among others, used pen, ink, and engraving tools to express pointed political views.[2] Moreover, their hapless targets have been acutely aware of the presence of these "annoying little pups, nipping at the heels. . . ."[3] Politicians crave the attention, knowing they have arrived when a cartoonist can draw them without having to indicate their names, but at the same time they dread the sharp sting of the cartoonist's pen.

In the 1870s, Boss Tweed of Tammany Hall (a powerful New York City politician who dominated local party politics) reportedly offered cartoonist Thomas Nast $100,000 to stop drawing cartoons about him (such as the one on page 451 in Chapter 12),[4] saying: "Stop them damn pictures. I don't care so much what the papers write about me. My constituents can't read. . . . But, damn it, they can see pictures."[5] By the early 1900s, legislatures in four states—Pennsylvania, California, Indiana, and Alabama—had introduced anti–cartoon censorship bills to protect the First Amendment freedoms of the political cartoonist.[6]

Political cartoons do more than elicit a laugh or a chuckle. Frequently they avoid humor altogether, going for outrage, indignation, ridicule, or scathing contempt. Their goal is to provoke a reaction from their audience, and they use the tools of irony, sarcasm, symbolism, and shock as well as humor. With this barrage of weapons aimed at you, your critical skills are crucial.[7]

WHAT TO WATCH OUT FOR

- **What is the event or issue that inspired the cartoon?** Political cartoonists do not attempt to inform you about current events; they assume that you already know what has happened. Their job is to comment on the news, and so your first step in savvy cartoon readership is to be up on what's happening in the world. The cartoon shown here assumes that you are familiar with enough American politics to know that Hillary Clinton is a front-runner for the 2016 democratic nomination—and that opponents were thinking about strategies for unseating her long before the party primaries.

- **Are there any real people in the cartoon? Who are they?** Cartoonists develop caricatures of prominent politicians that exaggerate some gesture or facial feature (often the nose, the ears, or the eyebrows, although cartoonists had a field day with Ronald Reagan's hair) that makes them immediately identifiable.[8] Richard Nixon's ski jump nose and swarthy complexion were frequently lampooned, as was his habit of raising his hands over his head in a victory salute. Clinton often appeared as a bulbous-nosed, chubby-cheeked, childlike figure, while George W. Bush was often drawn as a small figure with a monkey-like face, often with huge ears. The cartoonist version of Obama appears to have inherited his predecessor's exaggerated ears, along with Jimmy Carter's toothy grin. Here, all it takes is Clinton's first name, carved into a pedestal, for readers to understand who this cartoonist believes is the candidate to beat in 2016; the glimpse of a pair of high-heeled shoes and the cuffs of one of Clinton's signature pant suits serves to remind them of the gender barrier that a Clinton candidacy would break. Many cartoonists do not confine their art to real people. Some will use a generic person sometimes labeled to represent a group: big business, the U.S. Senate, environmentalists, or in this case the Republican Party, also known as the Grand Old Party, or G.O.P. Other cartoonists draw stereotypically middle-class citizens, talking television sets, or multipaneled "talking head" cartoons to get their views across.[9]

- *Are there symbols in the cartoon? What do they represent?* Without a key to the symbols cartoonists use, their art can be incomprehensible. Uncle Sam stands in for

© Dave Granlund/Cagle Cartoons Inc.

DAVE GRANLUND© www.davegranlund.com

the United States, donkeys are Democrats, and elephants are Republicans. Tammany Hall frequently appeared as a tiger in political cartoons of the time. Often these symbols are combined in unique ways. However, as politics has focused more on image and personality, symbols, although still important, have taken a back seat to personal caricature.[10]

- **What is the cartoonist's opinion about the topic of the cartoon?** Do you agree with it or not? Why? A cartoon is an editorial as surely as are the printed opinion pieces we focused on in Chapter 4 (in fact, they are often referred to as "editorial cartoons"). The cartoon has no more claim to objective status than does someone else's opinion, and you need to evaluate it critically before you take what it says to be accurate. In the drawing here, for instance, the cartoonist expresses the view that Hillary Clinton is a force to contend with—and that Republicans may have a difficult time chipping away at her. Often evaluation is harder with a cartoon than with text, because the medium can be so effective in provoking a reaction from us, whether it is shock, laughter, or scorn. Furthermore, adding to the difficulty, a single cartoon can be interpreted in multiple ways.

1. *Kirkus Reviews,* review of *Them Damned Pictures: Explorations in American Political Cartoon Art,* by Roger A. Fischer, January 15, 1996.

2. Richard E. Marschall, "The Century in Political Cartoons," *Columbia Journalism Review,* May–June 1999, 54.

3. Richard Ruelas, "Editorial Cartoonists Nip at the Heels of Society," *Arizona Republic,* June 9, 1996, A1.

4. Marschall, "The Century."

5. Ira F. Grant, "Cartoonists Put the Salt in the Stew," *Southland* (New Zealand) *Times,* February 20, 1999, 7.

6. Marschall, "The Century."

7. Questions are based on the PoliticalCartoons.com teachers' guide, www.cagle.com/teacher.

8. Robert W. Duffy, "Art of Politics: Media With a Message," *St. Louis Post-Dispatch Magazine,* September 2, 1992, 3D.

9. Marschall, "The Century."

10. Marschall.

THINKING OUTSIDE THE BOX

Should the president represent the interests of the people who voted for him, or of all Americans?

THE EVOLUTION OF THE AMERICAN PRESIDENCY
From restrained administrator to energetic problem-solver

The framers designed a much more limited presidency than the one we have today. The constitutional provisions give most of the policymaking powers to Congress, or at least require power sharing and cooperation. For most of our history, this arrangement was not a problem. As leaders of a rural nation with a relatively restrained governmental apparatus, presidents through the nineteenth century were largely content with a limited authority that rested on the grants of powers provided in the Constitution. But the presidency of Franklin Roosevelt, beginning in 1932, ushered in a new era in presidential politics.

THE FRAMERS' DESIGN FOR A LIMITED EXECUTIVE

Since the legislature was presumed by all to be the real engine of the national political system, the presidency was not a preoccupation of the framers when they met in Philadelphia in 1787. The breakdown of the national government under the Articles of Confederation, however, demonstrated the need for some form of a central executive. Nervous about trusting the general public to choose the executive, the founders provided for an Electoral College, a group of people who would be chosen by the states for the sole purpose of electing the president. The assumption was that this body would be made up of leading citizens who would exercise care and good judgment in casting their ballots and who would not make postelection claims on him. Because of their experience with King George III, the founders also wished to avoid the concentration of power that could be abused by a strong executive.

Although the majority's concept of a limited executive is enshrined in the Constitution, many of the arguments we hear today for a stronger executive were foreshadowed by the case that Alexander Hamilton made in *Federalist* No. 70 for a more "energetic" president.

QUALIFICATIONS AND CONDITIONS OF OFFICE

The framers' conception of a limited presidency can be seen in the brief attention the office receives in the Constitution. Article II is short and not very precise. It provides some basic details on the office of the presidency:

- The president is chosen by the Electoral College to serve four-year terms. The number of terms was unlimited until 1951 when, in reaction to Roosevelt's unprecedented four terms in office, the Constitution was amended to limit the president to two terms.

- The president must be a natural-born citizen of the United States, at least thirty-five years old, and a resident for at least fourteen years.

- The president is succeeded by the vice president if he dies or is removed from office. The Constitution does not specify who becomes president in the event that the vice president, too, is unable to serve, but in 1947 Congress passed the Presidential Succession Act, which establishes the order of succession after the vice president (see Table 8.1). While the rules for succession following vacancies are clear, the rules for replacing a president because of disability are not. The Twenty-fifth Amendment states that a vice president can take over when either a president himself or the vice president and a majority of the cabinet report to Congress that the president is unable to serve. If reports are contradictory, two-thirds of Congress must agree that the president is incapacitated.[8] But putting this into practice can be complicated. President Woodrow Wilson, for example, suffered an incapacitating stroke. Because no one wanted to remove a sitting president, his vice president, Thomas Riley Marshall, never came forward, leaving the executive branch essentially unable to function.

- The president can be removed from office for reasons of "Treason, Bribery, or other High Crimes and Misdemeanors." The process of removal involves two steps: First, after an in-depth investigation, the House votes to impeach by a simple majority vote, which charges the president with a crime. Second, the Senate tries the president on the articles of **impeachment** and can convict by a two-thirds majority vote. Only two American presidents, Andrew Johnson and Bill Clinton, have been impeached (in 1868 and 1998, respectively), but neither was convicted. The Senate failed, by one vote, to convict Johnson and could not

assemble a majority against Clinton. The power of impeachment is meant to be a check on the president, but it is most often threatened for partisan purposes. Impeachment resolutions were filed against Reagan (over the invasion of Grenada and the Iran-contra affair), George H. W. Bush (over Iran-contra), and George W. Bush (for a host of offenses ranging from falsifying evidence justifying the war in Iraq to failing to respond adequately to Hurricane Katrina). Republicans have called for President Obama's impeachment for causes ranging from supposedly lacking a birth certificate; to covering up what the administration knew about the terrorist attack on the U.S. consulate in Benghazi, Libya; to trading Taliban combatants for captive U.S. soldier Bowe Bergdahl; to taking executive actions regarding, among other things, recent EPA regulations on power plants.[9] To date, none of the charges against Obama have been filed as impeachment resolutions, however, and few of the resolutions filed about other presidents made it to the floor for a vote in the House, in part because such actions virtually bring governing to a halt and are not popular with the public.[10]

- While impeachment has come to be wielded as a weapon in partisan political battles, the president does sometimes commit actions worthy of impeachment. Nixon would have been impeached had he not resigned in 1974 (the House Judiciary Committee had passed the resolution and there were enough votes to pass the measure on the House floor and to gain conviction in the Senate). In that case there was clear evidence, in the form of conversations taped by the president himself, that Nixon had been involved directly in the cover-up of a burglary at Democratic National Committee headquarters in the Watergate Hotel. During the Reagan administration, a seven-year investigation by an independent counsel revealed that many members of Reagan's national security staff directed or knew about a plan to sell arms to Iran in exchange for American hostages, and to use the proceeds from the sale to assist "contra rebels" fighting against the Marxist Sandinista government in Nicaragua, in direct contradiction to Congress' wishes. While the so-called Iran-contra scandal damaged Reagan's legacy, Reagan himself claimed he knew nothing about it, and no solid evidence surfaced that he did. President George H. W. Bush, calling the investigation a partisan witch-hunt, pardoned six of the fourteen people indicted in the incident.

> **impeachment** a formal charge by the House that the president (or another member of the executive branch) has committed acts of "Treason, Bribery, or other high Crimes and Misdemeanors," which may or may not result in removal from office

TABLE 8.1

WHO DOES THE PRESIDENT'S JOB WHEN THE PRESIDENT CANNOT?

PRESIDENTIAL ORDER OF SUCCESSION

1. Vice president
2. Speaker of the House
3. President pro tempore of the Senate
4. Secretary of state
5. Secretary of the treasury
6. Secretary of defense
7. Attorney general
8. Secretary of the interior
9. Secretary of agriculture
10. Secretary of commerce
11. Secretary of labor
12. Secretary of health and human services
13. Secretary of housing and urban development
14. Secretary of transportation
15. Secretary of energy
16. Secretary of education
17. Secretary of veterans affairs
18. Secretary of homeland security

Note: It seems impossible that all in the line of succession could die simultaneously. Nevertheless, during the State of the Union address, when Congress and the cabinet are present with the president and vice president, one cabinet member does not attend in order to ensure that a catastrophe could not render our government leaderless. Some members of Congress have pushed legislation that would leapfrog the secretary of homeland security to eighth in line (one behind the attorney general), arguing that because of that secretary's particular familiarity with crises, he or she would be best able to lead the country.

Impeachment is more of a political than a legal process. The definition of an impeachable offense, as laid out in the Constitution, is so vague that it can mean anything a majority of the House of Representatives and two-thirds of the Senate are willing to vote on.

chief administrator the president's executive role as the head of federal agencies and the person responsible for the implementation of national policy

cabinet a presidential advisory group selected by the president, made up of the vice president, the heads of the federal executive departments, and other high officials to whom the president elects to give cabinet status

commander-in-chief the president's role as the top officer of the country's military establishment

THE CONSTITUTIONAL POWER OF THE PRESIDENT

The Constitution uses vague language to discuss some presidential powers and is silent on the range and limits of others. It is precisely this ambiguity that allowed the Constitution to be ratified by both those who wanted a strong executive power and those who did not. In addition, this vagueness has allowed the powers of the president to expand over time without constitutional amendment. We can think of the president's constitutional powers as falling into three areas: executive authority to administer government, and legislative and judicial powers to check the other two branches.

EXECUTIVE POWERS Article II, Section 1, of the Constitution begins, "The executive power shall be vested in a president of the United States of America." However, the document does not explain exactly what "executive power" entails, and scholars and presidents through much of our history have debated the extent of these powers.[11] Section 3 states the president "shall take care that the laws be faithfully executed." Herein lies much of the executive authority; the president is the **chief administrator** of the nation's laws. This means that he is the chief executive officer of the country, the person who, more than anyone else, is held responsible for agencies of the national government and the implementation of national policy.

The Constitution also specifies that the president, with the approval of the majority of the Senate, will appoint the heads of departments, who will oversee the work of implementation. These heads, who have come to be known collectively as the **cabinet**, report to the president. Today the president is responsible for the appointments of more than 3,500 federal employees: cabinet and lower administrative officers, federal judges, military officers, and members of the diplomatic corps. His responsibilities place him at the top of a vast federal bureaucracy. But his control of the federal bureaucracy is limited, as we will see in Chapter 9, because although he can make a large number of appointments, he is not able to fire many of the people he hires.

Other constitutional powers place the president, as **commander-in-chief**, at the head of the command structure for the entire military establishment. The Constitution gives Congress the power to declare war, but as the commander-in-chief, the president has the practical ability to wage war. These two powers, meant to check each other, instead provide for a battleground on which Congress and the president struggle for the power to control military operations. Congress passed the War Powers Act of 1973 after the controversial Vietnam War, which was waged by Presidents Lyndon Johnson and Richard Nixon but never officially declared by Congress. The act was intended to limit the president's power to send troops abroad without congressional approval. Most presidents have ignored it, however, when they wished to engage in military action abroad, and since public opinion tends to rally around the president at such times, Congress has declined to challenge popular presidential actions. The War Powers Act remains more powerful on paper than in reality.

Finally, under his executive powers, the president is the **chief foreign policy maker**. This role is not spelled out in the Constitution, but the foundation for it is laid in the provision that the president negotiates **treaties**—formal international agreements with other nations—with the approval of two-thirds of the Senate. The president also appoints ambassadors and receives ambassadors of other nations, a power that essentially amounts to determining what nations the United States will recognize.

While the requirement of Senate approval for treaties is meant to check the president's foreign policy power, much of U.S. foreign policy is made by the president through **executive agreements** with other heads of state, which avoids the slower and more cumbersome route of treaty making.[12] Executive agreements are used much more frequently than treaties; over 10,000 have been executed since 1970, compared to fewer than 1,000 treaties.[13] This heavy reliance on executive agreements gives the president considerable power and flexibility in foreign policy. Executive agreements are used not only to get around the need for Senate approval. Often they concern routine matters and are issued for the sake of efficiency. If the Senate had to approve each agreement, it would have to act at the rate of one per day, tying up its schedule and keeping it from many more important issues.[14] However, even though the executive agreement is a useful and much-used tool, Congress may still thwart the president's intentions by refusing to approve the funds needed to put an agreement into action.

The framers clearly intended that the Senate would be the principal voice and decision maker in foreign policy, but that objective was not realized even in George Washington's presidency. At subsequent points in our history, Congress has exerted more authority in foreign policy, but for the most part, particularly in the twentieth century, presidents have taken a strong leadership role in dealing with other nations. Part of the reason for this is that Congress has guarded its prerogatives in domestic policy because those are so much more crucial in its members' reelection efforts. This has changed somewhat in recent years as the worldwide economy has greatly blurred the line between domestic and foreign affairs, and in instances where domestic constituencies have a strong interest overseas, as in the Israeli-Palestinian conflict in the Middle East.

LEGISLATIVE POWERS Even though the president is the head of the executive branch of government, the Constitution also gives him some legislative power to check Congress. He "shall from time to time give to the Congress information of the state of the union, and recommend to

their consideration such measures as he shall judge necessary and expedient." Although the framers' vision of this activity was quite limited, today the president's **State of the Union address**, delivered before the full Congress every January, is a major statement of the president's policy agenda. In *The Big Picture*, you can see "wordle" images for key State of the Union addresses from different presidents. Notice how this form of rendering the speech allows you to compare the issues that were important to each administration.

The Constitution gives the president the nominal power to convene Congress and, when there is a dispute about when to disband, to adjourn it as well. Before Congress met regularly, this power, though limited, actually meant something. Today we rarely see it invoked. Some executives, such as the British prime minister, who can dissolve Parliament and call new elections, have a much more formidable convening power than that available to the U.S. president.

The principal legislative power given the president by the Constitution is the **presidential veto**. If the president objects to a bill passed by the House and the Senate, he can veto it, sending it back to Congress with a message indicating his reasons. Congress can override a veto with a two-thirds vote in each house, but because mustering the two-thirds support is quite difficult, the presidential veto is a substantial power. Even the threat of a presidential veto can have a major impact in getting congressional legislation to fall in line with the administration's preferences.[15] Table 8.2 shows the number of bills vetoed since 1933 and the number of successful veto overrides by Congress.

As can be seen in the first column of figures in Table 8.2, the number of vetoes has varied a great deal from one president to the next. Most of the time, presidents are successful in having the vetoes sustained. The least successful was President George W. Bush. Although he joined John Quincy Adams and Thomas Jefferson as the only presidents who did not veto a bill during their first terms,[16] following

---

chief foreign policy maker the president's executive role as the primary shaper of relations with other nations

treaties formal agreements with other countries; negotiated by the president and requiring approval by two-thirds of the Senate

executive agreements presidential arrangements with other countries that create foreign policy without the need for Senate approval

State of the Union address a speech given annually by the president to a joint session of Congress and to the nation announcing the president's agenda

presidential veto a president's authority to reject a bill passed by Congress; may be overridden only by a two-thirds majority in each house

TABLE 8.2

PRESIDENTIAL VETOES, ROOSEVELT TO OBAMA

YEARS	PRESIDENT	TOTAL VETOES	REGULAR VETOES	POCKET VETOES	VETOES OVERRIDDEN	VETO SUCCESS RATE
1933–1945	Franklin Roosevelt	635	372	263	9	97.6%
1945–1953	Harry Truman	250	180	70	12	93.3
1953–1961	Dwight Eisenhower	181	73	108	2	97.3
1961–1963	John F. Kennedy	21	12	9	0	100.0
1963–1969	Lyndon Johnson	30	16	14	0	100.0
1969–1974	Richard Nixon	43	26	17	7	73.1
1974–1977	Gerald Ford	66	48	18	12	75.0
1977–1981	Jimmy Carter	31	13	18	2	84.6
1981–1989	Ronald Reagan	78	39	39	9	76.9
1989–1993	George H. W. Bush	46	29	17*	1	96.6
1993–2001	Bill Clinton	37	36	1	2	96.4
2001–2009	George W. Bush	12	11	1	4	66.7
2009–present	Barack Obama	2	2	0	0	100.0

Source: "Summary of Bills Vetoed: 1789–Present," www.senate.gov/reference/legislation/vetoes/vetocounts.htm.

*Although they are counted here, Congress did not recognize two of Bush's pocket vetoes and considered the legislation enacted.

the 2006 midterm elections, Bush vetoed dozens of the new Democratic majority's bills. These were overridden at a record rate that can partially be explained by Bush's falling popularity and by public disenchantment with the war in Iraq. The Democrats in Congress had little concern about their challenging an unpopular president.

Congress has regularly sought to get around the obstacle of presidential vetoes by packaging a number of items together in a bill. Traditionally, presidents have had to sign a complete bill or reject the whole thing. Thus, for example, Congress regularly adds such things as a building project or a tax break for a state industry onto, say, a military appropriations bill that the president wants. Often presidents calculate that it is best to accept such add-ons, even if they think them unjustified or wasteful, in order to get passed what they judge to be important legislation.

Before it was ruled unconstitutional by the Supreme Court in 1998, the short-lived *line-item veto* promised to provide an important new tool for presidents. Favored by conservatives and by President Clinton, the 1996 line-item veto was supposed to save money by allowing presidents to cut some items, like pork barrel projects, from spending bills without vetoing the entire package. The Supreme Court declared the law unconstitutional because the Constitution says that all legislation is to be passed by both houses and then presented as a whole to the president for his approval.

THE BIG PICTURE: HOW PRESIDENTS TALK TO THE NATION

Seeing Presidential Rhetoric

GEORGE WASHINGTON (1790)

Just after his inauguration, the first American president carefully shepherds the new nation over rocky terrain.

ABRAHAM LINCOLN (1862)

In the second year of the Civil War, the president who hadn't been able to save the Union tries to hold the remnants of his country together.

LYNDON B. JOHNSON (1965)

In the first year of his own term, the president who came to office because of the murder of another seeks to raise the spirits of a nation and secure his legacy.

RONALD REAGAN (1985)

After a landslide reelection, the president who became a conservative icon lays out his agenda for his second term.

New Technology and New Ways to Talk to the Nation

First presidential public address (1789)

First presidential press conference (1913)

First presidential radio address (1923)

Fireside chats (1933–44)

First televised presidential speech (1947)

First presidential whistlestop tour (1948)

The founders created a constitutionally limited executive and even though the people holding the job have tried to expand those powers in various ways, sometimes it must have seemed as though the power of their words was the most effective tool they possessed. The power of presidents to persuade the public has always depended on the technology at hand and as that technology has grown, so has the public nature of the office. Here you can see some critical moments in presidential history reflected in the word clouds of the state of the union messages they used to communicate to the nation they led.

FRANKLIN D. ROOSEVELT (1944)

The year before he died, the president who saw the country through the Great Depression and into World War II reassures and encourages Americans to hold the course.

JOHN F. KENNEDY (1962)

In the middle of his short time in office, the first president born in the 20th century faces new challenges.

GEORGE W. BUSH (2002)

The year after 9/11, the president who had come to office objecting to nation building rallies the country for war.

OBAMA (2011)

Facing opposition on legislation to jump-start a stagnant economy, the nation's first black president urges the country to rally behind a bipartisan program for growth.

First televised presidential debate (1960)

First televised State of the Union (1965)

First White House website (1994)

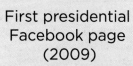

First presidential Facebook page (2009)

First presidential tweet (2010)

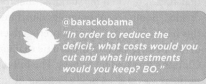

@barackobama
"In order to reduce the deficit, what costs would you cut and what investments would you keep? BO."

First live streamed debate (2012)

Speaking From the Bully Pulpit

President Theodore Roosevelt—who famously used the term "Bully!" the way we might use "excellent" or "awesome" today—coined the phrase "bully pulpit" to describe the office of the president. Roosevelt was one of the first to exploit the presidency as a platform from which to leverage both public and legislative support for his policy agenda. He used it to push for Progressive movement reforms and earned his reputation as the "trust buster" for his fight to ensure the rights of the common working man by pushing back against large corporate monopolies.

Another of the president's key legislative powers comes from the vice president's role as presiding officer of the Senate. Although the vice president rarely presides over the Senate, Article I, Section 3, says that he may cast a tie-breaking vote when the hundred-member Senate is evenly divided. Some recent examples illustrate just how important this has been to presidential prerogatives. In 1993 Vice President Al Gore voted to break a tie that enabled President Clinton's first budget to pass. The bill included controversial tax increases and spending cuts but ultimately helped create a budget surplus. Eight years later, Vice President Dick Cheney broke a tie vote on Bush's first budget, which ironically undid some of the Clinton tax increases but also included numerous other tax reductions. Both of these pieces of legislation were hallmarks of their respective presidents' agendas. The fact that a president can count on his vice president to break a tie when the Senate is split over controversial legislation is an often underappreciated legislative power.

Although the Constitution does not grant the president the power to make law, his power to do so has grown over time and now is generally accepted. As we saw in *What's at Stake. . . ?*, presidents can issue executive orders (not to be confused with the executive agreements he can make with other nations), which are supposed to be clarifications of how laws passed by Congress are to be implemented by specific agencies. Some of the most significant presidential actions have come from executive orders, including President Franklin Roosevelt's order to hold Japanese Americans in internment camps in World War II, President Truman's order that black and white military troops be integrated, President John F. Kennedy's and President Lyndon Johnson's affirmative action programs, and many of the post–September 11 security measures such as the establishment of military tribunals for cases against terrorists. Together with executive agreements, and even signing statements, these quasi-legislative powers, what one author calls presidential "unilateralist politics," significantly increase the president's role as a policymaker, independent of Congress.[17]

Frustrated by the partisan divide in Congress and unable to get much beyond absolute emergency legislation through the Republican-controlled House of Representatives following the 2010 election, President Obama launched a conscious and explicit program to expand the use of executive orders and other executive authority, under a campaign labeled "We Can't Wait."

Although Obama has been an exception, executive orders tend to be released at a higher rate at the beginning of a president's term as he immediately implements key policies and at the end of his term as he tries to leave his legacy.[18] Indeed, presidents often release particularly symbolic executive orders on their first days in office. Since executive orders are not Congress-made laws, a new president can reverse any of his predecessor's orders that he wants to.[19]

JUDICIAL POWERS Presidents can have tremendous long-term impact on the judiciary, but in the short run their powers over the courts are meager. Their continuing impact comes from nominating judges to the federal courts, including the Supreme Court. The political philosophies of individual judges influence significantly how they interpret the law, and this is especially important for Supreme Court justices, who are the final arbiters of constitutional meaning. Since judges serve for life, presidential appointments have a long-lasting effect. For instance, today's Supreme Court is distinctly more conservative than its

> **executive orders** clarifications of congressional policy issued by the president and having the full force of law
>
> **signing statements** statements recorded along with signed legislation clarifying the president's understanding of the constitutionality of the bill

immediate predecessors due to the appointments made by Presidents Reagan and Bush in the 1980s and early 1990s. Moreover, President Reagan is credited by many observers with having ushered in a "judicial revolution." He, together with his successor, George H. W. Bush, appointed 550 of the 837 federal judges, most of them conservatives. Clinton appointed moderates to the courts, angering many Democrats, who felt that his appointees should have been more liberal. President George W. Bush revived the conservative trend that was halted under Clinton.[20] Although President Obama's pick of Sonia Sotomayor for the Supreme Court pleased liberals, his nomination of Elena Kagan caused some to worry that his selections would follow Clinton's more moderate record.[21] In general, Obama's choices for the judiciary are fairly liberal, but because he has been slower than Bush to make appointments and the appointments he has made have often been blocked by Republicans in the Senate, he has not made a distinctive ideological shift in the federal courts.[22] Obama's nominations have, however, produced a more diverse federal judiciary: he has appointed more women, Asian, and Hispanics than any previous president as well as twelve openly gay federal judges and the first ever Native American female judge in the country's history.[23]

Presidents cannot always gauge the judicial philosophy of their appointees, however, and they can be sadly disappointed in their choices. Republican president Dwight Eisenhower appointed Chief Justice Earl Warren and Justice William Brennan, both of whom turned out to be more liberal than the president had anticipated. When asked if he had any regrets as president, Eisenhower answered, "Yes, two, and they are both sitting on the Supreme Court."[24]

The presidential power to appoint is limited to an extent by the constitutional requirement for Senate approval of federal judges. Traditionally, most nominees have been approved, with occasional exceptions. Sometimes rejection stems from questions about the candidate's competence, but in other instances rejection is based more on style and judicial philosophy. The Democratic-led Senate's rejection of President Reagan's very conservative Supreme Court nominee Robert Bork in 1987 is one of the more controversial cases.[25] Some observers believe that the battle over the Bork nomination signaled the end of deference to presidents and opened up the approval process to endless challenges and partisan bickering.[26] Some of the harshest battles

between the president and Congress in recent years came from partisan Senate challenges to judicial nominations. The political polarization we discussed in Chapter 7 has infected the nomination process. The frequent threat of the filibuster and the use of anonymous holds in the Senate allow the party opposing the president to hold up nominations so that many federal judgeships remain open, causing a backlog of cases. Both parties play the game as they try to prevent undesired ideological shifts in the federal courts.[27]

A president's choice of judges for the federal district courts is also limited by the tradition of **senatorial courtesy**, whereby a senior senator of the president's party or both senators of either party from the state in which the appointees reside have what amounts to a veto power over the president's choice. If presidents should ignore the custom of senatorial courtesy and push a nomination unpopular with one of the home state senators, fellow senators will generally refuse to confirm the appointee.[28]

Although presidents can leave a lasting imprint on the judiciary, in the short run they do little to affect court decisions. They do not contact judges to plead for decisions; they do not offer them inducements as they might a fence-sitting member of Congress. When, as happens rarely, a president criticizes a federal judge for a decision, the criticism is usually poorly received. For example, when President Obama used his State of the Union address in 2010 to criticize the Supreme Court majority for its landmark campaign finance decision (*Citizens United v. Federal Election Commission*), a flood of blogs and editorials suggested that the president had been unduly disrespectful, and one justice, Samuel Alito, sat shaking his head and mouthing the words "not true" as the president spoke.[29]

The least controversial way a president can try to influence a court decision is to have the Justice Department invest resources in arguing a case. The third-ranking member of the Justice Department, the **solicitor general**, is a presidential appointee whose job it is to argue cases for the government before the Supreme Court. The solicitor general is thus a bridge between the executive and the judiciary, not only deciding which cases the government will appeal to the Court, but also filing petitions stating the government's (usually the president's) position on cases to which the government is not even a party. These petitions, called *amicus curiae* ("friend of the court") briefs, are taken very seriously by the Court. The government is successful in its litigation more often than any other litigant, winning over two-thirds of its cases in the past half-century, and often having its arguments cited by the justices themselves in their opinions.[30] Elena Kagan, President Obama's second appointment to the Supreme Court, served as his solicitor general before her nomination.

One additional judicial power granted to the president by the Constitution is the **pardoning power**, which allows a president to exempt a person, convicted or not, from punishment for a crime. This power descends from a traditional power of kings as the court of last resort and thus a check on the courts. Pardons can backfire in dramatic ways.

senatorial courtesy tradition of granting senior senators of the president's party considerable power over federal judicial appointments in their home states

solicitor general the Justice Department officer who argues the government's cases before the Supreme Court

pardoning power a president's authority to release or excuse a person from the legal penalties of a crime

● Alito Gaffe

After President Gerald Ford pardoned Richard Nixon, in the hopes that the nation would heal from its Watergate wounds more quickly if it didn't have to endure the spectacle of its former president on trial, Ford experienced a tremendous backlash that may have contributed to his 1976 loss to Jimmy Carter. Subsequent presidents have each run into problems with unpopular pardons. Bill Clinton, in his last day in office, issued an unusually large number of pardons. Some were widely unpopular—like that for fugitive Marc Rich, who was residing in Switzerland, owed millions in taxes, and was charged with multiple counts of tax fraud—but nevertheless were entirely legal. When pardons like this are motivated by personal, political, or partisan considerations, rather than as a check on the power of the courts, they tend to be seen by the public and the media as presidential abuses of the public trust.[31]

THE TRADITIONAL PRESIDENCY

The presidency that the founders created and outlined in the Constitution is not the presidency of today. In fact, so clearly have the effective rules governing the presidency changed that scholars speak of the era of the *traditional presidency*, from the founding to the 1930s, and the era of the *modern presidency*, from the 1930s to the present. Although the constitutional powers of the president have been identical in both eras, the interpretation of how far the president can go beyond his constitutional powers has changed dramatically.

The founders' limited vision of the office survived more or less intact for a little over one hundred years. There were exceptions, however, to their expectations that echoed Hamilton's call for a stronger executive. Several early presidents exceeded the powers granted in the Constitution. Washington expanded the president's foreign policy powers, Jefferson entered into the Louisiana Purchase, and Andrew Jackson developed the role of president as popular leader. In one of the most dramatic examples, Abraham Lincoln, during the emergency conditions of the Civil War, stepped outside his constitutional role to call up state militias, to enlarge the army and use tax money to pay for it, to blockade the southern ports, and to suspend the writ of habeas corpus. (See *CLUES to Critical Thinking*.) He claimed that his actions, though counter to the Constitution, were necessary to save the nation.[32]

These presidents believed that they had what modern scholars call **inherent powers** to fulfill their constitutional duty to "take care that the laws be faithfully executed." Some presidents, like Lincoln, claimed that national security required a broader presidential role. Others held that the president, as our sole representative in foreign affairs, needed a stronger hand abroad than at home. Inherent powers are not listed explicitly in the Constitution but are implied by the powers that are granted, and they have been supported, to some extent, by the Supreme Court.[33] But

most nineteenth- and early-twentieth-century presidents, conforming to the founders' expectations, took a more retiring role, causing one observer to claim that "twenty of the twenty-five presidents of the nineteenth century were lords of passivity."[34] The job of the presidency was seen as a primarily administrative office, in which presidential will was clearly subordinate to the will of Congress.

THINKING OUTSIDE THE BOX

What political impact might it have if, following Washington's wishes, the president were known as "His High Mightiness"?

THE MODERN PRESIDENCY

The simple rural nature of life in the United States changed rapidly in the century and a half after the founding. The country grew westward, and the nation became more industrialized. More people worked in factories, fewer on the land. The postal system expanded greatly, and the federal government became involved in American Indian affairs, developed national parks, and enacted policies dealing with transportation, especially the railroads. Government in the nineteenth century sought bit by bit to respond to the new challenges of its changing people and economy, and as it responded, it grew beyond the bounds of the rudimentary administrative structure supervised by George Washington. With the crisis of the Great Depression and Franklin Roosevelt's New Deal solution, the size of government exploded and popular ideas about government changed radically. From being an exception, as it was in our early history, the use of strong presidential power became an expectation of the modern president.

THE GREAT DEPRESSION Nothing in their prior experience had prepared Americans for the calamity of the Great Depression. Following the stock market crash of October 1929, the economy went into a tailspin. Unemployment soared to 25 percent while the gross national product plunged from around $100 billion in 1928 to under $60 billion in 1932.[35] President Herbert Hoover held that government had only limited powers and responsibility to deal with what was, he believed, a private economic crisis. There was no widespread presumption, as there is today, that

> **inherent powers** presidential powers implied but not stated explicitly in the Constitution

government was responsible for the state of the economy or for alleviating the economic suffering of its citizens.

Roosevelt's election in 1932, and his three reelections, initiated an entirely new level of governmental activism. For the first time, the national government assumed responsibility for the economic well-being of its citizens on a substantial scale. Relying on the theory mentioned earlier, that foreign affairs are thought to justify greater presidential power than do domestic affairs, Roosevelt portrayed himself as waging a war against the Depression and sought from Congress the powers "that would be given to me if we were in fact invaded by a foreign foe."[36] The New Deal programs he put in place tremendously increased the size of the federal establishment and its budget. The number of civilians (nonmilitary personnel) working for the federal government increased by over 50 percent during Roosevelt's first two terms (1933–1939). The crisis of the Great Depression created the conditions for extraordinary action, and Roosevelt's leadership created new responsibilities and opportunities for the federal government. Congress delegated a vast amount of discretionary power to Roosevelt so that he could implement his New Deal programs.

The Policies and Persona of the Modern Presidency
The challenges of the Great Depression and World War II were met with a greatly increased role of the national government in American lives, the economy, and the world. Franklin Roosevelt's New Deal policies, and his central leadership role in the war effort, combined with his use of radio to speak directly to the public, transformed the nature of the office. The president became the central figure in American politics, and politics became more central to the lives of Americans.

THINKING OUTSIDE THE BOX

How might presidential behavior change if we once again allowed presidents to serve more than two terms?

PRESIDENTIAL PROMISES, POPULAR EXPECTATIONS The legacy of the New Deal is that Americans now look to their president and their government to regulate their economy, solve their social problems, and provide political inspiration. No president has had such a profound impact on how Americans live their lives today.[37] Roosevelt's New Deal was followed by Truman's Fair Deal. Eisenhower's presidency was less activist, but it was followed by Kennedy's New Frontier and Johnson's Great Society. All of these comprehensive policy programs did less than they promised, but they reinforced Americans' belief that it is government's and, in particular, the president's job to make ambitious promises. While presidents from Carter to Reagan to Clinton enthusiastically promoted plans for cutting back the size of government, few efforts were successful. Not even President Reagan, more conservative and therefore more hostile to "big government," was able to significantly reduce government size and popular expectations of government action.

"THE IMPERIAL PRESIDENCY" The growth of domestic government is not the only source of the increased power of the modern president, however. As early

as 1936, the Supreme Court confirmed in *United States v. Curtiss-Wright Corporation* the idea that the president has more inherent power in the realm of foreign affairs than in domestic politics.[38]

These decisions became more significant as the U.S. role in world politics expanded greatly in the post–World War II years. The ascendance of the United States as a world power, its engagement in the Cold War, and its participation in undeclared wars such as Korea and Vietnam made the office very powerful indeed—what historian Arthur Schlesinger called, in a 1973 book, "the imperial presidency."[39] The philosophy behind the imperial presidency was summed up neatly by Richard Nixon, ironically several years after he was forced to resign, when he declared, "When the president does it, that means it's not illegal."[40]

THE PRESIDENCY TODAY

Whether or not the power of the modern presidency ever approached "imperial" status at one time, there is no doubt that the political reaction to the Vietnam War and the Watergate scandal in the 1970s made it harder for the modern president to act. Congress, the media, and the

CLUES
TO CRITICAL THINKING

Abraham Lincoln

Excerpt From Speech to Congress, September 15, 1863

In a list of restrictions on the powers of Congress, Article I, Section 9, of the U.S. Constitution says, "The Privilege of the Writ of Habeas Corpus shall not be suspended, unless when in Cases of Rebellion or Invasion the public Safety may require it." Habeas corpus, meaning literally "to have the body," is a way of protecting someone from being arrested and held for political reasons. A judge can issue a writ of habeas corpus and have the prisoner delivered before him, to inquire into the legality of the charge. For some people this writ is so essential to our notion of due process of law that they call it the "writ of liberty."

As the Civil War began, President Abraham Lincoln struggled to suppress the rebellion in the southern states and the activities of

its northern sympathizers in the Democratic Party. In April 1861 he was fearful that the state of Maryland, leaning toward secession, would act to prevent the federal army from passing through the state. To control what he believed to be the subversive speech and actions of Maryland politicians, he suspended the writ of habeas corpus.

John Merryman was arrested in May of the same year. U.S. Supreme Court justice Roger B. Taney issued a writ of habeas corpus to the military to show cause for Merryman's arrest. Under Lincoln's orders, the military refused. Taney issued a judgment saying that under the Constitution only Congress had the power to suspend the writ, and that by taking that power on himself, Lincoln was taking not only the legislative power, but also the judicial power, to arrest and imprison without due process of law. Taney granted that he could not enforce his judgment against the power of the military but said that if the military were allowed to take judicial power in that way, then the people of the United States had ceased to live under the rule of law.

On July 4, Lincoln appeared before Congress and, among other things, attempted to defend his assumption of the power to suspend habeas corpus and his defiance of the Supreme Court's ordering him to stop. The following is an excerpt from his speech.

Obviously we have survived what Taney saw as an overzealous power grab. Although Lincoln expanded the suspension of habeas corpus in 1862, Congress finally acted to approve it in 1863, and it remained suspended until a Supreme Court ruling in 1866 (Ex Parte Milligan) officially restored it. What did Lincoln risk in defying the Supreme Court? Was it worth it?

Soon after the first call for militia it was considered a duty to authorize the commanding general in proper cases according to his discretion, to suspend the privilege of the writ of habeas corpus, or in other words to arrest and detain, without resort to the ordinary processes and forms of law, such individuals as he might deem dangerous to the public safety. This authority has purposely been exercised but very sparingly. Nevertheless the legality and propriety of what has been done under it are questioned and the attention of the country has been called to the proposition that one who is sworn to "take care that the laws be faithfully executed" should not himself violate them. Of course some consideration was given to the questions of power and propriety before this matter was acted upon. The whole of the laws which were required to be faithfully executed were being resisted and failing of execution in nearly one-third of the States. Must they

courts check the president in ways they had not done earlier in the era of the modern presidency. Many in Congress felt that neither the Johnson nor the Nixon administrations had been sufficiently forthcoming over the Vietnam War. Frustration with that, as well as with Nixon's abuse of his powers during Watergate and his unwillingness to spend budgeted money as Congress had appropriated it, led Congress to develop its own mechanisms for getting information about public policy to use as a check on presidential power.[41] Congress also weakened the office of the presidency with the passage of the War Powers Act (1973), which we discussed earlier; the Foreign Intelligence and Surveillance Act (1978), designed to put a check on the government's ability to spy on people within the United States; and the Independent Counsel Act (1978), which was intended to provide an impartial check on a president's

activities but which was ultimately left open to abuse by his opponents.

At the same time, fresh from the heady success of the *Washington Post*'s discovery of the Watergate scandal, the Washington press corps abandoned the discretion that had kept them from reporting Franklin Roosevelt's inability to walk or John F. Kennedy's extramarital affairs, and began to subject the president to closer scrutiny. Reporters, eager to make their names as investigative journalists, became far more aggressive in their coverage of the White House.

Even the Supreme Court served to limit the power and stature of the presidency, as when it ruled unanimously in 1997 that a sitting president does not have immunity from civil lawsuits while he is in office, adding that the process of such a case was unlikely to prove a

be allowed to finally fail of execution, even had it been perfectly clear that by the use of the means necessary to their execution some single law, made in such extreme tenderness of the citizen's liberty that practically it relieves more of the guilty than of the innocent, should to a very limited extent be violated? To state the question more directly, are all the laws but one to go unexecuted and the Government itself go to pieces lest that one be violated? Even in such a case would not the official oath be broken if the Government should be overthrown, when it was believed that disregarding the single law would tend to preserve it? But it was not believed that this question was presented. It was not believed that any law was violated. The provision of the Constitution that "the privilege of the writ of habeas corpus shall not be suspended unless when in cases of rebellion or invasion the public safety may require it," is equivalent to a provision—is a provision—that such privilege may be suspended when in cases of rebellion or invasion the public safety does require it. It was decided that we have a case of rebellion, and that the public safety does require the qualified suspension of the privilege of the writ which was authorized to be made. Now, it is insisted that Congress and not the Executive is vested with this power. But the Constitution itself is silent as to which, or who, is to exercise the power; and as the provision was plainly made for a dangerous emergency, it cannot be believed the framers of the instrument intended that in every case the danger should run its course until Congress could be called together, the very assembling of which might be prevented, as was intended in this case, by the rebellion.

Source: Federal Judicial Center, http://www.fjc.gov/history/home.nsf/page/tu_merryman_doc_5.html.

Consider the source and the audience: Lincoln is speaking to Congress under a state of emergency. How does that fact affect the terms in which he casts his argument? When does urgency become panic? How far should it be resisted?

Lay out the argument and the underlying values and assumptions: What is Lincoln's essential purpose here, which he believes justifies some reduction in due process? What does he see as the trade-off facing him as executor of the laws? Why doesn't he mention the name of the person who has challenged his actions? How does he reason that the founders must not have intended members of Congress to be the ones to decide whether habeas corpus should be suspended?

Uncover the evidence: What does a reading of the Constitution tell us about this matter? Is the Constitution indeed silent?

Evaluate the conclusion: How persuasive is the "ends justify the means" argument in this context? What are its limits? What means might not be justified by a worthy end?

Sort out the political implications: Is Lincoln's argument relevant to the beefing up of executive power after 9/11? What are the similarities between the two situations? What are the differences?

disruption of his duties.[42] Paula Jones's lawsuit against Bill Clinton, of course, proved to be disruptive of his presidency in the extreme, and ended up leading to his impeachment, although on grounds that had nothing to do with the case. Had the Court not made that decision, Clinton's affair with Monica Lewinsky would not have come to light, and he would most likely not have been impeached.

THE BUSH-CHENEY RESTORATION OF THE IMPERIAL PRESIDENCY
The modern presidency had been weakened by post-Watergate developments and the Clinton impeachment. When the George W. Bush administration came to power, Bush and his vice president, Dick Cheney, were determined to restore the luster and power of the office. Cheney had been a young staffer in the Nixon White House and chief of staff to Gerald Ford before embarking on a career in Congress. He had seen firsthand the changes in the executive and felt they had gone too far. Thus, many of Bush's early executive orders were designed to bolster presidential powers, as were claims of executive privilege made by his administration.

In addition, Bush expanded the practice of using signing statements, issued on the signing of a bill, that were intended to "clarify" the president's understanding of what the bill meant and how he believed it ought to be enforced. Bush did not invent the signing statement. Since the 1800s, presidents had been issuing statements if they thought a part of a bill they signed was unconstitutional, especially if they thought it unconstitutionally restricted executive power; but these signing statements, recorded in the *Federal Register*, along with the legislation they refer to,

AP Photo/Pablo Martinez Monsivais

The Post 9/11 Presidency
As the public united behind the president in the aftermath of the terror attacks of 2001, the Bush-Cheney administration was able to take on a more active role in governing and increased the power of the office through the use of presidential signing statements, executive orders, and claims of executive privilege.

had been used only sparingly. Typically, presidents used the presidential veto to block legislation they didn't like, whereupon Congress could override the veto if the bill had sufficient support. But unlike his predecessors, Bush had not vetoed a single bill by the time he had been in office for five years. Instead he had issued a huge number of signing statements, over 750, compared to 232 by his father in his four years in the White House, and only 140 issued by Bill Clinton in his eight years.

Many of Bush's signing statements reflected a strong commitment to the theory of the unitary executive, a controversial legal view held by members of the Bush administration that the Constitution requires that all executive power be held only by the president and, therefore, that it cannot be delegated to or wielded by any other branch. Consequently, Bush's signing statements reserved the right to ignore, among other things, an antitorture law, a law forbidding him to order troops into combat in Colombia, a law requiring him to inform Congress if he

wanted to divert funds from congressionally authorized programs to start up secret operations, a law preventing the military from using intelligence about Americans that was gathered unconstitutionally, a law that required the Justice Department to inform Congress about how the FBI was using domestic wiretapping, laws that created whistle-blower protection for federal employees, and laws that required the federal government to follow affirmative action principles.[43]

Critics of the Bush administration howled when they realized what was going on, accusing Bush of doing an end-run around Congress and claiming that he was setting up himself, and thus the executive branch, as the ultimate decider of what is constitutional, a function generally thought to belong to the Supreme Court. "There is no question that this administration has been involved in a very carefully thought-out, systematic process of expanding presidential power at the expense of the other branches of government," said one scholar.[44]

The terror attacks of September 11, 2001, provided Bush and Cheney with a strong and persuasive rationale for their desire to create a more muscular presidency. Bush's extraordinarily high approval ratings in the days following September 11 made Congress unwilling to take him on. The Republicans in Congress were supportive of the administration's efforts, and the Democrats feared being seen as soft on terrorism and so went along with Bush's plans. He was able to initiate the wars in Afghanistan and Iraq, and the Patriot Act passed handily in 2001, and only the Supreme Court, in the 2004 case *Hamdi v. Rumsfeld* and the 2006 case *Hamdan v. Rumsfeld*, attempted to put on the brakes. As we argue in this chapter, high approval ratings can give a president more power than the Constitution allows him.

Only after Bush's reelection in 2004, with waning approval ratings, was he seen as vulnerable enough for Congress to criticize him seriously. By 2006 his approval was so low that Democrats easily won back control of both the House and the Senate and began to undertake the job of congressional oversight that had been largely lacking for the previous six years.

The fate of the Bush administration illustrates the basic themes of this chapter. The Constitution does not give presidents sufficient power to meet their promises and to match expectations of domestic and world leadership, so presidents curry public support to engender a more compliant Congress. Bush chose to stick with his ideological agenda and his slim but cooperative majorities in Congress, and to use the levers available to act unilaterally: signing statements, executive orders, claims of executive privilege, and politicizing the bureaucracy to achieve policy compliance, especially in regard to the Department of Justice. With the decline in his popularity and his party's losses in Congress, his powers waned and he was a reclusive lame duck during the final months of his presidency.

THE OBAMA PRESIDENCY Overall, it is unlikely that the Bush-Cheney efforts to bulk up the executive will have lasting effect. Obama wrestles with the same challenges of office as have all presidents in the modern age, but he is on the record as supporting the traditional checks and balances that limit the president's power. Obama continued the use of signing statements, though initially only on a limited basis to protect the president's constitutional prerogatives.[45] Although liberal critics have called out his use of these statements, as well as his failure to close the prison at Guantánamo Bay, his efforts to pursue the war in Afghanistan, and his continuance of some of the Bush administration's national security practices (like secret wiretapping) that they claim infringe on civil liberties,[46] in general Obama has rejected his predecessor's bulked-up presidential aspirations. A former constitutional law professor, Obama seems to be aware of the necessity of maintaining checks and balances, and he has shown no signs of embracing the Bush philosophy of the unitary executive. However, as we saw in *What's at Stake…?*, following the Democrats' loss of control of the House of Representatives in the 2010 election, the Obama administration did develop an explicit strategy of exercising executive power to a much greater extent than he did in his first two years in office, which is what presidents typically do when blocked by Congress.[47] His use of executive orders picked up in his second administration, when his reelection failed to break what he had referred to as the "fever" of opposition among Republicans.

PAUSE AND REVIEW:

WHO, WHAT, HOW

The politicians who initially had something important at stake in the rules governing the executive were the founders themselves. Arranged by those, like Alexander Hamilton, who wanted a strong leader and by others who preferred a multiple executive to ensure checks on the power of the office, the constitutional compromise provides for a stronger position than many wanted, but one still limited in significant ways from becoming overly powerful and independent.

Until the 1930s, presidents were mostly content to live within the confines of their constitutional restrictions, with only occasional excursions into the realm of inherent powers. But since the 1930s, presidents and citizens have entered into a complex relationship. Seeking effective leadership in an increasingly sophisticated world, citizens have been willing to expand the informal rules of presidential power provided they approve of the ways in which the president uses it. When the powers of the presidency have seemed to have gotten out of hand, however, Congress, the courts, and the media have been quick to limit it, showing how well the founders' system of checks and balances functions.

IN YOUR OWN WORDS » Compare the modern presidency with the founders' expectations for a limited executive.

PRESIDENTIAL POLITICS
The struggle for power in a constitutionally limited office

Presidential responsibilities and the public's expectations of what the president can accomplish have increased greatly since the start of the twentieth century, but as we have discussed, the Constitution has not been altered to give the president more power. To avoid failure, presidents have to seek power beyond that which is explicitly granted by the Constitution, and even beyond what they can claim as part of their inherent powers, and they do that with varying degrees of success.

THE EXPECTATIONS GAP AND THE NEED FOR PERSUASIVE POWER

Even presidents who have drawn enthusiastically on their inherent powers to protect national security or conduct foreign policy or who support the theory of the unitary executive still cannot summon the official clout to ensure that their legislation gets through Congress, that the Senate approves their appointments, and that other aspects of their campaign promises are fulfilled. Some scholars believe that presidents should be given the power necessary to do the job correctly. Others argue that no one can do the job; it is not a lack of power that is the problem, but rather, no human being is up to the task of solving everyone's problems on all fronts. The solution according to this view is to lower expectations and return the presidency to a position of less prominence.[48]

New presidents quickly face the dilemma of high visibility and status, and limited constitutional authority. Of course, they do not want to fail. It would be political suicide for them to say, "Gee, America, this job is a lot tougher than I thought it would be. The truth is, I don't have the power to do all the stuff I promised." Presidential frustration with the limits of the office is captured nicely by President Truman's remarks about his successor, President Eisenhower, a former general. "He'll sit here," Truman would remark (tapping his desk for emphasis), "and he'll say, 'Do this! Do that!' *And nothing will happen.* Poor Ike—it won't be a bit like the Army. He'll find it very frustrating."[49]

Yet people continue to run for and serve as president, and as we have seen, they deal with the expectations gap by attempting to augment their power with executive orders, executive agreements, claims of executive privilege, signing statements, and the like. All of these give the president some ability to act unilaterally. However, to be successful

AP Photo/Pablo Martinez Monsivais

Going Public by Going Viral

Concerned that not enough young people were enrolling on HealthCare.gov, President Obama played straight man to comedian Zach Galifianakis, pitching his health care plan on the Funny or Die web site's popular *Between Two Ferns* in 2013. The video went viral, leading to a sizable bump in traffic at the site—and an increase in enrollments—as the deadline for enrollment approached.

with larger policy initiatives, presidents seek to develop their primary extraconstitutional power, which is, in one scholar's phrase, the **power to persuade**.[50] To achieve what is expected of them, the argument goes, presidents must persuade others to cooperate with their agendas—most often members of Congress, but also the courts, the media, state and local officials, bureaucrats, foreign leaders, and especially the American public.

Other scholars, however, doubt that it is really persuasion alone that allows a president to get things done. They argue that little evidence indicates that presidents are able to influence important actors, or even the public, to change their policy priorities or preferences, and that presidents' substantial policy successes are due primarily to their ability to see and exploit existing opportunities. These may be political ambitions of members of Congress; latent concerns or yearnings in the public; or changes in public mood or media attention about unexpected events, such as the economic collapse of the 2008 Great Recession or the attacks of September 11, 2001. Presidents vary in their ability to capitalize on the political context they face as much as on their ability to single-handedly change minds, either in Washington or in the country at large.[51] Whether they seek to persuade or to take advantage of potential opportunities, presidents have to go beyond their relatively modest constitutional powers if they want to fulfill voter expectations and bring about major policy changes in America.

GOING PUBLIC

One central strategy that presidents follow in their efforts to influence people "inside the Beltway" (that is, the Washington insiders) to go along with their agenda is to

reach out and appeal to the public directly for support. This strategy of **going public** is based on the expectation that public support will put pressure on other politicians to give the president what he wants.[52] Presidents use their powers as both head of government and head of state to appeal to the public.[53] A president's effort to go public can include a trip to an international summit, a town meeting–style debate on a controversial issue, or even the president's annual State of the Union address or other nationally televised speeches.

Another aspect of going public is drawing experts and leaders to conferences or especially the White House to draw attention to and to gain support for presidential initiatives. This became part of an explicit Obama administration strategy following the 2010 elections in which Republicans gained control of the House of Representatives. It involved inviting groups as varied as university presidents, to discuss ways to increase enrollments of low-income and minority students, and business executives, to develop ideas for dealing with the long-term unemployed. The intention is to garner support among specific and strategically situated leaders who have the capacity to move on problems even in the face of continued congressional gridlock.[54]

THE PRESIDENCY AND THE MEDIA At the simplest level of the strategy of going public, the president just takes

> **power to persuade** a president's ability to convince Congress, other political actors, and the public to cooperate with the administration's agenda
>
> **going public** a president's strategy of appealing to the public on an issue, expecting that public pressure will be brought to bear on other political actors

his case to the people. Consequently, presidential public appearances have increased greatly in the era of the modern presidency. Recent presidents have had some sort of public appearance almost every day of the week, year round. Knowing that the White House press corps will almost always get some airtime on network news, presidents want that coverage to be favorable. Shaping news coverage so that it generates favorable public opinion for the president is now standard operating procedure.[55]

THE RATINGS GAME Naturally, only a popular president can use the strategy of going public effectively, so popularity ratings become crucial to how successful a president can be. Since the 1930s the Gallup Organization has been asking people, "Do you approve or disapprove of the way [*name of the current president*] is handling his job as president?" The public's ratings of the president—that is, the percentage saying they approve of how the president is handling his job—varies from one president to the next and also typically rises and falls within any single presidential term. The president's ratings are a kind of political barometer: the higher they are, the more effective the president is with other political and economic actors; the lower they are, the harder he finds it to get people to go along. For the modern presidency, the all-important power to persuade is intimately tied to presidential popularity.

Three factors in particular can affect a president's popularity: a cycle effect, the economy, and unifying or divisive current events:[56]

- The **cycle effect** refers to the tendency for most presidents to begin their terms of office with relatively high popularity ratings, which decline as they move through their four-year terms (see Figure 8.1). During the very early months of this cycle, often called the **honeymoon period**, presidents are frequently most effective with Congress. Often, but not always, presidential ratings rise going into reelection, but this seldom approaches the popularity the president had immediately after being elected the first time.

  The post-honeymoon drop in approval demonstrated in Figure 8.1 may occur because, by then, presidents have begun to try to fulfill the handsome promises on which they campaigned. Fulfilling promises requires political action, and as presidents exercise their head-of-government responsibilities, they lose the head-of-state glow they bring with them from the election. Political change seldom favors everyone equally, and when someone wins, someone else usually loses. Some citizens become

disillusioned as the president makes divisive choices, acts as a partisan, or is attacked by Congress and interests that do not favor his policies. For some citizens, the president then becomes "just another politician," not the dignified head of state they thought they were electing. The cycle effect means that presidents need to present their programs early, while they enjoy popular support. Unfortunately, much opportunity available during the honeymoon period can be squandered because of inexperience, as it was at the start of the Clinton administration. In contrast, President Obama chose as his first chief of staff Rahm Emanuel, a veteran Clinton White House staffer then serving in Congress (see *Profiles in Citizenship* in Chapter 16). Emanuel, who in now mayor of Chicago, was able to help Obama accomplish an unusually ambitious legislative agenda in the early years of his presidency. Obama continued to be effective with Congress long after his approval ratings left the honeymoon stage, passing in his first two years a major economic stimulus plan, health care reform, and a financial reform bill, along with many less comprehensive pieces of legislation. In fact, his achievements, coming in the context of a highly polarized political environment, probably helped to drive down his approval ratings.

- The second important factor that consistently influences presidential approval is the state of the economy. At least since Franklin Roosevelt, the government has taken an active role in regulating the national economy, and every president promises economic prosperity. In practice, however, presidential power over the economy is quite limited, though we nevertheless hold our presidents accountable for economic performance. President George H. W. Bush lost the presidency in large measure because of the prolonged recession in the latter part of his administration. Clinton won it with a campaign focused on his plan for economic recovery. President Obama came into office during the worst economic recession to hit the nation since the Great Depression of the 1930s. His ratings reflected a traditional honeymoon effect, but they dropped as unemployment rose and continued to decline as the economic recovery was slower than the public hoped.

- Newsworthy current events can also influence presidential approval. Sometimes events occur beyond the president's control and he is judged by his response to them. For example, the public and the media looked to President Obama for a response to the BP Gulf oil disaster in 2010. Although the government could do little about the spill because it was dependent on BP for equipment and technological know-how to find a solution, Obama's ratings still took a hit as the oil continued to spill into the Gulf. Events like these are opportunities for establishing presidential leadership,

---

cycle effect the predictable rise and fall of a president's popularity at different stages of a term in office

honeymoon period the time following an election when a president's popularity is high and congressional relations are likely to be productive

FIGURE 8.1 AVERAGE QUARTERLY PRESIDENTIAL APPROVAL RATINGS, EISENHOWER TO OBAMA

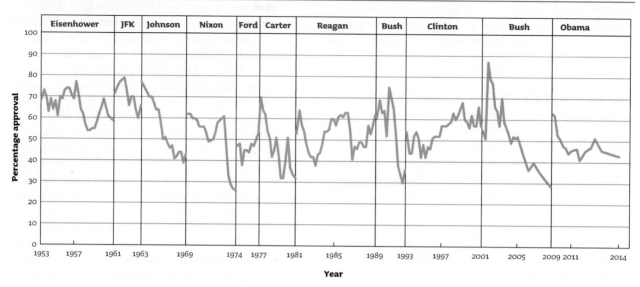

Sources: Quarterly data for 1953–2000 provided by Robert S. Erikson; developed for Robert S. Erikson, James A. Stimson, and Michael B. MacKuen, *The Macro Polity* (Cambridge: Cambridge University Press, 2002); data for 2001–2014 calculated by authors from the Gallup Organization.

Note: Respondents were asked, "Do you approve or disapprove of the way [*name of the current president*] is handling his job as president?"

and how presidents perform under such unexpected pressures influences their standing with the public and their long-term effectiveness.

Besides being tests of a president's leadership, newsworthy events can be both divisive and unifying. Political controversy, almost by definition, is divisive and generally hurts presidential ratings. And, of course, controversy in politics is unavoidable even though the public at large is reluctant to accept this fact of democratic governance.[57] This is part of the reason that presidents' approval ratings seldom maintain their honeymoon highs. Eventually presidents must veto bills, take stands on abortion or stem cell research, raise taxes or oppose a tax break, or call for more, or less, regulation. All of these everyday acts of governing give rise to political friction, and this wears down the ratings of a public who prefer not to see their president as a politicking head of government. The drop in ratings for Barack Obama, who was unusually successful at getting his legislative agenda passed during his first two years in office, is a textbook example of what happens when a president takes on a political role. Knowing that their cooperation would only bolster Obama, congressional Republicans have made a concerted effort to deny him support wherever they could, ensuring that bills that passed on a party-line vote would look controversial and thus unpopular. This, coupled with their intense criticism of the administration's handling of both domestic and foreign

affairs, ensured that Obama would be seen as a partisan figure and contributed to the steady decline in his job approval ratings.[58]

On the flip side, unifying events can help presidential ratings. Television footage of the president signing agreements with other heads of state looks "presidential." Similarly, when a president leads the nation in conflict with other countries, at least initially, the public rallies and his approval ratings improve. President George H. W. Bush's rating soared during the 1990–1991 Gulf War, but those were topped by his son's ratings following the terrorist attacks of 2001 (see Figure 8.1). George W. Bush's administration framed subsequent legislation in terms of the war on terror, including tax cuts, energy policy, and military spending, all of which were on his agenda before September 11, and his high approval ratings helped him garner support for his agenda even from congressional Democrats. President Obama experienced a small bump in his approval ratings in spring 2011 after he announced the killing of Osama bin Laden, but it did not translate into leverage with the Republican Congress, which soon helped to send Obama's numbers south again in the wake of the debt ceiling crisis later that summer. The capture of Ahmed Abu Khattala, a senior leader believed to have major responsibility for the attacks on the U.S. diplomatic mission in Benghazi, Libya, passed without barely a blip in the president's approval ratings.

Thus modern presidents necessarily play the ratings game.[59] Those who choose not to play suffer the consequences: Truman, Johnson, and Ford tended not to heed the polls so closely, and they either had a hard time in office or were not reelected.[60]

WORKING WITH CONGRESS

Presidents do not always try to influence Congress by going public. They must often deal directly with Congress itself, and sometimes they combine strategies and deal with the public and Congress at the same time. The Constitution gives the primary lawmaking powers to Congress. Thus, to be successful with his policy agenda, the president has to have congressional cooperation. This depends in part on the reputation he has with members of that institution and other Washington elites for being an effective leader.[61] Such success varies with several factors, including the compatibility of the president's and Congress' goals and the party composition of Congress.

SHARED POWERS AND CONFLICTING POLICY
GOALS Presidents and members of Congress usually define the nation's problems and possible solutions in different ways. In addition to the philosophical and partisan differences that may exist between the president and members of Congress, each has different constituencies to please. The president, as the one leader elected by the whole nation, needs to take a wider, more encompassing view of the national interest. Members of Congress have relatively narrow constituencies and tend to represent their particular interests. Thus, in many cases, members of Congress do not want the same things the president does.

What can the president do to get his legislation through a Congress made up of members whose primary concern is with their individual constituencies? For one thing, presidents have a staff of assistants to work with Congress. The legislative liaison office specializes in determining what members of Congress are most concerned about, what they need, and how legislation can be tailored to get their support. In some cases, members just want their views to be heard; they do not want to be taken for granted. In other cases, the details of the president's program have to be explained adequately. It is electorally useful for members to have this done in person, by the president, complete with photo opportunities for release to the papers back home.

Presidential candidates often claim to be running for office as "outsiders," politicians removed from the

> **legislative liaison** executive personnel who work with members of Congress to secure their support in getting a president's legislation passed
>
> **divided government** political rule split between two parties, in which one controls the White House and the other controls one or both houses of Congress

politics-as-usual world of Washington and therefore untainted by its self-interest and strife. This can just be a campaign ploy, but when presidents such as Jimmy Carter and Bill Clinton are elected who truly *do* lack experience in Washington politics, they may fail to understand the sensitivities of members of Congress and the dynamics of sharing powers. President Carter, even though he had a healthy Democratic majority, had a very difficult time with Congress because he did not realize that, from the perspective of Capitol Hill, what Jimmy Carter believed was good for the nation might not be considered best for each member.[62] Subsequent presidents seem to have learned from Carter's experience. In just the latest example, as we mentioned earlier, President Obama, himself a former senator, initially picked a legislature-savvy chief of staff to help shepherd his agenda through the lawmaking process.

PARTISANSHIP AND DIVIDED GOVERNMENT
When the president and the majority of Congress are of the same party, the president is more successful at getting his programs passed. When the president faces **divided government**—that is, when he is of a different party than the majority in one or both houses—he does not do as well.[63] Part of the problem is that in our highly polarized politics today, passage of a bill supported by the president is evaluated not only in terms of policy impact, but also as giving a victory to the president, which is something the opposition is loath to do. An equally important part of the problem of divided government is that members of different parties stand for different approaches and solutions to the nation's problems. Democratic presidents and members of Congress tend to be more liberal than the average citizen, and Republican presidents and members of Congress tend to be more conservative.

Figure 8.2 shows a hypothetical example of the position that a Democratic president would take in dealing with a Democratic-led Congress. When the same party controls Congress and the presidency, the two institutions can cooperate relatively easily on ideological issues because the majority party wants to go in the same direction as the president. The president offers his own position, but he is happy to cooperate with the Democratic majority on proposal A because this is much closer to what he wants than is the status quo or the opposition party's proposal. This reflects the situation for two years after the 2008 election, when the Democrats had won the presidency along with continuing control of both houses of Congress. With substantial and sympathetic Democratic majorities in Congress, President Obama set a record for getting his bills through Congress (see Figure 8.3). Consider how drastically the situation changes under divided government. Of course, after the 2010 midterms, with the House in Republican hands and the Senate under Democratic control, very little legislation moved one way or the other, but imagine if the Republicans had gained control of the Senate as well as the House. If Obama were to support a bill similar to

FIGURE 8.2 HYPOTHETICAL POLICY ALTERNATIVES UNDER UNIFIED AND DIVIDED GOVERNMENT

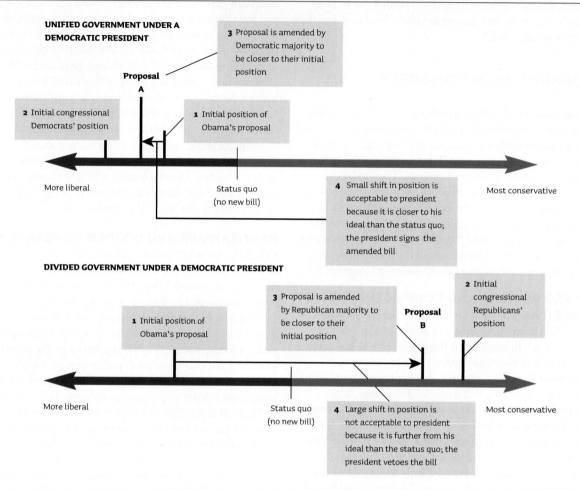

UNIFIED GOVERNMENT UNDER A DEMOCRATIC PRESIDENT

Proposal A

3 Proposal is amended by Democratic majority to be closer to their initial position

2 Initial congressional Democrats' position

1 Initial position of Obama's proposal

More liberal

Status quo (no new bill)

4 Small shift in position is acceptable to president because it is closer to his ideal than the status quo; the president signs the amended bill

Most conservative

DIVIDED GOVERNMENT UNDER A DEMOCRATIC PRESIDENT

2 Initial congressional Republicans' position

3 Proposal is amended by Republican majority to be closer to their initial position

Proposal B

1 Initial position of Obama's proposal

More liberal

Status quo (no new bill)

4 Large shift in position is not acceptable to president because it is further from his ideal than the status quo; the president vetoes the bill

Most conservative

It is much easier to pass legislation under unified government, where the president's position and that of Congress start out relatively close together, than under divided government, where a large gap exists between the initial positions of the president and Congress. Presidential success in getting bills passed is much higher under unified government than it is when the opposition party has a majority in Congress.

---

proposal A, Congress would ignore it or amend it to fit more conservative ideological preferences. If the Republican Congress sent a bill like proposal B to the president, he would veto it, preferring the alternative of no bill, the status quo, to what Congress passed. Thus, under divided government, Congress tends to ignore what the president wants, and the president tends to veto what the opposition majority party in Congress offers.

Under divided government, presidential success is likely to falter. Figure 8.3 shows the percentage of bills passed that were supported by each president from Eisenhower to Obama. Notice that the success rate is consistently higher under unified government (orange bars). Dramatic examples of the impact of divided government can be seen in both Clinton's and George W. Bush's administrations. For his first two years in office, Clinton worked with a Democratic majority in both houses, and Congress passed 86 percent of the bills he supported. The next two years (1995–1996) the

Republicans had a majority in both houses, and Clinton's success rate dropped to 46 percent.[64] Bush enjoyed impressive success, with an average of more than three-quarters of his favored bills enacted into law, when he had Republican majorities in Congress. But when Bush had to deal with a Democratic Congress after the 2006 midterm election, his success rate dropped dramatically. With 96.7 percent of his preferred bills making it into law, Obama in 2009 had the most successful year of any president in the fifty-six years that *Congressional Quarterly* has been keeping track. These results are attributable to the large Democratic majorities in the House and the Senate, coupled with the president's ambitious agenda and a tanking economy that required action.[65] The 2010 midterm elections, which replaced the Democratic majority in the House of Representatives with a conservative Republican majority, spelled an end to Obama's high rate of success, dropping from an average of 91 percent under the Democratic majority to

FIGURE 8.3 PRESIDENTIAL SUCCESS UNDER UNIFIED AND DIVIDED GOVERNMENT, EISENHOWER TO OBAMA

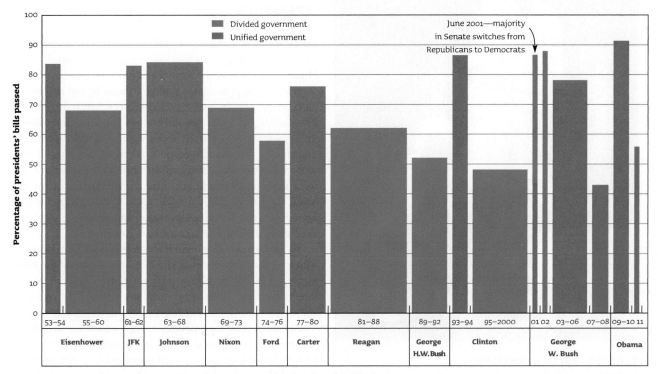

When the president faces a divided government—that is, when the opposing party controls one or both houses of Congress—he usually finds it harder to get his bills passed.

Source: Data from "Presidential Support Background," CQ *Weekly*, January 11, 2010, 117; "Table 6-7: Presidential Victories on Votes in Congress, 1953–2010," in Harold W. Stanley and Richard G. Niemi, eds., *Vital Statistics on American Politics 2011-2012* (Washington, D.C.: CQ Press, 2011), 246–248; Sam Goldfarb, "2011 Vote Studies: Presidential Support," CQ *Weekly*, January 16, 2012, 98–104; Shawn Zeller, "2012 Vote Studies: Presidential Support," CQ *Weekly*, January 21, 2013; Emily Ethridge "2013 Vote Studies: Presidential Support," CQ *Weekly*, February 3, 2014.

just over 55 percent in his years facing a Republican House. Divided government, however, does not doom Washington to inaction. When national needs are pressing or the public mood seems to demand action, the president and opposition majorities have managed to pass important legislation.[66] For example, the government was divided with a Democrat in the White House and Republicans in control of both houses of Congress when major welfare reform was passed with the Personal Responsibility and Work Opportunity Act of 1996. But national needs do not always cause Congress to step up. In 2011 and 2012, Congress was unable to agree on policies to deal with revenue shortfalls and the budget, or even the previously routine extension of the national debt limit to enable it to pay its bills. Congress has managed at best stop-gap temporary measures to stave off impending crises, like a national default on debt payments. Members failed to bridge the ideological divide in October 2013, when House Republicans' insistence on defunding Obamacare resulted in a government shutdown for sixteen days. Congress

remains so ideologically divided that progress on longer-term solutions is not likely in the near future, certainly not while Obama remains in office.

PAUSE AND REVIEW:

WHO, WHAT, HOW

The president wants to get his policy agenda enacted with congressional cooperation and to get and maintain the public approval necessary to keep the expanded powers he needs to do his job. He tries to accomplish these goals with his constitutional powers, by maintaining his reputation among Washington elites as an effective leader, by building coalitions among members of Congress, by going public, by skillfully using the media, and by trying to keep the economy healthy.

AP Photo/Charles Dharapak

Teed Off, But in a Good Way

Responding to critics who claim he doesn't do enough schmoozing, President Obama, known for his love of the links, invited Speaker of the House John Boehner, a fellow avid golfer, and Ohio governor John Kasich to join him and Vice President Joe Biden for a round of golf at Andrews Air Force Base. Though no "grand bargains" were hatched that sunny June day in 2011, the media couldn't get enough of the political camaraderie, promptly dubbing the event a "golf summit."

Citizens have an enormous amount of power in this regard because, distant though Washington may seem to most citizens, presidents are driven by the need for public approval to get most of the things that they want. Congress too has goals: members want to get policy passed so that they may go home to the voters and claim to have supported their interests and to have brought home the bacon. Legislators need to meet the expectations of a different constituency than does the president, but few members of Congress want to be seen by the voters as an obstacle to a popular president. A president who has a strong reputation inside Washington and who has broad popularity outside comes to Congress with a distinct advantage, and members of Congress will go out of their way to cooperate and compromise with him.

IN YOUR OWN WORDS ≫ Identify strategies and tools presidents employ to overcome the constitutional limitations of the office.

MANAGING THE PRESIDENTIAL ESTABLISHMENT
The challenges of supervising an unwieldy bureaucracy

We tend to think of the president as one person—what one presidential scholar calls the "single executive image."[67] However, despite all the formal and informal powers of the presidency, the president is limited in what he can accomplish on his own. In fact, the modern president is one individual at the top of a large and complex organization called the presidency, which itself heads the even larger executive branch of government. George Washington got by with no staff to speak of and consulted with his small cabinet of just three department heads, but citizens' expectations of government, and consequently the sheer size of the government, have grown considerably since then, and so has the machinery designed to manage that government.

Today the executive branch is composed of the cabinet with its fifteen departments, the Executive Office of the President, and the White House staff, amounting altogether to hundreds of agencies and two million civilian employees and almost a million and a half active-duty military employees. The modern president requires a vast bureaucracy to help him make the complex decisions he faces daily, but at the same time the bureaucracy itself presents a major management challenge for the president. The reality of the modern presidency is that the president is limited in his ability to accomplish what he wants by the necessity of dealing with this complex bureaucracy. The executive bureaucracy becomes part of the "how" through which the president tries to get what he wants—for the country, his party, or himself as a politician. But at the same time it becomes another "who," a player in government that goes after its own goals and whose goals can conflict with those of the president.

THE CABINET

Each department in the executive branch is headed by a presidential appointee; collectively these appointees form the president's cabinet. Today the cabinet comprises fifteen posts heading up fifteen departments. The newest cabinet-level department is the Department of Homeland Security, created in 2003. The cabinet is not explicitly set up in the Constitution, though the founders were well aware that the president would need specialty advisers in certain areas. President Washington's cabinet included just secretaries of state, treasury, and war (now called the secretary of defense). The original idea was for the cabinet members to be the president's men overseeing areas for which the president was responsible but that he was unable to supervise personally.

All of that has changed. Today the president considers the demands of organized interests and the political groups and the stature of his administration in putting together his cabinet. The number of departments has grown as various interests (for example, farmers, veterans, workers) have pressed for cabinet-level representation. Appointments to the cabinet have come to serve presidential political goals after the election rather than the goal of helping to run the government. Thus the cabinet secretaries typically are chosen to please—or at least not alienate—the organized interests of the constituencies most affected by the departments. Democrats and Republicans will not always choose the same sort of person to fill a cabinet post, however. For example, a Democratic president would be likely to choose a labor leader for secretary of labor, whereas a Republican president would be more likely to fill the post with a representative of the business community.

Presidents may also seek ethnic and gender balance in their cabinet choices. Bill Clinton followed through on his promise to appoint a cabinet of exceptional diversity, and George W. Bush's first- and second-term cabinets followed suit. Bush had two Hispanics, two African Americans, and two Asian Americans serving in his second-term cabinet; four cabinet members were women. In addition, the president chooses cabinet members who have independent stature and reputation before their appointments. President Obama borrowed from Abraham Lincoln's notion of building a "team of rivals" when he appointed Hillary Clinton (whom he defeated for the 2008 Democratic Party nomination) to be his first secretary of state and when he retained Bush's secretary of defense, Robert Gates. The president's sense of legitimacy is underscored by having top-quality people working in his administration. Last, but certainly not least, a president wants people who are ideologically similar to him in the policy areas they will be handling.[68] This is not easily achieved (and may not be possible) given the other considerations presidents must weigh.

The combination of these factors in making cabinet choices—political payoffs to organized interests, and the legitimacy provided by top people in the area—often results in a "team" that may not necessarily be focused on carrying out the president's agenda. There are exceptions to the typically guarded relationship between cabinet members and the president, but they prove the rule. President Kennedy

appointed his brother Robert as attorney general. George H. W. Bush appointed his very close friend and personal adviser James Baker as treasury secretary. In these cases, however, the close relationship with the president preceded appointment to the cabinet. In general, the political considerations of their appointment, coupled with their independent outlook, mean that cabinet members will provide the president with a variety of views and perspectives. They do not usually, as a group, place loyalty to the president's agenda above other considerations in their advice to the president. Consequently presidents tend to centralize their decision making by relying more on their advisers in the Executive Office of the President for advice they can trust.[69]

EXECUTIVE OFFICE OF THE PRESIDENT

The **Executive Office of the President** (EOP) is a collection of organizations that form the president's own bureaucracy. Instituted by Franklin Roosevelt in 1939, the EOP was designed specifically to serve the president's interests, supply information, and provide expert advice.[70] Among the organizations established in the EOP is the **Office of Management and Budget** (OMB), which helps the president exert control over the departments and agencies of the federal bureaucracy by overseeing all their budgets. The director of OMB works to ensure that the president's budget reflects his own policy agenda. Potential regulations created by the agencies of the national government must be approved by OMB before going into effect. This gives the president an additional measure of control over what the bureaucracy does.

Because modern presidents are held responsible for the performance of the economy, all presidents attempt to bring about healthy economic conditions. The job of the **Council of Economic Advisers** is to predict for presidents where the economy is going and to suggest ways to achieve economic growth without much inflation.

Other departments in the EOP include the **National Security Council** (NSC), which gives the president daily updates about events around the world. The NSC's job is to provide the president with information and advice about foreign affairs; however, the council's role has expanded at times into actually carrying out policy—sometimes illegally, as in the Iran-contra affair.[71] When the existing federal bureaucracy is less than fully cooperative with the president's wishes, some presidents have simply bypassed the agencies by running policy from the White House. One strategy that presidents since Nixon have followed is to appoint so-called policy czars who have responsibility for supervising policy across agencies. Obama has used this strategy extensively to coordinate policy in such areas as health care, energy, and the economy. He made over forty of these appointments in his first term, to establish firm White House control over the bureaucracy.[72]

Executive Office of the President collection of nine organizations that help the president with policy and political objectives

Office of Management and Budget organization within the EOP that oversees the budgets of departments and agencies

Council of Economic Advisers organization within the EOP that advises the president on economic matters

National Security Council organization within the EOP that provides foreign policy advice to the president

PROFILES IN CITIZENSHIP:
JOE BIDEN

NBC Universal/Getty Images

In the cold December that followed the 2010 midterm elections—with the 111th Congress in the waning days of its lame-duck session before the members headed home for their holiday break—the Obama administration still had a long Christmas wish list. Senate ratification of the New START Treaty with Russia was on its agenda, as were extending the tax cuts for those making under $250,000 a year and getting unemployment insurance extended for those especially hard hit by the recession. The administration

wanted to repeal the "don't ask, don't tell" policy in the military and get the DREAM Act passed, which would allow kids brought to this country by parents who entered illegally to find a path to citizenship through education or military service. After what President Obama described as the "shellacking" the Democrats took in the elections, no one thought he had a chance of getting any of those things done, but his administration was scrambling to end the year on a positive note.

Our interview with Vice President Joe Biden took place in the thick of the administration's negotiations with congressional Republicans over extending the tax cuts, and Biden was the negotiator-in-chief. We were slotted in for an appointment in his White House office between cabinet members who wanted to discuss the implications of agreeing to extend the Bush tax cuts for the country's wealthiest citizens, and Nancy Pelosi, then the Speaker of the House, and Harry Reid, the Senate majority leader, who were adamantly opposed to extending the tax cuts for the wealthy. The air in his White House office fizzed with power and excitement as Biden waited for a call from Senate minority leader Mitch McConnell to cement a deal that would, he argued, "save the economy from a double dip recession, make a compromise where the working poor continue to get their tax cuts even though we have to give temporarily on the upper end, where you see an increase in the stimulus that you'll end up with a million and a half more jobs than you would've next year, and where in the process we get the arms control treaty ratified and the trade deal."

Though the call didn't come while we were there, by late afternoon it would be announced that, due in large part to Biden's bargaining, the White House had gotten much of what it wanted in the tax cut deal. The repeal of "don't ask, don't tell" followed days later, as did ratification of the New START Treaty and passage of several other key pieces of legislation. While the administration didn't get everything it wanted—the tax cuts were extended for the wealthiest Americans as well as for those in the middle class and the DREAM Act did not pass—no one argued when President Obama hailed the lame-duck session as the most productive in decades.

That day in early December, the vice president clearly relished his role in brokering the deal that would make it possible for the rest to follow, and he was eloquent and hopeful about the possibilities of using power to good purpose. It's a great time to be in service, he says, what he calls "the single greatest opportunity" in his forty years of public life. "We are in one of those inflection points in history," he says, "I don't think it's occurred in American history but three times, where . . . if we do nothing, the momentum is going to drag us in the direction that makes it increasingly more difficult to correct the course." He discusses some of the biggest challenges we face—global warming, inequalities in education, our changing economy, and our standing in the world. "So you are at one of those moments where if we get it right, this can be a truly transformational moment where you look back twenty years from now and say, we had set the course of the nation, we put it on a trajectory that puts us in

WHITE HOUSE STAFF

Closest to the president, both personally and politically, are the members of the **White House Office**, which is included as a separate unit of the EOP. White House staffers have offices in the White House, and their appointments do not have to be confirmed by the Senate. Just as the public focus on the presidency has grown, so

has the size of the president's staff. The White House staff, around 60 members under Roosevelt, grew to the 300–400 range under Eisenhower and in 2013 rested at

> **White House Office** the approximately four hundred employees within the EOP who work most closely and directly with the president

the position to be able to lead the world in the twenty-first century or not."

> "I'VE BEEN HERE FOR EIGHT PRESIDENTS, AND I'M AN OPTIMIST BECAUSE I KNOW THE HISTORY OF THE STORY OF AMERICAN PROGRESS. I MEAN THE AMERICAN PEOPLE HAVE NEVER EVER, NEVER SHIED AWAY WHEN YOU'VE GIVEN THEM A VISION, A CHALLENGE . . . ."

Being a key actor in a transformational moment is a pretty heady place to be for someone who started life, as Biden often reminds people, as a working-class kid from Scranton, Pennsylvania. How he got from there to here is an unlikely story but in some ways a quintessentially American one. Biden was born to a large Irish-Catholic family that moved, in time, to Delaware, but it was in his "Grandpop" Finnegan's kitchen in Scranton that he learned the first principles of politics: that no one and no group is above any other and that politics was a matter of personal honor.[1] Those themes have guided Biden's career, through his college years, law school, a stint on the New Castle County Council, and a long-shot candidacy for the U.S. Senate when he was only twenty-nine years old that launched the thirty-six years he spent in that institution before he joined the Obama ticket and ascended to the vice presidency in 2009.

You can tell by his face, as he talks about his career, that it has been fun. He's been thrilled at the experiences it has brought his family (a granddaughter, for instance, plays basketball with the president and his daughters), and he has the satisfaction of knowing that what he does on a daily basis makes a difference in people's lives. He says, "My dad used to have an expression, he'd say it's a lucky person that gets up in the morning, puts both feet on the floor, knows what they are about to do, and thinks it still matters."

Today, at the pivotal moment in which he serves, he is enormously hopeful that the things he will help do will matter immensely both domestically and globally. He has more power than the traditional vice president, serving as an essential liaison with Congress for the Obama administration (witness his work with McConnell on the tax cut extension) and as a key adviser to the president on foreign policy and issues facing the middle class. Asked whether he can stay optimistic in the face of partisan battles at home and dire challenges abroad, he lights up. "Absolutely, I am absolutely optimistic," he says. "I've been here for eight presidents, and I'm an optimist because I know the history of the story of American progress. I mean the American people have never ever, never shied away when you've given them a vision, a challenge, and you know where you want to take it. They've never let the country down, never. That's not American exceptionalism. I would argue, as a student of history, that that's literally true, literally true; we rise to the occasion."

And the boy from Scranton is right in the middle of it. Here are some other words of advice from the vice president:

On the importance of confidence:

Look, . . . there are a lot of advantages, people don't all show up on the playing field with the same equipment, and I'm not talking intellect. The great advantage I had is that I don't ever remember a time my parents not drilling into me—"You're a man of your word, without your word you're not a man. Joey, nobody is better than you in the whole world, you're no better but nobody is better than you." My mother gave me absolute confidence. It was a gigantic, gigantic asset.

On keeping the republic:

I'd tell [students] to be engaged. . . . [Y]ou know that old quote from Plato, the penalty good men pay for not being engaged in politics is being governed by men worse than themselves. [Students] have nobody to blame but themselves, zero. My dad used to say never complain and never explain, and . . . that's exactly what I'd tell them . . . stop whining, get engaged. Number two, the political system is so wide open you can drive a Mack truck through it, so the idea that "Oh, God, I have to come from influence and money to have an impact?" Simply not true.

1. Joe Biden, *Promises to Keep.* (New York: Random House, 2007), xv.

Source: Joe Biden talked with Christine Barbour, Gerald Wright, and Patrick Haney on December 6, 2010.

about 460.[73] The organization of the White House Office has also varied greatly from administration to administration. Presidential scholar James P. Pfiffner has described

> **chief of staff** the person who oversees the operations of all White House staff and controls access to the president

this organization generally in terms of the following three functional categories: policymaking and coordination, outreach and communications, and internal coordination (see Figure 8.4).

Central to the White House Office is the president's **chief of staff**, who is responsible for the operation of all White House personnel (see "*Profiles in Citizenship:* Rahm Emanuel" in Chapter 16 for a conversation with President

FIGURE 8.4 **ORGANIZATION OF THE WHITE HOUSE OFFICE**

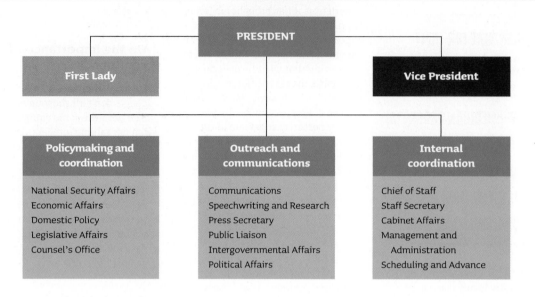

Obama's first chief of staff). Depending on how much power the president delegates, the chief of staff may decide who gets appointments with the president and whose memoranda he reads. The chief of staff also has a big hand in hiring and firing decisions at the White House. Critics claim that the chief of staff isolates the president by removing him from the day-to-day control of his administration, but demands on the president have grown to the point that a chief of staff is now considered a necessity. Presidents Carter and Ford tried to get by without a chief of staff, but each gave up and appointed one in the middle of his term to make his political life more manageable.[74]

The chief of staff and the other top assistants to the president have to be his eyes and ears, and they act on his behalf every day. The criteria for a good staffer are very different from those for a cabinet selection. First and foremost, the president demands loyalty. That is why presidents typically bring along old friends and close campaign staff as personal assistants. For instance, Barack Obama brought with him several longtime close associates: Rahm Emanuel, who was a friend and colleague from Chicago politics; and three senior advisers, David Axelrod, Valerie Jarrett, and Pete Rouse, who replaced Emanuel when he left Washington to run for mayor of Chicago. Rouse was replaced in 2011 by William Daley, son of a former Chicago mayor and himself a former commerce secretary in the Clinton administration. When Daley resigned he was replaced by Jack Lew, who had long experience on Capitol Hill, on Wall Street, and as OMB director under Clinton and Obama.[75] Lew subsequently took over as secretary of the treasury following the resignation of Timothy

Geithner, who had the top job in the treasury during Obama's first term.

A general principle that presidents employ is that their staffs exist only to serve them. When things go well, the president gets the credit; when they do not, the staff take the blame, sometimes even being fired or asked to resign. Such replacements are not unusual at all as presidents change personnel and management strategies to maximize their policy effectiveness and political survival.

The different backgrounds and perspectives of the White House staff and the cabinet mean that the two groups are often at odds. The cabinet secretaries, dedicated to large departmental missions, want presidential attention for those efforts; the staff want the departments to put the president's immediate political goals ahead of their departmental interests. As a result, the past several decades have seen more and more centralization of important policymaking in the White House, and more decisions being taken away from the traditional turf of the departments.[76]

THE VICE PRESIDENT

For most of our history, vice presidents have not been important actors in presidential administrations. Because the original Constitution awarded the vice presidency to the second-place presidential candidate, these officials were seen as potential rivals to the president and were excluded from most decisions and any meaningful policy responsibility. That was corrected with the Twelfth Amendment (1804), which provided for electors to select both the president and the vice president. However, custom for most of the period since then has put a premium on balancing the ticket in terms of regional, ideological, or political interests, which has meant that the person in the second spot is typically not close to the president. In fact, the vice president has sometimes been a rival even in modern times, as when John F. Kennedy appointed Lyndon Johnson, the Senate majority leader from Texas, as his vice president in 1960 in an effort to gain support from the southern states.

Since the Constitution provides only that the vice president act as president of the Senate, which carries no power unless there is a tie vote, most vice presidents have tried to make small, generally insignificant jobs seem important, often admitting that theirs was not an enviable post. Thomas Marshall, Woodrow Wilson's vice president, observed in his inaugural address that "I believe I'm entitled to make a few remarks because I'm about to enter a four-year period of silence."[77] Roosevelt's first vice president, John Nance Garner, expressed his disdain for the office even more forcefully, saying that the job "is not worth a pitcher of warm piss."[78]

Ultimately, however, the job of vice president is what the president wants it to be. President Reagan largely ignored George H. W. Bush, for instance, whereas Al Gore, serving under President Clinton, had a central advisory role.[79] Dick Cheney brought a good deal of Washington experience upon which President George W. Bush relied heavily, so much so that many observers have portrayed Cheney as the real power behind the throne.[80]

President Obama's vice president, Joe Biden, brought the heft of a lengthy résumé from six terms in the U.S. Senate and his longtime service on the Senate Foreign Relations Committee. Obama did not relinquish as much authority to his vice president as Bush did, but Biden proved to be an effective, independent, and valued policy adviser to the president. He is used as an administration spokesperson on a wide range of issues, including his specialty area of foreign relations.[81]

Thus, even though the office of the vice presidency is not a powerful one, vice presidents who establish a relationship of trust with the president can have a significant impact on public policy. The office is important as well, of course, because it is the vice president who assumes the presidency if the president dies, is incapacitated, resigns, or is impeached. Many vice presidents also find the office a good launching pad for a presidential bid. Four of the last ten vice presidents—Lyndon Johnson, Richard Nixon, Gerald Ford, and George H. W. Bush—ended up in the

Right-Hand Man

In any administration the vice president has only as much power and influence as his or her president allows, and vice presidents traditionally were relegated to ceremonial duties. But that trend has changed significantly in recent administrations. Former vice president Al Gore served as a key advisor to President Bill Clinton in the 1990s, a trend that has continued in the Bush and Obama administrations.

Oval Office, although Al Gore did not enjoy similar success in 2000.

THE FIRST SPOUSE

The office of the "first lady" is undergoing immense changes that reflect the tremendous flux in Americans' perceptions of the appropriate roles for men and women. Even the term "first lady" seems strangely antiquated in an age when a woman almost won a major party's nomination for the presidency and another was a vice presidential candidate, and particularly so when the runaway favorite for the 2016 Democratic nomination is Hillary Clinton, making the "first spouse" also an ex-president.

But the office of first lady has always contained controversial elements, partly the result of conflict over the role of women in politics, but also because the intimate relationship between husband and wife gives the presidential spouse, an unelected position, unique insight into and access to the president's mind and decision-making processes. For all the checks and balances in the American system, there is no way to check the influence of the first spouse. It will be interesting to see whether "first gentlemen" become as controversial as their female counterparts (see the box "Madam President?" for the prospects of a woman president).

MADAM PRESIDENT?

In the United States the idea of Madam President is just that—still an idea—although the 2008 election brought it closer to reality than ever before and Hillary Clinton is widely expected to run again in 2016. In many other countries, however, women chief executives are business as usual. Women have served as elected national leaders or appointed prime ministers in more than fifty countries, beginning in 1960 with Sirimavo Bandaranaike of Sri Lanka, the first elected woman prime minister; in 1980 Vigdis Finnbogadottir of Iceland became the first elected woman head of state.[1]

Why has the United States lagged behind other nations in electing a woman to its highest political office? American women were among the first women in the world to gain the right to vote, in 1920, but women leaders have served or are serving in countries such as Pakistan and Senegal, where women currently have fewer civil rights than do women in the United States. Culture does not seem to offer an explanation, because women have been chief executives in Islamic, South American, southern European, Asian, and African countries, where the social and cultural separation between male and female roles has been most

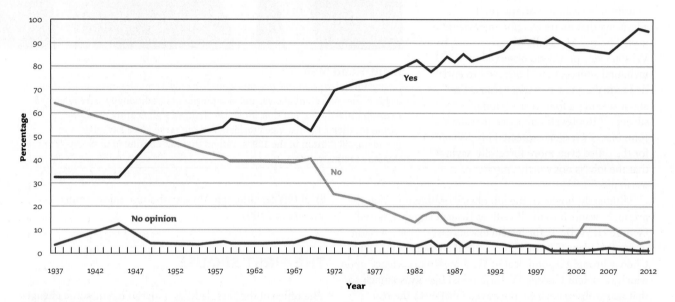

Note: Respondents were asked, "If your party nominated a generally well-qualified person for president who happened to be . . . a woman, would you vote for that person?"

Sources: Authors' update of data from the California State University Social Sciences Research and Instructional Council, www.csubak.edu/ssric/Modules/Others/disk1/gallup.htm; and Gallup polls accessed through the Roper Center for Public Opinion Research.

First ladies' attempts to play a political role are almost as old as the Republic. In fact, as her husband, John, was preparing to help with the writing of the Constitution, future first lady Abigail Adams admonished him to "remember the ladies," although there is no evidence that he actually did. Much later, in 1919, first lady Edith Bolling Galt Wilson virtually took over the White House following the illness of her husband, Woodrow, controlling who had access to him and perhaps even issuing presidential decisions in his name. And Eleanor Roosevelt, like her husband, Franklin, took vigorously to political life and kept up an active public role even after his death.

But since the 1960s and the advent of the women's movement, the role of the first lady is seen by the public as less an issue of individual personality and quirks, and more a national commentary on how women in general should behave. As a surrogate for our cultural confusion on what role women should play, the office of the first lady has come under uncommon scrutiny, especially when she takes on a more overtly political role, as did Rosalyn Carter, who even attended cabinet meetings at her husband's request. Public

pronounced. Furthermore, countries with social and cultural traditions more similar to the United States, such as Britain and Canada, have also had women as national leaders.

So why has the United States not had a female president? In public opinion polls, Americans seem to indicate that they are willing to give it a try. In 2012 a Gallup poll found that 95 percent of Americans would vote for a "well-qualified woman" for president,[2] up from 78 percent in 1984 and only 53 percent in 1969.[3] (See figure.) Some people question whether Americans really would support a woman for president, however. One experimental survey found that 26 percent of those polled felt angry about the prospect of a woman president, leading the researchers to believe that some Americans report supporting a woman for president only because they know it is a socially desirable answer.[4]

Another likely explanation for the lack of a woman leader in the United States is that there aren't many women in the pipeline, in jobs like vice president, senator, or state governor, which generate presidential candidates. This is partly because women enter politics on average a decade later than do men, meaning they begin climbing the political ladder later, as well.[5] The number of female senators from both parties continues to rise, but it remains well below the average percentage of women in American society. Perhaps more important, the number of female governors (four of our past five presidents were governors)

has remained limited. Only six women (three Democrats and three Republicans) currently serve as governors. In some ways, 2008 was a groundbreaking year for women candidates. Before then, the only woman candidate for vice president for either party was Geraldine Ferraro, who ran with Walter Mondale in 1984, and only a handful of women (for example, Carol Moseley Braun and Elizabeth Dole) had tried to win the presidential nomination. In 2008 Hillary Clinton nearly won the Democratic nomination, and Sarah Palin, then governor of Alaska, was chosen as the vice presidential candidate for the Republicans. Though these breakthroughs put, as Clinton stated, cracks in the glass ceiling, they also underscore the paucity of women candidates in the pool; there were no serious contenders for the presidency in 2012. Stay tuned, though. It is entirely likely that 2016 will see Clinton running on the Democratic ticket, and perhaps a Republican woman may run again as a vice presidential candidate if New Mexico governor Susana Martinez can be persuaded to enter the race. (See *Profiles in Citizenship* on pp. 122–123.)

Nevertheless, several researchers point to important advances for women in prominent political positions that may lead to a deeper pool of women candidates for president in the future. Nancy Pelosi, D-Calif., served as Speaker of the House of Representatives, the highest leadership position in the House. The continued appointment of women to key executive posts dealing with international affairs, especially

including two secretaries of state, also demonstrates that women can handle crisis-filled political situations. As more women like Clinton and Palin become involved in presidential elections, Americans will grow more accustomed to seeing women in these positions of power.

Several organizations are working toward the goal of electing more women to office, and to the office of president, in the United States. Political action committees like EMILY's List and WISH List work with the primary aim of raising money for women candidates for major political offices. The White House Project was a nonpartisan initiative dedicated to raising the public's awareness of women political leaders in the United States and to putting a woman in the White House, but it folded in 2013 for financial reasons.

1. The History Net, "Women Prime Ministers and Presidents—20th Century Heads of State," womenshistory.about.com/od/rulers20th/a/women_heads.htm.

2. Andrew Kohut, "Are Americans Ready to Elect a Female President," Pew Research Center, pewresearch.org/pubs/474/female-president.

3. California State University Social Sciences Research and Instructional Council, "65 Years of Gallup Polling. Mystery Table Three: Willingness to Support a Woman for President," www.csubak.edu/ssric/modules/other/disk1/gallup.htm.

4. "Americans' Support for a Female President Is Significantly Exaggerated" (news release), www.niu.edu/pubaffairs/releases/2007/jan/research.shtml.

5. Eleanor Clift and Tom Brazaitis, *Madam President* (New York: Routledge, 2003), 227.

objections to her activities and her position as informal presidential adviser showed that the role of the first lady was controversial even in the late 1970s. Hillary Rodham Clinton shook up public expectations of the first lady's role even more. A successful lawyer who essentially earned the family income while her husband, Bill, served four low-paid terms as governor of Arkansas, Hillary was the target of both public acclaim and public hatred. Her nontraditional tenure as first lady was capped in 2000, at the end of Clinton's second term, by her election as the junior senator from New York. Eight years later she made her own nearly

successful run for the Democratic nomination for president and then became Obama's secretary of state.

The politically safest strategy for a first lady appears to be to stick with a noncontroversial moral issue and ask people to do what we all agree they ought to do. Lady Bird Johnson beseeched us to support highway beautification; Nancy Reagan suggested, less successfully, that we "just say no" to drugs; and Laura Bush focused on the issues of education, youth, and literacy.

First lady Michelle Obama said flatly that she did not intend to take on an active policymaking role. "I can't do everything,"

Alex Wong/Getty Images News/Getty Images

Writing Their Own Job Description

First Lady Michelle Obama shares a giggle with Hillary Rodham Clinton at an event in 2010. Clinton redefined the role of first lady, taking on policy issues during her husband's administration. She later served as a U.S. senator and ran a formidable campaign for president, eventually being appointed secretary of state. Michelle Obama has for the most part chosen a more traditional path, raising public awareness about health and nutrition and reaching out to military families.

she explained. A committed and active mother to two children still at home, she wants to keep their lives as normal as possible while living in the White House. Insofar as she takes on a public role, it has thus far been in the noncontroversial styles of Reagan and Bush, as an advocate for working parents, particularly those in the military, who juggle career loads with the demands of raising families, and as a strong supporter of a healthy diet as an antidote to rising childhood obesity rates.[82] Avoiding policy and partisan conflict, Michelle Obama has had popularity ratings much higher than the president's.[83]

PAUSE AND REVIEW:

WHO, WHAT, HOW

The purpose of the executive bureaucracy is to help the president do his job by providing information, expertise, and advice. But while the president's closest advisers are usually focused on his interests, various cabinet officers, staff members, and agency heads may develop agendas of their own that may be at odds with those of the president. He has an easier time controlling members of the EOP, whose job is more clearly to serve him. The vice president and first lady are also more likely to find an agenda that is consistent with the president's.

IN YOUR OWN WORDS » Describe the organization and functions of the executive office.

THE PRESIDENTIAL PERSONALITY
Translating leadership style and image into presidential power

Effective management of the executive branch is one feature of a successful presidency, but there are many others. Historians and presidential observers regularly distinguish presidential success and failure, even to the extent of actually rating presidential greatness.[84] Political scientists also assess presidential success, usually in terms of how frequently presidents can get their legislative programs passed by Congress.[85] We have already discussed the powers of the president, the challenges to success provided by the need for popularity, the difficulties of dealing with Congress, and the enormous management tasks faced by the president. In this section we look at the personal resources of a president that lead to success or contribute to failure. We begin by exploring what kinds of people are driven to become president in the first place.

CLASSIFYING PRESIDENTIAL CHARACTER

Most presidents share some personality characteristics—giant ambition and large egos, for instance—but this does not mean that they are carbon copies of one another. They clearly differ in fundamental ways. A number of scholars have developed classification schemes of presidential personalities. Each of these schemes is based on the expectation that knowing key dimensions of individual presidential personalities will help explain, or even predict, how presidents will behave in certain circumstances. The most famous of these schemes was developed by James David Barber, who classified presidents on two dimensions: their energy level (passive or active) and their orientation toward life (positive or negative).[86]

Some of our best and most popular presidents have been active-positives. They have had great energy and a very positive orientation toward the job of being president. Franklin Roosevelt, John F. Kennedy, Bill Clinton, and

Barack Obama represent this type. Others have had less energy (passives) or have been burdened by the job of being president (negatives). They have acted out their roles, according to Barber, as they thought they should, out of duty or obligation. Ronald Reagan and George W. Bush fit the model of the passive-positive president. They liked being leaders but believed that the job was one of delegating and setting the tone rather than of taking an active policymaking role. Richard Nixon is usually offered as one of the clearest examples of an active-negative president; he had lots of energy but could not enjoy the job of being president.

Assessing individual personalities is a fascinating enterprise, but it is fraught with danger. Few politicians fit neatly into Barber's boxes (or the categories of other personality theorists) in an unambiguous way. Although some scholars find that personality analysis adds greatly to their understanding of the differences among presidencies, others discount it altogether, claiming that it leads one to overlook the ways in which rules and external forces have shaped the modern presidency.[87]

PRESIDENTIAL STYLE

In addition to their personality differences, each president strives to create a **presidential style**, or an image that captures symbolically who he is for the American people and for leaders of other nations. These personal differences in how presidents present themselves are real, but they are also carefully cultivated. Each also strives to distinguish himself from his predecessors, to set himself apart, and to give hope for new, and presumably better, presidential leadership.[88]

For example, Harry Truman was known for his straight, sometimes profane, talk and no-nonsense decision making. In contrast, Dwight Eisenhower developed his "Victorious General" image as a statesman above the fray of petty day-to-day politics. John F. Kennedy, whose term followed Eisenhower's, evoked a theme of "getting the country moving again" and embodied this with a personal image of youth and energy.

In the wake of Watergate and Richard Nixon's disgrace, Jimmy Carter hit a winning note with a style promising honesty and competent government. Carter was honest, but his self-doubts and admissions that the United States faced problems that government might not be able to solve disappointed many Americans. In contrast, Ronald Reagan's "it's-morning-in-America" optimism and his calming, grandfatherly presence were soaked up by an eager public.

> **presidential style** image projected by the president that represents how he would like to be perceived at home and abroad

Courtesy of Ronald Reagan Library

The Great Communicator
This was the label many people applied to President Ronald Reagan because of his ability to connect with the American public. His effectiveness as a communicator had little to do with explaining complex policy decisions. Rather, he conveyed a sense of confidence, trustworthiness, and warmth. He made people feel good.

Bill Clinton's style combined the image of the highly intellectual Rhodes scholar with that of a compassionate leader, famous for "feeling America's pain." That carefully managed image could not disguise the fact that Clinton was also a man of large appetites, however, from his jogging breaks to eat at McDonald's to his extramarital affairs. While people approved of Clinton's leadership through the end of his presidency, a majority of citizens noted concerns about his honesty and moral character.

George W. Bush came into office with an opposite set of characteristics. Widely perceived as a nonintellectual who joked that C students could grow up to be president, he cultivated the image of the chief executive officer he was: a president primarily interested in results, not academic debates, who was willing to set a course and leave others to get the job done. Despite a reputation for hard drinking and high living in his youth, including a drunk driving arrest, Bush's pledge of abstinence, traditional marriage,

FIGURE 8.5　PRESIDENTIAL STYLE: A COMPARISON OF THE PUBLIC'S IMAGE OF CLINTON, BUSH, AND OBAMA

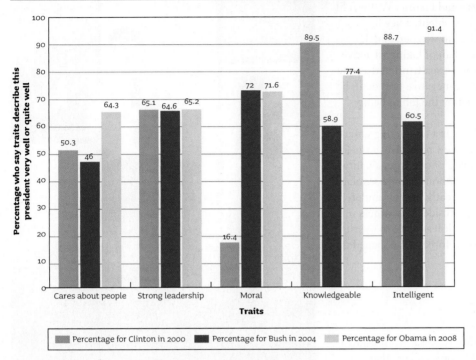

Source: Calculated by authors from the American National Elections Studies Cumulative File.

and frequent references to Jesus Christ helped to put a moral tone on his presidency that Clinton's had lacked. Figure 8.5 compares public opinion about presidential character for Clinton, as he left office in 2000; Bush, during his 2004 reelection campaign; and Obama, after the 2008 election.

Barack Obama brings an even-keeled disposition to the White House. His calm demeanor (symbolized by the unofficial slogan of his first campaign—"No Drama Obama") remained consistent through the economic and environmental crises of the first term of his presidency. As he says of himself, "I don't get too high when things are going well, and I don't get too low when things are going tough."[89] Obama's image incorporates elements of the styles of several of his predecessors, combining Ronald Reagan's optimism, Bill Clinton's braininess, and George W. Bush's faith and commitment to family.

At least one part of his presidential style seems to be uniquely Obama's own. In his first term, he brought to office a deep commitment to bipartisanship that at least one observer said "had all the markings of an obsessive disorder" given the president's persistence in attempting to find common ground with an opposition party that had made defeating him its chief goal.[90] Many of Obama's own supporters were infuriated by what they viewed as too conciliatory an approach on his part, and were heartened to

see that, by 2011, Obama was taking a more confrontational stance toward his own campaign and negotiations with congressional Republicans.

Presidential style is an important but subtle means by which presidents communicate. It can be an opportunity for enhancing public support and thereby the president's ability to deal effectively with Congress and the media. But any style has its limitations, and the same behavioral and attitudinal characteristics of a style that help a president at one juncture can prove a liability later. Furthermore, as Clinton's experience shows, the president does not always have total control over the image of him that the public sees. Political enemies and an investigative press can combine to counter the image the president wants to project. Because public perception is tied so closely to leadership ability, a significant portion of the president's staffers end up concerning themselves with "image management."

PAUSE AND REVIEW:

WHO, WHAT, HOW

In the matter of presidential style and personality, the person with the most at stake is undoubtedly the president. His goals are popularity, legislative success, support for his party, and a favorable judgment in the history books. He functions in a number of policy roles as the head of government, but he also serves as our head of state, a role that is merely symbolic at times but that can be of tremendous importance for presidential power in times of national crisis or in conflicts with other nations. Because presidents' formal powers to fulfill these functions are limited, and their informal powers depend on their popularity with citizens and with the Washington elite, the personality and style that allow them to win popularity are crucial.

IN YOUR OWN WORDS ➤➤ Evaluate the importance of leadership style and image as they relate to presidential power.

The Presidents Club

» THE CITIZENS AND THE PRESIDENCY

"Rolling election" by public opinion poll

There are more than 300 million American citizens and only one president. While we all have a reasonable chance of meeting our members of Congress, only the luckiest few will actually shake hands with the president of the United States. With connections this remote, how can we talk about the relationship between the citizens and the president?

Perhaps in the days before technology made mass communication so easy and routine, we could not. But today, while we may never dance at an inaugural ball or even wave at the president from afar, we can know our presidents intimately (and often far more intimately than we want to!). Through the medium of television, we can watch them board airplanes, speak to foreign leaders, swing golf clubs or play basketball, dance with their wives, and speak directly to us. Skilled communicators, especially like Ronald Reagan and Barack Obama, can touch us personally—inspiring us and infuriating us as if we were family and friends.

So it is fitting, in a way, that the citizens of the United States have the ultimate power over the president. We elect him (and someday her), it is true, but our power goes beyond a once-every-four-years vote of approval or disapproval. Modern polling techniques, as we have seen, allow us to conduct a "rolling election," as the media and the politicians themselves track popular approval of the president throughout his term. The presidential strategy of going public is made possible because all Americans—citizens, president, and members of Congress—know just where the president stands with the public and how much political capital he has to spend.

In 1998 and 1999 we saw perhaps the clearest example of the power that citizens' support can give to a president in the fate of Bill Clinton's imperiled presidency. After a lengthy investigation, independent prosecutor Kenneth Starr sent a report to Congress on September 9, 1998, that he claimed provided grounds for Clinton's impeachment on perjury and obstruction-of-justice charges. As graphic details of Clinton's behavior were made public, Clinton's personal approval ratings sank, yet his job approval ratings stayed high. Questioned on specifics, people said they disapproved of Clinton's moral character and found his

© Ken Cedeno/Corbis

A Very Exclusive Club

One of the great innovations of modern democracy is the peaceful transfer of power. In 2008, presidents past, present, and future met amiably in the Oval Office. From left to right are George H. W. Bush, Barack Obama, George W. Bush, Bill Clinton, and Jimmy Carter. Said the younger Bush to the incoming president, Obama, "We want you to succeed. . . . Whether we're Democrat or Republican, we all care deeply about this country. . . . All of us who have served in this office understand that the office transcends the individual."

behavior (having an affair with a White House intern) repellent, but they thought the impeachment movement was politically motivated and that Clinton's private behavior had no impact on his ability to do his job. They seemed to find him wanting in the symbolic head-of-state role we discussed earlier in this chapter but continued to approve of him as the head of government. In clear rejection of the investigation of the president, Americans went against tradition on Election Day 1998: instead of handing the president's party its usual midterm loss, they supported the Democrats so strongly that they gained five seats in Congress. The day after Clinton was impeached, on December 11, his approval ratings with the American public hit a high of 73 percent.[91] Had they fallen it would have been much harder for Democrats and moderates in the House and the Senate to support him and the president may well have lost his job.

In a similar vein, although the details are strikingly different, the presidency of George W. Bush also came to depend on unusually high opinion ratings where one might not have expected to find them. Bush claimed the presidency after a contested election in which he received fewer popular votes than his opponent and that was resolved by the Supreme Court in a five-to-four vote that many believed was politically motivated. Many pundits predicted that his presidency would be a one-term failure. While his early approval ratings showed he was enjoying something on the low end of a traditional honeymoon, by the summer of 2001, his ratings were clearly sinking. In September, however, the unthinkable happened. When terrorists flew hijacked planes into the World Trade Center and the Pentagon and launched America into the war on terrorism, Bush was given a clean slate on which to write his presidential legacy. Making the war against terrorism the keystone of his presidency, his portrayal of the conflict in simple terms reassured Americans, and his early military successes solidified their support for him. His approval rating hit 90 percent—higher than any other president since records have been kept. With high ratings, Bush was as powerful as, if not more powerful than, if he had won the election in a landslide, and the 2002 election again failed to show the traditional midterm loss as Bush's efforts swept Republicans into Congress—building slightly the majority in the House of Representatives and creating a Republican majority in the Senate.

In President Obama's case, he rode in to office with high approval numbers, perhaps due to the historic nature of his election, but with the economy in crisis they soon slipped. Within a year he had used what political capital they gave him in getting his health care bill passed, a contentious and partisan period in which Republicans said that if they could just defeat the bill it would prove to be his Waterloo.[92] They didn't defeat it, but they campaigned against it and won handily in the midterm election of 2010. Having made the defeat of Obama a priority,[93] they undertook a concerted policy of ensuring that he had no legislative successes to run on and could not be seen as an effective president, motivating him to undertake the "We Cannot Wait" campaign of executive actions to do what he could without Congress. With no legislative success to speak of after 2009 and with an economy he could not stimulate and a workforce he could not support, Obama's opinion ratings languished. The fact that they were not lower caused some analysts, as we saw, to speculate that perhaps his personal likeability and the fact that Americans still blamed Bush for the economy gave him a margin for error.

Clinton's approval ratings eventually sank back to normal; Bush's ended up dropping steadily into the low 30s, the worst of any president except Richard Nixon. Obama's fell after he failed to achieve a "grand bargain" to resolve the debt ceiling crisis in the summer of 2011, but gradually crept back up to hover around 50 percent by the time of the 2012 election, when he was reelected with 51 percent of the popular vote. Subsequently, the political malaise that plagues Washington, D.C., continued to take a toll on the president's job approval ratings as they slipped into the middle and low 40s. How can we understand the very unusual reaction of Americans who seem to approve of presidents they don't like, like presidents they don't approve of, and reelect both?

For one thing, the public judges presidents on different criteria in part because the office has different roles to fill. On which of the president's roles is the public being asked its opinion? Americans may have disapproved of President Clinton as head of state, but they certainly supported him as head of government. The opposite might be more the case for President Bush. Second, under everyday circumstances, questions concerning presidential job and personal approval seem straightforward, but the strength of the economy, current political conflicts, external events, and the personal foibles of the president can alter the public's assessment in complex ways that either enhance or limit the president's power. Finally, the institution of the American presidency, like most of the rest of the government designed by the framers, was meant to be insulated from the whims of the public. It is an irony that in contemporary politics the president is often more indebted to the citizens for his power than he is to the Electoral College, Congress, the courts, or any of the political elites the founders trusted to stabilize American government.

IN YOUR OWN WORDS >> Give examples of ways in which public opinion affects the relationship between citizens and the president.

LET'S REVISIT: WHAT'S AT STAKE...

The Constitution may be a study in ambiguity on some issues, but on others it is crystal clear. Congress makes the laws. Presidents can veto or they can sign laws, but when they do the latter, it is their job to enforce the law that Congress passed. The principle of checks and balances depends on this back-and-forth power-wielding arrangement. If one branch could impose its will on the others without limit, checks and balances would disappear.

Still, controversy remains about how strong the executive power should be. Obama and Bush faced different Congresses with different motives for complaint. Although both were attempting to bypass an institution that the founders had intended as a check, for each the stakes were different.

When Obama threatened to act if Congress would not, what he had at stake was the legacy of his presidency. His actions were intended to goad a Congress to action that had determined not to give him any legislative victories and to keep campaign promises he had made that were at risk of being thwarted by that inactive Congress. His preference was for bipartisan congressional action and his actions came from frustration that Congress was doing nothing, not from any conviction that the president should have more powers than the Constitution gave him.

George W. Bush on the other hand was dealing with a Congress bending over backward to work with him in the difficult days after 9/11. His aggressive use of signing statements had a different purpose. For the Bush administration, as we saw, what was at stake was a more muscular presidency, one that wasn't, as they thought, emasculated in the wake of the Watergate scandal. Signing statements were not the only strategy Bush pursued to strengthen the office, but they were a clear attempt to move the presidency beyond its constitutional limits. Other presidents have used signing statements to assert their right to preserve their constitutional powers, but they have not used the statements to expand them.[94]

For Congress, the stakes in dealing with each president were high, but different. For the Congress that Obama faced the stakes were partisan—how the Republican Party could maintain internal partisan harmony while pursuing long-term partisan objectives. Constitutional issues were almost afterthoughts because Obama's actions were all arguably inside the limits of what the Constitution allowed, even if Congress didn't like them. Said one expert on presidential power: "This is what presidents do. . . . It's taken Obama two years to get there, but this has happened throughout history. You can't be in that office with all its enormous responsibilities—when things don't happen, you get blamed for it—and not exercise all the powers that have accrued to it over time."[95] Additionally, Obama's executive actions were transparent—Congress could see them and take action if it liked, the Supreme Court could rule on the executive actions if they were challenged, and the public could respond by holding the president accountable if they disagreed.

In the case of Bush's signing statements, constitutional issues were central because his actions essentially allowed the executive to rewrite the bills, ignoring what he didn't like and keeping what he did, and keeping it as quiet as possible, with no way for Congress to respond legislatively. As Bruce Fein, a former official in the Reagan Justice Department, said, "This is an attempt by the president to have the final word on his own constitutional powers, which eliminates the checks and balances that keep the country a democracy. There is no way for an independent judiciary to check his assertions of power, and Congress isn't doing it either. So this is moving us toward an unlimited executive power."[96]

And, of course, the stakes could not have been higher for the American public. The point of checks and balances is to limit the power wielded by any one branch, so that the government as a whole would stay limited in power, and to ensure that individual liberties would be safe from government encroachment. Very high stakes, indeed.

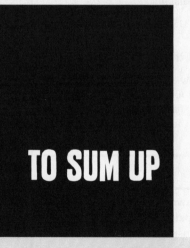

TO SUM UP

for CQ Press

Sharpen your skills with **SAGE edge** at http://edge.sagepub.com/barbour7e. **SAGE edge for students** provides a personalized approach to help you accomplish your coursework goals in an easy-to-use learning environment.

The Double Expectations Gap

Presidents face a double expectations gap when it comes to their relationship with the American public. The first gap is between what the president must promise in order to gain office and the limitations put on the president by the powers granted by the Constitution. The second gap occurs between conflicting roles. An American president must function as both a political head of government and an apolitical head of state, and often these two roles conflict.

head of state (p. 282)
head of government (p. 283)

The Evolution of the American Presidency

When it came to defining the functions and powers of the president, the founders devised rules that both empowered and limited the president. While some of the founders argued for a strong leader with far-reaching powers, others argued for several executives who would check each other's power. The constitutional compromise gives us an executive that has certain powers and independence, yet is checked by congressional and judicial power.

impeachment (p. 286)
chief administrator (p. 287)
cabinet (p. 287)
commander-in-chief (p. 287)
chief foreign policy maker (p. 288)
treaties (p. 288)
executive agreements (p. 288)
State of the Union address (p. 288)
presidential veto (p. 288)
signing statements (p. 292)
executive orders (p. 292)
senatorial courtesy (p. 293)
solicitor general (p. 293)
pardoning power (p. 294)
inherent powers (p. 292)

Presidential Politics

The president is in a constant struggle with Congress and the public for the furthering of his legislative agenda. The president needs both congressional cooperation and public approval in order to fulfill campaign promises. The chief executive uses several strategies to achieve these goals, including going public and building coalitions in Congress.

power to persuade (p. 300)
going public (p. 300)
cycle effect (p. 301)
honeymoon period (p. 301)
legislative liaison (p. 303)
divided government (p. 303)

Managing the Presidential Establishment

The presidential establishment includes the cabinet, the Executive Office of the President, and the White House Office—a huge bureaucracy that has grown considerably since the days of George Washington's presidency. Although the resources are vast, managing such a large and complex organization presents its own problems for the president. The president's closest advisers are generally focused on his interests, but the variety of other staff and agency heads—often with their own agendas and often difficult to control—can make life difficult for the chief executive.

Executive Office of the President (p. 307)
Office of Management and Budget (p. 307)
Council of Economic Advisors (p. 307)
National Security Council (p. 307)
White House Office (p. 308)
chief of staff (p. 309)

The Presidential Personality

We have seen two periods of presidential leadership so far. The first period, called the traditional presidency, which lasted until the 1930s, describes chief executives who mainly lived within the limits of their constitutional powers. Since then, in the modern presidency, a more complex relationship has existed between the president and the American citizens, in which presidents branch out to use more informal powers yet remain indebted to public approval for this expansion.

presidential style (p. 315)

The Citizens and the Presidency

Americans get to know their presidents via the media as much as through any policy they make. Public opinion polling functions as a "rolling election," connecting the president to citizens on an ongoing basis.

ENGAGE

Visit a presidential library.
There are thirteen presidential libraries, each dedicated to preserving "the raw materials of history." Visit one to get a look at the legacies that our leaders have chosen to leave behind. You can find information and links to online exhibits via the **National Archives**.

Visit the White House.
The White House home page provides recent presidential addresses, pictures, information on key administration officials and presidential and vice presidential family members, as well as facts about the White House and the executive branch.

Get involved with a presidential campaign.
Presidential primaries and elections provide a great opportunity to engage in the political process. Research the candidates, and decide on one who you feel you can support. Then put yourself to work by volunteering for a campaign.

EXPLORE

Gibbs, Nancy, and Michael Duffy. 2012. *The President's Club: Inside the World's Most Exclusive Fraternity.* New York: Simon & Schuster. This book offers a fascinating glimpse into the nature of the most powerful position in the world, and how the men who have filled it since World War II have both shaped and been shaped by it.

McClellan, Scott. 2008. *What Happened: Inside the Bush White House and Washington's Culture of Deception.* New York: PublicAffairs. The author, who served as White House press secretary during the tenure of George W. Bush, charts the administration's controversial behavior in the run-up to the war in Iraq, and offers an incisive analysis of the well-known "Plame incident."

***Lincoln.* 2012.** Based on historian Doris Kearns Goodwin's biography *Team of Rivals,* this film (directed by Steven Spielberg) examines Abraham Lincoln's relationship with his somewhat adversarial cabinet in the waning years of the Civil War.

***The West Wing* (TV series). 1999–2006.** This award-winning television series was about a fictitious U.S. president and the political issues he and the members of his administration must address.

Miller Center of Public Affairs. The Miller Center's American President Online Reference Resource is an information clearinghouse on the U.S. presidency. Profiles of each U.S. president include an at-a-glance section and links to essays, speeches, and additional resources on the president and his administration.

9

THE BUREAUCRACY

IN YOUR OWN WORDS   After you've read this chapter, you will be able to

»   Explain how the characteristics and features of bureaucracy influence decision making.

»   Outline the organization and roles of the federal bureaucracy.

»   Describe power struggles between political appointees and professional bureaucrats.

»   Describe the relationship between the federal agencies and the three branches of the federal government.

»   Analyze the tension between transparency and efficiency in the federal bureaucracy.

WHAT'S AT STAKE...IN FEDERAL REGULATION OF THE ORGANIC FOOD INDUSTRY?

WHAT DID THE CHICKEN THAT LAID YOUR breakfast egg have for its breakfast? Was your hamburger once on drugs? And just what is the pedigree of the french fries you ate at lunch? Do you care? Some people do. Those who worry about eating vegetables that have been grown with the aid of pesticides or chemical fertilizers, or meat from animals that were given hormones or antibiotics—or those who are concerned about the environmental effects of such practices—form part of a growing number of consumers who look for the label *organic* before they buy food. One estimate says that Americans spent more than $29 billion on organic foods in 2011.[1]

What does it mean to be organic? There is no standardized definition, so states, localities, and private agencies are free to define organic as they wish. Usually the standards are stringent. For example, many groups require organic farmers to use land on which no artificial or synthetic fertilizers, pesticides, or herbicides have been used for five years. Such farming techniques favor the small,

committed organic farmer and are difficult for large agribusinesses to apply.[2]

In an effort to eliminate the patchwork of local regulations and to assure consumers that organic food purchased anywhere in the country was equally safe, the organic food industry repeatedly asked the U.S. Department of Agriculture (USDA) to nationalize standards. When the USDA revealed its standardized definition of organic, however, it was a definition traditional organic farmers and consumers didn't recognize. USDA standards proposed in December 1997 would have allowed the use of genetic engineering, irradiation, antibiotics and hormones, and sewage sludge—techniques that run directly counter to the values of organic farming—in the production of foods to be labeled organic. Though strongly supported by the conventional food manufacturers and the developers of biotechnology, these standards were bitterly opposed by the organic food industry and its consumers.

Before they issue new regulations, however, all federal agencies must give interested parties and the public the

AP Photo/Tony Avelar

a quirky tale about a handful of food fanatics. What is really at stake in the issue of whether the organic food industry should be regulated by the USDA? «

Organic Is Big Business
Organic farmers Drew and Myra Goodman's small roadside farm has blossomed into the country's largest grower of organic produce, with more than 28,000 acres in the United States and abroad. Despite the growing popularity (and profitability) of organic produce, large agribusiness farms still dominate the landscape and bring their political influence to the table over regulatory processes such as defining what constitutes "organic" food.

opportunity to be heard. In the battle to win USDA support, the conventional food industry and the food preparers associations had—and used—all the resources of big business; the organic food industry had none. Searching for another strategy for influencing the enormous bureaucracy of the USDA, they began a grassroots campaign, encouraging consumers to write to the USDA objecting to the new standards. Natural food stores posted information and distributed fliers on the proposed regulation, and Horizon Organic Dairy used the back panels of its milk cartons to pass on the information and urge consumer action.[3]

The campaign was successful. The USDA received nearly 300,000 letters and emails opposing the proposal. Even Congress went on record against it.[4] The result was that Secretary of Agriculture Dan Glickman eliminated the provision allowing genetic engineering, crop irradiation, and the use of sewage sludge as fertilizer. Said Glickman, "Democracy will work. We will listen to the comments and will, I am sure, make modifications to the rule."[5]

Depending on where you stand, the moral of this story varies. It might be a David-and-Goliath success, or just

KIDS have dramatic aspirations for their futures: they want to be adventurers or sports stars, doctors or lawyers, even president of the United States. Almost no one aspires to be what so many of us become: bureaucrats. But bureaucrats are the people who make national, state, and local government work for us. They are the people who give us our driving tests and renew our licenses, who deliver our mail, who maintain our parks, who order books for our libraries. Bureaucrats send us our Social Security checks, find us jobs through the unemployment office, process our student loans, and ensure that we get our military benefits. In fact, bureaucrats defend our country from foreign enemies, chase our crooks at home, and get us aid in times of natural disasters. We know them as individuals. We greet them, make small talk, laugh with them. They may be our neighbors or friends. But as a profession, civil servants are seldom much admired or esteemed in this country. Indeed, they are often the targets of scorn or jokes, and the people who work in the organizations we call bureaucracies are derided as lazy, incompetent, power hungry, and uncaring.

Such a jaded view, like most other negative stereotypes, is based on a few well-publicized bureaucratic snafus and the frustrating experiences we all have at times with the bureaucracy. Waiting in endless lines at the post office or driver's license bureau, expecting in the mail a government check that never arrives, reading about USDA definitions of *organic* that seem preposterous—all these things can drive us crazy. In addition, as demonstrated by the organic food example, the bureaucracy is the source of many of the rules that can help us get what we want from government but that often irritate us with their seeming arbitrariness and rigidity. Though they aren't elected, bureaucrats can have a great deal of power over our lives.

Bureaucracies are essential to running a government. Bureaucracy, in fact, is often the only ground on which citizens and politics meet, the only contact many Americans have with government except for their periodic trips to the voting booth. Bureaucrats are often called "civil servants" because, ultimately, their job is to serve the civil society in which we all live.

WHAT IS BUREAUCRACY?

A top-down organizational system aiming for competence and fairness

In simplest terms, a **bureaucracy** is any organization that is structured hierarchically: those at the top—with responsibility for the organization's success—give the orders, and those on the bottom follow them. The classic definition comes to us from German sociologist Max Weber. Weber's model of bureaucracy features the following four characteristics:[6]

ASSISTANT TO THE AIDE OF THE DEPUTY VICE CHAIRMAN OF THE COMMITTEE TO REDUCE PENTAGON BUREAUCRACY

BENNETT THE CHRISTIAN SCIENCE MONITOR

- *Hierarchy.* A clear chain of command exists in which all employees know who their bosses or supervisors are, as well as whom they in turn are responsible for.

- *Specialization.* The effectiveness of the bureaucracy is accomplished by having tasks divided and handled by expert and experienced full-time professional staffs.

- *Explicit rules.* Bureaucratic jobs are governed by rules rather than by bureaucrats' own feelings or judgments about how the job should be done. Thus bureaucrats are limited in the discretion they have, and one person in a given job is expected to make pretty much the same decisions as another. This leads to standardization and predictability.

- *Merit.* Hiring and promotions are often based on examinations but also on experience or other objective criteria. Politics, in the form of political loyalty, party affiliation, or dating the boss's son or daughter, is not supposed to play a part.

> **bureaucracy** an organization characterized by hierarchical structure, worker specialization, explicit rules, and advancement by merit
>
> **neutral competence** the principle that bureaucracy should be depoliticized by making it more professional
>
> **spoils system** nineteenth-century practice of firing government workers of a defeated party and replacing them with loyalists of the victorious party
>
> **patronage** system in which a successful candidate rewards friends, contributors, and party loyalists for their support with jobs, contracts, and favors

Political scientist Herbert Kaufman says that the closer governments come to making their bureaucracies look more like Weber's model, the closer they are to achieving "neutral competence."[7] **Neutral competence** represents the effort to depoliticize the bureaucracy, or to take politics out of administration, by having the work of government done expertly, according to explicit standards rather than personal preferences or party loyalties. The bureaucracy in this view should not be a political arm of the president or of Congress, but rather it should be neutral, administering the laws of the land in a fair, evenhanded, efficient, and professional way.

THE SPOILS SYSTEM

Americans have not always been so concerned with the norm of neutral competence in the bureaucracy. Under a form of bureaucratic organization called the **spoils system**, practiced through most of the nineteenth century in the United States, elected executives—the president, governors, and mayors—were given wide latitude to hire their own friends, family, and political supporters to work in their administrations. The spoils system is often said to have begun with the administration of President Andrew Jackson and gets its name from the adage "To the victor belong the spoils of the enemy," but Jackson was neither the first nor the last politician to see the acquisition of public office as a means of feathering his cronies' nests. Such activity, referred to as **patronage**, allowed the elected executive to use jobs to pay off political debts as well as to gain cooperation from the officials who were hired this way, thereby strengthening his base of power.

Filling the bureaucracy with political appointees almost guarantees incompetence because those who get jobs for political reasons are more likely to be politically motivated than genuinely skilled in a specific area. Experts who are devoted to the task of the agency soon become discouraged because advancement is based on political favoritism rather than on how well the job is done. America's disgust with the corruption and inefficiency of the spoils system, as well as our collective distrust of placing too much power in the hands of any one person, led Congress to institute various reforms of the American **civil service**, as it is sometimes called, aimed at achieving a very different sort of organization.

One of the first reforms, and certainly one of the most significant, was the Civil Service Reform Act of 1883. This act, usually referred to as the **Pendleton Act**, created the initial Civil Service Commission, under which federal employees would be hired and promoted on the basis of merit rather than patronage. It prohibited firing employees for failure to contribute to political parties or candidates. Civil service coverage increased until President Harry Truman in 1948 was successful in getting 93 percent of the federal work force covered under the merit system.

Protection of the civil service from partisan politicians got another boost in 1939 with the passage of the **Hatch Act**. This act was designed to take the pressure off civil servants to work for the election of parties and candidates. It forbids pressuring federal employees for contributions to political campaigns, and it prohibits civil servants from taking leadership roles in campaigns. They cannot run for federal political office, head up an election campaign, or make public speeches on behalf of candidates. However, they are permitted to make contributions, to attend rallies, and to work on registration or get-out-the-vote drives that do not focus on just one candidate or party. The Hatch Act thus seeks to neutralize the political effects of the bureaucracy. However, in doing so, it denies federal employees a number of activities that are open to other citizens.

WHY IS BUREAUCRACY NECESSARY?

Much of the world is organized bureaucratically. Large tasks require organization and specialization. The Wright brothers may have been able to construct a rudimentary airplane, but no two people or even small group could put together a Boeing 747. Similarly, though we idolize individual American heroes, we know that efforts like the D-Day invasion of Europe, putting a man on the moon, or the war on terrorism take enormous coordination and planning. Smaller in scale, but still necessary, are routine tasks like delivering the mail, evaluating welfare applications, ensuring that Social Security recipients get their checks, and processing student loans.

Obviously many bureaucracies are public, like those that form part of our government. But the private sector has the same demand for efficient expertise to manage large organizations. Corporations and businesses are bureaucracies, as are universities and hospitals. It is not being public or private that distinguishes a bureaucracy; rather, it is the need for a structure of hierarchical, expert decision making. In this chapter we focus on public bureaucracies, in particular, the federal bureaucracy.

BUREAUCRACY AND DEMOCRACY

Decision making by experts may seem odd to Americans, who cherish the idea of democracy, and it may be why so many Americans dislike so much of our public bureaucracy. If we value democracy and the corresponding idea that public officials should be accountable, or responsible, to the people, how can we also value bureaucracy, in which decisions are often made behind closed doors by unelected "experts" who, because of civil service protections, are difficult to hold accountable?

Bureaucratic decision making in a democratic government presents a real puzzle unless we consider that democracy may not be the best way to make every kind of decision. If we want to ensure that many voices are heard from, then democracy is an appropriate way to make decisions. But those decisions will be made slowly (it takes a long time to poll many people on what they want to do), and though the decisions are likely to be popular, they are not necessarily made by people who know what they are doing. When we're deciding whether to have open heart surgery, we don't want to poll the American people, or even the hospital employees. Instead we want an expert, a heart surgeon, who can make the "right" decision, not the popular decision, and make it quickly.

Democracy could not have designed the rocket ships that formed the basis of America's space program, or decided the level of toxic emissions allowable from a factory smokestack, or determined the temperature at which beef must be cooked in restaurants to prevent food poisoning. Bureaucratic decision making, by which decisions are made at upper levels of an organization and

> **civil service** nonmilitary employees of the government who are appointed through the merit system
>
> **Pendleton Act** 1883 civil service reform that required the hiring and promoting of civil servants to be based on merit, not patronage
>
> **Hatch Act** 1939 law limiting the political involvement of civil servants to protect them from political pressure and keep politics out of the bureaucracy

Spoils System ● Jackson's Kitchen Cabinet ●

carried out at lower levels, is essential when we require expertise and dispatch.

ACCOUNTABILITY AND RULES

Bureaucratic decision making does leave open the problem of **accountability**: Who is responsible for seeing that things get done, and to whom does that person answer? Where does the buck stop? Unlike private bureaucracies, where the need to turn a profit usually keeps bureaucrats relatively accountable, the lines of accountability are less clear in public bureaucracies. Because the Constitution does not provide specific rules for the operation of the bureaucracy, Congress has filled in a piecemeal framework for it that, generally speaking, ends up promoting the goals of members of Congress and the interests they represent.[8] The president of the United States, nominally the head of the executive branch of government, also has goals and objectives he would like the bureaucracy to serve. Thus at the very highest level, the public bureaucracy must answer to several bosses who often have conflicting goals.

THINKING OUTSIDE THE BOX

When does bureaucratic decision making become a threat to democracy?

The problem of accountability exists at a lower level as well. Even if the lines of authority from the bureaucracy to the executive and legislative branches were crystal clear, no president or congressional committee has the interest or time to supervise the day-to-day details of bureaucratic operations. To solve the problem of accountability within the bureaucracy and to prevent the abuse of public power at all levels, we again resort to rules. If the rules of bureaucratic policy are clearly defined and well publicized, it is easier to tell if a given bureaucrat is doing his or her job, and doing it fairly.

What does fairness mean in the context of a bureaucracy? It means, certainly, that the bureaucrat should not play favorites. The personnel officer for a city is not supposed to give special consideration to her neighbors or to her boyfriend's brother. We do not want employees to give preferential treatment to people like themselves, whether that likeness is based on race, ethnicity, religion,

> **accountability** the principle that bureaucratic employees should be answerable for their performance to supervisors, all the way up the chain of command

Study Now, Pay Later

If there is one part of the federal bureaucracy many students are familiar with, it's the arm that handles student loans. Dealing with the forms and red tape of applying for a loan might be a royal pain, but can you imagine what the experience would be like if student loan awards were made democratically, rather than through the neutral and impartial bureaucracy that is tasked with the job?

partisanship, or even sexual orientation, or to discriminate against people who are different from them. And we do not want people to run their organizations at the expense of the public good. In these and many additional ways, we do not want the people carrying out jobs in any bureaucracy to take advantage of the power they have.

CONSEQUENCES OF A RULE-BASED SYSTEM

The centrality of rules in bureaucracies has important trade-offs. According to the goals of neutral competence, we try to achieve fairness and predictability by insisting that the bureaucrats do their work according to certain rules. If everyone follows his or her job description, the supervisor, boss, or policymaker can know what, within some limits, is likely to happen. Similarly, if an important task is left undone, it should be possible to determine who did not do his or her job.

On the negative side, the bureaucrats' jobs can quickly become rule-bound; that is, deviations from the rules become unacceptable, and individuality and creativity are stifled. Sometimes the rules that bind bureaucrats do not seem relevant to the immediate task at hand, and the workers are rewarded for following the rules, not for fulfilling the goals of the organization. Rigid adherence to rules designed to protect the bureaucracy often results in outcomes that have the opposite effect. Furthermore, compliance with rules has to be monitored, and the best way we have developed to guarantee compliance is to generate a paper or, these days, an electronic record of what has been done. To be sure that all the necessary information will be available if needed, it has to be standardized—hence the endless forms for which the bureaucracy is so famous.

For the individual citizen applying for a driver's license, a student loan, or food stamps, the process can become a morass of seemingly unnecessary rules, regulations, constraints, forms, and hearings. We call these bureaucratic hurdles **red tape**, after the red tape that seventeenth-century English officials used to bind legal documents.

Rules thus generate one of the great trade-offs of bureaucratic life. If we want strict fairness and accountability, we must tie the bureaucrat to a tight set of rules. If we allow the bureaucrat discretion to try to reach goals with a looser set of rules, or to waive a rule when it seems appropriate, we may gain some efficiency, but we lose accountability. Given the vast number of people who work for the federal government, we have opted for the accountability, even while we howl with frustration at the inconvenience of the rules.[9]

PAUSE AND REVIEW:

WHO, WHAT, HOW

The American public is strongly committed to democratic governance, but sometimes decisions need to be made that do not lend themselves to democracy. When complex, technical decision making is needed, some form of specialization and expertise is required. Because we also want accountability and fairness among our decision makers, we want them to stick to a prescribed set of rules. Bureaucratic decision making and administration offer possibilities in governance that democracy cannot, but they also bring their own difficulties and challenges.

IN YOUR OWN WORDS » Explain how the characteristics and features of bureaucracy influence decision making.

THE AMERICAN FEDERAL BUREAUCRACY
A patchwork of agencies and commissions to meet growing public demands

In 2012 more than two million civilians worked for the federal government,[10] excluding U.S. Postal Service employees, with another approximately 1.2 million in the armed forces.[11] Only a relative handful, approximately 65,000 employees, work in the legislative branch or the judiciary. The rest are in the executive branch, home of the federal bureaucracy.[12] In this section we look at the evolution of the federal bureaucracy, its present-day organization, and its basic functions.

EVOLUTION OF THE FEDERAL BUREAUCRACY

The central characteristic of the federal bureaucracy is that most of its parts developed independently of the others in a piecemeal and political fashion, rather than emerging from a coherent plan. Some government activities are fundamental; from the earliest days of the republic, the government had departments to handle foreign relations, money, and defense. But other government tasks have developed over time as the result of historical forces, as solutions to particular problems, or as a response to different groups who want government to do something for them. The emerging picture is more like a patchwork quilt than the streamlined efficient government structure we would like to have. Thus the nature and duties of the agencies reflect the politics of their creation and the subsequent politics of their survival and growth.[13] We can understand federal agencies as falling into three categories: those designed to serve essential government functions, those crafted to meet the changing needs and problems of the country, and those intended to serve particular clientele groups.[14]

SERVING ESSENTIAL GOVERNMENT FUNCTIONS Some departments are created to serve essential government functions, the core operations that any viable government performs. For example, the Departments of State, War, and the Treasury were the first cabinet offices because the activities they handle are fundamental to the smooth functioning of government. The Department of State exists to handle diplomatic relations with other nations. When diplomacy fails, national interests must be protected by force; the Department of Defense (formerly War) supervises the air force, army, navy, marines, and, in time of war, the coast guard. All nations have expenses and must extract resources in the form of taxes from their citizens to pay for them. The Department of the Treasury, which oversees the Internal Revenue Service (IRS), performs this key tax collection function. Treasury also prints the money we use and oversees the horrendous job of managing the national debt. Imagine the effort to manage a debt that increases $2.3 billion a day![15]

RESPONDING TO CHANGING NATIONAL NEEDS Other departments and agencies were created to meet the changing needs of the country as we industrialized and evolved into a highly urbanized society. For example,

> **red tape** the complex procedures and regulations surrounding bureaucratic activity

with westward expansion, the growth of manufacturing, and increased commerce came demands for new roles for government. The Department of the Interior was created in 1848 to deal with some of the unforeseen effects of the move westward, including the displacement of Native Americans and the management of western public lands and resources.

Similarly, a number of the negative aspects of industrialization, including child labor abuses, filthy and dangerous working conditions, unsanitary food production, and price gouging by the railroads, led to calls for government intervention to manage the burgeoning marketplace of an industrialized society. Thus began the development of the independent regulatory commissions starting in the late nineteenth century with the Interstate Commerce Commission and continuing into the twentieth century with the Federal Trade Commission, the Federal Reserve System, and others.

Under the New Deal, several new agencies were created and new programs put into place. The federal government's largest single program today, Social Security, was organized under the Social Security Administration as a supplement for inadequate and failed old-age pensions. For the first time, the national government became directly involved in the economic well-being of individual citizens. Related programs like the Works Progress Administration and the Civilian Conservation Corps were sometimes called government "make-work" programs because their primary purpose was to create jobs and get people back to work. The new obligations of the national government did not vanish with postwar prosperity. Americans came to expect that government would play a large role in managing the economy and in ensuring that people could work, eat, and live in decent housing. President Lyndon Johnson's War on Poverty resulted in the creation of the Office of Economic Opportunity in 1964 and the Department of Housing and Urban Development (HUD) in 1965.

A changing international environment also created needs that required government to grow. The Cold War between the United States and the Soviet Union launched a multipronged policy effort that included investment in military research, science (the National Science Foundation), education (the National Defense Education Act), and space exploration (the National Aeronautics and Space Administration). Much more recently, the September 11, 2001, terror attacks on the United States led to the establishment of a new cabinet-level Department of Homeland Security to coordinate efforts to protect the country. The new department created a new bureaucratic structure, but also organized under its

> clientele groups groups of citizens whose interests are affected by an agency or a department and who work to influence its policies

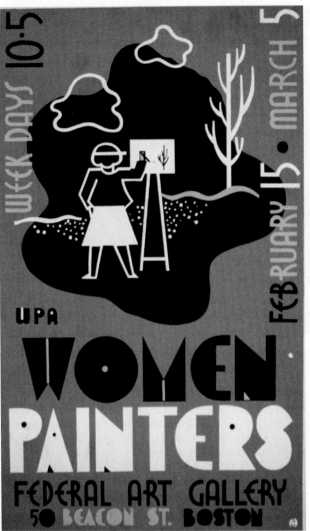

Uncle Sam Lends a Hand (and a Brush)
The federal government's response to the Great Depression was Roosevelt's New Deal, which provided assistance to anxious Americans of all professions in need of stable work. The Federal Art Project provided support to struggling artists between 1935 and 1943, creating more than 200,000 works of art for public buildings. This poster is both a product of and publicity for the project.

authority some preexisting agencies and bureaus, including those controlling the U.S. Secret Service, immigration, and emergency management.

RESPONDING TO THE DEMANDS OF CLIENTELE GROUPS A number of departments and agencies either were created or have evolved to serve distinct clientele groups. These may include interest groups—groups of citizens, businesses, or industry members who are affected by government regulatory actions and who organize to try to influence policy. Or they may include unorganized groups, such as poor people, to which the government has decided to respond. Such departments are sensitive to the

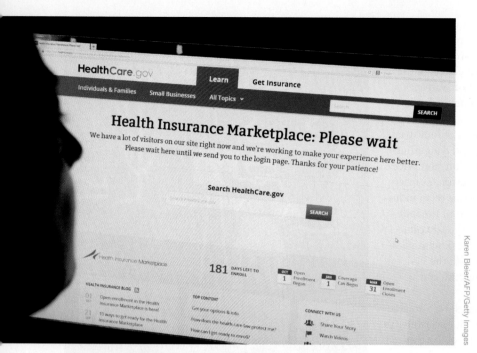

one of those classifications. The difficulty in classifying an agency as one type or another stems partly from Congress' habit of creating hybrids: agencies that act like government corporations, for instance, or cabinet-level departments that regulate. The overall organizational chart of the U.S. government makes this complex bureaucracy look reasonably orderly, but to a large extent the impression of order is an illusion.

DEPARTMENTS The federal government currently has fifteen **departments**. *The Big Picture* on page 332 shows how and when these departments were created. The heads of departments are known as secretaries—for example, the secretary of state or the secretary of defense—except for the head of the Department of Justice, who is called the attorney general. These department heads collectively make up the president's cabinet, appointed by the president, with the consent of the Senate, to provide advice on critical areas of government affairs such as foreign relations, agriculture, education, and so on. These areas are not fixed, and presidents may propose different cabinet offices. Although the secretaries are political appointees who usually change when the administration

A Bureaucrative Snafu

The roll-out of HealthCare.gov—the online avenue for the public to sign up for health care insurance as part of the Patient Protection and Affordable Care Act—was a giant bust. It could not handle the immense traffic and left hundreds of thousands of potential applicants frustrated while feeding the Republican opposition line that the program was a disaster. Part of the reason for the breakdown was the tremendous complexity of the program, magnified by the government procurement process that favors hiring those best at applying for government contracts over the most talented and skilled, and the common (and this time highly consequential and visible) bureaucratic habit of not passing bad news up the chain of command. Recovery was politically costly for the administration, but the glitches were worked out by year's end.

concerns of those specific groups rather than focusing on what is good for the nation as a whole. The Department of Agriculture, among the first of these, was set up in 1862 to assist U.S. agricultural interests. It began by providing research information to farmers and later arranged subsidies and developed markets for agricultural products. Politicians in today's budget-cutting climate talk about cutting back on agricultural subsidies, but no one expects the USDA to change its focus of looking out, first and foremost, for the farmer. Similar stories can be told of the Departments of Labor, Commerce, Education, and Veterans Affairs.

ORGANIZATION OF THE FEDERAL BUREAUCRACY

The federal bureaucracy consists of four types of organizations: (1) cabinet-level departments, (2) independent agencies, (3) regulatory boards and commissions, and (4) government corporations. To make the job of understanding the bureaucracy more complicated, some agencies can fit into more than

changes (or even more frequently), they sit at the heads of the large, more or less permanent, bureaucracies we call departments. Cabinet heads may not have any more actual power than other agency leaders, but their posts do carry more status and prestige.

When a cabinet department is established, it is a sign that the government recognizes its policy area as a legitimate and important political responsibility. Therefore, groups fight hard to get their causes represented at the cabinet level. During the Clinton administration, environmental groups tried to get the Environmental Protection Agency (EPA) raised to the cabinet level. The fact that it was not elevated, despite President Bill Clinton's campaign promises on the matter, was a sign that the business and development interests that opposed environmental regulation were stronger politically. Even though the EPA is not a cabinet-level agency, its director has been asked by some

---

departments one of the major subdivisions of the federal government, represented in the president's cabinet

---

presents to meet with the cabinet, giving him or her cabinet rank and thus more status, even if the agency is not so elevated. In the Obama administration, the EPA director has cabinet-level rank, as does the White House chief of staff, the director of the Office of Management and Budget, the U.S. trade representative, the ambassador to the United Nations, and the chair of the Council of Economic Advisers.[16]

INDEPENDENT AGENCIES Congress has established a host of agencies outside the cabinet departments. The **independent agencies** are structured like the cabinet departments, with a single head appointed by the president. Their areas of jurisdiction, however, tend to be narrower than those of the cabinet departments. Congress does not follow a blueprint for how to make an independent agency or a department. Instead, it expands the bureaucracy to fit the case at hand, given the mix of political forces of the moment—that is, given what groups are demanding what action, and with what resources. As a result, the independent agencies vary tremendously in size, ranging from fewer than 350 employees in the Federal Election Commission (FEC) to over 66,000 in the Social Security Administration.[17]

These agencies are called independent because of their independence from cabinet departments, but they vary in their independence from the president. This is not accidental, but political. When Congress is not in agreement with the current president, it tends to insulate new agencies from presidential control by making the appointments for fixed terms that do not overlap with the president's, or they remove budgetary oversight from the Office of Management and Budget.[18] Thus some agency heads serve at the president's discretion and can be fired at any time; others serve fixed terms, and the president can appoint a new head or commissioner only when a vacancy occurs. Independent agencies also vary in their freedom from judicial review. Congress has established that some agencies' rulings cannot be challenged in the courts, whereas others' can be.[19]

INDEPENDENT REGULATORY BOARDS AND COMMISSIONS Independent regulatory boards and commissions make regulations for various industries, businesses, and sectors of the economy. **Regulations** are simply limitations or restrictions on the behavior of an individual or a business; they are bureaucratically determined

independent agencies government organizations independent of the departments but with a narrower policy focus

independent regulatory boards and commissions government organizations that regulate various businesses, industries, or economic sectors

regulations limitations or restrictions on the activities of a business or an individual

prescriptions for how business is to take place. This chapter opened with the battle over a regulation: the guidelines that must be followed for a product to be labeled *organic*. Regulations usually seek to protect the public from some industrial or economic danger or uncertainty. The Securities and Exchange Commission, for example, regulates the trading of stocks and bonds on the nation's stock markets, while the Food and Drug Administration regulates such things as how drugs must be tested before they can be marketed safely and what information must appear on the labels of processed foods and beverages sold throughout the country. Regulation usually pits the individual's freedom to do what he or she wants, or a business's drive to make a profit, against some vision of what is good for the public. As long as there are governments, there will be trade-offs between the two because it is for the purpose of managing citizens' collective lives that governments are formed. How each trade-off is made between individual freedom and public safety is a question of public policy (see *CLUES to Critical Thinking*).

There are thirty-eight agencies of the federal government whose principal job it is to issue and enforce regulations about what citizens and businesses can do, and how they have to do it. This effort cost on average between $57 billion and $84 billion per year between 2003 and 2013.[20] Given the scope of the undertaking, it is not surprising that regulation occasionally gets out of hand. If an agency exists to regulate, regulate it probably will, whether or not a clear case can be made for restricting action. The average cheeseburger in America, for instance, is the subject of over 40,000 federal and state regulations, specifying everything from the vitamin content of the flour in the bun, to the age and fat content of the cheese, to the temperature at which the burger must be cooked, to the speed at which the ketchup must flow to be certified Grade A Fancy.[21] Some of these rules are undoubtedly crucial; we all want to be able to buy a cheeseburger without risking food poisoning and possible death. Others are informative; those of us on restrictive diets need to know what we are eating, and none of us likes to be ripped off by getting something other than what we think we are paying for. Others seem merely silly. When we consider that adult federal employees are paid to measure the speed of ketchup, we readily sympathize with those who claim that the regulatory function is getting out of hand in American government.

The regulatory agencies are set up to be largely independent of political influence, though some are bureaus within cabinet departments—the federal Food and Drug Administration, for example, is located in the Department of Health and Human Services. Most independent regulatory agencies are run by a commission of three or more people who serve overlapping terms, and the terms of office, usually between three and fourteen years, are set so that they do not coincide with presidential terms. Commission members are nominated by the president and confirmed by Congress, often with a bipartisan vote. Unlike

THE BIG PICTURE: HOW THE FEDERAL BUREAUCRACY GOT SO BIG

The country started out with a minimum of agencies needed to support a nation: The departments of State (diplomacy with other nations), War (now defense, for when diplomacy fails), and Treasury (to collect taxes). As the nation grew, greater industrialization and urbanization inevitably produced new problems, which have resulted in a greater role for government—and new agencies—to regulate and maintain an increasing complex society.

Annual Spending in Billions, 2013

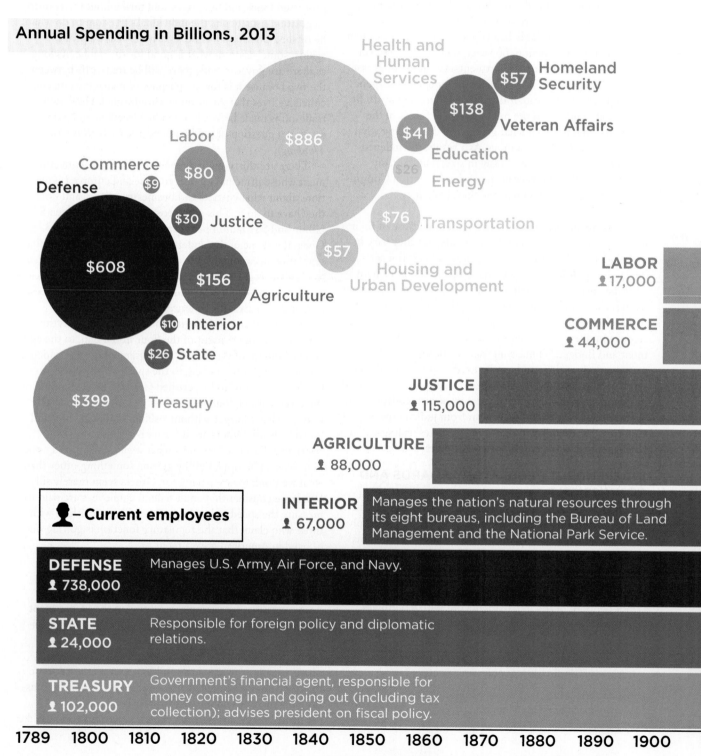

Health and Human Services $886

Homeland Security $57

Veteran Affairs $138

Education $41

Energy $26

Transportation $76

Labor $80

Commerce $9

Defense $608

Justice $30

Agriculture $156

Housing and Urban Development $57

Interior $10

State $26

Treasury $399

🯅 – Current employees

LABOR 🯅 17,000

COMMERCE 🯅 44,000

JUSTICE 🯅 115,000

AGRICULTURE 🯅 88,000

INTERIOR 🯅 67,000 — Manages the nation's natural resources through its eight bureaus, including the Bureau of Land Management and the National Park Service.

DEFENSE 🯅 738,000 — Manages U.S. Army, Air Force, and Navy.

STATE 🯅 24,000 — Responsible for foreign policy and diplomatic relations.

TREASURY 🯅 102,000 — Government's financial agent, responsible for money coming in and going out (including tax collection); advises president on fiscal policy.

| 1789 | 1800 | 1810 | 1820 | 1830 | 1840 | 1850 | 1860 | 1870 | 1880 | 1890 | 1900 |

Sources: Table Ea636-643, Table Aa6-8, hsus.cambridge.org/HSUSWeb/HSUSEntryServlet, Office of Management and Budget, "Historcal Tables: Table 1.1, www.whitehouse.gov/omb/budget/historicals,

HOMELAND SECURITY
👤 184,000

Created to prevent terrorist attacks within the United States, make the country less vulnerable to terrorism, and help the nation survive attacks that do occur.

VETERANS AFFAIRS
👤 313,000

Administers programs to help veterans and their families, including pensions, medical care, disability, and death benefits.

EDUCATION
👤 5,000

Provides federal aid to local school districts and colleges and student college loans.

ENERGY
👤 16,000

Oversees national activities relating to the production, regulation, marketing, and conservation of energy.

TRANSPORTATION
👤 56,000

Administers overall transportation policy, including highways, urban mass transit, railroads, aviation, and waterways.

HOUSING AND URBAN DEVELOPMENT
👤 11,000

Administers housing and community development programs.

HEALTH AND HUMAN SERVICES
👤 76,000

Administers government health and security programs; includes Centers for Disease Control and Prevention and Food and Drug Administration.

Responsible for work force safety and employment standards.

Responsible for economic and technological development; includes Census Bureau.

Legal arm of the executive branch, responsible for enforcement of federal laws, including civil rights and antitrust laws.

Administers federal programs related to food production and rural life, including price support programs and soil conservation.

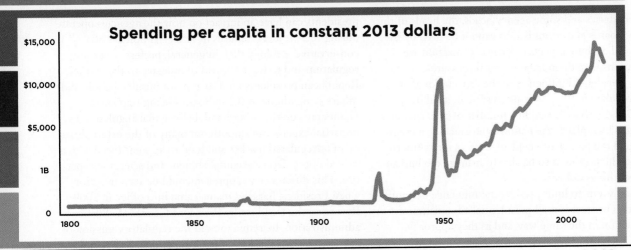

Spending per capita in constant 2013 dollars

$15,000				
$10,000				
$5,000				
1B				
0				

1800   1850   1900   1950   2000

1910 1920 1930 1940 1950 1960 1970 1980 1990 2000 2010 2020

and U.S. Bureau of the Census, "Annual Population Estimates," NST-EST2012-01, www.census.gov/popest/data/national/totals/2012/index.html.

CLUES
TO CRITICAL THINKING

"50 Years After Thalidomide: Why Regulation Matters"

By Margaret Hamburg, M.D., commissioner of the U.S. Food and Drug Administration

FDAVoice, **February 7, 2012**

Thalidomide was a drug widely prescribed in Europe in the 1960s to alleviate morning sickness in pregnant women, but it was never approved for use in the United States. Tragically, the drug was found to cause severe birth defects. The market alone was not sufficient to prevent such a tragedy from occurring. Writing in the U.S. Food and Drug Administration blog FDAVoice, this author makes the case for what she calls "smart" government regulation. What are the uses and limits to government regulation?

Fifty years ago, the vigilance of FDA medical officer Dr. Frances Kelsey prevented a public health tragedy of enormous proportion by ensuring that the sedative thalidomide was never approved in the United States. As many remember, in the early 1960s, reports were coming in from around the world of countless women who were giving birth to children with extremely deformed limbs and other severe birth defects. They had taken thalidomide. Although it was being used in many countries, Dr. Kelsey discovered that it hadn't even been tested on pregnant animals.

Dr. Kelsey's reaction to thalidomide exemplifies the FDA's mission: protecting and promoting the health of the American people, using science for regulatory decision-making.

Now I know that in some circles regulation is viewed as a roadblock to innovation and economic growth. But in actuality, when done right, regulation isn't a roadblock; it's the actual pathway to achieving real and lasting innovation.

Smart, science-based regulation instills consumer confidence in products and treatments. It levels the playing field for businesses. It decreases the threat of litigation. It prevents recalls that threaten industry reputation and consumer trust, not to mention levying huge preventable costs on individual companies and entire industries. And it spurs industry to excellence.

The tragedy of thalidomide led to changes that strengthened both the regulatory and scientific environment for medical product development and review.

In response to the public uproar, in 1962 Congress enacted the Kefauver-Harris amendments to the Federal Food, Drug and Cosmetic Act. Thanks to these new amendments, manufacturers had to prove that a drug was not only safe, but also effective. Approvals had to be based on sound science. Companies had to monitor safety reports that emerged postmarket and adhere to good manufacturing practices that would lead to consistently safe products. And there were new protections for patients.

The amendments not only benefited patients, they helped industry, raising scientific standards that eventually ushered in today's sophisticated, science-based life sciences industry.

For the very first time, many companies put in place research and development programs, including the design and implementation of controlled clinical trials. Major therapeutic breakthroughs resulted, including the use of beta blockers in patients after a heart attack and angiotensin-converting enzyme

cabinet secretaries and some agency heads, the heads of the regulatory boards and commissions cannot be fired by the president. All of these aspects of their organization are intended to insulate them from political pressures, including presidential influence, in the expectation that they will regulate in the public interest unaffected by current partisan preferences. The number of such agencies is growing, which places the national bureaucracy increasingly beyond the president's control, even as most Americans expect the president to be able to manage the bureaucracy to get things done.[22]

Congress wants to limit presidential influence of regulatory agencies because not all presidential administrations view regulation in the same way, and as they approach the job of appointing regulatory officials accordingly,

presidents can have an impact on how the agencies operate during their leaders' tenures in office. As holders of a conservative ideology that, in general, prefers to see less regulation and to leave control of industry to the market, Republican presidents tend to appoint businesspeople and others sympathetic to the industries being regulated. Democrats, on the other hand, believe that regulation by impartial experts can smooth out many of the externalities of an unregulated market and tend to appoint those with a record of regulatory accomplishment and scientific expertise. This difference in approach could be seen in action when President Barack Obama came into office in 2009. Reversing the trend set by President George W. Bush's administration, he reinvigorated the regulatory mission of agencies such as the EPA, the Occupational Safety and

inhibiters to improve survival in patients with heart failure. All of these were good news for public health and for corporate bottom lines. The best drugs and treatments rose to the top, not simply those that were most heavily marketed.

The Harris-Kefauver Amendments created a culture of quality and innovation that laid the foundation for our current regulatory environment which fosters a domestic pharmaceutical industry that is second to none.

Going forward, smart regulation requires regulatory flexibility that responds to changing situations, new information and new challenges. It also demands that we advance regulatory science: the knowledge and tools necessary for the meaningful and timely review of products for safety, efficacy, quality and performance.

Thalidomide, once again, is a good example. It came back on the U.S. market in 1998 after data showed it was safe and effective to treat a complication of leprosy. In an appropriate balancing of benefit and risk, FDA required strong safety monitoring and a strict dispensing plan before approving the drug.

Regulation such as this requires a strong, robust FDA, one endowed with the necessary resources to ensure smart, sound, science-based regulation.

Source: FDA Voice, http://blogs.fda.gov/fdavoice/index.php/2012/02/50-years-after-thalidomide-why-regulation-matters.

Consider the source and the audience: Dr. Hamburg is the commissioner of the FDA, writing a post on the official FDA blog. What is her perspective toward government regulation likely to be? Does it cause you to disbelieve what she says, or does it strengthen her authority?

Lay out the argument and the underlying values and assumptions: Hamburg clearly believes government can be an effective actor in solving social problems, in particular in putting limits on and giving guidelines to corporations in order to ensure public safety. She argues for what she calls "smart" regulation. What does she mean by "smart"? How does she feel such regulation can increase innovation and development?

Uncover the evidence: Hamburg essentially relies on anecdotal evidence to make her case. The thalidomide tragedy occurred in the absence of government regulation, and government regulation now in place makes the public safer and has resulted in the discovery of new drugs. Is that one example shocking enough to make her case? Would you like to see any statistical or other data? What kind?

Evaluate the conclusion: Are people better off because of government regulation? Can we ensure the "smart" regulation Hamburg wants to see, as she thinks we can? What would "dumb" regulation look like?

Sort out the political significance: Hamburg is doing more here than making an abstract case for government regulation—she is arguing for the future of the FDA's funding. Why in the political climate of 2012 would she have found that necessary? Would this argument be persuasive to those who would want to cut the agency's funding?

Health Administration, and the Securities and Exchange Commission, in what one progressive author called "the quiet revolution."[23]

GOVERNMENT CORPORATIONS We do not often think of the government as a business, but public enterprises are, in fact, big business. The U.S. Postal Service is one of the larger businesses in the nation in terms of sales and personnel. The Tennessee Valley Authority and the Bonneville Power Administration of the northwestern states are both in the business of generating electricity and selling it to citizens throughout their regions. If you ride the rails as a passenger, you travel by Amtrak, a government-owned corporation (technically called the National Railroad Passenger Corporation). All these businesses are set up to be largely independent of both congressional and presidential influence. This independence is not insignificant. Consider, for example, how angry citizens are when the postal rates go up. Because the Postal Commission is independent, both the president and Congress avoid the political heat for such unpopular decisions.

Congress created these publicly owned **government corporations** primarily to provide a good or service that is not profitable for a private business to provide. The Federal Deposit Insurance Corporation (FDIC) is a good example.

> **government corporations** companies created by Congress to provide to the public a good or service that private enterprise cannot or will not profitably provide

Following the Great Depression, during which financial institutions failed at an alarming rate, citizens were reluctant to put their money back into banks. A "government guarantee," through FDIC, of the safety of savings gave, and continues to give, citizens much more confidence than if the insurance were provided by a private company, which itself could go broke. The government's ownership of Amtrak came about because a national rail service did not prove profitable for private industry but was seen by Congress as a national resource that should not be lost. Similarly, the post office guarantees that mail reaches the most remote corners of the country, where delivery service might not be profitable for a private company. With competition from the private companies that do exist, like FedEx and UPS, however, as well as the declining demand for mail service as the country conducts more and more of its business electronically, the post office is in financial trouble. In 2012 the postal service announced plans to downsize in an effort to save money.[24]

The rationale is that providing these services entails not just making a profit but also serving the public interest. However, as in so many other aspects of American government, the public is relatively quiet in speaking up for its interests, and so the politics of government corporations become the politics of interested bureaucrats, clientele groups, and congressional subcommittees.

THINKING OUTSIDE THE BOX

Are some essential services now provided by the federal bureaucracy better left to the private sector?

ROLES OF THE FEDERAL BUREAUCRACY

Federal bureaucrats at the broadest level are responsible for helping the president to administer the laws, policies, and regulations of government. The actual work the bureaucrat does depends on the policy area in which he or she is employed. Take another look at the titles of the cabinet departments and independent agencies displayed in *The Big Picture*. Some part of the bureaucracy is responsible for administering rules and policies on just about every imaginable aspect of social and economic life.

Bureaucrats are not confined to administering the laws, however. Although the principle of separation of powers—by which the functions of making, administering, and interpreting the laws are carried out by the legislative, executive, and judicial branches—applies at the highest level of government, it tends to dissolve at the level of the bureaucracy. In practice, the bureaucracy is an all-in-one policymaker. It administers the laws, but it also effectively makes and judges compliance with laws. It is this wide scope of bureaucratic power that creates the problems of control and accountability that we discuss throughout this chapter.

BUREAUCRACY AS ADMINISTRATOR We expect the agencies of the federal government to implement the laws passed by Congress and signed by the president. Operating under the ideal of neutral competence, a public bureaucracy serves the political branches of government in a professional, unbiased, and efficient manner. In many cases this is exactly what bureaucrats do, and with admirable ability and dedication. The rangers in the national parks help citizens enjoy our natural resources, police officers enforce the statutes of criminal law, social workers check for compliance with welfare regulations, and postal workers deliver letters and packages in a timely way. All these bureaucrats are simply carrying out the law that has been made elsewhere in government.

BUREAUCRACY AS RULE MAKER The picture of the bureaucrat as an impartial administrator removed from political decision making is a partial and unrealistic one. The bureaucracy has a great deal of latitude in administering national policy. Because it often lacks the time, the technical expertise, and the political coherence and leverage to write clear and detailed legislation, Congress frequently passes laws that are vague, contradictory, and overly general. In order to carry out or administer the laws, the bureaucracy must first fill in the gaps. Congress has essentially delegated some of its legislative power to the bureaucracy. Its role here is called **bureaucratic discretion**. Bureaucrats must use their own judgment, which under the ideal of neutral competence should remain minimal, in order to carry out the laws of Congress. Congress does not say how many park rangers should be assigned to Yosemite versus Yellowstone, for instance; the Park Service has to interpret the broad intent of the law and make decisions on this and thousands of other specifics. Bureaucratic discretion is not limited to allocating personnel and other "minor" administrative details. Congress cannot make decisions on specifications for military aircraft, dictate the advice the agricultural extension agents should give to farmers, or determine whether the latest sugar substitute is safe for our soft drinks. The appropriate bureaucracy must fill in all those details. For example, when Congress passed the Patient Protection and Affordable Care Act in 2010, a key provision barred insurers from implementing "unreasonable premium increases" unless they first submit justifications to federal and state officials. But Congress left it up to the

bureaucratic discretion bureaucrats' use of their own judgment in interpreting and carrying out the laws of Congress

Vaping Rules ● Pump My Ride ●

bureaucracy to define "unreasonable," which would have enormous impact on how the law was implemented.

The procedures of administrative rule making are not completely insulated from the outside world, however. Before they become effective, all new regulations must first be publicized in the *Federal Register*, which is a primary source of information for thousands of interests affected by decisions in Washington. Before adopting the rules, agencies must give outsiders—the public and interest groups—a chance to be heard, as we saw in the examination of organic farming regulation that began this chapter. Similarly, in the case of the rule making concerning the 2010 health care act, the bureaucracy became the focus of intense lobbying efforts by the health insurance industry, which wanted the rule to be defined as favorably for it as possible.[25]

BUREAUCRACY AS JUDGE The third major function of governments is adjudication, or the process of interpreting the law in specific cases for potential violations and deciding the appropriate penalties when violations are found. This is what the courts do. However, a great deal of adjudication in America is carried out by the bureaucracy. For example, regulatory agencies not only make many of the rules that govern the conduct of business but also are responsible for seeing that individuals, but more often businesses, comply with their regulations. Tax courts, under the IRS, for instance, handle violations of the tax codes.

The adjudication functions of the agencies, while generally less formal than the proceedings of the courts, do have formal procedures, and their decisions have the full force of law. In most cases if Congress does not like an agency ruling, it can work to change it, either by passing new legislation or by more subtle pressures. Nevertheless, agencies often issue rulings that could never have overcome the many hurdles of the legislative process in Congress.

WHO ARE THE FEDERAL BUREAUCRATS?

The full civilian work force of the federal bureaucracy reflects the general work force fairly accurately. For example, 46.9 percent of the U.S. civilian labor force is female and 42.7 percent of the civil service is female. African Americans make up 11.9 percent of the civilian work force and 18.3 percent of the civil service.[26] The distributions are similar for other demographic characteristics such as ethnic origin or level of education. This representative picture is disturbed, however, by the fact that not all bureaucratic positions are equal. Policymaking is done primarily at the highest levels, and the upper grades are

> *Federal Register* publication containing all federal regulations and notifications of regulatory agency hearings

staffed predominantly by well-educated white males. As illustrated in "*Snapshot of America*: Who Are Our Federal Bureaucrats?", women and minorities are distinctly underrepresented in the policymaking (and higher-paying) levels of the bureaucracy.[27]

PAUSE AND REVIEW:

WHO, WHAT, HOW

Government exists, among other reasons, to solve citizens' common problems and to provide goods and services that the market does not or cannot provide. The apparatus for problem solving and service providing is primarily the bureaucracy. Congress and the president define the problems, make the initial decisions, and assign responsibility for solving them to a department, an agency, or a regulatory board.

Citizens or groups of citizens who want something from the government must deal with the bureaucracy as well. Finally, the bureaucrats themselves have a stake in performing their mandated jobs in a political context where Congress and the president may hedge on the details of what that job actually is. Consequently, bureaucrats need to go beyond administering the laws to making them and judging compliance with them as well. Though we cautiously separate power, and check and balance it among all our elected officials, it is curious that where the officials are unelected and thus not accountable to the people, powers are fused and to a large extent unchecked. The bureaucracy is therefore a very powerful part of the federal government.

IN YOUR OWN WORDS » Outline the organization and roles of the federal bureaucracy.

POLITICS INSIDE THE BUREAUCRACY
Power struggles between political appointees and professional bureaucrats, constrained by cultural norms

Politicians and bureaucrats alike are wary about the effects of politics on decision making. They act as if fairness and efficiency could always be achieved if only the struggle over competing interests could be set aside through an emphasis on strict rules and hierarchical organization. We know, of course, that the struggle can't be set aside. As a fundamental human activity, politics is always with us, and it is always shaped by the particular rules and institutions in which it is played out. Politics within bureaucracies is a subset of politics generally, but it takes on its own cast according to the context in which it takes place.

SNAPSHOT OF AMERICA: WHO ARE OUR FEDERAL BUREAUCRATS?

Federal Workers by Gender

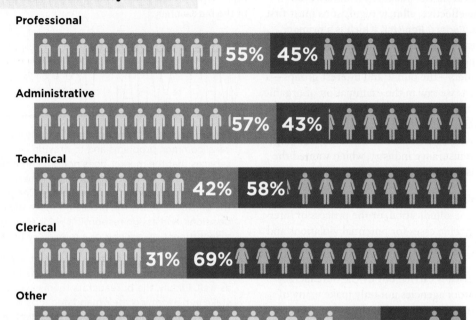

Professional
55% 45%

Administrative
57% 43%

Technical
42% 58%

Clerical
31% 69%

Other
88% 12%

Demographics in the Civil Service

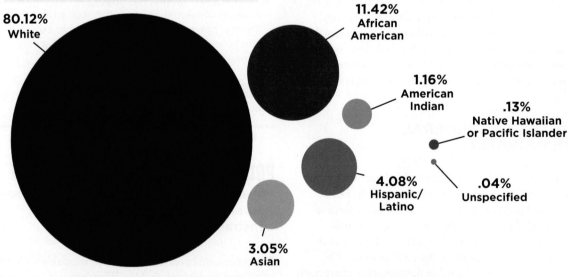

80.12% White

11.42% African American

1.16% American Indian

.13% Native Hawaiian or Pacific Islander

4.08% Hispanic/ Latino

.04% Unspecified

3.05% Asian

BEHIND THE NUMBERS

The federal bureaucrats who work for the U.S. government represent a fair cross-section of the American population. But relatively few women, African Americans, or Hispanics reach the highest grade levels of the civil service ladder. Does this "glass ceiling" make a difference in the way the bureaucracy does its job?

Source: Office of Personnel Management, *Common Characteristics of the Government* , Fiscal Year 2013, www.opm.gov/policy-data-oversight/ data-analysis-documentation/federal-employment-reports/common-characteristics-of-the-government/ccog2013.pdf; and Data, Analysis & Documentation, FEDERAL EMPLOYMENT REPORTS Profile of Federal Civilian Non-Postal Employees, September 30, 2013.

BUREAUCRATIC CULTURE

The particular context in which internal bureaucratic politics is shaped is called bureaucratic culture—the accepted values and procedures of an organization. Consider any place you may have been employed. When you began your job, the accepted standards of behavior may not have been clear, but over time you figured out who had power, what your role was, which rules could be bent and which had to be followed strictly, and what the goals of the enterprise were. Chances are you came to share some of the values of your colleagues, at least with respect to your work. Those things add up to the culture of the workplace. Bureaucratic culture is just a specific instance of workplace culture.

Knowing the four main elements of bureaucratic culture will take us a long way toward understanding why bureaucrats and bureaucracies behave the way they do. Essentially these elements define what is at stake within a bureaucracy, and what bureaucrats need to do to ensure that they are winners and not losers in the bureaucratic world. To explore bureaucratic culture, let's imagine that you have landed a job working in the U.S. Department of Agriculture. Over time, if you are successful in your job, you will come to share the values and beliefs of others working in your department; that is, you will come to share their bureaucratic culture.

POLICY COMMITMENT As a good bureaucrat in training, the first thing you will do is develop a commitment to the policy issues of agriculture. No matter if you've never thought much about farming before. As an employee of the USDA, you will eventually come to believe that agricultural issues are among the most important facing the country, just as those working at the National Aeronautics and Space Administration place a priority on investigating outer space, and bureaucrats at the National Institutes of Health believe fervently in health research. You will share a commitment to your policy area not only because your job depends on it but also because all the people around you believe in it.

ADOPTION OF BUREAUCRATIC BEHAVIOR Not long after you join your department, you will start to see the logic of doing things bureaucratically; you may even start to sound like a bureaucrat. Bureaucratese, the formal and often (to outsiders) amusing and sometimes confusing language that many bureaucrats use in their effort to convey information without controversy, may become your second tongue (see *Don't Be Fooled by…Bureaucratese*). Part of the reason for the development of bureaucratese is that the use of

bureaucratic culture the accepted values and procedures of an organization

bureaucratese the often unintelligible language used by bureaucrats to avoid controversy and lend weight to their words

acronyms and other linguistic shortcuts can make communication more efficient for those in the know, but use of bureaucratese also seems to be an effort to avoid responsibility (for example, use of the passive voice means you don't say who performed the action) or to make the author appear more authoritative by using more and longer words than are really necessary. The elaborate rule structure that defines the bureaucracy will come to seem quite normal to you. You will even depend on it because relying on the rules relieves you of the responsibility of relying on your own judgment. You will learn that exercising such bureaucratic discretion, as we discussed earlier, can leave you vulnerable if your decisions are not clearly within the rules.

The hierarchical organization of authority will also make a good deal of sense, and you will, in fact, find yourself spending a lot of your time helping to make your superiors look good to their superiors, even as the people working under you will be helping you to look good to your bosses. Remember that in a hierarchy most of your rewards will come from those over you in the power structure; you will be dependent on your superiors for work assignments, promotions, budget allotments, and vacation authorizations. Your superiors will have the same relationships with their bosses.

As you become committed to the bureaucratic structure, you will learn that conformity to the rules and norms of the enterprise is the name of the game. Free spirits are not likely to thrive in a bureaucratic environment where deference, cooperation, and obedience are emphasized and rewarded, and the relentless rule orientation and hierarchy can wear down all but the most committed independent souls.

SPECIALIZATION AND EXPERTISE Early on in your career, you will realize that departments, agencies, and bureaus have specific areas of responsibility. There is not a great deal of interagency hopping; most bureaucrats spend their whole professional lives working in the same area, often in the same department. The lawyers in the Justice Department, scientists at the National Science Foundation, physicians at the National Institutes of Health, and even you as a soybean expert at the USDA all have specialized knowledge as the base of your power. Your power comes from your expertise, and that is tied to the specific policy areas of your agency. To move, you would give that up— and so, not surprisingly, few do.

Because of specialization and expertise, bureaucrats come to know a lot more about their policy areas than do the public or even politicians who must make decisions relevant to those areas. Their possession of critical information gives bureaucrats considerable power in policymaking situations.

IDENTIFICATION WITH THE AGENCY All three of the characteristics of bureaucratic culture discussed so far lead to the fourth: identification with and protection of the agency. As you become attached to the interests of agriculture, committed to the rules and structures of the bureaucracy, concerned with the fortunes of your superiors, and

DON'T BE FOOLED BY...
BUREAUCRATESE

The tortured and twisted language our government bureaucrats seem to love can be so awful that it's actually amusing—if you have nothing at stake in figuring out what it means. Try this on for size: "The metropolitan Washington region's transportation system will promote economic sustainability and quality of life through a facilitation of inter- and intra-jurisdictional connectivity of employment and population centers, with a comprehensive multi-modal approach to mobility and utilize available tools to reduce congestion."[1] What a windy way to say that the Washington transportation system will relieve traffic jams by using a variety of methods of transit!

It's no wonder that people have trouble paying attention to what their government says. But what might be merely irritating, or laughable, or just plain stupid when it comes to transportation can assume a lot more importance when it's something we need to know about. If you've ever applied for a student loan, chances are you've already spent some time scratching your head over phrases like "For loans first disbursed on or after October 1, 2011, the school in which the student is enrolled has a cohort default rate, calculated under either subpart M or subpart N of 34 CFR part 668 of less than 15 percent for each of the three most recent fiscal years for which data are available. . . ." Isn't that just the kind of language you want to see when signing a binding legal agreement? It's no wonder that the Center for Plain Language, a nonprofit group dedicated to the idea that "Plain Language Is a Civil Right," chose that particular loan document as one of the worst of the year in 2010.[2]

The truth is, translating bureaucratese, the bewildering way that government officials often speak, can be quite a project. It would be nice if we could just avoid dealing with government language altogether, but most of us can't. At some time in our lives we register a car, apply for a student loan, get a marriage license, or file a building permit. We may need to register for Social Security benefits or apply for Medicaid or food stamps. We may fill out a passport application or a form to bring purchases back through customs after traveling abroad. We may want to read a report from the local school committee or the public transportation board. And one thing is certain: we all have to pay taxes. With these facts of life in mind, it's good to get a firm handle on government jargon.

WHAT TO WATCH OUT FOR

- **Overly complicated terms that refer to common objects and events.** In bureaucratese, "means of egress" are exits, a "grade separation structure" can turn out to be a bridge, "rail movements" are train trips, "agricultural specialists" are farmers, and an application for an "unenclosed premise permit" is a request to build a patio.[3] Such language may result from an effort to be more specific, from a wish to be less specific, or just from a desire to make something sound more important than it is. Don't be fooled by lofty or euphemistic language.

- **Passive voice.** Bureaucrats often speak passively: "Action is taken," or "Resources are acquisitioned." The passive voice allows the author to avoid saying who is taking the action or acquiring the resources, often key pieces of information you need or want to know.

- **Insider language.** Every line of work, from ditch digging to software engineering, has its own unique jargon. Government workers are no exception: Police talk about "perps" and "collars" (perpetrators and arrests); an aide to your senator might refer to a bill that "died in committee" (that is, was prevented from going to the Senate floor for a vote). Don't be intimidated by the insider language that bureaucrats sometimes use. If you don't understand what you are being told, seek out—or demand—an explanation.

- **Redundant language.** Phrases that are unnecessarily repetitive can make even a relatively simple concept sound incredibly complicated. Bureaucrats are not the only ones guilty of this. An article on writing for lawyers (many of whom go on to work in the government, of course) points out that it is unnecessary to say "green in color," "consensus of opinion," "free gift," or "final outcome."[5] Such wordiness is not only wrong, but it clutters up the language, making it hard to understand what is being said.

- **Nouns that have been turned into verbs.** Bureaucrats are famous for this. *Impact*, *acquisition*, and *dialogue*, for instance, are used as nouns in everyday language but as verbs in bureaucratese. If a word seems out of place, it probably is. Think creatively when translating government documents.

- **Never speak or write like this yourself!** Bureaucratese is bad enough coming from bureaucrats and lawyers. There is no substitute for good, clear, crisp writing.

Reading and understanding the bloated jargon of government bureaucratese can be quite a challenge. Those of you with a sweet tooth can practice on Official Government Bureaucracy Cookies.[6]

Official Government Bureaucracy Cookies

Output:	six dozen cookie units
Inputs:	1 cup packed brown sugar
	1/2 cup butter, softened
	2 eggs
	2 1/2 cups all purpose flour
	1/2 teaspoon salt
	1 cup chopped pecans or walnuts

1/2 cup white sugar

1/2 cup shortening

1 1/2 teaspoons vanilla

1 teaspoon baking soda

12 ounces semisweet chocolate chips

Guidance:

After procurement actions, decontainerize inputs. Perform measurement tasks on a case-by-case basis:

1. In a mixing-type bowl, impact heavily on brown sugar, white sugar, butter, and shortening. Coordinate the interface of eggs and vanilla, avoiding an overrun scenario to the best of your skills and abilities.

2. At this point in time, leverage flour, baking soda, and salt into a bowl and aggregate. Equalize with prior mixture and develop intense and continuous liaison among inputs until well coordinated. Associate with chocolate and nut subsystems and execute stirring options.

3. Within this time frame, take action to prepare the heating environment for throughput by manually setting the oven baking unit to a temperature of 375 degrees F.

4. Drop mixture in an ongoing fashion from a teaspoon implement onto an ungreased cookie sheet at intervals sufficiently apart to permit total and permanent throughputs to the maximum extent particular under operating conditions. Position cookie sheet in a bake situation for 8 to 10 minutes or until cooking action terminates.

5. Initiate coordination of outputs with the cooling rack function. Containerize, wrap in red tape and disseminate to authorized staff personnel on a timely and expeditious basis.

iStockphoto

1. Walden Siew, "Ready Readers Respond to Our Gibberish Alert," *Washington Times,* December 1, 1997, 1, web version.

2. U.S. Department of Education, Federal Family Education Loan Program (*Federal Register* 2009 § 682.604 Processing the borrower's loan proceeds and counseling borrowers), as presented by the Center for Plain Language, 2010 Wondermark Awards, centerforplainlanguage.org/awards/past-years/wondermark2010/.

3. Laurel Walker, "Functionaries Should Better Utilize Lexicon: Why Do Bureaucrats Insist on Using So Much Unintelligible Jargon?" *Milwaukee Journal Sentinel,* July 5, 1997, 1–2.

4. Bill McAllister and Maralee Schwartz, "'A Pony to Ride': Freshly Minted Bureaucratese," *Washington Post,* May 8, 1990, 1.

5. Tom Goldstein and Jethro K. Lieberman, "Double Negative Use Is Not Unavoidable," *Texas Lawyer,* May 28, 1990, 2.

6. Material reprinted with the express permission of "Ottawa Citizen Group Inc.," a division of Postmedia Network Inc.

appreciative of your own and your colleagues' specialized knowledge, your estimation of the USDA will rise. You will begin to think that what is good for Agriculture is good for you, and that threats to the department's well-being become threats to you. You will identify with the department, not just because your job depends on it but because you believe in what it does.

CONSEQUENCES OF THE BUREAUCRATIC CULTURE

This pervasive bureaucratic culture breeds a number of political consequences. On the plus side, it holds the bureaucracy together, fostering values of commitment and loyalty to what could otherwise be seen as an impersonal and alienating work environment. It means that the

people who work in the federal government, for the most part, really believe in what they do. Members of the Federal Bureau of Investigation (FBI), for example, are strongly attached to the agency's law enforcement mission and are steeped in one of the most distinctive bureaucratic cultures in the nation. This strong commitment to its law enforcement mission has led to major successes, such as the exposure and arrest of major organized crime figures across the country.

But bureaucratic culture can lead to negative consequences as well. As former FBI agent Coleen Rowley pointed out in testimony before the Senate Judiciary Committee in June 2002, this culture very likely had a role in the failure of our law enforcement and intelligence agencies to foresee and

enforcement agency; agents are rewarded for making arrests. Its antiterrorist activities prior to September 11 were focused on after-the-fact investigations of terrorist attacks (leading to convictions) but not on preventing such attacks against domestic targets.[29]

The CIA, on the other hand, is focused on clandestine activity to develop information about non-American groups and nations. It is more secretive and less rule-bound, more focused on plans and intentions than on after-the-fact evidence and convictions. Agents focus on relationships, not individual achievement. One reporter covering the two agencies wrote that though the two agencies need to work with each other, "they have such different approaches to life that they remain worlds apart. In fact, they speak such different languages that they can barely even communicate."[30]

When an agency is charged with making the rules, enforcing them, and even adjudicating them, it is relatively easy to cover up less catastrophic agency blunders. If Congress, the media, or the public had sufficient information and the expertise to interpret it, this would not be as big a problem. However, specialization necessarily concentrates the expertise and information in the hands of the agencies. Congress and the media are generalists. They can tell something has gone wrong when terrorists attack the United States seemingly without warning, but they cannot evaluate the hundreds of less obvious problems that may have led to the failure to warn that only an expert would even recognize.

Congress has tried to check the temptation for bureaucrats to cover up their mistakes by offering protection to whistleblowers. **Whistleblowers** are employees who expose instances or patterns of error, corruption, or waste in their agencies. They are just good citizens whose consciences will not permit them to protect their agencies and superiors at the expense of what they believe to be the public good. Coleen Rowley, for instance, was asked to testify before the Senate Judiciary Committee because someone had leaked to the media a memo she had written to FBI director Robert Mueller detailing her concerns about the failure of upper-level agency officials to heed her office's worries and to give permission for the search of Moussaoui's computer. Writing that memo was difficult for her because it required her to break with her loyalty to an agency she loved in order to hold it to standards she believed it should meet.

Whistleblowers are not popular with their bosses, as you can well imagine. The Whistleblower Protection Act of 1989 established an independent agency to protect employees from being fired, demoted, or otherwise punished for exposing wrongdoing. The act's intention to protect whistleblowers is certainly a step in the direction of counteracting a negative tendency of organizational behavior, but it does little to offset the pervasive pressure to protect the programs and the agencies from harm,

Repeating Historic Mistakes

NASA associate administrator William Readdy examines debris from the Space Shuttle *Columbia,* which broke apart upon reentry into the Earth's atmosphere in 2003. Similar bureaucratic failures that were responsible for the explosion of the shuttle *Challenger* thirteen years earlier—including an entrenched culture that stifled engineers who were concerned about safety—were blamed for this second tragedy.

Getty Images News/Getty Images

prevent the attacks of September 11, 2001. Rowley's office, in Minneapolis, had known that a possible terrorist, Zacarias Moussaoui, was seeking to take flying lessons. Finding his activities suspicious and worrisome, Minneapolis agents tried to get a warrant to search his computer but were unable to do so. In her testimony, Rowley targeted the FBI's hierarchical culture, with its implicit norm that said field agents did not go over the heads of their superiors, who frequently second-guessed their judgment. "There's a certain pecking order, and it's real strong," she told the committee. "Seven to nine levels is really ridiculous."[28]

Not only did bureaucratic culture keep the FBI from knowing what information it had prior to September 11, but it also kept the FBI and the Central Intelligence Agency (CIA) from communicating with each other about the various pieces of the puzzle they had found. Between them they had much of the information needed to have discovered the plot, but no one "connected the dots." Why? The cultures are different. The FBI is primarily a law

> **whistleblowers** individuals who publicize instances of fraud, corruption, or other wrongdoing in the bureaucracy

embarrassment, and budget cuts. Moreover, the law has not worked anything like its supporters had hoped. Over the past ten years, complaints of agency punishment by whistle-blowers have averaged 835 a year. In almost all these cases, the agency's decisions support the bureaucracy rather than the whistleblower, creating a great career disincentive to speak out when one's agency is guilty of corruption, wrong-doing, or simple incompetence.[31]

One problem with the phenomena of whistleblowers is separating valid claims of governmental wrongdoing from illegal behavior (see our discussion of Edward Snowden in Chapter 5), or distinguishing insider information that is used to feed partisan attacks on an administration from valid information about cover-ups or bureaucratic wrong-doing. An ongoing example in the Obama administration are the claims about whether the administration impeded the House Republican-led investigations into the September 11, 2012, attacks on the U.S. consulate in Beng-hazi, Libya.[32] The partisan noise makes it difficult to deter-mine if there is merit in any of the claims.

THINKING OUTSIDE THE BOX

When is rocking the bureaucratic boat (blowing the whistle) a good thing, and when is it not?

PRESIDENTIAL APPOINTEES AND THE CAREER CIVIL SERVICE

Another aspect of internal bureaucratic politics worth noting is the giant gulf between those at the very top of the department or agency who are appointed by the president and those in the lower ranks who are long-term civil service employees. Of the two million civilian employees in the U.S. civil service, about 3,500 are appointed by the presi-dent or his immediate subordinates.

CONFLICTING AGENDAS Presidential appointees are sometimes considered "birds of passage" by the career service because of the regularity with which they come and go. Though generally quite experienced in the agency's policy area, appointees have their own careers or the presi-dent's agenda as their primary objective rather than the long-established mission of the agency. The rank-and-file civil service employees, in contrast, are wholly committed to their agencies. Minor clashes are frequent, but they can intensify into major rifts when the ideology of a newly elected presi-dent varies sharply from the central values of the operating agency. Researchers have found that presidents seek to put their own people, rather than career civil service managers, in the higher ranks of agencies that do not agree with their policy preferences. Some observers claim this is unjustified

"politicization" of the agencies, whereas others contend that it is one of the necessary levers presidents use to achieve some control over the vast federal bureaucracy.[33]

When Ronald Reagan was elected president in 1980, he brought in a distinctly conservative ideology. His appoin-tees to agencies such as the Department of Education and the EPA were charged with reversing the growing federal presence in education and countering the EPA's advocacy of environmental protection over business interests. While President Reagan succeeded in making changes, they were not as extensive as conservatives had hoped, partly because the agencies resisted all the way. President George W. Bush engaged in much the same effort to make bureaucratic appointments loyal to his conservative agenda, and many observers concluded that his efforts were more successful than Reagan's.[34] While President Obama made an effort to make appointments that reversed the conservative trend of his predecessor, some liberal critics felt he was still too business friendly in many areas.[35]

CONFLICTING TIME FRAMES Political appointees have short-term outlooks; they are viewed by career bureaucrats as "birds of passage."[36] The professionals, in contrast, serve long tenures in their positions; the average upper-level civil servant has worked in his or her agency for over seventeen years, and expects to remain there.[37] Chances are the professionals were there before the current president was elected, and they will be there after he leaves office. Thus, while the political appointees have the advan-tage of higher positions of authority, the career bureaucrats have time working on their side. Not surprisingly, the bureaucrat's best strategy when the political appointee presses for a new but unpopular policy direction is to stall. This is easily achieved by consulting the experts on feasi-bility, writing reports, drawing up implementation plans, commissioning further study, doing cost-benefit analyses, consulting advisory panels of citizens, and on and on.

PRESIDENTIAL STRATEGIES Given the difficulty that presidents and their appointees can have in dealing with the entrenched bureaucracy, presidents who want to institute an innovative program are better off starting a new agency than trying to get an old one to adapt to new tasks. In the 1960s, when President John F. Kennedy wanted to start the Peace Corps, a largely volunteer organization that provided assistance to developing countries by working at the grassroots level with the people themselves, he could have added it to any number of existing departments. He might have argued to have it placed in the State Depart-ment (which traditionally works through diplomacy at the highest levels of international politics), or in the CIA (which employs people in other countries in its intelli-gence-gathering operations), or in the Agency for Interna-tional Development (which consists of experts at adminis-tering foreign aid). The problem was that either these existing agencies were unlikely to accept the idea that nonprofessional volunteers could do anything useful, or

they were likely to subvert them to their own purposes, such as spying or managing aid. Thus President Kennedy was easily persuaded to have the Peace Corps set up as an independent agency, a frequent occurrence in the change-resistant world of bureaucratic politics.[38]

PAUSE AND REVIEW:

WHO, WHAT, HOW

Life inside the bureaucracy is clearly as political as life outside. Many actors attempt to use the rules to advance themselves and the interests of their agency or clientele group, but the bureaucracy has its own culture in which the rules are played out.

Individual bureaucrats want to succeed in their jobs and promote their agencies. Here time, bureaucratic culture, and the rigid nature of bureaucratic rules are in their favor. Congress has helped bureaucrats who wish to challenge an agency to correct a perceived wrong or injustice by passing the Whistleblower Protection Act.

The president has an enormous stake in what the bureaucracy does, and so do his political appointees, who have their own agendas for advancement. But the entrenched civil service can often and easily outlast them, and ultimately prevail.

IN YOUR OWN WORDS » Describe power struggles between political appointees and professional bureaucrats.

EXTERNAL BUREAUCRATIC POLITICS
Turf wars among agencies and with the three branches of government

Politics affects relationships not only within bureaucratic agencies but also between those agencies and other institutions. While the bureaucracy is not one of the official branches of government, since it falls technically within the executive branch, it is often called the fourth branch of government because it wields so much power. It can be checked by other agencies, by the executive, by Congress, by the courts, or even by the public, but it is not wholly

d'Alene, Idaho, with occasional forays into the wilds of Washington, D.C. After years of managing hundreds of miles of trails from Montana to Alaska, Jaime now spends her time shaping national policy and programs and helping trail managers agency-wide in their work.

She so clearly loves her job that it's easy to forget that she is in fact a government employee—not something that fills every heart with joy and satisfaction. But for Jaime, the two go hand in hand.

> WE EACH HAVE A RESPONSIBILITY TO DO SOMETHING POSITIVE TOWARD OUR FUTURE, WHATEVER IT IS.

About government service she says:

The students I went to school with and that I deal with now are generally conservation or environmentally-oriented. So they tend to see government as a mechanism to help manage public lands and effect change. They see government as one major way to get in there and make a difference. And if you don't like what government's doing, then get in there and help change it.

Which might be different from other students who, in general, might look from the outside towards the government and go 'ewwww… bureaucracy.' I guess what I would say to folks is, well, I see it as *our* government and we need government. Government gets us roads and health standards and great education systems. And if you don't like it or if you see problems, I think there's tremendous opportunity to get in there and help improve it.

And on keeping the republic:

We're all part of the Republic; we're each fortunate to be part of this Republic and we have a responsibility to contribute. I'm really big on service in any dimension, in any area of interest. For me, it's about the concept of citizen advocacy and citizen stewardship—to contribute to the greater good. And I think that we have a responsibility to do that, as opposed to the opposite of simply watching or criticizing.

Stewardship is recognizing and enjoying the opportunities and responsibilities we've inherited. For me, it's the great public lands and natural resources, clean air and healthy water, our trails and wilderness areas, our wild and scenic rivers. And knowing that, while we've inherited these resources, we also have a responsibility to take care of them and help make decisions that inform wise choices for their future management. We each have a responsibility to do something positive toward our future, whatever it is—our work, choices we make in the things we buy or don't buy, how we spend our weekends, how we vote. For the future—for our children, but also for the country and for the globe. That's the big piece. That's the hard piece. That's the important piece.

Source: Jaime Schmidt spoke with Christine Barbour in the summer of 2014.

under the authority of any of those entities. In this section we examine the political relationships that exist between the bureaucracy and the other main actors in American politics.

INTERAGENCY POLITICS

As we have seen, agencies are fiercely committed to their policy areas, their rules and norms, and their own continued existence. The government consists of a host of agencies, all competing intensely for a limited amount of federal resources and political support. They all want to protect themselves and their programs, and they want to grow, or at least to avoid cuts in personnel and budgets.

To appreciate the agencies' political plight, we need to see their situation *as they see it.* Bureaucrats are a favorite target of the media and elected officials. Their budgets are periodically up for review by congressional committees and the president's budget department, the Office of Management and Budget. Consequently, agencies are compelled to work for their survival and growth. They have to act positively in an uncertain and changing political environment in order to keep their programs and their jobs.

CONSTITUENCY BUILDING One way agencies compete to survive is by building groups of supporters. Members of Congress are sensitive to voters' wishes, and because of this, support among the general public as well as interest groups is important for agencies. Congress will not want to cut an agency's budget, for instance, if doing so will anger a substantial number of voters or important interests.

As a result, agencies try to control some services or products that are crucial to important groups. In most cases, the groups are obvious, as with the clientele groups of, say, the USDA. Department of Agriculture employees work hard for farming interests, not just because they believe in the programs but also because they need strong support from agricultural clienteles to survive. Agencies whose work does not earn them a lot of fans—like the IRS, whose mission is tax collection—have few groups to support them. When Congress decided to reform the IRS in 1998, there were no defenders to halt the changes.[39] The survival incentives for bureaucratic agencies do not encourage agencies to work for the broader public interest but rather to cultivate special interests that are likely to be more politically active and powerful.

This turf jealousy can undermine good public policy. Take, for example, the military: for years, the armed services successfully resisted a unified weapons procurement, command, and control system. Each branch wanted to maintain its traditional independence in weapons development, logistics, and communications technologies, costing the taxpayers millions of dollars. Getting the branches to give up control of their turf was politically difficult, although it was accomplished eventually.

When Things Go Really Wrong

After tornadoes tore through the Midwest in March 2012, governors from several states requested that the president declare the damaged localities to be federal disaster areas. Inspectors from the Federal Emergency Management Agency arrived soon after to assess the damage and coordinate relief and aid.

THE BUREAUCRACY AND THE PRESIDENT

As we discussed in Chapter 8, one of the president's several jobs is that of chief administrator. In fact, organizational charts of departments and agencies suggest a clear chain of command, with the cabinet secretary at the top reporting directly to the president. But in this case, being "the boss" does not mean that the boss always, or even usually, gets his way. The long history of the relationship between the president and the bureaucracy is largely one of presidential frustration. President Kennedy voiced this exasperation when he said that dealing with the bureaucracy "is like trying to nail jelly to the wall." Presidents have more or less clear policy agendas that they believe they have been elected to accomplish, and with amazing consistency presidents complain that "their own" departments and agencies are uncooperative and unresponsive. The reasons for presidential frustration lie in the fact that, although the president has some authority over the bureaucracy, the bureaucracy's different perspectives and goals often thwart the chief administrator's plans.

Even independent regulatory commissions run into this problem. Numerous observers have noted the phenomenon of **agency capture**, whereby commissions tend to become creatures of the very interests they are supposed to regulate. In other words, as the regulatory bureaucrats become more and more immersed in a policy area, they come to share the views of the regulated industries. The larger public's preferences tend to be less well formed and certainly less well expressed because the general public does not hire teams of lawyers, consultants, and lobbyists to represent its interests. An excellent case in point is the USDA's proposed definition of *organic*, which seemed designed to benefit big food industries and agribusiness rather than the public and small farmers. The regulated industries have a tremendous amount at stake. Over time, regulatory agencies' actions may become so favorable to regulated industries that in some cases the industries themselves have fought deregulation, as did the airlines when Congress and the Civil Aeronautics Board deregulated air travel in the 1980s.[40]

GUARDING THE TURF Agencies want to survive, and one way to stay alive is to offer services that no other agency provides. Departments and agencies are set up to deal with the problems of fairly specific areas. They do not want to overlap with other agencies because duplication of services might indicate that one of them is unnecessary, inviting congressional cuts. Thus, in many instances, agencies reach explicit agreements about dividing up the policy turf in an only partly successful effort to avoid competition and duplication.

APPOINTMENT POWER Presidents have some substantial powers at their disposal for controlling the bureaucracy. The first is the power of appointment. For the departments, and for quite a few of the independent agencies, presidents appoint the heads and the next layer or two of undersecretaries and deputy secretaries. These cabinet secretaries and agency administrators are responsible for running the departments and agencies. The president's

> **agency capture** process whereby regulatory agencies come to be protective of and influenced by the industries they were established to regulate

VA Disaster

formal power, though quite significant, is often watered down by the political realities of the appointment and policymaking processes.

Cabinet secretaries are supposed to be "the president's men and women," setting directions for the departments and agencies that serve the president's overall policy goals. The reality is that although the president does select numerous political appointees, many also have to be approved by the Senate. The process begins at the start of the president's administration when he is working to gain support for his overall program, so he doesn't want his choices to be too controversial. This desire for early widespread support means presidents tend to play it safe and to nominate individuals with extensive experience in the policy areas they will oversee. Their backgrounds mean that the president's men and women are only partially his. They arrive on the job with some sympathy for the special interests and agencies they are to supervise on the president's behalf, as well as loyalty to the president.

As we mentioned, recent presidents have sought to achieve political control over agencies by expanding the numbers of their appointees at the top levels of agencies, especially those agencies whose missions are not consistent with the administration's policy agenda.[41] President George W. Bush was especially adept at this politicization of the bureaucracy. For instance, in his second term, he appointed one of his most trusted personal advisers to head the Department of Justice. Officials in the Justice Department fired existing U.S. attorneys and replaced them with conservatives who would be more sympathetic to Republican policy concerns, which blunted the agency's traditionally aggressive enforcement of civil rights laws.[42] This effort was not restricted to Justice, but a similar political housecleaning occurred followed in the wake of the September 11 attacks and criticisms of the CIA's anti-terrorist preparations.[43]

President Obama's appointees have been named with less of an eye to their ideological views than to their scientific expertise. As a Democrat, Obama has attempted to reinvigorate the regulatory purpose and effective competence of the agencies in the bureaucracy, but Senate Republicans still refused to approve many of his recommendations because they disapprove generally of the agencies' regulatory mission. Rather than let agencies languish, Obama sought to get his nominations through with the use of recess appointments, a practice authorized by the Constitution that allows the president to make appointments without Senate approval when Congress is not in session. Intended to allow the president to deal with emergency appointments when the Senate cannot meet, presidents of both parties have used the strategy to get around recalcitrant Senates. In Obama's case the Republican House refused to agree to recess to thwart an impending Obama recess appointment, keeping both itself and the Senate in nominal session even while taking breaks. Challenged, the Supreme Court sided unanimously with the Senate, thus invalidating the president's appointment to the agency in question, the National Labor Relations Board, and tipping the balance toward Congress in the ongoing presidential-congressional battle for control of the bureaucracy.[44]

THE BUDGET PROPOSAL The president's second major power in dealing with the bureaucracy is his key role in the budget process. About fifteen months before a budget request goes to Congress, the agencies send their preferred budget requests to the Office of Management and Budget, which can lower, or raise, departmental budget requests. Thus the president's budget, which is sent to Congress, is a good statement of the president's overall program for the national government. It reflects his priorities, new initiatives, and intended cutbacks. His political appointees and the civil servants who testify before Congress are expected to defend the president's budget.

And they do defend the president's budget, at least in their prepared statements. However, civil servants have contacts with interest group leaders, congressional staff, the media, and members of Congress themselves. Regardless of what the president wants, the agencies' real preferences are made known to sympathetic members of the key authorizations and appropriations committees. Thus the president's budget is a beginning bargaining point, but Congress can freely add to or cut back presidential requests, and most of the time it does so. The president's budget powers, while not insignificant, are no match for an agency with strong interest group and congressional support. Presidential influence over the bureaucratic budget is generally more effective in terminating an activity that the president opposes than in implementing a program that the agency opposes.[45]

THE PRESIDENTIAL VETO The third major power of the president is the veto. As we argued in Chapter 8, the presidential veto can be an effective weapon for derailing legislation, but it is a rather blunt tool for influencing the bureaucracy. First, many spending bills are bundled together. The president may want a different set of funding priorities for, say, mass transit systems, but such funding is buried in a multibillion-dollar multiagency appropriation. He may not like everything in the bill, but he does not want to risk shutting down the government or starting a public battle. Without a line-item veto, the veto can be used only as a threat in political bargaining. By itself, it does not guarantee the president what he wants.

GOVERNMENT REORGANIZATION In addition to his other efforts, the president can try to reorganize the bureaucracy, combining some agencies, eliminating others, and generally restructuring the way government responsibilities are handled. Such reorganization efforts have become a passion with some presidents, but they are limited in their efforts by the need for congressional approval.[46]

One recent effort at reorganization was the creation of the Department of Homeland Security in response to the terrorist attacks of September 11, 2001. The goal of the new department was to refocus the activities of multiple agencies whose jurisdictions touched on security issues, bringing them under the leadership of a single organization. More typical of reorganization efforts, in the sense that it was intended to make government leaner and more efficient, was President Clinton's National Performance Review, which later became the National Partnership for Reinventing Government. The goal of this commission, headed by Vice President Al Gore, was to trim the federal payroll by a quarter of a million jobs and to produce savings of $100 billion by decentralizing, deregulating, and freeing government employees to show more initiative in getting their jobs done. More recently, in 2012, President Obama announced a plan to merge agencies that exist to help the private sector and to downsize the government, which he claimed would save upwards of $3 billion over ten years. Because it would have required the cooperation of Congress to grant him the authority to accomplish it, the effort was unlikely to go anywhere in an election year.[47]

POWERS OF PERSUASION The president's final major power over the bureaucracy is an informal one, the prestige of the office itself. The Office of the President impresses just about everyone. If the president is intent on change in an agency, his powers of persuasion and the sheer weight of the office can produce results. Few bureaucrats could stand face to face with the president of the United States and ignore a legal order. But the president's time is limited, his political pressures are many, and he needs to choose his priorities very carefully. The media, for example, will not permit him to spend a good part of every day worrying about a program that they think is trivial. He will be publicly criticized for wasting time on "minor matters." Thus the president and his top White House staff have to move on to other things. The temptation for a bureaucracy that does not want to cooperate with a presidential initiative is to wait it out, to take the matter under study, to be "able" to accomplish only a minor part of the president's agenda. The agency or department can then begin the process of regaining whatever ground it lost. It, after all, will be there long after the current president is gone.

THE BUREAUCRACY AND CONGRESS

Relationships between the bureaucracy and Congress are not any more clear-cut than those between the agencies and the president, but in the long run individual members of Congress, if not the whole institution itself, have more control over what specific bureaucracies do than does the executive branch. This is not due to any particular grant of power by the Constitution, but rather to informal policy-making relationships that have grown up over time and are now all but institutionalized. That is, much of the influence over the bureaucracy is exercised by Congress, but in highly decentralized agency-by-agency and subcommittee-by-subcommittee sets of relationships.

IRON TRIANGLES Much of the effective power in making policy in Washington is lodged in what political scientists call **iron triangles**. An iron triangle is a tight alliance among congressional committees, interest groups or representatives of regulated industries, and bureaucratic agencies, in which policy comes to be made for the benefit of the shared interests of all three, not for the benefit of the greater public. Politicians are themselves quite aware of the pervasive triangular monopoly of power. Former secretary of health, education, and welfare John Gardner once declared before the Senate Government Operations Committee, "As everyone in this room knows but few people outside of Washington understand, questions of public policy nominally lodged with the Secretary are often decided far beyond the Secretary's reach by a trinity—not exactly a holy trinity—consisting of (1) representatives of an outside lobby, (2) middle-level bureaucrats, and (3) selected members of Congress."[48]

A good example of an iron triangle is the natural resources policy shown in Figure 9.1. In 2010, as oil gushed into the Gulf of Mexico from the ruined oil rig *Deepwater Horizon*, the Minerals Management Service (MMS), an obscure agency that few citizens had heard of, was blasted into the news. The MMS, which was in charge of issuing leases, collecting royalties, and overseeing the dangerous work of offshore drilling for oil and gas on America's continental shelf, was accused of having cozy and even illegal relationships with the industry it was charged with regulating. Agency employees were said to have accepted meals, gifts, and sporting trips from the oil industry, and some agency staff were accused of having had sex and using drugs with industry employees.

At the agency's top sat people like J. Steven Griles, who had worked as an oil industry lobbyist before joining the government. In middle management, the line between the industry and its regulators in the field was blurred.[49] As one MMS district manager put it, "Obviously we're all oil industry. . . . We're all from the same part of the country. Almost all our inspectors have worked for oil companies out on the [Gulf] platforms. They grew up in the same towns."[50] The industry and agency shared a goal of maximizing oil and gas production with hardly more than a whisper of concern for the effects of what was believed to be an unlikely accident. Not surprisingly, many key congressional leaders of the committees with jurisdiction over oil and gas drilling policies are from states with large petroleum interests. The House

> **iron triangles** the phenomenon of a clientele group, congressional committee, and bureaucratic agency cooperating to make mutually beneficial policy

FIGURE 9.1 THE OIL INDUSTRY–BOEMRE IRON TRIANGLE

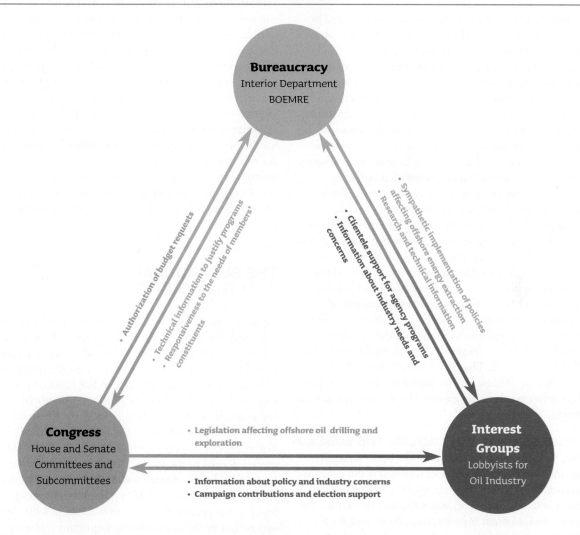

Iron triangles (involving Congress, the bureaucracy, and special interest groups) exist on nearly every subgovernment level. In this example, you can see how the BOEMRE (the Bureau of Ocean Energy Management, Regulation and Enforcement), which depends on the House and the Senate for its budget, influences and is influenced by oil company lobbyists, who in turn influence and are influenced by House and Senate committees and subcommittees. This mutual interdependence represents a monopoly of power.

Committee on Natural Resources and its subcommittee on Energy and Mineral Resources have several members whose districts have major financial interests in oil and gas production, and most of these members receive substantial contributions from the oil and gas industry. The oil- and gas-producing states of Louisiana, Texas, Oklahoma, Colorado, and New Mexico all have members of Congress who receive major contributions from oil and gas industry sources.[51]

Thus the oil industry, the MMS, and members of Congress with responsibility for overseeing the agency all possessed interests in protecting energy production that reinforced one another in a cozy triangle and disregarded

the general public's interests in avoiding environmental catastrophe and receiving the appropriate royalties from oil and gas use. The drug and sex scandals, along with the media's relentless coverage of the *Deepwater Horizon* disaster, focused national attention on the problem and spurred the Obama administration to reorganize the agency, now called the Bureau of Ocean Energy Management, Regulation and Enforcement (BOEMRE). However, the forces that created this situation—that is, the intertwined interests among members of Congress who serve on committees that oversee agencies that regulate the industries that affect voters in their districts—are a fundamental part of our political-economic system. As long as citizens and industry are free to "petition Congress for redress of grievances," as the First Amendment guarantees, iron triangles will remain.

The metaphor of the iron triangle has been refined by scholars, who speak instead of **issue networks**.[52] The iron triangle suggests a particular relationship among a fixed interest group and fixed agencies and fixed subcommittees. The network idea suggests that the relationships are more complex than a simple triangle. There are really clusters of interest groups, policy specialists, consultants, and research institutes ("think tanks") that are influential in policy areas. To continue with the offshore drilling example, environmental groups such as the League of Conservation Voters monitor the environmental records of members of Congress, and outside groups use existing laws to force agencies like the BOEMRE to change their procedures. So, for example, the Center for Biological Diversity sought to sue the Department of the Interior (of which the MMS was part) for failing to get appropriate environmental permits required by the Marine Mammal Protection Act and the Endangered Species Act.[53] Thus "outsiders" can use the courts, and they often lobby sympathetic members of Congress to contest the relationships that develop as iron triangles. Their participation shows that the concept of an iron triangle does not always incorporate all the actors in a particular policy area. That is, while the relationships identified by the iron triangle remain important, the full range of politics is frequently better captured by the concept of issue networks.

CONGRESSIONAL CONTROL OF THE BUREAUCRACY Congressional control of the bureaucracy is found more in the impact of congressional committees and subcommittees than in the actions of the institution as a whole. Congress, of course, passes the laws that create the agencies, assigns them their responsibilities, and funds their operations. Furthermore, Congress can, and frequently does, change the laws under which the agencies operate. Thus Congress clearly has the formal power to control the bureaucracy. It also has access to a good deal of information that helps members monitor the bureaucracy. This monitoring process is called **congressional oversight**. Members learn about agency behavior through required reports, oversight hearings and testimony by experts, and reports by congressional agencies such as the Government Accountability Office, and from constituents and organized interests.[54] But Congress is itself often divided about what it wants to do and is unable to set clear guidelines for agencies. During the first six years of the Bush administration, for example, the Republican majority was more intent on supporting the president than on protecting congressional prerogatives in the policy process. This aided the president's expansion of control of the bureaucracy.[55] Only when a congressional consensus exists on what an agency should be doing, or at least that Congress should monitor what the agency does, is congressional control fully effective.

In general, agencies are quite responsive to the congressional committees most directly involved with their authorizations and appropriations. The congressional control that committees and subcommittees exert on the bureaucracy is not the same as the control exercised by Congress as a whole. This is because the subcommittee policy preferences do not always reflect accurately the preferences of the full Congress. Members of Congress gravitate to committees in which they have a special interest—either because of the member's background and expertise or because of the committee's special relevance for the home constituency.[56] Thus, in being responsive to the relevant committees and subcommittees, usually with the support of the organized interests served by the agencies, bureaucrats are clearly less sensitive to the preferences of Congress as a whole, the president, and the general public.

THE BUREAUCRACY AND THE COURTS

Agencies can be sued by individuals and businesses for not following the law. If a citizen disagrees with an agency ruling on welfare eligibility, or the adequacy of inspections of poultry processing plants, or even a ruling by the IRS, he or she can take the case to the courts. In some cases the courts have been important. A highly controversial example involves the timber industry. Environmentalists sued the Department of the Interior and the U.S. Forest Service to prevent logging in some of the old-growth forests of the Pacific Northwest. They sought protection for the spotted owl under the terms of the Endangered Species Act. After a decade-long struggle, logging was greatly restricted in the area in 1992, despite opposition by the economically important timbering interests of the region. However, under the more business-friendly Bush administration, the issue was once again on the agenda and, as the timber industry gained ground, the environmental groups were back in court. In 2009 the Obama administration reversed the Bush administration policy that had doubled the amount of logging allowed.[57]

More often, though, the courts play only a modest role in controlling the bureaucracy. One of the reasons for this limited role is that, since the Administrative Procedure

> **issue networks** complex systems of relationships among groups that influence policy, including elected leaders, interest groups, specialists, consultants, and research institutes
>
> **congressional oversight** efforts by Congress, especially through committees, to monitor agency rule making, enforcement, and implementation of congressional policies

Iron Triangle ●

Act of 1946, the courts have tended to defer to the expertise of the bureaucrats when agency decisions are appealed. That is, unless a clear principle of law is violated, the courts usually support administrative rulings.[58] So, for example, while the Supreme Court did restrict some aspects of the Bush administration's policies of unlimited detention of "enemy combatants" held at Guantánamo Bay, it did not go nearly as far as civil liberties advocates wanted.[59]

Another reason is that Congress explicitly puts the decisions of numerous agencies, such as the Department of Veterans Affairs, beyond the reach of the courts. They do this, of course, when members expect they will agree with the decisions of an agency but are uncertain about what the courts might do. Finally, even without these restrictions, the courts' time is extremely limited. The departments and independent agencies make thousands and thousands of important decisions each year; the courts can act on only those decisions about which someone feels sufficiently aggrieved to take the agency to court. Court proceedings can drag on for years, and meanwhile the agencies go about their business making new decisions. In short, the courts can, in specific instances, decide cases that influence how the bureaucracy operates, but such instances are the exception rather than the rule.

PAUSE AND REVIEW:

WHO, WHAT, HOW

All of Washington and beyond have something at stake in bureaucratic politics. The agencies themselves battle over scarce resources, using the tools of constituency building to keep pressure on Congress to maintain their funding levels, and keeping their functions separate from other agencies even if the result is redundancy and inefficiency.

The president can employ a variety of techniques to control the bureaucracy, but given time constraints and the weight of bureaucratic norms, he is generally unsuccessful at wresting control from the bureaucrats.

Congress has much at stake in its interactions with the bureaucracy. The bottom line in bureaucratic politics is that the bureaucracy is ultimately responsible to Congress. It is difficult to speak of Congress as a whole institution guided by a common interest, but individual members of Congress certainly have identifiable interests. Because policymaking in Congress so often takes place at the committee and subcommittee levels, and because those committees develop iron triangle relationships with interest groups and the bureaucracies that serve them, members of Congress have quite a lot of input into what the bureaucracy does.

AP Photo/ Pablo Martinez Monsivais

Partisanship Can Fuel Oversight
The traditional role of oversight is for Congress to check on the executive branch, but partisan differences can also influence these investigations. Here, then–secretary of state Hillary Clinton reacts to questions about the 2012 attacks on the U.S. diplomatic mission in Benghazi, Libya, during a highly charged exchange with the Republican-controlled Senate Foreign Relations Committee.

IN YOUR OWN WORDS >> Describe the relationship between the federal agencies and the three branches of the federal government.

>> THE CITIZENS AND THE BUREAUCRACY
The tension between transparency and efficiency

The picture that emerges from a look at the politics of the bureaucracy is one of a powerful arm of government, somewhat answerable to the president, more responsible to Congress, but with considerable discretion to do what it wants, often in response to the special interests of clientele groups or regulated industry. If anyone is forgotten in this policymaking arrangement, it is the American public, the average citizens and consumers who are not well organized and who may not even know that they are affected by an issue until the policy is already law. We can look at the relationship between the bureaucracy and the public to determine how the public interest is considered in bureaucratic policymaking.

First, we should figure out what the "public interest" in a democracy really means. Is it the majority preference? If so, then what happens to the minority? Is it some unknown, possibly unpleasant goal that we would favor unanimously if only we could be detached from our particular interests—a sort of national equivalent of eating our spinach because it's good for us? We can imagine some interests that would be disadvantaged by any notion of the public good, no matter how benign. Industries that pollute are disadvantaged by legislation promoting clean air and water; manufacturers of bombs, warplanes, and tanks are disadvantaged by peace. The point here is not to argue that there is no such thing as a "public interest" but to point out that in a democracy it may be difficult to reach consensus on it. To that end, the public interest can probably best be determined by increasing the number of people who have input into deciding what it is. The facts of political life are that the most organized, vocal, and well-financed interests usually get heard by politicians, including bureaucrats. When we speak of the public interest, we usually refer to the interest that would be expressed by the unorganized, less vocal, poorer components of society, if they would only speak. In this final section we look at efforts to bring more people into the bureaucratic policymaking process so as to make policy more responsive to more citizens.

To help increase bureaucratic responsiveness and sensitivity to the public, Congress has made citizen participation a central feature in the policymaking of many agencies. This frequently takes the form of **citizen advisory councils** that, by statute, subject key policy decisions of agencies to outside consideration by members of the public. There are more than 1,200 such committees and councils in the executive branch. The people who participate on these councils are not representative of the citizenry; rather, they are typically chosen by the agency and have special credentials or interests relevant to the agencies' work. Thus citizen advisory councils are hardly a reflection of the general population.

Seven different types of citizen advisory councils have been called over the years (1937 through 1996) to make recommendations on the Social Security system. All have favored the existing programs and recommended expansion. Why? Because members of the councils were carefully selected from among people who already thought highly of Social Security. What political scientist Martha Derthick concluded about the Social Security councils is probably true generally: "The outsiders tended to become insiders as they were drawn into the council's deliberations. . . . Typically, advisory council reports paved the way for program executives' own current recommendations."[60]

Given the chance, such groups can generally be counted on to praise existing efforts—unless they are genuinely flawed or the council is investigating some policy

disaster—and then to call for a greater commitment and more resources to deal with whatever problems they are considering. This arrangement serves the interests of the bureaucracy, interest groups, Washington consultants, and elected officials. It probably does not achieve the goal of making public policy more responsive to the broader public interest.

Other reform efforts have attempted to make the bureaucracy more accessible to the public. Citizen access is enhanced by the passage of **sunshine laws** that require that meetings of policymakers be open to the public. Thus the Open Meeting Law was passed in 1976, requiring important agency reviews, hearings, and decision-making sessions to be open to the public, along with most congressional committee and subcommittee meetings. However, most national security and personnel meetings and many criminal investigative meetings are exempted. The right to attend a meeting is of little use unless one can find out that it is being held. The Administrative Procedures Act requires advanced published notices of all hearings, proposed rules, and new regulations so that the public can attend and comment on decisions that might affect them. These announcements appear in the *Federal Register*. In a separate section, the *Federal Register* also contains major presidential documents, including executive orders, proclamations, transcripts of speeches and news conferences, and other White House releases.

With all this information about every meeting, every proposed regulation, and more, the *Federal Register* becomes very large—more than 70,000 pages a year. Such size makes it quite forbidding to the average citizen; fortunately, a government booklet, "The *Federal Register*: What It Is and How to Use It," is generally available in libraries and on the Internet, and it greatly eases the task of navigating the *Register*. An online edition of the *Federal Register* is also available (www.gpoaccess.gov/fr/).

A related point of access is the **Freedom of Information Act (FOIA)**, which was passed in 1966 and has been amended several times since. This act provides citizens with the right to copies of most public records held by the agencies. These records include the evidence used in agency decisions, correspondence pertaining to agency business, research data, financial records, and so forth. The agency has to provide the information requested or let the applicant know which provisions of the FOIA allow the agency to withhold the information.

citizen advisory councils citizen groups that consider the policy decisions of an agency; a way to make the bureaucracy responsive to the general public

sunshine laws legislation opening the process of bureaucratic policymaking to the public

Freedom of Information Act (FOIA) 1966 law that allows citizens to obtain copies of most public records

Net Neutrality Rules ●   Coding a Better Government ●

Citizens also receive protection under the **Privacy Act of 1974**, which gives them the right to find out what information government agencies have about them. It also sets up procedures so that erroneous information can be corrected and ensures the confidentiality of Social Security, tax, and related records.

These reforms may provide little practical access for most citizens. Few of us have the time, the knowledge, or the energy to plow through the *Federal Register* and to attend dull meetings. Similarly, while many citizens no doubt feel they are not getting the full story from government agencies, they also do not have much of an idea of what it is they don't know. Hence, few of us ever use the FOIA.

In fact, few Americans try to gain access to the bureaucracy because of negative images that tell us that it is too big, too remote, too complex, and too devoted to special interests. The public does not think well of the bureaucracy or the government, although it does report favorably on its interactions with individual bureaucrats and agencies.[61] One reason for the public disaffection with the bureaucracy may be that it is so constantly under attack by a frustrated president and by members of Congress who highlight the failings of some aspects of government to divert attention from those that are serving their interests only too well.

Political scientist Kenneth Meier suggests that although countries usually get bureaucracies no worse than they deserve, the United States has managed to get one that is much better than it deserves, given citizen attitudes and attentiveness toward it. He says that in terms of responsiveness and competency, the U.S. federal bureaucracy is "arguably the best in the world."[62] He places the responsibility for maintaining the quality of the system squarely with the citizens and, to some extent, with the media, suggesting that citizens contact bureaucratic

AP Photo/Dee Marvin

"Freedom" of Information

The 1966 Freedom of Information Act (FOIA) allows citizens access to declassified documents at the state and federal levels. However, provisions contained within the act allow authorities to refuse access to specific information for various reasons. Officials can do this by blacking out content, as in the documents shown here, or by refusing to release them entirely. Critics say that it can be next to impossible to piece together the actual events or facts surrounding an event when access is denied so frequently, and that declassified should mean just that—that it is open to the public for review.

agencies about issues of concern, vote with an elected official's bureaucratic appointments in mind, keep realistic expectations of what government can do, and encourage the media in its watchdog role. Keeping the republic may require public participation in bureaucracy as well as in democracy.

Privacy Act of 1974 a law that gives citizens access to the government's files on them

IN YOUR OWN WORDS » Analyze the tension between transparency and efficiency in the federal bureaucracy.

LET'S REVISIT: **WHAT'S AT STAKE...**

Let's go back to the question of what's at stake in the dispute over the USDA's organic food regulation. Remember that regulations are a form of rules, and rules determine who the winners and losers are likely to be. Regulations can serve a variety of interests. They could serve the public interest, simply making it easier for consumers to buy organic food by standardizing what it means to be organic. But regulations can also serve interests besides the public interest. In this case, there were competing business interests as well. Agribusiness and the food preparation industry wanted to use regulations to break into a lucrative market previously closed to them because of the labor-intensive nature of organic farming. For the traditional organic farmers, the proposed regulations spelled disaster.

As far as big business was concerned, this case was like many others. Businesses in the United States are able to lobby the government freely to try to get rules and regulations passed that enhance their positions, and to try to stop those that will hurt them. As we will see in Chapter 11's discussion of interest groups, the larger sums of money that big business can bring to the lobbying effort usually give them an edge in influencing government. If the larger businesses were allowed to compete as organic food producers, the small businesses would lose the only advantage they had, and they would have been forced out of business. In this case, the small businesses were aided by citizen action. This example shows that it is possible to energize a public audience to respond to the bureaucracy. Because those consumers who choose to eat organic foods were a focused, committed, and assertive segment of the population, they were able to follow through with political action.

TO SUM UP

Sharpen your skills with **SAGE edge** at **http://edge.sagepub.com/barbour7e**. **SAGE edge for students** provides a personalized approach to help you accomplish your coursework goals in an easy-to-use learning environment.

REVIEW

What Is Bureaucracy?

Bureaucracies are everywhere today, in the private as well as the public spheres. They create a special problem for democratic politics because the desire for democratic accountability often conflicts with the desire to take politics out of the bureaucracy. We have moved from the spoils system of the nineteenth century to a civil service merit system with a more professionalized bureaucracy.

bureaucracy (p. 325)
neutral competence (p. 325)
spoils system (p. 325)

patronage (p. 325)
civil service (p. 326)
Pendleton Act (p. 326)
Hatch Act (p. 326)
accountability (p. 327)
red tape (p. 328)

The American Federal Bureaucracy

The U.S. bureaucracy has grown from just three cabinet departments at the founding to a gigantic apparatus of fifteen cabinet-level departments and hundreds of independent agencies, regulatory commissions, and government corporations. This growth has been in response to the expansion of the nation, the politics of special economic and social groups, and the emergence of new problems.

clientele groups (p. 329)
departments (p. 330)
independent agencies (p. 331)
independent regulatory boards and commissions (p. 331)
regulations (p. 331)
government corporations (p. 335)
bureaucratic discretion (p. 336)
Federal Register (p. 337)

Politics Inside the Bureaucracy

The culture of bureaucracy refers to how agencies operate—their assumptions, values, and habits. The bureaucratic culture increases employees' belief in the programs they administer, their commitment to the survival and growth of their agencies, and the tendency to rely on rules and procedures rather than goals.

Many observers believe that the bureaucracy should simply administer the laws the political branches have enacted. In reality, the agencies of the bureaucracy make government policy, and they play the roles of judge and jury in enforcing those policies. These activities are in part an unavoidable consequence of the tremendous technical expertise of the agencies because Congress and the president simply cannot perform many technical tasks.

bureaucratic culture (p. 339)
bureaucratese (p. 339)
whistleblowers (p. 342)

External Bureaucratic Politics

Agencies work actively for their political survival. They attempt to establish strong support outside the agency, to avoid direct competition with other agencies, and to jealously guard their own policy jurisdictions. Presidential powers are only modestly effective in controlling the bureaucracy. The affected clientele groups working in close cooperation with the agencies and the congressional committees that oversee them form powerful iron triangles.

agency capture (p. 346)
iron triangles (p. 348)
issue networks (p. 350)
congressional oversight (p. 350)

The Citizens and the Bureaucracy

Regardless of what the public may think, the U.S. bureaucracy is actually quite responsive and competent when compared with the bureaucracies of other countries. Citizens can increase this responsiveness by taking advantage of opportunities for gaining access to bureaucratic decision making.

citizen advisory councils (p. 352)
sunshine laws (p. 352)
Freedom of Information Act (FOIA) (p. 352)
Privacy Act of 1974 (p. 353)

Reach out to your agencies.
Have an opinion or a question for or about a federal agency? **USA .gov** is the front door to the executive branch, with links and contact information for all federal agencies. These agencies make rules that affect your life every day—from what you eat to how you get your Internet services— and every citizen is entitled to review and comment on new and proposed rules. Take a look at

what decisions are being made, and make your opinion clear.

Become a bureaucrat.
It may not seem glamorous, but in fact there are many fantastic job opportunities with the federal government. You can search **usajobs.gov** by location or keyword to find openings in everything from the FBI to the National Park Service, and get on track for a great career.

Find out what the government knows.
Want to know if the FBI's got a file on you? Or just how that big-box store in your town was able to get its hand on public land? The Freedom of Information Act (FOIA) is your ticket to public records. Visit the **FOIA website** to peruse FOIA data or make a FOIA request.

ENGAGE

Helco, Hugh. 1977. *A Government of Strangers: Executive Politics in Washington.* Washington, DC: **Brookings Institution**. A classic book that details the conflict between appointed officials and career bureaucrats.

Reich, Robert. 1997. *Locked in the Cabinet.* **New York: Knopf.** Bill Clinton's longtime friend and first secretary of labor gives a firsthand look at the politics behind the Clinton administration.

EXPLORE

National Whistleblowers Center. The National Whistleblowers Center is an advocacy organization that aims to protect the rights of individuals who speak out against wrongdoing and who fear retaliation from their employers. The site contains information on whistleblowers, advocacy efforts, resources, and press releases.

The Wire. 2002–2008. This acclaimed HBO drama takes a hard look at how bureaucratic structures affect politics, policing, labor, education, crime—and even the internal working workings of organized drug cartels—in a fictionalized version of Baltimore, Maryland.

The Insider. 1999. This film is based on a true story about a 1994 *60 Minutes* report on malpractices in the tobacco industry that was never aired because Westinghouse, the parent company of CBS, objected.

Silkwood. 1983. Also based on a true story, this film is about a plutonium plant worker who died mysteriously after blowing the whistle on the dangerous conditions in the plant.

10

THE AMERICAN LEGAL SYSTEM AND THE COURTS

IN YOUR OWN WORDS   After you've read this chapter, you will be able to

» Describe the role that law plays in democratic society.

» Explain the role of Congress and the courts in establishing the judiciary.

» Evaluate Hamilton's claim that the judiciary was the "least dangerous branch of government" in light of the power it wields.

» Outline the institutional rules and political influences that shape the Supreme Court and the decisions it makes.

» Describe the relationship between citizens and the courts in America.

WHAT'S AT STAKE... WHEN THE SUPREME COURT GETS INVOLVED IN PARTISAN POLITICS?

THE 2000 PRESIDENTIAL ELECTION BETWEEN
George W. Bush and Al Gore must have set Alexander Hamilton spinning in his grave. In the *Federalist Papers* the American founder wrote confidently that the Supreme Court would be the least dangerous branch of government. Having the power of neither the sword nor the purse, it could do little other than judge, and Hamilton blithely assumed that those judgments would remain legal ones, not matters of raw power politics.

More than two hundred years later, however, without military might or budgetary power, the Supreme Court took into its own hands the very political task of deciding who would be the next president of the United States and, what's more, made that decision right down party lines. On a five-to-four vote (five more conservative justices versus four more liberal ones), the Supreme Court overturned the decision of the Florida Supreme Court to allow a recount of votes in the contested Florida election and awarded electoral victory to Bush.

How had it come to this? The presidential vote in Florida was virtually tied, recounts were required by law in some locations, and voting snafus in several other counties had left untold numbers of votes uncounted. Whether those votes should, or even could, be counted or whether voter error and system failure had rendered them invalid was in dispute. Believing that a count of the disputed ballots would give him the few hundred votes he needed for victory, Al Gore wanted the recount. Bush did not. The Florida secretary of state, a Republican appointed by the governor, Bush's brother, ordered the vote counting finished. The Florida Supreme Court, dominated heavily by Democrats, ruled instead that a recount should go forward.

Bush appealed to the U.S. Supreme Court, asking it to overturn the Florida Supreme Court's decision and to stay, or suspend, the recount pending its decision. A divided Court issued the stay. Justice John Paul Stevens took the unusual route of writing a dissent from the stay, arguing that it was unwise to "stop the counting of legal votes."

Stevens, "the loser is perfectly clear. It is the nation's confidence in the judge as an impartial guardian of the rule of law."

Who was right here? The issue was debated by everyone from angry demonstrators outside the Court to learned commentators in scholarly journals, from families at the dinner table to editorial writers in the nation's press. Was Scalia correct that Bush had really already won and that it was up to the Court to save the legitimacy of his claim to power? Or was Stevens right: that by engaging in politics so blatantly, the Court had done itself irremediable damage in the eyes of the public? What was really at stake for the Court and for America in the five-to-four decision of *Bush v. Gore?* **«**

Reuters/Larry Downing

Taking It to the Court

With the presidential election between George W. Bush and Al Gore hinging on the outcome in too-close-to-call Florida, demonstrators on both sides of the partisan divide rallied as the U.S. Supreme Court decided whether to allow a recount in that state.

Justice Antonin Scalia wrote in response that the recount would pose "irreparable harm" to Bush by "casting a cloud on what he claims to be the legitimacy of his election."

The split between the justices, so apparent in the order for the stay, reappeared in the final decision, where six separate opinions ended up being written. On a five-to-four vote, the majority claimed that if the recount went forward under the Florida Supreme Court's order with different standards for counting the vote in different counties, it would amount to a denial of equal protection of the laws. The amount of work required to bring about a fair recount could not be accomplished before the December 12 deadline. A three-person subset of the majority added that the Florida court's order was illegal in the first place.

The dissenters argued instead that the December 12 deadline was not fixed and that the recount could have taken place up to the meeting of the Electoral College on December 18, that there was no equal protection issue, that the Supreme Court should defer to the Florida Supreme Court on issues of state law, and that by involving itself in the political case, the Court risked losing public trust. While the winner of the election was in dispute, wrote

IMAGINE a world without laws. You careen down the road in your car, at any speed that takes your fancy. You park where you please and enter a drugstore that sells drugs of all sorts, from Prozac to LSD to vodka and beer. You purchase what you like—no one asks you for proof of your age or for a prescription—and there are no restrictions on what or how much you buy. There are no rules governing the production or usage of currency either, so you hope that the dealer will accept what you have to offer in trade.

Life is looking pretty good as you head back out to the street, only to find that your car is no longer there. Theft is not illegal, and you curse yourself for forgetting to set the car alarm and for not using your wheel lock. There are no police to call, and even if there were, tracking down your car would be virtually impossible since there are no vehicle registration laws to prove you own it in the first place.

Rather than walk—these streets are quite dangerous, after all—you spot a likely car to get you home. You have to wrestle with the occupant, who manages to clout you over the head before you drive away. It isn't much of a prize, covered with dents and nicks from innumerable clashes with other cars jockeying for position at intersections where there are neither stop signs nor lights and the right of the faster prevails. Arriving home to enjoy your beer in peace and to gain a respite from the war zone you call your local community, you find that another family has moved in while you were shopping. Groaning with frustration, you think that surely there must be a better way!

And there is. As often as we might rail against restrictions on our freedom, such as not being able to buy beer if we are under twenty-one, or having to wear a motorcycle helmet, or not being able to speed down an empty highway, laws actually do us much more good than harm. British philosophers Thomas Hobbes and John Locke, whom we discussed in Chapter 1, both imagined a "prepolitical" world without laws. Inhabitants of Hobbes's state of nature found life without laws to be dismal or, as he put it, "solitary, poor, nasty, brutish and short." And although residents of Locke's state of nature merely found the lawless life to be "inconvenient," they had to mount a constant defense of their possessions and their lives. One of the reasons both Hobbes and Locke thought people would be willing to leave the state of nature for civil society, and to give up their freedom to do whatever they wanted, was to gain security, order, and predictability in life. Because we tend to focus on the laws that stop us from doing the things we want to do, or that require us to do things we don't want to do, we often forget the full array of laws that make it possible for us to live together in relative peace and to leave behind the brutishness of Hobbes's state of nature and the inconveniences of Locke's.

Laws occupy a central position in any political society, but especially in a democracy, where the rule is ultimately by law and not the whim of a tyrant. Laws are the "how" in the formulation of politics as "who gets what, and how"—they dictate how our collective lives are to be organized, what rights we can claim, what principles we should live by, and how we can use the system to get what we want. Laws can also be the "what" in the formulation, as citizens and political actors use the existing rules to create new rules that produce even more favorable outcomes.

LAW AND THE AMERICAN LEGAL SYSTEM
Rules of the game that make collective living possible

Thinking about the law can be confusing. On the one hand, laws are the sorts of rules we have been discussing: limits and restrictions that get in our way, or that make life a little easier. But on the other hand, we would like to think that our legal system is founded on rules that represent basic and enduring principles of justice, that create for us a higher level of civilization. Laws are products of the political process, created by political human beings to help them get valuable resources. Those resources may be civil peace and security, or a particular moral order, or power and influence, or even goods or

entitlements. Thus, for security, we have laws that eliminate traffic chaos, enforce contracts, and ban violence. For moral order (and for security as well!), we have laws against murder, incest, and rape. And for political advantage, we have laws like those that give large states greater power in the process of electing a president and those that allow electoral districts to be drawn by the majority party. Laws dealing with more concrete resources are those that, for example, give tax breaks to homeowners or subsidize dairy farmers.

Different political systems produce different systems of laws as well. In small communities where everyone shares values and experiences, formal legal structures may be unnecessary since everyone knows what is expected of him or her, and the community can force compliance with those expectations, perhaps by ostracizing nonconformists. In authoritarian systems, like those of the former Soviet Union, or North Korea or China, laws exist primarily to serve the rulers and the state, and they are subject to sudden change at the whim of the rulers. In systems that merge church and state, such as the Holy Roman Empire, pre-Enlightenment Europe, or some Islamic countries today, laws are assumed to be God-given, and violations of the law are analogous to sin against an all-powerful creator. These sorts of legal systems are not much more convenient for the "ruled" than is Locke's state of nature, though they may be more secure.

In nonauthoritarian countries, where citizens are more than mere subjects and can make claims of rights against the government, laws are understood to exist for the purpose of serving the citizens. That is, laws make life more convenient, even if they have to restrict our actions to do so. But laws, and the courts that interpret and apply them, perform a variety of functions in a democratic society, some of which we commonly recognize, and others of which are less obvious.

THE ROLE OF LAW IN DEMOCRATIC SOCIETIES

For the purpose of understanding the role of law in democratic political systems, we can focus on five important functions of laws:[1]

- The first, and most obvious, function follows directly from Hobbes and Locke: laws *provide security* (for people and their property) so that we may go about our daily lives in relative harmony.

- Laws *provide predictability*, allowing us to plan our activities and go about our business without fearing a random judgment that tells us we have broken a law we didn't know existed.

- The fact that laws are known in advance and identify punishable behaviors leads to the third function of laws in a democracy, that of *conflict resolution*, through neutral third parties known as **courts**.

- A fourth function of laws in a democratic society is *to reflect and enforce conformity to society's values*—for instance, that murder is wrong or that parents should not be allowed to abuse their children.

- A fifth function of laws in a democracy is *to distribute the benefits and rewards society has to offer and to allocate the costs of those good things*, whether they are welfare benefits, civil rights protection, or tax breaks.

THE AMERICAN LEGAL TRADITION

We mentioned earlier that different political systems have different kinds of legal systems—that is, different systems designed to provide order and resolve conflict through the use of laws. Most governments in the industrialized world, including many European countries, South America, Japan, the province of Quebec in Canada, and the state of Louisiana (because of its French heritage), have a legal system founded on a **civil-law tradition**, based on a detailed, comprehensive legal code usually generated by the legislature. Some of these codes date back to the days of Napoleon (1804). Such codified systems leave little to the discretion of judges in determining what the law is. Instead, the judge's job is to take an active role in getting at the truth. He or she investigates the facts, asks questions, and determines what has happened. The emphasis is more on getting the appropriate outcome than on maintaining the integrity of the procedures, although fair procedures are still important. While this system is well entrenched in much of the world, and has many defenders, the legal system in the United States is different in three crucial ways.

THE COMMON-LAW TRADITION
To begin, the U.S. legal system, and that of all the states except Louisiana, is based on common law, which developed in Great Britain and the countries that once formed the British Empire. The **common-law tradition** relied on royal judges making decisions based on their own judgment and on previous legal decisions, which were applied uniformly, or *commonly*, across the land. The emphasis was on preserving the decisions that had been made before, what is called relying on **precedent**, or *stare decisis* (Latin for "let the decision stand"). Judges in such a system have far more power in determining what the law is than do judges in civil-law systems, and their job is to determine and apply the law as an impartial referee, not to take an active role in discovering the truth.

The legal system in the United States, however, is not a pure common-law system. Legislatures do make laws, and attempts have been made to codify, or organize, them into a coherent body of law. American legislators, however, are less concerned with creating such a coherent body of law

than with responding to the various needs and demands of their constituents. As a result, American laws have a somewhat haphazard and hodgepodge character. But the common-law nature of the legal system is reinforced by the fact that American judges still use their considerable discretion to decide what the laws mean, and they rely heavily on precedent and the principle of *stare decisis*. Thus, when a judge decides a case, he or she will look at the relevant law but will also consult previous rulings on the issue before making a ruling of his or her own.

THE UNITED STATES AS AN ADVERSARIAL SYSTEM
Related to its origins in the British common-law tradition, a second way in which the American legal system differs from many others in the world is that it is an adversarial system. By **adversarial system**, we mean that our trial procedures are "presumed to reveal the truth through the clash of skilled professionals vigorously advocating competing viewpoints."[2] The winner may easily be the side with the most skilled attorneys, not the side that is "right" or "deserving" or that has "justice" on its side. Judges have a primarily passive role; they apply the law, keep the proceedings fair, and make rulings when appropriate, but their role does not include that of active "truth seeker."

Other legal systems offer an alternative to the adversarial system, and a comparison with these **inquisitorial systems** can help us understand the strengths and weaknesses of our own. The difference can be summed up this way: adversarial systems are designed to determine whether a particular accused person is guilty, whereas inquisitorial systems are intended to discover "who did it."[3] While Britain shares our adversarial tradition, many civil-law European countries, like France and Germany, have trial procedures that give a much more active role to the judge as a fact-finder. In these systems, the judge questions witnesses and seeks evidence,

courts institutions that sit as neutral third parties to resolve conflicts according to the law

civil-law tradition a legal system based on a detailed comprehensive legal code, usually created by the legislature

common-law tradition a legal system based on the accumulated rulings of judges over time, applied uniformly—judge-made law

precedent a previous decision or ruling that, in common-law tradition, is binding on subsequent decisions

adversarial system trial procedures designed to resolve conflict through the clash of opposing sides, moderated by a neutral, passive judge who applies the law

inquisitorial system trial procedures designed to determine the truth through the intervention of an active judge who seeks evidence and questions witnesses and the prosecution (the side bringing the case) and the defense have comparatively minor roles.

In an era when American courtrooms have become theatrical stages and trials are often media extravaganzas, the idea of a system that focuses on finding the truth, that reduces the role of lawyers, that limits the expensive process of evidence gathering, and that makes trials cheaper and faster in general sounds very appealing. For both cultural and political reasons, we are unlikely to switch to a more inquisitorial system, however. It can be argued, for instance, that the adversarial system makes it easier to maintain that key principle of American law, "innocent until proven guilty." Once a judge in an inquisitorial system has determined that there is enough evidence to try someone, he or she is in fact assuming that the defendant is guilty.[4] In addition, the adversarial system fits with our cultural emphasis on individualism and procedural values, and it gives tremendous power to lawyers, who have a vested interest in maintaining such a system.[5]

THE UNITED STATES AS A LITIGIOUS

SYSTEM Not only is the U.S. system adversarial, but it is also *litigious*, which is another way of saying that American citizens sue one another, or litigate, a lot. Legal scholars differ on whether Americans are more litigious than citizens of other nations. Certainly there are more lawyers per capita in the United States than elsewhere (three times as many as in England, for instance, and twenty times as many as in Japan), but other countries have legal professionals other than lawyers who handle legal work, and the number of actual litigators (lawyers who practice in court) is sometimes limited by professional regulations.

Some evidence, however, suggests that Americans do file civil suits—that is, cases seeking compensation from actions that are not defined as crimes, such as medical malpractice or breach of contract—more often than do citizens of many other countries. While the American rate of filing civil suits is roughly the same as that of the English, Americans file 25 percent more civil cases per capita than do the Germans, and 30 to 40 percent more cases per capita than do the Swedes.[6] Comparisons aside, it remains true that forty-four lawsuits are filed annually for every thousand people in the population.[7]

Why do Americans spend so much time in the courtroom? Scholars argue that the large number of lawsuits in the United States is a measure of our openness and democratic concern for the rights of all citizens,[8] and that litigation is unavoidable in democracies committed to individuals' freedoms and to citizens' rights to defend themselves from harm by others.[9] Americans also sue one another a lot because our society has traditionally failed to provide other mechanisms for providing compensation and security from risk. For instance, until health care reform kicked in fully in 2014, many Americans lacked health insurance, a basic security that in many other countries is provided by the government. When disaster strikes, in the form of a car accident or a doctor's error or a faulty product, the only way many individuals can cover expenses has been to sue.

The large number of lawsuits in America, however, has a negative as well as a positive side. Some experts argue that Americans have come to expect "total justice," that everything bad that happens can be blamed on someone, who should compensate them for their harm.[10] In addition, our propensity to litigate means that the courts get tied up with what are often frivolous lawsuits, as when a prisoner filed a million-dollar lawsuit against New York's Mohawk Correctional Facility claiming "'cruel and unusual' punishment for incidents stemming from a guard's refusal to refrigerate the prisoner's ice cream."[11] Such suits are costly not only to the individuals or institutions that must defend themselves, but also to taxpayers, who support the system as a whole, paying the salaries of judges and legal staff. Politicians make occasional attempts to limit lawsuits (for instance, the recent Republican effort to cap medical malpractice awards), but these efforts often have political motivations and usually come to nothing.

© Patricia Mann

"So Sue Me . . ."
Litigation is one avenue Americans sometimes take to address the risks of everyday life. The label on this coffee cup, "Caution...I'm Hot," is the result of one such lawsuit, in which a customer sued a chain for serving coffee that was determined to have been dangerously hot. The case was highly publicized in the media, drawing criticism that the verdict, which favored the plaintiff, was a gross representation of Americans' propensity for frivolous lawsuits. But others pointed to evidence that the elderly plaintiff suffered severe burns from the coffee, requiring skin grafts, and sued only after the company refused to pay her related medical bills.

DON'T BE FOOLED...
WHEN GOING TO COURT

A cherished principle of our legal system is that everyone is entitled to his or her day in court. If you get into trouble, you are guaranteed access to the courts to redress your wrongs or to defend yourself against false claims. And the way life is in America these days, you are increasingly likely to end up there. If you don't find yourself in court physically, you will certainly watch legal proceedings on television or read about someone's legal travails in a book, newspaper, or magazine. In a society with a heavy emphasis on due process rights, with a litigious disposition to boot, the legal system plays a prominent role in many of our lives at one time or another.

But the legal system is run by lawyers, and legal jargon, like the bureaucratese we studied in Chapter 9, is not easy to understand. In fact, lawyers have a vested interest in our not understanding legalese in the same way that accountants benefit from an incomprehensible tax code. The more we cannot understand the language of the law, the more we need lawyers to tell us what it all means. We cannot condense three years of law school vocabulary here, but we can arm you with some basics to keep in mind if (or when!) you have your day in court.

Entry-Level or Appeals Court?

One critical question, when trying to sort out what is happening in a court of law, is whether we are looking at a proceeding in an entry-level or an appeals court. The personnel and the procedures differ, depending on what kind of court it is.

- **Entry-level court.** This is the court in which a person is initially accused of breaking a criminal or a civil law. The questions to be decided in this court are (1) what is the relevant law and (2) is the person accused guilty of a crime or responsible for violating the civil law? The first question is a question of law, the second a question of fact. The entry-level court produces a verdict based on the application of law to a finding of fact.

- **Appeals court.** This is a court that handles cases when one party to an entry-level proceeding feels that a point of law was not properly applied. Cases are appealed only on points of law, not on interpretations of facts. If new facts are shown to be present, a new trial at the entry level can be ordered.

Who's Who?

It's almost impossible to follow the legal action if you aren't familiar with the players. Here we have grouped them under three headings: the people who are themselves involved in the dispute, the people who represent them in court, and the people who make the decisions.

People Involved in the Dispute

The parties to the dispute have different names, depending on whether the case is being heard for the first time or on appeal.

- **Plaintiff.** The person bringing the charges or the grievance if the case is in its original, or entry-level, court. If the case is a criminal case, the plaintiff will always be the government, because crimes are considered to be injuries to the citizens of the state, no matter who is really harmed.

- **Defendant.** The person being accused of a crime or of injuring someone.

- **Petitioner.** The person filing an appeal. The petitioner can be either the plaintiff or the defendant from the lower court trial. It is always the loser of that trial, however.

- **Respondent.** The other party in an appeal. As there may be several layers of appeals, the petitioner in one case may later find himself or herself the respondent in a further appeal.

When you see a case name written out it will look like this: *Name of Plaintiff v. Name of Defendant*, or *Name of Petitioner v. Name of Respondent*. The names of the cases may switch back and forth as the case moves its way through various appeals. The historic case known as *Gideon v. Wainwright*, for example, began as a simple criminal case of Wainwright, the prosecutor for Florida, as the plaintiff, against Clarence Gideon, the defendant. When Gideon decided to file his appeal with the Supreme Court, he became the petitioner against Wainwright, now the respondent.

People Who Represent the Parties in Court

- **Lawyers or attorneys.** Professionals who represent the two sides in a dispute. Unlike in other countries, in the United States the same lawyer who works on the case behind the scenes will also represent the client in court.

- **Prosecuting attorney.** The lawyer for the plaintiff. In criminal cases the prosecutor is always a representative of the government—a district or prosecuting attorney at the state level, and a U.S. attorney at the federal level.

- On appeal the government's case is argued by the **state attorney general** (at the state level), the **U.S. attorney** (at the federal level), and the solicitor general (if the case goes all the way to the Supreme Court).

- **Defense attorney** (also called a defense counsel). The representative of the defendant. In a criminal case, the Constitution guarantees that a poor defendant be provided with an attorney free of charge, so it can happen that both the prosecutor and the defense counsel are being paid by the same government to represent the two opposing interests in the case.

People Who Make the Decisions

The final group of players are the decision makers. Two kinds of decisions have to be made in a court of law: decisions about facts (what actually happened) and decisions about law. Generally the facts are decided on by citizens, and the law is applied by legal professionals.

- **Juries.** Groups of citizens who decide on the facts in a case. Juries are intended to be a check by citizens on the power of the courts. The Constitution guarantees us a jury of our peers, or equals, although we can waive our right to a jury trial, in which case the judge will make the findings of fact. Lawyers representing the two sides choose from a pool that is representative of the general population, according to a detailed set of rules. In recent years, lawyers have become expert at picking juries that they believe will give maximum advantage to their clients. Questions of fact arise only in entry-level cases, so there are no juries in appeals courts. Citizens can be asked to sit on grand juries (to decide if there is enough factual evidence to warrant bringing a case to trial) or trial juries (to decide whether or not someone is guilty as charged).

- **Jurors.** Participants on a jury, either trial or grand, chosen from a pool of citizens on jury duty at the time.

- **Judges.** Deciders of questions of law. In entry-level courts, judges make rulings on points of law and instruct the jury on the law, so that they know how to use the facts they decide on. If there is no jury, the judge finds facts and applies the law as well. In appeals courts, panels of judges rule on legal questions that are alleged to have arisen from an earlier trial (for example, if a defendant was not given the opportunity to speak to a lawyer, was that a violation of due process?).

- **Justices.** Panels of justices in appeals courts in a state court or the federal Supreme Court. There are no witnesses, and no evidence is presented that would raise any factual questions. If new evidence is thought to be present, the justices order a new trial at the entry level.

WHAT TO WATCH OUT FOR (SHOULD YOU BE UNLUCKY ENOUGH TO FIND YOURSELF HAVING A DAY IN COURT)

- **Does the dispute I am involved in need to be solved in a court of law?** If you have been arrested, you probably have little choice about whether you go to court, but if you are involved in a civil dispute, there are ways to solve conflicts outside the courtroom. Explore options involving mediation and arbitration if you want to avoid a lengthy and possibly acrimonious legal battle.

- **Do I need a lawyer?** Americans are increasingly getting into the do-it-yourself legal business, but before you take on such a project, carefully evaluate whether hiring a lawyer will serve your interests. Remember that the legal system has been designed by lawyers, and they are trained to know their way around it. Will you be at a disadvantage in resolving your dispute if you don't have a lawyer? It's one thing to draw up your own will, but quite another to undertake your own criminal defense. Disputes such as divorce, child custody, and small claims fall somewhere in between, but as a general rule, if the person whose claims you are contesting has a lawyer, you might want one, too.

- **Is the case worth the potential cost in money, time, and emotional energy?** Again, if you are in criminal court, you may not have any choice over whether you go to court, but often people enter into civil disputes without a clear idea of the costs involved, seeing them sometimes as a "get-rich-quick" option. Will your lawyer work on a contingency basis (taking a percentage, usually 30 percent, of the settlement he or she wins for you), or will you have to pay an hourly rate? Billable hours can add up quite quickly. Is there a higher principle involved, or is it all about money? Will it be worth it to bring or contest a losing case, only to be left with substantial attorney's fees? You might be willing to sacrifice more for an important cause than for a monetary settlement. Cases can drag on for years, through multiple levels of appeals, and can become a major drain on one's energy and resources.

- **Should I serve on a jury if called?** Serving on a jury is a good opportunity to see how the system works from the inside, as well as to make a contribution to the nation. Finding a reason to be excused from jury duty sometimes seems like an attractive option when you are besieged by the demands of daily life, but there are real costs to avoiding this civic duty. Since all citizens are entitled to a jury trial, having an active pool of willing jurors is important to the civic health of the nation.

KINDS OF LAW

Laws are not all of the same type, and distinguishing among them can be very difficult. It's not important that we understand all the shades of legal meaning; in fact, it often seems that lawyers speak a language all their own. Nevertheless, most of us will have several encounters with the law in our lifetime, and it's important that we know what laws regulate what sorts of behavior. To get a better understanding of the various players in the court's legal arena, see *Don't Be Fooled . . . When Going to Court.*

SUBSTANTIVE AND PROCEDURAL LAWS We have used the terms *substantive* and *procedural* elsewhere in this book, and though the meanings we use here are related to the earlier ones, these are precise legal terms that describe specific kinds of laws. **Substantive laws** are those whose actual content or "substance" defines what we can and cannot legally do. **Procedural laws**, on the other hand, establish the procedures used to conduct the law—that is, how the law is used, or applied, and enforced. Thus a substantive law spells out what behaviors are restricted—for instance, driving over a certain speed or killing someone. Procedural laws refer to how legal proceedings are to take place: how evidence will be gathered and used, how defendants will be treated, and what juries can be told during a trial. Because our founders were concerned with limiting the power of government to prevent tyranny, our laws are filled with procedural protections for those who must deal with the legal system—what we call guarantees of **procedural due process**. Given their different purposes, these two types of laws sometimes clash. For instance, someone guilty of breaking a substantive law might be spared punishment if procedural laws meant to protect him or her were violated because the police failed to read the accused his or her rights or searched the accused's home without a warrant. Such situations are complicated by the fact that not all judges interpret procedural guarantees in the same way.

CRIMINAL AND CIVIL LAWS

Criminal laws prohibit specific behaviors that the government (state, federal, or both) has determined are not conducive to the public peace, behaviors as heinous as murder or as relatively innocuous as stealing an apple. Since these laws refer to crimes against the state, it is the government that prosecutes these cases rather than the family of the murder victim or the owner of the apple. The penalty, if the person is found guilty, will be some form of payment to the public—for example, community service, jail time, or even death, depending on the severity of the crime and the provisions of the law. In fact, we speak of criminals having to pay their "debt to society" because, in a real sense, their actions are seen as a harm to society.

Civil laws, on the other hand, regulate interactions between individuals. If one person sues another for damaging his or her property, or causing physical harm, or failing to fulfill the terms of a contract, it is not a crime

against the state that is alleged but rather an injury to a specific individual. A violation of civil law is called a *tort* instead of a crime. The government's purpose here is not to prosecute a harm to society but to provide individuals with a forum in which they can peacefully resolve their differences. Apart from peaceful conflict resolution, government has no stake in the outcome.

Sometimes a person will face both criminal charges and a civil lawsuit for the same action. An example might be a person who drives while drunk and causes an accident that seriously injures a person in another car. The drunk driver would face criminal charges for breaking laws against driving while intoxicated and might also be sued by the injured party to receive compensation for medical expenses, missed income, and pain and suffering. Such damages are called *compensatory damages*. The injured person might also sue the bar that served the alcohol to the drunk driver in the first place; this is because people suing for compensation often target the involved party with the deepest pockets—that is, the one with the best ability to pay. A civil suit might also include a fine intended to punish the individual for causing the injury. These damages are called *punitive damages*. Reflecting our notion that government poses a bigger threat to our liberties than we do to each other, the burden of proof is easier to meet in civil trials.

CONSTITUTIONAL LAW One kind of law we have discussed often in this book so far is **constitutional law**. This refers, of course, to the laws that are in the Constitution, that establish the basic powers of and limitations on governmental institutions and their interrelationships, and that guarantee the basic rights of citizens. In addition, constitutional law refers to the many decisions that have been made by lower court judges in America, as well as by the justices on the Supreme Court, in their attempts to decide precisely what the Constitution means and how it should be interpreted. Because of our common-law tradition, these decisions, once made, become part of the vast foundation of American constitutional law.

---

substantive laws laws whose content, or substance, defines what we can or cannot do

procedural laws laws that establish how laws are applied and enforced—how legal proceedings take place

procedural due process procedural laws that protect the rights of individuals who must deal with the legal system

criminal laws laws prohibiting behavior the government has determined to be harmful to society; violation of a criminal law is called a crime

civil laws laws regulating interactions between individuals; violation of a civil law is called a tort

constitutional law law stated in the Constitution or in the body of judicial decisions about the meaning of the Constitution handed down in the courts

All the cases discussed in Chapters 5 and 6, on civil liberties and equal rights, are part of the constitutional law of this country. As we have seen, constitutional law evolves over time as circumstances change, justices are replaced, cases are overturned, and precedent is reversed.

STATUTORY LAW, ADMINISTRATIVE LAW, AND EXECUTIVE ORDERS Most laws in the country are made by Congress and the state legislatures, by the bureaucracy under the authority of Congress, and even by the president. **Statutory laws** are those laws that legislatures make at either the state or the national level. Statutes reflect the will of the bodies elected to represent the people, and they can address virtually any behavior. Statutes tell us to wear seatbelts, pay taxes, and stay home from work on Memorial Day. According to the principle of judicial review, judges may declare statutes unconstitutional if they conflict with the basic principles of government or the rights of citizens established in the Constitution.

Because legislatures cannot be experts on all matters, they frequently delegate some of their lawmaking power to bureaucratic agencies and departments. When these bureaucratic actors exercise their lawmaking power on behalf of Congress, they are making **administrative law**. Administrative laws include the thousands of regulations that agencies make concerning how much coloring and other additives can be in the food we buy, how airports will monitor air traffic, what kind of material can be used to make pajamas for children, and what deductions can be taken legally when figuring your income tax. These laws, although made under the authority of elected representatives, are not, in fact, made by people who are directly accountable to the citizens of America. The implications of the undemocratic nature of bureaucratic decision making were discussed in Chapter 9.

Finally, some laws, called **executive orders**, are made by the president himself. These laws, as we explained in Chapter 8, are made without any participation by Congress

AP Photo/Andy Colwell/The Patriot-News

More Than One Day in Court
The American justice system not only makes decisions on criminal cases, but also allows citizens to seek compensation for injury or damage. Retired Penn State assistant football coach Jerry Sandusky, charged with multiple counts of child abuse, faced not just a battery of criminal charges. Both Sandusky and the university also were named in more than thirty civil lawsuits filed by victims and their families, with the university agreeing to pay almost $60 million to twenty-six plaintiffs in the first round of settlements.

and need be binding only during the issuing president's administration. Famous executive orders include President Harry Truman's desegregation of the armed forces in 1948 and President Lyndon Johnson's initiation of affirmative action programs for companies doing business with the federal government in 1967.

THINKING OUTSIDE THE BOX

Is justice a matter of enduring principles or the product of a political process?

PAUSE AND REVIEW:
WHO, WHAT, HOW

Citizens have a broad stake in a lawful society. They want security, predictability, peaceful conflict resolution, conformity to social norms, and a nondisruptive

---

statutory laws laws passed by a state or the federal legislature

administrative law law established by the bureaucracy, on behalf of Congress

executive orders clarifications of congressional policy issued by the president and having the full force of law

distribution of social costs and benefits, and they use laws to try to achieve these things. They use the full array of laws and legal traditions available to them in the American legal system to accomplish their goals. The results of the legal process are shaped by the distinctive nature of the American system—its common-law roots and its adversarial and litigious nature.

IN YOUR OWN WORDS ›› Describe the role that law plays in democratic society.

CONSTITUTIONAL PROVISIONS AND THE DEVELOPMENT OF JUDICIAL REVIEW
The role of Congress and the courts in establishing the judiciary

Americans may owe a lot of our philosophy of law (called *jurisprudence*) to the British, but the court system we set up to administer that law is uniquely our own. Like every other part of the Constitution, the nature of the judiciary was the subject of hot debate during the nation's founding. Large states were comfortable with a strong court system as part of the strong national government they advocated; small states, cringing at the prospect of national dominance, preferred a weak judiciary. Choosing a typically astute way out of their quandary, the authors of the Constitution postponed it, leaving it to Congress to settle later.

Article III, Section 1, of the Constitution says simply this about the establishment of the court system: "The judicial power of the United States, shall be vested in one supreme court, and in such inferior courts as Congress may from time to time ordain and establish." It goes on to say that judges will hold their jobs as long as they demonstrate "good behavior"—that is, they are appointed for life—and that they will be paid regularly and cannot have their pay reduced while they are in office. The Constitution does not spell out the powers of the Supreme Court. It only specifies which cases must come directly to the Supreme Court (cases affecting ambassadors, public ministers and consuls, and states); all other cases come to it only on appeal. It was left to Congress to say how. By dropping the issue of court structure and power into the lap of a future Congress, the writers of the Constitution neatly sidestepped the brewing controversy. It would require an act of Congress, the Federal Judiciary Act of 1789, to begin to fill in the gaps on how the court system would be organized. We turn to that act and its provisions shortly. First, we look at the controversy surrounding the birth of the one court that Article III does establish, the U.S. Supreme Court.

THE LEAST DANGEROUS BRANCH

The idea of an independent judiciary headed by a supreme court was a new one to the founders. No other country had one, not even England. Britain's highest court was also its Parliament, or legislature. To those who put their faith in the ideas of separation of powers and checks and balances, an independent judiciary was an ideal way to check the power of the president and the Congress. But to others it represented an unknown threat. To put those fears to rest, Alexander Hamilton penned *Federalist* No. 78, arguing that the judiciary was the least dangerous branch of government. It lacked the teeth of the other branches; it had neither the power of the sword (the executive power) nor the power of the purse (the legislative budget power), and consequently it could exercise "neither force nor will, but merely judgment."[12]

For a while, Hamilton was right. The Court was thought to be such a minor player in the new government that several of George Washington's original appointees to that institution turned him down.[13] Many of those who served on the Court for a time resigned prematurely to take other positions thought to be more prestigious. Further indicating the Court's lack of esteem was the fact that when the capital was moved to Washington, D.C., city planners forgot to design a location for it. As a result, the highest court in the land had to meet in the basement office of the clerk of the U.S. Senate.[14]

JOHN MARSHALL AND JUDICIAL REVIEW

The low prestige of the Supreme Court was not to last for long, however, and its elevation was due almost single-handedly to the work of one man. John Marshall was the third chief justice of the United States and an enthusiastic Federalist. During his tenure in office, he found several ways to strengthen the Court's power, the most important of which was having the Court create the power of **judicial review**. This is the power that allows the Court to review acts of the other branches of government and to invalidate them if they are found to run counter to the principles in the Constitution. For a man who attended law school for only six months (as was the custom in his day, he learned the law by serving as an apprentice), his legacy to American law is truly phenomenal.

***FEDERALIST* NO. 78** Marshall was not the first American to raise the prospect of judicial review. While the Constitution was silent on the issue of the Court's power and Hamilton had been quick to reassure the public that he envisioned only a weak judiciary, he dropped a hint in *Federalist* No. 78 that he would approve of a much stronger role for the Court. Answering critics who declared that judicial review would give too much power to a group of

> **judicial review** the power of the courts to determine the constitutionality of laws

unelected men to overrule the will of the majority as expressed through the legislature, Hamilton said that in fact the reverse was true. Since the Constitution was the clearest expression of the public will in America, by allowing that document to check the legislature, judicial review would actually place the true will of the people over momentary passions and interests that were reflected in Congress.

MARBURY V. MADISON The Constitution does not give the power of judicial review to the Court, but it doesn't forbid the Court to have that power either. Chief Justice John Marshall shrewdly engineered the adoption of the power of judicial review in *Marbury v. Madison* in 1803. This case involved a series of judicial appointments to federal courts made by President John Adams in the final hours of his administration. Most of those appointments were executed by Adams's secretary of state, but the letter appointing William Marbury to be justice of the peace for the District of Columbia was overlooked and not delivered. (In an interesting twist, John Marshall, who was finishing up his job as Adams's secretary of state, had just been sworn in as chief justice of the United States; he would later hear the case that developed over his own incomplete appointment of Marbury.) These "midnight" (last-minute) appointments irritated the new president, Thomas Jefferson, who wanted to appoint his own candidates, so he had his secretary of state, James Madison, throw out the letter, along with several other appointment letters. According to the Judiciary Act of 1789, it was up to the Court to decide whether Marbury got his appointment, which put Marshall in a fix. If he exercised his power under the act and Jefferson ignored him, the Court's already low prestige would be severely damaged. If he failed to order the appointment, the Court would still look weak.

From a legal point of view, Marshall's solution was breathtaking. Instead of ruling on the question of Marbury's appointment, which was a no-win situation for him, he instead focused on the part of the act that gave the Court authority to make the decision. This he found to go beyond what the Constitution had intended; that is, according to the Constitution, Congress didn't have the power to give the Court that authority. So Marshall ruled that although he thought Marbury should get the appointment (he had originally made it, after all), he could not enforce it because the relevant part of the Judiciary Act of 1789 was unconstitutional and therefore void. He justified the Court's power to decide what the Constitution meant by saying "it is emphatically the province of the judicial department to say what the law is."[15]

THE IMPACT OF JUDICIAL REVIEW With the *Marbury* ruling, Marshall chose to lose a small battle in order to win a very large war. By creating the power of judicial review, he vastly expanded the potential influence

> *Marbury v. Madison* the landmark case that established the U.S. Supreme Court's power of judicial review

Library of Congress

Freedom Fighter

Thurgood Marshall (center) secured his place in legal history when, as special counsel for the National Association for the Advancement of Colored People (NAACP), he convinced the Supreme Court to overturn segregation with the landmark 1954 ruling *Brown v. Board of Education*. In 1967, Marshall himself became a Supreme Court justice, appointed by President Lyndon Johnson.

of the Court and set it on the road to being the powerful institution it is today. While Congress and the president still have some checks on the judiciary through the powers to appoint, to change the number of members and jurisdiction of the Court, to impeach justices, and to amend the Constitution, the Court now has the ultimate check over the other two branches: the power to declare what they do to be null and void. What is especially striking about the gain of this enormous power is that the Court gave it to itself. What would have been the public reaction if Congress had voted to make itself the final judge of what is constitutional?

Aware of just how substantially their power was increased by the addition of judicial review, justices have tended to use it sparingly. The power was not used from its inception in 1803 until 1857, when the Court struck down the Missouri Compromise.[16] Since then it has been used only 158 times to strike down acts of Congress, although it has been used much more frequently (1,261 times) to invalidate acts of the state legislatures.[17]

┌─────────────────────────────────┐
│ THINKING OUTSIDE THE BOX   │
└─────────────────────────────────┘

What would American politics look like today if Chief Justice John Marshall hadn't adopted the power of judicial review?

PAUSE AND REVIEW:
WHO, WHAT, HOW

The Constitution is largely silent about the courts, leaving to Congress the task of designing the details of the judicial system. It was not the Constitution or Congress but John Marshall, the third chief justice, who used the common-law tradition of American law to give the Court the extraconstitutional power of judicial review. Once Marshall had claimed the power and used it in a ruling (*Marbury v. Madison*), it became part of the fundamental judge-made constitutional law of this country.

IN YOUR OWN WORDS » Explain the role of Congress and the courts in establishing the judiciary.

FEDERALISM AND THE AMERICAN COURTS
The structure and organization of the dual court system

In response to the Constitution's open invitation to design a federal court system, Congress immediately got busy putting together the Federal Judiciary Act of 1789. The system created by this act was too simple to handle the complex legal needs and the growing number of cases in the new nation, however, and it was gradually crafted by Congress into the very complex network of federal courts we have today. But understanding just the federal court system is not enough. Our federal system of government requires that we have two separate court systems, state and national—and, in fact, most of the legal actions in this country take place at the state level. Because of the diversity that exists among the state courts, some people argue that in truth we have fifty-one court systems. Since we cannot look into each of the fifty state court systems, we will take the "two-system" perspective and consider the state court system as a whole (see Figure 10.1).

UNDERSTANDING JURISDICTION

A key concept in understanding our dual court system is the issue of **jurisdiction**, the courts' authority to hear particular cases. Not all courts can hear all cases. In fact, the rules regulating which courts have jurisdiction over which cases are very specific. Most cases in the United States fall under the jurisdiction of state courts. As we will see, cases go to federal courts only if they qualify by virtue of the kind of question raised or the parties involved.

The choice of a court, though dictated in large part by constitutional rule and statutory law (both state and federal), still leaves room for political maneuvering. Four basic characteristics of a case help determine which court has jurisdiction over it: the involvement of the federal government (through treaties or federal statutes) or the Constitution, the parties to the case (if, for instance, states are involved), where the case arose, and how serious an offense it involves.[18]

Once a case is in either the state court system or the federal court system, it almost always remains within that system. It is extremely rare for a case to start out in one system and end up in the other. Just about the only time this occurs is when a case in the highest state court is appealed to the U.S. Supreme Court, and this can happen only for cases involving a question of federal law.

Cases come to state and federal courts under either their original jurisdiction or their appellate jurisdiction. A court's **original jurisdiction** refers to those cases that can come straight to it without being heard by any other court first. The rules and factors just discussed refer to original jurisdiction. **Appellate jurisdiction** refers to those cases that a court can hear on **appeal**—that is, when one of the parties to a case believes that some point of law was not applied properly at a lower court and asks a higher court to review it. Almost all the cases heard by the U.S. Supreme Court come to it on appeal. The Court's original jurisdiction is limited to cases that concern ambassadors and public ministers and to cases in which a state is a party—usually amounting to no more than two or three cases a year.

All parties in U.S. lawsuits are entitled to an appeal, although more than 90 percent of losers in federal cases accept their verdicts without appeal. After the first appeal, further appeals are at the discretion of the higher court; that is, the court can choose to hear them or not. The

> **jurisdiction** a court's authority to hear certain cases
>
> **original jurisdiction** the authority of a court to hear a case first
>
> **appellate jurisdiction** the authority of a court to review decisions made by lower courts
>
> **appeal** a rehearing of a case because the losing party in the original trial argues that a point of law was not applied properly

highest court of appeals in the United States is the U.S. Supreme Court, but its appellate jurisdiction is also discretionary. When the Court refuses to hear a case, it may mean, among other things, that the Court regards the case as frivolous or that it agrees with the lower court's judgment. Just because the Court agrees to hear a case, though, does not mean that it is going to overturn the lower court's ruling, although it does so about 70 percent of the time. Sometimes the Court hears a case in order to rule that it agrees with the lower court and to set a precedent that other courts will have to follow.

STATE COURTS

Although each state has its own constitution, and therefore its own set of rules and procedures for structuring and organizing its court system, the state court systems are remarkably similar in appearance and function (see Figure 10.1). State courts generally fall into three tiers, or layers. The lowest, or first, layer is the trial court, including major trial courts and courts where less serious offenses are heard. The names of these courts vary—for example, they may be called county and municipal courts at the minor level and superior or district courts at the major level. Here cases are heard for the first time, under original jurisdiction, and most of them end here as well.

Occasionally, however, a case is appealed to a higher decision-making body. In about three-fourths of the states, intermediate courts of appeals hear cases appealed from the lower trial courts. In terms of geographic organization, subject matter jurisdiction, and number of judges, courts of appeals vary greatly from state to state. The one constant is that these courts all hear appeals directly from the major trial courts and, on very rare occasions, directly from the minor courts as well.

Each of the fifty states has a state supreme court, although again the names vary. Since they are appeals courts, no questions of fact can arise, and there are no juries. Rather, a panel of five to nine *justices*, as supreme court judges are called, meet to discuss the case, make a decision, and issue an opinion. As the name suggests, a state's supreme court is the court of last resort, or the final court of appeals, in the state. All decisions rendered by these courts are final unless a case involves a federal question and can be heard on further appeal in the federal court system.

Judges in state courts are chosen through a variety of procedures specified in the individual state constitutions. The procedures range from appointment by the governor

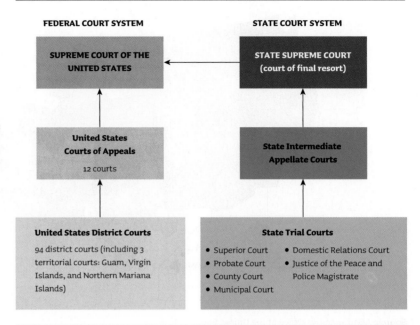

FIGURE 10.1 **THE DUAL COURT SYSTEM**

or election by the state legislature to the more democratic method of election by the state population as a whole. Thirty-nine states hold elections for at least some of their judges. Judicial elections are controversial, however. Supporters argue that they give people a voice, while holding judges accountable and keeping them in line with public opinion. Critics, however, say judicial elections can create a conflict of interest. For example, in 2002 the U.S. Chamber of Commerce and the Business Roundtable, two organizations that regularly appear in court, spent $25 million to influence judicial elections across the country.[19] Others argue that few people are able to cast educated votes in judicial elections and that the threat of defeat may influence judges' rulings.

FEDERAL COURTS

The federal system is also three-tiered. There is an entry-level tier called the district courts, an appellate level, and the Supreme Court at the very top (see Figure 10.1). In this section we discuss the lower two tiers and how the judges for those courts are chosen. Given the importance of the Supreme Court in the American political system, we discuss it separately in the following section.

DISTRICT COURTS The lowest level of the federal judiciary hierarchy consists of ninety-four U.S. federal district courts. These courts are distributed so that each state has at least one and the largest states each have four. The district courts have original jurisdiction over all cases

FIGURE 10.2 THE FEDERAL JUDICIAL CIRCUITS

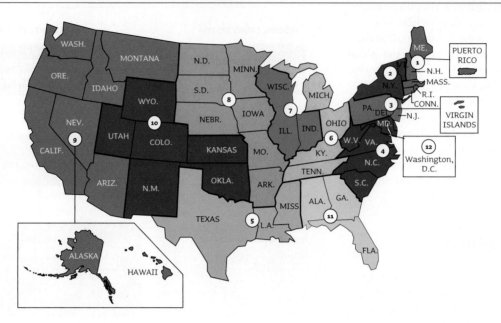

Source: Administrative Office of the United States Courts.

involving any question of a federal nature or any issue that involves the Constitution, Congress, or any other aspect of the federal government. Such issues are wide-ranging but might include, for example, criminal charges resulting from a violation of the federal anticarjacking statute or a lawsuit against the Environmental Protection Agency.

The district courts hear both criminal and civil-law cases. In trials at the district level, evidence is presented, and witnesses are called to testify and are questioned and cross-examined by the attorneys representing both sides. In criminal cases the government is always represented by a U.S. attorney. U.S. attorneys, one per district, are appointed by the president, with the consent of the Senate. In district courts, juries are responsible for returning the final verdict.

U.S. COURTS OF APPEALS Any case appealed beyond the district court level is slated to appear in one of the U.S. courts of appeals. These courts are arranged in twelve circuits, essentially large superdistricts that encompass several of the district court territories, except for the twelfth, which covers just Washington, D.C. (see Figure 10.2). This Twelfth Circuit Court hears all appeals involving government agencies, and so its caseload is quite large even though its territory is small. (A thirteenth Federal Circuit Court hears cases on such specialized issues as patents and copyrights.) Cases are heard in the circuit that includes the district court where the case was heard originally. Therefore, a case that was tried initially in Miami, in the southern district in Florida, would be appealed to the Court of Appeals for the Eleventh Circuit, located in Atlanta, Georgia.

The jurisdiction of the courts of appeals, as their name suggests, is entirely appellate in nature. The sole function of these courts is to hear appeals from the lower federal district courts and to review the legal reasoning behind the decisions reached there. As a result, the proceedings involved in the appeals process differ markedly from those at the district court level. No evidence is presented, no new witnesses called, and no jury impaneled. Instead, the lawyers for both sides present written briefs summarizing their arguments and make oral arguments as well. The legal reasoning used to reach the decision in the district court is scrutinized, but the facts of the case are assumed to be the truth and are not debated.

The decisions in the courts of appeals are made by a rotating panel of three judges who sit to hear the case. Although many more than three judges are assigned to each federal appeals circuit (the Court of Appeals for the Ninth Circuit, based in San Francisco, has twenty-nine active judges), the judges rotate in order to provide a decision-making body that is as unbiased as possible. In rare cases where a decision is of crucial social importance, all the judges in a circuit will meet together, or *en banc*, to render a decision. Having all the judges present, not just three, gives a decision more legitimacy and sends a message that the decision was made carefully.

SELECTION OF FEDERAL JUDGES The Constitution is silent about the qualifications of federal judges. It specifies only that they shall be appointed by the president, with the advice and consent of the Senate, and that they shall serve lifetime terms under good behavior. They can be removed from office only if impeached and convicted by the House of Representatives and the Senate, a process that has resulted in only thirteen impeachments and seven convictions in more than two hundred years.

Traditionally, federal judgeships have been awarded on the basis of several criteria, including rewarding political friendship, supporting and cultivating future support, especially of a gender or ethnic or racial group, and ideology (see "*Snapshot of America:* Who Has Been Appointed to the Federal Courts?"). Throughout most of the country's history, the courts have been demographically uniform—white, male, and predominantly Christian. President Jimmy Carter broke that trend, vowing to use his nominations to increase the diversity in the federal courts. President Bill Clinton renewed that commitment: nearly half of his appointees were women and minorities, compared to 35 percent under Carter, 14 percent under Ronald Reagan, and 27 percent under George H. W. Bush.[20] President George W. Bush, while not quite emulating Clinton's record, still made a point of nominating a diverse slate of candidates, especially increasing the number of Hispanics on the bench.[21] Barack Obama has also made increasing the diversity on the courts a top priority. According to the White House counsel, "The president wants the federal courts to look like America."[22] As of April 2014, 238 of President Barack Obama's nominees to the federal bench had been confirmed. Of those, two-thirds were women and/or minorities, among them Supreme Court justices Sonia Sotomayor and Elena Kagan.[23] The president's nominees have included several openly gay candidates as well. Because the Obama administration has cast a wider net, looking for diverse candidates but also for those with less traditional backgrounds (more government lawyers and law professors, for instance, than litigators), it has been slower to fill the openings on the bench than liberal critics would like.[24]

These days an increasingly important qualification for the job of federal judge is the ideological or policy positions of the appointee. Beginning with Richard Nixon in the 1970s, presidents have become more conscious of the political influence of these courts and have tried to use the nomination process to further their own political legacies. As presidents have taken advantage of the opportunity to shape the courts ideologically, the Senate confirmation process has become more rancorous. While Republican presidents Richard Nixon, Ronald Reagan, and George H. W. Bush made a conscious effort to redirect what they saw as the liberal tenor of court appointments in the years since the New Deal, and Democrat Jimmy Carter countered with liberal appointees, the moderate ideology of most of Democratic president Bill Clinton's appointees meant that the courts did not swing back in a radically liberal direction.[25] Clinton's appointees were what one observer called "militantly moderate"—more liberal than Reagan's and Bush's, but less liberal than Carter's, and similar ideologically to the appointments of Republican president Gerald Ford.[26] In conjunction with the fact that, by the end of George W. Bush's second term, 56.2 percent of the authorized judicial positions had been filled by Republicans,[27] this means that

today's federal bench tilts in a solidly conservative direction. President Barack Obama, focused on the diversity of his appointees, has come under criticism from liberals for not filling seats quickly enough, and thus for failing to build a liberal judicial legacy.[28]

The increasing politicization of the confirmation process means that many of a president's nominees face a grueling battle in the Senate, and even if they get through the Senate Judiciary Committee hearings, they are lucky if they can get as far as a vote on the floor. Senators of the opposing party can put a hold on a nomination, requiring a vote of sixty senators to bring the nomination to a vote. While both parties use this tactic to stall those nominations of the other party's president to which they object, the Republicans have recently been more effective. Observers chalk this up to the greater discipline among Republican senators. Said one liberal advocate during George W. Bush's administration, "Republican senators have voted in lock step to confirm every judge that Bush has nominated. The Democrats have often broken ranks."[29] That Republican unity has continued into the Obama years. While the politicization of the process means that each party has objected to the more ideological appointments of the other side, Republicans were blocking votes on all Obama nominations, even moderate ones that would typically have enjoyed bipartisan support, in order to stall the Obama administration's efforts and to gain leverage for other things they wanted.[30] Ironically, when those nominations do eventually come to a vote, they pass with the support of many of the Republicans who supported a filibuster to delay the vote in the first place. While these delay tactics may have helped the party score a short-term political victory, many federal judgeships went unfilled as a consequence, contributing to a backlog of cases in the courts. As we saw in *What's at Stake . . . ?* in Chapter 7, Senate majority leader Harry Reid eventually invoked what is known as the nuclear option, eliminating the filibuster on non–Supreme Court federal nominees.

Another, related influence on the appointment of federal judges is the principle of **senatorial courtesy**, which we discussed in Chapter 8. In reality, senators do most of the nominating of district court judges, often aided by applications made by lawyers and state judges. Traditionally, a president who nominated a candidate who failed to meet with the approval of the state's senior senator was highly unlikely to gain Senate confirmation of that candidate, even if he was lucky enough to get the Senate Judiciary Committee to hold a hearing on the nomination. The practice of senatorial courtesy was weakened somewhat by the Bush administration and Senate Republicans, who forced confirmation hearings despite the objections of Democratic home state senators.[31] Once President Barack Obama was elected, however, Senate Republicans sought to restore the

> **senatorial courtesy** tradition of granting senior senators of the president's party considerable power over federal judicial appointments in their home states

SNAPSHOT OF AMERICA: WHO HAS BEEN APPOINTED TO THE FEDERAL COURTS?

Apointees by Race/Ethnicity

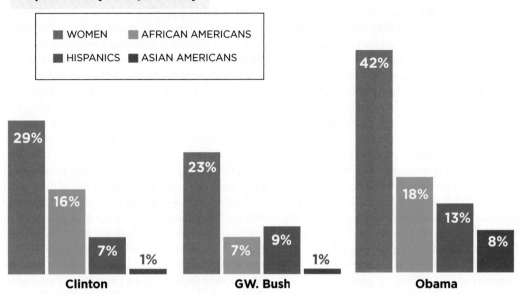

- ■ WOMEN
- ■ AFRICAN AMERICANS
- ■ HISPANICS
- ■ ASIAN AMERICANS

Clinton: 29% | 16% | 7% | 1%

GW. Bush: 23% | 7% | 9% | 1%

Obama: 42% | 18% | 13% | 8%

Presidential Confirmation Rates

Confirmation rate of district and circuit court judges and average number of confirmations per year

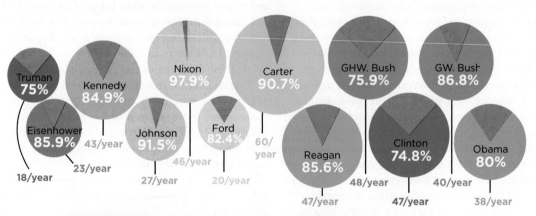

Truman 75% — 18/year
Eisenhower 85.9% — 23/year
Kennedy 84.9% — 43/year
Johnson 91.5% — 27/year
Nixon 97.9% — 46/year
Ford 82.4% — 20/year
Carter 90.7% — 60/year
Reagan 85.6% — 47/year
GHW. Bush 75.9% — 48/year
Clinton 74.8% — 47/year
GW. Bush 86.8% — 40/year
Obama 80% — 38/year

BEHIND THE NUMBERS

Just as America is becoming more diverse, so is our federal judiciary. President Obama has nominated significantly more women and minorities to the federal bench than his predecessors. Does it increase the legitimacy of the courts when citizens see people like themselves in judges' robes? Are the decisions likely to be different?

Source: Mitchell Sollenberger, "Judicial Nomination Statistics: U.S. District and Circuit Courts, 1945–1976," Congressional Research Service, October 22, 2003; Denis Rutkus and Mitchell Sollenberger, "Judicial Nomination Statistics: U.S. District and Circuit Courts, 1977–2003," Congressional Research Service, February 23, 2004; Denis Steven Rutkus, Kevin M. Scott, and Maureen Bearden, "U.S. Circuit and District Court Nominations by President George W. Bush during 107th– 109th Congresses," Congressional Research Service, January 23, 2007; "Judicial Nominations: 110th Congress," U.S. Department of Justice Archive, www.justice.gov/archive/olp/judicialnominations.htm; "Federal Judicial Nomination Statistics," July 11, 2012, judicialnominations.org/wp-content/uploads/2012/07/judicial-nominations-stats-07.11.12.pdf.

Note: Data from CRS Reports include nominations to territorial district courts in the U.S. Virgin Islands, Guam, and Northern Mariana Islands, as well as resubmitted nominations.

"Record Judicial Diversity, Record Judicial Delays," www.whitehouse.gov/blog/2011/08/18/infographic-record-judicial-diversity-record-judicial-delays.

Alliance for Justice, The State of the Judiciary, Judicial selection During the 113th Congress, October 24, 2013 [http://www.afj.org/wp-content/uploads/2013/10/Judicial-Selection-During-President-Obamas-Second-Term.pdf].

Brookings, Judicial Nominations and Confirmations: Fact and Fiction, December 30, 2013 [http://www.brookings.edu/blogs/fixgov/posts/2013/12/30-staffing-federal-judiciary-2013-no-breakthrough-year].

policy, sending a letter to the White House promising to block any appointments that didn't meet with the home state senator's approval.[32]

The growing influence of politics in the selection of federal judges does not mean that merit is unimportant. As the nation's largest legal professional association, the American Bar Association (ABA) has had the informal role since 1946 of evaluating the legal qualifications of potential nominees. While poorly rated candidates are occasionally nominated and confirmed, perhaps because of the pressure of a senator or a president, most federal judges receive the ABA's professional blessing. The ABA's role has become more controversial in recent years, as Republicans are convinced that it has a liberal bias. In 2001 the Bush administration announced that it would no longer seek the ABA's ratings of its nominees, breaking a tradition that goes back to Dwight Eisenhower. The ABA continued to rate the nominees (and the Bush White House boasted that the vast majority of its nominees were rated qualified or well qualified), but it did so independently.[33] In March 2009 the Obama administration restored the ABA's traditional role in the nomination process, only to find, ironically, that a number of Obama's potential nominees failed to rank as qualified, perhaps because they were less likely to have the traditional backgrounds as litigators that the litigator-heavy ABA panel may be looking for.[34] Because the administration has dropped those nominees who were not ranked as qualified, it has had a slower nominating process than its predecessors.

Steve Petteway, Collection of the Supreme Court of the United States

More Than Half of the Population, Only a Third of the Court
Before Sandra Day O'Connor (left) became the first woman appointed to the U.S. Supreme Court in 1981, no woman had ever served on the nation's highest court. Today, a full third of the court is female. Some observers note that women come to decisions differently than men, but the impact of the gender shift on the court will not be clear for several years. Here, O'Connor joins current justices Sotomayor, Ginsberg, and Kagan at the Court for Kagan's formal investiture ceremony in 2010.

THINKING OUTSIDE THE BOX

How would the federal judiciary be different if judges were elected rather than appointed?

PAUSE AND REVIEW:
WHO, WHAT, HOW

The dual court system in America is shaped by rules that ultimately determine who will win and lose in legal disputes. Because our common-law tradition gives the judge a great deal of power to interpret what the law means, the selection of judges is critical to how the rules are applied. Both the president and the Senate are involved in the selection of federal judges, and both have a stake in creating a federal judiciary that reflects the views they think are important—and that rewards the people they feel should be rewarded. The rules that determine whether the president or the Senate is successful come partly from the Constitution (the nomination and confirmation processes) and partly from tradition (senatorial courtesy).

IN YOUR OWN WORDS >> Evaluate Hamilton's claim that the judiciary was the "least dangerous branch of government" in light of the power it wields.

THE SUPREME COURT
A political institution

At the very top of the nation's judicial system reigns the Supreme Court. While the nine justices do not wear the elaborate wigs of their British colleagues in the House of Lords, the highest court of appeals in Britain, they do don long black robes to hear their cases and sit against a majestic background of red silk, perhaps the closest thing to the pomp and circumstance of royalty that we have in American government. Polls show that even after its role in the contested presidential election of 2000, the Court gets higher ratings from the public than does Congress or the president, and that it doesn't suffer as much from the popular cynicism about government that afflicts the other branches.[35]

The American public seems to believe that the Supreme Court is indeed above politics, as the founders wished it to be. Such a view, while gratifying to those who want to believe in the purity and wisdom of at least one aspect of their government, is not strictly accurate. The members of the Court themselves are preserved by the rule of lifetime tenure from continually having to seek reelection or reappointment, but they are not removed from the political world around them. It is more useful, and closer to reality, to regard the Supreme Court as an intensely political institution. In at least four critical areas—how its members are chosen, how those members choose which cases to hear, how they make decisions, and the effects of the decisions they make—the Court is a decisive allocator of who gets what, when, and how. Reflecting on popular idealizing of the Court, scholar Richard Pacelle says that "not to know the Court is to love it."[36] In the remainder of this chapter, we get to know the Court, not to stop loving it but to gain a healthy respect for the enormously powerful political institution it is.

HOW MEMBERS OF THE COURT ARE SELECTED

In a perfect world, the wisest and most intelligent jurists in the country would be appointed to make the all-important constitutional decisions faced by members of the Supreme Court. In a political world, however, the need for wise and intelligent justices needs to be balanced against the demands of a system that makes those justices the choice of an elected president, and confirmed by elected senators. The need of these elected officials to be responsive to their constituencies means that the nomination process for Supreme Court justices is often a battleground of competing views of the public good. Merit is certainly important, but it is tempered by other considerations resulting from a democratic selection process.

On paper, the process of choosing justices for the Supreme Court is not a great deal different from the selection of other federal judges, though no tradition of senatorial courtesy exists at the high court level. Far too much is at stake in Supreme Court appointments to even consider giving any individual senator veto power. Because the job is so important, the president himself gets much more involved than he does in other federal judge appointments. As the box "Packing the Courts" highlights, the composition of the Court has serious political consequences.

The Constitution, silent on so much concerning the Supreme Court, does not give the president any handy list of criteria for making these critical appointments. But the demands of his job suggest that merit, shared ideology, political reward, and demographic representation all play a role in this choice.[37] We can understand something about the challenges that face a president making a Supreme Court appointment by examining each of these criteria briefly.

MERIT The president will certainly want to appoint the most qualified person and the person with the highest ethical standards who also meets the other prerequisites. Scholars agree that most of the people who have served the Court over the years have been among the best legal minds available, but they also know that sometimes presidents have nominated people whose reputations have proved questionable.[38] The ABA passes judgment on candidates for the Supreme Court, as it does for the lower courts, issuing verdicts of "well qualified," "qualified," "not opposed," and "not qualified." The Federal Bureau of Investigation (FBI) also checks out the background of nominees, although occasionally critical information is missed. In 1987 the Reagan administration, which had widely publicized its "Just Say No" campaign against drug use, was deeply embarrassed when National Public Radio reporter Nina Totenberg broke the story that its Supreme Court nominee, appeals court judge Douglas Ginsburg, had used marijuana in college and while on the Harvard Law School faculty. Ginsburg withdrew his name from consideration. More controversial was the 1991 case of Clarence Thomas, already under attack for his lack of judicial experience and low ABA rating, who was accused of sexual harassment by a former employee, law professor Anita Hill. Although Thomas was confirmed, the hearings brought to center stage ethical questions about Court nominees.

POLITICAL IDEOLOGY Although a president wants to appoint a well-qualified candidate to the Court, he is constrained by the desire to find a candidate who shares his views on politics and the law. Political ideology here involves a couple of dimensions. One is the traditional liberal–conservative dimension. Supreme Court justices, like all other human beings, have views on the role of government, the rights of individuals, and the relationship between the two. Presidents want to appoint justices who look at the world the same way they do, although they are occasionally surprised when their nominee's ideological stripes turn out to be different than they had anticipated. Republican president Dwight Eisenhower called the appointment of Chief Justice Earl Warren, who turned out to be quite liberal in his legal judgments, "the biggest damn fool mistake I ever made."[39] Although there have been notable exceptions, most presidents appoint members of their own party in an attempt to get ideologically compatible justices. Overall, roughly 90 percent of Supreme Court nominees belong to the president's party.

PACKING THE COURTS

The Supreme Court was a thorn in President Franklin Roosevelt's side. Faced with the massive unemployment and economic stagnation that characterized the Great Depression of the 1930s, Roosevelt knew he would have to use the powers of government creatively, but he was hampered by a Court that was ideologically opposed to his efforts to regulate business and industry and skeptical of his constitutional power to do so. In Roosevelt's view, he and Congress had been elected by the people, and public opinion favored his New Deal policies, but a majority of the "nine old men," as they were called, on the Supreme Court consistently stood in his way. Six of the justices were over age seventy, and Roosevelt had appointed none of them.

Roosevelt proposed to change the Court that continually thwarted him. The Constitution allows Congress to set the number of justices on the Supreme Court, and indeed the number has ranged from six to ten at various times in our history. Roosevelt's answer to the recalcitrant Court was to ask Congress to allow him to appoint a new justice for every justice over age seventy who refused to retire, up to a possible total of fifteen. Thus he would create a Court whose majority he had chosen and that he confidently believed would support his New Deal programs.

Most presidents try to pack the Court, building their own legacies with appointees who they hope will perpetuate their vision of government and politics. But Roosevelt's plan was dangerous because it threatened to alter the two constitutional principles of separation of powers and checks and balances. Roosevelt would have made into a truism Hamilton's claim that the judiciary was the least dangerous branch of government, while raising the power of the presidency to a height even Hamilton had not dreamed of. The American people reacted with dismay. Public opinion may have backed his policies, but it turned on him when he tried to pack the Court.

No other president has attempted to pack the Court as blatantly as Roosevelt did, and none has failed so ignominiously. The public backlash may have contributed to the slowing of the New Deal and the Republican victories in 1938 that left Roosevelt with a weakened Democratic majority in Congress. His audacious plan had risked the very policy success he was trying so hard to achieve.

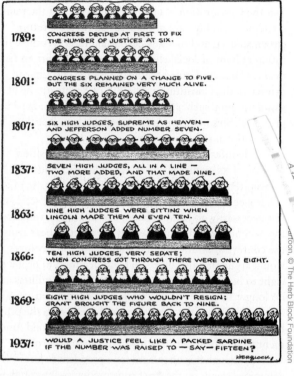

Precedent for the President
Historical Figures—a 1937 Herblock cartoon.

In the end, Roosevelt was reelected two more times. The Court, ironically, did an about-face. One justice started voting with the Roosevelt supporters; another retired. Eventually he made eight appointments to the Supreme Court, putting his stamp on it more effectively than any other president since Washington. The Court was, in essence, packed by Roosevelt after all.

But ideology has another dimension when it refers to the law. Justices can take the view that the Constitution means exactly what it says it means and that all interpretations of it must be informed by the founders' intentions. This approach, called **strict constructionism**, holds that if the

> **strict constructionism** a judicial approach holding that the Constitution should be read literally, with the framers' intentions uppermost in mind

meaning of the Constitution is to be changed, it must be done by amendment, not by judicial interpretation. Judge Robert Bork, a Reagan nominee who failed to be confirmed by the Senate, is a strict constructionist. During his confirmation hearings, when he was asked about the famous reapportionment ruling, in *Baker v. Carr*, that the Constitution effectively guarantees every citizen one vote, Bork replied that if the people of the United States wanted their Constitution to guarantee "one man one vote," they were free to amend the document to say so. In Bork's judgment, without that amendment, the principle was simply the result of justices' rewriting of the Constitution. When the senators asked him about the right to privacy, another right enforced by the Court but not specified in the Constitution, Bork simply laughed.[40] The opposite position to strict constructionism, what might be called **judicial interpretivism**, holds that the Constitution is a living document, that the founders could not possibly have anticipated all possible future circumstances, and that justices should interpret the Constitution in light of social changes. When the Court, in *Griswold v. Connecticut*, ruled that while there is no right to privacy in the Constitution, the Bill of Rights can be understood to imply such a right, it was engaging in judicial interpretation. Strict constructionists would deny that there is a constitutional right to privacy.

While interpretivism tends to be a liberal position because of its emphasis on change, and strict constructionism tends to be a conservative position because of its adherence to the status quo, the two ideological scales do not necessarily go hand in hand. For instance, even though the Second Amendment refers to the right to bear arms in the context of militia membership, many conservatives would argue that this needs to be understood to protect the right to bear arms in a modern context, when militias are no longer necessary or practical—not a strict constructionist reading of the Constitution. Liberals, on the other hand, tend to rely on a strict reading of the Second Amendment to support their calls for tighter gun controls.

Even though it is often hard for a president to know where a nominee stands on the strict constructionist–interpretivist scale, especially if that nominee does not have a large record of previous decisions in lower courts, this ideological placement can be very important in the decision-making process. This was the case, for instance, with President Richard Nixon, who was convinced that interpretivist justices were rewriting the Constitution to give too many protections to criminal defendants, and with President Reagan, who faulted interpretivist justices for the *Roe v. Wade* decision legalizing abortion on the grounds of the right to privacy. But in neither case have all of these presidents' appointees adhered to the desired manner of interpreting the Constitution.

In the George W. Bush administration, another ideological element rose in importance along with the strict constructionist–interpretivist divide. Bush was concerned with finding nominees who not only would interpret the Constitution strictly but also would support a strengthening of executive power. As we saw in Chapter 8, many members of the Bush administration supported the unitary theory of the executive, which claims that the Constitution permits only the president to wield executive power. Under this theory, efforts by Congress to create independent agencies outside of the president's purview are unconstitutional. The administration also objected to efforts by Congress and the courts to limit or interpret executive power in matters of national security. Both of the men Bush appointed to the Court, Chief Justice John Roberts and

Samuel Alito, are supporters of a strong executive office.

President Obama's Supreme Court nominees thus far reflect his own center-left, interpretivist ideology. His first nomination, Sonia Sotomayor, who joined the Court in September 2009, was more controversial for remarks she had made about her ethnicity and gender than for her judicial views. When former solicitor general Elena Kagan was nominated by Obama for the Court in 2010, however, her lack of a history of clear judicial rulings left her ideology something of a mystery, and many liberals feared that she would end up being a moderate voice on the Court.[41]

The trend over the past few decades, since Nixon made a campaign issue of not appointing justices who were "soft on crime," is for Republican presidents to carefully pick conservative nominees, to avoid disappointments of the Eisenhower-Warren variety. Democratic presidents, however, particularly Clinton and Obama, have not seemed to share the urgency to put liberals on the Court, perhaps because neither man is particularly liberal himself. The upshot is a Court that has moved to the right; scholars have noted that both conservative and liberal justices have grown more conservative over time, shifting the Court to the right (see Figure 10.3).[42]

REWARD More than half of the people who have been nominated to the Supreme Court have been personally acquainted with the president.[43] Often nominees are either friends of the president, or his political allies, or other people he wishes to reward in an impressive fashion. Harry Truman knew and had worked with all four of the men he appointed to the Court, Franklin Roosevelt appointed people he knew (and who were loyal to his New Deal), John F. Kennedy appointed his longtime friend and associate Byron White, and Lyndon Johnson appointed his good friend Abe Fortas.[44] While several FOBs (Friends of Bill) appeared on Clinton's short lists for his appointments, none was actually appointed. Though George W. Bush tried to appoint his friend and White House counsel Harriet Miers to the Court, she was forced to withdraw her name amid criticism that she wasn't sufficiently qualified. Barack Obama had a longtime working relationship with one of his nominees, Elena Kagan, who had been his first solicitor general.

REPRESENTATION Finally, the president wants to appoint people who represent groups he feels should be included in the political process, or whose support he wants to gain. Lyndon Johnson appointed Thurgood Marshall at least in part because he wanted to appoint an African American to the Court. After Marshall retired, President George H. W. Bush appointed Clarence Thomas to fill his seat. While Bush declared that he was making the appointment because Thomas was the person best qualified for the job, and not because he was black, few believed him. In earlier

> **judicial interpretivism** a judicial approach holding that the Constitution is a living document and that judges should interpret it according to changing times and values

FIGURE 10.3 CHANGES IN IDEOLOGY OF SUPREME COURT JUSTICES, 1937-2013

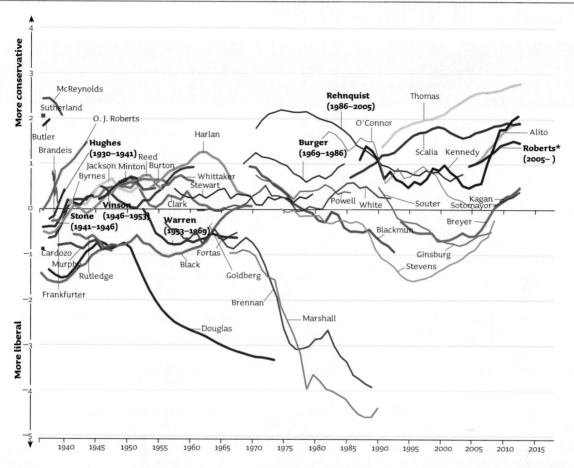

Source: "The 2013 Justice Data Files," Martin-Quinn Scores, Andrew W. Martin and Kevin M. Quinn, http://mqscores.berkeley.edu/measures.php

Note: Sotomayor and Kagan's 2010 ratings overlap. Justices' ideological ratings measured as Martin-Quinn scores. These calculations are due to Andrew Martin (Washington University School of Law) and Kevin M. Quinn (UC Berkeley School of Law) based on the Supreme Court Database (scdb.wustl.edu/documentation.php?var=decisionDirection). All cases before the Court are coded for liberal-conservative direction and outcomes, and justices' ideological voting scores over time are calculated based on their votes on the cases and relative to other justices. Dates in bold indicate time as chief justice.

*Roberts's Court is growing more conservative.

years, presidents also felt compelled to ensure that there was at least one Catholic and one Jew on the Court. This necessity has lost much of its force today as interest groups seem more concerned with the political than the denominational views of appointees, but Hispanic groups rejoiced when President Obama made Sonia Sotomayor the first Hispanic member of the Court in 2009. The issue of ethnic representation on the Court was put front and center during Sotomayor's confirmation hearings when she drew fire from Republicans who noted a line in a speech she had given in 2001, where she had argued that "I would hope that a wise Latina woman with the richness of her experiences would more often than not reach a better conclusion than a white male who hasn't lived that life."[45]

Table 10.1 shows the composition of the Supreme Court. There are six men on the Court and three women.

Six justices are Catholic, and three Jewish; only Judeo-Christian religions have been represented on the Court so far. Five of the justices were appointed by Republicans, four by Democrats. They have attended an elite array of undergraduate institutions and law schools. In 2014 their ages ranged from fifty-four to eighty-one, with the average being sixty-eight. There have never been any Native Americans or Asian Americans on the Court, and only two African Americans, whose terms did not overlap, and one Hispanic. The overwhelmingly elite, white male Christian character of the Court raises interesting questions. We naturally want our highest judges to have excellent legal educations (although John Marshall barely had any). But should the nation's highest court represent demographically the people whose Constitution it guards? Some observers (including Justice Sotomayor) have suggested that women

TABLE 10.1

COMPOSITION OF THE SUPREME COURT, 2014

JUSTICE	YEAR BORN	YEAR APPOINTED	POLITICAL PARTY	APPOINTING PRESIDENT	HOME STATE	COLLEGE/ LAW SCHOOL	RELIGION	POSITION WHEN APPOINTED
John G. Roberts Jr.	1955	2005	Rep.	W. Bush	Maryland	Harvard/ Harvard	Catholic	U.S. Appeals Court Judge
Antonin Scalia	1936	1986	Rep.	Reagan	D.C.	Georgetown/ Harvard	Catholic	U.S. Appeals Court Judge
Anthony M. Kennedy	1936	1988	Rep.	Reagan	California	Stanford/ Harvard	Catholic	U.S. Appeals Court Judge
Clarence Thomas	1948	1991	Rep.	Bush	Georgia	Holy Cross/ Yale	Catholic	U.S. Appeals Court Judge
Ruth Bader Ginsburg	1933	1993	Dem.	Clinton	New York	Cornell/ Columbia	Jewish	U.S. Appeals Court Judge
Stephen G. Breyer	1938	1994	Dem.	Clinton	California	Stanford, Oxford/ Harvard	Jewish	U.S. Appeals Court Judge
Samuel A. Alito Jr.	1950	2006	Rep.	W. Bush	New Jersey	Princeton/ Yale	Catholic	U.S. Appeals Court Judge
Sonia Sotomayor	1954	2009	Ind.	Obama	New York	Princeton/ Yale	Catholic	U.S. Appeals Court Judge
Elena Kagan	1960	2010	Dem.	Obama	New York	Oxford/ Harvard	Jewish	Solicitor General

Source: Supreme Court of the United States, "The Justices of the Supreme Court," www.supremecourtus.gov/about/biographies.aspx.

judges may be sensitive to issues that have not been salient to men and may alter behavior in the courtroom; the same may be true of minority judges. In a different vein, what message is sent to citizens when the custodians of national justice are composed primarily of a group that is itself fast becoming a minority in America?

CONFIRMATION BY THE SENATE As with the lower courts, the Senate must approve presidential appointments to the Supreme Court. Here again, the Senate Judiciary Committee plays the largest role, holding hearings and inviting the nominee, colleagues, and concerned interest groups to testify. Sometimes the hearings, and the subsequent vote in the Senate, are mere formalities, but increasingly, as the appointments have become more ideological and when the Senate majority party is not the party of the president, the hearings have had the potential to become political battlefields. Even when the president's party controls the Senate, the minority party can still influence the choice through the filibuster unless the Senate Republicans

renew their 2005 effort to halt this tradition. The Bork and Thomas hearings are excellent examples of what can happen when interest groups and public opinion get heavily involved in a controversial confirmation battle. These political clashes are so grueling because so much is at stake.

CHOOSING WHICH CASES TO HEAR

The introduction of political concerns into the selection process makes it almost inevitable that political considerations will also arise as the justices make their decisions. Politics makes an appearance at three points in the decision-making process, the first of which is in the selection of the cases to be heard.

The Supreme Court could not possibly hear the roughly eight thousand petitions it receives each year.[46] Intensive screening is necessary to reduce the number to the more manageable eighty to ninety that the Court finally hears. This screening process, illustrated in *The Big Picture* on page 382, is a political one; having one's case heard by the Supreme Court is a scarce resource. What rules and which people determine who gets this resource and who doesn't?

PETITIONING THE SUPREME COURT

Almost all the cases heard by the Court come from its appellate, not its original, jurisdiction, and of these virtually all arrive at the Court in the form of petitions for **writs of certiorari**, in which the losing party in a lower court case explains in writing why the Supreme Court should hear its case. Petitions to the Court are subject to strict length, form, and style requirements, and must be accompanied by a $300 filing fee. Those too poor to pay the filing fee are allowed to petition the Court *in forma pauperis*, which exempts them not only from the filing fee but also from the stringent style and form rules. In the 2012 term, 6,005 of the 7,509 case filings were *in forma pauperis*.[47] The Court's jurisdiction here is discretionary; it can either grant or deny a writ of certiorari. If it decides to grant certiorari and review the case, then the records of the case will be called up from the lower court where it was last heard.

For a case to be heard by the Court, it must be within the Court's jurisdiction, and it must present a real controversy that has injured the petitioner in some way, not just request the Court's advice on an abstract principle. In addition, it must be an appropriate question for the Court—that is, it must not be the sort of "political question" usually dealt with by the other two branches of government. This last rule is open to interpretation by the justices, however, and they may not all agree on what constitutes a political question. But these rules alone do not narrow the Court's caseload to a sufficiently small number of cases, and an enormous amount of work remains for the justices and their staffs, particularly their law clerks.

THE ROLE OF LAW CLERKS

Law clerks, usually recent graduates from law school who have served a year as clerk to a judge on a lower court, have tremendous responsibility over certiorari petitions, or "cert pets," as they call

' 'Congress shall make no law'. . . now, I wonder what they meant by that . . .?'

them. They must read all the petitions (thirty pages in length plus appendixes) and summarize each in a two- to five-page memo that includes a recommendation to the justices on whether to hear the case, all with minimal guidance or counsel from their justices.[48] Some justices join a "cert pool"—each clerk reads only a portion of the whole number of submitted petitions and shares his or her summaries and evaluations with the other justices. Currently eight of the nine justices of the Court are in a pool; one justice, Justice Samuel Alito, requires his clerks to read and evaluate all the petitions.

The memos are circulated to the justices' offices, where clerks read them again and make comments on the advisability of hearing the cases. The memos, with the clerks' comments, go on to the justices, who decide which cases they think should be granted cert and which denied. The chief justice circulates a weekly list of the cases he thinks should be discussed, which is known unimaginatively as the "discuss list." Other justices can add to that list the cases they think should be discussed in their Friday afternoon meetings.

THE RULE OF FOUR

Once a case is on the discuss list, it takes a vote of four justices to agree to grant it certiorari. This **Rule of Four** means that it takes fewer people to decide to hear a case than it will eventually take to decide the case itself, and thus it gives some power to a minority on the Court. The denial of certiorari does not necessarily signal that the Court endorses a lower court's ruling. Rather, it simply means that the case was not seen as important or special enough to be heard by the highest court. Justices who believe strongly that a case should not be denied have, increasingly in recent years, engaged in the practice of

---

writs of certiorari formal requests by the U.S. Supreme Court to call up the lower court case it decides to hear on appeal

Rule of Four the unwritten requirement that four Supreme Court justices must agree to grant a case certiorari in order for the case to be heard

THE BIG PICTURE: HOW A CASE GETS TO THE SUPREME COURT

The Justices of the Supreme Court

Justice:	Sonia Sotomayor	Ruth Bader Ginsburg	Stephen Breyer	Elena Kagan
Appointed by:	Obama	Clinton	Clinton	Obama
Appointed in:	2009	1993	1994	2009
Martin-Quinn Score*:	.787	.803	.954	.981

Martin-Quinn scores use voting records to rate how liberal or conservative each justice is, with the lower number being more liberal and the higher more conservative.

Influence of executive branch (solicitor general)

Precedent

Opinion writing
Debates about wording, arm twisting, occasional vote-changing

Justices' personal beliefs and attitudes

Supreme Court conference
preliminary vote, opinion assigned

Public opinion

Amicus curiae briefs filed by interest groups

Influence of other justices /small group dynamics

Oral arguments before the Court

Cases come to the Supreme Court from federal district courts of appeals, state supreme courts, and its original jurisdiction

Petitions to the Court for a writ of certiorari
(Approx. 10,000/year)
Reviewed by law clerks, briefs circulated to justices

The Supreme Court is the final court of appeal in the United States. Don't be fooled by the marble columns and velvet drapes—the Court is a political institution. Power is injected into the process when the justices decide which cases to hear, when they decide cases, and in the impact that those cases have on American lives. This is the political process by which a case gets to the Court.

Anthony Kennedy	John Roberts	Antonin Scalia	Samuel Alito	Clarence Thomas
Reagan	GW Bush	Reagan	GW Bush	GHW Bush
1988	2005	1986	2005	1991
2.037	2.943	3.822	3.874	5.566
(Median Justice)				

Opinion
(majority, concurring, dissenting) **published**
Approx. 80 signed opinions/year

Opinion
(majority, concurring, dissenting) **published**
Approx. 80 signed opinions/year

How frequently the justices voted with each other in 2

	AS	AK	CT	RBG	SB	SA	SS	EK
JR	90%	92%	88%	77%	85%	85%	79%	83%
AS		85%	95%	81%	78%	90%	78%	85%
AK			82%	79%	85%	88%	79%	86%
CT				75%	78%	96%	75%	79%
RBG					89%	75%	90%	94%
SB						77%	89%	90%
SA							75%	79%
SS								91%
EK								

Written briefs presented to the court

Justices' personal beliefs and attitudes

Error correction & lower court disputes

Amicus curiae briefs filed by interest groups

Law and precedent

"Discuss list" is reviewed in conference
Rule of Four

The docket is established
Approx. 100 cases accepted/year

Source: Administrative Office of the United States Courts

PROFILES IN CITIZENSHIP: SANDRA DAY O'CONNOR

© Marc Royce/Corbis Outline

Even though she'd told the story many times, Sandra Day O'Connor's voice still echoed with the frustration of that first job hunt. But there was irony in her voice, too—after all, the story had a happy ending, though it's one she never imagined when she graduated from law school back in 1952.

Really, all she wanted then was to work as a lawyer. She was getting married that summer, and her husband-to-be still had a year left in law school. Since, she said dryly, they both liked to eat, she thought getting a job would be a good idea.

But she reckoned without the prejudice against hiring women that pervaded the country in those days. Positions galore were posted on the jobs board at Stanford Law School, where she'd graduated third in her class of 102, but none of the firms was willing to hire a woman. She'd even parlayed an undergraduate friendship into an interview at a friend's father's firm, but all that resulted were questions about her office skills.

The former Supreme Court justice's story sounded both ludicrous and poignant when we interviewed her the year before her retirement in her impressive law chambers, with their rich polished woods and warm leather furniture, the walls lined with thick volumes of legal wisdom. As this most distinguished of American women recounted that long-ago interview in her precise, forceful voice, her snowy white hair and soft blue suit not blunting at all the effect of the power she radiated, it was hard not to find the incongruity a little amusing, even as one imagined the bitter disappointment of the young lawyer she once was.

"Well, Miss Day, how do you type?" asked the partner who interviewed her.

Just so-so, she replied. "If you can type well enough, maybe I can get you a job here as a legal secretary," he suggested. "But, Miss Day, our firm has never hired a woman as a lawyer. I don't see the day when we will—our clients wouldn't accept it."

Having run into a brick wall in the private sector, Sandra Day, soon to be Sandra Day O'Connor, set to work convincing the San Mateo County attorney to hire her; because he was engaged in public law, "he wasn't afraid to have a woman in his office." With that first job—initially undertaken without pay and in a shared office—she launched herself on a public career that coursed through years in the state attorney general's office in Arizona, the Arizona senate, and the state bench, and would finally hit its dramatic peak twenty-nine years later, when President Ronald Reagan appointed her as the first female justice on the U.S. Supreme Court.

Don't you just wish you could have seen her girlfriend's father's partner's face when that announcement was made?

But maybe it's too easy to blame Sandra Day O'Connor's extraordinary career in public law on the stubborn sexism of the private legal profession in 1950s America. She might have taken that path anyway—her decision to go to law school in the first place was in part idealistic, inspired by a professor

---

"dissenting from the denial" in an effort to persuade other justices to go along with them (since dissension at this stage makes the Court look less consensual) and to put their views on record. Fewer than 5 percent of cases appealed to the Supreme Court survive the screening process to be heard by the Court.

OTHER INFLUENCES The decisions to grant cert, then, are made by novice lawyers without much direction, who operate under enormous time and performance pressures, and by the justices, who rely on the evaluations of these young lawyers while bringing to the process the full array of values and ideologies for which they were, in part, chosen. Naturally the product of this process will reflect these characteristics, but there are other influences on

the justices and the decision-making process at this point as well.

One factor is whether the United States, under the representation of its lawyer, the **solicitor general**, is party to any of the cases before it. Between 70 and 80 percent of the appeals filed by the federal government are granted cert by the justices, a far greater proportion than for any other group.[49] Researchers speculate that this is because of the stature of the federal government's interests, the justices' trust in the solicitor general's ability to weed out frivolous

> **solicitor general** Justice Department officer who argues the government's cases before the Supreme Court

she'd taken a law class from as an undergraduate. "He was the first one who persuaded me that the individual could make a difference in this big world of ours," she remembered. By "the individual" he meant not just a president or governor or other person with power, but even someone "at the bottom of the totem pole." "The person at the bottom will sometimes have the best understanding of how to make something work. If you are sincere about it and determined enough, you can hang in there and see to it that it happens."

> "... EVERY NEW GENERATION HAS TO LEARN ALL OVER AGAIN THE FOUNDATIONS OF OUR GOVERNMENT ... AND EVERY INDIVIDUAL'S ROLE IN IT."

And those are the recurring themes in the life of Sandra Day O'Connor: sincerity in her efforts, determination to make a difference, persistence in the face of opposition, and independence in charting her path.

Perhaps all these qualities were honed from an early age, as she grew up on her family's Lazy B Ranch on the border of New Mexico and Arizona. There the fact that their herd grazed on federal land taught her early about the interrelationship between citizens and government. The harsh, isolated beauty of the land taught her other things as well. As she has written, the ranch was "a place where the wind always blows, the sky forms a dome overhead, and the clouds make changing patterns against the blue, and where the stars at night are brilliant and constant, a place to see the sunrise and sunset, and always to be reminded how small we are in the universe but, even so, how one small voice can make a difference."[1]

And there is that idealism again, an optimism about the potential of human beings that is tempered, when she talks, with a strong no-nonsense manner and a brisk practicality, a moderation and pragmatism that was reflected in her judgments on the Court. She's clearly never suffered fools gladly but at the same time is not without hope that we can save ourselves from foolishness. Here is some of her advice:

On what she'd tell today's students about how one person can make a difference:

Of course [you] have to have courage, you have to learn to believe in yourself, and to do that you have to develop some skills. So learn to read fast, and to write well, that's what you need to learn to do as a student. I have to read something like 1,500 pages a day. Now I couldn't do that if I hadn't taken speed reading. And that's important. I'm serious. You don't realize how important it is to be able to read fast. Because if you can read fast, think of all you can learn . . . . And then have courage to believe that, yes, you are equipped to do something, and go do it.

On keeping the republic:

You know, I've always said that we don't inherit our knowledge and understanding through the gene pool. And every new generation has to learn all over again the foundations of our government, how it was set up and why, and what is every individual's role in it. And we have to convey that to every generation . . . [i]f every young generation of citizens [doesn't] have an understanding of this, we can't keep our nation in decent order for the future.

1. Sandra Day O'Connor and H. Alan Day, *Lazy B: Growing Up on a Cattle Ranch in the American Southwest* (New York: Random House 2002), 302.

Source: Sandra Day O'Connor talked with Christine Barbour on March 3, 2005.

---

lawsuits, and the experience the solicitor general brings to the job.[50] Justices are also influenced by **amicus curiae briefs**, or "friend of the court" documents, that are filed in support of about 8 percent of petitions for certiorari by interest groups that want to encourage the Court to grant or deny cert. The amicus briefs do seem to affect the likelihood that the Court will agree to hear a case, and since economic interest groups are more likely to be active here than are other kinds of groups, it is their interests that most often influence the justices to grant cert.[51] As we will see, amicus curiae briefs are also used further on in the process.

DECIDING CASES

Once a case is on the docket, the parties are notified and they prepare their written briefs and oral arguments for their Supreme Court appearance. Lawyers for each side get only a half-hour to make their cases verbally in front of the Court, and they are often interrupted by justices who seek clarification, criticize points, or offer supportive arguments. The half-hour rule is generally followed strictly. In one case, two justices got up and walked out as the oral argument cut

> **amicus curiae briefs** "friend of the court" documents filed by interested parties to encourage the Court to grant or deny certiorari or to urge it to decide a case in a particular way

into their lunch hour, even though the lawyer who was speaking had been granted an extension by the chief justice.[52]

The actual decision-making process occurs before and during the Supreme Court conference meeting. Conference debates and discussions take place in private, although justices have often made revealing comments in their letters and memoirs that give insight into the dynamics of conference decision making. A variety of factors affect the justices as they make decisions on the cases they hear. Some of those factors come from within the justices—their attitudes, values, and beliefs—and some are external.

JUDICIAL ATTITUDES

Justices' attitudes toward the Constitution and how literally it is to be taken are clearly important, as we saw earlier in our discussion of strict constructionism and interpretivism. Judges are also influenced by the view they hold of the role of the Court: whether it should be an active lawmaker and policymaker, or should keep its rulings narrow and leave lawmaking to the elected branches of government. Those who adhere to **judicial activism** are quite comfortable with the idea of overturning precedents, exercising judicial review, and otherwise making decisions that shape government policy. Practitioners of **judicial restraint**, on the other hand, believe more strongly in the principle of *stare decisis* and reject any active lawmaking by the Court as unconstitutional.

These positions seem at first to line up with the positions of interpretivism and strict constructionism, and often they do. But exceptions exist, as when liberal justice Thurgood Marshall, who had once used the Constitution in activist and interpretivist ways to change civil rights laws, pleaded for restraint among his newer and more conservative colleagues who were eager to roll back some of the earlier decisions by overturning precedent and creating more conservative law.[53]

In recent years, especially in the wake of a Massachusetts Supreme Court decision that said forbidding gays the right to marry violates the Massachusetts constitution, conservatives have lambasted what they call the activism or "legislating from the bench" of courts who they say take decision making out of the hands of the people. But activism is not necessarily a liberal stance, and restraint is not necessarily conservative. Activism or restraint often seems to be more a function of whether a justice likes the status quo than it does of any steady point of principle.[54] A justice seeking to overturn the *Roe v. Wade* ruling allowing women to have abortions during the first trimester of pregnancy would be an activist conservative justice; Justice Thurgood Marshall ended his term on the Court as a liberal restraintist.

In addition to being influenced by their own attitudes, justices are influenced in their decision making by their backgrounds (region of residence, profession, place of education, and the like), their party affiliations, and their political attitudes, all of which the president and the Senate consider in selecting future justices.[55]

EXTERNAL FACTORS

Justices are also influenced by external factors.[56] Despite the founders' efforts to make justices immune to politics and the pressures of public opinion by giving them lifetime tenure, political scientists have found that they usually tend to make decisions that are consistent with majority opinion in the United States. Of course, this doesn't mean that justices are reading public opinion polls over breakfast and incorporating their findings into judicial decisions after lunch. Rather, the same forces that shape public opinion also shape the justices' opinions, and people who are elected by the public choose the justices they hope will help them carry out their agenda, usually one that is responsive to what the public wants.

Political forces other than public opinion exert an influence on the Court, however. The influence of the executive branch, discussed earlier, contributes to the high success rate of the solicitor general. Interest groups also put enormous pressure on the Supreme Court, although with varying success. Interest groups are influential in the process of nomination and confirmation of the justices, they file amicus curiae briefs to try to shape the decisions on the certiorari petitions, and they file an increasingly large number of briefs in support of one or the other side when the case is actually reviewed by the Court. According to one scholar, the number of amicus briefs filed by interest groups is increasing, although the Court does not release official numbers. *Bloomberg News* notes that the unofficial record for amicus briefs filed was 102 (for the 2003 affirmative action cases we discussed in Chapter 6) until the 2012 health care case, which inspired a whopping 136.[57] Interest groups also have a role in sponsoring cases when individual petitioners do not have the resources to bring a case before the Supreme Court. The National Association for the Advancement of Colored People (NAACP), the American Civil Liberties Union (ACLU), and the Washington Legal Foundation are examples of groups that have provided funds and lawyers for people seeking to reach the Court. While interest group activity has increased tremendously since the 1980s, researchers are uncertain whether it has paid off in Court victories. Their support does seem to help cases get to the Court, however, and they may reap other gains, such as publicity.

A final influence on the justices worth discussing here is the justices' relationships with one another. While they usually (at least in recent years) arrive at their conference meeting with their minds already made up, they cannot afford to ignore one another. It takes five votes to decide a case, and the justices need each other as allies. One scholar

judicial activism view that the courts should be lawmaking, policymaking bodies

judicial restraint view that the courts should reject any active lawmaking functions and stick to judicial interpretations of the past

John Oliver's #RealAnimalsFakePaws ● Cameras in Court

who has looked at the disputes among justices over decisions, and who has evaluated the characterization of the Court as "nine scorpions in a bottle," says that the number of disagreements is not noteworthy.[58] On the contrary, what is truly remarkable is how well the justices tend to cooperate, given their close working relationship, the seriousness of their undertaking, and the varied and strong personalities and ideologies that go into the mix.

WRITING OPINIONS Once a decision is reached, or sometimes as it is being reached, the writing of the opinion is assigned. The **opinion** is the written part of the decision that states the judgment of the majority of the Court; it is the lasting part of the process, read by law students, lawyers, judges, and future justices. As the living legacy of the case, the written opinions are vitally important for how the nation will understand what the decision means. If, for instance, the opinion is written by the least enthusiastic member of the majority, it will be weaker and less authoritative than if it is written by the most passionate member. The same decision can be portrayed in different ways, stated broadly or narrowly, with implications for many future cases or for fewer. If the chief justice is in the majority, it is his or her job to assign the opinion-writing task. Otherwise, the senior member in the majority assigns the opinion. So important is the task that chief justices are known to manipulate their votes, voting with a majority they do not agree with in order to keep the privilege of assigning the opinion to the justice who would write the weakest version of the majority's conclusion.[59] Those justices who agree with the general decision, but who do so for reasons other than or in addition to those stated in the majority opinion, may write **concurring opinions**, and those who disagree may write **dissenting opinions**. These other opinions often have lasting impact as well, especially if the Court changes its mind, as it often does over time and as its composition changes. When such a reversal occurs, the reasons for the about-face are sometimes to be found in the dissent or the concurrence for the original decision.

> **opinion** the written decision of the Court that states the judgment of the majority
>
> **concurring opinions** documents written by justices expressing agreement with the majority ruling but describing different or additional reasons for the ruling
>
> **dissenting opinions** documents written by justices expressing disagreement with the majority ruling

The Least Visible Branch: Who Are These People?
Because members of the Supreme Court are appointed for life, and therefore do not need to curry favor with the public, what we know about them is limited largely by what they choose to say and their official Court opinions. From left to right are Clarence Thomas, Sonia Sotomayor, Antonin Scalia, Stephen Breyer, Chief Justice John Roberts, Samuel Alito, Anthony Kennedy, Elena Kagan, and Ruth Bader Ginsburg.

THE POLITICAL EFFECTS OF JUDICIAL DECISIONS

The last area in which we can see the Supreme Court as a political actor is in the effects of the decisions it makes. These decisions, despite the best intentions of those who adhere to the philosophy of judicial restraint, often amount to the creation of public policies as surely as do acts of Congress. Chapters 5 and 6, on civil liberties and the struggle for equal rights, make clear that the Supreme Court, at certain points in its history, has taken an active lawmaking role. The history of the Supreme Court's policymaking role is the history of the United States, and we cannot possibly recount it here, but a few examples should show that rulings of the Court have had the effect of distributing scarce and valued resources among people, affecting decisively who gets what, when, and how.[60]

It was the Court, for instance, under the early leadership of John Marshall, that greatly enhanced the power of the federal government over the states by declaring that the Court itself has the power to invalidate state laws (and acts of Congress as well) if they conflict with the Constitution;[61] that state law is invalid if it conflicts with national law;[62] that Congress' powers go beyond those listed in Article I, Section 8, of the Constitution;[63] and that the federal government can regulate interstate commerce.[64] In the early years of the twentieth century, the Supreme Court was an ardent defender of the right of business not to be regulated by the federal government, striking down laws providing for

CLUES
TO CRITICAL THINKING

"Welcome to the Roberts Court: How the Chief Justice Used Obamacare to Reveal His True Identity"

By Jeffrey Rosen, *The New Republic*, June 29, 2012

In the wake of the Supreme Court's five-to-four decision upholding most of President Obama's health care bill, Chief Justice John Roberts was praised by liberals and lambasted by conservatives. In this article, Professor Jeffrey Rosen explains that Roberts's vote was more complex than either side knew.

In 2006, at the end of his first term as Chief Justice, John Roberts told me that he was determined to place the bipartisan legitimacy of the Court above his own ideological agenda. But he recognized the difficulty of the task. "It's sobering to think of the seventeen chief justices," he said. "Certainly a solid majority of them have to be characterized as failures."

Specifically, he was concerned that his colleagues were too often handing down 5–4 decisions that divided along predictable party lines, which made it hard for the public to maintain faith in the Court as an institution that transcends politics. Roberts pledged to try to persuade his colleagues to avoid party line votes in the most divisive cases. Roberts said he would embrace as his model his judicial hero, John Marshall, who sometimes engaged in legal "twistifications," to use Thomas Jefferson's derisive phrase, in order to achieve results that would strengthen the institutional legitimacy of the Court.

In the health care case, Roberts produced a twistification of which Marshall would have been proud. He joined the four liberals in holding that the Affordable Care Act's individual mandate was justified by Congress's taxing power even though he also joined the four conservatives in holding that the mandate was not justified by Congress's power to regulate interstate commerce.

For bringing the Court back from the partisan abyss, Roberts deserves praise not only from liberals but from all Americans who believe that it's important for the Court to stand for something larger than politics. On Thursday, Roberts did precisely what he said he would do when he first took office: He placed the bipartisan legitimacy of the Court above his own ideological agenda. Seven years into his Chief Justiceship, the Supreme Court finally became the Roberts Court.

It would be easy, of course, to question the coherence of the combination of legal arguments that Roberts embraced, but it would also be beside the point: Roberts's decision was above all an act of judicial statesmanship. On both the left and the right commentators are praising his "political genius" in handing the president the victory he sought even as he laid the groundwork for restricting congressional power in the future.

That's why it was foolish for conservatives to worry that Roberts could be intimidated by President Obama and other liberals who warned that a 5–4 Republican-Democratic vote striking down health care would represent a failure of Roberts's bipartisan vision. Roberts understood this on his own: Anyone who cared enough about his legacy to discuss it at the beginning of his tenure is far too savvy to be swayed by warnings from the left or right. Whether or not Roberts voted to uphold the mandate after the

initial decisions were drafted, as some commentators are now suggesting, Roberts knew that the health care decision would be the defining moment of his early tenure, and he rose to the occasion.

That's not to say that Roberts has reinvented himself as a liberal: He has strong views that he's unwilling to compromise, and with his strategic maneuvering in the health care case, he has now increased the political capital that will allow him to continue to move the Court in a conservative direction in cases involving affirmative action and the voting rights act, both of which he may well strike down next year by 5–4 votes. Marshall achieved a similar act of judicial jujitsu in *Marbury v. Madison*, when he refused to confront president Jefferson over a question of executive privilege but laid the groundwork for expanding judicial power in the future.

But Roberts's career defining choice in the health care case calls to mind the bipartisan ambitions not only of John Marshall but also Barack Obama. Like Roberts, Obama came to Washington as a Harvard educated lawyer who was strongly identified with one side of the political spectrum but believed in the virtues of bipartisanship. Obama expressed that belief by endorsing a version of the health care mandate that had the imprimatur of conservatives ranging from Mitt Romney to the Heritage Foundation. But despite strenuously reaching out to Republicans in the health care debate, Obama was able to win only one Republican vote (that of Joseph Cao (R-LA)). And Obama found himself assailed on both his left and right flanks from ideological purists who saw any kind of moderation as a form of apostasy.

Roberts now faces similar attacks from the left and right over the health care case for the compromise he forged with the pragmatic liberals, Elena Kagan and Stephen Breyer, over the Medicaid expansion. All three justices concluded that it violated the Constitution by threatening states with the loss of their existing Medicaid funding, but could be saved by removing the threat. But by joining the liberals in upholding the mandate, Roberts was able to persuade them to join him in restricting Congressional power. On health care, both Obama and Roberts exercised something increasingly rare in a polarized age: bipartisan leadership, which inherently requires compromise.

In a sense, all of the justices in the health care case reached decisions that coincide with their judicial philosophies and temperaments. Roberts was more interested in institutional legitimacy than philosophical purity. The pragmatic liberals, Kagan and Breyer, were willing to meet him half way. The more civil libertarian liberals, Ginsburg and Sotomayor, were not. Among the conservative dissenters, the romantic libertarian, Anthony Kennedy, proved as unalterably opposed as ever to incursions on liberty, regardless of whether they came, in his view, from the right as from the left. The tea party conservative Clarence Thomas filed a separate statement making clear how radically he wanted to restrict federal power. And the newly minted devotee of states rights, Antonin Scalia, included sclerotic rhetoric warning of the apocalypse. Scalia, increasingly, sounds more like an angry pundit than a neutral judge, and in the process, he gives us a vision of what both the liberal and conservative wings might have sounded like if Roberts hadn't prevented them from polarizing entirely.

Of course, it didn't all come down to judicial temperament. In the most divisive constitutional cases, the substance of legal arguments will always play a part. Arguments by liberal scholars who care about constitutional text and history, such as Neil Siegel of Duke Law School, were reflected in Chief Justice Roberts's

opinion about the taxing power. Justice Ginsburg's defense of Congress's power to pass the mandate under the commerce clause adopted New Textualists arguments by Jack Balkin of Yale Law School about how the framers of Article VI of the Virginia Plan during the Constitutional Convention would have wanted Congress to coordinate economic action in areas where the states were powerless to act on their own. The majority opinion also vindicated Solicitor General Don Verrilli's decision to emphasize the breadth of Congress's taxing power. But in the end, there are good arguments on both sides of any constitutional question, and justices have broad discretion to pick and choose among competing legal arguments based on a range of factors—including concerns about text, history, precedent, or institutional legitimacy. The fact that Roberts chose to place institutional

legitimacy front and center is the mark of a successful Chief.

As Roberts recognized, faith in the neutrality of the law and the impartiality of judges is a fragile thing. When I teach constitutional law, I begin by telling students that they can't assume that it's all politics. To do so misses everything that is constraining and meaningful and inspiring about the Constitution as a framework for government. There will be many polarizing decisions from the Roberts Court in the future, and John Roberts will be on the conservative side of many of them. But with his canny performance in the health care case, Roberts has given the country a memorable example of what it means to be a successful Chief Justice.

Source: Copyright Jeffrey Rosen. This article originally appeared in *The New Republic* and is reprinted by permission.

Consider the source and the audience: Jeffrey Rosen is a law professor at Georgetown University who supported the nomination of John Roberts as chief justice. He is writing in *The New Republic,* a longstanding center-left journal about politics. How are Rosen's own views reflected in this article?

Lay out the argument, the values, and the assumptions: This article is about Chief Justice Roberts's efforts to be a "successful" chief justice. How do Roberts (and Rosen) define "success" in this context? How is it related to "institutional legitimacy"? And what does Rosen mean that the Court is now "the Roberts Court"?

Uncover the evidence: Rosen bases his insights into Roberts's thinking on his own interviews of Roberts, as well as his analysis of what Roberts argued in the health care case. Is that persuasive to you?

Evaluate the conclusion: Rosen argues that Roberts has used a "twistification" to get his way in the long run (reduced powers for Congress) while avoiding seeming like a partisan in the short run. Liberal critics like the short-term result but fear the long-term result. Conservative critics have the opposite view. Did Roberts's "nonpartisan" solution avoid politics?

Sort out the political implications: Roberts's decision here certainly sidestepped the kind of political controversy the Court generated when it decided *Bush v. Gore* in 2000 (see *What's at Stake...?*). Is avoiding that kind of dramatic taking-of-sides all that is necessary to restore "faith in the neutrality of the law and the impartiality of judges"?

maximum working hours,[65] regulation of child labor,[66] and minimum wages.[67] The role of the Court in making civil rights policy is well known. In 1857 it decided that slaves, even freed slaves, could never be citizens;[68] in 1896 it decided that separate accommodations for whites and blacks were constitutional;[69] and then it reversed itself, declaring separate but equal to be unconstitutional in 1954.[70] It is the Supreme Court that has been responsible for the expansion of due process protection for criminal defendants,[71] for instituting the principle of one person–one vote in drawing legislative districts,[72] and for establishing the right of a woman to have an abortion in the first trimester of pregnancy.[73] And, of course, there was the case of *Bush v. Gore*, with which we began this chapter. Each of these actions has altered the distribution of power in American society in ways that some would argue should be done only by an elected body.

In many ways the Roberts Court promises to be as political as those that have come before, although there have been some surprising twists that keep Court-watchers guessing. In 2010 the Court ruled five to four that campaign finance legislation could not limit the money spent by corporations on electioneering broadcasts because corporations have First Amendment protections.[74] Although we don't yet understand the full impact of this case, as we will see in Chapter 14, the Super PACs it allows have changed the campaigning landscape. In 2012 the Court handed down rulings that, among other things, struck down most of Arizona's immigration law and upheld the constitutionality of President Obama's health care bill, albeit not on grounds that observers had anticipated. In that ruling Chief Justice Roberts used creative reasoning to save the president's signature legislation, concluding the individual mandate in the bill was not a mandate, which would have fallen outside Congress's commerce clause power, but a tax, which was indisputably within Congress's tool box (see *CLUES to Critical Thinking*).[75] In 2013 the Court rolled back parts of the historic Voting Rights Act and then the next week struck down the Defense of Marriage Act that defined marriage as being between a man and a woman. And in 2014 the Court limited the president's ability to make appointments during congressional recesses, struck down overall limits by individuals to campaigns, and ruled in a split decision that family-owned corporations do not have to provide health insurance that covers birth control to employees if it offends their religious beliefs. While this is by no means a comprehensive list of Supreme Court cases during Roberts's tenure, it shows that these decisions get right in the thick of determining who gets what and how they get it.

PAUSE AND REVIEW:

WHO, WHAT, HOW

The Supreme Court is a powerful institution, and all Americans have a great stake in what it does. Citizens want to respect the Court and to believe that it is the guardian of American justice and the Constitution.

The president wants to create a legacy and to build political support with respect to his Supreme Court appointments, and he wants to place justices on the Court who reflect his political views and judicial philosophy. Occasionally he also wants to influence the decisions made by the Court.

Members of the Senate also have an interest in getting justices on the Court who reflect their views and the views of their parties. They are also responsive to the wishes of their constituents and to the interest groups that support them. Confirmation hearings can consequently be quite divisive and acrimonious. Interest groups, which want members on the Court to reflect their views, can lobby the Senate before and during the confirmation hearings, and can prepare amicus curiae briefs in support of the parties they endorse in cases before the Court.

Finally, the justices themselves have a good deal at stake in the politics of the Supreme Court. They want a manageable caseload and are heavily reliant on their law clerks and the rules of court procedure. They want to make significant and respected decisions, which means they have to weigh their own decision-making criteria carefully.

IN YOUR OWN WORDS » Outline the institutional rules and political influences that shape the Supreme Court and the decisions it makes.

» THE CITIZENS AND THE COURTS
Equal treatment and equal access?

In this chapter we have been arguing that the legal system and the American courts are central to the maintenance of social order and conflict resolution, and are also a fundamental component of American politics—who gets what, and how they get it. This means that a crucial question for American democracy is, Who takes advantage of this powerful system for allocating resources and values in society? An important component of American political culture is the principle of equality before the law, which we commonly take to mean that all citizens should be treated equally *by* the law, but which also implies that all citizens should have equal access *to* the law. In this concluding section we look at the questions of equal treatment *and* equal access.

EQUAL TREATMENT BY THE CRIMINAL JUSTICE SYSTEM

In Chapter 6, on civil rights, we examined in depth the issue of equality before the law in a constitutional sense. But what about the day-to-day treatment of citizens by the law enforcement and legal systems? Citizens *are* treated

Kennedy's Swing Vote ● Roberts' Decision

differently by these systems according to their race, their income level, and the kinds of crimes they commit. That African Americans and whites have very different views of their treatment by law enforcement and the courts is not news but it was brought home to Americans, most recently in the summer of 2014 by the very different reactions whites and blacks had to the shooting of Michael Brown, an unarmed teenager, by a police officer in Ferguson, Missouri. In the week following the killing, amid riots and demonstrations, curfews and the calling in of the National Guard by the governor, 80 percent of African Americans said they thought the incident raised important ideas about race. In contrast, 47 percent of whites said the issue of race was getting more attention than it deserved.[76] For African Americans, Brown was but the latest young man to be shot by police in suspect circumstances, highlighting the fear that many have that their sons are often targeted by the police out of fear or prejudice. Whites, on the other hand, are accustomed to seeing the police as a source of safety rather than danger, and often fail to understand what such incidents look like from the other side of the racial divide. In fact, as Ferguson struggled for calm, sympathy for the police officer who shot Brown generated several online efforts to raise support and funds for him and his family.

African Americans and white Americans do not experience our criminal justice system in the same ways, beginning with what is often the initial contact with the system, the police. Blacks are often harassed by police or treated with suspicion without any real cause—consider the practice of "stop-and-frisk" tactics in black neighborhoods in New York City, for example, technically random in nature but affecting mostly black men. As a result, blacks, and black men especially, tend to perceive the police as persecutors rather than protectors. In New York, specifically, reactions to stop-and-frisk tended to reflect race, with 48 percent of whites calling the practice "acceptable," compared to a mere 35 percent of blacks.[77] Federal courts weighed in on the practice in 2013, ruling that stop-and-frisk violated the constitutional rights of minorities in the city and amounted to "indirect racial profiling." Stopping short of ending the practice entirely, Justice Shira A. Sheindlin called for a range of reforms and a federal monitor to oversee them.[78]

Today the fact remains that blacks are more likely to be arrested than whites, and they are more likely to go to jail,

Scott Olson/Getty Images

Emotions, Boiling Over

After local police shot and killed an unarmed teenager in August 2014, protestors, both peaceful and disruptive, took to the streets of Ferguson, Missouri, to express their anger over what they saw as a pattern of unfair—and at times fatal— treatment along racial lines. The response from law enforcement and the National Guard was overwhelming but did little to quell the unrest, and reactions from the public only highlighted tensions on issues of race relations in the United States.

where they serve harsher sentences. A study of marijuana use and arrests, for example, shows that while young whites use marijuana at higher rates than blacks, blacks are three times more likely to be arrested for marijuana possession.[79] Clearly, initial interactions with police play a role here—they are more likely to stop and frisk a black person. But race is not the only factor that divides American citizens in their experience of the criminal justice system. Income also creates a barrier to equal treatment by the law. Over half of those convicted of felonies in the United States were defended by court-appointed lawyers.[80] These lawyers are likely to be less than enthusiastic about these assignments: the pay is modest and sometimes irregular. Many lawyers do not like to provide free services *pro bono publico* ("for the public good") because they are afraid it will offend their regular corporate clients. Consequently the quality of the legal representation available to the poor is not of the same standard available to those who can afford to pay well. Yale law professor John H. Langbein is scathing on the role of money in determining the legal fate of Americans. He says, "Money is the defining element of our modern American criminal-justice system." The wealthy can afford crackerjack lawyers who can use the "defense lawyer's bag of tricks for sowing doubts, casting aspersions, and coaching witnesses," but "if you are not a person of means, if you cannot afford to engage the elite defense-lawyer industry—and that means most of us—you will be cast into a different system, in which the financial advantages of the state will overpower you and leave you effectively at the mercy of prosecutorial whim."[81]

EQUAL ACCESS TO THE CIVIL JUSTICE SYSTEM

While the issue with respect to the criminal justice system is equal treatment, the issue for the *civil* justice system is equal access. Most of us in our lifetimes will have some legal problems. While the Supreme Court has ruled that low-income defendants must be provided with legal assistance in state and federal criminal cases, there is no such guarantee for civil cases. That doesn't mean, however, that less affluent citizens have no recourse for their legal problems. Both public and private legal aid programs exist. Among others, the Legal Services Corporation (LSC), created by Congress in 1974, is a nonprofit organization that provides resources to over 138 legal aid programs around the country with more than 900 local offices. The LSC helps citizens and some immigrants with legal problems such as those concerning housing, employment, family issues, finances, and immigration. This program has been controversial, as conservatives have feared that it has a left-wing agenda and

Republicans have tried to limit it when they have been in the congressional majority.

Does the fact that these services exist mean that more citizens get legal advice? Undoubtedly it does. Every year LSC programs handle nearly a million cases.[82] Still, there is no question that many of the legal needs of the less affluent are not being addressed through the legal system.[83]

Clearly a bias in the justice system favors those who can afford to take advantage of lawyers and other means of legal assistance. And since people of color and women are much more likely to be poor than are white males (although white men are certainly represented among the poor), the civil justice system ends up discriminating as well.

These arguments do not mean that the U.S. justice system has made no progress toward a more equal dispensation of justice. Without doubt, we have made enormous strides since the days of *Dred Scott*, when the Supreme Court ruled that blacks did not have the standing to bring cases to court, and since the days when lynch mobs dispensed their brand of vigilante justice in the South. The goal of equal treatment *by* and equal access *to* the legal system in America, however, is still some way off.

IN YOUR OWN WORDS » Describe the relationship between citizens and the courts in America.

LET'S REVISIT: **WHAT'S AT STAKE...**

In the years since the divisive outcome of *Bush v. Gore*, the nation has calmed down. The stunning national crisis that began with the terrorist attacks on September 11, 2001, put things into a broader perspective, and a Court-decided election no longer seemed as great a danger as the possibility of being caught without any elected leader at all at a critical time. Public opinion polls show that trust in all institutions of government, including the Supreme Court, ran high after September 11, and Bush's legitimacy no longer rested with the Court's narrow majority but rather with the approval ratings that hit unprecedented heights in the aftermath of the terrorist attacks and with his successful reelection in 2004.

But changed national circumstances and subsequent elections do not mean that the Court's unusual and controversial move in resolving the 2000 election should go unanalyzed. What was at stake in this extraordinary case?

First, as Justice Stevens pointed out at the time, the long-term consequences of people's attitudes toward the Court were at risk. Indeed, polls have shown a somewhat steady decline in people's perceptions of the highest court in the land in the years since, but whether that is due to the Court's finding in *Bush v. Gore* or to later rulings—or to an overall decrease in faith in government institutions—remains unclear.[84] The Court, as we have seen, has often engaged in policymaking, and to believe that it is not a political

institution would be a serious mistake. But part of its own legitimacy has come from the fact that most people do not perceive it as political, and it is far more difficult now to maintain that illusion. In the immediate aftermath of the decision, the justices, speaking around the country, tried to contain the damage and reassure Americans; even some of the dissenting justices emphasized that the decision was not made on political or ideological grounds. But fifteen years later, retired Justice Sandra Day O'Connor expressed some regrets, not about the ruling itself or her vote in it, but about the Court's decision to get involved at all. Noting that the case had earned the court "a less-than-perfect reputation," O'Connor wondered if "maybe the court should have said, 'We're not going to take it, goodbye.'"[85]

Also at stake in such a deeply divided decision was the Court's own internal stability and ability to work together. While the confidentiality of the justices' discussions in arriving at the decision has been well guarded, the decision itself shows that they were acrimonious. Again, in the aftermath, the justices have tried to put a unified front on what was clearly a bitter split. Members of the majority have continued to socialize with dissenters, and as Justice Scalia himself told one audience, "If you can't disagree without hating each other, you better find another profession other than the law."[86] While the stakes in this case may have been more directly political than in most other cases, the members of the Supreme Court are used to disagreeing over important issues and probably handle the level of conflict more easily than do the Americans who look up to them as diviners of truth and right.

Another stake in the pivotal decision was the fundamental issue of federalism itself. The federal courts, as Justice Ruth Bader Ginsburg wrote in her dissent, have a long tradition of deferring to state courts on issues of state law. Indeed, many observers were astounded that the Court agreed to hear the case in the first place, assuming that the justices would have sent it back to be settled in Florida. Normally it would have been the ardent conservatives on the Court— Rehnquist, Scalia, and Thomas— whom one would have expected to leap to the defense of states' rights. Subsequent decisions have made clear, however, that the *Bush v. Gore* decision did not signal a reversal on their part. If the opinions of the Court about federalism have changed at all since 2000, it is probably due more to the imperatives of the war on terrorism,

as we suggested in Chapter 2, than to the dictates of the election case.

Some observers argue that the majority of the Court saw something else at stake that led them to set aside their strong beliefs in states' rights and to run the risk that they might be seen as more Machiavelli than King Solomon, more interested in power than wisdom. The majority saw the very security and stability of the nation at stake. Anticipating a long recount of the votes that might even then be inconclusive, they thought it was better to act decisively at the start rather than to wait until a circus-like atmosphere had rendered impossible the most important decision a voting public can make. Whether they were right in doing so, and whether the stakes justified the risks they took, politicians, partisans, and historians will continue to debate for years to come.

TO SUM UP

for CQ Press

Sharpen your skills with **SAGE edge** at http://edge.sagepub.com/barbour7e. **SAGE edge for students** provides a personalized approach to help you accomplish your coursework goals in an easy-to-use learning environment.

REVIEW

Law and the American Legal System

Laws serve five main functions in a democratic society. They offer security, supply predictability, provide for conflict resolution, reinforce society's values, and provide for the distribution of social costs and benefits. American law is based on legislation, but its practice has evolved from a tradition of common law and the use of precedent by judges. The American legal system is considered to be both adversarial and litigious in nature. The adversarial nature of our system implies that two opposing sides advocate their position with lawyers in the most prominent roles, while the judge has a relatively minor role, in comparison.

Laws serve many purposes and are classified in different ways. Substantive laws cover what we can or cannot do, while procedural laws establish the procedures used to enforce law generally. Criminal laws concern specific behaviors considered undesirable by the government, while civil laws cover interactions between individuals. Constitutional law refers to laws included in the Constitution as well as the precedents established over time by judicial decisions relating to these laws. Statutory laws, administrative laws, and executive orders are established by Congress and state legislatures, the bureaucracy, and the president, respectively.

courts (p. 362)
civil-law tradition (p. 362)
common-law tradition (p. 362)
precedent (p. 362)
adversarial system (p. 362)
inquisitorial system (p. 362)
substantive laws (p. 366)
procedural laws (p. 366)
procedural due process (p. 366)
criminal laws (p. 366)
civil laws (p. 366)
constitutional law (p. 366)
statutory laws (p. 367)
administrative law (p. 367)
executive orders (p. 367)

Constitutional Provisions and the Development of Judicial Review

The founders were deliberately vague in setting up a court system so as to avoid controversy during the ratification process. The details of design were left to Congress, which established a layering of district, state, and federal courts with differing rules of procedure. The Constitution never stated that courts could decide the constitutionality of legislation. The courts gained the extraconstitutional power of judicial review when Chief Justice John Marshall created it in *Marbury v. Madison*.

judicial review (p. 368)
Marbury v. Madison (p. 369)

Federalism and the American Courts

The political views of the judge and the jurisdiction of the case can have great impact on the verdict. The rules of the courtroom may vary from one district to another, and the American dual court system often leads to more than one court's having authority to deliberate.

jurisdiction (p. 370)
original jurisdiction (p. 370)
appellate jurisdiction (p. 370)
appeal (p. 370)
senatorial courtesy (p. 373)

The Supreme Court

The U.S. Supreme Court reigns at the top of the American court system. It is a powerful institution, revered by the American public but as political an institution as the other two branches of government. Politics is involved in how the Court is chosen and how it decides a case, and in the effects of its decisions.

strict constructionism (p. 377)
judicial interpretivism (p. 378)
writs of certiorari (p. 381)
Rule of Four (p. 381)
solicitor general (p. 384)
amicus curiae briefs (p. 385)
judicial activism (p. 386)
judicial restraint (p. 386)
opinion (p. 387)
concurring opinions (p. 387)
dissenting opinions (p. 387)

The Citizens and the Courts

While the U.S. criminal justice system has made progress toward a more equal dispensation of justice, minorities and poor Americans have not always experienced equal treatment by the courts or had equal access to them.

ENGAGE

Be a juror.
If you were on trial, whom would you want deciding your fate? Most Americans are registered for jury duty when they register to vote, but most will jump through hoops to avoid serving when a juror questionnaire or summons arrives in the mail. The justice system depends on citizens to serve as the fair and impartial jurors; if you are called, consider it your civic duty to be one of them.

Spend a day in court.
Watching the justice process in action can be an eye-opening experience. Head down to your local courthouse and sit in on a trial or hearing to see how the courts work in your municipality.

Listen to oral arguments.
Cameras are not allowed in most courtrooms, and especially not in the U.S. Supreme Court. But thanks to streaming audio, you can hear the cases—and justices' questions and concerns— firsthand without having to travel to Washington, D.C.

Read court decisions and learn court history.
You can find decisions easily at **Findlaw.com.**

Baum, Lawrence. 2013. *The Supreme Court*, 11th ed. Washington, DC: CQ Press. The definitive book for understanding the Supreme Court as a political institution.

Carp, Robert A., Ronald Stidham, and Kenneth L. Manning. 2013. *Judicial Processes in America*, 9th ed. Washington, DC: CQ Press. The Constitution was written so that judges would be impartial observers and not be influenced by politics. The authors, however, argue that justices are actually quite involved in the policymaking process.

Shesol, Jeff. 2010. *Supreme Power: Franklin Roosevelt Versus the Supreme Court*. New York: Norton. Shesol offers a detailing of Roosevelt's efforts to reorganize the federal judiciary, set into the political context of the day, and the battle that ensued.

***Recount*. 2008.** This critically acclaimed HBO film depicts the disputed 2000 presidential election, and includes dramatizations of oral arguments before the Supreme Court (as well as the reading of opinions) in *Bush v. Gore*.

***A Civil Action*. 1999.** This film offers a captivating account of a court case detailing lawyer Jan Schlichtmann's maddening legal battle against two corporations accused of industrial pollution.

***Twelve Angry Men*. 1957.** This classic movie examines the tough decisions that a jury has to make as it deliberates the verdict in a murder trial.

EXPLORE

You and 1,000,000 people like this.

11 PUBLIC OPINION

IN YOUR OWN WORDS   After you've read this chapter, you will be able to

» Explain the role of public opinion in a democracy.

» Evaluate how well American citizens measure up to notions of an "ideal democratic citizen."

» Identify key factors that influence our individual and collective political opinions.

» Describe different techniques used to gauge public opinion.

» Give examples of ways in which public opinion enhances or diminishes the relationship between citizens and government.

WHAT'S AT STAKE...WHEN WE MOVE TO MORE DIRECT DEMOCRACY?

IN FEBRUARY 2012 THE NEW JERSEY legislature passed a bill legalizing gay marriage and sent it to Gov. Chris Christie for his signature. Christie vetoed it, saying, "An issue of this magnitude and importance, which requires a constitutional amendment, should be left to the people of New Jersey to decide."[1]

"Letting the people decide" is an attractive idea in a country like the United States that prides itself on its democracy. But how much responsibility do you want to take for the way you are governed? Most of us are pretty comfortable with the idea that we should vote for those who make our rules (although we don't all jump at the chance to do it), but how about voting on the rules themselves? Citizens of some states—California, for instance—have become used to being asked for their votes on new state laws through referenda and voter initiatives. But what about national politics—do you know enough or care enough to vote on laws for the country as a whole, just as if you were a member of Congress or a senator? Should we be governed more by public opinion than by the opinions of our elected leaders? This is the question that drives the debate about

whether U.S. citizens should be able to participate in such forms of direct democracy as the national referendum or initiative.

Not only do many states (twenty-seven out of fifty) employ some form of direct democracy, but many other countries do as well. In the past several years alone, voters in Slovenia were asked to decide about the establishment of a tribunal to resolve a border dispute with Croatia, in Bolivia about whether there should be limits to individual landholdings, in Azerbaijan about amending the constitution, in Sierra Leone about choosing a president (in the first democratic elections since 1967), and in Iceland about terms of payment on the national debt.

In 1995 former senator Mike Gravel, D-Alaska, proposed that the United States join many of the world's nations in adopting a national plebiscite, or popular vote on policy. He argued that Americans should support a national initiative he called "Philadelphia II" (to evoke "Philadelphia I," which was, of course, the Constitutional Convention), which would set up procedures for direct popular participation in national lawmaking.[2] Such participation could take place

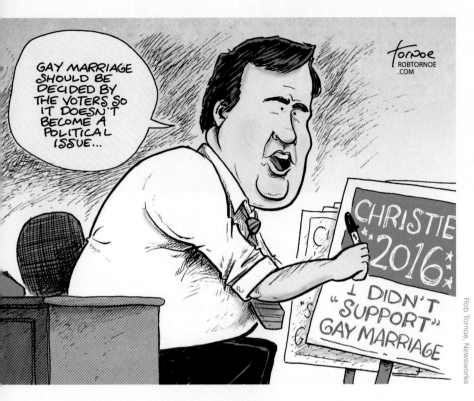

them think that the polls are "right only some of the time" or "hardly ever right."[4] (You might believe that finding, or you might not.) Politicians can be leery of polls, too—or even downright scornful of them. Disdainful of the Bill Clinton years, when the president's team of pollsters openly tested the public on various issues, including his approval ratings, the George W. Bush administration was cagey about the fact that they watched polls at all. Bush himself frequently said things like, "I really don't worry about polls or focus groups; I do what I think is right."[5] Matthew Dowd, the Bush administration's chief of polling at the Republican National Committee, echoed that stance with an emphatic "We don't poll policy positions. Ever."[6] Of course, the Bush administration did look at polls, and conducted them, too, just like every other administration has since the advent of modern polling, and just as the Obama administration continues to do today.[7]

These reactions to public opinion raise an interesting question. What is so bad about being ruled by the polls in a democracy, which, after all, is supposed to be ruled by the people? If politics is about who gets what, and how they get it, shouldn't we care about what the "who" thinks? **Public opinion** is just what the public thinks. It is the aggregation, or collection, of individual attitudes and beliefs on one or more issues at any given time. **Public opinion polls** are nothing more than scientific efforts to measure that opinion—to estimate what an entire group of people thinks about an issue by asking a smaller sample of the group for its opinions. If the sample is large enough and chosen properly, we have every reason to believe that it will provide a reliable estimate of the whole. With today's technology, we can keep a constant finger on the pulse of America and know what its citizens are thinking at almost any given time. And yet, at least some Americans seem torn about the role of public opinion in government today. On the one hand, we want to believe that what we think matters, but on the other hand, we'd like to think that our

Punting—At Least Until the Primary

As a Republican from a moderate northeastern state, New Jersey governor Chris Christie faces a challenge in seeking his party's nomination to the presidency in 2016. An endorsement of same-sex marriage might have won him support in his state, where public opinion favors the measure, but would likely have cost him the votes of the party's powerful conservative base when the presidential primary rolls around.

through the ballot box (the Swiss go to the polls four times a year to vote on national policy) or even electronically, as some have suggested, with people voting on issues by computer at home. Experts agree that the technology exists for at-home participation in government. And public opinion is overwhelmingly in favor of proposals to let Americans vote for or against major national issues before they become law.[3]

Do you agree with Gravel and the roughly three-quarters of Americans who support more direct democracy at the national level? Should we have rule by public opinion in the United States? How would the founders have responded to this proposal? And what would be the consequences for American government if a national plebiscite were passed? Just what is at stake in the issue of direct democracy at the national level? «

It is fashionable these days to denounce the public opinion polls that claim to tell us what the American public thinks about this or that political issue. The American people themselves are skeptical—65 percent of

elected officials are guided by unwavering principles.

In this chapter we argue that public opinion *is* important for the proper functioning of democracy, that the expression of what citizens think and what they want is a prerequisite for their ability to use the system and its rules to get what they want from it. But the quality of the public's opinion on politics, and the ways that it actually influences policy, may surprise us greatly.

THE ROLE OF PUBLIC OPINION IN A DEMOCRACY
Keeping the government of the people informed by the people

Public opinion is important in a democracy for at least two reasons. The first reason is normative: we believe public opinion *should* influence what government does. The second is empirical: a lot of people behave as if public opinion does matter, and to the degree that they measure, record, and react to it, it does become a factor in American politics.

WHY PUBLIC OPINION OUGHT TO MATTER

The presence of "the people" is pervasive in the documents that create and support the American government. In the Declaration of Independence, Thomas Jefferson wrote that a just government must get its powers from "the consent of the governed." Our Constitution begins, "We, the People. . . ." And Abraham Lincoln's Gettysburg Address hails our nation as "government of the people, by the people, and for the people." What all of this tells us is that the very legitimacy of the U.S. government, like that of all other democracies, rests on the idea that government exists to serve the interests of its citizens.

Since the beginning of the republic, there has been a shift in our institutions toward a greater role for the citizenry in politics. We can see this in the Seventeenth Amendment to the Constitution (1913), which took the election of the U.S. Senate from the state legislatures and gave it to the citizens of the states. We can see it in the altered practice of the Electoral College. Once supposed to be a group of enlightened citizens who would exercise independent judgment, in recent decades it almost always follows the vote of the people (with the dramatic exception of the 2000 election).

Tell Me What You Really Think
Our elected officials may seem disconnected from popular opinion, but they are in fact are keenly sensitive to their constituents, knowing that their votes on major bills may come back to haunt them when it's time for reelection. Members of Congress pay attention to public opinion polls, and most try to provide some face time in their districts as well. Here, Rep. Joe Wilson, R-S.C., hears from staff at Holland Hill Elementary School during his annual district bus tour.

We can see it in state politics, where the instruments of direct democracy—the initiative, referendum, and recall—allow citizens to vote on policies and even remove officials from office before their terms are up. These changes reflect views like those of political scientist V. O. Key, who observed, "Unless mass views have some place in the shaping of policy, all talk about democracy is nonsense."[8]

But how to determine whose views should be heard? As we saw in Chapter 1, different theories of democracy prescribe different roles for "the people," in part because these theories disagree about how competent the citizens of a country are to govern themselves. Elitists suspect that citizens are too ignorant or ill-informed to be trusted with major political decisions; pluralists trust groups of citizens to be competent on those issues in which they have a stake, but they think that individuals may be too busy to gather all the information they need to make informed decisions, and proponents of participatory democracy have faith that the people are both smart enough and able to gather enough information to be effective decision makers.

As Americans, we are also somewhat confused about what we think the role of the democratic citizen should be.

We introduced these conflicting notions of citizenship in Chapter 1. One view, which describes what we might call the *ideal democratic citizen*, is founded on the vision of a virtuous citizen activated by concern for the common good, who recognizes that democracy carries obligations as well as rights. In this familiar model a citizen should be attentive to and informed about politics, exhibit political tolerance and a willingness to compromise, and practice high levels of participation in civic activities.

A competing view of American citizenship holds that Americans are *apolitical, self-interested actors*. According to this view, Americans are almost the opposite of the ideal citizen: inattentive and ill informed, politically intolerant and rigid, and unlikely to get involved in political life.

We argue in this chapter, as we have earlier, that the American public displays both of these visions of citizenship. But we also argue that there are mechanisms in American politics that buffer the impact of apolitical, self-interested behavior, so that Americans as a *group* often behave as ideal citizens, even though as *individuals* they do not.

WHY PUBLIC OPINION DOES MATTER

Politicians and media leaders act as though they agree with Key's conclusion, which is the practical reason why public opinion matters in American politics. Elected politicians, for example, overwhelmingly believe that the public is keeping tabs on them. When voting on major bills, members of Congress worry quite a lot about public opinion in their districts.[9] Presidents, too, pay close attention to public opinion. In fact, recent presidents have had in-house public opinion experts whose regular polls are used as an important part of presidential political strategies. And, indeed, the belief that the public is paying attention is not totally unfounded. Although the public does not often act as if it pays attention or cares very much about politics, it can act decisively if the provocation is sufficient. For instance, in the 2006 midterm election, voters showed their frustration with Republicans' support for the war in Iraq (despite polls that said a majority of Americans had come to oppose the war) by handing the Democrats enough seats in the House and the Senate to give them control in both chambers.[10] And in 2008 and 2010, elections were primarily about voter angst over a depressed economy, a worry that first enhanced and then diminished the Democrats' control of Congress.

Politicians are not alone in their tendency to monitor public opinion as they do their jobs. Leaders of the media also focus on public opinion, making huge investments in polls and devoting considerable coverage to reporting what the public is thinking. Polls are used to measure public attitudes toward all sorts of things. Of course, we are familiar with "horse race" polls that ask about people's voting intentions and lend drama to media coverage of electoral races. Sometimes these polls themselves become the story the media covers. With the availability of a twenty-four-hour news cycle and the need to find something to report on all the time, it is not surprising that the media have fastened on their own polling as a newsworthy subject. Public opinion, or talk about it, seems to pervade the modern political arena.

PAUSE AND REVIEW:

WHO, WHAT, HOW

Public opinion is important in theory—in our views about how citizens and politicians *should* behave—and in practice—how they actually *do* behave. American political culture contains two views of citizenship, an idealized view and a self-interested view. These two views seem to be at odds, and Americans are ambivalent about the role public opinion should play in politics. The founders of the American polity developed constitutional rules to hold the power of citizens in check. Many of those rules, however, have changed over the intervening two hundred years as consensus has grown that citizens should play a stronger role in government.

Politicians and the media act as if they think the public is very powerful indeed. Politicians usually try to play it safe by responding to what the public wants, or what they think it will want in the future, while the media often cover public opinion as if it were a story in itself, and not just the public's reaction to a story.

IN YOUR OWN WORDS ›› Explain the role of public opinion in a democracy.

CITIZEN VALUES
How do we measure up?

At the beginning of this chapter we reminded you of the two competing visions of citizenship in America: one, the ideal democratic citizen who is attentive and informed, holds reasoned and stable opinions, is tolerant and participates in politics, and two, the apolitical, self-interested actor who does not meet this ideal. As we might expect from the fact that Americans hold two such different views of what citizenship is all about, our behavior falls somewhere in the middle. For instance, some citizens tune out political news but are tolerant of others and vote regularly. Many activist citizens are informed, opinionated, and participatory but are intolerant of others' views, which can make the give and take of democratic politics difficult. We are not ideal democratic citizens, but we know our founders did not expect us to be. As we will see by the end of this chapter, our democracy survives fairly well despite our lapses.

POLITICAL KNOWLEDGE AND INTEREST

The ideal democratic citizen understands how government works, who the main actors are, and what major principles underlie the operation of the political system. Public opinion pollsters periodically take readings on what the public knows about politics, and the conclusion is always the same: Americans are not very well informed about their political system.[11]

Knowledge of key figures in politics is important for knowing whom to thank—or blame—for government policy, key information if we are to hold our officials accountable. Virtually everyone (99 percent of Americans) can name the president, but knowledge falls sharply for less central offices.[12] In 2011 most respondents to a national survey (82 percent) could pick out Hillary Clinton as secretary of state from a choice of four national politicians that included their pictures, fewer than half (47 percent) knew that Chief Justice John Roberts is generally regarded as conservative (the survey told respondents that Roberts was the chief justice, a role that other surveys have shown Americans cannot always identify), and only 38 percent knew that the Republicans controlled the House of Representatives.[13] Americans have a reasonable understanding of the most prominent aspects of the governmental system and the most visible leaders—and frequently about issues that receive a lot of media coverage—but they are ignorant about other central actors and key principles of political life.

Efforts to follow politics are also highly variable in the United States. For example, just 26 percent of the public in 2011 said they follow what is going on in government and public affairs "most of the time," whereas 42 percent said "only now and then" or "hardly at all."[14] Taken together the moderate levels of political knowledge and interest indicate that the American public does not approach the high levels of civic engagement recommended by civics texts, but neither is it totally ignorant and unconcerned. In fact, as we will see, the public separates itself into different strata of political engagement, with only a minority who are seriously involved in following and trying to influence politics and government.

TOLERANCE

A key democratic value is tolerance. In a democracy, with many people jockeying for position and competing visions of the common good, tolerance for ideas different from

US Navy Photo by Mass Communication Specialist 1st Class Chad J. McNeeley/Released

Learning While You Laugh

Comedy Central's *The Daily Show With Jon Stewart* lampoons current political news nightly. Despite the show's irreverent tone, studies show that *Daily Show* viewers are relatively knowledgeable about political news and events. Here, chairman of the Joint Chiefs of Staff Mike Mullen discusses the role of private contractors and CIA agents in military operations with Jon Stewart in 2010.

one's own and respect for the rights of others provide oil to keep the democratic machinery running smoothly. It is a prerequisite for compromise, an essential component of politics generally, and democratic politics particularly.

How do Americans measure up on the important democratic requirement of respect for others' rights? The record is mixed. As we saw in Chapters 5 and 6, America has a history of denying basic civil rights to some groups, but clearly tolerance is on the increase since the civil rights movement of the 1960s. Small pockets of intolerance persist, primarily among extremist groups such as those who advocate violence against doctors who perform abortions, the burning of black churches in the South, or anti-Arab and anti-Muslim incidents following the terrorist attacks on the World Trade Center and the Pentagon on September 11, 2001.[15] Such extremism, however, is the exception rather than the rule in contemporary American politics.

In terms of general principles, Most Americans support the values of freedom of speech, religion, and political equality. For instance, 90 percent of respondents told researchers they believed in "free speech for all, no matter what their views might be." Subsequent studies, such as those by the First Amendment Center, show similar data. However, when citizens are asked to apply these principles to particular situations in which specific groups have to be tolerated (especially unpopular groups like the American Nazi Party preaching race hatred or atheists preaching against God and religion), the levels of political tolerance drop dramatically.[16]

FIGURE 11.1 **COMPARISON OF VOTER TURNOUT AMONG SELECT NATIONS**

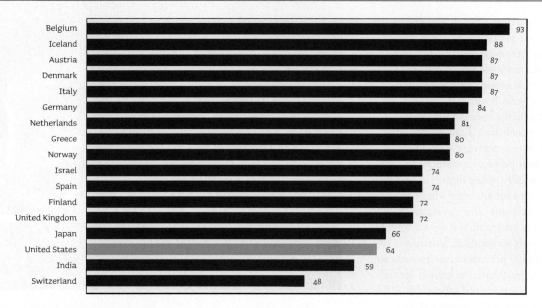

Belgium 93
Iceland 88
Austria 87
Denmark 87
Italy 87
Germany 84
Netherlands 81
Greece 80
Norway 80
Israel 74
Spain 74
Finland 72
United Kingdom 72
Japan 66
United States 64
India 59
Switzerland 48

Source: Data calculated by authors with data from the Institute for Democracy and Electoral Assistance, www.idea.int/vt/.

In studies of political tolerance, the least politically tolerant are consistently the less educated and less politically sophisticated. For example, one study found that on a civil liberties scale designed to measure overall support for First Amendment rights, only 24 percent of high school graduates earned high scores, compared with 52 percent of college graduates.[17]

Such findings have led some observers to argue that elites are the protectors of our democratic values. According to this view, the highly educated and politically active are the ones who guard the democratic process from the mass of citizens who would easily follow undemocratic demagogues (like Adolf Hitler). Critics of this theory say that educated people simply know what the politically correct responses to polls are and therefore can hide their intolerance better. In practice, the mass public's record has not been bad, and some of the worst offenses of intolerance in our history, from slavery to the incarceration of the Japanese in America during World War II, were led by elites, not the mass public. Nevertheless, the weight of the evidence does indicate that democratic political tolerance increases with education.

PARTICIPATION

One of the most consistent criticisms of Americans by those concerned with the democratic health of the nation is that we do not participate enough. And indeed, as participation is usually measured, the critics are right. Figure 11.1 shows that for voter turnout in national elections, the United

States ranks almost last among industrialized nations. Various explanations have been offered for the low U.S. turnout, including the failure of parties to work to mobilize turnout and obstacles to participation such as restrictive registration laws, limited voting hours, and the frequency of elections. We examine who votes and why in Chapter 14, but for now the fact remains that, among industrialized nations, the United States has one of the lowest levels of voter turnout in national elections.

PAUSE AND REVIEW:

WHO, WHAT, HOW

In a nation that claims to be ruled by the people, all American citizens have a stake in ensuring that "the people" are as close to being public-spirited ideal democratic citizens as they can be. It is also the case, however, that the primary incentive that drives each citizen is concern for his or her own interests, and that although many citizens do exhibit some of the characteristics of the ideal democratic citizen, they rarely exhibit all of them. Consequently, most citizens do not fit the model of the theoretical ideal. Those who do fit the model achieve that status through political education, the practice of toleration, and political participation.

IN YOUR OWN WORDS » Evaluate how well American citizens measure up to notions of an "ideal democratic citizen."

WHAT INFLUENCES OUR OPINIONS ABOUT POLITICS?
Sources of continuity and division in the American public

So far, we have learned that many, but by no means all, Americans exhibit the characteristics of our so-called ideal democratic citizen, and we have discovered that the elements of ideal democratic citizenship are not distributed equally across the population. The implication of our analysis, that education and socioeconomic status have something to do with our political opinions and behaviors, still does not tell us where our opinions come from. In this section we look at several sources of public opinion: political socialization, economic self-interest, partisanship and ideology, education, demographics, and geographic region of residence. All these things affect the way we come to see politics, what we believe we have at stake in the political process, and the kind of citizenship we practice.

Of the three elements of the ideal citizen we discuss here—political knowledge, tolerance, and participation—which is most important for the health of democracy?

POLITICAL SOCIALIZATION: HOW WE LEARN THE RULES OF THE GAME

Democracies and, indeed, all other political systems depend for their survival on each new generation's picking up the values and allegiances of previous generations—beliefs in the legitimacy of the political system and its leaders, and a willingness to obey the laws and the commands of those leaders. You can well imagine the chaos that would result if each new generation of citizens, freshly arrived at adulthood, had to be convinced from scratch to respect the system and obey its laws. In fact, that doesn't happen because we all learn from our cradles to value and support our political systems, which is why the children in France or China support their leaders as surely as the children of

> **political socialization** the process by which we learn our political orientations and allegiances
>
> **patriotism** a strong emotional attachment to one's political community

Courtesy of Ann West

Little Patriots
Early political socialization can happen unintentionally. Parents take youngsters to parades to enjoy the music and the colorful pageantry. Once there, though, children begin to develop an emotional response to political celebrations (like the Fourth of July) and national symbols (like the American flag).

the United States support theirs. The process by which we learn our political orientations and allegiances is called **political socialization**, and it works through a variety of agents, including family, schools, group memberships, and the major public events of our lives.

FAMILY The family, of course, has a tremendous opportunity to influence political development. Children typically develop an emotional response to some fundamental objects of government before they really understand much about those objects. Thus one of the important orientations that develops in the preschool years is **patriotism**, a strong emotional attachment to the political community. Children saluting the flag or watching fireworks at Independence Day celebrations easily absorb the idea that being American is something special. The greatest impact of the family—though one that has weakened somewhat in recent years—is on party identification.[18] Children tend to choose the same political party as their parents.[19] Interestingly, when parents disagree in their partisanship, the child identifies more often with the party affiliation of the mother. The family has a weaker effect on attitudes such as racial relations or welfare.

SCHOOLS AND EDUCATION Schools, where many children begin their day with the Pledge of Allegiance, and where schoolbooks emphasize stories of patriotism and national heroes, are an important agent of political learning and the development of citizen orientations. Most school districts include as part of their explicit mission that the schools should foster good citizenship.[20] In many districts, U.S. history or civics is a required course, and some state legislatures require a course or two in U.S. and state politics for all college students in the state system.

Early on in school, children develop basic citizenship skills, such as learning fundamental civic precepts—like "Always obey the laws" and "Be helpful to others."[21] Political training also continues in the schools with the establishment of class officers, mock presidential elections, and, at the upper grades, a widening array of clubs and extracurricular activities whose byproducts include training in leadership and group skills, group decision making, cooperation, and problem solving. All these experiences help foster essential citizenship skills in a society that depends largely on grassroots organization and voluntary compliance with political decisions.

GROUPS Shared values and experiences help define families, friends, and social groups, and research backs up the common notion that peer groups have a lot of influence on individuals' social and political attitudes. People who attend the same church tend to have similar political attitudes, as do individuals who live in the same neighborhoods. These tendencies can be traced in part to the ways people select themselves into groups, but they are reinforced by social contacts. The processes of talking, working, and worshiping together lead people to see the world similarly.[22]

Groups can also influence members by simple peer pressure. Researchers have documented the effects of peer pressure as a phenomenon they call the **spiral of silence**, a process by which a majority opinion becomes exaggerated.[23] In many contexts, when there is a clearly perceived majority position, those holding minority positions generally do not speak up or defend their views. This relative silence tends to embolden the advocates of the majority opinion to speak even more confidently. Thus what may begin as a bare majority for a group's position can become the overwhelming voice of the group through this spiral of silence.

POLITICAL AND SOCIAL EVENTS Major political and social events can have a profound socializing influence on the political orientations of the public and, because most of us experience these events largely, if not exclusively, through the filter of the media, those in the news and entertainment business have a potentially strong influence over how our views are shaped.

Divisive political events can cause levels of trust in government to decline; unifying events can cause them to rise. For example, coming out of World War II and into the prosperity of the 1950s, many Americans had a rosy picture of the United States; their good feelings were manifested as strong approval of government. However, the divisive events of the 1960s, including the civil rights movement and the unpopular Vietnam War, followed by the scandal of Watergate and the resignation of President Richard Nixon in the 1970s, had visible consequences in declining levels of trust in government, as Figure 11.2 shows.[24]

The partisan politics of the 1990s, including the impeachment of President Bill Clinton and the contested presidential election of 2000, should have caused levels of trust to fall even further. That they did not probably reflects citizens' generally positive assessment of government's role in the economic prosperity of the era. The events of September 11, 2001, and the ensuing war on terror caused Americans to see their government in an even more positive light. As is evident from Figure 11.2, however, as Americans' attention focused on domestic issues and partisan politics returned to business as usual, expressions of trust fell to their pre–September 11 levels.

SOURCES OF DIVISIONS IN PUBLIC OPINION

Political socialization produces a citizenry that largely agrees with the rules of the game and accepts the outcomes of the national political process as legitimate. That does not mean, however, that we are a nation in agreement on most or even very many things. There is a considerable range of disagreement in the policy preferences of Americans, and those disagreements stem in part from citizens' self-interests, ideology, education, age, gender, race, and religion—even the area of the country in which they live.

ECONOMIC SELF-INTEREST People's political preferences often come from an assessment of what is best for them economically, from asking, "What's in it for me?" So, for instance, those in the lowest income brackets are the least likely to agree that too much is being spent on welfare, while those with more income are more likely to agree. Similarly, as incomes increase so does the feeling that one is paying too much in taxes. These patterns are only tendencies, however. Some wealthy people favor the redistribution of wealth and more spending on welfare; some people living in poverty oppose these policies. Even on these straightforward economic questions, other factors are at work. Similarly, those with lower incomes are generally more favorable than

> **spiral of silence** the process by which a majority opinion becomes exaggerated because minorities do not feel comfortable speaking out in opposition

Meet Your Federal Government, 1946 ● Nature or Nurture? ●

FIGURE 11.2 TRUST IN GOVERNMENT, 1958-2013

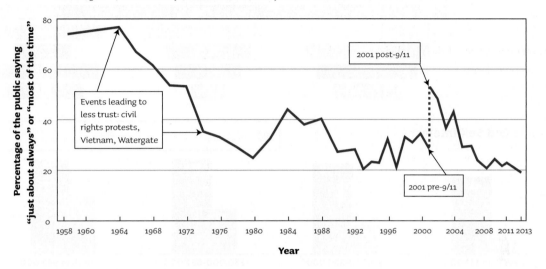

Question: How much of the time do you trust the government in Washington to do what is right?—Just about always, most of the time, or only some of the time?

Public levels of trust in government response to major political events

Sources: National Election Studies, 1958–2000; various polls from the Roper Center, 1994–2004. Yearly averages calculated by the authors with separate averages for 2001 (before and after September 11). Data from 2005 are gathered from seventy-one national polls accessed from the Roper Center. These include polls from CBS News/*New York Times,* CNN/Opinion Research/*USA Today,* NBC/*Wall Street Journal,* Pew Research Center, Quinnipiac University Polls, Kaiser/NPR, and AP/Gfk Polls.

the wealthy to government attempts to narrow the income gap between rich and poor. (See *"Snapshot of America:* What Do We Think, by Income and Education?".)

PARTISANSHIP AND IDEOLOGY Much of the division in contemporary American public opinion can be described in ideological (liberal or conservative) or partisan (Democrat or Republican) terms. How we adopt the labels of current political conflict has a good deal of influence on the policy positions we take, and even on how we perceive political personalities and events.

As we saw in Chapter 2, ideologies are sets of ideas about politics, the economy, and society that help us deal with the political world. For many Americans today, liberalism stands for faith in government action to bring about equitable outcomes and social tolerance, while conservatism for many represents a preference for limited government and traditional social values. A whole host of policy controversies in contemporary American politics are widely discussed in liberal-conservative terms.

Party identification, as we will see in Chapter 12, refers to our relatively enduring allegiances to one of the major political parties; for many of us it is part of what defines us.[25] Party labels provide mental cues that we use in interpreting and responding to personalities and news.

Identification as a Democrat or Republican strongly influences how we see the political world. Research shows

that uncertainty about new policies or personalities is usually resolved to be consistent with our partisanship. Even our view of objective events is affected by partisanship. Toward the end of Republican president Ronald Reagan's second term in office, a poll asked Americans whether inflation and unemployment had gotten better or worse over the eight years of his administration. In fact, both had improved, but Democrats and Republicans were miles apart in their perceptions of the objective facts: a majority of the Democrats said inflation was worse and only 8 percent acknowledged it was better. Among Republicans only 13 percent thought it had gotten worse, and fully 47 percent thought it had improved.[26] In a more recent example, just fourteen days into the Obama administration, a poll asked if Americans approved or disapproved of the way Obama was handling his job as president. Objectively, it would be hard for anyone to tell much after only two weeks, but partisans had formed their opinions: fully half of the Republicans polled already disapproved, compared to only 2 percent of Democrats.[27] Clearly we see the world through a partisan lens.

Because, as we have noted throughout this book, party elites and candidates have become ideologically polarized in recent decades—that is, Republicans are increasingly associated with a very conservative ideology and Democrats with a liberal one, with less common ground left in the middle—citizens have found it increasingly easy to sort

SNAPSHOT OF AMERICA: WHAT DO WE THINK, BY EDUCATION AND INCOME?

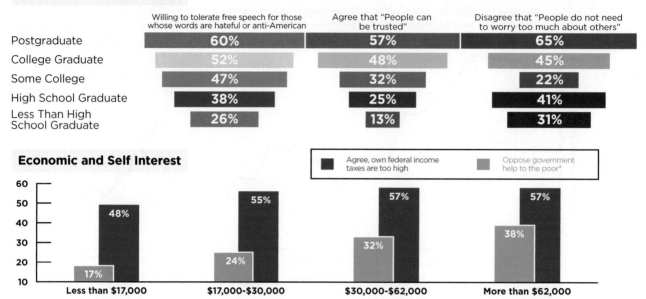

Democratic Enlightenment

	Willing to tolerate free speech for those whose words are hateful or anti-American	Agree that "People can be trusted"	Disagree that "People do not need to worry too much about others"
Postgraduate	60%	57%	65%
College Graduate	52%	48%	45%
Some College	47%	32%	22%
High School Graduate	38%	25%	41%
Less Than High School Graduate	26%	13%	31%

Economic and Self Interest

Legend: ■ Agree, own federal income taxes are too high   ■ Oppose government help to the poor*

	Less than $17,000	$17,000–$30,000	$30,000–$62,000	More than $62,000
Oppose government help to the poor	17%	24%	32%	38%
Agree own federal income taxes are too high	48%	55%	57%	57%

*Some people think that the government in Washington should do everything possible to improve the standard of living of all poor Americans; other people think it is not the government's responsibility, and that each person should take care of himself. Table shows those on side of people taking care of themselves.

BEHIND THE NUMBERS

American's exercise of citizenship has long reflected a mix of concerns about community and self-interest. How do the democratic values of knowledge, participation, enlightenment vary with levels of education? And can self-interest explain the differences in feelings about taxes and welfare among income groups?

Source: Calculated by authors from the 2010 General Social Survey and the 2010 Cooperative Congressional Election Survey.

---

themselves into one party or the other.[28] This process of **partisan sorting** means that average Democrats and Republicans are much further apart ideologically than was the case in previous decades (see Figure 12.3). The impact on politics has been quite profound. For one thing, fewer people are likely to swing between candidates because fewer come to contemporary elections with a fully open mind. More and more voters are predisposed one way or the other by the combination of ideological and partisan identifications. We see this in the "red state versus blue state" phenomenon in presidential elections where the outcomes of all but a handful of states are perfectly predictable due to the states' being predominately Republican and conservative, or Democratic and liberal.[29] Another consequence of the great partisan sort is that citizens (following the lead of politicians and commentators) find it much easier to demonize the opposition. This has contributed to the nastiness, anger, and general incivility of contemporary politics, which in turn has contributed to citizens' disgust with politics in general.[30]

An important ideological group in the electorate includes those who are "philosophical conservatives" but "operational liberals." When asked, they identify themselves as conservatives, attached to the concept of limited government and an unregulated market, but they also support many of the programs that accompany contemporary liberalism, such as Social Security, Medicare, and environmental protection. Of course, politicians try to play on this, with Republicans appealing to such citizens' loyalty to "conservative principles" while Democrats avoid ideological labels and try to focus attention on specific favored programs.

EDUCATION As we suggested earlier in our discussion of the ideal democratic citizen, a number of political orientations

> **partisan sorting** the process through which citizens align themselves ideologically with one of the two parties, leaving fewer citizens remaining in the center and increasing party polarization

Birth Year Influences Political Views

Policy Preference Difference and Age

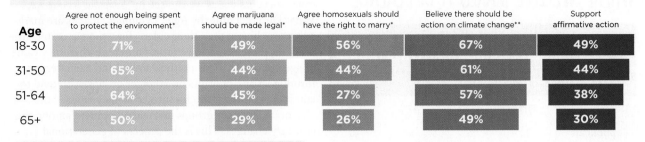

Age	Agree not enough being spent to protect the environment*	Agree marijuana should be made legal*	Agree homosexuals should have the right to marry*	Believe there should be action on climate change**	Support affirmative action
18-30	71%	49%	56%	67%	49%
31-50	65%	44%	44%	61%	44%
51-64	64%	45%	27%	57%	38%
65+	50%	29%	26%	49%	30%

On Some Policies, Age Does Not Matter Much

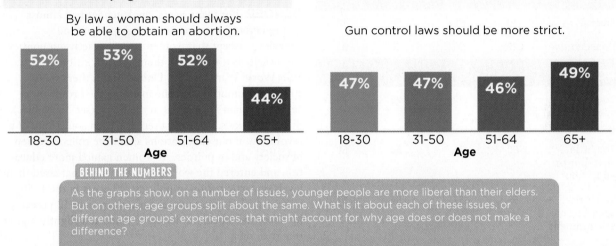

By law a woman should always be able to obtain an abortion.

18-30	31-50	51-64	65+
52%	53%	52%	44%

Age

Gun control laws should be more strict.

18-30	31-50	51-64	65+
47%	47%	46%	49%

Age

BEHIND THE NUMBERS

As the graphs show, on a number of issues, younger people are more liberal than their elders. But on others, age groups split about the same. What is it about each of these issues, or different age groups' experiences, that might account for why age does or does not make a difference?

Source: Calculated by authors from *Cumulative Social Survey (2008, 2010, 2012); **Cooperative Congressional Survey, 2012.

---

change as a person attains more education. One important study looked in depth at how education influences aspects of citizenship, separating citizen values into "democratic enlightenment" and "democratic engagement."[31] *Democratic enlightenment* refers to a citizen's ability to hold democratic beliefs, including the acceptance that politics is about compromise and that sometimes the needs of the whole community will conflict with and override one's individual preferences. *Democratic engagement* refers to a citizen's ability to understand his or her own interests and how to pursue those interests in politics. Both democratic dimensions are tied to education: better-educated citizens are more likely to be tolerant and committed to democratic principles and are more likely to vote, to be informed about politics, and to participate at all levels of the political system (see "*Snapshot of America:* What Do We Think, by Income and Education?" on page 406).[32] In short, those who graduate from college have many more of the attributes of the idealized active democratic citizen than do those who do not graduate from high school.

AGE We might expect that people change their opinions as they age, that our experiences over time affect how we see the political world. There is, however, precious little evidence for the common view that masses of people progress from youthful idealism to mature conservatism.

Indeed, extensive research shows that, on most political issues, only small differences in policy preferences are related to age.[33] One exception is the finding of consistent age differences in political engagement. Middle-age and older citizens are typically more attentive to and more active in politics: they report more frequent efforts to persuade others, they vote more often, and they are more likely to write letters to public officials and to contribute to political campaigns. It seems that acting out one's political role may be part and parcel of the array of activities that we associate with "settling down," such as marrying, having children, and establishing a career. This exception was mitigated somewhat in 2008 with the unusual response of young people to Barack Obama's candidacy for president.

TABLE 11.1

WHERE WE LIVE MAKES A DIFFERENCE

	BIG CITY	SUBURBS	SMALL TOWN	RURAL
PARTY IDENTIFICATION				
Democrat	59%	47%	42%	39%
Republican	22	35	38	40
Ideology				
Liberal	40	28	26	18
Conservative	29	35	36	33
POLICY				
Too little spending to help blacks	46	32	26	28
Too little spending on education	80	75	66	68
Too little spending on environment	65	57	54	57
Allow abortion for any reason	52	49	37	29
Agree that homosexuals should have the right to marry	56	48	44	33

Source: Calculated by authors from the 2010 General Social Survey.

Note: The middle categories of "independent" and "moderate" are not shown for party identification and ideology but are included in the calculations.

The Obama candidacy brought record numbers of young people to the polls, and at the same time created one of the sharpest age-vote relationships we have seen, with younger voters supporting Obama in overwhelming numbers.[34]

Another area in which age plays a role in public opinion is in the creation of political generations, groups of citizens who have been shaped by particular events, usually in their youth, and whose shared experience continues to identify them throughout their lives. One of the most distinctive of such groups is the New Deal generation—those who came of age during the Great Depression. They are distinctly more Democratic in their party orientations than preceding generations.[35] Young people are likely to be more influenced by current political trends since they carry less political baggage to offset new issues that arise. Thus, for example, environmental issues and gay rights are currently prominent on the political agenda. On these and other social issues, as we can see in "*Snapshot of America: What Do We Think, by Age?*", younger citizens are markedly more liberal than their elders, for whom accepted attitudes on these issues were rather different when they came of age politically. Thus political events and age intersect, forming lasting imprints on younger groups, who tend to continue with the attitudes formed as they entered the electorate. As older groups die, overall opinion among the citizenry changes. This is the process of generational replacement.

GENDER For many years, one's gender had almost no predictive power in explaining opinions and behavior—except that women were less active in politics and usually less warlike in their political attitudes. Just after World War II, in the United States there was a strong presumption that the man was the breadwinner and the woman's place was in the home (see Table 11.1). Since the 1960s, however, there has been something of a revolution in our expectations about the role of women in society and in politics. As women gained more education and entered the work force, they also increased their levels of participation in politics. Whereas in the 1950s women trailed men in voter turnout by over 12 percent, by 2006, and since, women have voted at a slightly higher rate than men.[36]

Interestingly, in the last quarter of the twentieth century, as men and women approached equality in their levels of electoral participation, their attitudes on issues diverged. This tendency for men and women to take different issue positions or to evaluate political figures differently is called the gender gap. In almost all cases, it means that women are more liberal than men. The ideological stances of women overall have not changed significantly since the 1970s, but those of men have shifted steadily, as more call themselves conservatives (see "*Snapshot of America: What Do We Think, by Gender [and Marriage]?*"). On a number of specific policy issues the gender gap is substantial, particularly on compassion issues and on issues involving the use of force: females are more liberal on social welfare policies, that is, programs of aid for children, the elderly, and the poor; and females are less favorable to the death penalty and less willing than men to go war. Interestingly, the direction of differences is opposite on moral issues; men are more favorable to marijuana

> **political generations** groups of citizens whose political views have been shaped by the common events of their youth
>
> **gender gap** the tendency of men and women to differ in their political views on some issues

Millennials Don't Make Sense ●

SNAPSHOT OF AMERICA: WHAT DO WE THINK, BY GENDER (AND MARRIAGE)?

The Gender Gap in Political Ideology

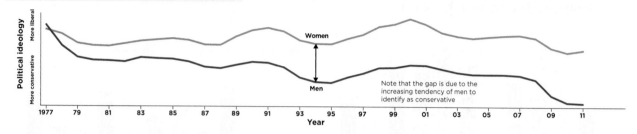

Marital Status, Attitudes Toward Gay Marriage, and Party Identification

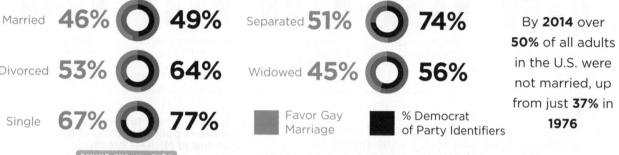

Married   46%   49%   Separated   51%   74%

Divorced   53%   64%   Widowed   45%   56%

Single   67%   77%

Favor Gay Marriage   % Democrat of Party Identifiers

By **2014** over **50%** of all adults in the U.S. were not married, up from just **37%** in **1976**

BEHIND THE NUMBERS

Consider how the structure of American households are changing with fewer headed by married man and woman. What does this mean for our policy and partisan preferences going forward?

Source: 2012 Cooperative Congressional Surveys, calculated by authors.

---

legalization and banning prayer in schools. On so-called women's issues, such as abortion or women having an equal role in business (where we might expect the greatest gender gap), the differences between the sexes are surprisingly small.[37] The gender gap also has electoral consequences. Women are more likely than men to vote for Democratic candidates. In fact, in every presidential election from 1980 to 2012, women have been more supportive of the Democratic candidate than have men, and interestingly, in recent elections, this gap has been largest among young people (those aged eighteen to twenty-nine).[38] Clearly there is something of a gender divide in U.S. national elections, and it appears to be growing as it is compounded by the effects of age.

> **marriage gap** the tendency for married people to hold political opinions that differ from those of people who have never married

The differences between men and women might be explained by their different socialization experiences and by the different life situations they face. The impact of one's life situation has emerged recently in what observers are calling the **marriage gap**. This refers to the tendency for different opinions to be expressed by those who are married or widowed versus those who have never been married. "Marrieds" tend toward more traditional and conservative values; "never marrieds" tend to have a more liberal perspective. The "never marrieds" are now sufficiently numerous that in many localities they constitute an important group that politicians must consider in deciding which issues to support.

RACE AND ETHNICITY Race has been a perennial cleavage in American politics. Only in recent decades have blacks achieved the same political rights as the white majority, and yet disparity in income between whites and blacks continues. When we compare by race the answers to a question about spending to improve the condition of blacks, the responses are quite different. African Americans

What Influences Our Opinions About Politics?   **409**

SNAPSHOT OF AMERICA: WHAT DO WE THINK, BY RACE AND ETHNICITY?

Policies Supported, by Race

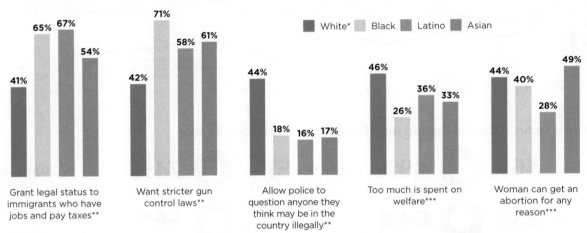

Legend: White* ■ Black ■ Latino ■ Asian

Grant legal status to immigrants who have jobs and pay taxes
- 41%
- 65%
- 67%
- 54%

Want stricter gun control laws**
- 42%
- 71%
- 58%
- 61%

Allow police to question anyone they think may be in the country illegally**
- 44%
- 18%
- 16%
- 17%

Too much is spent on welfare***
- 46%
- 26%
- 36%
- 33%

Woman can get an abortion for any reason***
- 44%
- 40%
- 28%
- 49%

*Non-Hispanic whites.**Source: Cooperative Congressional Survey, 2012. ***Source: Cumulative Social Survey, 2008–20012,

Michael Brown, a young unarmed African American male was shot by the police in Ferguso, Missouri. Whites and African Americans differ greatly on their views of the incident.

Agree "great deal" or "fair amount" of confidence in police handling of the shooting of Michael Brown

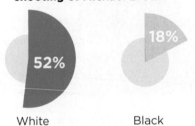

White 52% Black 18%

Source: Pew Research Center, "Stark Racial Division in Reactions to Ferguson Police Shooting," August 18, 2014, www.people-press.org/2014/08/18/stark-racial-divisions-in-reactions-to-ferguson-police-shooting.

Race/Ethnicity and Preferences for Government Spending

When asked whether "Government should improve the standard of living of the poor" we see significant racial/ethnic group differences...but nevertheless we agree on where government needs to spend.

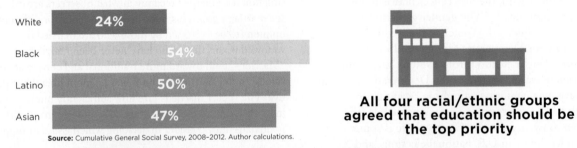

- White 24%
- Black 54%
- Latino 50%
- Asian 47%

Source: Cumulative General Social Survey, 2008–2012. Author calculations.

All four racial/ethnic groups agreed that education should be the top priority

BEHIND THE NUMBERS

Race and ethnicity stand for more than kinship; they also are markers for people's experiences in American society and politics. These experiences give rise to our policy preferences and even how we perceive the world. Looking at the differences in these charts, how can groups' experiences account for the differences you see?

are more favorable to such spending than are whites. We see a similar pattern in whether respondents would support a community bill to bar discrimination in housing. African Americans tend to favor such a law; whites are more likely to side with the owner's right to sell a house to whomever he or she chooses. These differences, some of which are shown in "*Snapshot of America:* What Do We Think, by Race and Ethnicity?", are typical of a general pattern. On issues of economic policy and race, African Americans are substantially more liberal than whites. However, on social issues like abortion and prayer in schools, the racial differences are more muted.

The root of the differences between political attitudes of blacks and whites most certainly lies in the racial discrimination historically experienced by African Americans. Blacks tend to see much higher levels of discrimination and racial bias in the criminal justice system, in education, and in the job market. Undeniably a large gulf exists between the races in their perceptions about the continuing frequency and severity of racial discrimination.[39]

Finally, reflecting the very different stands on racial and economic issues the parties have taken, African Americans are the most solidly Democratic group in terms of both party identification and voting. Interestingly, as income and other status indicators rise for whites, they become more conservative and Republican. The same does not happen among African Americans. Better-educated and higher-income blacks actually have stronger racial identifications, which results in distinctly liberal positions on economic and racial issues and solid support for Democratic candidates.[40]

Some signs indicate that this may be changing, however. The increasing number of black conservatives shows that the assumptions once made about African Americans and the Democratic Party are not universally true. This small but emerging pattern is exemplified by former secretary of state Condoleezza Rice; Supreme Court Justice Clarence Thomas; former California Board of Regents member Ward Connerly (see *Profiles in Citizenship* in Chapter 6); former head of the Republican National Committee Michael Steele; and most recently, Herman Cain, who briefly led in the polls for the Republican presidential nomination in 2012, and Senator Tim Scott, R-S.C., who threatened to impeach President Obama over the debt limit controversy.[41] Nevertheless, the rise of Democrat Barack Obama to become the first black president of the United States has undoubtedly reinforced the bond between African Americans and the Democratic Party.

Of course Americans differ by ethnicity as well as by race, and these factors interact in interesting ways to influence the opinions we hold on different policies. The *Snapshot of America* on page 410 compares the views of non-Hispanic whites, blacks, and Hispanics or Latinos. Unfortunately, the numbers of Asians in typical national surveys are too small to achieve reliable estimates, but studies have shown that there is little consensus among Asians as a group across a wide range of issues. In general, whites, blacks, and Latinos

are not consistent in terms of contemporary liberalism-conservatism. For example, whites are most conservative on the death penalty, with almost three-quarters favoring capital punishment, compared to about half of African Americans and Latinos. Blacks are most liberal in the belief that too little is spent on health care, but most conservative in favoring prayer in the schools. Latinos stand out in their opposition to abortion and in not favoring a reduction in the numbers of immigrants allowed into the country. Although the pattern is not one of ideological consistency, these differences make sense in terms of the particular histories and contexts of America's racial and ethnic mix.

RELIGION Many political issues touch on matters of deep moral conviction or values. In these cases the motivation for action or opinion formation is not self-interest but one's view of what is morally right. The question of morals and government, however, is tricky. Many people argue that it is not the government's business to set moral standards, although it is increasingly becoming the position of conservatives that government policy ought to reflect traditional moral values. In addition, government gets into the morals business by virtue of establishing policies on issues of moral controversy, like abortion, assisted suicide, and organ transplants. These questions are often referred to as social issues, as opposed to economic issues, which center more on how to divide the economic pie.

Our views of morality and social issues are often rooted in our differing religious convictions and the values with which we were raised. We often think of religion in terms of the three major faiths in America: Protestantism, Catholicism, and Judaism. Following the New Deal realignment, there were major political differences in the preferences of these groups, with non-southern Protestants being predominantly Republican, and Catholics and Jews being much more likely to be Democrats and to call themselves liberals. Over the years those differences have softened quite a bit, but today Catholics are less conservative than Protestants, and more Democratic, while Jews and the not religious are clearly more liberal and Democratic than the other groups. Specific religious affiliations may no longer be the most important religious cleavage for understanding citizen opinions on social issues. Since the 1970s a new distinction has emerged in U.S. politics, between those in whose lives traditional religion plays a central role and those for whom it is less important. In this alignment, those who adhere to traditional religious beliefs and practices (frequent churchgoers, regular Bible readers, "born-again Christians," and those who pray frequently) tend to take conservative positions on an array of social issues (such as homosexuality and abortion), compared with more liberal positions taken on those issues by what may be called "seculars," those who say they have no religious affiliation. Among those who say they are agnostic, Democrats far outnumber Republicans and liberals outnumber conservatives.

GEOGRAPHIC REGION Where we live matters in terms of our political beliefs. People in the Farm Belt talk about different things than do city dwellers on the streets of Manhattan. Texans appreciate subtle assumptions that are not shared by Minnesotans. Politicians who come from these areas represent people with different preferences, and much of the politics in Congress is about being responsive to differing geography-based opinions.[42] For instance, scholars have long argued that "the South is different." The central role of race and its plantation past for a long time gave rise to different patterns of public opinion compared to the non-southern states. The South today is not the Old South, but the region does retain some distinctive values. Opinions in the South—by which we mean the eleven states of the Confederacy—remain more conservative on civil rights but also on other social issues. (See the "*Snapshot of America:* How Do We Differ From State to State?" feature in Chapter 4, which shows how the states vary in terms of political ideology.)

Whether we live in the city, the suburbs, or the country also has an effect on our opinions. City dwellers are more Democratic in their political preferences and more liberal on issues like spending to help minorities and to improve education. On other issues, such as the environment, abortion, and a proposed constitutional amendment to ban same-sex marriages, rural residents stand out as distinctly conservative compared to other residential groups (see Table 11.1). In fact, analyses show that rural areas have become the anchor for the contemporary Republican Party, with its stress on limited government, individual responsibility, and traditional values.[43]

PAUSE AND REVIEW:

WHO, WHAT, HOW

Political socialization helps to fuel and maintain the political system by transferring fundamental democratic values from one generation to the next. More specific values come from demographic characteristics—our age, race, and gender—and from our life experiences—education, religious affiliation, and where we live.

As citizens find themselves in different circumstances, with differing political ideas, these differences are mined by interest groups, political parties, and candidates for office who are looking for support, either to further their causes or to get elected. Thus the differences in policy preferences that a complex society inevitably produces become the stuff of political conflict.

IN YOUR OWN WORDS » Identify key factors that influence our individual and collective political opinions.

MEASURING AND TRACKING PUBLIC OPINION
Using science to discover what people are thinking about political issues

Given the central role that public opinion plays in democracy, finding out what the public thinks is an important business, and one at which social scientists have gotten very adept over the years. While public opinion polls are sometimes discounted by politicians who don't like their results, the truth is that today most social scientists and political pollsters conduct public opinion surveys according to the highest standards of scientific accuracy, and their results are for the most part reliable. In this section we look at the ways that we are able to gauge what the public thinks about issues important to our civic and political lives.

LEARNING ABOUT PUBLIC OPINION WITHOUT POLLS

You undoubtedly know what your friends and family think about many issues, even though you have never conducted an actual poll on their beliefs. We all reside in social communities that bring us into contact with various types of people. Simply by talking with them, we get a sense of their ideas and preferences. Politicians, whose careers depend on voters, are necessarily good talkers and good listeners. They learn constituent opinion from the letters, phone calls, and emails they receive. They visit constituents, make speeches, attend meetings, and talk with community leaders and interest group representatives. Elected politicians also pick up signals from the size of the crowds that turn out to hear them speak and from the way those crowds respond to different themes. All these interactions give them a sense of what matters to people and how citizens are reacting to news events, economic trends, and social changes. Direct contact with people puts politicians in touch with concerns that could be missed entirely by the most scientifically designed public opinion poll. That poll might focus on issues of national news that are on the minds of national politicians or pollsters, while citizens may be far more concerned about the building of a dam upriver from their city or about teacher layoffs in their school district.

Thus politicians are fond of saying that they do not believe in polls or that they do not trust them. Perhaps what they are actually saying is that polls are no substitute for their own sampling of what is on their constituents' minds. It is natural to want to rely on our personal experiences with people. Members of Congress say they use a mix of sources to learn about public opinion, relying primarily on personal contacts including telephone calls and mail from constituents much more than opinion polls.[44]

While informal soundings of public opinion may be useful to a politician for some purposes, they are not very reliable for gauging how everyone in a given population thinks because they are subject to sampling problems. A **sample** is the portion of the population a politician or pollster surveys on an issue. Based on what that sample says, the surveyor then makes an estimation of what everyone else thinks. This may sound like hocus-pocus, but if the sample is scientifically chosen to be representative of the whole population, it actually works very well. Pollsters are trained to select a truly representative sample—that is, one that does not overrepresent any portion of the population and whose responses can therefore be safely generalized to the whole. When a sample is not chosen scientifically and has too many people in it from one portion of the population, we say it has a problem of **sample bias**. When trying to judge public opinion from what they hear among their supporters and friendly interest groups, politicians must allow for the bias of their own sampling. If they are not effective at knowing how those they meet differ from the full public, they will get a misleading idea of public opinion.

Library of Congress

Pollsters Get a Black Eye

Harry Truman laughed last and loudest after one of the biggest mistakes in American journalism. The *Chicago Daily Tribune* relied on a two-week-old Gallup poll to predict the outcome of the 1948 presidential race, damaging the image of polling for decades. With polls today conducted all the way up to Election Day—and exit polls tracking how ballots are actually cast—similar goofs are much less likely.

THE DEVELOPMENT OF MODERN PUBLIC OPINION POLLS

The scientific poll as we know it today was developed in the 1930s (for a history of polling, see this chapter's *Big Picture*). However, newspapers and politicians have been trying to read public opinion as long as we have had democracies. The first efforts at actually counting opinions were the **straw polls**, dating from the first half of the nineteenth century and continuing in a more scientific form today.[45] The curious name for these polls comes from the fact that a straw, thrown up into the air, will indicate which way the wind is blowing.[46] These polls were designed to help politicians predict which way the political winds were blowing and, more specifically, who would win an upcoming election. Before the modern science of

sampling was well understood, straw polls were conducted by a variety of hit-or-miss methods, and though their results were often correct, they were sometimes spectacularly wrong.

The experience of the *Literary Digest* illustrates this point dramatically. The *Literary Digest* was a highly popular magazine that conducted straw polls in the 1920s and 1930s. It mailed millions of questionnaires during presidential election campaigns asking recipients who they planned to vote for and then tabulated the mailed-in results. The *Digest* polls were quite successful in predicting the election winners in 1920 through 1932 and received wide recognition and publicity. However, in 1936 the magazine predicted that President Franklin Roosevelt would be defeated by Alf Landon by a wide margin. Instead, Roosevelt won handily. The poll was wrong for several reasons. First, some people change their minds often during an election campaign, with some remaining undecided until the final days, and the *Digest* poll was unable to record last-minute voting decisions. Second, there was a clear (in retrospect) sample bias: the *Digest* poll had included too many Republican voters in its sample because it drew names from lists of automobile registrations, telephone directories, and different clubs and organizations. The sample thus overrepresented the middle-class,

sample the portion of the population that is selected to participate in a poll

sample bias the effect of having a sample that does not represent all segments of the population

straw polls polls that attempt to determine who is ahead in a political race

● Poll Accuracy and Bias

Measuring and Tracking Public Opinion **413**

THE BIG PICTURE: HOW WE KNOW WHAT THE PUBLIC REALLY THINKS

Public opinion polling is hard to get our heads around—how can we know what the public thinks without asking everyone? It seems beyond counterintuitive that we can estimate what an entire nation thinks by asking as few as 1,500 people, and yet, so we can. While polling can feel mysterious, the truth is it is anything but—the science of polling allows us to make very educated estimates of what the public thinks.

The History of Polling

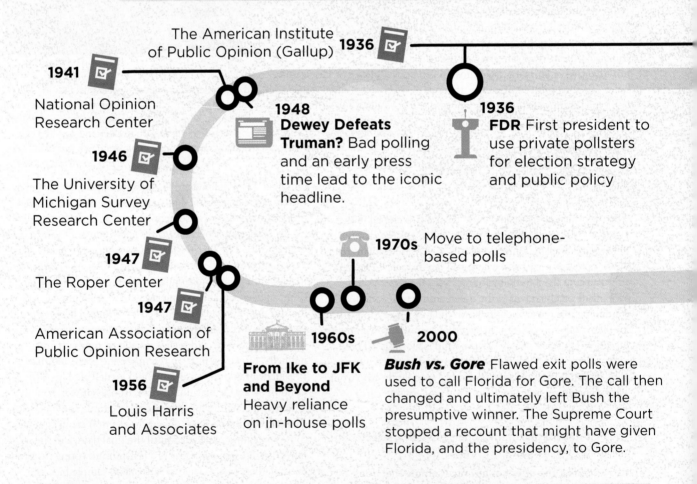

JULY 4, 1776

"When in the course of human events, it becomes necessary for one people to dissolve the political bands that have connected them with another...a decent respect to the opinions of mankind requires that they should declare the causes that impel them to the separation."

1936 The American Institute of Public Opinion (Gallup)

1941 National Opinion Research Center

1946 The University of Michigan Survey Research Center

1947 The Roper Center

1947 American Association of Public Opinion Research

1956 Louis Harris and Associates

1948 Dewey Defeats Truman? Bad polling and an early press time lead to the iconic headline.

1936 FDR First president to use private pollsters for election strategy and public policy

1970s Move to telephone-based polls

1960s From Ike to JFK and Beyond Heavy reliance on in-house polls

2000 _Bush vs. Gore_ Flawed exit polls were used to call Florida for Gore. The call then changed and ultimately left Bush the presumptive winner. The Supreme Court stopped a recount that might have given Florida, and the presidency, to Gore.

 "We all do no end of feeling and we mistake it for thinking. And out of it we get an aggregation which we consider a boon. Its name is public opinion. It is held in reverence. It settles everything. Some think it is the voice of God." —Mark Twain, "Corn-pone Opinions," 1900

"In a government based on suffrage the question is not whether the opinion of any one person is intelligent, but whether the collective judgment of all the people is intelligent. Democracy doesn't require that every man be a philosopher; it only requires that the sum total of all opinions be sound." —George Gallup, 1943

1824

First Straw Poll The poll showed a lead for Andrew Jackson over John Quincy Adams and two others. Jackson did then win the popular vote but failed to get a majority in the Electoral College. The race was thrown to the House of Representatives, which picked Adams as the next president.

 "What I want to get done is exactly what the people desire to have done, and the question for me is how to find that out exactly." —Abraham Lincoln, 1861

 1936 George Gallup calls election correctly for FDR, using probability theory to generalize from a small sample

1920s–1930st
The Blossoming of Market Research Opinion researchers used sampling, survey techniques, and statistical methods to delve into consumers' minds.

 ## 1916–1936
Literary Digest Straw Poll The bigger the sample size, the better? The poll was sent to 10 million people in 1936, and the 2 million who responded indicated that Republican Alf Landon was winning the presidency. But it was a bad sample, drawn from a list of people more likely to be Republican.

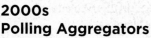 ## 2000s
Polling Aggregators Pollster.com and fivethirtyeight.com reduce the margin of error in polls by combining multiple polls and/or running simulations

2010s
Polling Techniques in Flux Cell-phone only households, call screening, low response rates, the rise of Internet polling, robo polling, and online panels are among the new considerations.

 ## 2012
Unskewing the Polls Convinced that turnout would not match 2008's, Romney's pollsters assumed that polls showing an Obama lead must be wrong and altered their polls' turnout model. Romney was reportedly "shell shocked" when he lost.

 "The private citizen, beset by partisan appeals for the loan of his Public Opinion, will soon see, perhaps, that these appeals are not a compliment to his intelligence, but an imposition on his good nature and an insult to his sense of evidence. —Walter Lippman, *Public Opinion,* 1922

financially well-off population, since at that time most families could not afford cars or telephones. Although this bias had not been a problem in the past, by 1936 these voters were becoming more identified with the Republican Party.[47] The sample bias was compounded because respondents had to mail in their questionnaires. Not only were they not representative to begin with, but the more political, intense, and involved voters who self-selected themselves by mailing back the questionnaire further skewed the results.

Polling errors led to an even more well-known polling fiasco in 1948, one whose results were captured in a photograph of a smiling and victorious President Harry Truman holding up a copy of the *Chicago Daily Tribune*, whose headline declared "Dewey Defeats Truman." By this time, pollsters had learned more about sampling requirements but not enough about the changing minds of voters. Having polled the public early on and established that Dewey held a substantial lead, few polling organizations bothered to follow up. The *Tribune* used old data, and polls again failed to capture last-minute changes in voters' decisions.

THE QUALITY OF OPINION POLLING TODAY

Today, polling is big business and a relatively precise science. Political polls are actually a small portion of the marketing business, which tries to gauge what people want and are willing to buy. Many local governments also conduct surveys to find out what their citizens want and how satisfied they are with various municipal services. All polls face the same two challenges, however: (1) getting a good sample, which entails both sampling the right number of people and eliminating sample bias, and (2) asking questions that yield valid results.

HOW BIG DOES A SAMPLE NEED TO BE? No sample is perfect in matching the population from which it is drawn, but it should be close. Confronted with a critic who did not trust the notion of sampling, George Gallup is said to have responded, "Okay, if you do not like the idea of a sample, then the next time you go for a blood test, tell them to take it all!" It might seem counterintuitive, but statisticians have determined that a sample of only one thousand to two thousand people can be very representative of the entire United States with its more than 300 million residents.

Sampling error is a number that indicates how reliable the poll is; based on the size of the sample, it tells within what range the actual opinion of the whole population would fall. Typically a report of a poll will say that its "margin of error" is plus or minus 3 percent. This means that, based on sampling theory, there is a 95 percent chance that the real figure for the whole population is within 3 percent of that reported. For instance, when a poll reports a presidential approval rating of 60 percent and a 3 percent margin of error, there is a 95 percent chance that between 57 and 63 percent of the population approve of the president's

job performance. A poll that shows one candidate leading another by 2 percent of the projected vote is really too close to call since the 2 percent might be due to sampling error. The larger the sample, the smaller the sampling error, but samples larger than two thousand add very little in the way of reliability. Surveying more people, say five thousand, is much more expensive and time-consuming but does not substantially reduce the sampling error.

DEALING WITH THE PROBLEM OF SAMPLE BIAS Because of fiascos like the *Literary Digest* poll, modern polls now employ systematic **random samples** of the populations whose opinions they want to describe. In a systematic random sample, everyone should have the same chance to be interviewed. Since almost all households now have telephones, it is possible to get a representative sample in telephone polls. Some pollsters argue that respondents are more candid and cooperative when they are interviewed in person. But achieving a representative sample for in-person interviewing is much more difficult since it requires interviewers to make personal contact with specific individuals chosen in advance.

Because reputable survey firms use scientific sampling strategies, sampling bias is not generally a problem that plagues modern pollsters, but there is one way it can sneak in through the back door. The chief form of sample bias in current surveys is nonresponse. Response rates to telephone surveys have dropped considerably over the years; in current surveys sometimes as few as one-quarter of those intended to be included in surveys actually participate. The reasons for this drop include hostility to telemarketers; the increasing use of caller ID; the growing use of cell phones (which are more difficult for pollsters to call since they are not allowed to autodial them); and the simple fact that people are busier, are working more, and have less time and inclination to talk to strangers on the phone.[48] As a result, most telephone polls, unless corrected, will have too many elderly women and too few younger men because the former are typically at home to answer the phone when the interviewer calls, and the latter are more frequently out. One consequence of the nonresponse problem is that the most reluctant respondents—those likely to be missed in a typical survey—seem to be less racially tolerant than the average population, meaning that a standard survey might yield responses that are slightly more liberal on racial matters than might be the population as a whole.[49]

Pollsters deal with the problem of differential response rates, which yield a sample that does not look demographically like the population that is being sampled—perhaps there are too many whites or old people, or not enough

> **sampling error** a number that indicates within what range the results of a poll are accurate
>
> **random samples** samples chosen in such a way that any member of the population being polled has an equal chance of being selected

FIGURE 11.3 ASKING THE RIGHT QUESTION

Version A

Question: Do you favor or oppose allowing students and parents to choose a private school to attend at public expense?

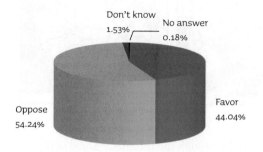

Don't know 1.53%
No answer 0.18%
Oppose 54.24%
Favor 44.04%

Version B

Question: A proposal has been made that would allow parents to send their school-age children to any public, private, or church-related school they choose. For those parents choosing non-public schools, the government would pay all or part of the tuition. Would you favor or oppose this proposal in your state?

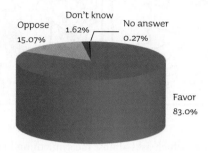

Oppose 15.07%
Don't know 1.62%
No answer 0.27%
Favor 83.0%

Comparison of results from two versions of school choice questions

Source: PDK/Gallup 33rd Annual Survey of the Public's Attitude Towards Public Schools, 2001.

---

college graduates or young adults—by **weighting** the sample to match what the census says the population looks like. This is done during the analysis of the results; under- or overrepresented groups are multiplied by values that bring them into line with their actual numbers in the population. Surprisingly, though, studies of differential response rates, which one might think would cause serious sample biases, find that well-constructed telephone polls continue to provide accurate information on citizens' responses to most questions about politics and issues.

THE IMPORTANCE OF ASKING THE RIGHT QUESTIONS
Asking the right questions in surveys is a surprisingly tricky business. Researchers have emphasized three main points with respect to constructing survey questions:

- *Respondents should be asked about things they know and have thought about.* Otherwise, they will often try to be helpful but will give responses based on whatever cues they can pick up from the context of the interview or the particular question. For example, some researchers from the University of Cincinnati did a local survey in which they asked respondents whether they favored a nonexistent "Public Affairs Act of 1974." Almost a quarter of the respondents were willing to give an opinion![50] Researchers have also found that including a "don't know" category in the list of possible answers matters to how respondents think about a question. In a study concerning legislation

> **weighting** adjustments to surveys during analysis so that selected demographic groups reflect their values in the population, usually as measured by the census

about which few people would have any knowledge, about 30 percent offered an opinion; however, this dropped to about 10 percent when respondents were offered "don't know" as one of the valid responses along with agree or disagree.[51] Moreover, the level of seeming non-opinions increases for less familiar topics and decreases markedly for more familiar topics.[52]

- *Questions should not be ambiguous.* One highly controversial example comes from a 1992 survey that reported that over a third of the American public either did not believe or doubted that the Holocaust had even happened.[53] One newspaper called the American public "willfully stupid"; Holocaust survivor, author, and Nobel laureate Elie Wiesel was "shocked" by the results.[54] The uproar, however, was largely the product of a bad question. Respondents were asked, "Does it seem possible or does it seem impossible to you that the Nazi extermination of the Jews never happened?" To say that one believed the Holocaust happened, the respondent had to agree to a double negative—that it was "impossible" that it "never" happened. There was plenty of room for confusion. Other respondents were asked a more straightforward version of the question: "The term Holocaust usually refers to the killing of millions of Jews in Nazi death camps during World War II. Do you doubt that the Holocaust actually happened, or not?" With this wording, only 9 percent doubted the Holocaust and 4 percent were unsure.[55]

- *Similar questions can yield surprisingly different answers.* For instance, do a majority of Americans support school choice, in which the government will pay the costs of children attending the schools the parents select? Notice in Figure 11.3 how two rather similar questions on this topic yield very different conclusions. In the shorter version, a majority are opposed to school choice, whereas in the

Doonesbury

BY GARRY TRUDEAU

longer version, which asks almost the same thing but with greater detail, an overwhelming majority are in favor of it. Words like *proposal* may connote some legitimacy in respondents' minds, or perhaps the injection of religion or the mention of "school-age children" brings to mind different "considerations" that affect how the questions are interpreted.[56] Why do you think people would be more likely to answer more positively to the second wording?

There are still other considerations that pollsters should take into account. Studies have shown, for instance, that the order in which questions are asked can change the results, as can such a simple factor as the number of choices offered for responses. Clearly, good surveys can tell us a lot about public opinion, but they will hardly ever produce the final word. And, of course, just as soon as they might, public opinion would probably shift again in any case.

TYPES OF POLLS

Many people and organizations report the results of what they claim are measures of public opinion. To make sense of this welter of claims, it is useful to know some basic polling terminology and the characteristics of different types of polls.

NATIONAL POLLS National polls are efforts to measure public opinion within a limited period of time using a national representative sample. The time period of interviewing may be as short as a few hours, with the results reported the next day, or extended over a period of weeks, as in academic polls. The underlying goal, however, is the same: to achieve scientifically valid measures of the knowledge, beliefs, or attitudes of the adult population.

Many national polls are conducted by the media in conjunction with a professional polling organization. These polls regularly measure attitudes on some central item, such as how the public feels about the job that the president or Congress is doing. Several of these organizations make

their polls available through the Internet.[57] Some of the polls that regularly collect data in large national samples include the following: the ABC News/*Washington Post* poll, the CBS News/*New York Times* poll, the NBC News/*Wall Street Journal* poll, and the CNN/*USA Today*/Gallup poll. With the growing numbers of polls have come "polls of polls," which seek to average the results of multiple polling organizations' efforts. These can be found online, at sites like www.pollster.com, www.pollingreport.com, www.fivethirtyeight.com, and www.realclearpolitics.com. Other polling organizations provide more in-depth surveys than these media polls. Some are designed to see how people feel about particular topics or to find out how people develop attitudes and evaluate politics more generally. Two of these in particular, the General Social Survey and the National Election Studies, provide much of the data for academic research on public opinion in America (and much of what we say in this chapter about public opinion).[58]

CAMPAIGN POLLS A lot of polling is done for candidates in their efforts to win election or reelection. Most well-funded campaigns begin with a **benchmark poll**, taken of a sample of the population, or perhaps just of the potential voters, in a state or district to gather baseline information on how well the candidate is known, what issues people associate with the candidate, and what issues people are concerned about, as well as assessments of the opposition, especially if the opponent is an incumbent. Benchmark polls are instrumental in designing campaign strategy.

Presidential campaigns and a few of the better-funded statewide races (for example, those for governor or U.S. senator) conduct **tracking polls**. These follow changes in attitudes toward the candidates by having ongoing sets of

> **benchmark poll** initial poll on a candidate and issues on which campaign strategy is based and against which later polls are compared
>
> **tracking polls** ongoing series of surveys that follow changes in public opinion over time

interviews. Such daily samples are too small to allow reliable generalization, but groups of these interviews averaged over time are extremely helpful. The oldest interviews are dropped as newer ones are added, providing a dynamic view of changes in voters' preferences and perceptions.

A sudden change in a tracking poll might signal that the opponent's new ads are doing damage or that interest group endorsements are having an effect. Campaign strategies can be revised accordingly. More recently, the news media have undertaken tracking polls as part of their election coverage. By 2008 there were up to nine pollsters reporting daily results, and several websites were aggregating the polls. The averaging process of the aggregators helps smooth out individual pollsters' house effects (biases or patterns that might be built into an individual pollster's methodology) and differences in their assumptions about turnout. Their "track record" was a good one—the folks at the Huffington Post site (which was then called pollster.com) and fivethirtyeight .com missed the individual state results by less than 2.5 points. In 2012 there were at least ninety polls in the field at least once, and twenty-four trackers were in the field at least five times in the last three weeks of the campaign. Most of these underestimated Obama's support, though some, like the well-known Gallup and Rasmussen, were particularly off-base. While there was a good deal of back and forth in the media about what the electorate was likely to look like, with some Republicans arguing that the public polls were "skewed" because there were too many Democrats in the samples (a demographic distribution that proved correct on Election Day, however), it was the polling aggregators that got it right again. As in 2008, pollster.com and fivethirtyeight.com, along with some newer modelers, were good predictors of the results, with Nate Silver's fivethirtyeight .com nailing it almost exactly (see *Profiles in Citizenship*).[59]

On election night the media commentators often "call" a race, declaring one candidate a winner, sometimes as soon as the voting booths in a state are closed but well before the official vote count has been reported. These predictions are made, in part, on the basis of **exit polls**, which are short questionnaires administered to samples of voters in selected precincts after they vote. Exit polls focus on vote choice, a few demographic questions, some issue preferences, and evaluations of candidates. In addition to helping the networks predict the winners early, exit polls are used by network broadcasters and journalists to add explanatory and descriptive material to their election coverage. Because exit polls are expensive to conduct, media organizations have banded together in recent years to share the costs of conducting national exit polls.

Exit polls, however, have a mixed record in recent elections, leading news agencies to become cautious about how the results are used.[60] For example, in 2000 flawed data led the networks to mistakenly "call" Florida for Vice President Al Gore (which would have meant that he'd won the presidency); then to switch the call to George W. Bush; and finally, late in the evening, to conclude that the state was too close to call at all. Exit poll defenders argue that these polls are being misused by the public and the media; they are not intended to predict the elections in progress but to explain the vote after the election by providing information on what groups voted for which candidates. The challenges faced by those conducting exit polls are the same as those the preelection pollsters must contend with: it is very difficult to obtain a fully representative sample of voters. As a result of these problems, networks are now relatively cautious in declaring winners without corroborating evidence from the actual vote returns; there were no mistakes in "calling" the states in the 2004 presidential election, although exit poll results led the Kerry campaign to think they had won early in the evening.[61] In 2008 and 2012 the exit polls did not lead to any surprises, although by 2012 the media consortium sponsoring the polls had decided not to poll some of the less populated and less competitive states.

PSEUDO-POLLS A number of opinion studies are wrongly presented as polls. More deceptive than helpful, these pseudo-polls range from potentially misleading entertainment to outright fraud. Self-selection polls are those, like the *Literary Digest*'s, in which respondents, by one mechanism or another, select themselves into a survey rather than being chosen randomly. Examples of self-selection polls include viewer or listener call-in polls and Internet polls. These polls tell you only how a portion of the media outlet's audience (self-selected in the first place by their choice of a particular outlet) who care enough to call in or click a mouse (self-selected in the second place by their willingness to expend effort) feel about an issue.

When the CNN web site asks users to record their views on whether the United States should engage in military action with Iraq, for instance, the audience is limited, first, to those who own or have access to computers; second, to those who care enough about the news to be on the CNN site; and third, to those who want to pause in their news viewing for the short time it takes for their vote to be counted and the results to appear on the screen. Further, nothing stops individuals from recording multiple votes to make the count seem greater than it is. Results of such polls are likely to be highly unrepresentative of the population as a whole. They should be presented with caution and interpreted with a great deal of skepticism.

Another, increasingly common kind of pseudo-poll is the push poll, which poses as a legitimate information-seeking effort but is really a shady campaign trick to change people's attitudes. **Push polls** present false or highly negative information, often in a hypothetical form, and ask respondents to react to it. The information, presented as if

---

exit polls election-related questions asked of voters right after they vote

push polls polls that ask for reactions to hypothetical, often false, information in order to manipulate public opinion

PROFILES IN CITIZENSHIP: NATE SILVER

© Melissa Ann Pinney

Public opinion polls generated a lot of controversy in the days leading up to the 2012 presidential election. Most professional pollsters and the Obama campaign said that their polls forecast an Obama victory; the Romney campaign claimed those polls over-sampled Democrats. At the center of the controversy was Nate Silver, whose forecasting model steadily predicted a likely win for Obama. Republicans said he was shilling for the Democrats, but he ultimately nailed the Electoral College vote.

But then, Nate Silver is a very smart guy, a guy who deals in numbers and mathematical models and predictions all the time. He wasn't long out of college before he had developed the PECOTA (Player Empirical Comparison and Optimization Test Algorithm) system—a model for predicting the performance of baseball players that became associated with a web site called Baseball Prospectus that Silver managed. Baseball is a long way from politics, however, and by 2008 Silver had given up Baseball Prospectus and was concentrating his mathematical prowess on primaries and electoral votes, writing on the new blog that he called fivethirtyeight.com (after the total number of votes in the Electoral College).

If you ask him how he got to here from there, the answer is about what you'd expect from this young, brilliant, and quirky man. He got into politics because of Internet poker, of course. Doesn't everyone?

Some context here is that Silver is the son of a political scientist, so the world was one he was well familiar with and he liked it. "I was more into politics as compared to a normal person," he says, "because it was interesting, kind of like a big game show." But still, Internet poker?

"In 2006 I was playing poker mostly online. The outgoing Republican Congress passed a law where they basically made online poker illegal, but it was not very effective. What they technically did, more or less, is say you can play poker, but you can't deposit money in and out, so that had a chilling effect on the game . . . that got me following congressional procedure." Besides, he had gone to the University of Chicago, and a member of the Chicago law faculty, Sen. Barack Obama, was running for

---

true or at least possible, can raise doubts about a candidate and even change a voter's opinion about him or her. Insofar as they have a legitimate function, "push questions" are used on a limited basis by pollsters and campaign strategists to find out how voters might respond to negative information about the candidate or the opposition. This is the kind of information that might be gathered in a benchmark poll, for example. Less scrupulous consultants, working for both political parties, however, sometimes use the format as a means of propaganda. As an example, a pollster put this question to Florida voters:

> Please tell me if you would be more likely or less likely to vote for Lt. Governor Buddy MacKay if you knew that Lt. Gov. Buddy MacKay plans to imple-ment a new early-release program for violent offenders who have served a mere 60 percent of their sentences if he is elected governor?[62]

MacKay had no such plans, and to imply that he did was false. Moreover, the goal of this "poll" was not to learn anything but rather to plant negative information in the minds of thousands of people. By posing as a legiti-mate poll, the push poll seeks to trick respondents into accepting the information as truthful and thereby to influ-ence the vote. Such polls are often conducted without any acknowledgment of who is sponsoring them (usually the opponents of the person being asked about). The target candidate often never knows that such a poll is being conducted, and because push polls frequently pop up the weekend before an election, he or she cannot rebut the lies or half-truths. A key characteristic of push polls is that they seek to call as many voters as they can with little regard to the usual care and quality of a legitimate repre-sentative sample. "Push polling for me is marketing," said Floyd Ciruli, a Denver-based pollster. "You call everybody you can call and tell them something that may or may not be true."[63]

Legislation against push polling has been introduced in several state legislatures, and the practice has been condemned by the American Association of Political Consultants.[64] There is a real question, however, about

president. "That was kind of cool," he says. "I actually had like a hometown candidate now."

Goodbye baseball, hello politics.

"DON'T UNDERESTIMATE YOUR ABILITY TO COME UP WITH AN IDEA THAT NOBODY ELSE HAS. IT HAPPENS ALL THE TIME. QUIT BEING A CONSUMER AND BE A PRODUCER."

Silver started blogging on the liberal Daily Kos site under the pseudonym Poblano, and then he started fiverthirtyeight.com. What Silver added that other analysts didn't was a model that aggregated the existing polling and, based on those numbers as well as demographic and other data, ran computerized simulations of the various primary and general election races. If Obama and Hillary Clinton were facing off in a primary in North Carolina, for instance, Silver could simulate the election one hundred times and tell you what percentage of the time Obama would win and what percentage Clinton would. His predictions were uncannily accurate, and soon Silver's readership soared and he was on cable TV, analyzing polls and races.

In 2010 Silver signed a three-year contract with the *New York Times*, and then left to start his own web empire at ESPN, where you can currently find fivethirtyeight.com. There, he blogs regularly on politics and elections—with occasional forays into sports, economics, and popular culture. He's also written a book, *The Signal and the Noise: Why So Many Predictions Fail—But Some Don't*, published in 2012.

What does he want people to get from his work? "I want to inform people, I want people to think more critically about things. Basically, I want people to not be intimidated by numbers and statistics, to not just assume that something that they hear, whether it's from a politician or from Fox News or from [another] writer in the *New York Times*, is necessarily true. I just want to encourage people to use their brains."

Here's some other advice from Nate Silver:

On patriotism:

You probably have some family members who have their flaws and idiosyncrasies and probably a few distant relatives who are even fairly screwed-up people, but you still love them, anyway. I think that's what patriotism is really, saying, "Look, this is where I was born, or I migrated to the United States, this is where my loyalty is. . . ." You don't have a choice, it doesn't matter how unhappy you are, you know? It's your family, and you are stuck with it.

On keeping the republic:

People just have to be willing to put in the work. It's a big, complicated world now, and as many people that there are, there are more things to be done. Don't underestimate your ability to come up with an idea that nobody else has. It happens all the time. Quit being a consumer and be a producer. Start your own blog, start your own political organization. Have fun with it—there is nothing wrong with that at all.

Source: Nate Silver spoke with Christine Barbour in July 2010.

---

whether efforts to regulate push polls can survive a First Amendment test before the Supreme Court.

SURVEY EXPERIMENTS A final category of polls are those conducted by social scientists not so much to gauge and measure public opinion about elections or current events as to deepen our understanding of public attitudes, especially on controversial issues such as race, gender, and civil liberties, where respondents know what the socially acceptable answer to the survey questions is and so are less likely to disclose their true opinions. In survey experiments, the survey questions are manipulated in an effort to get respondents to disclose more information than they think they are disclosing.

A pioneering example of such work is an experiment in the study of racial attitudes in which researchers sought to find out if the way a question is framed affects how respondents feel about a particular group. In this case, researchers wondered if the mention of affirmative action, which many people do not like, would influence respondents' attitudes toward African Americans. A sample of white respondents were randomly put into two groups, a control group that was only asked a question about their feelings toward blacks, and a group that first was asked about their view of affirmative action and then their attitude toward blacks. The mere mention of affirmative action excited more negative responses toward blacks in the second group,[65] which helped researchers to understand the complex sets of issues that lie behind racial attitudes in American public opinion and told them something about the impact of framing on racial attitudes. The numbers of survey experiments is increasing because the technology of the Internet allows the use of images, sounds, and other multimedia in addition to the words used in a typical survey.[66]

NEW TECHNOLOGIES AND CHALLENGES IN POLLING

Technology is a pollster's friend, but it can also create unexpected challenges. In the early days of polls, surveys were done in-person, on the door stoop or in the living room.

DON'T BE FOOLED BY...
PUBLIC OPINION POLLS

In the heat of the Clinton impeachment hearings, angry conservative Republicans could not believe the polls: over 65 percent of Americans still approved of the job the president was doing and did not want to see him removed from office. Their conclusion? The polls were simply wrong. "The polls are targeted to get a certain answer," said one Floridian. "There are even T-shirts in South Florida that say 'I haven't been polled'."[1]

Do we need to know people personally who have been polled in order to trust poll results? Of course not. But there are lots of polls out there, not only those done carefully and responsibly by reputable polling organizations but also polls done for marketing and overtly political purposes—polls with an agenda, we might say. How are we, as good scholars and citizens, to know which results are reliable indications of what the public thinks, and which are not? One thing we can do is bring our critical thinking skills to bear by asking some questions about the polls reported in the media.

WHAT TO WATCH OUT FOR[2]

- **Who is the poll's sponsor?** Even if the poll was conducted by a professional polling company, it may still have been commissioned on behalf of a candidate or company. Does the sponsor have an agenda? How might that agenda influence the poll, the question wording, or the sponsor's interpretation of events?

- **Is the sample representative?** That is, were proper sampling techniques followed? What is the margin of error?

- **From what population was the sample taken?** There is a big difference, for instance, between the preference of the general public for a presidential candidate and the preference of likely voters, especially if one is interested in predicting the election's outcome! Read the fine print. Sometimes a polling organization will weight responses according to the likelihood that the respondent will actually vote in order to come up with a better prediction of the election result. Some polls survey only the members of one party, or the readers of a particular magazine, or people of a certain age, depending on the information they are seeking to discover. Be sure the sample is not self-selected. Always check the population being sampled, and do not assume it is the general public.

- **How are the questions worded?** Are loaded, problematic, or vague terms used? Could the questions be confusing to the average citizen? Are the questions available with the poll results? If not, why not? Do the questions seem to lead you to respond one way or the other? Do they oversimplify issues or complicate them? If the survey claims to have detected change over time, be sure the same questions were used consistently. All these things could change the way people respond.

- **Are the survey topics ones that people are likely to have information and opinions about?** Respondents rarely admit that they don't know how to answer a question, so responses on obscure or technical topics are likely to be more suspect than others.

- **What is the poll's response rate?** A lot of "don't knows," "no opinions," or refusals to answer can have a decided effect on the results.

- **Do the poll results differ from those of other polls, and if so, why?** Check out elections.huffingtonpost.com/pollster, www.fivethirtyeight.com, or www.realclearpolitics.com for some context. Don't necessarily assume that a change in individual poll numbers means that public opinion has changed. What is it about this poll that might have caused the discrepancy?

- **What do the results mean?** Who is doing the interpreting? What are that person's motives? For instance, pollsters who work for the Democratic Party will have an interpretation of the results that is favorable to Democrats, and a Republican interpretation will favor Republicans. Try interpreting the results yourself.

1. Melinda Henneberger, "Where G.O.P. Gathers, Frustration Does Too," *New York Times,* February 1, 1999, 3.

2. Some of these questions are based in part on similar advice given to poll watchers in Herbert Asher, *Polling and the Public: What Every Citizen Should Know,* 7th ed. (Washington, DC: CQ Press, 2007), 206–209.

That method was superseded by telephone interviewing as almost all households got telephones and in light of the obvious efficiency of calling people on the phone versus sending interviewers to far-flung places for face-to-face interviews. With the advent of computer technology has come the substitution of computers for humans to do the interviewing. The computers dial the numbers (autodialing) and deliver recorded messages, even "interacting" by asking questions that are answered by pushing buttons on a touch-tone phone. This technology, called "robo calling," is much cheaper than using human interviewers, but it is also controversial. It is easily abused, especially when combined with push poll methods.[67] Legitimate polling firms also use robo calls and have collected more information on more political subjects than has been available in the past, such as the state-by-state results provided by SurveyUSA.[68]

Computers provide another challenge (and opportunity) for pollsters in the form of online surveys. Here we do not mean the polls that CNN or others put up asking for volunteers to click in their opinions on some issue. Pollsters create panels of Internet users who regularly log in to deliver their opinions on matters the pollsters select. Although some critics argue that the online polls have no scientific basis because they do not rely on strict probability samples, proponents argue that with appropriate adjustments, the Internet polls nicely match results from traditional telephone interviewing. They have the advantage of garnering fewer refusals, and for some kinds of questions, respondents to online surveys appear to be more candid in admitting to things that might be embarrassing to confess to a human interviewer.[69]

Pollsters also face a growing challenge as increasing numbers of citizens, especially younger people, rely on cell phones. The U.S. Telephone Consumer Protection Act limits the technologies that can be used in contacting cell phone users—forbidding autodialing, for instance. Those contacted by cell phones are also more likely to refuse to answer polls. As pollsters adapt to these newer technologies, research and regulations are likely to lead to changes in contacting cell phone users.[70]

HOW ACCURATE ARE POLLS?

For many issues, such as attitudes toward the environment or presidential approval, we have no objective measure against which to judge the accuracy of public opinion polls. With elections, however, polls do make predictions, and we can tell by the vote count whether the polls are correct. The record of most polls is, in general, quite good. For example, almost all the major polls have predicted the winner of presidential elections correctly since 1980, except in the incredibly close 2000 election. They are not correct to the percentage point, nor would we expect them to be, given the known levels of sampling error, preelection momentum shifts, and the usual 15 percent of voters who claim to

remain undecided up to the last minute. Polls taken closer to Election Day typically become more accurate as they catch more of the late deciders.[71] Even in the 2000 presidential election, most of the polls by the election's eve had done a fairly good job of predicting the tightness of the race. Read *Don't Be Fooled by…Public Opinion Polls* for some tips on how you can gauge the reliability of poll results you come across.

PAUSE AND REVIEW:

WHO, WHAT, HOW

Citizens, politicians and their staffs, the media, and professional polling organizations are all interested in the business of measuring and tracking public opinion. Citizens rely on polls to monitor elections and get a sense of where other Americans stand on particular issues. Their interest is in fair polling techniques that produce reliable results.

To win elections, politicians must know what citizens think and what they want from their officials. They need to know how various campaign strategies are playing publicly and how they are faring in their races against other candidates. Politicians and their campaign consultants evaluate face-to-face contact with voters and their correspondence and calls, but they also pay attention to national media and party or campaign polls.

The media want current and accurate information on which to base their reporting. They also have an interest in keeping and increasing the size of their audiences. To build their markets, they create and publish polls that encourage their audiences to see elections as exciting contests.

Finally, professional pollsters have an interest in producing accurate information for their clients. The quality of their surveys rests with good scientific polling techniques.

IN YOUR OWN WORDS ›› Describe different techniques used to gauge public opinion.

›› THE CITIZENS AND PUBLIC OPINION
Informational shortcuts that save democracy from our lack of care and attention

We have seen ample evidence that although politicians may act as if citizens are informed and attentive, only some Americans live up to our model of good citizenship, and those who do often belong disproportionately to the ranks of the well-educated, the well-off, and the older portions of the population. This disparity between our ideal citizen and

CLUES TO CRITICAL THINKING

"How Much Do Voters Know?"

By Alexander Burns, *Politico*, March 13, 2012

This article shows the American voter's intelligence in a less-than-flattering light. Should we be insulted?

Voters are appalled at President Barack Obama's handling of gas prices, even though virtually every policy expert in both parties says there's little a president can do to affect the day-to-day price of fuel in a global market.

Americans are disgusted at Washington's bailout culture, and especially the 2008 rescue of the financial services industry. They're so fed up with bailouts, in fact, that a majority of them now think federal intervention in the auto industry was a good idea that helped the country.

They're aghast at the trajectory of the war in Afghanistan, which Obama helped escalate and extend, and they don't think the war was worth it in the first place. And many also think Obama is handling the conflict acceptably well.

That's presumably a different set of voters than the ones who routinely tell pollsters that they still believe the president is a Muslim, despite all public evidence to the contrary.

Add up that litany of contradictory, irrational or simply silly opinions, and it's enough to make a political professional suspect the electorate is, well, not entirely sophisticated about the choices it's facing in 2012.

"The first lesson you learn as a pollster is that people are stupid," said Tom Jensen of Public Policy Polling, a Democratic polling firm. "I tell a client trying to make sense of numbers on a poll that are inherently contradictory that at least once a week."

Jensen, a Democrat, pointed to surveys showing that voters embraced individual elements of the Affordable Care Act, while rejecting the overall law, as an example of the political schizophrenia or simple ignorance that pollsters and politicians must contend with.

©2014 iStockphoto LP

"We're seeing that kind of thing more and more. I think it's a function of increased political polarization and voters just digging in their heels and refusing to consider the opposing facts once they've formed an opinion about something," said Jensen, who has generated eye-catching data showing many GOP primary voters still question the president's religion and nationality. "I also think voters are showing a tendency to turn issues that should be factual or non-factual into opinions. If you show a Tennessee birther Obama's birth certificate, they're just going to say 'well in my opinion he's not a real American.' It's not about the birth certificate; it's about expressing hatred for Obama in any form they can."

But irrationality on policy issues transcends party lines and cuts across groups that feel differently about the president. Taken all together, the issue polling compiled so far in the 2012 cycle presents a sharp corrective to the candidates' description of the race as a great debate placing two starkly different philosophies of government before an informed electorate.

In reality, the contest has been more like a game of Marco Polo, as a hapless gang of Republican candidates and a damaged, frantic incumbent try to connect with a historically fickle and frustrated electorate.

And "fickle" is a nice way of describing the voters of 2012, who appear to be wandering, confused and Forrest Gump–like through the experience of a presidential campaign. It isn't just unclear which party's vision they'd rather embrace; it's entirely questionable whether the great mass of voters has even the most basic grasp of the details—or for that matter, the most elementary factual components—of the national political debate.

The present furor over gas prices is a case in point: Obama's job approval dropped 9 points over the last month, according to a CBS/New York Times poll, as the cost of fuel has risen abruptly. The survey found that 54 percent of Americans believe that the president can do a lot to combat high gas prices.

That's not really true, but it's a dynamic that's shown up in other polls too: 26 percent of respondents told an ABC News/Washington Post poll that they approve of Obama's handling of gas prices, versus 65 percent who disapprove.

For voters to disapprove of Obama's energy and economic policies may be completely rational. But to reassess a president's performance in the context of a short-term increase in gas prices is more of a tantrum-like response to a new feeling of discomfort over which the president has relatively little control.

"Gas prices are a surrogate for Obama performance and evaluations of his job performance," said Steve Lombardo, who worked for Mitt Romney's presidential campaign in 2008 and is the head of the research and consulting firm StrategyOne. "Might not be fair but that is the way it is. The higher the gas prices the lower Obama's approval rating."

That calculus is fairly straightforward, though it's one that has frustrated presidents of both parties for decades. Other examples of the befuddlement of the 2012 voter are tougher to decode.

Take bailouts, for example. Today, Americans loathe the Troubled Assets Relief Program even more than they did in 2008. In the thick of the '08 financial crisis, 57 percent of respondents told Pew that government intervention was appropriate. Now, that number is 39 percent, extending an anti-bailout craze that helped drive the 2008 election.

But Americans aren't opposed to all bailouts, apparently. Amid a flurry of positive earnings reports from GM and Chrysler—and a comeback story told enthusiastically by public figures from Obama to Clint Eastwood—a 56 percent majority of Americans now think bailing out the auto industry was good for the economy. That's up from 37 percent in 2009, according to Pew.

Never mind the fact that the bank bailout has been at least as successful at reviving the financial sector as the auto rescue has been for Detroit.

A similar level of capriciousness is evident in foreign affairs. Americans' views of their overseas entanglements has been on the decline. According to Gallup, just 54 percent of Americans now view the United States as the world's preeminent military power—a 10-point drop since 2010. Last spring, Gallup tracked a quick reversal of public opinion on the intervention in Libya, going from a 10-point net positive public view to a 7-point net negative one over the course of a month. Sixty percent of voters now believe that the war in Afghanistan was not worth fighting, according to ABC News and the Washington Post.

And yet, Obama—who escalated the Afghan war with a temporary troop surge—continues to break even or fare a bit better than that when it comes to foreign policy and national security. The ABC/Washington Post poll found 46 percent of voters approve of his handling of the war, while 47 percent disapprove. Those aren't great numbers—except they look pretty good when three-fifths of the country think the war was a waste of time and effort.

Gallup analyst Jeffrey Jones said the seeming inconsistencies can come from the fact that voters "probably don't have a whole lot of detailed and specific information about the policies that are being put forward."

"When people evaluate presidents on certain issues, they're probably starting with a pretty global view of how he's doing and then adjust that for how he's doing in a particular area," Jones said. Applying that explanation to the drop in U.S. military confidence, Jones suggested: "It may stem in part from a global view, that things aren't going that well in the U.S."

Republican presidential strategist Mary Matalin gave a similar explanation for why public opinion often adds up to something different than the sum of its parts. As voters take stock of public events, there's often tension between their feelings about granular policy topics and the overarching principles that encompass those issues.

Like Jensen, she pointed to the debate over health care, suggesting that voters' support for goals like containing the cost of care ended up getting overwhelmed by their distaste for government power—giving rise to an apparent contradiction.

"In large measure, they're often not contradictions," she said. "There was a time when health care, Obamacare, just transcended health care and it became a proxy for counterproductive government expansion. When that flipped from coverage, or cost-cutting of coverage—all the issues that Obama said it was, which people like . . . it has now transcended that."

For voters and politicians and analysts who would prefer to see a more logical, coherent set of public responses to public problems, the good news is this: much of the day-to-day variation in policy polling will not, ultimately, have a major impact on the result of the 2012 election.

Indeed, the sheer irrationality and volatility of voters' views on most issues ends up giving disproportionate weight to the few issues where their opinions are strong and basically stable.

In 2012, that would not necessarily include the auto bailout or the intervention in Libya, or even gas prices as an issue in itself. It would include the larger state of the economy—and maybe nothing else.

"If the economy is bad, that's going to be the single issue and it's almost like nothing else matters," Jones said.

(Continued)

(Continued)

And besides, said Quinnipiac pollster Peter Brown, if voters seem to the political class like they are temperamental or unreasonable, it's sort of beside the point. Americans may change their policy views as they learn more or as events change, or for no good reason at all. But in the end, those views are the only metric in electoral politics that really matters.

"Just because someone's not familiar with something doesn't mean they won't give you their opinion. And just because they don't know a lot about it—their vote still counts as much as someone who does know a lot about it," Brown said.

"In the business of politics, voters are always right. Just like on Wall Street, the market is always right," he said. "You don't fight the market."

Source: *Politico*, Copyright 2012 by POLITICO, LLC. Reproduced with permission of POLITICO, LLC in the format Other Book via Copyright Clearance Center.

Consider the source and the audience: Alexander Burns writes for *Politico,* a Washington-insider kind of newspaper—read by a who's-who roster of people who make the federal government tick. Why might this somewhat condescending view of the American voter be of interest to such readers?

Lay out the argument, the values, and the assumptions: Burns is not writing an opinion piece, but he certainly seems to be implying that American voters aren't the brightest bulbs around. What does the pollster he quotes mean by saying that the American voter is "stupid"? What would "smart" look like for the analysts quoted here?

Uncover the evidence: Burns cites a lot of inconsistent positions held by Americans. Is that enough to persuade you that voters aren't very smart? What is the defense brought by people like Jones and Matalin? Are there other ways of being smart politically that aren't covered here?

Evaluate the conclusion: Burns implies that American voters hold many contradictory positions that don't rationally fit together, but at the end of his piece he quotes a pollster who says "the voters are always right" in a democratic system, and everyone's votes count the same. What does that mean?

Sort out the political implications: On the whole, is this an optimistic or a pessimistic take on the American system? If we are "stupid," are we doomed?

reality raises some provocative questions about the relationships among citizens, public opinion, and democracy. Were the founders right to limit the influence of the masses on government? Do we want less informed and coherent opinions represented in politics? Can democracy survive if it is run only by an educated elite?

Earlier in this chapter we suggested that all would not be lost for American democracy if only some of us turned out to be ideal citizens, and that although Americans as individuals might not fit the ideal, Americans as a group might behave as that ideal would predict. How is such a trick possible? The argument goes like this.

It may not be rational for all people to be deeply immersed in the minutiae of day-to-day politics. Our jobs, families, hobbies, and other interests leave us little time for in-depth study of political issues, and unless we get tremendous satisfaction from keeping up with politics (and some of us certainly do), it might be rational for us to leave the political information gathering to others. Social scientists call this idea **rational ignorance**.

This does not mean that we are condemned to make only ignorant or mistaken political decisions. Citizens are generally pretty smart. In fact, studies show that voters can

behave much more intelligently than we could ever guess from their answers to surveys about politics (see *CLUES to Critical Thinking*). A great many of us, sometimes without thinking about it, use shortcuts, called *heuristics*, to get political information. Such heuristics often serve us quite well, in the sense that they help us make the same decisions we might have made had we invested considerable time and energy in collecting that political information ourselves.[72]

SHORTCUTS TO POLITICAL KNOWLEDGE

One such shortcut is the **on-line processing** of information.[73] (*On-line* here does not refer to time spent on the

> **rational ignorance** the state of being uninformed about politics because of the cost in time and energy
>
> **on-line processing** the ability to receive and evaluate information as events happen, allowing us to remember our evaluation even if we have forgotten the specific events that caused it

Internet, as you will see.) Many of the evaluations we make of people, places, and things in our lives (including political figures and ideas) are made on the fly. We assemble impressions and reactions while we are busy leading our lives. When queried, we might not be able to explain why we like or dislike a thing or a person, and we might sound quite ignorant in the sense of not seeming to have reasons for our beliefs. But we do have reasons, and they may make a good deal of sense, even if we can't identify what they are.

A second important mental shortcut that most of us use is the **two-step flow of information**. Politicians and the media send out massive amounts of information. We can absorb only a fraction of it, and even then it is sometimes hard to know how to interpret it. In these circumstances, we tend to rely on **opinion leaders**, who are more or less like ourselves but who know more about the subject than we do.[74] Opinion leaders and followers can be identified in all sorts of realms besides politics. When we make an important purchase, say, a computer or a car, most of us do not research all the scientific data and technical specifications. We ask people who are like us, who we think should know, and whom we can trust. We compile their advice, consult our own intuition, and buy. The result is that we get pretty close to making an optimal purchase without having to become experts ourselves. The two-step flow allows us to behave as though we were very well informed without requiring us to expend all the resources that being informed entails.

A new wrinkle on the two-step flow is the practice of going online for others' opinions, whether this is feedback ratings on eBay or the "Likes" of Facebook, the process uses technology to gather information from "experts" (or at least those with a bit of experience and an opinion) about everything from airlines to zoos.[75] Interestingly, however,

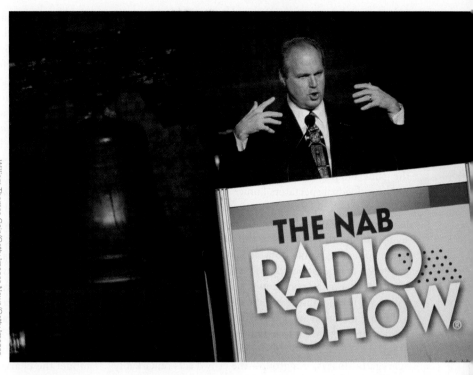

William Thomas Cain/Getty Images News/Getty Images

"Ditto, Rush"

With an audience of 15 million, talk show host and opinion leader Rush Limbaugh offers his "ditto heads" (as he calls his listeners) strong, and frequently inflammatory, conservative commentary aimed at an array of liberal targets. Limbaugh carries a lot of weight among conservative politicians, in part because he is credited with mobilizing supporters in the 1994 and 2010 congressional elections that resulted in Republican landslides. As a result, they try not to cross him, giving him considerable clout within the Republican Party, even when the candidates he promotes do not win.

while many observers hoped that a computer-literate younger generation would become more politically engaged as a result of its heavy use of social media, it does not seem that users of Facebook or other new media are any more likely to participate or express opinions than those who do not engage the digital social world.[76]

THINKING OUTSIDE THE BOX

Is a democracy that depends on citizen "shortcuts" weaker than one that does not?

THE RATIONAL ELECTORATE

Politicians deal with citizens mostly in groups and only rarely as individuals. Elected officials think about constituents as whole electorates ("the people of the great state of Texas") or as members of groups (women, environmentalists, developers, workers, and so forth). Groups, it turns

two-step flow of information the process by which citizens take their political cues from more well-informed opinion leaders

opinion leaders people who know more about certain topics than we do and whose advice we trust, seek out, and follow

out, appear to be better behaved, more rational, and better informed than the individuals who make up the groups, precisely because of the sorts of shortcuts we discussed in the previous section. This doesn't seem to make sense, so perhaps a nonpolitical example will clarify what we mean.

Consider the behavior of fans at a football game. People seem to cheer at the appropriate times; they know pretty much when to boo the referees; they oooh and aaaah more or less in unison. We would say that the crowd understands the game and participates effectively in it. However, what do the individual spectators know? If we were to do a football survey, we might ask about the players' names, the teams' win-loss records, the different offensive and defensive positions, the meaning of the referees' signals, and so forth. Some fans would do well, but many would probably get only a few questions right. From the survey, we might conclude that many people in this crowd do not know football at all. But because they take their cues from others, following the behavior of those who cheer for the same team, they can act as if they know what they are doing. Despite its share of football-ignorant individuals, in the aggregate—that is, as a group—the crowd acts remarkably football-intelligent.

THINKING OUTSIDE THE BOX

Do frequent opinion polls enhance or diminish democracy?

Similarly, if we were to ask people when national elections are held, for instance, only a handful would be able to say it is the Tuesday after the first Monday in November of evenly numbered years. Some people would guess that they occur in November, others might say in the fall sometime, and others would admit they don't know. Based on the level of individual ignorance in this matter, it would be surprising if many people ever voted at all, since you can't vote if you don't know when Election Day is. But somehow, as a group, the electorate sorts it out, and almost everyone who is registered and wants to vote finds his or her way to the polling place on the right day. By using shortcuts and taking cues from others, the electorate behaves just as if it knew all along when the election was. More substantively, even though many voters may be confused about which candidates stand where on specific issues, groups of voters do a great job of sorting out which party or candidate best represents their interests. Members of the religious right vote for Republicans, and members of labor unions vote for Democrats, for instance. Even though there are undoubtedly quite a few confused voters in the electorate in any particular election, they tend to cancel each other out in the larger scheme of things,

although understandably, some biases remain.[77] As a whole, from the politician's point of view, the electorate appears to be responsive to issues and quite rational in evaluating an incumbent's performance in office.[78]

So even though citizens do not spend a lot of time learning about politics, politicians are smart to assume that the electorate is attentive and informed. In fact, this is precisely what most of them do. For example, studies have shown that state legislators vote in accordance with the ideological preferences of their citizens, just as if the citizens were instructing them on their wishes.[79] The states with the most liberal citizens—for example, New York, Massachusetts, and California—have the most liberal policies. And the most conservative states, those in the South and the Rocky Mountains, have the most conservative policies. Other studies confirm a similar pattern in national elections.[80]

We began this chapter by asking why polling is routinely disparaged by politicians. Why don't we have more confidence in being ruled by public opinion? After all, in a democracy where the people's will is supposed to weigh heavily with our elected officials, we have uncovered some conflicting evidence. Many Americans do not model the characteristics of the ideal democratic citizen, but remember that the United States has two traditions of citizenship—one much more apolitical and self-interested than the public-spirited ideal. The reality in America is that the ideal citizen marches side by side with the more self-interested citizen, who, faced with many demands, does not put politics ahead of other daily responsibilities. But we have also argued that there are mechanisms and shortcuts that allow even some of the more apolitical and self-interested citizens to cast intelligent votes and to have their views represented in public policy. This tells us that at least one element of democracy—responsiveness of policies to public preferences—is in good working order.

We should not forget that political influence goes hand in hand with opinion formation. Those who are opinion leaders have much more relative clout than do their more passive followers. And opinion leaders are not distributed equally throughout the population. They are drawn predominantly from the ranks of the well-educated and the well-off. Similarly, even though the shortcuts we have discussed allow many people to vote intelligently without taking the time to make a personally informed decision, many people never vote at all. Voters are also drawn from the more privileged ranks of American society. The poor, the young, and minorities—all the groups who are underrepresented at the voting booth—are also underrepresented in policymaking. There cannot help but be biases in such a system.[81]

IN YOUR OWN WORDS ›› Give examples of ways in which public opinion enhances or diminishes the relationship between citizens and government.

LET'S REVISIT: **WHAT'S AT STAKE...**

We have argued in this chapter that public opinion is important in policymaking and that politicians respond to it in a variety of ways. But what would happen if we more or less bypassed elected officials altogether and allowed people to participate directly in national lawmaking through the use of a national referendum or initiative? What is at stake in rule by public opinion?

On the one hand, voters would seem to have something real to gain in such lawmaking reform. It would give new meaning to government "by the people," and decisions would have more legitimacy with the public. Certainly it would be harder to point the finger at those in Washington as being responsible for bad laws. In addition, as has been the experience in states with initiatives, citizens might succeed in getting legislation passed that legislators themselves refuse to vote for. Prime examples are term limits and balanced budget amendments. Term limits would cut short many congressional careers and balanced budget amendments would force politicians into hard choices about taxation and spending cuts that they prefer to avoid.

On the other side of the calculation, however, voters might be worse off. While policies like the two mentioned above clearly threaten the jobs of politicians, they also carry unintended consequences that might not be very good for the nation as a whole. Who should decide—politicians who make a career out of understanding government, or people who pay little attention to politics and current events and who vote from instinct and outrage? Politicians who have a vested interest in keeping their jobs, or the public who can provide a check on political greed and self-interest? The answer changes with the way you phrase the question, but the public might well suffer if left to its own mercy on questions of policy it does not thoroughly understand.

Not only policymaking but the protection of individual freedoms might suffer under increased direct democracy; the majority is not always the best safeguard of civil liberties and civil rights. When New Jersey governor Chris Christie defended his veto of the New Jersey gay marriage legislation, and declared that the matter should be decided by a direct vote of the people, he added, "The fact of the matter is, I think people would have been happy to have a referendum on civil rights rather than fighting and dying in the streets in the South." As Newark mayor Cory Booker quickly pointed out, if civil rights for African Americans had been left to a popular vote, they might never have happened: "I shudder to think what would have happened if the civil rights gains, heroically established by courageous lawmakers in the 1960s, were instead conveniently left up

to popular votes in our 50 states."[82] Ironically, the marriage equality issue in New Jersey was not settled by the people after all, but by the courts. Following a state superior court ruling, New Jersey became the fourteenth state to allow gays to marry in October 2013. Governor Christie originally tried to appeal the ruling but, in the middle of a heated battle for reelection, withdrew his appeal and allowed gay marriages to proceed.

There is no doubt that the founders of the Constitution, with their limited faith in the people, would have rejected such a national referendum wholeheartedly. Not only does it bring government closer to the people, but it wreaks havoc with their system of separation of powers and checks and balances. Popular opinion was supposed to be checked by the House and the Senate, which were in turn to be checked by the other two branches of government. Bringing public opinion to the fore upsets this delicate balance.

In addition, many scholars warn that the hallmark of democracy is not just hearing what the people want, but allowing the people to discuss and deliberate over their political choices. Home computer voting or trips to the ballot box do not necessarily permit such key interaction.[83] Majority rule without the tempering influence of debate and discussion can deteriorate quickly into majority tyranny, with a sacrifice of minority rights.

The flip side may also be true, however. Since voters tend to be those who care more intensely about political issues, supporters of a national referendum also leave themselves open to the opposite consequence of majority tyranny: the tyranny of an intense minority who care enough to campaign and vote against an issue that a majority prefer, but only tepidly.

Finally, there are political stakes for politicians in such a reform. As we have already seen, the passage of laws they would not have themselves supported would make it harder for politicians to get things done. But on the positive side, a national referendum would allow politicians to avoid taking the heat for decisions that are bound to be intensely unpopular with some segment of the population. One of the reasons why national referenda are often used in other countries is to diffuse the political consequences for leaders of unpopular or controversial decisions.

Direct democracy at the national level would certainly have a major impact on American politics, but it is not entirely clear who the winners and losers would be, or even if there would be any consistent winners. The new rules would benefit different groups at different times. The American people believe they would enjoy the power, and various groups are confident they would profit, but in the long run the public interest might be damaged in terms of the quality of American democracy and the protections available to minorities. Politicians have very little to gain. If such a reform ever does come about, it will be generated not by the elite but by public interest groups, special interest groups, and reformers from outside Washington.

TO SUM UP

Sharpen your skills with **SAGE edge** at http://edge.sagepub.com/ barbour7e. **SAGE edge for students** provides a personalized approach to help you accomplish your coursework goals in an easy-to-use learning environment.

The Role of Public Opinion in a Democracy

The role of public opinion in politics has been hotly debated throughout American history. The founders devised a Constitution that would limit the influence of the masses. Today, some changes in the rules have given the public a greater role in government.

Politicians and the media watch public opinion very closely. Elected officials look for job security by responding to immediate public desires or by skillfully predicting future requests. The media make large investments in polls, sometimes covering public attitudes on a candidate or an issue as a story in itself.

public opinion (p. 398)
public opinion polls (p. 398)

Citizen Values

There are two competing visions of citizenship in America. The ideal democratic citizen demonstrates political knowledge, possesses an ideology (usually liberal or conservative), tolerates different ideas, and votes consistently. At the other extreme lies the apolitical, self-interested citizen. Most Americans fall somewhere between these extremes, but factors such as age, higher education, and improved socioeconomic status seem to contribute to behavior that is closer to the ideal.

What Influences Our Opinions About Politics?

Political socialization—the transfer of fundamental democratic values from one generation to the next—is affected by demographic characteristics such as race and gender, and by life experiences such as education and religion. Interest groups, political parties, and candidates all attempt to determine the political ideas shared by various groups in order to gain their support.

political socialization (p. 403)
patriotism (p. 403)
spiral of silence (p. 404)
partisan sorting (p. 406)
political generations (p. 408)
gender gap (p. 408)
marriage gap (p. 409)

Measuring and Tracking Public Opinion

While most politicians pay attention to their own informal samplings of opinion, they have also come to rely on professional polling. Such polls are based on scientific polling methods that focus on getting a good sample and asking questions that yield valid results.

sample (p. 413)
sample bias (p. 413)
straw polls (p. 413)

sampling error (p. 416)
random samples (p. 416)
weighting (p. 417)
benchmark polls (p. 418)
tracking polls (p. 418)
exit polls (p. 419)
push polls (p. 419)

The Citizens and Public Opinion

Even though Americans do not measure up to the ideal of the democratic citizen, there is much

evidence to support the idea that public opinion does play a large role in government policy. While some citizens may seem apolitical and disinterested, many use rational information shortcuts to make their voting decisions. Policymakers have responded by staying generally responsive to public preferences.

rational ignorance (p. 426)
on-line processing (p. 426)
two-step flow of information (p. 427)
opinion leaders (p. 427)

ENGAGE

Read the data yourself.
News media love to report on polls—but they rarely give the whole picture. Take some time to check out results of respected polling organizations and see the numbers for yourself. Prepare to get lost in a sea of fascinating data at the Gallup Organization; the Pew Research Center for the People and the Press; ABC News/*Washington Post* polls; *Los Angeles Times* polls; and the *New York Times* polls.

Take the long view.
If you're curious why Truman wound up beating Dewey despite

what the polls said, the **Roper Center for Public Opinion Research** is a great place to start. With archives going back to the 1930s, it is one of the world's leading repositories of public opinion and other social science data. If you find yourself really digging data, follow **Historical Opinion (@HistOpinion)** on Twitter for a daily glimpse at archival polling data that is surprisingly illuminating.

Take the broad view.
How do Americans' opinions compare with the rest of the

world's? **World Public Opinion's "Americans and the World Digest"** is a repository of U.S. public opinion on issues of international concern ranging from globalization and trade to biotechnology and human rights.

Follow FiveThirtyEight.com.
Nate Silver and company crunch numbers and make projections on everything from politics to sports. Follow the blog (fivethirtyeight.com) or on Twitter (@FiveThirtyEight) for daily updates.

EXPLORE

Asher, Herbert. 2010. *Polling and the Public: What Every Citizen Should Know*, 8th ed. Washington, DC: CQ Press. This book is an easy-to-understand and extremely informative source on the problems with public opinion polling undertaken by both candidates and the news media.

Gallup, George, and Saul Forbes Rae. 1940. *The Pulse of Democracy*. New York: Simon & Schuster. This mid-twentieth-century classic work is a hopeful account of the processes and promise of polling by perhaps the most important figure behind the development of the polling industry as we know it today. Gallup provides an insightful and candid view of polling in its infancy and with it wonderful insights into the politics of the early days of the New Deal era.

Greenberg, Stanley. 2009. *Dispatches From the War Room: In the Trenches With Five Extraordinary Leaders*. New York: St. Martin's Press. In this memoir, pollster and political strategist Stanley Greenberg offers insights into his work with President Bill Clinton, British prime minister Tony Blair, Israeli prime minister Ehud Barak, Bolivian president Gonzalo Sanchez de Lozada, and South African president Nelson Mandela.

Silver, Nate. 2012. *The Signal and the Noise: Why So Many Predictions Fail—But Some Don't*. New York: Penguin Press HC. In this examination of the subtle science of drawing truth from numbers, the noted statistician draws on his own groundbreaking work making predictions.

Magic Town. 1947. This classic film tells the tale of a rookie pollster (James Stewart) who finds a small town that he believes accurately reflects American public opinion. Dating from the early days of polling, it's one of the first films to delve into the then-new science of public opinion polling.

12

POLITICAL PARTIES

IN YOUR OWN WORDS After you've read this chapter, you will be able to

» Describe the role parties play in making government policy.

» Explain the tension between the party base and the general electorate regarding their influence on issue positions.

» Outline the evolution of the party system in the United States.

» Explain how parties connect citizens and government.

» Describe the way in which the American party system works.

» Give examples of ways in which parties serve (or fail to serve) citizens in American politics.

WHAT'S AT STAKE... WHEN A PARTY BECOMES TIED TO ITS MOST EXTREME MEMBERS?

OCCASIONALLY THE THIRD TIME REALLY IS the charm. After defying smart predictions that Republicans would take back the Senate in 2010, and again, high expectations that it would happen in 2012, Republican Senator Mitch McDonnell finally got to add "Majority Leader" to his resume in January, 2015. What took him so long?

In 2010, Republicans were pretty sure they were on a path to taking back the Senate. They didn't think they could do it all at once; they had a good shot at seats in Nevada, where incumbent Harry Reid was unpopular, and in South Carolina. Wins there would leave them needing to pick off just a few more in 2012, a year in which Democrats would be defending more vulnerable seats than they had in 2010. Republicans and independent analysts believed a good showing in 2010, along with 2012 pickup opportunities in Missouri, Montana, North Dakota, and Connecticut, could put Republicans in the majority come January 2013. Democrats were afraid that they were right.

The first step in giving Senate Minority Leader Mitch McConnell the majority leader's job was to get rid of the current holder of that seat, Nevada Democrat Harry Reid. In the spring of 2010, pundits said Reid was a dead man walking. Seen as one of the Democrats' most vulnerable incumbents, his poll numbers were sinking fast. Reid had done much of the heavy work of getting President Barack Obama's agenda passed through the Senate, and some of those policies, notably the stimulus bill and health care reform, were not popular in Nevada, where the economic recovery was dragging its feet and unemployment was higher than the national average. Sue Lowden, a Nevada state senator and businesswoman with a moderately conservative record, looked likely to win the Republican primary, and the Reid camp was seriously worried that Reid would lose the election to her in the fall.

But Harry Reid got lucky. When the dust cleared the day after the Republican primary, Tea Party favorite Sharron Angle was the winner by fourteen points; Angle was a woman whom the *New York Times* called "a largely unknown former state lawmaker with 10 grandchildren, whose fondness for weightlifting and for her .44 Magnum won the ardor of the Republican Party base."[1] In the

Party–favored Marco Rubio defeated moderate governor Charlie Crist in the Republican Senate primary. Although both primary results turned what were seen as certain Republican wins to races in which the outcome was up for grabs, both Rand and Rubio won. South Carolina Senator Jim DeMint, who had backed many of the Tea Party candidates, said, "You can't change Washington unless you change people who are here. People are ready to throw out the bums."[5]

While Rand Paul and Rubio both won on Election Day, other candidates supported by DeMint did not. Harry Reid lived to fight another day. So did another Democrat who was supposed to lose. Chris Coons of Delaware expected to face off against Michael Castle, a nine-term congressman and former governor, but instead faced Tea Party candidate Christine O'Donnell, whose most famous campaign commercial began with the words

AP Photo/Rogelio V. Solis

The Enemy of My Enemy Is My Friend

Republican Senator Thad Cochran from Mississippi courted African American voters, who turned out in large numbers in the primary runoff to help defeat Cochran's Tea Party challenger, Chris McDaniel.

primary, Angle had supported the privatization of Social Security and Medicare, a Scientology-based program that would have provided massages to prisoners, the elimination of the Departments of Education and Energy, the United States' withdrawal from the United Nations, unregulated oil drilling within the United States and off its shores, and the shipping of nuclear waste to Nevada for reprocessing.[2] Those positions appealed strongly to her Tea Party base but were not as popular throughout the state, even among Republicans.

Shortly after her primary win, mention of these positions was scrubbed from her web site. Reid's campaign, however, had captured the missing pages and published them on a site it called TheRealSharronAngle.com. Angle sent Reid's campaign a cease-and-desist letter, claiming Reid was seeking to deceive voters, but after briefly taking down the archived information, Reid's people resurrected it and continued to run an aggressive advertising campaign, painting Angle as a fringe candidate, too conservative for Nevada.[3] Reid began to pull even in the polls, and by July 2010 one of them showed him with a seven-point lead.[4]

Still, these were heady days for the Tea Partiers. In Kentucky the mainstream candidate for the Republican Senate nomination, who had been backed by Senate minority leader Mitch McConnell, lost to libertarian and Tea Party–backed Rand Paul. In Florida, the Tea

"I am not a witch." Due in large part to candidates like Angle and O'Donnell, the Republicans did not make the electoral headway in the Senate that they had hoped to in 2010.

After the election, Minnesota representative Michele Bachmann formed a Tea Party Caucus in the House and invited fellow conservatives to join. Some did with enthusiasm, but some mainstream Republicans cringed, and analysts pointed out that what were seen as victories for the Tea Party in the Republican primaries of 2010 might not turn into victories for the Republican Party in the longer term. One article said of the fervor that "the Tea Party movement is a loaded political weapon for Republicans heading into the midterm elections."[6]

But heading into the 2012 election, Republican hopes were once again high. With economic growth painfully slow and President Obama's reelection anything but certain, many thought the Republicans had a good shot to win the Senate, despite the losses in 2010. But that loaded political weapon seemed to have the Republicans, not the Democrats, in its sights.

In Missouri, taking back the seat of Democratic Senate incumbent Claire McCaskill had been seen as a good bet for the Republicans, until ultra-conservative Todd Akin won the primary. Another supposedly sure thing for the Republicans, the Indiana Senate seat that the party had held since the election of Dick Lugar in 1976, was suddenly in jeopardy when the six-term senator lost a primary challenge to Tea Party candidate Richard Mourdock, who declared that his idea of compromise was to get the Democrats to move to the Republican side of the issues. Both Akin and Mourdock later made headlines, and not in a good way, after each publicly made comments about rape that flabbergasted many and made mainstream Republicans quake. (Akin suggested that in cases of what he called "legitimate rape" women could not get pregnant, thereby obviating the need for allowing abortion in the case of rape, and Mourdock suggested that should a woman get pregnant following a rape, it was "God's will" that the pregnancy be carried to term.[7])

The bright hopes that Republicans held in 2010 and 2012, were finally realized in 2014. What was different this time around? The political environment had changed, to be sure, but so had the candidate selection strategy of the Republicans. What is really at stake for a political party in tying its fortunes to its more ideologically extreme members? We will return to these questions after we learn more about how political parties work. **《**

AMERICANS have always been of two minds about political parties. Partisan passions can burn long and brightly, fueling public service and civic action. But we are also cynical about partisan bickering and the **political gridlock**, or stalemate, that can result when rival parties stubbornly refuse to budge from their positions to achieve a compromise in the public interest. Skepticism about political parties, in fact, has been a major feature of American politics since the drafting of the Constitution. When James Madison wrote in *Federalist* No. 10 that "liberty is to faction what air is to fire," he conceded that factions, whether in the form of interest groups or political parties, are a permanent fixture within our representative system, but he hoped to have limited their effects by creating a large republic with many and varied interests. President George Washington echoed Madison's concerns when he warned "against the baneful effects of the spirit of party generally" in his farewell address as president in 1796.

> **political gridlock** the stalemate that occurs when political rivals, especially parties, refuse to budge from their positions to achieve a compromise in the public interest
>
> **political party** a group of citizens united by ideology and seeking control of government in order to promote their ideas and policies

But it was already too late. In the presidential election of 1796, Washington's vice president, John Adams, was backed by the Federalist Party, and his opponent, Thomas Jefferson, was supported by the Democratic-Republicans. The degree to which Madison, as primary author of the Constitution, overestimated the new republic's ability to contain the effects of faction is shown by the fact that the Constitution originally awarded the presidency to the top Electoral College vote-getter, and the vice presidency to the runner-up. In 1796 this meant that Federalist John Adams found himself with Democratic-Republican Jefferson as his vice president. (The Constitution was amended in 1804 to prevent this unhappy partisan consequence from becoming a regular occurrence.) Parties have been entrenched in American politics ever since.

Despite popular disenchantment with political parties and politicians' occasional frustration with them, most political observers and scholars believe that parties are essential to the functioning of democracy in general, and American democracy in particular. Despite Madison's opinion of factions, parties have not damaged the Constitution. They provide an extraconstitutional framework of rules and institutions that enhance the way the Constitution works. Who wins and who loses in American politics is determined not just by the Constitution but also by more informal rules, and chief among these are the rules produced by the political parties.

We can define a **political party** as a group of citizens united under a label who recruit, nominate, and elect candidates for office in order to control the government in accordance with their ideas and policies. In this chapter you will learn more about parties themselves, their role in American politics, their history, and the peculiar nature of American parties.

WHAT ARE POLITICAL PARTIES?
Organizations seeking to influence government policy by controlling the apparatus of government

Probably because Madison hoped that they would not thrive, political parties—unlike Congress, the presidency, the Supreme Court, and even the free press—are not mentioned in the Constitution. As we will see, in fact, many of the rules that determine the establishment and role of the parties have been created by party members themselves. Although the founding documents of American politics are silent on the place of political parties, keen political observers have long appreciated the fundamental role that political parties play in our system of government.[8] According to one scholar, "Political parties created democracy, and . . . democracy is unthinkable save in terms of parties."[9]

THE ROLE OF PARTIES IN A DEMOCRACY

Our definition of parties—as organizations that seek, under a common banner, to promote their ideas and policies by gaining control of government through the nomination and election of candidates for office—underscores a key difference between parties and interest groups. While both interest groups and parties seek to influence governmental policies, only parties gain this influence by sponsoring candidates in competitive elections. For political parties, winning elections represents a means to the end of controlling democratic government. Parties are crucial to the maintenance of democracy for three reasons:

- *Political linkage.* Parties provide a linkage between voters and elected officials, helping to tell voters what candidates stand for and providing a way for voters to hold their officials accountable for what they do in office, both individually and collectively.

- *Unification of a fragmented government.* Parties help overcome some of the fragmentation in government that comes from separation of powers and federalism. The founders' concern, of course, was to prevent government from becoming too powerful. But so successful were they in dividing up power that without the balancing effect of party to provide some connection between state and national government, for instance, or between the president and Congress, American government might find it very hard to achieve anything at all. Parties can lend this coherence, however, only when they control several branches or several levels of government.

- *A voice for the opposition.* Parties provide an articulate opposition to the ideas and policies of those elected to serve in government. Some citizens and critics may decry the **partisanship**, or taking of political sides, that sometimes seems to be motivated by possibilities for party gain as much as by principle or public interest. Others, however, see partisanship as providing the necessary antagonistic relationship that, like our adversarial court system, keeps politicians honest and allows the best political ideas and policies to emerge.

To highlight the multiple tasks that parties perform to make democracy work and to make life easier for politicians, political scientists find it useful to divide political parties into three separate components: the party organization, the party-in-government, and the party-in-the-electorate.[10]

PARTY ORGANIZATION
The **party organization** is what most people think of as a political party. The party organization represents the system of central committees at the national, state, and local levels. At the top of the Democratic Party organization is the Democratic National Committee, and the Republican National Committee heads the Republican Party. Underneath these national committees are state-level party committees, and below them are county-level party committees, or county equivalents (see Figure 12.1). These party organizations raise money for campaigns, recruit and nominate candidates, organize and facilitate campaigns, register voters, mobilize voters to the polls, conduct party conventions and caucuses, and draft party platforms. This may seem like a lot; however, this is only a fraction of what party organizations do, as we will see at the end of this chapter.

PARTY-IN-GOVERNMENT
The **party-in-government** comprises all the candidates for national, state, and local office who have been elected. The president, as the effective head of his party, the Speaker of the House of Representatives, the majority and minority leaders in the House and the Senate, the party whips in Congress, and state governors are all central actors in the party-in-government, which plays an important role in organizing government and in translating the wishes of the electorate into public policies.

PARTY-IN-THE-ELECTORATE
The **party-in-the-electorate** represents ordinary citizens who identify with or have some feeling of attachment to one of the political parties. Public opinion surveys determine **party identification**, or party ID, by asking respondents if they think of themselves as Democrats, Republicans, or independents. You can see two clear trends in party identification over time in Figure 12.2. Overall, voter attachments to the parties have declined; the percentage identifying as independent has increased slowly but steadily since the 1930s so that today more people consider themselves independents than identify with either of the political parties. The second trend to note in Figure 12.2 is the loss of the large numerical advantage the Democratic Party had among identifiers in the 1950s. The parties were about even by 2002, but the Democrats recovered a modest lead in party affiliation going into the 2012 presidential election.

Most voters who identify with one of the political parties "inherit" their party IDs from their parents, as we

> **partisanship** loyalty to a political cause or party
>
> **party organization** the official structure that conducts the political business of parties
>
> **party-in-government** members of the party who have been elected to serve in government
>
> **party-in-the-electorate** ordinary citizens who identify with the party
>
> **party identification** voter affiliation with a political party

FIGURE 12.1   ORGANIZATIONAL STRUCTURE OF THE PARTY SYSTEM

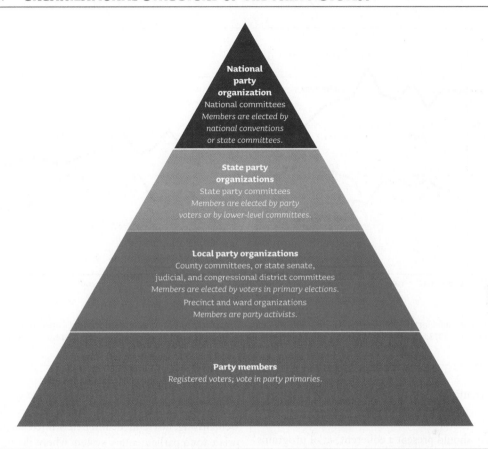

National party organization
National committees
Members are elected by national conventions or state committees.

State party organizations
State party committees
Members are elected by party voters or by lower-level committees.

Local party organizations
County committees, or state senate, judicial, and congressional district committees
Members are elected by voters in primary elections.
Precinct and ward organizations
Members are party activists.

Party members
Registered voters; vote in party primaries.

suggested in our discussion of political socialization in Chapter 11.[11] Party identifiers generally support the party's basic ideology and policy principles. These policy principles usually relate to each party's stance on the use of government to solve various economic and social problems.

Voters in most states can choose to register their party preferences for the purpose of voting in party primaries (elections to choose candidates for office). These voters are not required to perform any special activities, to contribute money to the political party, or for that matter, even to vote in the primaries. However, while voters do not have a strong formal role to play in the party organization, parties use identifiers as a necessary base of support during elections. In virtually every presidential election, both of the major-party candidates win the votes of an overwhelming percentage of those who identify with their respective parties. But just capturing one's **party base** is not sufficient to win a national election since neither party has a majority of the national

> **party base** members of a political party who consistently vote for that party's candidates

voters. As we will see later in this chapter, candidates are often pulled between the ideological preferences of their base and the more moderate preferences of independents.

THINKING OUTSIDE THE BOX

Can you have a democracy without political parties?

THE RESPONSIBLE PARTY MODEL

Earlier we said that one of the democratic roles of parties is to provide a link between the voters and elected officials, or, to use the terms we just introduced, between the party-in-the-electorate and the party-in-government. There are many ways in which parties can link voters and officials, but for the link to truly enhance democracy—that is, the control of leaders by citizens—certain conditions have to be

FIGURE 12.2 PARTY IDENTIFICATION, 1952–2013

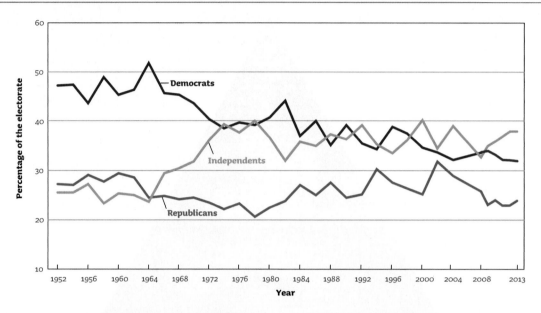

Sources: American National Election Studies, University of Michigan; data made available by the Inter-University Consortium for Political and Social Research; for 2009–2013, data from Pew Research Center, "Party Identification," www.pewresearch.org/data-trend/political-attitudes/party-identification/.

met. Political scientists call the fulfillment of the following conditions the **responsible party model:**[12]

- Each party should present a coherent set of programs to the voters, consistent with its ideology and clearly different from those of the other party.

- The candidates for each party should pledge to support their party's platform and to implement their party's program if elected.

- Voters should make their choices based on which party's program most closely reflects their own ideas and hold the parties responsible for unkept promises by voting their members out of office.

- While governing, each party should exercise control over its elected officials to ensure that party officials are promoting and voting for its programs, thereby providing accountability to the voters.

The responsible party model proposes that democracy is strengthened when voters are given clear alternatives and hold the parties responsible for keeping their promises. Voters can, of course, hold officials accountable without the assistance of parties, but it takes a good deal more of their time and attention. Furthermore, several political scientists have noted that while individuals can be held accountable for their own actions, many, if not most, government actions are the product of many officials. Political parties give us a way of holding officials accountable for what they do collectively as well as individually.[13]

The responsible party model fits some systems, especially parliamentary systems such as in Great Britain, quite well. Strong, disciplined, and determined parties are appropriate for a parliamentary system where the majority party controls, by definition, both the legislative and the executive branches, and can control the government without minority obstruction like our Senate filibuster. The model is more problematic when used, as political scientists in the past have done, to critique the American parties, which during the middle decades of the twentieth century were seen as too unfocused and undisciplined to fit the model.[14] Changes in our system over the past twenty years or so have brought the American parties closer to a responsible party model—especially in the distinctive policy programs the parties have come to represent. But even as the parties have become more highly polarized, there is a growing disconnect between their behavior and the demands of our constitutional system of checks and balances and separation of powers. This means that the parties often share power and must cooperate to get things done, yet such polarized parties in our system of shared powers is a recipe for gridlock and frustration—which is pretty much what most Americans see today in their national government.[15] In practice the American system also falls short of the idealized

> **responsible party model** party government when four conditions are met: clear choice of ideologies, candidates pledged to implement ideas, party held accountable by voters, and party control over members

responsible party model because American voters don't fit the model's conditions; they do not vote solely on party or issues, relying on other considerations like candidate experience and personality. Still, even though it doesn't fit the American case perfectly, the responsible party model is valuable because it underscores the importance of voters holding the parties accountable for governing, and it provides a useful yardstick for understanding fundamental changes in the U.S. two-party system.

PAUSE AND REVIEW:

WHO, WHAT, HOW

Political parties seek to control government and to promote their ideologies and policies. They do this by creating rules that allow them to control the nomination, campaign, and election processes and by trying to control the actions of their members elected to office. Politicians obviously have something at stake here, too. Parties provide a mechanism that helps them get nominated for office, win elections, and run government—but winning requires the support of nonparty members as well.

American citizens also have a big stake in what political parties do. Parties provide a link between citizens and government, cohesion among levels and branches of government, and an articulate opposition to government policy.

IN YOUR OWN WORDS >> Describe the role parties play in making government policy.

DO AMERICAN PARTIES OFFER VOTERS A CHOICE?
The party base and the general electorate as countervailing forces on a party's issue positions

A key feature of the responsible party model is that the parties should offer voters a choice between different visions of how government should operate. Barry Goldwater, the 1964 Republican presidential nominee, stated this more bluntly: political parties, he said, should offer "a choice, not an echo." Offering voters a choice is the

Melina Mara/The Washington Post via Getty Images

Getting the House in Order
Individual elections can affect the party as a whole. Here, Republicans face the media after secret ballot voting to determine leadership positions in the House of Representatives after Majority Leader Eric Cantor's unexpected defeat in the 2014 primary. Pictured are newly minted House majority whip Steve Scalise, R-La. (left); Rep. Greg Walden, R-Oreg.; Speaker of the House John Boehner, R-Ohio; and newly elected House majority leader Kevin McCarthy, R-Calif.

primary means through which parties make representative democracy work. In America the policy differences between the two major parties, the Democrats and the Republicans (often also called the GOP for "Grand Old Party"), are narrower than in some democracies around the world, particularly those with many parties spread across the ideological spectrum. Increasingly, however, voters do see clear policy choices between the Democratic and Republican Parties.[16] In this section we investigate what the two major parties stand for, including competing forces that draw the parties apart to ideologically distinct positions and push them together to take more moderate stances.

WHAT DO THE PARTIES STAND FOR?

Although it may seem to voters that members of the two parties are not very different once they are elected to office, the parties can be considered quite distinct in three areas: their ideologies, their memberships, and the policies they stand for.

PARTY IDEOLOGY Each major party represents a different ideological perspective about the way that government should be used to solve problems. Ideologies, as we have said before, are broad sets of ideas about politics

CLUES
TO CRITICAL THINKING

"Let's Just Say It: The Republicans Are the Problem"

By Thomas E. Mann and Norman J. Ornstein, *Washington Post*, April 27, 2012

Here's a provocative title! As we saw in Chapter 7, hyperpartisanship in recent years has just about brought congressional action to a halt. Thomas Mann, a political scientist who works at the Brookings Institute, a liberal think tank, and Norm Ornstein, who works at the American Enterprise Institute, a conservative think tank, chalk up the chief source of the problem to internal changes in the Republican Party. Are they right, or is this just another effort to point fingers and assign blame?

Rep. Allen West, a Florida Republican, was recently captured on video asserting that there are "78 to 81" Democrats in Congress who are members of the Communist Party. Of course, it's not unusual for some renegade lawmaker from either side of the aisle to say something outrageous. What made West's comment—right out of the McCarthyite playbook of the 1950s—so striking was the almost complete lack of condemnation from Republican congressional leaders or other major party figures, including the remaining presidential candidates.

It's not that the GOP leadership agrees with West; it is that such extreme remarks and views are now taken for granted.

We have been studying Washington politics and Congress for more than 40 years, and never have we seen them this dysfunctional. In our past writings, we have criticized both parties when we believed it was warranted. Today, however, we have no choice but to acknowledge that the core of the problem lies with the Republican Party.

The GOP has become an insurgent outlier in American politics. It is ideologically extreme; scornful of compromise; unmoved by conventional understanding of facts, evidence and science; and dismissive of the legitimacy of its political opposition.

When one party moves this far from the mainstream, it makes it nearly impossible for the political system to deal constructively with the country's challenges.

"Both sides do it" or "There is plenty of blame to go around" are the traditional refuges for an American news media intent on proving its lack of bias, while political scientists prefer generality and neutrality when discussing partisan polarization. Many self-styled bipartisan groups, in their search for common ground, propose solutions that move both sides to the center, a strategy that is simply untenable when one side is so far out of reach.

It is clear that the center of gravity in the Republican Party has shifted sharply to the right. Its once-legendary moderate and center-right legislators in the House and the Senate—think Bob Michel, Mickey Edwards, John Danforth, Chuck Hagel—are virtually extinct.

The post-McGovern Democratic Party, by contrast, while losing the bulk of its conservative Dixiecrat contingent in the decades after the civil rights revolution, has retained a more diverse base. Since the Clinton presidency, it has hewed to the center-left on issues from welfare reform to fiscal policy. While the Democrats may have moved from their 40-yard line to their 25, the Republicans have gone from their 40 to somewhere behind their goal post.

What happened? Of course, there were larger forces at work beyond the realignment of the South. They included the mobilization of social conservatives after the 1973 *Roe v. Wade* decision, the anti-tax movement launched in 1978 by California's Proposition 13, the rise of conservative talk radio after a congressional pay raise in 1989, and the emergence of Fox News and right-wing blogs. But the real move to the bedrock right starts with two names: Newt Gingrich and Grover Norquist.

From the day he entered Congress in 1979, Gingrich had a strategy to create a Republican majority in the House: convincing voters that the institution was so corrupt that anyone would be better than the incumbents, especially those in the Democratic majority. It took him 16 years, but by bringing ethics charges against Democratic leaders; provoking them into overreactions that enraged Republicans and united them to vote against Democratic initiatives; exploiting scandals to create even more public disgust with politicians; and then recruiting GOP candidates around the country to run against Washington, Democrats and Congress, Gingrich accomplished his goal.

Ironically, after becoming speaker, Gingrich wanted to enhance Congress's reputation and was content to compromise with President Bill Clinton when it served his interests. But the forces Gingrich unleashed destroyed whatever comity existed across party lines, activated an extreme and virulently anti-Washington base—most recently represented by tea party activists—and helped drive moderate Republicans out of Congress. (Some of his progeny, elected in the early 1990s, moved to the Senate and polarized its culture in the same way.)

Norquist, meanwhile, founded Americans for Tax Reform in 1985 and rolled out his Taxpayer Protection Pledge the following year. The pledge, which binds its signers to never support a tax increase (that includes closing tax loopholes), had been signed as of last year by 238 of the 242 House Republicans and 41 of the 47 GOP senators, according to ATR. The Norquist tax pledge has led to other pledges, on issues such as climate change, that create additional litmus tests that box in moderates and make cross-party coalitions nearly impossible. For Republicans concerned about a primary challenge from the right, the failure to sign such pledges is simply too risky.

Today, thanks to the GOP, compromise has gone out the window in Washington. In the first two years of the Obama administration, nearly every presidential initiative met with vehement, rancorous and unanimous Republican opposition in the House and the Senate, followed by efforts to delegitimize the results and repeal the policies. The filibuster, once relegated to a handful of major national issues in a given Congress, became a routine weapon of obstruction, applied even to widely supported bills or presidential nominations. And Republicans in the Senate have abused the confirmation process to block any and every nominee to posts such as the head of the Consumer Financial Protection Bureau, solely to keep laws that were legitimately enacted from being implemented.

In the third and now fourth years of the Obama presidency, divided government has produced something closer to complete gridlock than we have ever seen in our time in Washington, with partisan divides even leading last year to America's first credit downgrade.

On financial stabilization and economic recovery, on deficits and debt, on climate change and health-care reform, Republicans have been the force behind the widening ideological gaps and the strategic use of partisanship. In the presidential campaign and in Congress, GOP leaders have embraced fanciful policies on taxes and spending, kowtowing to their party's most strident voices.

Republicans often dismiss nonpartisan analyses of the nature of problems and the impact of policies when those assessments don't fit their ideology. In the face of the deepest economic downturn since the Great Depression, the party's leaders and their outside acolytes insisted on obeisance to a supply-side view of economic growth—thus fulfilling Norquist's pledge—while ignoring contrary considerations.

The results can border on the absurd: In early 2009, several of the eight Republican co-sponsors of a bipartisan health-care reform plan dropped their support; by early 2010, the others had turned on their own proposal so that there would be zero GOP backing for any bill that came within a mile of Obama's reform initiative. As one co-sponsor, Sen. Lamar Alexander (R-Tenn.), told The Washington Post's Ezra Klein: "I liked it because it was bipartisan. I wouldn't have voted for it."

And seven Republican co-sponsors of a Senate resolution to create a debt-reduction panel voted in January 2010 against their own resolution, solely to keep it from getting to the 60-vote threshold Republicans demanded and thus denying the president a seeming victory.

This attitude filters down far deeper than the party leadership. Rank-and-file GOP voters endorse the strategy that the party's elites have adopted, eschewing compromise to solve problems and insisting on principle, even if it leads to gridlock. Democratic voters, by contrast, along with self-identified independents, are more likely to favor deal-making over deadlock.

Democrats are hardly blameless, and they have their own extreme wing and their own predilection for hardball politics. But these tendencies do not routinely veer outside the normal bounds of robust politics. If anything, under the presidencies of Clinton and Obama, the Democrats have become more of a status-quo party. They are centrist protectors of government, reluctantly willing to revamp programs and trim retirement and health benefits to maintain its central commitments in the face of fiscal pressures.

No doubt, Democrats were not exactly warm and fuzzy toward George W. Bush during his presidency. But recall that they worked hand in glove with the Republican president on the No Child Left Behind Act, provided crucial votes in the Senate for his tax cuts, joined with Republicans for all the steps taken after the Sept. 11, 2001, attacks and supplied the key votes for the Bush

administration's financial bailout at the height of the economic crisis in 2008. The difference is striking.

The GOP's evolution has become too much for some longtime Republicans. Former senator Chuck Hagel of Nebraska called his party "irresponsible" in an interview with the *Financial Times* in August, at the height of the debt-ceiling battle. "I think the Republican Party is captive to political movements that are very ideological, that are very narrow," he said. "I've never seen so much intolerance as I see today in American politics."

And Mike Lofgren, a veteran Republican congressional staffer, wrote an anguished diatribe last year about why he was ending his career on the Hill after nearly three decades. "The Republican Party is becoming less and less like a traditional political party in a representative democracy and becoming more like an apocalyptic cult, or one of the intensely ideological authoritarian parties of 20th century Europe," he wrote on the Truthout Web site.

Shortly before Rep. West went off the rails with his accusations of communism in the Democratic Party, political scientists Keith Poole and Howard Rosenthal, who have long tracked historical trends in political polarization, said their studies of congressional votes found that Republicans are now more conservative than they have been in more than a century. Their data show a dramatic uptick in polarization, mostly caused by the sharp rightward move of the GOP.

If our democracy is to regain its health and vitality, the culture and ideological center of the Republican Party must change. In the short run, without a massive (and unlikely) across-the-board rejection of the GOP at the polls, that will not happen. If anything, Washington's ideological divide will probably grow after the 2012 elections.

In the House, some of the remaining centrist and conservative "Blue Dog" Democrats have been targeted for extinction by redistricting, while even

(Continued)

(Continued)

ardent tea party Republicans, such as freshman Rep. Alan Nunnelee (Miss.), have faced primary challenges from the right for being too accommodationist. And Mitt Romney's rhetoric and positions offer no indication that he would govern differently if his party captures the White House and both chambers of Congress.

We understand the values of mainstream journalists, including the effort to report both sides of a story. But a balanced treatment of an unbalanced phenomenon distorts reality. If the political dynamics of Washington are unlikely to change anytime soon, at least we should change the way that reality is portrayed to the public.

Our advice to the press: Don't seek professional safety through the even-handed, unfiltered presentation of opposing views. Which politician is telling the truth? Who is taking hostages, at what risks and to what ends?

Also, stop lending legitimacy to Senate filibusters by treating a 60-vote hurdle as routine. The framers certainly didn't intend it to be. Report individual senators' abusive use of holds and identify every time the minority party uses a filibuster to kill a bill or nomination with majority support.

Look ahead to the likely consequences of voters' choices in the November elections. How would the candidates govern? What could they accomplish? What differences

can people expect from a unified Republican or Democratic government, or one divided between the parties?

In the end, while the press can make certain political choices understandable, it is up to voters to decide. If they can punish ideological extremism at the polls and look skeptically upon

candidates who profess to reject all dialogue and bargaining with opponents, then an insurgent outlier party will have some impetus to return to the center. Otherwise, our politics will get worse before it gets better.

Source: Reprinted by permission of the authors.

Consider the source and the audience: This article has a bipartisan author team and appeared in the *Washington Post,* known for its mainstream coverage of national politics. They take to task not only national politicians but also the media that cover them, all people who read the *Post.* Was that a gutsy move, astonishingly foolish, or just wrong-headed?

Lay out the argument, the values, and the assumptions: Mann and Ornstein's primary concern seems to be that politics in Washington today resembles a game of dangerous brinkmanship. Why do they hold Gingrich and Norquist responsible? What do they see as the primary role of parties? And what is the role of the media in a democracy? How would politics in the United States work if Mann and Ornstein had their way? What is the Republican case for not cooperating with Democrats?

Uncover the evidence: Mann and Ornstein rely in part on historical events to make their case. Can those events be interpreted differently? They also use the words of disaffected Republicans to show how the party has changed. Does that help support their case? Are there any other kinds of evidence you would like to see?

Evaluate the conclusion: Do you agree with Mann and Ornstein that politics-as-brinkmanship is a problem? Are they correct to blame changes within the Republican Party for that? How would Republicans respond to that? Do you agree that in American politics the effort to be "neutral" means that sometimes analysts and reporters fail to tell the whole story?

Sort out the political implications: The authors essentially say that it is up to the media and the voters to fix this situation if we want a government that can solve problems effectively. Are those two groups of people up to the task? How might Republicans be expected to react?

that help to organize our views of the political world, the information that regularly bombards us, and the positions we take on various issues. As we saw in Chapter 2, liberalism and conservatism today are ideologies that divide the country sharply over issues such as the role of government in the economy, in society, and in citizens' private lives. In general, conservatives look to government to provide social and moral order, but they want the economy to remain as unfettered as possible in the distribution of material resources. Liberals encourage government action to solve economic and social problems but want government to stay

out of their personal, religious, and moral lives, except as a protector of their basic rights.

At least since the New Deal of the 1930s, the Democratic Party, especially outside the South, has been aligned with a liberal ideology and the Republican Party with a conservative perspective.[17] Since the 1960s the parties have become more consistent internally with respect to their ideologies. The most conservative region in the country is the South, but because of lingering resentment of the Republican Party for its role in the Civil War, the South was for decades tied tightly to the Democratic

Party. In the 1960s, however, conservative southern Democratic voters began to vote for the Republican Party, and formerly Democratic politicians were switching their allegiances as well. By the 1990s the South had become predominantly Republican. This swing made the Democratic Party more consistently liberal and the Republicans more consistently conservative and, as we explained in Chapter 7, the parties became more polarized. To illustrate, so-called "consistents," liberal Democrats and conservative Republicans, made up only 33 percent of party identifiers in 1977, while "inconsistents," conservative Democrats and liberal Republicans, made up 21 percent. Consistency between party ideology and beliefs of party members has increased over the years so that, by 2012, consistents made up 53 percent of party identifiers and inconsistents made up only 9 percent.[18]

As we saw in *What's at Stake...?*, this greater ideological consistency within each of the parties gives the party activist bases more power because they do not have to do battle with people of different ideological persuasions. The stronger activist core is able to exert more internal pressure within the parties, nominating candidates through primaries but also calling for ideological conformity in the parties in Congress, leading to the phenomenon of hyperpartisanship that we discussed in Chapter 7 (see *CLUES to Critical Thinking*). As we saw, there is no overlap in the House of Representatives between the parties: all Republicans are more conservative than the most conservative Democrat, yielding two completely distinct ideological encampments with little basis for compromise. The differences among the public are not as great, but they are still notable. Figure 12.3 shows the ideological composition of Democrats and Republicans. Notice that although the conservative label is more popular, the likelihood of identifying oneself as a conservative is much greater among Republicans. It is not, of course, the case that all Democrats think the same or that all Republicans think the same. Each party has its ideological and moderate factions, but the divisions between partisans in the electorate are greater today.[19]

PARTY MEMBERSHIP Party ideologies attract and are reinforced by different coalitions of voters. This means that the Democrats' post–New Deal liberal ideology reflects the preferences of its coalition of working- and lower-class voters, including union members, minorities, women, the elderly, and more educated urban dwellers. The Republicans' conservative ideology, on the other hand, reflects the preferences of upper- to middle-class whites, those who are in evangelical and Protestant religions, and rural and suburban voters. The "*Snapshot of America*: Who Belongs to What

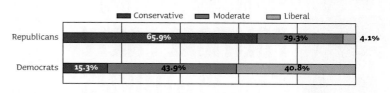

FIGURE 12.3 PARTY IDENTIFICATION AND IDEOLOGY

■ Conservative ■ Moderate ▨ Liberal

Republicans: 65.9% | 29.3% | 4.1%
Democrats: 15.3% | 43.9% | 40.8%

Source: CBS News/*New York Times* polls, 2008–2012. Calculated by authors.

Party?" shows how each party's coalition differs based on group characteristics. There is nothing inevitable about these coalitions, however, and they are subject to change as the parties' stances on issues change and as the opposing party offers new alternatives. Working-class whites (non-Hispanic whites without a college education) were once the bedrock constituency of the Democratic Party. However, the Republicans' more conservative appeals on racial and social issues have won over enough of this group that are they are as likely to support Republicans in a given election.[20]

POLICY DIFFERENCES BETWEEN THE PARTIES When the parties run slates of candidates for office, those candidates run on a **party platform**—a list of policy positions the party endorses and pledges its elected officials to enact as policy. A platform is the national party's campaign promises, usually made only in a presidential election year. If the parties are to make a difference politically, then the platforms have to reflect substantial differences that are consistent with their ideologies. The responsible party model requires that the parties offer distinct platforms, that voters know about them and vote on the basis of them, and that the parties ensure that their elected officials follow through in implementing them.

The two major parties' stated positions on some key issues from their 2012 platforms appear in *Don't Be Fooled by . . . Political Party Platforms*. These differences between the Democratic and Republican platforms in 2012 are typical, and they are what make it possible for the electorate to bring about meaningful policy changes. When the parties' programs are clearly different, electing a new majority party to Congress can result in substantial changes in the policy directions pursued by the national government. That is, party differences are necessary for popular control of the overall directions of government policy.

FORCES DRAWING THE PARTIES APART AND PUSHING THEM TOGETHER

Political parties in our system have a dilemma—how to keep the core ideological base satisfied while appealing to enough more moderate voters that they can win elections in diverse constituencies. In a small, homogeneous district this is not

> **party platform** a list of policy positions a party endorses and pledges its elected officials to enact

DON'T BE FOOLED BY...
POLITICAL PARTY PLATFORMS

Think of it as an invitation to a party—so to speak. In their platforms, political parties make a broad statement about who they are and what they stand for in the hope that you will decide to join them. The excerpts below from the Democratic and Republican platforms of 2012 show differing positions on several key issues. The full text of these platforms can be found on the web sites of the parties' national committees.

WHAT TO WATCH OUT FOR

When you read a party's platform, keep these questions in mind:

- **Whose platform is it, and what do you know about that party's basic political positions?** Understanding the basics will help you to interpret key phrases. For instance, how might terms like *class warfare* be defined differently in the Democratic and Republican platforms?

- **Who is the audience?** Parties direct their platforms to two different groups—the party faithful and potential new supporters. For example, Democrats want to keep their traditional supporters, like union members, but they also want to broaden their appeal to the middle class and to small-business owners. Republicans want to keep their base (including pro-life activists) happy but also want to attract more women in an effort to close the gender gap. How does this dual audience affect how parties portray themselves?

- **Which statements reflect values, and which are statements of fact?** First, get clear about the values you are being asked to support. Parties tend to sprinkle their platforms liberally with terms like *fundamental rights*. Which rights do they actually mean, and do you consider them fundamental rights? What are the costs and benefits of agreeing to their value claims? Then evaluate the facts. Are they accurate? Check out statistics. Do they seem reasonable? If not, look them up.

- **Do you think the party can deliver on its policy proposals?** What resources (money, power, and so on) would it need? Can it get them? Would enacting the promised policies achieve what the party claims it would? Who would win, and who would lose?

- **What is your reaction to the platform?** Could you support it? How does it fit with your personal values and political beliefs? Is the appeal of this platform emotional? Intellectual? Ideological? Moral? Remember that party platforms are not just statements of party principles and policy proposals; they are also advertisements. Read them with all the caution and suspicion you would bring to bear on any other ad that attempts to convince you to buy, or buy into, something. *Caveat emptor!* (Let the buyer beware!)

ISSUE	DEMOCRATIC PLATFORM	REPUBLICAN PLATFORM
Abortion	The Democratic Party strongly and unequivocally supports *Roe v. Wade* and a woman's right to make decisions regarding her pregnancy, including a safe and legal abortion, regardless of ability to pay. We oppose any and all efforts to weaken or undermine that right.	We support a human life amendment to the Constitution and endorse legislation to make clear that the Fourteenth Amendment's protections apply to unborn children. We oppose using public revenues to promote or perform abortion or fund organizations which perform or advocate it and will not fund or subsidize health care which includes abortion coverage. We support the appointment of judges who respect traditional family values and the sanctity of innocent human life.

ISSUE	DEMOCRATIC PLATFORM	REPUBLICAN PLATFORM
Gay Rights (Marriage)	We support the right of all families to have equal respect, responsibilities, and protections under the law. We support marriage equality and support the movement to secure equal treatment under law for same-sex couples. We also support the freedom of churches and religious entities to decide how to administer marriage as a religious sacrament without government interference. . . . We support the full repeal of the so-called Defense of Marriage Act and the passage of the Respect for Marriage Act.	We reaffirm our support for a Constitutional amendment defining marriage as the union of one man and one woman. We applaud the citizens of the majority of States which have enshrined in their constitutions the traditional concept of marriage, and we support the campaigns underway in several other States to do so.
Gun Control	We recognize that the individual right to bear arms is an important part of the American tradition, and we will preserve Americans' Second Amendment right to own and use firearms. We believe that the right to own firearms is subject to reasonable regulation. . . . [W]e can work together to enact commonsense improvements—like reinstating the assault weapons ban and closing the gun show loophole—so that guns do not fall into the hands of those irresponsible, law-breaking few.	We uphold the right of individuals to keep and bear arms, a right which antedated the Constitution and was solemnly confirmed by the Second Amendment. . . . This also includes the right to obtain and store ammunition without registration. We support the fundamental right to self-defense wherever a law-abiding citizen has a legal right to be . . . , and we support federal legislation that would expand the exercise of that right by allowing those with state-issued carry permits to carry firearms in any state that issues such permits to its own residents.
War on Terror/ Afghanistan	[We support President Obama's shift] away from the Bush administration's sweeping and internationally divisive rhetoric of a "global war on terrorism" to a more focused effort against an identifiable network of people: al-Qaeda and its affiliates. That has allowed us to target force with greater precision against those who want to harm Americans and attack the United States and move away from the type of large-scale military deployments characteristic of the previous administration and favored by many Republicans today.	We must deter any adversary who would attack us or use terror as a tool of government. Every potential enemy must have no doubt that our capabilities, our commitment, and our will to defeat them are clear, unwavering, and unequivocal. We must immediately employ a new blueprint for a National Military Strategy that is based on an informed and validated assessment of the potential threats we face, one that restores as a principal objective the deterrence using the full spectrum of our military capabilities. As Ronald Reagan proved by the victorious conclusion of the Cold War, only our capability to wield overwhelming military power can truly deter the enemies of the United States from threatening our people and our national interests.
Energy Policy	It's not enough to invent clean energy technologies here; we want to make them here and sell them around the world. . . . We support more infrastructure investment to speed the transition to cleaner fuels in the transportation sector. And we are expediting the approval process to build out critical oil and gas lines essential to transporting our energy for consumers. . . .	The Republican Party is committed to domestic energy independence. The United States and its neighbors to the North and South have been blessed with abundant energy resources, tapped and untapped, traditional and alternative, that are among the largest and most valuable on earth. . . . Unlike the current Administration, we will not pick winners and losers in the energy marketplace. Instead, we will let the free market and the public's preferences determine the industry outcomes.
Environmentalism	We affirm the science of climate change, commit to significantly reducing the pollution that causes climate change, and know we have to meet this challenge by driving smart policies that lead to greater growth in clean energy generation and result in a range of economic and social benefits.	. . . [W]e believe people are the most valuable resource, and human health and safety are the most important measurements of success. A policy protecting these objectives, however, must balance economic development and private property rights in the short run with conservation goals over the

(Continued)

(Continued)

ISSUE	DEMOCRATIC PLATFORM	REPUBLICAN PLATFORM
		long run. Also, public access to public lands for recreational activities such as hunting, fishing, and recreational shooting should be permitted on all appropriate federal lands.
Taxes	We believe in deficit reduction not by placing the burden on the middle class and the poor, but by cutting out programs we can't afford and asking the wealthiest to again contribute their fair share.	We oppose tax policies that divide Americans or promote class warfare. . . . In any restructuring of federal taxation, to guard against hypertaxation of the American people, any value added tax or national sales tax must be tied to the simultaneous repeal of the Sixteenth Amendment, which established the federal income tax.
Workplace Rights	Democrats believe that the right to organize and collectively bargain is a fundamental American value. . . . We will continue to fight for the right of all workers to organize and join a union. . . . We will continue to vigorously oppose "Right to Work" and "paycheck protection" efforts, and so-called "Save Our Secret Ballot" measures whenever they are proposed.	We salute the Republican Governors and State legislators who have saved their States from fiscal disaster by reforming their laws governing public employee unions. We urge elected officials across the country to follow their lead in order to avoid State and local defaults on their obligations and the collapse of services to the public.
Voter Rights	We believe the right to vote and to have your vote counted is an essential American freedom, and we oppose laws that place unnecessary restrictions on those seeking to exercise that freedom. . . . Democrats know that voter identification laws can disproportionately burden young voters, people of color, low-income families, people with disabilities, and the elderly, and we refuse to allow the use of political pretexts to disenfranchise American citizens.	We support State laws that require proof of citizenship at the time of voter registration to protect our electoral system against a significant and growing form of voter fraud. . . . We call for vigorous prosecution of voter fraud at the State and federal level. . . . We recognize that having a physical verification of the vote is the best way to ensure a fair election.
Health Care	We believe accessible, affordable, high quality health care is part of the American promise, that Americans should have the security that comes with good health care, and that no one should go broke because they get sick.	We believe that taking care of one's health is an individual responsibility. Chronic diseases, many of them related to lifestyle, drive healthcare costs, accounting for more than 75 percent of the nation's medical spending. To reduce demand, and thereby lower costs, we must foster personal responsibility while increasing preventive services to promote healthy lifestyles.

Source: Democratic Party platform: assets.dstatic.org/dnc-platform/2012-National-Platform.pdf; Republican Party platform: www.gop.com/wp-content/uploads/2012/08/2012GOPPlatform.pdf.

likely to be a problem. Conservative Republicans and liberal Democrats can be nominated and elected and party members are happy. As constituencies get larger and more diverse, parties have a choice. They can be moderate and win elections, or stay ideologically pure and lose. In other words, there are internal forces that draw the parties away from each other, to the opposite ends of the ideological spectrum, but external, electoral forces can push them together. These forces are central to understanding electoral politics in America today. In this section we look more closely at these complex relationships.

THE PULL TOWARD EXTREMISM As we have seen so far in this chapter, there are major forces within the

Republican Party Platform   Democratic Party Platform ●

SNAPSHOT OF AMERICA: WHO BELONGS TO WHAT PARTY?

■ Female Democrats

■ Female Republicans

Democratic Party

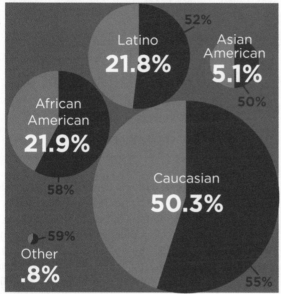

Latino
21.8%
52%

Asian American
5.1%
50%

African American
21.9%
58%

Caucasian
50.3%
55%

Other
.8%
59%

Republican Party

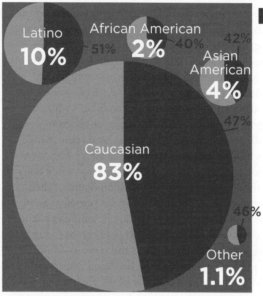

Latino
10%
51%

African American
2%
40%
42%

Asian American
4%
47%

Caucasian
83%

Other
1.1%
46%

BEHIND THE NUMBERS

The chart shows that our two political parties are made up of different proportions of the nation's racial and ethnic groups. The fast growing of these are Latinos, and today they are twice as likely to identify Democrats rather than Republicans. Experts predict this will hurt Republican's electoral chances in coming decades. Of course, these patterns can change. What might the parties do that could change racial and ethnic partisan loyalties?

Source: American National Election Studies time series, 2012 survey. Authors' calculations with racial and ethnic groups weighted to match 2013 census data (U.S. Census Bureau's American Community Survey, 2013, http://factfinder2.census.gov/faces/nav/jsf/pages/searchresults.xhtml?refresh=t].

parties that keep them distinct: the needs to placate party activists, to raise money, and to keep the candidates true to their own beliefs as well as to those of their base. On key issues, although presidents seek to portray their proposals as serving the interests of the general public, in fact the specific policy solutions are almost always consistent with their party's ideological perspective and policy agenda.

The main players in political parties are often called the "party faithful," or **party activists**, people who are especially committed to the values and policies of the party, and who devote more of their resources, in both time and money, to the party's cause. The activists are part of the party base, but their support for the party goes beyond simply voting. They also volunteer their time, donate their money, and stay actively involved in party politics. Although these party activists are not an official organ of the party, they represent

party activists the "party faithful"; the rank-and-file members who actually carry out the party's electioneering efforts

a party's lifeblood. Compared to the average voter, party activists tend to be more ideologically extreme (more conservative or more liberal even than the average party identifier) and to care more intensely about the party's issues. Their influence can have significant effects on the ideological character of both parties.[21]

Party activists play a key role in keeping the parties ideologically distinct because one of the primary goals of their participation and support is to ensure that the party advocates their issue positions. Because they tend to be concerned with keeping the party pure, they can be reluctant to compromise on their issues,[22] although they also care a great deal about winning.[23] Liberal activists kept the Democratic Party to the left of most Americans during the 1970s and 1980s; the only Democratic candidate who won a presidential election during that time was Jimmy Carter, in the immediate aftermath of the Watergate scandal that drove Republican Richard Nixon from office. Republicans sought to keep alive the impression that the Democrats were a party of crazed left-wing activists in 1988 by making *liberal*, or "the L-word" as they referred to it, such a derogatory term that Democrats would not use it to describe themselves for fear of

● Partisanship Is Good

turning off voters. The Democratic Party dealt with this problem by restructuring its internal politics and giving more weight to moderates like Bill Clinton and Al Gore. They also responded by relabeling themselves as "progressives" with fewer and fewer candidates and on-air leftists embracing the "liberal" label.[24] The Republicans got caught in the same trap of appearing to be as conservative as their most activist members in the religious right and, later, in the Tea Party.

The need to please party activists gives candidates a powerful incentive to remain true to the party's causes. Activists are poised to work hard for candidates who promote their political, social, economic, or religious agendas and, conversely, to work just as hard against any candidate who does not pass their litmus test.[25] This means that candidates who moderate too much or too often risk alienating the activists who are a key component of their success. For instance, John McCain, in his primary race to become the 2008 Republican presidential nominee, was seen as an outsider by many of the Republican base and was not able to generate the enthusiasm and contributions he probably would have received if he had been consistently appealing to the party base over the years. His pick of Sarah Palin as his running mate went some way to healing that breach, but at the cost of alienating many voters in the middle of the ideological spectrum.

Active support and contributions by those with strong ideological policy preferences help to keep candidates from converging to the ideological position of the moderate voter (see Figure 12.4, bottom). Thus the likely winner of most Democratic primaries is going to be more liberal than the average voter in the general election, and the likely winner of most Republican primaries will be more conservative. Even though candidates do win some votes by taking more moderate stands, they are nevertheless mindful of their bases and tend not to stray very far from their roots once in office.[26] This means that few politicians are willing to be truly moderate and work with the other side. Since the 1980s an increased ideological polarization between the parties has yielded more intense partisan conflict and sometimes policy gridlock.

THE PUSH TOWARD MODERATION Ideological purists do not always win the day, however. Obviously, if a candidate is going to win an election, he or she must appeal to more voters than does the opposing candidate. On any policy or set of policies, voters' opinions range from very liberal to very conservative; however, in the American two-party system, most voters tend to be in the middle, holding a moderate position between the two ideological extremes (see Figure 12.4, top). In diverse districts, the party that appeals best to the moderate and independent voters usually wins most of the votes. Thus, even though the ideologies of the parties are distinct, the pressures related to winning a majority of votes can lead both parties to campaign on the same issue positions, making them look similar to voters.[27] As a result, at various times the Republicans moved from their initial opposition

to join the majority of voters in supporting Social Security, Medicare, and Medicaid. Similarly, the Democrats, while wanting to expand health care coverage, did not embrace a government "single-payer" plan that would necessarily cover everyone.

THINKING OUTSIDE THE BOX

Does partisanship have to lead to divisiveness?

The parties can deal with the tension between activists and the larger body of moderates in ways other than by changing the party positions. One strategy is simply to emphasize issues that are popular with moderates. In the 2004 election, George W. Bush focused on the dangers inherent in the war on terror, on which moderates favored him strongly over John Kerry; however, in 2008 and 2012 the need to appease the party base kept John McCain and Mitt Romney to the right of center for most of their campaigns. In 2008 Barack Obama appealed to moderates with his insistence that politics need not be ideological and divisive, but in 2012, after four years of partisan gridlock in Washington, he ran instead on helping the middle class, and his campaign focused on turning out the Democratic base.

Another way parties can make their programs attractive to moderates while keeping their bases happy is to reframe the issues in ways that are palatable to more voters. In the 2010 midterm elections, Republicans opposed to financial reform and regulation, losing positions at a time when many Americans were angry at corporate America, couched their stance not as probusiness but as antigovernment, since polls showed that government was also the target of voter anger. Both parties, of course, attempt to present their policies in ways that will get the widest possible acceptance among the public.

PAUSE AND REVIEW:

WHO, WHAT, HOW

The rules of electoral politics create incentives for the parties to take moderate positions that appeal to the majority of voters, but party activists, primary voters, and big-money donors, who tend to be more ideological and issue oriented, push party policy agendas back toward their extremes. As a consequence, parties and their candidates tend to remain true to their respective party's ideological perspective, promoting policy solutions that are consistent with the party's ideology. Thus Democratic candidates espouse a

FIGURE 12.4 **EXTERNAL AND INTERNAL FORCES ON THE PARTIES**

THE PUSH TOWARD MODERATION

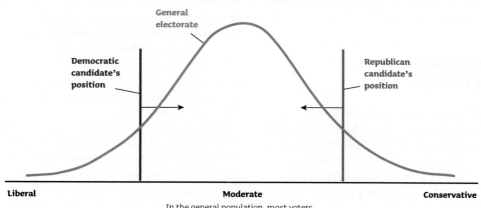

General
electorate

Democratic
candidate's
position

Republican
candidate's
position

Liberal | Moderate | Conservative

In the general population, most voters
are moderate; their preferences push
candidates toward political moderation.

THE PULL TOWARD EXTREMISM

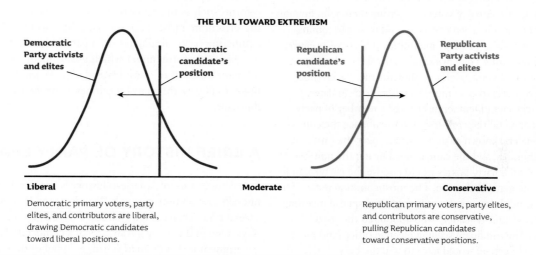

Democratic
Party activists
and elites

Democratic
candidate's
position

Republican
candidate's
position

Republican
Party activists
and elites

Liberal | Moderate | Conservative

Democratic primary voters, party
elites, and contributors are liberal,
drawing Democratic candidates
toward liberal positions.

Republican primary voters, party elites,
and contributors are conservative,
pulling Republican candidates
toward conservative positions.

policy agenda that reflects the liberal interests of the coalition of groups that represent their most ardent supporters. Likewise, Republican candidates advocate a policy agenda that reflects the conservative interests of the coalition of groups that are their most ardent supporters. In this way, both parties, in most elections, offer voters "a choice, not an echo," but they also contribute to the growing partisanship of American politics. The real losers in this situation may be the party moderates and independents who, less intense and active than the party base, find themselves poorly represented at the end of the day.[28]

IN YOUR OWN WORDS » Explain the tension between the party base and the general electorate regarding their influence on issue positions.

THE HISTORY OF PARTIES IN AMERICA
From party machines to effective political organizations

For James Madison, parties were just an organized version of that potentially dangerous political association, the faction. He had hopes that their influence on American politics would be minimal, but scarcely was the ink dry on the Constitution before the founders were organizing themselves into groups to promote their political views. In the 1790s a host of disagreements among these early American politicians led Alexander Hamilton and John Adams to organize the Federalists, the group of legislators who supported their views. Later, Thomas Jefferson and James Madison would do the same with the

Democratic-Republicans. Over the course of the next decade, these organizations expanded beyond their legislative purposes to include recruiting candidates to run as members of their party for both Congress and the presidency. The primary focus, however, was on the party-in-government and not on the voters.[29]

THE EVOLUTION OF AMERICAN PARTIES

The history of political parties in the United States is dominated by ambitious politicians who have shaped their parties in order to achieve their goals.[30] Chief among those goals, as we have seen, are getting elected to office and running government once there. In 1828 Martin Van Buren and Andrew Jackson turned the Democratic Party away from a focus on the party-in-government, creating the country's first mass-based party and setting the stage for the development of the voter-oriented party machine. **Party machines** were tightly organized party systems at the state, city, and county levels that kept control of voters by getting them jobs, helping them out financially when necessary, and in fact becoming part of their lives and their communities. This mass organization was built around one principal goal: taking advantage of the expansion of voting rights to all white men (even those without property) to elect more Democratic candidates.[31]

The Jacksonian Democrats enacted a number of party and governmental reforms designed to enhance the control of party leaders, known as **party bosses**, over the candidates, the officeholders, and the campaigns. During the nomination process the party bosses would choose the party's candidates for the general election. The most common means for selecting candidates was the party caucus, a special meeting of hand-picked party leaders who appointed the party's nominees. Any candidate seeking elective office (and most offices were elective) would have to win the boss's approval by pledging his loyalty to the party boss and supporting policies that the party boss favored.

Winning candidates were expected to hire only other party supporters for government positions and reward only party supporters with government contracts. This largesse expanded the range of people with a stake in the party's electoral success. The combination of candidates and people who had been given government jobs and contracts meant that the party had an army of supporters to help recruit and mobilize voters to support the party. Moreover, because party bosses controlled the nomination process, any candidate who won elective office but did not fulfill his pledges to the party boss would be replaced by someone who would. This system of **patronage**, which we discussed in Chapter 9 (on bureaucracy), rewarded faithful party supporters with public office, jobs, and government contracts and ensured that a party's candidates were loyal to the party or at least to the party bosses.

Because the Democratic Party machine was so effective at getting votes and controlling government, the Whig

Party (1830s through 1850s), and later the Republican Party (starting in the mid-1850s), used these same techniques to organize. Party bosses and their party machines were exceptionally strong in urban areas in the East and Midwest. The urban machines, while designed to further the interests of the parties themselves, had the important democratic consequence of integrating into the political process the masses of new immigrants coming into the urban centers at the turn of the twentieth century. Because parties were so effective at mobilizing voters, the average participation rate exceeded 80 percent in most U.S. elections prior to the 1900s.

However, the strength of these party machines was also their weakness. In many cases, parties would do almost anything to win, including directly buying the votes of people, mobilizing new immigrants who could not speak English, and resurrecting dead people from their graves to vote in the elections. In addition, the whole system of patronage, based on doling out government jobs, contracts, and favors, came under attack by reformers in the early 1900s as representing favoritism and corruption. Political reforms such as the **party primary**, in which the party-in-the-electorate rather than the party bosses chose between competing party candidates for a party's nomination, and civil service reform, under which government jobs were filled on the basis of merit instead of party loyalty, did much to ensure that party machines went the way of the dinosaur.

A BRIEF HISTORY OF PARTY ERAS

A striking feature of American history is that, while we have not had a revolutionary war in America since 1776, we have several times changed our political course in rather dramatic ways. One of the many advantages of a democratic form of government is that dramatic changes in policy direction can be effected through the ballot box rather than through bloody revolution. Over the course of two centuries, the two-party system in the United States has been marked by periods of relative stability lasting twenty-five to forty years, with one party tending to maintain a majority of congressional seats and controlling the presidency. These periods of stability are

party machines mass-based party systems in which parties provided services and resources to voters in exchange for votes

party bosses party leaders, usually in an urban district, who exercised tight control over electioneering and patronage

patronage system in which successful party candidates reward supporters with jobs or favors

party primary nomination of party candidates by registered party members rather than party bosses

called **party eras**. Short periods of large-scale change—peaceful revolutions, as it were, signaled by one major **critical election** in which the majority of people shift their political allegiance from one party to another—mark the end of one party era and the beginning of another. Scholars call such a shift in party dominance a **realignment**. In these realignments the coalitions of groups supporting each of the parties change to a new alignment of groups. Though it is not always the case, realignments generally result in parallel changes in governmental policies, reflecting the policy agenda of each party's new coalition. Realignments have been precipitated by major critical events like the Civil War and the Great Depression. Sometimes decisive realignments are not apparent, but rather the old period of stability gradually breaks down without a critical precipitating event in a period of **dealignment**, slowly re-forming into a new and different party era. The United States has gone through six party eras in its two-hundred-years-plus history. *The Big Picture* in this chapter summarizes the six party eras and the realigning elections associated with the transitions between them.

THE PARTIES TODAY

As *The Big Picture* in this chapter indicates, the New Deal coalition supporting the Fifth Party Era has changed, but no single critical election has marked a clear realignment. Rather, we have had an incremental realignment across a relatively long series of elections that has included the massive migration of white southerners to the Republican Party and the less massive but still notable trend for

"THAT'S WHAT'S THE MATTER."

BOSS TWEED. "As long as I count the Votes, what are you going to do about it? say?"

The Granger Collection, New York

Set to Win
Party bosses, like New York City's Boss Tweed, controlled the political process and ruled the ballot box.

party eras extended periods of relative political stability in which one party tends to control both the presidency and Congress

critical election an election signaling a significant change in popular allegiance from one party to another

realignment a substantial and long-term shift in party allegiance by individuals and groups, usually resulting in a change in policy direction

dealignment a trend among voters to identify themselves as independents rather than as members of a major party

Catholics to be less solidly Democratic than they were at the formation of the New Deal. Similarly, African Americans have shifted from somewhat favoring the Democratic Party to overwhelming Democratic identification, a trend solidified with Barack Obama's nomination as the Democratic candidate for the presidency in 2008. The geographic bases of the parties have also changed: the South used to be referred to as the "Solid South," meaning solidly Democratic; it is now the most dependable region for the Republican Party in presidential elections. In recent elections, Democrats have been more likely to win in New England and the mid-Atlantic states—areas where the Republicans were stronger in the 1940s. However, since the 1980s, party identification has strengthened, but along more consistent ideological and less regional lines.[32] In recent years these changes have been labeled as differences between "Red" and "Blue" America, which refers to the southern, midwestern, and mountain support for the Republican Party set against a pattern of coastal and industrial Northeast support for Democrats (see *Snapshot of America:* How Did We Vote in the 2012 Presidential Election?" in Chapter 14).

THE BIG PICTURE: HOW THE AMERICAN POLITICAL PARTIES HAVE EVOLVED

James Madison may have been suspicious of political parties, lumping them in with the dreaded "factions" that he thought were so destructive to liberty, but the fact is that they have always been with us, even in Madison's time. What has varied over time is not the tendency of Americans to form umbrella groups with their ideological fellows to try to affect political change from inside the system, but the particular configurations of those parties. This Big Picture shows how American parties have evolved over time and, since 1879, when data on the current parties begin, just how polarized those parties have been at various times in our history.

First Party Era

In the U.S. party system's elite-driven formative stage, the issue of federal versus states' rights provided the central political cleavage. The Federalists, supporters of a stronger national government, were led by John Adams and Alexander Hamilton, while the Democratic-Republicans (also called Jeffersonian Republicans) supported states' rights and were led by Thomas Jefferson and James Madison.

Second Party Era

Buoyed by an explosion in the number of voters—which swelled from 350,000 in 1824 to well over a million in 1828—Jackson prevailed in the bitter election of 1828, solidifying the coalition of states' rights supporters (lower classes and southern states) over those advocating more power for the national government (business interests and northern states). From the ashes of Adams's failed candidacy came a new party—the Whigs, led by Henry Clay and Daniel Webster, who competed with the Democrats until the mid-1850s.

Third Party Era

Republicans took control of the House of Representatives in 1858, and by 1860 the party's presidential candidate, Abraham Lincoln, had won the presidency as well. After the Civil War, an era of regionalism pitted Republicans (northern and western states) against Democrats (southern and pro-slavery states). Presidential elections were closely contested, but the Republicans tended to hold the edge.

Political Parties in Power

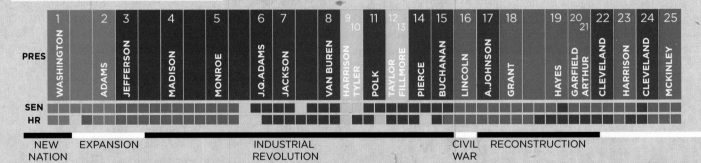

PRES	1 WASHINGTON · 2 ADAMS · 3 JEFFERSON · 4 MADISON · 5 MONROE · 6 J.Q.ADAMS · 7 JACKSON · 8 VAN BUREN · 9 HARRISON 10 TYLER · 11 POLK · 12 TAYLOR 13 FILLMORE · 14 PIERCE · 15 BUCHANAN · 16 LINCOLN · 17 A.JOHNSON · 18 GRANT · 19 HAYES · 20 GARFIELD 21 ARTHUR · 22 CLEVELAND · 23 HARRISON · 24 CLEVELAND · 25 MCKINLEY
SEN	
HR	

NEW NATION | EXPANSION | INDUSTRIAL REVOLUTION | CIVIL WAR | RECONSTRUCTION

1789   **1879**

Ideological Difference Between Parties in Congress

HOUSE 1879-2013

1.0

.5

0

.5

1.0

Party Means on Liberal-Conservative Dimension

Fourth Party Era

Although William Jennings Bryan, a Nebraska Democrat, attempted to merge the Democratic Party with the People's Party in the presidential elections of 1896, he failed to amass enough farmers and industrial labor voters to win. The splitting of votes between the People's Party and the Democrats strengthened the Republican Party. As economic issues subsided in the late 1890s, the regional bases of Republicans and Democrats intensified.

Fifth Party Era

The coalition of voters supporting the New Deal included southern Democrats, Catholic immigrants, blue collar workers, and farmers. Republicans maintained support among business owners and industrialists, and strengthened their regional support in the Northeast and Plains states.

Sixth Party Era

While there is much controversy about whether we have entered a new partisan era at all, and no single critical election has marked the realignment, incremental changes have occurred that are large and so far long-lasting. A realigning process has mobilized African Americans and other minorities into the Democratic Party and southern whites into the Republican Party, creating a greater consistency between partisanship and ideological and issue preferences. The current era is characterized by a narrowly divided nation, intense party competition, and increased gridlock in government.

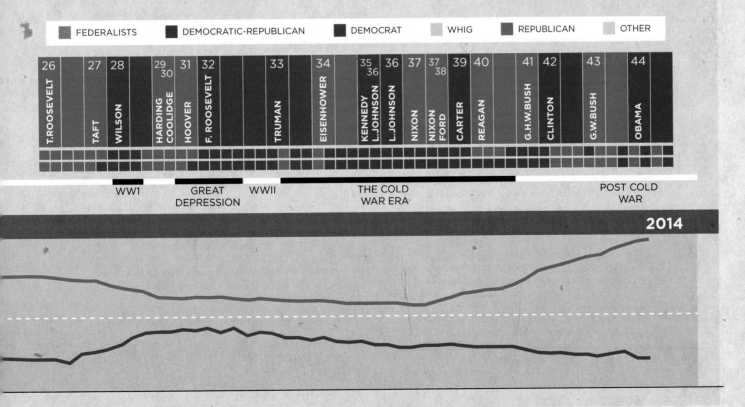

FEDERALISTS · DEMOCRATIC-REPUBLICAN · DEMOCRAT · WHIG · REPUBLICAN · OTHER

26 T.ROOSEVELT · 27 TAFT · 28 WILSON · 29 30 HARDING COOLIDGE · 31 HOOVER · 32 F.ROOSEVELT · 33 TRUMAN · 34 EISENHOWER · 35 36 KENNEDY L.JOHNSON · 36 L.JOHNSON · 37 NIXON · 37 38 NIXON FORD · 39 CARTER · 40 REAGAN · 41 G.H.W.BUSH · 42 CLINTON · 43 G.W.BUSH · 44 OBAMA

WW1 · GREAT DEPRESSION · WWII · THE COLD WAR ERA · POST COLD WAR

2014

The current party era is thus characterized by major changes that have mobilized African Americans and other minorities into the Democratic Party and southern whites into the Republican Party, and a system in which neither party has a clear, enduring majority. These phenomena have led to a much higher incidence of divided government at the national and state levels, with the executive and legislative branches in the hands of different parties. One consequence of divided government is that it makes it difficult for voters to know which party to hold accountable.

The gradual transformation of the New Deal era has helped political scientists see party change as a process of **conflict extension**, rather than one of conflict displacement. The earlier understanding of party change was that a new issue cleavage (say, one that split voters along the lines of businesses and corporations versus workers) would come along and displace older cleavages (for instance, one that divided Americans by industrial versus agrarian interests). Now scholars believe that the process involves new issues coming to be seen as an extension of the original issues. For instance, more recent controversies (over race beginning in 1960s and social issues since the 1970s) have been incorporated into the long-existing Democratic-Republican economic cleavage dating from the formation of the New Deal era in the 1930s.[33] The result is that multiple differences in American politics are now aligned on the partisan divide, making partisanship more meaningful in policy terms, but also more intense as the stakes are higher for more people in terms of which party wins.

PAUSE AND REVIEW:

WHO, WHAT, HOW

Early political leaders designed parties as elite-driven institutions that served their own interests in governing. Laws that gave the vote to all white males, however, meant that politics was less of an elite activity and inspired leaders to create the mass-based political machine. These machines continued to allow leaders total control over the party, but with the perhaps unexpected consequence of politicizing new generations of American immigrants and strengthening American democracy.

Reformers wanted more political accountability—more power for the voters and less for the party bosses. They broke the machines with civil service reform and primary elections. The American party system, though not perfect, has allowed citizens to repeatedly change their government, at times radically, without resort to violence or bloodshed.

IN YOUR OWN WORDS ≫ Outline the evolution of the party system in the United States.

WHAT DO PARTIES DO?
Enhancing democracy by linking citizens and government

We have said that, in general, parties play an important role in American democracy by providing a link between citizens and government, coherence in government, and a vocal opposition. These roles are tied closely to the two main activities of parties: electioneering and governing. Generally, party organizations handle tasks related to electioneering, and the party-in-government handles tasks related to governing. In this section we look at each of these two party functions.

ELECTIONEERING

Electioneering involves recruiting and nominating candidates, defining policy agendas, and getting candidates elected. According to an old saying in politics, "before you can save the world, you must save your seat." One of the primary reasons for the existence of party organizations is to help candidates get and save their seats.

WHO SHOULD RUN? RECRUITING CANDIDATES
Each party's electioneering activities begin months before the general election with the first step of finding candidates to run. There is usually no shortage of ambitious politicians eager to run for high-profile offices like state governor and U.S. senator, but the local parties have to work hard to fill less visible and desirable elective offices like those in the state legislature and county government. It is especially difficult to recruit candidates to run against a current officeholder because incumbents enjoying the advantages of having previously assembled a winning coalition and having a name voters recognize are hard to beat. Incumbents also tend to have a financial advantage; donors and interest groups are more likely to give money to candidates who have proven themselves by winning than to challengers who are largely untested. Unless there is a strong indication that an incumbent is vulnerable, it is hard to recruit opposing candidates.[34]

In response to this reality, parties have begun to target races they think they can win and to devote their resources to those elections. Although they generally try to run candidates in most races, they will target as especially winnable those contests where the seat is open (no incumbent is

conflict extension a theory of party change that sees new issues reinforcing rather than supplanting existing party differences

electioneering the process of getting a person elected to public office

running), or where the incumbent has done something to embarrass himself or herself (perhaps a scandal), or where strong electoral indicators suggest that the party has a good chance of winning the seat (perhaps the party's previous gubernatorial candidate won a strong majority of votes in the district). In these targeted races the party attempts to recruit quality candidates—perhaps known community leaders—and to direct campaign contributions and aid to the targeted contests.[35]

NOMINATING CANDIDATES

The nomination phase is a formal process through which the party chooses a candidate for each elective office to be contested that year. The nomination phase can unite the party behind its candidates, or it can lead to division within the party among the competing factions that support different candidates and different policy agendas. For this reason the nomination phase is one of the most difficult and important tasks for the party.

Today, as we have seen, party primaries are the dominant means for choosing candidates for congressional, statewide, state legislative, and local offices. In most states the primary election occurs three to four months prior to the general election. In these primaries, party members select their party's nominees for the offices on the ballot. There are a number of different types of primaries. Generally, in **closed primaries**, only voters who have registered as a member of a given party are allowed to vote in that party's primary. In **open primaries**, voters simply request one party's ballot on the day of the primary or choose which party's primary they wish to participate in after they enter the polling booth.[36]

Many party officials complain about the open primary system because it permits members of the other party to get

The Granger Collection, New York

Mudslinging Back in the Fourth Party Era

Tough campaigns aren't new to American politics. During the 1896 presidential race, one very partisan novelty item attempted to show what a vote for either candidate would mean: a vote for William McKinley, "Protection to American Industries"; a vote for William Jennings Bryan, "Repudiation, Bankruptcy, and Dishonor."

involved in the nomination process. This occurred on an organized basis in the 2008 presidential primaries, when conservative radio talk show host Rush Limbaugh launched his "Operation Chaos," encouraging Republican voters to cross over and vote in the Democratic primary for Senator Hillary Clinton since McCain was already clearly the Republican nominee. People disagree whether the goal was simply to prolong the battle for the Democratic nomination or to promote the election of the candidate many conservatives thought would be easier to defeat. Regardless, there is some evidence that Limbaugh's electoral mischief may have cost Barack Obama primary wins in Texas and Indiana.[37] Because voters who are not necessarily loyal to a party are allowed to vote, open primaries can weaken political parties.[38]

In presidential primaries, voters do not choose the actual candidates they want to run for president; rather, they elect delegates. Delegates are usually party activists who support a candidate and run for the opportunity to go to the party's national **nominating convention** the summer before the election and cast a vote for him or her. We discuss the mechanics of presidential election nominating conventions in more detail in Chapter 14.

> **closed primaries** primary elections in which only registered party members may vote
>
> **open primaries** primary elections in which eligible voters do not need to be registered party members
>
> **nominating convention** formal party gathering to choose candidates

It's a Party for the Party
The national nominating conventions have evolved into full-blown spectacles, with balloons, streamers, celebrities, and 24-7 information, action, and events. President Barack Obama and Vice President Joe Biden accepted their nominations for reelection at the Democratic National Convention in Charlotte, North Carolina.

In addition to nominating candidates, party conventions have the important function of bringing the party faithful together to set the policy priorities of the party, to elect party officers, and, not least, to provide a sense of solidarity and community for the activists. After working long and hard all year in their communities, party activists find it restoring and rejuvenating to come together with like-minded people to affirm the principles and policies they hold in common.

The primary process and the practice of televising convention proceedings have dramatically changed the nature of these national conventions. Before reforms in the late 1960s that ensured that candidates would be chosen by elected delegates rather than party bosses, national conventions were filled with political bargaining and intrigue and conflict over platform issues. Delegates going into the convention did not always know who would be the party's nominee.[39] By 1972, when many states had adopted the primary system, delegates were committed to presidential candidates before the convention began, meaning that there was little question about who would get the nomination. Floor battles at the convention can still happen, however, as they did in 1980 during the late Massachusetts senator Ted Kennedy's challenge to President Jimmy Carter for the Democratic nomination. The prospect of such a divisive move can throw party members into a panic, as it did toward the end of the primaries in 2008, when Democrats feared Senator Clinton would take her battle for the

nomination all the way to the August convention. But generally speaking, today's presidential nominating conventions merely rubber-stamp the primary victor.

The influence of television on the national conventions has been considerable as well. In the 1950s the new medium of television began covering the national conventions. With a national audience watching, the parties began to use these conventions as a public springboard for the presidential campaign. It was important that the party appear to be strong and unified, to maximize its electoral chances. The riot-torn 1968 Democratic convention in Chicago highlights the importance of party unity: young people, most of them Democrats, protested the Vietnam War and the selection process that led to the nomination of Vice President Hubert H. Humphrey, a supporter of U.S. involvement in the war. The protests, conflict, and disarray of the Democratic convention, which television brought into America's living rooms, may have played a role in Humphrey's loss to Richard Nixon in the general election.

Even though skirmishes between the ideological wings within both parties flare up occasionally, for the most part, conventions have turned into choreographed events, designed to show, in prime time, that the party is unified behind its presidential candidate. In fact, conventions have generally become so routine and predictable that since 2000 the networks have devoted very little prime-time coverage to them, although the cable stations have picked up the slack. In 2008, however, things were a little more exciting and networks and cable stations alike showed the major convention speeches, with Obama's and McCain's acceptance speeches garnering more than 38 million viewers each.[40] The 2012 election returned to the status quo—the networks showed only one hour of prime-time convention coverage per party, forcing the Republicans to move Ann Romney's speech so that it would be covered. Viewership was down as well; only 57 percent of households watched at least one convention, rather than the 64.5 percent who tuned in in 2008.[41]

DEFINING POLICY AGENDAS After a political party nominates its candidates, one of the party's main roles is to develop a policy agenda, which represents policies that a party's candidates agree to promote when campaigning and to pursue when governing. The development of such an agenda involves much politicking and gamesmanship as each faction of the party tries to get its views written into the party platform, which we discussed earlier. Whoever wins control over the party platform has decisive input on how the campaign proceeds.

GENERAL ELECTIONS In the election phase the role of the party changes from choosing among competing candidates within the party and developing policy agendas to getting its nominated candidates elected. Traditionally the party's role here was to "organize and mobilize" voters, but increasingly they are becoming the providers of extensive services to candidates.

The advent of mass communication—radio, television, and most recently the Internet—has changed the way a party and its candidates relate to voters. When party organizations were the major source of information about a candidate, elections were party centered. Now, with mass communication, elections are more candidate centered. Candidates can effectively run their own campaigns with their own staffs—buying television and radio ad time and presenting themselves on their own terms—and party affiliation is just one of the many characteristics of a candidate, not the sole identifying feature. This shift toward candidate-centered politics is part of a larger transformation in campaigning from the labor-intensive campaigns of the past, which depended on party workers getting out the vote for the party's candidates, to today's capital-intensive campaigns, which depend on the tools of mass communication and money to buy airtime.[42] It does depend, however, on the candidate. In 2008 Barack Obama's unprecedented fundraising ability meant that he had the wherewithal to conduct his own campaign, whereas John McCain, until his choice of Sarah Palin as his running mate energized his base, was more dependent on his party's efforts on his behalf.[43]

Consistent with this change toward capital-intensive campaigns, today's political parties primarily offer candidate services, including fundraising and training in campaign tactics, instruction on compliance with election laws, and public opinion polling and professional campaign assistance.[44]

Money, of course, is central in a capital-intensive campaign, and the parties are major fundraising organizations. Because of a loophole in the campaign finance laws that allowed parties to collect contributions of unlimited size from donors, parties became major banks for candidates in the 1990s (see Chapter 14). These unlimited funds, called **soft money**, were used by the parties for party-building

efforts such as voter registration and issue development activities.[45] Both parties distributed money to candidates either by giving cash directly to the candidates or by supplementing the campaign efforts of candidates with television and radio issue advertising. Although this issue advertising was supposed to represent an "independent" expenditure of money—candidates were not allowed to participate in the decisions about how the money was spent or direct the content of the issue ads—in practice, there was generally much correspondence between the issue ads of the party and the campaign ads of the candidates, because parties simply mimicked the ads of their candidates.

Soft money raising was seriously limited in 2002 by the Bipartisan Campaign Reform Act, or BCRA. Especially important to the parties was the provision that did away with their ability to collect unlimited soft money contributions. Nevertheless, practices like "bundling"—the collection of many individual contributions by political action committees (PACs)—and other apparent loopholes allowed the parties to continue their role as major providers of campaign services to candidates.[46]

In 2010, however, the Supreme Court fundamentally changed the financial and political landscape of electoral politics in America with its decision in *Citizens United v. Federal Elections Commission*. As we will discuss in Chapter 14, the Court's decision allows individuals and organizations to give unlimited amounts of money to so-called Super PACs, which are independent of the candidates' and even the parties' campaign efforts. It means that those with deep pockets and a willingness to spend have the ability to exercise enormous influence in the electoral arena—and to do so anonymously. It is too early to gauge the full impact of the decision, but legions of critics argue that the Court's *Citizens United* decision is a fundamental threat to democratic equality.[47]

In congressional elections, both parties spend a great deal of money on the targeted contests we discussed earlier.[48] For targeted seats the parties supplement their

soft money unregulated campaign contributions by individuals, groups, or parties that promote general election activities but do not directly support individual candidates

FrumForum.com

David Frum is a waiter. And no, that doesn't mean the former Bush speechwriter, author of eight books and editor of the *Frum Forum,* a web site "dedicated to the modernization and renewal of the Republican party and the conservative movement,"[1] has opted for a second career in restaurant service.

According to Frum the political world is divided into two types of people: waiters and chasers. "A waiter is somebody who has a vision of where his country is going and parks himself at that position to wait for the country. Churchill was a waiter, Reagan was a waiter, but also Lyndon LaRouche was a waiter—it's not necessarily a good thing to be a waiter. Every crackpot, crank, and lunatic is also a waiter. The chasers are those always trying to catch up to where they think the people are at that moment." Chasers—Frum mentions Newt Gingrich, Bill Clinton, and Rush Limbaugh—adopt the values of the constituency they want to lead; waiters believe the world will eventually come around to adopting their view.

It is being a waiter that enables Frum to be at once an ardent member of the Republican Party and also one of its toughest critics. At least one criticism recently cost him a job. In the wake of the passage of the Obama health care bill, he argued publicly that by refusing to work with Democrats on the bill in hopes of denying Obama a victory, Republicans ended up having to swallow a more liberal policy than they would have if they had negotiated with Democrats. In response, he was fired from his position as a fellow at the American Enterprise Institute, which caused him to be even more critical of the party, arguing that the Republican practice of not tolerating dissent among its members was leading to a closed system that would ultimately weaken the party.

It wasn't a comfortable position for Frum, but discomfort is part of the job of being a waiter.

Born into a liberal Canadian family (he became a U.S. citizen in 2007), Frum moved right in college "under the impact of events." He says, "The late 1970s felt like the end of the world, the end of western civilization. . . . Then came the Reagan years and the battle to turn that situation around, and all of us young Reaganites felt that the Reagan people did a very good job of keeping us mobilized and motivated. . . ." He went on to law school at Harvard, and by the late 1980s he had become an editorial writer at the *Wall Street Journal.* It was there that he got his first taste of running counter to party orthodoxy, exploring the criticism of U.S. economic trends that it had benefited the wealthiest Americans but had left the least wealthy falling farther behind. "It was a very important debate, and as I plunged into the study of this thing, it became very clear to me that it was true. . . . And then I was also struck by the inability of my conservative colleagues to process this information. That is, if something is true, you can either say, 'it's a bad thing,' in which case you need to figure what we do about it, or 'it doesn't matter, we don't care whether it is true,' but you don't have the option of just saying, 'I don't see it, it's not there'." His work on the successes and limits of the Reagan Revolution resulted in his first book, *Dead Right.*

issue ads by sending party leaders into the district to raise money for the candidate. This move has the added benefit of giving the candidate greater media visibility. When the president's popularity is high, he is a positive campaign presence for his party's congressional candidates. If his approval ratings have fallen by the midterm, his congressional campaign appearances are more limited to fundraising events for his party's congressional candidates in closed gatherings of the party faithful with whom he typically remains a big draw. For the party that does not control the presidency, congressional leaders and presidential hopefuls (sometimes one and the same) usually fill this void.

GOVERNING

Once a party's candidates have been elected to office, attention turns to the matter of governance. **Governing** involves the two major jobs of controlling government by organizing and providing leadership for the legislative and/or

> **governing** activities directed toward controlling the distribution of political resources by providing executive and legislative leadership, enacting agendas, mobilizing support, and building coalitions

His writing brought him to the attention of the incoming George W. Bush administration in 2000, and he was offered a job as a White House speechwriter, where he was credited with the famous "axis of evil" phrase that justified Bush's foreign policy. His service put him in an uncomfortable position again when, in 2005, Bush nominated Harriet Miers to fill a vacancy on the Supreme Court. Frum's work with Miers in the White House, where she served as staff secretary, convinced him that she was not Supreme Court caliber. "It reflected a deep problem," he says. "[Bush] nominates her in October 2005, so this is after that bloody summer in Iraq, and after Hurricane Katrina, and it begins to raise the question—are these things all accidents? Or is something going wrong with the way this administration makes decisions?"

His willingness to criticize the administration of which he had once been a part made him a target in Republican circles, chiefly on Fox News, where the attacks got personal. And it cemented Frum's role as a waiter, a role he maintains today. Unlike some disaffected Republicans, like Andrew Sullivan (see *Profiles in Citizenship* in Chapter 15), who continue to call themselves conservative but who have left the Republican Party behind, Frum says, "I have not given up on the movement. I am not going to." Though he adds ruefully, "They may give up on me." Even if that

happens, however, Frum knows what to do.

While he waits, here are some of his observations on American politics:

> "IT'S NOT THAT PARTISANSHIP IS INTRINSICALLY EVIL; IN BRITAIN IT'S FINE. . . . BUT IN AMERICA, PARTISANSHIP IS A PROBLEM BECAUSE THE GOVERNMENT CAN'T GOVERN."

On partisanship:

It's a question about in whose interest do you govern, how do you govern, how do you solve problems, how do you work with people that disagree with you? How important is consensus? This is not a parliamentary political system, and if you try to run it like a parliamentary system, you wreck it. In a parliamentary system the government has enormous power. . . . The job of the other side is to shoot you down, embarrass you, and trip you up—but the other side of the political aisle cannot interfere with the working of the government. There's no filibuster, there's no veto, and the government governs. The other side tries to bring them down and they usually succeed, and at that point you

have these very rapid alternations of power. . . .

In the congressional system, the ability to sabotage, to stop the government from governing is very great, and the American system appears to work best with a high degree of consensus. It's not that partisanship is intrinsically evil; in Britain it's fine. In Britain it's indispensable; if you didn't have intense partisanship in Britain, the government would be too strong. But in America, partisanship is a problem because the government can't govern.

On keeping the republic:

Do not entrap yourself in a closed information system. Closed information systems require the complicity of the audience because information now is so abundant that it takes great effort to avoid coming into contact with it. Political science suggests that people are working harder and harder to avoid coming into contact with unwelcome information. And as I look at the Republican Party, many of these problems are not problems of leadership but of followership and the citizens also need to work harder at their job.

1. "About," *FrumForum*, www.frumforum.com/about.

Source: David Frum spoke with Christine Barbour and Gerald Wright on September 17, 2010.

---

executive branches and enacting the party's policy agendas. Party governance gives voters a means to make office-holders accountable for failed and successful governing policies,[49] and it can provide an extraconstitutional framework that can lend some coherence to the fragmentation produced by separation of powers and federalism.

CONTROLLING GOVERNMENT
When a party "controls" government at the national level and in the states, it means that the party determines who occupies the leadership positions in the branch of government in which the party has a majority. Thus, when Barack Obama won the presidency in 2008, he—and, by extension, the

Democrats—controlled the top leadership positions in the executive branch of the government (cabinet secretaries and undersecretaries of agencies and the White House staff). For the first two years of Obama's administration, his party also controlled the legislative branch. This means the Democrats selected the majority leader in the Senate and the Speaker of the House, controlled committee assignments, selected chairs of legislative committees, and had a majority of seats on each committee. Controlling government also means that the legislative leadership controls the legislative calendar and the rules governing legislative debate and amendments (especially in the House).

AP Photo/Charles Dharapak

Leader of the Nation, Leader of the Party

The president acts as official head of his or her party and the party leadership handles prioritizing of policy and corralling of votes, but the day-to-day activities of party strategy—from fundraising to recruiting to acting as party spokesperson—falls to the party chair. Here, Obama meets with Rep. Debbie Wasserman Schultz, of Florida, who also serves as chair of the Democratic Party.

The job of party governance in Congress has been made more challenging in recent years by the increasingly frequent use of the filibuster by the minority party in the Senate to stop everything from simple nominations to fill executive agency offices and staff the federal courts to legislation with clear majority (but less than three-fifths) support in the chamber. It is much more difficult to govern with polarized parties in a system in which power is checked at almost every turn. When then–Pennsylvania senator Arlen Specter left the Republican Party in April 2009, Democrats gained a filibuster-proof majority in the Senate for a brief period of time, until Sen. Ted Kennedy's seat was filled by Republican Scott Brown in January 2010. After the 2010 midterm elections, Democrats still maintained a small majority in the Senate, but Republicans were able to filibuster almost any legislation or nominations that reached the Senate. In addition, control of the House of Representatives passed to the Republicans, and with a divided government, the job of governing became even more difficult for both parties.

EXECUTION OF POLICY AGENDAS AND ACCOUNTABILITY Of course the ultimate goal of a political party is not only to choose who occupies the leadership positions in government but also to execute its policy agenda—the party's solutions to the nation's problems. Whether the problem is defined as a lack of affordable health care, insufficient national security, high taxes,

distressed communities, unemployment, illegal immigration, or a failing economy, each party represents an alternative vision for how to approach and solve problems.

We have already noted that significant differences exist between the platforms and policy agendas of the two major parties. The question here is whether the parties actually implement their policy agendas. On this score, parties do fairly well. About two-thirds of the platform promises of the party that controls the presidency are implemented.[50]

The classic example of a party fulfilling its campaign promises was the first hundred days of the New Deal under the Democratic Party. Running on a platform that called for an activist national government, Franklin Roosevelt and the congressional Democrats were elected in a landslide in 1932. Under Roosevelt's leadership, Congress proceeded to pass New Deal legislation designed to regulate the economy and banking industry, and to provide government programs to help farmers and the unemployed. After maintaining control of Congress in 1934, the Democrats went on to pass one of the most important pieces of legislation in American history, the Social Security Act (1935). Similarly, recent presidents have been successful in passing the signature issues of their campaigns. Important examples include President George W. Bush's tax cuts and the No Child Left Behind Act, and President Obama's Patient Protection and Affordable Care Act and the financial reform bill. These were major changes in the direction of national policy.

The greater competitiveness of the parties in the current era, however, means that divided government happens much more frequently than in earlier party systems, and as we saw in Chapter 8, presidential success typically plummets when the president's party loses control of Congress. This was certainly the case for Presidents Bush and Clinton following the midterm elections that brought them divided government for parts of their administrations and was the case for President Obama as well following the 2010 midterms.

Within the context of the responsible party model, the ability of a party to accomplish its stated agenda is extremely important for voter accountability. As the party in power promotes its policy agenda and its ideas for how government should solve problems, it provides voters with an opportunity to hold the party responsible for its successes or failures. Voters then determine if a party's candidates should be rewarded through reelection or punished by "throwing the rascals out." In 1932 the persistence of the Depression convinced voters that the GOP policies had failed and led them to replace the Republicans with the Democrats and their solutions. After seeing Democrats implement the New Deal in 1933 and 1934, the voters cast their ballots to keep Roosevelt and his party in power, thus rewarding the party for its efforts to deal with the Great Depression. As we have pointed out, such clear accountability is more difficult under divided government, when voters do not know which party to hold accountable.

PAUSE AND REVIEW:

WHO, WHAT, HOW

It is hard to imagine any actors in American politics *not* having a stake in the activities of electioneering and governing. For political parties, the stakes are high. They want electoral victory for their candidates and control of government. They try to achieve these goals by using the rules they themselves have created, as well as the electoral rules imposed by the state and federal governments.

Candidates seeking to get elected to office, and to build a reputation once there, engage in candidate-centered campaigns with the assistance of the party organization and the party-in-the-electorate. They also encourage the election of other members of their party.

Party activists want to gain and keep control of the party's agenda, to ensure that it continues to serve the causes they believe in. They participate in primaries and hold the elected officials accountable.

Citizens value their limited government, but paradoxically they also get impatient when government seems to grind to a halt in a morass of partisan bickering. The policy efficiency and coherence that parties can create can dissolve the gridlock, but this comes at the potential cost of a more powerful government. When voters elect a divided government, gridlock is almost inevitable.

IN YOUR OWN WORDS >> Explain how parties connect citizens and government.

CHARACTERISTICS OF THE AMERICAN PARTY SYSTEM
Ideologically moderate and decentralized

Party systems vary tremendously around the world. In some countries, the governmental structure has only one major party. This single party usually maintains its power through institutional controls that forbid the development of

opposition parties (totalitarian states like China and the old Soviet Union), or through corruption and informal means of physical coercion (Mexico, until recently), or through military control (Burma, Libya, and Sudan). These systems essentially prevent any meaningful party competition. Without choices at the ballot box, democracy is impossible. Some countries, on the other hand, have so many parties that often no single party can amass enough votes to control government. When that happens, the parties may try to cooperate with other parties, governing together as a coalition. Parties can represent ideological positions, social classes, or even more informal group interests. Parties can put tight constraints on what elected leaders can do, making them toe the "party line," or they can give only loose instructions that leaders can obey as they please. The truth is, there is no single model of party government.

Among all the possibilities, the American party system is distinctive, but it too fails to fit a single model. It is predominantly a two-party system, although third-party movements have come and gone throughout our history. For decades political scientists observed that the American system tended toward ideological moderation, at least compared with other multiple-party countries. However, the parties have changed and today they are at least as far apart ideologically as they have been at any point in our long national history. This polarization has grown in a highly decentralized party system with fluctuating levels of party discipline. We explore each of these characteristics in this section.

TWO PARTIES

As we have seen, the United States has a two-party system. Throughout most of the United States' history, in fact, two specific parties, the Democrats and the Republicans, have been the only parties with a viable chance of winning the vast majority of elective offices. As a consequence, officeholders representing these two parties dominate the governing process.

WHY A TWO-PARTY SYSTEM? The United States—along with countries like Great Britain and New Zealand—stands in sharp contrast to other democratic party systems around the world, such as those found in Sweden, France, Israel, and Italy, which have three, four, five, or more major political parties, respectively. The United States has experienced few of the serious political splits—stemming from such divisive issues as language, religion, or social conflict—that are usually responsible for multiple parties. The lack of deep and enduring cleavages among the American people is reinforced by the longevity of the Democratic and Republican Parties themselves. Both parties predate the Industrial Revolution, the urbanization and suburbanization of the population, and the rise of the information age, and they have weathered several wars, including the Civil War and two world wars, as well as numerous economic recessions and depressions. One scholar compared each party to a "massive geological formation composed of different strata, with each representing a constituency or group added to the party in one political era and then subordinated to new strata produced in subsequent political eras." Proponents from one era may continue to support a political party even if it undergoes changes in issue positions. These political parties persist not just because of the support they can attract today but because of the accumulation of support over time.[51]

But the most important reason that the United States maintains a two-party system is that the rules of the system, in most cases designed by members of the two parties themselves, make it very difficult for third parties to do well on a permanent basis.[52] As we saw in Chapter 4, for instance, democracies that have some form of proportional representation are more likely to have multiple parties. These governments distribute seats in the legislature to parties by virtue of the proportion of votes that each party receives in the election. For example, if a party receives 20 percent of the vote, it will receive roughly 20 percent of the seats in the legislature. Countries with proportional representation systems have more parties than those with single-member plurality-vote systems, because small parties can still participate in government even though they do not get a majority of the votes. In the United States, in contrast, we use the single-member district electoral system. This means that the candidate who receives the most votes in a defined district (generally with only one seat) wins that seat, and the loser gets nothing, except perhaps some campaign debt. This type of winner-take-all system creates strong incentives for voters to cast their ballots for one of the two established parties because voters know they are effectively throwing away their votes when they vote for a third-party candidate.

The United States has other legal barriers that reinforce the two-party system. In most states, legislators from both parties have created election laws that regulate each major party's activities, but these laws also protect the parties from competition from other parties. For example, state election laws ensure the place of both major parties on the ballot and make it difficult for third parties to gain ballot access. Many states require that potential independent or third-party candidates gather a large number of signature petitions before their names can be placed on the ballot. Another common state law is that before a third party can conduct a primary to select its candidate, it must have earned some minimum percentage of the votes in the previous election.

Third parties are also hampered by existing federal election laws. These laws regulate the amount of campaign contributions that presidential candidates can receive from individuals and PACs and provide dollar-for-dollar federal matching money for both major parties' presidential campaigns, if the candidates agree to limit their spending to a predetermined amount. However, third-party candidates cannot claim federal campaign funds until after the election is over, and even then their funds are limited by the percentage of past and current votes they received. As an additional hurdle, they need to have gained about 5 percent or more of the national vote in order to be eligible for federal funds.[53]

Access to the national media can also be a problem for third parties. Even though regulations are in place to ensure that the broadcast media give candidates equal access to the airwaves, Congress has insisted on a special exception that limits participation in televised debates to candidates from the two major parties, which kept Ross Perot out of the debates in 1996,[54] Ralph Nader and Patrick Buchanan out in 2000, Nader out again in 2004 and 2008, and Bob Barr out in 2008.

THIRD-PARTY MOVEMENTS Just because the Democrats and the Republicans have dominated our party system does not mean that they have gone unchallenged. Over the years, numerous third-party movements have tried to alter the partisan make-up of American politics. These parties have usually arisen either to represent specific issues that the parties failed to address, like Prohibition in 1869, or to promote ideas that were not part of the ideological spectrum covered by the existing parties, like socialist parties, never very popular here, or the Libertarian Party. In general, third parties have sprung up from the grassroots or have broken off from an existing party (the latter are referred to as splinter parties). In the case of the current Tea Party movement, the new party is not actually distinct from the Republican Party (most Tea Party members identify themselves as conservative Republicans), and as long as the Republican Party adopts most of the issues the Tea Partiers care about, they are not likely to separate and form an organized party of their own. In many cases third parties have been headed up by a strong leader who carries much of the momentum for the party's success on his or her own shoulders (for example, Teddy Roosevelt, George Wallace, and Ross Perot).

Third parties can have a dramatic impact on presidential election outcomes. When the winning margins are large, third parties may be merely a blip on the screen, but when the electorate is narrowly divided, the presence of third-party candidates is fraught with peril for Democrats and Republicans. After he voted for Nader in 2000, Green Party member Matt Duss got telephone calls from Democrats. "Are you !#%!b GREENS out of your !# minds?" they screamed into his ear.[55] Some joked that GREEN stood for "Get Republicans Elected Every November." Did Ralph Nader cost Al Gore the election? Perhaps he did, but that oversimplifies a complex event. As one analyst put it, Nader undoubtedly cost Gore many votes, but Pat Buchanan's Reform Party candidacy cost Bush as well. Although Buchanan won only 450,000 votes overall, had he not been in the race, Bush arguably could have won narrow victories in Iowa, New Mexico, Oregon, and Wisconsin, and won the Electoral College without the help of Florida.[56] Many Republicans believe that Bush's father was also hurt in his 1992 reelection bid against Bill Clinton by the candidacy of Ross Perot. Third-party challenges are not just a lose-lose proposition for the major parties, however. In an effort to prevent third parties from taking crucial support away from them, many major-party candidates, as we saw earlier, try to appropriate their issues, thereby broadening their base of support. Thus, although third parties are, in most cases, short lived, they nonetheless fill a significant role in the American party system.

THINKING OUTSIDE THE BOX

Are the American people well represented by a two-party system?

© David J. & Janice L. Frent Collection/Corbis

INCREASING IDEOLOGICAL POLARIZATION

Compared to many other party systems—for instance, the Italian system, which offers voters a variety of choice ranging from the communist-based Democratic Left Party to the ultra-conservative neo-Fascist National Alliance Party—the United States has traditionally had a rather limited menu of viable parties: the moderately liberal Democratic Party versus a moderately conservative Republican Party. Both parties continue to agree on the fundamental features of American politics—including the Bill of Rights, the Constitution, and a capitalist free-enterprise system—but the policy differences between the parties have grown. Rather than the 1950s characterization of the parties as "tweedledum and tweedledee," today there stands, as we saw in Chapter 2, an ideological gulf between the parties on a host of central issues of the economy, the distribution of the nation's resources, and the role of government in our private lives. As much as ever in our history, the Democratic Party holds that government policy should actively promote the welfare of the middle class and the poor, largely by extending the enlarged role of the state that defined the New Deal. Today's Republicans, in contrast, want to greatly reduce the role of government in the market and let individual initiative and the workings of unfettered capitalism settle questions of resource allocation while giving the state a stronger role in legislating conformance to "traditional family values." The result is a country that has consensus on the fundamentals of government structure but with parties that are divided sharply over the role of government in the economy and our lives.

DECENTRALIZED PARTY ORGANIZATIONS

In American political parties, local and state party organizations make their own decisions. They have affiliations with the national party organization but no obligations to obey its dictates other than selecting delegates to the national

When It Comes to Parties, Three's a Crowd

No third-party candidate has ever been elected president, but that does not mean they are without significant impact. In 2000, Green Party candidate Ralph Nader was on the ballot in forty-four states, and carried 2.7 percent of the popular vote, which may have had an impact on the outcome in very close states like Florida. If Nader had not run, experts agree that Al Gore would have won the presidency.

convention. Decision making is dispersed across the organization rather than centralized at the national level; power tends to move from the bottom up instead of from the top down. This means that local concerns and politics dominate the lower levels of the party, molding its structure, politics, and policy agendas. Local parties and candidates can have a highly distinctive character and may look very different from the state or national parties. Political scientists refer to this as a *fragmented party organization*.

American parties are organized (or disorganized) into several major divisions spread across the national, state, and local levels. Most visible are the national committees, the Republican National Committee (RNC) and the Democratic National Committee (DNC). They are responsible for taking care of the national parties' business between their national presidential nominating conventions. They provide a good deal of campaign support and fundraising assistance, especially to presidential candidates. After these are the congressional campaign committees, one for each party in the House and in the Senate, which are responsible for trying to elect party members with the goal of keeping or gaining party control.

At the subnational level are state and local party organizations. Since the 1970s the state organizations have become more professionally organized and staffed, providing increased levels of support, often with funds from the national committees. Increasingly, the state legislative leaders have what are called "leadership PACs," which they use to gather funds from activists and interest groups and funnel those into competitive contests in their efforts to gain partisan majorities in the state legislatures. Finally, there are local party organizations, which are generally much weaker,

BIPARTISANSHIP

often existing only on a part-time basis staffed by volunteers. The local organizations have such a structure because the vast majority of local elections, like those for city councils and school boards, are nonpartisan.[57]

The decentralized character of American parties means that the national organization does not have financial or, especially, ideological control of the state and local organizations. This makes it possible for new factions within the parties to capture local and then state organizations as a base for influencing the directions of the parties more generally. Consider, for example, the successful efforts of the Christian Right in the Republican Party in the late 1980s. Building on dedicated local volunteers and church networks, the movement established itself as a powerful force in the Republican Party nationally. The Tea Party movement today is attempting to follow a similar strategy, although national media attention helps it focus its efforts at nonlocal levels as well.

The consequences of decentralization can also be seen in the occasional frustration of national officials when an embarrassing candidate is able to pull off a primary victory. Among many examples is David Duke, a former Ku Klux Klan member who ran for governor of Louisiana in 1991, and Alvin Greene, an unemployed army veteran without a campaign or even a web site, who captured the Democratic nomination for the U.S. Senate in South Carolina in 2010. In these cases the national organizations are powerless to do anything other than withhold support. Usually, as in these cases, the embarrassing candidate just loses and is forgotten.

The biggest reason for the fragmentation of control of American parties is federalism and political reforms like the direct primary. All of our candidates, even the president and vice president, are elected in state (or local) elections that are to some extent governed by state laws. Thus members of the state legislatures and Congress are attached primarily to the state parties that constitute much of the electoral base. Of course, even their ability to run depends on their surviving the

local context of contested district or state primary elections, and the national parties have at best only indirect influence on these.

Decentralization, however, does not mean that local parties are necessarily different from their national counterparts. Consider the possible effect of party activists. While their influence means that the base may control the leadership (decentralization), rather than the other way around, power may be less fragmented as the base strengthens its hold on the entire party. The more conservative base of the Republican Party has long had greater control at the local level, but national Republican policy was tempered by the need to get along with Democrats in Congress and to appeal to the moderate voter in national elections. When the party took control of Congress in 1994, however, members of Congress were better able to impose their more ideological perspective at the upper levels of the party.

CHANGES IN PARTY DISCIPLINE OVER TIME

Historically, American party organizations have been notable for their lack of a hierarchical (top-down) power structure, and the officials elected to government from the two parties have not felt compelled to take their orders from the top. This looseness within the parties was a continuing source of frustration for the advocates of the responsible party model of government. They wished for greater **party discipline**—the ability of party leaders to keep members voting together in a cohesive way—which was more typical of European parliamentary parties. This lack of party unity among legislators in the United States reflected the diversity of opinions within the parties, among both activists and rank-and-file identifiers. We have seen, however, that significant changes have occurred in the parties' base coalitions, especially in the movement of southern conservatives from the Democratic to the Republican Party. This shift, with similar but less dramatic ideological alignment in the non-southern states, has resulted in a party system in which we have greater ideological agreement within the parties and greater ideological distance between them.

These changes in the electoral environment of Congress have helped create the conditions for greatly heightened partisanship in Congress. One factor is simply the greater ideological agreement within the parties coupled with an increased (and seemingly increasing) ideological gulf between the parties. This is reinforced by stronger party leadership made possible by rules changes in the House of Representa-

> **party discipline** ability of party leaders to bring party members in the legislature into line with the party program

Republican National Committee ● Democratic National Committee ●

tives in the 1970s.[58] For example, in 2006, Democrat Nancy Pelosi became the first woman Speaker of the House and led the Democrats with a firm and expert hand. She gained a reputation among some as "one of the most powerful Speakers in modern history."[59] Pelosi's ability to lead the House Democrats and to pass President Obama's program was made possible by the increased ideological homogeneity within the Democratic Party that is an important aspect of the polarized political parties of the contemporary era.[60] The Republican victories in 2010 made John Boehner, R-Ohio, the new Speaker of the House. His freshman class was largely supported by the Tea Party movement, and their energy and unbending commitment to conservative principles repeatedly made it difficult for Boehner to reach compromises with his Democratic colleagues or the Obama administration, frequently causing him to back off of positions he had taken to keep his party base happy.[61]

PAUSE AND REVIEW:

WHO, WHAT, HOW

The United States' two-party system is a direct result of, first, the kind of electoral system that the founders designed and, second, the rules that lawmakers in the two parties have put into place to make it difficult for third parties to thrive. This does not stop the drive for third parties, however, when dissatisfied voters seek representation of ideas and issues that the two major parties do not address.

The American parties are, in general, ideologically moderate. Activists want parties to take more extreme stances and to act on their principles. Voting in primaries has enabled them to pull the parties in a more extreme, but also more disciplined, direction. The losers here are the general voting public, who cannot always find a moderate alternative to vote for. Some scholars argue that these voters may register their wishes for moderation by splitting their tickets, resulting in a divided government that is less able to act decisively.[62]

IN YOUR OWN WORDS >> Describe the way in which the American party system works.

>> THE CITIZENS AND POLITICAL PARTIES
Learning to tolerate the messiness of democracy

We began this chapter by noting that, for all their importance to the success of democracy, political parties have

been perennially unpopular with the public. Scholars tell us that one reason for this unpopularity is that voters are turned off by partisan bickering and each party's absorption with its own ideological agenda instead of a concern for the public interest.[63] In this section we suggest the possibility that politics is *about* bickering, and that bickering may itself be a major safeguard of American democracy.

We defined politics at the start of this book as the struggle over who gets what and how they get it in society, a process that involves cooperation, bargaining, compromise, and trade-offs. We remarked at the outset that Americans often see politics as a dirty business, but that it is really our saving grace since it allows us to resolve conflict without violence. The difficulty is that Americans do not see politics as our saving grace. Perhaps we have enjoyed relative domestic tranquility for so long that we do not know what it is like to have to take our disagreements to the streets and the battlefields to resolve them. Some researchers have found that when Americans look at government, they do not focus primarily on the policy *outcomes* but on the political *process* itself. Although policies themselves are increasingly complex and difficult to grasp, most of us are able to understand the way in which the policies are created, the give and take, the influence of organized interests, and the rules of the game. In other words, finding the *what* of politics to be complicated, most citizens focus their attention and evaluation on the *how*. We are not helped out here by the media, which, rather than explaining the substance of policy debate to American citizens, instead treat politics like one long, bitterly contested sporting event.

Given citizen dissatisfaction with partisan politics in America, where do we go from here? What is the citizen's role in all this, if it is not to stand on the sidelines and be cynical about partisan politics? Political scientists John Hibbing and Elizabeth Theiss-Morse argue that the problem lies with a lack of citizen education—education not about the facts of American government but about the process. "Citizens' big failure," they claim, "is that they lack an appreciation for the ugliness of democracy."[64] Democratic politics is messy by definition; it is authoritarian government that is neat, tidy, and efficient. Perhaps the first thing we as citizens should do is to recognize that partisanship is not a failure of politics; it is the heart of politics.

At the beginning of this chapter, we said there were three ways in which parties enhanced democracy in America. We have given considerable attention to the first two: the linkage between citizen and government and the coherence among the branches of government that parties can provide. The third way parties serve democracy is in providing for a vocal opposition, an adversarial voice that scrutinizes and critiques the opposite side, helping to keep the process and the people involved honest. This is akin to the watchdog function the media are said to serve, but it is more institutionalized, a self-monitoring process that keeps both parties on their toes. To be sure, this self-monitoring certainly can, and does, deteriorate into some of the uglier aspects of American democracy, but it also serves as the guardian of political freedom. Where such partisan squabbling is not allowed, political choice and democratic accountability cannot survive either.

There are three things citizens can do to offset their frustration with the partisan course of American politics:

1. *Get real.* Having realistic expectations of the process of democratic government can certainly help head off disillusionment when those expectations are not met.

2. *Get involved.* Parties, because of their decentralized nature, are one of the places in American politics to which citizens have easy access. The only reason the more extreme ideologues hold sway in American politics is that the rest of us allow them to, by leaving the reins in their hands.

3. *Don't split your ticket.* If you are truly disturbed at what you see as government paralysis, try voting for a straight party ticket. Even if you vary the party from election to election, you will be able to hold the party accountable for government's performance.

IN YOUR OWN WORDS >> Give examples of ways in which parties serve (or fail to serve) citizens in American politics.

LET'S REVISIT: **WHAT'S AT STAKE...**

We began this chapter by looking at the Republican struggles to take back control of the U.S. Senate, an effort that had been doomed to failure in 2010 and 2012 but finally came to fruition in 2014, and we asked what was at stake when a party ties itself to its most conservative members.

It took a while in the wake of 2010 and 2012 for the party to ask themselves that question. Some Republicans believed that it was just a matter of candidates expressing themselves badly.[65] Others, however, believed that the problems went deeper than cosmetics and went right to the ideology of the candidates themselves. We have argued in this chapter that the Republican Party has moved far to the right in recent years, and that the hyperpartisanship has meant that legislators have more trouble compromising in the national interest of getting things done. After the 2012 election, some Republicans agreed, arguing that their party had moved too far to the extremes and needed to moderate some of its positions to appeal more to women, Latino, and African American voters.

And so the party began, at least at the Senate level, to recruit quality nominees and to weed out the Tea Party candidates they felt might be popular with primary voters but would be nonstarters with state electorates, candidates like Mississippi state senator Chris McDaniel, who was trying to oust veteran Republican senator Thad Cochran, and Liz Cheney, who was trying to push aside incumbent senator Mike Enzi of Wyoming as not conservative enough. Both failed in their primary efforts to unseat long-established, non-extremist Republicans.

That those insurgent candidates did not succeed was no accident. As writers for the New York Times put it, " Republican leaders knew that if they wanted to win the Senate, they needed to crush the enemy: not Democrats, but the rebels within their own party." Thus began a concerted effort of candidate selection, training, and donor-education in what was electable behavior and what was not. "Little was left to chance: Republican operatives sent fake campaign trackers — interns and staff members brandishing video cameras to record every utterance and move — to trail their own candidates. In media training sessions, candidates were forced to sit through a reel of the most self-destructive moments of 2012, when Todd Akin and Richard Mourdock's comments on rape and pregnancy helped sink the party."[66]

And in the long run, it paid off. Tea Party challenges to establishment candidates lost, good candidates were recruited, and they avoided making the kinds of gaffes that play endlessly on the media loop before an election. And in the end, Senator McConnell was able to claim the mantle he'd wanted for six years.

Whether the Republican's have solved their extremism problem is not yet clear. There are still flamethrowers in the House and at least three Senators with Tea Party backgrounds and 2016 presidential aspirations who can make McConnell's life a majority leader difficult.

Further, not all Republicans diagnose their electoral problems the same way. Former South Carolina Republican Senator Jim DeMint, the Tea Party stalwart who said that he would rather have "thirty Republicans in the Senate who believe in principles of freedom than sixty who don't believe in anything,"[67] decided to resign his Senate seat in 2012 to take on the leadership of a conservative think tank called the Heritage Foundation, saying, "I'm leaving the Senate now, but I'm not leaving the fight. . . . I've decided to join the Heritage Foundation at a time when the conservative movement needs strong leadership in the battle of ideas."[68]

The Republican experience of the last three election cycles suggests that what is at stake when a party is captive to its more extreme members is that it puts itself outside the comfort zone of most mainstream Americans, who remain much closer to the middle ideologically. The party may win elections that take place in ideologically homogeneous congressional districts, but when you move to the state or national level, it's harder to sell those more extreme ideas to moderate voters. But for the ideological purists such as DeMint, a larger cause is at stake. In the present case, what is at stake is no less than a struggle to define the soul of the Republican Party. Stay tuned as the party continues to work it out.

REVIEW

What Are Political Parties?

Political parties make a major contribution to American government by linking citizens and government, overcoming some of the fragmentation of government that separation of powers and federalism can produce, and creating an articulate opposition.

political gridlock (p. 435)
political party (p. 435)
partisanship (p. 436)
party organization (p. 436)
party-in-government (p. 436)
party-in-the-electorate (p. 436)
party identification (p. 436)
party base (p. 437)
responsible party model (p. 438)

Do American Parties Offer Voters a Choice?

American political parties offer the average voter a choice in terms of ideology, membership, and policy positions (platform). The differences may not always be evident, however, because electoral forces create incentives for parties to take moderate positions, drawing the parties together. At the same time, party activists who are committed to the values and policies of a particular party play a key role in pushing the parties apart and keeping them ideologically distinct.

party platform (p. 443)
party activists (p. 447)

The History of Parties in America

American history reveals at least five distinct party eras. These are periods of political stability when one party has a majority of congressional seats and controls the presidency. A realignment, or new era, occurs when a different party assumes control of government. Party politics

today may be undergoing both a realignment and a dealignment, resulting in greater numbers of voters identifying themselves as independents.

party machines (p. 450)
party bosses (p. 450)
patronage (p. 450)
party primary (p. 450)
party eras (p. 451)
critical election (p. 451)
realignment (p. 451)
dealignment (p. 451)
conflict extension (p. 454)

What Do Parties Do?

The two primary activities of parties are electioneering (getting candidates elected) and governing (all the activities related to enacting party policy agendas in government).

electioneering (p. 454)
closed primaries (p. 455)
open primaries (p. 455)
nominating convention (p. 455)
soft money (p. 457)
governing (p. 458)

Characteristics of the American Party System

America's two-party system is relatively moderate, decentralized, and increasingly disciplined. The rules are designed to make it hard for third parties to break in, but numerous third-party movements have arisen at different times to challenge the two dominant parties.

party discipline (p. 464)

The Citizens and Political Parties

Although public disenchantment with political parties may be on the increase, parties remain one of the most accessible avenues for citizen participation in government.

ENGAGE

Join the party.
There is strength in numbers, and becoming a card-carrying member of a political party can allow you to increase the volume of your own voice, especially in states with closed primaries. Not sure which party suits you? Sites like **iSideWith.com** offer political quizzes that can help you to see which party best reflects your personal views.

Do some recon.
Take some time to explore where the parties stand on issues that are important to you. You can find answers to all your questions about the two major parties via the Republican and Democratic National Committees. There you'll find a little history on some of the lesser-known parties in the United States, with links to their web sites. Want to know how policy issues are being framed in congressional campaign and fundraising efforts? A few key sites provide the partisan line: **National Republican Senatorial Committee, National Republican Congressional Committee, Democratic Senatorial Campaign Committee, and Democratic Congressional Campaign Committee.**

Take a look at the alternatives.
Don't fit in with the big two? Take a look at where the most viable (and the most out-there) third parties stand at **Politics 1's Directory of U.S. Political Parties.** Project Vote Smart provides a comprehensive directory of all U.S. parties, big and small.

EXPLORE

Abramowitz, Alan I. 2011. *The Disappearing Center: Engaged Citizens, Polarization, and American Democracy.* **New Haven: Yale University Press.** Abramowitz argues that today's hyperpartisanship is a response not to anger in the fringes of the electorate, but to apathy and disengagement among those who would form the center of it.

Aldrich, John H. 2011. *Why Parties? A Second Look.* **Chicago: University of Chicago Press.** In this follow up to his insightful 1995 classic, Aldrich offers a thorough reexamination of the party system.

Hetherington, Marc J., and Bruce Larson. 2012. *Parties, Politics, and Public Policy in America,* 11th ed. **Washington, DC: CQ Press.** This text examines the continued vitality of American political parties.

Mann, Thomas E., and Norman J. Ornstein. 2012. *It's Even Worse Than It Looks: How the American Constitutional System Collided With the New Politics of Extremism.* **New York: Basic Books.** Congressional scholars Thomas Mann and Norman Ornstein identify overriding problems that have led Congress—and the United States—to the brink of institutional collapse, including the serious mismatch between our vehemently adversarial political parties.

Nader, Ralph. 2002. *Crashing the Party: How to Tell the Truth and Still Run for President.* **New York: St. Martin's Press.** The vigilant muckraker and Green Party candidate gives a blow-by-blow account of his 2000 run for the White House and offers theories on what he sees as the failure of the two-party system.

13 INTEREST GROUPS

IN YOUR OWN WORDS   After you've read this chapter, you will be able to

» Explain how and why interest groups form.

» Identify four types of interest groups and the kinds of interests they represent.

» Describe how interest groups use lobbying and campaign activities to get the public policy they want.

» Identify specific resources that interest groups bring to bear when attempting to influence public policy.

» Summarize the relationship among citizens, interest groups, and government.

WHAT'S AT STAKE...IN WORKING WITH INTEREST GROUPS EARLY IN THE POLICYMAKING PROCESS?

HARRY AND LOUISE KILLED HEALTH CARE reform in 1994, and in 2009 President Barack Obama's then–chief of staff, Rahm Emanuel, was determined that they wouldn't do it again.

Emanuel had been working in the Clinton White House when the insurance industry set out to stop health care reform in 1994, spending millions on TV advertising, including a series of commercials that featured a worried couple—Harry and Louise—sitting at their kitchen table, discussing their fears over government-run health care plans, which aired on major networks during prime time (back in the days before DVRs and streaming media). An apprehensive public was easily persuaded to share Harry and Louise's concerns, and the health care industry scored a major victory. Health care reform was dead for at least the next sixteen years.

Emanuel had watched the Clintons in 1994, and he thought he knew where they had gone wrong. President Bill Clinton had assigned his wife, Hillary, the task of coming up with a comprehensive health care plan. Hillary Clinton consulted

experts and worked for a year before delivering a hefty plan to her husband, who in turn gave it to Congress with instructions to pass the bill. Congress, however, doesn't take that kind of instruction well. Allegedly the late senator Daniel Patrick Moynihan (the New York democrat whose seat Hillary Clinton would later occupy) took one look and said, "I'm not even going to read it."[1]

Members of Congress weren't the only powerful opponents of the Clinton bill. The insurance, medical, and pharmaceutical industries were all opposed and immediately spent millions on an advertising campaign to defeat it, as well as on intensive lobbying efforts to convince an already skeptical Congress to ignore the bill. It never even came up for a vote.

As far as Emanuel was concerned, the lessons learned were, first, get Congress involved from the start, and, second, do something to bring the relevant interest groups to the table. The Obama team took these lessons to heart. From the beginning, Congress invested heavily in the reform bill's design. And in March 2009 the White

Getting Everyone on Board
President Barack Obama speaks about health care in May 2009 while leaders from the insurance, hospital, and other medical industries stand with him. Earlier efforts at health care reform floundered, in part because Congress and relevant interest groups were excluded from the process.

who had promised a change in the way Washington did business, alienated many in his own party. Some of the strongest criticism of his plan came from disillusioned liberals who were resentful that the bill would require them to buy insurance from private companies, and who believed that Obama had sold out the so-called "public option" and the opportunity to accrue cost savings by reducing drug costs further. The clamor of criticism nearly drowned out the victory celebration when the president finally signed the law on March 23, 2010.

Was it worth it? Was Emanuel's calculation correct that the bill would not pass at all if special interest groups torpedoed it? Was the political cost of seeming to be "consorting with the enemy" too great to bear? Just what was at stake in the Obama administration's decision to bring health groups into the reform process at an early stage? **«**

House invited members of all the affected industries to meet with President Obama and members of Congress. Out of the public eye, the president's negotiators met with representatives of the health care industry and deals were made. For example, America's Health Insurance Plans, an industry interest group that represents the insurance companies, agreed to sign on to a plan of universal insurance coverage for all Americans, regardless of preexisting health conditions, in exchange for the White House's agreement that any plan it endorsed would require every American who could afford it to buy insurance and would not include a public competitor to the private health insurance plans. Similarly, the representatives of the pharmaceutical industry agreed to make $80 billion in cuts on drug prices in exchange for the White House's agreement not to push for further cuts. Though this situation would change before the health care reform bill became law, the Obama administration had, at least initially, coopted two of the loudest and richest voices that had brought down the Clinton health care plan.

But at what cost? Republicans had already determined that their strategy would be to deny Obama any legislative victories they could, so they were all opposed to health care reform for political, if not policy, reasons. In addition, by making deals with the health care industry, Obama,

F R E N C H observer Alexis de Tocqueville, traveling in America in the early 1830s, noted a peculiar (he thought) tendency of Americans to join forces with their friends, neighbors, and colleagues. He said, "Americans of all ages, all conditions, and all dispositions, constantly form associations. They have not only commercial and manufacturing companies, in which all take part, but associations of a thousand other kinds—religious, moral, serious, futile, general or restricted, enormous or diminutive."[2] As the "*Snapshot of America:* How Many of Us Belong, and to What?" shows, Americans are indeed among the top "joiners" in the world.

While Tocqueville's remarks did not refer specifically to political groups, James Madison was concerned about the American propensity to form political associations, or what he called factions. As we saw in Chapter 3, Madison defined a **faction** as a group of citizens united by some common passion or interest, and opposed to the rights of other citizens or to the interests of the whole community.[3] He feared that factions would weaken and destabilize a republic, but he also believed, as he argued in *Federalist* No. 10 (see *CLUES to Critical Thinking*), that a large republic could contain the

> **faction** a group of citizens united by some common passion or interest and opposed to the rights of other citizens or to the interests of the whole community

Harry and Louise ●

SNAPSHOT OF AMERICA: HOW MANY OF US BELONG, AND TO WHAT?

Americans Active in a Group

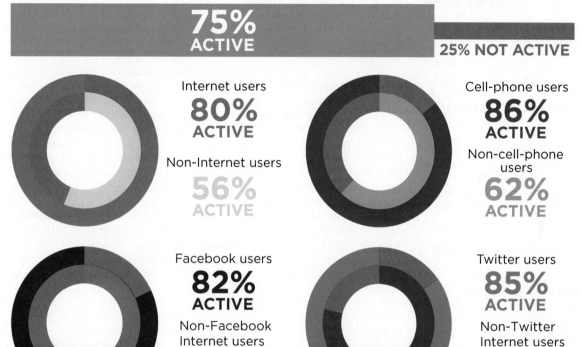

Total Americans

75% ACTIVE

25% NOT ACTIVE

Internet users
80% ACTIVE

Non-Internet users
56% ACTIVE

Cell-phone users
86% ACTIVE

Non-cell-phone users
62% ACTIVE

Facebook users
82% ACTIVE

Non-Facebook Internet users
77% ACTIVE

Twitter users
85% ACTIVE

Non-Twitter Internet users
79% ACTIVE

Source: Research Center, "Stark Racial Division in Reactions to Ferguson Police Shooting," August 18, 2014, www.people-press.org/2014/08/18/stark-racial-divisions-in-reactions-to-ferguson-police-shooting.

What kinds of groups are American adults active in?

Church Groups **40%**
Volunteer Groups **22%**
Trade Associations **20%**
Political Parties **15%**
Book Clubs **11%**
Environmental Groups **7%**
Gaming Communities **6%**
Cultural Groups **5%**

Sports Groups **24%**
Community Groups **19%**
Alumni Associations **14%**
Art Clubs **10%**
Labor Unions **8%**
Veterans Organizations **7%**
Farm Organizations **4%**

Source: Cumulative General Social Survey, 2008–2012. Author calculations.

BEHIND THE NUMBERS

Americans are active in groups. And internet users we can see in the chart are more active than most. Notice the wide range of types of groups we join. What sorts of issues or controversies might cause the members each of these groups to become active in local, state, or even national politics?

Source: Lee Rainie, Kristen Purcell and Aaron Smith, "The Social Side of the Internet," Pew Research Internet Project, January 18, 2011. [http://www.pewinternet.org/2011/01/18/the-social-side-of-the-internet/]

CLUES TO CRITICAL THINKING

Federalist No. 10

By James Madison, November 23, 1787

Of all the Federalist Papers, perhaps none has received as much scrutiny and discussion as Madison's Federalist No. 10 and his claim that interest groups—or factions, as he calls them—can potentially threaten the very health of a society.

To the People of the State of New York:

Among the numerous advantages promised by a well constructed Union, none deserves to be more accurately developed than its tendency to break and control the violence of faction. The friend of popular governments never finds himself so much alarmed for their character and fate, as when he contemplates their propensity to this dangerous vice. . . .

By a faction, I understand a number of citizens, whether amounting to a majority or a minority of the whole, who are united and actuated by some common impulse of passion, or of interest, adversed to the rights of other citizens, or to the permanent and aggregate interests of the community.

There are two methods of curing the mischiefs of faction: the one, by removing its causes; the other, by controlling its effects.

There are again two methods of removing the causes of faction: the one, by destroying the liberty which is essential to its existence; the other, by giving to every citizen the same opinions, the same passions, and the same interests.

It could never be more truly said than of the first remedy, that it was worse than the disease. Liberty is to faction what air is to fire, an aliment without which it instantly expires. But it could not be less folly to abolish liberty, which is essential to political life, because it nourishes faction, than it would be to wish the annihilation of air, which is essential to animal life, because it imparts to fire its destructive agency.

The second expedient is as impracticable as the first would be unwise. As long as the reason of man continues fallible, and he is at liberty to exercise it, different opinions will be formed. As long as the connection subsists between his reason and his self-love, his opinions and his passions will have a reciprocal influence on each other; and the former will be objects to which the latter will attach themselves. The diversity in the faculties of men, from which the rights of property originate, is not less an insuperable obstacle to a uniformity of interests. The protection of these faculties is the first object of government. From the protection of different and unequal faculties of acquiring property, the possession of different degrees and kinds of property immediately results; and from the influence of these on the sentiments and views of the respective proprietors, ensues a division of the society into different interests and parties.

The latent causes of faction are thus sown in the nature of man; and we see them everywhere brought into different degrees of activity, according to the different circumstances of civil society. . . . But the most common and durable source of factions has been the various and unequal distribution of property. Those who hold and those who are without property have ever formed distinct interests in society. Those who are creditors, and those who are debtors, fall under a like discrimination. A landed interest, a manufacturing interest, a mercantile interest, a moneyed interest, with many lesser interests, grow up of necessity in civilized nations, and divide them into different classes, actuated by different sentiments and views. The regulation of these various and interfering interests forms the principal task of modern legislation, and involves the spirit of party and faction in the necessary and ordinary operations of the government. . . .

It is in vain to say that enlightened statesmen will be able to adjust these clashing interests, and render them all subservient to the public good. Enlightened statesmen will not always be at the helm. Nor, in many cases, can such an adjustment be made at all without taking into view indirect and remote considerations, which will rarely prevail over the immediate interest which one party may find in disregarding the rights of another or the good of the whole.

The inference to which we are brought is, that the CAUSES of faction cannot be removed, and that relief is only to be sought in the means of controlling its EFFECTS.

If a faction consists of less than a majority, relief is supplied by the republican principle, which enables the majority to defeat its sinister views by regular vote. It may clog the administration, it may convulse the society; but it will be unable to execute and mask its violence under the forms of the Constitution. When a majority is included in a faction, the form of popular government, on the other hand, enables it to sacrifice to its ruling passion or interest both the public good and the rights of other citizens. To secure the public good and private rights against the danger of such a faction, and at the same time to preserve the spirit and the form of popular government, is then the great object to which our inquiries are directed. Let me add that it is the great desideratum by which this form of government can be rescued from the opprobrium under which it has so long labored, and be recommended to the esteem and adoption of mankind.

By what means is this object attainable? Evidently by one of two only. Either the existence of the same passion or interest in a majority at the same time must be prevented, or the majority, having such coexistent passion or interest, must be rendered, by their number and local situation, unable to concert and carry into effect schemes of oppression. If the impulse and the opportunity be suffered to coincide, we well know that neither moral nor religious motives can be relied on as an adequate control. They are not found to be such on the injustice and violence of individuals, and lose their efficacy in proportion to the number combined together, that is, in proportion as their efficacy becomes needful.

From this view of the subject it may be concluded that a pure democracy, by which I mean a society consisting of a small number of citizens, who assemble and administer the government in person, can admit of no cure for the mischiefs of faction. A common passion or interest will, in almost every case, be felt by a majority of the whole; a communication and concert result from the form of government itself; and there is nothing to check the inducements to sacrifice the weaker party or an obnoxious individual. Hence it is that such democracies have ever been spectacles of turbulence and contention; have ever been found incompatible with personal security or the rights of property; and have in general been as short in their lives as they have been violent in their deaths. Theoretic politicians, who have patronized this species of government, have erroneously supposed that by reducing mankind to a perfect equality in their political rights, they would, at the same time, be perfectly equalized and assimilated in their possessions, their opinions, and their passions.

A republic, by which I mean a government in which the scheme of representation takes place, opens a different prospect, and promises the cure for which we are seeking. Let us examine the points in which it varies from pure democracy, and we shall comprehend both the nature of the cure and the efficacy which it must derive from the Union.

The two great points of difference between a democracy and a republic are: first, the delegation of the government, in the latter, to a small

number of citizens elected by the rest; secondly, the greater number of citizens, and greater sphere of country, over which the latter may be extended.

The effect of the first difference is, on the one hand, to refine and enlarge the public views, by passing them through the medium of a chosen body of citizens, whose wisdom may best discern the true interest of their country, and whose patriotism and love of justice will be least likely to sacrifice it to temporary or partial considerations. Under such a regulation, it may well happen that the public voice, pronounced by the representatives of the people, will be more consonant to the public good than if pronounced by the people themselves, convened for the purpose. On the other hand, the effect may be inverted. Men of factious tempers, of local prejudices, or of sinister designs, may, by intrigue, by corruption, or by other means, first obtain the suffrages, and then betray the interests, of the people. The question resulting is, whether small or extensive republics are more favorable to the election of proper guardians of the public weal; and it is clearly decided in favor of the latter by two obvious considerations:

In the first place, it is to be remarked that, however small the republic may be, the representatives must be raised to a certain number, in order to guard against the cabals of a few; and that, however large it may be, they must be limited to a certain number, in order to guard against the confusion of a multitude. Hence, the number of representatives in the two cases not being in proportion to that of the two constituents, and being proportionally greater in the small republic, it follows that, if the proportion of fit characters be not less in the large than in the small republic, the former will present a greater option, and consequently a greater probability of a fit choice.

In the next place, as each representative will be chosen by a greater number of citizens in the large than in the small republic, it will be more difficult for unworthy candidates to practice

with success the vicious arts by which elections are too often carried; and the suffrages of the people being more free, will be more likely to centre in men who possess the most attractive merit and the most diffusive and established characters.

It must be confessed that in this, as in most other cases, there is a mean, on both sides of which inconveniences will be found to lie. By enlarging too much the number of electors, you render the representatives too little acquainted with all their local circumstances and lesser interests; as by reducing it too much, you render him unduly attached to these, and too little fit to comprehend and pursue great and national objects. The federal Constitution forms a happy combination in this respect; the great and aggregate interests being referred to the national, the local and particular to the State legislatures.

The other point of difference is, the greater number of citizens and extent of territory which may be brought within the compass of republican than of democratic government; and it is this circumstance principally which renders factious combinations less to be dreaded in the former than in the latter. The smaller the society, the fewer probably will be the distinct parties and interests composing it; the fewer the distinct parties and interests, the more frequently will a majority be found of the same party; and the smaller the number of individuals composing a majority, and the smaller the compass within which they are placed, the more easily will they concert and execute their plans of oppression. Extend the sphere, and you take in a greater variety of parties and interests; you make it less probable that a majority of the whole will have a common motive to invade the rights of other citizens; or if such a common motive exists, it will be more difficult for all who feel it to discover their own strength, and to act in unison with each other. Besides other impediments, it may be remarked that, where there is a consciousness of unjust or dishonorable purposes, communication is always checked by

(Continued)

(Continued)

distrust in proportion to the number whose concurrence is necessary.

Hence, it clearly appears, that the same advantage which a republic has over a democracy, in controlling the effects of faction, is enjoyed by a large over a small republic,—is enjoyed by the Union over the States composing it. Does the advantage consist in the substitution of representatives whose enlightened views and virtuous sentiments render them superior to local prejudices and schemes of injustice? It will not be denied that the representation of the Union will be most likely to possess these requisite endowments. Does it consist in the greater security afforded by a greater variety of parties, against the event of any one party being able to outnumber and oppress the rest? In an equal degree does the increased variety of parties comprised within the Union, increase this security? Does it, in fine, consist in the greater obstacles opposed to the concert and accomplishment of the secret wishes of an unjust and interested majority? Here, again, the extent of the Union gives it the most palpable advantage.

The influence of factious leaders may kindle a flame within their particular States, but will be unable to spread a general conflagration through the other States. A religious sect may degenerate into a political faction in a part of the Confederacy; but the variety of sects dispersed over the entire face of it must

secure the national councils against any danger from that source. A rage for paper money, for an abolition of debts, for an equal division of property, or for any other improper or wicked project, will be less apt to pervade the whole body of the Union than a particular member of it; in the same proportion as such a malady is more likely to taint a particular county or district, than an entire State.

In the extent and proper structure of the Union, therefore, we behold a republican remedy for the diseases most incident to republican government. And according to the degree of pleasure and pride we feel in being republicans, ought to be our zeal in cherishing the spirit and supporting the character of Federalists.

PUBLIUS.

Source: Thomas, The Library of Congress, http://thomas.loc.gov/home/histdox/fed_10 .html.

Consider the source and the audience: The *Federalist Papers* were anonymous editorials, written to persuade the citizens of New York to sign on to the Constitution. *Federalist* No. 10 was especially aimed at people who feared the possibilities for corruption in a large country. How is Madison responding to those fears?

Lay out the argument, the values, and the assumptions: How does Madison define factions and why are they problematic? Why does he think the root causes of factions cannot be controlled, but the effects of factions can? How will the new republic do that?

Uncover the evidence: Does Madison provide any evidence to support his arguments? Is there any other type of evidence he could have added to make his argument more persuasive?

Evaluate the conclusion: Was Madison right? Are factions the source of instability in American politics? Can they be contained?

Sort out the political implications: What would Madison say if he could come back today? Would he think his expectations in *Federalist* No. 10 had been borne out? Would his argument change in the altered technological environment of today?

effects of factions by making it hard for potential members to find one another and by providing for so many potential political groups that, if they did find each other and organize, their very numbers would cancel each other out.

Modern political scientists have a different take on factions, which they call by the more neutral term *interest groups*. An **interest group** is an organization of individuals who share a common political goal and unite for the purpose of influencing public policy decisions.[4] (Parties, as you may recall from the previous chapter, also seek to influence policy, but they do so by sponsoring candidates in elections.) The one major difference between this definition and Madison's

is that many political scientists do not believe that all interest groups are opposed to the broad public interest. Rather, they hold that interest groups play an important role in our democracy, ensuring that the views of organized interests are heard in the governing process.[5] That is, interest groups are an essential part of the "who" in our formulation of politics as who gets what and how. We saw in Chapter 1 that interest

interest group an organization of individuals who share a common political goal and unite for the purpose of influencing government decisions

groups play a central role in the pluralist theory of democracy, which argues that democracy is enhanced when citizens' interests are represented through group membership. The group interaction ensures that members' interests are represented but also that no group can become too powerful.

Although they have long existed, interest groups, unlike political parties, were not a major force in American politics until the beginning of the twentieth century. When the Progressive reformers at the turn of the century opened up the political process to the people, political parties were weakened and interest groups were correspondingly strengthened. By the 1960s, Washington, D.C., was awash in interest group activity as the federal government continued to expand its New Deal and Great Society programs,[6] and the growth has continued to the present day. While precise data on the number of interest groups do not exist, according to one author, from 1970 to 1990, an average of ten interest groups were formed every week.[7]

The increase in the number of interest groups accelerated after 1974, when the Federal Election Campaign Act was passed in an effort to curb campaign spending abuses. Seeking to regulate the amount of money an interest group could give to candidates for federal office, the law provided for **political action committees (PACs)** to serve as fundraisers for interest groups. As we will see later in this chapter, PACs are limited in how much money they can donate to a candidate, but a number of loopholes allow them to get around some of the restrictions, and recent court cases have lifted limitations on how much money these groups can spend on a candidate's behalf.[8] Although many PACs are creatures of interest groups, others are independent and act as interest groups in their own right. Though their activities are limited to collecting and distributing money, PACs have become extremely powerful players in American politics. Today there are about 4,210 PACs,[9] and they typically contribute a substantial portion of candidates' campaign funds, although Barack Obama broke the pattern of campaign reliance on PACs in 2008.

The explosion of interest group activity has probably caused Madison and the other founders to roll over in their graves. After all, Madison believed that he had secured the republic against what he called the "mischiefs of faction." He could not have envisioned a day when mass transportation and communication systems would virtually shrink the large size of the republic that he had believed would isolate interest groups. In today's world, dairy farmers in Wisconsin can easily form associations with dairy farmers in Pennsylvania; coal producers in the East can organize with coal producers in the Midwest; citrus growers in Florida can plan political strategy with citrus growers in California. Nor would Madison have foreseen the development of the Internet, which allows hundreds of thousands of people to organize and to voice their concerns to their representatives almost instantaneously.

Critics argue that interest groups have too much power, that they don't effectively represent the interests of groups that don't organize (the poor, the homeless, or the young, for instance), and that they clog up the vital arteries of American democracy, leading to gridlock and stagnation.[10] Supporters echo Madison's pluralist hopes—that group politics can preserve political stability by containing and regulating conflict and by providing checks on any one group's power.

THE ROLES AND FORMATION OF INTEREST GROUPS
Organizing around common political goals to influence policy from outside the apparatus of government

Whether we approve or disapprove of the heavy presence of interest groups in the United States, it is undeniable that they play a significant role in determining who gets what in American politics. In this section we consider the various political roles that interest groups play, and the conditions and challenges they have met in order to organize in the first place.

ROLES OF INTEREST GROUPS

Negative images of interest groups abound in American politics and the media. Republicans speak of the Democrats as "pandering" to special interest groups like labor unions and trial lawyers; in their turn, Democrats claim that the Republican Party has been captured by big business and the religious right. In both cases, the parties charge each other with giving special treatment to some groups at the expense of the public good. The truth is that, as Madison guessed, interest groups have become an integral part of American politics, and neither party can afford to ignore them. In this section we go beyond the negative stereotypes of interest groups to discuss the important roles they play in political representation, participation, education, agenda building, provision of program alternatives, and program monitoring.[11]

- *Representation.* Interest groups play an important role in representing their members' views to Congress, the executive branch, and administrative agencies. Whether they represent teachers, manufacturers of baby food, people concerned with the environment, or the elderly, interest groups ensure that their members' concerns are adequately heard in the policymaking process. The activity of persuading policymakers to support their members' positions is

political action committees (PACs) the fundraising arms of interest groups

called **lobbying**. Lobbying is the central activity of interest groups.

- *Participation.* Interest groups provide an avenue for citizen participation in politics that goes beyond voting in periodic elections. They are a mechanism for people sharing the same interests or pursuing the same policy goals to come together, pool resources, and channel their efforts for collective action. Whereas individual political action might seem futile, participation in the group can be much more effective.

- *Education.* One of the more important functions of interest groups is to educate policymakers regarding issues that are important to the interest group. Members of Congress must deal with many issues and generally cannot hope to become experts on more than a few. Consequently they are often forced to make laws in areas where they have scant knowledge. Interest groups can fill this void by providing details on issues about which they are often the experts. In addition, sometimes interest groups must educate their members about important issues that may affect them.

- *Agenda building.* We can think of those issues that Congress, the executive branch, or administrative agencies will address as an informal political agenda. It is the role of an interest group to alert the proper government authorities about its issue; get the issue on the political agenda; and, finally, make the issue a high priority for action.

- *Provision of program alternatives.* Interest groups can be effective at supplying alternative suggestions for how issues should be dealt with once they have been put on the agenda. From this mix of proposals, political actors choose a solution.[12]

- *Program monitoring.* Once laws are enacted, interest groups keep tabs on their consequences, informing Congress and the regulatory agencies about the effects, both expected and unexpected, of federal policy. For example, the Children's Defense Fund has been active in drawing the attention of the national government to the effect of federal policies on the well-being of children.[13] Program monitoring helps the government decide whether to continue or change a policy, and it also helps to keep politicians accountable by ensuring that someone is paying attention to what they do.

WHY DO INTEREST GROUPS FORM?

Many of us can imagine public problems that we think need to be addressed. But despite our country's reputation as a nation of joiners, most of us never act, never organize a group, and never even join one. Social scientists call this the *problem of collective action:* the difficulty of getting people to work together to achieve a common goal. The problem of collective action can be overcome, in part, by the shared perception of a serious common problem or threat, an abundance of time and money to support a cause, and effective leadership.

COMMON PROBLEM OR THREAT Most interest groups seem to be organized around shared interests, but many people who share interests never come together at all. What causes some groups to organize? For one noted scholar, the key triggering mechanism for interest group formation is a disturbance in the political, social, or economic environment that threatens the members of a group—for instance, governmental action to regulate businesses and professions.[14] This threat alerts the group's members that they need to organize to protect their interests through political action.

RESOURCE ADVANTAGE While this explanation helps us understand interest group formation, it focuses on the external threats to a group rather than the internal resources that the potential group has. Researchers have long observed that some interest groups organize more easily than others and that some interest groups have formed without an external threat.[15] The resources available to prospective interest group members seem to be the key. Those with more money can pay for the direct-mail campaigns, publicity, legal assistance, and professional lobbying help that get the message to Washington and the public that the group means business. Perhaps just as important, those with greater resources are more likely to understand the political process, to have the confidence to express their views, and to appreciate the value of organizing into an interest group to push their policy positions.[16] This suggests that individuals with more wealth and more knowledge of the political system have a natural advantage in using the interest group process to pursue their policy goals. This also can explain why business and professional groups are more prevalent than those that represent the homeless, welfare recipients, and the unemployed.

EFFECTIVE LEADERSHIP Even though wealthy groups have an advantage over groups whose pockets are not as well lined, an effective and charismatic leader can

> **lobbying** interest group activities aimed at persuading policymakers to support the group's positions

help redress the imbalance. The strong, effective leadership of what one scholar has called **interest group entrepreneurs** can be crucial to a group's ability to organize, no matter what its resources are.[17] These entrepreneurs have a number of important characteristics, among them that they shoulder much of the initial burden and costs of organizing the group, and that they can convince people that the interest group will be able to promote the group's interests and influence the policies that affect it.[18] Such inspirational leaders have included César Chavez, who organized the United Farm Workers; Ralph Nader, who began a number of consumer interest groups; and Candy Lightner, who established Mothers Against Drunk Driving (MADD).

THE FREE RIDER PROBLEM

External threats, financial resources, and effective leadership can spur interest group formation, but they are usually not enough to overcome what we called earlier the problem of collective action. Another name for this is the **free rider problem**: Why should people join you to solve the problem when they can free ride—that is, reap the benefits of your action whether they join or not?[19] The free rider problem affects interest groups because most of the policies that interest groups advocate involve the distribution of a collective good. A **collective good** is a good or benefit that, once provided, cannot be denied to others. Public safety, clean air, peace, and lower consumer prices are all examples of collective goods that can be enjoyed by anyone. When collective goods are involved, it is difficult to persuade people to join groups because they are going to reap the benefits anyway. The larger the number of potential members involved, the more this holds true, because each will have trouble seeing that his or her efforts will make a difference.

Many groups overcome the free rider problem by supplying **selective incentives**—benefits available to their

Slow Food Nation

Slow Food USA is an interest group that represents people who want to preserve local, authentic ways of growing and preparing food. An offshoot of the international Slow Food movement, and the brainchild of interest group entrepreneur Carlo Petrini, Slow Food advocates eating regionally, seasonally, and convivially.

members that are not available to the general population. There are three types of these incentives:[20]

- **Material benefits** are tangible rewards that members can use. One of the most common material benefits is information. For example, many groups publish a magazine or a newsletter packed with information about issues important to the group and pending legislation relevant to the group's activities. In addition to information, interest groups often offer material benefits in the form of group activities, group benefit policies, or gifts. The National Rifle Association (NRA) sponsors hunting and shooting competitions and offers discounted insurance policies. The Sierra Club offers a package of benefits that includes over 250 nature treks throughout the United States. The Arbor Day Foundation gives members ten free trees when they join.

---

interest group entrepreneurs effective group leaders who are likely to have organized the group and can effectively promote its interests among members and the public

free rider problem the difficulty groups face in recruiting when potential members can gain the benefits of the group's actions whether they join or not

collective good a good or service that, by its very nature, cannot be denied to anyone who wants to consume it

selective incentives benefits that are available only to group members as an inducement to get them to join

material benefits selective incentives in the form of tangible rewards

---

Store Home | Login

SPONSOR A WILD PLACE
Great gifts that help protect the wild...

SIERRA CLUB
FOUNDED 1892
Explore, enjoy and protect the planet

ABOUT US ⌄   PLACES ⌄   GIFT OPTIONS ⌄   SHOPPING CART 🛒   CHECKOUT ◎

LIMITED EDITION: EXPLORER GIFT PACK

This limited edition Sierra Club Explorer Gift Pack is perfect for the outdoors person in your family. They will be equipped with a Sierra Club expedition pack, water bottle and organic-cotton hat all gift-wrapped in our reusable Sierra Club tote bag.

With your $50 Donation

- Sierra Club Black Expedition Pack
- Green Sierra Club Water Bottle
- Organic-Cotton Black Sierra Club Baseball Cap
- Reusable Red Sierra Club Tote Bag

Hiker Gift Pack $50

Gift Amount

Price	$50.00
* Quantity:	

Free Riders Don't Get Backpacks

The Sierra Club works to protect the environment, a goal that benefits members and nonmembers alike. Like other interest groups, the organization offers selective incentives—in this case material benefits, such as logo-bearing backpacks and water bottles—to lure individuals to support their cause formally (and financially).

- **Solidary benefits** come from interaction and bonding among group members. For many individuals, politics is an enjoyable activity, and the social interactions occurring through group activities provide high levels of satisfaction and, thus, are a strong motivating force. Solidary incentives can come from local chapter meetings, lobbying missions to Washington or the state capital, or group-sponsored activities. The significant point is that the interest group provides the venue through which friendships are made and social interactions occur.

- **Expressive benefits** are those rewards that come from doing something that you strongly believe in, from affiliating yourself with a purpose to which you are deeply committed—essentially from the *expression* of your values and interests. Many people, for example, are attracted to the American Civil Liberties Union (ACLU) because they passionately believe in protecting individual civil liberties. People who join the National Right to Life Committee believe strongly in making all abortions illegal in the United States. Their membership in the group is a way of expressing their views and ideals.

Group leaders often use a mixture of incentives to recruit and sustain members. Thus the NRA recruits many of its members because they are committed to the cause of protecting an individual's right to bear arms. The NRA reinforces this expressive incentive with material incentives like its magazine and with solidary incentives resulting from group fellowship. The combination of these incentives helps make the NRA one of the strongest interest groups in Washington.

PAUSE AND REVIEW:

WHO, WHAT, HOW

While they may have any number of goals, interest groups primarily want to influence policy. To accomplish this goal, they employ representation, participation, education, agenda building, alternative policy proposals, and program monitoring. To get anything done at all, however, they must organize and convince members to join. If all of the benefits of membership are collective goods, then potential

solidary benefits selective incentives related to the interaction and bonding among group members

expressive benefits selective incentives that derive from the opportunity to express values and beliefs and to be committed to a greater cause

Small Groups, Big Impact ⬤   Membership Has Privileges ⬤

members may free ride on the efforts of others while still enjoying the product of the group's success. Thus interest groups offer selective benefits to entice members: material benefits, solidary benefits, and expressive benefits.

IN YOUR OWN WORDS » Explain how and why interest groups form.

TYPES OF INTEREST GROUPS
Organizing around shared interests, passions, and identities

There are potentially as many interest groups in America as there are interests, which is to say the possibilities are unlimited. Therefore, it is helpful to divide them into different types, based on the kind of benefit they seek for their members. Here we distinguish among economic, equal opportunity, public, and government (both foreign and domestic) interest groups. Depending on the definitions that they use, scholars have come up with different schemes for classifying interest groups, so do not be too surprised if you come across these groups with different labels at various times.

ECONOMIC INTEREST GROUPS

Economic interest groups seek to influence government for the economic benefit of their members. Generally these are players in the productive and professional activities of the nation—businesses, unions, other occupational associations, agriculturalists, and so on. The economic benefits they seek may be higher wages for a group or an industry, lower tax rates, bigger government subsidies, or more favorable regulations. What all economic interest groups have in common is that they are focused primarily on pocketbook issues.

CORPORATIONS AND BUSINESS ASSOCIATIONS Given that government plays a key role in regulating the economy and defining the ground rules for economic competition, it should not surprise us that 70 percent of all the interest groups that have their own lobbies in Washington, D.C., or hire professionals there, are business related.[21] Corporations and business groups, which have huge stakes in the outcome of the economic-policymaking process and spend heavily to influence it, are the most numerous and the most powerful of all interest groups (see Figure 13.1). An example of what this means in

> **economic interest groups** groups that organize to influence government policy for the economic benefit of their members

practical terms is Wall Street's average of $1.5 million a day to influence the implementation of the Dodd-Frank Wall Street Reform and Consumer Protection Act (passed in 2010).[22] The primary issues that these interest groups pursue involve taxes, labor, and regulatory issues. However, business interests have also been active in the areas of education, welfare reform, and health insurance.

Economic interest groups may be corporations like BP or Monsanto, which lobby government directly. More than six hundred corporations keep full-time Washington offices to deal with government relations, and that doesn't count the companies that hire out this function to independent lobbyists, or whose attempts to influence policy are made in cooperation with other businesses.[23] Such cooperation may take the form of industry associations, like the Tobacco Institute, the American Sportfishing Association, or the National Frozen Pizza Institute.

At a more general level, businesses may join together in associations like the National Association of Manufacturers or the Business Roundtable, representing major corporations.[24] The most diverse of these major business lobbies is the Chamber of Commerce, which represents a whole host of businesses (over three million) ranging from small mom-and-pop stores to large employers.[25] The Chamber spent heavily, almost $70 million, on congressional races in the last two elections, and with some considerable success in electing Republicans it believed would support its legislative agenda. Ironically, however, the organization's success was limited as many of the conservative Republicans it helped to elect worked against some of the Chamber's legislative priorities such as immigration reform and increased appropriations for infrastructure. Making campaign contributions, while a powerful tool, is not always a surefire way for groups to get what they want from politicians.[26]

UNIONS AND PROFESSIONAL ASSOCIATIONS
Interest groups often organize in response to one another. The business groups we just discussed organized not only as a way to deal with the increased regulatory powers of the federal government but also because labor was organized. Although labor organizations do not represent the force in society that they once did (membership has declined dramatically since the early 1950s, when over 35 million workers were unionized),[27] they can still be a formidable power when they decide to influence government, especially at the state level. The American Federation of Labor–Congress of Industrial Organizations (AFL-CIO) is by far the largest American union organization, with over 12 million members from fifty-six trade and industrial unions.[28] In 2005, the year of the AFL-CIO's fiftieth anniversary, two of its most influential member unions, the Brotherhood of Teamsters and Service Employees International Union, left the AFL-CIO with two other unions, depriving the organization of one-third of its members.[29] The United Auto Workers and the United Mine Workers of America also represent major segments of the labor force.[30]

FIGURE 13.1 CONTRIBUTIONS TO POLITICAL PARTIES, BY ECONOMIC SECTOR, 2013-2014

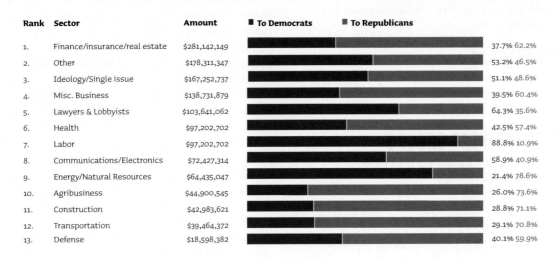

Rank	Sector	Amount	To Democrats	To Republicans
1.	Finance/insurance/real estate	$281,142,149	37.7%	62.2%
2.	Other	$178,311,347	53.2%	46.5%
3.	Ideology/Single issue	$167,252,737	51.1%	48.6%
4.	Misc. Business	$138,731,879	39.5%	60.4%
5.	Lawyers & Lobbyists	$103,641,062	64.3%	35.6%
6.	Health	$97,202,702	42.5%	57.4%
7.	Labor	$97,202,702	88.8%	10.9%
8.	Communications/Electronics	$72,427,314	58.9%	40.9%
9.	Energy/Natural Resources	$64,435,047	21.4%	78.6%
10.	Agribusiness	$44,900,545	26.0%	73.6%
11.	Construction	$42,983,621	28.8%	71.1%
12.	Transportation	$39,464,372	29.1%	70.8%
13.	Defense	$18,598,382	40.1%	59.9%

Which economic sectors are financing our elected officials? This figure shows how much different sectors of the economy are contributing to which political parties. While contributions do not necessarily guarantee politicians' votes or support, they certainly let politicians know what issues their political friends are concerned about. Notice that the finance/insurance/real estate sector outspends any other group by a wide margin. What is this likely to mean when issues of financial reform or consumer protection legislation are considered?

Source: Center for Responsive Politics, "Sector Totals, 2013–2014," https:// www.opensecrets.org/industries/. Accessed August 4, 2014.

Public employees are another large segment of America's union-represented work force. The American Federation of Government Employees represents federal workers, while the American Federation of State, County and Municipal Employees represents workers at lower levels of government. Teachers, firefighters, police, and postal workers, among others, also have large unions that wield significant influence on matters of policy in their particular areas of interest. In recent years, however, public employee unions have taken a hit as Republican governors like Wisconsin's Scott Walker have targeted them as part of a budget-cutting strategy. Because unions have been a legendary force in organizing and getting out the vote for the Democrats, the Republican restrictions on public unions have had the side benefit (for them) of reducing Democratic resources as well as cutting the budget. The resulting reduction in union power was demonstrated in June 2012, when a recall election failed to remove Walker from power.[31]

Unions are not the only organizations to represent economic interests along occupational lines. Many occupations that require much training or education have formed professional associations. Their basic purposes are to protect the profession's interests and to promote policies that enhance its position. For example, the American Medical Association has lobbied vigorously to lower the amount of medical malpractice awards.[32] The American Bar Association not only represents attorneys' interests (as do groups like the Association of Trial Lawyers of America) but, over the years,

also has actively promoted structural and procedural reforms of the courts.

AGRICULTURAL INTEREST GROUPS Farming occupies an unusual place in American labor politics. It is the one occupation on which everyone in the nation depends for food, but it is also the one most subject to the vagaries of climate and other forces beyond human control. To keep farmers in business and the nation's food supply at affordable levels, the U.S. government has long regulated and subsidized agriculture. Consequently, although less than 2 percent of the U.S. work force is involved in farming, a large network of interest groups has grown up over the years to pursue policies favorable to agriculture. These include the American Farm Bureau, the largest national organization representing farmers, and other groups like the American Agriculture Movement and the National Farmers Union, which represents the interests of small-scale farmers.[33]

The agricultural community has evolved over the years to include agribusiness interests ranging from growers' associations (wheat, corn, fruit) to large multinational corporations like Archer Daniels Midland (ADM is a major grain processor), Altria (made up of the Philip Morris tobacco company and Kraft Foods), and ConAgra Foods, Inc. These agribusiness interests are not very different from the corporate interests we discussed earlier, even though their business is agriculture.

United Federation of Teachers ● Look for the Union Label, 1978 ●

EQUAL OPPORTUNITY INTEREST GROUPS

Equal opportunity interest groups organize to promote the civil rights of groups that do not believe that their members' interests are being adequately represented and protected in national politics through traditional means. Because in many cases these groups are economically disadvantaged, or are afraid that they might become disadvantaged, these groups also advocate economic rights for their members. Equal opportunity groups believe that they are underrepresented not because of *what they do* but because of *who they are*. They may be the victims of discrimination, or see themselves as threatened. These groups have organized on the basis of age, race, ethnic group, gender, and sexual orientation. Membership is not limited to people who are part of the demographic group because many people believe that promoting the interests and rights of various groups in society is in the broader interest of all. For this reason, some scholars classify these groups as public interest groups, a type we explore in the next section.

Doug Beltel/The Oregonian/Landov

The Dwindling Voice of the Working Class

Private-sector union membership has been in a long, steady decline, and municipal unions—which represent public school teachers, police, firefighters, and others employed by state and local governments—are under attack in several cash-strapped states, especially ones with Republican administrations hostile to the goals of the union movement. Organized labor unions don't carry the same clout they did in the 1950s and 1960s, and the result is that workers, union and nonunion, have less of an organized presence expressing their concerns. Here, teachers in Wisconsin rally against Gov. Scott Walker's plan to limit their right to bargain collectively with the state in 2011.

THINKING OUTSIDE THE BOX

Are there ways to get people to pay for collective goods?

AGE One of the fastest-growing segments of the U.S. population is composed of people aged sixty-five and older, as we saw in Chapter 2. Established in 1961, the American Association of Retired Persons (now known simply as AARP) has a membership of more than 40 million Americans, more than one-half of all Americans over fifty years old. Despite its original name, ironically, almost half of AARP's members still work.[34] Why does a group that

claims to represent retired Americans have so many workers? Because a mere $16 a year is all it takes to become a member of AARP and to enjoy its numerous material benefits, like reduced health insurance rates and travel discounts.

With the motto of "Leave No Child Behind," the Children's Defense Fund (CDF) is strikingly different from AARP, and not just in the ages of those it represents. The CDF is funded from foundation grants and private donations. Indeed, because its constituents are not adults, it does not have any formal members. To combat this, the CDF regularly holds media events in which it issues reports and displays the results of its sponsored research. Through these media events, the CDF hopes to draw the public's attention to the plight of children in poverty and enhance the public's support for programs that address their needs.[35] The CDF does not have the support of a legion of dues-paying members to get its proposed legislation passed. Supporters of children's rights and well-being suggest that this lack of effective advocates is precisely the reason that children are the largest group in the United States living in poverty.

> **equal opportunity interest groups** groups that organize to promote the civil and economic rights of underrepresented or disadvantaged groups

RACE AND ETHNICITY Many equal opportunity groups promote the interests of racial or ethnic minorities. Among such groups, none can match the longevity and success of the National Association for the Advancement of Colored People (NAACP). Founded in 1909 in response to race riots in Springfield, Illinois (the home of Abraham Lincoln), the NAACP has had a long history of fighting segregation and promoting the cause of equal opportunity and civil rights for African Americans. Its Legal Defense and Educational Fund is responsible for litigating most of the precedent-setting civil rights cases, including the famous *Brown v. Board of Education.* (See Chapter 6 for details on the struggle for equal rights.) Today the NAACP is by far the largest race-based equal opportunity group, with a membership of over 500,000.[36]

Many other equal opportunity interest groups are similar to the NAACP but focus on the civil rights of other races or ethnic minorities. The League of United Latin American Citizens (LULAC) has worked for over eighty-five years to advocate the rights of Hispanics in the United States with respect to such issues as education, employment, voter registration, and housing.[37] The Mexican American Legal Defense and Educational Fund (MALDEF) is dedicated to the protection of Latinos in the United States, working through the courts and the legislatures on issues of language, immigration, employment, and education.[38] In a similar vein, the American Indian Movement (AIM) has for over forty years promoted and protected the interests of Native Americans. Founded on a philosophy of self-determination, AIM has worked to support legal rights, educational opportunities, youth services, job training, and other programs designed to eliminate the exploitation and oppression of Native Americans.[39] Likewise, numerous groups represent the concerns of Asian Americans. For example, the Southeast Asia Resource Action Center (SEARAC) is an umbrella organization coordinating the efforts of several networks supporting Asian Americans. SEARAC is a national and regional advocate for Cambodian, Laotian, and Vietnamese Americans on public policies concerning health care, economic growth, civil rights, and increased political participation.[40]

GENDER Issues dealing with the equal treatment of women are a major feature of the American political landscape. Among women's groups, the National Organization for Women (NOW) is the largest, with over 500,000 members nationwide.[41] Funded by membership dues, NOW maintains an active lobbying effort in Washington and in many state capitals, builds coalitions with other women's rights groups, and conducts leadership training for its members. NOW has been a lightning rod for controversy among women because of its strong support for women's reproductive rights. Other groups that have drawn fire for having a feminist ideological agenda

include EMILY's List, which stands for Early Money Is Like Yeast (it makes the dough rise). EMILY's List is a PAC that contributes money to Democratic women candidates.

Whereas NOW and groups like EMILY's List have ties to liberal interests, other groups, like the National Women's Political Caucus, have sprung up to support the efforts of all women to be elected to public office, no matter what their partisan affiliation. Still others are conservative. For every group like NOW or EMILY's List, there is a conservative counterpart that actively opposes most, if not all, of what is seen as a liberal feminist agenda. For instance, Republican women have formed WISH (Women in the Senate and House). Other prominent conservative women's group are the Eagle Forum, which since 1972 has campaigned against reproductive rights, the Equal Rights Amendment, and the societal trend of women working outside the home; and the Susan B. Anthony List, which supports antiabortion candidates.[42]

In addition to these women's groups, there are groups that promote equal opportunity for men. The American Coalition for Fathers and Children, for example, has formed around the issue of promoting divorced men's custodial rights.[43] The men's groups pale in comparison, however, to the women's groups when it comes to funding, membership, and national exposure.

SEXUAL ORIENTATION With the sexual revolution of the late 1960s and early 1970s, a number of gay and lesbian groups formed to fight discriminatory laws and practices based on sexual orientation. Their activities represent a two-tier approach to advocating equal opportunities for gays and lesbians. First, there is a focus on local and state governments to pass local ordinances or state laws protecting the civil rights of gays and lesbians. Groups that have made efforts at the local and state levels include the Gay and Lesbian Activists Alliance, which has been active in the mid-Atlantic states around Washington, D.C., since 1971, and the Gay and Lesbian Advocates and Defenders, a group composed of individuals from New England. On the national level, groups like the National Gay and Lesbian Task Force and the Human Rights Campaign tend to focus their efforts on opposing federal policies that are intolerant of gays and lesbians (for example, exclusion of gays and lesbians from the military or a constitutional amendment to ban gay marriage) and on promoting funding for AIDS research.

While most gay and lesbian groups are officially nonpartisan, many have close ties to the Democratic Party. To promote gay and lesbian issues within the Republican Party, activists within the GOP have formed groups like the Log Cabin Republicans and the now-defunct GOProud to provide campaign contributions to GOP candidates who support equal opportunity for gays and lesbians, and to lobby Republican representatives and senators on gay and lesbian issues.[44]

PUBLIC INTEREST GROUPS

Public interest groups try to influence government to produce noneconomic benefits that cannot be restricted to the interest groups' members or denied to any member of the general public. The benefits of clean air, for instance, are available to all, not just the members of the environmental group that fought for them. In a way, all interest group benefits are collective goods that all members of the group can enjoy, but public interest groups seek collective goods that are open to all members of society or, in some cases, the entire world.

Public interest group members are usually motivated by a view of the world that they think everyone would be better off to adopt. They believe that the benefit they seek is good for everyone, even if individuals outside their group may disagree or even reject the benefit. While few people would dispute the value of clean air, peace, and the protection of human rights internationally, there is no such consensus about protecting the right to an abortion, or the right to carry concealed weapons, or the right to smoke marijuana. Yet each of these issues has public interest groups dedicated to procuring and enforcing these rights for all Americans. Because they are involved in the production of collective goods for very large populations and the individual incentive to contribute may be particularly difficult to perceive, public interest groups are especially vulnerable to the free rider problem. That has not stopped them from organizing, however. The number of these groups grew dramatically in the 1960s and again in the 1980s.[45]

People are drawn to public interest groups because they support the groups' values and goals; that is, expressive benefits are the primary draw for membership. Often when events occur that threaten the goals of a public interest group, membership increases. For example, fearing that the Republicans would dismantle environmental laws after Ronald Reagan was elected president, new members flocked to environmental interest groups like the Sierra Club and the National Wildlife Federation; these organizations gained about 150,000 members from 1980 to 1985.[46]

> **public interest groups** groups that organize to influence government to produce collective goods or services that benefit the general public

AP Photo/Jim Cole

Raising the Bar, and the Money

Former Michigan governor Jennifer Granholm (left, alongside EMILY's List president Stephanie Schriock, center, and moderator Tiffany Eddy) speaks at a 2013 town hall discussion entitled "Madam President." EMILY's List is a gender-equality-focused interest group that works toward a very specific goal: to encourage—both socially and financially—women to run for public office, including the office of the presidency.

Likewise, after President Clinton signed the Brady Bill in 1993—which required a waiting period before gun purchases, among other regulations—the NRA saw its membership increase by half a million, and it shot up again in 2008 when, in anticipation of Barack Obama's election to the presidency, the NRA claimed that Obama would ban guns if elected (even though Obama's record on gun rights is hardly one designed to please gun control advocates).[47]

While many members are initially attracted by expressive benefits, public interest groups seek to keep them active by offering material benefits and services ranging from free subscriptions to the group's magazine to discount insurance packages.

ENVIRONMENTAL GROUPS Starting with Earth Day in 1970, environmentally based interest groups have been actively engaged in promoting environmental policies. The Clean Air and Water Acts, the Endangered Species Act, and the creation of the Environmental Protection Agency all represent examples of their successes during the 1970s. Today the Sierra Club, National Audubon Society, and Natural Resources Defense Council maintain active and professional lobbying efforts in Washington, as do environmental groups such as Greenpeace. On the extreme fringes of the environmental movement are more confrontational groups like Earth First! Their members take a dim view of attempts to lobby members of Congress for "green" laws. Instead, their calls for direct action have included building and living in aerial platforms in old-growth redwood forests in California so as to dissuade the timber industry from felling the trees. Activists have also protested by taking over the offices of local members of Congress.[48]

CONSUMER GROUPS The efforts of Ralph Nader and his public interest group Public Citizen have become synonymous with the cause of consumer protectionism. Since his path-breaking book *Unsafe at Any Speed* (1965) documented the safety problems with Chevrolet's Corvair, Nader has been exposing the hazards of a variety of other consumer products and addressing unsafe practices in the nuclear power, airline, and health care industries.[49] Another consumer advocacy group is Consumers Union, the nonprofit publisher of *Consumer Reports* magazine. Consumers Union testifies before state and federal government agencies, petitions government, and files lawsuits to protect consumer interests.[50]

RELIGIOUS GROUPS Religious groups in America have had a long history of interest group activity, dating back to the abolitionist movement. In more recent times, religious groups have developed and grown in response to what they describe as the moral decay and decadence of American society. The Christian Coalition, for example, with two million members the most powerful religious fundamentalist group in American politics,[51] lobbies on political issues and provides members with voters' guides. Pat Robertson, who had chaired the Christian Coalition's board, also developed the Christian Broadcasting Network in 1976, which, along with other large Christian media sources like James Dobson's *Focus on the Family* radio broadcast, helps to educate and mobilize evangelical Christians on political issues nationwide. These groups have become a major force in national politics and an important part of the coalition supporting the Republican Party.[52]

Fundamentalist Christian groups are not the only religiously affiliated interest groups. The United States Conference of Bishops also lobbies on particular issues like health care and birth control, and the Anti-Defamation League promotes a broad set of foreign, domestic, and legal issues that combat worldwide anti-Semitism and discrimination against Jewish Americans.

SECOND AMENDMENT GROUPS Based on its interpretation of the Second Amendment to the Constitution, the NRA is opposed to almost any effort to control and regulate the sale and distribution of firearms. As we saw in Chapter 5, overall, the NRA has had considerable policy success. Despite public opinion polls that show a clear majority of Americans favoring gun control, the level of regulation of gun purchases remains minimal. The NRA's success can be credited to its highly dedicated members who are willing to contribute their time,

resources, and votes to those candidates who support the NRA's positions—and, conversely, to a credible threat of retribution to officeholders who cross the NRA. In the 1994 elections, one year after passage of the Brady Bill, NRA voters contributed to the coalition of voters who ousted moderate Democratic representatives, and Brady supporters, across the South.[53]

One group that has challenged the power of the NRA is Handgun Control, Inc., an interest group founded by Brady Bill namesake James Brady, who was severely wounded in the 1981 attempted assassination of President Reagan, and his wife, Sarah. Handgun Control, Inc., now known as the Brady Campaign to Prevent Gun Violence, was instrumental in getting the waiting-period legislation passed in 1993. In 1994 Congress followed the Brady Bill with the Violent Crime Control and Law Enforcement Act, which banned nineteen types of automatic or semiautomatic assault rifles.[54] With the election of a Republican majority in 1994, gun control efforts had less success in Congress and when the assault weapons ban lapsed in 2004, they were able to keep it from being renewed.[55]

REPRODUCTIVE RIGHTS GROUPS The Supreme Court's decision in *Roe v. Wade* (1973), granting women the right to an abortion, generated a number of interest groups. On the pro-choice side of this debate are the National Abortion Rights Action League (NARAL) and Planned Parenthood. These groups have mounted a public relations campaign aimed at convincing policymakers that a majority of Americans want women to have the right to choose safe and legal abortions.[56] In 2012 many of these same groups were involved in defending the Obama administration's position that health care plans had to include birth control coverage.

On the pro-life side of the debate are the National Right to Life Committee and its more confrontational partner, Operation Rescue. The National Right to Life Committee lobbies Congress and state legislatures to limit abortions, hoping ultimately to secure the passage of a constitutional amendment banning them altogether. Operation Rescue attempts to prevent abortions by blocking access to abortion clinics, picketing clinics, and intercepting women who are considering abortions. In recent years, pro-life groups have shifted from a single focus on abortion to other issues they see as similar, such as opposing stem cell research.

Conservative groups won an important victory in a 2014 Supreme Court ruling in favor of Hobby Lobby. The family-held corporation had argued that the Affordable Care Act's requirement that insurance coverage must include birth control coverage violated its religious values because they perceived some forms of birth control as causing very early abortions.[57] The case illustrated how interest groups can use the courts as well as the legislative process to achieve their policy goals.

OTHER PUBLIC INTEREST GROUPS

Other public interest groups target the issue of human rights. The ACLU is a nonprofit, nonpartisan defender of individual rights against the encroachment of a powerful government. The ACLU supports the rights of disadvantaged minorities and claims to be the "nation's guardian of liberty."[58] Another human rights group, Amnesty International, promotes human rights worldwide, with over three million members in 150 countries. In the United States, Amnesty International lobbies on issues such as the death penalty, arms control, and globalization.[59]

Interest groups have also taken up the cause of animal rights. The most well-known of these groups is the Humane Society. Beyond providing local animal shelters, the Humane Society researches animal cruelty and lobbies governments at all levels on issues ranging from domestic pet over-population and adoption to farm animal treatment and wildlife habitat protection (see "*Profiles in Citizenship:* Wayne Pacelle"). In recent years a number of actors and actresses have used their celebrity status to protect animals. People for the Ethical Treatment of Animals (PETA) is a leading national interest group promoting the rights of animals. Its grassroots campaigns include attacking major health and beauty corporations like Procter & Gamble for using animals for product testing, assailing circuses and rodeos for using animals as entertainment, and condemning fur coat manufacturers for the cruel ways they kill animals.[60] Other groups like the Animal Liberation Front also advocate animal rights. Animal rights activists often use civil disobedience in their attempts to stop hunting and end the use of animals for biomedical and product safety tests.[61]

GOVERNMENT INTEREST GROUPS

Foreign governments also lobby Congress and the president. Typically some lobbyists' most lucrative contracts come from foreign governments seeking to influence foreign trade policies. The Japanese government maintains one of the more active lobbying efforts in Washington, hiring former members of Congress and bureaucrats to aid in their efforts to keep U.S. markets open to Japanese imports.[62] In recent years, ethics rules have been initiated to prevent former government officials from working as foreign government lobbyists as soon as they leave office,

Chris Maddaloni/CQ Roll Call

Student Loan Super Group

Interest groups can amplify their voices when they coalesce around specific cause. In 2012 the United States Public Interest Research Group (US PIRG, a coalition of dozens of state PIRGs operating on hundreds of college campuses), along with other groups and individual students, collected more than 130,000 letters in support of the Student Loan Affordability Act, which sought to prevent onerous increases in interest rates on certain student loans.

but lobbying firms continue to hire them when they can because of their contacts and expertise.[63]

PAUSE AND REVIEW:

WHO, WHAT, HOW

All citizens stand to win or lose a great deal from government action. If it goes their way, producing policy that benefits them, they win. But if it produces policy that helps other citizens at their expense, or passes the cost of expensive policy onto them, or reduces their ability to use the system to get what they want, then they lose. Economic actors want to protect their financial interests; members of disadvantaged or threatened groups want to protect their legal and economic interests; ideologically motivated people want to promote their vision of the good society; and governments want a good relationship with the U.S. federal government. All these actors promote their goals through the formation of different types of interest groups.

IN YOUR OWN WORDS » Identify four types of interest groups and the kinds of interests they represent.

PROFILES IN CITIZENSHIP:
WAYNE PACELLE

In the midst of one of his finest moments, Wayne Pacelle got himself thrown out of the gallery of the House of Representatives.

He was watching the vote on a budget amendment he had lobbied hard for, an amendment to cut millions of dollars of taxpayer money spent to promote the sale of U.S.-made mink coats in Italy, China, and France. He needed 218 votes to win, and everyone thought they were going to be trounced. He watched the scoreboard light up with vote after vote. When they got to 232, he couldn't help it. He let out a yell and pumped his fist. But the House frowns on emotional displays in the gallery, and out he went. Was he abashed? Hardly. "It didn't take the smile off my face," he says, grinning even now at the memory.

It was a great win, but every single triumph matters to Pacelle—it's how he feeds his spirit and keeps himself going in the face of the often daunting odds and unimaginable stories of animal abuse he confronts daily in his job as CEO of the Humane Society of the United States. Each law enacted by Congress to protect animals (15 in the past few years), each state bill passed (more than 150), each statewide ballot measure approved (15 so far), each animal life saved, each creature relieved of pain and suffering—he tallies them all. "I celebrate the positive action because it's easy to get burned out," he says. "It's easy to get demoralized.... And for me, I just tell people you've got to celebrate every little victory, it makes a big difference."

"For us, it's not an all-or-nothing game," he explains. "We can't solve all of the issues in the world, we never will. . . But if we solve it for a million, or 10 million, or a billion creatures, that's a 100-percent victory for each of those animals. And just that one act of merciful behavior or the shielding of an animal from abuse or cruelty can mean all the difference between a good quality of life and a miserable, tormented existence for that creature."

Pacelle has felt that kind of enormous, compassionate connection to animals ever since he was two or three years old. "It was a purely emotional, altruistic response that I had toward other creatures. I just saw them as powerless and I saw them as peers at that age, and they looked to me like they were composed of the same spark of life that people were."

He carried that empathy and awareness with him as he got older and, as he read philosophy and learned more about the world, he began to fit it into a broader context of what it meant to him to be a responsible citizen. He started an animal rights group in college in the 1980s, at the same time that he was active in the antiapartheid movement to limit U.S. investment in South Africa and in protests of U.S. involvement in Central

INTEREST GROUP POLITICS
Strategies for influencing different branches of government

The term *lobbying* comes from seventeenth-century England, where representatives of special interests would meet members of the English House of Commons in the large anteroom, or lobby, outside the Commons floor to plead their cases.[64] Contemporary lobbying, however, reaches far beyond the lobby of the House or Senate. Interest groups do indeed contact lawmakers directly, but they no longer confine their efforts to chance meetings in the legislative lobby.

Today, lobbyists target all branches of government and the American people as well. The ranks of those who work with lobbyists have also swelled. Beginning in the 1980s, interest groups, especially those representing corporate interests, have been turning to a diverse group of political consultants, including professional Washington lobbyists, campaign specialists, advertising and media experts, pollsters, and academics. Lobbying today is a big business in its own right.

There are two main types of lobbying. **Direct lobbying** (sometimes called inside lobbying) is interaction with actual decision makers within government institutions. While we tend to think of Congress as the typical recipient of lobbying efforts, the president, the bureaucracy,

> **direct lobbying** direct interaction with public officials for the purpose of influencing policy decisions

America. Ask him what the common thread is and he is clear: "I'm broadly interested in making the world a better place," he says. "That's the bottom line. Public policy is just the means to achieve the end of a more fair, a more just society."

A huge and saintly ambition, but Pacelle doesn't look like a zealot or a crusader when he says it. Actually, he looks like, well, a movie star, or a relative of a famous American political family (possessing what the *Washington Post* once called "John Kennedy, Jr. good looks"). He is polished, articulate, and funny (it must run in the family—his brother, Richard, is the funniest political scientist we know), and the animals couldn't ask for a more dedicated or committed advocate.

How has he kept that idealism and commitment in the face of the giant sums of money that Washington lobbyists traffic in these days? He may be an optimist, but he's a realist, too. "You'd be naive to think money doesn't have an impact," he says. "It does. It gains access, and it builds loyalty. But, ultimately, money is a means to an end. Money is there to have resources to deliver a message to influence voting behavior. So if you've got people who can organize around

a principle and you can deliver votes based on that set of ideas, then you don't need money." Well, maybe not as much, anyway. Here are some of his thoughts:

"... MAKING THE WORLD A BETTER PLACE—THAT'S THE BOTTOM LINE."

On the positive side of lobbying:

There's a reason in Washington, D.C., that there are thousands of lobbyists and thousands of interest groups. They're not here for fun; it's not just a big party. They're here because it does make a difference, and participation can have a measurable impact on public policy. I think for me, just being determined and dogged about it, just not relenting, just basically treating this as if it's a full court press all the time. . . . I mean when we're not on defense, we're on the offense. It's almost a very crusading sort of attitude. I don't like to infuse it with religious sorts of notions, but it's a powerful, ethical construct. And having enough imagination

to see that things can be different. That we're not just locked into our present set of social relationships and circumstances, that we can aspire to do things better.

On keeping the republic:

No one's going to hand you a key to change everything, but if you're smart and if you're determined you can make a real difference in the world. I've seen it happen thousands and thousands of times. And anybody who tells me differently just isn't paying attention to what's going on. And don't count on somebody else to do it, you know, don't count on a group like the Humane Society of the United States to do it. When I go around and I talk to people I say, "Listen, we can help." And our staff of four hundred, we've got great experts and we do a lot of amazing stuff, but you make the difference. It's the collective action of people of conscience that really can have a meaningful impact on society. And again, the history is of people stepping up and calling themselves to action. And leadership and citizenship are such important values in this culture. And if not them, who?

Source: Wayne Pacelle talked with Christine Barbour on March 10, 2005.

---

and even the courts are also the focus of heavy efforts to influence policy. **Indirect lobbying** (or outside lobbying) attempts to influence policymakers by mobilizing interest group members or the general public to contact elected representatives on an issue. Some groups have resorted to more confrontational indirect methods, using political protests, often developing into full-blown social movements, to make their demands heard by policymakers. Recently, corporations and other, more traditional interest groups have been combining tactics—joining conventional lobbying methods with the use of

email, computerized databases, talk radio, and twenty-four-hour cable television—to bring unprecedented pressure to bear on the voting public to influence members of government.

DIRECT LOBBYING: CONGRESS

When interest groups lobby Congress, they rarely concentrate on all 435 members of the House or all 100 members of the Senate. Rather, lobbyists focus their efforts on congressional committees, where most bills are written and revised. Because the committee leadership is relatively stable from one Congress to the next (unless a different party wins a majority), lobbyists can develop long-term relationships with committee members and their staffs.

> **indirect lobbying** attempts to influence government policymakers by encouraging the general public to put pressure on them

STRATEGIES FOR CONGRESSIONAL LOBBYING Interest groups use many strategies to influence members of Congress:

- *Personal contacts.* Personal contacts, including appointments, banquets, parties, lunches, or simply casual meetings in the hallways of Congress, are the most common and the most effective form of lobbying.

- *Professional lobbyists.* Interest groups frequently need professional help to navigate the increasingly complex world of government regulations and benefits. As a result, much of modern lobbying involves the use of professional lobbyists, either in-house employees dedicated to advancing the interests of a particular group, or contract lobbyists who work for lobbying firms that address a variety of groups' needs.

Because access to power and knowledge about how government works is key to successful lobbying, some of the most effective lobbyists are former government officials. Rotating into lobbying jobs from elected or other government positions is known as passing through the **revolving door**, a concept we meet again in Chapter 15. It refers to public officials who leave their posts to become interest group representatives (or media figures), parlaying the special knowledge and contacts they gathered in government into lucrative salaries in the private sector. Such assistance can be so invaluable to their clients that even legislative aides can make their fortune lobbying, commanding starting salaries of more than $300,000 a year.[65] One study has found that 56 percent of the revenue generated by private lobbying firms can be traced to people who once had some involvement with the federal government.[66] Current law passed in 2007 requires that senators wait two years before lobbying Congress; members of the House must wait just one year. Former Senate staffers cannot lobby the Senate for a year after they leave their positions, and House staffers cannot lobby the actual offices or committees where they worked.

The Center for Responsive Politics has tracked the post-Congress careers of 416 former members of Congress, and found that 306—or almost three-quarters of those tracked—served as lobbyists or consultants to organizations that seek to influence Congress.[67] So even though there are waiting periods, clearly most members find using their knowledge and contacts on behalf of varied interests an attractive option after their terms of government service. In addition, former congressional staff frequently move from Capitol Hill to K Street for higher salaries. Between 2001 and 2011, 5,400 staffers resigned to capitalize on the contacts they had made working with Congress.[68]

Other government officials also face new restrictions on when they can lobby the agencies for which they once worked.[69] President Obama felt so strongly that the revolving door was a breach of the public trust that early in his administration he signed an executive order prohibiting presidential appointees from working as lobbyists for two years after leaving their posts and from returning to lobby the executive branch during his time in office.[70]

Examples of the revolving door abound. Famed Washington lobbying and legal firm Alston & Bird once simultaneously employed two one-time Senate majority leaders, former Republican senator Bob Dole and former Democratic senator Tom Daschle. Although neither of the retired senators actually went to the Hill to lobby directly for clients, they were available to dispense political wisdom; to share their experience, knowledge, and contacts; and to provide access to their one-time colleagues. It makes sense for lobbying firms to hire former officials from both parties so that they can maximize their access to the halls of power.

Revolving-door activity is subject to occasional attempts at regulation and frequent ethical debate, as it was in 2007, because it raises questions about whether people should be able to convert public service into private profit, and whether such an incentive draws people into public office for motives other than serving the public interest.

- *Expert testimony.* Interest groups lobby decision makers by providing testimony and expertise, and sometimes they even draft legislation on the many issue areas in which policymakers cannot take the time to become expert.[71] Information is one of the most important resources lobbyists can bring to their effort to influence Congress. Providing valid information to representatives and staffers becomes a tool that lobbyists use to build long-term credibility with members of Congress.

For example, in 2003, with support from a president and a vice president who were former energy company executives, Republicans in Congress worked closely with energy companies to develop legislation that would increase oil exploration, coal mining, and nuclear plant development. One industry lobbyist said of the energy bill: "This is the mother lode."[72] Democrats, locked out of the conference committee that was considering the bill, were so frustrated by the influence of the energy lobbyists that then-senator Bob Graham, D-Fla., fumed, "at this point, industry

> **revolving door** the tendency of public officials, journalists, and lobbyists to move between public- and private-sector (media, lobbying) jobs

lobbyists are effectively writing this bill."[73] Of course, in their turn energy companies had been frustrated with the Clinton administration's pro-environmental positions on energy exploration, claiming that they listened only to conservationists and environmental groups.[74]

- *Campaign contributions.* Giving money to candidates is another lobbying technique that helps interest groups gain access and a friendly ear. The 1974 Federal Election Campaign Act that was passed in an effort to curb campaign spending abuses was aimed at regulating the amount of money an interest group could give to candidates for federal office, by providing for PACs to serve as fundraisers for interest groups. Subsequent campaign finance legislation has limited how much money PACs can donate to candidates, but loopholes let them circumvent the restrictions in order to support the candidates of their choice. These loopholes have been enhanced since 2012, when the Supreme Court's ruling in the *Citizens United v. Federal Election Commission* case essentially removed any limits on political expenditures by corporations and unions. Figures 13.2 and 13.3 show how the major types of PACs divide their money between the Democratic and Republican Parties. As groups have adjusted to the new rules, expenditure have exploded. Going into the 2014 midterm elections, political advertising for congressional races was predicted to break $2 billion, an increase of almost $70 million from 2010.[75] These groups use the money not only to support or oppose specific candidates, but also to define the issues and tenor of the campaigns—which, given the volume of money at their disposal, they are increasingly able to do.

- *Coalition formation.* Interest groups attempt to bolster their lobbying efforts by forming coalitions with other interest groups. While these coalitions tend to be based on single issues, building coalitions in favor of or against specific issues has become an important strategy in lobbying Congress. In recent years, for instance, the liberal and conservative groups came together in an unlikely coalition to stop legislation in the House and the Senate that aimed to stop online piracy.[76]

ATTEMPTS AT LOBBYING REFORM Many attempts have been made to regulate the tight relationship between lobbyist and lawmaker. The difficulty, of course, is that lawmakers benefit from the relationship with lobbyists in many ways and are not enthusiastic about curtailing their opportunities to get money and support. In 1995 Congress completed its first attempt in half a century to regulate lobbying when it passed the Lobbying Disclosure Act. The act required lobbyists to report how much they are paid, by whom, and what issues they are promoting.[77] Also in 1995, the Senate and the House passed separate resolutions addressing gifts and travel given by interest groups to senators and representatives.[78] Partly in reaction, in September 2007, after the Democrats took back the majority in the House and the Senate in 2006, Congress passed and President George W. Bush signed the Honest Leadership and Open Government Act, which tightened travel and gift restrictions and included, among other things, the following provisions:[79]

- Prohibits senators, members of the House, and their aides from receiving any gifts, meals, or travel in violation of their chamber's rules. While these rules are complex, basically any gifts from registered lobbyists are forbidden and gifts from other sources must have a monetary value of under $50.

- Increases the frequency with which lobbyist disclosures must be filed.

- Requires lawmakers to disclose when lobbyists "bundle" or collect from clients more than $15,000 in campaign contributions in a six-month period.

- Requires disclosure of "earmarks"—that is, special projects of individual legislators often hidden in legislation, and their sponsors.

- Forbids members of Congress to influence lobbying firms to hire members of a particular party.

Ethics reforms can cast a definite chill on lobbyist activity. The combination of the 2007 reform and President Obama's limitations on lobbyists' access to the White House led to a significant drop in lobbying. The number of registered lobbyists dropped from 14,840 to 12,340 between 2007 and 2013.[80] Nevertheless members of Congress and lobbyists quickly learn where they can bend the rules.[81] As soon as the 2007 reform was passed, lobbying groups scrambled to find new ways to provide travel for lawmakers they wanted to influence, and ways to make free meals acceptable (perhaps calling them receptions, which are legal if widely attended, or fundraisers).[82]

DIRECT LOBBYING: THE PRESIDENT

As we saw in the *What's at Stake...?* that opened this chapter, lobbyists also target the president and the White House staff to try to influence policy. As with Congress, personal contacts within the White House are extremely important, and the higher up in the White House, the better. Nor has the White House been exempt from the revolving-door phenomenon. At least two Clinton cabinet members, the late secretary of commerce Ron Brown and trade representative Mickey Kantor, had been professional lobbyists, and this

THE BIG PICTURE: DARK MONEY IN THE 2012 ELECTION

As a result of two 2010 Supreme Court decisions money by outside groups—with an increasingly number funded by anonymous donors providing what is called "Dark Money"—have become a major factor in our elections. These organizations can spend unlimited amounts on campaigns, much of it in attack ads, as long as they do not contribute directly to a candidate's campaign.

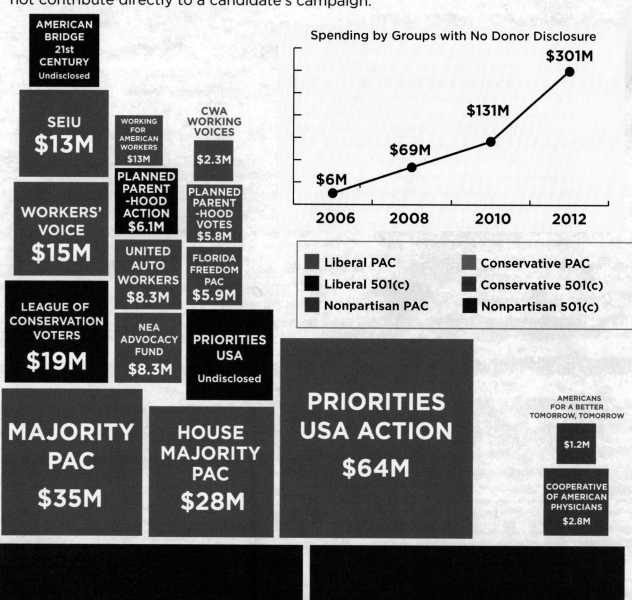

AMERICAN BRIDGE 21st CENTURY
Undisclosed

SEIU
$13M

WORKING FOR AMERICAN WORKERS
$13M

CWA WORKING VOICES
$2.3M

PLANNED PARENT-HOOD ACTION
$6.1M

PLANNED PARENT-HOOD VOTES
$5.8M

WORKERS' VOICE
$15M

UNITED AUTO WORKERS
$8.3M

FLORIDA FREEDOM PAC
$5.9M

LEAGUE OF CONSERVATION VOTERS
$19M

NEA ADVOCACY FUND
$8.3M

PRIORITIES USA
Undisclosed

Spending by Groups with No Donor Disclosure

$6M — 2006
$69M — 2008
$131M — 2010
$301M — 2012

Liberal PAC	Conservative PAC
Liberal 501(c)	Conservative 501(c)
Nonpartisan PAC	Nonpartisan 501(c)

MAJORITY PAC
$35M

HOUSE MAJORITY PAC
$28M

PRIORITIES USA ACTION
$64M

AMERICANS FOR A BETTER TOMORROW, TOMORROW
$1.2M

COOPERATIVE OF AMERICAN PHYSICIANS
$2.8M

AMERICAN FEDERATION OF STATE, COUNTY AND MUNICIPAL EMPLOYEES AFSCME
$160M

NATIONAL ASSOCIATION OF REALTORS
$160M

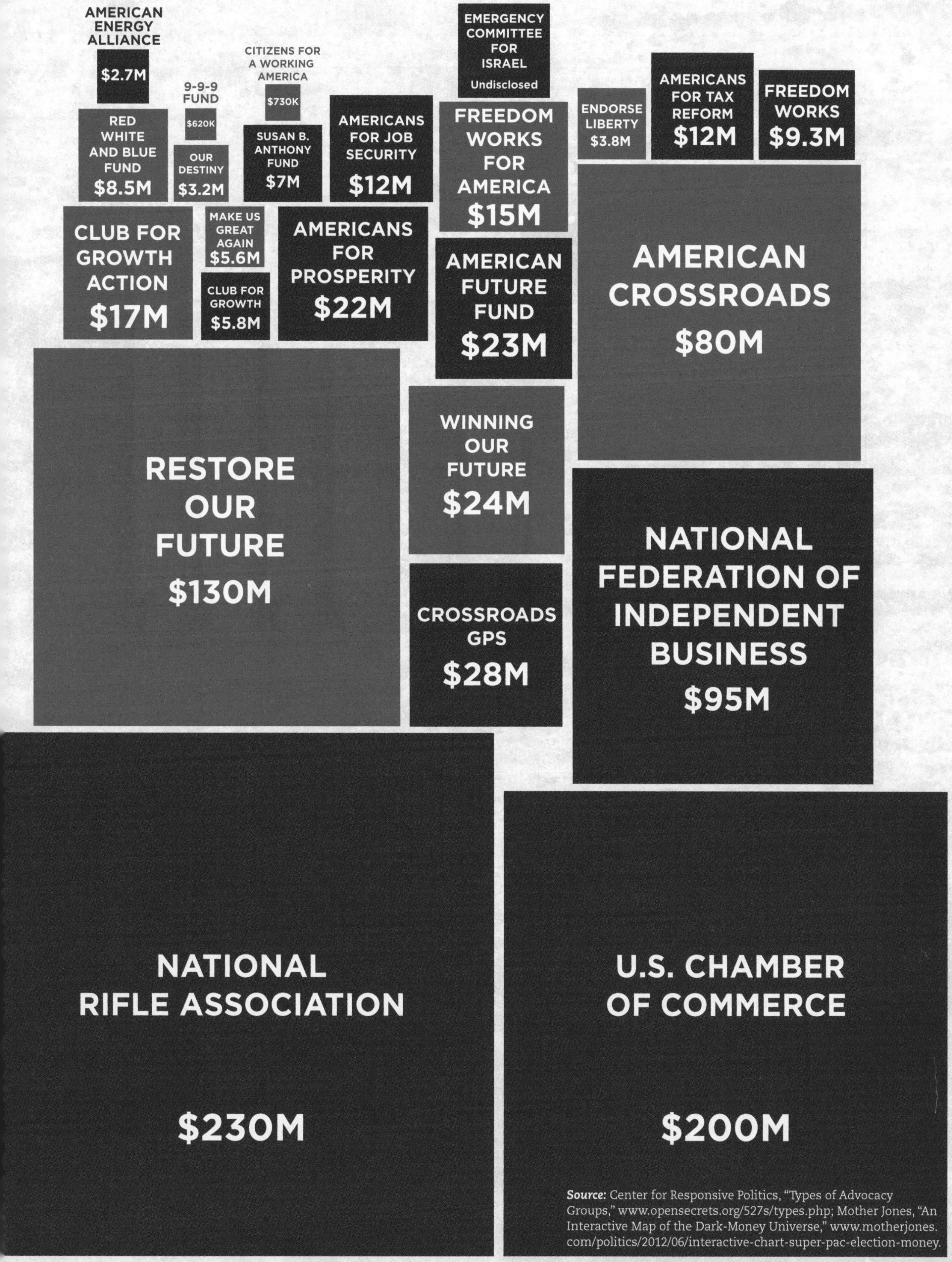

AMERICAN
ENERGY
ALLIANCE
$2.7M

RED
WHITE
AND BLUE
FUND
$8.5M

9-9-9
FUND
$620K

OUR
DESTINY
$3.2M

CITIZENS FOR
A WORKING
AMERICA
$730K

SUSAN B.
ANTHONY
FUND
$7M

AMERICANS
FOR JOB
SECURITY
$12M

EMERGENCY
COMMITTEE
FOR
ISRAEL
Undisclosed

FREEDOM
WORKS
FOR
AMERICA
$15M

ENDORSE
LIBERTY
$3.8M

AMERICANS
FOR TAX
REFORM
$12M

FREEDOM
WORKS
$9.3M

CLUB FOR
GROWTH
ACTION
$17M

MAKE US
GREAT
AGAIN
$5.6M

CLUB FOR
GROWTH
$5.8M

AMERICANS
FOR
PROSPERITY
$22M

AMERICAN
FUTURE
FUND
$23M

AMERICAN
CROSSROADS
$80M

RESTORE
OUR
FUTURE
$130M

WINNING
OUR
FUTURE
$24M

CROSSROADS
GPS
$28M

NATIONAL
FEDERATION OF
INDEPENDENT
BUSINESS
$95M

NATIONAL
RIFLE ASSOCIATION

$230M

U.S. CHAMBER
OF COMMERCE

$200M

Source: Center for Responsive Politics, "Types of Advocacy
Groups," www.opensecrets.org/527s/types.php; Mother Jones, "An
Interactive Map of the Dark-Money Universe," www.motherjones.
com/politics/2012/06/interactive-chart-super-pac-election-money.

FIGURE 13.2   SPENDING BY TYPE OF PAC, 1989–2012 (IN MILLIONS)

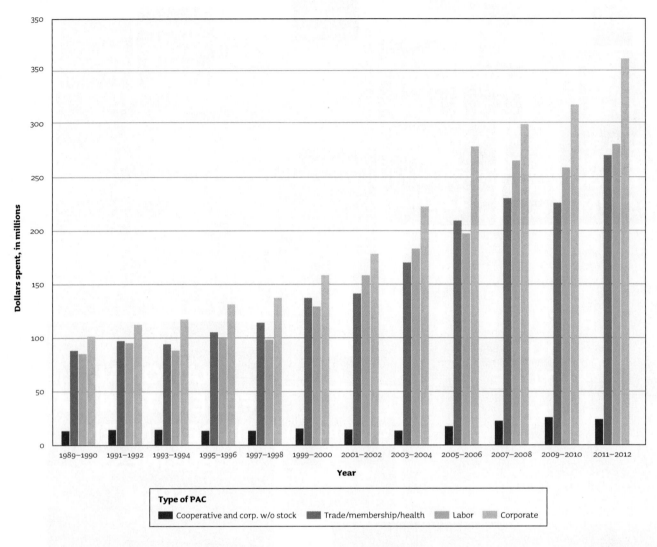

Source: Harold W. Stanley and Richard G. Niemi, "Table 2-12: Contributions and Independent Expenditures, by Type of PAC, 1999–2012," *Vital Statistics on American Politics 2013–2014* (Washington, DC: CQ Press, 2014), 96–97.

despite Clinton's unusually tough stance against lobbying.[83] Similarly, former senator Tom Daschle was in line to take a high-profile role in health care reform in the Obama administration until it became known that he had failed to disclose compensation (in the form of a car and driver) he received from a lobbying firm. Despite Obama's seemingly uncompromising stance against the revolving door, he had to relax his rules somewhat to fill some executive branch positions.[84] Part of the difficulty is that the practice of the revolving door is so pervasive—with one party's appointees joining lobbying forms while their party is out of power—that a president is hard pressed to find stellar appointees who *haven't* been lobbyists at some point.

The official contact point between the White House and interest groups is the Office of Public Liaison. Its basic purpose is to foster good relations between the White House and interest groups in order to mobilize these groups to support the administration's policies. Given the highly partisan and ideologically charged nature of most presidencies, it should not be surprising that each White House administration cultivates the groups with which it feels most ideologically comfortable.

DIRECT LOBBYING: THE BUREAUCRACY

While opportunities for lobbying the president may be somewhat limited, opportunities for lobbying the rest of the executive branch abound. Interest groups know that

FIGURE 13.3 PAC CONTRIBUTIONS TO ALL CONGRESSIONAL CANDIDATES, BY TYPE OF PAC AND CANDIDATE PARTY, 2011–2012

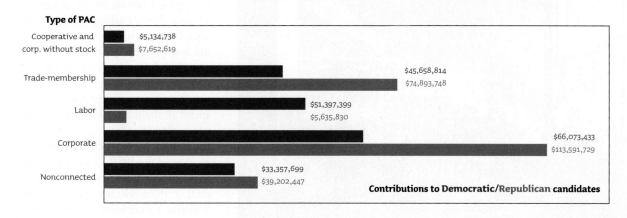

Type of PAC

Cooperative and corp. without stock: $5,134,738 / $7,652,619

Trade-membership: $45,658,814 / $74,893,748

Labor: $51,397,399 / $5,635,830

Corporate: $66,073,433 / $113,591,729

Nonconnected: $33,357,699 / $39,202,447

Contributions to Democratic/Republican candidates

Source: Federal Election Commission, "PAC Table 2: PAC Contributions to Candidates: January 1, 2011 through December 31, 2012," http: www.fec .gov/press/summaries/2012/tables/pac/PAC2_2012_24m.pdf.

winning the legislative battle is only the first step. The second, and sometimes most important, battle takes place in the bureaucracy, where Congress has delegated rule-making authority to federal agencies that implement the law.[85] When, for instance, the Occupational Safety and Health Administration (OSHA) decreed that workplace design must take into account the physical abilities of workers in order to avoid repetitive motion injuries, groups like organized labor supported the effort, although they believed the new standards did not go far enough, while business groups lobbied heavily against it, claiming that the standards were unnecessary, unsupported by medical evidence, and expensive to implement.[86]

Interest groups often try to gain an advantage by developing strong relations with regulating agencies. Because many of the experts on a topic are employed by the interests being regulated, it is not unusual to find lobbyists being hired by government agencies, or vice versa, in an extension of the revolving-door situation we discussed earlier. The close relationships that exist between the regulated and the regulators, along with the close relationships between lobbyists and congressional staffers, lead to the creation of the iron triangles we talked about in Chapter 9 (see especially Figure 9.1 on page 349). In addition to iron triangles working against an open policymaking environment by limiting the participation of actors not in the triangle, they also have the potential for presenting conflicts of interest. Although recent laws prevent former government employees from lobbying their former agencies for five years after they leave their federal jobs, government agencies are sometimes forced to recruit personnel from within the businesses they are regulating because that is often where the experts are to be found.

DIRECT LOBBYING: THE COURTS

Interest groups also try to influence government policy by challenging the legality of laws or administrative regulations in the courts. These legal tactics have been used by groups like the NAACP (challenging segregation laws), the ACLU (freedom of speech, religion, and civil liberties cases), the Sierra Club (environmental enforcement), and Common Cause (ethics in government). As soon as the Bipartisan Campaign Reform Act (BCRA) of 2002 was passed, the NRA, the ACLU, the AFL-CIO, and other groups immediately went into action to challenge the new law in court. Sometimes groups bring cases directly, and sometimes they file amicus curiae ("friend of the court") briefs asking the courts to rule in ways favorable to their positions. Many of the groups that challenged campaign finance reform returned to chime in with amicus briefs in the *Citizens United* case that ultimately rendered the heart of the BCRA unconstitutional.[87]

INDIRECT LOBBYING: THE PUBLIC

One of the most powerful and fastest-growing kinds of lobbying is indirect lobbying, in which the lobbyists use public opinion to put pressure on politicians to do what they want.[88] In this section we examine the various ways in which interest groups use the public to lobby and influence government decision makers. These efforts include educating the public by disseminating information and research, mobilizing direct citizen lobbying efforts, and organizing demonstrations or protests.

A popular way for interest groups to get out their message is through the use of **issue advocacy ads.** These commercials encourage constituents to support or oppose a certain policy or candidate without directly telling citizens how to vote. In the past, as long as these ads did not specifically promote the election or defeat of a particular candidate, issue advocacy ads were not subject to any limitations, meaning a PAC could spend all the money it wanted on ads promoting an issue and, by implication, the candidates of its choice. The passage of the BCRA (also called the McCain-Feingold Act) put a temporary chill on these ads, but several recent Supreme Court rulings, culminating with the 2010 decision in *Citizens United,* have lifted the restrictions, and in fact, issue advocacy ads can now directly advocate for or against candidates as well as for their issue positions.[91]

Even under the restraining hand of the McCain-Feingold Act, so-called **527 groups** like the Swift Boat Veterans for Truth, which effectively attacked John Kerry during his 2004 campaign for the presidency, are able to raise unlimited amounts of money from labor unions, corporations, and interest groups to mobilize voters with issue advocacy ads on television and radio, so long as they do not directly advocate the election or defeat of a candidate.[92] Organized under section 527 of the Internal Revenue Code, they are not subject to laws that the Federal Election Commission regulates.[93] In the wake of the *Citizens United* ruling, these groups are less important than they were because the 527 loophole is no longer needed for groups to spend unlimited money, but they still exist.

Groups can also get information to the public through the skillful use of the Internet, whether through carefully designed advocacy web sites and blogs, through social networks, or through web-based videos, creating messages that go "viral," spreading quickly by email and hitting targeted audiences. Internet-savvy interest groups are increasingly turning to YouTube for a cheap and efficient way to get their message out.

Power Lunch

Rules and regulations may prevent lobbyists from treating lawmakers and government workers to free meals, but there's still enough wheeling and dealing over drinks and dinner to support a thriving restaurant industry in Washington, D.C. High-end establishments that offer privacy as well as fine dining are favored by K Street firms.

EDUCATING THE PUBLIC Interest groups must get their issues onto the public's agenda before they can influence how the public feels about them. Many interest group leaders are sure that the public will rally to their side once they know "the truth" about their causes.[89] Interest groups often begin their campaigns by using research to show that the problem they are trying to solve is a legitimate one. For example, the Tax Foundation is a conservative group promoting tax cuts. To dramatize its point that American taxes are too high, every year the foundation announces "Tax Freedom Day"—the day on which the average wage earner finishes paying the amount of taxes he or she will owe and starts working for his or her own profit. In 2014 that day was April 21.[90] The foundation believes that this information is so compelling that the public will jump to the conclusion that their taxes are too high.

Of course, all the research in the world by the Tax Foundation, or any other interest group, does no good if the public is unaware of it. For this reason, interest groups cultivate press coverage. They know that people are more likely to take their research seriously if it is reported by the media as legitimate news, but getting news coverage can be difficult for interest groups because they are in competition with every other group, not to mention with actual news stories. Many of them turn to expensive public relations firms to help them get their message out, using tactics ranging from TV commercials to direct-mail campaigns (see *Don't Be Fooled by . . . Direct Mail*).

> **issue advocacy ads** advertisements that support issues or candidates without telling constituents how to vote
>
> **527 groups** groups that mobilize voters with issue advocacy advertisements on television and radio but may not directly advocate the election or defeat of a particular candidate

DON'T BE FOOLED BY...
DIRECT MAIL

The NRA knows where you live—but it's not gunning for you; it's after your money. So are the Brady Campaign to Prevent Gun Violence, the Humane Society, the Sierra Club, and Save the Children. You can only be glad that you are probably too young for AARP to take an interest in you yet. Our mailboxes, once a repository for letters from mom and a handful of bills, have become a battleground for interest groups after our hard-earned cash, and now our email inboxes are filling fast, too. Welcome to the age of direct-mail solicitations.

If it hasn't happened to you yet, no doubt as you become gainfully employed, give money to a cause or two you admire, and become integrated into your community, you too will become the target of "personalized" written requests from interest groups for the donations that they need to keep financially afloat. Direct mail is big business, run by professionals whose job it is to design the impassioned pleas that encourage you to open your wallet or write that check. Because interest groups have so much at stake in their direct-mail solicitations (in many cases, their very survival depends on it), they pull out all the stops in their letters to you. How can you evaluate these dramatic requests so that you can in fact support the legitimate groups whose causes you believe in, but not fall (as they hope you will) for over-the-top exaggeration and provocatively embellished prose? When presented with a plea for funds, it is worth doing a little homework before you part with any cash.

WHAT TO WATCH OUT FOR

- **Hidden agendas.** Always ask yourself, "What is this group? What does it stand for?" Sometimes direct-mail writers spend the majority of their time telling you what they are against, or whom they oppose, in the hopes that you will share their animosities and therefore support them. Many groups give a web address. Check them out, but remember that the web content is also written by supporters and may not give you a full or unbiased view. Look up the group in a newspaper archive and get some objective information (that is, information not written by the group itself!).

- **Vague connections.** A letter might address you as though you were a long-lost friend, but it pays to take a little time to figure out exactly how the organization came to think of you as a potential donor. Often a group will buy a mailing list from some other group. You can occasionally trace your name by the particular spelling (or misspelling), use of a maiden name or nickname, or some other characteristic that does not appear on your standard mailing address. Knowing how a group got your name can sometimes tell you what its connections are and what it is about. A simple mail order purchase of hiking boots can get you on the mailing lists of sports outfitters, and a short step later onto the lists of the NRA or the Sierra Club, both of which hope that outdoorsy people support their causes. In addition, as mailing techniques get more sophisticated, interest groups are able to personalize their requests for support. If you belong to the local Humane Society and other groups that would indicate your love for animals, and if the interest group got your name from their lists, it can target you with a fundraising letter that plays on your concern for animal life. If the letter seems to be directed to your deepest values, harden your heart until you have checked out the group independently.

- **Unverified claims.** Direct mail is designed to make you sit down and write a check now. From some letters, you get the sense that Armageddon is at hand and the world will soon self-destruct without your donation. Do not believe everything you read in a fundraising letter. Verify the facts before you send any money. The more persuasive and amazing the claim appears to be, the more it requires verification!

- **Check out their record.** Be clear about what you are being asked for—it is almost always money, but a group may also ask you to write your congressperson, make a phone call, wear a ribbon, or otherwise show support for a cause. Make sure you know what you are committing to do. If possible, check out the interest group's record for effective action. If most of the money it gets goes to administrative costs, you won't be furthering your cause much by contributing your dollars.

- **What's in it for you?** What material benefits does the group offer? Do you receive a newsletter? Discounts on products or services? Special offers for the group? We are not advising free ridership here, but it is wise to know exactly what you are getting before you part with your cash.

MOBILIZING THE PUBLIC The point of disseminating information, hiring public relations firms, creating web sites, and running issue ads is to motivate the public to lobby politicians themselves. On most issues, general public interest is low, and groups must rely on their own members for support. As you might suspect, groups like AARP, the Christian Coalition, and the NRA, which have large memberships, have an advantage because they can mobilize a large contingent of citizens from all over the country to lobby representatives and senators. Generally this mobilization involves

Ralph Fresco/Getty Images Sport/Getty Images

Going to Bat Against Breast Cancer

Interest groups don't just lobby government—they lobby the public, too, in hopes of educating us about (and rallying us behind) their causes. The Susan J. Komen Foundation for Breast Cancer Research has increased public awareness of breast cancer largely through public events like Major League Baseball's annual Mother's Day event, during which players, coaches, and umpires across the league sport pink bats, gloves, and other equipment.

encouraging members to write letters, send emails or faxes, or make phone calls to legislators about a pending issue.

Professional lobbyists freely admit that their efforts are most effective when the people "back home" are contacting representatives about an issue.[94] Although considerable evidence indicates that members of Congress do monitor their mail and respond to the wishes of their constituents, there is also some evidence that as these tactics have become more prevalent, they are being met with increasing skepticism and resistance on Capitol Hill.[95] To combat congressional skepticism, many interest groups have begun to deliver on their threats to politicians by mobilizing their members to vote. The religious right has long been able to do this, mobilizing conservative voters from the pulpit, but more recently liberals—for example, the "netroots," liberal

activist groups like MoveOn.org and ActBlue that challenge establishment politicians and interest groups—have gotten into the game via the Internet.

UNCONVENTIONAL METHODS, SOCIAL PROTEST, AND MASS MOVEMENTS A discussion of interest group politics would not be complete without mention of the unconventional technique of social protest. Throughout our history, groups have turned to **social protest**—activities ranging from planned, orderly demonstrations to strikes and boycotts, to acts of civil disobedience—when other techniques have failed to bring attention to their causes. The nonviolent civil rights protests—beginning with the Montgomery, Alabama, bus boycott discussed in Chapter 6—illustrate the types of actions such groups have used to bring their concerns to national attention.

Like other grassroots lobbying techniques, the techniques of social protest provide a way for people to publicly express their disagreement with a government policy or action. At the same time, their use often signals the strength of participants' feelings on an issue—and, often, outrage over being closed out from more traditional avenues of political action. Thus demonstrations and protests have frequently served an important function for those who have been excluded from the political process because of their minority, social, or economic status. While social protest may have the same objective as other types of indirect lobbying—that is, educating the public and mobilizing the group's members—demonstrations and spontaneous protests also aim to draw in citizens who have not yet formed an opinion or to change the minds of those who have. Such actions may turn a political action into a mass movement, attracting formerly passive or uninterested observers to the cause.

Social protest in the United States did not begin with the civil rights movement, although many activists since then have followed the strategies used by civil rights leaders. The labor movement of the late nineteenth century used demonstrations and strikes to attract more members to unions, with the goal of improving working conditions and wages. The women's suffrage movement of the late nineteenth and early twentieth centuries, discussed in Chapter 6, used social protest to fight for voting rights for women. Social movements have been used to change both private and government behavior. The prohibition (or temperance) movement of the late nineteenth and early twentieth centuries, for example, was aimed at stopping one particular behavior: the drinking of alcohol.

Modern mass movements employ many of the same tactics as those used in earlier days, but they have also

> **social protest** public activities designed to bring attention to political causes, usually generated by those without access to conventional means of expressing their views

benefited greatly from the opportunities offered by the modern media. The increasingly widespread medium of television was important to the success of the civil rights movement in the 1950s and early 1960s, as the protests and demonstrations brought home the plight of southern blacks to other regions of the country. Especially significant to the TV audience was the coverage of police brutality. Viewers were shocked by the beatings with nightsticks and the use of high-pressure hoses on demonstrators. In the 1970s mass demonstration was used effectively by peace groups protesting American involvement in the Vietnam War. Americans at home could not help but be impressed by the huge numbers of students gathered at such protests—burning draft cards, marching on the Pentagon, or staging college sit-ins or teach-ins to protest the government's policy. Month after month, a complete recap of the day's major protest activities on the evening news forced most people to at least confront their own views on the situation.

The possibilities for using the media to support mass movements have exploded with the advent of the Internet. High-tech flash campaigns have helped groups like Censure and Move On (now MoveOn.org, a citizen action group formed in 1998 to pressure Congress not to impeach President Clinton) to mobilize hundreds of thousands of citizens to lobby Congress by setting up relatively inexpensive and efficient "cyberpetitions" on their web sites.[96] Less conventional outlets of the traditional media can also get involved in social protest. Since the beginning of the Obama administration, Fox News has helped to foment protest on the right with publicity for and encouragement of the Tea Party movement.[97] In response, in 2010 Jon Stewart and Stephen Colbert staged a dual Rally for Sanity/Keep Fear Alive event, drawing an estimated 215,000 people to Washington's National Mall.

Today a number of groups continue in the tradition of unconventional social protest. Operation Rescue, which opposes abortion rights, tends to be the most active in using unconventional techniques to influence public opinion and, through harassment and intimidation, to discourage both providers and those seeking abortions. The group also extended its tactics to similar issues, for instance protesting the termination of medical treatment to a brain-damaged woman.[98] Although Operation Rescue's tactics tend to be the most extreme, even more traditional mainstream abortion groups like the National Right to Life Committee (on the pro-life side) and NOW (a pro-choice group) take an active role in organizing annual marches in Washington to promote their respective causes.

> **grassroots lobbying** indirect lobbying efforts that spring from widespread public concern
>
> **astroturf lobbying** indirect lobbying efforts that manipulate or create public sentiment, "astroturf" being artificial grassroots

"ASTROTURF" POLITICAL CAMPAIGNS: DEMOCRATIC OR ELITE DRIVEN?

The indirect lobbying we have discussed is often called **grassroots lobbying**, meaning that it addresses people in their roles as ordinary citizens. It is the wielding of power from the bottom (roots) up, rather than from the top down. Most of what we refer to as grassroots lobbying, however, does not spring spontaneously from the people but is orchestrated by elites, leading some people to call it **astroturf lobbying**—indicating that it is not really genuine. Often the line between real grassroots and astroturf lobbying is blurred, however. A movement may be partly spontaneous but partly orchestrated. After MoveOn.org's success as a spontaneous expression of popular will spread by "word of mouse" over the Internet, its organizers began other flash campaigns, notably one called "Gun Safety First," urging people to support gun control measures. This was less clearly a spontaneous popular movement, but it still involved mobilizing citizens to support a cause they believed in. Similarly, the current Tea Party movement has been, in part, the project of Dick Armey, a former Republican House majority leader whose organization, FreedomWorks for America, promotes low taxes and small government. FreedomWorks and several other conservative groups, as well as prominent individuals including some commentators at Fox News, have lent their organizational expertise to the Tea Partiers but deny that they are orchestrating an astroturf movement.[99] Regardless of how it started out, the Tea Party movement has certainly acquired a life and mind, perhaps several minds, of its own.

At the astroturf extreme, there was nothing spontaneous at all about the pharmaceutical industry's 2003 efforts to oppose the importation of cheaper drugs from Canada. The Pharmaceutical Research and Manufacturers Association (PhRMA), the industry's lobbying group, spent over $4 million on such tactics as persuading seniors that their access to medicine would be limited if reimportation of these American-made drugs were allowed and convincing members of a Christian advocacy group that prescription drug importation might lead to easier access to the controversial morning-after pill.[100] Concerned citizens were then coached by a PhRMA-hired public relations firm on how to contact legislators to weigh in against the proposed law. Such a strategy is obviously an attempt to create an opinion that might not otherwise even exist, playing on popular fears about drug availability and sentiments about abortion to achieve corporate ends.

While pure grassroots efforts are becoming increasingly rare, a good deal of indirect lobbying is done to promote what a group claims is the public interest, or at least the interest of the members of some mass-based group like AARP. One observer who works for a public interest group says, "Grassroots politics has become a top-down corporate enterprise," and speculates that there is very little genuine grassroots-type lobbying left.[101] More often than not, astroturf lobbying uses the support of the public to promote the

Are there any lobbying techniques that should be off limits in a democracy?

interest of a corporation or business. In many cases the clients of astroturf lobbying efforts are large corporations seeking tax breaks, special regulations, or simply the end of legislation that may hurt the corporation's interest. To generate public support, clients employ armies of lobbyists, media experts, and political strategists to conduct polls, craft multimedia advertising campaigns, and get the message out to "the people" through cable and radio news talk shows, the Internet, outbound call centers, fax machines, or some combination of these. Astroturf campaigns are very expensive.

One prominent campaign media consultant predicts that direct lobbying will become less important as indirect lobbying gains in effectiveness and popularity.[102] While indirect lobbying seems on its face to be more democratic, to the extent that it manipulates public opinion, it may in fact have the opposite effect. And as multimedia campaigns get more and more expensive, the number of groups that can afford to participate will undoubtedly decline. Ironically, as lobbying moves away from the closed committee rooms of Congress and into the realm of what appears to be popular politics, it may not get any more democratic than it has traditionally been.

PAUSE AND REVIEW:

WHO, WHAT, HOW

Interest groups exist to influence policy. Because of the complexity of the American system, these groups can accomplish their goals in a number of ways. They can engage in direct lobbying, by working from inside the government to influence what the government does, or by working on the public rather than on government officials to influence policy. Sometimes interest group organizers will inspire their members to use unconventional methods to try to influence government, including social protests, mass resistance or demonstrations, and Internet communication. Increasingly, lobbyists are combining strategies and taking advantage of the new communication technologies to create innovative, expensive, and often successful campaigns to influence public policy.

IN YOUR OWN WORDS » Describe how interest groups use lobbying and campaign activities to get the public policy they want.

INTEREST GROUP RESOURCES
Using money, leadership skills, size, and intensity to make their voices heard

Interest group success depends in large part on the resources a group can bring to the project of influencing government (see Table 13.1). The pluralist defense of interest groups is that all citizens have the opportunity to organize, and thus all can exercise equal power. But all interest groups are not created equal. Some have more money, more effective leadership, more members, or better information than others, and these resources can translate into real power differences that give groups a better chance of influencing government policy than, say, the Children's Defense Fund. In this section we examine the resources that interest groups can draw on to exert influence over policymaking: money, leadership, membership, and information.

MONEY

Interest groups need money to conduct the business of trying to influence governmental policymakers. Money can buy an interest group the ability to put together a well-trained staff, to hire outside professional assistance, and to make campaign contributions in the hopes of gaining access to government officials. Having money does not guarantee favorable policies, but not having money just about guarantees failure.

STAFF One of the reasons money is important is that it enables an interest group to hire a professional staff, usually an executive director, assistants, and other office support staff. The main job of this professional staff is to take care of the day-to-day operations of the interest group, including pursuing policy initiatives; recruiting and maintaining membership; providing membership services; and, of course, getting more money through direct mailings, telemarketing, web site donations, and organizational functions. Money is important for creating an organizational infrastructure that can in turn be used to raise additional support and resources.

PROFESSIONAL ASSISTANCE Money also enables the interest group to hire the services of professionals, such as a high-powered lobbying firm. These firms have invested heavily to ensure that they have connections to members of Congress.[103] A well-endowed group can also hire a public relations firm to help shape public opinion on a policy, as was done with the Harry and Louise campaign discussed in *What's at Stake. . . ?*, and a skilled person to handle Internet operations.

CAMPAIGN CONTRIBUTIONS Interest groups live by the axiom that to receive, one must give—and give a lot to important people. The maximum that any PAC can give

TABLE 13.1

TEN OF THE MOST INFLUENTIAL LOBBIES IN WASHINGTON

INDUSTRY OR GROUP	MAJOR PLAYERS	KEY POLICY AREAS	LOBBYING EXPENDITURES FOR 2012
Finance	Insurance, securities and investing, real estate, banks, finance/credit companies	Financial regulation and reforms	$487.5 million
Oil	Exxon Mobile, Koch Industries, Chevron Corporation; Royal Dutch Shell	Environmental regulation	$140.7 million
Agribusiness	Food industry (Kraft, Unilever, Monsanto); tobacco companies (Phillip Morris); biofuel producers and logging companies	Food labeling, environmental regulation, biofuel production	$139.7 million
Defense	Lockheed Martin, Boeing, General Dynamics	Defense, military	$136 million
Technology	Apple, Microsoft, Google, Amazon, Facebook	Corporate tax rates, cybersecurity, Net neutrality	$133.2 million
Pharmaceuticals	Pfizer, Eli Lilly & Co., Merck	Health care regulation	$119.5 million
Mining	The coal industry	Environmental regulation	$32.6 million
Retirees	AARP	Health care, Medicare, Social Security, retirement and age discrimination	$9.9 million
Gun rights	National Rifle Association (NRA)	Second Amendment rights, gun control and regulation	$6.1 million
Pro-Israel	American Israel Public Affairs Committee	Foreign policy	$3.6 million

Sources: Compiled by the authors using rankings by BusinessPundit.com, www.businesspundit.com/10-of-the-biggest-lobbies-in-washington/, April 26, 2011, and figures from the Center for Responsive Politics, www.opensecrets.org/lobby/top.php?indexType=c&showYear=2012.

to a congressional campaign is $5,000 for each separate election. While some PACs give millions to campaigns, most PACs give less than $50,000 to candidates for each election cycle, focusing their contributions on members of the committees responsible for drafting legislation important to their groups.[104] In the wake of the *Citizens United* decision, however, considerable money can be spent by groups on a candidate's behalf, and the groups don't have to disclose the donors' identities. It has become apparent that although the *Citizens United* decision made only small changes to campaign finance law, it had the psychological

effect of giving a "green light" to those who wanted to spend lavishly on an election.[105] In 2012 the so-called Super PACs unleashed by *Citizens United* spent more than one billion dollars, though it wasn't clear that all that money had a real impact on the outcome of the election, at least in the presidential and Senate races.[106]

PAC spending is usually directed toward incumbents of both parties, with incumbents in the majority party, especially committee chairs, getting the greatest share. This dramatic difference is shown in Figure 13.4, which illustrates not only that most of the PAC money goes to

FIGURE 13.4 PAC CONTRIBUTIONS TO CONGRESSIONAL CAMPAIGNS BY TYPE OF CONTEST, 1998–2012

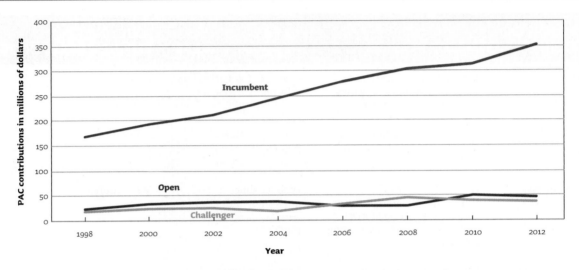

Source: Federal Election Commission, "Campaign Finance Statistics," http: www.fec.gov/press/campaign_finance_statistics.shtml.

incumbents, but also that this huge imbalance has increased over the past decade. About 80 percent of PAC contributions go to incumbent members of Congress.[107] While most PACs want to curry favor with incumbents of either party, some tend to channel their money to one party. For instance, business interests, the American Medical Association, pro-life groups, Christian groups, and the NRA tend to support Republican candidates; and labor groups, the Association of Trial Lawyers of America, the National Education Association, and environmental and pro-choice groups give primarily to Democrats.

The ability to make sizable and strategically placed campaign contributions buys an interest group access to government officials.[108] Access gives the interest group the ability to talk to a representative and members of his or her staff and to present information relevant to the policies they seek to initiate, change, or protect. Access is important because representatives have any number of competing interests vying for their time. Money is meant to oil the door hinge of a representative's office so that it swings open for the interest group. For instance, the Clinton administration was well known in its early years for allowing major donors to stay in the Lincoln bedroom of the White House. The access bought by campaign contributions is usually less blatant, but officials know who has supported their campaigns, and they are unlikely to forget it when the interest group comes knocking at their doors.

The relationship between money and political influence is extremely controversial. Many critics argue that this money buys more than just access; rather, they charge, it buys votes. The circumstantial evidence is strong. For

instance, in the Senate deliberations on a public option in health care, which would have provided individuals with an alternative to private health care insurance, the thirty senators who supported the public option had received an average of $15,937 in contributions from the health care industry in the previous six years, compared to the $37,322 that was received, on average, by the seventy senators who opposed it.[109]

However, in the matter of vote buying, systematic studies of congressional voting patterns are mixed. These studies show that the influence of campaign contributions is strongest in committees, where most bills are drafted. However, once the bill reaches the floor of the House or the Senate, there is no consistent link between campaign contributions and roll-call voting.[110] This suggests that campaign contributions influence the process of creating and shaping the legislation, and thus defining the policy alternatives. Nonetheless, the final outcome of a bill is determined by political circumstances that go beyond the campaign contributions of interest groups.

LEADERSHIP

Leadership is an intangible element in the success or failure of an interest group. We mentioned earlier that an effective and charismatic leader or interest group entrepreneur can help a group organize even if it lacks other resources. In the same way, such a leader can keep a group going when it seems to lack the support from other sources. Candy Lightner's role in MADD and César Chavez's leadership of the United Farm Workers are excellent cases in point. But professional interest group leadership can come at a cost. As the mass membership interest groups that characterized this country in the past century give way to highly professional groups whose power comes more from their organizational skills than from their active members, some observers have argued that the groups no longer serve as training grounds for citizenship and are more elite driven than democratic. Says one, "The result is a new civic America largely run by advocates and managers without members and marked by yawning gaps between immediate involvements and larger undertakings."[111] Ultimately, professional group leadership can leave the mass citizenry with fewer paths to civic engagement, eliminating one of the characteristics of interest group politics that leads pluralists, for instance, to claim that interest groups can enhance democracy.

Michael Rougier/The LIFE Picture Collection/Getty Images

Leaders Inspire Leaders
The success of the United Farm Workers Union rested largely on the shoulders of Cesar Chavez, whose charismatic and effective leadership caught the attention of powerful Americans like Robert F. Kennedy and brought national attention to the plight of farm workers. Here, Kennedy lends his support to Chavez (center) during the activist's prolonged hunger strike in 1968.

MEMBERSHIP: SIZE AND INTENSITY

The membership of any interest group is an important resource in terms of its size, but the level of intensity that members exhibit in support of the group's causes is also critical. Members represent the lifeblood of the interest group because they generally fund its activities. When an interest group is trying to influence policy, it can use its members to write letters, send emails, and engage in other forms of personal contact with legislators or administrative officials. Often interest groups try to reinforce their PAC contributions by encouraging their members to give personal campaign contributions to favored candidates.

Larger groups generally have an advantage over smaller ones. For instance, with more than 40 million members, AARP can mobilize thousands of people in an attempt to influence elected officials' decisions regarding issues like mandatory retirement, Social Security, or Medicare. In addition, if an interest group's members are spread throughout the country, as are AARP's, that group can exert its influence on almost every member of Congress.

If a group's members are intensely dedicated to the group's causes, then the group may be far stronger than its numbers would indicate. Intense minorities, because of their willingness to devote time, energy, and money to a cause they care passionately about, can outweigh more apathetic majorities in the political process. For instance, although a majority of Americans favor some form of gun control, they are outweighed in the political process by the intense feeling of the just over four million members of the NRA, who strongly oppose gun control.[112]

INFORMATION

Information is one of the most powerful resources in an interest group's arsenal. Often the members of the interest group are the *only* sources of information on the potential or actual impact of a law or regulation. The long struggle to regulate tobacco is a case in point. While individuals witnessed their loved ones and friends suffering from lung diseases, cancer, and heart problems, it took public health interest groups like the American Cancer Society, the Public Health Cancer Association, and the American Heart Association to conduct the studies, collect the data, and show the connection between these life-threatening illnesses and smoking habits. Of course the tobacco industry and its interest group, the Tobacco Institute, presented their own research to counter these claims. Not surprisingly, the tobacco industry's investigations showed "no causal relationship" between tobacco use and these illnesses.[113] Eventually, the volume of information showing a strong relationship overwhelmed industry research suggesting otherwise. In 1998 the tobacco industry reached a settlement with states to pay millions of dollars for the treatment of tobacco-related illnesses.

WHO, WHAT, HOW

Again, there is no mystery about what interest groups want: they seek to influence the policymaking process. Some interest groups are clearly more successful than others because the rules of interest group politics reward some group characteristics—such as size, intensity, money, effective leadership, and the possession of information—more than others (perhaps social conscience or humanitarianism). It is certainly possible to imagine reforms or rule changes that would change the reward structure and, in so doing, change the groups that would be successful.

IN YOUR OWN WORDS » Identify specific resources that interest groups bring to bear when attempting to influence public policy.

» THE CITIZENS AND INTEREST GROUPS
The people versus the powerful

Defenders of pluralism believe that interest group formation helps give more power to more citizens, and we have seen that it certainly can enhance democratic life. Interest groups offer channels for representation, participation, education, defining policy solutions, and public agenda building, and they help to keep politicians accountable. Pluralists also believe that the system as a whole benefits from interest group politics. They argue that if no single interest group commands a majority, interest groups will compete with one another and ultimately must form coalitions to create a majority. In the process of forming coalitions, interest groups compromise on policy issues, leading to final policy outcomes that reflect the general will of the people as opposed to the narrow interests of specific interest groups.[114] In this final section we examine the claims of critics of interest group politics who argue that it skews democracy—giving more power to some people than to others—and particularly discriminates against segments of society that tend to be underrepresented in the first place (the poor and the young, for instance).

We have seen in this chapter that a variety of factors—money, leadership, membership, and information—can make an interest group successful. But this raises red danger flags for American democracy. In American political culture, we value political equality, which is to say the principle of one person, one vote. And as far as voting goes, this is how we practice democracy. Anyone who attempts to visit the polls twice on Election Day is turned away, no matter how rich that person is, how intensely he or she feels about the election, or how eloquently he or she begs for another

vote. But policy is made not only at the ballot box. It is also made in the halls and hearing rooms of Congress; in the conference rooms of the bureaucracy; and in corporate boardrooms, private offices, restaurants, and bars. In these places interest groups speak loudly, and since some groups are vastly more successful than others, they have the equivalent of extra votes in the policymaking process.

We are not terribly uncomfortable with the idea that interest groups with large memberships should have more power. After all, democracy is usually about getting the most votes in order to win. But when it comes to the idea that the wealthy have an advantage, or those who feel intensely, or those who have more information, we start to balk. What about the rest of us? Should we have relatively less power over who gets what because we lack these resources?

It is true that groups with money, and business groups in particular, have distinct advantages of organizational access. Many critics suggest that business interests represent a small, wealthy, and united set of elites who dominate the political process,[115] and much evidence supports the view that business interests maintain a special relationship with government and tend to unite behind basic conservative issues (less government spending and lower taxes). Other evidence, however, suggests that business interests are often divided regarding governmental policies and that other factors can counterbalance their superior monetary resources.

Because business interests are not uniform and tightly organized, groups with large memberships can prevail against them. Corporate money may buy access, but politicians ultimately depend on votes. Groups with large memberships have more voters. A good example of this principle occurred in 1997 when President Clinton proposed trimming $100 billion in Medicare spending over five years. Instead of raising premiums on the elderly, the Clinton administration proposed cuts in Medicare reimbursements to hospitals and doctors. This proposal sparked an intensive lobbying campaign pitting the American Medical Association and the American Hospital Association, two of the most powerful and well-financed lobbies in Washington, against AARP, representing more than 40 million older Americans. Fearing the voting wrath of AARP, the Republican-led Congress struck a deal with the administration to cut Medicare reimbursements for hospitals and doctors.[116] As this example suggests, when a group's membership is highly motivated and numerous, it can win despite the opposition's lavish resources.[117]

Interest group politics in America clearly contains some biases, but it is not the case that any one group or kind of group always gets its way. After years of collecting government subsidies and benefiting from favorable policies, the tobacco industry has at last been stripped of its privilege, illustrating that even corporate giants can be brought low.[118] Similarly the less wealthy but very intense NRA, which kept gun control off the American law books for decades, has finally been confronted by angry citizens' groups that have put the issue of gun control firmly on the public's agenda, though with mixed success.[119]

What has helped to equalize the position of these groups in American politics is the willingness on the part of citizens to fight fire with fire, politics with politics, organization with organization—an effort made more accessible with the widespread use of the Internet. It is, finally, the power of participation and democracy that can make pluralism fit the pluralists' hopes. For some groups, such as the poor, such advice may be nearly impossible to follow. Lacking knowledge of the system and the resources to organize in the first place, poor people are often the last to be included in interest group politics. Neighborhood-level organizing, however, such as that done by the Southwest Voter Registration Education Project and Hermandad Mexicana Latinoamericana, can counteract this tendency. Other groups left out of the system, such as the merely indifferent, or young people who often regard current issues as irrelevant, will pay the price of inattention and disorganization when the score cards of interest group politics are finally tallied.

IN YOUR OWN WORDS » Summarize the relationship among citizens, interest groups, and government.

LET'S REVISIT: **WHAT'S AT STAKE...**

In this chapter we have seen that Madison's fear of factions was not unfounded. Interest groups may not be able to buy votes, per se, but they certainly can buy access and influence, and the politician who ignores them does so at his or her peril.

Having seen what happened when President Clinton failed to get the health industry groups on board, the Obama team was determined to avoid Clinton's mistakes. What was at stake for the Obama administration, for interest groups, for the political parties, and for the nation as a whole in the White House's decision to bring these groups in at the ground level in the effort to reform the country's health care system?

The stakes for the White House were huge. President Obama had made health care a signature issue of his campaign and had promised as well a new way of governing—lean, effective, and bipartisan. Republicans could deny him the "bipartisan label," but he didn't want to cede ground on whether government could be an effective actor as well. Most observers agreed that if health care reform failed to pass this time around, it could be years before it had another shot. White House communications director Dan Pfeiffer said that what was on the line was whether government could still solve big problems, whereas former Senate majority leader Tom Daschle said that a failure to get the bill passed would amount to a failure to govern. The way to succeed was to get all the concerned actors on board. "The President said that having people at the table is better than having them throw stuff at the table," said Pfeiffer.[120]

For industry interest groups, the stakes were substantial as well. If they stayed outside of the process but were unable to stop health care reform, they risked being stuck with a policy they hated. And many groups agreed with one of the basic tenets of the reformers—that the status quo in health care, with its rising costs, was unsustainable. If they joined the reform effort, they could have a say in shaping the solution to the problem. America's Health Insurance Plans, recognizing that its members would be required to cover preexisting conditions, made the "universal mandate"— the condition that all who could afford it be required to buy insurance—the price of their cooperation. The drug companies were able to head off more severe cuts in drug coverage and competition from cheaper drug companies abroad by voluntarily offering to reduce costs. As *New Republic* writer Jonathan Cohn put it, for interest groups the choice was simple: you can be at the table or you can be on the menu.[121]

The value of the strategy the interest groups followed is suggested by the fate of the Republican Party, which did stay outside the process and refused to compromise. After reform passed, conservative author and former George W. Bush speechwriter David Frum criticized the Republican strategy, saying that Republican participation could have pulled the plan in a direction more consistent with conservative principles. By refusing to play at all, the Republicans ceded influence over the final product—they went for all the marbles and ended with none.[122] By getting involved early, interest groups got a good share of the marbles.

Which, of course, is what so annoyed President Obama's liberal critics. Obama gave away the store, they argued, making concessions before he had to and giving up the public option, a key element of reform near and dear to their hearts.[123] For them, what was at stake in Obama's deal-making with the health care industry was the very integrity of reform. No less than the Republicans, Democratic critics believed that to compromise was to water down their principles. Had they insisted on purity, however, there likely would have been no health care bill at all. Though the House of Representatives managed to pass a bill with a weak version of the public option, without Republican support, Senate majority leader Harry Reid needed every Democrat on board, as well as independent senator Joe Lieberman of Connecticut. Lieberman tends to vote with the Democrats, but he made it clear that he would not support a public option, and the legislative effort to provide it died.[124]

The political stakes were high for the actors, like the president, who stood to face a crippled agenda if he could not bring off the reform he had promised, and for the Republicans, who had sworn to bring Obama to his Waterloo over the issue. For the health care industry, the stakes were more substantive—how much would they have to give away to keep reform within tolerable limits? The stakes for the American people were more substantive as well. For the uninsured and the uninsurable, the stakes were the difference between regular access to quality care and a patchwork of critical care cobbled together in emergency rooms and free clinics. For all Americans, the insured as well as the uninsured, the stakes were runaway health care costs that limit our ability to spend money on other necessities, or costs brought under control, with savings ultimately reducing the federal deficit. Those on the left and the right seem to believe that, by holding out, their side could have achieved all their goals, but the truth is that American politics is about compromise, and a health care reform proposal that didn't try to incorporate multiple views and goals was probably not going to be passed at all, especially given the tenuous nature of the Democratic majority in the Senate. What was at stake in bringing the industry groups to the table in the health care reform effort was the very fate of health care in America. Whether or not the reform was strong enough to improve it remains to be seen.

Sharpen your skills with **SAGE edge** at http://edge.sagepub.com/barbour7e. **SAGE edge for students** provides a personalized approach to help you accomplish your coursework goals in an easy-to-use learning environment.

TO SUM UP

REVIEW

The Roles and Formation of Interest Groups

Government will always distribute resources in ways that benefit some at the expense of others. People form interest groups in order to influence the way that government policy decisions are made. To accomplish their goals, interest groups lobby elected officials, rally public opinion, offer policy suggestions, and keep tabs on policy once enacted. Interest groups also must organize and convince others to join, often offering selective benefits to members.

faction (p. 472)
interest group (p. 476)
political action committees (PACs) (p. 477)
lobbying (p. 478)

interest group entrepreneurs (p. 479)
free rider problem (p. 479)
collective good (p. 479)
selective incentives (p. 479)
material benefits (p. 479)
solidarity benefits (p. 480)
expressive benefits (p. 480)

Types of Interest Groups

Interest groups come in all different types. Economic groups like business associations or trade unions want to protect and improve their status. Public interest groups advocate their vision of society, and equal opportunity groups organize to gain, or at least improve, economic status and civil rights. Governments form associations to improve relations among their ranks.

Interest Group Politics

Lobbyists are the key players of interest groups. They influence public policy either by approaching the three branches of government (direct lobbying) or by convincing the people to pressure the government (indirect lobbying).

Interest Group Resources

The success of individual interest groups is often affected by factors like funding, quality of leadership, membership size and intensity, and access to information.

The Citizens and Interest Groups

Critics of interest groups fear that the most powerful groups are simply those with the most money, and that this poses a danger to American democracy. However, interest group formation may also be seen as a way to give more power to more citizens, offering a mechanism to keep politicians accountable by offering additional channels for representation, participation, education, creation of policy solutions, and public agenda building.

ENGAGE

Follow the money.
Find out who the biggest donors are—and where their money is going. There's no better place to start than **The Center for Responsive Politics**, which provides up-to-the-minute data on money and politics and contains a wealth of information on lobbyists and PACs, politician and congressional committee profiles, campaign donation lists, and much more.

Do some investigating.
Want to dig further? The **Federal Election Commission** lists the official reports regarding campaign finance. With a little research, the user can gain access to how much PAC money was spent in recent as well as past elections. You can also check out the **Senate Office of Public Records**, where you can find Lobbying Disclosure Reports for all the interests that have lobbied Congress.

Find the groups that are lobbying for you.
Everyone has an interest, and love them or hate them, interest groups have a loud voice in Washington. Consider the issues that are important to you, and see who is speaking up on them on Capitol Hill. **Political Advocacy Groups: A Directory of U.S. Lobbyists** is a frequently updated directory of U.S. interest groups and lobby organizations that includes, for each interest group entry, contact information and a copy of the group's mission statement.

Don't be a free rider.
Found a group that lobbies on your behalf? Don't be afraid to become a card-carrying (and dues-paying) member to help ensure that your voice is heard. Chances are you can join some really potent interest groups right on your college campus, including your state chapter of the **Public Interest Research Group (PIRG)**, a self-styled "advocate for the public interest" that seeks to combat the actions of special interest lobbyists.

EXPLORE

Cigler, Allan J., and Burdett A. Loomis, eds. 2012. *Interest Group Politics*, 8th ed. Washington, DC: CQ Press. This noteworthy collection deals with the many facets of interest group politics.

Feldman, Richard. 2007. *Ricochet: Confessions of a Gun Lobbyist*. Hoboken, NJ: Wiley. Written by a former NRA regional political director and gun lobbyist, this book offers an unprecedented insider's view of the National Rifle Association.

***The Best Congress Money Can Buy*. 2007.** *Dan Rather Reports* (New York: CBS). This film analyzes the extent of interest groups' control over congressional decision making. A unique look at how much government legislation money can really buy.

***Thank You for Smoking*. 2006.** This Golden Globe–nominated film follows the efforts of Nick Naylor—chief spokesperson for a major tobacco lobby—to paint cigarette use in a more positive light, and the heated public debate that ensues.

14 VOTING, CAMPAIGNS, AND ELECTIONS

IN YOUR OWN WORDS After you've read this chapter, you will be able to

» Explain the function of elections, both as intended by the founders and in practice.

» Analyze the reasons why Americans vote—or don't vote.

» Identify four factors that influence voters' decisions.

» Describe the organizational and strategic tactics involved in presidential campaigns.

» Summarize the importance of elections for citizens.

WHAT'S AT STAKE...IN HOW A CAMPAIGN GETS OUT ITS VOTE?

WHEN ELECTION DAY 2012 ROLLED AROUND, both major party campaigns were feeling optimistic. The Obama campaign had been quietly confident for months. Its polls and most of the public polls showed a small but steady lead for the president, and the forecasting models that averaged all the polls together and added economic variables showed a good chance for an Obama win. The campaign was especially confident about its ground game—its ability to mobilize supporters and get out the vote. For over a year the campaign had been working on a system that aggregated all the data it had on potential voters, and it had constructed a massive electronic system for microtargeting voters, directing ads to them, soliciting money from them, and getting them to vote. The campaign had been working the early voting states, and the totals of the votes the campaign saw there reassured it that its statistical models of which voters would actually turn out on Election Day were sound.

But the members of the Romney campaign were equally confident. They dismissed polls showing a

lead for Obama, claiming that the public polls were overestimating the numbers of Democrats who would show up on Election Day. Traditionally Democratic voters are younger than the Republican base and less white; young people and minorities tend not to vote at the rates that the Republicans' older and whiter base does. Consequently the Romney campaign based its own polls on a different turnout model, reducing the percentage of Democratic voters expected to vote. Its polls found growing momentum for Romney because he was supported by Republicans as well as a majority of voters identifying as independents. The campaign felt good about its get-out-the-vote (GOTV) effort, too; it had a hugely expensive and technologically advanced system that would channel information about who voted on Election Day from volunteers on the ground, via their cell phones, to campaign headquarters in Boston. Armed with that information, volunteers could be dispatched to call or encourage the nonvoters to get to the polls in the swing states before they closed.

© Daniel Shea Photography

Nerd Cave

Sequestered in a back room they dubbed the "Cave" in President Obama's campaign headquarters in Chicago, the young number crunchers took voter data gathering and analysis to a new level and reset the standard for future campaigns. The chief analytics officer said of his fellow workers, "We're kind of a weird bunch of kids. I haven't seen the sun for a while."

The Romney campaign had given interviews the day before Election Day, touting the system that it called the Orca Project (because the Orca whale is the natural predator of the Narwhal, the name for the Obama data management system). Romney's communications director said, "At 5 o'clock when the exit polls come out, we won't pay attention to that. We will have had much more scientific information just based on the political operation we have set up."[1] While the Romney campaign was talking up the virtues of Orca, the Obama campaign was much more silent about Narwhal, and about the program called Gordon, which was actually more comparable to Orca. Still, the Obama people insisted that they were going to win, and so did the Romney people.

What happened? Well of course, the president of the United States is still Barack Obama, so obviously he won. But the news took a while to sink in at the Romney campaign gathering at the Westin Boston Waterfront Hotel. An adviser for the campaign said that Mitt Romney was "shell-shocked" at the results. He delayed making a concession speech to President Obama, even after all the networks had called the election. The campaign had ordered an eight-minute fireworks display to celebrate its victory, and Romney had prepared a victory speech but no concession speech (candidates generally prepare both, just in case

either outcome occurs). Another adviser said, "There is nothing worse than when you think you are going to win, and you don't. It was like a sucker punch."[2]

At Obama's postelection gathering in Chicago's McCormick Place, the mood was considerably better. There were no fireworks, but Obama, who had prepared two speeches, got to give the victory version. Behind the scenes there was a less visible but no less heartfelt celebration, and the in-house technical people who had been hired over a year before to design Narwhal and Gordon (and several other systems) heaved a sigh of relief.

"I think the Republicans f**ked up in the hubris department," said Harper Reed, the chief technology officer of the Obama campaign. "I know we had the best technology team I've ever worked with, but we didn't know if it would work. I was incredibly confident it would work. I was betting a lot on it. We had time. We had resources. We had done what we thought would work, and it still could have broken. Something could have happened."[3]

And, in fact, for the Republicans, something did happen. On the day of the election, with more than 30,000 volunteers ready to gather information on who had voted and send it back to the campaign electronically, Orca crashed. The system had not been tried out in the field until that day; it hadn't been checked for bugs, and there had been no dry run.

Said one Romney volunteer who repeatedly tried to access the system all day on November 6:

> So, the end result was that 30,000+ of the most active and fired-up volunteers were wandering around confused and frustrated when they could have been doing anything else to help. Like driving people to the polls, phone-banking, walking door-to-door, etc. We lost by fairly small margins in Florida, Virginia, Ohio, and Colorado. If this had worked, could it have closed the gap? I sure hope not, for my sanity's sake.[4]

The Romney camp was reduced to following CNN and calling county election offices for its turnout information, and without detailed information, was unable to direct its volunteers to get out their votes. Still, the campaign thought it was winning. It was only as the reports indicated that turnout was high in areas that favored Obama that the campaign realized that its own turnout model had been flawed. The campaign had counted on turnout looking like it had in 2004, when participation of young people and minorities had not been high. Instead, it was looking more like 2008. Although apparently fewer voters overall had turned out, the demographic profile of the electorate looked like 2008, except that the percentage of young voters and minorities was slightly higher. While the Romney GOTV effort was not stellar, it looked like the Obama effort was.

In fact, the Obama team had prepared for the catastrophe that had befallen the Romney system. They had gamed out the system repeatedly, simulating every kind of crash and failure they could think of. The massive amounts of data that had been collected were analyzed by number crunchers sitting in a Chicago room known as the "Cave," who used the data to construct a model that predicted turnout all over the nation. Volunteers had converged on the swing states from around the country, canvassing neighborhoods, ready to follow up with potential voters who had not voted early or gotten to the polls on Election Day. Thanks to the data, the campaign knew exactly where those voters were.

Wrote one Obama volunteer from Idaho who had relocated to the swing state of Ohio for the four weeks preceding the election,

> For the last four days of the election, we helped manage a staging location for GOTV in one ward of a city in the eastern suburbs of Cleveland. I imagine that the campaign will never release the total number of people who worked or volunteered in Ohio; they might not even know. But extrapolating from our experience, I estimate that there might have been close to 50,000 people on the ground in one way or another during GOTV in Ohio, including 700 lawyers, 300 in the Cleveland area alone, protecting our vote.[5]

As the calendar ticked over to November 6, the tiny town of Dixville Notch, New Hampshire, which always votes at midnight, cast half of its votes (five) for the president and half for Romney. The kids in the Cave were thrilled. Their forecast model had predicted exactly that result, and as the day progressed, other turnout figures confirmed their model's forecast as well. As they had expected, Obama ended up winning handily; the turnout machinery had done its work well.

Once upon a time, getting out the vote meant making phone calls, knocking on doors, and hoping for the best. Systems didn't crash on Election Day because there were no systems. Clearly the effort has gotten far more sophisticated. Technology has changed the playing field. Just what is at stake in how a campaign mobilizes its supporters and gets out the vote? **«**

ALTHOUGH we pride ourselves on our democratic government, Americans seem to have a love-hate relationship with the idea of campaigns and voting. On the one hand, many citizens believe that elections do not accomplish anything, that elected officials ignore the wishes of the people, and that government is run for the interests of the elite rather than the many. Voters in 2008 were unusually motivated, with a turnout rate of higher than 60 percent, but typically only about half of the eligible electorate votes.

On the other hand, when it is necessary to choose a leader, whether the captain of a football team, the president of a dorm, or a local precinct chairperson, the first instinct of most Americans is to call an election. Even though there are other ways to choose leaders—picking the oldest, the wisest, or the strongest; holding a lottery; or asking for volunteers—Americans almost always prefer an election. We elect over half a million public officials in America.[6] This means we have a lot of elections—more elections more often for more officials than in any other democracy. In this chapter we examine the complicated place of elections in American politics and American culture.

VOTING IN A DEMOCRATIC SOCIETY
A nonviolent means for political change

Up until the last couple hundred years, it was virtually unthinkable that the average citizen could or should have any say in who would govern. Rather, leaders were chosen by birth, by the church, by military might, by the current leaders, but not by the mass public. Real political change, when it occurred, was usually ushered in with violence and bloodshed.

Today, global commitment to democracy is on the rise. Americans and, increasingly, other citizens around the world believe that government with the consent of the governed is superior to government imposed on unwilling subjects and that political change is best accomplished through the ballot box rather than on the battlefield or in the streets. The mechanism that connects citizens with their governments, by which they signify their consent and through which they accomplish peaceful change, is elections. Looked at from this perspective, elections are an amazing innovation—they provide a method for the peaceful transfer of power. Quite radical political changes can take place without blood being shed, an accomplishment that would confound most of our political ancestors.

As we saw in Chapter 1, however, proponents of democracy can have very different ideas about how much power citizens should exercise over government. Elite theorists believe that citizens should confine their role to choosing among competing elites; pluralists think citizens should join groups that fight for their interests in government on their behalf; and participatory democrats call for more active and direct citizen involvement in politics. Each of these views has consequences for how elections should be held. How many officials should be chosen by the people? How often should elections be held? Who should be allowed to vote? Should people choose officials directly, or through representatives whom they elect? How accountable should officials be to the people who elect them?

We have already seen, in Chapter 11, that though Americans hardly resemble the informed, active citizens prescribed by democratic theory, that does not mean they are unqualified to exercise political power. At the end of this chapter, when we have a clearer understanding of the way that elections work in America, we will return to the question of how much power citizens should have and what different answers to this question mean for our thinking about elections. We begin our study of elections, however, by examining the functions that they can perform in democratic government. First we look at the very limited role that the founders had in mind for popular elections when they designed the American Constitution, and then we evaluate the claims of democratic theorists more generally.

THE FOUNDERS' INTENTIONS

The Constitution reflects the founding fathers' fears that people could not reliably exercise wise and considered judgment about politics. Consequently the founders built a remarkable layer of insulation between the national government and the will of the people. The president was to be elected not directly by the people but by an Electoral College, which was expected to be a group of wiser-than-average men who would use prudent judgment. In fact, only the House of Representatives, one-half of one-third of the government, was to be popularly elected. The Senate and the executive and judicial branches were to be selected by different types of political elites who could easily check any

A Hard-Won Right
Democracy is nothing if it is not about citizens choosing their leaders. In 1966 black voters in Peachtree, Alabama, lined up to vote for the first time since passage of the Voting Rights Act of 1965.

moves that might arise from the whims of the masses. In the founders' view, the government needed the support of the masses, but it could not afford to be led by what they saw as the public's shortsighted and easily misguided judgment.

THE FUNCTIONS OF ELECTIONS

Despite the founders' reluctance to entrust much political power to American citizens, we have since altered our method of electing senators to make these elections direct, and the Electoral College, as we shall see, almost always endorses the popular vote for president. As we said in the introduction to this chapter, elections have become a central part of American life, even if our participation in them is somewhat uneven. Theorists claim that elections fulfill a variety of functions in modern democratic life: selecting leaders, giving direction to policy, developing citizenship, informing the public, containing conflict, and legitimizing and stabilizing the system. Here we examine and evaluate how well elections fill some of those functions.

SELECTION OF LEADERS Like our founders, many philosophers and astute political observers have had doubts about whether elections are the best way to choose wise and capable leaders. Philosophers from Plato to John Stuart Mill have expressed doubts about citizen capability, arguing that you cannot trust the average citizen to make wise choices in the voting booth.[7] More recent critics also focus on the other side of the equation, claiming that democratic

elections often fail to produce the best leaders because the electoral process scares off some of the most capable candidates. Running for office is a hard, expensive, and bruising enterprise. Many qualified people are put off by the process, though they might be able to do an excellent job and have much to offer through public service. The simple truth is that elections ensure only that the leader chosen is the most popular on the ballot. There is no guarantee that the best candidate will run, or that the people will choose the wisest, most honest, or most capable leader from the possible candidates.

THINKING OUTSIDE THE BOX

Are elections the best way to choose our leaders?

POLICY DIRECTION Democracy and elections are only partially about choosing able leadership. The fears of the founders notwithstanding, today we also expect that the citizenry will have a large voice in what the government actually does. Competitive elections are intended in part to keep leaders responsive to the concerns of the governed, since they can be voted out of office if voters are displeased.

The policy impact of elections, however, is indirect. For instance, at the national level, we elect individuals, but we do not vote on policies. Although citizens in about half the

Enter a politician's name or zip code

| BIO | VOTES | POSITIONS | RATINGS | SPEECHES | FUNDING |

40,000 POLITICIANS, MILLIONS OF FACTS

VOTE EASY — Find your political soulmate

POLITICAL GALAXY — Any Politician, Any Issue

My VOTE SMART — Beta

Courtesy of Project Vote Smart

Vote Smart
Volunteer members of Project Vote Smart, liberals and conservatives alike, reach out to citizens to inform them about the voting records and backgrounds of thousands of candidates and elected officials so that voters can make informed decisions. The group accepts no funding from any organization, special interest group, or industry as part of its effort to maintain its neutral, nonbiased platform.

● Contested Election

Voting in a Democratic Society **513**

CLUES
TO CRITICAL THINKING

Al Gore's Concession Speech, December 13, 2000

The 2000 presidential election was unusual on several counts (see What's at Stake . . . ? in Chapter 10). A state's election results were contested, amid accusations of fraud and misleading ballot design; that state's supreme court was overruled by the U.S. Supreme Court in the matter of recounts; and the results of that contested state election gave an Electoral College victory to a candidate who had lost the popular vote. This concession speech by Al Gore, who won the popular vote even as he lost the Electoral College, highlights how elections, even as odd as this one, serve to legitimate government when people agree on the rules.

Good evening.

Just moments ago, I spoke with George W. Bush and congratulated him on becoming the 43rd president of the United States, and I promised him that I wouldn't call him back this time.

I offered to meet with him as soon as possible so that we can start to heal the divisions of the campaign and the contest through which we just passed.

Almost a century and a half ago, Senator Stephen Douglas told Abraham Lincoln, who had just defeated him for the presidency, "Partisan feeling must yield to patriotism. I'm with you, Mr. President, and God bless you."

Well, in that same spirit, I say to President-elect Bush that what remains of partisan rancor must now be put aside, and may God bless his stewardship of this country.

Neither he nor I anticipated this long and difficult road. Certainly neither of us wanted it to happen. Yet it came, and now it has ended, resolved, as it must be resolved, through the honored institutions of our democracy.

Over the library of one of our great law schools is inscribed the motto, "Not under man but under God and law." That's the ruling principle of American freedom, the source of our democratic liberties. I've tried to make it my guide throughout this contest as it has guided America's deliberations of all the complex issues of the past five weeks.

Now the U.S. Supreme Court has spoken. Let there be no doubt, while I strongly disagree with the court's decision, I accept it. I accept the finality of this outcome which will be ratified next Monday in the Electoral College. And tonight, for the sake of our unity of the people and the strength of our democracy, I offer my concession.

I also accept my responsibility, which I will discharge unconditionally, to honor the new president elect and do everything possible to help him bring Americans together in fulfillment of the great vision that our Declaration of Independence defines and that our Constitution affirms and defends.

Let me say how grateful I am to all those who supported me and supported the cause for which we have fought. Tipper and I feel a deep gratitude to Joe and Hadassah Lieberman who brought passion and high purpose to our partnership and opened new doors, not just for our campaign but for our country.

This has been an extraordinary election. But in one of God's unforeseen paths, this belatedly broken impasse can point us all to a new common ground, for its very closeness can serve to remind us that we are one people with a shared history and a shared destiny.

Indeed, that history gives us many examples of contests as hotly debated, as fiercely fought, with their own challenges to the popular will.

Other disputes have dragged on for weeks before reaching resolution. And each time, both the victor and the vanquished have accepted the result peacefully and in the spirit of reconciliation.

So let it be with us.

I know that many of my supporters are disappointed.

I am too. But our disappointment must be overcome by our love of country.

And I say to our fellow members of the world community, let no one see this contest as a sign of American weakness. The strength of American democracy is shown most clearly through the difficulties it can overcome.

Some have expressed concern that the unusual nature of this election might hamper the next president in the conduct of his office. I do not believe it need be so.

President-elect Bush inherits a nation whose citizens will be ready to assist him in the conduct of his large responsibilities.

states can make policy directly through initiatives and referenda, the founders left no such option at the national level. Rather, they provided us with a complicated system in which power is divided and checked. Those who stand for election have different constituencies and different terms of office. Thus the different parts of the national government respond to different publics at different times. The voice of the people is muted and modulated. At times,

I personally will be at his disposal, and I call on all Americans—I particularly urge all who stood with us to unite behind our next president. This is America. Just as we fight hard when the stakes are high, we close ranks and come together when the contest is done.

And while there will be time enough to debate our continuing differences, now is the time to recognize that that which unites us is greater than that which divides us.

While we yet hold and do not yield our opposing beliefs, there is a higher duty than the one we owe to political party. This is America and we put country before party. We will stand together behind our new president.

As for what I'll do next, I don't know the answer to that one yet. Like many of you, I'm looking forward to spending the holidays with family and old friends. I know I'll spend time in Tennessee and mend some fences, literally and figuratively.

Some have asked whether I have any regrets and I do have one regret: that I didn't get the chance to stay and fight for the American people over the next four years, especially for those who need burdens lifted and barriers removed, especially for those who feel their voices have not been heard. I heard you and I will not forget.

I've seen America in this campaign and I like what I see. It's worth fighting for and that's a fight I'll never stop.

As for the battle that ends tonight, I do believe as my father once said, that no matter how hard the loss, defeat might serve as well as victory to shape the soul and let the glory out.

So for me this campaign ends as it began: with the love of Tipper and our family; with faith in God and in the country I have been so proud to serve, from Vietnam to the vice presidency; and with gratitude to our truly tireless campaign staff and volunteers, including all those who worked so hard in Florida for the last 36 days.

Now the political struggle is over and we turn again to the unending struggle for the common good of all Americans and for those multitudes around the world who look to us for leadership in the cause of freedom.

In the words of our great hymn, "America, America": "Let us crown thy good with brotherhood, from sea to shining sea."

And now, my friends, in a phrase I once addressed to others, it's time for me to go.

Thank you and good night, and God bless America.

Source: CNN.com Transcripts, http://transcripts.cnn.com/TRANSCRIPTS/0012/14/se.06.html.

Consider the source and the audience: Gore is speaking to several audiences here. Who are they? Why does he address "our fellow members of the world community"? At the time, Gore was certainly considering a run for the presidency in the future. How might that have shaped his message? How could he have used this speech to rally supporters if he had wanted to?

Lay out the argument and the underlying values and assumptions: What personal values of Gore's become apparent in this speech? How do they affect his political views? What is Gore's view of the common good here? How does that differ from partisan advantage, and when should the former take precedence over the latter? When should a political outcome be accepted even when one doesn't like it? How do the "honored institutions of our democracy" help to resolve contests like this? In what context does Gore refer to the Supreme Court and the Electoral College?

Uncover the evidence: What kinds of evidence does Gore use to support his argument that the result of the election process should be accepted even if one doesn't agree with it, and that George W. Bush is the legitimate president of the United States?

Evaluate the conclusion: Did Gore's use of symbolism and references to history, law, and religion convince supporters to accept the election result? Did they convince the world that the United States was a stable and solid nation? Did they convince the nation to put the trauma of the partisan backbiting behind it and move on?

Sort out the political implications: Many electoral reforms were debated following the election, but few were enacted. Who would have resisted reform, and why?

however, especially when there is a change in the party that controls the government, elections do produce rather marked shifts in public policy.[8] The New Deal of the 1930s is an excellent case in point. The election of a Democratic president and Congress allowed a sweeping political response to the Depression, in sharp contrast to the previous Republican administration's hands-off approach to the crisis.

The electoral process actually does a surprisingly good job of directing policy in less dramatic ways as well. A good deal of research demonstrates, for example, that in the states, elections achieve a remarkable consistency between the general preferences of citizens and the kinds of policies that the states enact.[9] At the congressional level, members of the House and the Senate are quite responsive to the overall policy wishes of their constituents, and those who are not tend to suffer at the polls.[10] At the presidential level, through all of the hoopla and confusion of presidential campaigns, scholars have found that presidents do, for the most part, deliver on the promises that they make and that the national parties do accomplish much of what they set out in their platforms.[11] Finally, elections speed up the process by which changes in public preferences for a more activist or less activist (more liberal or more conservative) government are systematically translated into patterns of public policy.[12]

CITIZEN DEVELOPMENT Some theorists argue that participation in government in and of itself—regardless of which leaders or policy directions are chosen—is valuable for citizens and that elections help citizens feel fulfilled and effective.[13] When individuals are unable to participate in politics, their sense of **political efficacy**, of being effective in political affairs, suffers. In studies of the American electorate, people who participate more, whether in elections or through other means, have higher senses of political efficacy.[14] From this perspective, then, elections provide a mechanism by which individuals can move from passive subjects who see themselves pushed and pulled by forces larger than themselves to active citizens fulfilling their potential to have a positive effect on their own lives.

INFORMING THE PUBLIC When we watch the circus of the modern presidential campaign, it may seem a bit of a stretch to say that an important function of elections, and the campaigns that precede them, is to educate the public. But ideally the campaign is a time of deliberation when alternative points of view are aired openly so that the citizenry can judge the truth and desirability of competing claims and the competence of competing candidates and parties. The evidence is that campaigns do in fact have this impact. People learn a good deal of useful political information from campaign advertisements and for the most part choose the candidates who match their values and policy preferences.[15] As citizens, we probably know and understand a lot more about our government because of our electoral process than we would without free and competitive elections.

CONTAINING CONFLICT Elections help us influence policy, but in other ways they also limit our options for political influence.[16] When groups of citizens are unhappy about their taxes, or the quality of their children's schools, or congressional appropriations for cancer research or any other matter, the election booth is their primary avenue of influence. Of course, they can write letters and sign petitions, but those have an impact only because the officials

they try to influence must stand for reelection. Even if their candidate wins, there is no guarantee that their policy concerns will be satisfied. And those who complain are likely to hear the systemwide response: If you don't like what's going on, vote for change.

If elections help reduce our political conflicts to electoral contests, they also operate as a kind of safety valve for citizen discontent. There is always a relatively peaceful mechanism through which unhappy citizens can vent their energy. Elections can change officials, replacing Democrats with Republicans or vice versa, but they do not fundamentally alter the underlying character of the system. Without the electoral vent, citizens might eventually turn to more threatening behaviors like boycotts, protests, civil disobedience, and rebellion.

LEGITIMATION AND SYSTEM STABILITY A final important function of elections is to make political outcomes acceptable to participants. By participating in the process of elections, we implicitly accept, and thereby legitimize, the results. The genius here is that participation tends to make political results acceptable even to those who lose in an immediate sense. They do not take to the streets, set up terrorist cells, or stop paying their taxes. Rather, in the overwhelming majority of instances, citizens who lose in the electoral process shrug their shoulders, obey the rules made by the winning representatives, and wait for their next chance to elect candidates whose policies are more to their liking. Even many supporters of Al Gore in 2000 came to accept George W. Bush's Electoral College victory as conferring legitimacy on him, despite his loss of the popular vote (see *CLUES to Critical Thinking*). The beauty of elections is that they can bring about change but without grave threats to the stability of the system.

PAUSE AND REVIEW:

WHO, WHAT, HOW

Those with the greatest stake in the continued existence of elections in America are the citizens who live under their rule. At stake for citizens is, first, the important question of which candidates and parties will govern. However, by viewing elections in a broader perspective, we can see that elections also contribute to the quality of democratic life: they help to define a crucial relationship between the governed and those they choose as leaders, to influence public policy, to educate the citizenry, to contain conflict, and to legitimize political outcomes and decisions.

political efficacy citizens' feelings of effectiveness in political affairs

IN YOUR OWN WORDS » Explain the function of elections, both as intended by the founders and in practice.

EXERCISING THE RIGHT TO VOTE IN AMERICA
The costs of not voting

We argued in Chapter 11 that even without being well informed and following campaigns closely, Americans can still cast intelligent votes reflecting their best interests. But what does it say about the American citizenry when, in a typical presidential election, barely half of the adult population votes? In off-year congressional elections, in primaries, and in many state and local elections held at different times from the presidential contest, the rates of participation drop even lower.

How do we explain this low voter turnout? Is America just a nation of political slackers? This is a serious and legitimate question in light of the important functions of democracy we have just discussed, and in light of the tremendous struggle many groups have had to achieve the right to vote. Indeed, as we saw in Chapter 6, the history of American suffrage—the right to vote—is one struggle after another for access to the ballot box.

Voting varies dramatically in its importance to different citizens. For some, it is a significant aspect of their identities as citizens. Eighty-seven percent of American adults believe that voting in elections is a "very important obligation" for Americans.[17] Thus many people vote because they believe they should and because they believe the vote gives them a real influence on government. However, only about half the electorate has felt this way strongly enough to vote in recent presidential elections.

WHO VOTES AND WHO DOESN'T?

Many political observers, activists, politicians, and political scientists worry about the extent of nonvoting in the United States.[18] When people do not vote, they have no voice in choosing their leaders, their policy preferences are not registered, and they do not develop as active citizens. Some observers fear that their abstention signals an alienation from the political process.

From survey data, we know quite a lot about who votes and who doesn't in America in terms of their age, gender, income, education, and racial and ethnic make-up:

- *Age.* Older citizens consistently vote at higher rates. For example, 72 percent of those aged sixty-five to seventy-four years reported voting in the 2012 election, compared to 41.2 percent of those aged eighteen to twenty-four years. This gap of 31 percent, however, is a bit larger than it had been in 2008 but not as large as the 40 percent gap in the 2010 midterm when older voters turned out and younger voters stayed home.[19]

- *Gender.* Since 1984 women have been voting at a higher rate than men, although the differences are typically only 3 or 4 percent. For example, in the 2012 presidential election the turnout rates for women and men were 63.7 and 59.7 percent, respectively, higher than the 46.2 and 44.8, respectively, in 2010.

- *Income.* The likelihood of voting goes up steadily with income. For example, in 2012 only 46.9 percent of those making $10,000 or less reported voting, compared to 80.2 percent of those earning $150,000 or more.

- *Education.* Education is consistently one of the strongest predictors of turnout. For instance, in the 2012 election, only 38 percent of those with less than a high school education voted, compared to almost 75 percent of those with a bachelor's degree; 81.3 percent of those with advanced degrees voted.

- *Race and ethnicity.* Turnout among members of racial and ethnic minority groups has traditionally been lower than that of whites. But that changed in 2008 (and 2012), with an African American as the Democratic nominee. Turnout for blacks was 65 percent, virtually tied with non-Hispanic whites in 2008 (66 percent) and even surpassing the white turnout in 2012 (66.2 versus 62.2 percent). Hispanic turnout increased in 2008 to 50 percent, surpassing turnout among Asians for that year, but dropped like most groups in 2012 (48 percent). In the 2010 midterm, racial and ethnic differences were larger, with turnout among non-Hispanic whites surpassing African American turnout by 5 percent and Latino turnout by 17 percent.

When we add these characteristics together, the differences are substantial. Compare, for example, the turnout among eighteen- to twenty-four-year-old males with less than a high school education (only 24.8 percent) with the turnout rate for females aged sixty-five to seventy-four years with advanced degrees (85.4 percent).[20] By virtue of their different turnout rates, some groups in American society are receiving much better representation than others. The same patterns hold true and are even more pronounced for types of political engagement other than voting, such as actively working for a party or candidate in distributing literature, staffing the phone banks during a get-out-the-vote drive, or making financial contributions.[21] The upshot is that our elected officials are indebted to and hear much more from the higher socioeconomic ranks in

FIGURE 14.1 VOTER TURNOUT IN PRESIDENTIAL AND MIDTERM HOUSE ELECTIONS, 1932-2014

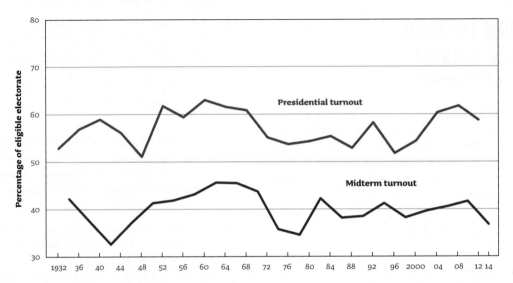

Sources: Presidential data from 2000 through 2005, *The New York Times Almanac*, 114; midterm data through 1998 from U.S. Census Bureau, *2000 Statistical Abstract*, 291; 2004 data and beyond from United States Election Project, http://www.electproject.org/home/voter-turnout/voter-turnout-data.

Note: Data for 2014 is an estimate.

society. They do not hear from and are not elected by the low-participation "have nots."[22]

WHY AMERICANS DON'T VOTE

As we have noted elsewhere, compared with other democratic nations, the United States has low voter turnout levels (see Figure 11.1, on page 402). Despite overall increases in education, age, and income, which generally increase the number of voters, presidential election turnout rates have barely gotten over the 60-percent mark for more than thirty years (and midterm congressional turnout rates have been much lower)[23] (see Figure 14.1). What accounts for such low turnout rates in a country where 82 percent of adults say voting is important to democracy[24]—indeed, in a country that often prides itself on being one of the best and oldest examples of democracy in the world? The question of low voter turnout in the United States poses a tremendous puzzle for political scientists, who have focused on six factors to try to explain this mystery.

THINKING OUTSIDE THE BOX

Should there be penalties for those who don't vote?

LEGAL OBSTACLES: REGULATING THE ELECTORATE Voter turnout provides a dramatic illustration of our theme that rules make a difference in who wins and who loses in politics. Election rules define who *can* vote and how easy it will be for those legally eligible to vote to actually do so. In many countries the government takes responsibility for registering citizens to vote, and in some—Australia, Belgium and Italy, for example—voting is required by law. As a result, turnout rates in these countries are high.[25] Traditionally the United States has had a set of rules that put a brake on voting participation by placing the burden to register on the citizen and by making voting more difficult than it is in other places. We can think of the rules of elections as a set of valves that make it easier or harder for people to vote, a process we call **regulating the electorate**. These rules include requiring citizens to register to vote and restricting voting to a single weekday when most people have to work.

Although constitutional amendments set fundamental voting protections based on race, gender, and age, the Constitution gives to the states the primary responsibility for determining how elections are held. Most of the rules that regulate the electorate—how early and where voters need to register, whether early voting or voting by mail is permitted, how long polls are open, and the like—are made at the state

> **regulating the electorate** the process of setting rules that define who can vote and how difficult or easy it will be to cast a ballot in an election

level, and over time we have seen substantial fluctuations in how easy various states make it for citizens to exercise their constitutional right to vote.

Underlying these changes are conflicting goals. One the one hand, Americans hold generally that every citizen has the right to vote, that in a healthy democracy most will exercise this right, and that by doing so they will legitimate public policy and feel happier about obeying the laws they helped to make. Voting is a central part of being a democratic citizen, and Americans pride themselves on living in a democracy. Still, even people who are deeply committed to democratic norms debate whether voting ought to be made so easy that uninformed voters go to the polls. For those who think voters should pass some minimum threshold of involvement in the system, the existence of some hurdles, in the form of registration laws and limited voting opportunities, helps to weed out those who really do not know much about the issues or the candidates they are voting for. Those who reject this idea say that everyone who is obligated under the law ought to have easy access to making that law, and that individuals might not know the nuances of public policy but they do know their own interests best. This is a philosophical debate that is unlikely to be solved any time soon.

Alongside this philosophical debate is an ongoing and recently intensified partisan battle about who should be encouraged to vote. At the heart of this debate (if not in its rhetoric) is not so much what is good for the democracy as a whole, as much as what is most beneficial to each political party. Substantial demographic differences are found in the primary supporters of the parties: Republicans are wealthier, whiter, and better educated; Democrats are less wealthy, less educated, and have many more African Americans and Latinos among their core supporters. As a result, all other things being equal, Republicans are more likely to vote, and restrictions on voting like voter ID laws, fewer voting hours, or longer registration periods are widely believed to have a greater impact on Democratic supporters. Thus, at least since the battle over the Voting Rights Act of 1965, there has been a rather consistent split between Democrats, who tend to favor laws that make voting easier, since their voters are those most likely to be dissuaded by cumbersome regulations, and Republicans, who favor tighter rules, knowing that most of their voters will turn out anyway. This battle has intensified in recent years as the parties have become more polarized.

And so, the debate over how easy it should be to exercise one's right to vote, instead of being fought over philosophical grounds about the nature of democracy, has become a partisan power struggle. When Democrats were in charge of Congress, in the 1990s, we saw an effort to make voting more widely accessible. For instance, Congress

passed the National Voter Registration Act of 1993, or the **Motor Voter Bill** as it is more commonly called, which requires the states to take a more active role in registering people to vote, including providing registration opportunities when people are applying for driver's licenses or at the welfare office. A number of states followed up with laws that allowed extended periods of early voting, same-day registration and, in the case of Oregon, voting by mail. Each reform has marginally increased the numbers of people voting, but on the whole the results have been a disappointment to Democratic reformers. An exhaustive review of the research concluded that, even with obstacles to voting removed, "for many people, voting remains an activity from which there is virtually no gratification—instrumental, expressive, or otherwise."[26]

Even though regulating the electorate makes little apparent difference to electoral outcomes, it has not gone away as a partisan issue. Since 2008, and especially following the 2010 Republican successes in state elections, laws have been passed that require various forms of identification to vote and that cut back on the existing trend of permitting early voting. The Supreme Court cleared the way for the election rule battles in its 2008 decision that Indiana's voter ID law—at the time the strictest in the nation—does not violate the Constitution. Encouraged by that decision, almost half of the states, mostly those under Republican control, have instituted voting restrictions. These include various voter ID requirements, restrictions of voter registration drives, elimination of election-day registration, and a cutting back on opportunities for early voting.[27] (See "*Snapshot of America:* How Did We Vote in the 2012 Presidential Election?")

The drive to tighten the voting rules was made much easier by the Supreme Court's decision in *Shelby County v. Holder* (2013), which blunted the Voting Right Act's requirement for states with histories of racial discrimination to have changes in their election laws cleared by the federal courts or the Department of Justice. Following that decision, a number of states in the deep South implemented restrictive provisions that would be or had been denied under the preclearance requirement. Recent changes in Virginia provide an illustration of the measures the Republican-controlled state governments have adopted: the state eliminated same-day registration, reduced the early voting period, ended preregistration for sixteen- and seventeen-year-olds, and instituted a photo ID requirement. Republicans insist that these measures are intended to reduce voter fraud, but there is little or no evidence that such fraud exists and the real agenda is clearly to restrict the voting of constituents (minorities, the poor, and the young) who are seen as sympathetic to Democrats.

But the electoral rules are not settled. Citizen and partisan groups are contesting efforts to restrict voting in the legislatures and in the courts. Although the justification for greater restrictions is generally stated in terms of ensuring the integrity of the electoral process—a goal few would disagree with, whether Democrats or

---

Motor Voter Bill legislation allowing citizens to register to vote at the same time they apply for a driver's license or other state benefit

SNAPSHOT OF AMERICA: HOW DID WE VOTE IN THE 2012 PRESIDENTIAL ELECTION?

2012 Election Results, by County

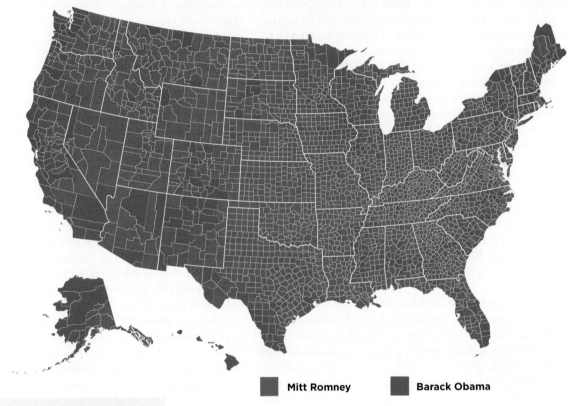

■ Mitt Romney   ■ Barack Obama

Purple America?

Who Were the Voters?

Gender:

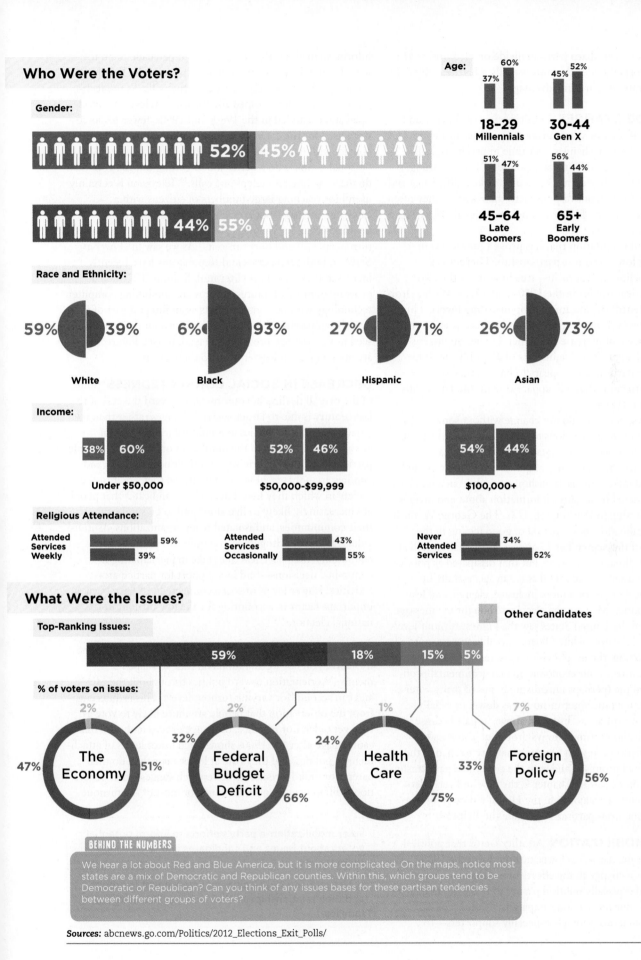

52% 45%

44% 55%

Age:

37% **60%**	45% **52%**
18–29 Millennials	**30–44** Gen X
51% 47%	56% 44%
45–64 Late Boomers	**65+** Early Boomers

Race and Ethnicity:

White	Black	Hispanic	Asian
59% 39%	6% 93%	27% 71%	26% 73%

Income:

Under $50,000	$50,000-$99,999	$100,000+
38% 60%	52% 46%	54% 44%

Religious Attendance:

Attended Services Weekly	Attended Services Occasionally	Never Attended Services
59% / 39%	43% / 55%	34% / 62%

What Were the Issues?

Other Candidates

Top-Ranking Issues:

59%   18%   15%   5%

% of voters on issues:

The Economy — 2% / 47% / 51%

Federal Budget Deficit — 2% / 32% / 66%

Health Care — 1% / 24% / 75%

Foreign Policy — 7% / 33% / 56%

BEHIND THE NUMBERS

We hear a lot about Red and Blue America, but it is more complicated. On the maps, notice most states are a mix of Democratic and Republican counties. Within this, which groups tend to be Democratic or Republican? Can you think of any issues bases for these partisan tendencies between different groups of voters?

Sources: abcnews.go.com/Politics/2012_Elections_Exit_Polls/

Republicans—the sharp partisan divide on electoral restrictions supports the idea that this is really a battle to regulate the electorate for partisan advantage.

ATTITUDE CHANGES Political scientists have found that some of the low voter turnout we can see in Figure 14.1 is accounted for by changes over time in psychological orientations or attitudes toward politics.[28] For one thing, if people feel that they do not or cannot make a difference and that government is not responsive to their wishes, they often don't bother to vote. Lower feelings of political efficacy lead to less participation.

A second orientation that has proved important in explaining low turnout is partisanship. There was a distinct decline in Americans' attachments to the two major political parties in the 1960s and 1970s. With a drop in party identification came a drop in voting levels. This decline, however, has leveled off, and in recent years there has even been an increase in the percentage of citizens saying they identify as Democrats or Republicans. This increase in partisanship appears to have reversed the decline in turnout that was apparent from the late 1960s through the 1980s.

Attitudes, of course, do not change without some cause; they reflect citizens' reactions to what they see in the political world. It is easy to understand why attitudes have changed since the relatively tranquil 1950s. Amid repeated scandal and increasing partisanship, our public airwaves have been dominated by negative information about and images of the leadership in Washington, D.C. The George W. Bush administration did enjoy a period of good feeling in the aftermath of the September 11 attacks, as the nation rallied against the threat of terrorism, but that dissipated as politics got back to usual. President Obama ran successfully by raising expectations for a more inclusive, cleaner, and less partisan politics. Many in the electorate bought the message of hope, and the United States saw the highest turnout levels in decades. However, while Obama was able to pass quite a bit of legislation, the deep division between the parties and the complexities of our economic and environmental problems dashed the (perhaps unrealistic) hopes of many voters. In 2010 Democratic voter turnout was down, especially among young voters, as discussed above, in part because midterm election turnout always drops but also possibly reflecting frustration with Obama's inability to change the tone as he had promised and with the continued partisanship in politics. As we saw in Chapter 7, the new and very ideological Republican majority in the House did nothing to quell the rancorous partisanship inside the Beltway.

VOTER MOBILIZATION Another factor that political scientists argue has led to lower turnout from the 1960s into the 2000s is a change in the efforts of politicians, interest groups, and especially political parties to make direct contact with people during election campaigns.[29] **Voter mobilization** includes contacting people—especially supporters—to inform them about the election and to persuade them to vote. It can take the form of making phone calls, knocking on doors, or even supplying rides to the polls. As the technology of campaigns, especially the use of television, developed and expanded in the 1980s and 1990s, fewer resources were used for the traditional shoe-leather efforts of direct contact with voters, but solid evidence now indicates that personal contacts do a better job of getting out the vote than do mass mailing and telephone calls.[30] Television is certainly useful for reaching large numbers of citizens with a campaign message, but it is less effective at motivating people to vote. In fact, negative television attack ads tend to turn people off and hurt turnout.[31] As we saw in *What's at Stake...?*, both Democrats and Republicans have recently increased their efforts at voter mobilization. They and a growing number of interest groups are combining computer technology with personal contacts as an integral part of their overall campaigns.[32] The increases in turnout that we have seen in the past few presidential elections (see Figure 14.1) are attributable, at least in part, to these efforts.[33]

DECREASE IN SOCIAL CONNECTEDNESS Some of the overall decline in voter turnout toward the end of the last century is due to larger societal changes rather than to citizen reactions to parties and political leaders. **Social connectedness** refers to the number of organizations people participate in and how tightly knit their communities and families are—that is, how well integrated they are into the society in which they live. The evidence indicates that people are increasingly likely to live alone and to be single, new to their communities, and isolated from organizations. As individuals loosen or altogether lose their ties to the larger community, they have less of a stake in participating in communal decisions—and less support for participatory activities. Lower levels of social connectedness have been an important factor in accounting for the low turnout in national elections.[34]

GENERATIONAL CHANGES Events occurring in the formative years of a generation continue to shape its members' orientation toward politics throughout their lives, and can account for varying turnout levels. This is different from the observation that people are more likely to vote as they get older. For instance, those age groups (cohorts) that came of age after the 1960s show much lower levels of attachment to politics, and they vote at lower rates than do their parents or grandparents. Some research suggests that generational differences account for much or most of the turnout

---

voter mobilization a party's efforts to inform potential voters about issues and candidates and to persuade them to vote

social connectedness citizens' involvement in groups and their relationships to their communities and families

decline at the end of the 1990s. That is, people who once voted have not stopped voting; rather, they are dying and are being replaced by younger, less politically engaged voters. The result is lower turnout overall.[35] Of course it is possible for this trend to be reversed as events and personalities politicize and mobilize new generations of citizens.

THE RATIONAL NONVOTER

A final explanation for the puzzle of low voter turnout in America considers that, for some people, not voting may be the rational choice. This explanation suggests that the question to ask is not "Why don't people vote?" but rather "Why does anyone vote?" The definition of *rational* means that the benefits of an action outweigh the costs. It is rational for us to do those things from which we get back more than we put in. Voting demands our resources, time, and effort. Given those costs, if someone views voting primarily as a way to influence government and sees no other benefits from it, it becomes a largely irrational act.[36] That is, no one individual's vote can change the course of an election unless the election would otherwise be a tie, and the probability of that happening in a presidential election is small (though, as the 2000 election showed, it is not impossible).

For many people, however, the benefits of voting go beyond the likelihood that they will affect the outcome of the election. In fact, studies have demonstrated that turnout decisions are not really based on our thinking that our votes will determine the outcome. Rather, we achieve other kinds of less tangible benefits from voting. Just like the expressive benefits that many people get from joining an interest group, there are expressive benefits from voting as well. It feels good to do what we think we are supposed to do or to help, however little, the side or the causes we believe in.[37] Plus, we get social rewards from our politically involved friends for voting (and avoid sarcastic remarks for not voting). These benefits accrue no matter which side wins.

It is useful to remember, however, that even these psychological benefits are not distributed equally in the electorate. For example, the social pressures to be engaged and the rewards from voting are substantially higher for those in the middle class than the working class and the unemployed. That is, the socially (and economically) connected receive greater expressive as well as "instrumental" or policy benefits from voting.

Reuters/Steven Johnson

Souls to the Polls

Seeking to increase turnout among their congregants, black churches in many states have organized "souls to the polls" events, providing transportation to early-voting sites after Sunday services. Here, congregants from Day Springs Missionary Baptist Church in Gainesville, Florida, head to polling sites to cast their ballots in October 2012. Recent measures that tighten voting rules may have an impact on the effectiveness of such efforts in many states.

DOES NONVOTING MATTER?

What difference does it make that some people vote and others do not? There are two ways to tackle this question. One approach is to ask whether election outcomes would be different if nonvoters were to participate. The other approach is to ask whether higher levels of nonvoting indicate that democracy is not healthy. Both questions, of course, concern important potential consequences of low participation in our elections.

CONSEQUENCES FOR ELECTION OUTCOMES

Studies of the likely effects of nonvoting come up with contradictory answers. A traditional, and seemingly logical, approach is to note that nonvoters, being disproportionately poor and less educated, and racial or ethnic minorities, have social and economic characteristics that are more common among Democrats than among Republicans. Therefore, were these people to vote, we could expect that Democratic candidates would do better. Some polling results support this thinking. Pollsters asked registered voters a number of questions to judge how likely it was that they would actually vote in elections for House members. When the voting intentions of all registered voters and the subset of likely voters were compared, the likely voters were distinctly more Republican. If this were to hold true generally, we could conclude that nonvoting works to the disadvantage of Democratic candidates. One political scholar found some evidence of this for the 1980 presidential election and concluded that a much higher turnout among nonvoters would have made the election closer and that Jimmy Carter might even have won reelection.[38] Similarly, when political scientists have run simulations to test whether full turnout would alter the results in elections for the U.S. Senate, the share of the vote for Democratic candidates is increased, but given that these elections are not particularly close, the extra votes would seldom change the winner of the elections.[39]

Undermining this interpretation are findings from most other presidential elections that nonvoters' preferences are quite responsive to short-term factors, so they go disproportionately for the winning candidate. Because these voters are less partisan and have less intensely held issue positions, they are moved more easily by the short-term campaign factors favoring one party or the other. In most presidential elections, nonvoters' participation would have increased the winner's margin only slightly or not changed things at all.[40] Interviews taken shortly after the two most recent presidential elections suggest that those who did not vote would have broken for the winner, Bush in 2004 and Obama in 2008.[41]

We are left with an interesting inconsistency: Research suggests that the potential effects of mobilizing nonvoters are probably not as consistently pro-Democratic as popular commentary suggests. But at the same time, in one voting reform rule after another, we see Democrats consistently favoring measures to increase turnout and Republicans just as consistently favoring more restrictive rules.[42] Thus the politics of regulating the electorate is intensely partisan, even while the actual consequences remain somewhat uncertain.

CONSEQUENCES FOR DEMOCRACY Low turnout might not affect who wins an election, but elections do more than simply select leaders. How might nonvoting affect the quality of democratic life in America? Nonvoting can influence the stability and legitimacy of democratic government. The victor in close presidential elections, for example, must govern the country, but as critics often point out, as little as 25 percent of the eligible electorate may have voted for the winner. When a majority of the electorate sits out of an election, the entire governmental process may begin to lose legitimacy in society at large. Nonvoting can also have consequences for the nonvoter. To the extent that nonvoters have different policy goals, they are underrepresented by not voting. Politicians are more

attentive to the voice of voters (and contributors). And then psychologically, as we have noted, failure to participate politically can aggravate already low feelings of efficacy and produce higher levels of political estrangement. To the extent that being a citizen is an active pursuit, unhappy, unfulfilled, and unconnected citizens seriously damage the quality of democratic life for themselves and for the country as a whole.

PAUSE AND REVIEW:

WHO, WHAT, HOW

All political actors are not equal on Election Day. Some reduce their power considerably by failing to turn out to vote. Two things are at stake in these turnout patterns. The first is a question of representation and political power: while many politicians would like to attend to the needs of all constituents equally, when push comes to shove and they have to make hard choices, voters are going to be heeded more than silent nonvoters. A second issue at stake in low and declining turnout rates is the quality of democratic life—and the stability and legitimacy of the system. Nonvoting is tied to citizen estrangement from the political process, and in this view the quality of democratic life itself depends on active citizen participation.

IN YOUR OWN WORDS » Analyze the reasons why Americans vote—or don't vote.

HOW THE VOTER DECIDES
Many factors determine the final choice

Putting an X next to a name on a ballot or pulling a lever on a voting machine or even putting your finger on a party icon on a touch-screen monitor to register a preference would seem like a pretty simple act. Although the action itself may be simple, the decision process behind the choice is anything but. A number of considerations go into our decision about how to vote, including our partisan identification and social group membership; our gender, race, and ethnicity; our stance on the issues and our evaluation of the job government has been doing generally; and our opinions of the candidates. In this section we examine how these factors play out in the simple act of voting.

PARTISANSHIP AND SOCIAL GROUP MEMBERSHIP

The single biggest factor accounting for how people decide to vote is *party identification*, a concept we discussed in

Chapter 12. For most citizens, party ID is relatively stable, carrying over from one election to the next in what one scholar has called "a standing decision."[43] In 2012, for example, 92 percent of those identifying with the Democratic Party voted for Barack Obama, and 93 percent of those identifying with the Republican Party voted for Mitt Romney.[44]

Clearly, party ID has a strong and direct influence on identifiers' voting decisions. Scholars have demonstrated that party ID also has an important indirect influence on voting decisions, because voters' party ID also colors their views on policy issues and their evaluation of candidates, leading them to judge their party's candidate and issue positions as superior.[45] Under unusual circumstances, social group characteristics can exaggerate or override traditional partisan loyalties. The 1960 election, for instance, was cast in terms of whether the nation would elect its first Catholic president. In that context, religion was especially salient, and fully 82 percent of Roman Catholics supported John F. Kennedy, compared to just 37 percent of Protestants—a difference of 45 percentage points. Compare that to 1976, when the Democrats ran a devout Baptist, Jimmy Carter, for president. The percentage of Catholics voting Democratic dropped to 58 percent, while Protestants voting Democratic increased to 46 percent. The difference shrank to just 12 percent.

GENDER, RACE, AND ETHNICITY

The impact of gender on voting decisions is not clear. In Chapter 11 we discussed the gender gap in the positions men and women take on the issues, which has generally led women to be more likely to support the Democratic candidate. Since 1964, women have been more supportive of the Democratic candidate in every presidential election but one (they were not more likely to support Carter in 1976), and the Democrats clearly wanted to put women's issues at the forefront on the 2012 campaign.[46] But women do not vote monolithically; for instance, married women are more conservative than single women.

It's an open question whether the gender of a candidate affects the women's vote. In statewide races, there is some evidence that Republican and independent women will cross party lines to vote for Democratic women candidates, though the opposite is not true for Republican women candidates.[47] In the Super Tuesday 2008 Democratic primaries, a larger percentage of women than men voted for Hillary Clinton in fourteen out of sixteen states.[48] However, despite the speculation that the nomination of Sarah Palin as the Republican vice presidential candidate might have swayed some women to support the McCain-Palin ticket, there was little evidence in the 2008 exit polls to support that idea.

African Americans have tended to vote Democratic since the civil rights movement of the 1960s. In fact, African Americans have averaged just under 90 percent of the two-party vote for the Democratic candidate in recent presidential elections (1988 to 2004).[49] The nomination of Barack Obama, the first black to receive a major party's presidential nomination, increased the solidarity of the African American vote even further in 2008. This was evident in the Democratic primaries, where the African American vote was a major factor, with 82 percent of it going for Obama, compared to 16 percent for Hillary Clinton. Having a black presidential candidate heightened the role of race in the general election as well. African American support for the Democratic ticket reached a record 95 percent in 2008 and 93 percent in 2012.[50]

Ethnicity is less predictive of the vote than race, partly because ethnic groups in the United States become politically diverse as they are assimilated into the system. Although immigrant groups have traditionally found a home in the Democratic Party, dating back to the days when the party machine would provide a one-stop shop for new immigrants seeking jobs, homes, and social connections, recent immigrant groups today include Asians and Hispanics, both of which comprise diverse ethnic communities with distinct identities and varying partisan tendencies.[51] These diverse groups tend to support the Democratic Party, but each has subgroups that are distinctly more Republican: Vietnamese, in the case of Asians, and Cubans, among Latino groups.[52] That said, in 2012, Obama received the overwhelming majority of Hispanic votes. Nationally 71 percent of Latino voters supported Obama (up from 67 percent in 2008), as did 73 percent of Asian Americans, and 58 percent of all other racial and ethnic minorities. One observer calls these groups the "coalition of the ascendant," meaning that these are growing portions of the population whose support for the Democratic Party spells trouble for the Republicans if they cannot broaden their appeal.[53]

ISSUES AND POLICY

An idealized view of elections would have highly attentive citizens paying careful attention to the different policy positions offered by the candidates and then, perhaps aided by informed policy analyses from the media, casting their ballots for the candidates who best represent their preferred policy solutions. In truth, as we know by now, American citizens are not "ideal," and the role played by issues is less obvious and more complicated than the ideal model would predict. The apparent role of issues in electoral decision making is limited by the following factors:

- People are busy and, in many cases, rely on party labels to tell them what they need to know about the candidates.[54]

- People know where they stand on "easy" issues like capital punishment or gay marriage, but some issues, like economic and tax policy, health care, Social Security reform, or foreign policy in the Middle East, are complicated. Many citizens tend to tune out these more complicated issues or, confused, fail to vote in their own interests.[55]

- The media do not generally cover issues in depth. Instead, they much prefer to focus on the horse-race aspect of elections, looking at who is ahead in the polls rather than what substantive policy issues mean for the nation.[56]

- As we discussed in Chapter 11, people process a lot of policy-relevant information in terms of their impressions of candidates (on-line processing) rather than as policy information. They are certainly influenced by policy information, but they cannot necessarily articulate their opinions and preferences on policy.

Although calculated policy decisions by voters are rare, policy considerations do have a real impact on voters' decisions. To see that, it is useful to distinguish between prospective and retrospective voting. The idealized model of policy voting with which we opened this section is **prospective voting**, in which voters base their decisions on what will happen in the future if they vote for a candidate—what policies will be enacted, what values will be emphasized in policy. Prospective voting requires a good deal of information that average voters, as we have seen, do not always have or even want. While all voters do some prospective voting and, by election time, are usually aware of the candidates' major issue positions, it is primarily party activists and political elites who engage in the full-scale policy analysis that prospective voting entails.

Instead, most voters supplement their spotty policy information and interest with their evaluation of how they think the country is doing, how the economy has performed, and how well the incumbents have carried out their jobs. They engage in **retrospective voting**, casting their votes as signs of approval based on past performance to signal their desire for more of the same or for change.[57]

In presidential elections this means that voters look back at the state of the economy, at perceived successes or failures in foreign policy, and at domestic issues like education, gun control, or welfare reform. In 1980 Ronald Reagan skillfully focused on voter frustration in the presidential debate by asking voters this question: "[A]re you better off than you were four years ago?"[58] Politicians have been reprising that question ever since. In 2008 the situation was more complicated, as no incumbent was running, but nonetheless Democrat Barack Obama tried to make the election a retrospective referendum on the Bush years, tying Republican John McCain to Bush's record whenever he could. The effort was partially successful; fully 67 percent of the almost three-quarters of the electorate who disapproved of how Bush was handling his job voted for Obama.

But in the 2010 midterm elections Republicans managed to turn the strategy back on Obama, pegging the stubbornly bad economy to his policies and tapping into voter angst about the economy to turn Democrats out of office.

In 2012 the central strategic campaign objective of the Republican challenger, Mitt Romney, was to cast the election as a referendum on Obama's culpability for a slow economic recovery, hoping that this strategy would push voters to cast a ballot for change. The Obama campaign had the challenge of changing the subject and making the election a choice between the president's and Romney's visions for the country. The Obama campaign began a concerted effort to shape public views of Romney in the summer of 2012, running commercials that painted the Republican as a rich venture capitalist who was out of touch with middle-class America. By the time Romney began to answer those ads in the fall campaign, many people had made up their minds. Gaffes on Romney's part, particularly his statement caught on videotape that 47 percent of Americans would never vote for him because they were dependent on government and took no responsibility for their lives, cemented his fate. Although the election was close, exit polls showed that most voters did not hold Obama responsible for the economy and thought he cared more about their concerns than Romney did.

Retrospective voting is considered to be "easy" decision making as opposed to the more complex decision making involved in prospective voting because one only has to ask, "How have things been going?" as a guide to whether to support the current party in power. Retrospective voting is also seen as a useful way of holding politicians accountable, not for what they said or are saying in a campaign, but for what they or members of their party in power *did*. Some scholars believe that this type of voting is all that is needed for democracy to function well.[59] In practice, voters combine elements of both voting strategies.

THE CANDIDATES

In addition to considerations of party, personal demographics, and issues, voters also base their decisions on judgments about candidates as individuals. What influences voters' images of candidates? Some observers have claimed that voters view candidate characteristics much as they would a beauty or personality contest. There is little support,

prospective voting basing voting decisions on well-informed opinions and consideration of the future consequences of a given vote

retrospective voting basing voting decisions on reactions to past performance; approving the status quo or a desire for change

however, for the notion that voters are won over merely by good looks or movie-star qualities. Consider, for example, that Richard Nixon almost won against John F. Kennedy, who had good looks, youth, and a quick wit in his favor. Then, in 1964, the awkward, gangly Lyndon Johnson defeated the more handsome and articulate Barry Goldwater in a landslide. In fact, ample evidence indicates that voters form clear opinions about candidate qualities that are relevant to governing, such as trustworthiness, competence, experience, and sincerity. Citizens also make judgments about the ability of the candidates to lead the nation and withstand the pressures of the presidency. Ronald Reagan, for example, was admired widely for his ability to stay above the fray of Washington politics and to see the humor in many situations. By contrast, his predecessor, Jimmy Carter, seemed overwhelmed by the job.

The 2012 campaign allowed voters to develop distinct images of Barack Obama and Mitt Romney. First, voters had four years of almost daily experience with Obama as president, and one thing that the polls showed was that voters generally liked him, even in an economy that virtually everyone agreed had not recovered fast enough. In January 2012 one poll found that fully 71 percent agreed that the president was "warm and friendly" rather than "cold and aloof."[60] Similarly, Obama stacked up well as a "good communicator" and one who "cares about people like me." Among voters who valued this attribute most in their voting decisions, 81 percent cast their ballots for Obama.[61] Obama's challenger, Mitt Romney, decided early on to stress his success in business as qualification for dealing with the economy. He did manage to hold an edge on who could manage the economy better (just 49 percent to Obama's 48 percent in the exit polls), but, with the help of a lot of Democratic and Obama ads, he came to be seen as a rich plutocrat who was unconcerned about the average person. Pundits and late-night comedians got a lot of mileage out of Romney's off-the-cuff offer of a $10,000 wager during a primary debate, his remark that he liked to fire people who perform services for him, and his remarks to his contributors about the 47 percent who do not pay income taxes. Clearly there was a substantial difference in perceptions of the candidates in 2012: both candidates were seen as competent to deal with the most important problem, the economy, but Obama was perceived as also caring more about the average citizen.

PAUSE AND REVIEW:

WHO, WHAT, HOW

Citizens have a strong interest in seeing that good and effective leaders are elected and that power transfers peacefully from losers to winners. By the standard of highly informed voters carefully

weighing the alternative policy proposals of competing candidates, the electorate may seem to fall short. However, by a realistic standard that considers the varying abilities of people and the frequent reluctance of candidates and the media to be fully forthcoming about policy proposals, the electorate does not do too badly. Voters come to their decisions through a mix of partisan considerations, membership in social groups, policy information, and candidate image.

IN YOUR OWN WORDS » Identify four factors that influence voters' decisions.

PRESIDENTIAL CAMPAIGNS
The long, expensive
road to the White House

Being president of the United States is undoubtedly a difficult challenge, but so is getting the job in the first place. In this section we examine the long, expensive, and grueling "road to the White House," as the media like to call it.

GETTING NOMINATED

Each of the major parties (and the minor parties, too) needs to come up with a single viable candidate from the long list of party members with ambitions to serve in the White House. How the candidate is chosen will determine the sort of candidate chosen. Remember, in politics the rules are always central to shaping the outcome. Prior to 1972, primary election results were mostly considered "beauty contests" because their results were not binding. But since 1972, party nominees for the presidency have been chosen in primaries, taking the power away from the party elite and giving it to the activist members of the party who care enough to turn out and vote in the party primaries.

THE PRE-PRIMARY SEASON It is hard to say when a candidate's presidential campaign actually begins. Potential candidates may begin planning and thinking about running for the presidency in childhood. Bill Clinton is said to have wanted to be president since high school, when he shook President Kennedy's hand. At one time or another, many people in politics consider going for the big prize, but there are several crucial steps between wishful thinking and running for the nomination. Candidates vary somewhat in their approach to the process, but most of those considering a run for the White House go through the following steps:

The Shake That Launched a Dream?
What inspires a person to want to become president? Having the opportunity to shake the hand of a sitting president—especially one he particularly admired—clearly meant a lot to the teenaged Bill Clinton.

1. Potential candidates usually test the waters unofficially. They talk to friends and fellow politicians to see just how much support they can count on, and they often leak news of their possible candidacy to the press to see how it is received in the media. This period of jockeying for money, lining up top campaign consultants, generating media buzz, and getting commitments of potential support from party and interest group notables even before candidates announce they are running is called the **invisible primary**. Some candidates may have an interest but find during the invisible primary that there is not enough early support among the powerful or the public to support a presidential run.[62] News reports of candidate trips to Iowa or New Hampshire (the early

caucus and primary states) even a year or two before the primaries (see below) is taken by some commentators to indicate that a potential candidate is well into his or her own invisible primary.

2. If the first step has positive results, candidates file with the Federal Election Commission (FEC) to set up a committee to receive funds so that they can officially explore their prospects. The formation of an **exploratory committee** legally allows the candidate to collect money to determine if he or she wants to run, but it is also useful as a form of campaigning itself. Announcing the creation of such a committee can be exploited as a media event by the candidate, using the occasion to get free publicity for the launching of the still-unannounced campaign and for signaling to the political community that the presidential primary landscape has changed.

3. It costs a lot of money for a candidate to be taken seriously. Some well-positioned candidates are able to raise large amounts of money before they officially enter the race, whereas others are forced to scramble to catch up. Those with the most pre-primary funds are more likely to win.[63] The 2012 Republican primary nicely illustrated this general truth about presidential primaries: Mitt Romney's campaign had raised over $90 million before the primaries even began, vastly more than his several competitors. While others rose and fell in popularity, Romney, thanks in large part to his substantial war chest, was able to outlast all of them. Former Clinton campaign advisor and CNN analyst Paul Begala notes that "Napoleon said god is on the side of big battalions. Voters are usually on the side of big money."[64] This is especially the case in party primaries where the ideological differences between candidates are not huge, and often the candidates are not well-known.

4. The potential candidate must use the pre-primary season to position himself or herself as a credible prospect with the media. It is no coincidence that, in the last nine elections, the parties' nominees have all held prominent government offices and have entered the field with some media credibility. Incumbents especially have a huge advantage here.

> **invisible primary** early attempts to raise money, line up campaign consultants, generate media attention, and get commitments for support even before candidates announce they are running
>
> **exploratory committee** formed to determine the viability of one's candidacy for office; activities may include polling, travel, and other communications relevant to the purpose

5. The final step of the pre-primary season is the official announcement of candidacy. Like the formation of the exploratory committee, this statement is part of the campaign itself. Promises are made to supporters, agendas are set, media attention is captured, and the process is under way.

PRIMARIES AND CAUCUSES The actual fight for the nomination takes place in the state party caucuses and primaries in which delegates to the parties' national conventions are chosen. In a **party caucus**, grassroots members of the party in each community gather in selected locations to discuss the current candidates. They then vote for delegates from that locality who will be sent to the national convention, or who will go on to larger caucuses at the state level to choose the national delegates. Attending a caucus is time consuming, and participation rates are frequently in the single digits,[65] although an especially heated battle, like that in 2008 between Barack Obama and Hillary Clinton, saw much higher turnout. Most states still hold primary elections, but in recent years there has been a trend toward caucuses, the method used in fifteen states.[66]

The most common device for choosing delegates to the national conventions is the **presidential primary**. Primary voters cast ballots that send delegates committed to voting for a particular candidate to the conventions. Presidential primaries can be either open or closed, depending on the rules the state party organizations adopt, and these can change from year to year. Any registered voter may vote in an **open primary**, regardless of party affiliation. At the polling place, the voter chooses the ballot of the party whose primary he or she wants to vote in. Only registered party members may vote in a **closed primary**. A subset of this is the semi-open primary, open only to registered party members and those not registered as members of other parties. The Democrats also send elected state officials, including Democratic members of Congress and governors, to their national conventions. Some of these

Tom Williams/CQ Roll Call/Getty Images

Challengers Launching the Campaign
Republican presidential candidate Mitt Romney and his running mate, Wisconsin representative Paul Ryan, greet the crowd at the Republican National Convention in Tampa in September 2012. Facing an incumbent president during an economic downturn, Romney's choice of Ryan as a running mate signaled that he was staking out positions on fiscal issues important to the party's conservative base.

officials are "superdelegates," able to vote as free agents, but the rest must reflect the state's primary vote.[67]

In addition to varying in terms of whom they allow to vote, the parties' primary rules also differ in how they distribute delegates among the candidates. The Democrats generally use a method of proportional representation, in which the candidates get the percentage of delegates equal to the percentage of the primary vote they win (provided they get at least 15 percent). Republican rules run from proportional representation, to winner-take-all (the candidate with the most votes gets all the delegates, even if he or she does not win an absolute majority), to direct voting for delegates (the delegates are not bound to vote for a particular candidate at the convention), to the absence of a formal system (caucus participants may decide how to distribute the delegates).

State primaries also vary in the times at which they are held, with various states engaged in **front-loading**, vying to hold their primaries first in order to gain media maximum exposure and influence over the nomination. By tradition and state law, the Iowa caucus and the New Hampshire primary are the first contests for delegates. As a result, they get tremendous attention, from both candidates and the media—much more than their contribution to the delegate count would justify. This is why in 1998 other states began moving their primaries earlier in the season.[68] The process of moving up primary dates continued in 2012 with the Iowa caucuses held on January 3 and twenty-three states having held primaries or caucuses by March 6, 2012, the day of Super Tuesday, on which the largest number of primaries are held.

---

party caucus local gathering of party members to choose convention delegates

presidential primary an election by which voters choose convention delegates committed to voting for a certain candidate

open primary primary election in which eligible voters need not be registered party members

closed primary primary election in which only registered party members may vote

front-loading the process of scheduling presidential primaries early in the primary season

It Always Starts in Iowa
Candidates eyeing the presidential nominations of their parties often begin their unofficial campaigns by touring Iowa, where crucial first votes take place. Here, senator and likely presidential hopeful Rand Paul, R-Ky., fields questions from the Westside Conservative Club in Urbandale, Iowa, in August 2014—more than two years before the state caucus.

Scott Olson/Getty Images

former or incumbent vice presidents, five were senators, and six were governors. Governors, with executive experience and the ability to claim that they are untainted by the gridlock politics of Washington, have recently had the edge, with four of those six former governors going on to win the presidency.

In most of the crowded primaries in recent years there has been a clear **front-runner**, a person who many assume will win the nomination before the primaries even begin. Early front-runner status is positive because it means the candidate has raised significant money, has a solid organization, and receives more media coverage than his or her opponents. But success in primaries comes not just from getting a majority of the votes but also from being perceived as a winner, and front-runners are punished if they fail to live up to lofty expectations—the fate shared by Republican Rudy Giuliani and Democrat Hillary Clinton in 2008. The goal for all the other candidates is to attack the front-runner so as to drive down his or her support, while maneuvering into position as the chief alternative. Then if the front-runner stumbles, as often happens, each of the attacking candidates hopes to emerge from the pack.

Generally a candidate's campaign strategy becomes focused on developing **momentum**, the perception by the press, the public, and the other candidates in the field that one is on a roll, and that polls, primary victories, endorsements, and funding are all coming one's way. Considerations of electability—which candidate has the best chance to triumph in November—are important as voters decide whom to support, and here candidates who seem to have momentum can have an advantage.

Interestingly, who actually "wins" in the primaries is not always the candidate who comes in first in the balloting. An equally critical factor is whether the candidate is seen to be improving or fading—the matter of momentum and expectations. Much of the political credit that a candidate gets for an apparent "win" depends on who else is running in that primary and the media expectations of that candidate's performance.

The primary campaigns involve a lot of speeches and television ads, but increasingly important are the debates among the contenders for a party's nomination. These are televised nationally, giving the whole country exposure to each party's candidates. It is arguable that the many debates among candidates for the 2008 Democratic nomination gave Barack Obama national media exposure and the united effort of the

The consequence of such front-loading is that candidates must have a substantial war chest and be prepared to campaign nationally from the beginning. Traditionally, winners of early primaries could use that success to raise more campaign funds to continue the battle. With the primaries stacked at the beginning, however, this becomes much harder. When the winner can be determined within weeks of the first primary, it is less likely that a dark horse, or unknown candidate, can emerge. The process favors well-known, well-connected, and, especially, well-funded candidates. Again, incumbents have an enormous advantage here.

The heavily front-loaded primary has almost no defenders, but it presents a classic example of the problems of collective action that politics cannot always solve.[69] No single state has an incentive to hold back and reduce its power for the good of the whole; each state is driven to maximize its influence by strategically placing its primary early in the pack. Since states make their own laws, subject to only a few regulations laid down by the parties, they are able to schedule the primary season pretty much as they want, regardless of what system would produce the best nominees for national office.

In the fierce battle that the primaries have become, incumbents, of course, have a tremendous advantage. No incumbent has been seriously challenged since Ronald Reagan gave Gerald Ford a good scare in 1976. While the incumbent's advantage is most powerful here, most serious presidential contenders have held at least some major elected office. Of the two major parties' nominees over the past eleven presidential elections, eight were incumbent presidents, three were

> **front-runner** the leading candidate and expected winner of a nomination or an election
>
> **momentum** the widely held public perception that a candidate is gaining electoral strength

candidates to weaken Hillary Clinton in those debates was costly to her as well. In 2012 the complex ups and downs of the Republican candidates' fortunes can be traced, in part, to debate performances. As with presidential debates, a gaffe can be costly, as when in a November 2011 primary debate Texas governor Rick Perry could name only two of the three cabinet departments he said he would abolish.

THE CONVENTION

Since 1972, delegates attending the national conventions have not had to decide who the parties' nominees would be. However, two official actions continue to take place at the conventions. First, as we discussed in Chapter 12, the parties hammer out and approve their platforms, the documents in which parties set out their distinct issue positions. Second, the vice presidential candidate is named officially. The choice of the vice president is up to the presidential nominee. Traditionally the choice was made to balance the ticket (ideologically, regionally, or even, when Democrat Walter Mondale chose Geraldine Ferraro in 1984, by gender). Bill Clinton's choice of Al Gore was a departure from this practice, as he tapped a candidate much like himself—a Democratic moderate from a southern state. In 2000 George W. Bush picked Dick Cheney, a man whose considerable experience in the federal government could be expected to offset Bush's relative lack of it. In 2004 liberal Bostonian John Kerry returned to the regional and ideological balancing principle, choosing moderate North Carolina senator John Edwards as his running mate, though he broke with tradition by announcing his choice three weeks before his party's convention.

In 2008 Barack Obama chose Delaware senator Joe Biden as his running mate, going for an experienced hand with a foreign policy background to shore up his own—at that time relatively thin—record. Democrats applauded his pick of Biden as one that balanced the ticket and showcased Obama's own judgment and decision-making skills. They had barely finished cheering their new nominee, however, when John McCain upstaged Obama with his own pick, Alaska governor Sarah Palin, who he felt would bolster his maverick credentials, help him energize his base, and bolster his standing with women. The choice was immediately controversial; wildly popular with religious conservatives, it was viewed with surprise and skepticism by Democrats and media commentators.

There is no clear evidence that the vice presidential choice has significant electoral consequences, but the presidential nominees weigh it carefully nonetheless. If nothing else, the caliber of the nominee's choice for vice president is held to be an indication of the kind of appointments the nominee would make if elected. Although McCain's pick of Palin as his running mate was popular initially, with 20 percent more of the public having positive than negative feelings toward her, a cascade of bad news stories about her soon engulfed the McCain campaign. By the time of the election, Palin's

Stan Honda/AFP/Getty Images

Improv at the Convention

Nominating conventions are usually well-orchestrated and predictable affairs, but they have their viral moments. One of the standouts of the 2012 campaigns occurred when Clint Eastwood surprised the Romney campaign with an eccentric bit of improv during prime time at the Republican National Convention, lecturing an empty chair on the inadequacies of the Obama presidency. The performance prompted Obama to tweet a picture of his cabinet room chair labeled "The President" with the caption "This seat's taken."

negatives were 7 percent higher than her positives. This all rebounded on the campaign amid charges that McCain could hardly have been following his slogan of "putting country first" with such a selection.

In 2012 Mitt Romney also stepped on his own campaign message a bit, with his pick of Wisconsin congressman Paul Ryan. Throughout the primary season, Romney had emphasized his business credentials as his major qualification for office, claiming that a president should have private-sector experience. In choosing Ryan, who had no such experience, he, like McCain, was forced to alter his message. Nonetheless, Ryan was a popular choice with the Republican base and helped to fill a hole in Romney's own resume by putting someone with Tea Party credentials on the ticket.

The conventions typically provide the nominee with a "convention bump" in the preelection polls. Media coverage of the carefully orchestrated party harmony, the enthusiasm of party supporters, and even the staged theatrics seem to have a positive impact on viewers. The result is that candidates have usually, though not always, experienced a noticeable rise in the polls immediately following the conventions. Both Obama and McCain received bounces from their

THE BIG PICTURE: HOW THE ELECTORAL COLLEGE WORKS, AND HOW IT MIGHT WORK

The founding fathers intended the Electoral College to be a compromise between direct election of the president (they weren't sure they trusted us!) and selection of the president by Congress (they didn't want him to be indebted). Consequently, the Electoral College is selected once every four years, those members meet in November to choose the president, and then they disband, never to meet again. Good idea, or bad? Look at how it works and decide for yourself.

How It Works

Each state is allotted a set number of electors but can decide how to allocate them among the presidential candidates.

 **+** **=** **#**

| # of Representatives | 2 Senators | Total Allotted Votes Per State |

538 Votes in total

What Your Vote Means

When you cast your vote you are really voting for an elector chosen by the state party who will cast a vote for president on your behalf.

109p6.05

Electors pledged to a candidate are chosen by state parties

Citizens vote for electors pledged to their preferred candidate

States allocate their electoral votes to the candidate(s) according to that state's formula

How the States Allocate Their Votes

48 states have a winner-take-all system where the candidate who wins the popular vote in the state gets ALL the state's electoral votes. But Maine and Nebraska award their votes proportionally.

NE   ME

In 2012, the Electoral Vote Looked Like This...

12, 3, 3, 10, 4
7, 4, 3, 3, 10, 10, 29, 3/4, 11 (MA)
6, 16, 20, 4 (RI)
6, 5 ①②③, 20, 11, 18, 5, 14 (NJ)
55, 6, 9, 6, 10, 8, 13, 3 (DE)
11, 5, 7, 6, 11, 15, 10 (MD)
6, 9, 16, 9, 3 (DC)
38, 8
3, 29
4

The winner is...

On election night, news networks use returns and exit poll interviews to estimate who won each state and its electoral votes. A simple majority, or 270, is sufficient to win.

270

| Obama 332 ☑ | Romney 206 |

Source: 270toWin [http://www.270towin.com/alternative-electoral-college-allocation-methods/]

But It Could Be Different

The winner-take all system seems unfair to some people, and it concentrates presidential contests in just a few "battleground states." But states could allocate their votes differently. Here are a few of the options, with a look at how they would have affected the results of the 2012 election.

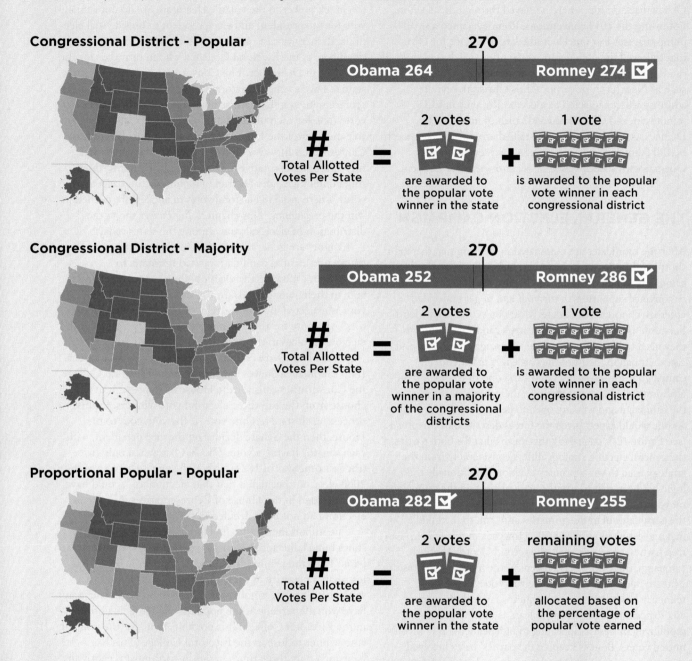

Congressional District - Popular

270

Obama 264 | Romney 274 ☑

Total Allotted Votes Per State **=** **2 votes** are awarded to the popular vote winner in the state **+** **1 vote** is awarded to the popular vote winner in each congressional district

Congressional District - Majority

270

Obama 252 | Romney 286 ☑

Total Allotted Votes Per State **=** **2 votes** are awarded to the popular vote winner in a majority of the congressional districts **+** **1 vote** is awarded to the popular vote winner in each congressional district

Proportional Popular - Popular

270

Obama 282 ☑ | Romney 255

Total Allotted Votes Per State **=** **2 votes** are awarded to the popular vote winner in the state **+** **remaining votes** allocated based on the percentage of popular vote earned

Popular Vote - Eliminate the Electoral College (because the popular vote winner has lost 4 times!)

Obama 65,918,507 (51.01%) ☑ | Romney 60,934,407 (47.15%)

National Popular Vote Interstate Compact A budding agreement among the states would commit each state to cast all of their electoral votes for the national popular vote winner, ensuring that the popular vote winner becomes president, but without amending the Constitution. It will take effect if states with 270 combined electoral votes commit to be bound by it. As of 2014, ten states plus the District of Columbia, accounting for nearly a third of the required 270 votes, had passed legislation to join the compact.

conventions in 2008, though McCain's was slightly larger. McCain briefly achieved a lead in the polls after his convention, but the negative publicity surrounding Palin and then the economic crisis that began in mid-September put Obama back on top, where he stayed through the election. Following the 2012 conventions, Romney gained a small bump that was lost quickly in the larger bounce for Obama that followed the Democratic convention. Media coverage of the Republican convention was dominated by odd moments such as New Jersey governor Chris Christie's keynote address, which neglected to mention Romney until 18 minutes in, and Clint Eastwood's turn of improv. The Democrats, on the other hand, rallied around an epic speech by Bill Clinton that energized the party, even though Obama's own speech was seen as a more somber moment.

THE GENERAL ELECTION CAMPAIGN

After the candidates are nominated in late summer, there is a short break, at least for the public, before the traditional fall campaign. When the campaign begins, the goal of each side is to convince supporters to turn out and to get undecided voters to choose its candidate. Most voters, the party identifiers, will usually support their party's candidate, although they need to be motivated by the campaign to turn out and cast their ballots. Most of the battle in a presidential campaign is for the swing voters, the one-third or so of the electorate who have not made up their minds at the start of the campaign and who are open to persuasion by either side. As one would expect given the forces described in Chapter 12 (see Figure 12.3, page 443), this means that for both parties, the general election strategy differs considerably from the strategy used to win a primary election. Traditionally the logic has been that to win the general election the campaigns move away from the sharp ideological tone used to motivate the party faithful in the primaries and "run to the middle" by making less ideological appeals. However, in this era of polarized parties, especially since the second George W. Bush campaign, there are fewer citizens in the middle, and those who are there are much less likely to vote.[70] Thus the tendency has been for a campaign to stay with the party's ideological message, putting at least as much emphasis on mobilizing its base as appealing to independents and uncommitted voters. Besides keeping the parties' bases involved, staying with more ideological appeals can help candidates avoid being charged with "flip-flopping" on the issues.

In the general campaign, each side seeks to get its message across, to define the choice in terms that give its candidate the advantage. This massive effort to influence the information to which citizens are exposed requires a clear strategy, which begins with a plan for winning the states where the candidate will be competitive.

THE ELECTORAL COLLEGE The presidential election is not a national race; it is a race between the candidates in each of the fifty states and the District of Columbia (see

"*Snapshot of America:* How Did We Vote in the 2012 Presidential Election?"). The reasons for the Electoral College's existence may seem outdated sometimes, but it nevertheless drives campaign strategy. Because our founders feared giving too much power to the volatile electorate, we do not actually vote for the president and vice president in presidential elections. Rather, we cast our votes in November for electors (members of the Electoral College), who in turn vote for the president in December. The Constitution provides for each state to have as many electoral votes as it does senators and representatives in Congress. Thus Alaska has three electoral votes (one for each of the state's U.S. senators and one for its sole member of the House of Representatives). By contrast, California has fifty-five electoral votes (two senators and fifty-three representatives). In addition, the Twenty-third Amendment gave the District of Columbia three electoral votes. There are 538 electoral votes in all; 270 are needed to win the presidency. This chapter's *Big Picture* shows the distribution of electoral votes among the states today.

Electors are generally activist members of the party whose presidential candidate carried the state. In December, following the election, the electors meet and vote in their state capitals. In the vast majority of cases, they vote as expected, but there are occasional "faithless electors" who vote for their own preferences. The results of the electors' choices in the states are then sent to the Senate, where the ballots are counted when the new session opens. If no candidate achieves a majority in the Electoral College, the Constitution calls for the House of Representatives to choose from the top three electoral vote winners. In this process, each state has one vote. If the vote goes to the House, then the Senate decides on the vice president, with each senator having a vote. This has happened only twice (the last time was in 1824), although some observers of the 2000 election speculated that that election, too, could have been decided in the House of Representatives if Florida's election had not been decided in the courts.

The importance of the Electoral College is that all the states but Maine and Nebraska operate on a winner-take-all basis. Thus the winner in California, even if he or she has less than a majority of the popular vote, wins all of the state's fifty-five electoral votes. The loser in California may have won 49 percent of the popular vote but gets nothing in the Electoral College. It is possible, then, for the popular vote winner to lose in the Electoral College. This has happened only three times in our history, most recently in 2000, when Bush received an Electoral College majority even though Gore won the popular vote by more than half a million votes. Usually, however, the opposite happens: the Electoral College exaggerates the candidate's apparent majority. The 2012 election is typical of this exaggeration of the victory margin in the Electoral College. Obama got

---

> **swing voters** the approximately one-third of the electorate who are undecided at the start of a campaign

more than 51 percent of the two-party popular vote, but his majority in the Electoral College was 61.7 percent. This exaggeration of the winning margin has the effect of legitimizing the winner's victory and allowing him to claim that he has a mandate—a broad popular endorsement—even if he won by a smaller margin of the popular vote.

The rules of the Electoral College give greater power to some states over others. The provision that all states get at least three electoral votes in the Electoral College means that citizens in the smaller-population states get proportionately greater representation in the Electoral College. Alaska, for example, sent one elector to the Electoral College for every 240,000 people, while California had one elector for every 679,000 residents.

However, this "advantage" is probably offset by the practice of winner-take-all, which focuses the candidates' attention on the largest states with the biggest payoffs in electoral votes, especially the competitive, or "battleground," states. Small states with few electoral votes or those that are safely in the corner of one party or the other are ignored (although California, a reliably Democratic state, still received twenty-two visits by the Romney campaign, twenty of which were for fundraising).[71] Battlegrounds get the most candidate attention. Ohio was the primary focus in 2012 (as it often is) and saw a total of 148 visits by the candidates and their wives (68 for the Obama campaign, and 80 for the Romney campaign; of those visits, only a total of 7 involved fundraising). Campaign spending figures tell the same story of unequal activity: our largest state of California saw the campaigns spend a total of $320 (two ads in tiny media markets), whereas in competitive Florida they spent $173 million on television ads ($78 million by the Obama campaign and $95 million by the Romney campaign).[72]

Over the years, hundreds of bills have been introduced in Congress to reform or abolish the Electoral College, an especially urgent project for many Democrats after the 2000 election.[73] Major criticisms of the current system include the following:

- The Electoral College is undemocratic because it is possible for the popular winner not to get a majority of the electoral votes.

- In a very close contest, the popular outcome could be dictated by a few "faithless electors" who vote their consciences rather than the will of the people of their states.

- The Electoral College distorts candidates' campaign strategies. The winner-take-all provision in all but two states puts a premium on a few large, competitive states, which get a disproportionate share of the candidates' attention.

> **oppo research** investigation of an opponent's background for the purpose of exploiting weaknesses or undermining credibility

Few people deny the truth of these charges, and hardly anyone believes that if we were to start all over, the current Electoral College would be chosen as the best way to elect a president. Nevertheless, all the proposed alternatives also have problems, or at least serious criticisms.

In 2008 and 2012 Barack Obama turned the conventional wisdom about red and blue America on its head. While the states of the deep South and some of the western states stayed red, Obama targeted and won states that Democrats rarely carry, chalking up victories in Indiana, Virginia, North Carolina, Florida, and Nevada in 2008, and losing only two of those, Indiana and North Carolina, in 2012. Demographic changes in those states make them potentially more favorable territory for Democrats.

Fearing that the future electoral math is going to work against them, Republicans in some blue states such as Pennsylvania and Wisconsin have begun to talk about dividing up their Electoral College votes by congressional district, as is done in Maine and Nebraska. In Pennsylvania, for example, Obama won all of the state's twenty electoral votes. If the electoral vote had been allocated by who won the states' heavily gerrymandered congressional districts, the Republicans would have won thirteen of the twenty electoral votes.[74]

WHO RUNS THE CAMPAIGN? Running a modern presidential campaign has become a highly specialized profession. Most presidential campaigns are led by an "amateur," a nationally prestigious chairperson who may serve as an adviser and assist in fundraising. However, the real work of the campaign is done by the professional staff the candidate hires, and who themselves become important figures not only in the campaigns but often in the administrations as advisers and, later, as political commentators. For example, James Carville, Bill Clinton's campaign strategist, continues to appear frequently on television as a campaign commentator, as has Karl Rove, who ran both of George W. Bush's successful campaigns and worked as a policy adviser in the Bush White House. Obama's campaign trust included David Axelrod, who continued as a political adviser in the White House (see *Profiles in Citizenship*); Robert Gibbs, who took the job as Obama's first press secretary; and David Plouffe, who served as the 2008 Obama campaign manager and then White House adviser. Jim Messina, an Obama White House staffer, joined on as campaign manager in 2012. Campaign work at the beginning of the twenty-first century is big business.

Some of the jobs include not only the well-known ones of campaign manager and strategist but also more specialized components tailored to the modern campaign's emphasis on information and money. For instance, candidates need to hire research teams to prepare position papers on issues so that the candidate can answer any question posed by potential supporters and the media. But researchers also engage in the controversial but necessary task of **oppo research**—delving into the background and vulnerabilities of the opposing candidate with an eye to exploiting his or her weaknesses. Central to the modern campaign's efforts to get and control the flow of

PROFILES IN CITIZENSHIP:
DAVID AXELROD

Courtesy of Jamie Manley and Axelrod Strategies.

David Axelrod got involved in his first campaign pamphleteering for Bobby Kennedy when he was nine years old, and from then through his days as communications director for Barack Obama's senate and presidential campaigns, to a stint in the White House as senior advisor to the president, to his current gig as founding director at the University of Chicago's Institute of Politics, he has pretty much lived his dream. Sometimes it is tempting to look at a person as successful as Axelrod has

been and think, "Boy, did he get lucky." In Axelrod's case, however, it's clear he made it happen, every single step of the way, through an unlikely combination of starry-eyed idealism and dogged determination.

Though he grew up in New York, Axelrod has been an adopted Chicagoan since his days as an undergrad at University of Chicago. He quickly fell in love with the city and with Chicago politics—talking himself into an internship at the *Chicago Tribune*, where he spent two and a half years covering local politics on the night shift, and more years in the trenches before landing a coveted column. Watching '70s Chicago in transition from the old political machine and the evolution of the black independent political movement embodied by Harold Washington was a formative experience. When Axelrod left the paper to set up his own consulting business, it was a leap of faith; he had been bitten, hard, by the campaign bug.

Campaigns are like a narcotic, says the man who has been instrumental in running so many of them. "They are these existential experiences, where you are running full speed for months, sometimes years, and all for one day. And when they end, you feel let down and you're looking for the next challenge... There is something really invigorating, inspiring about being part of an effort too, to make change, to make a difference. Where you feel like you're doing something that's bigger than yourself and you're surrounded by people who share that [emotion] and that experience. I just love the feel of campaign headquarters. I love being among people, many of whom volunteer, there because they want to make their community and the country stronger. And they're inspiring to me.

They're often young people... and I love being among young people because you know even in the most cynical of times they're inspiring. They're properly skeptical but they're not cynical."

Axelrod's story is all about finding inspiration not just in volunteers and students but in the authentic figures who can see themselves clearly in relation to their times, and who believe in the transformative power of good government to make people's lives better—figures from Illinois Senator Paul Simon, to Massachusetts Governor Deval Patrick, to the young Illinois state legislator who Axelrod helped to put in the White House.

For him, authenticity is the key to making a public figure inspiring and, indeed, electable. "I think that authenticity is an essential ingredient for successful candidates and successful leaders," he says. "If you don't feel comfortable in your own skin then voters are not going to feel comfortable with you."

In fact, it was the seeming lack of authenticity he was finding in those seeking out his services that caused him to hook up with Barack Obama. "He was considering a race for the Senate—this seemed to me like a way to recharge my batteries... I always liked him. He was very public spirited, he seemed like a good guy. He always knew why he wanted to be in public life and what he wanted to do. And I really admired him and that became a great partnership." A partnership, of course, that made history

In his post–White House days Axelrod is looking forward to spending more time with the family he feels has given him

---

information, oppo research has become a central component in all elections, contributing to the negative campaigning so prevalent in recent years.[75] Astute candidates also have oppo research done on themselves; knowing that their opponent will be studying them, they work to be prepared to deal with attacks that might be coming. With his checkered youth in mind, Texas governor George W. Bush hired people to do oppo research on him twice during his runs for governor. The benign results then convinced him later that he had nothing to fear from the close scrutiny of a national campaign.

Candidates also need advance teams to plan and prepare their travel agendas, to arrange for crowds (and the signs they wave) to greet the candidates at airports, and even to

reserve accommodations for the press. Especially in the primaries, staff devoted to fundraising are essential to ensure the constant flow of money necessary to grease the wheels of any presidential campaign. They work with big donors and engage in direct-mail and Internet campaigns to solicit money from targeted groups. Much of the success of the Obama campaign rested on its effectiveness at communicating with and mobilizing its supporters electronically. Assisted by Mark Zuckerberg, the inventor of Facebook, among others, the Obama campaign raised more money and had many more volunteers than its competitor campaigns, which did not benefit from such skilled use of the Internet.[76]

Finally, of course, candidates need to hire a legal team to keep their campaigns in compliance with the regulations of

leeway to indulge the work he loves. He also has high hopes for the Institute of Politics he founded at the University of Chicago. There, he wants to give students a connection to the vibrant, engaging world of politics and to awaken them to the stakes he sees for them in the current political world.

THAT'S HOW DEMOCRACY'S SUPPOSED TO WORK, BY SEIZING CONTROL OF THE FUTURE.

He says, "My job whenever I talk to young people, but certainly at the University, is to make the point that whatever equity you care about, whether it's human rights, climate change, deficits, education... it's going to be impacted dramatically by the decisions that are made in Washington, in state capitals, and in capitals around the world. And you can walk away and let other people make those decisions, but then you have to live with the consequences of those."

On patriotism:

I was the son of an immigrant who came here with nothing; I ended up as the Senior Advisor to the President. I grew up in a housing development and my sister and I shared a room in a rental apartment that was probably about as big as from here to the kitchen. And I've lived my dreams. My father came here in 1922. If he'd tried to come in '23 when the very harsh immigration laws were put in place, he probably wouldn't have been here.

And his life would have been different and I think less good. So I believe in America. I believe in what America has been. I believe in the values that have been time honored and I think fighting for those is a worthy cause. And I hope young people pick that torch up because they're the ones who are going to have the greatest—by far the greatest—stake here.

On keeping the republic:

The greatest admonition I can give to young people is don't take what we have for granted. Democracy requires participation. I'm biased in this regard because I'm devoting my life to it—to this project—but I think they should get in the arena. And getting in the arena doesn't necessarily mean running for public office, although it could. It doesn't necessarily mean working in campaigns, although I think that's a good thing to do. You know my sister is an educational psychologist. She helps kids with learning disabilities deal with school systems in Massachusetts. And she was not political at all. And she got involved in politics through school board elections in her community because she was very concerned about policies there. And from there she was the one who called me and said I should work for Deval Patrick, because she was so inspired by him.

That's how democracy's supposed to work, by seizing control of the future. Seize control of the decisions that are made in your communities. Seize control of it or at least a piece of it, understanding that the outcome is not always going to be what you want; the second thing that we need

to understand is that compromise is a necessary ingredient. This whole country was founded on compromise. *The Federalist Papers* are full of compromise. The Constitution is a big compromise. And it's a work in progress, you know. But, you can't be an absolutist and engage in a healthy democracy.

As messy and as troubled and as challenged as it is, I really believe it's the best path forward. . . . This is the best vehicle to influence your future and the future of your community, the country, and the world. So my advice is to get in the arena—be a candidate, work for a candidate. Be a policy advisor, a speech writer. Go to work for a not-for-profit that is trying to push for public policy. Be a journalist and communicate in a thoughtful way what's going on in the world.

But be involved in it; don't, don't surrender to the cynicism. That would be a tragic thing to do because I've seen it. You *can* bring about real fundamental change. I know that there are people who now have healthcare who wouldn't have. There are soldiers who are home with their families who are not at risk today because of what we've done. There are autoworkers on the line that would be unemployed today but for what we've done. There are gay people who would be still unable to serve in the military, still unable to marry, still unable to live their full lives but for what we have done. . . . So my message is make a difference, get involved.

Source: David Axelrod spoke with Christine Barbour and Gerald C. Wright on August 18, 2014.

the FEC and to file the required reports. In general, campaign consultants are able to provide specialized technical services that the parties' political committees cannot.[77]

PRESENTING THE CANDIDATE An effective campaign begins with a clear understanding of how the candidate's strengths fit with the context of the times and the mood of the voters. To sell a candidate effectively, the claims to special knowledge, competence, or commitment must be credible.[78] In 1992 the Clinton campaign contrasted its candidate's fresh, young, energetic image with the public's perceptions of the incumbent, President George H. W. Bush, as lacking a clear policy direction or vision. The Clinton campaign headquarters (which staffers

called "The War Room") prominently displayed a sign—"It's the Economy, Stupid"—to help keep the campaign on track. In 2000 and 2004 George W. Bush's campaign staff were able to portray him as an effective "decider," as opposed to the more ineffective and flip-flopping images they created of Al Gore and John Kerry.

The 2008 Obama presidential campaign is considered by many observers to be one of the best-run campaigns in modern American politics. It paired near complete message control with an unprecedented use of technology and a massive and very well-organized volunteer component. The campaign capitalized on a national weariness with the Bush years and crafted a campaign theme emphasizing change that was well suited to Obama's apparent competence, his skills as a speaker, and his relative outsider status (he had served only two years in the U.S. Senate when he decided to run for president). He highlighted his change theme by continually linking McCain to the unpopular Bush administration and its policies, arguing that McCain was running for Bush's third term.

In 2012 the Obama campaign again won plaudits for its organization and excellent technological innovation. Sometimes lost in the general awe of the data-crunching and get-out-the-vote operation is the strategic effort the campaign made early on to frame the election as a choice between two candidates offering very different visions for America rather than as a referendum on the president. Given slow economic growth and the Republicans' success in denying the president any legislative victories in the two years preceding the election, the campaign felt it would lose the latter, so as soon as the campaign was sure that Romney would be the Republican nominee, it began to define him as a wealthy plutocrat out of touch with middle-class American concerns. Inexplicably, the Romney campaign let the Obama campaign have the stage to itself in the summer before the election. By the time Romney's campaign began to introduce Romney as it wanted voters to see him, as a bipartisan economic problem solver, it was too late. Many voters' perceptions were locked in, and the release of the tape with Romney's "47 percent" comments only reinforced them.

THE ISSUES Earlier we indicated that issues matter to voters as they decide how to vote. This means that issues must be central to the candidate's strategy for getting elected. From the candidate's point of view, there are two kinds of issues to consider when planning a strategy: valence issues and position issues.

Valence issues are policy matters on which the voters and the candidates share the same preference. These are what we might call "motherhood and apple pie" issues, because no one opposes them. Everyone is for a strong, prosperous economy; for America having a respected leadership role in the world; for fighting terrorism; for thrift in government; and for a clean environment. Similarly, everyone opposes crime and drug abuse, government waste, political corruption, and immorality.

Position issues have two sides. On abortion, there are those who are pro-life and those who are pro-choice. On military engagements such as Vietnam, Iraq, or Afghanistan, there are those who favor pursuing a military victory and those who favor just getting out. Many of the hardest decisions for candidates are on position issues—although a clear stand means that they will gain some friends, it also guarantees that they will make some enemies. Realistic candidates who want to win as many votes as possible try to avoid being clearly identified with the losing side of important position issues. For instance, activists in the Republican Party fought to keep their strong pro-life plank in the party platform in 2000. However, because a majority of the electorate is

opposed to the strong pro-life position, George W. Bush seldom mentioned the issue during the campaign, even though one of his first acts as president was to cut federal funding to overseas groups that provide abortions or abortion counseling. John McCain, needing to solidify his Republican base in 2008, was more explicit about his party's pro-life stance, and it appeared to cost him with independent voters, as it did with Mitt Romney in 2012. When two Republican senate candidates made news by arguing that abortion should not be legal even in the case of rape, President Obama was able to paint Romney as extreme on the issue by association.

When a candidate or party does take a stand on a difficult position issue, the other side often uses it against them as a wedge issue. A **wedge issue** is a position issue on which the parties differ and that proves controversial within the ranks of a particular party. For a Republican, an anti–affirmative action position is not dangerous, since few Republicans actively support affirmative action. For a Democrat, though, it is a very dicey issue, because liberal party members endorse it but more moderate members do not. An astute strategy for a Republican candidate is to raise the issue in a campaign, hoping to drive a wedge between the Democrats and to recruit to his or her side the Democratic opponents of affirmative action.

The idea of **issue ownership** helps to clarify the role of policy issues in presidential campaigns. Because of their past stands and performance, each of the parties is widely perceived as better able to handle certain kinds of problems. For instance, the Democrats may be seen as better able to deal with education matters, and the Republicans as more effective at solving crime-related problems. The voter's job then is not so much to evaluate positions on education and crime, but rather to decide which problem is more important. If education is pressing, a voter might go with the Democratic candidate; if crime is more important, the voter might choose the Republican.[79] From the candidate's point of view, the trick is to convince voters that the election is about the issues that his or her party "owns."

An example of how issue ownership operated in the 2008 presidential election can be seen in exit poll data. Voters were asked which of five issues was the most important facing the country. Three of those issues worked to the advantage of Barack Obama. Two of them—the economy and health care—are Democratic-owned issues, and Obama

---

valence issues issues on which most voters and candidates share the same position

position issues issues on which the parties differ in their perspectives and proposed solutions

wedge issue a controversial issue that one party uses to split the voters in the other party

issue ownership the tendency of one party to be seen as more competent in a specific policy area

It's the Economy . . . Again ● Oppo Depot ●

received clear majorities on both. John McCain owned just one issue, terrorism. Unfortunately for McCain, only 9 percent of the electorate felt that was the most important issue. We might have suspected that McCain would also command an advantage on the war in Iraq issue, but by 2008 the war was relatively unpopular and Obama had initially claimed attention in the Democratic field by being an early critic of the war, and thus got the support of most of these voters. What is clear is that Obama benefited electorally from the economic crisis that directed voters' attention to that issue.

Because valence issues are relatively safe, candidates stress them at every opportunity. They also focus on the position issues that their parties "own" or on which they have majority support. What this suggests is that the real campaign is not about debating positions on issues—how to reduce the deficit or whether to restrict abortion—but about which issues should be considered. Issue campaigning is to a large extent about setting the agenda.

THE MEDIA It is impossible to understand the modern political campaign without appreciating the pervasive role of the media. Even though many voters tend to ignore campaign ads—or at least they tell survey interviewers that they do—we know that campaign advertising matters. It has increased dramatically with the rise of television as people's information source of choice. Studies show that advertising provides usable information for voters. Political ads can heighten the loyalty of existing supporters, and they can educate the public about what candidates stand for and what issues candidates believe are most important. Ads also can be effective in establishing the criteria on which voters choose between candidates.

One of the best examples of this effective advertising came from the 1988 presidential campaign. Because George H. W. Bush was behind in the polls and perceived as not very sympathetic to average citizens, his campaign sought to change the way people were thinking about him and his opponent, Michael Dukakis. The campaign came up with an effective ad showing criminals walking in and out of a prison through a turnstile. A voice-over claimed that Dukakis's "revolving door prison policy" had permitted first-degree murderers to leave on weekend furloughs. At the same time, a pro-Bush group called the National Security PAC ran the more controversial Willie Horton ad, which focused on the mug shot of Horton, showing (without

AP Photo/Charles Dharapak

Who Owns This Issue?
Women demonstrate outside the Supreme Court in March 2014, as the justices heard arguments on the health care law requirement that businesses provide contraceptive coverage to female employees. The justices (who struck down the requirement five to four) were just as divided on the issue as the public. Those on the right claim that closely held corporations should not have to pay for treatments that violate the religious beliefs of business owners, whereas those on the left insist that contraceptive care is a private health care matter.

saying so) that he was African American. Implying that Dukakis bore some responsibility for the events described, the commercial coolly told how Horton, who was serving a life sentence for murder, had stabbed a man and raped his girlfriend while on a weekend pass.[80] The Dukakis campaign failed to respond to this one-two punch, and subsequent surveys showed that those who saw the commercials came to think of crime as an important issue in the campaign. Bush's standings began to climb, and, of course, he went on to win the election.[81] (See *Don't Be Fooled by…Campaign Advertising* for some advice on how to critically evaluate the political ads that come your way.) Although **negative advertising** may turn off some voters and give the perception that politics is an unpleasant business, the public accepts accurate attacks on the issues. As long as it does not go too far, an attack ad that highlights negative aspects of an opponent's record actually registers more quickly and is remembered more frequently and longer by voters than are positive ads.[82] Experts have suggested that requiring candidates to appear in their own ads would discourage negativity. Negative ads, however, continue to be the rule, rather than the exception, though not all candidates resort to them equally. During the heat of the 2008 campaign, in one week, nearly 100 percent of the McCain campaign's ads were negative, compared to 34 percent of Obama's ads during the same time period.[83]

negative advertising campaign advertising that emphasizes the negative characteristics of opponents rather than one's own strengths

DON'T BE FOOLED BY...
CAMPAIGN ADVERTISING

"Sticks and stones may break my bones," goes the old childhood rhyme, "but words can never hurt me." Try telling that to the innumerable targets of negative advertising, sloganeering that emphasizes the negative characteristics of one's opponents rather than one's own strengths. Negative advertising has characterized American election campaigns since the days of George Washington. *George Washington?* His opponents called him a "dictator" who would "debauch the nation."[1] Thomas Jefferson was accused of having an affair with a slave, a controversy that has outlived any of the people involved; Abraham Lincoln was claimed to have had an illegitimate child; and Grover Cleveland, who admitted to fathering a child out of wedlock, was taunted with the words, "Ma, Ma, where's my Pa?"[2] (His supporters had the last laugh, however: "Gone to the White House, ha, ha, ha.")

Like it or not (and most Americans say they do not), the truth is that negative campaign advertising works, and in the television age it is far more prevalent than anything that plagued Washington, Jefferson, Lincoln, or Cleveland. People remember it better than they do positive advertising; tracking polls show that after a voter has seen a negative ad eight times, he or she begins to move away from the attacked candidate.[3] Some candidates claim that their advertising is not really negative but rather "comparative," and indeed a candidate often needs to compare his or her record with another's in order to make the case that he or she is the superior choice. Negative advertising is nonetheless unpopular with voters, who often see it as nasty, unfair, and false. In fact, advertising that is proved to be false can frequently backfire on the person doing the advertising.

WHAT TO WATCH OUT FOR

How is a savvy media consumer to know what to believe? Be careful, be critical, and be fair in how you interpret campaign ads. Here are some tips. Ask yourself these questions:

- **Who is running the ad?** What do they have to gain by it? Look to see who has paid for the ad. Is it the opponent's campaign? An interest group? A political action committee (PAC) or a 527 group? What do they have at stake, and how might that affect their charges? If the ad's sponsors do not identify themselves, what might that tell you about the source of the information? About the information itself?

- **Are the accusations relevant to the campaign or the office in question?** If character is a legitimate issue, questions of adultery or drug use might have bearing on the election. If not, they might just be personal details used to smear this candidate's reputation. Ask yourself, What kind of person should hold the job? What kinds of qualities are important?

- **Is the accusation or attack timely?** If a person is accused of youthful experimentation with drugs or indiscreet behavior in his or her twenties but has been an upstanding lawyer and public servant for twenty-five years, do the accusations have bearing on how the candidate will do the job?

- **Does the ad convey a fair charge that can be answered, or does it evoke unarticulated fears and emotions?** A 1964 ad for Lyndon Johnson's presidential campaign showed a little girl counting as she plucked petals from a daisy. An adult male voice gradually replaced hers, counting down to an explosion of a mushroom cloud that obliterated the

"Long History" of Attack Ads
Candidates on both sides use negative ads to paint their opponents in an unfavorable light. In 2012 the Romney campaign's "Long History" ad painted President Barack Obama as unfavorable to the welfare reforms enacted during the Clinton administration, claims that fact checkers said were false.

picture. The daisy commercial never even mentioned Johnson's opponent, Barry Goldwater, though the clear implication was that the conservative, promilitary Goldwater was likely to lead the nation to a nuclear war. Amid cries of "Foul!" from Goldwater's Republican supporters, the ad was aired only once, but it became a classic example of the sort of ad that seeks to play on the fears of its viewers.

- **Is the ad true?** FactCheck.org, a project of the Annenberg Public Policy Center, is an excellent resource for monitoring factual accuracy in campaign ads. Other media outlets like the *New York Times* will often run "ad watches" to help viewers determine if the information in an advertisement is true. If it is not (and sometimes even if it is), you can usually count on hearing a response from the attacked candidate rebutting the charges. Occasionally candidates have chosen not to respond, claiming to take the high road, but as Michael Dukakis's dismal performance in the 1988 election showed, false attacks left unanswered can be devastating. Try to conduct your own "ad watch." Study the campaign ads and evaluate their truthfulness.

1. Alexandra Marks, "Backlash Grows Against Negative Political Ads," *Christian Science Monitor*, September 28, 1995, 1.

2. Roger Stone, "Positively Negative," *New York Times*, February 26, 1996, 13.

3. Ibid.

Because paid media coverage is so expensive, a campaign's goal is to maximize opportunities for free coverage while controlling, as much as possible, the kind of coverage it gets. The major parties' presidential candidates are accompanied by a substantial entourage of reporters who need to file stories on a regular basis, not only for the nation's major newspapers and television networks but also to keep reporters and commentators on the cable news stations, like CNN, MSNBC, and Fox, busy. These media have substantial influence in setting the agenda—determining what issues are important and, hence, which candidates' appeals will resonate with voters.[84] As a result, daily campaign events are planned more for the press and the demands of the evening news than for the actual in-person audiences, who often seem to function primarily as a backdrop for the candidates' efforts to get favorable airtime each day. The campaigns also field daily conference calls with reporters to attack their opponents and defend their candidates and to try to control, or "spin," the way they are covered. In the last couple of election cycles, a strategy for getting on the news without spending a lot of money has been to produce negative "web ads" designed for Internet circulation, which, if catchy enough, could get endless coverage by the networks, the cable stations, and the blogs.

Although the candidates want the regular exposure, they do not like the norms of broadcast news, which they see as perpetuating horse-race journalism, focusing on who is ahead rather than on substantive issues.[85] In addition, the exhausting nature of campaigns, and the mistakes and gaffes that follow, are a source of constant concern because of the media's tendency to zero in on them and replay them endlessly. The relationship between the campaigns and the media is testy. Each side needs the other, but the candidates want to control the message, and the media want stories that are "news"—controversies, changes in the candidates' standings, or stories of goofs and scandals. We discuss the complex relationship between the media and the candidates at greater length in Chapter 15.

Candidates in recent elections have turned increasingly to "soft news" and entertainment programming to get their messages across. Candidates have been especially effective at appealing across party lines to reach the less engaged voters in the soft news formats. Many 2008 candidates, including John McCain, Barack Obama, Ron Paul, and Hillary Clinton, appeared on NBC's *Saturday Night Live* and Comedy Central's *The Daily Show With Jon Stewart* and *The Colbert Report* (even Michelle Obama made a stop at the latter two). Obama kept up the tradition in 2012, but Mitt Romney chose to avoid the informal appearances, playing it safe but missing an opportunity to show himself in a more relaxed light.

In 2008 the Internet really came into its own as a source of news. Mainstream media outlets like the *New York Times*, the *Washington Post*, *Time* magazine, and the major networks maintained blogs that joined independent bloggers like Josh Marshall of Talkingpointsmemo.com and National Review Online in updating campaign news and poll results throughout the day. And with everyone having a cell phone camera or a video camera in his or her pocket, YouTube has helped to transform the electoral landscape as well. A

Presidential Debates, Then and Now

The 1960 presidential debate between Vice President Richard Nixon and Sen. John F. Kennedy was the first to be televised—and many believe that it benefitted the young, charismatic Kennedy, who appeared poised and relaxed in comparison to a brooding Nixon. A half-century later, many analysts argue that debates have little influence on election outcomes. The election of 2012, however, may have proved to be the exception: a very strong performance by Mitt Romney in the first debate and an unusually lively and testy face-off in the second town hall meeting made for great television, and certainly affected the momentum of the contest.

recorded gaffe or misstatement by a candidate or a campaign surrogate could go viral—reaching millions of viewers with the quick clicks of many mouses. Politicians accustomed to a more conventional way of campaigning were often caught in the YouTube trap. Bill Clinton, for instance, campaigning for his wife in the Democratic primary, was several times captured on tape saying something ill-advised that spread quickly before he could attempt damage control. Even the media-savvy Obama found a tape of his words about frustrated voters becoming bitter, spoken at what he thought was a closed fundraiser, making the Internet and then the mainstream media rounds at lightning speed. And as we have seen, in 2012 Mitt Romney was recorded at a private fundraiser speaking about how 47 percent of Americans, who pay no taxes, would never vote for him or be persuaded to take responsibility for their lives. His poll numbers dipped after this, and although they improved after the first debate, he was haunted by the image of being unsympathetic to the plight of almost half of Americans.

PRESIDENTIAL DEBATES Since 1976 the presidential debates have become one of the major focal points of the campaign. The first televised debate was held in 1960 between Sen. John F. Kennedy and Vice President Richard Nixon. The younger and more photogenic Kennedy came out on top in those televised debates, but interestingly, those who heard the debates on the radio thought that Nixon did a better job.[86] In general, leading candidates find it less in their interest to participate in debates because they have more to lose and less to win, and so for years debates took place on a sporadic basis.

More recently, however, media and public pressure have all but guaranteed that at least the major-party candidates will participate in debates, although the number, timing, and format of the debates are renegotiated for each presidential election season. Recent elections have generated two or three debates, with a debate among the vice presidential contenders worked in as well. Third-party candidates, who have the most to gain from the free media exposure and the legitimacy that debate participation confers on a campaign, lobby to be included but rarely are. Ross Perot was invited in 1992 because both George H. W. Bush and Bill Clinton hoped to woo his supporters. Ralph Nader and Pat Buchanan were shut out of all three debates in 2000.

Do the debates matter? Detailed statistical studies show, not surprisingly, that many of the debates have been stand-offs. However, some of the debates, especially those identified with significant candidate errors or positive performances, have moved vote intentions 2 to 4 percent, which in a close race could be significant.[87] In addition, a good deal of evidence indicates that citizens learn about the candidates and their issue positions from the debates.[88] In 2012 President Obama was familiar to voters, but his challenger, Mitt Romney, was known mostly as the plutocratic caricature that had been painted of him in Obama advertisements. During their first debate, Romney looked relaxed, confident, and presidential, while the president looked grumpy and passive. Polls showed a huge win for Romney, and many of the Republican-leaning voters who had been turned off by Romney's 47 percent gaffe returned to his camp. Obama's poll numbers dipped, and Romney even took the lead in the polls for a short while. Mad at himself for his sleepy performance in the first debate,

Presidential Campaign Ad Database ●

Obama snapped back in the second and third debates, and polls showed that voters considered him the winner. By Election Day he had returned to his pre-debate standing in the polls.

MONEY Winning—or even losing—a presidential campaign involves serious money. The presidential candidates in 2012 spent a total of more than $2 billion, almost double what was spent by the presidential candidates in 2004, which had doubled what was spent in 2000. The data in Figure 14.2 show this striking upward trend, which came about despite significant fundraising limits put into place by the Bipartisan Campaign Reform Act (BCRA).

This torrent of cash is used to cover the costs of all the activities just discussed: campaign professionals, polling and travel for the candidates and often their spouses (along with the accompanying staff and media), with the biggest share going to the production and purchase of media advertising. The campaign costs for all federal offices in 2008 came in at about $5.3 billion, or just over $18 for every man, woman, and child in the country.[89] Of course, the 2012 expenditures easily top all previous records.

Where does all this money come from? To make sense of the changing world of election campaign finance, we need to start by defining the different kinds of campaign contributions, each with different sources and regulations:

- **Government matching funds** are given, in the primary and general election campaigns, to qualified presidential candidates who choose to accept them and to spend only that money. The funds come from citizens who have checked the box on their tax returns that sends $3 ($6 on joint returns) to fund presidential election campaigns. The idea behind the law is to more easily regulate big money influence on campaign finances, to ensure a fair contest, and to free up candidates to communicate with the public. For primary elections, if a candidate raises at least $5,000 in each of twenty states and agrees to abide by overall spending limits (almost $55 million in 2012), as well as state-by-state limits, the federal government matches every contribution up to $250.

This same fund has in the past fully financed both major-party candidates' general election campaigns and continues to subsidize the two national party

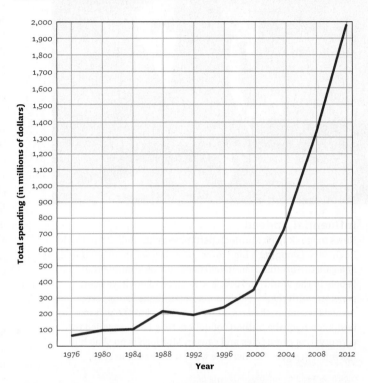

FIGURE 14.2 **INCREASE IN TOTAL SPENDING IN PRESIDENTIAL CAMPAIGNS, 1976-2012**

Source: Center for Responsive Politics, "Presidential Fund-raising and Spending, 1976–2008," www.opensecrets.org/pres08/totals.php?cycle=2008; "Banking on Becoming President," www.opensecrets.org/pres08/index.php; and "2012 Presidential Race," www.opensecrets.org/pres12/index.php?ql3.

nominating conventions. John McCain opted to participate in the 2008 federal campaign financing and faced a spending limit of $84.1 million. Barack Obama was the first presidential nominee not to participate in the general election federal financing, arguing that by relying on small donors, his campaign was essentially publicly funded anyway. This meant that his campaign had to raise all the funds it would spend rather than receiving the federal subsidy, but it also meant that the Obama campaign was not limited in the amount it could spend. If presidential candidates accept this public funding, they may not raise any other funds or use any leftover funds raised during the primary campaign.

In 2012 both parties' candidates anticipated raising and spending at least $1 billion each, so their campaigns refused the option of government matching funds (about $94 million available in 2012) and the limited spending that accepting those funds would impose. This may well spell the death of public funding of presidential general election campaigns.[90] Third parties that received at least 5 percent of the vote in the previous presidential

---

government matching funds money given by the federal government to qualified presidential candidates in the primary and general election campaigns

be unconstitutional in a 1999 Colorado district federal court decision but was later upheld in a five-to-four Supreme Court decision.[93]

However, in the 2010 decision in *Citizens United v. Federal Election Commission*,[94] the Supreme Court struck down a provision of BCRA that prohibited corporations (and, by implication, unions and interest groups) from sponsoring broadcast ads for or against specific candidates. Corporations, unions, and individual citizens are thus free to engage in broadcast campaigns, although provisions requiring disclosure and limitations on direct contributions to candidates were retained. A new loophole is being exploited by what are called 501c groups (after the section of the tax codes under which they are chartered). Experts disagreed about the likely consequences of the far-reaching decision, but mirroring the Court's five-to-four breakdown on the ruling, it was generally decried by liberals and supported by conservatives.[95] What is not controversial is that the decision opened the floodgates for vast sums of money, much of it coming through what are known as Super PACs funded by very wealthy individuals, corporations, and unions.[96]

- **Soft money** is unregulated money collected by parties and interest groups in unlimited amounts to spend on party-building activities, get-out-the-vote drives, voter education, or issue position advocacy. Prior to the passage of campaign finance reform in 2002, as long as the money was not spent to tell people how to vote or coordinated with a specific candidate's campaign, the FEC could not regulate soft money. This allowed corporate groups, unions, and political parties to raise unlimited funds often used for television and radio advertising, especially in the form of issue advocacy ads. As we discussed in Chapter 13, **issue advocacy ads** are television or radio commercials run during an election campaign that promote a particular issue, usually by attacking the character, views, or position of the candidate the group running the ad wishes to defeat. The courts have considered these ads protected free speech and have held that

Influential, Indeed

News mogul Rupert Murdoch (left) poses with billionaire David Koch, who (along with his brother, Charles) was being honored at a gala celebrating *Time* magazine's "100 Most Influential People in the World" in 2014. The Koch brothers have been generous with their wealth, donating millions to support medical research, the arts, and education—but the pair is best known for the millions of dollars they have provided to conservative candidates and causes. Murdoch is no slouch in the influence game, either—he was on *Time's* list in 2008.

campaign may also collect public financing. Unlike the two major parties, however, the money a third party receives depends on the number of votes the party received in the previous election. Ross Perot was eligible to receive $29 million for his 1996 presidential campaign after his party won 19 percent of the vote in 1992, while the two major parties received $61.8 million each.[91]

- **Hard money** refers to the funds given *directly* to candidates by individuals, political action committees (PACs), the political parties, and the government. The spending of hard money is under the control of the candidates, but its collection is governed by the rules of the Federal Election Campaign Act (FECA) of 1971, 1974, and its various amendments. This act established the FEC and was intended to stop the flow of money from large contributors (and thus limit their influence) by outlawing contributions by corporations and unions, and by restricting contributions from individuals. The campaign finance reform bill passed in 2002 actually raised the hard money limits. Under that law, individuals can give a federal candidate up to $2,300 per election and can give a total of $108,200 to all federal candidates and parties in a two-year election cycle.[92] The limit on the parties' hard money contributions to candidates was held to

hard money campaign funds donated directly to candidates; amounts are limited by federal election laws

soft money unregulated campaign contributions by individuals, groups, or parties that promote general election activities but do not directly support individual candidates

issue advocacy ads advertisements paid for by soft money, and thus not regulated, that promote certain issue positions but do not endorse specific candidates

individuals and organizations could not be stopped from spending money to express their opinions about issues, or even candidates, so long as they did not explicitly tell viewers how to vote.

Most observers thought that BCRA would remove unregulated money from campaigns and curb negative advertising. While it limited the spending of PACs and parties, new groups, called 527 groups after the loophole (section 527) in the Internal Revenue Code that allows them to avoid the regulations imposed by BCRA, sprang up in their stead (see Chapter 13). Like groups that raised and spent soft money prior to BCRA, 527s can raise unlimited funds for issue advocacy or voter mobilization so long as they do not openly promote any candidate or openly try to defeat any particular candidate. BCRA does forbid all groups, even 527s, from running such ads funded by soft money within sixty days of a general election, or within thirty days of a primary election. The 2010 *Citizens United* case loosened the regulations further, lifting the sixty-day limit. For upcoming elections it appears that interest groups, corporations, and unions will have greater leeway in how and when they campaign for candidates. Even so, they are still limited in making direct (hard money) contributions; most of their efforts will be as independent expenditures (efforts that cannot be coordinated with the candidates' campaigns). Moreover, it can be argued that the new decision will not affect our elections in a major way as these entities found plenty of ways to attempt to influence campaigns under the old laws. In any case, given that such contributors do not share a single common ideology or set of issue preferences, some observers argue that any effects will largely cancel each other out. Only with the unfolding of future elections will we know for sure.[97]

GETTING OUT THE VOTE Get-out-the-vote (GOTV) drives refer to the voter mobilization efforts we discussed earlier in this chapter. As we saw in *What's at Stake...?*, voter mobilization efforts are an increasingly important part of any presidential campaign. As we noted, in the 1980s and 1990s such efforts concentrated mostly on television advertising. The expense of these "air wars" meant that parties and campaigns worried less about knocking on doors and the shoe-leather efforts associated with a campaign's "ground war." Parties mistakenly associated GOTV with "get on television" rather than its traditional

meaning of "get out the vote."[98] Beginning in 1998 the campaigns renewed efforts to contact potential voters face-to-face. This is consistent with research that shows that decreased party mobilization efforts were a substantial part of the reason that voter turnout had been decreasing.[99]

In 2008 and 2012, however, the Obama campaign rewrote the strategy book for modern campaigns. Not only did it reawaken efforts at direct contacting, but it tied such contact to advances in Internet technology and social networking, from regular ads on YouTube, to recurring emails and text messages to contributors, to highly sophisticated and coordinated volunteer efforts at voter mobilization.[100] The Obama team had paid staff, hundreds of offices, and thousands of volunteers in place across all the battleground states. One high-level Republican campaign official said in 2008, "This is the greatest ground game they've ever put together. It's scary."[101] As we have seen, the 2012 campaign improved on the innovations of 2008, engaging everyday citizens as integral parts of the campaigns rather than just as spectators and voters. The Obama campaign's successful mobilization efforts were able to turn typically Republican states such as Indiana to the Democratic column in 2008, and to keep all the states they won in 2008 except North Carolina in 2012.[102]

What is particularly interesting about these grassroots efforts is that they are not just a return to a bygone era. Rather, mobilization efforts combine old-school door-to-door campaigning with modern technology.[103] Vast computer databases tell volunteers whose doors to knock on, and these volunteers often have hand-held personal electronic devices that have detailed information on each voter.[104] This allows parties and groups to target swing voters and their base voters. Campaigns and interest groups also flood supporters' email in-boxes and tie up the phone lines. Seventy-six percent of voters in battleground states reported that they had been contacted and urged to vote a particular way.[105] In their zeal to seek out all possible voters, campaigns have reached out to poorer voters in both urban and rural areas who have not received either party's attention in recent decades.[106]

INTERPRETING ELECTIONS

After the election is over, when the votes are counted, and we know who won, it would seem that the whole election season is finally finished. In reality, the outcomes of our collective decisions cry for interpretation. Probably the most important interpretation is the one articulated by the victor. The winning candidate in presidential elections inevitably claims an **electoral mandate**, maintaining that the people want the president to do the things he campaigned on and that the election is all about the voters' preference for his leadership and policy programs. Presidents who can

get-out-the-vote (GOTV) drives efforts by political parties, interest groups, and the candidate's staff to maximize voter turnout among supporters

electoral mandate the perception that an election victory signals broad support for the winner's proposed policies

sell the interpretation that their election to office is a ringing endorsement of their policies can work with Congress from a favored position.[107] To the extent that the president is able to sell his interpretation, he will be more successful in governing. In contrast, the losing party will try to argue that its loss was due to the characteristics of its candidate or specific campaign mistakes. Party members will, predictably, resist the interpretation that the voters rejected their message and their vision for the nation. In general, Congress responds less to presidential declarations of a mandate and more to indications of changes in public preferences signaled by a change in which party wins the presidency or a large legislative seat turnover, especially one that produces a change in party control of Congress.[108]

The media also offer their interpretations of elections. In fact, research shows that of the many possible explanations that are available, the mainstream media quickly—in just a matter of weeks—hone in on an agreed-upon standard explanation of the election.[109] In 2000 the media, in explaining the closeness of the race, focused on how much more likable voters found George W. Bush, despite the majority's agreement with Al Gore on the issues, and on what they claimed to be Gore's badly run campaign. In 2004 the media decided quickly that, although the nation was closely divided, moral-values voters in red states put Bush over the top. In 2008 the media story was that President Bush's rock-bottom approval ratings were dragging down McCain and that, with the economy in collapse, the Republican was facing insurmountable odds while the voters were hungry for change. The media, assisted by the left-leaning blogosphere, also maintained that Obama had run a reasonably positive campaign, but that Republicans were stirring up anger and mob-like sentiments with their insinuations that Obama was "un-American" and "risky." These explanations offer parts of the truth, but they oversimplify reality and do not give us a complete understanding of the complex decisions made by the American electorate.

PAUSE AND REVIEW:

WHO, WHAT, HOW

In the matter of presidential elections, the parties, their elites, party activists, and the candidates all have something vital at stake. The traditional party leaders fared best under the old rules and closed-door decision making that yielded seasoned and electable politicians as the parties' nominees. Activists, with a broader agenda than simply winning power, seek control of the platform and the nomination, and may well have goals other than electability in mind. The primary system allows them to reap the fruits of the considerable time and resources they are willing to invest in politics.

Candidates seeking the nomination must answer to both the traditional party leaders and the activist members. This often puts them in a difficult position. Once nominated and pursuing a national bipartisan victory, the candidate needs to hold on to party supporters while drawing in those not already committed to the other side. Here the candidate makes use of the rules of the Electoral College, professional staff, strategic issue positions, the media, fundraising, and voter mobilization.

IN YOUR OWN WORDS >> Describe the organizational and strategic tactics involved in presidential campaigns.

>> THE CITIZENS AND ELECTIONS
Do too many informed voters lead to too much conflict?

At the beginning of this chapter we acknowledged that the American citizen does not look like the ideal citizen of classical democratic theory. Nothing we have learned in this chapter has convinced us otherwise, but that does not mean that Americans are doomed to an undemocratic future. In the first chapter of this book we considered three models of citizen activity in democracies, which we revisit here.

The first model we discussed is the elite model, which argues that as citizens we can do no more (or are fitted to do no more) than choose the elites who govern us, making a rather passive choice from among remote leaders. The second model of democratic politics, the pluralist model, sees us as participating in political life primarily through our affiliation with different types of groups. Finally, the participatory model of democracy is perhaps more prescriptive than the other two models, which it rejects because it believes that it is unsatisfactory for the majority of the citizenry to play a largely passive role in the political system. This model holds that we grow and develop as citizens through being politically active. In fact, rather than fitting any of these models exclusively, the American citizen's role in elections seems to borrow elements from all three models in a way that might be called a fourth model. As we shall see, American citizens, though they do not meet the ideals of democratic theory, do make a difference in American politics through the mechanism of elections.

A FOURTH MODEL?

The early studies of voting that used survey research found that most citizens had surprisingly low levels of interest in presidential election campaigns. These studies of the 1944 and 1948 presidential elections found that most citizens had their minds made up before the campaigns began and that opinions changed only slightly in response to the efforts of the parties and candidates. Instead of people relying on new information coming from the campaigns, people voted according to the groups to which they belonged. That is, income, occupation, religion, and similar factors structured who people talked to, what they learned, and how they voted.

The authors of these studies concluded that democracy is probably safer without a single type of citizen who matches the civics ideal of high levels of participation, knowledge, and commitment.[110] In this view, such high levels of involvement would indicate a citizenry fraught with conflict. Intense participation comes with intense commitment and strongly held positions, which make for an unwillingness to compromise. This revision of the call for classic "good citizens" holds that our democratic polity is actually better off when it has lots of different types of citizens: some who care deeply, are highly informed, and participate intensely; many more who care moderately, are a bit informed, and participate as much out of duty to the process as commitment to one party or candidate; and some who are less aware of politics until some great issue or controversy awakens their political slumber.

The virtue of modern democracy in this *political specialization view* is that citizens play different roles and that together these roles combine to form an electoral system that has the attributes we prefer: it is reasonably stable; it responds to changes of issues and candidates, but not too much; and the electorate as a whole cares, but not so intensely that any significant portion of the citizenry will challenge the results of an election. Its most obvious flaw is that it is biased against the interests of those who are least likely to be the activist or pluralist citizens—the young, the poor, the uneducated, and minorities.[111]

DO ELECTIONS MAKE A DIFFERENCE?

If we can argue that most Americans do take more than a passive role in elections and that, despite being less-than-ideal democratic citizens, most Americans are involved "enough," then we need to ask whether the elections they participate in make any difference. We would like to think that elections represent the voice of the people in charting the directions for government policy. Let us briefly discuss how well this goal is attained. At a minimal but nevertheless important level, elections in the United States do achieve electoral accountability. By this we mean only that by having to stand for reelection, our leaders are more or less constantly concerned with the consequences of what they do for their next election. The

Reuters/Larry Downing

Unpleasant October Surprise

Just weeks before the 2012 election, Hurricane Sandy devastated parts of the nation's east coast. Both President Obama and his Republican challenger Mitt Romney suspended campaign activities in the storm's immediate aftermath, but Obama, shown here touring the damage and comforting the storm's victims with Republican governor Chris Christie of New Jersey, was able to stay in the public eye. Many in Romney's campaign felt that the storm sapped any momentum he might have gathered after the first presidential debate.

fact that citizens tend to vote retrospectively provides incumbent administrations with a lot of incentive to keep things running properly, and certainly to avoid policies that citizens may hold against them. Thus we begin by noting that elections keep officeholders attentive to what they are doing.

We can also ask if elections make a difference in the sense that it matters who wins. The answer is yes. Today the parties stand on opposite sides of many issues, and given the chance, they will move national policy in the direction they believe in. Thus in 1980 the election of Ronald Reagan ushered in conservative policies—especially his tax cuts and domestic spending reductions—that Jimmy Carter, whom Reagan defeated, would never have even put on the agenda. Looking at elections over time, scholars Robert S. Erikson, Michael MacKuen, and James A. Stimson observe a direct relationship between national elections and the policies that government subsequently enacts. Electing Democrats results in more liberal policies; electing Republicans results in more conservative policies.[112] This same generalization can be seen in the politics of the American states, where we find that more liberal states enact more liberal policies and more conservative states enact more conservative policies. Policy liberalism, which is a composite measure of things like the tax structure, welfare benefits, educational spending, voting for the Equal Rights Amendment, and so forth, is higher as the states become more liberal.[113] There is much solid evidence that elections are indeed crucial in bringing about a degree of policy congruence between the electorate and what policymakers do.

Just because elections seem to work to bring policy into rough agreement with citizen preferences does not mean that all citizens know what they want and that candidates know this and respond. Some citizens do know what they want; others do not. Some candidates heed the wishes of constituents; others pay more attention to their own consciences or to the demands of ideological party activists and contributors. Averaged over all these variables, however, we do find that policy follows elections. Citizens, even with the blunt instrument of the ballot, can and do change what government does.[114]

IN YOUR OWN WORDS » Summarize the importance of elections for citizens.

LET'S REVISIT: **WHAT'S AT STAKE...**

You could call it the revenge of the nerds: the triumph of geeky science over faith and finger-crossing. The chief analytics officer for the Obama campaign said of the young data crunchers tasked with coming up with a turnout forecast in the Cave in the campaign's Chicago office, "We're kind of a weird bunch of kids. I haven't seen the sun for a while."[115] An article about the campaign's tech team was called "When the Nerds Go Marching In."[116] And one campaign official said, "It's about turning over control to some nerds. And more than any other year, campaign leadership really took that leap of faith."[117]

Getting out the vote, which used to be a matter of old-fashioned, face-to-face retail politics, now begins in dark rooms filled with glowing computer screens. The personal touch is still important, but the science of campaigning has come a long way even from the beginning of this century. It was 2004 when Republican political guru Karl Rove broke new ground in the George W. Bush reelection campaign by microtargeting supporters and mobilizing a strong turnout for the incumbent. Democrats were caught off guard, but by 2012 they had caught up.

One writer who has studied the science of campaigning says that the Obama campaign was better than its opponents in getting out the vote because the entire door-to-door element of the campaign was backed up by powerful data analysis that told the canvassers who to target and how to persuade. A campaign doesn't want to waste time on the unpersuadable, and the nerdy Obama analytics team had eliminated the guesswork. This writer says,

> With an eager pool of academic collaborators in political science, behavioral psychology, and economics linking up with curious political operatives and hacks, the left has birthed an unexpected subculture. It now contains a

full-fledged electioneering intelligentsia, focused on integrating large-scale survey research with randomized experimental methods to isolate particular populations that can be moved by political contact.[118]

The Romney campaign had tried to construct a system that would help garner information on Election Day, but it was years behind the Obama team, in part because it had rejected what science could do for it. One analysis points out three miscalculations the campaign made.[119] First, when the polls said that the electorate had a lot of Democrats in it, but the Romney campaign members' impressions of the enthusiasm on their side made them doubt the polls, they rejected the science and altered the partisan balance in their model to fit their intuition. Second, they believed that doing well with independents meant they were bound to win, without researching who the independent voters were. In hindsight, it became apparent that fewer voters were self-identifying as Republicans in the polls and were calling themselves independents instead. By adopting voter models that subtracted Democrats and bolstered the percentages of Republicans while also counting independents, the Romney campaign model was essentially double-counting some of its voters. And, finally, the campaign members were confident that the voters who said they were undecided would break for Romney at the last minute, again basing their expectations on what they guessed would happen.

The geeky Obama campaign, having cast its lot with science, knew that none of those things were true. What's at stake in how a campaign gets out its vote is winning, and the mistakes of the Romney campaign will be ones no campaign can afford to make in the future.

TO SUM UP

REVIEW

Voting in a Democratic Society

Elections represent the core of American
democracy, serving several functions: selecting
leaders, giving direction to policy, developing
citizenship, informing the public, containing
conflict, and stabilizing the political system.

political efficacy (p.516)

Exercising the Right to Vote in America

Voting enhances the quality of democratic life by
legitimizing the outcomes of elections. However,
American voter turnout levels are typically
among the lowest in the world and may endanger
American democracy. Factors such as age,
income, education, and race affect whether a
person is likely to vote.

regulating the electorate (p. 518)
Motor Voter Bill (p. 519)
voter mobilization (p. 522)
social connectedness (p. 522)

How the Voter Decides

Candidates and the media often blur issue
positions, and voters realistically cannot
investigate policy proposals on their own.
Therefore, voters make a decision by considering
party identification and peer viewpoints,
prominent issues, and campaign images.

prospective voting (p. 526)
retrospective voting (p. 526)

Presidential Campaigns

The "road to the White House" is long, expensive,
and grueling. It begins with planning and early
fundraising in the pre-primary phase and
develops into more active campaigning during
the primary phase, which ends with each party's
choice of a candidate, announced at the party
conventions. During the general election the
major-party candidates are pitted against
each other in a process that relies increasingly
on the media and getting out the vote. Much of
the battle at this stage is focused on attracting
voters who have not yet made up their
minds.

The Electoral College demonstrates well the
founders' desire to insulate government from
public whims. Citizens do not vote directly for
the president or vice president but rather for an
elector who has already pledged to vote for that
candidate. Except in Maine and Nebraska, the
candidate with the majority of votes in a state
wins all the electoral votes in that state.

invisible primary (p. 528)
exploratory committee (p. 528)
party caucus (p. 529)
presidential primary (p. 529)
open primary (p. 529)
closed primary (p. 529)
front-loading (p. 529)
front-runner (p. 530)
momentum (p. 530)
swing voters (p. 534)
oppo research (p. 535)
valence issues (p. 538)
position issues (p. 538)
wedge issue (p. 538)
issue ownership (p. 538)
negative advertising (p. 539)
government matching funds (p. 543)
hard money (p. 544)
soft money (p. 544)
issue advocacy ads (p. 544)
get-out-the-vote (GOTV) drives (p. 545)
electoral mandate (p. 545)

The Citizens and Elections

Although American citizens do not fit the
mythical ideal of the democratic citizen,
elections still seem to work in representing the
voice of the people in terms of citizen policy
preferences.

ENGAGE

Register to vote—and don't let anything stop you from voting. You can register to vote at your local department of motor vehicles, or if you prefer to do it online, **Rock the Vote** makes it easy. But registering is not enough: college students are among the most likely to be affected by voter ID laws being enacted in many states. Stay on top of the changing requirements, and find out what you'll need in order to vote in your state so that nothing stands in your way when you get to the polls.

Be an informed voter. It's hard to know where every candidate stands on every issue. **Project Vote Smart** is dedicated to providing clear, unbiased information on current elections and candidates and is a great resource for anyone who wants to, well, vote smart.

Don't be a misinformed voter. Anyone who's running for office is bound to stretch the truth—if not outright lie—from time to time. **FactCheck.org,** a project of the Annenberg Public Policy Center, site separates fact from fiction in campaigns and everyday politics. Both articles and podcasts are available at their web site.

Take a look back at presidential campaigns. From the happy-go-lucky Kennedy jingle of the 1960s to the notorious "Willie Horton" ads of the 1980s to a few that you'll surely remember from the 2000s, the changing nature of campaign advertising tells, in many ways, the story of presidential politics since the dawn of television. Visit **The Living Room Candidate** to get a glimpse of the campaign commercials that have shaped elections—and history—and compare them with the ones you'll be seeing in the run-up to 2016.

EXPLORE

Anonymous (Joe Klein). 1996. *Primary Colors: A Novel of Politics*. New York: Random House. This "fictional" account of a southern governor running for president whose campaign is constantly plagued by scandal is fun to read—and the film version (1998) is almost as fun to watch.

Heilemann, John, and Mark Halperin. 2010. *Game Change: Obama and the Clintons, McCain and Palin, and the Race of a Lifetime*. New York: HarperCollins. Two veteran political reporters unearth the inside story on the historic 2008 campaign, detailing Barack Obama's meteoric rise, Hillary Clinton's unexpected fall, and struggles within John McCain's camp surrounding the selection of Sarah Palin as his running mate. The Emmy-winning HBO film of the same name (2012) is based on the part of the book that dealt with McCain's choice of Palin as running mate, and it provides a penetrating look at the consequences of the unrelenting pressure to win that campaign staffers face.

Raymond, Allen (author), and Ian Spiegelman (contributor). 2008. *How to Rig an Election: Confessions of a Republican Operative*. New York: Simon & Schuster. Written by Republican campaign adviser Allen Raymond, this highly acclaimed book offers an insider's perspective on the "dark" side of electoral campaigns.

Semiatin, Richard J., ed. 2012. *Campaigns on the Cutting Edge*, 2nd ed. Washington, DC: CQ Press. Semiatin offers a detailed look at the changing face of modern political campaigns, with an emphasis on the increasingly prominent role played by digital media.

15

THE MEDIA

IN YOUR OWN WORDS   After you've read this chapter, you will be able to

» Describe the main sources from which Americans get their news and information.

» Summarize the evolution of the modern news media.

» Explain the roles and responsibilities of journalists.

» Describe the link between media and politics.

» Discuss the relationship between citizens and the media.

WHAT'S AT STAKE...IN THE DEMISE OF THE PRINT NEWS MEDIA?

ONCE UPON A TIME, NEWS ENTERED THE
average American's life at only a couple of neatly defined
and very predictable points during the day. The local
morning paper arrived before dawn, there to be read over
coffee and breakfast. The afternoon paper (yes, most cities
had two papers back then) was waiting for you when you
came home from work. Big city papers like the *New York
Times* and the *Washington Post* were available only to those
who lived in New York or Washington, D.C., unless you
ordered a copy of the paper to be mailed to you, at great
expense, arriving several days late (no FedEx, no overnight
delivery). In 1960 the evening news came on all three TV
stations at 7:30 p.m., and TV-owning America (87 percent
of households in 1960) got their last news of the day from
Chet Huntley and David Brinkley on NBC, John Daly on
ABC, or Douglas Edwards on CBS (Edwards was to be
followed two years later by Walter Cronkite, also known as
"Uncle Walter," the most trusted face in news). That was
pretty much it for news in 1960s America, unless a special
event (a space shot, for instance) or a tragedy (like JFK's
assassination) occurred that required a special bulletin.

That was then. More than fifty years later, readership
of newspapers is way, way down. Whereas a third of

Americans bought a daily paper in 1941, only 13 percent did
so in 2009.[1] From 1991 to 2012, the number of Americans
who said they bought a newspaper the previous day
plummeted by 50 percent, from 56 percent to 23 percent.[2]
Readership continued to fall through 2011, although the
pace of decline has moderated somewhat as the economy
picked up, mostly due to new, unearned revenue, such as
venture capital investments and philanthropy.[3] While this
influx of cash, much of it from the tech industry (such as
the sale of the *Washington Post* to Amazon.com founder and
CEO Jeff Bezos in 2013[4]) signals the potential for a shift in
the news model, print editions continue to struggle (see
CLUES to Critical Thinking). Many venerable newspapers have
ceased publication or moved to a print-online hybrid or
simply an online existence, among them, the *Tucson Citizen,*
the *Rocky Mountain News,* the *Baltimore Examiner,* the *Seattle
Post-Intelligencer,* the *Detroit News/Free Press,* and the *Christian
Science Monitor.*[5] Today, most towns have only one paper, if
they have any at all.

Meanwhile, in addition to the three original networks,
which continue to broadcast news as well as a variety of
programming, there are now more than a dozen television
stations around the world that are devoted to nothing but

CLUES
TO CRITICAL THINKING

"The Strange, Sad Death of Journalism"

By Michael Gerson, *Washington Post*, **November 27, 2009**

In this article a conservative laments changes in the profession of journalism. Is this a partisan or a bipartisan issue?

Like the nearby Smithsonian National Museum of Natural History, the Newseum—Washington's museum dedicated to journalism—displays dinosaurs. On a long wall near the entrance, the front pages of newspapers from around the country are electronically posted each morning—the artifacts of a declining industry. Inside, the high-tech exhibits are nostalgic for a lower-tech time when banner headlines and network news summarized the emotions and exposed the scandals of the nation. Lindbergh Lands Safely. One Small Step. Nixon Resigns. Cronkite removes his glasses to announce President Kennedy's death at 1 p.m. Central Standard Time.

Behind a long rack of preserved, historic front pages, there is a kind of journalistic mausoleum, displaying the departed. The Ann Arbor News, closed July 23 after 174 years in print. The Rocky Mountain News, taken at age 150. The Seattle Post-Intelligencer, which passed quietly into the Internet.

What difference does this make? For many conservatives, the "mainstream media" is an epithet. Didn't the Internet expose the lies of Dan Rather? Many on the left also shed few tears, preferring to consume their partisanship raw in the new media.

But a visit to the Newseum is a reminder that what is passing is not only a business but also a profession—the journalistic tradition of nonpartisan objectivity. Journalists, God knows, didn't always live up to that tradition. But they generally accepted it, and they felt shamed when their biases or inaccuracies were exposed. The profession had rules about facts and sources and editors who enforced standards. At its best, the profession of journalism has involved a spirit of public service and adventure— reporting from a bomber during a raid in World War II, or exposing the suffering of Sudan or Appalachia, or rushing to the site of the World Trade Center moments after the buildings fell.

By these standards, the changes we see in the media are also a decline. Most cable news networks have forsaken objectivity entirely and produce little actual news, since makeup for guests is cheaper than reporting. Most Internet sites display an endless hunger to comment and little appetite for verification. Free markets, it turns out, often make poor fact-checkers, instead feeding the fantasies of conspiracy theorists from "birthers" to Sept. 11, 2001, "truthers." Bloggers in repressive countries often show great courage, but few American bloggers have the resources or inclination to report from war zones, famines and genocides.

The democratization of the media— really its fragmentation—has encouraged ideological polarization. Princeton University professor Paul Starr traced this process recently in the Columbia Journalism Review. After the captive audience for network news was released by cable, many Americans did not turn to other sources of news. They turned to entertainment. The viewers who remained were more political and more partisan. "As Walter Cronkite prospered in the old environment," says Starr, "Bill O'Reilly and Keith Olbermann thrive in the new one. As the diminished public for journalism becomes more partisan, journalism itself is likely to shift further in that direction."

Cable and the Internet now allow Americans, if they choose, to get their information entirely from sources

news, 24-7, many of which can be accessed from the United States. In addition, there are hundreds of talk radio stations around the country, and of course there is the glorious, chaotic marketplace of ideas and information called the Internet.

Today we take for granted that we can access most information sources not only from newspapers, magazines, books, radio, and the television, but also from our digital devices. We can be linked to the world of information from our phones, tablets, or computers, which we can use to read the news, follow a blog, download a book, or watch a movie. Carry around a newspaper? Why on Earth would we want to do that?

Midway through the second decade of the century, it is not unusual to hear people say that the day of the print

media is over.[6] If you are feeling inclined to irony, you can Google "the newspaper is dead" and you will get almost 150,000 hits, all with people insisting (1) that it is true, (2) that it isn't, (3) that it matters, and (4) that it doesn't. In further irony, many of the most thriving news web sites— from "viral news sites" like Buzzfeed to online journals like the *Drudge Report* and the *Huffington Post* that traffic in "breaking news"—are often merely linking to the reporting of others—often to reporting done by those same dinosaur newspapers whose deaths they are quick to proclaim.

What's the truth here? Is the newspaper an anachronism, a dinosaur left over from another era, or an essential institution whose demise is unimaginable? A writer at *LA Observed,* an online site that touts its independent

that agree with them—sources that reinforce and exaggerate their political predispositions.

And the whole system is based on a kind of intellectual theft. Internet aggregators (who link to news they don't produce) and bloggers would have little to collect or comment upon without the costly enterprise of newsgathering and investigative reporting. The old-media dinosaurs remain the basis for the entire media food chain. But newspapers are expected to provide their content free on the Internet. A recent poll found that 80 percent of Americans refuse to pay for Internet content. There is no economic model that will allow newspapers to keep producing content they don't charge for, while Internet sites repackage and sell content they don't pay to produce.

I dislike media bias as much as the next conservative. But I don't believe that journalistic objectivity is a fraud. I was a journalist for a time, at a once-great, now-diminished newsmagazine. I've seen good men and women work according to a set of professional standards I respect—standards that serve the public. Professional journalism is not like the buggy-whip industry, outdated by economic progress, to be mourned but not missed. This profession has a social value that is currently not reflected in its market value.

What is to be done? A lot of good people are working on it. But if you currently have newsprint on your hands, thank you.

Consider the source and the audience: Michael Gerson, as he indicates in his column, is a conservative. A former speechwriter and adviser to President George W. Bush (as well as other Republicans), he now writes a syndicated column that appears, among other places, in the widely read *Washington Post*. How might this background affect his views of the media and journalism?

Lay out the argument, the values, and the assumptions: Gerson is nostalgic in this column for the *profession* of journalism. How does he define that? What does he mean by the "democratization" of the media? What damage does he think it has done? In what way is it based on "intellectual theft"?

Uncover the evidence: Does Gerson offer any evidence for his view in this column? Does the fact that most of his audience probably watches TV, reads some news, and participates in social media mean that he doesn't need to do more than to refer to their shared culture?

Evaluate the conclusion: Gerson, like many others, concludes that objective news gathering as an honorable profession is getting lost in the scrum of sloppy and parasitic cable TV shows, blogs, and tweets. Is he right? Can the profession of journalism endure in that environment?

Sort out the political significance: If Gerson is right, what is to be done? Is there a business model that will keep journalism alive while allowing the myriad voices that have been generated in the modern media to thrive? If it is in all of our interests to have people doing good, solid reporting on the events of the day, how is it to be paid for?

reporting and commentary, jumped in with both feet: "Not that I'm happy about this, but I'll say it. Newspapers don't matter. Otherwise people would be reading them."[7] Less cavalierly, a journalist writing in *USA Today* (one of the endangered papers) speculated recently that "[s]ometime soon, millions of people may find themselves unwittingly involved in a test that could profoundly change their daily routines, local economies and civic lives. They'll have to figure out how to keep up with City Hall, their neighborhoods and their kids' schools—as well as store openings, new products and sales—without a 170-year-old staple of daily life: a local newspaper."[8]

Does it matter? No less a grand thinker than Thomas Jefferson said, "The basis of our governments being the opinion of the people, the very first object should be to keep that right; and were it left to me to decide whether we should have a government without newspapers or newspapers without a government, I should not hesitate a moment to prefer the latter."[9] Are newspapers that fundamental? Can a democratic world survive without newsprint? Just what is at stake in the declining importance of the American newspaper? «

IT'S hard to imagine anyone today voting for a presidential candidate without checking out the candidate's web site or Facebook page, seeing him or her give a speech on streaming video, or watching a fundraising pitch on YouTube. But most of those who voted for George

I DON'T UNDERSTAND— I'VE WATERED DOWN CONTENT, REDESIGNED WHAT WAS LEFT AND GAVE IT ALL AWAY FOR FREE ON THE INTERNET AND YET I STILL CAN'T GET ANYBODY TO READ A NEWSPAPER...

METRO NEWSPAPER PUBLISHERS

CLICKITY CLACK CLICK

www.MILTPRIGGEE.com

CAGLECARTOONS

Washington for president, or for Abraham Lincoln, had never even heard the voice of the candidate they chose, and they might have had only a vague idea of what the candidate looked like. By the 1930s, Franklin Roosevelt's voice reached millions in his radio "fireside chats" and his face was widely familiar to Americans from newspaper and magazine photographs, but his moving image was restricted to newsreels that had to be viewed in the movie theater. Not until the advent of television in the mid-twentieth century were presidents, senators, and representatives beamed into the living rooms of Americans, and their smiling, moving images made a part of the modern culture of American politics.

Fast forward more than fifty years. The electronic age in which we live today has made politics immediate and personal in a way that would leave even these later politicians stunned and bemused. Our information-oriented culture means we are bombarded 24-7 with news flashes, sound bites, web ads, blog posts, commercials, comedy routines, text messages, podcasts, and requests to join networks of those who want our friendship and support. Today we do far more than just watch and listen to the media, which are increasingly multimedia, digital, available on demand, and often interactive in nature. Communication scholars refer to this merging of traditional and digital media as **media convergence**, and it has implications for our political as well as social lives.[10] Politicians scramble to stay on top of electronic innovations that continually shape and alter the political world. President George W. Bush's use of the words *internets* and *the Google* signaled his discomfort with the changing electronic world, much as his father's unfamiliarity with a grocery scanner revealed his eight years before. Then-candidate Barack Obama's confident use of networking strategies and text messaging in his campaign for the presidency put him at an advantage over his older and less tech-savvy opponent, John McCain, and posed a

formidable challenge for Mitt Romney four years later.[11]

Democracy demands that citizens be informed about their government, that they be able to criticize it, deliberate about it, and change it if it doesn't do their will. Information, in a very real sense, is power. Information must be available, and it must be disseminated widely. This was fairly easy to accomplish in the direct democracy of ancient Athens, where the small number of citizens were able to meet together and debate the political issues of the day. Because their democracy was direct and they were, in effect, the government, there was no need for anything to mediate *between* them and government, to keep them informed, to publicize candidates for office, to identify issues, and to act as a watchdog for their democracy.

In some ways our own democratic political community has been harder to achieve. For much of our history, we haven't known our fellow citizens outside of our own communities, we have been unable to directly investigate the issues ourselves, and we've had no idea what actions our government has taken to deal with issues unless the media told us. We are still dependent on the mass media to connect us to our government, and to create the only real space we have for public deliberation of issues. But increasing technological developments make possible ever-newer forms of political community and more immediate access to information. Government officials can communicate with us directly, bypassing the traditional press. Networking sites like Facebook, LinkedIn, and Twitter allow people to reach out and interact socially, and politicians have not been shy about using such strategies to create networks of supporters. Chat rooms and blogs allow people with common interests to find each other from the far reaches of the world, and allow debate and discussion on a scale never before imagined.

Some visionaries talk of the day when we will all vote electronically on individual issues from our home computers (or maybe even our phones). If we have not yet arrived at that day of direct democratic decision making, changes in the media are nonetheless revolutionizing the possibilities of democracy, much as the printing press and television did earlier, bringing us closer to the Athenian ideal of political community in cyberspace, if not in real space.

> **media convergence** the merging of traditional media with digital communication technologies such as telecommunications and the Internet

WHERE DO WE GET OUR INFORMATION?
Increasingly from multiple sources

Media is the plural of *medium*, meaning in this case an agency through which communication between two different entities can take place. Just as a medium can be a person who claims to transmit messages from the spiritual world to earthbound souls, today's **mass media**, whether through printed word or electronic signal, convey information cheaply and efficiently from the upper reaches of the political world to everyday citizens. And what is just as important in a democratic society, the media help carry information back from citizens to the politicians who lead, or seek to lead, them.

The news media in the twenty-first century increasingly rely on new technology. The printing press may have been invented in China over a thousand years ago, but almost all of the truly amazing innovations in information technology—telegraphs, telephones, photography, radio, television, computers, faxes, cell phones, and the Internet—have been developed in the past two hundred years, and just over half of them have come into common use only in the past fifty. What that means is that our technological capabilities sometimes outrun our sophistication about how that technology ought to be used or how it may affect the news it transfers.

Understanding who gets information, where it comes from, and how that information is affected by the technology that brings it to us is crucial to being a knowledgeable student of politics, not to mention an effective democratic citizen. In this section we examine the sources that we in America turn to for the news and the consequences that follow from our choices.

WHO GETS WHAT NEWS FROM WHERE?

In a recent study, most Americans (80 percent) reported that they enjoyed keeping up with the news, but fewer than half (40 percent) enjoyed it a lot. Young people were less likely to feel this way—only 24 percent of those aged eighteen to twenty-nine fell into the "a lot" category, compared to about half of those aged fifty and older.[12] Even though about 83 percent of Americans will get some news on a given day, only 26 percent say they get it from reading a newspaper (down from 48 percent a dozen years earlier). Television news watchers are holding relatively steady at about 55 percent of the public, but radio listeners have dropped to 33 percent, down from 49 percent ten years ago.[13] The news source that shows growth is the

> **mass media** means of conveying information to large public audiences cheaply and efficiently

From Three Networks to Nonstop Social Networks
In 1968 television news was limited to evening broadcasts on the three networks—only a few relatively powerful people, like President Lyndon Johnson, had the luxury of tuning in to all three of them simultaneously. By the 1990s cable news networks like CNN and Fox News had ushered in the era of twenty-four-hour news. Today, it's possible to create your own custom media diet from a variety of sources—and carry them all around in your pocket.

SNAPSHOT OF AMERICA: WHERE DO WE GET OUR NEWS?

News Consumers

Traditionalists	Integrators	Net-Newsers	Disengaged
45%	23%	13%	18%

Traditionalists
- Older, less educated, and less affluent
- Heavy reliance on television news
- Most have computer, but few get news online
- Understand news better by seeing pictures
- Strong interest in weather; little interest in science or technology

Integrators
- Middle aged, well educated, and affluent
- Television is their main source of news, but they also get news online on a typical day
- Spend the most time with the news on a typical day
- Greater interest in political news and sports

Net-Newsers
- Relatively young, well educated, and affluent
- Regularly read political blogs and watch television news
- Web news use soars during the day
- Frequent online news viewers
- Strong interest in technology news

Disengaged
- Less educated and less affluent
- Do not follow the news closely on a daily basis
- More likely to follow weather and local news

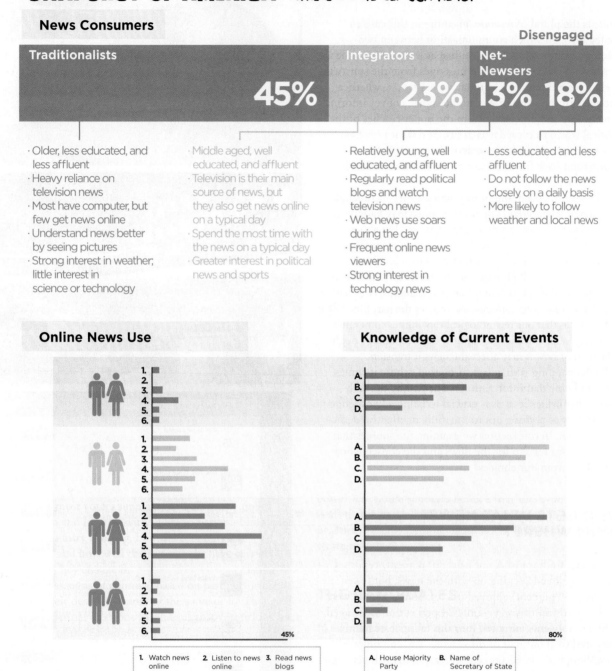

Online News Use

Knowledge of Current Events

1. Watch news online
2. Listen to news online
3. Read news blogs
4. Get news emails
5. Send news emails
6. Have RSS feed with news

45%

A. House Majority Party
B. Name of Secretary of State
C. Name of British PM
D. All Three

80%

BEHIND THE NUMBERS

The Pew Research Center derived these categories of news consumers from their surveys. Given the descriptions of each, where do you fit? In what ways does where one gets one's news affect one's knowledge of political leaders?

Source: Pew Media Consumption Survey [http://www.people-press.org/2012/09/27/about-the-media-consumption-survey-data/]

Internet—at least half of the public consider the Web a main source of their news in 2014, up from only 24 percent in 2003.[14] Many of those who do get their news online combine the Internet with more traditional sources and those who use mobile devices to access the Internet are spending more time reading the news and checking it more often.[15] The "*Snapshot of America:* Where Do We Get Our News?" shows the demographics behind this changing media landscape.

Despite the fact that most of the American public is exposed to some news, and some people are exposed to quite a lot of it, levels of political information in this country are not high. In one study, only about half of the public could correctly answer questions about domestic politics and public figures.[16] These politically informed people are not evenly distributed throughout the population, either. Older Americans, those with more education, and men were more likely to answer the questions correctly.[17]

NEWSPAPERS AND MAGAZINES

As we indicated in *What's at Stake . . . ?*, American newspaper readership is currently at a historical low and it is also lower than in most other industrialized nations.[18] Today only about a dozen cities have more than one daily paper. But several major newspapers—the *Wall Street Journal*, *USA Today*, the *New York Times*, and the *Washington Post*—have achieved what amounts to national circulation, providing even residents of single-daily cities with an alternative. Those major papers gather their own news, and some smaller papers that cannot afford to station correspondents around the world can subscribe to their news services. Practically speaking, this means that most of the news that Americans read on a daily basis comes from very few sources: these outlets or wire services like the Associated Press (AP) or Reuters.

Newspapers cover political news, of course, but many other subjects also compete with advertising for space in a newspaper's pages. Business, sports, entertainment (movies and television), religion, weather, book reviews, comics, crossword puzzles, advice columns, classified ads, and travel information are just some of the kinds of content that most newspapers provide in an effort to woo readers, although increasingly many of these are available online. Craigslist, for instance, has done much to make the classified sections of newspapers redundant, and data show that as public engagement with online classifieds more than doubled from 2005 to 2009, newspaper revenues from classified ads plummeted.[19] Generally the front section and especially the front page are reserved for major current events, but these need not be political in nature. Business deals, sporting events, and even sensational and unusual weather conditions can push politics farther back in the paper.

Magazines can often be more specialized than newspapers. While the standard weekly news magazines (*Time*, *U.S. News and World Report*, and the new, weekly *Christian Science Monitor*, for example) carry the same eclectic mix of subjects as major newspapers, they can also offer more comprehensive news coverage because they do not need to meet daily deadlines, giving them more time to develop a story. These popular news magazines tend to be middle of the road in their ideological outlook. Other magazines appeal specifically to liberal readers—for instance, the *New Republic* and the *Nation*—or to conservatives—for instance, the *National Review* and the *American Spectator.*

RADIO

The decline in the number of newspapers that began in the early 1900s was probably due in part to the emergence of radio. Although radios were expensive at first, one in six American families owned one by 1926,[20] and the radio had become a central part of American life. Not only was radio news more up-to-the-minute, it was also more personal. Listeners were able to hear a session of Congress for the first time in 1923 and a presidential inauguration in 1925.[21] Disasters such as the 1937 crash of the airship *Hindenburg* were brought into Americans' homes with an immediacy that newspapers could not achieve. Franklin Roosevelt was the first president to fully embrace the medium, and used his "fireside chats" to sell his New Deal policies directly to the public, circumventing reporters he viewed as hostile to his ideas.[22]

Today, most American households have at least one radio, and 90 percent of Americans say they listen to radio weekly.[23] More than 15,000 radio stations broadcast over the airwaves in the United States, offering entertainment and news shows through commercial networks and their local affiliates.[24] There are also two noncommercial networks, National Public Radio and Public Radio International, funded in small part by the U.S. government but also by private donations from corporations and individuals. Since the 1980s the radio call-in talk show has grown in popularity, allowing the radio hosts and their guests, as well as the audience, to air their opinions on politics and creating a sense of political community among their primarily conservative listeners. In addition to broadcast radio, Internet radio and satellite radio stations (tuned in via Internet streaming or through paid subscription services such as Sirius XM) offer an endless variety of audio feeds that cover everything from sports, to politics, to music for every taste, and allow once local stations to reach national audiences.

TELEVISION

The impact of radio on the American public, however dramatic initially, cannot compare with the effects of television, which grew into a national medium almost immediately thanks to the previously established radio networks.

Bill O'Reilly and Fake Bill O'Reilly

Fox News pundit Bill O'Reilly is known for making grand political statements on his evening program—delivering his "talking points" and opinions to loyal fans of his show, *The O'Reilly Factor*. Comedian Stephen Colbert was long known for favoring "truthiness" over truth, and for mimicking O'Reilly on the *Colbert Report* before moving to CBS's *Late Show* in 2014. The two men appeared on each other's shows on January 18, 2007.

American ownership of television sets skyrocketed from 9 percent of households in 1950 to 97 percent in 1975, a statistic that continues to hold firm. In fact, 82 percent of American homes have more than one TV set and 54 percent own three or more; over 80 percent receive cable or satellite transmission.[25]

Politicians were quick to realize that, like radio, television allowed them to reach a broad audience without having to deal with print reporters and their adversarial questions. The Kennedy administration was the first to make real use of television, a medium that might have been made for the young, telegenic president. And it was television that brought the nation together in a community of grief when Kennedy was assassinated.

Television carried the Vietnam War (along with its protesters) and the civil rights movement into Americans' homes, and the images that it created helped build popular support to end the war abroad and segregation at home. Television can create global as well as national communities, an experience many Americans shared as they sat captive before their television sets in the days following the terrorist attacks on New York and Washington, D.C., in 2001, or watching victory celebrations around the world following the election of President Barack Obama in 2008.

Live television viewership has declined over the past several years, but Americans remain voracious viewers of

videos, whether live on television, delayed on a digital recording device, or streamed from the Internet. Neilson reports that the average American watches nearly five hours of video each day, 98 percent of which they watch on a traditional TV set.[26] Given that most Americans spend six to eight hours a day at school or at work, this is an astounding figure, accounting for much of America's leisure time. Television is primarily an entertainment medium; news has always been a secondary function. While the earliest news offerings consisted simply of "talking heads" (reporters reading their news reports), many newscasts now fall into the category of "infotainment," news shows dressed up with drama and emotion to entice viewers to tune in. Once given a choice of only three networks, the typical American home today receives nearly 189 television channels. It is interesting to note, however, that most viewers consistently tune to only an average of seventeen channels regularly.[27] Rather than pursuing broad markets, stations are now often focusing on specific audiences such as people interested in health and fitness, sports, or travel. This practice of targeting a small, specialized broadcast market is called **narrowcasting**.[28] The competition for viewers is fierce, and as we will see, the quality of the news available can suffer as a consequence.

There are many television shows whose primary subject is politics. Many cable stations and C-SPAN, sometimes called "America's Town Hall," offer news around the clock, although not all the news concerns politics. Weekend shows like *Meet the Press* highlight the week's coverage of politics, and the cable news stations frequently showcase debates between liberals and conservatives on current issues. Some stations, such as the music channel MTV, direct their political shows to a specific age group (here, young people), and others, like *America's Voice*, to those holding particular ideologies (conservatism, in this case).

Like radio, television has its call-in talk shows. And politics is often the subject of the jokes on such shows as *Saturday Night Live*, *The Daily Show With Jon Stewart*, *The Late Show With Stephen Colbert*, and *The Tonight Show*. Since at least 2000 the major presidential candidates and their wives have regularly sat down to chat with the likes of Larry King, David Letterman, and Oprah Winfrey (who

> **narrowcasting** the targeting of specialized audiences by the media

took the unprecedented step of endorsing Barack Obama in 2008). Sometimes the performance is forced, but candidates who can convey an image of themselves as a regular, likable person can win in a big way. The habit of appearing on popular TV shows was so established by 2012 that President Obama decided to appear on *The View* with the first lady rather than engage in bilateral talks during the United Nations General Assembly Meeting, rightly calculating that he would reach more voters on the daytime talk show. During the 2012 election season, President Obama hit most of the late-night comedy shows, stopping in to talk with Jon Stewart, Jay Leno, David Letterman, and Jimmy Fallon in the months before the election, in what his campaign said was an effort to speak to undecided voters. To the frustration of the TV hosts, Republican candidate Mitt Romney was absent from the comedy lineups except for an appearance on *The Tonight Show* in March.[29]

Craig Ruttle/Redux

A Few Tweets Over the Line

Many government leaders and agencies circumvent traditional press by making use of social media, but acting as one's own gatekeeper can be risky. Former representative Anthony Weiner was a rising star in Congress who made great use of social media to drum up support for his legislative agenda and a likely run for the New York City mayor's office, only to see it all fall apart when he mistakenly posted a private (and appalling) photo to his 45,000 followers. Here, Weiner checks his phone on his way to a campaign event in 2013, during an ill-fated attempt at a political comeback.

THE INTERNET

The most recent new medium to revolutionize the way we get political news is the Internet, or the web (for World Wide Web), which connects home or business computers to a global network of digital sites and an ever-expanding array of media content. In 2014 some 87 percent of American adults used the Internet (up from 46 percent in 2000).[30] A full 70 percent of households have a broadband connection at home, and more than half of Americans are able to access the Internet from smartphones and other devices.[31] Sixty-one percent of Americans in 2010 said they got some news from the Internet on a typical day—more than five times the number from a decade ago—and 25 percent did so from their phones. Fifty-nine percent of adult Americans say they get their news from a combination of on- and offline sources. Twenty-eight percent of Americans have a customizable web page that feeds them news, and 37 percent of Internet users have socially interacted with others concerning the news—creating it, commenting on it, or disseminating it through social

networking sites like Facebook or Twitter.[32] It is not too much to say that the Internet is revolutionizing the way we get information.

Today, most major **news organizations**—including all the major newspapers and broadcast news organizations—are multimedia ventures. All the major newspapers, magazines, and news networks, along with news services like the AP, have web sites where all or most of the news in their print versions can be found, often with additional links and information. Access to these sites is sometimes available for free, although that clearly provides a disincentive for people to subscribe, thus damaging these news organizations' bottom line and hindering their ability to report the news. Increasingly, they are putting most of their content behind a pay wall, like the *New York Times* and *Wall Street Journal* have done, as they search for a viable business model that will keep them solvent. By searching for the topics we want and connecting to links with related sites, we can customize our web news. Politics buffs can bypass nonpolitical news, and vice versa. True politics junkies can go straight to the source: the federal government makes enormous amounts of information available at its www.whitehouse.gov, www.house.gov, and www.senate.gov sites.

The web has also provided fertile ground for myriad other sources of news to take root. For example, online sources like *Slate*, *Salon*, the *Huffington Post*, and the *Drudge*

> **news organizations** businesses (and occasionally nonprofits) devoted to reporting and disseminating news via print, broadcast, or digital media—or a multimedia combination.

SNAPSHOT OF AMERICA: WHO PARTICIPATES IN SOCIAL MEDIA?

Social Networking Use, by Age

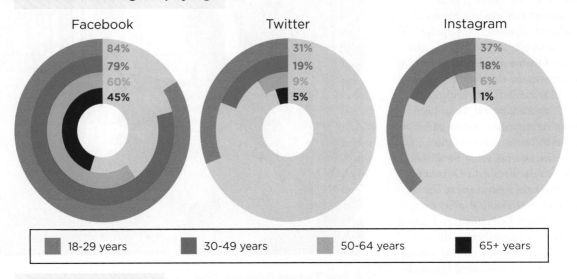

Facebook	Twitter	Instagram
84%	31%	37%
79%	19%	18%
60%	9%	6%
45%	5%	1%

■ 18-29 years   ■ 30-49 years   ■ 50-64 years   ■ 65+ years

Monthly Active Users

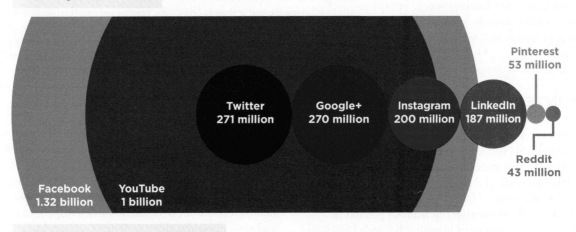

Facebook 1.32 billion

YouTube 1 billion

Twitter 271 million

Google+ 270 million

Instagram 200 million

LinkedIn 187 million

Pinterest 53 million

Reddit 43 million

Overall Use Over Time, by Age

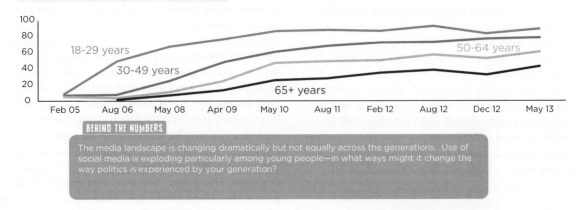

18-29 years

30-49 years

50-64 years

65+ years

Feb 05   Aug 06   May 08   Apr 09   May 10   Aug 11   Feb 12   Aug 12   Dec 12   May 13

BEHIND THE NUMBERS

The media landscape is changing dramatically but not equally across the generations. Use of social media is exploding particularly among young people—in what ways might it change the way politics is experienced by your generation?

Pew Internet & American Life Project, Dec 20, 2013. [http://www.pewinternet.org/2013/12/30/demographics-of-key-social-networking-platforms/]

Source: for avg monthly users: company filings, Forbes 6/24/14 [http://www.forbes.com/sites/jeffbercovici/2014/06/24/still-more-data-shows-pinterest-passing-twitter-in-popularity/]; TechCrunch, [http://techcrunch.com/2014/04/18/linkedin-hits-300-million-users/]; Business Insider [http://www.businessinsider.com/google-plus-three-years-later-2014-6]; Mashable [http://mashable.com/2012/10/31/reddit-valuation/]

Report exist solely on the Internet and may or may not adopt the conventions, practices, and standards of the more traditional media.

Web logs, or **blogs**, have become increasingly popular as well. Blogs—online journals, like the one discussed by Andrew Sullivan in this chapter's *Profiles in Citizenship* on page 586—can be set up by anyone with access to the Internet. (Sullivan's is so popular that he can now charge for some content and pay himself a salary.) Blogs can be personal, political, cultural, or anything in between; they run the gamut from individual diaries to investigative journalism. The fact that anyone can put up a blog or a web page and distribute information on any topic makes the task of using the information on the web challenging. Also in the mix are **news aggregators**—sites and software that cull content from other web sites to produce "newsfeeds." Some news aggregators, like Google News, the *Huffington Post*, and Buzzfeed, have editors who choose articles from other sites to share with their readers, sometimes with original content as well. Other news aggregators allow readers to customize their own news feeds through web-based applications.

All of these overlapping sources give us access to more information than ever before, but the task of sorting and evaluating that information is solely our own responsibility (see *Don't Be Fooled by . . . the World Wide Web* in Chapter 5).

Not only does the web provide information, but it is also interactive to a degree that far surpasses talk radio or television. The social networking sites Facebook, MySpace, and Twitter, as well as many other web sites and blogs, have chat rooms or discussion opportunities where all sorts of information can be shared, topics debated, and people met. (See "*Snapshot of America:* Who Participates in Social Media?") Likewise, most online news sources enable readers to comment on articles and posts. Although this can allow the formation of communities based on specialized interests or similar views, it can also make it very easy for people with fringe or extreme views to find each other and organize.[33] Political campaigns began to take advantage of this in 2008, using online technology and social networking principles to organize, raise funds, and get out the vote. Barack Obama's campaign proved to be skilled at using the new technology, setting the gold standard for future candidates to beat.[34] The Internet has the potential to increase the direct participation of citizens in political communities and political decisions, though the fact that not all Americans have equal access to the web means that multiple classes of citizenship could form.[35]

---

blogs web logs, or online journals, that can cover any topic, including political analysis

news aggregators web sites, applications, and software that cull content from other digital sources

---

From newspapers to radio, television, and, most recently, the Internet, Americans have moved eagerly to embrace the new forms of technology that entertain them and bring new ways of communicating information. But the deluge of political information requires consumers to sort through and critically analyze the news they get—often a costly exercise in terms of time, effort, and financial resources. Consequently, although the amount of political information available to Americans has increased dramatically, Americans do not seem to be particularly well informed about their political world.

IN YOUR OWN WORDS ≫ Describe the main sources from which Americans get their news and information.

WHO OWNS THE MEDIA, AND HOW DOES THAT AFFECT OUR NEWS?
From government control to corporate control

The ownership structure of the American media has changed dramatically since the days of the nation's founding. The media have gone from dependence on government for their very existence to massive corporate ownership that seems to rival government for its sheer power and influence on the citizenry. In this section we look at the ways in which the ownership of those media has changed the kind of news we get.

THE EARLY AMERICAN PRESS

In its earliest days, the press in America was dependent on government officials for its financial, and sometimes political, survival. Under those circumstances, the press could hardly perform either the watchdog function of checking up on government or the democratic function of empowering citizens. It served primarily to empower government or, during the Revolution, the patriots who had seized control of many of the colonial presses.

During colonial times, printers were required to obtain government approval and thus tended to avoid controversial political reporting so that they could stay in business. But the radical patriot movement was aggressive and violent in its methods of securing a supportive press. As public opinion swung toward independence, printers who favored British rule or aimed to treat both sides objectively were targeted with letters and criticism, and their print shops were raided, vandalized, and burned. Angry mobs burned the loyalist printers in effigy and frequently forced them to change their viewpoints or shut down their presses.

After the American Revolution, with independence firmly in hand, Americans celebrated their "freedom of the press," which they enshrined in the First Amendment to the Constitution. The debates over the Constitution itself took place in newspapers and pamphlets, producing works such as the *Federalist Papers*. Most revolutionaries concluded that, without the press, independence could not have been won and liberty could not survive. It is ironic that the victory they celebrated was founded on the vigorous suppression of their opponents' freedom of the press.

The press that grew up in the early American republic continued to be anything but free and independent. Because the newspaper business was still a risky financial proposition, it was an accepted practice for a politician or a party to set up a newspaper and support it financially—and expect it to support the appropriate political causes in return. Andrew Jackson, elected in 1828, carried the patronage of the press to new lengths. Like his predecessors, he offered friendly papers the opportunity to print government documents and denied it to his critics. But Jackson's administration heralded an age of mass democracy. Voter turnout doubled between 1824 and 1828.[36] People were reading newspapers in unheard of numbers, and those papers were catering to their new mass audiences with a blunter and less elite style than they had used in the past.

GROWING MEDIA INDEPENDENCE

The newspapers after Jackson's day were characterized by larger circulations, which drew more advertising and increased their financial independence. As newspapers sought to increase their readership, they began to offer more politically impartial news coverage in the hope that they would not alienate potential readers. This effort to be objective, which we see as a journalistic virtue today, came about at least partly as the result of the economic imperatives of selling newspapers to large numbers of people who do not share the same political views.

Prior to 1833, newspapers had been expensive; a year's subscription cost more than the average weekly wages of a skilled worker.[37] But in that year, the *New York Sun* began selling papers at only a penny a copy. Its subject matter was not an intellectual treatment of complex political and economic topics, but rather more superficial political reporting of crime, human interest stories, humor, and advertising. As papers began to appeal to mass audiences rather than partisan supporters, they left behind their opinionated reporting and strove for more objective, "fairer" treatment of their subjects that would be less likely to alienate the readers and the advertisers on whom they

depended for their livelihood. This isn't to say that newspaper editors stayed out of politics, but they were not seen as being in the pocket of one of the political parties, and the news they printed was considered to be evenhanded. In 1848 the AP was organized as a wire service to collect foreign news and distribute it to member papers in the United States. This underscored the need for objectivity in political reporting so that the news would be acceptable to a variety of papers.[38]

After the Civil War, the need for newspapers to appeal to a mass audience resulted in the practice of *yellow journalism*, the effort to lure readers with sensational reporting on topics like sex, crime, gossip, and human interest. With the success of such techniques, newspapers became big business in the United States. Newspaper giant Joseph Pulitzer's *World* was challenged by William Randolph Hearst's New York *Journal*, and the resulting battle for circulation drew the criticism that there were no depths to which journalists wouldn't sink in their quest for readers. The irony, of course, is that sensationalism did win new readers and allowed papers to achieve independence from parties and politicians, even as they were criticized for lowering the standards of journalism.

THE MEDIA TODAY

Today the media continue to be big business, but on a scale undreamed of by such early entrepreneurs as Pulitzer and Hearst. No longer does a single figure dominate a paper's editorial policy; rather, all the major circulation newspapers in this country, as well as the national radio and television stations, are owned by major conglomerates. Often editorial decisions are matters of corporate policy, not individual judgment. And if profit was an overriding concern for the editor-entrepreneurs, it is gospel for the conglomerates. Interestingly, journalists freed themselves from the political masters who ruled them in the early years of this country, only to find themselves just as thoroughly dominated by the corporate bottom line.

MEDIA MONOPOLY The modern media get five times as much of their revenue from advertising as from circulation. Logic dictates that advertisers will want to spend their money where they can get the biggest bang for their buck: the papers with the most readers and the stations with the largest audiences. Because advertisers go after the most popular media outlets, competition is fierce, and outlets that cannot promise advertisers wide enough exposure fail to get the advertising dollars and go out of business. Competition drives out the weaker outlets, corporations seeking to maximize market share gobble up smaller outlets, and to retain viewers, they all stick to the formulas that are known to produce success. What this means for the media world today is that there are fewer and fewer outlets, they are owned by fewer and fewer corporations, and the content they offer is more and more the same.[39]

Freedom of the Press ● The Information Free-for-All ●

In fact, today, just six corporations—Time-Warner, Disney, Viacom, CBS Corporation, News Corporation Limited, and General Electric—own most of the major national newspapers, the leading news magazines, the national television networks including CNN and other cable stations, as well as publishing houses, movie studios, telephone companies, entertainment firms, and other multimedia operations. Most of these corporations are also involved in other businesses, as their familiar names attest. *The Big Picture* shows in detail the media empires that own the major television networks. These giant corporations cross national lines, forming massive global media networks, controlled by a handful of corporate headquarters. Media critic Ben Bagdikian calls these media giants a "new communications cartel within the United States," with the "power to surround every man, woman, and child in the country with controlled images and words, to socialize each new generation of Americans, to alter the political agenda of the country."[40] What troubles him and other critics is that many Americans don't know that most of the news and entertainment comes from just a few corporate sources and are unaware of the consequences that this corporate ownership structure has for all of us.

IMPLICATIONS OF CORPORATE OWNERSHIP FOR THE NEWS WE GET

What does the concentrated corporate ownership of the media mean to us as consumers of the news? We should be aware of at least four major consequences:

- There is a **commercial bias** in the media today toward what will increase advertiser revenue and audience share. People tune in to watch scandals and crime stories, so extensive coverage of nonnewsworthy events, like John Edwards's extramarital affair and Sarah Palin's teenaged daughter's pregnancy, appear relentlessly on the front pages of every newspaper in the country, not just the gossip-hungry tabloids but also the more sober *New York Times* and *Wall Street Journal*. It may not be because an editor has decided that the American people need to know the latest developments, but because papers that don't reveal those developments may be passed over by consumers for those that do. Journalistic judgment and ethics are often at odds with the imperative to turn a profit.

- The effort to get and keep large audiences, and to make way for increased advertising, means a reduced emphasis on political news. This is especially true at the local level, which is precisely where the political events that most directly affect most citizens occur. More Americans watch local television news than

watch national news, and yet one political scientist, drawing on his research of local news in North Carolina, has shown that local news shows spend an average of only six out of thirty minutes on political news, compared with hot topics like weather, sports, disasters, human interest stories, and "happy talk" among the newscasters.[41]

- The content of the news we get is lightened up and dramatized to keep audiences tuned in.[42] As in the days of yellow journalism, market forces encourage sensational coverage of the news. Television shows often capitalize on the human interest in dramatic reenactments of news events, with a form of journalism that has come to be called "infotainment" because of its efforts to make the delivery of information more attractive by dressing it up as entertainment. To compete with such shows, the mainstream network news broadcasts increase the drama of their coverage as well. Sensational newscasts focus our attention on scandalous or tragic events rather than on the political news that democratic theory argues citizens need.

- The corporate ownership of today's media means that the media outlets frequently face conflicts of interest in deciding what news to cover or how to cover it. As one critic asks, how can NBC's anchor report critically on nuclear power without crossing the network's corporate parent, General Electric, or how can ABC give fair treatment to Disney's business practices?[43] The question is not hypothetical: after Disney acquired ABC, several ABC employees, including a news commentator who had been critical of Disney in the past, were fired.[44] And with Rupert Murdoch's News Corporation giving a million dollars to the Republican Governors Association in 2010, who would be surprised at the Republican-friendly coverage of its news operations like Fox News, the *New York Post*, and the *Wall Street Journal*?[45] In fact, 33 percent of newspaper editors in America said they would not feel free to publish news that might harm their parent company,[46] a statistic that should make us question what is being left out of the news we receive. A further conflict of interest arises in advertising matters. Note, as just one example, the media's slowness to pick up on stories critical of the tobacco industry, a major advertiser.[47]

- Breaking a news story—that is, being the first to publish new information—has always been a point of pride for editors and journalists (nobody remembers the second newspaper to report on the Watergate scandal, after all). Thus journalists have always had to walk a fine line between the time spent reporting—that is, investigating and verifying stories—and getting those stories published before their competition does. This tension has become even more intense as daily

> **commercial bias** the tendency of the media to make coverage and programming decisions based on what will attract a large audience and maximize profits

THE BIG PICTURE: WHO OWNS (AND CONTROLS) TODAY'S INFORMATION NETWORKS

Today most of our news comes from a handful of powerful sources. While some, like the New York Times are still independent, others are part of massive media conglomerates or, like the Washington Post, owned by Amazon's Jeff Bezos, tied in other ways to the information world. What implication does this ownership structure have for the news we get?

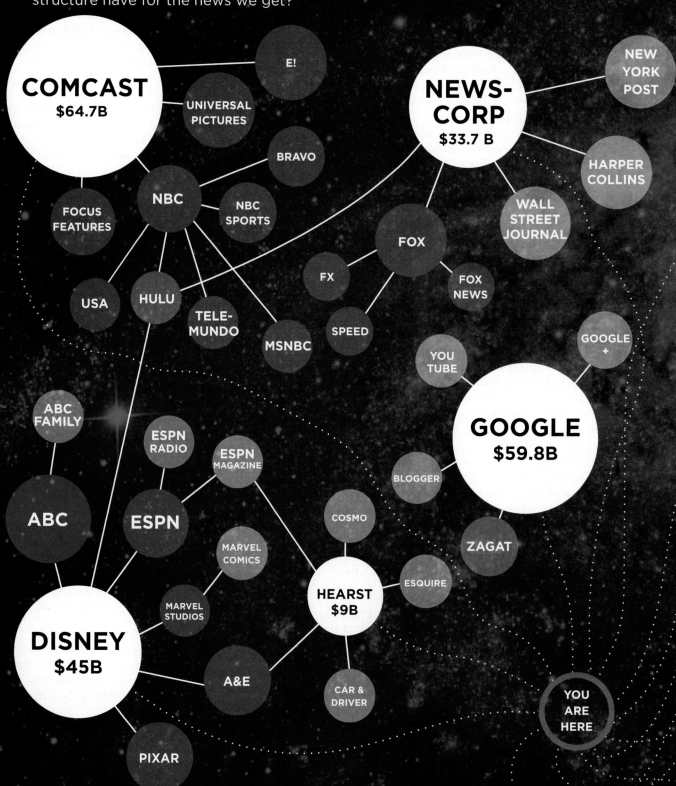

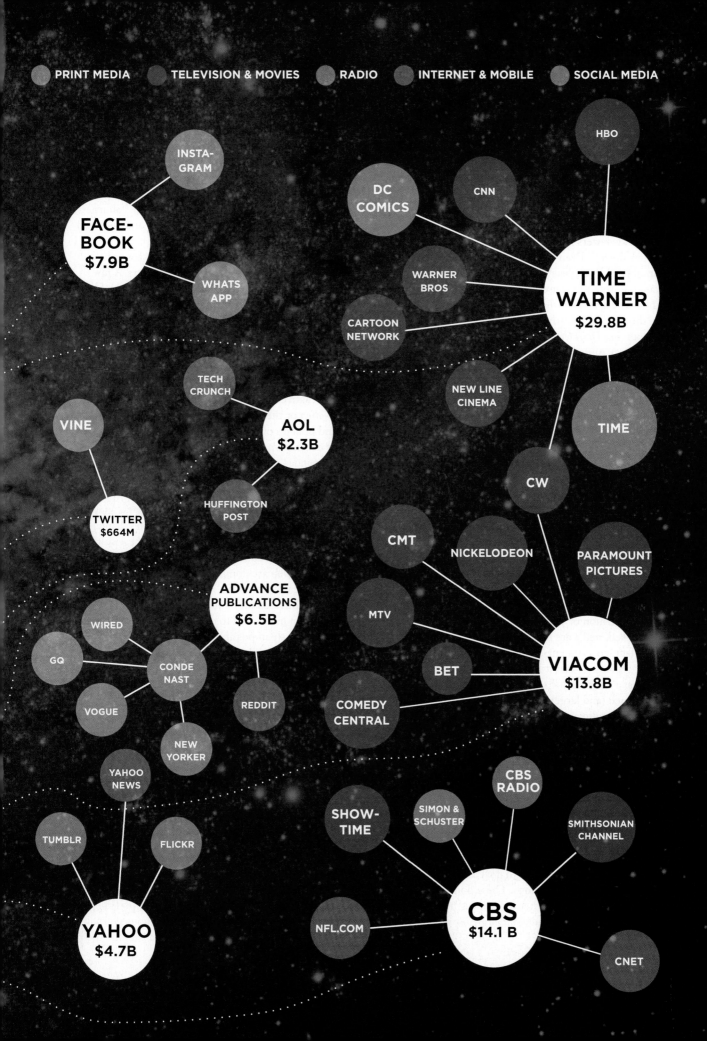

PRINT MEDIA   TELEVISION & MOVIES   RADIO   INTERNET & MOBILE   SOCIAL MEDIA

INSTA-GRAM

FACE-BOOK $7.9B

WHATS APP

DC COMICS

CNN

HBO

WARNER BROS

CARTOON NETWORK

TIME WARNER $29.8B

NEW LINE CINEMA

TECH CRUNCH

AOL $2.3B

TIME

VINE

HUFFINGTON POST

CW

TWITTER $664M

CMT

NICKELODEON

PARAMOUNT PICTURES

ADVANCE PUBLICATIONS $6.5B

MTV

WIRED

GQ

CONDE NAST

VOGUE

REDDIT

BET

VIACOM $13.8B

NEW YORKER

COMEDY CENTRAL

YAHOO NEWS

CBS RADIO

TUMBLR

FLICKR

SHOW-TIME

SIMON & SCHUSTER

SMITHSONIAN CHANNEL

YAHOO $4.7B

NFL.COM

CBS $14.1 B

CNET

deadlines for print or nightly broadcast have given way to the modern twenty-four-hour news cycle. In the rush to avoid getting "scooped" by another station or newspaper, reporters and editors alike have sometimes jumped the gun, disseminating incorrect information or flat-out lies without taking the time to fact check or analyze them. For example, when the U.S. Supreme Court's hotly anticipated decision on the Affordable Care Act was handed down in 2012, both Fox and CNN rushed to report on it without having read Chief Justice John Roberts's decision in its entirety—and told viewers incorrectly that Obamacare had been struck down.[48] Even more troubling, perhaps, is the number of journalists and editors at online outlets ranging from the conservative blog Breitbart.com to the *Washington Post* who have retweeted or reblogged to their readers clearly made-up stories from the news parody site *Daily Current* (think *The Onion*, without the jokes). Among these stories were completely false reports that Sarah Palin had joined the Arab news network Al-Jazeera, and that Nobel Prize–winning economist (and *New York Times* columnist) Paul Krugman had filed for bankruptcy. [49]

ALTERNATIVES TO THE CORPORATE MEDIA

The corporate media monopoly affects the news we get in serious ways. Citizens have some alternative news options, but few are truly satisfactory as a remedy, and most require more work than switching on the television in the evening. One alternative is public radio and television. Americans tend to assume that media wholly owned or controlled by the government serve the interests of government rather than the citizens. This was certainly true in our early history and is true in totalitarian countries such as the former Soviet Union or today's China. But as we have seen, privately owned media are not necessarily free either.

And, in fact, government-controlled media are not necessarily repressive. Great Britain and other European countries have long supported a media system combining privately owned (and largely partisan) newspapers with publicly owned radio and television stations. Although such stations now find themselves competing with cable rivals, some, including the British Broadcasting Company (BBC), are renowned for their programming excellence. Sometimes, then, publicly owned media may be even "freer" than privately owned media if they allow producers to escape the commercial culture in which most media shows exist. The United States has public radio and television networks, but they are not subsidized by the government at sufficient levels to allow them complete commercial freedom. Rather, they are funded by a combination of government assistance and private or corporate donations. These donations sound very much like commercials when announced at the start and finish of programming and could arguably affect the content of the shows.

Another choice for citizens is the *alternative press*. Born of the counterculture and antiwar movement in the 1960s, these local weekly papers, like the (New York) *Village Voice* and the *SF* (San Francisco) *Weekly*, were intended to offer a radical alternative to the mainstream media. Usually free and dependent on advertising, these papers have lost their radical edge and become so profitable that, in an ironic turn of events, they themselves are now getting bought up by chains like New Times, Inc.[50] Rejecting the alternative press as too conventional, there is now even an "alternative to the alternative press" aimed at a younger audience and coveted by advertisers.[51]

Nevertheless, an independent press does continue to thrive without the support of corporate owners. A few investigative magazines, like *Mother Jone*s (published by the Foundation for National Progress) and *Consumer Reports* (published by Consumers Union), rely on funding from subscribers and members of their nonprofit parent organizations. However, unless they are completely free from advertising (as is *Consumer Reports*), even these independent publications are not entirely free from corporate influence. Other alternative newsletters and magazines, such as the liberal *Nation* or the conservative *National Review*, cover issues and policies often ignored by the mainstream press, but they do so from a perspective that supports their own political agendas.

A final, but rapidly growing, alternative to the mainstream corporate media is, of course, the Internet. The Internet offers myriad sources for political news. As we saw in *Don't Be Fooled by . . . the World Wide Web* in Chapter 5, it takes time and effort to figure out which of these sources are accurate and trustworthy—and in many cases the news options on the web are dominated by the same corporate interests as are the rest of the media—but the Internet enables the motivated individual to get around the biases of the mainstream media and to customize the news in a way that was previously impossible. Not only are there news feeds and web portals that allow users to get the news they want, when they want it, but the growing number of blogs presents news readers with a new and independent option for finding news online—one that allows them to go around the corporate barriers in their quest for news. Although in 2008 only 10 percent of the public reported regularly reading blogs for information about current events and politics, that remains a huge number of Americans who are logging on to get their political news from this alternative source.[52]

Social media such as Facebook, Twitter, and YouTube are also rapidly becoming favored news sources in addition to ways of keeping up with friends. The Pew Center's Project for Excellence in Journalism, which has studied YouTube in particular, finds that "the data reveal that a complex, symbiotic relationship has developed between citizens and news organizations on YouTube, a relationship that comes close to the continuous journalistic 'dialogue' many observers predicted would become the new journalism online. Citizens are creating their own videos about news and posting them. They are also actively sharing news videos produced by journalism professionals. And news organizations are taking advantage of citizen content and incorporating it into their journalism. Consumers, in turn, seem to be embracing the interplay in what they watch and share, creating a new kind of television news."[53] In addition, the growing number of cell phone users offers another way for people to access this customized news, with owners of smart phones notable for their heavy news consumption, and as we mentioned earlier, people who access their news on mobile devices are spending longer with the news and getting it from more sources.[54] The fact that these tech-savvy news readers are disproportionately well educated and young suggests that America's news-reading habits may be changing dramatically, and that the web may come closer to realizing its potential for offering a truly democratic, practical, and "free" alternative to the corporate-produced news we now receive.

THINKING OUTSIDE THE BOX

Can a corporately owned press be a free press?

REGULATION OF THE MEDIA

The media in America are almost entirely privately owned, but they do not operate without some public control. Although the principle of freedom of the press keeps the print media almost free of restriction (see Chapter 5), the broadcast media have been treated differently. In the early days of radio, great public enthusiasm for the new medium resulted in so many radio stations that signal interference threatened to damage the whole industry. Broadcasters asked the government to impose some order, which it did with the passage of the Federal Communications Act, creating the Federal Communications Commission (FCC), an independent regulatory agency, in 1934.

Because access to the airwaves was considered a scarce resource, the government acted to ensure that radio and television serve the public interest by representing a variety of viewpoints. Accordingly, the 1934 bill contained three provisions designed to ensure fairness in broadcasting:

- *The equal time rule.* The *equal time rule* means that if a station allows a candidate for office to buy or use airtime outside of regular news broadcasts, it must allow all candidates that opportunity. On its face, this provision seems to give the public a chance to hear from candidates of all ideologies and political parties, but in actuality, it often has the reverse effect.

Confronted with the prospect of allowing every candidate to speak, no matter how slight the chance of his or her victory and how small an audience is likely to tune in, many stations instead opt to allow none to speak at all. This rule has been suspended for purposes of televising political debates. Minor-party candidates may be excluded and may appeal to the FCC if they think they have been unfairly left out.

- *The fairness doctrine.* The *fairness doctrine* extended beyond election broadcasts; it required that stations give free airtime to issues that concerned the public and to opposing sides when controversial issues were covered. Like the equal time rule, this had the effect of encouraging stations to avoid controversial topics. The FCC ended the rule in the 1980s, and when Congress tried to revive it in 1987, President Ronald Reagan vetoed the bill, claiming it led to "bland" programming.[55]

- *The right of rebuttal.* The *right of rebuttal* says that individuals whose reputations are damaged on the air have a right to respond. This rule is not strictly enforced by the FCC and the courts, however, for fear that it would quell controversial broadcasts, as the other two rules have done.

All of these rules remain somewhat controversial. Politicians would like to have the rules enforced because they help them to air their views publicly. Theoretically, the rules should benefit the public, though as we have seen, they often do not. Media owners see these rules as forcing them to air unpopular speakers who damage their ratings and as limiting their abilities to decide station policy. They argue that given all the cable and satellite outlets, access to broadcast time is no longer such a scarce resource and that the broadcast media should be subject to the same legal protections as the print media.

Many of the limitations on station ownership that the original act established were abolished with the 1996 Telecommunications Act in order to open up competition and promote diversity in media markets. The act failed to rein in the media giants, however, and, in fact, ended up facilitating mergers that concentrated media ownership even more. The law permits ownership of multiple stations as long as they do not reach more than 35 percent of the market, and nothing prevents the networks themselves from reaching a far larger market through their collective affiliates. The 1996 legislation also opened up the way for ownership of cable stations by network owners, and it allows cable companies to offer many services previously supplied only by telephone companies. The overall effect of this deregulation has been to increase dramatically the possibilities for media monopoly.

Some users favor a policy of *net neutrality* that would ensure that telecommunication companies cannot use their control over Internet access to restrict or limit content with

requires a free press to which all citizens have access. We have a free press in this country, and we also have a free market, and these two worlds produce clashing rules in which the press has largely been the loser to economic imperative.

IN YOUR OWN WORDS >> Summarize the evolution of the modern news media.

WHO ARE THE JOURNALISTS?
Gatekeepers who decide what news gets covered and how

Corporate ownership does not tell the whole story of modern journalism. Although the mass media are no longer owned primarily by individuals, individuals continue to be the eyes, ears, nose, and, in fact, legs of the business. Journalists are the people who discover, report, edit, and publish the news in newspapers and magazines and on the radio, television, and the Internet. To understand the powerful influence the media exert in American politics, we need to move beyond the ownership structure to the question of who American journalists are and how they do their jobs.

WHAT ROLES DO JOURNALISTS PLAY?

Journalism professors David Weaver and Cleveland Wilhoit have asked journalists about their perceptions of the roles they play in American society. Based partly on their work, we can distinguish four journalistic roles: the gatekeeper, the disseminator, the interpretive/investigator, and the public mobilizer.[58] Often these roles coexist in a single journalist.

- **Gatekeepers** decide, in large part, the details about what news gets covered (or not) and how. Not all journalists share this enormous power of gatekeeping equally. Managers of the wire services, which determine what news gets sent on to member papers; editors who decide what stories should be covered or what parts of a story should be cut; and even

> **gatekeepers** journalists and media elite who determine which news stories are covered and which are not

Richard B. Levine/Newscom

Marketplace of Ideas, or Black Market?
Lawmakers struggle between keeping the Internet open and free, and protecting copyright holders from online piracy, a costly form of intellectual theft. In 2012, the Stop Online Piracy Act (SOPA)—which would have increased penalties for unauthorized streaming of copyrighted content—prompted unprecedented protests from the tech world, with Wikipedia and some seven thousand other sites going dark for twenty-four hours.

price discrimination, and would keep the Internet unfettered and open to innovation. Opponents argue such a policy would reduce incentives for companies to innovate. In 2007 the Federal Trade Commission declined to recommend regulation, issuing a report disparaging the subject of regulation generally and arguing that the industry is a young one and the effects of regulation on consumers and providers are unknown.[56] In 2008, however, several net neutrality bills were introduced in Congress (of which the "netroots," such as the posters at *Daily Kos*, were in favor, and the telecom and cable companies in opposition), and in December 2010, the FCC approved rules of net neutrality along party lines, Democrats on the commission voting in favor, Republicans opposed.[57]

PAUSE AND REVIEW:

WHO, WHAT, HOW

The ownership of the media has historically influenced whether the news is objective, and thus serves the public interest, or is slanted to serve a particular political or economic interest. Democratic theory and American political tradition tell us that democracy

reporters who decide how to pitch a story are all gatekeepers, though to varying degrees.

- *Disseminators* confine their role to getting the facts of the story straight and moving the news out to the public quickly, avoiding stories with unverified content, and reaching as wide an audience as possible. The disseminator role is open to the criticism that, in a complex society, simple dissemination does nothing to help citizens understand the news. In the words of veteran journalist Eric Sevareid, in merely reporting the facts, journalists "have given the lie the same prominence and impact the truth is given."[59]

- *Interpretive/investigators* developed their role in reaction to this criticism and to the growing sophistication of the issues confronting the American public. This role combines the functions of investigating government's claims, analyzing and interpreting complex problems, and discussing public policies in a timely way. Such interpretation is related to investigation, or the actual digging for information that is not readily apparent or available. Such a role is not new to journalism. The muckrakers of the early twentieth century exposed abuses of public and private power ranging from corporate monopolies, to municipal corruption, to atrocious conditions in meatpacking plants, to political dishonesty, and their work inspired a wide array of political reforms. Bob Woodward and Carl Bernstein, the two young reporters for the *Washington Post* who uncovered the Watergate scandal in the 1970s, brought the spirit of investigative journalism to the present day. The public legacy of muckraking is alive in journalism today as reporters uncover shameful migrant worker conditions, toxic waste dumps near residential areas, and corruption in local officials. Many online journalists, like blogger Josh Marshall of *Talking Points Memo*, carry on the muckraking tradition.

- *Public mobilizers* develop the cultural and intellectual interests of the public, set the political agenda, and let the people express their views. This role is closely aligned with a contemporary movement in the American media called public or civic journalism. Civic journalism is a movement among journalists to be responsive to citizen input in determining what

news stories to cover. It is a reaction to the criticism that the media elite report on their own interests and holds that, instead, the media ought to be driven by the people and their interests. The movement is controversial in American journalism because, while on its face it is responsive to the citizens, it is also seen as condescending to them, with the potential for manipulation. With the growing presence of the Internet as a space where people can communicate and organize, public mobilization is becoming a much more grassroots affair.

WHO CHOOSES JOURNALISM?

The vast majority of journalists in this country (just over two-thirds) work in the print media, and about one-third are in broadcast journalism. Journalists live throughout the country, although those with more high-powered jobs tend to be concentrated in the Northeast. The gender, education, ethnic backgrounds, and religious affiliations of American journalists are examined in "*Snapshot of America:* Who Are the Journalists?"

Does this demographic profile of journalism make any difference? Does a population need to get its news from a group of reporters that mirrors its own gender, ethnic, and religious characteristics in order to get an accurate picture of what is going on? Not surprisingly, this question generates controversy among journalists. Some insist that the personal profile of a journalist is irrelevant to the quality of his or her news coverage, but some evidence suggests that the life experiences of journalists do influence their reporting. For instance, most mainstream media focus on issues of concern to white middle-class America and reflect the values of that population, at the expense of minority issues and the concerns of poor people. General reporting also emphasizes urban rather than rural issues and concentrates on male-dominated sports. Women journalists, on the other hand, tend to report more on social issues that are of more concern to women.[60] And while recent layoffs in the news industry have hit blacks harder than whites, more women are in top editing jobs than ever before.[61]

WHAT DO JOURNALISTS BELIEVE?

It is not the demographic profile of journalists, but their ideological profile—that is, the political views that they hold—that concerns many observers. Political scientists know that the more educated people are, the more liberal their views tend to be. Because professional journalists are a well-educated lot on the whole, their views tend to be to the left of the average American's, particularly on social issues.[62] Women and minority journalists are more likely to be Democrats than the average American, though of course there are Republicans and independents in the profession as

---

muckrakers investigative reporters who search for and expose misconduct in corporate activity or public officials

civic journalism a movement among journalists to be responsive to citizen input in determining what news stories to cover

---

● Black Reporters Declining ● More Women in Charge

SNAPSHOT OF AMERICA: WHO ARE THE JOURNALISTS?

Journalists Compared to Overall U.S. Population

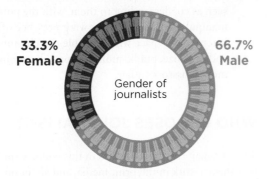

33.3% Female

Gender of journalists

66.7% Male

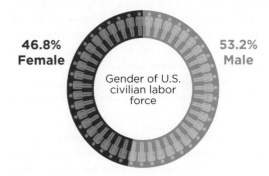

46.8% Female

Gender of U.S. civilian labor force

53.2% Male

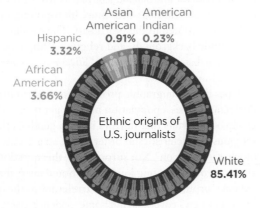

Asian American **0.91%**

American Indian **0.23%**

Hispanic **3.32%**

African American **3.66%**

Ethnic origins of U.S. journalists

White **85.41%**

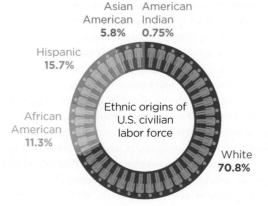

Asian American **5.8%**

American Indian **0.75%**

Hispanic **15.7%**

African American **11.3%**

Ethnic origins of U.S. civilian labor force

White **70.8%**

Party Identification

Political Leanings Democrat

36%
Journalists

31%
U.S. adult population

Political Leanings Republican

19%
Journalists

31%
U.S. adult population

BEHIND THE NUMBERS

Compare the backgrounds and political leanings of journalists with the larger U.S population. Who is underrepresented? Is this a problem for the kind of news that America hears and reads? Would greater diversity among journalists affect the how events and people are reported and interpreted in the news?

Source: Lars Willnat and David H. Weaver, *The American Journalist in the Digital Age: Key Findings* (Bloomington: School of Journalism, Indiana University, 2014).

well (see "*Snapshot of America:* Who Are the Journalists?").[63]

Still, even though they have ideological inclinations of their own, most members of the "mainstream media" in the United States strive to leave their values outside the newsroom and to do objective work. Indeed, studies show that there is no discernible overall ideological bias in the media. To the extent that some outlets are tilted slightly to the left, they are offset by others that lean slightly to the right.[64] Most journalists, aware that their values are more liberal than the average American's, try hard to keep their coverage of issues balanced. Some Democratic candidates for president have even accused the press of being harder on them to compensate for their personal preferences. Ben Bradlee, then–executive editor of the *Washington Post*, said that when Ronald Reagan became president, the journalists at the *Post* thought, "Here comes a true conservative. . . . And we are known—though I don't think justifiably—as the great liberals. So [we thought] we've got to really behave ourselves here. We've got to not be arrogant, make every effort to be informed, be mannerly, be fair. And we did this. I suspect in the process that this paper and probably a good deal of the press gave Reagan not a free ride, but they didn't use the same standards on him that they used on Carter and Nixon."[65] In addition to this sort of self-restraint, the liberal tendencies of many journalists are tempered by the undoubtedly conservative nature of news ownership and management we have already discussed. The editorial tone of many papers is conservative; for instance, generally more papers endorse Republican candidates for president than they do Democrats (see Figure 15.1). For instance, in the run-up to the 2012 presidential election, Mitt Romney beat Barack Obama in endorsements 45 to 40 percent (although, unusually, Obama did lead John McCain in 2008).[66]

Interestingly, despite the studies showing no discernible partisan bias in the media, people today, both liberals and conservatives, tend to perceive a bias against their own views, especially to the extent that they talk with others with similar views about that bias.[67] Until the mid-1980s, citizens were not convinced that there was an ideological bias in the media—55 percent believed that the media were basically accurate and only 45 percent thought the press was biased in its reporting. Today large percentages are skeptical about the media sources they follow—both print and broadcast.[68]

Not surprisingly, the rise in the perception that the media are biased coincides with the growth of a more partisan tone in the media. A concerted conservative effort to bring what they believe is a much-needed balance to the news has resulted in a host of talk radio shows, including those of Rush Limbaugh and Glenn Beck, the Fox News Channel on TV, and the online *Drudge Report*, to join

FIGURE 15.1 **NEWSPAPER ENDORSEMENTS OF PRESIDENTIAL CANDIDATES, 1932–2012**

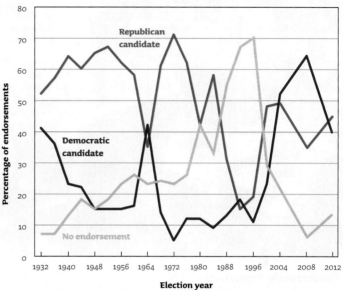

Sources: Harold W. Stanley and Richard G. Niemi, *Vital Statistics on American Politics, 2009–2010* (Washington, D.C.: CQ Press, 2010), Table 14.7; 2012 data from editorandpublisher.com/election/.

already existing conservative media outlets like the *Wall Street Journal* editorial page. The rise of the conservative media has led to what two scholars call a conservative "echo chamber," "a self-protective enclave hospitable to conservative beliefs" that "reinforces the views of these outlets' like-minded audience members, helps them maintain ideological coherence, protects them from counterpersuasion, reinforces conservative values and dispositions . . . and distances listeners, readers, and viewers from 'liberals' in general and Democrats in particular."[69]

The increasing effectiveness of this Republican media machine has led liberals to argue that the media are biased against them, especially after media coverage of the Clinton impeachment, the 2000 election recount, the Swift Boat attacks on John Kerry, and the rise of the Tea Party movement.[70] Their response—in the form of shows like the *Rachel Maddow Show* and *Up With Chris Hayes* on MSNBC; Current TV, a cable station started in 2005 by former vice president Al Gore; and the online *Huffington Post* (among other blogs and liberal web sites)—now contributes a powerful liberal voice, but one nowhere nearly as effective politically as the conservative voice already in place. This is due partly to the different values that conservatives and liberals bring to the table. Liberals can't settle on a single truth to promote and often argue as much among themselves as with their ideological opponents. Conservatives, on the other hand, are more willing to silence their own party members who don't conform to the conservative ideal they believe Ronald

in the 1960s, political news about women was rare. When the National Organization for Women was formed in 1966, the *Washington Post* did not mention it and the *New York Times* ran its story on the "Food, Fashion, Family, and Furnishings" page under a recipe for roasting turkey.[72]

The beat system, however, is well entrenched in American journalism, and at the top echelon of American journalists are those who cover the national political beat in Washington. National politics takes place in Washington—not just the interactions of Congress, the president, and the courts but also the internal workings of political parties and the rival lobbying of interest groups, including states, major corporations, and other national organizations. For a political reporter, Washington is the coveted place to be.

Tomorrow's Reporters
Statistically, journalists have always been primarily male and usually white—but that demographic is shifting as the next generation takes the reigns. Here, student journalists reporting on tuition hikes are working in the *California Aggie* newsroom at the University of California–Davis.

Reagan embodied, even when it is far removed from the actual Ronald Reagan's words and visions.[71]

When Americans, most of whom hold moderate views somewhere in the political center, listen to these overtly partisan media sources, it is no wonder that they perceive the media as biased in one direction or another. In 2010, at his "Rally to Restore Sanity and/or Fear," held on the Washington Mall, comedian Jon Stewart blasted what he called the "24-hour political pundit perpetual panic conflictinator," accusing cable news outlets on both sides of demonizing each other so severely that they were creating a political environment in which compromise and cooperation are well-nigh impossible.

THE GROWTH OF THE WASHINGTON PRESS CORPS

From a news-gathering perspective, America is organized into beats, identifiable areas covered by reporters who become familiar with their territories, get to know the sources of their stories, and otherwise institutionalize their official bit of journalistic "turf." Typical beats include the police, politics, business, education, and sports, and these can be broken down into even more specialized areas, such as the White House, Congress, and the Supreme Court. News that doesn't fit neatly into a preexisting beat may not get well covered or may turn up in unexpected places. For instance,

THE REVOLVING DOOR As the *Washington Post*'s David Broder points out, the concentration of politics, politicians, and reporters in Washington leads to "a complex but cozy relationship between journalists and public officials."[73] Washington journalists share an interest in politics with politicians, they have similar educations, they often make about the same amount of money, and they are in many ways natural colleagues and friends. So much do journalists and politicians have in common that they often exchange jobs with ease, in a trend that Broder calls the "revolving door."

The **revolving door**, like the interest group phenomenon we discussed in Chapter 13, refers to the practice of journalists taking positions in government and then returning to journalism again, or vice versa, perhaps several times over. The number of prominent journalists who have gone through this revolving door is legion, including such notables as George Stephanopoulos, a Clinton adviser who now hosts *Good Morning America* on ABC; Karl Rove, President George W. Bush's political adviser who is now a commentator on Fox; and Jay Carney, who went from a career in print journalism to being Obama's press secretary, to name only a few.[74]

THE ROLE OF THE PUNDIT Many of those who return to the media through the revolving door find themselves joining the ranks of the journalists and academics who have earned the unofficial and slightly tongue-in-cheek

> **revolving door** the tendency of public officials, journalists, and lobbyists to move between public and private sector (media, lobbying) jobs

title of **pundit**. A pundit is traditionally a learned person, someone professing great wisdom. In contemporary media parlance, it has come to mean a professional observer and commentator on politics—a person skilled in the ways of the media and of politics who can make trenchant observations and predictions about the political world and help us untangle the complicated implications of political events. The twenty-four-hour news cycle and the growth in cable news shows means there is a nearly insatiable demand for bodies to fill the political "panels," and sometimes the ones who appear have pretty tenuous claims to expertise. Because of the media attention they get, many pundits join the unofficial ranks of the celebrity journalists who cross over from reporting on public figures to being public figures themselves, thus raising a host of questions about whether they themselves should be subject to the same standards of criticism and scrutiny that they apply to politicians. Because they receive wide media coverage from their fellow journalists, the pronouncements of the punditry carry considerable power. The pundits, as journalists, are meant to be a check on the power of politicians, but who provides a check on the pundits?

PAUSE AND REVIEW:

WHO, WHAT, HOW

American journalists do not mirror American society; they are more male, more white, and more liberal than the average population, although some elements of that picture are changing. It is not clear, however, how much difference this profile makes in the public's perception of the news it gets. In the high-stakes world of Washington journalism, the tight relationship between journalists and politicians provides citizens with more information and a more complete context in which to understand it. But the link also requires citizens to be skeptical about what they hear and who they hear it from.

IN YOUR OWN WORDS >> Explain the roles and responsibilities of journalists.

THE MEDIA AND POLITICS
Manipulating information to influence who gets what, and how

As we have seen, the American media make up an amazingly complex institution. Once primarily a nation of print

> **pundit** a professional observer and commentator on politics

journalism, the United States is now in the grip of the electronic media. Television has changed the American political landscape, and now the Internet promises, or threatens, to do the same. Privately owned, the media have a tendency to represent the corporate interest, but that influence is countered to some extent by the professional concerns of journalists. Still, some of those at the upper levels of the profession, those who tend to report to us on national politics, have very close links with the political world they cover, and this too influences the news we get. What is the effect of all this on American politics? In this section we look at four major areas of media influence on politics: the shaping of public opinion, the portrayal of politics as conflict and image, the use of public relations strategies by politicians, and the reduction in political accountability.

THE SHAPING OF PUBLIC OPINION

As we saw in Chapter 11, the media are among the main agents of political socialization: they help to transfer political values from one generation to the next and to shape political views in general. We have already looked at the question of bias in the media and noted that not only is there a corporate or commercial bias, but that Americans are also increasingly convinced that the news media are ideologically biased. Political scientists acknowledge that ideological bias may exist, but they conclude that it isn't so

DON'T BE FOOLED BY...
THE NEWS MEDIA

Do you read the newspaper? Watch the news? Follow newsfeeds on Twitter? If so, you might consider yourself a well-informed citizen. But are you? That depends on where you get your news—and on how carefully you consume it.

Back in 2003, with the United States in the early months of the war in Iraq, a series of polls revealed that a surprising number of U.S. adults had the following misperceptions on aspects of the situation in Iraq:

- Evidence of links between Iraq and al Qaeda has been found. [No evidence has been found.]

- Weapons of mass destruction have been found in Iraq. [No such weapons have been found.]

- World public opinion favored the United States going to war with Iraq. [World opinion was strongly opposed to the U.S. invasion of Iraq.]

What's the matter with these people? Didn't they watch the news? Well, it turns out that they did: 80 percent of respondents noted that they get most of their news from TV and radio, while 20 percent cited print media as their primary news source. When researchers inquired further about viewing habits, they found the highest rates of misperceptions occurred among Fox News viewers, among whom 80 percent had at least one of the above items wrong. The most accurate perceptions were among the Public Broadcasting System (PBS) and National Public Radio (NPR) audience, in which just 23 percent had any misperceptions on the above items (see figure). Interestingly, these media source effects held up even when levels of education and partisanship were taken into account. Researchers have not been able to determine causality here. That is, while Fox News was a staunch supporter of the Bush administration's war effort, they do not know whether Fox's stance on the war effort led to the misperceptions being held, or whether supporters of the president who already held the misperceptions decided to watch Fox. Ten years later, not much has changed: Recent research shows that NPR listeners remain the best informed, while Fox News viewers are the worst-informed.[1]

Public Misperceptions and Primary Media Sources

As we have seen throughout this chapter, many forces are working to make the citizen's job difficult when it comes to getting, following, and interpreting the news. But forewarned is forearmed, and the knowledge you have gained can turn you into the savviest of media consumers. Journalist Carlin Romano notes, "What the press covers matters less in the end than how the public reads. Effective reading of the news requires not just a key—a Rosetta stone by which to decipher current clichés—but an activity, a regimen."[2] You need to be not just a consumer of information, but an active, critical consumer.

WHAT TO WATCH OUT FOR

- **Who owns the media source where you accessed the information?** Look at the page in newspapers and magazines that lists the publisher and editors. Take note of radio and television call letters. Check out *The Big Picture* on page 566 and see if the source is owned by one of the media conglomerates shown there. Look to see who takes credit for a web site. What could be this owner's agenda? Is it corporate, political, ideological? How might that agenda affect the news?

- **Where did the story originate?** In addition to considering who owns the site on which a story is posted, you should consider where the story itself came from. These days, the two can be very different, as many "news sites" are actually just news aggregators that share stories from other sites for their own readers. As a result, news reports—and in some cases, only small portions of news reports—are passed along from one source to another like a game of telephone, often with individual writers and bloggers adding their own headline and spin to the story as they repost. If the source where you find a story is not responsible for reporting the story, should you trust it? Did the source contribute to the expense of reporting the story, and can the source verify the quality of the story? What happens when a source cherry-picks snippets and reposts with its own headlines—and how

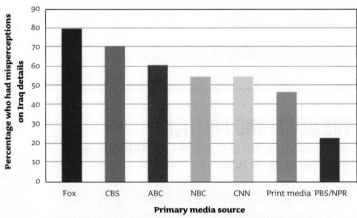

Source: Data from Steve Kull, "Misperceptions, the Media and the Iraq War," the PIPA/Knowledge Networks Poll, October 2, 2003, www.pipa.org.

might a source's agenda play a role in how it presents the stories it reposts?

- **Who is this journalist (reporter, anchor, webmaster, etc.)?** Does he or she share the characteristics of the average American or of the media elite? How might that affect his or her perspective on the news? Has he or she been in politics? In what role? How might that affect how he or she sees current political events? Some of this information might be hard to find at first, but if a particular journalist appears to have a special agenda, it might be worth the extra research to find out.

- **Is this news, or opinion?** Not every article or segment presented in the news media is actually news—the line between reporting and editorializing has become increasingly blurry. Take a moment to think about the nature of what you're watching or reading. Is the source a journalist, or a columnist or pundit? Is the source reporting facts, or presenting arguments?

- **What's the quality of the reporting?** When news breaks, twenty-four-hour news organizations often emphasize speed over accuracy. Sources that take the time to investigate claims, confirm facts, and verify sources may not be the fastest to report the news, but they are often more accurate than those that react immediately. Watch out, too, for the poorly thought out retweet: even the most reputable news sources have succumbed to the temptation to repeat a fact without verifying it.

- **What is the news of the day?** How do the news stories covered by your source (radio, TV, newspaper, magazine, or web) compare to the stories covered elsewhere? Why are these stories covered and not others? Who makes the decisions? How are the stories framed? Are positive or negative aspects emphasized? What standards do the journalists suggest you use to evaluate the story—that is, what standards do they seem to focus on?

- **What issues are involved?** Can you get beyond the "horse race"? For instance, if reporters are focusing on the delivery of a politician's speech and his or her opponent's reactions to it, try reading the speech yourself (the *New York Times* will usually provide a transcript for major speeches). Similarly, when the media emphasize conflict, ask yourself what underlying issues are involved. Look for primary (original) sources whenever possible, ones that have not been processed by the media for you. If conflicts are presented as a choice between two sides, ask yourself if there are other sides that might be relevant.

- **Who are the story's sources?** Are they "official" sources? Whose point of view do they represent? Are their remarks attributed to them, or are they speaking "on background" (anonymously)? Such sources frequently show up as "highly placed administration officials" or "sources close to the senator." Why would people not want their names disclosed? How should that affect how we interpret what they say? Do you see the same sources appearing in many stories in different types of media? Have these sources been through the "revolving door"? Are they pundits? What audience are they addressing?

- **Is someone putting spin on this story?** Is there visible news management? Is the main source the politician's press office? Is the story based on a leak? If so, can you guess the motivation of the leaker? What evidence supports your guess? What is the spin? That is, what do the politician's handlers want you to think about the issue or event?

- **Who are the advertisers?** How might that affect the coverage of the news? What sorts of stories might be affected by the advertisers' presence? Are there potential stories that might hurt the advertiser?

- **What are the media doing to get your attention?** Is the coverage of a news event detailed and thorough, or is it "lightened up" to make it faster and easier for you to process? If so, what are you missing? What is on the cover of the newspaper or magazine? What is the lead story on the network? How do the media's efforts to get your attention affect the news you get? Would you have read or listened to the story if the media had not worked at getting your attention?

- **What values and beliefs do you bring to the news?** What are your biases? Are you liberal? Conservative? Do you think government is too big, or captured by special interests, always ineffective, or totally irrelevant to your life? Do you have any pet peeves or special interests that direct your attention? How do your current life experiences affect your political views or priorities? How do these values, beliefs, and ideas affect how you see the news, what you pay attention to, and what you skip? Think about all the articles or stories you tuned out, and ask yourself why you did so.

- **Can you find a news source that you usually disagree with, that you think is biased or always wrong?** Read it now and again. It will help you keep your perspective and ensure that you get a mix of views that will keep you thinking critically. We are challenged not by ideas we agree with but by those that we find flawed. Stay an active media consumer.

1. Andrew Beaujon, "Survey: NPR's Listeners Best Informed, Fox News Viewers Worst Informed," May 23, 2012, www.poynter.org/latest-news/mediawire/174826/survey-nprs-listeners-best-informed-fox-news-viewers-worst-informed/.

2. Carlin Romano, "What? The Grisly Truth About Bare Facts," in Robert Karl Manoff and Michael Schudson, eds., *Reading the News* (New York: Pantheon Books, 1986), 78.

much that the media tell us what to think as that they tell us what to think *about*. These scholars have documented four kinds of media effects on our thinking: agenda setting, priming, framing, and persuasion by professional communicators.[75]

AGENDA SETTING Most of us get most of our news from television, but television is limited in the number of the many daily political events it can cover. As political scientists Shanto Iyengar and Donald Kinder say, television news is "news that matters,"[76] which means that television reporters perform the function of agenda setting. When television reporters choose to cover an event, they are telling us that out of all the events happening, this one is important and we should pay attention. A classic example of agenda setting in television news concerns the famine in Ethiopia that hit the American airwaves in 1984 in the form of a freelance film that NBC's Tom Brokaw insisted on showing on *The Nightly News*. Although the Ethiopian famine had been going on for over a decade, it became news only after NBC chose to make it news, and the famine was a major concern for the American public for almost a year. U.S. government food aid rose from $23 million in 1984 to $98 million after the NBC broadcast.[77]

The agenda-setting role of the media is not the last word, however. When Americans lost interest in the famine, the network coverage ceased, although the famine itself did not. Often the media will be fascinated with an event that simply fails to resonate with the public. Despite extensive media coverage of President Bill Clinton's affair with White House intern Monica Lewinsky in 1998, public opinion polls continued to show that the public did not think it was an issue worthy of the time the media spent on it.

PRIMING Closely related to agenda setting, priming refers to the ways that the media influence how people and events should be evaluated by things that they emphasize as important. The theory of priming says that if the media are constantly emphasizing crime, then politicians, and particularly the president, will be evaluated on how well they deal with crime. If the media emphasize the environment, then that will become the relevant yardstick for evaluation. During George W. Bush's presidential campaign, the media emphasized the intelligence of the candidates, causing many of Bush's verbal gaffes to be seen as indications of his intelligence. He continued to misspeak in the same ways after he became president, but once the war on terrorism began, those in the media chose to emphasize different yardsticks—such as leadership and calmness—for evaluating Bush's performance, and his intelligence was no longer seen as an issue. In effect, according to this concept, the media tell us not only what to think about but also how to think about those things. Priming has been supported with empirical evidence,[78] although it is clearly not in effect all the time on all the issues.

FRAMING A third media effect on our thinking is called framing. Just as a painting's appearance can be altered by changing its frame, a political event can look different to us depending on how the media frame it—that is, what they choose to emphasize in their coverage. For example, people view a war differently depending on whether the coverage highlights American casualties or military victories. Similarly, the story of a mother on welfare can emphasize the circumstances of her personal life, leading to the conclusion that she is responsible for her plight, or it can emphasize national data on education, poverty levels, and unemployment, implying that social forces are to blame. The important point about framing is that how the media present a political issue or event may affect how the public perceives that issue, whether they see it as a problem, and who they view as responsible for solving it.

PERSUASION BY PROFESSIONAL COMMUNICATORS Finally, some political scientists argue that the media affect public opinion because viewers, who often don't have the time or background to research the issues themselves, sometimes change their minds to agree with trusted newscasters and expert sources.[79] Familiar with this phenomenon, when President Lyndon Johnson heard popular CBS news anchor Walter Cronkite take a stand against American involvement in Vietnam, he told an aide it was "all over." Predicting that the public would follow the lead of one of the most trusted figures in America, he knew there would be little support for a continued war effort. Often, however, especially in the age of cable news and multiple broadcast choices, the communicators on whom the media rely are not revered figures like "Uncle Walter," but people who regularly pass through the revolving door and whose objectivity cannot be taken for granted.

DO MEDIA EFFECTS MATTER? The effects of agenda setting, priming, framing, and expert persuasion should not be taken to mean that we are all unwitting dupes of the media. In the first place, these are not iron-clad rules; they are tendencies that scholars have discovered and confirmed with experimentation and public opinion surveys. That means that they hold true for many but not all people. Members of the two major political parties, for instance, are less affected by agenda setting than are independents, perhaps because the latter do not have a party to rely on to tell them what is important.[80]

Second, we bring our own armor to the barrage of media effects we face regularly. We all filter our news watching through our own ideas, values, and distinct perspectives.

> **priming** the way in which the media's emphasis on particular characteristics of people, events, or issues influences the public's perception of those people, events, or issues
>
> **framing** process through which the media emphasize particular aspects of a news story, thereby influencing the public's perception of the story

Scholars who emphasize that audiences are active, not passive, consumers of the media say that people counter the effects of the media by setting their own agendas and processing the news in light of those agendas. That is, viewers exercise **selective perception**; they filter information through their own values and interests, thereby determining the news items they will pay attention to, the items they will remember, and the items they will forget.[81] If people do not seem to be well informed on the issues emphasized by the media, it may be that they do not see them as having an effect on their lives. The point is that as consumers, we do more than passively absorb the messages and values provided by the media.

This same point can be made with respect to ideological bias in the news. While researchers have tried to look at whether the ideological slant of a news source makes a difference to one's perception of the news, it is a difficult question to answer since people seem to gravitate to the sources that they agree with. Are their views shaped by bias in the news, or do they choose the bias they prefer to be exposed to? A 2003 study looking at misperceptions about the Iraq war (specifically, beliefs that there was evidence of links between al Qaeda and Saddam Hussein, that weapons of mass destruction had been found in Iraq, and that world opinion favored U.S. action in Iraq) concluded that the frequency with which those beliefs were held varied dramatically with the primary source of a person's news. Watchers of the Fox News Channel (which tended to be more supportive of the Bush administration) held those misperceptions much more frequently than did those who got their news from other sources.[82] (See *Don't Be Fooled by . . . the News Media.*)

THE PORTRAYAL OF POLITICS AS CONFLICT AND IMAGE

In addition to shaping public opinion, the media also affect politics by their tendency to portray complex and substantive political issues as questions of personal image and contests between individuals. Rather than examining the details and nuances of policy differences, the media tend to focus on image and to play up personalities and conflicts even when their readers and viewers say they want something quite different. The effect of this, according to some researchers, is to make politics seem negative and to increase popular cynicism.

> **selective perception** the phenomenon of filtering incoming information through personal values and interests
>
> **horse-race journalism** the media's focus on the competitive aspects of politics rather than on actual policy proposals and political decisions

HORSE-RACE JOURNALISM Horse-race journalism refers to the media's tendency to see politics as competition between individuals. Rather than reporting on the policy differences between politicians or the effects their proposals will have on ordinary Americans, today's media tend to report on politics as if it were a battle between individual gladiators or a game of strategy and wit but not substance. This sort of journalism not only shows politics in the most negative light, as if politicians cared only to score victories off one another in a never-ending fight to promote their own self-interests, but it also ignores the concerns that citizens have about politics.

As journalist James Fallows points out, when citizens are given a chance to ask questions of politicians, they focus on all the elements of politics that touch their lives: taxes, wars, Social Security, student loans, education, and welfare.[83] But journalists focus on questions of strategy, popularity, and relative positioning in relation to real or imagined rivals. Fallows gives the following example of coverage of the 1996 presidential campaign. When interviewed by former CBS anchor Dan Rather about Bill Clinton's reelection campaign, the late Sen. Ted Kennedy, D-Mass., started to speak about the balanced budget amendment, which was supported by many Americans but not by the president. Rather responded, "Senator, you know I'd talk about these things the rest of the afternoon, but let's move quickly to politics. Do you expect Bill Clinton to be the Democratic nominee for reelection in 1996?"[84] The obsession with who is winning makes the coverage of campaigns, or of partisan battles in Congress, or of disputes between the president and Congress far more trivial than it needs to be, and far less educational to the American public. (*Don't Be Fooled . . . by the News Media* will help you get beyond the horse-race coverage in much of today's media.)

THE EMPHASIS ON IMAGE Television is primarily an entertainment medium and, by its nature, one that is focused on image: what people look like, what they sound like, and how an event is staged and presented. Television, and to some extent its competition in the print media, concentrates on doing what it does well: giving us pictures of politics instead of delving beneath the surface. This has the effect of leading us to value the more superficial aspects of politics, even if only subconsciously. An early and telling example was the 1960 presidential debate between Richard Nixon and John F. Kennedy, when the young and telegenic Kennedy presented a more presidential image than the swarthy and sweating Nixon and won both the debate and the election. Combine this emphasis on image with horse-race journalism, and the result is a preoccupation with appearance and strategy at the cost of substance. In the 2000 debates, the media focused on candidate Al Gore's impatient behavior while George W. Bush was speaking, rather than on the substance of what either candidate had to say. History repeated itself in the coverage of the 2008 debates, when commentators fixed on the visible contempt

THE CHRISTIAN SCIENCE MONITOR BENNETT

'...Political campaigns have become so simplistic and superficial... In the 20 seconds we have left, could you explain why?..

features—such as medical advances, pet stories, and scandals—that they believe will attract viewers, networks must reduce the time available for the major news events of the day—what one critic calls an effort to "dumb down the content" of news.[87]

SCANDAL WATCHING Reporters also tend to concentrate on developing scandals to the exclusion of other, possibly more relevant, news events. At the end of the summer of 2008, when former Democratic candidate John Edwards revealed that he had had an affair with a campaign staffer, media attention focused immediately and obsessively on Edwards, who had been out of the race for months, rather than on the two candidates, Obama and McCain, who were still contending for the presidency. Political scientist Larry Sabato refers to this behavior as a **feeding frenzy**: "the press coverage attending any political event or circumstance where a critical mass of journalists leap to cover the same embarrassing or scandalous subject and pursue it intensely, often excessively, and sometimes uncontrollably."[88] Many such feeding frenzies have been over scandals that have proved not to be true or seemed insignificant with the passing of time, and yet the media have treated them with the seriousness of a world crisis. Reputations have been shredded, justly or unjustly, but once the frenzy has begun, it is difficult to bring rational judgment to bear on the case. After such attacks, the media frequently indulge in introspection and remorse, until the next scandal starts to brew.

GROWING NEGATIVISM, INCREASED CYNICISM Political scientist Thomas Patterson attributes the phenomenon of the feeding frenzy to an increased cynicism among members of the media. He argues that it is not a liberal or a conservative bias among reporters that we ought to worry about. Rather, it is their antigovernment views—focusing on the adversarial and negative aspects of politics to the exclusion of its positive achievements—that foster a cynical view of politics among the general public. Most presidents and presidential candidates are treated by the press as fundamentally untrustworthy, when in fact most do precisely what they say they are going to do.

that John McCain showed for Barack Obama. Viewers named the calmer, more comfortable-looking Obama the winner of the debates by a large margin. Similarly, Mitt Romney benefited from his first debate appearance in 2012, when his competent and presidential demeanor convinced watchers that he'd won the debate over a more subdued Obama and persuaded wavering Republicans to support him—although it wasn't sufficient to win the election for him, especially in light of Obama's much stronger performance in the last two debates.

The words of politicians are being similarly reduced to the audio equivalent of a snapshot, the **sound bite**. A sound bite is a short block of speech by a politician that makes it on the news. Like the film clips of Gore's debate behavior, these are often played repetitively and can drown out the substance of the message a politician wishes to convey. Occasionally they can come back to haunt a politician, as did George H. W. Bush's famous 1988 promise, "Read my lips, no new taxes," broken in 1992 when, as president, he did, in fact, support a tax hike. The amount of time that the electronic media devote to the actual words a politician utters is shrinking. In 2000 the average length for a sound bite from a presidential candidate on the nightly network news was 7.3 seconds, down from 10 seconds in 1992 and 42 seconds in 1968.[85] Journalists use the extra time to interpret what we have heard and often to put it into the horse-race metaphor we just discussed.[86]

The emphasis on superficial image is exacerbated by the competition among media outlets. Ratings wars have led television news shows to further reduce the substance of their coverage under the assumption that audiences want more "light" news. To make way for the human interest

> **sound bite** a brief, snappy excerpt from a public figure's speech that is easy to repeat on the news
>
> **feeding frenzy** excessive press coverage of an embarrassing or scandalous subject

Soundbite Journalism

Clinton, in his first year, was plagued by press criticism despite the fact that he kept a majority of his campaign promises and was more successful in getting his legislative packages through Congress that year than Kennedy, Nixon, Ford, Carter, Reagan, or Bush had been in their best years. Yet in the first six months of his presidency, 66 percent of his news evaluations were negative.[89] Since it takes time and energy to investigate all the claims that a president or a candidate makes, the media evaluate political claims not with their own careful scrutiny but with statements from political opponents. This makes politics appear endlessly adversarial and, as Patterson says, replaces investigative journalism with attack journalism.[90]

Nixon Presidential Library and Museum

News That Would Not Be Managed

The Nixon administration ran a tight ship when it came to managing the president's image, but even they could not spin the story after Watergate broke. Here, Nixon press secretary Ron Ziegler and staffers Frank Gannon and Diane Sawyer catch their breath after the president announced his resignation in 1974. (Sawyer passed through the revolving door to journalism and is former the anchor of *ABC World News*.)

CONSEQUENCES OF THE EMPHASIS ON CONFLICT AND IMAGE A consequence of the negative content of political coverage is that voters' opinions of candidates have sunk, and citizen dissatisfaction with the electoral process has risen.[91] Not only is the public becoming more cynical about the political world, but it is also becoming more cynical about the media. A recent public opinion poll shows that half or more of the American public now thinks that the news is too biased, sensationalized, and manipulated by special interests, and that reporters offer too many of their own opinions, quote unnamed sources, and are negative.[92] Two scholars argue that the "conflict-driven sound-bite-oriented discourse of politicians," in conjunction with the "conflict-saturated strategy-oriented structure of press coverage," creates a mutually reinforcing lack of confidence in the system that they call the "spiral of cynicism."[93] But as we argued at the beginning of this chapter, the media have a real and legitimate role to play in a democracy: disseminating information, checking government, and creating political community. If people cease to trust the media, the media become less effective in playing their legitimate roles as well as their more controversial ones, and democracy becomes more difficult to sustain.

Another consequence, and one that may alleviate the first somewhat, is that new forms of the media are opening up to supplement or even replace the older ones. Television talk shows, radio call-in shows, and other outlets that involve public input and bypass the adversarial questions and negative comments of the traditional media allow the public, in some ways, to set the agenda. In fact, a study of the 1992 election showed that television talk shows focused more on substantive policy issues and presented more balanced and positive images of the candidates than did the mainstream media.[94]

POLITICS AS PUBLIC RELATIONS

There is no doubt that the media portray politics in a negative light, that news reporting emphasizes personality, superficial image, and conflict over substantive policy issues. Some media figures argue, however, that this is not the media's fault, but rather the responsibility of politicians and their press officers who are so obsessed with their own images on television that they limit access to the media, speak only in prearranged sound bites, and present themselves to the public in carefully orchestrated "media events."[95] Media events are designed to limit the ability of reporters to put their own interpretation on the occasion. The rules of American politics, which require a politician to have high public approval to maximize his or her clout, mean that politicians have to try to get maximum exposure for their ideas and accomplishments while limiting the damage the media can do with their intense scrutiny, investigations, and critical perspectives. This effort to control the media can lead to an emphasis on short-term gain over long-term priorities and the making of policy decisions with an eye to their political impact—a tendency that has come to be known as the **permanent campaign**.[96] A first-rate example of how the permanent campaign drove events in the George W. Bush administration can be found in *What Happened: Inside the Bush White House and Washington's Culture of Deception*, the memoirs of Bush's former press secretary, Scott McClellan.[97]

NEWS MANAGEMENT News management describes the chief mechanism of the permanent campaign, the efforts of a politician's staff—media consultants, press secretaries, pollsters, campaign strategists, and general advisers—to control the news about the politician. The staff want to put their own issues on the agenda, determine for themselves the standards by which the politician will be evaluated, frame the issues, and supply the sources for reporters, so that they will put their client, the politician, in the best possible light. In contemporary political jargon, they want to put a **spin**, or an interpretation, on the news that will be most flattering to the politician whose image is in their care. To some extent, modern American politics has become a battle between the press and the politicians and among the politicians themselves to control the agenda and the images that reach the public. It has become a battle of the "spin doctors." The classic example of news management is the rehabilitation of the image of Richard Nixon after he lost the 1960 election to the more media-savvy Kennedy campaign. Inspired by the way the Kennedy administration had managed the image of Kennedy as war hero, patriot, devoted father, and faithful husband, when at least one of those characterizations wasn't true, Nixon speechwriter Ray Price saw his mission clearly. Noting that Nixon was personally unpopular with the public, he wrote in a 1967 memo, "We have to be very clear on this point: that the response is to the image, not to the man, since 99 percent of the voters have no contact with the man. It's not what's there that counts, it's what's projected—and it's not what he projects but rather what the voter receives. It's not the man we have to change, but rather the received impression."[98] With the help of an advertising executive and a television producer, among others, Nixon was repackaged and sold to voters as the "New Nixon." He won election as president in 1968 and 1972, and that he had to resign in 1974 is perhaps less a failure of his image makers than the inevitable revelation of the "real" Nixon underneath.

NEWS MANAGEMENT TECHNIQUES

The techniques that Nixon's handlers developed for managing his image have become part of the basic repertoire of political staffs, particularly in the White House but even to some extent for holders of lesser offices. They can include any or all of the following:[99]

- *Tight control of information.* Staffers pick a "line of the day"—for instance, a focus on education or child care—and orchestrate all messages from the administration around that theme. This strategy frustrates journalists who are trying to follow independent

stories. But it recognizes that the staff must "feed the beast" by giving the press something to cover, or they may find the press rebelling and covering stories they don't want covered at all.[100]

- *Tight control of access to the politician.* If the politician is available to the press for only a short period of time and makes only a brief statement, the press corps is forced to report the appearance as the only available news.

- *Elaborate communications bureaucracy.* The Nixon White House had four offices handling communications. In addition to the White House press secretary, who was frequently kept uninformed so that he could more credibly deny that he knew the answers to reporters' questions, there was an Office of Communications, an Office of Public Liaison, and a speechwriting office.

- *A concerted effort to bypass the White House press corps.* During Nixon's years this meant going to regional papers that were more easily manipulated. Today it can also include the so-called new media of television talk shows and late-night television, and other forums that go directly to the public, such as town hall meetings. Part and parcel of this approach is the strategy of rewarding media outlets that provide friendly coverage and punishing those that do not.

- *Prepackaging the news in sound bites.* If the media are going to allow the public only a brief snippet of political language, the reasoning goes, let the politician's staff decide what it will be. In line with this, the press office will repeat a message often, to be sure the press and the public pick up on it, and it will work on phrasing that is catchy and memorable.

- *Leaks.* A final and effective way that politicians attempt to control the news is with the use of leaks, secretly revealing confidential information to the press. **Leaks** can serve a variety of purposes. For instance, a leak can be a **trial balloon**, in which an official leaks a policy or plan in order to gauge public reaction to it. If the reaction is negative, the official

---

permanent campaign the idea that governing requires a continual effort to convince the public to sign on to the program, requiring a reliance on consultants and an emphasis on politics over policy

news management the efforts of a politician's staff to control news about the politician

spin an interpretation of a politician's words or actions, designed to present a favorable image

leaks confidential information secretly revealed to the press

trial balloon an official leak of a proposal to determine public reaction to it without risk

denies he or she ever mentioned it, and if it is positive, the policy can go ahead without risk. Bureaucrats who want to anonymously stop a practice they believe is wrong may use a "whistleblower leak." Information can be leaked to settle grudges, or to curry favor, or just to show off.[101] The George W. Bush administration, for instance, annoyed at former ambassador Joe Wilson's views on the Iraq war, leaked the identity of his wife, Valerie Plame, as a CIA agent to discredit Wilson's opinions on the Iraq war, a classic example of leaking information in an effort to control the news.

Not all presidential administrations are equally accomplished at using these techniques of news management, of course. Nixon's was successful, at least in his first administration, and Reagan's has been referred to as a model of public relations.[102] President Clinton did not manage the media effectively in the early years of his first administration; consequently, he was at the mercy of a frustrated and annoyed press corps. Within a couple of years, however, the Clinton staff had become much more skilled, and by his second administration they were adeptly handling scandals that would have daunted more seasoned public relations experts.

THINKING OUTSIDE THE BOX

Should journalists rely on anonymous sources?

NEWS MANAGEMENT IN THE BUSH ADMINISTRATION AND BEYOND The George W. Bush administration did a superb job of news management, especially in Bush's first term. For instance, most of Bush's public events were open only to Bush supporters; where there was audience interaction, he received questions only from those who endorsed his programs and goals. In addition, in 2005 it was revealed that the Bush administration had paid several journalists to report favorably on the president's policies, and the administration expanded a Clinton-era program of government-produced videos touting administration achievements that were distributed to local television stations, which showed them as actual news.[103] The Government Accountability Office has said that such videos may be "covert propaganda" and cannot be made if they do not disclose who made them, but the Department of Justice and the Office of Management and Budget has

said that the agencies may ignore that finding.[104] Finally, reporters who could be trusted to ask supportive questions were favored in White House news briefings and press conferences.[105] Supporters defended the Bush White House's news management strategy as efficient and praiseworthy. Critics, on the other hand, claimed that the White House had become a "propaganda machine" to serve the president's political goals.[106] "George W. Bush doesn't really want people to get the news unfiltered. He wants people to get the news filtered by George W. Bush," said one.[107]

Barack Obama's White House has been as disciplined as Bush's was, although his public events are not vetted for supporters and the president faces more negative questions because of it. During the presidential campaign, the Obama camp was famous for avoiding leaks and controlling its message and, although that perfect discipline has not been maintained in the White House, it is still remarkably free of public infighting and leaks. Obama's first press secretary, Robert Gibbs, was a senior adviser to the president and had uncommon access and a dedication to protecting Obama's interests, though his second, Jay Carney, and his third, Josh Earnest, are more traditional spokespeople.[108] One difference between the Obama administration and its predecessors is the elaborate electronic communication network it has set up, which allows administration officials to talk directly to supporters and to bypass the traditional media if they want to, texting and tweeting as well as sending emails and posting information, videos, and pictures to the White House web site. Still, many critics have noted that for all his eloquent speaking ability, Obama seems strangely reluctant to use it to advance or explain his agenda.[109]

There is a real cost to the transformation of politics into public relations, no matter whose administration is engaging in the practice (and with varying degrees of expertise, they all do). Not only does the public suffer from not getting the straight story to evaluate government policies that affect their lives, but politicians must spend time and energy on image considerations that do not really help them serve the public. And the people who are skilled enough at managing the press to get elected to office have not necessarily demonstrated any leadership skills. The skills required by an actor and a statesperson are not the same, and the current system may encourage us to choose the wrong leaders for the wrong reasons and discourage the right people from running at all.

REDUCTION IN POLITICAL ACCOUNTABILITY

A final political effect of the media, according to some scholars, is a reduction in political accountability. **Political accountability** is the very hallmark of democracy: political leaders must answer to the public for their actions. If our leaders do something we do not like, we can make them bear the consequences of their actions by voting them out of office. The threat of being voted out of office is supposed to encourage them to do what we want in the first place.

> **political accountability** the democratic principle that political leaders must answer to the public for their actions

political actions, and harder to make politicians behave responsibly.

Selling It on Sunday Morning

Politicians seeking to round up support for, or clarify their position on, particular issues are able to sound off to the press—and a large and politically engaged audience—by appearing on popular Sunday morning political programs on major networks. Sen. John McCain, R-Ariz., shown here with NBC's Andrea Mitchell on *Meet the Press*, has proven to be one of the most prolific news program guests, making twenty-four appearances on the Sunday morning circuit in 2013 alone.

Some political scientists, however, argue that Americans' reliance on television for their news has weakened political accountability, and thus democracy as well.[110] Their arguments are complex but compelling.

First, they say that television has come to reduce the influence of political parties, since it allows politicians to take their message directly to the people. Parties are no longer absolutely necessary to mediate politics—that is, to provide a link between leaders and the people—but parties have traditionally been a way to keep politicians accountable.

Second, television covers politicians as individuals, and as individuals, they have incentives to take credit for what the public likes and to blame others for what the public doesn't like. And because they are covered as individuals, they have little reason to form coalitions to work together.

Third, television, by emphasizing image and style, allows politicians to avoid taking stances on substantive policy issues; the public often does not know where they stand and cannot hold them accountable.

Finally, the episodic way in which the media frame political events makes it difficult for people to discern what has really happened politically and whose responsibility it is.

The result is that the modern media, and especially television, have changed the rules of politics. Today it is harder for citizens to know who is responsible for laws, policies, and

PAUSE AND REVIEW:

WHO, WHAT, HOW

Where the worlds of politics and the media intersect, there are many actors with something serious at stake. Journalists, of course, want bylines or airtime, the respect of their peers, and professional acclaim, at the same time that they want to help keep their news organizations competitive and profitable. Their goals and rules clash with those of politicians, who need to communicate with the public; to present themselves as attractive, effective leaders; and to make their ideas and proposed policies clear to voters. The clash of journalists' and politicians' goals means that each side often feels exploited or treated unfairly by the other, making for an uneasy relationship between the two.

What is at stake for citizens is not only their ability to get information on which to base their political decisions, but also their ability to see good as well as bad in government, to know their leaders as they really are and not just their public relations images, and to hold them accountable. The rules put the burden of responsibility on citizens to be critical consumers of the media.

IN YOUR OWN WORDS » Describe the link between media and politics.

» THE CITIZENS AND THE MEDIA

Growing citizen access increases engagement but blurs lines of journalism

We have been unable to talk about the media in this chapter without talking about citizenship. Citizens have been a constant "who" in our analysis because the media exist, by definition, to give information to citizens and to mediate their relationship to government. But if we evaluate the traditional role of the media with respect to the public, the relationship that emerges is not a particularly responsive one. Almost from the beginning, control of the American media has been in the hands of an elite group, whether party leaders, politicians, wealthy entrepreneurs, or corporate owners. Financial

Journalism's Highest Cost

The abduction and brutal murder of American journalist James Foley at the hands of Islamic State militants in 2014 (after holding him hostage for nearly two years) highlights the risks involved in reporting news. Right, a man lays flowers near a photo of Foley during a memorial service held in Irbil, Iraq, a few days after his death. On the left, Foley meets with students who had worked to free him after he was taken captive in Libya and held for forty-four days in 2011.

concerns have meant that the media in the United States have been driven more by profit motive than by public interest. Not only are ownership and control of the media far removed from the hands of everyday Americans, but the reporting of national news is done mostly by reporters who do not fit the profile of those "average" citizens and whose concerns often do not reflect the concerns of their audience.

Citizens' access to the media has been correspondingly remote. The primary role available to them has been passive: that of reader, listener, or watcher. The power they wield is the power of switching newspapers or changing channels, essentially choosing among competing elites; but this is not an active, participatory role. While freedom of the press is a right technically held by all citizens, there is no right of access to the press. Citizens have difficulty making their voices heard, and, of course, most do not even try. Members of the media holler long and loud about their right to publish what they want, but only sporadically and briefly do they consider their obligations to the public to provide the sort of information that can sustain a democracy. If active democracy requires a political community in which the public can deliberate about important issues, it would seem that the American media are failing miserably at creating that community.

The rapid changes in information technology that we have discussed throughout this chapter offer some hope that the media can be made to serve the public interest more effectively. As we saw in this chapter's *What's at Stake...?* feature, the media are in flux and, while the future of the print media is in question, some of the new media that are replacing it are remarkably more open and responsive. Along with social networks, some of these new media—such as cable news, specialized television programs, and Internet news—allow citizens to get fast-breaking reports of events as they occur and even to customize the news that they get. Talk radio and call-in television

shows—new uses of the "old" media—allow citizen interaction, as do Internet chat rooms and other online forums. Many web sites allow users to give their opinions of issues in unscientific straw polls. Some analysts speculate that it is only a matter of time until we can all vote on issues from our home computers. The one thing that these new forms of media have in common is that they bypass the old, making the corporate journalistic establishment less powerful than it was but perhaps giving rise to new elites and raising new questions about participation and how much access we really want citizens to have.

One of the most significant developments in the new media is the proliferation of web logs, or blogs (see *"Profiles in Citizenship:* Andrew Sullivan"), which we mentioned earlier. It is truly citizen journalism—the cyber-equivalent of giving everyday people their own printing presses and the means to publish their views. While blogs can be on any subject, the ones that interest us here are the ones that focus on politics and media criticism. As is true of any unregulated media source, there is a good deal of inaccurate and unsubstantiated information in the so-called blogosphere. There is no credentialing process for bloggers, they are not usually admitted to the White House or other official news conferences unless they also report for a more traditional media outlet, and they generally lack the resources required to do a great deal of investigative reporting.

But blogs can also do many things that their more mainstream brethren cannot, and there is some truly first-rate journalism to be found on blogs. Since bloggers are not (usually) indebted to deep corporate pockets, they can hold the mainstream media accountable. For example, when CBS's Dan Rather reported in the fall of 2004 on documents that seemed to support the claim that George W. Bush had used influence to escape the draft, it was bloggers who discovered that the evidence was fraudulent. It is the job of

PROFILES IN CITIZENSHIP:
ANDREW SULLIVAN

Andrew H. Walker/Getty Images Entertainment/Getty Images

It's hard not to feel like a stalker when you are meeting a blogger whose work you have followed for a decade. You have seen his wedding pictures, laughed at his dogs' antics, know all about his health status, and keep up with his political views. He, on the other hand, may have read and even answered some of your emails over the years but, really, he has no clue who you are. So, getting the chance to sit down for coffee with Andrew

Sullivan, the founder and editor of the *Daily Dish* (www.andrewsullivan.com), which marked its ten-year anniversary in 2010, is just a little creepy, in a nice and reassuring way—like meeting a total stranger who has the face of an old friend.

But Sullivan, the man who describes his job as "having a conversation with 1.2 million people a month," totally gets that. He knows that his job is breaking down traditional boundaries between journalism and political activism, between reporting and analysis, between the personal and the public, and yes, between stranger and friend.

But blogging seems to be a perfect medium for Sullivan, who has in his time aspired to be both politician and writer. He is Oxford educated, with a Ph.D. in government from Harvard, and before turning thirty, he was the editor of the *New Republic*. But his academic heft and considerable brilliance is balanced with a passionate zeal for the issues he cares about. Blogging lets him combine advocacy and fact-sifting in a form of journalism that, when done well, breaks with the old models of news-gathering and dissemination in startling ways.

So, Sullivan is not at all shy about airing his opinions—he is a pro-life Catholic, a conservative, British-born, America-loving, married gay man who is a civil libertarian and a fiscal conservative with a deep thread of compassion and humanitarianism running through it

all. But while opinionated, he is not a partisan (though he claims an affinity for British Toryism). He refuses to appear on partisan cable television shows (though he is a frequent guest on *Real Time With Bill Maher*), and he shows a remarkable ability to change his mind about deeply held views if new evidence appears or he meets a persuasive counterargument. He was a strong supporter of George W. Bush and the Iraq war in its early years, for instance, and then an even stronger opponent of both when he began to doubt the evidence that had brought us to invade Iraq. Likewise, he is pro-life, but when his readers' stories convinced him that his position against late-term abortion was wrong, he changed his position on that, too.

What Sullivan calls his "readership of extraordinarily smart and humane and interesting people" is the lifeblood of his blog. When he seeks information, they provide it; when he is wrong, they correct him; when something is happening in the world that he cares about, they gather round in a virtual community to share the incoming news. After the 2009 Iranian election resulted in streets full of green-garbed protesters demonstrating against the regime, his site became the go-to place for updates on what was happening. Facing local news blackouts, demonstrators blogged, tweeted, and texted information that found its way to Sullivan and, in solidarity with a revolution he supported passionately, he turned his site green for the duration.

---

the consumer to scrutinize the reporting of bloggers as scrupulously as they do the rest of the media, however. There is no substitute for critical evaluation of the news, but blogs are a media form that is truly independent, open, and democratic in a way that no other media source can be.

IN YOUR OWN WORDS » Discuss the relationship between citizens and the media.

THINKING OUTSIDE THE BOX

Should the media be driven by what consumers want to know or what they need to know?

Media With Meaning ●

He says: "We were also, amazingly, the prime source of information for people in Iran itself because their networks were being stymied. People who were in Lebanon and Syria who couldn't get to their news sites went to me. My colleagues Patrick and Chris, we took eight-hour shifts around twenty-four hours. . . . And in one of the more iconic moments when Neda [Agha-Soltan, a bystander at the protests] was shot by a government sniper and fell to the ground, I got this staggering picture on the blog. We were among the first to broadcast it within minutes of it occurring. Now that's to bring a moment in a revolution instantly to a global audience of millions . . . it was totally an organic process in which we were essentially a filter and I think it was a breakthrough moment for the media."

For Sullivan, blogging is a democratic as well as a journalistic phenomenon. In 2002 he wrote in the *London Times* that "what bloggers do is completely new—and cannot be replicated on any other medium. It's somewhere in between writing a column and talk radio. It's genuinely new. And it harnesses the web's real genius—its ability to empower anyone to do what only a few in the past could genuinely pull off. In that sense, blogging is the first journalistic model that actually harnesses rather than merely exploits the true democratic nature of the web. It's a new medium finally finding a unique voice.

"Stay tuned as that voice gets louder and louder."[1]

Here are some other thoughts from Andrew Sullivan:

On patriotism:

It's not the same thing as nationalism. It is not that your country is always right. . . . I think at some level it is simply loving—and I mean that in a deep sense—the culture, tradition, constitution, and people of the place you call home. In a way I must say I have two patriotisms—of the country I came from and the country I'm still trying to become a citizen of. And patriotism, yes, does mean sometimes dissenting from one's country's leadership, but I think it's too facile to say it's the highest form. I think another equally valid form is supporting your country when the chips are down, even when it isn't perfect, even when it does make mistakes, because it's yours.

On keeping the republic:

America is actually in I think a quite extraordinary crisis right now—spiritually, politically, and economically. I don't think it's been this acute since maybe the late 70s or 60s. . . . I do think people have to understand if they are not there the discourse will be captured by someone else. And you have a responsibility—I've lived long enough to understand that. And it's easy to insulate oneself and delude oneself into thinking it doesn't really matter or I don't have to do something—but in fact you do.

One of the ways this really struck home for me was, personally, in the late 80s, early 90s, the AIDS crisis. I realized if I didn't help these people who were dying no one would. . . . And then when I contracted it, and thought I was given a few years, I sat down and wrote [his book] *Virtually Normal*, because I wanted to leave behind a contribution to an argument [about gay rights]. . . . I had nothing to lose because I thought I was going to die. But why should I have had to get to that point? So imagine that you have a couple of years left on this Earth, what are you waiting for?

1. Andrew Sullivan, "A Blogger's Manifesto," *Sunday Times of London*, February 24, 2002.

Source: Andrew Sullivan talked with Christine Barbour in August 2010.

LET'S REVISIT: **WHAT'S AT STAKE...**

In this chapter we have seen that the world of information has undergone enormous, one might almost say revolutionary, change in the past half-century, and the rollercoaster ride hasn't come to an end. There are so many new ways to get information that the real challenge seems to be to processing it and evaluating it. Worrying about the fate of something as old-fashioned as a newspaper seems almost beside the point.

But what is at stake in the impending demise of newspapers as a business model is more than it might seem on its face. The issue is not about newspapers, per se—but about the news they report. As Clay Shirky, an Internet expert and writer, says, "Society doesn't need newspapers. What we need is journalism."[111] By this he means information, well researched and objective, about the world we live in, about the things our elected officials are doing in our name, about the consequences of the public choices we make.

Journalism has traditionally been paid for by newspapers that have either had their own news bureaus around the world or subscribed to and supported a news service like the AP. The money they paid for news-gathering came from advertisers who paid their rates because they had no other way to reach their markets. Now that those advertisers have multiple, cheap outlets in which to market their wares, newspapers, and thus journalism, are in danger. But journalism today is also in danger from forces within. As we have seen, the mainstream media, the conventional media of which print has always been the backbone, are concentrated in corporate ownership and driven by their quest for advertising dollars to simplify and "dummy down" the news, often becoming uncomfortably close to their sources in the process. The quality of journalism has been threatened by more than the decline of the print media.

Shirky argues that we are in the midst of a revolution, "where the old stuff gets broken faster than the new stuff is put in its place,"[112] so we don't know what journalism will look like in a new, post-newspaper age. But Shirky thinks it's a mistake to assume that we aren't transitioning to such an age, that those who proclaim loudly that the old newspaper model can be saved are whistling past the graveyard, refusing to acknowledge that printing presses are costly to run and that the model of newspaper-centered news is obsolete in a world where the Internet makes it impossible for them to charge for or to retain control over the work they do.

And as we saw, some observers believe that the revolution is bringing positive changes. Media critic Dan Gillmor argues that a powerful, citizen-driven journalism is taking the place of a complacent, ratings-driven corporate journalism, that information is gathered and disseminated in real time with multiple researchers on the job to correct and assist each other, a sort of Wikipedia journalism, perhaps.[113] This is the model, for instance, of Andrew Sullivan, who "live blogged" the Iranian uprising in 2009, passing on to his readers information tweeted to him from the front lines, information that could not have been easily gathered even with a news bureau in Tehran. Sullivan would agree with Gillmor, arguing that blogging is "the first journalistic model that actually harnesses rather than exploits the true democratic nature of the web."[114]

For Sullivan, the demise of the old media and the rise of the new is a positive development, making him more hopeful for democracy, not less. He says,

> But what distinguishes the best of the new media is what could still be recaptured by the old: the mischievous *spirit* of journalism and free, unfettered inquiry. Journalism has gotten too pompous, too affluent, too self-loving, and too entwined with the establishment of both wings of American politics to be what we need it to be.
>
> We need it to be fearless and obnoxious, out of a conviction that more speech, however much vulgarity and nonsense it creates, is always better than less speech. In America, this is a liberal spirit in the grandest sense of that word—but also a conservative one, since retaining that rebelliousness is tending to an ancient American tradition, from the Founders onward.[115]

Shirky is optimistic as well:

> For the next few decades, journalism will be made up of overlapping special cases. Many of these models will rely on amateurs as researchers and writers. Many of these models will rely on sponsorship or grants or endowments instead of revenues. Many of these models will rely on excitable 14 year olds distributing the results. Many of these models will fail. No one experiment is going to replace what we are now losing with the demise of news on paper, but over time, the collection of new experiments that do might give us the journalism we need.[116]

And then again, they may not—Shirky's optimism does not seem misplaced in light of the work of writers such as Gillmor and Sullivan, but the truth is that what's at stake in the end of the newspaper model may be the very information we need to make the intelligent decisions that allow democracy to thrive. The jury is out on this one, but the open, innovative nature of the medium allows each of us to engage in the experimentation and work that might bring the answers. The late media critic Marshall McLuhan wrote in the 1960s that "the medium is the message." In the Internet age, that has the potential to be true as never before.

SAGE edge™
for CQ Press

Sharpen your skills with **SAGE edge** at http://edge.sagepub.com/barbour7e. **SAGE edge for students** provides a personalized approach to help you accomplish your coursework goals in an easy-to-use learning environment.

Where Do We Get Our Information?

An increasing number of Americans have access to the web via any number of devices, and the convergence of mass media in the digital age means that we have more information at our fingertips than ever before. More media outlets and more information means that Americans must devote ever-increasing amounts of time and effort to sorting out what is relevant to them. Traditional news media—especially newspapers—must struggle to survive in an era of free online content.

media convergence (p. 556)
mass media (p. 557)
narrowcasting (p. 560)
news organziations (p. 561)
blogs (p. 563)
news aggregators (p. 563)

Who Owns the Media, and How Does That Affect Our News?

The early American press was highly partisan, but when newspapers suddenly became cheap and thus accessible to the general public in the 1830s, papers aimed for objectivity as a way to attract more readers. Later, newspaper owners used sensationalist reporting to sell more newspapers and gain independence from political interests. Today's media is largely still profit driven, and while small and independent news sources are gaining traction through digital media, the biggest news organizations are still owned by a few large corporate interests. The 1934 Federal Communications Act, which created the Federal Communications Commission, imposed order on multiple media outlets and attempted to serve the public interest through three provisions: the equal time rule, the fairness doctrine, and the right of rebuttal.

commercial bias (p. 565)

Who Are the Journalists?

Journalists, playing four roles, have great influence over news content and presentation.

Gatekeepers decide what is news and what is not. Disseminators determine relevant news and get it out to the public quickly. The investigator role involves verifying the truth of various claims or analyzing particular policies. Finally, as public mobilizers, journalists try to report the people's interests rather than their own.

gatekeepers (p. 570)
muckrakers (p. 571)
civic journalism (p. 571)
revolving door (p. 574)
pundit (p. 575)

The Media and Politics

Public skepticism of the media has increased in recent decades. Some critics believe the homogeneous background of journalists—mostly male, white, well educated, with northeastern roots—biases the press, as does their predominantly liberal ideology. Others claim that the revolving door, the practice of journalists taking government positions but later returning to reporting, severely damages news objectivity.

priming (p. 578)
framing (p. 578)
selective perception (p. 579)
horse-race journalism (p. 579)
sound bite (p. 580)
feeding frenzy (p. 580)
permanent campaign (p. 582)
news management (p. 582)
spin (p. 582)
leaks (p. 582)
trial balloon (p. 582)
political accountability (p. 583)

The Citizens and the Media

Citizen historically have played a passive role in the media as consumers of information. But the rise of new, interactive media and the growth of the civic journalism movement may help to transform citizens into more active media participants.

REVIEW

ENGAGE

Understand journalism better. Despite journalism's sometimes shabby reputation, the truth is that it is can, and should, be an honorable and ethical profession. Get to know what the best reporters and editors think by following the **Columbia Journalism Review,** which bills itself as "a watchdog and a friend of the press in all its forms," and frequently publishes articles on issues that lie right at the intersection of media and politics. Another great resource is the **Poynter Institute**, a nonprofit school for journalists and teachers of journalists, which offers useful information on issues of diversity, ethics, and interpreting the media. Interested in the history of journalism? **PBS's media timeline** provides a quick but intensive overview.

Be a critical news consumer. Whenever you read, watch, listen, or click on a news story, remind yourself of the CLUES questions posed throughout this book: Consider the source and the audience; Lay out the argument and the underlying values and assumptions; Uncover the evidence; Evaluate the conclusion, and Sort out the implications.

Arm yourself to understand breaking news. National Public Radio's *On the Media* provides ongoing coverage of media issues ranging from blockbuster films to interactive journalism. Subscribe to the podcast for regular doses of media news, and take a few minutes to check out their downloadable guide, *The Breaking News Consumers Handbook,* for a useful set of guidelines for understanding news as it is happening.

EXPLORE

Schaefer, Todd, and Thomas Birkland. 2007. *Encyclopedia of Media and Politics.* **Washington, DC: CQ Press.** An authoritative guide to the relationship between media and politics, this reference covers diverse topics ranging from media-related legislation to profiles of influential media outlets.

West, Darrell M. 2013. *Air Wars: Television Advertising and Social Media in Election Campaigns, 1952–2012,* **6th ed. Washington, D.C.: CQ Press.** West's book is a comprehensive and informative source on the use of television and social media advertising in campaigns and how political ads have changed over time.

ETalkingHeads' Political Blog Directory. Are you interested in exploring how pundits and novices alike use new forms of digital media to talk politics? This comprehensive political blog directory offers links to political blogs sorted by political orientation (for example, left-leaning, right-leaning, moderate).

A Mighty Heart. **2007.** This well-received film artfully explores the relationship between media and politics through the real-life story of Daniel Pearl, a *Wall Street Journal* reporter who was brutally murdered at the hands of Pakistani militants in 2002.

Good Night and Good Luck. **2006.** George Clooney directed this fascinating portrayal of CBS newscaster Edward R. Murrow's fight against McCarthyism and the wave of anticommunist sentiment that pervaded American society in the early 1950s.

All the President's Men. **1976.** This film tells the story of how investigative reporting by two young *Washington Post* journalists led to the downfall of Richard Nixon. After the movie (as well as the book) was released, the number of people entering the field of journalism increased dramatically.

The Daily Show with Jon Stewart **(Comedy Central).** Four nights a week, Stewart offers solid satire of the news media and politics, coupled with insightful interviews with guests from across the political and cultural spectrum.

The Newsroom **(HBO).** This dramatic series envisions the not-so-recent past from the vantage point of a struggling cable news network.

APPENDIX MATERIAL

ARTICLES OF CONFEDERATION

To all to whom these Presents shall come, we the under-signed Delegates of the States affixed to our Names send greeting.

Articles of Confederation and perpetual Union between the states of New Hampshire, Massachusetts-bay Rhode Island and Providence Plantations, Connecticut, New York, New Jersey, Pennsylvania, Delaware, Maryland, Virginia, North Carolina, South Carolina and Georgia.

ARTICLE I

The Stile of this Confederacy shall be "The United States of America".

ARTICLE II

Each state retains its sovereignty, freedom, and independence, and every power, jurisdiction, and right, which is not by this Confederation expressly delegated to the United States, in Congress assembled.

ARTICLE III

The said States hereby severally enter into a firm league of friendship with each other, for their common defense, the security of their liberties, and their mutual and general welfare, binding themselves to assist each other, against all force offered to, or attacks made upon them, or any of them, on account of religion, sovereignty, trade, or any other pretense whatever.

ARTICLE IV

The better to secure and perpetuate mutual friendship and intercourse among the people of the different States in this Union, the free inhabitants of each of these States, paupers, vagabonds, and fugitives from justice excepted, shall be entitled to all privileges and immunities of free citizens in the several States; and the people of each State shall free ingress and regress to and from any other State, and shall enjoy therein all the privileges of trade and commerce, subject to the same duties, impositions, and restrictions as the inhabitants thereof respectively, provided that such restrictions shall not extend so far as to prevent the removal of property imported into any State, to any other State, of which the owner is an inhabitant; provided also that no imposition, duties or restriction shall be laid by any State, on the property of the United States, or either of them.

If any person guilty of, or charged with, treason, felony, or other high misdemeanor in any State, shall flee from justice, and be found in any of the United States, he shall, upon demand of the Governor or executive power of the State from which he fled, be delivered up and removed to the State having jurisdiction of his offense.

Full faith and credit shall be given in each of these States to the records, acts, and judicial proceedings of the courts and magistrates of every other State.

ARTICLE V

For the most convenient management of the general interests of the United States, delegates shall be annually appointed in such manner as the legislatures of each State shall direct, to meet in Congress on the first Monday in November, in every year, with a power reserved to each State to recall its delegates, or any of them, at any time within the year, and to send others in their stead for the remainder of the year.

No State shall be represented in Congress by less than two, nor more than seven members; and no person shall be capable of being a delegate for more than three years in any term of six years; nor shall any person, being a delegate, be capable of holding any office under the United States, for which he, or another for his benefit, receives any salary, fees or emolument of any kind.

Each State shall maintain its own delegates in a meeting of the States, and while they act as members of the committee of the States.

In determining questions in the United States in Congress assembled, each State shall have one vote.

Freedom of speech and debate in Congress shall not be impeached or questioned in any court or place out of Congress, and the members of Congress shall be protected in their persons from arrests or imprisonments, during the time of their going to and from, and attendence on Congress, except for treason, felony, or breach of the peace.

ARTICLE VI

No State, without the consent of the United States in Congress assembled, shall send any embassy to, or receive any embassy from, or enter into any conference, agreement, alliance or treaty with any King, Prince or State; nor shall any person holding any office of profit or trust under the United States, or any of them, accept any present, emolument, office or title of any kind whatever from any King, Prince or foreign State; nor shall the United States in Congress assembled, or any of them, grant any title of nobility.

No two or more States shall enter into any treaty, confederation or alliance whatever between them, without the consent of the United States in Congress assembled, specifying accurately the purposes for which the same is to be entered into, and how long it shall continue.

No State shall lay any imposts or duties, which may interfere with any stipulations in treaties, entered into by the United States in Congress assembled, with any King, Prince or State, in pursuance of any treaties already proposed by Congress, to the courts of France and Spain.

No vessel of war shall be kept up in time of peace by any State, except such number only, as shall be deemed necessary by the United States in Congress assembled, for the defense of such State, or its trade; nor shall any body of forces be kept up by any State in time of peace, except such number only, as in the judgement of the United States in Congress assembled, shall be deemed requisite to garrison the forts necessary for the defense of such State; but every State shall always keep up a well-regulated and disciplined militia, sufficiently armed and accoutered, and shall provide and constantly have ready for use, in public stores, a due number of filed pieces and tents, and a proper quantity of arms, ammunition and camp equipage.

No State shall engage in any war without the consent of the United States in Congress assembled, unless such State be actually invaded by enemies, or shall have received certain advice of a resolution being formed by some nation of Indians to invade such State, and the danger is so imminent as not to admit of a delay till the United States in Congress assembled can be consulted; nor shall any State grant commissions to any ships or vessels of war, nor letters of marque or reprisal, except it be after a declaration of war by the United States in Congress assembled, and then only against the Kingdom or State and the subjects thereof, against which war has been so declared, and under such regulations as shall be established by the United States in Congress assembled, unless such State be infested by pirates, in which case vessels of war may be fitted out for that occasion, and kept so long as the danger shall continue, or until the United States in Congress assembled shall determine otherwise.

ARTICLE VII

When land forces are raised by any State for the common defense, all officers of or under the rank of colonel, shall be appointed by the legislature of each State respectively, by whom such forces shall be raised, or in such manner as such State shall direct, and all vacancies shall be filled up by the State which first made the appointment.

ARTICLE VIII

All charges of war, and all other expenses that shall be incurred for the common defense or general welfare, and allowed by the United States in Congress assembled, shall be defrayed out of a common treasury, which shall be supplied by the several States in proportion to the value of all land within each State, granted or surveyed for any person, as such land and the buildings and improvements thereon shall be estimated according to such mode as the United States in Congress assembled, shall from time to time direct and appoint.

The taxes for paying that proportion shall be laid and levied by the authority and direction of the legislatures of the several States within the time agreed upon by the United States in Congress assembled.

ARTICLE IX

The United States in Congress assembled, shall have the sole and exclusive right and power of determining on peace and war, except in the cases mentioned in the sixth article—of sending and receiving ambassadors—entering into treaties and alliances, provided that no treaty of commerce shall be made whereby the legislative power of the respective States shall be restrained from imposing such imposts and duties on foreigners, as their own people are subjected to, or from prohibiting the exportation or importation of any species of goods or commodities whatsoever—of establishing rules for deciding in all cases, what captures on land or water shall be legal, and in what manner prizes taken by land or naval forces in the service of the United States shall be divided or appropriated—of granting letters of marque and reprisal in times of peace—appointing courts for the trial of piracies and felonies commited on the high seas and establishing courts for receiving and determining finally appeals in all cases of captures, provided that no member of Congress shall be appointed a judge of any of the said courts.

The United States in Congress assembled shall also be the last resort on appeal in all disputes and differences now subsisting or that hereafter may arise between two or more States concerning boundary, jurisdiction or any other causes whatever; which authority shall always be exercised in the manner following. Whenever the legislative or executive authority or lawful agent of any State in controversy with another shall present a petition to Congress stating the matter in question and praying for a hearing, notice thereof shall be given by order of Congress to the legislative or executive authority of the other State in controversy, and a day assigned for the appearance of the parties by their lawful agents, who shall then be directed to appoint by joint consent, commissioners or judges to constitute a court for hearing and determining the matter in question: but if they cannot agree, Congress shall name three persons out of each of the United States, and from the list of such persons each party shall alternately strike out one, the petitioners beginning, until the number shall be reduced to thirteen; and from that number not less than seven, nor more than nine names as Congress shall direct, shall in the presence of Congress be drawn out by lot, and the persons whose names shall be so drawn or any five of them, shall be commissioners or judges, to hear and finally determine the controversy, so always as a major part of the judges who shall hear the cause shall agree in the determination: and if either party shall neglect to attend at the day appointed, without showing reasons, which Congress shall judge sufficient, or being present shall refuse to strike, the Congress shall proceed to nominate three persons out of each State, and the secretary of Congress shall strike in behalf of such party absent or refusing; and the judgement and sentence of the court to be appointed, in the manner before prescribed, shall be final and conclusive; and if any of the parties shall refuse to submit to the authority of such court, or to appear or defend their claim or cause, the court shall nevertheless proceed to pronounce sentence, or judgement, which shall in like manner be final and decisive, the judgement or sentence and other proceedings being in either case transmitted to Congress, and lodged among the acts of Congress for the security of the parties concerned: provided that every commissioner, before he sits in judgement, shall take an oath to be administered by one of the judges of the supreme or superior court of the State, where the cause shall be tried, 'well and truly to hear and determine the matter in question, according to the best of his judgement, without favor, affection or hope of reward': provided also, that no State shall be deprived of territory for the benefit of the United States.

All controversies concerning the private right of soil claimed under different grants of two or more States, whose jurisdictions as they may respect such lands, and the States which passed such grants are adjusted, the said grants or either of them being at the same time claimed to have originated antecedent to such settlement of jurisdiction, shall on the petition of either party to the Congress of the United States, be finally determined as near as may be in the same manner as is before prescribed for deciding disputes respecting territorial jurisdiction between different States.

The United States in Congress assembled shall also have the sole and exclusive right and power of regulating the alloy and value of coin struck by their own authority, or by that of the respective States—fixing the standards of weights and measures throughout the United States—regulating the trade and managing all affairs with the Indians, not members of any of the States, provided that the legislative right of any State within its own limits be not infringed or violated—establishing or regulating post offices from one State to another, throughout all the United States, and exacting such postage on the papers passing through the same as may be requisite to defray the expenses of the said office—appointing all officers of the land forces, in the service of the United States, excepting regimental officers—appointing all the officers of the naval forces, and commissioning all officers

whatever in the service of the United States—making rules for the government and regulation of the said land and naval forces, and directing their operations.

The United States in Congress assembled shall have authority to appoint a committee, to sit in the recess of Congress, to be denominated 'A Committee of the States', and to consist of one delegate from each State; and to appoint such other committees and civil officers as may be necessary for managing the general affairs of the United States under their direction—to appoint one of their members to preside, provided that no person be allowed to serve in the office of president more than one year in any term of three years; to ascertain the necessary sums of money to be raised for the service of the United States, and to appropriate and apply the same for defraying the public expenses—to borrow money, or emit bills on the credit of the United States, transmitting every half-year to the respective States an account of the sums of money so borrowed or emitted—to build and equip a navy—to agree upon the number of land forces, and to make requisitions from each State for its quota, in proportion to the number of white inhabitants in such State; which requisition shall be binding, and thereupon the legislature of each State shall appoint the regimental officers, raise the men and cloath, arm and equip them in a solid-like manner, at the expense of the United States; and the officers and men so cloathed, armed and equipped shall march to the place appointed, and within the time agreed on by the United States in Congress assembled. But if the United States in Congress assembled shall, on consideration of circumstances judge proper that any State should not raise men, or should raise a smaller number of men than the quota thereof, such extra number shall be raised, officered, cloathed, armed and equipped in the same manner as the quota of each State, unless the legislature of such State shall judge that such extra number cannot be safely spread out in the same, in which case they shall raise, officer, cloath, arm and equip as many of such extra number as they judge can be safely spared. And the officers and men so cloathed, armed, and equipped, shall march to the place appointed, and within the time agreed on by the United States in Congress assembled.

The United States in Congress assembled shall never engage in a war, nor grant letters of marque or reprisal in time of peace, nor enter into any treaties or alliances, nor coin money, nor regulate the value thereof, nor ascertain the sums and expenses necessary for the defense and welfare of the United States, or any of them, nor emit bills, nor borrow money on the credit of the United States, nor appropriate money, nor agree upon the number of vessels of war, to be built or purchased, or the number of land or sea forces to be raised, nor appoint a commander in chief of the army or navy, unless nine States assent to the same: nor shall a question on any other point, except for adjourning from day to day be determined, unless by the votes of the majority of the United States in Congress assembled.

The Congress of the United States shall have power to adjourn to any time within the year, and to any place within the United States, so that no period of adjournment be for a longer duration than the space of six months, and shall publish the journal of their proceedings monthly, except such parts thereof relating to treaties, alliances or military operations, as in their judgement require secrecy; and the yeas and nays of the delegates of each State on any question shall be entered on the journal, when it is desired by any delegates of a State, or any of them, at his or their request shall be furnished with a transcript of the said journal, except such parts as are above excepted, to lay before the legislatures of the several States.

ARTICLE X

The Committee of the States, or any nine of them, shall be authorized to execute, in the recess of Congress, such of the powers of Congress as the United States in Congress assembled, by the consent of the nine States, shall from time to time think expedient to vest them with; provided that no power be delegated to the said Committee, for the exercise of which, by the Articles of Confederation, the voice of nine States in the Congress of the United States assembled be requisite.

ARTICLE XI

Canada acceding to this confederation, and adjoining in the measures of the United States, shall be admitted into, and entitled to all the advantages of this Union; but no other colony shall be admitted into the same, unless such admission be agreed to by nine States.

ARTICLE XII

All bills of credit emitted, monies borrowed, and debts contracted by, or under the authority of Congress, before the assembling of the United States, in pursuance of the present confederation, shall be deemed and considered as a charge against the United States, for payment and satisfaction whereof the said United States, and the public faith are hereby solemnly pledged.

ARTICLE XIII

Every State shall abide by the determination of the United States in Congress assembled, on all questions which by this confederation are submitted to them. And the Articles of this Confederation shall be inviolably observed by every State, and the Union shall be perpetual; nor shall any alteration at any time hereafter be made in any of them; unless such alteration be agreed to in a Congress of the United States, and be afterwards confirmed by the legislatures of every State.

And Whereas it hath pleased the Great Governor of the World to incline the hearts of the legislatures we respectively represent in Congress, to approve of, and to authorize us to ratify the said Articles of Confederation and perpetual Union. Know Ye that we the undersigned delegates, by virtue of the power and authority to us given for that purpose, do by these presents, in the name and in behalf of our respective constituents, fully and entirely ratify and confirm each and every of the said Articles of Confederation and perpetual Union, and all and singular the matters and things therein contained: And we do further solemnly plight and engage the faith of our respective constituents, that they shall abide by the determinations of the United States in Congress assembled, on all questions, which by the said Confederation are submitted to them. And that the Articles thereof shall be inviolably observed by the States we respectively represent, and that the Union shall be perpetual.

In Witness whereof we have hereunto set our hands in Congress. Done at Philadelphia in the State of Pennsylvania the ninth day of July in the Year of our Lord One Thousand Seven Hundred and Seventy-Eight, and in the Third Year of the independence of America.

Agreed to by Congress 15 November 1777

In force after ratification by Maryland, 1 March 1781

DECLARATION OF INDEPENDENCE

On June 11, 1776, the responsibility to "prepare a declaration" of independence was assigned by the Continental Congress, meeting in Philadelphia, to five members: John Adams, Benjamin Franklin, Thomas Jefferson, Robert Livingston, and Roger Sherman. Impressed by his talents as a writer, the committee asked Jefferson to compose a draft. After modifying Jefferson's draft the committee turned it over to Congress on June 28. On July 2 Congress voted to declare independence; on the evening of July 4, it approved the Declaration of Independence.

In Congress, July 4, 1776.

The unanimous Declaration of the thirteen United States of America,

When in the Course of human events, it becomes necessary for one people to dissolve the political bands which have connected them with another, and to assume among the Powers of the earth, the separate and equal station to which the Laws of Nature and of Nature's God entitle them, a decent respect to the opinions of mankind requires that they should declare the causes which impel them to the separation.

We hold these truths to be self-evident, that all men are created equal, that they are endowed by their Creator with certain unalienable Rights, that among these are Life, Liberty and the pursuit of Happiness. That to secure these rights, Governments are instituted among Men, deriving their just powers from the consent of the governed. That whenever any form of Government becomes destructive of these ends, it is the Right of the People to alter or to abolish it, and to institute new Government, laying its foundation on such principles and organizing its powers in such form, as to them shall seem most likely to effect their Safety and Happiness. Prudence, indeed, will dictate that Government long established should not be changed for light and transient causes; and accordingly all experience hath shown, that mankind are more disposed to suffer, while evils are sufferable, than to right themselves by abolishing the forms to which they are accustomed. But when a long train of abuses and usurpations, pursuing invariably the same Object evinces a design to reduce them under absolute Despotism, it is their right, it is their duty, to throw off such Government, and to provide new Guards for their future security. Such has been the patient sufferance of these Colonies; and such is now the necessity which constrains them to alter their former Systems of Government. The history of the present King of Great Britain is a history of repeated injuries and usurpations, all having in direct object the establishment of an absolute Tyranny over these States. To prove this, let Facts be submitted to a candid world.

He has refused his Assent to Laws, the most wholesome and necessary for the public good.

He has forbidden his Governors to pass Laws of immediate and pressing importance, unless suspended in their operation till his Assent should be obtained; and when so suspended, he has utterly neglected to attend to them.

He has refused to pass other Laws for the accommodation of large districts of people, unless those people would relinquish the right of Representation in the Legislature, a right inestimable to them and formidable to tyrants only.

He has called together legislative bodies at places unusual, uncomfortable, and distant from the depository of their Public Records, for the sole purpose of fatiguing them into compliance with his measures.

He has dissolved Representative Houses repeatedly, for opposing with manly firmness his invasions on the rights of the people.

He has refused for a long time, after such dissolutions, to cause others to be elected; whereby the Legislative Powers, incapable of Annihilation, have returned to the People at large for their exercise; the State remaining in the mean time exposed to all the dangers of invasion from without, and convulsions within.

He has endeavored to prevent the population of these States; for that purpose obstructing the Laws of Naturalization of Foreigners; refusing to pass others to encourage their migration hither, and raising the conditions of new Appropriations of Lands.

He has obstructed the Administration of Justice, by refusing his Assent to Laws for establishing Judiciary Powers.

He has made Judges dependent on his Will alone, for the tenure of their offices, and the amount and payment of their salaries.

He has erected a multitude of New Offices, and sent hither swarms of Officers to harass our People, and eat out their substance.

He has kept among us, in times of peace, Standing Armies without the Consent of our legislature.

He has affected to render the Military independent of and superior to the Civil Power.

He has combined with others to subject us to a jurisdiction foreign to our constitution, and unacknowledged by our laws; giving his Assent to their acts of pretended legislation:

For quartering large bodies of armed troops among us:

For protecting them, by a mock Trial, from Punishment for any Murders which they should commit on the Inhabitants of these States:

For cutting off our Trade with all parts of the world:

For imposing taxes on us without our Consent:

For depriving us in many cases, of the benefits of Trial by Jury:

For transporting us beyond Seas to be tried for pretended offences:

For abolishing the free System of English Laws in a neighbouring Province, establishing therein an Arbitrary government, and enlarging its Boundaries so as to render it at once an example and fit instrument for introducing the same absolute rule into these Colonies:

For taking away our Charters, abolishing our most valuable Laws, and altering fundamentally the Forms of our Governments:

For suspending our own Legislature, and declaring themselves invested with Power to legislate for us in all cases whatsoever.

He has abdicated Government here, by declaring us out of his Protection and waging War against us.

He has plundered our seas, ravaged our Coasts, burnt our towns, and destroyed the lives of our people.

He is at this time transporting large armies of foreign mercenaries to compleat the works of death, desolation and tyranny, already begun with circumstances of Cruelty & perfidy scarcely parallel in the most barbarous ages, and totally unworthy the Head of a civilized nation.

He has constrained our fellow Citizens taken Captive on the high Seas to bear Arms against their Country, to become the executioners of their friends and Brethren, or to fall themselves by their Hands.

He has excited domestic insurrections amongst us, and has endeavoured to bring on the inhabitants of our frontiers, the merciless Indian Savages, whose known rule of warfare, is an undistinguished destruction of all ages, sexes and conditions.

In every stage of these Oppressions We have Petitioned for Redress in the most humble terms: Our repeated Petitions have been answered only by repeated injury. A Prince, whose character is thus marked by every act which may define a Tyrant, is unfit to be the ruler of a free People.

Nor have We been wanting in attention to our British brethren. We have warned them from time to time of attempts by their legislature to extend an unwarrantable jurisdiction over us. We have reminded them of the circumstances of our emigration and settlement here. We have appealed to their native justice and magnanimity, and we have conjured them by the ties of our common kindred to disavow these usurpations, which would inevitably interrupt our connections and correspondence. They too have been deaf to the voice of justice and of consanguinity. We must, therefore, acquiesce in the necessity, which denounces our Separation, and hold them, as we hold the rest of mankind, Enemies in War, in Peace Friends.

We, therefore, the Representatives of the United States of America, in General Congress, Assembled, appealing to the Supreme Judge of the world for the rectitude of our intentions, do, in the Name, and by Authority of the good People of these Colonies, solemnly publish and declare, That these United Colonies are, and of Right ought to be Free and Independent States; that they are Absolved from all Allegiance to the British Crown, and that all political connection between them and the State of Great Britain, is and ought to be totally dissolved; and that as Free and Independent States, they have full Power to levy War, conclude Peace, contract Alliances, establish Commerce, and to do all other Acts and Things which Independent States may of right do. And for the support of this Declaration, with a firm reliance on the Protection of Divine Providence, we mutually pledge to each other our Lives, our Fortunes and our sacred Honor.

John Hancock

New Hampshire:
Josiah Bartlett,
William Whipple,
Matthew Thornton.
Massachusetts-Bay:
Samuel Adams,
John Adams,
Robert Treat Paine,
Elbridge Gerry.

Rhode Island:
Stephen Hopkins,
William Ellery.

Connecticut:
Roger Sherman,
Samuel Huntington,
William Williams,
Oliver Wolcott.

New York:
William Floyd,
Philip Livingston,
Francis Lewis,
Lewis Morris.

Pennsylvania:
Robert Morris,

Benjamin Harris,
Benjamin Franklin,
John Morton,
George Clymer,
James Smith,
George Taylor,
James Wilson,
George Ross.

Delaware:
Caesar Rodney,
George Read,
Thomas McKean.

Georgia:
Button Gwinnett,
Lyman Hall,
George Walton.

Maryland:
Samuel Chase,

William Paca,
Thomas Stone,
Charles Carroll of
Carrollton.

Virginia:
George Wythe,
Richard Henry Lee,
Thomas Jefferson,
Benjamin Harrison,
Thomas Nelson Jr.,

Francis Lightfoot Lee,
Carter Braxton.

North Carolina:
William Hooper,
Joseph Hewes,
John Penn.

South Carolina:
Edward Rutledge,
Thomas Heyward Jr.,

Thomas Lynch Jr.,
Arthur Middleton.

New Jersey:
Richard Stockton,
John Witherspoon,
Francis Hopkinson,
John Hart,
Abraham Clark.

CONSTITUTION OF THE UNITED STATES

The United States Constitution was written at a convention that Congress called on February 21, 1787, for the purpose of recommending amendments to the Articles of Confederation. Every state but Rhode Island sent delegates to Philadelphia, where the convention met that summer. The delegates decided to write an entirely new constitution, completing their labors on September 17. Nine states (the number the Constitution itself stipulated as sufficient) ratified by June 21, 1788.

The framers of the Constitution included only six paragraphs on the Supreme Court. Article III, Section 1, created the Supreme Court and the federal system of courts. It provided that "[t]he judicial power of the United States, shall be vested in one supreme Court," and whatever inferior courts Congress "from time to time" saw fit to establish. Article III, Section 2, delineated the types of cases and controversies that should be considered by a federal—rather than a state—court. But beyond this, the Constitution left many of the particulars of the Supreme Court and the federal court system for Congress to decide in later years in judiciary acts.

We the People of the United States, in Order to form a more perfect Union, establish Justice, insure domestic Tranquility, provide for the common defence, promote the general Welfare, and secure the Blessings of Liberty to ourselves and our Posterity, do ordain and establish this Constitution for the United States of America.

ARTICLE I

Section 1. All legislative Powers herein granted shall be vested in a Congress of the United States, which shall consist of a Senate and House of Representatives.

Section 2. The House of Representatives shall be composed of Members chosen every second Year by the People of the several States, and the Electors in each State shall have the Qualifications requisite for Electors of the most numerous Branch of the State Legislature.

No Person shall be a Representative who shall not have attained to the age of twenty five Years, and been seven Years a Citizen of the United States, and who shall not, when elected, be an Inhabitant of that State in which he shall be chosen.

[Representatives and direct Taxes shall be apportioned among the several States which may be included within this Union, according to their respective Numbers, which shall be determined by adding to the whole Number of free Persons, including those bound to Service for a Term of Years, and excluding Indians not taxed, three fifths of all other Persons.][1] The actual Enumeration shall be made within three Years after the first Meeting of the Congress of the United States, and within every subsequent Term of ten Years, in such Manner as they shall by Law direct. The Number of Representatives shall not exceed one for every thirty Thousand, but each State shall have at Least one Representative; and until such enumeration shall be made, the State of New Hampshire shall be entitled to chuse three, Massachusetts eight, Rhode-Island and Providence Plantations one, Connecticut five, New-York six, New Jersey four, Pennsylvania eight, Delaware one, Maryland six, Virginia ten, North Carolina five, South Carolina five, and Georgia three.

When vacancies happen in the Representation from any State, the Executive Authority thereof shall issue Writs of Election to fill such Vacancies.

The House of Representatives shall chuse their Speaker and other Officers; and shall have the sole Power of Impeachment.

Section 3. The Senate of the United States shall be composed of two Senators from each State, [chosen by the Legislature thereof,][2] for six Years; and each Senator shall have one Vote.

Immediately after they shall be assembled in Consequence of the first Election, they shall be divided as equally as may be into three Classes. The Seats of the Senators of the first Class shall be vacated at the Expiration of the second Year, of the second Class at the Expiration of the fourth Year, and of the third Class at the Expiration of the sixth Year, so that one third may be chosen every second Year; [and if Vacancies happen by Resignation, or otherwise, during the Recess of the Legislature of any State, the Executive thereof may make temporary Appointments until the next Meeting of the Legislature, which shall then fill such Vacancies.][3]

No Person shall be a Senator who shall not have attained to the Age of thirty Years, and been nine Years a Citizen of the United States, and who shall not, when elected, be an Inhabitant of that State for which he shall be chosen.

The Vice President of the United States shall be President of the Senate, but shall have no Vote, unless they be equally divided.

The Senate shall chuse their other Officers, and also a President pro tempore, in the Absence of the Vice President, or when he shall exercise the Office of President of the United States.

The Senate shall have the sole Power to try all Impeachments. When sitting for that Purpose, they shall be on Oath or Affirmation. When the President of the United States is tried, the Chief Justice shall preside: And no Person shall be convicted without the Concurrence of two thirds of the Members present.

Judgment in Cases of Impeachment shall not extend further than to removal from Office, and disqualification to hold and enjoy any Office of honor, Trust or Profit under the United States: but the Party convicted shall nevertheless be liable and subject to Indictment, Trial, Judgment and Punishment, according to Law.

Section 4. The Times, Places and Manner of holding Elections for Senators and Representatives, shall be prescribed in each State by the Legislature thereof; but the Congress may at any time by Law make or alter such Regulations, except as to the Places of chusing Senators.

The Congress shall assemble at least once in every Year, and such Meeting shall [be on the first Monday in December],[4] unless they shall by Law appoint a different Day.

Section 5. Each House shall be the Judge of the Elections, Returns and Qualifications of its own Members, and a Majority of each shall constitute a Quorum to do Business; but a smaller Number may adjourn from day to day, and may be authorized to compel the Attendance of absent Members, in such Manner, and under such Penalties as each House may provide.

Each House may determine the Rules of its Proceedings, punish its Members for disorderly Behaviour, and, with the Concurrence of two thirds, expel a Member.

Each House shall keep a Journal of its Proceedings, and from time to time publish the same, excepting such Parts as may in their Judgment require Secrecy; and the Yeas and Nays of the Members of either House on any question shall, at the Desire of one fifth of those Present, be entered on the Journal.

Neither House, during the Session of Congress, shall, without the Consent of the other, adjourn for more than three days, nor to any other Place than that in which the two Houses shall be sitting.

Section 6. The Senators and Representatives shall receive a Compensation for their Services, to be ascertained by Law, and paid out of the Treasury of the United States. They shall in all Cases, except Treason, Felony and Breach of the Peace, be privileged from Arrest during their Attendance at the Session of their respective Houses, and in going to and returning from the same; and for any Speech or Debate in either House, they shall not be questioned in any other Place.

No Senator or Representative shall, during the Time for which he was elected, be appointed to any civil Office under the Authority of the United States, which shall have been created, or the Emoluments whereof shall have been increased during such time; and no Person holding any Office under the United States, shall be a Member of either House during his Continuance in Office.

Section 7. All Bills for raising Revenue shall originate in the House of Representatives; but the Senate may propose or concur with Amendments as on other Bills.

Every Bill which shall have passed the House of Representatives and the Senate, shall, before it become a Law, be presented to the President of the United States; If he approve he shall sign it, but if not he shall return it, with his Objections to that House in which it shall have originated, who shall enter the Objections at large on their Journal, and proceed to reconsider it. If after such Reconsideration two thirds of that House shall agree to pass the Bill, it shall be sent, together with the Objections, to the other House, by which it shall likewise be reconsidered, and if approved by two thirds of that House, it shall become a Law. But in all such Cases the Votes of both Houses shall be determined by yeas and Nays, and the Names of the Persons voting for and against the Bill shall be entered on the Journal of each House respectively. If any Bill shall not be returned by the President within ten Days (Sundays excepted) after it shall have been presented to him, the Same shall be a Law, in like Manner as if he had signed it, unless the Congress by their Adjournment prevent its Return, in which Case it shall not be a Law.

Every Order, Resolution, or Vote to which the Concurrence of the Senate and House of Representatives may be necessary (except on a question of Adjournment) shall be presented to the President of the United States; and before the Same shall take Effect, shall be approved by him, or being disapproved by him, shall be repassed by two thirds of the Senate and House of Representatives, according to the Rules and Limitations prescribed in the Case of a Bill.

Section 8. The Congress shall have Power To lay and collect Taxes, Duties, Imposts and Excises, to pay the Debts and provide for the common Defence and general Welfare of the United States; but all Duties, Imposts and Excises shall be uniform throughout the United States;

To borrow Money on the credit of the United States;

To regulate Commerce with foreign Nations, and among the several States, and with the Indian Tribes;

To establish an uniform Rule of Naturalization, and uniform Laws on the subject of Bankruptcies throughout the United States;

To coin Money, regulate the Value thereof, and of foreign Coin, and fix the Standard of Weights and Measures;

To provide for the Punishment of counterfeiting the Securities and current Coin of the United States;

To establish Post Offices and post Roads;

To promote the Progress of Science and useful Arts, by securing for limited Times to Authors and Inventors the exclusive Right to their respective Writings and Discoveries;

To constitute Tribunals inferior to the supreme Court;

To define and punish Piracies and Felonies committed on the high Seas, and Offences against the Law of Nations;

To declare War, grant Letters of Marque and Reprisal, and make Rules concerning Captures on Land and Water;

To raise and support Armies, but no Appropriation of Money to that Use shall be for a longer Term than two Years;

To provide and maintain a Navy;

To make Rules for the Government and Regulation of the land and naval Forces;

To provide for calling forth the Militia to execute the Laws of the Union, suppress Insurrections and repel Invasions;

To provide for organizing, arming, and disciplining, the Militia, and for governing such Part of them as may be employed in the Service of the United States, reserving to the States respectively, the Appointment of the Officers, and the Authority of training the Militia according to the discipline prescribed by Congress;

To exercise exclusive Legislation in all Cases whatsoever, over such District (not exceeding ten Miles square) as may, by Cession of particular States, and the Acceptance of Congress, become the Seat of the Government of the United States, and to exercise like Authority over all Places purchased by the Consent of the Legislature of the State in which the Same shall be, for the Erection of Forts, Magazines, Arsenals, dock-Yards, and other needful Buildings;—And

To make all Laws which shall be necessary and proper for carrying into Execution the foregoing Powers, and all other Powers vested by this Constitution in the Government of the United States, or in any Department or Officer thereof.

Section 9. The Migration or Importation of such Persons as any of the States now existing shall think proper to admit, shall not be prohibited by the Congress prior to the Year one thousand eight hundred and eight, but a Tax or duty may be imposed on such Importation, not exceeding ten dollars for each Person.

The Privilege of the Writ of Habeas Corpus shall not be suspended, unless when in Cases of Rebellion or Invasion the public Safety may require it.

No Bill of Attainder or ex post facto Law shall be passed.

No Capitation, or other direct, Tax shall be laid, unless in Proportion to the Census or Enumeration herein before directed to be taken.[5]

No Tax or Duty shall be laid on Articles exported from any State.

No Preference shall be given by any Regulation of Commerce or Revenue to the Ports of one State over those of another; nor shall Vessels bound to, or from, one State, be obliged to enter, clear, or pay Duties in another.

No Money shall be drawn from the Treasury, but in Consequence of Appropriations made by Law; and a regular Statement and Account of the Receipts and Expenditures of all public Money shall be published from time to time.

No Title of Nobility shall be granted by the United States: And no Person holding any Office of Profit or Trust under them, shall, without the Consent of the Congress, accept of any present, Emolument, Office, or Title, of any kind whatever, from any King, Prince, or foreign State.

Section 10. No State shall enter into any Treaty, Alliance, or Confederation; grant Letters of Marque and Reprisal; coin Money; emit Bills of Credit; make any Thing but gold and silver Coin a Tender in Payment of Debts; pass any Bill of Attainder, ex post facto Law, or Law impairing the Obligation of Contracts, or grant any Title of Nobility.

No State shall, without the Consent of the Congress, lay any Imposts or Duties on Imports or Exports, except what may be absolutely necessary for executing its inspection Laws: and the net Produce of all Duties and Imposts, laid by any State on Imports or Exports, shall be for the Use of the Treasury of the United States; and all such Laws shall be subject to the Revision and Controul of the Congress.

No State shall, without the Consent of Congress, lay any Duty of Tonnage, keep Troops, or Ships of War in time of Peace, enter into any Agreement or Compact with another State, or with a foreign Power, or engage in War, unless actually invaded, or in such imminent Danger as will not admit of delay.

ARTICLE II

Section 1. The executive Power shall be vested in a President of the United States of America. He shall hold his Office during the Term of four Years, and, together with the Vice President, chosen for the same Term, be elected, as follows:

Each State shall appoint, in such Manner as the Legislature thereof may direct, a Number of Electors, equal to the whole Number of Senators and Representatives to which the State may be entitled in the Congress: but no Senator or Representative, or Person holding an Office of Trust or Profit under the United States, shall be appointed an Elector.

[The Electors shall meet in their respective States, and vote by Ballot for two Persons, of whom one at least shall not be an Inhabitant of the same State with themselves. And they shall make a List of all the Persons voted for, and of the Number of Votes for each; which List they shall sign and certify, and transmit sealed to the Seat of the Government of the United States, directed to the President of the Senate. The President of the Senate shall, in the Presence of the Senate and House of Representatives, open all the Certificates, and the Votes shall then be counted. The Person having the greatest Number of Votes shall be the President, if such Number be a Majority of the whole Number of Electors appointed; and if there be more than one who have such Majority, and have an equal Number of Votes, then the House of Representatives shall immediately chuse by Ballot one of them for President; and if no Person have a Majority, then from the five highest on the list the said House shall in like Manner chuse the President. But in chusing the President, the Votes shall be taken by States, the Representation from each State having one Vote; A quorum for this Purpose shall consist of a Member or Members from two thirds of the States, and a Majority of all the States shall be necessary to a Choice. In every Case, after the Choice of the President, the Person having the greatest Number of Votes of the Electors shall be the Vice President. But if there should remain two or more who have equal Votes, the Senate shall chuse from them by Ballot the Vice President.][6]

The Congress may determine the Time of chusing the Electors, and the Day on which they shall give their Votes; which Day shall be the same throughout the United States.

No Person except a natural born Citizen, or a Citizen of the United States, at the time of the Adoption of this Constitution, shall be eligible to the Office of President; neither shall any Person be eligible to that Office who shall not have attained to the Age of thirty five Years, and been fourteen Years a Resident within the United States.

In Case of the Removal of the President from Office, or of his Death, Resignation, or Inability to discharge the Powers and Duties of the said Office,[7] the Same shall devolve on the Vice President, and the Congress may by Law provide for the Case of Removal, Death, Resignation or Inability, both of the President and Vice President, declaring what Officer shall then act as President, and such Officer shall act accordingly, until the Disability be removed, or a President shall be elected.

The President shall, at stated Times, receive for his Services, a Compensation, which shall neither be encreased nor diminished during the Period for which he shall have been elected, and he shall not receive within that Period any other Emolument from the United States, or any of them.

Before he enter on the Execution of his Office, he shall take the following Oath or Affirmation:—"I do solemnly swear (or affirm) that I will faithfully execute the Office of President of the United States, and will to the best of my Ability, preserve, protect and defend the Constitution of the United States."

Section 2. The President shall be Commander in Chief of the Army and Navy of the United States, and of the Militia of the several States, when called into the actual Service of the United States; he may require the Opinion, in writing, of the principal Officer in each of the executive Departments, upon any Subject relating to the Duties of their respective Offices, and he shall have Power to grant Reprieves and Pardons for Offences against the United States, except in Cases of Impeachment.

He shall have Power, by and with the Advice and Consent of the Senate, to make Treaties, provided two thirds of the Senators present concur; and he shall nominate, and by and with the Advice and Consent of the Senate, shall appoint Ambassadors, other public Ministers and Consuls, Judges of the supreme Court, and all other

Officers of the United States, whose Appointments are not herein otherwise provided for, and which shall be established by Law: but the Congress may by Law vest the Appointment of such inferior Officers, as they think proper, in the President alone, in the Courts of Law, or in the Heads of Departments.

The President shall have Power to fill up all Vacancies that may happen during the Recess of the Senate, by granting Commissions which shall expire at the End of their next Session.

Section 3. He shall from time to time give to the Congress Information of the State of the Union, and recommend to their Consideration such Measures as he shall judge necessary and expedient; he may, on extraordinary Occasions, convene both Houses, or either of them, and in Case of Disagreement between them, with Respect to the Time of Adjournment, he may adjourn them to such Time as he shall think proper; he shall receive Ambassadors and other public Ministers; he shall take Care that the Laws be faithfully executed, and shall Commission all the Officers of the United States.

Section 4. The President, Vice President and all civil Officers of the United States, shall be removed from Office on Impeachment for, and Conviction of, Treason, Bribery, or other high Crimes and Misdemeanors.

ARTICLE III

Section 1. The judicial Power of the United States, shall be vested in one supreme Court, and in such inferior Courts as the Congress may from time to time ordain and establish. The Judges, both of the supreme and inferior Courts, shall hold their Offices during good Behaviour, and shall, at stated Times, receive for their Services, a Compensation, which shall not be diminished during their Continuance in Office.

Section 2. The judicial Power shall extend to all Cases, in Law and Equity, arising under this Constitution, the Laws of the United States, and Treaties made, or which shall be made, under their Authority; —to all Cases affecting Ambassadors, other public Ministers and Consuls; —to all Cases of admiralty and maritime Jurisdiction; —to Controversies to which the United States shall be a Party; —to Controversies between two or more States; —between a State and Citizens of another State; —between Citizens of different States; —between Citizens of the same State claiming Lands under Grants of different States, and between a State, or the Citizens thereof, and foreign States, Citizens or Subjects.[8]

In all Cases affecting Ambassadors, other public Ministers and Consuls, and those in which a State shall be Party, the supreme Court shall have original Jurisdiction. In all the other Cases before mentioned, the supreme Court shall have appellate Jurisdiction, both as to Law and Fact, with such Exceptions, and under such Regulations as the Congress shall make.

The Trial of all Crimes, except in Cases of Impeachment, shall be by Jury; and such Trial shall be held in the State where the said Crimes shall have been committed; but when not committed within any State, the Trial shall be at such Place or Places as the Congress may by Law have directed.

Section 3. Treason against the United States, shall consist only in levying War against them, or in adhering to their Enemies, giving them Aid and Comfort. No Person shall be convicted of Treason unless on the Testimony of two Witnesses to the same overt Act, or on Confession in open Court.

The Congress shall have Power to declare the Punishment of Treason, but no Attainder of Treason shall work Corruption of Blood, or Forfeiture except during the Life of the Person attainted.

ARTICLE IV

Section 1. Full Faith and Credit shall be given in each State to the public Acts, Records, and judicial Proceedings of every other State. And the Congress may by general Laws prescribe the Manner in which such Acts, Records and Proceedings shall be proved, and the Effect thereof.

Section 2. The Citizens of each State shall be entitled to all Privileges and Immunities of Citizens in the several States.

A Person charged in any State with Treason, Felony, or other Crime, who shall flee from Justice, and be found in another State, shall on Demand of the executive Authority of the State from which he fled, be delivered up, to be removed to the State having Jurisdiction of the Crime.

[No Person held to Service or Labour in one State, under the Laws thereof, escaping into another, shall, in Consequence of any Law or Regulation therein, be discharged from such Service or Labour, but shall be delivered up on Claim of the Party to whom such Service or Labour may be due.]9

Section 3. New States may be admitted by the Congress into this Union; but no new State shall be formed or erected within the Jurisdiction of any other State; nor any State be formed by the Junction of two or more States, or Parts of States, without the Consent of the Legislatures of the States concerned as well as of the Congress.

The Congress shall have Power to dispose of and make all needful Rules and Regulations respecting the Territory or other Property belonging to the United States; and nothing in this Constitution shall be so construed as to Prejudice any Claims of the United States, or of any particular State.

Section 4. The United States shall guarantee to every State in this Union a Republican Form of Government, and shall protect each of them against Invasion; and on Application of the Legislature, or of the Executive (when the Legislature cannot be convened) against domestic Violence.

ARTICLE V

The Congress, whenever two thirds of both Houses shall deem it necessary, shall propose Amendments to this Constitution, or, on the Application of the Legislatures of two thirds of the several States, shall call a Convention for proposing Amendments, which, in either Case, shall be valid to all Intents and Purposes, as Part of this Constitution, when ratified by the Legislatures of three fourths of the several States, or by Conventions in three fourths thereof, as the one or the other Mode of Ratification may be proposed by the Congress; Provided [that no Amendment which may be made prior to the Year One thousand eight hundred and eight shall in any Manner affect the first and fourth Clauses in the Ninth Section of the first Article; and]10 that no State, without its Consent, shall be deprived of its equal Suffrage in the Senate.

ARTICLE VI

All Debts contracted and Engagements entered into, before the Adoption of this Constitution, shall be as valid against the United States under this Constitution, as under the Confederation.

This Constitution, and the Laws of the United States which shall be made in Pursuance thereof; and all Treaties made, or which shall be made, under the Authority of the United States, shall be the supreme Law of the Land; and the Judges in every State shall be bound thereby, any Thing in the Constitution or Laws of any State to the Contrary notwithstanding.

The Senators and Representatives before mentioned, and the Members of the several State Legislatures, and all executive and judicial Officers, both of the United States and of the several States, shall be bound by Oath or Affirmation, to support this Constitution; but no religious Test shall ever be required as a Qualification to any Office or public Trust under the United States.

ARTICLE VII

The Ratification of the Conventions of nine States, shall be sufficient for the Establishment of this Constitution between the States so ratifying the Same.

Done in Convention by the Unanimous Consent of the States present the Seventeenth Day of September in the Year of our Lord one thousand seven hundred and Eighty seven and of the Independence of the United States of

America the Twelfth. IN WITNESS whereof We have hereunto subscribed our Names,

George Washington, President and deputy from Virginia, and thirty-eight other delegates.

[The language of the original Constitution, not including the Amendments, was adopted by a convention of the states on September 17, 1787, and was subsequently ratified by the states on the following dates: Delaware, December 7, 1787; Pennsylvania, December 12, 1787; New Jersey, December 18, 1787; Georgia, January 2, 1788; Connecticut, January 9, 1788; Massachusetts, February 6, 1788; Maryland, April 28, 1788; South Carolina, May 23, 1788; New Hampshire, June 21, 1788.

Ratification was completed on June 21, 1788.

The Constitution subsequently was ratified by Virginia, June 25, 1788; New York, July 26, 1788; North Carolina, November 21, 1789; Rhode Island, May 29, 1790; and Vermont, January 10, 1791.]

AMENDMENTS

AMENDMENT I

(First ten amendments ratified December 15, 1791.)

Congress shall make no law respecting an establishment of religion, or prohibiting the free exercise thereof; or abridging the freedom of speech, or of the press; or the right of the people peaceably to assemble, and to petition the Government for a redress of grievances.

AMENDMENT II

A well regulated Militia, being necessary to the security of a free State, the right of the people to keep and bear Arms, shall not be infringed.

AMENDMENT III

No Soldier shall, in time of peace be quartered in any house, without the consent of the Owner, nor in time of war, but in a manner to be prescribed by law.

AMENDMENT IV

The right of the people to be secure in their persons, houses, papers, and effects, against unreasonable searches and seizures, shall not be violated, and no Warrants shall issue, but upon probable cause, supported by Oath or affirmation, and particularly describing the place to be searched, and the persons or things to be seized.

AMENDMENT V

No person shall be held to answer for a capital, or otherwise infamous crime, unless on a presentment or indictment of a Grand Jury, except in cases arising in the land or naval forces, or in the Militia, when in actual service in time of War or public danger; nor shall any person be subject for the same offence to be twice put in jeopardy of life or limb; nor shall be compelled in any criminal case to be a witness against himself, nor be deprived of life, liberty, or property, without due process of law; nor shall private property be taken for public use, without just compensation.

AMENDMENT VI

In all criminal prosecutions, the accused shall enjoy the right to a speedy and public trial, by an impartial jury of the State and district wherein the crime shall have been committed, which district shall have been previously ascertained by law, and to be informed of the nature and cause of the accusation; to be confronted with the witnesses against him; to have compulsory process for obtaining witnesses in his favor, and to have the Assistance of Counsel for his defence.

AMENDMENT VII

In Suits at common law, where the value in controversy shall exceed twenty dollars, the right of trial by jury shall be preserved, and no fact tried by a jury, shall be otherwise re-examined in any Court of the United States, than according to the rules of the common law.

AMENDMENT VIII

Excessive bail shall not be required, nor excessive fines imposed, nor cruel and unusual punishments inflicted.

AMENDMENT IX

The enumeration in the Constitution, of certain rights, shall not be construed to deny or disparage others retained by the people.

AMENDMENT X

The powers not delegated to the United States by the Constitution, nor prohibited by it to the States, are reserved to the States respectively, or to the people.

AMENDMENT XI (RATIFIED FEBRUARY 7, 1795)

The Judicial power of the United States shall not be construed to extend to any suit in law or equity, commenced or prosecuted against one of the United States by Citizens of another State, or by Citizens or Subjects of any Foreign State.

AMENDMENT XII (RATIFIED JUNE 15, 1804)

The Electors shall meet in their respective states and vote by ballot for President and Vice-President, one of whom, at least, shall not be an inhabitant of the same state with themselves; they shall name in their ballots the person voted for as President, and in distinct ballots the person voted for as Vice-President, and they shall make distinct lists of all persons voted for as President, and of all persons voted for as Vice-President, and of the number of votes for each, which lists they shall sign and certify, and transmit sealed to the seat of the government of the United States, directed to the President of the Senate; — The President of the Senate shall, in the presence of the Senate and House of Representatives, open all the certificates and the votes shall then be counted; — The person having the greatest number of votes for President, shall be the President, if such number be a majority of the whole number of Electors appointed; and if no person have such majority, then from the persons having the highest numbers not exceeding three on the list of those voted for as President, the House of Representatives shall choose immediately, by ballot, the President. But in choosing the President, the votes shall be taken by states, the representation from each state having one vote; a quorum for this purpose shall consist of a member or members from two-thirds of the states, and a majority of all the states shall be necessary to a choice. [And if the House of Representatives shall not choose a President whenever the right of choice shall devolve upon them, before the fourth day of March next following, then the Vice-President shall act as President, as in the case of the death or other constitutional disability of the President. —][11] The person having the greatest number of votes as Vice-President, shall be the Vice-President, if such number be a majority of the whole number of Electors appointed, and if no person have a majority, then from the two highest numbers on the list, the Senate shall choose the Vice-President; a quorum for the purpose shall consist of two-thirds of the whole number of Senators, and a majority of the whole number shall be necessary to a choice. But no person constitutionally ineligible to the office of President shall be eligible to that of Vice-President of the United States.

AMENDMENT XIII (RATIFIED DECEMBER 6, 1865)

Section 1. Neither slavery nor involuntary servitude, except as a punishment for crime whereof the party shall have been duly convicted, shall exist within the United States, or any place subject to their jurisdiction.

Section 2. Congress shall have power to enforce this article by appropriate legislation.

AMENDMENT XIV (RATIFIED JULY 9, 1868)

Section 1. All persons born or naturalized in the United States, and subject to the jurisdiction thereof, are citizens of the United States and of the State wherein they reside. No State shall make or enforce any law which shall abridge the privileges or immunities of citizens of the United States; nor shall any State deprive any person of life, liberty, or property, without due process of law; nor deny to any person within its jurisdiction the equal protection of the laws.

Section 2. Representatives shall be apportioned among the several States according to their respective numbers, counting the whole number of persons in each State, excluding Indians not taxed. But when the right to vote at any election for the choice of electors for President and Vice President of the United States, Representatives in Congress, the Executive and Judicial officers of a State, or the members of the Legislature thereof, is denied to any of the male inhabitants of such State, being twenty-one years of age,[12] and citizens of the United States, or in any way abridged, except for participation in rebellion, or other crime, the basis of representation therein shall be reduced in the proportion which the number of such male citizens shall bear to the whole number of male citizens twenty-one years of age in such State.

Section 3. No person shall be a Senator or Representative in Congress, or elector of President and Vice President, or hold any Office, civil or military, under the United States, or under any State, who, having previously taken an oath, as a member of Congress, or as an officer of the United States, or as a member of any State legislature, or as an executive or judicial officer of any State, to support the Constitution of the United States, shall have engaged in insurrection or rebellion against the same, or given aid or comfort to the enemies thereof. But Congress may by a vote of two-thirds of each House, remove such disability.

Section 4. The validity of the public debt of the United States, authorized by law, including debts incurred for payment of pensions and bounties for services in suppressing insurrection or rebellion, shall not be questioned. But neither the United States nor any State shall assume or pay any debt or obligation incurred in aid of insurrection or rebellion against the United States, or any claim for the loss or emancipation of any slave; but all such debts, obligations and claims shall be held illegal and void.

Section 5. The Congress shall have power to enforce, by appropriate legislation, the provisions of this article.

AMENDMENT XV (RATIFIED FEBRUARY 3, 1870)

Section 1. The right of citizens of the United States to vote shall not be denied or abridged by the United States or by any State on account of race, color, or previous condition of servitude.

Section 2. The Congress shall have power to enforce this article by appropriate legislation.

AMENDMENT XVI (RATIFIED FEBRUARY 3, 1913)

The Congress shall have power to lay and collect taxes on incomes, from whatever source derived, without apportionment among the several States, and without regard to any census or enumeration.

AMENDMENT XVII (RATIFIED APRIL 8, 1913)

The Senate of the United States shall be composed of two Senators from each State, elected by the people thereof, for six years; and each Senator shall have one vote. The electors in each State shall have the qualifications requisite for electors of the most numerous branch of the State legislatures.

When vacancies happen in the representation of any State in the Senate, the executive authority of such State shall issue writs of election to fill such vacancies: Provided, That the legislature of any State may empower the executive thereof to make temporary appointments until the people fill the vacancies by election as the legislature may direct.

This amendment shall not be so construed as to affect the election or term of any Senator chosen before it becomes valid as part of the Constitution.

AMENDMENT XVIII (RATIFIED JANUARY 16, 1919)

Section 1. After one year from the ratification of this article the manufacture, sale, or transportation of intoxicating liquors within, the importation thereof into, or the exportation thereof from the United States and all territory subject to the jurisdiction thereof for beverage purposes is hereby prohibited.

Section 2. The Congress and the several States shall have concurrent power to enforce this article by appropriate legislation.

Section 3. This article shall be inoperative unless it shall have been ratified as an amendment to the Constitution by the legislatures of the several States, as provided in the Constitution, within seven years from the date of the submission hereof to the States by the Congress.[13]

AMENDMENT XIX (RATIFIED AUGUST 18, 1920)

The right of citizens of the United States to vote shall not be denied or abridged by the United States or by any State on account of sex.

Congress shall have power to enforce this article by appropriate legislation.

AMENDMENT XX (RATIFIED JANUARY 23, 1933)

Section 1. The terms of the President and Vice President shall end at noon on the 20th day of January, and the terms of Senators and Representatives at noon on the 3d day of January, of the years in which such terms would have ended if this article had not been ratified; and the terms of their successors shall then begin.

Section 2. The Congress shall assemble at least once in every year, and such meeting shall begin at noon on the 3d day of January, unless they shall by law appoint a different day.

Section 3.[14] If, at the time fixed for the beginning of the term of the President, the President elect shall have died, the Vice President elect shall become President. If a President shall not have been chosen before the time fixed for the beginning of his term, or if the President elect shall have failed to qualify, then the Vice President elect shall act as President until a President shall have qualified; and the Congress may by law provide for the case wherein neither a President elect nor a Vice President elect shall have qualified, declaring who shall then act as President, or the manner in which one who is to act shall be selected, and such person shall act accordingly until a President or Vice President shall have qualified.

Section 4. The Congress may by law provide for the case of the death of any of the persons from whom the House of

Representatives may choose a President whenever the right of choice shall have devolved upon them, and for the case of the death of any of the persons from whom the Senate may choose a Vice President whenever the right of choice shall have devolved upon them.

Section 5. Sections 1 and 2 shall take effect on the 15th day of October following the ratification of this article.

Section 6. This article shall be inoperative unless it shall have been ratified as an amendment to the Constitution by the legislatures of three-fourths of the several States within seven years from the date of its submission.

AMENDMENT XXI (RATIFIED DECEMBER 5, 1933)

Section 1. The eighteenth article of amendment to the Constitution of the United States is hereby repealed.

Section 2. The transportation or importation into any State, Territory, or possession of the United States for delivery or use therein of intoxicating liquors, in violation of the laws thereof, is hereby prohibited.

Section 3. This article shall be inoperative unless it shall have been ratified as an amendment to the Constitution by conventions in the several States, as provided in the Constitution, within seven years from the date of the submission hereof to the States by the Congress.

AMENDMENT XXII (RATIFIED FEBRUARY 27, 1951)

Section 1. No person shall be elected to the office of the President more than twice, and no person who has held the office of President, or acted as President, for more than two years of a term to which some other person was elected President shall be elected to the office of the President more than once. But this Article shall not apply to any person holding the office of President when this Article was proposed by the Congress, and shall not prevent any person who may be holding the office of President, or acting as President, during the term within which this Article becomes operative from holding the office of President or acting as President during the remainder of such term.

Section 2. This article shall be inoperative unless it shall have been ratified as an amendment to the Constitution by the legislatures of three-fourths of the several States within seven years from the date of its submission to the States by the Congress.

AMENDMENT XXIII (RATIFIED MARCH 29, 1961)

Section 1. The District constituting the seat of Government of the United States shall appoint in such manner as the Congress may direct:

A number of electors of President and Vice President equal to the whole number of Senators and Representatives in Congress to which the District would be entitled if it were a State, but in no event more than the least populous State; they shall be in addition to those appointed by the States, but they shall be considered, for the purposes of the election of President and Vice President, to be electors appointed by a State; and they shall meet in the District and perform such duties as provided by the twelfth article of amendment.

Section 2. The Congress shall have power to enforce this article by appropriate legislation.

AMENDMENT XXIV (RATIFIED JANUARY 23, 1964)

Section 1. The right of citizens of the United States to vote in any primary or other election for President or Vice President, for electors for President or Vice President, or for Senator or Representative in Congress, shall not be denied or abridged by the United States or any State by reason of failure to pay any poll tax or other tax.

Section 2. The Congress shall have power to enforce this article by appropriate legislation.

AMENDMENT XXV (RATIFIED FEBRUARY 10, 1967)

Section 1. In case of the removal of the President from office or of his death or resignation, the Vice President shall become President.

Section 2. Whenever there is a vacancy in the offie of the Vice President, the President shall nominate a Vice President who shall take office upon confirmation by a majority vote of both Houses of Congress.

Section 3. Whenever the President transmits to the President pro tempore of the Senate and the Speaker of the House of Representatives his written declaration that he is unable to discharge the powers and duties of his office, and until he transmits to them a written declaration to the contrary, such powers and duties shall be discharged by the Vice President as Acting President.

Section 4. Whenever the Vice President and a majority of either the principal officers of the executive departments or of such other body as Congress may by law provide, transmit to the President pro tempore of the Senate and the Speaker of the House of Representatives their written declaration that the President is unable to discharge the powers and duties of his office, the Vice President shall immediately assume the powers and duties of the office as Acting President.

Thereafter, when the President transmits to the President pro tempore of the Senate and the Speaker of the House of Representatives his written declaration that no inability exists, he shall resume the powers and duties of his office unless the Vice President and a majority of either the principal officers of the executive departments or of such other body as Congress may by law provide, transmit within four days to the President pro tempore of the Senate and the Speaker of the House of Representatives their written declaration that the President is unable to discharge the powers and duties of his office. Thereupon Congress shall decide the issue, assembling within forty-eight hours for that purpose if not in session. If the Congress, within twenty-one days after receipt of the latter written declaration, or, if Congress is not in session, within twenty-one days after Congress is required to assemble, determines by two-thirds vote of both Houses that the President is unable to discharge the powers and duties of his office, the Vice President shall continue to discharge the same as Acting President; otherwise, the President shall resume the powers and duties of his office.

AMENDMENT XXVI
(RATIFIED JULY 1, 1971)

Section 1. The right of citizens of the United States, who are eighteen years of age or older, to vote shall not be denied or abridged by the United States or by any State on account of age.

Section 2. The Congress shall have power to enforce this article by appropriate legislation.

AMENDMENT XXVII
(RATIFIED MAY 7, 1992)

No law varying the compensation for the services of the Senators and Representatives shall take effect, until an election of Representatives shall have intervened.

Source: U.S. Congress, House, Committee on the Judiciary, The Constitution of the United States of America, as Amended, 100th Cong., 1st sess., 1987, H Doc 100–94.

NOTES

1. The part in brackets was changed by section 2 of the Fourteenth Amendment.
2. The part in brackets was changed by the first paragraph of the Seventeenth Amendment.
3. The part in brackets was changed by the second paragraph of the Seventeenth Amendment.
4. The part in brackets was changed by section 2 of the Twentieth Amendment.
5. The Sixteenth Amendment gave Congress the power to tax incomes.
6. The material in brackets was superseded by the Twelfth Amendment.
7. This provision was affected by the Twenty-fifth Amendment.
8. These clauses were affected by the Eleventh Amendment.
9. This paragraph was superseded by the Thirteenth Amendment.
10. Obsolete.
11. The part in brackets was superseded by Section 3 of the Twentieth Amendment.
12. See the Nineteenth and Twenty-sixth Amendments.
13. This amendment was repealed by Section 1 of the Twenty-first Amendment.
14. See the Twenty-fifth Amendment.

NOTES

Chapter 1

1. This quotation, as well as following quotations from Matthew Brandi, are taken from interviews conducted by the authors, February 2011.
2. Lucy Madison, "Obama: 'Occupy Wall Street' Reflects 'Broad-Based Frustration'," *Political Hotsheet*, CBS News, October 6, 2011, www.cbsnews.com/8301-503544_162-20116707-503544.html.
3. Douglas Rushkoff, "Think Occupy Wall St. Is a Phase? You Don't Get It," CNNOpinion, October 5, 2011, www.cnn.com/2011/10/05/opinion/rushkoff-occupy-wall-street/index.html.
4. Emily Hoban Kirby and Kei Kawashima-Ginsberg, "The Youth Vote in 2008," www.civicyouth.org/PopUps/FactSheets/FS_youth_Voting_2008_updated_6.2.pdf; www.civicyouth.org/quick-facts/youth-voting/#15, updated August 2009.
5. E. J. Dionne, *Why Americans Hate Politics* (New York: Simon & Schuster, 1991), 354, 355.
6. Harold D. Lasswell, *Politics: Who Gets What, When, How* (New York: McGraw-Hill, 1938).
7. Joseph A. Schumpeter, *Capitalism, Socialism, and Democracy*, 3rd ed. (New York: Harper Colophon Books, 1950), 269–296.
8. Robert A. Dahl, *Pluralist Democracy in the United States* (Chicago: Rand McNally, 1967).
9. Carole Pateman, *Participation and Democratic Theory* (New York: Cambridge University Press, 1970).
10. For an explanation of this view, see, for example, Russell L. Hanson, *The Democratic Imagination in America: Conversation With Our Past* (Princeton: Princeton University Press, 1985), 55–91; and Gordon Wood, *The Creation of the American Republic, 1776–1787* (New York: Norton, 1969).
11. Bruce E. Johansen, *Forgotten Founders: Benjamin Franklin, the Iroquois and the Rationale for the American Revolution* (Ipswich, Mass.: Gambit, 1982).
12. Dionne, 354, 355.
13. Alan Feuer, "Occupy Sandy: A Movement Moves to Relief," *New York Times*, November 9, 2012, www.nytimes.com/2012/11/11/nyregion/where-fema-fell-short-occupy-sandy-was-there.html?pagewanted=all.

Chapter 2

1. Chris Cilizza, "Three Sentences on Immigration Reform that will Haunt Republicans in 2016" The Washington Post, July 1, 2014, http://www.washingtonpost.com/blogs/the-fix/wp/2014/07/01/three-sentences-on-immigration-that-will-haunt-republicans-in-2016/
2. Jennifer Steinhauer, "Speaker 'Confident' of Deal With White House on Immigration," *New York Times*, November 8, 2012. http://www.nytimes.com/2012/11/09/us/politics/boehner-confident-of-deal-with-white-house-on-immigration.html?module=Search&mabReward=relbias%3Ar%2C{%221%22%3A%22RI%3A11%22}&_r=0

3. Ashley Parker and Jonathan Martin, "Senate, 68–32, Passes Overhaul for Immigration," *The New York Times,* June 27, 2013, www.nytimes.com/2013/06/28/us/politics/immigration-bill-clears-final-hurdle-to-senate-approval.html?pagewanted=all&module=Search&mabReward=relbias%3Ar%2C{%221%22%3A%22RI%3A11%22}
4. *Graham v. Richardson,* 403 U.S. 532 (1971).
5. See, for instance, Nicole Cusano, "Amherst Mulls Giving Non-Citizens Right to Vote," *Boston Globe,* October 26, 1998, B1; "Casual Citizenship?" Editorial, *Boston Globe,* October 31, 1998, A18.
6. David M. Kennedy et al., *The American Pageant,* 12th ed. (Boston: Houghton Mifflin, 2002), 731.
7. Randal C. Archibold, "Arizona Enacts Stringent Law on Immigration," *New York Times,* April 23, 2010, www.nytimes.com/2010/04/24/us/politics/24immig.html.
8. Brian Lawson, "UA Economist Finds Immigration Law Could Cost Alabama Millions in Lost Taxes, Billions in Lost GDP," *Huntsville Times,* January 31, 2012, blog.al.com/breaking/2012/01/ua_economist_finds_immigration.html.
9. Josh Gerstein, "Arizona Law to Be Heard by Supreme Court," *Politico,* December 12, 2011, www.politico.com/news/stories/1211/70293.html.
10. Adam Liptak, "Blocking Parts of Arizona Law, Justices Allow Its Centerpiece," *New York Times,* June 26, 2012, www.nytimes.com/2012/06/26/us/supreme-court-rejects-part-of-arizona-immigration-law.html?_r=1.
11. Kate Zernike and Megan Thee-Brenan, "Poll Finds Tea Party Backers Wealthier and More Educated," *New York Times,* April 14, 2010.
12. Benjamin R. Barber, "Foreword," in Grant Reeher and Joseph Cammarano, eds., *Education for Citizenship: Ideas and Innovations in Political Learning* (New York: Rowman & Littlefield, 1997), ix.
13. Chris Cilizza, "Three Sentences on Immigration Reform that Will Haunt Republicans in 2016," The Washington Post, July 1, 2014, www.washingtonpost.com/blogs/the-fix/wp/2014/07/01/three-sentences-on-immigration-that-will-haunt-republicans-in-2016/
14. Alexa Ura, "Fiery Anti-Immigration GOP Nominee Dan Patrick Shifts Tome to Appeal to Hispanic Voters. The Huffington Post, May 29, 2014.http://www.huffingtonpost.com/2014/05/29/dan-patrick-hispanic-voters-_n_5411060.html
15. Capital Report, "Immigration Reform is No Longer a Slam-dunk Issue for Democrats," Market Watch. September 10, 2014, http://blogs.marketwatch.com/capitolreport/2014/09/10/immigration-reform-is-no-longer-a-slam-dunk-issue-for-democrats/
16. Carrie Budoff Brown, Jake Sherman, and Manu Raju, "2012 Election Puts Spotlight on Immigration Reform," Politico, November 11, 2012, www.politico.com/news/stories/1112/83552.html

Chapter 3

1. David Barstow, "Tea Party Lights Fuse for Rebellion on Right," *New York Times,* February 15, 2010, www.nytimes.com/2010/02/16/us/politics/16teaparty.html?emc=eta1.
2. Richard A. Serrano, "Uneasy in Oklahoma: Fifteen Years After the McVeigh Bombing, Anger at Washington and Talk of a State Militia," *Los Angeles Times,* April 18, 2010.
3. Operation American Spring, operationamericanspring.org. Cheryl K. Chumley, "Operation American Spring to Hit D.C., to Oust Obama, Biden, Boehner, Holder," *Washington Times,* May 14, 2014, www.washingtontimes.com/news/2014/may/14/operation-american-spring-hitting-dc-to-oust-obama/; Cheryl K. Chumley, "Operation American Spring Falls Flat: 'This Is Very Disappointing,' Texan Says," *Washington Times,* Friday, May 16, 2014, www.washingtontimes.com/news/2014/may/16/operation-american-spring-falls-flat-very-disappoi/.
4. "Lubbock Co. Judge Warns of Potential Danger If Obama Is Re-elected," Fox 34 News, August 23, 2012, www.myfoxlubbock.com/news/local/story/Lubbock-tom-head-tax-rates-president-obama/PeO4Q8GeGEiy_FpxheUnmA.cspx.
5. Toni Lucy, "Anti-Government Forces Still Struggle to Recover From Oklahoma City Fallout," *USA Today,* May 9, 2000, 9A; Evan Thomas and Eve Conant, "Hate: Antigovernment Extremists Are on the Rise—and On the March," *Newsweek,* April 19, 2010.
6. Tea Party, "About Us," www.teaparty.org/about-us/.
7. There are many good illustrations of this point of view. See, for example, Gordon Wood, *The Creation of the American Republic, 1776–1787* (New York: Norton, 1969); Lawrence Henry Gipson, *The Coming of the Revolution, 1763–1775* (New York: Harper Torchbooks, 1962); Bernard Bailyn, *The Ideological Origins of the American Revolution* (Cambridge, Mass.: Belknap, 1967); and Jack P. Greene, ed., *The Reinterpretation of the American Revolution, 1763–1789* (New York: Harper & Row, 1968).
8. Robert Darcy, Susan Welch, and Janet Clark, *Women, Elections, and Representation* (Lincoln: University of Nebraska Press, 1994), 5–6.
9. Donald R. Wright, *African Americans in the Colonial Era* (Arlington Heights, Ill.: Harlan Davidson, 1990), 52.
10. Wright, 56.
11. Wright, 57–58.
12. Lawrence Henry Gipson, "The American Revolution as an Aftermath of the Great War for the Empire, 1754–1765," in Edmund S. Morgan, ed., *The American Revolution* (Englewood Cliffs, N.J.: Prentice Hall, 1965), 160.
13. Bailyn, 160–229.
14. Gipson, "The American Revolution," 163.
15. James L. Roark, et al., *The American Promise: A History of the United States*, 3rd ed. (Boston: Bedford/St. Martin's, 2005).
16. Thomas Paine, *Common Sense and Other Political Writings* (Indianapolis, Ind.: Bobbs-Merrill, 1953).

17. Cited in John L. Moore, *Speaking of Washington* (Washington, D.C.: Congressional Quarterly, 1993), 102–103.
18. John Locke, *Second Treatise of Government,* C. B. Macpherson, ed. (Indianapolis: Hackett, 1980), 31.
19. Garry Wills, *Inventing America* (New York: Doubleday, 1978), 377.
20. Wright, 122.
21. Wright, 152.
22. Mary Beth Norton et al., *A People and a Nation* (Boston: Houghton Mifflin, 1994), 159.
23. Darcy, Welch, and Clark, 8.
24. See, for example, Sally Smith Booth, *The Women of '76* (New York: Hastings House, 1973); and Charles E. Claghorn, *Women Patriots of the American Revolution: A Biographical Dictionary* (Metuchen, N.J.: Scarecrow Press, 1991).
25. Carl Holliday, *Woman's Life in Colonial Days* (Boston: Cornhill, 1922), 143.
26. Wood, 398–399.
27. Wood, 404.
28. Alexander Hamilton, James Madison, and John Jay, *The Federalist Papers,* Clinton Rossiter, ed. (New York: New American Library, 1961), 84.
29. Adrienne Koch, "Introduction," in James Madison, *Notes of Debates in the Federal Convention of 1787* (New York: Norton, 1969), xiii.
30. Moore, 9.
31. James Madison, *Notes of Debates in the Federal Convention of 1787 Reported by James Madison,* reissue ed. (New York: Norton, 1987).
32. There are many collections of Anti-Federalist writings. See, for example, W. B. Allen and Gordon Lloyd, eds., *The Essential Antifederalist* (Lanham, Md.: University Press of America, 1985); Cecilia Kenyon, ed., *The Antifederalists* (Indianapolis, Ind.: Bobbs Merrill, 1966); and Ralph Ketcham, *The Anti-Federalist Papers and the Constitutional Convention Debates* (New York: New American Library, 1986).
33. Hamilton, Madison, and Jay, 322.
34. Ketcham, 14.
35. James H. Kettner, *The Development of American Citizenship, 1608–1870* (Chapel Hill: University of North Carolina Press, 1978).
36. Carl Hulse, "Recalling 1995 Bombing, Clinton Sees Parallels," *New York Times,* April 16, 2010.

Chapter 4

1. Andrew Harris, "Marijuana Mayhem Splits U.S. in Two as States Like Idaho Bust Travelers," *Idaho Statesman,* August 22, 2014, www.idahostatesman.com/2014/08/22/3336621/marijuana-mayhem-splits-us-in.html.
2. Carrie Johnson, "U.S. Eases Stance on Medical Marijuana," *Washington Post,* October 20, 2009.
3. Dave Phillips, "Bid to Expand Medical Marijuana Business Faces Federal Hurdles," *New York Times,* August 23, 2014, www.nytimes.com/2014/08/24/us/bid-to-expand-medical-marijuana-business-faces-federal-hurdles.html.
4. Lindsey Seavert, "Mom Charged After Giving Son Medical Marijuana," KARE (NBC affiliate), Minneapolis, MN, August 20, 2014, www.kare11.com/story/news/local/2014/08/20/mn-mom-charged-after-giving-son-medical-marijuana/14372025/.
5. Juliet Lapidos, "The Public Lightens Up About Weed," *New York Times,* July 26,

2014, www.nytimes.com/2014/07/27/opinion/sunday/high-time-the-public-lightens-up-about-weed.html.
6. Alexander Hamilton, James Madison, and John Jay, *The Federalist Papers,* Clinton Rossiter, ed. (New York: New American Library, 1961), 82.
7. James Madison, *Notes of Debates in the Federal Convention of 1787,* reissue ed. (New York: Norton, 1987), 86.
8. David M. Olson, *The Legislative Process* (Cambridge, Mass.: Harper & Row, 1980), 21–23.
9. Richard F. Fenno Jr., *The United States Senate: A Bicameral Perspective* (Washington, D.C.: American Enterprise Institute for Public Policy Research, 1982), 5.
10. Madison, 136, 158.
11. Hamilton, Madison, and Jay, 465.
12. Lawrence S. Graham et al., *Politics and Government: A Brief Introduction,* 3rd ed. (Chatham, N.J.: Chatham House Publishers, 1994), 172–173.
13. Baron de Montesquieu, *The Spirit of the Laws,* Thomas Nugent, trans. (New York: Hafner Press, 1949), 152.
14. Hamilton, Madison, and Jay, 322.
15. Ibid., 84.
16. Ibid., 322.
17. Ibid., 321–322.
18. James C. McKinley Jr., "Agreement on Tougher Drunken-Driving Standard," *New York Times,* May 10, 2001, B5.
19. For a full explanation of the bakery metaphors, see Morton Grodzins, *The American System* (Chicago: Rand McNally, 1966). A more updated discussion of federalism can be found in Joseph Zimmerman, *Contemporary American Federalism: The Growth of National Power* (New York: Praeger, 1992).
20. Paul E. Peterson, *City Limits* (Chicago: University of Chicago Press, 1981).
21. Charles Mahtesian, "Romancing the Smokestack," *Governing* (November 1994): 36–40.
22. Harold Wolman, "Local Economic Development Policy: What Explains the Divergence Between Policy Analysis and Political Behavior?" *Journal of Urban Affairs* 10 (1988): 19–28; Martin Saiz and Susan Clarke, "Economic Development and Infrastructure Policy," in Virginia Gray and Russell Hanson, eds., *Politics in the American States,* 8th ed. (Washington, D.C.: CQ Press, 2004).
23. David Damon and Mark K. Matthews, "Tax Incentives to Lure Jobs Could Hit $31M," *Orlando Sentinel,* May 11, 2009, articles.orlandosentinel.com/2009-05-11/news/solar_1_willard-ohio-incentives.
24. Robert C. Turner, Patria Fleming, and Ben Kaufman, "The Political Economy of Trophy Industrial Recruitment Projects," paper for the Northeast Political Science Annual Conference, November 17–19, 2005.
25. Kierstan Gordan, "Scholars, Dollars and Sense," *Governing* (May 2000): 44.
26. Eliza Griswold, "The Fracturing of Pennsylvania" *New York Times,* November 11, 2011; Wenonah Hauter, "For Democrats Nationwide, Pennsylvania Offer a Lens on the Widening Rift over Fracking" The Bog, Huff Post Politics, September 25, 2013, www.huffingtonpost.com/wenonah-hauter/for-democrats-nationwide-_b_3981518.html.
27. The National Organization for the Reform of Marijuana Laws, "State Info," July 29, 2014, norml.org/states.
28. James Dao, "Red, Blue and Angry All Over," *New York Times,* January 16, 2005.
29. *McCulloch v. Maryland,* 4 Wheat. 316 (1819).
30. *Gibbons v. Ogden,* 9 Wheat. 1 (1824).

31. *Cooley v. Board of Wardens of Port of Philadelphia,* 53 U.S. (12 How.) 299 (1851).
32. *Dred Scott v. Sanford,* 60 U.S. 393 (1857).
33. *Pollock v. Farmer's Loan and Trust Company,* 1157 U.S. 429 (1895).
34. *Lochner v. New York,* 198 U.S. 45 (1905).
35. *Hammer v. Dagenhart,* 247 U.S. 251 (1918).
36. John Kincaid, "State-Federal Relations: Dueling Policies," in *The Book of the States 2008* (Lexington, Ky.: The Council of State Governments, 2008), 19.
37. Kincaid.
38. Morris Fiorina, *Congress: Keystone of the Washington Establishment,* 2nd ed. (New Haven: Yale University Press, 1989); John E. Chubb, "Federalism and the Bias for Centralization," in John E. Chubb and Paul E. Peterson, eds., *The New Directions in American Politics* (Washington, D.C.: Brookings Institution, 1985), 273–306.
39. U.S. Census Bureau, *Statistical Abstract of the United States, 2010* (Washington, D.C.: U.S. Census Bureau), Table 419.
40. Jason DeParle, "Welfare Limits Left Poor Adrift as Recession Hits," *New York Times,* April 8, 2012, www.nytimes.com/2012/04/08/us/welfare-limits-left-poor-adrift-as-recession-hit.html?hp.
41. Quote from Rochelle L. Stanfield, "Holding the Bag," *National Journal,* September 9, 1995, 2206.
42. Walker, 232–234; Kincaid, "State-Federal Relations: Dueling Policies."
43. Stephen Clark, "Homeland Security Delays Launch of 'Real ID'—Again," March 5, 2011, www.foxnews.com/politics/2011/03/05/homeland-security-delays-launch-real-id/3/28/2012; Priscilla M. Regan, "Opposition to REAL ID Act at the State Level: Privacy, Immigration or Unfunded Mandates," prepared for delivery at the annual meeting of the American Political Science Association, Boston, August 28–31, 2008; U.S. Department of Homeland Security, "REAL ID Final Rule," www.dhs.gov/files/laws/gc_1172765386179.shtm.
44. Martha Derthick, "Madison's Middle Ground in the 1980s," *Public Administration Review* (January–February 1987): 66–74.
45. Advisory Commission on Intergovernmental Relations, *Federal Mandate Relief for State, Local, and Tribal Governments* (Washington, D.C.: U.S. Government Printing Office, January 1995), 18.
46. Donald F. Kettl, "Mandates Forever," *Governing* (August 2003): 12; Tom Diemer, "Unfunded Mandate Bill Working Well," *Cleveland Plain Dealer,* February 8, 1998, 20A; Jonathan Walters, "The Accidental Tyranny of Congress," *Governing* (April 1997): 14.
47. "Keeping America Healthy," www.medicaid.gov/Medicaid-CHIP-Program-Information/By-Topics/Financing-and-Reimbursement/Financing-and-Reimbursement.html.
48. Stephen C. Fehr, "Recession Could Reshape State Governments in Lasting Ways," Pew Center for the States, February 11, 2010, www.stateline.org/live/details/story?contentId=454018.
49. Thomas Pugh, "Across America, Public-Sector Job Cuts Take a Heavy Toll," *Miami Herald,* April 4, 2012, www.miamiherald.com/2012/04/04/2733150/across-america-public-sector-job.html.
50. Fehr, "Recession Could Reshape State Governments in Lasting Ways."
51. Alison Vekshin, "Tea Party Opposition to Stimulus Will Harm States, Kramer Says," *Business Week,* September 15, 2010, www.businessweek.com/news/2010-09-15/tea-party-opposition-to-stimulus-will-harm-states-kramer-says.html; Jeff Brady, "Stimulus Money Meets Mixed Reactions

From States," *Weekend Edition*, National Public Radio, February 19, 2009, www.npr.org/templates/story/story.php?storyId=100731571.
52. National Conference of State Legislatures, "State Budget Update, March 2011," www.ncsl.org/issues-research/budget/state-budget-update-march-2011.aspx.
53. Hamilton, Madison, and Jay, 278.
54. *Gonzales v. Raich,* 545 U.S. 1 (2005).
55. Jerry Seper, "DEA Raids Medical Marijuana Centers," *Washington Times,* January 19, 2007, A9.
56. Carrie Johnson, "U.S. Eases Stance on Medical Marijuana," *Washington Post,* October 20, 2009.
57. Tim Dickinson, "Obama's War on Pot," *Rolling Stone,* February 16, 2012, www.rollingstone.com/politics/news/obamas-war-on-pot-20120216.
58. Jacob Sullum, "The Power to Regulate Anything," *Los Angeles Times,* April 22, 2008.
59. Warren Richey, "Showdown Over Medical Marijuana," *Christian Science Monitor,* November 29, 2004.

Chapter 5

1. Susan Candiotti, Greg Botelho, and Tom Watkins. "Newtown Shooting Details Revealed in Newly Released Documents," CNN, March 29, 2013. www.cnn.com/2013/03/28/us/connecticut-shooting-documents/
2. Full transcript of President Obama's Remarks at a Dec. 16 Prayer Vigil for the victims of the Shooting at Sandy Hook Elementary School, *Washington Post,* December 16, 2012. http://www.washingtonpost.com/politics/president-obamas-speech-at-prayer-vigil-for-newtown-shooting-victims-full-transcript/2012/12/16/f764bf8a-47dd-11e2-ad54-580638ede391_story.html
3. Karen McVeigh, "Sandy Hook: One Year on, Campaigners Prepare for New Push on Gun Control," *The Guardian,* December 13, 2013. www.theguardian.com/world/2013/dec/13/sandy-hook-campaigners-push-gun-control
4. Ted Barrett and Tom Cohen, "Senate Rejects Expanded Gun Background Checks," CNN, April 18, 2013. www.cnn.com/2013/04/17/politics/senate-guns-vote/
5. Ashley Fantz, Lindsey Knight, and Kevin Wang, "A Closer Look: How Many Newtown-like School Shootings Since Sandy Hook?" CNN, June 19, 2014. www.cnn.com/2014/06/11/us/school-shootings-cnn-number/
6. Darren K. Carlson, "Far Enough? Public Wary of Restricted Liberties," *Gallup Poll,* January 20, 2004.
7. *West Virginia Board of Education v. Barnette,* 319 U.S. 624 (1943).
8. *Hamdi v. Rumsfeld,* 124 S. Ct. 2633 (2004); *Rasul v. Bush,* 124 S. Ct. 2686 (2004).
9. *Hamdan v. Rumsfeld,* 548 U.S. 557 (2007).
10. *Korematsu v. United States,* 323 U.S. 214 (1944).
11. Associated Press, *The Cold War at Home and Abroad 1945–1953* (New York: Grollier, 1995), 145.
12. Robert Frederick Burk, *The Eisenhower Administration and Black Civil Rights* (Knoxville: University of Tennessee Press, 1984), 204.
13. Ben Conery, "Administration Seeks Patriot Act Extensions; Defies Liberties Groups," *Washington Times,* September 16, 2009, 1.
14. Jack N. Rakove, "James Madison and the Bill of Rights," in *This Constitution: From Ratification to the Bill of Rights,* American Political Science Association and American Historical Association (Washington, D.C.: Congressional Quarterly, 1988), 165.
15. David M. O'Brien, *Constitutional Law and Politics,* vol. 2 (New York: Norton, 1995), 300.
16. Ann Bowman and Richard Kearney, *State and Local Government,* 3rd ed. (Boston: Houghton Mifflin, 1996), 39.
17. *Barron v. The Mayor and City Council of Baltimore,* 7 Peters 243 (1833).
18. *Chicago, Burlington & Quincy Railroad Co. v. Chicago,* 166 U.S. 226 (1897).
19. *Gitlow v. New York,* 268 U.S. 652 (1920), cited in O'Brien, 304.
20. Peter Irons, *Brennan vs. Rehnquist: The Battle for the Constitution* (New York: Knopf, 1994), 116.
21. O'Brien, 646.
22. O'Brien, 647.
23. O'Brien, 645; Henry J. Abraham and Barbara A. Perry, *Freedom and the Court* (New York: Oxford University Press, 1994), 223.
24. O'Brien, 648.
25. Irons, 137.
26. *Abington School District v. Schempp,* 374 U.S. 203, 83 S. Ct. 1560 (1963).
27. *Abington School District v. Schempp; Murray v. Curlett,* 374 U.S. 203 (1963).
28. *Engel v. Vitale,* 370 U.S. 421, 82 S. Ct. 1261 (1962).
29. *Epperson v. Arkansas,* 393 U.S. 97 (1968).
30. *Lemon v. Kurtzman,* 403 U.S. 602, 91 S. Ct. 2105 (1971).
31. O'Brien, 661.
32. *Lynch v. Donnelly,* 465 U.S. 668 (1984).
33. *Wallace v. Jaffree,* 472 U.S. 38 (1985).
34. *Edwards v. Aguillard,* 482 U.S. 578 (1987).
35. *Board of Education of Westside Community Schools v. Mergens,* 496 U.S. 226 (1990).
36. *Lee v. Weisman,* 112 S. Ct. 2649 (1992).
37. *Santa Fe Independent School District v. Doe,* 530 U.S. 290 (2000).
38. *Locke v. Davey,* 124 S. Ct. 1307 (2004).
39. Charles C. Hayes, "State Lawmakers Reignite School Wars Over Religion," The First Amendment Center, at Vanderbilt University and the Newseum, April 6, 2012, www.firstamendmentcenter.org/state-lawmakers-reignite-school-wars-over-religion.
40. *Cantwell v. Connecticut,* 310 U.S. 296 (1940).
41. *Minersville School District v. Gobitis,* 310 U.S. 586 (1940).
42. *West Virginia State Board of Education v. Barnette,* 319 U.S. 624 (1943).
43. *McGowan v. Maryland,* 36 U.S. 420; *Two Guys From Harrison-Allentown, Inc., v. McGinley,* 366 U.S. 582; *Gallagher v. Crown Kosher Super Market of Massachusetts,* 366 U.S. 617; *Braunfield v. Brown,* 366 U.S. 599 (1961).
44. *Sherbert v. Verner,* 374 U.S. 398 (1963).
45. *Employment Division, Department of Human Resources v. Smith,* 494 U.S. 872 (1990).
46. *City of Boerne v. Flores,* 521 U.S. 507, 1997.
47. *Gonzales v. O Centro Espirata Beneficente Uniao do Vegetal,* 546 U.S. 418 (2006).
48. Adam Liptak, "Religious Groups Given 'Exception' to Work Bias Law," *New York Times,* January 11, 2012, www.nytimes.com/2012/01/12/us/supreme-court-recognizes-religious-exception-to-job-discrimination-laws.html.
49. Rodney K. Smith, "Does Obama Really Care About Religious Freedom in America?" *Christian Science Monitor,* February 17, 2012, www.csmonitor.com/Commentary/Opinion/2012/0217/Does-Obama-really-care-about-religious-freedom-in-America.
50. *Reynolds v. U.S.,* 98 U.S. 145 (1878).
51. *Welsh v. United States,* 398 U.S. 333 (1970).
52. John L. Sullivan, James Pierson, and George Marcus, *Political Tolerance and American Democracy* (Chicago: University of Chicago Press, 1982), 203.
53. John Cassidy, "Demonizing Edward Snowden: Which Side Are You On?" *New Yorker* blog, June 24, 2013, www.newyorker.com/online/blogs/johncassidy/2013/06/demonizing-edward-snowden-which-side-are-you-on.html.
54. O'Brien, 373; Samuel Walker, *In Defense of American Liberties: A History of the ACLU* (New York: Oxford University Press, 1990), 29.
55. Cited in Walker, 14.
56. *Schenck v. United States,* 249 U.S. 47 (1919); *Debs v. United States,* 249 U.S. 211 (1919); *Frowerk v. United States,* 249 U.S. 204 (1919); *Abrams v. United States,* 250 U.S. 616 (1919).
57. *Whitney v. California,* 274 U.S. 357 (1927).
58. *Brandenburg v. Ohio,* 395 U.S. 444 (1969).
59. *United States v. O'Brien,* 391 U.S. 367 (1968).
60. *Tinker v. Des Moines,* 393 U.S. 503 (1969).
61. *Street v. New York,* 394 U.S. 576 (1969).
62. *Texas v. Johnson,* 491 U.S. 397 (1989).
63. *United States v. Eichman,* 110 S. Ct. 2404 (1990).
64. *Virginia v. Black,* 538 U.S. 343 (2003).
65. *National Association for the Advancement of Colored People v. Alabama,* 357 U.S. 449 (1958).
66. *Sheldon v. Tucker,* 364 U.S. 516 (1960).
67. *Heart of Atlanta Motel v. United States,* 379 U.S. 241 (1964).
68. *Roberts v. United States Jaycees,* 468 U.S. 609 (1984).
69. *Jacobellis v. Ohio,* 378 U.S. 476 (1964).
70. *Miller v. California,* 413 U.S. 15 (1973).
71. *Cohen v. California,* 403 U.S. 15 (1971).
72. *Chaplinsky v. New Hampshire,* 315 U.S. 568 (1942).
73. *Terminello v. Chicago,* 337 U.S. 1 (1949).
74. *Cohen v. California,* 403 U.S. 15 (1971).
75. *Doe v. University of Michigan,* 721 F. Supp. 852 (E. D. Mich. 1989); *UMW Post v. Board of Regents of the University of Wisconsin,* 774 F. Supp. 1163, 1167, 1179 (E. D. Wis. 1991).
76. *R.A.V. v. City of St. Paul,* 60 LW 4667 (1992).
77. *Near v. Minnesota,* 283 U.S. 697 (1930).
78. *New York Times Company v. United States,* 403 U.S. 670 (1971).
79. Anthony Lewis, *Make No Law: The Sullivan Case and the First Amendment* (New York: Vintage Books/Random House, 1991).
80. *New York Times v. Sullivan,* 376 U.S. 254 (1964).
81. *Sheppard v. Maxwell,* 385 U.S. 333 (1966).
82. *Nebraska Press Association v. Stuart,* 427 U.S. 539 (1976).
83. *Reno v. ACLU,* 521 U.S. 1113 (1997).
84. *Ashcroft v. ACLU,* 124 S. Ct. 2783 (2004).
85. *United States v. American Library Association, Inc.,* 539 U.S. 194 (2003).
86. Pamela LiCalzi O'Connell, "Compressed Data: Law Newsletter Has to Sneak Past Filters," *New York Times,* April 2, 2001, C4.
87. Jeffery Selingo, "Student Writers Try to Duck the Censors by Going On-line," *New York Times,* June 7, 2001, G6.
88. Chloe Albanesius, "After Blackout, Congress Postpones Action on SOPA, PIPA," *PC Magazine,* January 20, 2012, www.pcmag.com/article2/0,2817,2399132,00.asp.
89. *United States v. Lopez,* 514 U.S. 549 (1995); *Printz v. United States,* 521 U.S. 898 (1997).
90. Robert J. Spitzer, *The Politics of Gun Control* (Chatham, N.J.: Chatham House, 1995), 49.

91. Spitzer, 47.
92. *United States v. Cruikshank*, 92 U.S. 542 (1876); *Presser v. Illinois*, 116 U.S. 252 (1886); *Miller v. Texas*, 153 U.S. 535 (1894); *United States v. Miller*, 307 U.S. 174 (1939).
93. *Printz v. United States*, 521 U.S. 898 (1997).
94. Warren Richey, "Supreme Court Asserts Broad Gun Rights," *Christian Science Monitor*, June 27, 2008.
95. Robert Barnes and Dan Eggen, "Supreme Court Affirms Fundamental Right to Bear Arms," *Washington Post*, June 29, 2010, www.washingtonpost.com/wp-dyn/content/article/2010/06/28/AR2010062802134.html.
96. *Olmstead v. United States*, 277 U.S. 438 (1928).
97. *Katz v. United States*, 389 U.S. 347 (1967).
98. *Berger v. State of New York*, 388 U.S. 41 (1967).
99. Adam Liptak, "Major Ruling Shields Privacy of Cellphones, *New York Times*, June 25, 2014, www.nytimes.com/2014/06/26/us/supreme-court-cellphones-search-privacy.html.
100. *Skinner v. Railway Labor Executive Association*, 489 U.S. 602 (1989).
101. *Veronia School District v. Acton*, 515 U.S. 646 (1995).
102. Associated Press, "Supreme Court Upholds Invasive Strip Searches," National Public Radio, April 2, 2012, www.npr.org/2012/04/02/149849568/supreme-court-upholds-invasive-strip-searches.
103. *Weeks v. United States*, 232 U.S. 383 (1914).
104. *Wolf v. Colorado*, 338 U.S. 25 (1949).
105. *Mapp v. Ohio*, 367 U.S. 643 (1961).
106. *United States v. Calandra*, 414 U.S. 338 (1974).
107. *United States v. Janis*, 428 U.S. 433 (1976).
108. *Massachusetts v. Sheppard*, 468 U.S. 981 (1984); *United States v. Leon*, 468 U.S. 897 (1984); *Illinois v. Krull*, 480 U.S. 340 (1987).
109. *Herring v. United States*, No. 07-513. Argued October 7, 2008—Decided January 14, 2009.
110. *Miranda v. Arizona*, 382 U.S. 925 (1965); *Dickerson v. United States*, 530 U.S. 428, 120 S. Ct. 2326; 2000 U.S. LEXIS 4305.
111. *Johnson v. Zerbst*, 304 U.S. 458 (1938).
112. *Gideon v. Wainwright*, 372 U.S. 335 (1963).
113. *Ross v. Mofitt*, 417 U.S. 600 (1974); *Murray v. Giarratano*, 492 U.S. 1 (1989).
114. Henry Weinstein, "Many Denied Right to Counsel, Group Says," *Los Angeles Times*, July 13, 2004, A10.
115. *In re Kemmler*, 136 U.S. 436 (1890).
116. *Atkins v. Virginia*, 536 U.S. 304 (2002).
117. *Roper v. Simmons*, 543 U.S. 551 (2005).
118. *Kennedy v. Louisiana*, No. 07-343. Argued April 16, 2008—Decided June 25, 2008; modified October 1, 2008.
119. *Furman v. Georgia, Jackson v. Georgia, Branch v. Texas*, 408 U.S. 238 (1972).
120. *Gregg v. Georgia*, 428 U.S. 153 (1976); *Woodson v. North Carolina*, 428 U.S. 280 (1976); *Roberts v. Louisiana*, 428 U.S. 325 (1976).
121. *McClesky v. Kemp*, 481 U.S. 279 (1987).
122. *McClesky v. Zant*, 111 S. Ct. 1454 (1991).
123. *Baze v. Rees*, 553 U.S. 35 (2008).
124. Jack Hitt, "The Moratorium Gambit," *New York Times Magazine*, December 9, 2001, 82.
125. Keith Richburg, "New Jersey Approves Abolition of Death Penalty," *Washington Post*, December 14, 2007, A3.
126. Frank Newport, "In U.S., Two-Thirds Continue to Support Death Penalty," October, 13, 2009, www.gallup.com/poll/123638/In-U.S.-Two-Thirds- Continue-Support-Death-Penalty.aspx.
127. Samuel D. Warren and Louis D. Brandeis, "The Right to Privacy," *Harvard Law Review* 4 (1890).
128. *Griswold v. Connecticut*, 391 U.S. 145 (1965).
129. *Eisenstadt v. Baird*, 405 U.S. 438 (1972).
130. *Roe v. Wade*, 410 U.S. 113 (1973).
131. *Harris v. McRae*, 448 U.S. 297 (1980).
132. See, for example, *Webster v. Reproductive Health Services*, 492 U.S. 4090 (1989) and *Rust v. Sullivan*, 111 S. Ct. 1759 (1991).
133. *Gonzales v. Carhart*, 550 U.S. 124 (2007).
134. Erik Eckholm, "Push for 'Personhood' Amendment Represents New Tack in Abortion Fight," *New York Times*, October 25, 2011, www.nytimes.com/2011/10/26/us/politics/personhood-amendments-would-ban-nearly-all-abortions.html?pagewanted=all.
135. Andrew Sullivan, "An Anti-Abortion Frenzy in the States," *The Daily Dish*, April 25, 2012, andrewsullivan.thedailybeast.com/2012/04/an-anti-abortion-frenzy-in-the-states.html; Erik Eckholm and Kim Severson, "Virginia Senate Passes Ultrasound Bill as Other States Take Notice," *New York Times*, February 28, 2012, www.nytimes.com/2012/02/29/us/virginia-senate-passes-revised-ultrasound-bill.html?pagewanted=all.
136. Lydia Saad, "U.S. Abortion Attitudes Closely Divided," August 4, 2009, www.gallup.com/poll/122033/U.S.-Abortion-Attitudes-Closely-Divided.aspx.
137. *Bowers v. Hardwick*, 478 U.S. 186 (1986).
138. *Commonwealth of Kentucky v. Wasson*, 842 S.W.2d 487 (1992).
139. *Lawrence v. Texas*, 539 U.S. 558 (2003).
140. *Romer v. Evans*, 517 U.S. 620 (1996).
141. *Cruzan v. Director, Missouri Department of Health*, 497 U.S. 261 (1990).
142. Frank Newport, "The Terri Schiavo Case in Review: Support for Her Being Allowed to Die Consistent," April 1, 2005, www.gallup.com.
143. *Washington v. Glucksberg*, 521 U.S. 702 (1997); *Vacco v. Quill*, 521 U.S. 793 (1997).
144. Stephen Adler and Wade Lambert, "Just About Everyone Violates Some Laws, Even Model Citizens," *Wall Street Journal*, March 12, 1993, 1.
145. Thomas Janoski, *Citizenship and Civil Society: A Framework of Rights and Obligations in Liberal, Traditional and Social Democratic Regimes* (Cambridge, U.K.: Cambridge University Press, 1998), 53–54.
146. Full transcript of President Obama's Remarks at a Dec. 16 Prayer Vigil for the victims of the Shooting at Sandy Hook Elementary School. http://www.washingtonpost.com/politics/president-obamas-speech-at-prayer-vigil-for-newtown-shooting-victims-full-transcript/2012/12/16/f764bf8a-47dd-11e2-ad54-580638ede391_story.html
147. Peter Rugg and James Nye, "'The Most Revolting, Tone Deaf Statement I've Ever Seen': NRA Condemned After Its Astonishing Response to Sandy Hook Massacre Calling for Schools to Arm Themselves," *The Daily Mail*, December 21, 2013. www.dailymail.co.uk/news/article-2251762/NRA-condemned-astonishing-response-Sandy-Hook-massacre-calling-schools-arm-themselves.html#ixzz3HAeAoM2k
148. Walter Hickey, "How the NRA Became the Most Powerful Interest in Washington," *Business Insider,* December 18, 2012. www.businessinsider.com/nra-lobbying-money-national-rifle-association-washington-2012-12
149. Ted Barrett and Tom Cohen, Senate Rejects Expanded Gun Background Checks. CNN April 18, 2013. http://www.cnn.com/2013/04/17/politics/senate-guns-vote/

Chapter 6

1. Jackie Calmes and Peter Baker, "Obama Says Same-Sex Marriage Should Be Legal," *New York Times*, May9, 2012, www.nytimes.com/2012/05/10/us/politics/obama-says-same-sex-marriage-should-be-legal.html?pagewanted=all.
2. Jacob Combs and Scottie Thomaston, "DOMA Ruled Unconstitutional in Connecticut Case Pedersen v. OPM," *Huffington Post*, August 1, 2012, www.huffingtonpost.com/jacob-combs.
3. Kathy Kiely, "These Are America's Governors. No Blacks. No Hispanics," *USA Today,* January 21, 2002, 1A.
4. David O'Brien, *Constitutional Law and Politics*, vol. 2 (New York: Norton, 1991), 1265.
5. American Civil Liberties Union, "Felon Enfranchisement and the Right to Vote," www.aclu.org/votingrights/exoffenders/index.html.
6. *Dred Scott v. Sanford,* 19 How. (60 U.S.) 393 (1857).
7. Scholars are divided about Lincoln's motives in issuing the Emancipation Proclamation; whether he genuinely desired to end slavery or merely used political means to shorten the war is hard to tell at this distance. Donald G. Nieman, *Promises to Keep: African-Americans and the Constitutional Order, 1776 to the Present* (New York: Oxford University Press, 1991), 55.
8. Bernard A. Weisberger, *Many Papers, One Nation* (Boston: Houghton Mifflin Company, 1987), 200.
9. Nieman, 107.
10. *The Civil Rights Cases*, 109 U.S. 3 (1883).
11. *Plessy v. Ferguson*, 163 U.S. 537 (1896).
12. Weisberger, 205–206.
13. *Guinn v. United States*, 238 U.S. 347 (1915).
14. *Missouri ex rel Gaines v. Canada*, 305 U.S. 337 (1938).
15. *Sweatt v. Painter*, 339 U.S. 629 (1950).
16. *Korematsu v. United States*, 323 U.S. 214 (1944).
17. *Brown v. Board of Education of Topeka (I)*, 347 U.S. 483 (1954).
18. *Brown v. Board of Education of Topeka (II)*, 349 U.S. 294 (1955).
19. *Gayle v. Browder*, 352 U.S. 903 (1956).
20. *Heart of Atlanta Motel, Inc. v. United States*, 379 U.S. 241 (1964); *Katzenbach v. McClung*, 379 U.S. 294 (1964); *Harper v. Virginia Board of Elections*, 383 U.S. 663 (1966).
21. Nieman, 179.
22. Nieman, 180.
23. *Swann v. Charlotte-Mecklenberg Board of Education*, 402 U.S. 1 (1971).
24. *Milliken v. Bradley*, 418 U.S. 717 (1974).
25. "*Brown v. Board*'s Goals Unrealized," *Atlanta Journal-Constitution*, May 16, 2004, 6C; Gary Orfield and Chungmei Lee, "*Brown* at 50: King's Dream or *Plessy*'s Nightmare?" Report conducted by the Harvard Civil Rights Project, 2004, www.civilrightsproject.harvard.edu/research/reseg04/brown50.pdf.
26. *Regents of the University of California v. Bakke*, 438 U.S. 265 (1978).
27. See, for example, *United Steelworkers of America v. Weber*, 443 U.S. 193 (1979); *Fullilove v. Klutznick*, 448 U.S. 448 (1980); *Firefighters Local Union No. 1784 v. Stotts*, 467 U.S. 561 (1984); and *Wygant v. Jackson Board of Education*, 476 U.S. 267 (1986).
28. *Patterson v. McLean Credit Union*, 491 U.S. 164 (1989).
29. *Wards Cove Packing, Inc. v. Atonio*, 490 U.S. 642 (1989).
30. *City of Richmond v. J. A. Croson*, 488 U.S. 469 (1989).
31. Darryl Fears, "A Diverse—and Divided—Black Community," *Washington Post*, February 24, 2002, A1.

32. Carmen DeNavas-Walt, Bernadette D. Proctor, and Jessica C. Smith, "Income, Poverty, and Health Insurance Coverage in the United States, 2012," www.census.gov/prod/2013pubs/p60-245.pdf.

33. Jonathan D. Glater, "Racial Gap in Pay Gets a Degree Sharper, a Study Finds," *Washington Post*, November 2, 1995, 13.

34. Joel Dresang, "Black Professional Men Paid Less Than White Peers," *Milwaukee Journal Sentinel*, August 16, 2001, 1D.

35. Andrea Orr, "Why Do Black Men Earn Less?" Economic Policy Institute, March 3, 2011, www.epi.org/publication/why_do_black_men_earn_less/.

36. Adam Liptak, "Supreme Court Invalidates Key Part of Voting Rights Act," *New York Times*, June 25, 2013, www.nytimes.com/2013/06/26/us/supreme-court-ruling.html?pagewanted=all.

37. National Conference of Black Mayors, "Leadership Development Program," www.aphia06dbl.org/files/NCBM.pdf.

38. CNNPolitics.com, "Poll: 76 Percent Say U.S. Ready for Black President," April 4, 2008, edition.cnn.com/2008/POLITICS/04/03/poll.black.president/index.html.

39. U.S. Census Bureau, "Voter Turnout Increases by 5 Million in 2008 Presidential Election U.S. Census Reports," July 20, 2009, www.census.gov/Press-Release/www/releases/archives/voting/013995.html.

40. Pew Research Center for the People and the Press, "Blacks Upbeat About Black Progress, Prospects," January 12, 2010, www.people-press.org/reports/576; Gallup, "One Third in US See Improved Race Relations Under Obama," August 24, 2011, www.gallup.com/poll/149141/one-third-improved-race-relations-obama.aspx; "Race in America: Key Data Points," Pew Research Center, August 27, 2013, www.pewresearch.org/key-data-points/race-in-america-key-data-points/.

41. Kathy Kiely, "National Elite Political Circles Lack Minorities," *USA Today Online*, January 21, 2002.

42. Pew Research Center for the People and the Press, "Public Backs Affirmative Action but Not Minority Preferences," June 2, 2009, pewresearch.org/pubs/1240/sotomayor-supreme-court-affirmative-action-minority-preferences.

43. Jodi Wilgoren, "U.S. Court Bars Race as Factor in School Entry," *New York Times*, March 28, 2001, A1.

44. Jacques Steinberg, "Redefining Diversity," *New York Times*, August 29, 2001, A14.

45. *Gratz v. Bollinger*, 539 U.S. 244 (2003).

46. *Grutter v. Bollinger*, 539 U.S. 306 (2003).

47. Nick Anderson, "How Supreme Court's Michigan Affirmative Action Ruling Affects Colleges," *Washington Post*, April 23, 2014, www.washingtonpost.com/local/education/how-supreme-courts-michigan-affirmative-action-ruling-affects-colleges/2014/04/23/7b0c79ae-cad7-11e3-93eb-6c0037dde2ad_story.html.

48. Ward Connerly, "Up From Affirmative Action," *New York Times*, April 29, 1996.

49. David K. Shipler, "My Equal Opportunity, Your Free Lunch," *New York Times*, March 5, 1995.

50. *Cherokee Nation v. Georgia*, 30 U.S. (5 Pet.) 1, 20 (1831).

51. Vine Deloria Jr. and Clifford M. Lytle, *The Nations Within: The Past and Future of American Indian Sovereignty* (New York: Pantheon, 1984), 17.

52. J. Bretting and B. Morris, "Fry-Bread Federalism Revisited: A Model of American Indian Intergovernmental Relations," paper presented at the 2005 annual meeting of the Western Political Science Association, Oakland, Calif.

53. *Lyng v. Northwest Indian Cemetery Protective Association*, 485 U.S. 439 (1988).

54. *Employment Division v. Oregon*, 494 U.S. 872 (1990).

55. U.S. Census Bureau, "American Indian and Alaskan Native Heritage Month," November 2013, www.census.gov/newsroom/releases/archives/facts_for_features_special_editions/cb13-ff26.html.

56. U.S. Census Bureau, "American Indian and Alaskan Native Heritage Month."

57. Nicholas Kristof, "Poverty's Poster Child," May 10, 2012, www.nytimes.com/2012/05/10/opinion/kristof-poverty sposter-child.html.

58. *Seminole Tribe of Florida v. Butterworth*, 658 F.2d 310 (1981), cert. denied, 455 U.S. 1020 (1982); *State of California v. Cabazon Band of Mission Indians*, 480 U.S. 202 (1987).

59. National Indiana Gaming Commission web site, "Gaming Revenue Reports," www.nigc.gov/Gaming_Revenue_Reports.aspx.

60. Adrian Sainz, "Indian Gambling Revenues Up in 2006, But Growth Slows," *North County Times*, June 28, 2007; National Indian Gaming Commission, "Tribal Gaming Revenues (in thousands) by Region Fiscal Year 2003 and 2002," n.d., www.nigc.gov/nigc/tribes/tribaldata2003/gamerevenue.jsp.

61. National Caucus of Native American State Legislators web site, www.nativeamericanlegislators.org/Public%20Documents/Caucus%20Membership.aspx.

62. U.S. Census Bureau, "Hispanic Heritage Month Quick Facts" August 66, 2012, www.census.gov/newsroom/releases/archives/facts_for_features_special_editions/cb12-ff19.html.

63. U.S. Census Bureau, "2010 Census Shows Nation's Hispanic Population Grew Four Times Faster Than US Population" May 26, 2011, www.census.gov/newsroom/releases/archives/2010_census/cb11-cn146.html.

64. Pew Hispanic Center, "Country of Origin Profiles," May 26, 2011, www.pewhispanic.org/2011/05/26/country-of-origin-profiles/.

65. Mark Falcoff, "Our Language Needs No Law," *New York Times*, August 5, 1996.

66. Rene Sanchez, "Both Parties Courting Latinos Vigorously," *Washington Post Online*, October 26, 1998, 2.

67. Douglas R. Hess and Jody Herman, "Representational Bias in the 2008 Electorate," November 2009, www.projectvote.org.

68. U.S. Census Bureau, "Asian/Pacific American Heritage Month," Profile America: Facts for Features, April 23, 2014, www.census.gov/newsroom/releases/pdf/cb14-ff13_asian.pdf.

69. Ronald Takaki, *Strangers From a Different Shore* (Boston: Little, Brown, 1989), 363-364.

70. *Hirabayashi v. United States*, 320 U.S. 81 (1943); *Korematsu v. United States*, 323 U.S. 214 (1944).

71. U.S. Census Bureau, "Income, Poverty and Health Insurance Coverage: 2010," www.census.gov/newsroom/releases/archives/income_wealth/cb11-157.html.

72. Data from harvard.edu, stanford.edu, mit.edu, and berkeley.edu.

73. Takaki.

74. Norimitsu Onishi, "Affirmative Action: Choosing Sides," *New York Times* Education Life Supplement, March 31, 1996, 27.

75. Mark Hugo Lopez, "In 2014, Latinos Will Surpass Whites as Largest Racial/Ethnic Group in California," Pew Research Center, January 24, 2014, www.pewresearch.org/fact-tank/2014/01/24/in-2014-latinos-will-surpass-whites-as-largest-racialethnic-group-in-california/.

76. Lena H. Sun, "Getting Out the Ethnic Vote," *Washington Post*, October 7, 1996, B5; K. Connie Kang, "Asian Americans Slow to Flex Their Political Muscle," *Los Angeles Times*, October 31, 1996, A18.

77. Sun, B5; Kang, A18.

78. Sun, B5.

79. Paul Van Slambrouck, "Asian-Americans' Politics Evolving," *Christian Science Monitor*, September 8, 1998, 2.

80. Eleanor Flexner, *Century of Struggle: The Woman's Rights Movement in the United States* (New York: Atheneum, 1973), 148-149.

81. Nancy E. McGlen and Karen O'Connor, *Women's Rights: The Struggle for Equality in the 19th and 20th Centuries* (New York: Praeger, 1983), 272-273.

82. *Bradwell v. Illinois*, 16 Wall. 130 (1873).

83. Quoted in Flexner, 178.

84. Flexner, 296.

85. McGlen and O'Connor, 83.

86. Jane Mansbridge, *Why We Lost the ERA* (Chicago: Chicago University Press, 1986), 13.

87. *Reed v. Reed*, 404 U.S. 71 (1971); *Craig v. Boren*, 429 U.S. 190 (1976).

88. *Weinberger v. Wiesenfeld*, 420 U.S. 636 (1975); *Califano v. Goldfarb*, 430 U.S. 199 (1977); *Califano v. Westcott*, 443 U.S. 76 (1979); *Orr v. Orr*, 440 U.S. 268 (1979).

89. Shelley Donald Coolidge, "Flat Tire on the Road to Pay Equity," *Christian Science Monitor*, April 11, 1997, 9; National Committee on Pay Equity, "The Wage Gap Over Time; In Real Dollars, Women See a Continuing Gap," www.pay-equity.org/info-time.html.

90. *Ledbetter v. Goodyear Tire & Rubber Co.*, 550 U.S. 618 (2007).

91. *Johnson v. Transportation Agency, Santa Clara, California*, 480 U.S. 616 (1987).

92. Barbara Noble, "At Work: And Now the Sticky Floor," *New York Times*, November 22, 1992, 23.

93. Kenneth Gray, "The Gender Gap in Yearly Earnings: Can Vocational Education Help?" Office of Special Populations' Brief, vol. 5, no. 2. National Center for Research in Vocational Education, University of California, Berkeley, Office of Special Populations, University of California, Berkeley.

94. Stephanie Armour, "Pregnant Workers Report Growing Discrimination," *USA Today*, February 16, 2005.

95. Barbara Burrell, "Campaign Finance: Women's Experience in the Modern Era," in Sue Thomas and Clyde Wilcox, eds., *Women and Elective Office: Past, Present, and Future* (New York: Oxford University Press, 1998), 27.

96. Gary F. Moncrief, Peverill Squire, and Malcolm E. Jewell, *Who Runs for the Legislature?* (Upper Saddle River, N.J.: Prentice Hall, 2001), 98-99.

97. CQ Weekly, "Guide to the New Congress," November 6, 2014. www.cq.com/graphics/weekly/2014/11/06/wr20141106_CQWeekly.pdf; Center for American Women and Politics, fact sheets, www.cawp.rutgers.edu/fast_facts/

98. Center for American Women and Politics, "Women Mayors in U.S. Cities 2014." www.cawp.rutgers.edu/fast_facts/levels_of_office/Local-WomenMayors.php

99. Rasmussen Reports, "77% Think Woman President Likely in Next 10 Years," January 15, 2014, www.rasmussenreports.com/public_content/politics/general_politics/january_2014/77_think_woman_president_likely_in_next_10_years.

100. Hillary Clinton, "Hillary's Remarks in Washington, DC," June 7, 2008, www.hillaryclinton.com.

101. Amy Caiazza, "Does Women's Representation in Elected Office Lead to Women-Friendly Policy?" Research in Brief, Institute for Women's Policy Research, May 2002, www.thecocklebur.com/wp-content/uploads/2010/12/One-2002-report.pdf; Kimberly Cowell-Meyers and Laura Langbein, "Linking Women's Descriptive and

Substantive Representation in the United States," *Politics and Gender*, 5 (2009): 491–518.

102. Kristin Eliasberg, "Making a Case for the Right to Be Different," *New York Times*, June 16, 2001, B11.
103. *Bowers v. Hardwick*, 478 U.S. 186 (1986).
104. *John J. Hurley, and South Boston Allied War Veterans Council v. Irish-American Gay, Lesbian, and Bisexual Group of Boston*, 115 S. Ct. 714 (1995).
105. *Romer v. Evans*, 115 S. Ct. 1092 (1996).
106. Linda Greenhouse, "The Supreme Court: The New Jersey Case; Supreme Court Backs Boy Scouts in Ban of Gays From Membership," *New York Times*, June 29, 2000, A1.
107. *Lawrence v. Texas*, 539 U.S. 558 (2003).
108. *Goodridge v. Dept. of Pub. Health*, 440 Mass. 309 (2003).
109. David W. Dunlap, "Gay Survey Raises a New Question," *New York Times*, October 18, 1994, B8.
110. National Gay and Lesbian Task Force, "The Gay, Lesbian, and Bisexual Vote: As Much as 5% of Presidential and Congressional Voters," 2004, www.thetaskforce.org/theissues/issue.cfm?issueID=32.
111. OpenSecrets.org, *Human Rights Campaign: Summary 2008,* www.opensecrets.org/orgs/all_summary.php?id=D000000158&nid=1276.
112. "Military Misguidance," *Chicago Sun Times*, November 20, 2002, 51.
113. Nathaniel Frank, "What the Changes to DADT Mean: The Good, the Bad and the Politically Dangerous," *Huffington Post*, March 25, 2010, www.huffingtonpost.com/nathaniel-frank/what-the-changes-to-dadt_b_513665.html
114. Nate Silver, "Public Opinion on Don't Ask Don't Tell," *New York Times*, November 30, 2010, fivethirtyeight.blogs.nytimes.com/2010/11/30/public-opinion-on-dont-ask-dont-tell/.
115. Public Religion Institute/Religion Services, "Same Sex Marriage, Gay Rights," March 7–11, 2012, pollingreport.com/civil.htm.
116. Gallup, "Half of Americans Support Legal Gay Marriage," May 8, 2012, www.gallup.com/poll/154529/HalfAmericans-Support-Legal-Gay-Marriage.aspx.
117. USA Today, "Obama's Gay Marriage Evolution Mirrors Nation's," May 10, 2012, www.usatoday.com/news/opinion/editorials/story/2012-05-09/Obama-same-sex-marriage/54865732/1.
118. *Massachusetts Board of Retirement v. Murgia*, 427 U.S. 307 (1976).
119. *Massachusetts Board of Retirement v. Murgia; Vance v. Bradley*, 440 U.S. 93 (1979); *Gregory v. Ashcroft*, 501 U.S. 452 (1991).
120. *Alabama v. Garrett*, 531 U.S. 356 (2001).
121. *Graham v. Richardson*, 403 U.S. 365 (1971).
122. *Pyler v. Doe*, 457 U.S. 202 (1982).
123. Robert J. Samuelson, "Immigration and Poverty," *Newsweek*, July 15, 1996, 43.
124. Sanford J. Ungar, "Enough of the Immigrant Bashing," *USA Today*, October 11, 1995, 11A.
125. Theda Skocpol, "Advocates Without Members: The Recent Transformation of American Civil Life," in Theda Skocpol and Morris P. Fiorina, eds., *Civic Engagement in American Democracy* (Washington, D.C., and New York: Brookings Institution and the Russell Sage Foundation, 1999), 470–472.
126. Andrew Sullivan, "Why Gay Marriage Is Good for Straight America," *Newsweek*, July 18, 2011, www.thedailybeast.com/newsweek/2011/07/17/andrew-sullivan-why-gay-marriage-is-good-for-america.html.

127. Andrew Sullivan, "Did Gay Marriages Ruin Straight Ones?" *The Dish*, May 25, 2012, andrewsullivan.thedailybeast.com/2012/05/do-gay-marriages-ruin-straight-ones.html.
128. Molly Ball, "Poll of the Day: America's Gay-Marriage Evolution," *The Atlantic*, May 8, 2012, www.theatlantic.com/politics/archive/2012/05/poll-of-the-day-americas-gay-marriage-evolution/256878/#slide1.

Chapter 7

1. David Herszenhorn, "How the Filibuster Became the Rule," *New York Times*, December 3, 2007, www.nytimes.com/2007/12/02/weekinreview/02herszenhorn.html?scp=1&sq=McConnell%20umpteenth& st=cse.
2. David Welna, "With Nominees Stalled, Democrats Reprise Filibuster Threat," NPR, November 20, 2013, www.npr.org/blogs/itsallpolitics/2013/11/20/246394094/with-nominees-stalled-democrats-reprise-filibuster-threat
3. Suzy Khimm, "Harry Reid Promises Filibuster Reform if Dems Win the Election," *Washington Post*, July 17, 2012, www.washingtonpost.com/blogs/ezra-klein/wp/2012/07/17/harry-reid-promises-filibuster-reform-if-dems-win-the-election/; Jillian Rayfield, "Harry Reid: Senate Will Pursue Filibuster Reform," Salon, November 9, 2012, www.salon.com/2012/11/09/harry_reid_senate_will_pursue_filibuster_reform/
4. Burgess Everett and Seung Min Kim, "Senate Goes for `Nuclear Option,'" *Politico*, November 21, 2013, www.politico.com/story/2013/11/harry-reid-nuclear-option-100199.html
5. Sahil Kapur, "Nuclear Option Triggered: Dems Make Historic Change to Filibuster Rules," *Talking Points Memo*, November 21, 2013, http://talkingpointsmemo.com/dc/harry-reid-nuclear-option-senate
6. John R. Hibbing and Elizabeth Theiss-Morse, *Congress as Public Enemy* (New York: Cambridge University Press, 1995), chs. 2, 3.
7. Glenn R. Parker and Roger H. Davidson, "Why Do Americans Love Their Congressmen So Much More Than Their Congress?" *Legislative Studies Quarterly* (February 1979): 52–61.
8. Pew Research Center poll, cited in John Avalon, "Hyper-partisanhip Dragging Down Nation," June 7, 2012, www.cnn.com/2012/06/07/opinion/avlon-partisan-pew/index.html.
9. Keith Poole and Howard Rosenthal, "The Polarization of the Political Parties," May 10, 2012, voteview.com/political_polarization.asp.
10. David W. Brady, Hahrie Han, and Jeremy C. Pope, "Primary Elections and Candidate Ideology: Out of Step With the Primary Electorate?" *Legislative Studies Quarterly* 32 (2007): 79–105.
11. Heinz Eulau and Paul D. Karps, "The Puzzle of Representation: Specifying Components of Responsiveness," *Legislative Studies Quarterly* 2 (1977): 233–254.
12. Richard Fenno, *Homestyle* (Boston: Little, Brown, 1978), ch. 3.
13. Gary Jacobson, *The Politics of Congressional Elections*, 4th ed. (New York: Longman, 1997), ch. 8.
14. Thomas E. Mann and Norman J. Ornstein, *It's Even Worse Than It Looks: How the American Constitutional System Collided With the New Politics of Extremism* (New York: Basic Books, 2012); Thomas E. Mann and Norman J. Ornstein, "Let's Just Say It: The Republicans Are the Problem,"

Washington Post, April 27, 2012, www.washingtonpost.com/opinions/lets-just-say-it-the-republicans-are-the-problem/2012/04/27/gIQAxCVUIT_print.html.
15. Mann and Ornstein, "Let's Just Say It."
16. Mann and Ornstein, "Let's Just Say It."
17. Charles Mahtesian and Jim VandeHei, "Congress: It's Going to Get Worse," *Politico*, May 1, 2012, www.politico.com/news/stories/0412/75771.html; Steve LaTourette, "The Senate's 'Manchurian Candidates,'" *Politico*, November 11, 2012, www.politico.com/news/stories/1112/83703.html.
18. Megan Slack, "Here's How a Government Shutdown Hurts the American People," *The White House Blog,* September 30, 2013, www.whitehouse.gov/blog/2013/09/30/heres-how-government-shutdown-hurts-american-people; Jonathan Weisman and Ashley Parker, "Republicans Back Down, Ending Crisis Over Shutdown and Debt Limit," *New York Times*, October 16, 2013, www.nytimes.com/2013/10/17/us/congress-budget-debate.html?pagewanted=all&_r=0.
19. Jonathan Miller, "Mourdock: Compromise Is Democrats Agreeing With Republicans," *National Journal*, May 9, 2012, www.nationaljournal.com/congress/mourdock-compromise-is-democrats-agreeing-with-republicans-20120509.
20. Frank Thorp, "Moderate GOP Rep. LaTourette Announces Retirement," July 31, 2012, firstread.msnbc.msn.com/_news/2012/07/31/13052993-moderate-gop-rep-latourette-announces-retirement?lite.
21. Ross K. Baker, *House and Senate* (New York: Norton, 1989).
22. D. C. W. Parker and M. Dull, "Divided We Quarrel: The Politics of Congressional Investigations, 1947–2004," *Legislative Studies Quarterly* 34 (2009): 319–345.
23. Lyle Denniston, "GAO Sues for Access to Cheney Records," *Boston Globe*, February 23, 2002, A1; Adam Cohen, "Bush v. Congress: The Looming Battle of Executive Privilege," *New York Times*, April 10, 2007, 20; Bruce Fein, "Restoring Congressional Oversight," *Washington Times*, November 28, 2006; Sheryl Gay Stolberg, "Bush Moves Toward Showdown With Congress on Executive Privilege," *New York Times*, June 29, 2007, 23.
24. Parker and Dull.
25. Jonathan Alter, "Obama Miracle Is White House Free of Scandal," Bloomberg News, October 27, 2011, www.bloomberg.com/news/2011-10-27/obama-miracle-is-white-house-free-of-scandal-commentary-by-jonathan-alter.html.
26. Tim Fernholz, "Democrats, Meet Darrell Issa, Likely the Man With the Subpoena," *Newsweek*, September 7, 2010, www.thedailybeast.com/newsweek/2010/09/07/darrell-issa-could-investigate-president-obama.html; Paul Waldman, "What Benghazi Is About: Scandal Envy," *The American Prospect,* November 15, 2012, prospect.org/article/what-benghazi-about-scandal-envy.
27. CBS News, "The House GOP's Benghazi Investigations: Who's Who?" May 19, 2014, www.cbsnews.com/news/whos-who-on-the-gops-benghazi-investigation/.
28. Neil A. Lewis, "Justice Dept. Nominee Avoids Confrontation at Hearing," *New York Times*, February 26, 2009, 23; Charlie Savage, "Long After Nomination, An Obama Choice Withdraws," *New York Times*, April 10, 2010, 16.
29. Gail Russell Chaddock, "Congress Girds Up for Return to Oversight," *Christian Science Monitor*, April 9, 2007, 1; Elizabeth Williamson, "Revival of Oversight Role Sought; Congress Hires More Investigators, Plans Subpoenas," *Washington Post*, April 25, 2007, A1.

30. Richard Painter and Michael Gerhardt, "Time to Support the President on Judicial Nominations," *The Hill's Congress Blog*, March 12, 2012, thehill.com/blogs/congress-blog/judicial/215445-time-to-support-the-president-on-judicial-nominations.

31. Adam Liptak, "Supreme Court Rebukes Obama on Right of Appointment," *New York Times*, June 24, 2014, www.nytimes.com/2014/06/27/us/supreme-court-president-recess-appointments.html.

32. Charles Cameron, Albert Cover, and Jeffrey Segal, "Senate Voting on Supreme Court Nominations," *American Political Science Review* 84 (1990): 525–534.

33. David Mayhew, *Congress: The Electoral Connection* (New Haven: Yale University Press, 1974).

34. *Baker v. Carr*, 396 U.S. 186 (1962); *Westberry v. Sanders*, 376 U.S. 1 (1964).

35. Sandhya Somashekhar and Aaron Blake, "Census Data Realigns Congressional Districts in Key Political States," *Washington Post*, December 21, 2010, www.washingtonpost.com/wp-dyn/content/article/2010/12/21/AR2010122103084.html.

36. Sam Wang, "The Great Gerrymander of 2012," *New York Times*, February 2, 2013, www.nytimes.com/2013/02/03/opinion/sunday/the-great-gerrymander-of-2012.html?pagewanted=all.

37. Roger H. Davidson and Walter J. Oleszek, *Congress and Its Members*, 9th ed. (Washington, D.C.: CQ Press, 2004), 48.

38. Charles Cameron, David Epstein, and Sharyn O'Halloran, "Do Majority-Minority Districts Maximize Substantive Black Representation in Congress?" *American Political Science Review* 90 (December 1996): 794–812; Kevin Hill, "Does the Creation of Majority Black Districts Aid Republicans? An Analysis of the 1992 Congressional Election in Eight Southern States," *Journal of Politics* 57 (May 1995): 384–401; D. Lublin, "Racial Redistricting and African-American Representation: A Critique of 'Do Majority-Minority Districts Maximize Substantive Black Representation in Congress?'" *American Political Science Review* 93 (1999): 183–186.

39. "How to Rig an Election," *The Economist*, April 25, 2002; Aaron Blake, "Name That District! (Gerrymandering Edition)," *Washington Post*, July 22, 2011, www.washingtonpost.com/blogs/the-fix/post/name-that-district-gerrymandering-edition/2011/07/25/gIQA17HucI_blog.html.

40. *Shaw v. Reno*, 509 U.S. 630 (1993); *Miller v. Johnson*, 115 S. Ct. 2475 (1995).

41. *Shaw v. Hunt*, 116 S. Ct. 1894 (1996); *Bush v. Vera*, 116 S. Ct. 1941 (1996); *Hunt v. Cromartie et al.*, 532 U.S. 534 (2001).

42. Peter Urban, "Congress Gets Lavish Benefits," *Connecticut Post*, January 16, 2005; Debra J. Saunders, "Perks of Office" Editorial, *San Francisco Chronicle*, November 19, 2000, 9.

43. Commission on the Executive, Legislative and Judicial Salaries, *Fairness for Public Servants* (Washington, D.C.: U.S. Government Printing Office, 1988), 23.

44. Eric Uslaner, *The Decline of Comity in Congress* (Ann Arbor: University of Michigan Press, 1993); Ezra Klein "Olympia Snowe Is Right About American Politics. Will We Listen?" Wonkblog, *Washington Post*, February 28, 2012.

45. Gary Jacobson, *The Politics of Congressional Elections*, 3rd ed. (New York: HarperCollins, 1992); Peverill Squire, "Challengers in Senate Elections," *Legislative Studies Quarterly* 14 (1989): 531–547; David Cannon, *Actors, Athletes and Astronauts: Political Amateurs in the United States Congress* (Chicago: University of Chicago Press, 1990).

46. Norman J. Ornstein, Thomas E. Mann, and Michael J. Malbin, *Vital Statistics on Congress, 2001–2002* (Washington, D.C.: AEI Press, 2002), 69; Davidson and Oleszek, 60; Peter E. Harrell, "A Slightly Redder Hue," *CQ Weekly*, November 6, 2004, 2621–2625; *Vital Statistics on American Politics* Online Edition, "Table 1-15: Mean Turnover in the House of Representatives From Various Causes, by Decade and by Party System, 1789–2008," CQ Press Electronic Library. Originally published in Harold W. Stanley and Richard G. Niemi, *Vital Statistics on American Politics, 2007–2008* (Washington, D.C.: CQ Press, 2008); Kyle *Kondik*, "So Much for That Anti-incumbent Wave," Sabato's Crystal Ball, March 15, 2012, www.centerforpolitics.org/crystalball/articles/nsp2012031502/.

47. Benjamin Knoll, "2012 House Incumbent Reelection Rates" Information Knoll, November 8, 2012, informationknoll.wordpress.com/2012/11/08/2012-house-incumbent-reelection-rates/.

48. Calculated by the authors from the Campaign Finance Institute data table, "Expenditures of House Incumbents and Challengers, by Election Outcome, 1974–2008," www.cfinst.org/pdf/vital/VitalStats_t3.pdf.

49. Harold Stanley and Richard Niemi, *Vital Statistics on American Politics*, 5th ed. (Washington, D.C.: CQ Press, 1995).

50. Michal McDonald, Twitter @ElectProject "Suspect when more data analyzed we'll see not so much a Republican wave, but more a Democratic trough," November 5, 2014.

51. Edward R. Tufte, *Political Control of the Economy* (Princeton: Princeton University Press, 1978); Robert S. Erikson, "The Puzzle of the Midterm Loss," *Journal of Politics* 50 (November 1988): 1011–1029; Robert S. Erikson and Gerald C. Wright, "Voters, Candidates, and Issues in Congressional Elections," in Lawrence Dodd and Bruce Oppenheimer, eds., *Congress Reconsidered*, 9th ed. (Washington, D.C.: CQ Press, 2005), 13271–14096.

52 John Adams, "Thoughts on Government," cited in Gordon S. Wood, *The Creation of the American Republic, 1776–1787* (New York: Norton, 1969), 165.

53. Manning.

54. Alexander Bolton and Tom Sullivan, "Not All Lawmakers Are Millionaires—Shock! More Than 1 in 4 in House Have 7-Figure Assets," *The Hill*, June 17, 2004, 1; "Guide to the New Congress," *CQ Roll Call*.

55. Kathleen Dolan, "Voting for Women in the 'Year of the Woman'," *American Journal of Political Science* 42 (1998): 272–293.

56. Jennifer Lawless and Richard Fox, *It Takes a Candidate: Why Women Don't Run for Office* (New York: Cambridge University Press, 2005).

57. Richard E. Cohen, "Is It an Earthquake, or Only a Tremor?" *National Journal*, July 8, 1995, 1786; K. Tate, *Black Faces in the Mirror: African Americans and Their Representatives in the U.S. Congress* (Princeton: Princeton University Press, 2003); K. J. Whitby, *The Color of Representation: Congressional Behavior and Black Interests* (Ann Arbor: University of Michigan Press, 1997); D. Lublin, *The Paradox of Representation: Racial Gerrymandering and Minority Interests in Congress* (Princeton: Princeton University Press, 1997).

58. Arian Campo-Flores, "Will Arizona's Tough Immigration Law Fuel Hispanic Turnout for Democrats?" *Newsweek*, May 20, 2010, www.newsweek.com/authors/arian-campo-flores.html; Michael Gerson, "The GOP's Harsh Immigration Stance Will Cost It," *Washington Post*, May 14, 2010; Daniel C. Vock, "Alabama Immigration Debate Heats Up," May 7, 2012, www.pewstates.org/projects/stateline/headlines/alabama-immigration-debate-heats-up-85899385104; Paul Begala, "No Republican Casa Blanca: Have Romney's Relentless Attacks on Latinos Sent the Right Off an Electoral Cliff?" *Newsweek*, March 19, 2012.

59. Peter Whoriskey, "Growing Wealth Widens Distance Between Lawmakers and Constituents," *Washington Post*, December 26, 2011.

60 Kay Lehman Schlozman, Sidney Verba, and Henry E. Brady, "Civic Participation and the Inequality Problem," in Theda Skocpol and Morris Fiorina, eds., *Civic Engagement in American Democracy* (New York: Russell Sage, 1999), ch. 12; Martin Gilens, "Inequality and Democratic Responsiveness," *Public Opinion Quarterly* 69 (2005): 778–796; Larry Bartels, *Unequal Democracy: The Political Economy of the New Gilded Age* (New York: Russell Sage, 2008), ch. 9.

61. Claudine Gay, "The Effect of Black Congressional Representation on Political Participation," *American Political Science Review* 95 (2001): 589–602; Cindy Simon Rosenthal, "The Role of Gender in Descriptive Representation," *Political Research Quarterly* 48 (1995): 599–611; Jennifer L. Lawless, "Politics of Presence? Congresswomen and Symbolic Representation," *Political Research Quarterly* 57 (2004): 81–99.

62. Michele Swers, *The Difference Women Make: The Policy Impact of Women in Congress* (Chicago: University of Chicago Press, 2002).

63. Tate; Whitby; Lublin, *The Paradox of Representation*.

64. David Canon, *Race, Redistricting, and Representation: The Unintended Consequences of Black Majority Districts* (Chicago: University of Chicago Press, 1999); Lublin, *The Paradox of Representation*.

65. Jane Mansbridge, "Should Blacks Represent Blacks and Women Represent Women? A Contingent 'Yes'," *Journal of Politics* 61 (1999): 628–657.

66. Nicholas Carnes, "Does the Numerical Underrepresentation of the Working Class in Congress Matter?" *Legislative Studies Quarterly* 37 (February 2012): 5–34.

67. Mann and Ornstein, *It's Even Worse Than It Looks*.

68. Glenn Parker, *Characteristics of Congress: Patterns in Congressional Behavior* (Englewood Cliffs, N.J.: Prentice Hall, 1989), 17–18, ch. 9.

69. Davidson and Oleszek, 155–156.

70. Leroy Rieselbach, *Congressional Reform in the Seventies* (Morristown, N.J.: General Learning Press, 1977); Leroy Rieselbach, *Congressional Reform* (Washington, D.C.: CQ Press, 1986).

71. Ed Gillespie and Bob Schellhas, eds., *Contract With America: The Bold Plan by Rep. Newt Gingrich, Rep. Dick Armey and the House Republicans to Change the Nation* (New York: Random House, 1994); James G. Gimpel, *Legislating the Revolution* (Boston: Allyn & Bacon, 1996).

72. Perry Bacon Jr., "Don't Mess With Nancy Pelosi," *Time*, August 27, 2006.

73. Edward Epstein, "Pelosi's Action Plan for Party Unity," *CQ Weekly*, March 30, 2009, 706.

74. Ronald Peters, coauthor of *Speaker Nancy Pelosi and the New American Politics*,

quoted in Edward Epstein, "Pelosi Gets Good Marks in Two New Books," *CQ Weekly*, May 10, 2010, 1128.

75. Bill Weiss, "Call for Resignation of Speaker John Boehner," MoveOn.org petitions petitions.moveon.org/sign/call-for-resignation; Sean Davis, "Is It Time for John Boehner to Resign as Speaker?" *The Federalist*, October 16, 2013, thefederalist.com/2013/10/16/time-john-boehner-resign-speaker/.

76. Alex Wayne, "Senate Passes Sweeping Health Overhaul," *CQ Weekly*, December 28, 2009, 2944.

77. Davidson and Oleszek, 193.

78. Matthew McCubbins and Thomas Schwartz, "Congressional Oversight Overlooked: Police Patrols Versus Fire Alarms," *American Journal of Political Science* (February 1984): 165–179.

79. Barbara Sinclair, "Party Leaders and the New Legislative Process," in Lawrence Dodd and Bruce Oppenheimer, eds., *Congress Reconsidered*, 6th ed. (Washington, D.C.: CQ Press, 1997), 229–245.

80. Richard Fenno, *Congressmen in Committees* (Boston: Little, Brown, 1973); Glenn R. Parker, *Characteristics of Congress* (Englewood Cliffs, N.J.: Prentice Hall, 1989).

81. Davidson and Oleszek, 204.

82. Steven Smith and Eric Lawrence, "Party Control of Committees in the Republican Congress," in Lawrence Dodd and Bruce Oppenheimer, eds., *Congress Reconsidered*, 6th ed. (Washington, D.C.: CQ Press, 1997), 163–192.

83. Davidson and Oleszek, 219–220.

84. Copies of these and hundreds of other GAO reports are available online at www.gao.gov.

85. Ramsey Cox, "Senate Rejects Amendment to End Tobacco Farm Subsidies," *The Hill*, May 23, 2013, thehill.com/blogs/floor-action/senate/301645-senate-rejects-amendment-to-end-tobacco-farm-subsidies.

86. Barbara Sinclair, *The Transformation of the U.S. Senate* (Baltimore: Johns Hopkins University Press, 1989).

87. Susan Herbst, *Rude Democracy: Civility and Uncivility in American Politics* (Philadelphia: Temple University Press, 2010).

88. Roger H. Davidson, Walter J. Oleszek, and Frances E. Lee, eds., *Congress and Its Members*, 11th ed. (Washington, D.C.: CQ Press, 2008), 276.

89. John Stewart, "A Chronology of the Civil Rights Act of 1964," in Robert Loevy, ed., *The Civil Rights Act of 1964: The Passage of the Law That Ended Racial Segregation* (Albany: SUNY Press, 1997), 358.

90. Stewart, 358–360.

91. Barbara Sinclair, "The New World of U.S. Senators," in Lawrence C. Dodd and Bruce I. Oppenheimer, eds., *Congress Reconsidered*, 8th ed. (Washington, D.C.: CQ Press, 2005), 11; Richard Beth and Stanley Bach, "Filibusters and Cloture in the Senate," Congressional Research Service, March 28, 2003, www.senate.gov/reference/resources/pdf/RL30360.pdf.

92. Emily Pierce, "Cloture, Filibusters Spur Furious Debate," *Roll Call*, March 5, 2008; U.S. Senate Virtual Reference Desk, "Senate Action on Cloture Motions," www.senate.gov/pagelayout/reference/cloture_motions/clotureCounts.htm.

93. Barbara Sinclair, *Unorthodox Lawmaking: New Legislative Processes in the U.S. Congress*, 4th ed. (Washington, D.C: CQ Press, 2011).

94. Donald R. Matthews and James A. Stimson, *Yeas and Nays* (New York: Wiley, 1975).

95. Richard Smith, "Interest Group Influence in the U.S. Congress," *Legislative Studies Quarterly* 20 (February 1995): 89–140.

96. Richard S. Dunham, "Power to the President—Courtesy of the GOP," *Business Week*, October 20, 1997, 51.

97. Stephen C. Craig, *The Malevolent Leaders: Popular Discontent in America* (Boulder: Westview Press, 1993); David Easton, "A Reassessment of the Concept of Political Support," *British Journal of Political Science* 5 (1975): 435–457; Glenn Parker, "Some Themes in Congressional Unpopularity," *American Journal of Political Science* 21 (1977): 93–110; E. J. Dionne Jr., *Why Americans Hate Politics* (New York: Simon & Schuster, 1991).

98. Seymour M. Lipset and William Schneider, *The Confidence Gap: Business, Labor, and Government in the Public Mind* (Baltimore: Johns Hopkins University Press, 1987).

99. Parker and Davidson; Richard F. Fenno Jr., "If, as Ralph Nader Says, Congress Is 'the Broken Branch,' How Come We Love Our Congressmen So Much?" in Norman J. Ornstein, ed., *Congress in Change* (New York: Praeger, 1975), 277–287.

100. David Herszenhorn, "How the Filibuster Became the Rule." *The New York Times*, December 2, 2007. http://www.nytimes.com/2007/12/02/weekinreview/02herszenhorn.html.

101. Herszenhorn.

Chapter 8

1. Michael R. Crittenden and Colleen McCain Nelson, "House Votes to Authorize Boehner to Sue Obama," *Wall Street Journal*, July 30, 2014. http://online.wsj.com/articles/house-votes-to-authorize-boehner-to-sue-obama-1406760762

2. Jennifer Epstein, "State of the Union 2014: Obama Calls for 'Year of Action,'" *Politico*, January 28, 2014. www.politico.com/story/2014/01/state-of-the-union-2014-address-barack-obama-102752.html

3. Carrie Budoff Brown and Jennifer Epstein, "President Obama's 'Year of Action' Falls Short," *Politico*, October 8, 2014. www.politico.com/story/2014/10/president-obama-executive-action-111687.html

4. Charlie Savage, "Bush Shuns Patriot Act," *Boston Globe*, March 24, 2006. A1; Charlie Savage, "Bush Challenges Hundreds of Laws," *Boston Globe*, April 30, 2006.

5. Charlie Savage, "Bush Shuns Patriot Act," *Boston Globe*, March 24, 2006. A1; Charlie Savage, "Bush Challenges Hundreds of Laws," *Boston Globe*, April 30, 2006.

6. Bruce Miroff, "Monopolizing the Public Space: The President as a Problem for Democratic Politics," in Bruce Miroff, Raymond Seidelman, and Todd Swanstrom, eds., *Debating Democracy* (Boston: Houghton Mifflin, 1997), 294–303.

7. Max Farrand, *The Framing of the Constitution of the United States* (New Haven: Yale University Press, 1913), 163.

8. Skip Thurman, "One Man's Impeachment Crusade," *Christian Science Monitor*, November 18, 1997, 4.

9. David Montgomery, "S.D. Republican Party Calls for Obama Impeachment," *Sioux Falls Argus Leader*, June 23, 2014; Impeach Obama Petition, www.teaparty.org/impeach-obama-petition/; Reid J. Epstein, "Impeach Obama, Says Michael Burgess," *Politico*, August 9, 2011; Igor Volsky, "Top Republican Senator Suggests Impeaching Obama Over Immigration Policies." Thinkprogress, June 26, 2012, thinkprogress.org/politics/2012/06/26/506195/top-republican-senator-suggests-impeaching-obama-over-immigration-policies/; Jennifer Steinhauer, "Ignoring

Qualms, Some Republicans Nurture Dreams of Impeaching Obama," *New York Times*, August 24, 2013; Tal Kopan, "Kerry Bentivolio: Impeachment 'a Dream'," *Politico*, August 21, 2013.

10. Robert DiClerico, *The American President*, 4th ed. (Englewood Cliffs, N.J.: Prentice Hall, 1995), 374; Susan Milligan, "Democrats Scuttle Proposal to Impeach Bush: Move Avoids House Debate," *Boston Globe*, June 12, 2008, A5.

11. Joseph A. Pika and John Anthony Maltese, *The Politics of the Modern Presidency*, 6th ed. (Washington, D.C.: CQ Press, 2004), 3; Jeffrey K. Tulis, "The Two Constitutional Presidencies," in Michael Nelson, ed., *The Presidency and the Political System* (Washington, D.C.: CQ Press, 1994), 91–123.

12. Loch Johnson and James M. McCormick, "The Making of International Agreements: a Reappraisal of Congressional Involvement," *Journal of Politics* 40 (1978): 468–478.

13. Pika and Maltese, 374; and author calculations from Library of Congress, thomas.loc.gov/home/treaties/treaties.html.

14. Lawrence Margolis, *Executive Agreements and Presidential Power in Foreign Policy* (New York: Praeger, 1985).

15. D. Roderick Kiewiet and Mathew D. McCubbins, "Presidential Influence on Congressional Appropriations Decisions," *American Political Science Review* 32 (1988): 713–736.

16. Joseph J. Schatz, "With a Deft and Light Touch, Bush Finds Ways to Win," *CQ Weekly*, December 11, 2004, 2900–2904.

17. William G. Powell, *Power Without Persuasion: The Politics of Direct Presidential Action* (Princeton: Princeton University Press, 2003).

18. Kenneth R. Mayer, *With the Stroke of a Pen: Executive Orders and Presidential Power* (Princeton: Princeton University Press, 2002), 88–89.

19. Adam L. Warber, *Executive Orders and the Modern Presidency: Legislating From the Oval Office* (Boulder, Colo.: Lynne Rienner Publishers, 2006); William G. Howell, *Power Without Persuasion: The Politics of Direct Presidential Action* (Princeton: Princeton University Press, 2003).

20. Robert A. Carp, Ronald Stidham, and Kenneth L. Manning, *Judicial Process in America*, 6th ed. (Washington, D.C.: CQ Press, 2004), 168.

21. Amy Goldstein, "Civil Rights Organizations Question Nominee Elena Kagan's Record on Race," *Washington Post*, June 27, 2010.

22. Charlie Savage, "Obama Backers Fear Opportunities to Reshape Judiciary Are Slipping Away," *New York Times*, November 14, 2009, www.nytimes.com/2009/11/15/us/politics/15judicial.html?scp=3&sq=Obama%20judicial%20appointments&st=cse.

23. Jennifer Bendery, "Obama Leaving His Mark on Judiciary as Senate Confirms Gay, Black Judges," Huffington Post, June 24, 2014, www.huffingtonpost.com/2014/06/17/obama-judges_n_5503075.html.

24. Quoted in Henry Abramson, *Justices and Presidents: A Political History of Appointments to the Supreme Court*, 2nd ed. (New York: Oxford University Press, 1985), 263.

25. Gerald Boyd, "White House Hunts for a Justice, Hoping to Tip Ideological Scales," *New York Times*, June 30, 1987; Alan I. Abramowitz and Jeffrey A. Segal, *Senate Elections* (Ann Arbor: University of Michigan Press, 1992), 1–6.

26. David Plotz, "Advise and Consent (Also, Obstruct, Delay, and Stymie): What's Still Wrong With the Appointments Process," *Slate Magazine*, March 19, 1999, www.slate.com/StrangeBedfellow/99-03-19/

StrangeBedfellow.asp.

27. Plotz.

28. Jennifer Bendery, "As Senate Runs Out of Judges to Confirm, Dozens of Courts Still Sit Empty With No Nominees," *Huffington Post*, June 4, 2014, www.huffingtonpost.com/2014/06/04/obama-judicial-nominees_n_5439100.html.

29. Mary Kate Cary, "Obama Wrong to Criticize the Supreme Court," *USNews.com* blog, www.usnews.com/opinion/blogs/mary-kate-cary/2010/01/29/obama-was-wrong-to-criticize-the-supreme-court.

30. Rebecca Mae Salokar, *The Solicitor General: The Politics of Law* (Philadelphia: Temple University Press, 1992), 29.

31. Bob Woodward, *Shadow: Five Presidents and the Legacy of Watergate* (New York: Simon & Schuster, 1999), 212–217.

32. Cited in David O'Brien, *Constitutional Law and Politics* (New York: Norton, 1991), vol. 1, 218.

33. *In re Neagle*, 135 U.S. 546 (1890); *In re Debs*, 158 U.S. 564 (1895); *United States v. Curtiss-Wright Export Corp.*, 299 U.S. 304, 57 S. Ct. 216 (1936); *Youngstown Sheet & Tube v. Sawyer*, 343 U.S. 579 (1952).

34. Lyn Ragsdale, *Presidential Politics* (Boston: Houghton Mifflin, 1993), 55.

35. *Historical Statistics of the United States: Colonial Times to 1970* (Washington, D.C.: U.S. Government Printing Office, 1975).

36. *Inaugural Addresses of the United States* (Washington, D.C.: U.S. Government Printing Office, 1982), quoted in Ragsdale, 71.

37. Suzanne Bilyeu, "FDR: How He Changed America—and Still Affects Your Life Today," *New York Times Upfront*, January 14, 2008.

38. *United States v. Curtiss-Wright Export Corp.*, 299 U.S. 304, 57 S. Ct. 216 (1936).

39. Arthur M. Schlesinger Jr., *The Imperial Presidency* (Boston: Mariner Books, 2004).

40. Richard Nixon interview with David Frost, May 20, 1977, cited in Charles Savage, *Takeover: The Return of the Imperial Presidency and the Subversion of American Democracy* (New York: Little, Brown, 2007), 21.

41. Roger H. Davidson and Walter J. Oleszek, *Congress and Its Members*, 9th ed. (Washington, D.C.: CQ Press, 2004), 407.

42. *Clinton v. Jones*, 520 U.S. 681 (1997).

43. Charlie Savage, "Bush Challenges Hundreds of Laws," *Boston Globe*, April 30, 2006, www.bostonglobe.com.

44. Philip Cooper, cited in Savage, "Bush Challenges Hundreds of Laws."

45. Vikki Gordon, "The Law: Unilaterally Shaping U.S. National Security Policy: The Role of the National Security Directives," *Presidential Studies Quarterly* (June 2008): 368–370; Christopher S. Kelley, "The Law: Contextualizing the Signing Statement," *Presidential Studies Quarterly* (December 2007): 737–749; Louis Fisher, "Invoking Inherent Powers: A Primer," *Presidential Studies Quarterly* (March 2007): 1–22; Charlie Savage, "Candidates on Executive Power: A Full Spectrum," *Boston Globe*, December 22, 2007.

46. See, for example, Peter Jamison, "Obama 'Even Worse' Than Bush on Secret Wiretapping Case, Says S.F. Lawyer," *The Snitch*, April 1, 2010, blogs.sfweekly.com/thesnitch/2010/04/obama_wiretap_ruling.php; Editorial, "We Can't Tell You," *New York Times*, April 3, 2010, www.nytimes.com/2010/04/04/opinion/04sun1.html.

47. Eric Posner, "The Presidency Comes With Executive Power. Deal With It: Obama's Just Doing What He's Empowered to Do," *New Republic*, February 3, 2014; Richard Wolf, "Obama Uses Executive Powers to Get Past Congress," *USA Today*, October 27, 2011.

48. Jeffrey Tulis, *The Rhetorical Presidency* (Princeton: Princeton University Press, 1987).

49. Richard E. Neustadt, *Presidential Power and the Modern Presidents* (New York: Free Press, 1990), 10.

50. Neustadt.

51. George Edwards III, *The Strategic President: Persuasion and Opportunity in Presidential Leadership* (Princeton: Princeton University Press, 2009).

52. Samuel Kernell, *Going Public: New Strategies of Presidential Leadership*, 2nd ed. (Washington, D.C.: CQ Press, 1996).

53. Barbara Hinckley, *The Symbolic Presidency* (London: Routledge, 1990), ch. 2.

54. Jackie Calmes, "Obama Counts on Power of Convening People for Change," *New York Times*, January 11, 2014, A10.

55. See Hedrick Smith, *The Power Game: How Washington Works* (New York: Random House, 1988), 405–406, for similar reports on the Nixon and Reagan administrations.

56. Lee Sigelman, "Gauging the Public Response to Presidential Leadership," *Presidential Studies Quarterly* 10 (Summer 1980): 427–433; James A. Stimson, "Public Support for American Presidents: A Cyclical Model," *Public Opinion Quarterly* 40 (Spring 1976): 1–21; Michael MacKuen, "Political Drama, Economic Conditions, and the Dynamics of Presidential Popularity," *American Journal of Political Science* 27 (February 1983): 165–192.

57. John R. Hibbing and Elizabeth Theiss-Morse, *Stealth Democracy: Americans' Beliefs About How Government Should Work* (New York: Cambridge University Press, 2002).

58. Almost weekly examples relating events to presidential job approval ratings can be found in the ongoing Gallup press releases interpreting their polls: www.gallup.com/tag/Presidential%2bJob%2bApproval.aspx

59. Paul Brace and Barbara Hinckley, *Follow the Leader: Opinion Polls and the Modern Presidents* (New York: Basic Books, 1992), ch. 5.

60. Brace and Hinckley, ch. 6.

61. Neustadt, 50–72.

62. Mark A. Peterson, *Legislating Together: The White House and Capitol Hill From Eisenhower to Reagan* (Cambridge, Mass.: Harvard University Press, 1990); George Edwards, *At the Margins: Presidential Leadership of Congress* (New Haven: Yale University Press, 1989), ch. 9.

63. James L. Sundquist, "Needed: A Political Theory for a New Era of Coalition Government in the United States," *Political Science Quarterly* 103 (Winter 1988–1989): 613–635.

64. *Congressional Quarterly Weekly Report*, December 21, 1996, 3455.

65. Shawn Zeller, "Historic Success, at No Small Cost," *CQ Weekly*, January 11, 2010, 112.

66. David Mayhew, *Divided We Govern: Party Control, Lawmaking, and Investigations, 1946–1990* (New Haven: Yale University Press, 1991).

67. Ragsdale, 1–4.

68. Terry Moe, "Presidents, Institutions, and Theory," in George C. Edwards III, John H. Kessel, and Bert A. Rockman, eds., *Researching the Presidency: Vital Questions, New Approaches* (Pittsburgh: University of Pittsburgh Press, 1993), 370.

69. Moe.

70. The President's Committee on Administrative Management, *Report of the Committee* (Washington, D.C.: U.S. Government Printing Office, 1937).

71. Jane Meyer and Doyle McManus, *Landslide: The Unmaking of the President, 1984–1988* (Boston: Houghton Mifflin, 1988).

72. Tom Hamburger and Christi Parsons, "President Obama's Czar System Concerns Some," *Los Angeles Times*, March 5, 2009; Zachary Coile, "Obama's Big Task: Managing the Best, Brightest," *San Francisco Chronicle*, January 11, 2009; James Risen , "Obama Takes on Congress Over Policy Czar Positions," *New York Times*, April 16, 2011.

73. White House, "2013 Annual Report to Congress on White House Staff," www.whitehouse.gov/briefing-room/disclosures/annual-records/2013.

74. James P. Pfiffner, *The Modern Presidency*, 2nd ed. (New York: St. Martin's, 1998), 91.

75. Devin Dwyer, "Obama's 4th Chief of Staff Rivals Modern Record for Single Term," January 9, 2012, abcnews.go.com/blogs/politics/2012/01/obamas-4th-chief-of-staff-rivals-modern-record-for-single-term/.

76. Harold Relyea, "Growth and Development of the President's Office," in David Kozak and Kenneth Ciboski, eds., *The American Presidency* (Chicago: Nelson Hall, 1985), 135; Pfiffner, 122.

77. Sid Frank and Arden Davis Melick, *The Presidents: Tidbits and Trivia* (Maplewood, N.J.: Hammond, 1986), 103.

78. Timothy Walch, ed., *At the President's Side: The Vice-Presidency in the Twentieth Century* (Columbia: University of Missouri Press, 1997), 45.

79. Ann Devroy and Stephen Barr, "Reinventing the Vice Presidency: Defying History, Al Gore Has Emerged as Bill Clinton's Closest Political Advisor," *Washington Post National Weekly Edition*, February 27–March 5, 1995, 6–7.

80. See, for example, Stephen F. Hayes, *Cheney: The Untold Story of America's Most Powerful and Controversial Vice President* (New York: HarperCollins, 2007); Bruce Kluger, David Slavin, and Tim Foley, *Young Dick Cheney: Great American* (San Francisco: AlterNet Books, 2008); John Nichols, *Dick: The Man Who Is President* (New York: The New Press, 2004); Lou Dubose and Jake Bernstein, *Vice: Dick Cheney and the Hijacking of the American Presidency* (New York: Random House, 2006).

81. Evan Thomas, "Inconvenient Truth Teller; From Health-Care Reform to Afghanistan, Joe Biden Has Bucked Obama—as Only a Good Veep Can," *Newsweek*, October 19, 2009, 30+; Howard Kurtz, "Finding Virtue in Vice; Despite Gaffes, Biden Has Blossomed as Obama's Most Recent Prime Spokesman," *Washington Post*, June 10, 2010, C01.

82. Michelle Obama, "As Barack's First Lady, I Would Work to Help Working Families and Military Families," *U.S. News & World Report*, October 1, 2008.

83. Jeffrey M. Jones, "Michelle Obama Remains Popular in U.S.," www.gallup.com/poll/154952/michelle-obama-remains-popular.aspx.

84. Robert K. Murray and Tim H. Blessing, "The Presidential Performance Study: A Progress Report," *Journal of American History* 70 (December 1983): 535–555.

85. Jon R. Bond and Richard Fleisher, *The President in the Legislative Arena* (Chicago: University of Chicago Press, 1990); George C. Edwards III, *Presidential Influence in Congress* (San Francisco: Freeman, 1980).

86. James David Barber, *The Presidential Character*, 4th ed. (Englewood Cliffs, N.J.: Prentice Hall, 1992).

87. See Michael Nelson, "James David Barber and the Psychological Presidency," in David Pederson, ed., *The "Barberian" Presidency:*

Theoretical and Empirical Readings (New York: Peter Lang, 1989), 93–110; Alexander George, "Assessing Presidential Character," *World Politics* (January 1974): 234–283; Jeffrey Tulis, "On Presidential Character," in Jeffrey Tulis and Joseph Bessette, eds., *Presidency and the Constitutional Order* (Baton Rouge: Louisiana State University Press, 1981).

88. Joseph Califano, *A Presidential Nation* (New York: Norton, 1975), 184–188.

89. Joel Achenbach, "In a Heated Race, Obama's Cool Won the Day," *Washington Post*, November 6, 2008, A47.

90. Justin Frank, "Has Obama Had a Psychological Breakthrough?" December 14, 2011, Time.com, ideas.time.com/2011/12/14/has-obama-had-a-psychological-breakthrough/.

91. Gallup poll, December 19, 1998, institution.gallup.com/documents/topics.aspx.

92. Ben Smith, "Health Reform Foes Plan Obama's Waterloo," *Politico*, July 17, 2009, www.politico.com/blogs/bensmith/0709/Health_reform_foes_plan_Obamas_Waterloo.html.

93. "GOP Leader's Top Goal: Make Obama 1-Term President," November 4, 2010, www.msnbc.msn.com/id/40007802/ns/politics-decision_2010/t/gop-leaders-top-goal-make-obama—term-president/#.UBLNunBXtxA.

94. Savage, "Obama's Embrace of a Bush Tactic Riles Congress."

95. Jack L. Goldsmith, Office of Legal Counsel under George W. Bush, quoted in Savage, "Shift on Executive Power Lets Obama Bypass Rivals"; see also Peter Baker, "Obama Making Plans to Use Executive Power," *The New York Times*, February 12, 2010, www.nytimes.com/2010/02/13/us/politics/130bama.html; Neela Banerjee, "EPA Seeks 30% Emissions Cut; a New Rule Targeting Carbon Dioxide From Existing Power Plants Faces a Yearlong Review and a Big Fight," *Los Angeles Times*, June 2, 2014, 1; Doyle McManus, "Obama's Era Of Limits," *Los Angeles Times*, January 29, 2014.

96. Quoted in Savage, "Bush Shuns Patriot Act."

Chapter 9

1. Organic Trade Association, "Consumer-Driven U.S. Organic Market Surpasses $31 Billion in 2011," press release, April 23, 2012, www.organicnewsroom.com/2012/04/us_consumerdriven_organic_mark.html.

2. Dann Denny, "Defining 'Organic,'" *Bloomington Herald Times*, April 16, 1998, D1.

3. Marian Burros, "Eating Well: U.S. Proposal on Organic Food Gets a Grass-Roots Review," *New York Times*, March 25, 1998, F10.

4. Gene Kahn, "National Organic Standard Will Aid Consumers," *Frozen Food Age* 47 (September 1998): 18.

5. Burros, F10.

6. H. H. Gerth and C. Wright Mills, eds., *From Max Weber* (New York: Oxford University Press, 1946), 196–199.

7. Herbert Kaufman, "Emerging Conflicts in the Doctrines of Public Administration," *American Political Science Review* 50 (December 1956): 1057–1073.

8. Morris P. Fiorina, *Congress: Keystone of the Washington Establishment* (New Haven: Yale University Press, 1977).

9. Herbert Kaufman, *Red Tape, Its Origins, Uses, and Abuses* (Washington, D.C.: Brookings Institution, 1977).

10. "Federal Civilian Employment in the Executive Branch," *Washington Post*, www.washingtonpost.com/wp-dyn/content/graphic/2011/02/14/GR2011021407001.html.

11. Bureau of Labor Statistics, *Guide to Military Careers*, www.bls.gov/ooh/military/military-careers.htm; August 2011 estimate.

12. Curtis Copeland, "The Federal Workforce: Characteristics and Trends," Congressional Research Service, April 19, 2011, assets.opencrs.com/rpts/RL34685_20110419.pdf.

13. Kenneth J. Meier and John Bohte, *Politics and the Bureaucracy*, 5th ed. (Belmont, CA: Thompson/Wadsworth), 2007.

14. Ibid.

15. U.S. National Debt Clock, accessed June 30, 2014, www.brillig.com/debt_clock/.

16. White House, "The Cabinet," www.whitehouse.gov/administration/cabinet.

17. Best Places to Work in the Federal Government, "FEC," bestplacestowork.org/BPTW/rankings/detail/LF00; "Social Security Administration," bestplacestowork.org/BPTW/rankings/detail/SZ00.

18. William G. Howell and David E. Lewis, "Agencies by Presidential Design," *Journal of Politics* 64 (2002): 1095–1114.

19. Dennis D. Riley, *Controlling the Federal Bureaucracy* (Philadelphia: Temple University Press, 1987), 139–142.

20. Office of Management and Budget, "2014 Report to Congress on the Benefits and Costs of Federal Regulations and Unfunded Mandates on State, Local and Tribal Entities," www.whitehouse.gov/sites/default/files/omb/inforeg/2011_cb/2011_cba_report.pdf.

21. *U.S. News and World Report*, February 11, 1980, 64.

22. David E. Lewis, "The Adverse Consequences of the Politics of Agency Design for Presidential Management in the United States: The Relative Durability of Insulated Agencies," *British Journal of Political Science* 34 (2004): 377–404.

23. John B. Judis, "The Quiet Revolution: Obama Has Reinvented the State in More Ways Than You Can Imagine," *New Republic*, February 1, 2010, www.tnr.com/article/politics/the-quiet-revolution.

24. Emily Stephenson, "Postal Service Downsizing Plan Cuts 35,000 Jobs," February 23, 2012, www.msnbc.msn.com/id/46501840/ns/business-us_business/t/postal-service-downsizing-plan-cuts-jobs/#.T80IVr9Xsb1.

25. Robert Pear, "Health Insurance Companies Try to Shape Rules," *New York Times*, May 15, 2010.

26. Bureau of Labor Statistics, "Employment Projections: Civilian Labor Force by Age, Sex, Race and Ethnicity," www.bls.gov/emp/ep_table_304.htm; FedSmith, Inc., "Federal Workforce 2014:Key Figures," www.scribd.com/doc/220100041/Federal-Workforce-2014-Key-Figures.

27. Ibid.

28. Quoted in Donald F. Kettl, *System Under Stress: Homeland Security and American Politics* (Washington, D.C.: CQ Press, 2004), 48.

29. "The 9/11 Commission Report: Final Report of the National Commission on Terrorist Attacks Upon the United States, Executive Summary," www.c-span.org/pdf/911finalreportexecsum.pdf.

30. Quoted in Kettl, 53.

31. Catherine Rampell, "Whistle-blowers Tell of Cost of Conscience," *USA Today*, November 24, 2006, 13A; Peter Eisler, "Whistle-blowers' Rights Get Second Look; Bills to Strengthen Protections Now Have Better Chance to Pass, Backers Say," *USA Today*, March 15, 2010, 6A.

32. Dana Hughes, "Obama Administration Denies Benghazi Whistleblowers Being Kept Quiet," ABC News, May 1, 2013, abcnews.go.com/blogs/politics/2013/05/obama-administration-denies-benghazi-whistleblowers-being-kept-quiet/; Adam Clark Estes, "Fox News Says Obama Muzzled Benghazi Whistleblowers," news.yahoo.com/fox-news-says-obama-muzzled-benghazi-whistleblowers-015810894.html.

33. David E. Lewis, "Staffing Alone: Unilateral Action and the Politicization of the Executive Office of the President, 1988–2004," *Presidential Studies Quarterly* 35 (2005): 496–514.

34. Dana Milbank, "Bush Seeks to Rule the Bureaucracy; Appointments Aim at White House Control," *Washington Post*, November 22, 2004, A4.

35. "The Phony Regulation Debate" (editorial), May 26, 2012, www.nytimes.com/2012/05/27/opinion/sunday/the-phony-regulation-debate.html.

36. Terry Moe, "The President's Cabinet," in James Pfiffer and Roger J. Davidson, eds., *Understanding the Presidency*, 3rd ed. (New York: Longman, 2003), 208.

37. Office of Personnel Management, *Federal Workforce Statistics: The Fact Book 2003 Edition* (Washington, D.C.: OPM, 2003), 10, www.opm.gov/feddata/03factbk.pdf.

38. Francis E. Rourke, *Bureaucracy, Politics and Public Policy*, 3rd ed. (Boston: Little, Brown, 1984), 106.

39. Albert B. Crenshaw, "Cash Flow," *Washington Post*, June 28, 1998, H1.

40. Anthony E. Brown, *The Politics of Airline Regulation* (Knoxville: University of Tennessee Press, 1987).

41. Lewis, 496–514.

42. Charlie Savage, "Bush Aide Admits Hiring Boasts; Says He Broke No Rules Giving Jobs to Conservatives," *Boston Globe*, June 6, 2007, A9; Charlie Savage, "Scandal Puts Spotlight on Christian Law School; Grads Influential in Justice Dept.," *Boston Globe*, April 8, 2007, A1; Eric Lipton, "Colleagues Cite Partisan Focus by Justice Officials," *New York Times*, May 12, 2007, A1.

43. Walter Pincus, "CIA Director Cuts Meetings on Terrorism; Coordinating Sessions Reduced to 3 a Week," *Washington Post*, January 10, 2005, A15; Walter Pincus, "Changing of the Guard at the CIA; Goss's Shake-Ups Leave Some Questioning Agency's Role," *Washington Post*, January 6, 2005, A3.

44. Robert Barnes, "Supreme Court Rebukes Obama on Recess Appointments," *Washington Post*, June 26, 2014.

45. Riley, ch. 2.

46. Harold Seidman and Robert Gilmour, *Politics, Position, and Power: From the Positive to the Regulatory State*, 4th ed. (New York: Oxford University Press, 1986), 3.

47. Mark Landler and Annie Lowrey, "Obama Bid to Cut Government Tests Congress," *New York Times*, January 13, 2012, www.nytimes.com/2012/01/14/us/politics/obama-to-ask-congress-for-power-to-merge-agencies.html?pagewanted=all.

48. Quoted in Riley, 43.

49. Edmund L. Andrews, "Blowing the Whistle on Big Oil," *New York Times*, December 3, 2006.

50. Quoted in Jason DeParle, "Minerals Service Had a Mandate to Produce Results," *New York Times*, August 7, 2010.

51. Center for Responsive Politics, "Oil and Gas," www.opensecrets.org/industries/indus.php?ind=e01.

52. Hugh Heclo, "Issue Networks and the Executive Establishment," in Anthony King, ed., *The New American Political System* (Washington, D.C.: American Enterprise Institute, 1978), 87–124.

53. Deborah Zabarenko, "Environmental Group to Sue U.S. Over Oil Permits," May 14, 2010, www.reuters.com/article/idUSTRE64D64320100515.

54. Matthew McCubbins and Thomas Schwartz, "Congressional Oversight Overlooked: Police Patrols Versus Fire Alarms," *American Journal of Political Science* 28 (1984): 16–79.

55. Thomas E. Mann, Molly Reynolds, and Peter Hoey, "Is Congress on the Mend?" *New York Times*, April 28, 2007.

56. Kenneth Shepsle and Barry Weingast, "The Institutional Foundations of Committee Power," *American Political Science Review* 81 (1987): 85–104.

57. Felicity Barringer, "Limits on Logging Are Reinstated," *New York Times*, July 16, 2009, www.nytimes.com/2009/07/17/science/earth/17forest.html?_r=1&ref=earth.

58. Matthew Crenson and Francis E. Rourke, "By Way of Conclusion: American Bureaucracy Since World War II," in Louis Galambois, ed., *The New American State: Bureaucracies and Policies Since World War II* (Baltimore: Johns Hopkins University Press, 1987), 137–177.

59. Charles Lane, "High Court Rejects Detainee Tribunals: 5 to 3 Ruling Curbs President's Claim of Wartime Power," *Washington Post*, June 30, 2006, A1; Robert Barnes, "Justices Say Detainees Can Seek Release," *Washington Post*, June 13, 2008, A1.

60. Martha Derthick, *Policymaking for Social Security* (Washington, D.C.: Brookings Institution, 1979), reprinted in "The Art of Cooptation: Advisory Councils in Social Security," in Francis E. Rourke, ed., *Bureaucratic Power in National Policy Making*, 3rd ed. (Boston: Little, Brown, 1986), 109.

61. Charles T. Goodsell, *The Case for Bureaucracy* (Chatham, N.J.: Chatham House, 1993), ch. 3; Robert L. Kahn, Barbara A. Gutek, Eugenia Barton, and Daniel Katz, "Americans Love Their Bureaucrats," in Francis E. Rourke, ed., *Bureaucracy, Politics, and Public Policy*, 4th ed. (Boston: Little, Brown, 1988).

62. Meier, 210–211.

Chapter 10

1. This list is based loosely on the discussion of the functions of law in James V. Calvi and Susan Coleman, *American Law and Legal Systems* (Upper Saddle River, N.J.: Prentice Hall, 1997), 2–4; Steven Vago, *Law and Society* (Upper Saddle River, N.J.: Prentice Hall, 1997), 16–20; and Lawrence Baum, *American Courts: Process and Policy*, 4th ed. (Boston: Houghton Mifflin, 1998), 4–5.

2. Christopher E. Smith, *Courts, Politics, and the Judicial Process* (Chicago: Nelson-Hall, 1993), 179.

3. Henry Abraham, *The Judicial Process* (New York: Oxford University Press, 1993), 97.

4. Abraham, 96–97.

5. Smith, 329.

6. Jethro K. Lieberman, *The Litigious Society* (New York: Basic Books, 1981), 6.

7. Smith, 324.

8. Ibid., 324, 327.

9. Lieberman, 168–190.

10. Lawrence Friedman, *Total Justice: What Americans Want From the Legal System and Why* (Boston: Beacon Press, 1985), 31–32, cited in Smith, 323.

11. "Prison Suits," *Reader's Digest*, August 1994, 96.

12. Alexander Hamilton, James Madison, and John Jay, *The Federalist Papers*, ed. Clinton Rossiter (New York: New American Library, 1961).

13. Robert A. Carp and Ronald Stidham, *The Federal Courts* (Washington, D.C.: CQ Press, 1991), 4.

14. Lawrence Baum, *The Supreme Court*, 5th ed. (Washington, D.C.: CQ Press, 1995), 13.

15. *Marbury v. Madison*, 5 U.S. (1 Cranch) 137 (1803).

16. *Dred Scott v. Sanford*, 60 U.S. (19 How.) 393.

17. Lawrence Baum, *The Supreme Court*, 8th ed. (Washington, D.C.: CQ Press, 2004), 170, 173.

18. Baum, *The Supreme Court*, 5th ed., 22–24.

19. Matthew J. Streb, "Just Like Any Other Election? The Politics of Judicial Elections," in Matthew J. Streb, ed., *Law and Election Politics: The Rules of the Game* (Boulder: Lynne Rienner, 2005).

20. Joan Biskupic, "Making a Mark on the Bench," *Washington Post National Weekly Edition*, December 2–8, 1996, 31.

21. Sheldon Goldman, Sara Schiavoni, and Elliot Slotnick, "George W. Bush's Judicial Philosophy: Mission Accomplished," *Judicature* 92 (May/June 2009): 276.

22. John Schwartz, "For Obama, a Record on Diversity but Delays on Judicial Confirmations," *New York Times*, August 6, 2011, www.nytimes.com/2011/08/07/us/politics/07courts.html?_r=2.

23. Mike Dorning, "Obama's Judicial Nominees: Liberals Are Upset With Them Too," *Bloomberg Businessweek*, May 1, 2014, www.businessweek.com/articles/2014-05-01/liberals-complain-obamas-judicial-nominees-are-too-conservative.

24. Charlie Savage, "Ratings Shrink President's List for Judgeships," *New York Times*, November 22, 2011, www.nytimes.com/2011/11/23/us/politics/screening-panel-rejects-many-obama-picks-for-federal-judgeships.html?emc=eta1.

25. Biskupic.

26. Ibid.

27. Goldman, Schiavoni, and Slotnick, 283.

28. Jeffrey Toobin, "Obama's Unfinished Judicial Legacy," *New Yorker*, July 31, 2012, www.newyorker.com/online/blogs/comment/2012/07/why-judges-matter.html; Charlie Savage, "Ratings Shrink President's List for Judgeships," *New York Times*, November 22, 2011, www.nytimes.com/2011/11/23/us/politics/screening-panel-rejects-many-obama-picks-for-federal-judgeships.html?emc=eta1.

29. David G. Savage, "Conservative Courts Likely Bush Legacy," *Los Angeles Times*, January 2, 2008, A11.

30. Doug Kendall, "The Bench in Purgatory: The New Republican Obstructionism on Obama's Judicial Nominees," *Slate*, October 26, 2009, www.slate.com/id/2233309/.

31. David M. O'Brien, "Ironies and Disappointments: Bush and Federal Judgeships," in Colin Campbell and Bert Rockman, eds., *The George W. Bush Presidency* (Washington, D.C.: CQ Press, 2004), 139–143.

32. Manu Raju, "Republicans Warn Obama on Judges," *Politico*, March 2, 2009, www.politico.com/news/stories/0309/19526.html.

33. Greg Gordon, "Federal Courts, Winner Will Make a Mark on the Bench," *Minneapolis Star Tribune*, September 27, 2004, 1A.

34. Charlie Savage, "Ratings Shrink President's List for Judgeships," *New York Times*, November 22, 2011, www.nytimes.com/2011/11/23/us/politics/screening-panel-rejects-many-obama-picks-for-federal-judgeships.html?emc=eta1.

35. The Gallup Organization, *Polls, Topics & Trends: Trust in Government*, various dates through 2004, www.gallup.com/poll/content/?ci=5392&pg=1; Linda Greenhouse, "The Nation: Vote Count Omits a Verdict on the Court," *New York Times*, November 18, 2001, sec. 4, 4.

36. Cited in Robert Marquand, "Why America Puts Its Supreme Court on a Lofty Pedestal," *Christian Science Monitor*, June 25, 1997, 14.

37. Although the president has no official "list" of criteria, scholars are mostly agreed on these factors. See, for instance, Henry J. Abraham, *The Judiciary* (New York: New York University Press, 1996), 65–69; Lawrence Baum, *American Courts: Process and Policy*, 4th ed. (Boston: Houghton Mifflin, 1998), 105–106; Philip Cooper and Howard Ball, *The United States Supreme Court: From the Inside Out* (Upper Saddle River, N.J.: Prentice Hall, 1996), 49–60; and Thomas G. Walker and Lee Epstein, *The Supreme Court of the United States* (New York: St. Martin's Press, 1993), 34–40.

38. Baum, *American Courts*, 4th ed., 105.

39. From the filmstrip *This Honorable Court* (Washington, D.C.: Greater Washington Educational Telecommunications Association, 1988), program 1.

40. Ibid.

41. Peter Baker, "Kagan Nomination Leaves Longing on the Left," *New York Times*, May 10, 2010, www.nytimes.com/2010/05/11/us/politics/11nominees.html?scp=1&sq=Elena%20Kagan%20liberal&st=cse.

42. Dave Gilson, "Charts: The Supreme Court's Rightward Shift," *Mother Jones*, June 29, 2012, www.motherjones.com/politics/2012/06/supreme-court-roberts-obamacare-charts.

43. Baum, *American Courts*, 4th ed., 105.

44. Walker and Epstein, 40.

45. Sonia Sotomayor, "A Latina Judge's Voice," address at U.C. Berkeley, October 26, 2001, www.berkeley.edu/news/media/releases/2009/05/26_sotomayor.shtml.

46. Baum, *The Supreme Court*, 8th ed., 103.

47. U.S. Supreme Court, "2013 Year-End Report on the Federal Judiciary," www.supremecourt.gov/publicinfo/year-end/2013year-endreport.pdf.

48. Philip Cooper and Howard Ball, *The United States Supreme Court: From the Inside Out* (Upper Saddle River, N.J.: Prentice Hall, 1996), 104.

49. Cooper and Ball, 134.

50. Walker and Epstein, 90.

51. Ibid., 91–92.

52. David O'Brien, *Storm Center* (New York: Norton, 1990), 272.

53. Walker and Epstein, 129–130.

54. Adam Cohen, "Psst…Justice Scalia…You Know, You're an Activist Too," *New York Times*, April 19, 2005, web version.

55. Walker and Epstein, 126–130.

56. What follows is drawn from the excellent discussion in Walker and Epstein, 131–139.

57. Greg Stohr, "Record Number of Amicus Briefs Filed in Health Care Cases," *Bloomberg News*, March 15, 2012, go.bloomberg.com/health-care-supreme-court/2012-03-15/record-number-of-amicus-briefs-filed-in-health-care-cases/.

58. Max Lerner, *Nine Scorpions in a Bottle: Great Judges and Cases of the Supreme Court* (New York: Arcade Publishing, 1994).

59. Philip J. Cooper, *Battles on the Bench: Conflict Inside the Supreme Court* (Lawrence: University Press of Kansas, 1995), 42–46.

60. For a provocative argument that the Court does not, in fact, successfully produce significant social reform and actually damaged the civil rights struggles in this country, see Gerald N. Rosenberg, *The Hollow Hope: Can Courts Bring About Social Change?* (Chicago: University of Chicago Press, 1991).

61. *Marbury v. Madison*, 1 Cr. 137 (1803).

62. *Martin v. Hunter's Lessee*, 14 U.S. 304 (1816).

63. *McCulloch v. Maryland*, 4 Wheat. 316 (1819).
64. *Gibbons v. Ogden*, 9 Wheat. 1 (1824).
65. *Lochner v. New York*, 198 U.S. 45 (1905).
66. *Hammer v. Dagenhart*, 247 U.S. 251 (1918).
67. *Adkins v. Children's Hospital*, 261 U.S. 525 (1923).
68. *Dred Scott v. Sanford*, 19 How. 393 (1857).
69. *Plessy v. Ferguson*, 163 U.S. 537 (1896).
70. *Brown v. Board of Education*, 347 U.S. 483 (1954).
71. For example, *Mapp v. Ohio*, 367 U.S. 643 (1961); *Gideon v. Wainwright*, 372 U.S. 335 (1963); and *Miranda v. Arizona*, 382 U.S. 925 (1965).
72. *Baker v. Carr*, 396 U.S. 186 (1962).
73. *Roe v. Wade*, 410 U.S. 113 (1973).
74. *Citizens United v. Federal Election Commission*, 558 U.S. —— (2010).
75. Jeffrey Rosen, "Welcome to the Roberts Court: How the Chief Justice Used Obamacare to Reveal His True Identity," *New Republic,* June 29, 2012, www.tnr.com/blog/plank/104493/welcome-the-roberts-court-who-the-chief-justice-was-all-along.
76. Pew Research Center for the People and the Press, "Stark Racial Divisions in Reactions to Ferguson Police Shooting," August 18, 2014, www.people-press.org/2014/08/18/stark-racial-divisions-in-reactions-to-ferguson-police-shooting/.
77. "New Yorkers' Views of the Mayor and the Police," August 20, 2012, www.nytimes.com/interactive/2012/08/20/nyregion/new-yorkers-views-of-the-mayor-and-the-police.html.
78. Joseph Goldstein, "Judge Rejects New York's Stop and Frisk Policy," *New York Times*, August 12, 2013, www.nytimes.com/2013/08/13/nyregion/stop-and-frisk-practice-violated-rights-judge-rules.html.
79. Dylan Matthews, "The Black/White Marijuana Arrest Gap, in Nine Charts," *Washington Post Wonkblog*, June 4, 2013, www.washingtonpost.com/blogs/wonkblog/wp/2013/06/04/the-blackwhite-marijuana-arrest-gap-in-nine-charts/.
80. Bureau of Justice Statistics, "Indigent Defense Systems," www.bjs.gov/index.cfm?ty=tp&tid=28#top.
81. John H. Langbein, "Money Talks, Clients Walk," *Newsweek*, April 17, 1995, 32.
82. Legal Services Corporation, "Fact Sheet: What Is LSC?", www.lsc.gov/about/factsheet_whatislsc.php.
83. Consortium on Legal Services and the Public, *Agenda for Success: The American People and Civil Justice* (Chicago: American Bar Association, 1996); see also Legal Services Corporation, "Serving the Civil Legal Needs of Low-Income Americans," April 30, 2000, www.lsc.gov/pressr/exsum.pdf.
84. Justin McCarthy, "Americans Losing Confidence in All Branches of U.S. Government," Gallup Politics, June 30, 2014, www.gallup.com/poll/171992/americans-losing-confidence-branches-gov.aspx.
85. Dahleen Glanton, "O'Connor Questions Court's Decision to Take Bush v. Gore," *Chicago Tribune*, April 27, 2013, articles.chicagotribune.com/2013-04-27/news/ct-met-sandra-day-oconnor-edit-board-20130427_1_o-connor-bush-v-high-court.
86. Linda Greenhouse, "*Bush v. Gore:* A Special Report," *New York Times,* February 20, 2001.

Chapter 11

1. Kate Zernike, "Christie Keeps His Promise to Veto Gay Marriage Bill," *New York Times*, February 17, 2012, www.nytimes.com/2012/02/18/nyregion/christie-vetoes-gay-marriage-bill.html.

2. Mike Gravel, "Philadelphia II: National Initiatives," *Campaigns and Elections* (December 1995/January 1996): 2.
3. According to a September 1994 Roper poll, 76 percent favor a national referendum.
4. Survey by Fox News and Opinion Dynamics, May 24–May 25, 2000, iPOLL database, Roper Center for Public Opinion Research, University of Connecticut, www.ropercenter.uconn.edu/ipoll.html.
5. "Exchange With Reporters in Waco, Texas, August 7, 2001," *Public Papers of the Presidents: George W. Bush—2001*, vol. 2, 945; U.S. Government Printing Office via GPO Access.
6. Joshua Green, "The Other War Room," *Washington Monthly*, April 2002, 16.
7. Sam Stein, "Obama Mocks Polls but Spends More on Them ($4.4M) Than Bush," *Huffington Post,* July 29, 2010, www.huffingtonpost.com/2010/07/29/obama-mocks-polls-but-spe_n_663553.html.
8. V. O. Key Jr., *Public Opinion and American Democracy* (New York: Knopf, 1961), 7.
9. John Kingdon, *Congressmen's Voting Decisions*, 2nd ed. (New York: Harper & Row, 1981), ch. 2.
10. Gary C. Jacobson, "The War, the President, and the 2006 Midterm Congressional Elections," paper presented at the annual meeting of the Midwest Political Science Association, Chicago, April 12–15, 2007.
11. Many works repeat this theme of the uninformed and ignorant citizen. See, for example, Bernard Berelson, Paul F. Lazarsfeld, and William N. McPhee, *Voting: A Study of Opinion Formation in a Presidential Campaign* (Chicago: University of Chicago Press, 1954); Angus Campbell, Philip E. Converse, Warren E. Miller, and Donald E. Stokes, *The American Voter* (New York: Wiley, 1960); W. Russell Neuman, *The Paradox of Mass Politics* (Cambridge: Harvard University Press, 1986); and Michael X. Delli Carpini and Scott Keeter, *What Americans Know About Politics and Why It Matters* (New Haven: Yale University Press, 1996).
12. Delli Carpini and Keeter, 70–75.
13. Pew Research Center for the People and the Press, October 2011 Knowledge Survey, www.people-press.org/files/legacy-questionnaires/Oct11%20Knowledge%20Topline.pdf.
14. Pew Research Center for the People and the Press, October 2011 Knowledge Survey.
15. John Marzulli and Michael Saul, "A Disturbing Wave of Hatred: Anti-Muslim, Anti-Arab Incidents in City, Nation," *New York Daily News*, September 19, 2001.
16. Herbert McClosky and Alida Brill, *Dimensions of Tolerance* (New York: Russell Sage Foundation, 1983), 50.
17. Ibid., 250.
18. Robert S. Erikson and Kent Tedin, *American Public Opinion*, 5th ed. (Boston: Allyn & Bacon, 1995), 127–128.
19. M. Kent Jennings and Richard G. Niemi, *The Political Character of Adolescence* (Princeton: Princeton University Press, 1974); Robert C. Luskin, John P. McIver, and Edward Carmines, "Issues and the Transmission of Partisanship," *American Journal of Political Science* 33 (May 1989): 440–458; Christopher H. Achen, "Parental Socialization and Rational Party Identification," *Political Behavior* 24 (June 2002): 151–170.
20. Shirley Engle and Anna Ochoa, *Education for Democratic Citizenship: Decision Making in the Social Studies* (New York: Teachers College of Columbia University, 1988).
21. Robert D. Hess and Judith V. Torney, *The Development of Political Attitudes in Children* (Chicago: Aldine, 1967).

22. Kenneth D. Wald, Dennis E. Owen, and Samuel S. Jill Jr., "Political Cohesion in Churches," *Journal of Politics* 52 (1990): 197–215; Robert Huckfeldt, Paul Allen Beck, Russell J. Dalton, and Jeffrey Levine, "Political Environments, Cohesive Social Groups, and the Communication of Public Opinion," *American Journal of Political Science* 39 (1995): 1025–1054; David C. Leege, Kenneth D. Wald, Brian S. Krueger, and Paul D. Mueller, *The Politics of Cultural Differences: Social Change and Voter Mobilization in the Post–New Deal Period* (Princeton: Princeton University Press, 2002).
23. Elisabeth Noelle-Neumann, *The Spiral of Silence: Public Opinion, Our Social Skin* (Chicago: University of Chicago Press, 1984).
24. Paul R. Abramson and Ada W. Finifter, "On the Meaning of Political Trust: New Evidence From Items Introduced in 1978," *American Journal of Political Science* 25 (May 1981): 295–306; Arthur H. Miller, "Is Confidence Rebounding?" *Public Opinion* (June/July 1983); Robert S. Erikson and Kent L. Tedin, *American Public Opinion*, 7th ed. (New York: Pearson-Longman, 2005), 162–166.
25. Angus Campbell, Philip E. Converse, Donald E. Stokes, and Warren E. Miller, *The American Voter* (New York: Wiley, 1960); Donald P. Green, Bradley Palmquist, and Eric Schickler, *Partisan Hearts and Minds: Political Parties and the Social Identities of Voters* (New Haven: Yale University Press, 2002).
26. Larry M. Bartels, "Beyond the Running Tally: Partisan Bias in Political Perceptions," *Political Behavior* 24 (June 2002).
27. CBS News poll, February 2–4, 2009. Telephone survey of 864 respondents. Calculated by the authors from data obtained from the Roper Center.
28. M. J. Hetherington, "Resurgent Mass Partisanship: The Role of Elite Polarization," *American Political Science Review* 95 (2001): 619–631; Alan Abramowitz, *The Disappearing Center: Engaged Citizens, Polarization and American Democracy* (New Haven: Yale University Press, 2010); Matthew S. Levendusky, *The Partisan Sort: How Liberals Became Democrats and Conservatives Became Republicans* (Chicago: University of Chicago Press, 2010).
29. Gerald C. Wright and Nathan Birkhead, "The Macro Sort of State Partisanship" *Political Research Quarterly* 67 (2014): 426–439.
30. Lilliana Mason, "The Rise of Uncivil Agreement: Issue Versus Behavioral Polarization in the American Electorate," *American Behavioral Scientist* 57 (2013): 140–159; Daniel M. Shea and Morris P. Fiorina, *Can We Talk? The Rise of Rude, Nasty, Stubborn Politics* (New York: Pearson, 2013).
31. Norman H. Nie, Jane Junn, and Kenneth Stehlik-Barry, *Education and Democratic Citizenship in America* (Chicago: University of Chicago Press, 1996).
32. For more on the effects of education, see Delli Carpini and Keeter, 188–189; Erikson and Tedin, 7th ed., 152–159; and Herbert H. Hyman, Charles R. Wright, and John Shelton Reed, *The Enduring Effects of Education* (Chicago: University of Chicago Press, 1975). For a dissenting view that formal education is just a mask for intelligence and native cognitive ability, see Robert Luskin, "Explaining Political Sophistication," *Political Behavior* 12 (1990): 3298–3409.

33. Christine L. Day, *What Older Americans Think: Interest Groups and Aging Policy* (Princeton: Princeton University Press, 1990).

34. Scott Helman, "Obama Strikes Chord With Generation Next: Campaign Targets Youth Vote in Ind," *Boston Globe*, May 3, 2008; Cynthia Burton and Joseph A. Gambardello, "Turnout for N.J. Primary Highest in Half a Century," *Philadelphia Inquirer*, February 7, 2008.

35. Warren E. Miller and J. Merrill Shanks, *The New American Voter* (Cambridge: Harvard University Press, 1996), ch. 7.

36. Figure calculated by the authors from National Election Studies data.

37. Rosalee A. Clawson and Zoe M. Oxley, *Public Opinion: Democratic Ideal and Democratic Practice*, 2nd ed. (Washington, D.C.: CQ Press, 2013).

38. "Trends in Voter Turnout," Social Science Data Analysis Network analysis of Current Population Survey data, www.ssdan.net/sites/default/files/briefs/vtbrief.pdf; Center for Information and Research on Civic Learning and Engagement, "Voter Turnout Among Young Women and Men in the 2012 Presidential Election," www.civicyouth.org/wp-content/uploads/2013/05/fs_gender_13_final.pdf.

39. Lee Sigelman and Susan Welch, *Black Americans' Views of Racial Equality—The Dream Deferred* (Cambridge: Cambridge University Press, 1991).

40. Katherine Tate, "Black Political Participation in the 1984 and 1988 Presidential Elections," *American Political Science Review* 85 (December 1991): 1159–1176.

41. Amanda Terkle, "Rep. Tim Scott Floats Impeachment If Obama Invokes 14th Amendment on Debt Limit (VIDEO)," HuffPost Politics, July 6, 2011, www.huffingtonpost.com/2011/07/06/tim-scott-impeachment-obama-14-amendment-debt_n_891521.html.

42. Robert S. Erikson, Gerald C. Wright, and John P. McIver, *Statehouse Democracy* (New York: Cambridge University Press, 1993), 18.

43. James G. Gimpel and Kimberly A. Karnes, "The Rural Side of the Urban-Rural Gap," *PS: Political Science & Politics* (July 2006).

44. Pew Research Center for People and the Press, "Public Appetite for Government Misjudged: Washington Leaders Wary of Public Opinion," www.people-press.org/files/legacy-pdf/92.pdf.

45. Susan Herbst, *Numbered Voices: How Opinion Polling Has Shaped American Politics* (Chicago: University of Chicago Press, 1993), ch. 4.

46. William Safire, *Safire's New Political Dictionary: The Definitive Guide to the New Language of Politics* (New York: Random House, 1993), 764.

47. Erikson and Tedin, 5th ed., 29–31.

48. Richard Morin, "Don't Ask Me: As Fewer Cooperate on Polls, Criticism and Questions Mount," *Washington Post*, October 28, 2004, C1.

49. Pew Research Center for the People and the Press, "Opinion Poll Experiment Reveals Conservative Opinions Not Underestimated, But Racial Hostility Missed," March 27, 1998, www.people-press.org/content.htm; Andrew Rosenthal, "The 1989 Elections: Predicting the Outcome; Broad Disparities in Votes and Polls Raising Questions," *New York Times*, November 9, 1989, A1; Adam Clymer, "Election Day Shows What the Opinion Polls Can't Do," *New York Times*, November 12, 1989, sec. 4, 4; George Flemming and Kimberly Parker, "Race and Reluctant Respondents: Possible Consequences of Non-Response for Pre-Election Survey," May 16, 1998, www.people-press.org/content.htm.

50. George F. Bishop et al., "Pseudo-Opinions on Public Affairs," *Public Opinion Quarterly* 44 (Summer 1980): 198–209.

51. Graham Kalton and Howard Schuman, "The Effect of the Question on Survey Responses: A Review," *Journal of the Royal Statistical Society. Series A (General)* 145 (1982): 42–73; Howard Schuman and Stanley Presser, *Questions and Answers in Attitude Surveys* (New York: Academic Press, 1981), 148–160.

52. George F. Bishop, Robert W. Oldendick, and Alfred J. Tuchfarber, "Experiments in Filtering Political Opinions," *Political Behavior* 2 (1980): 339–369.

53. This was a Roper Starch Worldwide poll conducted in November 1992 for the American Jewish Committee, and it was reported in conjunction with the dedication of the Holocaust Memorial Museum.

54. Debra J. Saunders, "Poll Shows Americans in Deep Dumbo," *San Francisco Chronicle*, April 23, 1993, A30; Leonard Larsen, "What's on Americans' Mind? Not Much, History Poll Finds," *Sacramento Bee*, June 2, 1993, B7, cited in David W. Moore and Frank Newport, "Misreading the Public: The Case of the Holocaust Poll," *Public Perspective* (March–April 1994).

55. Moore and Newport, 29.

56. John Zaller, *The Nature and Origins of Mass Opinion* (New York: Cambridge University Press, 1992).

57. See, for example, abcnews.go.com/blogs/politics/polls/, www.cbsnews.com/latest/opinion/, www.washingtonpost.com/politics/polling/, www.nytimes.com/pages/politics/index.html (click on "Poll Watch" to see recent polls), www.people-press.org, and for an excellent roundup of political polls, see www.pollingreport.com.

58. Two recent additions to the large-scale surveys are the National Annenberg Elections Surveys, which launched large, complex, in-person surveys of voter attitudes and decision making in the 2000, 2004, and 2008 elections (www.annenbergpublicpolicycenter.org/political-communication/naes/) and the recurring (since 2006) Cooperative Congressional Elections studies, which are Internet-based surveys. Each carries questions by teams of scholars from dozens of universities exploring a wide variety of questions about political behavior; see web.mit.edu/polisci/portl/cces/index.html.

59. Nate Silver, "Which Polls Fared Best, and Worst, in the 2012 Presidential Race," November 10, 2012, fivethirtyeight.blogs.nytimes.com/2012/11/10/which-polls-fared-best-and-worst-in-the-2012-presidential-race/.

60. Most of the exit poll reporting is based on surveys done by Edison Media Research and Mitofsky International for the National Election Pool. This is a consortium of ABC News, Associated Press, CBS News, CNN, Fox News, and NBC News. Each of the media organizations has its own analysts who then highlight different aspects of the exit poll data.

61. Adam Lisberg, "Exit Polls Out of Whack: Early Numbers Told Wrong Story," New York *Daily News*, November 4, 2002, 11; "Evaluation of Edison/Mitofsky Election System 2004," prepared by Edison Media Research and Mitofsky International for the National Election Pool (NEP), January 19, 2005.

62. Quoted in "Planting Lies With 'Push Polls,'" *St. Petersburg Times*, June 7, 1995, 10A.

63. Quoted in Betsy Rothstein, "Push Polls Utilized in Final Weeks," *The Hill*, October 28, 1998, 3.

64. "Pollsters Seek AAPC Action," *Campaigns and Elections* (July 1996): 55.

65. Paul Sniderman and Thomas Piazza, *The Scar of Race* (Cambridge: Harvard University Press, 1995).

66. TESS Time-Sharing Experiments for the Social Sciences, tessexperiments.org.

67. William Saletan, "Phoning It In," *Slate*, December 7, 2007, www.slate.com/iod/2179395/.

68. SurveyUSA home page, www.surveyusa.com.

69. David Sanders, Harold D. Clarke, Marianne C. Stewart, and Paul Whiteley, "Does Mode Matter for Modeling Political Choice? Evidence From the 2005 British Election Study," *Political Analysis* 15 (2007): 257–285; Robert P. Berrens, Alok K. Bohara, Hank Jenkins-Smith, Carol Silva, and David L. Weimer, "The Advent of Internet Surveys for Political Research: A Comparison of Telephone and Internet Samples," *Political Analysis* 11 (2003): 1–22; Taylor Humphrey, "The Case for Publishing (Some) Online Polls," *Polling Report*, January 15, 2007; Linchiat Chang and Jon A. Krosnick, "National Surveys via RDD Telephone Interviewing Versus the Internet," *Public Opinion Quarterly* 2009 (73): 641–678.

70. J. Michael Brick, Pat D. Brick, Sarah Dipko, Stanley Presser, Clyde Tucker, and Yangyang Yuan, "Cell Phone Survey Feasibility in the U.S.: Sampling and Calling Cell Numbers Versus Landline Numbers," *Public Opinion Quarterly* 71 (Spring 2007): 23–39. See the special issue of *Public Opinion Quarterly* (Winter 2007) for perspectives on the challenges that cell phones pose for surveys.

71. Erikson and Tedin, 5th ed., 42–47.

72. Research suggests that the use of information shortcuts does allow the electorate to make decisions that are more in line with their values than if they did not have such shortcuts; see Samuel Popkin, *The Reasoning Voter* (Chicago: University of Chicago Press, 1991); and Paul Sniderman, Richard Brody, and Philip Tetlock, *Reasoning and Choice: Exploration in Political Psychology* (New York: Cambridge University Press, 1991). However, this is not the same as saying that, if fully informed, everyone would make the same decision as they do without information. Indeed, information really does count; see Larry Bartels, "Uninformed Votes: Information Effects in Presidential Elections," *American Journal of Political Science* 40 (February 1996): 194–230; and Scott Althaus, "Information Effects in Collective Preferences," *American Political Science Review* 92 (September 1998): 545–558.

73. Milton Lodge, Kathleen McGraw, and Patrick Stroh, "An Impression-Driven Model of Candidate Evaluation," *American Political Science Review* 82 (June 1989): 399–419.

74. Berelson, Lazarsfeld, and McPhee, 109–115.

75. Philip Meyer, "The Elite Newspaper of the Future," *American Journalism Review*, October/November 2008, www.ajr.org/article.asp?id=4605.

76. J. C. Baumgartner and J. S. Morris, "MyFaceTube Politics: Social Networking Web Sites and Political Engagement of Young Adults," *Social Science Computer Review* 28 (2009): 24–44.

77. Larry M. Bartels, "Uninformed Votes: Information Effects in Presidential Elections," *American Journal of Political Science* 40 (1996): 194–230.

78. Gerald C. Wright, "Level of Analysis Effects on Explanations of Voting," *British Journal of Political Science* 18 (July 1989): 381–398; Samuel Popkin, *The Reasoning Voter* (Chicago: University of Chicago Press,

1991); Benjamin Page and Robert Shapiro, *The Rational Public* (Chicago: University of Chicago Press, 1993).

79. Erikson, Wright, and McIver.

80. Michael B. MacKuen, Robert S. Erikson, and James A. Stimson, "Macropartisanship," *American Political Science Review* 89 (December 1989): 1125–1142.

81. Larry Bartels, *Unequal Democracy: The Political Economy of the New Gilded Age* (Princeton: Princeton University Press, 2008), ch. 9; Martin Gilens, "Inequality and Democratic Responsiveness," *Public Opinion Quarterly* 69 (2005): 778–896.

82. Luke Johnson, "Chris Christie Links Civil Rights to Gay Marriage Vote, Draws Sharp Criticism," *Huffington Post*, February 1, 2012, www.huffingtonpost.com/2012/01/26/chris-christie-gay-marriage-civil-rights_n_1234276.html.

83. Jean Bethke Elshtain, "A Parody of True Democracy," *Christian Science Monitor*, August 13, 1992, 18.

Chapter 12

1. Jennifer Steinhauer, "Nevada Challenger Lifted by Tea Party Ardor," *New York Times*, June 9, 2010, www.nytimes.com/2010/06/10/us/politics/10nevada.html? scp=1&sq=sharron%20angle%20primary&st=cse.

2. Ibid.; Brian Stelter, "Reid and Angle Campaigns Fight Over Web Site," *The Caucus*, July 6, 2010, thecaucus.blogs.nytimes.com/2010/07/06/reidand-angle-campaigns-fight-over-website/?scp=1&sq=sharron%20angle%20website&st=cse; Adam Weinstein, "Nevada Tea Partiers' Memory Hole," *Mother Jones*, June 9, 2010, motherjones.com/mojo/2010/06/nevada-tea-partier-memoryhole-website-sharron-angle-harry-reidsenate.

3. Stelter.

4. Jessica Taylor, "Mason-Dixon Poll: Reid Rises Again," *Politico*, July 16, 2010, www.politico.com/news/stories/0710/39842.html.

5. "Jim DeMint: Tea Party Candidates Can Win Midterm Election Races," *The Huffington Post*, September 16, 2010, www.huffingtonpost.com/2010/09/16/jim-demint-tea-party-cand_n_719148.html.

6. Jonathan Allen and Jake Sherman, "GOP Leery of Tea Party Caucus," *Politico*, July 20, 2010, dyn.politico.com/members/forums/thread.cfm?catid=1&subcatid=1&threadid=42805501; Paul Kane, "Lieberman Savoring Life on Both Sides of the Aisle: Democrats Want Him in Caucus Despite His Backing of McCain," *Washington Post*, June 6, 2008, A17.

7. Liz Halloran, "Rape Comments Complicate But Don't End GOP Senate Takeover Chances," NPR, October 25, 2012, www.npr.org/blogs/itsallpolitics/2012/10/25/163636771/candidate-comments-complicate-but-dont-end-gop-senate-takeover-chances.

8. See, for example, James Bryce, *The American Commonwealth* (Chicago: Sergel, 1891), vol. 2, pt. 3.

9. E. E. Schattschneider, *Party Government* (New York: Holt, Rinehart, and Winston, 1942), 1.

10. This division and the following discussion are based on Frank Sorauf, *Party Politics in America* (Boston: Little, Brown, 1964), ch. 1; and V. O. Key Jr., *Politics, Parties, and Pressure Groups*, 5th ed. (New York: Corwell, 1964).

11. Richard G. Niemi and M. Kent Jennings, "Issues of Inheritance in the Formation of Party Identification," *American Journal of Political Science* 35 (1991): 970–988.

12. The discussion of the responsible party model is based on Austin Ranney, *The Doctrine of the Responsible Party Government* (Urbana: University of Illinois Press, 1962), chs. 1, 2.

13. Morris P. Fiorina, "The Decline of Collective Responsibility in American Politics," *Daedalus* 109 (Summer 1980): 25–45; John H. Aldrich, *Why Parties? The Origin and Transformation of Party Politics in America* (Chicago: University of Chicago Press, 1995), 3.

14. American Political Science Association, "Toward a More Responsible Two-Party System: A Report of the Committee on Political Parties of the American Political Science Association," *American Political Science Review* 44 (1950; 3, pt. 2): 1–99.

15. Thomas E. Mann and Norman J. Ornstein, *It's Even Worse Than It Looks: How the American Constitutional System Collided With the New Politics of Extremism* (New York: Basic Books, 2012).

16. Alan I. Abramowitz, "Exploring the Bases of Partisanship in the American Electorate: Social Identity vs. Ideology," *Political Research Quarterly* 59 (2006): 175–187.

17. Alan I. Abramowitz and Kyle L. Saunders, "Ideological Realignment in the U.S. Electorate," *Journal of Politics* 60 (1998): 634–652; Geoffrey C. Layman and Thomas M. Carsey, "Party Polarization and 'Conflict Extension' in the American Electorate," *American Journal of Political Science* 46 (2002): 786–802; Geoffrey C. Layman et al., "Activists and Conflict Extension in American Party Politics," *American Political Science Review* 104 (2010): 324–346.

18. Calculated by the authors using data from CBS News/*New York Times* national surveys; Abramowitz and Saunders report the same basic pattern in their analysis of white party identifiers using data from the American National Election Studies, Abramowitz and Saunders, "Ideological Realignment of the U.S. Electorate," 186.

19. Edward G. Carmines and Geoffrey C. Layman, "Issue Evolution in Postwar American Politics: Old Certainties and Fresh Tensions," in Byron E. Shafer, ed., *Present Discontents: American Politics in the Very Late Twentieth Century* (Chatham, N.J.: Chatham House, 1997), 89–134.

20. Ruy A. Teixeira and Joel Rogers, *America's Forgotten Majority: Why the White Working Class Still Matter* (New York: Basic Books, 2000); Thomas Frank, *What's the Matter With Kansas? How Conservatives Won the Heart of America* (New York: Metropolitan Books, 2004).

21. John H. Aldrich, "A Downsian Spatial Model With Party Activism," *American Political Science Review* 77 (1983): 974–990; David W. Brady, Hahrie Han, and Jeremy C. Pope, "Primary Elections and Candidate Ideology: Out of Step With the Primary Electorate?" *Legislative Studies Quarterly* 27 (2007): 79–105; Layman et al.; James L. Gibson and Susan E. Scarrow, "State Organizations in American Politics," in Eric M. Uslaner, ed., *American Political Parties: A Reader* (Itasca, Ill.: F. E. Peacock, 1993), 234.

22. James Q. Wilson, *The Amateur Democrat: Club Politics in Three Cities* (Chicago: University of Chicago Press, 1965).

23. Walter J. Stone and Alan I. Abramowitz, "Winning May Not Be Everything, But It's More Than We Thought: Presidential Party Activists in 1980," *American Political Science Review* 77 (1983): 945–956.

24. Godfrey Hodgson, *The Myth of American Exceptionalism* (New Haven: Yale University Press, 2009).

25. Joseph A. Aistrup, *The Southern Strategy Revisited: Republican Top-Down Advancement in the South* (Lexington: University of Kentucky Press, 1996), 148–151; Robert S. Erikson, Gerald C. Wright, and John P. McIver, *Statehouse Democracy: Public Opinion and Policy in the American States* (Cambridge: Cambridge University Press, 1993), ch. 5.

26. Gerald C. Wright and Michael B. Berkman, "Candidates and Policy in U.S. Senatorial Elections," *American Political Science Review* 80 (1986): 576–590.

27. Anthony Downs, *An Economic Theory of Democracy* (New York: Harper & Row, 1957).

28. Keith T. Poole and Howard Rosenthal, "The Polarization of American Politics," *Journal of Politics* 46 (1984): 1061–1079; Alan Abramowitz, *The Disappearing Center: Engaged Citizens, Polarization, and American Democracy* (New Haven: Yale University Press, 2010).

29. Aldrich, *Why Parties?*

30. Aldrich, *Why Parties?*, 5.

31. This discussion of the Jacksonian Democrats and machine politics and patronage is based on Aldrich, *Why Parties?*, ch. 4; Leon D. Epstein, *Political Parties in the American Mold* (Madison: University of Wisconsin Press, 1986), 134–143; and Frank J. Sorauf and Paul Allen Beck, *Party Politics in America*, 6th ed. (Glenview, Ill.: Scott, Foresman, 1988), 83–91.

32. Gerald C. Wright, John P. McIver, Robert S. Erikson, and David B. Holian, "Stability and Change in State Electorates, Carter Through Clinton," paper presented at the Midwest Political Science Association meetings, Chicago, 2000; Larry Bartels, "Partisanship and Voting Behavior, 1952–1996," *American Journal of Political Science* 44 (2000): 35–50.

33. Layman and Carsey.

34. Gary C. Jacobson, *The Electoral Origins of Divided Government* (Boulder: Westview Press, 1990), and *The Politics of Congressional Elections*, 6th ed. (New York: Longman, 2003).

35. Xandra Kayden and Eddie Mahe Jr., "Back From the Depths: Party Resurgence," in Uslaner, 192, 196; Aistrup, ch. 4.

36. Sarah McCally Morehouse and Malcolm E. Jewell, *State Politics, Parties, & Policy*, 2nd ed. (Lanham, Md.: Rowman & Littlefield, 2003), 127–133.

37. Alec MacGillis and Peter Slevin, "Did Rush Limbaugh Tilt Result in Indiana? Conservative Host Urged 'Chaos' Votes," *Washington Post*, May 8, 2008, A01.

38. David E. Price, *Bring Back the Parties* (Washington, D.C.: Congressional Quarterly, 1984), 130–132.

39. Sorauf and Beck, 218–233.

40. Jill Serjeant, "John McCain Speech Draws Record TV Ratings," September 5, 2008, www.washingtonpost.com.

41. Dylan Byers, "Joe Biden Wins Highest Convention Ratings," *Politico*, September 21, 2012, www.politico.com/blogs/media/2012/09/joe-biden-wins-highest-convention-ratings-136256.html.

42. Benjamin Ginsberg, *Consequences of Consent* (New York: Random House, 1982), 128–133.

43. Michael Luo and Mike McIntyre, "McCain to Rely on Party Money Against Obama," *New York Times*, May 19, 2008.

44. C. P. Cotter, J. L. Gibson, J. F. Bibby, and R. J. Huckshorn, *Party Organizations in American Politics* (New York: Praeger, 1984); John J. Coleman, "Resurgent or Just Busy? Party Organizations in Contemporary America," in John Green and Daniel Shea, eds., *The State of the Parties* (Lanham, Md.: Rowman & Littlefield, 1996), ch. 22.

45. Jill Abramson, "Democrats and Republicans Step Up Pursuit of 'Soft Money'," *New York Times*, May 13, 1998, 2; Jill Abramson, "Cost of '96 Campaign Sets Record at $2.2 Billion," *New York Times*, November 25, 1997, 1.

46. Marjorie Randon Hershey, *Party Politics in America*, 13th ed. (New York: Pearson Longman, 2008), ch. 12.

47. "Living in a Citizens United World: When Other Voices Are Drowned Out," *New York Times*, March 26, 2012 (editorial); Adam Liptak, "Viewing Free Speech Through Election Law Haze," *New York Times*, May 4, 2010; Adam Liptak, "Former Justice O'Connor Sees Ill in Election Finance Ruling," *New York Times*, January 27, 2010; Rebekah Metzler , "Progressives Push Amendment to Overturn Citizens United," USNEWS.com, April 18, 2012; Jeffrey Tobin, "Money Talks," *New Yorker*, April 11, 2011; Jaime Fuller, "Big Sky's the Limit," *The American Prospect*, June 2012; Rebekah Metzler, "McCain Calls SCOTUS Decision on Campaign Spending 'Stupid'," USNEWS.com, March 27, 2012.

48. Aistrup, 76; Paul S. Herrnson, *Congressional Elections: Campaigning at Home and in Washington*, 2nd ed. (Washington, D.C.: CQ Press, 1998), ch. 4.

49. Sorauf and Beck.

50. Gerald Pomper with Susan Lederman, *Elections in America* (New York: Longman, 1980), 145–150, 167–173.

51. Samuel Huntington, "The Visions of the Democratic Party," *Public Interest* (Spring 1985): 64; Layman and Carsey.

52. This section is based on Alan Ware, *Political Parties and Party Systems* (New York: Oxford University Press, 1996).

53. L. Sandy Maisel, *Parties and Elections in America*, 2nd ed. (New York: McGraw-Hill, 1993), ch. 10; Epstein; Price, 284.

54. Nelson Polsby, *The Consequences to Party Reform* (New York: Oxford University Press, 1983), 83.

55. Michael Powell, "Seared but Unwilted: Democrats See Red but Green Party Faithful Say They Made Their Point," *Washington Post*, December 27, 2000, C1.

56. David Leonhardt, "The Election: Was Buchanan the Real Nader?" *New York Times*, December 10, 2000, sec. 4, 4.

57. Gerald C. Wright, "Charles Adrian and the Study of Nonpartisan Elections," *Political Research Quarterly* 61 (2008): 13–16.

58. Joseph Cooper and David W. Brady, "Institutional Context and Leadership Style: The House From Cannon to Rayburn," *American Political Science Review* 75 (1981): 411–425; John H. Aldrich and David W. Rohde, "The Logic of Conditional Party Government: Revisiting the Electoral Connection," in Lawrence Dodd and Bruce Oppenheimer, eds., *Congress Reconsidered*, 7th ed. (Washington, D.C.: CQ Press, 2001).

59. Michelle Cottle, "House Broker," *New Republic*, June 11, 2008, www.tnr.com.

60. Aldrich and Rohde.

61. Ed Hornick, "The 'Big Headache': Boehner Backed Into Corner by Tea Party, Obama," CNN News, July 26, 2011, articles.cnn.com/2011-07-26/politics/tea.party.boehner_1_tea-party-debt-ceiling-debt-limit-vote?_s=PM:POLITICS.

62. Morris Fiorina, *Divided Government* (New York: Macmillan, 1992).

63. See, for example, Fiorina, *Divided Government*; and John R. Hibbing and Elizabeth Theiss-Morse, *Congress as Public Enemy: Public Attitudes Toward American Political Institutions* (Cambridge: Cambridge University Press, 1995).

64. Hibbing and Theiss-Morse, 157.

65. Kevin Robillard, "Dick Armey: Boehner Should Vote on Fiscal Cliff Plan," *Politico*, December 10, 2012, http://www.politico.com/story/2012/12/armey-boehner-should-vote-on-fiscal-cliff-plan-84831.html.

66. Jeremy Peters and Carl Hulse, "Republicans' First Step was o Handle Extremists in Party." The New York Times, November 5, 2014. http://mobile.nytimes.com/2014/11/05/us/politics/-republicans-first-had-to-wrestle-with-their-own-poor-discipline-.html?action=click&pgtype=Homepage&module=span-abc-region%C2%AEion=span-abc-region&WT.nav=span-abc-region&_r=1&referrer=

67. Charles Babbington, "Analysis: DeMint Move Defies GOP Shift to the Center," The Associated Press, December 7, 2012, http://news.yahoo.com/analysis-demint-move-defies-gop-shift-center-090121543--politics.html.

68. Kevin Robillard, "Dick Armey: Boehner Should Vote on Fiscal Cliff Plan," *Politico*, December 10, 2012, www.politico.com/story/2012/12/armey-boehner-should-vote-on-fiscal-cliff-plan-84831.html.

Chapter 13

1. PBS, "Obama's Deal," Part I, *Frontline*, www.pbs.org/wgbh/pages/frontline/obamasdeal/.

2. Alexis de Tocqueville, *Democracy in America*, Richard D. Heffner, ed. (New York: New American Library, 1956), 198.

3. James Madison, "Federalist No. 10," in Roy P. Fairfield, ed., *The Federalist Papers*, 2nd ed. (Baltimore: Johns Hopkins University Press, 1981), 16.

4. This definition is based on Jeffrey M. Berry, *The Interest Group Society*, 3rd ed. (New York: Longman, 1997); and David Truman, *The Governmental Process: Political Interest and Public Opinion*, 2nd ed. (New York: Knopf, 1971).

5. Berry; Truman; Allan J. Cigler and Burdett A. Loomis, eds., *Interest Group Politics*, 6th ed. (Washington, D.C.: CQ Press, 2002).

6. Burdett A. Loomis and Allan J. Cigler, "Introduction: The Changing Nature of Interest Group Politics," in Cigler and Loomis, *Interest Group Politics*, 6th ed., 2–5, 21–22.

7. Jonathan Rauch, *Demosclerosis: The Silent Killer of American Government* (New York: Crown, 1994), 39.

8. Michael Luo, "Money Talks Louder Than Ever in Midterms," *New York Times*, October 7, 2010, www.nytimes.com/2010/10/08/us/politics/08donate.html?scp=1&sq=Luo%20Money%20talks%2010uder&st=cse.

9. Marian Currinder, Joanne Connor Green, and M. Margaret Conway, "Interest Group Money in Elections," in Allan J. Cigler and Burdett A. Loomis, eds., *Interest Group Politics*, 7th ed. (Washington, D.C.: CQ Press, 2007), 187.

10. On this last point, see Rauch.

11. Berry, 6–8; John W. Kingdon, *Agendas, Alternatives, and Public Policy* (Boston: Little, Brown, 1984).

12. Kingdon.

13. Children's Defense Fund, 2005, www.childrensdefense.org.

14. Truman, 66–108.

15. Berry, 66.

16. Jeffrey Berry, Kent E. Portney, and Ken Thomson, *The Rebirth of Urban Democracy* (Washington, D.C.: Brookings Institution, 1993).

17. Robert Salisbury, "An Exchange Theory of Interest Groups," *Midwest Journal of Political Science* 13 (1969): 1–32.

18. For a full description of these incentives, see Peter B. Clark and James Q. Wilson, "Incentive Systems: A Theory of Organizations," *Administrative Science Quarterly* 6 (1961): 129–166.

19. Mancur Olson Jr., *The Logic of Collective Action* (New York: Schocken, 1971).

20. The idea of selective incentives is Olson's (1971, 51). This discussion comes from the work of Clark and Wilson (1961), 129–166, as interpreted in Salisbury. Clark and Wilson use the terms *material, solidary,* and *purposive* benefits, while Salisbury prefers *material, solidary,* and *expressive.* We follow Salisbury's interpretation and usage here.

21. John P. Heinz et al., *The Hollow Core* (Cambridge: Harvard University Press, 1993), 1–3.

22. Benjamin Goad, "Wall Street Spending $1.5M a Day on Lobbying, Campaigns," *The Hill*, July 25, 2014, thehill.com/regulation/finance/213342-wall-street-spending-15m-a-day-on-lobbying-politics.

23. Ronald G. Shaiko, "Making the Connection: Organized Interests, Political Representation, and the Changing Rules of the Game in Washington Politics," in Paul S. Herrnson, Ronald G. Shaiko, and Clyde Wilcox, eds., *The Interest Group Connection* (Washington, D.C.: CQ Press, 2005), 6.

24. Foundation for Public Affairs, *Public Interest Group Profiles, 2004–2005* (Washington, D.C.: CQ Press, 2004), 486–488.

25. U.S. Chamber of Commerce, "About Us," www.uschamber.com/about.

26. Sabrina Siddiqui and Paul Blumenthal, "Lawmakers Backed by Chamber of Commerce Spending Stall Business Lobby's Legislative Priorities," *HuffPost Politics*, August 18, 2013, www.huffingtonpost.com/2013/08/18/chamber-of-commerce-spending_n_3769902.html.

27. Eggen.

28. AFL-CIO: America's Union Movement, "About Us: AFL-CIO Unions," www.aflcio.org/About/AFL-CIO-Unions.

29. "Labor Pains," *Houston Chronicle*, July 28, 2005, B10; Amanda Paulson, "Union Split: Sign of Decline or Revival," *Christian Science Monitor*, July 27, 2005, 2.

30. International Brotherhood of Teamsters, www.teamsters.org; United Auto Workers, www.uaw.org; United Mine Workers of America, www.umwa.org.

31. David Kocieniewski, "Unions at Center of Wisconsin Recall Vote, Suffer a New Setback in Its Outcome," *New York Times*, June 6, 2012, www.nytimes.com/2012/06/07/us/politics/scott-walkers-win-in-wisconsin-casts-doubts-on-union-power.html?ref=politics.

32. Steve Lohr, "Bush's Next Target: Malpractice Lawyers," *New York Times*, February 27, 2005, sec. 3, 1.

33. American Farm Bureau Federation, "We Are Farm Bureau," www.fb.org/index.php?action=about.home; American Agriculture Movement, www.aaminc.org; National Farmers Union, www.nfu.org.

34. AARP, "AARP History," www.aarp.org/about-aarp/info-2009/History.html.

35. Children's Defense Fund, www.childrensdefense.org.

36. Foundation for Public Affairs, 483–485; NAACP, www.naacp.org.

37. League of United Latin American Citizens, lulac.org/about/history/.

38. Foundation for Public Affairs, 460–462.

39. American Indian Movement, www.aimovement.org.

40. Southeast Asia Resource Action Center, www.searac.org.

41. National Organization for Women, "FAQs," now.org/about/faqs/.

42. Eagle Forum, www.eagleforum.org; Susan B. Anthony List, www.sba-list.org.

43. American Coalition for Fathers and Children, www.acfc.org; National Congress for Fathers and Children, www.fathersmanifesto.net/ncfc.htm.

44. Log Cabin Republicans, "About Log Cabin," www.logcabin.org/about-us/.

45. Allan J. Cigler and Anthony J. Nowns, "Public Interest Entrepreneurs and Group Patrons," in Allan J. Cigler and Burdett A. Loomis, eds., *Interest Group Politics*, 4th ed. (Washington, D.C.: CQ Press, 1995), 77–78.

46. Christopher J. Bosso, "The Color of Money," in Cigler and Loomis, *Interest Group Politics*, 4th ed., 104.

47. Ben Smith, "NRA: Obama Most Anti-Gun Candidate Ever; Will Ban Guns," *Politico*, August 6, 2008, www.politico.com/blogs/bensmith/0808/NRA_Obama_most_antigun_candidate_ever_will_ban_guns.html.

48. William Booth, "Logging Protester Killed by Falling Redwood Tree," *Washington Post*, September 19, 1998, A2; Ed Henry, "Earth First! Activists Invade Riggs's California Office. In Aftermath, Congressman Considers Bill to Strengthen Penalty for Assaulting Congressional Staffers," *Roll Call*, October 27, 1997.

49. For a discussion of coalition politics involving Ralph Nader, see Loree Bykerk and Ardith Maney, "Consumer Groups and Coalition Politics on Capitol Hill," in Cigler and Loomis, *Interest Group Politics*, 4th ed., 259–279.

50. Consumers Union, www.consumersunion.org.

51. Foundation for Public Affairs, 197–199.

52. See James Guth et al., "Onward Christian Soldiers: Religious Activist Groups in American Politics," in Cigler and Loomis, *Interest Group Politics*, 4th ed., 55–75; Guth et al., "A Distant Thunder?" in Cigler and Loomis, *Interest Group Politics*, 6th ed., 162–165.

53. Joseph A. Aistrup, *Southern Strategy Revisited* (Lexington: University Press of Kentucky, 1996), 56–61.

54. Adam Clymer, "Decision in the Senate: The Overview; Crime Bill Approved 61–38, but Senate Is Going Home Without Acting on Health Care," *New York Times*, August 26, 1994, 1.

55. Sheryl Gay Stolberg, "Effort to Renew Weapons Ban Falters on Hill," *New York Times*, September 9, 2004, A1; Edward Epstein, "Supporters of Gun Ban Lament Its Expiration," *San Francisco Chronicle*, September 10, 2004, A1.

56. Jon Jeter, "Jury Says Abortion Opponents Are Liable; Efforts to Close Clinics Violate Racketeering Law," *Washington Post*, April 21, 1998, A1; "Operation Rescue Founder Files for Bankruptcy Due to Lawsuits," *Washington Post*, November 8, 1998, A29.

57. Adam Liptak, "Court Limits Birth Control Rule," *New York Times*, July 1, 2014, 1.

58. American Civil Liberties Union, "About Us," www.aclu.org/about/aboutmain.cfm.

59. Amnesty International, "About Us," www.amnestyusa.org/about-us/who-we-are.

60. Loomis and Cigler, 22–23; People for the Ethical Treatment of Animals, www.peta.org.

61. Animal Rights Law Project, www.animal-law.org; Animal Liberation Front, www.animalliberationfront.com; "Deaths of More Baby Rats on Shuttle Prompt Protests," *Los Angeles Times*, April 29, 1998, A14; Daniel B. Wood, "Animal Activists vs. Furriers: Now It's All in the Label," *Christian Science Monitor*, November 27, 1998, 2; Brad Knickerbocker, "Activists Step Up War to 'Liberate' Nature," *Christian Science Monitor*, January 20, 1999, 4.

62. Ronald J. Hrebenar and Clive S. Thomas, "The Japanese Lobby in Washington: How Different Is It?" in Cigler and Loomis, *Interest Group Politics*, 4th ed., 349–368.

63. Judy Sarasohn, "For Lobbyists, the $65 Million List," *Washington Post*, March 17, 2005, A23; *Congressional Quarterly Weekly Report*, December 12, 1992, 3792; Allison Mitchell, "A New Form of Lobbying Puts Public Face on Private Interests," *New York Times*, September 30, 1998, web version.

64. William Safire, *Safire's New Political Dictionary* (New York: Random House, 1993), 417–418.

65. Jeffrey H. Birnbaum, "The Road to Riches Is Called K Street," *Washington Post*, June 22, 2005, A1; Matt Kelley, "Pull of Lobbyists' Revolving Door: Salary vs. Service," *USA Today*, December 25, 2008, www.usatoday.com/news/washington/2008-12-25-revolvingdoor-inside_N.htm.

66. Jeffrey H. Birnbaum, "When Candidates Decry Lobbying, Ex-Lawmakers Embrace It," *Washington Post*, January 8, 2008, A17; Jordi Blanes I Vidal, Mirko Draca, and Christian Fons-Rosen, "Revolving Door Lobbyists," May 2011, personal.lse.ac.uk/blanesiv/revolving.pdf.

67. Center for Responsive Politics, "Former Members," www.opensecrets.org/revolving/top.php?display=Z.

68. T. W. Farnam, "Study Shows Revolving Door of Employment Between Congress, Lobbying Firms," *Washington Post*, September 13, 2011; Jordi Blanes i Vidaly, Mirko Draca, and Christian Fons-Rosen, "Revolving Door Lobbyists," May 2011, personal.lse.ac.uk/blanesiv/revolving.pdf.

69. Bart Jansen, "Lobbying Bill Signed Into Law," *CQ Today*, CQPolitics.com, September 14, 2007; see also www.common cause.org.

70. Dan Eggen and R. Jeffrey Smith, "Lobbying Rules Surpass Those of Previous Administrations, Experts Say," *Washington Post*, January 22, 2009, www.washingtonpost.com/wp-dyn/content/article/2009/01/21/AR2009012103472.html.

71. See Diana M. Evans, "Lobbying the Committee: Interest Groups and the House Public Works and Transportation Committee," in Allan J. Cigler and Burdett A. Loomis, eds., *Interest Group Politics*, 3rd ed. (Washington, D.C.: CQ Press, 1991), 264–265. For a graphic example of this practice, see Michael Weisskopf and David Maraniss, "Forging an Alliance for Deregulation; Rep. DeLay Makes Companies Full Partners in the Movement," *Washington Post*, March 12, 1995, A1.

72. Carl Hulse, "Tough Going as Negotiators Hammer Out Energy Bill," *New York Times*, September 30, 2003, A20.

73. Ibid.

74. Mike Soraghan, "Measure Stresses Drilling in Rockies; Energy Bill Gets OK, May Go to House Today," *Denver Post*, November 18, 2003, A1.

75. Ashley Parker, "Outside Money Drives a Deluge of Political Ads," *New York Times*, July 27, 2014.

76. "Stopping SOPA: A Backlash From the Internet Community Against Attempts to Rein in Content Thieves," *The Economist*, January 21, 2012, www.economist.com/node/21543173.

77. Adam Clymer, "Congress Passes Bill to Disclose Lobbyists' Roles," *New York Times*, November 30, 1995, 1.

78. Adam Clymer, "Senate, 98-0, Sets Tough Restriction on Lobbyist Gifts," *New York Times*, July 29, 1995, 1; "House Approves Rule to Prohibit Lobbyists' Gifts," *New York Times*, November 17, 1995, 1.

79. Jeff Zeleny and David D. Kirkpatrick, "House, 411–8, Passes a Vast Ethics Overhaul," *New York Times*, August 1, 2007, www.nytimes.com.

80. Megan R., Wilson, "Bombshell: Ethics Office Alleges Illegal Lobbying," *The Hill*, July 25, 2014, thehill.com/business-a-lobbying/business-a-lobbying/213394-bombshell-ethics-office-alleges-illegal-lobbying.

81. Jeffrey H. Birnbaum, "Seeing the Ethics Rules, and Raising an Exception," *Washington Post*, October 23, 2007, A17.

82. Ibid.

83. Jeffrey H. Birnbaum, *The Lobbyists: How Influence Peddlers Work Their Way in Washington* (New York: Random House, 1992), vi, viii.

84. Kenneth P. Vogel, "President Obama's Lobbying Reforms Praised by Congressional Research Service," *Politico*, December 3, 2009, www.politico.com/news/stories/1209/30185.html; Peter Baker, "Obama's Pledge to Reform Ethics Faces an Early Test," *New York Times*, February 2, 2009, www.nytimes.com/2009/02/03/world/americas/03iht-0310bby.19884903.html?scp=3&sq=Obama%27s%20Pledge%20to%20Reform%20Ethics&st=cse.

85. See Douglas Yates, *Bureaucratic Democracy* (Cambridge: Harvard University Press, 1982), ch. 4.

86. Cindy Skrzcki, "OSHA Set to Propose Ergonomics Standards; Long-Studied Rules Repeatedly Blocked," *Washington Post*, February 19, 1999.

87. Supreme Court of the United States Blog, "Citizens United v. Federal Election Commission," www.scotusblog.com/case-files/cases/citizens-united-v-federal-election-commission/.

88. Samuel Kernell, *Going Public: New Strategies of Presidential Leadership* (Washington, D.C.: CQ Press, 1986), 34.

89. Berry, 121–122.

90. The Tax Foundation, "Tax Freedom Day® 2014 Is April 21, Three Days Later Than Last Year," taxfoundation.org/article/tax-freedom-day-2014-april-21-three-days-later-last-year.

91. Luo; *Citizens United v. Federal Election Commission*, 558 U.S. 50 (2010).

92. Diana Dwyre, "527s: The New Bad Guys of Campaign Finance," in Cigler and Loomis, *Interest Group Politics*, 7th ed., 212–232.

93. John Green, "John Green Discusses Differences Between 527 Groups and Political Action Committees" (interview), *All Things Considered*, National Public Radio, August 19, 2004.

94. William B. Browne, "Organized Interests, Grassroots Confidants, and Congress," in Cigler and Loomis, *Interest Group Politics*, 4th ed., 288; John W. Kingdon, *Congressmen's Voting Decisions*, 2nd ed. (New York: Harper & Row, 1981).

95. Evans, 269.

96. *Censure and Move On* (news release), October 15, 1998, www.moveon.org.

97. MediaMatters, "Report: 'Fair and Balanced' Fox News Aggressively Promotes 'Tea Party' Protests," MediaMatters for America, April 8, 2009, mediamatters.org/reports/200904080025.

98. Colleen O'Connor, "Prayer War: Civil Disobedience Is an Increasingly Popular Cross to Bear," *Denver Post*, December 23, 2004, F1; Anna Badkhen, "Protesters Drawn to Schiavo's Hospice; Christian Conservatives Sponsor Some, Others Say They're Following Their Hearts," *San Francisco Chronicle*, March 24, 2005, A1; Dennis Mahoney, "Christian Group Plans Rallies, Protests; Gay Rights, Abortion Focus of Weeklong Visit to Columbus," *Columbus Dispatch*, June 7, 2004, 5D.

99. Chris Good, "The Tea Party Movement: Who's In Charge?" *The Atlantic*, April 13, 2009, www.theatlantic.com/politics/archive/2009/04/the-tea-party-movement-whos-in-charge/13041/.

100. Mark Brunswick, "Prescription Politics; Drug Lobby Intensifies Fight on Price Controls and Imports," Minneapolis *Star Tribune*, November 16, 2003, 1A; Jim VandeHei and Juliet Eilperin, "Drug Firms Gain Church Group's Aid; Claim About Import Measure Stirs Anger," *Washington Post*, July 23, 2003, A1.

101. John Stauber, director of the Center for Media & Democracy, quoted in J. A. Savage, "Astroturf Lobbying Replaces Grassroots Organizing: Corporations Mask Their Interests by Supporting Supposed Grassroots Organizations," *Business and Society Review*, September 22, 1995, 8.

102. Mike Murphy in Mitchell, A1.

103. Bill McAllister, "Rainmakers Making a Splash," *Washington Post*, December 4, 1997, A21.

104. Federal Election Commission, "PAC's Grouped by Total Spent," April 13, 2005, www.fec.gov/press/press2005/20050412pac/groupbyspending2004.pdf; Richard L. Hall and Frank W. Wayman, "Buying Time: Money Interests and the Mobilization of Bias in Congressional Committees," *American Political Science Review* 84 (1990): 797–820.

105. Luo; *Citizens United v. Federal Election Commission*.

106. Dan Eggen and T. W. Farnam, "Spending by Independent Groups Had Little Election Impact, Analysis Finds," *Washington Post*, November 7, 2012, www.washingtonpost.com/politics/decision2012/spending-by-independent-groups-had-little-election-impact-analysis-finds/2012/11/07/15fd30ea-276c-11e2-b2a0-ae18d6159439_story.html.

107. Jeffrey H. Birnbaum, "To Predict Losers in a Power Shift, Follow the Money," *Washington Post*, October 16, 2006, D1.

108. Andrew Bard Schmookler, "When Money Talks, Is It Free Speech?" *Christian Science Monitor*, November 11, 1997, 15; Nelson W. Polsby, "Money Gains Access. So What?" *New York Times*, August 13, 1997, A19.

109. "Senators Supporting Public Option Received Half as Much Money From Health Insurers," October 9, 2009, maplight.org/senators-supporting-public-option-got-half-as-much-money-from-health-insurers.

110. See John R. Wright, *Interest Groups and Congress* (Boston: Allyn & Bacon, 1996), 136–145; "Contributions, Lobbying, and Committee Voting in the U.S. House of Representatives," *American Political Science Review* 84 (1990): 417–438; Richard L. Hall and Frank W. Wayman, "Buying Time: Money Interests and the Mobilization of Bias in Congressional Committees," *American Political Science Review* 84 (1990): 797–820.

111. Theda Skocpol, *Diminished Democracy: From Membership to Management in American Civic Life* (Norman: University of Oklahoma Press, 2003); Theda Skocpol, "Advocates Without Members: The Recent Transformation of American Civic Life," in Theda Skocpol and Morris Fiorina, eds., *Civic Engagement in American Democracy* (Washington, D.C.: Brookings Institution, 1999).

112. Kelly D. Patterson and Matthew M. Singer, "The National Rifle Association in the Face of the Clinton Challenge," in Cigler and Loomis, *Interest Group Politics*, 6th ed., 62–63.

113. Lee Fritschler and James M. Hoefler, *Smoking and Politics*, 5th ed. (Upper Saddle River, N.J.: Prentice Hall, 1996), 20–35.

114. Truman, 519.

115. See C. Wright Mills, *The Power Elite* (New York: Oxford University Press, 1956); G.

William Domhoff, *The Powers That Be* (New York: Vintage, 1979).

116. David S. Hilzenrath, "Health Care Factions Clashing on Medicare Battlefield," *Washington Post*, July 19, 1997, C1; Ruth Marcus, "Some Swat Home Runs, Others Strike Out on Budget Deal," *Washington Post*, August 3, 1997, A1; Jennifer Mattos, "Clinton Proposes Medicare Cuts," *Time Daily*, January 14, 1997.

117. The problem is that there are a relatively small number of groups with large memberships. Labor unions, some environmental groups like the Sierra Club, some social movements revolving around abortion and women's rights, and the NRA currently have large memberships spread across a number of congressional districts.

118. Linda Greenhouse, "Justices to Rule on Tobacco," *New York Times*, May 2, 1999, sec. 4, 2; David E. Rosenbaum, "The Tobacco Bill: The Overview," *New York Times*, June 18, 1999, 1.

119. Katie Hafner, "Screen Grab: Mobilizing on Line for Gun Control," *New York Times*, May 20, 1999, G5; Francis X. Clines, "Guns and Schools: In Congress—Sketchbook," *New York Times*, June 17, 1999, 30.

120. PBS, "Obama's Deal," Part I.

121. PBS, "Obama's Deal," Part II, *Frontline*, www.pbs.org/wgbh/pages/frontline/obamasdeal/.

122. David Frum, "Waterloo," *FrumForum*, March 21, 2010, www.frumforum.com/waterloo.

123. Jane Hamsher, "We Want the Public Option," *The Guardian*, September 9, 2009, www.guardian.co.uk/commentisfree/cifamerica/2009/sep/08/healthcare-public-option-barack-obama; David Dayen, "The Deal With the Hospital Industry to Kill the Public Option," October 5, 2010, news.firedoglake.com/2010/10/05/the-deal-with-the-hospital-industry-to-kill-the-public-option/.

124. Jonathan Cohn, "How They Did It, Part Four," *New Republic*, May 25, 2010, www.tnr.com/article/politics/75147/ow-they-did-it-part-four.

Chapter 14

1. Margaret Warner, "Romney Campaign Enlists Help of 'Killer Whale' Project to Get Out the Vote," *PBS Newshour,* November 5, 2012, www.pbs.org/newshour/rundown/2012/11/romney-campaign-enlists-help-of-killer-whale-project-to-get-out-the-vote.html.

2. Jan Crawford, "Advisor: Romney 'Shellshocked' by Loss," *CBS News*, November 8, 2012, www.cbsnews.com/8301-250_162-57547239/adviser-romney-shellshocked-by-loss/.

3. Alexis Madrigal, "When the Nerds Go Marching In," *The Atlantic,* November 16, 2012, www.theatlantic.com/technology/archive/2012/11/when-the-nerds-go-marching-in/265325/#.UKaSAjGhdIk.email.

4. John Ekdahl, "The Unmitigated Disaster Known as Project Orca," *Ace of Spades HQ,* November 8, 2012, ace.mu.nu/archives/334783.php.

5. Josh Marshall, "Just Read This," *Talking Points Memo,* November 16, 2012, talkingpointsmemo.com/archives/2012/11/just_read_this_1.php?ref=fpblg.

6. Gerald Pomper, *Elections in America* (New York: Dodd, Mead, 1970), 1.

7. John Stuart Mill, *Considerations on Representative Government* (New York: Liberal Arts Press, 1958), 114.

8. David W. Brady, *Critical Elections and Congressional Policy Making* (Palo Alto, Calif.: Stanford University Press, 1988); Barbara Sinclair, "Party Realignment and

the Transformation of the Political Agenda: The House of Representatives, 1925–1938," *American Political Science Review* 71 (September 1977): 940–954.

9. Robert S. Erikson, Gerald C. Wright, and John P. McIver, *Statehouse Democracy* (New York: Cambridge University Press, 1993).

10. Robert Erikson and Gerald Wright, "Voters, Candidates, and Issues in Congressional Elections," in Lawrence Dodd and Bruce Oppenheimer, *Congress Reconsidered*, 6th ed. (Washington, D.C.: CQ Press, 1997); Gerald C. Wright and Michael Berkman, "Candidates and Policy Position in U.S. Senate Elections," *American Political Science Review* 80 (June 1986): 576–590; Robert S. Erikson, Michael MacKuen, and James A. Stimson, *The Macro Polity* (New York: Cambridge University Press, 2002).

11. Gerald Pomper with Susan Lederman, *Elections in America*, 2nd ed. (New York: Longman, 1980), chs. 7 and 8; Benjamin Ginsberg, *The Consequences of Consent* (Reading, Mass.: Addison Wesley Longman, 1982); Ian Budge and Richard I. Hofferbert, "Mandates and Policy Outputs: U.S. Party Platforms and Federal Expenditures, 1950–1985," *American Political Science Review* 84 (March 1990): 248–261.

12. Erikson, MacKuen, and Stimson.

13. Carole Pateman, *Participation and Democratic Theory* (Cambridge: Cambridge University Press, 1970).

14. Sidney Verba and Norman H. Nie, *Participation in America* (New York: Harper, 1972).

15. Robert S. Erikson, Costas Panagopoulos, and Christopher Wlezien, "The Crystallization of Voter Preferences During the 2008 Presidential Campaign," *Presidential Studies Quarterly* 40 (2010): 482–496; Robert Andersen, James Tilley, and Anthony F. Heath, "Political Knowledge and Enlightened Preferences: Party Choice Through the Electoral Cycle," *British Journal of Political Science* 35 (2005): 285–302; Steven F. Finkel, "Reexamining the 'Minimal Effects' Model in Recent Presidential Elections," *Journal of Politics* 55 (February 1993): 1–21.

16. Ginsberg.

17. Roper Center for Public Opinion Research, Community Consensus Survey, February 12–14, 1999.

18. Steven J. Rosenstone and John Mark Hansen, *Mobilization, Participation, and Democracy in America* (New York: Macmillan, 1993); Ruy A. Teixeira, *The Disappearing American Voter* (Washington, D.C.: Brookings Institution, 1992); Raymond E. Wolfinger and Steven J. Rosenstone, *Who Votes?* (New Haven: Yale University Press, 1980); Richard J. Timpone, "Structure, Behavior, and Voter Turnout in the United States," *American Political Science Review* 92 (March 1998): 145–158.

19. All of the figures in this section are taken from, or calculated by, the authors from the tables in U.S. Bureau of the Census, "Voting and Registration," thedataweb.rm.census.gov/TheDataWeb_HotReport2/voting/voting.html.

20. Ibid.

21. Sidney Verba, Kay Lehman Schlozman, and Henry E. Brady, *Voice and Equality: Civic Voluntarism in American Politics* (Cambridge: Harvard University Press, 1995).

22. Kay Lehman Schlozman, Sidney Verba, and Henry E. Brady, "Civic Participation and the Inequality Problem," in *Civic Engagement in American Democracy,* Theda Skocpol and Morris P. Fiorina, eds. (New York: Russell Sage, 1999); Henry E. Brady, Kay Lehman Schlozman, and Sidney Verba, "Prospecting for Participants: Rational

Expectations and the Recruitment of Political Activists," *American Political Science Review* 93 (1999): 153–168.

23. Richard Brody, "The Puzzle of Political Participation in America," in Anthony King, ed., *The New American Political System* (Washington, D.C.: American Enterprise Institute, 1978), 287–324.

24. Stephen Knack, "Drivers Wanted: Motor Voter and the Election of 1996," *PS: Political Science & Politics* (June 1999): 237–243.

25. International Institute for Democracy and Electoral Assistance, "Turnout in the World, Country by Country Performance," 2005, www.idea.int/vt/survey/voter_turnout_pop2.cfm.

26. Benjamin Highton, "Voter Registration and Turnout in the United States," *Perspectives on Politics* 2 (2004): 507–515.

27. "States With New Voting Restrictions Since 2010 Election," www.brennancenter.org/new-voting-restrictions-2010-election.

28. Teixeira, ch. 2; Paul R. Abramson, John H. Aldrich, and David W. Rohde, *Change and Continuity in the 1996 and 1998 Elections* (Washington, D.C.: CQ Press, 1999).

29. Rosenstone and Hansen.

30. Alan S. Gerber and Donald P. Green, "The Effects of Canvassing, Direct Mail, and Telephone Contact on Voter Turnout: A Field Experiment," *American Political Science Review* 94 (2000): 653–663.

31. Stephen Ansolabehere and Shanto Iyengar, *Going Negative: How Political Ads Shrink and Polarize the Electorate* (New York: Free Press, 1995).

32. Jeff Mapes, "National Parties Try Personal Touch," *Oregonian*, December 23, 2003, A1; Sharon Schmickle and Greg Gordon, "Vying for Voters," Minneapolis *Star Tribune*, October 31, 2004, 13A; Thomas B. Edsall, "Labor Targets Nonunion Voters; $20 Million Turnout Effort Expands Effort to Regain Influence," *Washington Post*, February 27, 2003, A4.

33. Gerald Pomper, "The Presidential Election: The Ills of American Politics After 9/11," in Michael Nelson, ed., *The Elections of 2004* (Washington, D.C.: CQ Press, 2005), 46.

34. Teixeira, 36–50; Robert Putnam, *Bowling Alone: The Collapse and Revival of American Community* (New York: Simon & Schuster, 2000), 31–47.

35. Warren E. Miller and Merrill J. Shanks, *The New American Voter* (Cambridge: Harvard University Press, 1996); Kevin Chen, *Political Alienation and Voting Turnout in the United States, 1969–1988* (Pittsburgh: Mellon Research University Press, 1992).

36. Anthony Downs, *An Economic Theory of Democracy* (New York: Harper & Row, 1957), 260–276.

37. Morris P. Fiorina, "The Voting Decision: Instrumental and Expressive Aspects," *Journal of Politics* 38 (1976), 390–415.

38. John Petrocik, "Voter Turnout and Electoral Preference: The Anomalous Reagan Elections," in Kay Lehman Schlozman, ed., *Elections in America* (Boston: Allen & Unwin, 1987), 239–260.

39. Jack Citrin, Eric Schickler, and John Sides, "What If Everyone Voted? Simulating the Impact of Increased Turnout in Senate Elections," *American Journal of Political Science* 47 (January 2003): 75–90.

40. Petrocik, 243–251; Stephen Earl Bennett and David Resnick, "The Implications of Nonvoting for Democracy in the United States," *American Journal of Political Science* 34 (August 1990): 795.

41. Calculated by the authors from the 2004 and 2008 Pre- and Post-American National Election Studies.

42. For a catalog of the voter restrictions proposed and passed in Republican-controlled state legislatures, see Wendy R. Weiser and Lawrence Norden, "Voting Law Changes in 2012," Brennan Center for Justice, brennan.3cdn.net/92635ddafbc09e8d88_i3m6bjdeh.pdf. These restrictions include voter ID laws, as discussed in the text, but also requirements of proof of citizenship, limits on same-day registration, restricting early and absentee voting, and making it more difficult for former felons to vote.

43. V. O. Key Jr., *The Responsible Electorate: Rationality in Presidential Voting, 1936–1960* (Cambridge: Harvard University Press, 1966); Miller and Shanks.

44. "2012 Exit Polls," *Fox News*, www.foxnews.com/politics/elections/2012-exit-poll.

45. Angus Campbell, Phillip Converse, Warren Miller, and Donald Stokes, *The American Voter* (New York: Wiley, 1960); Donald Green, Bradley Palmquist, and Eric Schickler, *Partisan Hearts and Minds* (New Haven: Yale University Press, 2002); Larry M. Bartels, "Beyond the Running Tally: Partisan Bias in Political Perceptions," *Political Behavior* 24 (2002): 117–150.

46. M. Margaret Conway, Gertrude A. Steuernagel, and David W. Ahern, *Women and Political Participation: Cultural Change in the Political Arena*, 2nd ed. (Washington, D.C.: CQ Press, 2005).

47. Eric Plutzer and John Zipp, "Identity Politics, Partisanship and Voting for Women Candidates," *Public Opinion Quarterly* 60 (1996): 30–57.

48. Center for American Women and Politics, "Proportions of Women and Men Who Voted for Hillary Clinton in the Super Tuesday Races of February 5, 2008," www.cawp.rutgers.edu/fast_facts/voters/documents/SuperTuesday_Clinton.pdf.

49. Calculated from Harold W. Stanley and Richard G. Niemi, *Vital Statistics on American Politics, 2007–2008* (Washington, D.C.: CQ Press, 2008), 127.

50. These figures are taken from media exit polls for the 2004 and 2008 presidential elections; Ron Brownstein, "The American Electorate Has Changed, and There's No Turning Back," *National Journal*, November 8, 2012, www.nationaljournal.com/magazine/the-american-electorate-has-changed-and-there-s-no-turning-back-20121108.

51. Wendy K. Tam, "Asians—A Monolithic Voting Bloc?" *Political Behavior* 17 (1995): 223–249; Pie-Te Lein, M. Margaret Conway, and Janelle Wong, *The Politics of Asian-Americans: Diversity and Community* (New York: Routledge, 2004); Atiya Kai Stokes, "Latino Group Consciousness and Political Participation," *American Politics Research* 41 (2003): 361–378; Benjamin Highton and Arthur L. Burris, "New Perspectives on Latino Voter Turnout in the United States," *American Politics Research* 30 (2002): 285–306.

52. Pei-Te Lien, Christian Collet, Janelle Wong, and S. Karthick Ramakrishnan, "Asian Pacific American Public Opinion and Participation," *PS: Political Science and Politics* 34 (2001): 628; David L. Leal, Matt A. Barreto, Jongho Lee, and Rodolofo O. De la Graza, "The Latino Vote in the 2004 Election," *PS: Political Science and Politics* 38 (2005): 41–49.

53. Brownstein, "The American Electorate Has Changed."

54. Downs.

55. Edward Carmines and James Stimson, "Two Faces of Issue Voting," *American Political Science Review* 74 (March 1980): 78–91; Larry Bartels, *Unequal Democracy* (Princeton, N.J.: Princeton University Press, 2008).

56. James Fallows, "Why Americans Hate the Media," *Atlantic Monthly*, February 1996, 45–64.

57. Morris P. Fiorina, *Retrospective Voting in American National Elections* (New Haven: Yale University Press, 1981).

58. "The Candidates' Confrontation: Excerpts From the Debate," *Washington Post*, October 30, 1980, A14.

59. Fiorina; Benjamin I. Page, *Choice and Echoes in Presidential Elections* (Chicago: University of Chicago Press, 1978).

60. Pew Poll cited in John Sides and Lynn Vavreck, *The Gamble: Choice and Chance in the 2012 Presidential Election* (Princeton, N.J.: Princeton University Press, 2012), 28.

61. "2012 Exit Polls," *Fox News*.

62. Linda Feldmann, "Before Any Votes: A 'Money Primary'," *Christian Science Monitor*, February 26, 2007, 1; Craig Gilbert, "'Invisible Primary' Already Begun: Some Think Presidential Field Narrowing Too Soon," *Milwaukee Journal Sentinel*, March 5, 2007; Chris Cillizza and Michael A. Fletcher, "Candidates Woo Bush Donors for 'Invisible Primary'," *Washington Post*, December 10, 2006, A01.

63. Michael J. Goff, *The Money Primary: The New Politics of Early Presidential Nomination Process* (Lanham, Md.: Rowman & Littlefield, 2004); Randall E. Adkins and Andrew J. Dowdle, "The Money Primary: What Influences the Outcome of Pre-Primary Presidential Nominating Fundraising?" *Presidential Studies Quarterly* 32 (June 2002): 256–275.

64. Jonathan Mann, "Money Talks in Republican Presidential Primaries," CNN Politics, February 1, 2012, articles.cnn.com/2012-02-01/politics/politics_mann-florida-romney-money_1_mitt-romney-super-pacs-super-political-action-committees?_s=PM:POLITICS.

65. Thomas R. Marshall, "Turnout and Representation: Caucuses Versus Primaries," *American Journal of Political Science* 22 (1978): 169–182; Gerald C. Wright, "Rules and the Ideological Character of Primary Electorates," in Steven S. Smith and Melanie J. Springer, eds., *Reforming the Presidential Nomination Process* (Washington, D.C.: Brookings Institution, 2009).

66. Barry Burden, "The Nominations: Technology, Money, and Transferable Momentum," in Nelson, 21–22.

67. Max Follmer, "Everything You've Ever Wanted to Know About Delegates and Superdelegates," *Huffington Post*, February 13, 2008, www.huffingtonpost.com/2008/02/13/everything-youve-ever-wa_n_86335.html.

68. Burden, 21.

69. Jack Germond and Jules W. Witcover, "Front-Loading Folly: A Dash to Decision, at a Cost in Deliberation," *Baltimore Sun*, March 22, 1996.

70. Alan Abramowitz, *The Polarized Public?* (Upper Saddle River, N.J.: Pearson, 2013).

71. "Presidential Campaign Stops: Who's Going Where?" *Washington Post Campaign 2012 Web Site*, www.washingtonpost.com/wp-srv/special/politics/2012-presidential-campaign-visits/.

72. "Mad Money: TV Ads in the 2012 Presidential Campaign," *Washington Post 2012 Campaign Web Site*, www.washingtonpost.com/wp-srv/special/politics/track-presidential-campaign-ads-2012/.

73. Sholomo Slonim, "The Electoral College at Philadelphia," *Journal of American History* 73 (June 1986): 35.

74. This as well as other allocation plans have been introduced by Republicans in the

Pennsylvania state legislature. Speculation continued about whether any would pass. "Bill to Change Electoral College System in PA Introduced," *Philadelphia Inquirer,* February 26, 2013; Benjy Sarlin, "Electoral College Rigging Scheme Could Spill Into PA Governor Race" *Talking Points Memo,* May 1, 2013, talkingpointsmemo.com/dc/electoral-college-rigging-scheme-could-spill-into-pa-governor-race.

75. Ruth Shalit, "The Oppo Boom," *New Republic*, January 3, 1994, 16–21; Adam Nagourney, "Researching the Enemy: An Old Political Tool Resurfaces in a New Election," *New York Times*, April 3, 1996, D20.

76. Brian C. Mooney, "Technology Aids Obama's Outreach Drive: Volunteers Answer Call on Social Networking Site," *Boston Globe*, February 24, 2008, A1.

77. Robin Kolodny and Angela Logan, "Political Consultants and the Extension of Party Goals," *PS: Political Science & Politics* (June 1998): 155–159.

78. Patrick Sellers, "Strategy and Background in Congressional Campaigns," *American Political Science Review* 92 (March 1998): 159–172.

79. John Petrocik, "Issue Ownership in Presidential Elections, With a 1980 Case Study," *American Journal of Political Science* 40 (August 1996): 825–850.

80. American Museum of the Moving Image, "The Living Room Candidate: Presidential Campaign Commercials 1952–2004," livingroomcandidate.movingimage.us/index.php.

81. Darrell M. West, *Air Wars: Television Advertising in Election Campaigns, 1952–2004* (Washington, D.C.: CQ Press, 2005).

82. Kathleen Hall Jamieson, "Shooting to Win; Do Attack Ads Work? You Bet—and That's Not All Bad," *Washington Post*, September 26, 2004, B1.

83. Wisconsin Advertising Project, press release, through October 8, 2008, wiscadproject.wisc.edu/wiscads_release_100808.pdf.

84. Shanto Iyengar and Donald Kinder, *News That Matters: Television and American Opinion* (Chicago: University of Chicago Press, 1987); James N. Druckman, "Priming the Vote: Campaign Effects in a U.S. Senate Election," *Political Psychology* 25, no. 4 (2004): 577–594.

85. Thomas Patterson, *Out of Order* (New York: Knopf, 1993); Fallows, 45–64.

86. Elihu Katz and Jacob Feldman, "The Debates in Light of Research," in Sidney Kraus, ed., *The Great Debates* (Bloomington: Indiana University Press, 1962), 173–223.

87. Thomas Holbrook, "Campaigns, National Conditions, and U.S. Presidential Elections," *American Journal of Political Science* 38 (November 1994): 986–992; John Geer, "The Effects of Presidential Debates on the Electorate's Preferences for Candidates," *American Politics Quarterly* 16 (1988): 486–501; David Lanoue, "The 'Turning Point': Viewers' Reactions to the Second 1988 Presidential Debate," *American Politics Quarterly* 19 (1991): 80–89.

88. David Lanoue, "One That Made a Difference: Cognitive Consistency, Political Knowledge, and the 1980 Presidential Debate," *Public Opinion Quarterly* 56 (Summer 1992): 168–184; Carol Winkler and Catherine Black, "Assessing the 1992 Presidential and Vice Presidential Debates: The Public Rationale," *Argumentation and Advocacy* 30 (Fall 1993): 77–87; Lori McKinnon, John Tedesco, and Lynda Kaid,

"The Third 1992 Presidential Debate: Channel and Commentary Effects," *Argumentation and Advocacy* 30 (Fall 1993): 106–118; Mike Yawn, Kevin Ellsworth, and Kim Fridkin Kahn, "How a Presidential Primary Debate Changed Attitudes of Audience Members," *Political Behavior* 20 (July 1998): 155–164; Annenberg Public Policy Center, "Voters Learned Positions on Issues Since Presidential Debates," NAES04 National Annenberg Election Survey, www.annenbergpublicpolicycenter.org/Downloads/Political_Communication/naes/.

89. OpenSecrets.org, "Banking on Becoming President," www.opensecrets.org/pres08/index.php; and OpenSecrets.org, "U.S. Election Will Cost $5.3 Billion, Center for Responsive Politics Predicts," www.opensecrets.org/news/2008/10/us-election-will-cost-53-billi/.

90. Tarini Parti, "Will 2012 Be the End of the Presidential Public Financing System?" www.opensecrets.org/news/2011/08/the-end-of-presidential-public-financing.html.

91. Federal Election Commission, "Chapter Two: Presidential Public Funding," www.fec.gov/info/arch2.htm.

92. Federal Election Commission, "Contribution Limits Chart 2007-08," www.fec.gov/pages/brochures/contriblimits.shtml.

93. Susan Glasser, "Court's Ruling in Colorado Case May Reshape Campaign Finance; Limits on Political Parties' 'Hard Money' Spending Nullified," *Washington Post*, March 28, 1999, A6; *FEC v. Colorado Republican Federal Campaign Committee*, 121 S. Ct. 2351, 2371 (2001).

94. 558 U.S. 50 (2010).

95. "How Corporate Money Will Reshape Politics: Restoring Free Speech in Elections," *New York Times*, January 21, 2010, roomfordebate.blogs.nytimes.com/2010/01/21/how-corporate-money-will-reshape-politics.

96. Spencer MacColl, "Citizens United Decision Profoundly Affects Political Landscape," May 5, 2011, www.opensecrets.org/news/2011/05/citizens-united-decision-profoundly-affects-political-landscape.html.

97. "The Court's Blow to Democracy," *New York Times*, January 21, 2010; Warren Richey, "Supreme Court: Campaign-Finance Limits Violate Free Speech," *Christian Science Monitor*, January 21, 2010; John Samples and Ilya Shapiro, "Supreme Court: Free Speech for All," *Washington Examiner*, January 21, 2010.

98. Dan Balz and David S. Broder, "Close Election Turns on Voter Turnout," *Washington Post*, November 1, 2002, A1.

99. Steven J. Rosenstone and John Mark Hansen, *Mobilization, Participation, and Democracy in America* (New York: Macmillan, 1993).

100. Adam Nagourney, "The '08 Campaign: A Sea Change for Politics as We Know It," *New York Times*, November 4, 2008, A1.

101. Les Blumenthal, "Down to the Wire; Canvassers Set a Frenetic Pace to Get Out the Vote," *Sacramento Bee*, October 25, 2004, A1.

102. Sam Roberts, "2008 Surge in Black Voters Nearly Erased Racial Gap," *New York Times*, July 21, 2009, 14.

103. Craig Gilbert, "Personal Touch in Political Race; Bush, Kerry Sides Try to Rally Support Like Never Before," Milwaukee *Journal Sentinel*, June 28, 2004, 1A.

104. Blumenthal.

105. Pew Research Center for the People and the Press Survey Reports, "Voters Liked Campaign 2004, But Too Much

'Mud-Slinging'," November 11, 2004, people-press.org/reports/display.php3?ReportID=233.

106. Blumenthal.

107. Lawrence J. Grossman, David A. M. Peterson, and James A. Stimson, *Mandate Politics* (New York: Cambridge University Press, 2006).

108. Lawrence J. Grossback, David A. M. Peterson, and James A. Stimson, "Comparing Competing Theories on the Causes of Mandate Perceptions," *American Journal of Political Science* 49 (2005): 406–419.

109. Marjorie Hershey, "The Constructed Explanation: Interpreting Election Results in the 1984 Presidential Race," *Journal of Politics* 54 (November 1992): 943–976.

110. Bernard Berelson, Paul Lazarsfeld, and William N. McPhee, *Voting* (Chicago: University of Chicago Press, 1954), ch. 10.

111. Sidney Verba, Kay Lehman Schlozman, Henry Brady, and Norman H. Nie, "Race, Ethnicity and Political Resources: Participation in the United States," *British Journal of Political Science* 23 (1993): 453–497.

112. Erikson, MacKuen, and Stimson; James A. Stimson, Michael B. MacKuen, and Robert S. Erikson, "Dynamic Representation," *American Political Science Review* 89 (September 1995): 543.

113. Erikson, Wright, and McIver.

114. Paul Burstein, "The Impact of Public Opinion on Public Policy: A Review and an Agenda," *Political Research Quarterly* 56 (2003): 29–40; David Jones and Monika McDermott, *Americans, Congress, and Democratic Responsiveness: Public Evaluations of Congress and Electoral Consequences* (Ann Arbor: University of Michigan Press, 2009); Stephen Ansolabehere and Phillip Edward Jones, "Constituents' Responses to Congressional Roll Call Voting," *American Journal of Political Science* 54 (2010): 58–97.

115. Christi Parsons and Kathleen Hennessy, "Obama Campaign's Investment in Data Crunching Paid Off," *Los Angeles Times,* November 13, 2012, articles.latimes.com/2012/nov/13/nation/la-na-obama-analytics-20121113.

116. Madrigal.

117. Parsons and Hennessy.

118. Sasha Issenberg, "A Vast Left-Wing Conspiracy," Slate, November 7, 2012, www.slate.com/articles/news_and_politics/victory_lab/2012/11/obama_s_victory_how_the_democrats_burned_by_karl_rove_became_the_party_of.html.

119. Crawford.

Chapter 15

1. Frank Ahrens, "The Accelerating Decline of Newspapers," *Washington Post*, October 27, 2009, www.washingtonpost.com/wp-dyn/content/article/2009/10/26/AR2009102603272.html.

2. Pew Center for People and the Press, "In Changing News Landscape, Even Television Is Vulnerable," October 11, 2012, www.pewresearch.org/daily-number/number-of-americans-who-read-print-newspapers-continues-decline/.

3. Rick Edmonds, Emily Guskin, Tom Rosenstiel, and Amy Mitchell, "Newspapers: Building Digital Revenues Proves Painfully Slow," Pew Center Project for Excellence in Journalism, April 11, 2012, stateofthemedia.org/2012/newspapers-building-digital-revenues-proves-painfully-slow/; Pew Research Journalism Project, "State of the News Media 2014," March 26, 2014, www

.journalism.org/2014/03/26/state-of-the-news-media-2014-overview/.

4. Paul Farhi, "Washington Post to be sold to the founder of Amazon," *Washington Post*, August 5, 2013.

5. Newspaper Death Watch, newspaperdeathwatch.com.

6. Jack Shafer, "The Great Newspaper Liquidation," June 5, 2012, blogs.reuters.com/jackshafer/2012/06/05/the-great-newspaper-liquidation/; David Carr, "The Fissures Are Growing for Newspapers," *New York Times*, July 8, 2012, www.nytimes.com/2012/07/09/business/media/newspapers-are-running-out-of-time-to-adapt-to-digital-future.html?emc=eta1.

7. T. J. Sullivan, "Newspapers Don't Matter," *LA Observed*, December 15, 2008, www.laobserved.com/intell/2008/12/newspapers_dont_matter.php.

8. David Lieberman, "Extra! Extra! Are Newspapers Dying?" *USA Today*, March 18, 2009, www.usatoday.com/printedition/money/20090318/newspapers18_cv.art.htm.

9. Thomas Jefferson to Edward Carrington, 1787, ME 6:57, Thomas Jefferson on Politics and Government, etext.virginia.edu/jefferson/quotations/jeff1600.htm.

10. Dan O'Hair and Mary Weimann, *Real Communication*, 2nd ed. (New York: Bedford/St. Martin's, 2012), 543.

11. Philip Rucker, "Romney Advisors, Aiming to Pop Obama's Digital Balloon, Pump Up Online Campaign," *Washington Post*, July 13, 2012, www.washingtonpost.com/politics/romney-advisers-aiming-to-pop-obamas-digital-balloon-pump-up-online-campaign/2012/07/13/gJQAsbc4hW_story.html.

12. Pew Center for People and the Press, p. 4.

13. Ibid.

14. Andrea Caumont, "12 Trends Shaping Digital News," Pew Research Center, October 16, 2013, www.pewresearch.org/fact-tank/2013/10/16/12-trends-shaping-digital-news/.

15. Pew Research Center, "New Devices, Platforms Spur More News Consumption," March 19, 2012, pewresearch.org/pubs/2222/news-media-network-television-cable-audioo-radio-digital-platforms-local-mobile-devices-tablets-smartphones-native-american-community-newspapers.

16. Pew Research Center for the People and the Press, "The Times Mirror News Interest Index: 1989-1995," www.people-press.org.

17. Pew Research Center for the People and the Press, "Audience Segments in a Changing News Environment," August 17, 2008, www.people-press.org/files/legacy-pdf/444.pdf, 44.

18. Ben H. Bagdikian, *The Media Monopoly*, 5th ed. (Boston: Beacon Press, 1997), 203.

19. Greg Sandoval, "Pew Illustrates How Craigslist Is Killing Newspapers," CNET.com, May 22, 2009, www.cnet.com/news/pew-center-illustrates-how-craigslist-is-killing-newspapers/; Sydney Jones, "Online Classifieds," Pew Research Internet Project, May 22, 2009, pewinternet.org/2009/05/22/online-classifieds/; Philip Weiss, "A Guy Named Craig: How a Schlumpy IBM Refugee Found You Your Apartment, Your Boyfriend, Your New Couch, Your Afternoon Sex Partner—and Now Finds Himself Killing Your Newspaper," *New York Magazine*, January 8, 2006, nymag.com/nymetro/news/media/internet/15500/.

20. Richard Davis, *The Press and American Politics: The New Mediator* (Upper Saddle River, N.J.: Prentice Hall, 1996), 60.

21. Ibid., 63.

22. Ibid., 67.

23. Pew Research Journalism Project, "Weekly Radio Listenership," www.journalism.org/media-indicators/weekly-radio-listenership/.

24. Jennifer Waits, "FCC Reports That the Number of Radio Stations in the U.S. Increased Last Quarter," July 11, 2014, www.radiosurvivor.com/2014/07/11/fcc-reports-non-commercial-fm-stations-lpfm-stations-fm-translators-u-s-rise-last-quarter/.

25. "U.S. Homes Receive a Record 118.6 TV Channels on Average," Marketcharts.com, June 13, 2008, www.marketingcharts.com/television/us-homes-receive-a-record-1186-tv-channels-on-average-4929/; "Nielson Estimates Number of U.S. Television Homes to be 114.7 Million," Nielson Wire, May 3, 2011, blog.nielsen.com/nielsenwire/media_entertainment/nielsen-estimates-number-of-u-s-television-homes-to-be-114-7-million/; "More Than Half the Homes in U.S. Have Three or More TVs," Nielson Wire, July 20, 2009, blog.nielsen.com/nielsenwire/media_entertainment/more-than-half-the-homes-in-us-have-three-or-more-tvs/.

26. Brian Stetler, "Neilson Reports a Decline in Television Viewing," *New York Times Media Decoder*, May 3, 2012, mediadecoder.blogs.nytimes.com/2012/05/03/nielsen-reports-a-decline-in-television-viewing/?_php=true&_type=blogs&_r=0.

27. Nielson, "Changing Channels: Americans View Just 17 channels Despite Record Number to Choose From," May 6, 2014, www.nielsen.com/content/corporate/us/en/insights/news/2014/changing-channels-americans-view-just-17-channels-despite-record-number-to-choose-from.html.

28. For an in-depth study of the negative effects of this sort of advertising on national community, see Joseph Turow, *Breaking Up America: Advertisers and the New Media World* (Chicago: University of Chicago Press, 1997).

29. See, for example, Dana Davis Rehm, "Why Can't NPR Staff Go to 'Rally to Restore Sanity' or 'March to Keep Fear Alive?'," October 13, 2010, www.npr.org/blogs/thisisnpr/2010/10/13/130549777/why-can-t-npr-staff-go-to-stewart-s-rally-to-restore-sanity-or-colbert-s-march-to-keep-fear-alive.

30. Pew Research Internet Project, "Internet Use Over Time," www.pewinternet.org/data-trend/internet-use/internet-use-over-time/.

31. Pew Internet, "Broadband vs. Dialup Adoption Over Time," www.pewinternet.org/data-trend/internet-use/connection-type/; Pew Internet, "Cellphone and Smartphone Ownership Demographics," www.pewinternet.org/data-trend/mobile/cell-phone-and-smartphone-ownership-demographics/.

32. Pew Research Center for the People and the Press, "The New News Landscape: Rise of the Internet," March 1, 2010, pewresearch.org/pubs/1508/internet-cell-phone-users-news-social-experience; Kathryn Zickuhr and Aaron Smith, "Digital Differences," Pew Internet, April 13, 2012, pewinternet.org/Reports/2012/Digital-differences/Main-Report/Internet-adoption-over-time.aspx; Aaron Smith, "Nearly Half of American Adults Are Smartphone Owners," Pew Internet, March 1, 2012, pewinternet.org/Reports/2012/Digital-differences/Main-Report/Internet-adoption-over-time.aspx.

33. Robert Marquand, "Hate Groups Market to the Mainstream," *Christian Science Monitor*, March 6, 1998, 4.

34. Rucker.

35. Pew Internet, "Broadband vs. Dialup Adoption Over Time."

36. Davis, 27.

37. Michael Emery and Edwin Emery, *The Press and America* (Upper Saddle River, N.J.: Prentice Hall, 1988), 115.

38. David Broder, *Behind the Front Page* (New York: Simon & Schuster, 1987), 134-135.

39. Bagdikian, xv.

40. Bagdikian, ix.

41. Robert Entman, *Democracy Without Citizens* (New York: Oxford University Press, 1989), 110-111.

42. Walter Goodman, "Where's Edward R. Murrow When You Need Him?" *New York Times*, December 30, 1997, E2.

43. Mark Crispin Miller, "Free the Media," *Nation*, June 3, 1996, 9.

44. Bagdikian, xxii.

45. Neil King Jr. and Louise Radnofsky, "News Corp. Gives $1 Million to GOP," *Wall Street Journal*, August 18, 2010, online.wsj.com/article/SB10001424052748703824304575435922310302654.html.

46. Bagdikian, 217.

47. Miller, 2.

48. Brian Stetler, "CNN and Fox Trip Up in Rush to Get the News on the Air," *New York Times*, June 28, 2012, www.nytimes.com/2012/06/29/us/cnn-and-foxs-supreme-court-mistake.html?_r=0.

49. David Weigel, "I Want to Believe: Why Does the Media Keep Running Fake Stories From a Joke-Free Satire Site?" *Slate*, March 11, 2013, www.slate.com/articles/news_and_politics/politics/2013/03/daily_currant_satire_the_fake_news_website_keeps_fooling_journalists.html.

50. David Armstrong, "Alternative, Inc.," *In These Times*, August 21, 1995, 14-18.

51. Jeff Gremillion, "Showdown at Generation Gap," *Columbia Journalism Review* (July-August 1995): 34-38.

52. Pew Research Center for the People and the Press, "Audience Segments in a Changing News Environment," 26.

53. Pew Center's Project for Excellence in Journalism, "YouTube and the News," July 16, 2012, www.journalism.org/analysis_report/youtube_news.

54. Pew Research Center, "New Devices, Platforms."

55. Doris Graber, *Mass Media and American Politics*, 5th ed. (Washington, D.C.: CQ Press, 1997), 62.

56. Federal Trade Commission, "Broadband and Connectivity Competition Policy," June 2007, www.ftc.gov/reports/broadband/v070000report.pdf.

57. "Democracy and the Web," Editorial, *New York Times*, May 19, 2008, www.nytimes.com; "Net Neutrality," Times Topics, *New York Times*, December 20, 2010, topics.nytimes.com/topics/reference/timestopics/subjects/n/net_neutrality/index.html.

58. David H. Weaver and G. Cleveland Wilhoit, *The American Journalist in the 1990s* (Mahwah, N.J.: Erlbaum Associates, 1996), 133-141.

59. Cited in Broder, 138.

60. Graber, 95-96.

61. Pew Research, "As News Business Takes a Hit, Number of Black Journalists Declines," August 1, 2014, www.pewresearch.org/fact-tank/2014/08/01/as-news-business-takes-a-hit-the-number-of-black-journalists-declines/; Pew Research, "Two Thirds of US Newspapers Employ Women in Top Editing Jobs," July 7, 2014, www.pewresearch.org/fact-tank/2014/07/30/asne-two-thirds-of-u-s-newspapers-employ-women-in-top-editing-jobs/.

62. William Schneider and I. A. Lewis, "Views on the News," *Public Opinion* (August-September 1985): 6.

63. Data in Weaver and Wilhoit, 15–19.
64. Dave D'Alessio and Mike Allen, "Media Bias in Presidential Elections: A Meta-Analysis," *Journal of Communication* (Autumn 2000): 133–156.
65. Mark Hertsgaard, *On Bended Knee: The Press and the Reagan Presidency* (New York: Farrar, Straus & Giroux, 1988), 3.
66. Calculated by the authors from data at editorandpublisher.com/election/.
67. William P. Eveland Jr. and Dhavan V. Shah, "The Impact of Individual and Interpersonal Factors on Perceived News Media Bias," *Political Psychology* (2003): 101.
68. Pew Research Center for the People and the Press, "Audience Segments in a Changing News Environment: Key News Audiences Now Blend Online and Traditional Sources," Pew Research Center Biennial News Consumption Survey, August 17, 2008, www.people-press.org/reports/pdf/444.pdf, 56.
69. Kathleen Hall Jamieson and Joseph N. Cappella, "Preface," in *Echo Chamber: Rush Limbaugh and the Conservative Media Elite* (New York: Oxford University Press, 2008).
70. Michael Calderone, "How Dems Grew to Hate the Liberal Media," August 24, 2008, www.cbsnews.com/news/how-dems-grew-to-hate-the-liberal-media/.
71. Jamieson and Cappella, "Preface."
72. Broder, 126.
73. Broder, 148.
74. Dom Bonafede, "Crossing Over," *National Journal*, January 14, 1989, 102; Michael Kelly, "David Gergen, Master of the Game," *New York Times Magazine*, October 31, 1993, 64ff; Jonathan Alter, "Lost in the Big Blur," *Newsweek*, June 9, 1997, 43.
75. Shanto Iyengar, *Is Anyone Responsible?* (Chicago: University of Chicago Press, 1991), 2.
76. Shanto Iyengar and Donald R. Kinder, *News That Matters* (Chicago: University of Chicago Press, 1987).
77. Stephen Hess, *News and Newsmaking* (Washington, D.C.: Brookings Institution, 1996), 91–92.
78. Iyengar and Kinder, 72.
79. Benjamin I. Page, Robert Y. Shapiro, and Glenn R. Dempsey, "What Moves Public Opinion?" *American Political Science Review* (March 1987): 23–43. The term *professional communicator* is used by Benjamin Page, *Who Deliberates? Mass Media in Modern Democracy* (Chicago: University of Chicago Press, 1996), 106–109.
80. Iyengar and Kinder, 93.
81. W. Russell Neuman, Marion R. Just, and Ann N. Crigler, *Common Knowledge: News and the Construction of Political Meaning* (Chicago: University of Chicago Press, 1996), 106–119.
82. Steven Kull, "Misperceptions, the Media, and the Iraq War," the PIPA/Knowledge Networks Poll, Program on International Policy Attitudes, October 2, 2003, 13–16, www.pipa.org/OnlineReports/Iraq/Media_10_02_03_Report.pdf.
83. James Fallows, "Why Americans Hate the Media," *Atlantic Monthly*, February 1996, 16.
84. Fallows, "Why Americans Hate the Media," 5–6.
85. Center for Media and Democracy, "Sound Bites Get Shorter," O'Dwyer's PR Newsletter, November 11, 2000, www.prwatch.org/node/384.
86. Thomas E. Patterson, *Out of Order* (New York: Vintage Books, 1994), 74.
87. Goodman, E2.
88. Larry J. Sabato, *Feeding Frenzy: How Attack Journalism Has Transformed American Politics* (New York: Free Press, 1991), 6.
89. Patterson, 243.
90. Ibid., 245.
91. Ibid., 23.
92. Judith Valente, "Do You Believe What Newspeople Tell You?" *Parade Magazine*, March 2, 1997, 4.
93. Joseph N. Cappella and Kathleen Hall Jamieson, *Spiral of Cynicism: The Press and the Public Good* (New York: Oxford University Press, 1997), 9–10.
94. S. Robert Lichter and Richard E. Noyes, *Good Intentions Make Bad News: Why Americans Hate Campaign Journalism* (Lanham, Md.: Rowman & Littlefield, 1995), xix.
95. Walter Cronkite, "Reporting Political Campaigns: A Reporter's View," in Doris Graber, Denis McQuail, and Pippa Norris, eds., *The Politics of News, The News of Politics* (Washington, D.C.: CQ Press, 1998), 57–69.
96. Joe Klein, "The Perils of the Permanent Campaign," *Time*, October 30, 2005.
97. Scott McClellan, *What Happened: Inside the Bush White House and Washington's Culture of Deception* (New York: Public Affairs, 2008).
98. Kelly, 7.
99. Kelly, 7–10.
100. Kenneth T. Walsh, *Feeding the Beast: The White House Versus the Press* (New York: Random House, 1996).
101. Hess, 68–90.
102. Hertsgaard, 6.
103. Anne Kornblut, "Administration Is Warned About Its Publicity Videos," *New York Times*, February 19, 2005, 11.
104. David Barstow and Robin Stein, "Under Bush, a New Age of Prepackaged News," *New York Times*, March 13, 2005, 1.
105. Johanna Neuman, "An Identity Crisis Unfolds in a Not-So-Elite Press Corps," *Los Angeles Times*, February 25, 2005, 18.
106. Jack Shafer, "The Propaganda President: George W. Bush Does His Best Kim Jong-il," *Slate,* February 3, 2005, www.slate.com/articles/news_and_politics/press_box/2005/02/the_propaganda_president.html.
107. Michael Kinsley, "Filter Tips," *Slate,* October 16, 2003, www.slate.com/articles/news_and_politics/readme/2003/10/filter_tips.html.
108. Jeff Zeleny, "Robert Gibbs," *New York Times*, November 6, 2008.
109. John Dickerson, "Always Be Selling," *Slate*, December 4, 2013, www.slate.com/articles/news_and_politics/politics/2013/12/barack_obama_needs_to_sell_obamacare_again_the_president_is_trying_to_save.html.
110. Stephen Ansolabehere, Roy Beyr, and Shanto Iyengar, *The Media Game: American Politics in the Television Age* (New York: Macmillan, 1993); Iyengar, *Is Anyone Responsible?*
111. Clay Shirky, "Newspapers and Thinking the Unthinkable," March 13, 2009, www.shirky.com/weblog/2009/03/newspapers-and-thinking-the-unthinkable/.
112. Ibid.
113. Dan Gillmor, *We the Media: Grassroots Journalism by the People, for the People* (Sebastopol, Calif.: O'Reilly Media, 2008).
114. Andrew Sullivan, "A Blogger Manifesto: Why Online Weblogs Are One Future for Journalism," *Sunday Times of London*, February 24, 2002.
115. Andrew Sullivan, "Happy 4th," *Daily Dish*, July 4, 2010, andrewsullivan.theatlantic.com/the_daily_dish/2010/07/happy-4th.html.
116. Shirky.

GLOSSARY

accommodationists supporters of government nonpreferential accommodation of religion (5)

accountability the principle that bureaucratic employees should be answerable for their performance to supervisors, all the way up the chain of command (9)

administrative law law established by the bureaucracy, on behalf of Congress (10)

advanced industrial democracy a system in which a democratic government allows citizens a considerable amount of personal freedom and maintains a free-market (though still usually regulated) economy (1)

adversarial system trial procedures designed to resolve conflict through the clash of opposing sides, moderated by a neutral, passive judge who applies the law (10)

affirmative action a policy of creating opportunities for members of certain groups as a substantive remedy for past discrimination (6)

agency capture process whereby regulatory agencies come to be protective of and influenced by the industries they were established to regulate (9)

allocative representation congressional work to secure projects, services, and funds for the represented district (7)

amendability the provision for the Constitution to be changed, so as to adapt to new circumstances (4)

amicus curiae briefs "friend of the court" documents filed by interested parties to encourage the Court to grant or deny certiorari or to urge it to decide a case in a particular way (10)

anarchy the absence of government and laws (1)

Anti-Federalists advocates of states' rights who opposed the Constitution (3)

antiterrorism measures to protect and defend U.S. citizens and interests from terrorist attacks (19)

antitrust policies government regulations that try to keep monopolies from emerging (18)

appeal a rehearing of a case because the losing party in the original trial argues that a point of law was not applied properly (10)

appellate jurisdiction the authority of a court to review decisions made by lower courts (10)

Articles of Confederation the first constitution of the United States (1777) creating an association of states with weak central government (3)

astroturf lobbying indirect lobbying efforts that manipulate or create public sentiment, "astroturf" being artificial grassroots (13)

asylum protection or sanctuary, especially from political persecution (2)

authoritarian capitalism a system in which the state allows people economic freedom but maintains stringent social regulations to limit noneconomic behavior (1)

authoritarian governments systems in which the state holds all power over the social order (1)

authority power that is recognized as legitimate (1)

bad tendency test rule used by the courts that allows speech to be punished if it leads to punishable actions (5)

balanced budget a budget in which expenditures equal revenues (18)

benchmark poll initial poll on a candidate and issues on which campaign strategy is based and against which later polls are compared (11)

bicameral legislature legislature with two chambers (4, 7)

Bill of Rights a summary of citizen rights guaranteed and protected by a government; added to the Constitution as its first ten amendments in order to achieve ratification (3)

bills of attainder laws under which specific persons or groups are detained and sentenced without trial (5)

black codes a series of laws in the post–Civil War South designed to restrict the rights of former slaves before the passage of the Fourteenth and Fifteenth Amendments (6)

block grants federal funds provided for a broad purpose, unrestricted by detailed requirements and regulations (4, 16)

blogs web logs, or online journals, that can cover any topic, including political analysis (15)

boycott refusal to buy certain goods or services as a way to protest policy or force political reform (6)

Brown v. Board of Education of Topeka Supreme Court case that rejected the idea that separate could be equal in education (6)

bureaucracy an organization characterized by hierarchical structure, worker specialization, explicit rules, and advancement by merit (9)

bureaucratese the often unintelligible language used by bureaucrats to avoid controversy and lend weight to their words (9)

bureaucratic culture the accepted values and procedures of an organization (9)

bureaucratic discretion bureaucrats' use of their own judgment in interpreting and carrying out the laws of Congress (9)

Bush Doctrine policy that supports preemptive attacks as a legitimate tactic in the U.S. war on state-sponsored terrorism (19)

business cycle the peaks and valleys of the economy between boom and bust (18)

busing achieving racial balance by transporting students to schools across neighborhood boundaries (6)

cabinet a presidential advisory group selected by the president, made up of the vice president, the heads of the federal executive departments, and other high officials to whom the president elects to give cabinet status (8)

capital gains tax a tax levied on the returns that people earn from capital investments, like the profits from the sale of stocks or a home (18)

capitalist economy an economic system in which the market determines production, distribution, and price decisions, and property is privately owned (1)

casework legislative work on behalf of individual constituents to solve their problems with government agencies and programs (7)

categorical grant federal funds provided for a specific purpose, restricted by detailed instructions, regulations, and compliance standards (4, 16)

Central Intelligence Agency (CIA) the government organization that oversees foreign intelligence gathering and related classified activities (19)

checks and balances the principle that allows each branch of government to exercise some form of control over the others (4)

chief administrator the president's executive role as the head of federal agencies and the person responsible for the implementation of national policy (8)

chief foreign policy maker the president's executive role as the primary shaper of relations with other nations (8)

chief of staff the person who oversees the operations of all White House staff and controls access to the president (8)

citizen advisory councils citizen groups that consider the policy decisions of an agency; a way to make the bureaucracy responsive to the general public (9)

citizen legislators part-time state legislators, who also hold other jobs in their community while serving in the statehouse (16)

citizens members of a political community with both rights and responsibilities (1)

civic journalism a movement among journalists to be responsive to citizen input in determining what news stories to cover (15)

civil-law tradition a legal system based on a detailed comprehensive legal code, usually created by the legislature (10)

civil laws laws regulating interactions between individuals; violation of a civil law is called a tort (10)

civil liberties individual freedoms guaranteed to the people primarily by the Bill of Rights (5)

civil rights citizenship rights guaranteed to the people (primarily in the Thirteenth, Fourteenth, Fifteenth, Nineteenth, and Twenty-sixth Amendments) and protected by the government (5, 6)

civil service nonmilitary employees of the government who are appointed through the merit system (9)

Clean Air Act legislation that set emissions standards for companies (17)

clear and present danger test rule used by the courts that allows language to be regulated only if it presents an immediate and urgent danger (5)

clientele groups groups of citizens whose interests are affected by an agency or a department and who work to influence its policies (9)

closed primaries primary elections in which only registered party members may vote (12, 14)

cloture a vote to end a Senate filibuster; requires a three-fifths majority, or sixty votes (7)

coattail effect the added votes received by congressional candidates of a winning presidential party (7)

coercive diplomacy the calibrated use of threats of the use of force aimed to make another actor stop or undo an aggressive action (19)

Cold War the half-century of competition and conflict after World War II between the United States and the Soviet Union (and their allies) (19)

collective bargaining the ability of unions to determine wages, hours, and working conditions in conjunction with the employer (18)

collective good a good or service that, by its very nature, cannot be denied to anyone who wants to consume it (13)

commander-in-chief the president's role as the top officer of the country's military establishment (8)

commercial bias the tendency of the media to make coverage and programming decisions based on what will attract a large audience and maximize profits (15)

commission the basic component of the county form of government; combines executive and legislative functions over a narrow area of responsibility (16)

common-law tradition a legal system based on the accumulated rulings of judges over time, applied uniformly—judge-made law (10)

Common Sense 1776 pamphlet by Thomas Paine that persuaded many Americans to support the Revolutionary cause (3)

communist democracy a utopian system in which property is communally owned and all decisions are made democratically (1)

communitarians those who favor a strong, substantive government role in the economy and the social order in order so that their vision of a community of equals may be realized (2)

compellence using foreign policy strategies to persuade, or force, an actor to take a certain action (19)

compelling state interest a fundamental state purpose, which must be shown before the law can limit some freedoms or treat some groups of people differently (5)

concurrent powers powers that are shared by both the federal and state governments (4)

concurring opinions documents written by justices expressing agreement with the majority ruling but describing different or additional reasons for the ruling (10)

confederal system a government in which local units hold all the power (4)

confederation a government in which independent states unite for common purpose but retain their own sovereignty (3)

conference committees temporary committees formed to reconcile differences in House and Senate versions of a bill (7)

conflict extension a theory of party change that sees new issues reinforcing rather than supplanting existing party differences (12)

congressional oversight a committee's investigation of the executive and of government agencies to ensure they are acting as Congress intends (7); efforts by Congress, especially through committees, to monitor agency rule making, enforcement, and implementation of congressional policies (9)

conservatives people who generally favor limited government and are cautious about change (2)

constituency the voters in a state or district (7)

constitution the rules that establish a government (3)

Constitutional Convention the assembly of fifty-five delegates in the summer of 1787 to recast the Articles of Confederation; the result was the U.S. Constitution (3)

constitutional law law stated in the Constitution or in the body of judicial decisions about the meaning of the Constitution handed down in the courts (10)

consumption tax a plan in which people are taxed not on what they earn but on what they spend (18)

containment the U.S. Cold War policy of preventing the spread of communism (19)

cooperative federalism the federal system under which the national and state governments share responsibilities for most domestic policy areas (4, 16)

cost-benefit analysis an evaluation method in which the costs of the program are compared to the benefits of the policy (17)

Council of Economic Advisers organization within the EOP that advises the president on economic matters (8)

council-manager government form of local government in which a professional city or town manager is appointed by elected councilors (16)

counterterrorism activities to stop terrorists from using force and responding when they do (19)

courts institutions that sit as neutral third parties to resolve conflicts according to the law (10)

covert operations undercover actions in which the prime mover country appears to have had no role (19)

criminal laws laws prohibiting behavior the government has determined to be harmful to society; violation of a criminal law is called a crime (10)

crisis policy foreign policy, usually made quickly and secretly, that responds to an emergency threat (19)

critical election an election signaling a significant change in popular allegiance from one party to another (12)

critical thinking analysis and evaluation of ideas and arguments based on reason and evidence (1)

cybersecurity the safety of the technological infrastructure on which we rely for communication, transportation, power, government services, and so on (19)

cycle effect the predictable rise and fall of a president's popularity at different stages of a term in office (8)

de facto discrimination discrimination that is the result not of law but rather of tradition and habit (6)

de jure discrimination discrimination arising from or supported by the law (6)

dealignment a trend among voters to identify themselves as independents rather than as members of a major party (12)

Declaration of Independence the political document that dissolved the colonial ties between the United States and Britain (3)

deficits shortfalls in the budget due to the government spending more in a year than it takes in (18)

democracy government that vests power in the people (1)

department one of the major subdivisions of the federal government, represented in the president's cabinet (9)

Department of Defense the executive department charged with managing the country's military personnel, equipment, and operations (19)

Department of Homeland Security the executive department meant to provide a unifying force in the government's efforts to prevent attacks on the United States and to respond to such attacks through law enforcement and emergency relief should they occur (19)

Department of State the executive department charged with managing foreign affairs (19)

depression a sharp reduction in a nation's GDP for more than a year, accompanied by high unemployment (18)

deregulation the elimination of regulations in order to improve economic efficiency (18)

descriptive representation the idea that an elected body should mirror demographically the population it represents (7)

deterrence maintaining military might so as to discourage another actor from taking a certain action (19)

devolution the transfer of powers and responsibilities from the federal government to the states (4, 16)

diplomacy the formal system of communication and negotiation between countries (19)

direct lobbying direct interaction with public officials for the purpose of influencing policy decisions (13)

director of national intelligence overseer and coordinator of the activities of the many agencies involved in the production and dissemination of intelligence information in the U.S. government, as well as the president's main intelligence adviser (19)

dissenting opinions documents written by justices expressing disagreement with the majority ruling (10)

distributive policies policies funded by the whole taxpayer base that address the needs of particular groups (17)

divided government political rule split between two parties, in which one controls the White House and the other controls one or both houses of Congress (8)

divine right of kings the principle that earthly rulers receive their authority from God (1)

dual federalism the federal system under which the national and state governments are responsible for separate policy areas (4, 16)

due process of the law guarantee that laws will be fair and reasonable and that citizens suspected of breaking the law will be treated fairly (5)

economic boom a period of fast economic growth in GDP, signaling prosperity (18)

economic bust a period of steep decline in GDP, signaling recession (18)

economic conservatives those who favor a strictly procedural government role in the economy and the social order (2)

economic interest groups groups that organize to influence government policy for the economic benefit of their members (13)

economic liberals those who favor an expanded government role in the economy but a limited role in the social order (2)

economic policy all the different strategies that government officials employ to solve economic problems (18)

economic sanctions restrictions on trade imposed on one country by another state or a group of states, usually as a form of punishment or protest (19)

economics production and distribution of a society's material resources and services (1)

electioneering the process of getting a person elected to public office (12)

Electoral College an intermediary body that elects the president (4)

electoral mandate the perception that an election victory signals broad support for the winner's proposed policies (14)

elite democracy a theory of democracy that limits the citizens' role to choosing among competing leaders (1)

embargo the refusal by one country to trade with another in order to force changes in its behavior or to weaken it (19)

English-only movements efforts to make English the official language of the United States (6)

entitlement program a federal program that guarantees benefits to qualified recipients (17)

enumerated powers of Congress congressional powers specifically named in the Constitution (Article I, Section 8) (4)

environmental policy distributive, redistributive, and regulatory policy that seeks to improve the quality of the physical world in which we live (17)

equal opportunity interest groups groups that organize to promote the civil and economic rights of underrepresented or disadvantaged groups (13)

Equal Rights Amendment constitutional amendment passed by Congress but never ratified that would have banned discrimination on the basis of gender (6)

establishment clause the First Amendment guarantee that the government will not create and support an official state church (5)

ex post facto laws laws that criminalize an action after it occurs (5)

excise taxes consumer taxes levied on specific merchandise, such as cigarettes or alcohol (18)

exclusionary rule rule created by the Supreme Court that evidence seized illegally may not be used to obtain a conviction (5)

executive the branch of government responsible for putting laws into effect (4)

executive agreements presidential arrangements with another country that create foreign policy without the need for Senate approval (8)

Executive Office of the President collection of nine organizations that help the president with policy and political objectives (8)

executive orders clarifications of congressional policy issued by the president and having the full force of law (8, 10)

exit polls election-related questions asked of voters right after they vote (11)

exploratory committee formed to determine the viability of one's candidacy for office; activities may include polling, travel, and other communications relevant to the purpose (14)

expressive benefits selective incentives that derive from the opportunity to express values and beliefs and to be committed to a greater cause (13)

factions groups of citizens united by some common passion or interest and opposed to the rights of other citizens or to the interests of the whole community (3, 13)

Federal Register publication containing all federal regulations and notifications of regulatory agency hearings (9)

Federal Reserve System independent commission that controls the money supply through a system of twelve federal banks (18)

federalism a political system in which power is divided between the central and regional units (3)

The Federalist Papers a series of essays written to build support for ratification of the Constitution (3)

Federalists supporters of the Constitution who favored a strong central government (3)

feeding frenzy excessive press coverage of an embarrassing or scandalous subject (15)

feudalism a social system in which a rigid social and political hierarchy was based on the ownership of land (3)

fighting words speech intended to incite violence (5)

filibuster a practice of unlimited debate in the Senate in order to prevent or delay a vote on a bill (7)

fiscal policy economic policy in which government regulates the economy through its powers to tax and spend (18)

527 groups groups that mobilize voters with issue advocacy advertisements on television and radio but may not directly advocate the election or defeat of a particular candidate (13)

flat tax a tax system in which all people pay the same percentage of their income (18)

foreign aid assistance given by one country to another in the form of grants or loans (19)

foreign policy a country's official positions, practices, and procedures for dealing with actors outside its borders (19)

framing process through which the media emphasize particular aspects of a news story, thereby influencing the public's perception of the story (15)

franking the privilege of free mail service provided to members of Congress (7)

free exercise clause the First Amendment guarantee that citizens may freely engage in the religious activities of their choice (5)

free rider problem the difficulty groups face in recruiting when potential members can gain the benefits of the group's actions whether they join or not (13)

free trade economic system by which countries exchange goods without imposing excessive tariffs and taxes (19)

free trade policies policies that encourage open borders between trading partners by eliminating protectionist policies (18)

freedom of assembly the right of the people to gather peacefully and to petition government (5)

Freedom of Information Act (FOIA) 1966 law that allows citizens to obtain copies of most public records (9)

French and Indian War a war fought between France and England, and allied Indians, from 1754 to 1763; resulted in France's expulsion from the New World (3)

front-loading the process of scheduling presidential primaries early in the primary season (14)

front-runner the leading candidate and expected winner of a nomination or an election (14)

fusion of powers an alternative to separation of powers, combining or blending branches of government (4)

gatekeepers journalists and media elite who determine which news stories are covered and which are not (15)

gender gap the tendency of men and women to differ in their political views on some issues (11)

General Agreement on Tariffs and Trade (GATT) a series of agreements on international trading terms; now known as the World Trade Organization (WTO) (19)

gerrymandering redistricting to benefit a particular group (7)

get-out-the-vote (GOTV) drives efforts by political parties, interest groups, and the candidate's staff to maximize voter turnout among supporters (14)

Gibbons v. Ogden Supreme Court ruling (1824) establishing national authority over interstate business (4)

going public a president's strategy of appealing to the public on an issue, expecting that public pressure will be brought to bear on other political actors (8)

governing activities directed toward controlling the distribution of political resources by providing executive and legislative leadership, enacting agendas, mobilizing support, and building coalitions (12)

government a system or an organization for exercising authority over a body of people (1)

government corporations companies created by Congress to provide to the public a good or service that private enterprise cannot or will not profitably provide (9)

government matching funds money given by the federal government to qualified presidential candidates in the primary and general election campaigns (14)

grandfather clauses provisions exempting from voting restrictions the descendants of those able to vote in 1867 (6)

grassroots lobbying indirect lobbying efforts that spring from widespread public concern (13)

Great Compromise the constitutional solution to congressional representation: equal votes in the Senate, votes by population in the House (3)

gross domestic product (GDP) total market value of all goods and services produced by everyone in a particular country during a given year (18)

habeas corpus the right of an accused person to be brought before a judge and informed of the charges and evidence against him or her (5)

hard money campaign funds donated directly to candidates; amounts are limited by federal election laws (14)

Hatch Act 1939 law limiting the political involvement of civil servants in order to protect them from political pressure and keep politics out of the bureaucracy (9)

head of government the political role of the president as leader of a political party and chief arbiter of who gets what resources (8)

head of state the apolitical, unifying role of the president as symbolic representative of the whole country (8)

hegemon the dominant actor in world politics (19)

honeymoon period the time following an election when a president's popularity is high and congressional relations are likely to be productive (8)

horse-race journalism the media's focus on the competitive aspects of politics rather than on actual policy proposals and political decisions (15)

House Rules Committee the committee that determines how and when debate on a bill will take place (7)

hyperpartisanship a commitment to party so strong it can transcend other commitments (7)

ideologies sets of beliefs about politics and society that help people make sense of their world (2)

immigrants citizens or subjects of one country who move to another country to live or work (2)

imminent lawless action test rule used by the courts that restricts speech only if it is aimed at producing or is likely to produce imminent lawless action (5)

impeachment a formal charge by the House that the president (or another member of the executive branch) has committed acts of "Treason, Bribery, or other high Crimes and Misdemeanors," which may or may not result in removal from office (8)

incorporation Supreme Court action making the protections of the Bill of Rights applicable to the states (5)

incumbency advantage the electoral edge afforded to those already in office (7)

independent agencies government organizations independent of the departments but with a narrower policy focus (9)

independent regulatory boards and commissions government organizations that regulate various businesses, industries, or economic sectors (9)

indirect lobbying attempts to influence government policymakers by encouraging the general public to put pressure on them (13)

individualism belief that what is good for society is based on what is good for individuals (2)

individualistic political culture a political culture that distrusts government, expects corruption, downplays citizen participation, and stresses individual economic prosperity; mid-Atlantic region, lower Midwest, West Coast (16)

inflation an increase in the price of goods (18)

inherent powers presidential powers implied but not explicitly stated in the Constitution (8)

initiative citizen petitions to place a proposal or constitutional amendment on the ballot, to be adopted or rejected by majority vote, bypassing the legislature (4, 16)

inquisitorial systems trial procedures designed to determine the truth through the intervention of an active judge who seeks evidence and questions witnesses (10)

institutions organizations in which governmental power is exercised (1)

intelligence community the agencies and bureaus responsible for obtaining and interpreting information for the government (19)

interest group an organization of individuals who share a common political goal and unite for the purpose of influencing government decisions (13)

interest group entrepreneurs effective group leaders who are likely to have organized the group and can effectively promote its interests among members and the public (13)

interest rates the cost of borrowing money calculated as a percentage of the money borrowed (18)

intergovernmental organizations bodies, such as the United Nations, whose members are countries (19)

intermediate standard of review standard of review used by the Court to evaluate laws that make a quasisuspect classification (6)

International Monetary Fund (IMF) economic institution that makes short-term, relatively small loans to countries to help balance their currency flows (19)

internationalism a foreign policy based on taking an active role in global affairs; the predominant foreign policy view in the United States today (19)

interstate compacts agreements between two or more states, frequently formed to manage a common resource (16)

invisible primary early attempts to raise money, line up campaign consultants, generate media attention, and get commitments for support even before candidates announce they are running (14)

iron triangles the phenomenon of a clientele group, congressional committee, and bureaucratic agency cooperating to make mutually beneficial policy (9)

isolationism a foreign policy view that nations should stay out of international political alliances and activities, and focus on domestic matters (19)

issue advocacy ads advertisements that support issues or candidates without telling constituents how to vote (13, 14)

issue networks complex systems of relationships between groups that influence policy, including elected leaders, interest groups, specialists, consultants, and research institutes (9)

issue ownership the tendency of one party to be seen as more competent in a specific policy area (14)

Jim Crow laws southern laws designed to circumvent the Thirteenth, Fourteenth, and Fifteenth Amendments and to deny blacks rights on bases other than race (6)

Joint Chiefs of Staff the senior military officers from four branches of the U.S. armed forces (19)

joint committees combined House-Senate committees formed to coordinate activities and expedite legislation in a certain area (7)

judicial activism view that the courts should be lawmaking, policymaking bodies (10)

judicial interpretivism a judicial approach holding that the Constitution is a living document and that judges should interpret it according to changing times and values (10)

judicial power the power to interpret laws and judge whether a law has been broken (4)

judicial restraint view that the courts should reject any active lawmaking functions and stick to judicial interpretations of the past (10)

judicial review power of the Supreme Court to rule on the constitutionality of laws (4, 10)

jurisdiction a court's authority to hear certain cases (10)

Keynesianism an economic theory that government could stimulate a lagging economy by putting more money into it or cool off an inflationary economy by taking money out (18)

laissez-faire capitalism an economic system in which the market makes all decisions and the government plays no role (1)

laws of supply and demand basic principles that regulate the economic market and influence the price of a good (18)

leaks confidential information secretly revealed to the press (15)

legislative agenda the slate of proposals and issues that representatives think it worthwhile to consider and act on (7)

legislative liaison executive personnel who work with members of Congress to secure their support in getting a president's legislation passed (8)

legislative supremacy an alternative to judicial review, the acceptance of legislative acts as the final law of the land (4)

legislature the body of government that makes laws (4)

legitimate accepted as "right" or proper (1)

Lemon **test** three-pronged rule used by the courts to determine whether the establishment clause is violated (5)

libel written defamation of character (5)

liberals people who generally favor government action and view change as progress (2)

libertarians those who favor a minimal government role in any sphere (2)

literacy tests tests requiring reading or comprehension skills as a qualification for voting (6)

lobbying interest group activities aimed at persuading policymakers to support the group's positions (13)

majority party the party with the most seats in a house of Congress (7)

Marbury v. Madison the landmark case that established the U.S. Supreme Court's power of judicial review (10)

marriage gap the tendency for married people to hold political opinions that differ from those of people who have never married (11)

Marshall Plan America's massive economic recovery program for Western Europe following World War II (19)

mass media means of conveying information to large public audiences cheaply and efficiently (15)

material benefits selective incentives in the form of tangible rewards (13)

mayoral government form of local government in which a mayor is elected in a partisan election (16)

McCulloch v. Maryland Supreme Court ruling (1819) confirming the supremacy of national over state government (4)

means-tested programs social programs whose beneficiaries qualify by demonstrating need (17)

Medicaid a federally sponsored program that provides medical care to the poor (17)

Medicare the federal government's health insurance program for the elderly and disabled (17)

merit system of judicial selection the attempt to remove politics—either through elections or appointments—from the process of selecting judges (16)

metropolitan-wide government a single government that controls and administers public policy in a central city and its surrounding suburbs (16)

midterm loss the tendency for the presidential party to lose congressional seats in off-year elections (7)

Miller **test** rule used by the courts in which the definition of obscenity must be based on local standards (5)

minimum rationality test standard of review used by the Court to evaluate laws that make a nonsuspect classification (6)

momentum the widely held public perception that a candidate is gaining electoral strength (14)

monetary policy economic policy in which government regulates the economy by manipulating interest rates to control the money supply (18)

monopoly a situation in which a single producer dominates a market and there is no competition (18)

moralistic political culture a political culture that expects government to promote the public interest and the common good, sees government growth as positive, and encourages citizen participation; New England, upper Midwest, and Pacific Northwest (16)

most favored nation the status afforded to WTO trading partners; a country gives the same "deal" to member nations that it offers to its "most favored" friend (19)

Motor Voter Bill legislation allowing citizens to register to vote at the same time they apply for a driver's license or other state benefit (14)

muckrakers investigative reporters who search for and expose misconduct in corporate activity or public officials (15)

multinational corporations large companies that do business in multiple countries (19)

narrowcasting the targeting of specialized audiences by the media (15)

National Association for the Advancement of Colored People (NAACP) an interest group founded in 1910 to promote civil rights for African Americans (6)

national debt the total of the nation's unpaid deficits, or simply the sum total of what the national government owes (18)

national lawmaking the creation of policy to address the problems and needs of the entire nation (7)

National Security Council (NSC) the organization within the Executive Office of the President that provides foreign policy advice to the president (8, 19)

naturalization the legal process of acquiring citizenship for someone who has not acquired it by birth (2)

necessary and proper clause constitutional authorization for Congress to make any law required to carry out its powers (4)

negative advertising campaign advertising that emphasizes the negative characteristics of opponents rather than one's own strengths (14)

neutral competence the principle that bureaucracy should be depoliticized by making it more professional (9)

New Jersey Plan a proposal at the Constitutional Convention that congressional representation be equal, thus favoring the small states (3)

news aggregators web sites, applications, and software that cull content from other digital sources (15)

news management the efforts of a politician's staff to control news about the politician (15)

news organizations businesses (and occasionally nonprofits) devoted to reporting

and disseminating news via print, broadcast, or digital media—or a multimedia combination (15)

nominating convention formal party gathering to choose candidates (12)

nongovernmental organizations organizations comprising individuals or interest groups from around the world focused on a special issue (19)

normative describes beliefs or values about how things should be or what people ought to do rather than what actually is (2)

norms informal rules that govern behavior in Congress (7)

North American Free Trade Agreement (NAFTA) trade agreement that removed most of the barriers to trade and investment that existed among the United States, Mexico, and Canada (18)

North Atlantic Treaty Organization (NATO) multinational organization formed in 1949 to promote the Cold War defense of Europe from the communist bloc (19)

nuclear triad the military strategy of having a three-pronged nuclear capability, from land, sea, or air (19)

nullification declaration by a state that a federal law is void within its borders (4)

Office of Management and Budget organization within the Executive Office of the President that oversees the budgets of departments and agencies (8)

omnibus legislation a large bill that contains so many important elements that members can't afford to defeat it and the president can't afford to veto it, even if the bill contains elements they dislike (7)

on-line processing the ability to receive and evaluate information as events happen, allowing us to remember our evaluation even if we have forgotten the specific events that caused it (11)

open primaries primary elections in which eligible voters do not need to be registered party members (12, 14)

opinion the written decision of the court that states the judgment of the majority (10)

opinion leaders people who know more about certain topics than we do and whose advice we trust, seek out, and follow (11)

oppo research investigation of an opponent's background for the purpose of exploiting weaknesses or undermining credibility (14)

original jurisdiction the authority of a court to hear a case first (10)

pardoning power a president's authority to release or excuse a person from the legal penalties of a crime (8)

parliamentary system government in which the executive is chosen by the legislature from among its members and the two branches are merged (4)

participatory democracy a theory of democracy that holds that citizens should actively and directly control all aspects of their lives (1)

partisan sorting the process through which citizens align themselves ideologically with one of the two parties, leaving fewer citizens remaining in the center and increasing party polarization (11)

partisanship loyalty to a party that helps shape how members see the world, define problems, and identify appropriate solutions (7, 12)

party activists the "party faithful"; the rank-and-file members who actually carry out the party's electioneering efforts (12)

party base members of a political party who consistently vote for that party's candidates (12)

party bosses party leaders, usually in an urban district, who exercised tight control over electioneering and patronage (12)

party caucus local gathering of party members to choose convention delegates (14)

party discipline ability of party leaders to bring party members in the legislature into line with the party program (12)

party eras extended periods of relative political stability in which one party tends to control both the presidency and Congress (12)

party identification voter affiliation with a political party (12)

party-in-government members of the party who have been elected to serve in government (12)

party-in-the-electorate ordinary citizens who identify with the party (12)

party machines mass-based party systems in which parties provided services and resources to voters in exchange for votes (12)

party organization the official structure that conducts the political business of parties (12)

party platform list of policy positions a party endorses and pledges its elected officials to enact (12)

party polarization greater ideological (liberal versus conservative) differences between the parties and increased ideological consensus within the parties (7)

party primary nomination of party candidates by registered party members rather than party bosses (12)

patriotism a strong emotional attachment to one's political community (11)

patronage system in which successful party candidates reward supporters with jobs or favors (9, 12)

peace dividend the expectation that reduced defense spending would result in additional funds for other programs (19)

Pendleton Act 1883 civil service reform that required the hiring and promoting of civil servants to be based on merit, not patronage (9)

permanent campaign the idea that governing requires a continual effort to convince the public to sign onto the program, requiring a reliance on consultants and an emphasis on politics over policy (15)

Plessy v. Ferguson Supreme Court case that established the constitutionality of the principle "separate but equal" (6)

pluralist democracy a theory of democracy that holds that citizen membership in groups is the key to political power (1)

pocket veto presidential authority to kill a bill submitted within ten days of the end of a legislative session by not signing it (7)

polarization the ideological distance between the parties and the ideological homogeneity within them (7)

police power the ability of the government to protect its citizens and maintain social order (5)

policy entrepreneurship practice of legislators becoming experts and taking leadership roles in specific policy areas (7)

policy representation congressional work to advance the issues and ideological preferences of constituents (7)

political accountability the democratic principle that political leaders must answer to the public for their actions (15)

political action committees (PACs) the fundraising arms of interest groups (13)

political correctness the idea that language shapes behavior and therefore should be regulated to control its social effects (5)

political culture the broad pattern of ideas, beliefs, and values about citizens and government held by a population (2)

political efficacy citizens' feelings of effectiveness in political affairs (14)

political generations groups of citizens whose political views have been shaped by the common events of their youth (11)

political gridlock the stalemate that occurs when political rivals, especially parties, refuse to budge from their positions to achieve a compromise in the public interest (12)

political party a group of citizens united by ideology and seeking control of government in order to promote their ideas and policies (12)

political socialization the process by which we learn our political orientations and allegiances (11)

politics who gets what, when, and how; a process of determining how power and resources are distributed in a society without recourse to violence (1)

poll taxes taxes levied as a qualification for voting (6)

popular sovereignty the concept that the citizens are the ultimate source of political power (1, 3)

popular tyranny the unrestrained power of the people (3)

pork barrel public works projects and grants for specific districts paid for by general revenues (7)

position issues issues on which the parties differ in their perspectives and proposed solutions (14)

poverty threshold the income level below which a family is considered to be "poor" (17)

power the ability to get other people to do what you want (1)

power to persuade a president's ability to convince Congress, other political actors, and the public to cooperate with the administration's agenda (8)

precedent a previous decision or ruling that, in common-law tradition, is binding on subsequent decisions (10)

preemption action that strikes and eliminates an enemy before it has a chance to strike you (19)

presidential primary an election by which voters choose convention delegates committed to voting for a certain candidate (14)

presidential style image projected by the president that represents how he would like to be perceived at home and abroad (8)

presidential system government in which the executive is chosen independently of the legislature and the two branches are separate (4)

presidential veto a president's authority to reject a bill passed by Congress; may be overridden only by a two-thirds majority in each house (8)

preventive war to use force without direct provocation in order to ensure that a chain of events does not unfold that could put you at immediate risk at some later date (19)

priming the way in which the media's emphasis on particular characteristics of people, events, or issues influences the public's perception of those people, events, or issues (15)

prior restraint censorship of or punishment for the expression of ideas before the ideas are printed or spoken (5)

Privacy Act of 1974 a law that gives citizens access to the government's files on them (9)

procedural due process procedural laws that protect the rights of individuals who must deal with the legal system (10)

procedural guarantees government assurance that the rules will work smoothly and treat everyone fairly, with no promise of particular outcomes (1, 2)

procedural laws laws that establish how laws are applied and enforced—how legal proceedings take place (10)

progressive taxes taxes whose rates increase with income (18)

propaganda the promotion of information, which may or may not be correct, designed to influence the beliefs and attitudes of a foreign audience (19)

prospective voting basing voting decisions on well-informed opinions and consideration of the future consequences of a given vote (14)

protectionism the imposition of trade barriers, especially tariffs, to make trading conditions favorable to domestic producers (18, 19)

public interest groups groups that organize to influence government to produce collective goods or services that benefit the general public (13)

public opinion the collective attitudes and beliefs of individuals on one or more issues (11)

public opinion polls scientific efforts to estimate what an entire group thinks about an issue by asking a smaller sample of the group for its opinion (11)

public policy a government plan of action to solve a problem (17)

pundit a professional observer and commentator on politics (15)

push polls polls that ask for reactions to hypothetical, often false, information in order to manipulate public opinion (11)

racial gerrymandering redistricting to enhance or reduce the chances that a racial or ethnic group will elect members to the legislature (7)

racism institutionalized power inequalities in society based on the perception of racial differences (6)

random samples samples chosen in such a way that any member of the population being polled has an equal chance of being selected (11)

ratification the process through which a proposal is formally approved and adopted by vote (3)

rational ignorance the state of being uninformed about politics because of the cost in time and energy (11)

realignment substantial and long-term shift in party allegiance by individuals and groups, usually resulting in a change in policy direction (12)

reapportionment a reallocation of congressional seats among the states every ten years, following the census (7)

recall elections votes to remove elected officials from office (4, 16)

recession a decline in GDP for two consecutive quarters (18)

Reconstruction the period following the Civil War during which the federal government took action to rebuild the South (6)

red tape the complex procedures and regulations surrounding bureaucratic activity (9)

redistributive policies policies that shift resources from the "haves" to the "have-nots" (17)

redistricting process of dividing states into legislative districts (7)

referendum an election in which a bill passed by the state legislature is submitted to voters for approval (4, 16)

refugees individuals who flee an area or a country because of persecution on the basis of race, nationality, religion, group membership, or political opinion (2)

regressive taxes taxes that require poor people to pay a higher proportion of their income than do the well off (18)

regulated capitalism a market system in which the government intervenes to protect rights and make procedural guarantees (1)

regulating the electorate the process of setting rules that define who can vote and how difficult or easy it will be to cast a ballot in an election (14)

regulations limitations or restrictions on the activities of a business or an individual (9)

regulatory policies policies designed to restrict or change the behavior of certain groups or individuals (17)

representation the efforts of elected officials to look out for the interests of those who elect them (7)

republic a government in which decisions are made through representatives of the people (1, 4)

responsible party model party government when four conditions are met: clear choice of ideologies, candidates pledged to implement ideas, party held accountable by voters, and party control over members (12)

retrospective voting basing voting decisions on reactions to past performance; approving the status quo or signaling a desire for change (14)

revolving door the tendency of public officials, journalists, and lobbyists to move between public-sector and private-sector (media, lobbying) jobs (13, 15)

rogue states countries that break international norms and produce, sell, or use weapons of mass destruction (19)

roll call votes publicly recorded votes on bills and amendments on the floor of the House or the Senate (7)

Rule of Four the unwritten requirement that four Supreme Court justices must agree to grant a case certiorari in order for the case to be heard (10)

rules directives that specify how resources will be distributed or what procedures govern collective activity (1)

sample the portion of the population that is selected to participate in a poll (11)

sample bias the effect of having a sample that does not represent all segments of the population (11)

sampling error a number that indicates within what range the results of a poll are accurate (11)

sedition speech that criticizes the government (5)

segregation the practice and policy of separating races (6)

select committee a committee appointed to deal with an issue or problem not suited to a standing committee (7)

selective incentives benefits that are available only to group members as an inducement to get them to join (13)

selective incorporation incorporation of rights on a case-by-case basis (5)

selective perception the phenomenon of filtering incoming information through personal values and interests (15)

self-regulating market an ideal market that corrects itself when it moves in an inflationary or recessionary direction (18)

senatorial courtesy tradition of granting senior senators of the president's party considerable power over federal judicial appointments in their home states (8, 10)

seniority system the accumulation of power and authority in conjunction with the length of time spent in office (7)

separation of powers the institutional arrangement that assigns judicial, executive, and legislative powers to different persons or groups, thereby limiting the powers of each (4)

separationists supporters of a "wall of separation" between church and state (5)

sexual harassment unwelcome sexual speech or behavior that creates a hostile work environment (6)

Shays's Rebellion a grassroots uprising (1787) by armed Massachusetts farmers protesting foreclosures (3)

signing statements statements recorded along with signed legislation clarifying the president's understanding of the constitutionality of the bill (8)

slavery the ownership, for forced labor, of one people by another (3)

social connectedness citizens' involvement in groups and their relationships to their communities and families (14)

social conservatives those who endorse limited government control of the economy but

considerable government intervention to realize a traditional social order; based on religious values and hierarchy rather than equality (2)

social contract the notion that society is based on an agreement between government and the governed in which people agree to give up some rights in exchange for the protection of others (1)

social democracy a hybrid system combining a capitalist economy and a government that supports equality (1)

social insurance programs programs that offer benefits in exchange for contributions (17)

social liberals those who favor greater control of the economy and the social order to bring about greater equality and to regulate the effects of progress (2)

social order the way we organize and live our collective lives (1)

social policies distributive and redistributive policies that seek to improve the quality of citizens' lives (17)

social protest public activities designed to bring attention to political causes, usually generated by those without access to conventional means of expressing their views (13)

Social Security a social insurance program under which individuals make contributions during working years and collect benefits in retirement (17)

Social Security Act of 1935 the New Deal Act that created AFDC, Social Security, and unemployment insurance (17)

social welfare policies public policies that seek to meet the basic needs of people who are unable to provide for themselves (17)

socialist economy an economic system in which the state determines production, distribution, and price decisions and property is government owned (1)

soft money unregulated campaign contributions by individuals, groups, or parties that promote general election activities but do not directly support individual candidates (12, 14)

solicitor general Justice Department officer who argues the government's cases before the Supreme Court (8, 10)

solidary benefits selective incentives related to the interaction and bonding among group members (13)

sound bite a brief, snappy excerpt from a public figure's speech that is easy to repeat on the news (15)

Speaker of the House the leader of the majority party who serves as the presiding officer of the House of Representatives (7)

spin an interpretation of a politician's words or actions, designed to present a favorable image (15)

spiral of silence the process by which a majority opinion becomes exaggerated because minorities do not feel comfortable speaking out in opposition (11)

spoils system the nineteenth-century practice of rewarding political supporters with public office (9)

standing committees permanent committees responsible for legislation in particular policy areas (7)

State of the Union address a speech given annually by the president to a joint session of Congress and to the nation announcing the president's agenda (8)

statutory laws laws passed by a state or the federal legislature (10)

strategic policy foreign policy that lays out a country's basic stance toward international actors or problems (19)

strategic politicians office-seekers who base the decision to run on a rational calculation that they will be successful (7)

straw polls polls that attempt to determine who is ahead in a political race (11)

strict constructionism a judicial approach holding that the Constitution should be read literally, with the framers' intentions uppermost in mind (10)

strict scrutiny a heightened standard of review used by the Supreme Court to assess the constitutionality of laws that limit some freedoms or that make a suspect classification (6)

structural defense policy foreign policy dealing with defense spending, military bases, and weapons procurement (19)

subjects individuals who are obliged to submit to a government authority against which they have no rights (1)

subsidy financial incentive given by the government to corporations, individuals, or other governments (17)

substantive guarantees government assurance of particular outcomes or results (1)

substantive laws laws whose content, or substance, defines what we can or cannot do (10)

sunshine laws legislation opening the process of bureaucratic policymaking to the public (9)

super legislation the process of amending state constitutions to include interest groups' policy preferences (16)

Superfund legislation designed to oversee the cleanup of toxic waste disposal sites (17)

superterrorism the potential use of weapons of mass destruction in a terrorist attack (19)

Supplemental Nutrition Assistance Program (SNAP) a federal program that provides vouchers to the poor to help them buy food (17)

supply-side economics President Ronald Reagan's economic plan, by which tax cuts would ultimately generate more, not less, government revenues by allowing for increased investments and productivity (18)

supremacy clause constitutional declaration (Article VI) that the Constitution and laws made under its provisions are the supreme law of the land (4)

surpluses the extra funds available because government revenues are greater than its expenditures (18)

suspect classification classification, such as race, for which any discriminatory law must be justified by a compelling state interest (6)

swing voters the approximately one-third of the electorate who are undecided at the start of a campaign (14)

symbolic representation efforts of members of Congress to stand for American ideals or to identify with common constituency values (7)

Temporary Assistance to Needy Families (TANF) a welfare program of block grants to states that encourages recipients to work in exchange for time-limited benefits (17)

terrorism an act of violence that targets civilians for the purpose of provoking widespread fear that will force government to change its policies (19)

Three-fifths Compromise the formula for counting five slaves as three people for purposes of representation that reconciled northern and southern factions at the Constitutional Convention (3)

totalitarian a system in which absolute power is exercised over every aspect of life (1)

tracking polls ongoing series of surveys that follow changes in public opinion over time (11)

trade deficit the difference between the value of the goods a country imports and what it exports (18)

traditionalistic political culture a political culture that expects government to maintain existing power structures and sees citizenship as stratified, with politicians coming from the social elite; South and Southwest (16)

treaties formal agreements with other countries; negotiated by the president and requiring approval by two-thirds of the Senate (8)

trial balloon an official leak of a proposal to determine public reaction to it without risk (15)

triggering event an external event that puts an issue onto the policy agenda (17)

Truman Doctrine policy of the United States starting in 1947 that the United States would aid free peoples to maintain their freedom in the face of aggressive communist movements (19)

two-step flow of information the process by which citizens take their political cues from more well-informed opinion leaders (11)

unfunded mandate a federal order mandating that states operate and pay for a program created at the national level (4, 16)

unicameral legislature a legislature with one chamber (4)

unified state court systems court systems organized and managed by a state supreme court (16)

unitary system government in which all power is centralized (4)

valence issues issues on which most voters and candidates share the same position (14)

value-added tax (VAT) a consumption tax levied at each stage of production, based on the value added to the product at that stage (18)

values central ideas, principles, or standards that most people agree are important (2)

veto override reversal of a presidential veto by a two-thirds vote in both houses of Congress (7)

Virginia Plan a proposal at the Constitutional Convention that congressional representation be based on population, thus favoring the large states (3)

voter mobilization a party's efforts to inform potential voters about issues and candidates and persuade them to vote (14)

weapons of mass destruction nuclear, biological, or chemical weapons that can kill huge numbers of people at one time (19)

wedge issue a controversial issue that one party uses to split the voters in the other party (14)

weighting adjustments to surveys during analysis so that selected demographic groups reflect their values in the population, usually as measured by the census (11)

whistleblowers individuals who publicize instances of fraud, corruption, or other wrongdoing in the bureaucracy (9)

White House Office the approximately four hundred employees within the Executive Office of the President who work most closely and directly with the president (8)

World Bank economic institution that makes large, low-cost loans with long repayment terms to countries, primarily for infrastructure construction or repairs (19)

writs of certiorari formal requests by the U.S. Supreme Court to call up the lower court case it decides to hear on appeal (10)

INDEX

Bold typeface denotes defined terms. "*f*" and "*t*" indicate figures and tables. Italic typeface denotes illustrations or photos.

Bills of attainder, **138**
Bin Laden, Osama, 302
Bipartisan Campaign Reform Act (BCRA) of
    2002, 457, 495, 496, 543, 545
Birmingham, Alabama demonstrations, 194-195
Birth control, 148, 169-171
Black codes, **186**
Black Muslims, 195
Black Panthers, 195
Black power movement, 195
Blackwell, Elizabeth, 211
Bleaching, 247
Block grants, **115**
Blogs, 158, **563**, 585-587
Blue Dog Democrats, 441-442
Blue Law Cases, 147
Boehner, John, 53, 222, 244, 259, 261, *306,*
    439, 465
Bolivia, 397
Bonneville Power Administration, 335
Booker, Cory, 429
Bork, Robert, 293, 377-378
Boss Tweed, 284, *451*
Boston Massacre, 68
Boston Tea Party, 67, 68
Bowers v. Hardwick (1986), 171
Boycott, **192**
BP *Deepwater Horizon* disaster, 244, 266, 301,
    348, 349
Bradlee, Ben, 573
Bradwell, Myra, 211
Brady Bill of 1993, 162, 485, 486
Brandi, Matt, 1-2, 25
Braun, Carol Mosley, 313
Brennan, Walter, 293
Breyer, Stephen, *387*
Britain
    American history and, 64-65
    common-law tradition, 362
    government controlled media, 568
    judicial system, 375
    legislative supremacy doctrine, 100
    monarchy, 282
    parliamentary system, 95-96, 98
    unitary system, 107
British Broadcasting Company (BBC), 568
Broder, David, 574
Brokaw, Tom, 578
Brooks, David, 113
Brown, Michael, 391
Brown, Peter, 426
Brown, Ron, 491
Brown, Scott, 283, 460
Brown v. Board of Education of Topeka (1954),
    192, 484
Bryan, William Jennings, *455*
Buchanan, Patrick, 462, 542
Budget process, 242-243, 347
    Office of Management and Budget, 307, 331,
        347
    presidential role, 347
    See also Economic policy
Bundling, 457
Bureaucracy, 324-**325**
    democracy and, 326-327
    need for, 326
    See also Federal bureaucracy
Bureaucratese, **338**
    cookie recipe, 339-340
    critical thinking about, 339
Bureaucratic culture, **338**-343
Bureaucratic discretion, **336**
Bureau of Indian Affairs, 200
Bureau of Ocean Energy Management,
    Regulation and Enforcement
    (BOEMRE), 349
Burger, Warren, 166, 170
Burns, Alexander, 424-426
Bush, George H. W., *317*
    accommodationist perspective, 143
    approval ratings, 302
    cabinet, 307
    campaign ads, 539
    economy and, 301
    impeachment resolutions, 286

judicial appointments, 136, 293, 379
Roe v. Wade and, 170
Ross Perot and, 542
tax policy, 580
use of pardons, 286
vice presidency, 311
Bush, George W., *298, 317*
    abortion policy, 538
    accommodationist perspective, 143
    approval ratings, 302, 317-318, 523
    balance of state and federal powers, 126
    bureaucratic appointments, 343, 347
    cabinet, 307
    congressional oversight, 243
    Democrats working with, 441
    draft avoidance accusations, 585
    gaffes, 578
    Gore debate, 579
    ideological position of nonsupporters, 53
    immigration policy, 41
    impeachment resolutions, 286
    imperial presidency, 297-298
    Internet and, 556
    judicial appointments, 274, 293, 375, 378
    judicial ideology, 378
    language policy, 55
    legitimacy after 2000 election, 516
    media management and public relations, 583
    midterm loss, 251
    minority cabinet members, 181
    moderates and, 448
    No Child Left Behind Act, 111
    oppo research and, 536
    political cartoons, 284
    polls and, 398
    portrayal as candidate, 537, 546
    presidential personality and style,
        315-316
    relationship with Congress, 304
    same-sex marriage policy, 221
    signature campaign issues, 460
    unitary executive theory, 298, 378
    use of block grants, 115
    use of signing statements, 297-298
    veto success, 288-289
    vice president and, 311, 531
    war on terror, 135. *See also* War on terror
Bush, Laura, 313
Bush v. Gore (2000), 359-360, 390, 392-393
Business regulation, 111, 112
Business-related interest
    groups, 481
Business Roundtable, 371, 481
Busing, **196**

Cabinet, **287**, 306-307
    departments, **330**-331
    minority members, 181
    See also Federal bureaucracy
Cain, Herman, 411
California
    affirmative action and, 198
    constitutional amendments and, 123
    electoral votes, 534
    gay marriage law, 179
    immigration policy, 254
    initiatives (propositions), 124
Cameron, David, *99*
Cameroon, 95
Campaign advertising, 539-542
Campaign finance, 273, 457-458, 543-545
    BCRA, 457, 495, 496, 543, 545
    Citizens United case, 293, 457, 491, 495, 496,
        501, 544
    501c groups, 544
    527 groups, 496, 545
    government matching funds, 543-544
    hard money, 544
    incumbent advantage, 249, 502
    interest groups and, 491, 500-502. *See also*
        Political action committees
    pre-primary funding, 528
    reforms, 457, 477
    soft money, 457, 544-545
    third parties and, 462

unequal spending among the states, 535
    winning congressional elections, 249
Campaign managers, 535
Campaign polls, **418**-419
Canada, 110
Cannon, Joe, 259
Cantor, Eric, *235*
Capitalist economy, **5-6**, 11
Capital punishment, 168-169
Cardozo, Benjamin N., 142
Carney, Jay, 574, 583
Carter, Jimmy, 303, 310, 315, *317,* 447, 524,
        525, 527
Carter, Rosalynn, 312
Carville, James, 535
Casework, **237**-238
Casinos, 202
Categorical grants, **114**-115
Caucus system, 450
Censorship, 149
Censure, 499
Center for Biological Diversity, 350
Central Intelligence Agency (CIA), 342
Chavez, Cesar, 206, 479, 502, *503*
Checks and balances, **101**-104
    Congress and executive branch, 243-245, 296
    Congress and judicial branch, 245
    constitutional provision, 104
    judiciary and executive branch, 296-297
    Madison on, 83
    See also Separation of powers
Cheney, Dick, 292, 297-298, 311, 531
Chief administrator, **287**
Chief foreign policy maker, **288**
Chief of staff, 301, **308**-309
Child Online Protection Act, 157
Children's Defense Fund (CDF), 483
Children's Internet Protection Act, 160
China
    immigration from, 40
    socialist economy, 7
Chinese Exclusion Act of 1882, 207
Christian Coalition, 137, 143, 486
Christian Right, 464
    gay rights and, 222
    religious right ideology, 53
    reproductive rights and, 171
Christie, Chris, 179, 226, 397-398, *398,* 429, 534
Citizen advisory councils, **352**
Citizens, 3, **11**
    American political beliefs and, 54-55
    bureaucracy and, 351-353
    civic journalism, 571
    democracy and, 11-12, 399-400
    interest groups and, 504-505
    media and, 584-586
    noncitizens' rights, 224
    partisan politics and, 465-466
    party-in-the-electorate, 436-437
    political efficacy, 516
    political knowledge, 401,
        424-427
    political participation. *See* Voter turnout;
        Voting
    political specialization view of democracy,
        546-547
    rational electorate, 427-428
    resolving conflicts about rights, 137
    rights and power of, 134
    rights and responsibilities, 12
    subjects versus, 85
    the courts and, 390-392
    See also Constituency; Public opinion; Voter
        decision making
Citizenship
    American citizenship, 33
    competing visions of, 400
    culture and values, 43-44
    educational influences, 407
    Enlightenment era ideas, 14
    founding of the U.S. and, 85
    framework for evaluation, 24
    in contemporary U.S., 18
    Madison's vision of, 17-18
    need for informed citizenry, 149

Randolph, Edmund, 78, 79, 97
Random samples, **416**
Rather, Dan, 579, 585
Ratification, **82**–84
Rational choice and voting, 523
Rational electorate, 427–428
Rational ignorance, **426**
Readdy, William, *342*
Reagan, Nancy, 313
Reagan, Ronald, 527
   accommodationist perspective, 143
   affirmative action policy, 196
   "are you better off" question, 526
   attempted assassination, 486
   balance of state and federal powers, 112
   bureaucratic appointments, 343
   fairness doctrine and, 569
   government size and, 295
   impeachment resolutions, 286
   Iran-contra scandal, 286
   judicial appointments, 136, 170, 293, 376, 377
   judicial ideology, 378
   media management, 583
   new era of conservative policies, 547
   1980 election and, 530
   political cartoons, 284
   presidential personality and style, 315
   Roe v. Wade and, 170
   use of block grants, 115
   vice president and, 311
REAL ID Act of 2005, 115–116
Reapportionment, **245**–248, 377
   "one person, one vote" principle, 246, 377
Recall elections, **125**
Recess appointments, 244, 347
Recession, 117
Reconstruction, **186**–187
Redistricting, **246**–247
Red states versus blue states, 406, 451, 535
Red tape, **328**
Referendum, **124**–125. *See also* Direct democracy
Reformation, 12–13
Refugees, **37**
Regents of the University of California v. Bakke
   (1978), 196
Regulated capitalism, **6**
Regulating the electorate, **518**, 524
Regulatory agencies, 331, **334**–335
   iron triangles, 348–350
   lobbying and, 495
   presidential influence on,
      334–335
Regulatory policy
   administrative law, *367*
   congressional powers, 111, 126
   economic regulation. *See also* Economic
      regulatory policy
   Federal Register, 338
   national government influence on states, 114
   organic foods, 323, 354
   Supreme Court decisions, 112
   See also Economic policy; Environmental
      policy; Public policy; Regulatory
      agencies
Rehnquist, William, 112, 166, 170–171
Reid, Harry, 261, 274, 308, 506
Religion
   opinions about politics and, 411, 525
   voter decision making and, 525
Religious freedom, 142–148
   Affordable Care Act and, 148
   establishment clause, 143–146
   free exercise clause, 146–148
   gap between law and practice, 146
   Lemon test, 146
   social order and, 147
Religious Freedom Restoration Act (1993), 147
Religious interest groups, 486
Religious requirements for voting, 65
Religious right, 53. *See also* Christian Right
Representation, **233**
   allocative, 237
   colonial era political philosophies, 68
   descriptive, **251**, 255–256
   factions and, 83

   interest groups and, 477–478
   lawmaking and partisanship tensions,
      233–239
   policy, 237
   proportional, 462
   symbolic, 238
   types of, 237–238
   voter turnout and, 517
Reproductive rights, 169–171
   interest groups, 486
   social protest, 499
   See also Abortion
Republic, **94**
Republican government, 94
   separation of powers, 101, 104
Republican National Committee (RNC), 436, 463
Republican Party
   abortion policy, 171
   anti-Obama opposition, 239, 258, 302
   Christian Right and, 464
   conservative ideology, 47, 53, 256, 258,
      442–443, 463. *See also* Conservatives
      and conservative ideology
   constitutional amendments and, 119
   differences from Democrats, 439–448, 519
   dysfunctional partisanship, 238–239
   historical development, 450–451
   immigration policy, 206–207, 254
   Log Cabin Republicans, 222, 484
   membership demographics, 443
   opposition to federal growth, 117
   party primary rules, 529
   party solidarity, 258
   platform, 444–446
   "Republicans are the problem," 440–442
   Tea Party and. *See* Tea Party
   See also Political parties
Republican virtue, 17
Republics, **17**
Responsible party model, **438**–439
Retrospective voting, **526**
Revere, Paul, 68, 284
Reverse discrimination, 196
Revolving door, **490**, 494, **574**
Reynolds v. U.S. (1878), 148
Rice, Condeleezza, 181, 411
Richardson, Bill, *217*
Right of rebuttal, 569
Rights, 132–134
   citizenship and, 172–173
   conflicts of, 134
   national security versus, 134–136
   of citizens in democratic systems, 12
   power of the people and, 134
   reasons for denying, 182–183
   resolving conflicts about, 136–137
   See also Civil rights
Right to die, 171–172
Roberts, John, 114, 147, 164, 378, *387*, 388–389,
   401, 568
Robertson, Pat, 486
Robo calling, 423
Roe v. Wade (1973), 170–171, 214, 378, 386
Roll call votes, **271**
Roman Catholics, 525
Romney, Ann, 456
Romney, Mitt, *4,* 442
   abortion policy, 538
   as governor
   debates, 542–543, 580
   election defeat and, 510
   English only policy, 32
   gaffes, 526, 542
   getting out the vote, 510–511, 548
   Hispanic voters and, 206
   immigration policy, 254
   income inequality views, 26
   moderates and, 448
   Paul Ryan and, *529,* 531

   portrayal as candidate, 538
   public perceptions of personality, 527
   Tea Party and, 53, 62
   See also Presidential election, 2012
Roosevelt, Eleanor, 312
Roosevelt, Franklin D., 6, 292, 307, 312, 314
   campaign promises fulfillment, 460–461
   court packing scheme, 377
   fireside chats, 556, 559
   judicial appointments, 378
   1932 election poll and, 416
   See also New Deal
Roosevelt, Theodore, *292*
Rosenthal, Howard, 441
Rouse, Pete, 310
Rove, Carl, 535, 548, 574
Rowley, Coleen, 341–342, 344–345
Rubio, Marco, 206
Rule of Four, **381**
Rules, 4–**5**, 93
   bureaucracies and, 327–328
Ryan, George, 169
Ryan, Paul, *529,* 531

Salaries of congress members, 248
Same-sex marriage. *See* Marriage equality
Sample bias, **413**, 416–417
Samples, **413**
Sampling error, **416**
Sandusky, Jerry, *367*
Sanford, Edward, 139
Santiago, Esmeralda, 42–43
Santorum, Rick, 53
Saturday Night Live, 541, 560
Sawyer, Diane, 581
Scalia, Antonin, 170, *387*
Scalise, Steve, *439*
Scandinavian social democracy, 7, 44
Schenck v. United States (1919), 152
Schiavo, Terri, 171
Schlesinger, Arthur, 295
School desegregation, 188–196
Schriock, Stephanie, *485*
Schwarzenegger, Arnold, 179
Scott, Tim, 411
Search engines, 158
Searches and seizures
   exclusionary rule, 165–166
   Fourth Amendment protections, 164–165
   strip searches, 150–151, 165
Second Amendment, 63, 160–163, 378
   interest groups, 486. *See also* National Rifle
      Association
   party platforms, 445
Secretary of defense, 330
Secretary of state, 330
Securities and Exchange Commission (SEC),
   244, 331
Sedition, **149**
   anti-sedition laws, 149–153
Segregation, 187–**188**
   civil rights movement and desegregation,
      188–196
Select committee, **263**
Selective incentives, **479**–480
Selective incorporation, **142**
Selective perception, **579**
Self-incrimination protections, 166
Senate, 97
   Constitutional Convention plans, 79
   elections, 245, 399, 512. *See also*
      Congressional elections
   filibusters and, 231–232, 267–270, 274, 380
   House and Senate differences, 241–243
   impeachment and, 243, 286
   leadership organization, 259, 261
   organization. *See* Congressional committees;
      Congressional organization
   presidential appointment confirmation, 97,
      244, 293, 347, 380
   presidential election process, 534
   qualifications for office, 95, 242
   representation in, 96
   standing committees, 262
   term of office, 242

⑤SAGE researchmethods

The essential online tool for researchers from the world's leading methods publisher

Find exactly what you are looking for, from basic explanations to advanced discussion

More content and new features added this year!

"I have never really seen anything like this product before, and I think it is really valuable."

John Creswell, University of Nebraska–Lincoln

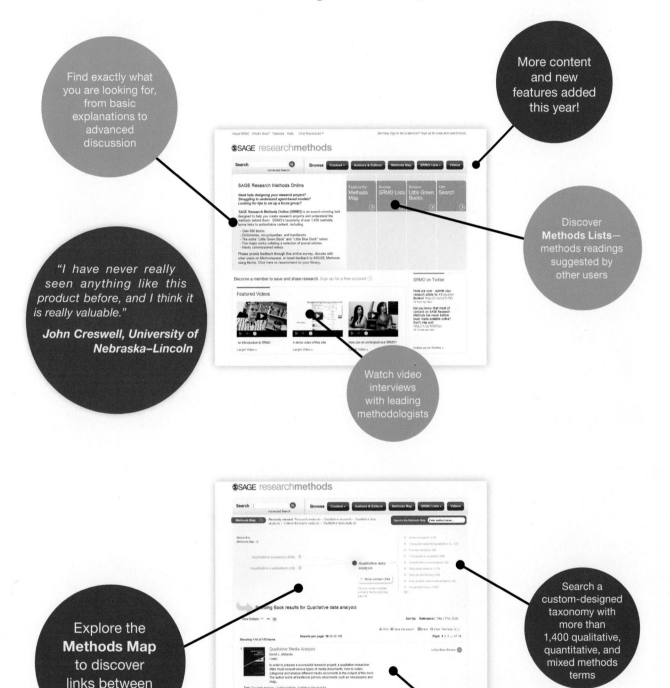

Discover **Methods Lists**— methods readings suggested by other users

Watch video interviews with leading methodologists

Explore the **Methods Map** to discover links between methods

Search a custom-designed taxonomy with more than 1,400 qualitative, quantitative, and mixed methods terms

Uncover more than 120,000 pages of book, journal, and reference content to support your learning

Find out more at
www.sageresearchmethods.com